HANDBOOK OF ECONOMETRICS
VOLUME 6B

HANDBOOKS IN ECONOMICS

2

Series Editors

KENNETH J. ARROW
MICHAEL D. INTRILIGATOR

ELSEVIER

AMSTERDAM • BOSTON • HEIDELBERG • LONDON
NEW YORK • OXFORD • PARIS • SAN DIEGO
SAN FRANCISCO • SINGAPORE • SYDNEY • TOKYO
North-Holland is an imprint of Elsevier

N·H

HANDBOOK OF ECONOMETRICS

VOLUME 6B

Edited by

JAMES J. HECKMAN
University of Chicago, Chicago
American Bar Foundation, USA
University College Dublin, Ireland

and

EDWARD E. LEAMER
University of California, Los Angeles

ELSEVIER

AMSTERDAM • BOSTON • HEIDELBERG • LONDON
NEW YORK • OXFORD • PARIS • SAN DIEGO
SAN FRANCISCO • SINGAPORE • SYDNEY • TOKYO
North-Holland is an imprint of Elsevier

N·H

North-Holland is an imprint of Elsevier
Radarweg 29, PO Box 211, 1000 AE Amsterdam, The Netherlands
The Boulevard, Langford Lane, Kidlington, Oxford OX5 1GB, UK

First edition 2007

Library of Congress Cataloging-in-Publication Data
A catalog record for this book is available from the Library of Congress

British Library Cataloguing in Publication Data
A catalogue record for this book is available from the British Library

ISBN: 978-0-444-50631-3 (Volume 6A)
ISBN: 978-0-444-53200-8 (Volume 6B)

ISSN: 0169-7218 (Handbooks in Economics series)
ISSN: 1573-4412 (Handbook of Econometrics series)

For information on all North-Holland publications
visit our website at books.elsevier.com

Printed and bound in the United Kingdom

Transferred to Digital Print 2010

INTRODUCTION TO THE SERIES

The aim of the *Handbooks in Economics* series is to produce Handbooks for various branches of economics, each of which is a definitive source, reference, and teaching supplement for use by professional researchers and advanced graduate students. Each Handbook provides self-contained surveys of the current state of a branch of economics in the form of chapters prepared by leading specialists on various aspects of this branch of economics. These surveys summarize not only received results but also newer developments, from recent journal articles and discussion papers. Some original material is also included, but the main goal is to provide comprehensive and accessible surveys. The Handbooks are intended to provide not only useful reference volumes for professional collections but also possible supplementary readings for advanced courses for graduate students in economics.

KENNETH J. ARROW and MICHAEL D. INTRILIGATOR

CONTENTS OF THE HANDBOOK

VOLUME 1

Part 1: MATHEMATICAL AND STATISTICAL METHODS IN ECONOMETRICS

PREFACE TO THE HANDBOOK

As conceived by the founders of the Econometric Society, econometrics is a field that uses economic theory and statistical methods to address empirical problems in economics. It is a tool for empirical discovery and policy analysis. The chapters in this volume embody this vision and either implement it directly or provide the tools for doing so. This vision is not shared by those who view econometrics as a branch of statistics rather than as a distinct field of knowledge that designs methods of inference from data based on models of human choice behavior and social interactions. All of the essays in this volume offer guidance to the practitioner on how to apply the methods they discuss to interpret economic data. The authors of the chapters are all leading scholars in the fields they survey and extend.

Auction theory and empirical finance are two of the most exciting areas of empirical economics where theory and data combine to produce important practical knowledge. These fields are well represented in this Handbook by Susan Athey and Philip Haile (auctions) and Lars Hansen, John Heaton, Nikolai Roussanov and Junghoon Lee (finance). Both papers present state of the art knowledge of their respective fields and discuss economic models for the pricing of goods and risk. These papers feature agent response to uncertainty as an integral part of the analysis. Work on the pricing of labor services lies at the core of empirical labor economics. Thomas MaCurdy surveys empirical methods for estimating wage equations from panel data in a way that is accessible to practitioners.

The econometrics of industrial organization (IO) is another vibrant area of applied econometrics. Scholars in the field of IO have embraced econometrics. The resulting symbiosis between theory and practice is a paragon for econometric research. Modern developments in game theory have been incorporated in econometric models that enrich both theory and empirical analysis. These developments are well-represented in this volume by the essays of Daniel Ackerberg, Lanier Benkard, Steven Berry, and Ariel Pakes and of Peter Reiss and Frank Wolak. Stephen Bond and John van Reenen summarize the related literature on modeling the dynamics of investment and employment, which is an integral part of macroeconomics and modern IO.

The essay by Erwin Diewert and Alice Nakamura surveys methods for measuring national productivity. They exposit a literature that provides the tools for comparing the economic performance of policies and of nations. The authors survey the methods that underlie this important field of economics. Edward Leamer's essay stresses the interplay between data and theory in the analysis of international trade patterns. In an increasingly global market, the measurement of trade flows and the study of the impact of trade on economic welfare is important for understanding recent economic trends.

Modern economics has come to recognize heterogeneity and diversity among economic agents. It is now widely acknowledged that the representative agent paradigm is an inaccurate and misleading description of modern economies. The essay by Richard Blundell and Thomas Stoker summarizes and synthesizes a large body of work on the aggregation of measurements across agents to produce reliable aggregate statistics and the pitfalls in the use of aggregates.

Consumer theory, including the theory of labor supply, is at the heart of empirical economics. The essay by Richard Blundell, Thomas MaCurdy, and Costas Meghir surveys a vast literature with an ancient lineage that has been at the core of empirical economics for over 100 years. They develop empirical models of consumer demand and labor supply in an integrated framework.

The evaluation of economic and social programs is a central activity in economics. It is the topic of three essays in this Handbook. James Heckman and Edward Vytlacil contribute two chapters. The first chapter moves the literature on program evaluation outside of the framework of conventional statistics to consider economic policy questions of interest, to incorporate agent choice behavior and the consequences of uncertainty, and to relate the recent work on policy evaluation in statistics to older and deeper frameworks developed in econometrics. Issues of causality and the construction of counterfactuals are addressed within the choice-theoretic framework of economics.

Their second chapter uses the *marginal treatment effect* to unify a diverse and disjointed literature on treatment effects and estimators of treatment effects. The marginal treatment effect can be interpreted as a willingness to pay parameter. This chapter focuses on mean treatment effects in static environments without explicit analysis of uncertainty.

The essay by Jaap Abbring and James Heckman surveys new methods for identifying *distributions* of treatment effects under uncertainty. It surveys and develops methods for the analysis of dynamic treatment effects, linking the statistical literature on dynamic sequential randomization to the econometric literature on dynamic discrete choices. It also surveys recent approaches to the general equilibrium evaluation of social programs.

One of the most important contributions of econometric theory to empirical knowledge is the analysis of the identifiability of econometric models – determining under what conditions a unique model describes the data being used in an empirical analysis. Cowles Commission analysts formalized these ideas, focusing largely on linear systems [Tjalling Koopmans, Herman Rubin, and Roy Leipnik (1950)]. Later work by Franklin Fisher (1966) extended the Cowles analysis to nonlinear, but parametric systems. Rosa Matzkin's contribution to this Handbook synthesizes and substantially extends these analyses to consider a large body of work on the identification of nonparametric models. The methods she surveys and extends underlie a large literature in applied economics.

Hidehiko Ichimura and Petra Todd present a guide to the recent literature on nonparametric and semiparametric estimators in econometrics that has been developed in the past 20 years. They conduct the reader through the labyrinth of modern nonparametric econometrics to offer both practical and theoretical guides to this literature.

Robert Moffitt and Geert Ridder address the important problem of how to combine diverse data sets to identify models and improve the precision of estimation of any model. This topic is of great importance because many data sets in many areas of economics contain valuable information on subsets of variables which, if they were combined in a single data set, would identify important empirical relationships. Moffitt and Ridder present the state of the art in combining data to address interesting economic questions.

Xiaohong Chen presents a detailed, informative survey of sieve estimation of semiparametric models. The sieve principle organizes many different approaches to nonparametric and semiparametric estimation within a common analytical framework. Her analysis clarifies an extensive and widely used literature. Marine Carrasco, Jean-Pierre Florens, and Eric Renault survey the literature on nonparametric and semiparametric econometrics that is based on inverse operators. Their analysis subsumes recent research on nonparametric instrumental variable methods as well as research on deconvolution of distributions. They present both theoretical and practical guides to this frontier area of econometrics.

JAMES J. HECKMAN
University of Chicago, Chicago, USA
American Bar Foundation, USA
University College Dublin, Dublin, Ireland

EDWARD E. LEAMER
University of California, Los Angeles, USA

Acknowledgements

We gratefully acknowledge support from the National Science Foundation, the University of Chicago, and University College London for conferences at which many of these papers were presented. We also thank the many referees and conference participants whose helpful comments have improved every chapter in this volume.

References

Fisher, F.M. (1966). The Identification Problem in Econometrics. McGraw–Hill, New York.

Koopmans, T.C., Rubin, H., Leipnik, R.B. (1950). "Measuring the equation systems of dynamic economics". In: Koopmans, T.C. (Ed.), Statistical Inference in Dynamic Economic Models. In: Cowles Commission Monograph, Number 10. John Wiley & Sons, New York, pp. 53–237. Chapter 2.

CONTENTS OF VOLUME 6B

PART 18

ECONOMETRIC EVALUATION OF SOCIAL PROGRAMS

Chapter 70

ECONOMETRIC EVALUATION OF SOCIAL PROGRAMS, PART I: CAUSAL MODELS, STRUCTURAL MODELS AND ECONOMETRIC POLICY EVALUATION*

JAMES J. HECKMAN

The University of Chicago, USA

American Bar Foundation, USA

University College Dublin, Ireland

EDWARD J. VYTLACIL

Columbia University, USA

Contents

* This research was supported by NSF: 9709873, 0099195, and SES-0241858 and NICHD: R01-HD32058, and the American Bar Foundation. The views expressed in this chapter are those of the authors and not necessarily those of the funders listed here. Handbook conferences in London and Chicago were supported by NSF grant SBR-9601142. We have benefited from comments received from Thierry Magnac and Costas Meghir at the UCL Handbook of Econometrics Conference, December 1998; general comments at the 2001 Chicago Handbook Conference and discussions with Jaap Abbring, Pedro Carneiro, Steve Durlauf, Hugo Garduño-Arredondo, Seong Moon, Salvador Navarro, Rodrigo Pinto, Peter Savelyev, G. Adam Savvas, Mohan Singh, John Trujillo, Semih Tumen, and Yu Xie. Jaap Abbring and T.N. Srinivasan made especially detailed and very helpful comments on the first draft of this chapter that greatly improved its content. Portions of this chapter first appeared in Heckman (2005) but are substantially revised here.

Handbook of Econometrics, Volume 6B

DOI: 10.1016/S1573-4412(07)06070-9

Abstract

This chapter relates the literature on the econometric evaluation of social programs to the literature in statistics on "causal inference". In it, we develop a general evaluation framework that addresses well-posed economic questions and analyzes agent choice rules and subjective evaluations of outcomes as well as the standard objective evaluations of outcomes. The framework recognizes uncertainty faced by agents and *ex ante* and *ex post* evaluations of programs. It also considers distributions of treatment effects. These features are absent from the statistical literature on causal inference. A prototypical model of agent choice and outcomes is used to illustrate the main ideas.

We formally develop models for counterfactuals and causality that build on Cowles Commission econometrics. These models anticipate and extend the literature on causal inference in statistics. The distinction between fixing and conditioning that has recently entered the statistical literature was first developed by Cowles economists. Models of simultaneous causality were also developed by the Cowles group, as were notions of invariance to policy interventions. These basic notions are updated to nonlinear and nonparametric frameworks for policy evaluation more general than anything in the current statistical literature on "causal inference". A formal discussion of identification is presented and applied to clearly formulated choice models used to evaluate social programs.

Keywords

causal models, counterfactuals, policy evaluation, policy invariance, structural models, identification

JEL classification: C10, C50

1. Introduction

Evaluating policy is a central problem in economics.[1] Evaluations entail comparisons of outcomes produced from alternative policies using different valuation criteria. Such comparisons often require constructing estimates of outcomes for policies that have never been implemented. They require that the economist construct counterfactuals.[2] Counterfactuals are required to forecast the effects of policies that have been tried in one environment but are proposed to be applied in new environments and to forecast the effects of new policies.

This chapter surveys recent approaches to the empirical construction of economic counterfactuals. The traditional approach to constructing policy counterfactuals in econometrics, first developed in the 1930s, builds econometric models using data, economic theory and statistical methods. The early econometric pioneers developed macroeconomic general equilibrium models and estimated them on aggregate time series data. Later on, economists used newly available microdata on families, individuals and firms to build microstructural models. This approach unites economics, statistics and microdata to build models to evaluate policies, to forecast the effects of extending the policies to new environments and to forecast the effects of new policies. It is exemplified in the chapters by Reiss and Wolak (Chapter 64); Ackerberg, Benkard, Berry and Pakes (Chapter 63); Athey and Haile (Chapter 60); Bond and Van Reenen (Chapter 65); Blundell, MaCurdy and Meghir (Chapter 69); and Blundell and Stoker (Chapter 68) of this Handbook.

More recently, some economists have adapted statistical "treatment effect" approaches that apply methods developed in statistics, educational research, epidemiology and biostatistics to the problem of evaluating economic policy. This approach takes the randomized trial as an ideal. It is much less explicit about the role of economic theory (or any theory) in interpreting evidence or in guiding empirical analyses. The goal of this chapter is to exposit, interpret and unite the best features of these two approaches.

The topics of econometric policy evaluation and policy forecasting are vast, and no chapter within the page limits of a Handbook chapter can cover all aspects of it. In this chapter we focus on microeconomic policy evaluation and policy forecasting.

We focus our discussion on the analysis of a class of latent variable (or "index") models that form the core of modern microeconometrics. Discrete choice theory [McFadden (1974, 1981, 1984, 1985, 2001)] and models of joint discrete and continuous variables [Heckman (1974, 1979, 2001), Heckman and MaCurdy (1986)] are based on latent variable models.[3] Such models provide a framework for integrating economic theory and statistical analysis. They are also frameworks for constructing policy counterfactuals.

[1] We use the term "policy" in a very general sense. It includes alternative actions which might be undertaken by organizations such as private businesses, governments or by family members.

[2] Counterfactuals are not necessarily contrary to fact. They are not directly observed.

[3] These models have their origins in mathematical psychology [Thurstone (1927), Bock and Jones (1968)].

Useful surveys of the econometrics of these models include Maddala (1983), Amemiya (1985), Ruud (2000) and Wooldridge (2002).

Microstructural models can be used to construct a wide variety of policy counterfactuals. They can also be used to evaluate existing policies and to forecast the effects of new policies. Embedded in general equilibrium models, they can also be used to evaluate the effects of changing the scale of existing policies or introducing new policies with substantial coverage [see, e.g., Heckman, Lochner and Taber (1998), Blundell et al. (2004)].

Applications of these models are legion. So are criticisms of this approach. Critics grant the interpretability of the economic frameworks and the parameters derived from them. At the same time, they question the strong functional form, exogeneity, support and exclusion assumptions used in classical versions of this literature, and the lack of robustness of empirical results obtained from them [see Goldberger (1983), Arabmazar and Schmidt (1982), Ruud (1981), Lewis (1986), Angrist and Krueger (1999) among many others].[4] While there have been substantial theoretical advances in weakening the parametric structure used to secure identification of the models used in the early work [see, e.g., Manski (1975, 1988), Heckman and Honoré (1990), Matzkin (1992, 1993, 1994, 2003, 2007), Powell (1994), and Chen (1999)], progress in implementing these procedures in practical empirical problems has been slow and empirical applications of semi-parametric methods have been plagued by issues of sensitivity of estimates to choices of smoothing parameters, trimming parameters, bandwidths and the like [see Chapter 74 (Ichimura and Todd); Chapter 76 (Chen); and Chapter 77 (Carrasco, Florens and Renault) of this Handbook]. The arbitrariness in the choice of parametric models that motivates recent work in semiparametric and nonparametric econometrics has its counterpart in the choice of nonparametric and semiparametric estimation parameters. Often, parametric structural models are computationally cumbersome [see Geweke and Keane (2001)] and identification in dynamic recursive models is often difficult to establish [see Rust (1994), Magnac and Thesmar (2002)], although progress has been made [see Taber (2001), Aguirregabiria (2004), Heckman and Navarro (2007)]. The curse of dimensionality and the complexity of computational methods plague high dimensional parametric models and nonparametric models alike. These considerations motivate pursuit of simpler, more transparent and more easily computed and replicable methods for analyzing economic data and for econometric policy analysis.

The recent literature on treatment effects emphasizes nonparametric identification of certain parameters, robustness, and simplicity (or transparency of identification) as its

[4] We note that most of this literature is based on Monte Carlo analysis or worst case analyses on artificial samples. The empirical evidence on nonrobustness of conventional parametric models is mixed. [See Heckman (2001)]. It remains to be established on a systematic basis that classical normality assumptions invariably produce biased estimates. The evidence in Heckman and Sedlacek (1985) and Blundell, Reed and Stoker (2003) shows that normality is an accurate approximation to log earnings data in economic models of self-selection. The analysis of Todd (1996) shows that parametric probit analysis is accurate for even extreme departures from normality.

main goals. In addition, it recognizes certain forms of heterogeneity in responses to treatment. These are major advances over the traditional structural literature. By focusing on one parameter instead of many, this approach can identify that parameter under weaker conditions than are required for structural parameters that answer many questions. At the same time, this literature is often unclear in stating what economic question the estimated parameters answer. Simplicity in estimation is often accompanied by obscurity in interpretation. The literature also ignores the problems of applying estimated "effects" to new environments or estimating the "effects" of new programs never previously implemented. A new language of counterfactuals and causality has been created. This chapter exposits the treatment effect models and relates them to more explicitly formulated structural econometric models.

Estimators for "causal effects" in the recent treatment effect literature make implicit behavioral assumptions that are rarely exposited. Many papers in the modern treatment effect literature, especially those advocating instrumental variables or natural experiments, proceed by picking an instrument or a natural experiment and defining the parameter of interest as the estimand corresponding to the instrument.[5] Economists using matching make the strong implicit assumption that the information acted on by the agents being studied is as good as that available to the analyst-economist. The literature is often unclear as to what variables to include in conditioning sets and what variables to exclude and the conditions under which an estimator identifies an economically interesting parameter.

The goal of this chapter and Chapter 71 of this Handbook is to integrate the treatment effect literature with the literature on micro-structural econometrics based on index models and latent variable models to create an economically interpretable econometric framework for policy evaluation and cost-benefit analysis that possesses the best features of the modern treatment effect literature: a clear statement of conditions required to secure identification, as well as robustness and transparency. "Causal effects" or "treatment parameters" are defined in terms of economically interpretable parameters. Counterfactuals and causality are interpreted within the framework of choice-theoretic economic models.

1.1. The relationship of this chapter to the literature on causal inference in statistics

The existing literature on "causal inference" in statistics is the source of inspiration for the recent econometric treatment effect literature and we examine it in detail. The literature in statistics on causal inference confuses three distinct problems that are carefully distinguished in this chapter and in the literature in economics:

[5] An estimand is the parameter defined by the estimator. It is the large sample limit of the estimator, assuming it exists.

Table 1
Three distinct tasks arising in the analysis of causal models

Task	Description	Requirements
1	Defining the set of hypotheticals or counterfactuals	A scientific theory
2	Identifying parameters (causal or otherwise) from hypothetical population data	Mathematical analysis of point or set identification
3	Identifying parameters from real data	Estimation and testing theory

- Definitions of counterfactuals.
- Identification of causal models from idealized data of population distributions (infinite samples without any sampling variation). The hypothetical populations may be subject to selection bias, attrition and the like. However, all issues of sampling variability are irrelevant for this problem.
- Identification of causal models from actual data, where sampling variability is an issue. This analysis recognizes the difference between empirical distributions based on sampled data and population distributions generating the data.

Table 1 delineates the three distinct problems.

The first problem is a matter of science, logic and imagination. It is also partly a matter of convention. A model of counterfactuals is more widely accepted, the more widely accepted are its ingredients:

- the rules used to derive a model including whether or not the rules of logic and mathematics are followed;
- its agreement with other theories; and
- its agreement with the evidence.

Models are descriptions of hypothetical worlds obtained by varying – hypothetically – the factors determining outcomes. Models are not empirical statements or descriptions of actual worlds. However, they are often used to make predictions about actual worlds.

The second problem is one of inference in very large samples. Can one recover counterfactuals (or means or distributions of counterfactuals) from data that are free of any sampling variation problems? This is the identification problem. Two distinct issues that are central to policy evaluation are (1) solving the problem of selection bias and (2) constructing counterfactual states from large samples of data.

The third problem is one of inference in practice. Can one recover a given model or the desired counterfactual from a given set of data? Solutions to this problem entail issues of inference and testing in real world samples. This is the problem most familiar to statisticians and empirical social scientists.[6] The boundary between problems two and three is permeable depending on how "the data" are defined.

This chapter focuses on the first two problems. Many applied economists would be unwilling to stop at step 2 and would seek estimators with desirable small sample properties. For a valuable guide to methods of estimation, we direct readers to Chapter 74 (Ichimura and Todd) of this Handbook.

Some of the controversy surrounding construction of counterfactuals and causal models is partly a consequence of analysts being unclear about these three distinct problems and often confusing them. Particular methods of estimation (e.g., matching or instrumental variable estimation) have become associated with "causal inference" and even the definition of certain "causal parameters" because issues of definition, identification and estimation have been confused in the recent literature.

The econometric approach to policy evaluation separates these problems and emphasizes the conditional nature of causal knowledge. Human knowledge advances by developing counterfactuals and theoretical models and testing them against data. The models used are inevitably provisional and conditional on *a priori* assumptions.[7] Blind empiricism leads nowhere. Economists have economic theory to draw on but recent developments in the econometric treatment effect literature often ignore it.

Current widely used "causal models" in epidemiology and statistics are incomplete guides to interpreting data or for suggesting estimators for particular problems. Rooted in biostatistics, they are motivated by the experiment as an ideal. They do not clearly specify the mechanisms determining how hypothetical counterfactuals are realized or how hypothetical interventions are implemented except to compare "randomized" with "nonrandomized" interventions. They focus only on outcomes, leaving the model for selecting outcomes only implicitly specified. The construction of counterfactual outcomes is based on appeals to intuition and not on formal models. Extreme versions of this approach deny causal status to any intervention that cannot in principle be implemented by a practical, real world experiment.

Because the mechanisms determining outcome selection are not modeled in the statistical approach, the metaphor of "random selection" is often adopted. This emphasis

[6] Identification in small samples requires establishing the sampling distribution of estimators, and adopting bias as the criterion for identifiability. This approach is conventional in classical statistics but has fallen out of favor in semiparametric and nonparametric econometrics [see, e.g., Manski (2003)].

[7] See Quine (1951). Thus to quote Quine, "The totality of our so-called knowledge or beliefs, from the most casual matters of geography or history to the profoundest laws of atomic physics ... is a man made fabric which impinges on experience only at the edges ... total science is like a field of force whose boundary conditions are experience ... A conflict with experience on the periphery occasions readjustments in the interior of the field. Reevaluation of some statements require reevaluation of others, because of their logical interconnections ... But the total field is so underdetermined by its boundary conditions, experience, that there is much latitude of choice as to what statements to re-evaluate in the light of any single contrary experience." [Quine (1951)]. We thank Steve Durlauf for suggesting this quote which suggests the awareness of the conditional nature of all knowledge, including causal knowledge, by a leading philosopher.

on randomization – or its surrogates like matching – rules out a variety of alternative channels of identification of counterfactuals from population or sample data. This emphasis has practical consequences because of the conflation of step one with steps two and three in Table 1. Since randomization is used to define the parameters of interest, this practice sometimes leads to the confusion that randomization is the only way – or at least the best way – to identify causal parameters from real data. In truth, this is not always so, as we show in this chapter.

One reason why epidemiological and statistical models are incomplete is that they do not specify the sources of randomness generating variability among agents, i.e., they do not specify why observationally identical people make different choices and have different outcomes given the same choice. They do not distinguish what is in the agent's information set from what is in the observing statistician's information set, although the distinction is fundamental in justifying the properties of any estimator for solving selection and evaluation problems. They do not distinguish uncertainty from the point of view of the agent whose behavior is being analyzed from variability as analyzed by the observing economist.

They are also incomplete because they are recursive. They do not allow for simultaneity in choices of outcomes of treatment that are at the heart of game theory and models of social interactions [see, e.g., Brock and Durlauf (2001), Tamer (2003)].

Economists since Haavelmo (1943, 1944) have recognized the value of precise models for constructing counterfactuals, for answering "causal" questions and addressing more general policy evaluation questions. The econometric framework is explicit about how models of counterfactuals are generated, the sources of the interventions (the rules of assigning "treatment"), and the sources of unobservables in treatment allocations and outcomes and their relationship. Rather than leaving the rules governing selection of treatment implicit, the econometric approach uses relationships between the unobservables in outcome and selection mechanisms to identify causal models from data and to clarify the nature of identifying assumptions.

The goal of the econometric literature, like the goal of all science, is to model phenomena at a deeper level, to understand the causes producing the effects so that one can use empirical versions of the models to forecast the effects of interventions never previously experienced, to calculate a variety of policy counterfactuals, and to use economic theory to guide the choices of estimators and the interpretation of the evidence. These activities require development of a more elaborate theory than is envisioned in the current literature on causal inference in epidemiology and statistics.

The recent literature sometimes contrasts structural and causal models.[8] The contrast is not sharp because the term "structural model" is often not precisely defined. There are multiple meanings for this term, which we clarify in this chapter. The essential contrast between causal models and explicit economic models as currently formulated is in the range of questions that they are designed to answer. Causal models as formulated

[8] See, e.g., Angrist and Imbens (1995) and Angrist, Imbens and Rubin (1996).

in statistics and in the econometric treatment effect literature are typically black-box devices designed to investigate the impact of "treatments" – which are often complex packages of interventions – on some observed set of outcomes in a given environment. Unbundling the components of complex treatments is rarely done. Explicit economic models go into the black box to explore the mechanism(s) producing the effects. In the terminology of Holland (1986), the distinction is between understanding the "effects of causes" (the goal of the treatment effect literature) and understanding the "causes of effects" (the goal of the literature building explicit economic models).

By focusing on one narrow black-box question, the treatment effect and natural experiment literatures can avoid many of the problems confronted in the econometrics literature that builds explicit economic models. This is its great virtue. At the same time, it produces parameters that are more limited in application. The parameters defined by instruments or "natural experiments" are often hard to interpret within any economic model. Without further assumptions, these parameters do not lend themselves to extrapolation out of sample or to accurate forecasts of impacts of other policies besides the ones being empirically investigated. By not being explicit about the contents of the blackbox (understanding the causes of effects), it ties its hands in using information about basic behavioral parameters obtained from other studies, as well as economic intuition to supplement available information in the data in hand. It lacks the ability to provide explanations for estimated "effects" grounded in economics or to conduct welfare economics. When the components of treatments vary across studies, knowledge does not cumulate across treatment effect studies whereas it accumulates across studies estimating common behavioral or technological parameters [see, e.g., the studies of labor supply in Killingsworth (1985), or the parameters of labor demand in Hamermesh (1993), or basic preference and income variability parameters as in Browning, Hansen and Heckman (1999)] which use explicit economic models to collate and synthesize evidence across apparently disparate studies. When the treatment effect literature is modified to address such problems, it becomes a nonparametric version of the literature that builds explicit economic models.

1.2. The plan of this chapter and our other contributions

Our contribution to this Handbook is presented in three chapters. Part I, Section 2, discusses core policy evaluation questions as a backdrop against which to compare alternative approaches to causal inference. A notation is developed and both individual level and population level causal effects are defined. Uncertainty at the individual level is introduced to account for one source of variation across agents in terms of outcomes and choices. We consider alternative criteria used to evaluate policies. We consider a wide variety of parameters of interest that arise in cost benefit analyses and more general analyses of the distribution of policy impacts. This section sets the stage for the rest of the chapter by defining the objects of interest that we study in this chapter.

Section 3 presents some prototypical econometric models that serve as benchmarks and reference points for the discussion throughout all three parts of this chapter. We review the normal theory model because it is familiar and still widely used and is the point of departure for both the treatment effect and "structural" literatures.

Section 4 defines and discusses causal models, treatment effects, structural models and policy invariant parameters, and analyzes both subjective and objective evaluations of interventions. We also discuss the Neyman (1923)–Rubin (1978) model of causal effects that is influential in statistics and epidemiology.

We review the conventional "structural" (i.e., explicit economic modelling) approach based on latent variable models and recent nonparametric extensions. We define "structural" models and policy-invariant structural parameters using the framework of Hurwicz (1962). A definition of causal models with simultaneous outcomes is presented. The Neyman (1923)–Rubin (1978) model advocated in statistics is compared to explicit econometric models. We discuss how econometric models can be used to construct counterfactuals and answer the range of policy questions discussed in Section 2. We discuss the strengths and limitations of this approach and review recent semiparametric advances in this literature that are relevant to constructing robust policy counterfactuals.

We introduce Marschak's Maxim, implicitly presented in his seminal 1953 paper on policy evaluation.[9] The goal of explicitly formulated econometric models is to identify *policy-invariant* or *intervention-invariant* parameters that can be used to answer classes of policy evaluation questions [see Marschak (1953), Hurwicz (1962), Hansen and Sargent (1980), Lucas and Sargent (1981)].[10] Policy invariance is defined for a class of policy interventions. Policy invariant economic parameters may or may not be interpretable economic parameters. The treatment-effect literature also seeks to identify intervention-invariant parameters for a class of interventions. In this sense the structural and treatment effect literatures share common objectives.

Marschak implicitly invoked a decision-theoretic approach to policy evaluation in noting that for many decisions (policy problems), only *combinations* of explicit economic parameters are required – no single economic parameter need be identified. Hurwicz (1962) refined this idea by noting that to be useful in forecasting policy, the combinations must be invariant to policy variation with respect to the policies being evaluated.

Following Marschak's Maxim, we postulate specific economic questions that are interesting to address and ask what *combinations* of underlying economic parameters or functionals are required to answer them. Answering one question well usually requires fewer assumptions, and places less demands on the data, than answering a wide array of questions – the original goal of structural econometrics. Our approach differs from the approach commonly pursued in the treatment effect and natural experiment literatures

[9] Marschak was a member of the Cowles Commission that developed the first econometric models of policy evaluation. The Cowles Commission approached the policy evaluation problem by constructing models of the economy and then using them to forecast and evaluate policies. This approach is still used today.

[10] The terms "policy invariant" and "structural" are defined precisely in Section 4.8.

by defining a parameter of interest in terms of what *economic question* it answers rather than as the estimand of a favored estimator or instrument.

Section 5 discusses the problem of identification, i.e., the problem of determining models from data. This is task 2 in Table 1. Section 6 exposits identification conditions for the normal model as presented in Section 3.3. It also discusses the recent literature that generalizes the normal model to address concerns raised about nonrobustness and functional form dependence yet preserves the benefits of a structural approach.

Part II of our contribution (Chapter 71 of this Handbook) extends the index function framework, which underlies the modern theory of microeconometrics, to unify the literature on instrumental variables, regression discontinuity methods, matching, control functions and more general selection estimators. Our approach is explicitly nonparametric. We present identifying conditions for each estimator relative to a well-defined set of economic parameters. We initially focus on a two outcome model and then present results for models with multiple outcomes. Bounds are developed for models that are not point identified. We show how these models can be used to address a range of policy problems. We also discuss randomized social experiments. Randomization is an instrumental variable. The focus of Chapter 71 is on mean treatment effects.

Part III, coauthored by Abbring and Heckman (Chapter 72 of this Handbook), considers recent analyses for identifying the distributions of treatment effects. It also discusses new issues that arise in dynamic frameworks when agents are making choices under various information sets that are revealed over time. This takes us into the analysis of dynamic discrete choice models and models for dynamic treatment effects. This section also discusses recent micro-based general equilibrium evaluation frameworks and deals with the important problems raised by social interactions among agents in both market and nonmarket settings.

2. Economic policy evaluation questions and criteria of interest

This section first presents the three central policy evaluation questions discussed in this chapter. We then introduce our notation and define individual level treatment effects. The evaluation problem is discussed in general terms. Population level mean treatment parameters are then defined. Criteria for evaluating distributions of outcomes are presented along with option values. We explicitly account for private and social uncertainty. We discuss, in general terms, the type of data needed to construct the evaluation criteria. Throughout this section we present concrete examples of general points.

2.1. Policy evaluation problems considered in this chapter

Three broad classes of policy evaluation questions are considered in this chapter. Policy evaluation question one is:

P-1 *Evaluating the impact of historical interventions on outcomes including their impact in terms of welfare.*

By historical, we mean interventions actually experienced and documented. A variety of outcomes and welfare criteria might be used to form these evaluations. It is useful to distinguish objective or public outcomes from "subjective" outcomes. Objective outcomes are intrinsically *ex post* in nature. Subjective outcomes can be *ex ante* or *ex post*. Thus the outcome of a medical trial produces both a cure rate and the pain and suffering of the patient. *Ex ante* expected pain and suffering may be different from *ex post* pain and suffering. Agents may also have *ex ante* evaluations of the objective outcomes that may differ from their *ex post* evaluations. By impact, we mean constructing either individual level or population level counterfactuals and their valuations. By welfare, we mean the valuations of the outcomes obtained from the intervention of the agents being analyzed or some other party (e.g., the parents of the agent or "society" at large). The welfare evaluations may be *ex ante* or *ex post*.

P-1 is the problem of *internal validity*. It is the problem of identifying a given treatment parameter or a set of treatment parameters in a given environment.[11] Focusing exclusively on objective outcomes, this is the problem addressed in the epidemiological and statistical literature on causal inference. A drug trial for a particular patient population is a prototypical problem in the literature. The econometric approach emphasizes valuation of the objective outcome of the trial (e.g., health status) as well as subjective evaluation of outcomes (patient's welfare), and the latter may be *ex post* or *ex ante*.

Most policy evaluation is designed with an eye toward the future and towards informing decisions about new policies and application of old policies to new environments. We distinguish a second task of policy analysis.

P-2 *Forecasting the impacts (constructing counterfactual states) of interventions implemented in one environment in other environments, including their impacts in terms of welfare.*

Included in these interventions are policies described by generic characteristics (e.g., tax or benefit rates, etc.) that are applied to different groups of people or in different time periods from those studied in implementations of the policies on which data are available. This is the problem of *external validity*: taking a treatment parameter or a set of parameters estimated in one environment to another environment.[12] The environment includes the characteristics of individuals and of the treatments.

Finally, the most ambitious problem is forecasting the effect of a new policy, never previously experienced.

P-3 *Forecasting the impacts of interventions (constructing counterfactual states associated with interventions) never historically experienced to various environments, including their impacts in terms of welfare.*

[11] The terminology originates with Campbell and Stanley (1963).

[12] Again, this term is due to Campbell and Stanley (1963).

This problem requires that we use past history to forecast the consequences of new policies. It is a fundamental problem in knowledge. Knight (1921, p. 313) succinctly states the problem:

"The existence of a problem in knowledge depends on the future being different from the past, while the possibility of a solution of the problem depends on the future being like the past."

P-3 is a problem that economic policy analysts have to solve daily. Appendix A shows the value of precisely formulated economic models in addressing problems P-2 and P-3. We now present a framework within which analysts can address these problems in a systematic fashion. It is also a framework that can be used for causal inference.

2.2. *Notation and definition of individual level treatment effects*[13]

To evaluate is to value and to compare values among possible outcomes. These are two distinct tasks, which we distinguish in this chapter. We define outcomes corresponding to state (policy, treatment) s for agent ω as $Y(s, \omega)$, $\omega \in \Omega$. The agent can be a household, a firm, or a country. One can think of Ω as a universe of agents with element ω.[14] The ω encompasses all features of agents that affect Y outcomes. $Y(\cdot, \cdot)$ may be generated from a scientific or economic theory. It may be vector valued. The components of $Y(s, \omega)$ may be discrete, continuous or mixed discrete-continuous random variables.

The $Y(s, \omega)$ are outcomes realized after treatments are chosen. In advance of treatment, agents may not know the $Y(s, \omega)$ but may make forecasts about them. These forecasts may influence their decisions to participate in the program or may influence the agents who make decisions about whether or not an individual participates in the program. Selection into the program based on actual or anticipated components of outcomes gives rise to the selection problem in the evaluation literature.

Let $\mathcal{S}$ be the set of possible treatments with elements denoted by s. For simplicity of exposition, we assume that this set is the same for all ω.[15] For each ω, we obtain a collection of possible outcomes given by $\{Y(s, \omega)\}_{s \in \mathcal{S}}$. The set $\mathcal{S}$ may be finite (e.g., there may be J states), countable, or may be defined on the continuum (e.g., $\mathcal{S} = [0, 1]$). For example, if $\mathcal{S} = \{0, 1\}$, there are two treatments, one of which may be a no-treatment state (e.g., $Y(0, \omega)$ is the outcome for an agent ω not getting a treatment like a drug, schooling or access to a new technology, while $Y(1, \omega)$ is the outcome in treatment

[13] Comments from Jaap Abbring were especially helpful in revising this section.

[14] Assume that $\Omega = [0, 1]$. We define random vectors $Y(\omega)$ for $\omega \in \Omega$. We can break out observed and unobserved values $X(\omega)$ and $U(\omega)$, for example.

[15] At the cost of more cumbersome notation, the $\mathcal{S}$ sets can be ω specific. This creates some measure-theoretic problems, and we do not take this more general approach in this chapter. Abbring and Heckman (Chapter 72) relax this assumption when they consider dynamic models and allow for person- and time-period-specific information sets.

state 1 for agent ω getting the drug, schooling or access). A two treatment environment receives the most attention in the theoretical literature, but the multiple treatment environment is the one most frequently encountered in practice.

Each "state" (treatment) may consist of a compound of subcomponent states. In this case, one can define s itself as a vector (e.g., $s = (s_1, s_2, \dots, s_K)$ for K components) corresponding to the different components that comprise treatment. Thus a job training program typically consists of a package of treatments. We might be interested in the package of one (or more) of its components. Thus s_1 may be months of vocational education, s_2 the quality of training and so forth.

The outcomes may be time subscripted as well, $Y_t(s, \omega)$ corresponding to outcomes of treatment measured at different times. The index set for t may be the integers, corresponding to discrete time, or an interval, corresponding to continuous time. In principle, one could index $\mathcal{S}$ by t, which may be defined on the integers, corresponding to discrete time, or an interval corresponding to continuous time. The $Y_t(s, \omega)$ are realized or *ex post* (after treatment) outcomes. When choosing treatment, these values may not be known. Gill and Robins (2001), Abbring and Van den Berg (2003), Abbring and Heckman (2007, Chapter 72), Lechner (2004) and Heckman and Navarro (2007) develop models for dynamic counterfactuals, where time-subscripted and ω-subscripted $\mathcal{S}$ arise as information accrues.

Under this assumption, the **individual treatment effect** for agent ω comparing objective outcomes of treatment s with objective outcomes of treatment s' is

$$Y(s, \omega) - Y(s', \omega), \quad s \neq s', \tag{2.1}$$

where we pick two elements $s, s' \in \mathcal{S}$. This is also called an **individual level causal effect**. This may be a nondegenerate random variable or a degenerate random variable. The causal effect is the Marshallian (1890) *ceteris paribus* change of outcomes for an agent across states s and s'. Only s and s' are varied.

Other comparisons are of interest in assessing a program. Economists are interested in the welfare of participants as well as the objective outcomes [see Heckman and Smith (1998)]. Although statisticians reason in terms of assignment mechanisms, economists recognize that agent preferences often govern actual choices. Comparisons across outcomes can be made in terms of utilities (personal, $R(Y(s, \omega), \omega)$, or in terms of planner preferences, R_G, or both types of comparisons might be made for the same outcome and their agreement or conflict evaluated). To simplify the notation, and at the same time allow for more general possibilities for arguments of the valuation function, we usually write $R(Y(s, \omega), \omega)$ as $R(s, \omega)$, suppressing the explicit dependence of R on $Y(s, \omega)$. In this notation, one can ask if $R(s, \omega) > R(s', \omega)$ or not (is the agent better off as a result of treatment s compared to treatment s'?). The difference in subjective outcomes is $[R(s, \omega) - R(s', \omega)]$, and is another possible treatment effect. Holding ω fixed holds all features of the agent fixed except the treatment assigned, s. Since the units of $R(s, \omega)$ are arbitrary, one could instead record for each s and ω an indicator if the outcome in s is greater or less than the outcome in s', i.e. $R(s, \omega) > R(s', \omega)$ or not. This is also a type of treatment effect.

These definitions of treatment effects embody Marshall's (1890) notion of *ceteris paribus* comparisons but now in utility space. A central feature of the econometric approach to program evaluation is the evaluation of subjective evaluations as perceived by decision makers and not just the objective evaluations focused on by statisticians.

The term "treatment" is used in multiple ways in this literature and this ambiguity is sometimes a source of confusion. In its most common usage, a treatment assignment mechanism is a rule $\tau : \Omega \to \mathcal{S}$ which assigns treatment to each ω. The consequences of the assignment are the outcomes $Y(s, \omega)$, $s \in \mathcal{S}$, $\omega \in \Omega$. The collection of these possible assignment rules is $\mathcal{T}$ where $\tau \in \mathcal{T}$. There are two aspects of a policy under this definition. The policy selects who gets what. More precisely, it selects individuals $\omega \in \Omega$ and specifies the treatment $s \in \mathcal{S}$ received.

In this chapter, we offer a more nuanced definition of treatment assignment that explicitly recognizes the element of choice by agent ω in producing the treatment assignment rule. Treatment can include participation in activities such as schooling, training, adoption of a particular technology, and the like. Participation in treatment is usually a choice made by agents. Under a more comprehensive definition of treatment, agents are assigned incentives like taxes, subsidies, endowments and eligibility that affect their choices, but the agent chooses the treatment selected. Agent preferences, program delivery systems, aggregate production technologies, market structures, and the like might all affect the choice of treatment. The treatment choice mechanism may involve multiple actors and multiple decisions that result in an assignment of ω to s. For example, s can be schooling while $Y(s, \omega)$ is earnings given schooling for agent ω. A policy may be a set of payments that encourage schooling, as in the Progressa program in Mexico, and the treatment in that case is choice of schooling with its consequences for earnings.

Our description of treatment assignment recognizes individual choices and constraints and is more suitable for policy evaluation by economists. We specify assignment rules $a \in \mathcal{A}$ which map individuals $\omega \in \Omega$ into constraints (benefits) $b \in \mathcal{B}$ under different mechanisms. In this notation, a constraint assignment mechanism a is a map

$$a : \Omega \to \mathcal{B}$$

defined over the space of agents. The constraints may include endowments, eligibility, taxes, subsidies and the like that affect agent choices of treatment.[16] The map a defines the rule used to assign $b \in \mathcal{B}$. It can include deterministic rules which give schedules mapping ω into $\mathcal{B}$, such as tax schedules or eligibility schedules. It can also include random assignment mechanisms that assign ω to an element of $\mathcal{B}$. Random assignment

[16] Elements of b can be parameters of tax and benefit schedules that affect individual incentives. A more general setup is possible where ω-specific schedules are assigned to person ω. The cost of this generality is more complicated notation. For simplicity we confine attention to a fixed – but possibly very large – set of parameters defined for all agents.

mechanisms add additional elements of randomness to the environment.[17] Abusing notation, when randomization is used, we will redefine Ω to include this new source of randomness.

Some policies may have the same overall effect on the aggregate distribution of b, but may treat given individuals differently. Under an anonymity postulate, some would judge such policies as equivalent in terms of the constraints (benefits) offered, even though associated outcomes for individuals may be different. Another definition of equivalent policies is in terms of the distribution of aggregate outcomes associated with the treatments. In this chapter, we characterize policies at the individual level, recognizing that sets of $\mathcal{A}$ that are characterized by some aggregate distribution over elements of $b \in \mathcal{B}$ may be what others mean by a policy.[18]

Given $b \in \mathcal{B}$ allocated by constraint assignment mechanism $a \in \mathcal{A}$, agents pick treatments. We define treatment assignment mechanism $\tau : \Omega \times \mathcal{A} \times \mathcal{B} \to \mathcal{S}$ as a map taking agent $\omega \in \Omega$ facing constraints $b \in \mathcal{B}$ assigned by mechanism $a \in \mathcal{A}$ into a treatment $s \in \mathcal{S}$.[19] In settings with choice, τ is the choice rule used by agents where $\tau \in \mathcal{T}$, a set of possible choice rules. It is conventional to assume a unique $\tau \in \mathcal{T}$ is selected by the relevant decision makers, although that is not required in our definition. A policy regime $p \in \mathcal{P}$ is a pair $(a, \tau) \in \mathcal{A} \times \mathcal{T}$ that maps agents denoted by ω into elements of s. In this notation, $\mathcal{P} = \mathcal{A} \times \mathcal{T}$.

Incorporating choice into the analysis of treatment effects is an essential and distinctive ingredient of the econometric approach to the evaluation of social programs. The traditional treatment-control analysis in statistics equates mechanisms a and τ. An assignment in that literature is an assignment to treatment, not an assignment of incentives and eligibility for treatment with the agent making treatment choices. In this notation, the traditional approach has only one assignment mechanism and treats noncompliance with it as a problem rather than as a source of information on agent preferences, as in the econometric approach.[20]

Policy invariance is a key assumption for the study of policy evaluation. It allows analysts to characterize outcomes without specifying how those outcomes are obtained. In our notation, policy invariance has two aspects. The first aspect is that, for a given $b \in \mathcal{B}$ (incentive schedule), the mechanism $a \in \mathcal{A}$ by which ω is assigned a b (e.g., random assignment, coercion at the point of a gun, etc.) and the incentive $b \in \mathcal{B}$ are assumed to be irrelevant for the values of realized outcomes for each s that is selected. Second, for a given s for agent ω, the mechanism τ by which s is assigned to the agent

[17] Formally, the probability system for the model without randomization is $(\Omega, \sigma(\Omega), \mathcal{F})$ where Ω is the probability space, $\sigma(\Omega)$ is the σ-algebra associated with Ω and $\mathcal{F}$ is the measure on the space. When we account for randomization we need to extend Ω to $\Omega' = \Omega \times \Psi$, where Ψ is the new probability space induced by the randomization, and we define a system $(\Omega', \sigma(\Omega'), \mathcal{F}')$.

[18] Anonymity is a central assumption in the modern income inequality literature. See Foster and Sen (1997).

[19] Note that including $\mathcal{B}$ in the domain of definition of τ is redundant since the map $a : \Omega \to B$ selects an element $b \in \mathcal{B}$. We make b explicit to remind the reader that agents are making choices under constraints.

[20] Thus, under full compliance, $a : \Omega \to \mathcal{S}$ and $a = \tau$, where $\mathcal{B} = \mathcal{S}$.

under assignment mechanism $a \in \mathcal{A}$ is irrelevant for the values assumed by realized outcomes. Both assumptions define what we mean by policy invariance.

Policy invariance allows us to describe outcomes by $Y(s, \omega)$ and ignore features of the policy and choice environment in defining outcomes. If we have to account for the effects of incentives and assignment mechanisms on outcomes, we must work with $Y(s, \omega, a, b, \tau)$ instead of $Y(s, \omega)$. The more complex description is the outcome associated with treatment state s for person ω, assigned incentive package b by mechanism a which are arguments of assignment rule τ. The following policy invariance assumptions justify collapsing these arguments of $Y(\cdot)$ down to $Y(s, \omega)$.

(PI-1) *For any two constraint assignment mechanisms* $a, a' \in \mathcal{A}$ *and incentives* $b, b' \in \mathcal{B}$, *with* $a(\omega) = b$ *and* $a'(\omega) = b'$, *and for all* $\omega \in \Omega$, $Y(s, \omega, a, b, \tau) = Y(s, \omega, a', b', \tau)$, *for all* $s \in \mathcal{S}_{\tau(a,b)}(\omega) \cap \mathcal{S}_{\tau(a',b')}(\omega)$ *for assignment rule* τ *where* $\mathcal{S}_{\tau(a,b)}(\omega)$ *is the image set for* $\tau(a, b)$. *For simplicity we assume* $\mathcal{S}_{\tau(a,b)}(\omega) = \mathcal{S}_{\tau(a,b)}$ *for all* $\omega \in \Omega$.[21]

This assumption says that for the same treatment s and agent ω, different constraint assignment mechanisms a and a' and associated constraint assignments b and b' produce the same outcome. For example, this assumption rules out the possibility that the act of randomization or the act of pointing a gun at the agent to secure cooperation with planner intentions has an effect on outcomes, given that the agent ends up in s. (PI-1) is a strong assumption and we discuss evidence against it in Chapter 71.

A second invariance assumption invoked in the literature is that for a fixed a and b, the outcomes are the same independent of the treatment assignment mechanism:

(PI-2) *For each constraint assignment* $a \in \mathcal{A}$, $b \in \mathcal{B}$ *and all* $\omega \in \Omega$, $Y(s, \omega, a, b, \tau) = Y(s, \omega, a, b, \tau')$ *for all* τ *and* $\tau' \in \mathcal{T}$ *with* $s \in \mathcal{S}_{\tau(a,b)} \cap \mathcal{S}_{\tau'(a,b)}$, *where* $\mathcal{S}_{\tau(a,b)}$ *is the image set of* τ *for a given pair* (a, b).

Again, we exclude the possibility of ω-specific image sets $\mathcal{S}_{\tau(a,b)}$ and $\mathcal{S}_{\tau'(a,b)}$. In principle, not all agents ω may be able to attain s for all (a, b) pairs. We invoke this assumption to simplify the analysis and to avoid excess notational and mathematical complexity. Assumption (PI-2) states that the actual mechanism used to assign treatment does not affect the outcomes. It rules out, among other things, social interactions and general equilibrium effects. Abbring and Heckman (Chapter 72) discuss evidence against this assumption.

These invariance postulates are best discussed in the context of specific economic models. We restate these conditions, which are closely related to the invariance conditions of Hurwicz (1962), when we discuss his treatment of policy invariance in Section 4.6 below, after we have specific economic models in hand.

[21] This final assumption can be easily relaxed, but at a major notational cost.

If treatment effects based on subjective evaluations are also considered, we need to broaden invariance assumptions (PI-1) and (PI-2) to produce invariance in rewards for certain policies and assignment mechanisms. It would be unreasonable to claim that utilities $R(\cdot)$ do not respond to incentives. Suppose, instead, that we examine subsets of constraint assignment mechanisms $a \in \mathcal{A}$ that give the same incentives (elements $b \in \mathcal{B}$) to agents, but are conferred by different delivery systems, a. For each $\omega \in \Omega$, define the set of mechanisms delivering the same incentive or constraint b as $\mathcal{A}_b(\omega)$:

$$\mathcal{A}_b(\omega) = \{a \mid a \in \mathcal{A}, a(\omega) = b\}, \quad \omega \in \Omega.$$

We allow for the possibility that the set of delivery mechanisms that deliver b may vary among the ω. Let $R(s, \omega, a, b, \tau)$ represent the reward to agent ω from a treatment s with incentive b allocated by mechanism a with an assignment to treatment mechanism τ. To account for invariance with respect to the delivery system, we assume (PI-1) and additional conditions:

(PI-3) *For any two constraint assignment mechanisms* $a, a' \in \mathcal{A}$ *and incentives* $b, b' \in \mathcal{B}$ *with* $a(\omega) = b$ *and* $a'(\omega) = b'$, *and for all* $\omega \in \Omega$, $Y(s, \omega, a, b, \tau) = Y(s, \omega, a', b', \tau)$ *for all* $s \in \mathcal{S}_{\tau(a,b)}(\omega) \cap \mathcal{S}_{\tau(a',b')}(\omega)$ *for assignment rule* τ, *where* $\mathcal{S}_{\tau(a,b)}(\omega)$ *is the image set of* $\tau(a, b)$ *and for simplicity we assume that* $\mathcal{S}_{\tau(a,b)}(\omega) = \mathcal{S}_{\tau(a,b)}$ *for all* $\omega \in \Omega$. *In addition, for any mechanisms* $a, a' \in \mathcal{A}_b(\omega)$, *producing the same* $b \in \mathcal{B}$ *under the same conditions postulated in the preceding sentence, and for all* ω, $R(s, \omega, a, b, \tau) = R(s, \omega, a', b, \tau)$.

This assumption says, for example, that utilities are not affected by randomization or the mechanism of assignment of constraints. We present evidence against this assumption in Chapter 71.

Corresponding to (PI-2) we have a policy invariance assumption for the utilities with respect to the mechanism of assignment:

(PI-4) *For each pair* (a, b) *and all* $\omega \in \Omega$,

$$Y(s, \omega, a, b, \tau) = Y(s, \omega, a, b, \tau'),$$
$$R(s, \omega, a, b, \tau) = R(s, \omega, a, b, \tau')$$

for all $\tau, \tau' \in \mathcal{T}$ *and* $s \in \mathcal{S}_{\tau(a,b)} \cap \mathcal{S}_{\tau'(a,b)}$.

This assumption rules out general equilibrium effects, social externalities in consumption, etc. in both subjective and objective outcomes. Observe that it is possible to satisfy (PI-1) and (PI-2) but not (PI-3) and (PI-4). For example, randomization may affect subjective evaluations through its effect of adding uncertainty into the decision process but it may not affect objective valuations. We discuss this possibility in Chapter 71 and show that it is empirically important.[22]

[22] We do not develop the third possible case when the roles of R and Y are reversed so that R is invariant and Y is not.

2.2.1. More general criteria

One might compare outcomes in different sets that are ordered. Thus if $Y(s,\omega)$ is scalar income and we compare outcomes for $s \in \mathcal{S}_A$ with outcomes for $s' \in \mathcal{S}_B$, where $\mathcal{S}_A \cap \mathcal{S}_B = \emptyset$, then one might compare Y_{s_A} to Y_{s_B}, where

$$s_A = \operatorname{argmax}_{s\in\mathcal{S}_A}\{Y(s,\omega)\} \quad \text{and} \quad s_B = \operatorname{argmax}_{s\in\mathcal{S}_B}\{Y(s,\omega)\},$$

where we suppress the dependence of s_A and s_B on ω. This compares the best in one choice set with the best in the other.[23] Another contrast compares the best choice with the next best choice. To do so, define $s' = \operatorname{argmax}_{s\in\mathcal{S}}\{Y(s,\omega)\}$ and $\mathcal{S}_B = \mathcal{S} \setminus \{s'\}$ and define the treatment effect as $Y_{s'} - Y_{s_B}$. This is the comparison of the highest outcome over $\mathcal{S}$ with the next best outcome. In principle, many different individual level comparisons might be constructed, and they may be computed using personal preferences, $R(\omega)$, using the preferences of the planner, R_G, or using the preferences of the planner over the preferences of agents.

Social welfare theory constructs aggregates over Ω or nonempty, nonsingleton subsets of Ω [see Sen (1999)]. Let $s_p(\omega)$ denote the $s \in \mathcal{S}_p$ that ω receives under policy p. This is a shorthand notation for the element in $\mathcal{S}_\tau$ determined by the map $p = (a,\tau)$ assigned to agent ω under policy p. A comparison of two policy outcomes $\{s_p(\omega)\}_{\omega\in\Omega}$ and $\{s_{p'}(\omega)\}_{\omega\in\Omega}$, where $p \neq p'$ for some $\omega \in \Omega$, using the social welfare function defined over outcomes $R_G(\{Y(s,\omega),\omega\}_{\omega\in\Omega})$ can be expressed as

$$R_G\big(\{Y(s_p(\omega),\omega)\}_{\omega\in\Omega}\big) - R_G\big(\{Y(s_{p'}(\omega),\omega)\}_{\omega\in\Omega}\big).$$

A special case of this analysis is cost-benefit analysis where willingness to pay measures $W(s_p(\omega),\omega)$ are associated with each agent using some compensating or equivalent variation measure for general preferences. The cost-benefit comparison of two policies p and p' is

Cost Benefit:

$$\mathbf{CB}_{p,p'} = \int_\Omega W\big(Y(s_p(\omega),\omega)\big)\,\mathrm{d}\mu(\omega) - \int_\Omega W\big(Y(s_{p'}(\omega),\omega)\big)\,\mathrm{d}\mu(\omega),$$

where p, p' are two different policies and p' may correspond to a benchmark of no policy and $\mu(\omega)$ is the distribution of ω.[24] The Benthamite criterion replaces $W(Y(s(\omega),\omega))$ with $R(Y(s(\omega),\omega))$ in the preceding expressions and integrates utilities across agents.

Benthamite:

$$\mathbf{B}_{p,p'} = \int_\Omega R\big(Y(s_p(\omega),\omega)\big)\,\mathrm{d}\mu(\omega) - \int_\Omega R\big(Y(s_{p'}(\omega),\omega)\big)\,\mathrm{d}\mu(\omega).$$

[23] This analysis could be done for vector $Y(s,\omega)$ provided that $\{Y(s,\omega)\}_{s\in\mathcal{S}}$ is an ordered set.

[24] These willingness-to-pay measures are standard in the social welfare evaluation literature. See, e.g., Boadway and Bruce (1984).

We now discuss the problems that arise in constructing these and other evaluation criteria. This takes us into the problem of causal inference, the second problem delineated in Table 1. We are discussing inference in a population and not in a sample so no issues of sampling variability arise.

2.3. The evaluation problem

Operating purely within the domain of theory, we have assumed a well defined set of individuals $\omega \in \Omega$ and a universe of counterfactuals or hypotheticals for each agent $Y(s, \omega)$, $s \in \mathcal{S}$. Different policies $p \in \mathcal{P}$ give different incentives by assignment mechanism a to agents who are allocated to treatment by a rule $\tau \in \mathcal{T}$. In the absence of a theory, there are no well defined rules for constructing counterfactual or hypothetical states or constructing the assignment to treatment rules.[25] Economic theories provide algorithms for generating the universe of internally consistent, theory-consistent counterfactual states.

These hypothetical states are possible worlds. They are products of a purely mental activity. No empirical problem arises in constructing these theoretically possible worlds. Indeed, in forecasting new policies, or projecting the effects of old policies to new environments, some of the $Y(s, \omega)$ may have never been observed for anyone. Different theories produce different $Y(s, \omega)$ and different assignment mechanisms.

The evaluation problem, in contrast with the model construction problem, is an identification problem that arises in constructing the counterfactual states and treatment assignment rules produced by these abstract models using data. This is the second problem presented in Table 1.

This problem is not precisely stated until the data available to the analyst are precisely defined. Different subfields in economics assume access to different types of data. They also make different assumptions about the underlying models generating the counterfactuals and mechanisms for selecting which counterfactuals are actually observed.

For each policy regime, at any point in time we observe agent ω in some state but not in any of the other states. Thus we do not observe $Y(s', \omega)$ for agent ω if we observe $Y(s, \omega)$, $s \neq s'$. Let $D_p(s, \omega) = 1$ if we observe agent ω in state s under policy regime p. Keeping the policy regime p implicit simplifies the notation so henceforth we work with $D(s, \omega)$ recognizing that it should always be understood as implicitly p subscripted with a constraint assignment mechanism (a) and a treatment assignment mechanism (τ). In this notation, $D(s, \omega) = 1$ implies that $D(s', \omega) = 0$ for $s \neq s'$.

[25] Efforts like those of Lewis (1974) to define admissible counterfactual states without an articulated theory as "closest possible worlds" founder on the lack of any meaningful metric or topology to measure "closeness" among possible worlds.

We observe $Y(s, \omega)$ if $D(s, \omega) = 1$ but we do not observe $Y(s', \omega)$, for $s \neq s'$. We keep the p implicit. We can define observed $Y(\omega)$ for a finite or countable $\mathcal{S}$ as

$$Y(\omega) = \sum_{s \in \mathcal{S}} D(s, \omega) Y(s, \omega).^{26} \tag{2.2}$$

Without further assumptions, constructing an empirical counterpart to the individual level causal effect (2.1) is impossible from the data on $(Y(\omega), D(\omega))$, $\omega \in \Omega$. This formulation of the evaluation problem is known as Quandt's switching regression model [Quandt (1958, 1974)] and is attributed in statistics to Neyman (1923), Cox (1958) and Rubin (1978). A version of it is formulated in a linear equations context for a continuum of treatments by Haavelmo (1943). The Roy model (1951) is another version of this framework with two possible treatment outcomes ($\mathcal{S} = \{0, 1\}$) and a scalar outcome measure and a particular assignment mechanism τ which is that $D(1, \omega) = \mathbf{1}[Y(1, \omega) \geqslant Y(0, \omega)]$.[27] The mechanism of selection depends on the potential outcomes. Agents choose the sector with the highest income so the actual selection mechanism is not a randomization.

The evaluation literature in macroeconomics analyzes policies with universal coverage at a point in time (e.g., a tax policy or social security) so that $D(s, \omega) = 1$ for some s and all ω. It uses time series data to evaluate the impacts of policies in different periods and typically uses mean outcomes (or mean utilities as in a Benthamite criterion) to evaluate policies.[28]

Social experiments attempt to create treatment assignment rules so that $D(s, \omega)$ is random with respect to $\{Y(s, \omega)\}_{s \in \mathcal{S}}$ (i.e., so that receipt of treatment is independent of the outcome of treatment). When agents self-select into treatment, rather than are randomly assigned to it, in general the $D(s, \omega)$ are not independent of $\{Y(s, \omega)\}_{s \in \mathcal{S}}$. Such selection arises in the Roy model example. This selection rule creates the potential for self-selection bias in inference.

The problem of self selection is an essential aspect of the evaluation problem when data are generated by the choices of agents. The agents making choices may be different from the agents receiving treatment (e.g., parents making choices for children). Such choices can include compliance with the protocols of a social experiment as well as ordinary choices about outcomes that people make in everyday life. As a consequence of self-selection, the distribution of the $Y(s, \omega)$ observed are not the population distribution of randomly sampled $Y(s, \omega)$.

Observe that in the Roy model, the choice of treatment (including the decisions not to attrite from the program) is informative on the relative evaluation of $Y(s, \omega)$. This

26 In the general case, $Y(\omega) = \int_{\mathcal{S}} D(s, \omega) Y(s, \omega)\, \mathrm{d}s$ where $D(s, \omega)$ is a Dirac function.

27 Thus $\tau(\omega) = 1$ for ω satisfying $Y(1, \omega) \geqslant Y(0, \omega)$ and $\tau(\omega) = 0$ for ω satisfying $Y(1, \omega) < Y(0, \omega)$.

28 One might argue that even a universal policy p like social security has different benefits $b \in \mathcal{B}$ (tax-benefit rates) for persons with different characteristics, so that there is not universal coverage in the sense that we have used it here.

point is more general and receives considerable emphasis in the econometrics literature.[29] Choices by agents provide information on subjective evaluations which are of independent interest.

A central problem analyzed in this chapter is the absence of information on outcomes for agent ω other than the outcome that is observed. Even a perfectly implemented social experiment does not solve this problem [Heckman (1992)]. Randomization identifies only one component of $\{Y(s,\omega)\}_{s\in\mathcal{S}}$ for any agent. In addition, even with large samples and a valid randomization, some of the $s \in \mathcal{S}$ may not be observed if one is seeking to evaluate new policies never experienced.

There are two main avenues of escape from this problem and we investigate both in this chapter. The first avenue, featured in explicitly formulated econometric models, often called "structural econometric analysis," is to model $Y(s,\omega)$ in terms of its determinants as specified by theory. This entails describing the random variables characterizing ω and carefully distinguishing what agents know and what the analyst knows. This approach also models $D(s,\omega)$ and the dependence between $Y(s,\omega)$ and $D(s,\omega)$ produced from variables common to $Y(s,\omega)$ and $D(s,\omega)$. The Roy framework models this dependence.[30] Like all scientific models, this approach stresses understanding the factors underlying outcomes and the choice of outcome equations and their dependence. Empirical models based on economic theory pursue this avenue of investigation.[31] Some statisticians call this the "scientific approach" and are surprisingly hostile to it [see Holland (1986)].

A second avenue of escape, and the one pursued in the recent treatment effect literature, redirects attention away from estimating the determinants of $Y(s,\omega)$ toward estimating some population version of (2.1), most often a mean, without modeling what factors give rise to the outcome or the relationship between the outcomes and the mechanism selecting outcomes. Agent valuations of outcomes are ignored. The treatment effect literature focuses exclusively on policy problem P-1 for the subset of outcomes that is observed. It ignores the problem of forecasting a new policy in a new environment (problem P-2), or a policy never previously experienced (problem P-3). Forecasting the effects of new policies is a central task of science, ignored in the treatment effect literature.

2.4. Population level treatment parameters

Constructing (2.1) or any of the other individual level parameters defined in Section 2.2 for a given agent is a difficult task because we rarely observe the same agent ω in distinct

[29] See, e.g., Heckman and Smith (1998).

[30] See Heckman and Honoré (1990) and Heckman (2001) for a discussion of this model.

[31] We include in this approach methods based on panel data or more generally the method of paired comparisons as applications of the scientific approach. Under special conditions discussed in Heckman and Smith (1998), we can observe the same agent in states s and s' in different time periods, and can construct (2.1) for all ω.

states s. In addition, some of the states in $\mathcal{S}$ may not be experienced by anyone. The conventional approach in the treatment effect literature is to reformulate the parameter of interest to be some summary measure of the population distribution of treatment effects like a mean or the distribution itself rather than attempting to identify individual treatment effects. It confines attention to subsets of $\mathcal{S}$ that are observed in a particular data set. Thus, the objects of interest are redefined to be distributions of $(Y(j,\omega) - Y(k,\omega))$ over ω or certain means (or quantiles) of the distribution of $(Y(j,\omega) - Y(k,\omega))$ over ω conditional on ω lying in a set $\{\omega\colon X(\omega) = x\}$, i.e., conditioning on $X(\omega)$ [Heckman, Smith and Clements (1997)]. They may instead consist of distributions of $Y(j,\omega)$ and $Y(k,\omega)$ separately [Abadie, Angrist and Imbens (2002), Chernozhukov and Hansen (2005)]. Depending on the conditioning sets used, different summary measures of the population distribution of treatment effects are produced. In addition, the standard implicit assumption in the treatment literature is that all states in $\mathcal{S}$ are observed and that assumptions (PI-1) and (PI-2) hold [Holland (1986), Rubin (1986)].

The conventional parameter of interest, and the focus of many investigations in economics and statistics is the average treatment effect or ATE. For program (state, treatment) j compared to program (state, treatment) k, it is

$$\text{ATE}(j,k) = E\big(Y(j,\omega) - Y(k,\omega)\big), \tag{2.3a}$$

where expectations are taken with respect to the distribution of ω. Conditioning on covariates X, which are associated with the observed components of ω, this parameter is

$$\text{ATE}(j,k \mid x) = E\big(Y(j,\omega) - Y(k,\omega) \mid X = x\big). \tag{2.3b}$$

It is the effect of assigning an agent to a treatment – taking someone from the overall population (2.3a) or a subpopulation conditional on X (2.3b) – and determining the mean gain of the move from base state k, averaging over the factors that determine Y but are not captured by X. This parameter is also the effect of moving the economy from a universal policy (characterized by policy k) and moving to a universal policy of j (e.g., from no social security to full population coverage). Such a policy would likely induce social interactions and general equilibrium effects which are assumed away in the treatment effect literature and which, if present, fundamentally alter the economic interpretation placed on the parameter.

A second conventional parameter in this literature is the average effect of treatment on the treated. Letting $D(j,\omega) = 1$ denote receipt of treatment j, the conventional parameter is

$$\text{TT}(j,k) = E\big(Y(j,\omega) - Y(k,\omega) \mid D(j,\omega) = 1\big). \tag{2.4a}$$

For a population conditional on $X = x$ it is

$$\text{TT}(j,k \mid x) = E\big(Y(j,\omega) - Y(k,\omega) \mid D(j,\omega) = 1, X(\omega) = x\big). \tag{2.4b}$$

We present precise models for decision rules below.

These parameters are the mean impact of moving agents from k to j for those people who get treatment, unconditional and conditional on X. It is the benefit part of the information needed to conduct a cost-benefit evaluation for an existing program. Under certain conditions, it is useful in making "up or out" decisions about an existing program – whether or not the program should be kept or terminated.[32]

A parallel pair of parameters for nonparticipants is treatment on the untreated, where $D(j,\omega) = 0$ denotes no treatment at level j:

$$\mathrm{TUT}(j,k) = E\big(Y(j,\omega) - Y(k,\omega) \mid D(j,\omega) = 0\big), \tag{2.5a}$$

$$\mathrm{TUT}(j,k \mid x) = E\big(Y(j,\omega) - Y(k,\omega) \mid D(j,\omega) = 0, X(\omega) = x\big). \tag{2.5b}$$

These parameters answer the question of how extension of a given program to nonparticipants as a group would affect their outcomes (unconditional and conditional on X, respectively).

The ATE parameter does not condition on a choice. It is policy invariant under conditions (PI-1) and (PI-2). The TT and TUT parameters condition on individual choices and are policy invariant only under the stronger conditions (PI-3) and (PI-4).

Analogous to the pairwise comparisons, we can define setwise comparisons for ordered sets. Thus, in the notation of Section 2.2, we can define the population mean version of the best in $\mathcal{S}_A$ compared with the best in $\mathcal{S}_B$ by

$$E\big(Y_{s_A}(\omega) - Y_{s_B}(\omega)\big),$$

where

$$s_A(\omega) = \operatorname{argmax}_{s\in\mathcal{S}_A}\big\{Y(s,\omega)\big\} \quad \text{and} \quad s_B(\omega) = \operatorname{argmax}_{s\in\mathcal{S}_B}\big\{Y(s,\omega)\big\},$$

or we can compare the mean best in the choice set with the mean second best, $E(Y_{s'}(\omega) - Y_{s_B}(\omega))$, where $s' = \operatorname{argmax}_{s\in\mathcal{S}}\{Y(s,\omega)\}$ and $\mathcal{S}_B = \mathcal{S} \setminus \{s'\}$. These parameters can be defined conditional on X.

The population treatment parameters just discussed are average effects: how the average in one treatment group compares to the average in another. The distinction between the marginal and average return is a central concept in economics. It is often of interest to evaluate the impact of marginal extensions (or contractions) of a program. Incremental cost-benefit analysis is conducted in terms of marginal gains and benefits. Let $R(Y(k,\omega), C(k,\omega), \omega)$ be the utility of person ω with outcome $Y(k,\omega)$ and cost $C(k,\omega)$. The **effect of treatment for people at the margin of indifference** (EOTM) between j and k, given that these are the best two choices available is, with respect to personal preferences, and with respect to choice-specific costs $C(j,\omega)$,

$$\begin{aligned}&\mathrm{EOTM}^R(j,k)\\ &\quad = E\left(Y(j,\omega) - Y(k,\omega) \;\middle|\; \begin{array}{l} R(Y(j,\omega), C(j,\omega), \omega) = R(Y(k,\omega), C(k,\omega), \omega); \\ \left.\begin{array}{l} R(Y(j,\omega), C(j,\omega), \omega) \\ R(Y(k,\omega), C(k,\omega), \omega)\end{array}\right\} \geqslant R(Y(l,\omega), C(l,\omega), \omega) \\ \hfill l \neq j,k \end{array}\right).\end{aligned} \tag{2.6}$$

[32] See, e.g., Heckman and Smith (1998).

This is the mean gain to agents indifferent between j and k, given that these are the best two options available. In a parallel fashion, we can define $\text{EOTM}^{R_G}(Y(j,\omega) - Y(k,\omega))$ using the preferences of another agent (e.g., the parent of a child; a paternalistic bureaucrat, etc.).

An analogous parameter can be defined for mean setwise comparisons. Thus we can define two versions of EOTM:

$$\text{EOTM}^R(s_A, s_B) = E\left(Y_{s_A} - Y_{s_B} \;\middle|\; \begin{array}{l} R(Y(s_A,\omega), C(s_A,\omega), \omega) \\ \quad = R(Y(s_B,\omega), C(s_B,\omega), \omega) \end{array}\right),$$

where s_A and s_B are distinct elements and $A \cap B = \emptyset$, and

$$\text{EOTM}^R\big(\{s'\}, \mathcal{S} \setminus \{s'\}\big) = E\left(Y_{s'} - Y_{s_B} \;\middle|\; \begin{array}{l} R(Y(s',\omega), C(s',\omega), \omega) \\ \quad = R(Y(s_B,\omega), C(s_B,\omega), \omega) \end{array}\right),$$

where s_B is the optimal choice in the set of $\mathcal{S} \setminus \{s'\}$. Again, these parameters can be defined conditional on $X = x$. Other setwise comparisons can be constructed. A generalization of this parameter called the **marginal treatment effect**, introduced into the evaluation literature by Björklund and Moffitt (1987), further developed in Heckman and Vytlacil (1999, 2000, 2005) and defined precisely in Chapter 71 of this Handbook, plays a central role in organizing and interpreting a wide variety of econometric estimators in this chapter.[33]

Many other mean treatment parameters can be defined depending on the choice of the conditioning set. Analogous definitions can be given for median and other quantile versions of these parameters [see Heckman, Smith and Clements (1997), Abadie, Angrist and Imbens (2002)]. Although means are conventional, distributions of treatment parameters are also of considerable interest. We consider distributional parameters in the next subsection.

Of special interest in policy analysis is the **policy relevant treatment effect**. It is the effect on aggregate outcomes of one policy regime $p \in \mathcal{P}$ compared to the effect of another policy regime. For it to be an interesting parameter, we assume (PI-1) and (PI-2) but not necessarily (PI-3) and (PI-4).

$$\textbf{PRTE:}\quad E_p\big(Y(s,\omega)\big) - E_{p'}\big(Y(s,\omega)\big), \quad \text{where } p, p' \in \mathcal{P},$$

where the expectations are taken over different spaces of policy assignment rules. This parameter is a version of a Benthamite policy criterion.

Mean treatment effects play a special role in the statistical approach to causality. They are the centerpiece of the Holland (1986)–Rubin (1978) model and in many other studies in statistics and epidemiology. Social experiments with full compliance and no disruption can identify these means because of a special mathematical property of means. If we can identify the mean of $Y(j,\omega)$ and the mean of $Y(k,\omega)$ from an experiment

[33] There are technical measure theoretic issues regarding whether EOTM is uniquely defined. They are discussed in Chapter 71.

where j is the treatment and k is the baseline, we can form the average treatment effect for j compared to k (2.3a). These can be formed over two different groups of agents. By a similar argument, we can form the treatment on the treated parameter (TT) (2.4a) or (TUT) (2.5a) by randomizing over particular subsets of the population (those who would select treatment and those who would not select treatment respectively), assuming full compliance and no Hawthorne effects or randomization (disruption) bias. See Heckman (1992) and the discussion in Chapter 71.

The case for randomization is weaker if the analyst is interested in other summary measures of the distribution or the distribution itself. In general, randomization is not an effective procedure for identifying median gains, or the distribution of gains or many other key economic parameters. The elevation of population means as the central population level "causal" parameters promotes randomization as an ideal estimation method. This focus on means converts a metaphor for outcome selection – randomization – into an ideal. We next turn to a discussion of distributions of counterfactuals.

2.5. *Criteria of interest besides the mean: Distributions of counterfactuals*

Although means are traditional, the answers to many interesting evaluation questions require knowledge of features of the distribution of program gains other than some mean. Thus modern political economy [Persson and Tabellini (2000)] seeks to know the proportion of agents who benefit from policy regime p compared with p'. Let s_p be shorthand notation for assignment of ω to outcome s under policy p and the associated set of treatment assignment mechanisms. For any two regimes p and p' the proportion who benefit is

$$\Pr\bigl(Y\bigl(s_p(\omega), \omega\bigr) \geqslant Y\bigl(s_{p'}(\omega), \omega\bigr)\bigr).$$

This is called the **voting criterion**. For particular treatments within a policy regime p, it is also of interest to determine the proportion who benefit from j compared to k as

$$\Pr\bigl(Y(j, \omega) \geqslant Y(k, \omega)\bigr).$$

Under (PI-1) and (PI-2) this is the same across all policy regimes.[34] We might be interested in the quantiles of $Y(s_p(\omega), \omega) - Y(s_{p'}(\omega), \omega)$ or of $Y(j, \omega) - Y(k, \omega)$ for $s_p(\omega) = j$ and $s_p(\omega) = k$ or the percentage who gain from participating in j (compared to k) under policy p. More comprehensive analyses would include costs and benefits. Distributional criteria are especially salient if program benefits are not transferrable or if restrictions on feasible social redistributions prevent distributional objectives from being attained.

The traditional literature on program evaluation focuses its attention on mean impacts. When the outcomes are in value units, these can be used to measure the effect of

[34] See Abbring and Heckman (Chapter 72). General equilibrium effects invalidate assumptions (PI-1) and (PI-2).

a program on total social output and are the basis of efficiency analyses. The implicit assumption of the traditional cost-benefit literature is that "a dollar is a dollar," regardless of who receives it.[35]

An emphasis on efficiency to the exclusion of distribution is not universally accepted.[36] An emphasis on efficiency is premised on the assumption that distributional issues are either irrelevant or that they are settled by some external redistribution mechanism using a family or a social welfare function.

Outcomes from many activities like health programs, educational subsidies and training programs are not transferrable. Moreover, even if all program outputs can be monetized, the assumption that a family or social welfare function automatically settles distributional questions in an optimal way is questionable. Many programs designed to supply publicly provided goods are properly evaluated by considering the incidence of their receipt and not the aggregate of the receipts. Hence counterfactual distributions are required. Distributions of counterfactuals are also required in computing option values of social programs, which we discuss next.

2.6. *Option values*

Voluntary social programs confer options, and these options can change threat points and bargaining power, even if they are not exercised.[37] It is, therefore, of interest to assess these option values. The most interesting versions of option values require knowledge of the joint distribution of potential outcomes. We consider the analysis of treatments offered within a policy regime. Persons offered a subsidized job may take it or opt for their best unsubsidized alternative. The option of having a subsidized alternative job will in general convey value. The option may be conferred simply by eligibility for a program or it may be conferred only on participants. The program creates an option for participants, if prior to participating in it, their only available option comes from the distribution of $Y(k, \omega)$, say F_k. Following or during participation in the program, the individual has a second option $Z(\omega)$ drawn from distribution F_Z. If both options are known prior to choosing between them, and agents are outcome maximizers, then the observed outcome $Y(j, \omega)$ is the maximum of the two options, $Y(j, \omega) = \max(Y(k, \omega), Z(\omega))$. The option $Z(\omega)$ may be available only during the period of program participation, as in a wage subsidy program, or it may become a permanent feature of the choice set as when a marketable skill is acquired. It is useful to distinguish the case where the program offers a distribution F_Z from which new offers are received each period from the case where a permanent $Z(\omega)$ value is created. Much of the literature on program evaluation implicitly equates $Z(\omega)$ with $Y(j, \omega)$. This is valid only if treatment is an irreversible condition that supplants $Y(k, \omega)$ or else

[35] See Harberger (1971).

[36] See Little and Mirrlees (1974).

[37] See, e.g., Osborne (2004).

$Z(\omega) \geqslant Y(k, \omega)$ for all ω so that agents who take the treatment use the skills conferred by it. In either case, agents offered $Z(\omega)$ always choose $Z(\omega)$ over $Y(k, \omega)$ or are indifferent, so $Y(j, \omega) \equiv Z(\omega)$ and the estimated distribution of $Y(j, \omega)$ is equivalent to the estimated distribution of $Z(\omega)$. In general it is useful to determine what a program offers to potential participants, what the offer is worth to them, and to distinguish the offered option from the realized choice.

The expected value of having a new option $Z(\omega)$ in addition to $Y(k, \omega)$ is

$$\text{(OP-1)} \quad E(\max(Y(k, \omega), Z(\omega))) - E(Y(k, \omega)),$$

assuming that potential participants in a program can choose freely between $Y(k, \omega)$ and $Z(\omega)$. This is the difference in expected outcomes between a two-option world and a one-option world, assuming that both are known at the time the choice between them is made. It is useful to distinguish the opportunities created from the program, $Z(\omega)$, from the options selected. The program extends opportunities to potential participants. Providing a new opportunity that may be rejected may improve the average outcome among agents who choose $Y(k, \omega)$ over $Z(\omega)$ through affecting the distribution of the $Y(k, \omega)$ offered to the agents.

For example, the outside option can improve bargaining power. If a housewife receives an outside job offer, her bargaining power at home may increase. If a program gives participants a second distribution from which they receive a new draw each period, and if realizations of the pair $(Y(k, \omega), Z(\omega))$ in each future period are independently and identically distributed, then the addition to future wealth of having access to a second option in every period is

$$\frac{1}{r}\big[E\big(\max\big(Y(k, \omega), Z(\omega)\big)\big) - E\big(Y(k, \omega)\big)\big],$$

where r is the interest rate. If Z is available only for a limited time period, as would be the case for a job subsidy, (OP-1) is discounted over that period and the expression should be appropriately modified to adjust for the finite life.

If the realizations $(Y(k, \omega), Z(\omega))$ are not known at the time when decisions to exercise the option are made, (OP-1) is modified to

$$\text{(OP-2)} \quad \max(E(Y(k, \omega) \mid \mathcal{I}_\omega), E(Y(j, \omega) \mid \mathcal{I}_\omega)) - E(Y(k, \omega) \mid \mathcal{I}_\omega),$$

where these expectations are computed against agent ω's information set $\mathcal{I}_\omega$.[38] Constructing these option values in general requires knowing the joint distribution of $Z(\omega)$ and $Y(k, \omega)$, and cannot be obtained from means or from social experiments which only identify marginal distributions. We now turn to a systematic accounting of uncertainty.

[38] A third definition of option value recognizes the value of having uncertainty resolved at the time decisions to choose between $Z(\omega)$ and $Y(k, \omega)$ are made. That definition is

$$\text{(OP-3)} \quad E(\max(Z(\omega), Y(k, \omega))) - \max(E(Z(\omega) \mid \mathcal{I}_\omega), E(Y(k, \omega) \mid \mathcal{I}_\omega)) = \text{(OP-1)–(OP-2)}.$$

2.7. Accounting for private and social uncertainty

Systematically accounting for uncertainty introduces additional considerations that are central to economic analysis but that are ignored in the treatment effect literature as currently formulated. Persons do not know the outcomes associated with possible states not yet experienced. If some potential outcomes are not known at the time treatment decisions are made, the best that agents can do is to forecast them with some rule. Even if, *ex post*, agents know their outcome in a benchmark state, they may not know it *ex ante*, and they may always be uncertain about what they would have experienced in an alternative state. This creates a further distinction: that between *ex post* and *ex ante* evaluations of both subjective and objective outcomes. The economically motivated literature on policy evaluation makes this distinction. The treatment effect literature does not.

In the literature on welfare economics and social choice, one form of decision-making under uncertainty plays a central role. The "Veil of Ignorance" of Vickrey (1945, 1961) and Harsanyi (1955, 1975) postulates that agents are completely uncertain about the positions of individuals in the distribution of outcomes under each policy, or should act as if they are completely uncertain, and they should use expected utility criteria (Vickrey–Harsanyi) or a maximin strategy [Rawls (1971)] to evaluate welfare under alternative policies. Central to this viewpoint is the anonymity postulate that claims the irrelevance of any particular agent's outcome to the overall evaluation of social welfare. This form of ignorance is sometimes justified as an ethically correct position that captures how an objectively detached observer should evaluate alternative policies, even if actual participants in the political process use other criteria. An approach based on the Veil of Ignorance is widely used in applied work in evaluating different income distributions [see Foster and Sen (1997)]. It is empirically easy to implement because it only requires information about the marginal distributions of outcomes produced under different policies. If the outcome is income, policy j is preferred to policy k if the income distribution under j stochastically dominates the income distribution under k.[39]

An alternative criterion is required if agents act in their own self-interest, or in the interest of certain other groups (e.g., the poor, the less able) and have at least partial knowledge about how they (or the groups they are interested in) will fare under different policies. The outcomes in different regimes may be dependent, so that agents who benefit under one policy may also benefit under another [see Carneiro, Hansen and Heckman (2001, 2003), Cunha, Heckman and Navarro (2005, 2006)].

Because agents typically do not possess perfect information, the simple voting criterion that assumes perfect foresight over policy outcomes that is discussed in Section 2.5 may not accurately characterize choices. It requires modification. Let $\mathcal{I}_\omega$ denote the information set available to agent ω. He or she evaluates policy j against k using that

[39] See Foster and Sen (1997) for a definition of stochastic dominance.

information. Under an expected utility criterion, agent ω prefers policy j over policy k if

$$E\big(R\big(Y(j,\omega),\omega\big) \mid \mathcal{I}_\omega\big) \geqslant E\big(R\big(Y(k,\omega),\omega\big) \mid \mathcal{I}_\omega\big).$$

The proportion of people who prefer j is

$$PB(j \mid j,k) = \int \mathbf{1}\big[E\big[R\big(Y(j,\omega),\omega\big) \mid \mathcal{I}_\omega\big] \geqslant E\big[R\big(Y(k,\omega),\omega\big) \mid \mathcal{I}_\omega\big]\big]\, \mathrm{d}\mu(\mathcal{I}_\omega), \tag{2.7}$$

where $\mu(\omega)$ is the distribution of ω in the population whose preferences over outcomes are being studied.[40,41] The voting criterion presented in Section 2.5 is the special case where the information set $\mathcal{I}_\omega$ contains $(Y(j,\omega), Y(k,\omega))$, so there is no uncertainty about $Y(j)$ and $Y(k)$. Abbring and Heckman (Chapter 72) offer an example of the application of this criterion.

Accounting for uncertainty in the analysis makes it essential to distinguish between *ex ante* and *ex post* evaluations. *Ex post*, part of the uncertainty about policy outcomes is resolved although agents do not, in general, have full information about what their potential outcomes would have been in policy regimes they have not experienced and may have only incomplete information about the policy they have experienced (e.g., the policy may have long run consequences extending after the point of evaluation). It is useful to index the information set $\mathcal{I}_\omega$ by t, $\mathcal{I}_{\omega,t}$, to recognize that information about the outcomes of policies may accrue over time. *Ex ante* and *ex post* assessments of a voluntary program need not agree.

Ex post assessments of a program through surveys administered to agents who have completed it [Katz et al. (1975), Hensher, Louviere and Swait (1999)], may disagree with *ex ante* assessments of the program. Both may reflect honest valuations of the program. They are reported when agents have different information about it or have their preferences altered by participating in the program. Before participating in a program, agents may be uncertain about the consequences of participation. An agent who has completed program j may know $Y(j,\omega)$ but can only guess at the alternative outcome $Y(k,\omega)$ which is not experienced. In this case, *ex post* "satisfaction" with j relative to k for agent ω who only participates in k is synonymous with the following inequality,

$$R\big(Y(j,\omega),\omega\big) \geqslant E\big(R\big(Y(k,\omega),\omega\big) \mid \mathcal{I}_\omega\big), \tag{2.8}$$

where the information is post-treatment. Survey questionnaires about "client" satisfaction with a program may capture subjective elements of program experience not captured by "objective" measures of outcomes that usually exclude psychic costs and benefits. Heckman, Smith and Clements (1997) present evidence on this question. Carneiro,

40 Agents would not necessarily vote "honestly", although in a binary choice setting they do and there is no scope for strategic manipulation of votes. See Moulin (1983). *PB* is simply a measure of relative satisfaction and need not describe a voting outcome when other factors come into play.

41 See Cunha, Heckman and Navarro (2006) for computations regarding both types of joint distributions.

Hansen and Heckman (2001, 2003), Cunha, Heckman and Navarro (2005, 2006) and Heckman and Navarro (2007) develop econometric methods for distinguishing *ex ante* from *ex post* evaluations of social programs, which are surveyed in Abbring and Heckman (Chapter 72).

2.8. *The data needed to construct the criteria*

Four ingredients are required to implement the criteria discussed in this section: (a) private preferences, including preferences over outcomes by the decision maker; (b) social preferences, as exemplified by the social welfare function; (c) distributions of outcomes in alternative states, and for some criteria, such as the voting criterion, *joint* distributions of outcomes *across* policy states; and (d) *ex ante* and *ex post* information about outcomes. Cost benefit analysis only requires information about means of measured outcomes and for that reason is easier to implement. The statistical treatment effect literature largely focuses on *ex post* means, but recent work in econometrics focuses on both *ex ante* and *ex post* distributions [see Carneiro, Hansen and Heckman (2001, 2003), Cunha, Heckman and Navarro (2005, 2006), Heckman, Smith and Clements (1997)]. This chapter focuses on methods for producing ingredients (c) and (d). There is a large literature on recovering private preferences [see, e.g., Chapter 67 (Blundell, MaCurdy and Meghir) of this Handbook] and on recovering technology parameters [see, e.g., Chapter 62 (Reiss and Wolak); and Chapter 61 (Ackerberg, Benkard, Berry and Pakes) of this Handbook]. The rich set of questions addressed in this section contrasts sharply with the focus on mean outcomes in epidemiology and statistics which ignores private and social preferences and distributions of outcomes. Carneiro, Hansen and Heckman (2001, 2003), Cunha, Heckman and Navarro (2005, 2006) and Heckman and Navarro (2007) present methods for extracting private information on outcomes and their evolution over time. We now present some examples of explicit economic models drawing on core elements of modern econometrics. We build on these examples throughout our chapter.

3. Roy and generalized Roy examples

To make the discussion more specific and to introduce a parametric version of the framework for discrete choice with associated outcomes that motivates the analysis in this chapter, we introduce versions of the Roy (1951) and generalized Roy models, define various treatment effects and introduce uncertainty into the analysis. We show how the Roy model and its extensions solve policy problems P-1–P-3 that are the focus of this chapter. We first develop the generalized Roy framework for a setting of perfect certainty, specialize it to the two-outcome case, and then introduce uncertainty. We produce some normal theory examples because normality is conventional and easy to link to standard regression theory. The analyses reported in Section 6, Appendix B and Chapter 71 relax the normality assumption.

3.1. A generalized Roy model under perfect certainty

Suppose that there are $\bar{S}$ states associated with different levels of schooling, or some other outcome such as residence in a region, or choice of technology. Associated with each choice s is a valuation of the outcome of the choice $R(s)$, where R is the valuation function and s is the state. Define Z as individual variables that affect choices. Each state may be characterized by a bundle of attributes, characteristics or qualities $Q(s)$ that fully characterize the state. If $Q(s)$ fully describes the state, $R(s) = R(Q(s))$. To simplify the notation, we do not use the ω notation in this section, but keep it implicit.

Suppose that $R(s)$ can be written in additively separable form in terms of deterministic and random components. We assume that the Z is observed. Let ν denote unobserved components as perceived by the econometrician. In this notation,

$$R(s) = \mu_R(s, Z) + \eta(s, Z, \nu), \tag{3.1}$$

where $\mu_R(s, Z)$ is the deterministic component of the utility function expressed in terms of observed variables Z and $\eta(s, Z, \nu)$ represents unobservables from the point of view of the econometrician (recall that we assume that there is no uncertainty facing the agent).[42] McFadden (1981) describes a large class of discrete choice models that can be represented in this form. Additive separability is convenient but not essential [Matzkin (1992, 1993, 1994)]. An example of these models is a random coefficient choice model where $R(s) = \gamma_s' z = \bar{\gamma}_s' z + \nu_s' z$, where $\bar{\gamma}_s$ is the mean of γ_s and ν_s is the deviation of γ_s from its mean. In the McFadden (1974) model, $\mu_R(s, z) = \bar{\gamma}_s' z + \nu_s$, where ν_s is independent of Z and also independent of s. In this abstract notation, the characteristics of choice s are embedded in the definition of γ_s. A more explicit version would write $\gamma_s = \gamma(Q(s))$, where $Q(s)$ are the characteristics of choice s. To simplify notation we write $\eta(s, Z, \nu)$ as $\eta(s)$.

Associated with each choice is outcome $Y(s)$ which may be vector valued. These outcomes can depend on X. For simplicity and familiarity we work with the scalar case. Following Carneiro, Hansen and Heckman (2003) and Heckman and Navarro (2007), we can accommodate the case where $Y(s)$ is a vector of continuous, discrete and mixed discrete-continuous outcomes. Again, for simplicity we drop "ω" and assume an additively separable case where $\mu_Y(s, X)$ is a deterministic function expressed in terms of observables and $U(s, X, \varepsilon)$, $s = 1, \ldots, \bar{S}$, are unobservables:

$$Y(s) = \mu_Y(s, X) + U(s, X, \varepsilon).$$

We leave the details of constructing the random variables $\eta(s, Z, \gamma)$ and $U(s, X, \varepsilon)$ for a later section of this chapter. For now one could work with the shorthand notation $U(s, X, \varepsilon) = U(s)$ and $\eta(s, Z, \gamma) = \eta(s)$.

[42] One definition of $\mu_R(s, Z)$ is $\mu_R(s, Z) = E[R(s) \mid Z]$, but other definitions are possible. The "structural" approach derives $\mu_R(s, Z)$ from economic theory.

This framework serves as a benchmark index model against which we can measure the recent contributions and limitations of the treatment effect literature. The chapters in the Handbook series by McFadden (1984), Heckman and MaCurdy (1986), Matzkin (1994), Blundell, MaCurdy and Meghir (2007), Reiss and Wolak (2007), Ackerberg et al. (2007), and Athey and Haile (2007) exposit detailed econometric analyses of specific economic models that are based on versions of this structure and extensions of it. Economically well-posed econometric models make explicit the assumptions used by analysts regarding preferences, technology, the information available to agents, the constraints under which they operate and the rules of interaction among agents in market and social settings. These explicit features make these models, like all scientific models, useful vehicles for interpreting empirical evidence using economic theory, for collating and synthesizing evidence across studies using economic theory, for measuring the welfare effects of policies, and for forecasting the welfare and direct effects of previously implemented policies in new environments and the effects of new policies.

The set of possible treatments $\mathcal{S}$ is $\{1, \ldots, \bar{S}\}$, the set of state labels. The set of counterfactual outcomes is $\{Y(s, X)\}_{s\in\mathcal{S}}$. The treatment assignment mechanism is produced by utility maximization:

$$D(j) = 1 \quad \text{if } \operatorname{argmax}_{s\in\mathcal{S}}\bigl\{R(s)\bigr\} = j, \tag{3.2}$$

where in the event of ties, choices are made by a flip of a coin. Thus agents *self select* into treatment and the probabilities of selection which are defined at the individual level are either zero or one for each agent (agents choose outcomes with certainty). Appendix B presents a proof of nonparametric identification of this generic model.

Other mechanisms for selection into sector s could be entertained. In the background, policy "p", under which choices are made, is kept implicit. Policies can operate to change Z, X, and the distributions $\eta(s, Z, \nu)$, $U(s, X, \varepsilon)$. Section 5 presents a more detailed analysis of policy regimes. Operating within a policy regime, and a particular treatment selection rule, we do not have to take a position on assumptions (PI-3) and (PI-4), which are assumptions about outcomes across policy regimes and across assignment rules within policy regimes. We next present examples of these models. We also introduce examples of models with uncertainty.

3.1.1. Examples of models that can be fit into this framework

Scalar income The original static Roy model (1951) writes $Y(j)$ as scalar income in sector j. For instance, sectors can be regions, industries [Heckman and Sedlacek (1985)], schooling levels [Willis and Rosen (1979), Carneiro, Hansen and Heckman (2003)] or union status [Lee (1978)]. See Heckman (2001) for a survey of these applications.

In the original setup, $R(j) \equiv Y(j)$, $Z = X$ and $Y(j)$ is scalar income in sector j so agents are income maximizers. In extensions of this model, there are sector-specific costs $C(j)$ which may depend on $Z = (X, W)$, $R(j) = Y(j) - C(j)$. This allows for nonpecuniary components as in Heckman and Sedlacek (1985), Carneiro, Hansen and Heckman (2003), Cunha, Heckman and Navarro (2005, 2006) and others, or tuition costs as in Willis and Rosen (1979). Policies may operate on costs or returns. Agents may be uncertain about future income when they make their choices so the decision rule is to go to the sector if $E(Y(1) - C(1) - Y(0) \mid \mathcal{I}) \geqslant 0$. *Ex post* returns are $(Y(1)-C(1)-Y(0))$. See Carneiro, Hansen and Heckman (2003), and Cunha, Heckman and Navarro (2005, 2006).

Choice of technology In this application, the profit-maximizing firm faces J technologies. $Y(j)$ is output. $F_j : X \to Y(j)$ maps inputs into outputs for technology j, assumed to be strictly concave and twice differentiable. There is a cost of inputs, $C(j)$, possibly including fixed cost components. As before, let $Z = (X, W)$. Assume that profit, $R(j)$, is maximized for each technology so $R(j) = \max_X\{F_j(X) - C(j, X, W)\}$, and

$$D(j) = 1 \quad \text{if } \operatorname{argmax}_\ell\{R(\ell)\} = j.$$

The potential outcome vector is $(Y(j), R(j), X(j), C(j))$ where $X(j)$ is the input vector chosen if j is chosen. In this example, utility, $R(j)$, is profit and firms are assumed to pick the technology with the highest profit. Policies operate on costs, profit taxes, and on returns [see Pitt and Rosenzweig (1989)].

Dynamic education choices Following Eckstein and Wolpin (1989, 1999), Keane and Wolpin (1997) and Heckman and Navarro (2007), we may explicitly account for information updating at attained schooling level s. We introduce uncertainty. Let $E(R(s, s+1) \mid \mathcal{I}_s)$ be the value of continuing on to the next schooling level given that an agent has already attained s and possesses information set $\mathcal{I}_s$. This value includes the options opened up by taking s. $D_{s,s+1}(\mathcal{I}_s) = 1$ if an agent continues from level s to level $s+1$. $D_{s,s+1}(\mathcal{I}_s) = \mathbf{1}[E(R(s, s+1) \mid \mathcal{I}_s) \geqslant 0]$ and equals 0 otherwise. Associated with each outcome is a payoff stream of future income and option values associated with the choice Y_{s+1}. Abbring and Heckman (Chapter 72) discuss dynamic counterfactuals and dynamic discrete choice.

Many other examples could be given. The literature on estimation and identification in structural models is active [see Rust (1994), Geweke and Keane (2001), Aguirregabiria (2004), Heckman and Navarro (2007)]. The unifying theme underlying all of these models is that latent variables (the utilities or value functions) generate observed outcomes. Since outcomes (or agent-predicted outcomes) affect choices, there is selection bias. To make the discussion specific and have a model in hand, we exposit a normal theory generalized Roy model in Section 3.3. First we use this framework to define treatment effects.

3.2. Treatment effects and evaluation parameters

The **individual level treatment effect** (2.1) for objective outcomes is

$$Y(s) - Y(s') = \mu_Y(s, X) - \mu_Y(s', X) + U(s) - U(s'). \tag{3.3}$$

The **subjective evaluation individual treatment effect** of program s compared to program s' is

$$R(s) - R(s') = \mu_R(s, Z) - \mu_R(s', Z) + \eta(s) - \eta(s')$$

in the metric of the valuation function. An alternative measure of the *relative* subjective evaluation of the program is

$$D(s, s', Z) = \mathbf{1}\big[R(s) \geqslant R(s')\big].$$

If $D(s, s') = 1$, the agent (weakly) prefers s over s'.

As in Section 2, one can define set-wise comparisons of treatment effects. Thus one can compare the outcome of the best with the outcome of the next best as in Dahl (2002), defining

$$s' = \operatorname{argmax}_{s \in \mathcal{S}}\big\{Y(s)\big\} \quad \text{and} \quad \mathcal{S}_B = \mathcal{S} \setminus \{s'\}$$

so that the treatment effect comparing the best to the next best is

$$Y(s') - Y(s_B).$$

Other comparisons can be made. Instead of private preferences, there may be social preferences of the "planner" defined over the choices of the individuals. Cost benefit criteria would be defined in a corresponding fashion.

The **evaluation problem** in this model is that we only observe each agent in one of $\bar{S}$ possible states. We do not know the outcome of the agent in other states and hence cannot directly form individual level treatment effects.

The **selection problem** arises because we only observe certain agents in any state. Thus we observe $Y(s)$ only for agents for whom $D(s) = 1$. In general, the outcomes of agents found in $S = s$ are not representative of what the outcomes of agents would be if they were randomly assigned to s.

We now define the population treatment parameters using this framework. Comparing s with s', $\text{ATE}(s, s' \mid X) = \mu_Y(s, X) - \mu_Y(s', X)$. Treatment on the treated for those choosing between s and s' given X, Z is

$$\begin{aligned} &E\big(Y(s) - Y(s') \mid X, Z, D(s) = 1\big) \\ &\quad = \text{TT}(s, s' \mid X, Z) \\ &\quad = \mu_Y(s, X) - \mu_Y(s', X) + E\big[U(s) - U(s') \mid X, Z, D(s) = 1\big], \end{aligned}$$

where the final term is the sorting gain that arises from agents selecting into the treatment. ATE and TT can be defined for the best compared to the next best.

$$\begin{aligned} \text{ATE}(s, s_B \mid X, Z) &= \mu_Y(s, X) - E\Big[\max_{j \in \mathcal{S} \setminus \{s\}} \big\{Y(j)\big\} \mid X, Z\Big], \\ \text{TT}(s, s_B \mid X, Z) &= \mu_Y(s, X) + E\big(U(s) \mid D(s) = 1, X, Z\big) \\ &\quad - E\Big[\max_{j \in \mathcal{S} \setminus \{s\}} \big\{Y(j)\big\} \mid D(s) = 1, X, Z\Big]. \end{aligned}$$

The effect of treatment given X for agents at the margin of participation between s and s' (EOTM) using the analysis of Section 2.4 is

$$\text{EOTM}(s, s') = \mu_Y(s, X) - \mu_Y(s', X) + E\big[U(s) - U(s') \mid R(s) = R(s')\big],$$

where $R(s), R(s') \geqslant R(k), s, s' \neq k$. We can define setwise versions of this parameter as well. Using the model, we can also compute the distributional criteria introduced in Section 2.5, e.g., the proportion of people who benefit from being in s compared to s':

$$\Pr\big(R(s) \geqslant R(s') \mid Z = z\big).$$

We can form quantiles of the outcome distribution and evaluate the quantile treatment effects [e.g., Chernozhukov and Hansen (2005)]. Letting $q^s(\nu)$ be the νth quantile of the $Y(s)$ distribution, the quantile treatment effects for a lth quantile are $q^s(l) - q^{s'}(l)$. From the agent preferences, and the outcome distributions we can form all of the treatment effects discussed in Section 2 for environments of perfect certainty.

For a known model, we can answer policy question P-1 within the sample used to fit the model. Thus we can solve the problem of internal validity by fitting the model (3.1) and (3.2). Policy question P-2 involves extrapolating the model to new regions of X, Z. This can be solved using parametric functional forms (e.g., $\mu_Y(s, X) = X\beta_s$ and $\mu_R(s, Z) = Z\gamma_s$). If $U(s)$ and $\eta(s)$ are independent of X, Z, the task is simplified. If they are not independent, then it is necessary to model the dependence of $U(s), \eta(s)$ on (X, Z) over the new support of (X, Z).

Policy problem P-3 entails the evaluation of new outcome states never previously experienced, for example a new element s. As suggested by the quotation from Frank Knight cited in Section 2, one avenue of solution is to characterize β_s and γ_s as functions of baseline characteristics that describe all programs $\beta_s = \beta(Q(s)), \gamma_s = \gamma(Q(s))$ and to characterize the dependence of $U(s), \eta(s)$ on $Q(s)$. Provided that we can define a new program s' as a combination of the characteristics of previous programs, and $\beta(Q(s)), \gamma(Q(s))$ (and the distributions of $U(s), \eta(s)$) are defined over supports that include $Q(s)$, we can solve P-3. We provide a specific example of this approach in the next subsection.

3.3. A two-outcome normal example under perfect certainty

To make the discussion concrete, it is helpful to exposit a prototypical model of choice and associated outcomes. The Roy model (1951) and its extensions [Gronau (1974), Heckman (1974), Willis and Rosen (1979), Heckman (1990), Carneiro, Hansen and Heckman (2003)] are at the core of microeconometrics.

Consider the following simple version of the Roy model. Persons start off in sector "0" (e.g., primary schooling). To simplify expressions, we write $Y(s)$ as Y_s in this section, and in other places where it is convenient to do so. We create parallel notation for $U(s) = U_s$. The variables Y_1 and Y_0 can be interpreted as the outcomes from being in sectors 1 and 0, respectively. We model these as

$$Y_1 = X\beta_1 + U_1, \tag{3.4a}$$

$$Y_0 = X\beta_0 + U_0, \tag{3.4b}$$

and associated costs (prices) as a function of W,

$$C = W\beta_C + U_C. \tag{3.4c}$$

In a schooling example, tuition and distance to school would be candidates for inclusion in W. The valuation of "1" relative to "0" is $R = Y_1 - Y_0 - C$. Substituting from (3.4a)–(3.4c) into the expression for R, we obtain the relative evaluation of outcome "1" versus outcome "0" as

$$R = X(\beta_1 - \beta_0) - W\beta_C + U_1 - U_0 - U_C.$$ [43]

Sectoral choice is indicated by D, where $D = 1$ if the agent selects 1, $D = 0$ otherwise:

$$D = \mathbf{1}[R \geqslant 0].$$

We define $\upsilon = (U_1 - U_0 - U_C)$, $Z = (X, W)$ and $\gamma = (\beta_1' - \beta_0', -\beta_C')$ so we can write $R = Z\gamma + \upsilon$. The generalized Roy model assumes that (recalling $Z = (X, W)$)

(i) $Z \perp\!\!\!\perp (U_0, U_1, U_C)$ (independence),
(ii) $(U_0, U_1, U_C) \sim \mathcal{N}(0, \Sigma_{\mathrm{GR}})$ (normality),

where $\mathcal{N}(0, \Sigma_{\mathrm{GR}})$ is normal with mean zero and variance–covariance matrix Σ_{GR} and "GR" stands for the generalized Roy model.

From its definition, $E(\upsilon) = 0$. The **Roy model** is the special case where $\beta_C = 0$ and $U_C = 0$, so choices are made solely on the basis of income, $R = Y_1 - Y_0$. The **extended Roy model** sets $\beta_C \neq 0$, but $U_C = 0$ so choices are made on net income subtracting costs but the determinants of the cost components (W) are observed by the analysts.

For the **generalized Roy model**, the probability of selecting treatment (outcome) 1 is

$$\Pr(R \geqslant 0 \mid Z = z) = \Pr(\upsilon \geqslant -z\gamma) = \Pr\left(\frac{\upsilon}{\sigma_\upsilon} \geqslant \frac{-z\gamma}{\sigma_\upsilon}\right) = \Phi\left(\frac{z\gamma}{\sigma_\upsilon}\right),$$

where Φ is the cumulative distribution function of the standard normal distribution and the last result follows from the symmetry of standard normal variables around zero. The choice probability is sometimes called the "propensity score" by statisticians. Higher values of the index lead to higher values of the probability of participation; $z\gamma$ is the mean scale utility function. Higher values of $z\gamma$ correspond to higher values of net utility from choosing treatment 1 over treatment 0.

[43] This use of R as a relative evaluation is a slight abuse of notation. Before we used R as absolute level of utility. However, choice valuations are always relative to some benchmark, so there is little possibility of confusion in this usage.

The variance–covariance matrix of (U_0, U_1, υ) is

$$\Sigma_\upsilon = \begin{pmatrix} \sigma_0^2 & \sigma_{01} & \sigma_{0\upsilon} \\ \sigma_{01} & \sigma_1^2 & \sigma_{1\upsilon} \\ \sigma_{0\upsilon} & \sigma_{1\upsilon} & \sigma_\upsilon^2 \end{pmatrix},$$

where σ_{ij} is the covariance between outcomes i and j.

In this model, the average treatment effect given $X = x$ is

$$\begin{aligned} \text{ATE}(x) &= E(Y_1 - Y_0 \mid X = x) \\ &= x(\beta_1 - \beta_0). \end{aligned}$$

Treatment on the treated is

$$\begin{aligned} \text{TT}(x, z) &= E(Y_1 - Y_0 \mid X = x, Z = z, D = 1) \\ &= x(\beta_1 - \beta_0) + E(U_1 - U_0 \mid \upsilon \geqslant -Z\gamma,\ Z = z) \\ &= x(\beta_1 - \beta_0) + E(U_1 - U_0 \mid \upsilon \geqslant -z\gamma), \end{aligned}$$

where the third equality follows from independence assumption (i). The **local average treatment effect** (LATE) of Imbens and Angrist (1994) is the average gain to program participation for those induced to receive treatment through a change in $Z[= (X, W)]$ by a component of W not in X. Such a change affects choices but not potential outcomes. Let $D(z)$ be the random variable D when we fix $W = w$ and let $D(z')$ be the random variable when we fix $W = w'$. The LATE parameter as defined by Heckman and Vytlacil (1999) is

$$\begin{aligned} \text{LATE}(z, z', x) &= E(Y_1 - Y_0 \mid D(z) = 0, D(z') = 1, X = x) \\ &= x(\beta_1 - \beta_0) + E\big(U_1 - U_0 \mid R(z) < 0, R(z') \geqslant 0, X = x\big) \\ &= x(\beta_1 - \beta_0) + E(U_1 - U_0 \mid -z'\gamma \leqslant \upsilon < -z\gamma), \end{aligned}$$

using independence assumption (i) and the index structure to obtain the final result.

A definition of LATE introduced by Heckman and Vytlacil (1999, 2000, 2005) can be made independent of the existence of any instrument. Imbens and Angrist (1994) define LATE by invoking an instrument and thereby apparently conflate tasks 1 and 2 in Table 1 (the tasks of definition and identification). We can define LATE as the mean return for agents with values of $\upsilon \in [\underline{\upsilon}, \bar{\upsilon}]$. Instruments W may not exist, yet LATE can still be defined as

$$\text{LATE}\big(x, \upsilon \in [\underline{\upsilon}, \bar{\upsilon}]\big) = x(\beta_1 - \beta_0) + E(U_1 - U_0 \mid \underline{\upsilon} \leqslant \upsilon < \bar{\upsilon}).$$

With this definition, we can separate task 1 of Table 1 from task 2. If $\underline{\upsilon} = -z'\gamma$ and $\bar{\upsilon} = -z\gamma$, we obtain the instrument-dependent version of LATE in the Roy model.

The **marginal treatment effect** (MTE) is defined conditional on X, Z, and $\upsilon = \upsilon^*$:

$$E(Y_1 - Y_0 \mid \upsilon = \upsilon^*,\ X = x,\ Z = z) = x(\beta_1 - \beta_0) + E(U_1 - U_0 \mid \upsilon = \upsilon^*).$$

This parameter is a generalization of a parameter introduced into the evaluation literature by Björklund and Moffitt (1987). It is the mean return for agents for whom $X = x$, $Z = z$, and $\upsilon = \upsilon^*$. It is defined independently of any instrument. At a special point of evaluation where $R = 0$ (i.e. $z\gamma + \upsilon = 0$), the MTE is a willingness to pay measure that informs us how much an agent at the margin of participation (in the indifference set) would be willing to pay to move from "0" to "1". This particular point of evaluation for the marginal treatment effect is what we called "EOTM" (the effect of treatment for agents at the margin of indifference) in Section 2.4.

Under regularity conditions satisfied by the normal distribution and expressing it in instrument-dependent form, EOTM can be defined as the limit form of LATE,

$$\begin{aligned}
&\lim_{z\gamma \to z'\gamma} \mathrm{LATE}(z, z', x) \\
&\quad = x(\beta_1 - \beta_0) + \lim_{z\gamma \to z'\gamma} E(U_1 - U_0 \mid -z'\gamma \leqslant \upsilon < -z\gamma) \\
&\quad = x(\beta_1 - \beta_0) + E(U_1 - U_0 \mid \upsilon = -z'\gamma).
\end{aligned}$$ [44]

LATE, as interpreted by Heckman and Vytlacil (1999, 2000, 2005), is the average return for agents with $\upsilon \in [-z'\gamma, -z\gamma]$. This parameter expresses the outcome of manipulating the values at which we set υ by manipulation of the mean scale utility $z\gamma$, but holding X fixed. The relative preferences for state 1 compared to state 0, but not the outcomes Y_1, Y_0, are affected by such changes because we fix X. An example of such a change in Z is a change in tuition but not a change in variables directly affecting Y_1, Y_0 (the X).

In the special case of the Roy model, $C = 0$, $R = Y_1 - Y_0$ and $\upsilon = U_1 - U_0$, the MTE is

$$E(Y_1 - Y_0 \mid U_1 - U_0 = u_1 - u_0,\ X = x) = x(\beta_1 - \beta_0) + (u_1 - u_0).$$

In the special case where $R = 0$, $x(\beta_1 - \beta_0) = -(u_1 - u_0)$ and MTE at this point of evaluation is zero (i.e. EOTM is zero).

We can work with $Z\gamma$ or with the propensity score $P(Z)$ interchangeably. Under our normality assumptions, ATE is defined as before. Treatment on the Treated can be defined using the standard selection formulae. We have already defined Φ as the distribution function for a standard unit normal random variable; $\phi(\psi) = \Phi'(\psi)$ is the density of this variable evaluated at ψ. Using results on the truncated normal surveyed in Heckman and Honoré (1990), and summarized in Appendix C, we can express treatment on the treated given Z, normalizing the variance of υ to 1 to simplify the notation,

$$\begin{aligned}
\mathrm{TT}(x, z) &= E(Y_1 - Y_0 \mid X = x, Z = z, \upsilon \geqslant -z\gamma) \\
&= x(\beta_1 - \beta_0) + \mathrm{Cov}(U_1 - U_0, \upsilon)\lambda(z\gamma),
\end{aligned}$$

[44] The regularity conditions apply to families of distributions that are more general than the normal ones. [These are discussed further in Chapter 71.]

where

$$\lambda(z\gamma) = \frac{\phi(z\gamma)}{\Phi(z\gamma)}.$$

λ is monotone decreasing in $z\gamma$ and $\lim_{z\gamma\to\infty}\lambda(z\gamma) = 0$ and $\lim_{z\gamma\to-\infty}\lambda(z\gamma) = \infty$. These and other properties of truncated normal random variables are presented in Appendix C.[45]

As noted by Heckman (1980) and Heckman and Robb (1985), because $\Phi(\psi)$ is monotone increasing in ψ, $z\gamma = \Phi^{-1}(\Pr(D(Z) = 1 \mid Z = z))$, and we can substitute everywhere for $z\gamma$ by $P(z) = \Pr(D(Z) = 1 \mid Z = z)$, the propensity score, to reach

$$\begin{aligned}\mathrm{TT}(x, z) &= \mathrm{TT}\big(x, P(z)\big)\\ &= x(\beta_1 - \beta_0) + \mathrm{Cov}(U_1 - U_0, \upsilon)K\big(P(z)\big).^{46}\end{aligned}$$

Observe that if $\mathrm{Cov}(U_1 - U_0, \upsilon) = 0$, ATE = TT. If $\mathrm{Cov}(U_1 - U_0, \upsilon) > 0$, TT > ATE because of purposive sorting into sector 1. A positive covariance is guaranteed by the Roy model because $\upsilon = U_1 - U_0$. As $z\gamma$ increases, more agents with low values of υ are drawn in to sector 1. If υ is positively correlated with $U_1 - U_0$, we lower the average quality of participants (agents for whom $R > 0$) as we increase $z\gamma$.

As $z\gamma \to \infty$, $P(z) \to 1$, and the distance between ATE and TT goes to zero. Agents with high values of the probability of participation are a random sample of the U_1 but obviously not a random sample of the $z\gamma$. Limit set arguments of the type that set $P(z)$ to one or zero play a crucial role in versions of semiparametric identification of economic choice models and in the entire treatment effect literature that seeks to identify ATE by the method of instrumental variables.

The LATE parameter for the generalized Roy model can be derived using the fact that if $(y, r) \sim N(\mu_y, \mu_r, \sigma_y, \sigma_r, \rho)$ and $b > a$, then

$$E(y \mid a \leqslant r < b) = \mu_y + \rho\sigma_y\left(\frac{\phi(\alpha) - \phi(\beta)}{\Phi(\beta) - \Phi(\alpha)}\right),$$

where $\alpha = (a - \mu_r)/\sigma_r$, $\beta = (b - \mu_r)/\sigma_r$. Using an instrument dependent definition of LATE and normalizing $\mathrm{Var}(\upsilon) = 1$,

$$\begin{aligned}\mathrm{LATE}(z, z', x) &= E(Y_1 - Y_0 \mid x, -z'\gamma \leqslant \upsilon < -z\gamma)\\ &= x(\beta_1 - \beta_0) + \mathrm{Cov}(U_1 - U_0, \upsilon)\left[\frac{\phi(z\gamma) - \phi(z'\gamma)}{\Phi(z'\gamma) - \Phi(z\gamma)}\right],\end{aligned} \tag{3.5}$$

where the final result uses the symmetry of the normal density. The Marginal Treatment Effect (MTE) corresponds to the expected outcome gain for those agents who are just indifferent to the receipt of treatment at the given value of the unobservable υ. Formally, recalling that we normalize $\mathrm{Var}(\upsilon) = 1$,

[45] Notice that $d = -z\gamma$ in the notation of Appendix C.

[46] $K(P(Z)) = \frac{\phi(\Phi^{-1}(P(z)))}{P(z)}$.

$$\begin{aligned}\text{MTE}(x, -z\gamma) &= x(\beta_1 - \beta_0) + E(U_1 - U_0 | \upsilon = -z\gamma)\\ &= x(\beta_1 - \beta_0) + \text{Cov}(U_1 - U_0, \upsilon)[-z\gamma].^{47}\end{aligned} \tag{3.6}$$

In terms of the propensity score, we can write $\text{MTE}(x, 1 - P(z)) = x(\beta_1 - \beta_0) + (\rho_1\sigma_1 - \rho_0\sigma_0)\Phi^{-1}(1 - P(z))$. As long as $\text{Cov}(U_1 - U_0, \upsilon) > 0$, those with high values of $P(z)$ (high values of $z\gamma$) have the *lowest* mean returns to participation. Evaluating MTE when $z\gamma$ is large corresponds to the case where the average outcome gain is evaluated for those agents with unobservables making them on average less likely to participate. Higher mean scale utilities draw in those agents with unobservables that make them less likely to participate. When $\upsilon = 0$, MTE = ATE as a consequence of the symmetry of the normal distribution.

The other evaluation criteria discussed in Section 2 can be formed using the normal model. The proportion of agents who benefit from the program in subjective terms is the propensity score $P(Z)$. In the special case of the Roy model where $C \equiv 0$, this is also the proportion of agents who benefit in "objective" terms ($\Pr(Y_1 \geqslant Y_0)$). The policy relevant treatment effect depends on the exact specification of policies. We develop versions of the policy relevant treatment effect in Chapter 71. Given the ingredients of the discrete choice model (3.1) with associated outcomes (3.3), we can generate all of the treatment effects and counterfactual distributions discussed in Section 2.

The linearity, exogeneity, separability and normality assumptions invoked in this section make it possible to solve policy problems P-1–P-3. We can solve policy problem P-2 (the extrapolation problem) using this model evaluated at new values of (X, Z). By construction the (U_1, U_0, υ) are independent of (X, Z), and given the functional forms all the mean treatment parameters can be generated for all (X, Z).

By parameterizing the β_i to depend only on measured characteristics, it is possible to forecast the demand for new goods and solve policy problem P-3. For example, suppose that β_1, β_0 and γ only depend on the characteristics of the policies. A special case would be

$$\beta_1(Q_1) = \Lambda Q_1', \tag{3.7a}$$

$$\beta_0(Q_0) = \Lambda Q_0', \tag{3.7b}$$

where Q_1 and Q_0 are $1 \times J$ vectors of characteristics of programs, and X is a $1 \times K$ vector of agent-specific characteristics, and Λ is a $K \times J$ matrix. Z is a $1 \times M$ vector

[47] Note that using L'Hôpital's Rule, MTE can be regarded as the limit form of LATE. Setting $\sigma_\upsilon = 1$, we obtain

$$\begin{aligned}\text{MTE}(x, -z\gamma) &= x(\beta_1 - \beta_0) + \text{Cov}(U_1 - U_0, \upsilon) \lim_{t \to -z\gamma}\left[\frac{\phi(-z\gamma) - \phi(t)}{\Phi(t) - \Phi(-z\gamma)}\right]\\ &= x(\beta_1 - \beta_0) + \text{Cov}(U_1 - U_0, \upsilon) \lim_{t \to -z\gamma}\left[\frac{(\phi(-z\gamma) - \phi(t))/(-z\gamma - t)}{(\Phi(t) - \Phi(-z\gamma))/(-z\gamma - t)}\right]\\ &= x(\beta_1 - \beta_0) + \text{Cov}(U_1 - U_0, \upsilon)[-z\gamma].\end{aligned}$$

and Γ is a $M \times J$ matrix of characteristics such that

$$\gamma(Q_1) - \gamma(Q_0) = \Gamma[Q_1' - Q_0'].$$

Under this assumption, all programs can be put on a common basis in terms of the characteristics they offer. The characteristics of agents are (X, Z). For a new program, generated by a new bundle of fixed characteristics, we can solve P-3 if we can also characterize the distributions of $\upsilon(s)$ and $U(s)$ in terms of the $Q(s)$. One special case is where the $\upsilon(s)$ and $U(s)$ do not depend on s, as in Quandt and Baumol (1966) or McFadden (1974). Then all effects of the new program come through the β and γ. We now consider some examples of the Roy model. It defines the economic choice framework used throughout this Handbook chapter, so it is useful to gain intuition about it.

3.3.1. Examples of Roy models

Figure 1, adapted from Heckman, Urzua and Vytlacil (2006), displays the distribution of gross gains $(Y_1 - Y_0)$ from adopting a treatment. The generating model is an extended Roy model with parameters given at the base of the table. The model builds in positive sorting on unobservables because $\upsilon = U_1 - U_0$ so $\text{Cov}(U_1 - U_0, \upsilon) > 0$. All agents face the same cost of treatment adoption C. The return to the treatment for the randomly selected agent is ATE ($= 0.2$). Given $C = 1.5$, the return to the agent at the margin is 1.5. The average return for the adopting agents is TT ($= 2.666$). Thus the agents adopting the treatment are the ones who benefit from it. This is a source of evaluation bias in evaluating programs.

Figure 2 plots the parameters ATE(p), TT(p), MTE(p) and TUT(p) (treatment on the untreated) that underlie the model used to generate Figure 1. Table 2 presents the formulae for the treatment parameters as a function of p. Here "p" denotes a value of $P(Z)$ and not a policy as in the previous sections. The declining MTE(p) is the prototypical pattern of diminishing returns that accompanies an expansion of treatment (MTE declines in $U_D = u_D = p$). Agents with low levels of $Z\gamma$ ($P(Z)$) that adopt the treatment must do so because their unobservables make them more likely to. They have high values of υ ($R = Z\gamma + \upsilon$) that compensate for the low values of $Z\gamma$. Since υ is positively correlated with $U_1 - U_0$ and Z does not enter $\mu_1(X) - \mu_0(X)$, the MTE is high for the low p agents at the margin of indifference. As cost C falls, more agents are drawn in to adopt treatment and the return falls. The pattern for treatment on the treated (TT(p)) is explained by similar considerations. As participation becomes less selective, the selected agent outcomes converge to the population average. As more agents participate, the stragglers are, on average, less effective adopters of the treatment. This explains the pattern for TUT(p). Observe that the slopes of these curves would reverse if there is negative sorting on unobservables ($\text{Cov}(U_1 - U_0, \upsilon) < 0$). In this case, participants in the program would be those with below-average unobservables. Figure 3 plots the trade-off in $Z\gamma$ and υ that make agents indifferent and the two regions demarcated by the line of indifference. Agents with $(Z\gamma, \upsilon)$ traits to the right of the line have $D = 1$. Agents with traits below the line have $D = 0$.

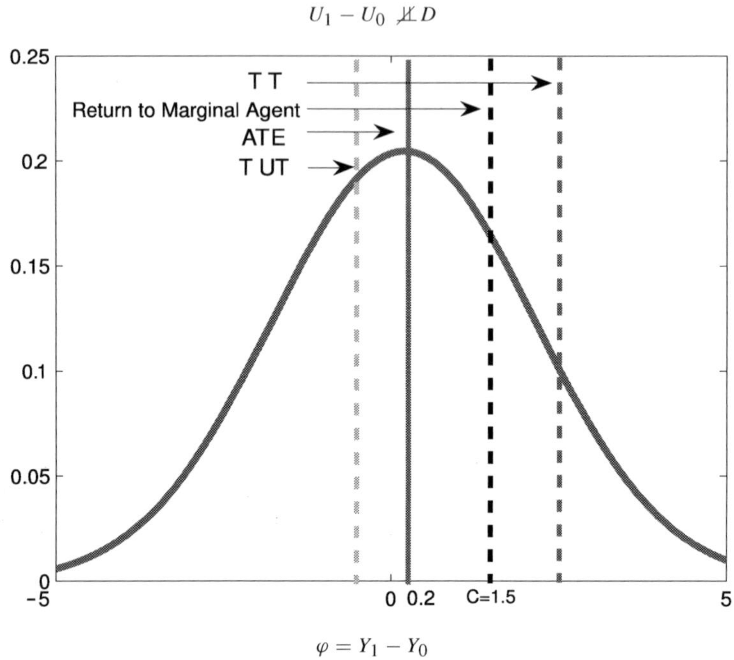

TT = 2.666, TUT = −0.632
Return to marginal agent = C = 1.5
ATE = $\mu_1 - \mu_0 = \bar{\varphi} = 0.2$

The model

Outcomes	Choice model
$Y_1 = \mu_1 + U_1 = \alpha + \bar{\varphi} + U_1$	$D = \begin{cases} 1 & \text{if } R \geqslant 0 \\ 0 & \text{if } R < 0 \end{cases}$
$Y_0 = \mu_0 + U_0 = \alpha + U_0$	

General case

$(U_1 - U_0) \not\perp\!\!\!\perp D$
ATE ≠ TT ≠ TUT

The researcher observes (Y, D, C)
$Y = \alpha + \varphi D + U_0$ where $\varphi = Y_1 - Y_0$

Parameterization

$\alpha = 0.67$ $(U_1, U_0) \sim N(\mathbf{0}, \mathbf{\Sigma})$ $\mu_Z = (2, -2)$ $R = Y_1 - Y_0 - C$

$\bar{\varphi} = 0.2$ $\mathbf{\Sigma} = \begin{bmatrix} 1 & -0.9 \\ -0.9 & 1 \end{bmatrix}$ $\mathbf{\Sigma}_Z = \begin{bmatrix} 9 & -2 \\ -2 & 9 \end{bmatrix}$ $C = 1.5$

Figure 1. Distribution of gains. The extended Roy economy. Adapted from Heckman, Urzua and Vytlacil (2006).

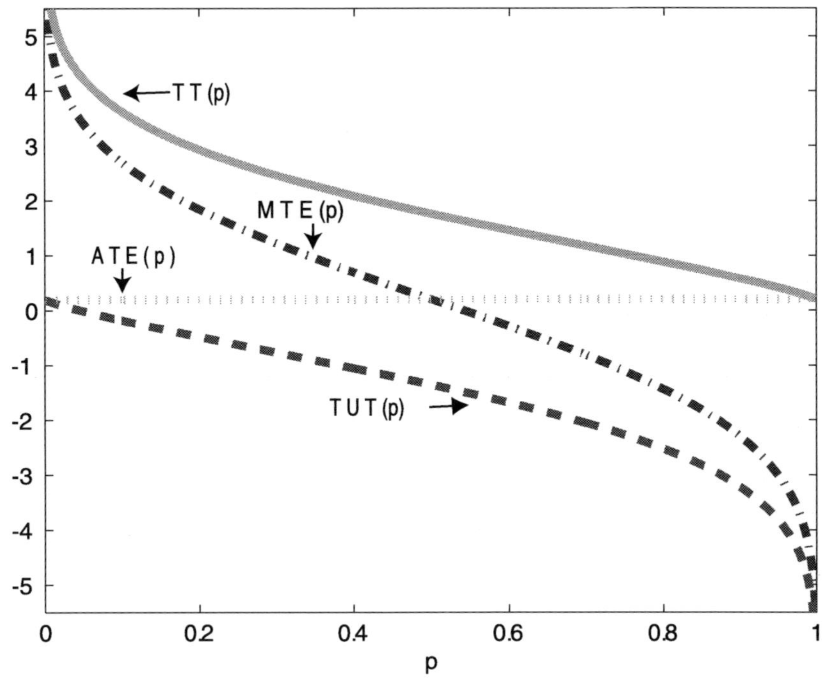

Figure 2. Treatment parameters as a function of $P(Z) = p$. Adapted from Heckman, Urzua and Vytlacil (2006).

Table 2
Treatment parameters evaluated at $P(Z) = p$

Parameter	Definition	Under assumptions (model below)
Marginal treatment effect	$E[Y_1 - Y_0 \mid R = 0, U_D = p]$	$\bar{\varphi} + \sigma_{U_1-U_0}\Phi^{-1}(1-p)$
Average treatment effect	$E[Y_1 - Y_0 \mid P(Z) = p]$	$\bar{\varphi}$
Treatment on the treated	$E[Y_1 - Y_0 \mid R > 0, P(Z) = p]$	$\bar{\varphi} + \sigma_{U_1-U_0}\frac{\phi(\Phi^{-1}(p))}{p}$
Treatment on the untreated	$E[Y_1 - Y_0 \mid R \leqslant 0, P(Z) = p]$	$\bar{\varphi} - \sigma_{U_1-U_0}\frac{\phi(\Phi^{-1}(p))}{p}$

Note. $\Phi(\cdot)$ and $\phi(\cdot)$ represent the cdf and pdf of a standard normal distribution, respectively. $\Phi^{-1}(\cdot)$ represents the inverse of $\Phi(\cdot)$.

This example shows how the extended Roy model can be used to define the distribution of treatment effects. Mean treatment parameters are derived from it. The Roy model and its extensions are examples of economic models that can be used to define counterfactuals (in this case Y_0 and Y_1). They are purely theoretical constructs. We discuss iden-

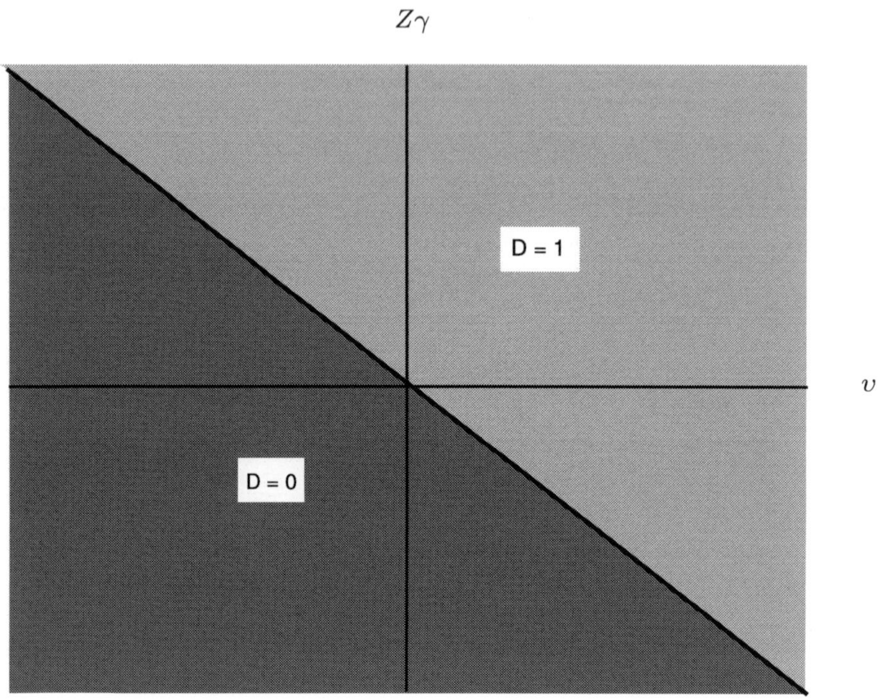

Figure 3. Partitions of $Z\gamma$ and υ into $D = 0$ and $D = 1$. The boundary $(Z\gamma + \upsilon = 0)$ is the margin of indifference.

tification of this model and its extensions in Section 6.1. In Chapter 71 and in Abbring and Heckman (Chapter 72), we consider how alternative evaluation estimators identify, or do not identify, the parameters of this basic economic model, and its extensions.

3.4. Adding uncertainty

Because it does not rely on explicitly formulated economic models, the treatment effect literature is not clear about the sources of variability and uncertainty that characterize choices and outcomes and their relationship. The econometric approach to program evaluation is very clear about the sources of uncertainty and variability in the econometric model.

In devising estimators and interpreting estimated parameters, it is helpful to distinguish the information available to the agent from the information available to the observing econometrician. In advance of choosing an activity, agents may be uncertain about the outcomes that will actually occur. They may also be uncertain about the full costs they bear. In general the agent's information is not the same as the econometrician's, and they may not be nested. The agent may know things in advance that the econometrician may never discover. On the other hand, the econometrician, benefitting from hindsight, may know some information that the agent does not know when he is making his choices.

Let $\mathcal{I}_{ea}$ be the information set confronting the agent at the time choices are made and before outcomes are realized. Agents may only imperfectly estimate consequences of their choices. In place of (3.1), we can write, using somewhat nonstandard notation,

$$R(s, \mathcal{I}_{ea}) = \mu_R(s, \mathcal{I}_{ea}) + \upsilon(s, \mathcal{I}_{ea})$$

reflecting that *ex ante* valuations are made on the basis of *ex ante* information where $\mu_R(s, \mathcal{I}_{ea})$ is determined by variables that are known to the econometrician and $\upsilon(s, \mathcal{I}_{ea})$ are components known to the agent but not the econometrician. *Ex post* evaluations can also be made using a different information set $\mathcal{I}_{ep}$ reflecting the arrival of information after the choice is realized. It is possible that

$$\operatorname{argmax}_{s \in \mathcal{S}}\{R(s, \mathcal{I}_{ea})\} \neq \operatorname{argmax}_{s \in \mathcal{S}}\{R(s, \mathcal{I}_{ep})\}$$

in which case there maybe *ex post* regret or elation about the choice made.

Determining agent information sets is a major research topic in structural econometrics [see Abbring and Campbell (2005), Miller (1984), Pakes (1986), Chan and Hamilton (2003), Carneiro, Hansen and Heckman (2003), Cunha, Heckman and Navarro (2005)]. The *ex ante* vs. *ex post* distinction is essential for understanding behavior. In environments of uncertainty, agent choices are made in terms of *ex ante* calculations. Yet the treatment effect literature largely reports *ex post* returns.[48] In this chapter, we analyze both *ex ante* and *ex post* objective outcomes and subjective valuations. Abbring and Heckman (Chapter 72) show how to implement these distinctions.

In the context of the simple two-outcome model developed in Section 3.3, we can define $R(\mathcal{I}_{ea})$ as

$$R(\mathcal{I}_{ea}) = E(Y_1 - Y_0 - C \mid \mathcal{I}_{ea}).$$

Under perfect foresight, the agent knows Y_1, Y_0 and C as in the classical generalized Roy model; $\mathcal{I}_{ea} \supseteq \{Y_1, Y_0, C\}$. More generally, the choice equation is generated by $D(\mathcal{I}_{ea}) = \mathbf{1}[R(\mathcal{I}_{ea}) \geqslant 0]$. *Ex post*, different choices might be made. *Ex ante*, agents may be uncertain about aspects of the choices that they made. For different specifications of the information set we obtain different choices.

The econometrician may possess yet a different information set $\mathcal{I}_e$. Choice probabilities computed against one information set are not generally the same as those computed against another information set. Operating with hindsight, the econometrician may be privy to some information not available to agents when they make their choices. Abbring and Heckman (Chapter 72) survey models with uncertainty.

[48] As Hicks (1946, p. 179) puts it, "*Ex post calculations of capital accumulation have their place in economic and statistical history; they are useful measure for economic progress; but they are of no use to theoretical economists who are trying to find out how the system works, because they have no significance for conduct.*"

We consider identifiability of the generalized Roy model under certainty in Section 6. The recent literature on semiparametric econometric models surveyed in Chapter 73 (Matzkin) of this Handbook enables economists to relax the normality, separability and functional form assumptions developed in the early literature on structural estimation while at the same time preserving the economic content of the structural literature.

Before developing this topic, we clarify the distinction between structural models and causal models and we relate the statistical treatment effect literature to the literature on structural economic models.

4. Counterfactuals, causality and structural econometric models

The literature on policy evaluation in economics sometimes compares "structural" approaches with "treatment effect" or "causal" models.[49] These terms are used loosely. This section formally defines "structural" models and uses them as devices for generating counterfactuals. We consider both outcome and treatment choice equations. We compare the econometric model for generating counterfactuals and causal effects with the Neyman (1923)–Rubin (1978) model of causality and compare "causal" parameters with "structural" parameters. We compare and evaluate the structural equations approach and the treatment effects approach. We restore the "ω" notation introduced in Section 2 because it clarifies our discussion.

4.1. Generating counterfactuals

The treatment effect approach and the explicitly economic approach differ in the detail with which they specify both observed and counterfactual outcomes $Y(s, \omega)$, for different treatments denoted by "s". The econometric approach models counterfactuals much more explicitly than is common in the application of the treatment effect approach. This difference in detail corresponds to the differing objectives of the two approaches. This greater attention to detail in the structural approach facilitates the application of theory to provide interpretation of counterfactuals and comparison of counterfactuals across data sets using the basic parameters of economic theory. These models also suggest strategies for identifying parameters (task 2 in Table 1). Models for counterfactuals are the basis for extending historically experienced policies to new environments and for forecasting the effects of new policies never previously experienced. These are policy questions P-2 and P-3 stated in Section 2. Comparisons are made across treatments to define the individual level (ω) causal effect of s relative to s' as in (2.1).

Models for counterfactuals are in the mind. They are internally consistent frameworks derived from theory. Verification and identification of these models are logically distinct tasks that should be carefully distinguished from the purely theoretical act of

[49] See, e.g., Angrist and Imbens (1995) and Angrist, Imbens and Rubin (1996).

constructing internally consistent models. No issue of sampling, inference or selection bias is entailed in constructing theoretical models for counterfactuals.

The traditional model of econometrics is the "all causes" model. It writes outcomes as a deterministic mapping of inputs to outputs:

$$y(s) = g_s(x, u_s), \tag{4.1}$$

where x and u_s are fixed variables specified by the relevant economic theory. This notation allows for different unobservables u_s to affect different outcomes.[50] $\mathcal{D}$ is the domain of the mapping $g_s : \mathcal{D} \to \mathcal{R}^y$, where $\mathcal{R}^y$ is the range of y. There may be multiple outcome variables. All outcomes are explained in a functional sense by the arguments of g_s in (4.1). If we model the *ex post* realizations of outcomes, it is entirely reasonable to invoke an all causes model. *Ex post*, all uncertainty has been resolved. Implicit in the definition of a function is the requirement that g_s be "stable" or "invariant" to changes in x and u_s. The g_s function remains stable as its arguments are varied. Invariance is a key property of a causal model.

Equation (4.1) is a production function relating inputs (factors) to outputs. The notation x and u_s anticipates the practical econometric problem that some arguments of functional relationship (4.1) are observed while other arguments may be unobserved by the econometrician. In the analysis of this section, their roles are symmetric. g_s maps (x, u_s) into the range of y or image of $\mathcal{D}$ under g_s, where the domain of definition $\mathcal{D}$ may differ from the empirical support.[51] Thus, Equation (4.1) maps admissible inputs into possible *ex post* outcomes. Our notation allows for different unobservables from a common list u to appear in different outcome equations.

A "deep structural" version of (4.1), discussed in Sections 3.2 and 3.3, models the variation of the g_s in terms of s as a map constructed from generating characteristics q_s, x and u_s into outcomes:

$$y(s) = g(q_s, x, u_s), \tag{4.2}$$

where now the domain of g, $\mathcal{D}$, is defined for q_s, x, u_s so that we have $g : \mathcal{D} \to \mathcal{R}^y$.[52] The components q_s provide the basis for generating the counterfactuals across treatments from a base set of characteristics. g maps (q_s, s, u_s) into the range of y, $g : (q_s, x, u_s) \to \mathcal{R}^y$, where the domain of definition $\mathcal{D}$ of g may differ from the empirical support. In this specification, different treatments s are characterized by different bundles of a set of characteristics common across all treatments. This framework provides the basis for solving policy problem P-3 since new policies (treatments) are generated from common characteristics, and all policies are put on a common basis.

[50] An alternative notation would use a common u and lets g_s select out s-specific components.

[51] The support is the region of the domain of definition where we have data on the function. Thus if $\mathcal{D}_x$ is the domain of x, the support of x is the region $\text{Supp}(x) \subset \mathcal{D}_x$ such that the data density $f(x)$ satisfies the condition $f(x) > 0$ for $x \in \text{Supp}(x)$.

[52] An example is given by Equations (3.7a) and (3.7b).

If a new policy is characterized by known transformations of (q_s, x, u_s) that lie in the domain of definition of g, policy forecasting problem P-3 can be solved. The argument of the maps g_s and g are part of the *a priori* specification of a causal model. Analysts may disagree about appropriate arguments to include in these maps.

One benefit of the statistical approach that focuses on problem P-1 is that it works solely with outcomes rather than inputs. However, it is silent on how to solve problems P-2 and P-3 and provides no basis for interpreting the population level treatment effects.

Consider alternative models of schooling outcomes of pupils where s indexes the schooling type (e.g., regular public, charter public, private secular and private parochial). The q_s are the observed characteristics of schools of type s. The x are the observed characteristics of the pupil. u_s are the unobserved characteristics of both the schools and the pupil. If we can characterize a proposed new type of school as a new package of different levels of the same ingredients x, q_s, and u_s and we can identify (4.2) over the domain of the function defined by the new package, we can solve problem P-3. If the same schooling input (same q_s) is applied to different students (those with different x) and we can identify (4.1) or (4.2) over the new domain of definition, we solve problem P-2. By digging deeper into the "causes of the effects" we can do more than just compare the effects of treatments in place with each other. In addition, as we show in Chapter 71, modeling the u_s and its relationship with the corresponding unobservables in the treatment choice equation, is highly informative on the choice of appropriate identification strategies.

Another example from the theory of labor supply writes hours of work h as a function of the before tax wage w, where s is the tax rate that is assumed common across all agents, and other characteristics are denoted u_s. Treatment in this example is the proportional tax rate s. We may write hours of work in tax regime s, for a person with wage w and characteristics x as

$$h_s = h\big(w(1-s), x, u_s\big)$$

as the labor supply for proportional tax rate s for an agent with characteristics (x, u_s).[53] This may be a factual (observed) quantity or a counterfactual quantity. Different tax rates (policies) produce different counterfactuals which are generated by a common function. We return to this example on several occasions throughout this chapter.

Our analysis in Section 3.3 provides a deep structural generalized Roy model example of causal functions. The outcome equations parameterized by (3.7a) and (3.7b) are examples of models with deep structural parameters that can be used to solve P-2 and P-3.

[53] This notation permits the unobservable to differ across tax regimes.

Equations (4.1) and (4.2) are sometimes called Marshallian causal functions [see Heckman (2000)]. Assuming that the components of (x, u_s) or (q_s, x, u_s) are variation-free,[54] a feature that may or may not be produced by the relevant theory, we may vary each argument of these functions to get a *ceteris paribus* causal effect of the argument on the outcome. Some components may be variation free while others are not. These thought experiments are conducted for hypothetical variations. Recall that the *a priori* theory specifies the arguments in the causal functions and the list of things held fixed when a variable is manipulated. Equations (3.4a)–(3.4b) are examples of Marshallian causal functions where (X, U) are the observed and unobserved variables.

Changing one coordinate while fixing the others produces a Marshallian *ceteris paribus* causal effect of a change in that coordinate on the outcome variables. Varying q_s fixes different treatment levels. Variations in u_s among agents explain why people with the same x characteristics respond differently to the same treatment s.

The *ceteris paribus* variation need not be for a single variable of the function. A treatment generally consists of a package of characteristics and if we vary the package from q_s to $q_{s'}$ we get different treatment effects.

We use the convention that lower case values are used to define fixed values and upper case notation denotes random variables. In defining (4.1) and (4.2), we have explicitly worked with fixed variables that are manipulated in a hypothetical way as in the algebra of elementary physics. In a purely deterministic world, agents act on these nonstochastic variables. If uncertainty is a feature of the environment, (4.1) and (4.2) can be interpreted as *ex post* realizations of the counterfactual. Even if the world is uncertain, *ex post*, after the realization of uncertainty, the outcomes of uncertain inputs are deterministic. Some components of u_s may be random shocks realized after decisions about treatment are made.

Thus if uncertainty is a feature of the environment, (4.1) and (4.2) can be interpreted as *ex post* realizations of the counterfactual as uncertainty is resolved. *Ex ante* versions may be different. From the point of view of agent ω with information set $\mathcal{I}_\omega$, the *ex ante* expected value of $Y(s, \omega)$ is

$$E\big(Y(s,\omega) \mid \mathcal{I}_\omega\big) = E\big(g\big(Q(s,\omega), X(\omega), U(s,\omega)\big) \mid \mathcal{I}_\omega\big),\ ^{55} \tag{4.3}$$

where $Q(s, \omega)$, $X(\omega)$, $U(s, \omega)$ are random variables generated from a distribution that depends on the agent's information set indexed by $\mathcal{I}_\omega$. This distribution may differ from the distribution produced by "reality" or nature if agent expectations are different from objective reality.[56] In the presence of intrinsic uncertainty, the relevant decision maker

[54] More precisely, if $\mathcal{X}, \mathcal{U}$ or $\mathcal{Q}, \mathcal{X}, \mathcal{U}$ are the domains of (4.1) and (4.2), $\mathcal{D} = (\mathcal{X}, \mathcal{U}) = \mathcal{X}_1 \times \cdots \times \mathcal{X}_N \times \mathcal{U}_1 \times \cdots \times \mathcal{U}_M$ or $(\mathcal{Q}, \mathcal{X}, \mathcal{U}) = \mathcal{Q}_1 \times \cdots \times \mathcal{Q}_K \times \mathcal{X}_1 \times \cdots \times \mathcal{X}_N \times \mathcal{U}_1 \times \cdots \times \mathcal{U}_M$ where we assume K components in $\mathcal{Q}$, N components in $\mathcal{X}$, and M components in $\mathcal{U}$.

[55] The expectation might be computed using the information sets of the relevant decision maker (e.g., the parents in the case of the outcomes of the child) who might not be the agent whose outcomes are measured. These random variables are drawn from agent ω's subjective distribution.

[56] Thus agents do not necessarily use rational expectations, so the distribution used by the agent to make decisions need not be the same as the distribution generating the data.

acts on (4.3) but the *ex post* counterfactual is

$$Y(s,\omega) = E\big(Y(s,\omega) \mid \mathcal{I}_\omega\big) + \nu(s,\omega), \tag{4.4}$$

where $\nu(s,\omega)$ satisfies $E(\nu(s,\omega) \mid \mathcal{I}_\omega) = 0$. In this interpretation, the information set of agent ω is part of the model specification but the realizations come from a probability distribution, and the information set includes the technology g. This representation clarifies the distinction between deterministic *ex post* outcomes and intrinsically random *ex ante* outcomes. Abbring and Heckman (Chapter 72) present Roy model examples of models accounting for uncertainty.

This statement of the basic deterministic model reconciles the all causes model (4.1) and (4.2) with the intrinsic uncertainty model favored by some statisticians [see, e.g., Dawid (2000) and the discussion following his paper]. *Ex ante*, there is uncertainty at the agent (ω) level but *ex post* there is not. The realizations of $\nu(s,\omega)$ are ingredients of the *ex post* all causes model, but not part of the subjective *ex ante* all causes model. The probability law used by the agent to compute the expectations of $g(Q(s,\omega), X(\omega), U_s(\omega))$ may differ from the objective distribution that generates the observed data, so no assumption of rational expectations is necessarily imposed. In the *ex ante* all causes model, manipulations of $\mathcal{I}_\omega$ define the *ex ante* causal effects.

Thus from the point of view of the agent we can vary elements in $\mathcal{I}_\omega$ to produce Marshallian *ex ante* causal response functions. The *ex ante* treatment effect from the point of view of the agent for treatment s and s' is

$$E\big(Y(s,\omega) \mid \mathcal{I}_\omega\big) - E\big(Y(s',\omega) \mid \mathcal{I}_\omega\big). \tag{4.5}$$

However, agents may not act in terms of these *ex ante* effects if they have decision criteria (utility functions) that are not linear in the outcomes but may form expectations of nonlinear functions of $Y(s,\omega)$, $s = 1,\dots,\bar{S}$. We discuss *ex ante* valuations of outcomes in the next section.

The value of the scientific (or explicitly structural) approach to the construction of counterfactuals is that it models the unobservables and the sources of variability among observationally identical people. Since it is the unobservables that give rise to selection bias and problems of inference that are central to empirically rigorous causal analysis, economists using the scientific approach can draw on economic theory to design and justify methods to control for selection bias. This avenue is not available to adherents of the statistical approach. Statistical approaches that are not explicit about the sources of the unobservables make strong implicit assumptions which, when carefully exposited, are often unattractive. We exposit these assumptions in Chapter 71 when we discuss specific policy evaluation estimators.

The models for counterfactuals (4.1) and (4.2) are based on theory. The arguments of these functions are varied by hypothetical manipulations. These are thought experiments. When analysts attempt to construct counterfactuals empirically, they must carefully distinguish between these theoretical relationships and the empirical relationships determined by conditioning only on the observables.

The data used to determine these functions may be limited in its support. In this case analysts cannot fully identify the theoretical relationships over hypothetical domains of definition. In addition, in the support, the components of X, $U(s)$ and $\mathcal{I}_\omega$ may not be variation free even if they are variation free in the hypothetical domain of definition of the function. A good example is the problem of multicollinearity. If the X in a sample are functionally dependent, it is not possible to identify the Marshallian causal function with respect to all variations in x over the available support even if one can imagine hypothetically varying the components of x over the domains of definition of the functions (4.1) or (4.2).

We next turn to an important distinction between fixing and conditioning on factors that gets to the heart of the distinction between causal models and correlational relationships. This point is independent of any problem with the supports of the samples compared to the domains of definition of the functions.

4.2. Fixing vs. conditioning

The distinction between *fixing* and *conditioning* on inputs is central to distinguishing true causal effects from spurious causal effects. In an important paper, Haavelmo (1943) made this distinction in linear equation models. Haavelmo's distinction is the basis for Pearl's (2000) book on causality that generalizes Haavelmo's analysis to nonlinear settings. Pearl defines an operator "do" to represent the mental act of fixing a variable to distinguish it from the action of conditioning which is a statistical operation. If the conditioning set is sufficiently rich, fixing and conditioning are the same in an *ex post* all causes model.[57] Pearl suggests a particular physical mechanism for fixing variables and operationalizing causality, but it is not central to his or any other definition of causality.

The distinction between fixing and conditioning is most easily illustrated in the linear regression model analyzed by Haavelmo (1943). Let $y = x\beta + u$. While y and u are scalars, x may be a vector. The linear equation maps every pair (x, u) into a scalar $y \in \mathbb{R}$. Suppose that the support of random variable (X, U) in the data is the same as the domain of (x, u) that are fixed in the hypothetical thought experiment and that the (x, u) are variation-free (i.e., can be independently varied coordinate by coordinate). We thus abstract from the problem of limited support that is discussed in the preceding section. We may write (dropping the "ω" notation for random variables, as we did in Section 3)

$$Y = X\beta + U.$$

Here "nature" or the "real world" picks (X, U) to determine Y. X is observed by the analyst and U is not observed, and (X, U) are random variables. This is an all causes

[57] Florens and Heckman (2003) distinguish conditioning from fixing, and generalize Pearl's analysis to both static and dynamic settings.

model in which (X, U) determine Y. The variation generated by the hypothetical model varies one coordinate of (X, U), fixing all other coordinates to produce the effect of the variation on the outcome Y. Nature (as opposed to the model) may not permit such variation.

Formally, we can write this model formulated at the population level as a conditional expectation,

$$E(Y \mid X = x, U = u) = x\beta + u.$$

Since we condition on both X and U, there is no further source of variation in Y. This is a deterministic model that coincides with the all causes model. Thus on the support, which is also assumed to be the domain of definition of the function, this model is the same model as the deterministic, hypothetical model, $y = x\beta + u$. Fixing X at different values corresponds to doing different thought experiments with the X. Fixing and conditioning are the same in this case.

If, however, we only condition on X, we obtain

$$E(Y \mid X = x) = x\beta + E(U \mid X = x).^{58} \tag{4.6}$$

This relationship does not generate U-constant (Y, X) relationships. It generates only an X-constant relationship. Unless we condition on all of the "causes" (the right-hand side variables), the empirical relationship (4.6) does not identify causal effects of X on Y. The variation in X also moves the conditional mean of U given X.

This analysis can be generalized to a nonlinear model $y = g(q, x, u)$. A model specified in terms of random variables Q, X, U with the same support as q, x, u has as its conditional expectation $g(Q, X, U)$ under general conditions. Conditioning only on Q, X does not in principle identify $g(q, x, u)$.

Conditioning and fixing on the arguments of g or g_s are the same operations in an "all causes" model if all causes are accounted for. In general, they are not the same. This analysis can be generalized to account for the temporal resolution of uncertainty if we include $\nu(s, \omega)$ as an argument in the *ex post* causal model. The outcomes can include both objective outcomes $Y(s, \omega)$ and subjective outcomes $R(Y(s, \omega), \omega)$.

Statisticians and epidemiologists often do not distinguish between fixing and conditioning because they typically define the models that they analyze in terms of some type of conditioning on observed random variables. However, thought experiments in models of hypotheticals that vary factors are distinct from variations in conditioning variables. The latter conflate the effects of variation in X, holding U fixed, with the effects of X in predicting the unobserved factors (the U) in the outcome equations. This is the crucial distinction introduced in Haavelmo's fundamental 1943 paper.

[58] We assume that the mean of U is finite.

4.3. Modeling the choice of treatment

Parallel to causal models for outcomes are causal models for the choice of treatment. Consider *ex ante* personal valuations of outcomes based on expectations of gains from receiving treatment s:

$$E\big(R\big(Y(s,\omega), C(s,\omega), Q(s,\omega), \omega\big) \mid \mathcal{I}_\omega\big), \quad s \in \mathcal{S},$$

where, as before, $C(s,\omega)$ is the price or cost agent ω must pay for participation in treatment s. We decompose $C(s,\omega)$ into observables and unobservables. We thus write $C(s,\omega) = K(W(s,\omega), \eta(s,\omega))$. We allow utility R to be defined over the characteristics that generate the treatment outcome (e.g., quality of teachers in a schooling choice model) as well as attributes of the agent. In parallel with the g_s function generating the $Y(s,\omega)$, we write

$$R\big(Y(s,\omega), C(s,\omega), Q(s,\omega), \omega\big) = f\big(Y(s,\omega), W(s,\omega), Q(s,\omega), \eta(s,\omega), \omega\big).$$

Parallel to the analysis of outcomes, we may keep $Q(s,\omega)$ implicit and use f_s functions instead of f. In the Roy model of Section 3.3, $R = Y_1 - Y_0 - C$ is the agent's subjective evaluation of treatment.

Our analysis includes both measured and unmeasured attributes as perceived by the econometrician. The agent computes expectations against his/her subjective distribution of information. We allow for imperfect information by postulating an ω-specific information set. If agents know all components of future outcomes, the upper case letters become lower case variables which are known constants. The $\mathcal{I}_\omega$ are the causal factors for agent ω. In a utility maximizing framework, choice $\hat{s}$ is made if $\hat{s}$ is maximal in the set of valuations of potential outcomes

$$\big\{E\big(R\big(Y(s,\omega), C(s,\omega), Q(s,\omega), \omega\big) \mid \mathcal{I}_\omega\big),\ s \in \mathcal{S}\big\}.$$

In this interpretation, the information set plays a key role in specifying agent preferences. Actual realizations may not be known at the time decisions are made. Accounting for uncertainty and subjective valuations of outcomes (e.g., pain and suffering for a medical treatment) is a major contribution of the econometric approach [see e.g., Carneiro, Hansen and Heckman (2003), Chan and Hamilton (2003), Heckman and Navarro (2007)]. The factors that lead an agent to participate in treatment s may be dependent on the factors affecting outcomes. Modeling this dependence is a major source of information used in the econometric approach to construct counterfactuals from real data as we demonstrate in Chapter 71. A parallel analysis can be made if the decision maker is not the same as the agent whose objective outcomes are being evaluated.

4.4. The econometric model vs. the Neyman–Rubin model

Many statisticians and social scientists invoke a model of counterfactuals and causality attributed to Donald Rubin by Paul Holland (1986) but which is actually due to Neyman

(1923).[59] This model arises from the statistical literature on the design of experiments.[60] It draws on hypothetical experiments to define causality and thereby creates the impression in the minds of many of its users that random assignment is the most convincing way to identify causal models. Some would say it is the only way to identify causal models.

Neyman and Rubin postulate counterfactuals $\{Y(s,\omega)\}_{s\in\mathcal{S}}$ without modeling the factors determining the $Y(s,\omega)$ as we have done in Equations (4.1)–(4.4), using the econometric or "structural" approach. Rubin and Neyman offer no model of the choice of which outcome is selected. Thus there is no "lower case", all causes model explicitly specified in this approach nor is there any discussion of the social science or theory producing the outcomes studied.

In our notation, Rubin assumes (PI-1) and (PI-2) as presented in Section 2.[61] Since he does not develop choice equations or subjective evaluations, he does not consider the more general invariance conditions (PI-3) and (PI-4) for both objective and subjective evaluations developed in Section 2.2. Assumptions (PI-1) and (PI-2) are versions of familiar invariance assumptions developed in Cowles Commission econometrics and formalized in Hurwicz (1962) but applied only to outcome equations and not to treatment choice equations. Assumption (PI-1) says that the objective outcomes are the same irrespective of the policy or assignment mechanism that implements it within a policy regime. (PI-2) assumes no general equilibrium effects or social interactions among agents for objective outcomes. Thus the outcomes for an agent are the same whether one agent receives treatment or many receive treatment.

More formally, the Rubin model assumes

(R-1) $\{Y(s,\omega)\}_{s\in\mathcal{S}}$, *a set of counterfactuals defined for* ex post *outcomes. It does not analyze agent valuations of outcomes nor does it explicitly specify treatment selection rules, except for contrasting randomization with nonrandomization*;

(R-2) (PI-1): *Invariance of counterfactuals for objective outcomes to the mechanism of assignment within a policy regime*;

(R-3) (PI-2): *No social interactions or general equilibrium effects for objective outcomes*;

and

(R-4) *There is no simultaneity in causal effects, i.e., outcomes cannot cause each other reciprocally.*

[59] The framework attributed to Rubin was developed in statistics by Neyman (1923), Cox (1958) and others. Parallel frameworks were independently developed in psychometrics [Thurstone (1927)] and economics [Haavelmo (1943), Roy (1951), Quandt (1958, 1972)].

[60] See Cox (1958) for a classic treatment of this subject.

[61] Rubin (1986) calls these assumptions "SUTVA" for Stable Unit Treatment Value Assumption.

Two further implicit assumptions in the application of the model are that P-1 is the only evaluation problem of interest and that mean causal effects are the only objects of interest.

The econometric approach is richer and deeper than the statistical treatment effect approach. Its signature features are:

1. Development of an explicit framework for outcomes $Y(s, \omega)$, $s \in \mathcal{S}$, measurements and the choice of outcomes where the role of unobservables ("missing variables") in creating selection problems and justifying estimators is explicitly developed.
2. The analysis of subjective evaluations of outcomes $R(s, \omega)$, $s \in \mathcal{S}$, and the use of choice data to infer them.
3. The analysis of *ex ante* and *ex post* realizations and evaluations of treatments. This analysis enables analysts to model and identify regret and anticipation by agents. Points 2 and 3 introduce agent decision making into the treatment effect literature.
4. Development of models for identifying entire distributions of treatment effects (*ex ante* and *ex post*) rather than just the traditional mean parameters focused on by many statisticians. These distributions enable analysts to determine the proportion of people who benefit from treatment, something not attempted in the statistical literature on treatment effects.
5. Development and identification of distributional criteria allowing for analysis of alternative social welfare functions for outcome distributions comparing different treatment states.
6. Models for simultaneous causality.
7. Definitions of parameters made without appeals to hypothetical experimental manipulations.
8. Clarification of the need for invariance of parameters with respect to classes of manipulations to answer classes of questions.[62]

We now amplify these points.

Selection models defined for potential outcomes with explicit treatment assignment mechanisms were developed by Gronau (1974) and Heckman (1974, 1976, 1978, 1979) in the economics literature before the Neyman–Rubin model was popularized in statistics. The econometric discrete choice literature [McFadden (1974, 1981)] uses counterfactual utilities or subjective evaluations as did its parent literature in mathematical psychology [Thurstone (1927, 1959)]. Unlike the Neyman–Rubin model, these models do not start with the experiment as an ideal but start with well-posed, clearly articulated models for outcomes and treatment choice where the unobservables that underlie the selection and evaluation problem are made explicit. The hypothetical manipulations

[62] This notion is featured in the early Cowles Commission work. See Marschak (1953) and Koopmans, Rubin and Leipnik (1950). It is formalized in Hurwicz (1962) as discussed below in Section 4.6. Rubin's "SUTVA" as embodied in (R-2) and (R-3) is a special case of the invariance condition formalized by Hurwicz and discussed in Section 4.6 below.

discussed in Section 3 define the causal parameters of the model. Randomization is a metaphor and not an ideal or "gold standard".

In contrast to the econometric model, the Holland (1986)–Rubin (1978) definition of causal effects is based on randomization. The analysis in Rubin's 1976 and 1978 papers is a dichotomy between randomization ("ignorability") and nonrandomization, and not an explicit treatment of particular selection mechanisms in the nonrandomized case as developed in the econometrics literature. Even under ideal conditions, randomization cannot answer some very basic questions such as what proportion of a population benefits from a program.[63] And in practice, contamination and cross-over effects make randomization a far from sure-fire solution even for constructing ATE.[64]

Statisticians sometimes conflate the three tasks delineated in Table 1. This problem is especially acute among the "causal analysts." The analysis of Holland (1986, 1988) illustrates this point and the central role of the randomized trial to the Holland–Rubin analysis. After explicating the "Rubin model", Holland gives a very revealing illustration that conflates the first two tasks of Table 1. He claims that there can be no causal effect of gender on earnings because analysts cannot randomly assign gender. This statement confuses the act of defining a causal effect (a purely mental act) with empirical difficulties in estimating it. These are tasks 1 and 2 in Table 1.

As another example of the same point, Rubin (1978, p. 39) denies that it is possible to define a causal effect of sex on intelligence because a randomization cannot *in principle* be performed.[65] In this and many other passages in the statistics literature, a causal effect is defined by a randomization. Issues of definition and identification are confused. This confusion continues to flourish in the literature in applied statistics. For example, Berk, Li and Hickman (2005) echo Rubin and Holland in insisting that if an experiment cannot "in principle" be performed, a causal effect cannot be defined.[66]

The act of definition is logically separate from the acts of identification and inference. A purely mental act can define a causal effect of gender. That is a separate task from identifying the causal effect. The claim that causality can only be determined by randomization glorifies randomization as the "gold standard" of causal inference.

[63] This point is made in Heckman (1992). See also Carneiro, Hansen and Heckman (2001, 2003), where this proportion is identified using choice data and/or supplementary proxy measures. See also Cunha, Heckman and Navarro (2005, 2006). Abbring and Heckman (Chapter 72) discuss this work.

[64] See the evidence on disruption bias and contamination bias arising in randomized trials that is presented in Heckman, LaLonde and Smith (1999), Heckman et al. (2000) and the discussion in Section 9 of Chapter 71.

[65] "Without treatment definitions that specify actions to be performed on experimental units, we cannot unambiguously discuss causal effects of treatments" [Rubin (1978, p. 39)].

[66] The LATE parameter of Imbens and Angrist (1994) is defined by an instrument and conflates task 1 and 2 (definition and identification). In Section 3.3 and in Chapter 71, we define the LATE parameter abstractly and separate issues of definition of parameters from issues of identification. Imbens and Angrist (1994) use instrumental variables as surrogates for randomization.

In the Neyman–Rubin model, the sources of variability generating $Y(s, \omega)$ as a random variable are not specified. The "causal effect" of s compared to s' is defined as the treatment effect (2.1). Holland (1986, 1988) argues that it is an advantage of the Rubin model that it is not explicit about the sources of variability among observationally identical agents, or about the factors that generate $Y(s, \omega)$. Holland and Rubin focus on mean treatment effects as the interesting causal parameters.

The econometric approach to causal inference supplements the model of counterfactuals with models of the choice of counterfactuals $\{D(s, \omega)\}_{s \in \mathcal{S}}$ and the relationship between choice equations and the counterfactuals. It moves beyond the dichotomy "missing at random" or "not missing at random". The $D(s, \omega)$ are explicitly modeled as generated by the collection of random variables $(Q(s, \omega), C(s, \omega), Y(s, \omega) \mid \mathcal{I}_\omega)$, $s \in \mathcal{S}$, where $Q(s, \omega)$ is the vector of characteristics of treatment s for agent ω, $C(s, \omega)$ are costs and $\{Y(s, \omega)\}_{s \in \mathcal{S}}$ are the outcomes and the "|" denotes that these variables are defined conditional on $\mathcal{I}_\omega$ (the agent's information set).[67] The variables determining choices are analyzed. Along with the *ex ante* valuations that generate $D(s, \omega)$ are the *ex post* valuations discussed in Section 2.6.[68,69]

Knowledge of the relationship between choices and counterfactuals suggests appropriate methods for solving selection problems. By analyzing the relationship of the unobservables in the outcome equation, and the unobservables in the treatment choice equation, the analyst can use *a priori* theory to devise appropriate estimators to identify causal effects.

The econometric approach, unlike the Neyman–Rubin model, emphasizes the welfare of the agents being studied (through R_G or $R(Y(s, \omega), \omega)$ or $R = Y_1 - Y_0 - C$ in the Roy model) – the "subjective evaluations" – as well as the objective evaluations. The econometric approach also distinguishes *ex ante* from *ex post* subjective evaluations, so it can measure both agent satisfaction and regret.[70]

In addition, modeling $Y(s, \omega)$ in terms of the characteristics of treatment, and of the treated, facilitates comparisons of counterfactuals and derived causal effects across studies where the composition of programs and treatment group members may vary. It also facilitates the construction of counterfactuals on new populations and the construction of counterfactuals for new policies. The Neyman–Rubin framework focuses exclusively on population level mean "causal effects" or treatment effects for policies actually experienced and provides no framework for extrapolation of findings to new environments

[67] If other agents make the treatment assignment decisions, then the determinants of $D(s, \omega)$ are modified according to what is in their information set.

[68] Corresponding to these random variables are the deterministic all causes counterparts $d(s), q_s, c(s), \{y(s)\}, i$, where the $(\{c(s)\}_{s \in \mathcal{S}}, \{q_s\}_{s \in \mathcal{S}}, \{y(s)\}_{s \in \mathcal{S}}, i)$ generate the $d(s) = 1$ if $(\{c(s)\}_{s \in \mathcal{S}}, \{q_s\}_{s \in \mathcal{S}}, \{y(s)\}_{s \in \mathcal{S}}) \in \Psi$, a subset of the domain of the generators of $d(s)$. Again the domain of definition of $d(s)$ is not necessarily the support of $c(s, \omega), q_s(\omega), \{Y(s, \omega)\}_{s \in \mathcal{S}}$ and $\mathcal{I}_\omega$.

[69] Random utility models generating $D(s, \omega)$ originate in the work of Thurstone (1927) and McFadden (1974, 1981).

[70] See Cunha, Heckman and Navarro (2005, 2006) for estimates of subjective evaluations and regret in schooling choices. Abbring and Heckman (Chapter 72) review their work.

or for forecasting new policies (problems P-2 and P-3). Its focus on population mean treatment effects elevates randomization and matching to the status of preferred estimators. Such methods cannot identify distributions of treatment effects or general quantiles of treatment effects.[71]

One major limitation of the Neyman–Rubin model is that it is recursive. It does not model causal effects of outcomes that occur simultaneously. We now present a model of simultaneous causality based on conventional simultaneous equations techniques that illustrate the power of the econometric approach. This analysis also illustrates one version of a "structural" economic model – the Cowles Commission model.

4.5. *Nonrecursive (simultaneous) models of causality*

A system of linear simultaneous equations captures interdependence among outcomes Y. For simplicity, we focus on *ex post* outcomes so in this subsection, we ignore revelation of information over time and we keep "ω" implicit. To focus the issue on nonrecursive causal models, in this subsection we also assume that the domain of definition of the model is the same as the support of the population data. Thus the model for values of upper-case variables has the same support as the domain of definition for the model in terms of lower-case variables.[72] The model developed in this section is rich enough to model interactions among agents. For simplicity we work with linear equations. We write this model in terms of parameters (Γ, B), observables (Y, X) and unobservables U as

$$\Gamma Y + BX = U, \quad E(U) = 0, \tag{4.7}$$

where Y is now a vector of endogenous and interdependent variables, X is exogenous $(E(U \mid X) = 0)$, and Γ is a full rank matrix. Equation systems like (4.7) are sometimes called "structural equations". A better nomenclature, suggested by Leamer (1985), is that the Y are internal variables determined by the model and the X are external variables specified outside the model.[73] This definition distinguishes two issues: (a) defining variables (Y) that are determined from inputs outside the model (the X) and (b) determining the relationship between observables and unobservables.[74] When the model is

[71] Angrist, Imbens and Rubin (1996) contrast structural models with causal models. The structural models they consider are the linear structural simultaneous equations models which we discuss as a special case of our analysis of nonrecursive models in Section 4.5. The appropriate comparison would be with nonseparable structural outcome models with correlated coefficients which is discussed in Heckman and Vytlacil (2001, 2005) and in Chapter 71. Angrist, Imbens and Rubin fail to note the recursive nature of Rubin model and the fundamentally nonrecursive nature of general structural models.

[72] This approach merges tasks 1 and 2 in Table 1. We do this in this section because the familiarity of the simultaneous equations model as a statistical model makes the all causes, fixed variable, *ex post* version confusing to many readers familiar with this model.

[73] This formulation is static. In a dynamic framework, Y_t would be the internal variables and the lagged Y, Y_{t-k}, $k > 0$, would be external to period t and be included in the X_t. Thus we could work with lagged dependent variables. The system would be $\Gamma Y_t + BX_t = U_t$, $E(U_t) = 0$.

[74] In a time series model, the internal variables are Y_t determined in period t.

of full rank (Γ^{-1} exists), it is said to be "complete". A complete model produces a unique Y from a given (X, U). A complete model is said to be in reduced form when structural equation (4.7) is multiplied by Γ^{-1}. The reduced form is $Y = \Pi X + \mathcal{E}$ where $\Pi = -\Gamma^{-1}B$ and $\mathcal{E} = \Gamma^{-1}U$.[75] This is a linear-in-the-parameters "all causes" model for vector Y, where the causes are X and $\mathcal{E}$. The "structure" is (Γ, B), Σ_U, where Σ_U is the variance–covariance matrix of U. In the Cowles Commission analysis it is assumed that Γ, B, Σ_U are invariant to general changes in X and translations of U. We discuss invariance of structural parameters further in the next subsection.

Π is assumed to be invariant. This is implied by the invariance of the structure but is a weaker requirement. The reduced form slope coefficients are Π, and $\Sigma_{\mathcal{E}}$ is the variance–covariance matrix of $\mathcal{E}$.[76] In the population generating (4.7), least squares recovers Π provided Σ_X, the variance of X, is nonsingular (no multicollinearity). In this linear-in-parameters equation setting, the full rank condition for Σ_X is a variation-free condition on the external variables. The reduced form solves out the Y to produce the net effect of X on Y. The linear-in-parameters model is traditional.[77] Nonlinear versions are available [Fisher (1966), Matzkin (2004, Chapter 73)]. For simplicity, we stick to the linear version, developing the nonlinear version in footnotes.[78]

The structural form (4.7) is an all causes model that relates in a deterministic way outcomes (internal variables) to other outcomes (internal variables) and external variables (the X and U). Without some restrictions, *ceteris paribus* manipulations associated with the effect of some components of Y on other components of Y are not possible within the model. We now demonstrate this point.

For specificity, consider a two-agent model of social interactions. Y_1 is the outcome for agent 1; Y_2 is the outcome for agent 2. This could be a model of interdependent consumption where the consumption of agent 1 depends on the consumption of agent 2 and other agent-1-specific variables (and possibly other agent-2-specific variables). It could also be a model of test scores. We can imagine populations of data generated from sampling the same two-agent interaction over time or sampling different two-agent couplings at a point in time.

Assuming that the preferences are interdependent, we may write the equations in structural form as

$$Y_1 = \alpha_1 + \gamma_{12} Y_2 + \beta_{11} X_1 + \beta_{12} X_2 + U_1, \tag{4.8a}$$

[75] In this section only, Π refers to the reduced form coefficient matrix and not the family of probabilities of treatment assignment Π_p, as in earlier sections.

[76] The original formulations of this model assumed normality so that only means and variances were needed to describe the joint distributions of (Y, X).

[77] The underlying all causes model writes $\Gamma y + Bx = u$, $y = \Pi x + \varepsilon$, $\Pi = -\Gamma^{-1}B$, $\varepsilon = \Gamma^{-1}u$. Recall that we assume that the domain of the all causes model is the same as the support of (X, U). Thus there is a close correspondence between these two models.

[78] Thus we can postulate a system of equations $G(Y, X, U) = 0$ and develop conditions for unique solution of reduced forms $Y = K(X, U)$ requiring that certain Jacobian terms be nonvanishing. See the contribution by Matzkin (Chapter 73) in this Handbook.

$$Y_2 = \alpha_2 + \gamma_{21} Y_1 + \beta_{21} X_1 + \beta_{22} X_2 + U_2. \tag{4.8b}$$

This model is sufficiently flexible to capture the notion that the consumption of 1 (Y_1) depends on the consumption of 2 if $\gamma_{12} \neq 0$, as well as 1's value of X if $\beta_{11} \neq 0$, X_1 (assumed to be observed), 2's value of X, X_2 if $\beta_{12} \neq 0$ and unobservable factors that affect 1 (U_1). The determinants of 2's consumption are defined symmetrically. We allow U_1 and U_2 to be freely correlated. We assume that U_1 and U_2 are mean independent of (X_1, X_2) so

$$E(U_1 \mid X_1, X_2) = 0 \tag{4.9a}$$

and

$$E(U_2 \mid X_1, X_2) = 0. \tag{4.9b}$$

Completeness guarantees that (4.8a) and (4.8b) have a determinate solution for (Y_1, Y_2).

Applying Haavelmo's (1943) analysis to (4.8a) and (4.8b), the causal effect of Y_2 on Y_1 is γ_{12}. This is the effect on Y_1 of fixing Y_2 at different values, holding constant the other variables in the equation. Symmetrically, the causal effect of Y_1 on Y_2 is γ_{21}. Conditioning, i.e., using least squares, in general, fails to identify these causal effects because U_1 and U_2 are correlated with Y_1 and Y_2. This is a traditional argument. It is based on the correlation between Y_2 and U_1. But even if $U_1 = 0$ and $U_2 = 0$, so that there are no unobservables, least squares breaks down because Y_2 is perfectly predictable by X_1 and X_2. We cannot simultaneously vary Y_2, X_1 and X_2. To see why, we derive the reduced form of this model.

Assuming completeness, the reduced form outcomes of the model after social interactions are solved out can be written as

$$Y_1 = \pi_{10} + \pi_{11} X_1 + \pi_{12} X_2 + \mathcal{E}_1, \tag{4.10a}$$

$$Y_2 = \pi_{20} + \pi_{21} X_1 + \pi_{22} X_2 + \mathcal{E}_2. \tag{4.10b}$$

Least squares can identify the *ceteris paribus* effects of X_1 and X_2 on Y_1 and Y_2 because $E(\mathcal{E}_1 \mid X_1, X_2) = 0$ and $E(\mathcal{E}_2 \mid X_1, X_2) = 0$. Simple algebra informs us that

$$\pi_{11} = \frac{\beta_{11} + \gamma_{12}\beta_{21}}{1 - \gamma_{12}\gamma_{21}}, \qquad \pi_{12} = \frac{\beta_{12} + \gamma_{12}\beta_{22}}{1 - \gamma_{12}\gamma_{21}},$$
$$\pi_{21} = \frac{\gamma_{21}\beta_{11} + \beta_{21}}{1 - \gamma_{12}\gamma_{21}}, \qquad \pi_{22} = \frac{\gamma_{21}\beta_{12} + \beta_{22}}{1 - \gamma_{12}\gamma_{21}}, \tag{4.11}$$

and

$$\mathcal{E}_1 = \frac{U_1 + \gamma_{12} U_2}{1 - \gamma_{12}\gamma_{21}}, \qquad \mathcal{E}_2 = \frac{\gamma_{21} U_1 + U_2}{1 - \gamma_{12}\gamma_{21}}.$$

Observe that because $\mathcal{E}_2$ depends on both U_1 and U_2 in the general case, Y_2 is correlated with U_1 through the direct channel of U_1 and through the correlation between U_1 and U_2. Without any further information on the variances of (U_1, U_2) and their relationship to the causal parameters, we cannot isolate the causal effects γ_{12} and γ_{21} from the reduced form regression coefficients. This is so because holding X_1, X_2, U_1 and U_2

fixed in (4.8a) or (4.8b), it is not *in principle* possible to vary Y_2 or Y_1, respectively, because they are exact functions of X_1, X_2, U_1 and U_2.

This exact dependence holds true even if $U_1 = 0$ and $U_2 = 0$ so that there are no unobservables.[79] In this case, which is thought to be the most favorable to the application of least squares to (4.8a) and (4.8b), it is evident from (4.10a) and (4.10b) that when $\mathcal{E}_1 = 0$ and $\mathcal{E}_2 = 0$, Y_1 and Y_2 are exact functions of X_1 and X_2. There is no mechanism yet specified within the model to independently vary the right hand sides of equations (4.8a) and (4.8b).[80] The X effects on Y_1 and Y_2, identified through the reduced forms, combine the direct effects (through β_{ij}) and the indirect effects (as they operate through Y_1 and Y_2, respectively).

If we assume exclusions ($\beta_{12} = 0$) or ($\beta_{21} = 0$) or both, we can identify the *ceteris paribus* causal effects of Y_2 on Y_1 and of Y_1 on Y_2, respectively, if $\beta_{22} \neq 0$ or $\beta_{11} \neq 0$, respectively. Thus if $\beta_{12} = 0$, from the reduced form

$$\frac{\pi_{12}}{\pi_{22}} = \gamma_{12}.$$

If $\beta_{21} = 0$, we obtain

$$\frac{\pi_{21}}{\pi_{11}} = \gamma_{21}.$$[81]

Alternatively, we could assume $\beta_{11} = \beta_{22} = 0$ and $\beta_{12} \neq 0$, $\beta_{21} \neq 0$ to identify γ_{12} and γ_{21}. These exclusions say that the social interactions only operate through the Y's.

[79] See Fisher (1966).

[80] Some readers of an earlier draft of this chapter suggested that the mere fact that we can write (4.8a) and (4.8b) means that we "can imagine" independent variation. By the same token, we "can imagine" a model

$$Y = \varphi_0 + \varphi_1 X_1 + \varphi_2 X_2,$$

but if part of the model is $(*) X_1 = X_2$, no causal effect of X_1 holding X_2 constant is possible in principle within the rules of the model. If we break restriction $(*)$ and permit independent variation in X_1 and X_2, we can define the causal effect of X_1 holding X_2 constant.

[81] In a general nonlinear model,

$$Y_1 = g_1(Y_2, X_1, X_2, U_1),$$
$$Y_2 = g_2(Y_1, X_1, X_2, U_2),$$

exclusion is defined as $\frac{\partial g_1}{\partial X_1} = 0$ for all (Y_2, X_1, X_2, U_1) and $\frac{\partial g_2}{\partial X_2} = 0$ for all (Y_1, X_1, X_2, U_2). Assuming the existence of local solutions, we can solve these equations to obtain

$$Y_1 = \varphi_1(X_1, X_2, U_1, U_2),$$
$$Y_2 = \varphi_2(X_1, X_2, U_1, U_2)$$

(which requires satisfaction of a local implicit function theorem). By the chain rule we can write

$$\frac{\partial g_1}{\partial Y_2} = \frac{\partial Y_1}{\partial X_1} \Big/ \frac{\partial Y_2}{\partial X_1} = \frac{\partial \varphi_1}{\partial X_1} \Big/ \frac{\partial \varphi_2}{\partial X_1}.$$

We may define causal effects for Y_1 on Y_2 using partials with respect to X_2 in an analogous fashion.

Agent 1's consumption depends only on agent 2's consumption and not on his value of X_2. Agent 2 is modeled symmetrically versus agent 1. Observe that we have *not* ruled out correlation between U_1 and U_2. When the procedure for identifying causal effects is applied to samples, it is called indirect least squares. The method traces back to Tinbergen (1930).[82]

The intuition for these results is that if $\beta_{12} = 0$, we can vary Y_2 in Equation (4.8a) by varying the X_2. Since X_2 does not appear in the equation, under exclusion, we can keep U_1, X_1 fixed and vary Y_2 using X_2 in (4.10b) if $\beta_{22} \neq 0$.[83] Symmetrically, by excluding X_1 from (4.8b), we can vary Y_1, holding X_2 and U_2 constant. These results are more clearly seen when $U_1 = 0$ and $U_2 = 0$.

Observe that in the model under consideration, where the domain of definition and the supports of the variables coincide, the causal effects of simultaneous interactions are defined if the parameters are identified in the sense of the traditional Cowles definition of identification [see, e.g., Ruud (2000), for a modern discussion of these identification conditions]. A hypothetical thought experiment justifies these exclusions. If agents do not know or act on the other agent's X, these exclusions are plausible.

An implicit assumption in using (4.8a) and (4.8b) for causal analysis is invariance of the parameters $(\Gamma, \beta, \Sigma_U)$ to manipulations of the external variables. This invariance embodies the key idea in assumptions (PI-1)–(PI-4), which are versions of Hurwicz's invariance condition discussed in Section 4.6. Invariance of the coefficients of equations to classes of manipulation of the variables is an essential part of the definition of structural models which we develop more formally below.

This definition of causal effects in an interdependent system generalizes the recursive definitions of causality featured in the statistical treatment effect literature [Holland (1988), and Pearl (2000)]. The key to this definition is manipulation of external inputs and exclusion, not randomization or matching.[84] We can use the population simultaneous equations model to define the class of admissible variations and address problems of definitions (task 1 of Table 1). If for a given model, the parameters of (4.8a) or (4.8b) shift when external variables are manipulated, or if external variables cannot be independently manipulated, causal effects of one internal variable on another cannot be defined *within that model*. If agents were randomly assigned to pair with their neighbors, and the parameters of (4.8a) were not affected by the randomization, then Y_2 would be ex-

[82] The analysis for social interactions in this section is of independent interest. It can be generalized to the analysis of N person interactions if the outcomes are continuous variables. For binary outcomes variables, the same analysis goes through for the special case analyzed by Heckman and MaCurdy (1986). However, in the general case, for discrete outcomes generated by latent variables, it is necessary to modify the system to obtain a coherent probability model. See Heckman (1978).

[83] Notice that we could also use U_2 as a source of variation in (4.10b) to shift Y_2. The roles of U_2 and X_2 are symmetric. However, if U_1 and U_2 are correlated, shifting U_2 shifts U_1 unless we control for it. The component of U_2 uncorrelated with U_1 plays the role of X_2.

[84] Indeed matching or, equivalently, OLS in this context, using the right-hand side variables of (4.8a) and (4.8b), does not identify causal effects as Haavelmo (1943) established long ago.

ogenous in Equation (4.8b) and one could identify causal effects by least squares.[85] At issue is whether such a randomization would recover γ_{12}. It might fundamentally alter agent 1's response to Y_2 if that agent is randomly assigned as opposed to being selected by the agent. Judging the suitability of an invariance assumption entails a thought experiment – a purely mental act.

4.5.1. Relationship to Pearl's analysis

Controlled variation in external forcing variables is the key to defining causal effects in nonrecursive models. It is of some interest to readers of Pearl's influential book on causality (2000) to compare our use of the standard simultaneous equations model of econometrics in defining causal parameters to his. In the context of Equations (4.8a) and (4.8b), Pearl defines a causal effect by "shutting one equation down" or performing "surgery".

He implicitly assumes that "surgery", or shutting down an equation in a system of simultaneous equations, uniquely fixes one outcome or internal variable (the consumption of the other agent in our example). In general, it does not. Putting a constraint on one equation places a restriction on the entire set of internal variables. In general, no single equation in a system of simultaneous equations uniquely determines any single outcome variable. Shutting down one equation might also affect the parameters of the other equations in the system and violate the requirements of parameter stability.

A clearer manipulation that can justify Pearl's approach but shows its special character is to assume that it is possible to fix Y_2 by assuming that it is possible to set $\gamma_{21} = 0$. Assume that U_1 and U_2 are uncorrelated.[86] This together with $\gamma_{21} = 0$ makes the model recursive.[87] It assumes that agent 1 is unaffected by the consumption of agent 2. Under these assumptions, one can regress Y_1 on Y_2, X_1, and X_2 in the population and recover all of the causal parameters of (4.8a). Variation in U_2 breaks the perfect collinearity among Y_2, X_1, and X_2. In general, as we discuss in the next subsection, it is often not possible to freely set some parameters without affecting the rest of the parameters of a model.

Shutting down an equation or fiddling with the parameters in Γ is not required to *define* causality in an interdependent, nonrecursive system or to identify causal parameters. The more basic idea is *exclusion* of different external variables from different equations which, when manipulated, allow the analyst to construct the desired causal quantities.

One can move from the problem of definition (task 1 of Table 1) to identification (task 2) by using population analog estimation methods – in this case the method of

[85] Note that we are breaking the rules we set out in Section 2 in this example and elsewhere in this section by discussing tasks 1 and tasks 2 interchangeably.

[86] Alternatively, one can assume that it is possible to measure U_1 and control for it.

[87] For a discussion of recursive systems as devices for defining causality, see Wold (1956).

indirect least squares.[88] There are many ways other than through exclusions of variables to identify this and more general systems. Fisher (1966) presents a general analysis of identification in both linear and nonlinear simultaneous equations systems. Matzkin (2004, Chapter 73) substantially extends this literature.

4.5.2. *The multiplicity of causal effects that can be defined from a simultaneous equations system*

In the context of the basic nonrecursive model, there are many possible causal variations, richer than what can be obtained from the reduced form. Using the reduced form ($Y = X\Pi + \mathcal{E}$), one can define causal effects as *ceteris paribus* effects of variables in X or $\mathcal{E}$ on Y. This definition solves out for all of the intermediate effects of the internal variables on each other. Using the structure (4.7), one can define the effect of one internal variable on another holding constant the remaining internal variables and (X, U). We have established that such causal effects may not be defined within the rules specified for a particular structural model. Exclusions and other restrictions discussed in Fisher (1966) make definitions of causal effects possible under certain conditions.

One can, in general, solve out from the general system of equations for a subset of the Y (e.g., Y^* where $Y = (Y^*, Y^{**})$), using the reduced form of the model, and use *quasi-structural* models to define a variety of causal effects that solve out for some but not all of the possible causal effects of Y on each other. These quasi-structural models may be written as

$$\Gamma^{**} Y^{**} = \Pi^{**} X + U^{**}.$$

This expression is obtained by using the reduced form for component Y^*: $Y^* = \Pi^* X + \mathcal{E}^*$ and substituting for Y^* in (4.7). U^{**} is the error term associated with this representation. There are many possible quasi-structural models. Causal effects of internal variables may or may not be defined within them, depending on the assumed *a priori* information.

The causal effect of one component of Y^{**} on another does not fix Y^* but allows the Y^* components to adjust as the components of Y^{**} and the X are varied. Thus the Y^* are not being held fixed when X and/or components of the Y^{**} are varied. Viewed in this way, the reduced form and the entire class of quasi-structural models do not define any *ceteris paribus* causal effect relative to all of the variables (internal and external) in the original system since they do not fix the levels of the other Y (in the case of reduced forms) or Y^* (in the case of the quasi-structural models). Nonetheless, the reduced form may provide a good guide to predicting the effects of certain interventions that affect the external variables. The quasi-structural models may also provide a useful guide for predicting certain interventions, where components of Y^{**} are fixed by policy. The reduced

[88] Two-stage least squares would work as well.

form defines a net causal effect of variations in X as they affect the internal variables. There are many quasi-structural models and corresponding thought experiments.

This discussion demonstrates another reason why causal knowledge is provisional in addition to the *a priori* specification of the internal and external variables in this system. Different analysts may choose different subsystems of equations derived from (4.7) to work with and define different causal effects within the different possible subsystems. Some of these causal effects may not be identified, while others may be. Systems smaller or larger than (4.7) can be imagined. The role of *a priori* theory is to limit the class of models and the resulting class of counterfactuals and to define which ones are interesting. *Ceteris paribus* manipulations of one variable are meaningfully defined only if we specify the variables being manipulated and the variables being held constant. This is the position we have taken in Section 4.1.

In this section, we have exposited the Cowles Commission definition of structure. We now present a basic definition of structure in terms of invariance of equations to classes of interventions. Invariance is a central idea in causal analysis and policy analysis.

4.6. Structure as invariance to a class of modifications

A basic definition of a system of structural relationships is that it is a system of equations invariant to a class of modifications or interventions. In the context of policy analysis, this means a class of policy modifications. This is the definition proposed by Hurwicz (1962). It is implicit in Marschak (1953) and it is explicitly utilized by Sims (1977), Lucas and Sargent (1981) and Leamer (1985), among others. This definition requires a precise definition of a policy, a class of policy modifications and specification of a mechanism through which policy operates.

The mechanisms generating counterfactuals and the choices of counterfactuals have already been characterized in Sections 4.1 and 4.3. Policies can act on preferences and the arguments of preferences (and hence choices), on outcomes $Y(s,\omega)$ and the determinants affecting outcomes or on the information facing agents. Recall that g_s, $s \in \mathcal{S}$, generates outcomes while f_s, $s \in \mathcal{S}$, generates subjective evaluations.[89] Specifically,

(i) *Policies can shift the distributions of the determinants of outcomes and choices* (Q, Z, X, U, η), *where* $Q = \{Q(s,\omega)\}_{s\in\mathcal{S}}$, $Z = \{Z(s,\omega)\}_{s\in\mathcal{S}}$, $X = \{X(s,\omega)\}_{s\in\mathcal{S}}$, $\eta = \{\eta(s,\omega)\}_{s\in\mathcal{S}}$ *and* $U = \{U_s(\omega)\}_{s\in\mathcal{S}}$ *in the population. This may entail defining the* g_s *and* f_s *over new domains. Let* $\mathcal{X} = (Q, Z, X, U, \eta)$ *be sets of arguments of the determinants of outcomes. Policies shifting the distributions of these variables are characterized by maps* $T_\chi : \chi \mapsto \chi'$.

(ii) *Policies can select new* f, g *or* $\{f_s, g_s\}_{s\in\mathcal{S}}$ *functions. In particular, new arguments (e.g., amenities or characteristics of programs) may be introduced as a result of policy actions creating new attributes. Policies shifting functions map*

[89] By f_s, we mean s-specific valuation functions.

f, g or $\{f_s, g_s\}_{s \in \mathcal{S}}$ into new functions $T_f : f_s \mapsto f_s'$; $T_g : g_s \mapsto g_s'$. This may entail changes in functional forms with a stable set of arguments as well as changes in arguments of functions.

(iii) *Policies may affect individual information sets $(\mathcal{I}_\omega)_{\omega \in \Omega}$. $T_{\mathcal{I}_\omega} : \mathcal{I}_\omega \mapsto \mathcal{I}_\omega'$.*

Clearly, any particular policy may incorporate elements of all three types of policy shifts.

Parameters of a model or parameters derived from a model are said to be policy invariant with respect to a class of policies if they are not changed (are invariant) when policies within the class are implemented. We have explicitly introduced such invariance in our discussion of the Cowles version of the structural model with respect to policies that change X, but not for policies that change the distribution of U. This notion is partially embodied in assumptions (PI-1) and (PI-2), which are defined solely in terms of *ex post* outcomes. More generally, policy invariance for f, g or $\{f_s, g_s\}_{s \in \mathcal{S}}$ requires for a class of policies $\mathcal{P}_A \subseteq \mathcal{P}$,

(PI-5) *The functions f, g or $\{f_s, g_s\}_{s \in \mathcal{S}}$ are the same for all values of the arguments in their domain of definition no matter how their arguments are determined, for all policies in $\mathcal{P}_A$.*

This definition is a version of (PI-3) and (PI-4) for the specific notation of the choice model developed in this chapter and for specific types of policies. This definition can be made separately for f, g, f_s, g_s or any function derived from them. It requires that when we change an argument of a function its value is the same for the same change of input irrespective of how we change it. It is defined relative to a class of policies and not necessarily for all policies.

In the econometric approach to policy evaluation, the analyst attempts to model how a policy shift affects outcomes without reestimating any model. Thus, for the tax and labor supply example presented in Section 4.1, with labor supply function $h_s = h(w(1-s), x, u_s)$, it is assumed that we can shift tax rate s without affecting the functional relationship mapping $(w(1-s), x, u_s)$ into h_s. If, in addition, the support of $w(1-s)$ under one policy is the same as the support determined by the available economic history, for a class of policy modifications (tax changes), the labor supply function can be used to accurately predict the outcomes for that class of tax policies. It would not be able to accurately forecast policies that extend the support of h_s to a new domain or if it shifts preferences in a way never previously experienced (e.g., by appealing to patriotism in time of war). In such cases, the domains of f and g would have to be extended to accurately forecast policy changes, and additional assumptions would have to be made. We discuss such assumptions in Chater 71 of our contribution to this Handbook.

In the simultaneous equations model analyzed in the last subsection, invariance requires stability of Γ, B and Σ_U to interventions. Such models can be used to accurately forecast the effects of policies that can be cast as variations in the inputs to that model that keep the parameters invariant. Policy invariant parameters are not necessarily causal parameters as we noted in our analysis of reduced forms in the preceding section. Thus, in the simultaneous equations model, depending on the *a priori* information available, it may happen that no causal effect of one internal variable on another may be defined but if Π is invariant to modifications in X, the reduced form is policy invariant for those modifications. The class of policy invariant parameters is thus distinct from the class of causal parameters, but invariance is an essential attribute of a causal model. For counterfactuals $Y(s, \omega)$, if assumption (PI-1) is not postulated for a class of policies $\mathcal{P}_A$, all of the treatment effects defined in Section 2 would be affected by policy shifts.

Rubin's SUTVA assumptions (R-2) and (R-3) are versions of Hurwicz's (1962) invariance assumptions for the functions generating objective outcomes. Thus Rubin's assumption (R-3) postulates that $Y(s, \omega)$ is invariant to all policies that change f but does not cover policies that change g or the support of Q. Within the treatment effects framework, a policy that adds a new treatment to $\mathcal{S}$ is not policy invariant for treatment parameters comparing the new treatment to any other treatment unless the analyst can model all policies in terms of a generating set of common characteristics specified at different levels, as in formulation (4.2) or our example in Section 3.3. The lack of policy invariance makes it potentially misleading to forecast the effects of new policies using treatment effect models.

"Deep structural" parameters generating the f and g are invariant to policy modifications that affect technology, constraints and information sets except when the policies extend the historical supports. Invariance can only be defined relative to a class of modifications and a postulated set of preferences, technology, constraints and information sets. Thus causal parameters can only be precisely identified within a class of modifications.

4.7. Alternative definitions of "structure"

The terms "structural equation" or "structure" are used differently by different analysts and are a major source of confusion in the policy analysis literature. In this section, we briefly distinguish three other definitions of structure besides our version of Hurwicz (1962). The traditional Cowles Commission structural model of econometrics was presented in Section 4.5. It is a nonrecursive model for defining and estimating causal parameters. It is a useful vehicle for distinguishing effects that can be defined in principle (through *a priori* theory) from effects that are identifiable from data. This is the contrast between tasks 1 and 2 of Table 1. The framework arose as a model to analyze the economic phenomenon of supply and demand in markets, and to analyze policies that affected price and quantity determination.

A second definition of structure, currently the most popular in the applied economics literature, defines an equation as structural if it is derived from an explicitly formulated economic theory. Consider a consumer demand problem where a consumer ω chooses among goods $X(\omega)$ given money income $M(\omega)$ and prices P, $P'X(\omega) \leqslant M(\omega)$. Preferences of ω, $R(X(\omega), \omega)$, are quasiconcave in $X(\omega)$ and twice differentiable. Many economists would say that $R(X(\omega), \omega)$ is structural because it describes the preferences of agent ω. There would be similar agreement that technology parameters are structural parameters.

When we solve for the demand functions, under standard conditions, we obtain $X(\omega) = X(\frac{P}{M(\omega)}, \omega)$. These are sometimes called "reduced form" expressions by analogy with the Cowles Commission simultaneous equations literature exposited in Section 4.5, assuming that prices normalized by income are exogenous. While any convention is admissible, this one is confusing since we can recover the preferences (up to a monotonic function) given the demand function under standard regularity conditions [see, e.g., Varian (1978)]. Is the indirect utility function $\widetilde{R}^*(\omega, \frac{P}{M(\omega)}) = R(X(\frac{P}{M(\omega)}), \omega) = R^*(\frac{P}{M(\omega)}, \omega)$ structural or reduced form?

While the notion of structure in this widely applied usage is intuitively clear, it is not the same notion of structure as used in Cowles Commission econometrics as defined in Section 4.5. It is structural in the sense that the internal variables (the X in this example) are substituted out for externally specified (to the consumer) P and M. At the market level, this distinction is not clear cut since X and P are jointly determined. The notion of a "reduced form" is not clearly specified until the statistical properties of X, P or M have been specified. Recall that the Cowles Commission definition of reduced form (a) solves out the X in terms of P and M and (b) assumes that P and M are "exogenous" relative to the unobserved variables. In current popular usage, a reduced form makes both assumptions.

A third definition of a structural model is as a finite parameter model. Structural in this sense means low dimensional and is not related to the endogeneity of any variable or the economic interpretation placed on the equations. Clearly the Cowles Commission model is finite dimensional if the dimensions of Y and X are finite. Nonlinear finite parameter versions of the Cowles Commission models as in Fisher (1966) are also structural in these systems. Systems that are structural in this sense are useful for extrapolation of functions out of their empirical supports.

A more basic definition of a system of structural equations, and the one featured in this chapter, is a system of equations invariant to a class of modifications. Without such invariance one cannot trust the models to forecast policies or make causal inferences. Invariance to modifications requires a precise definition of a policy, a class of policy modifications and specification of a mechanism through which policy operates. It makes clear that "structure" is a concept that is relative to the potential policy changes studied by the analyst. A system structural for one class of policy modifications may not be structural for another.

4.8. *Marschak's Maxim and the relationship between the structural literature and the statistical treatment effect literature*

The absence of explicit models of outcomes and choice is a prominent feature of the statistical treatment effect literature. A major goal of this chapter and our other chapter in this Handbook is to infuse economics into the treatment effect literature and to understand its achievements and implicit identifying assumptions in economic terms. Economically well-posed models make explicit the assumptions used by analysts regarding preferences, technology, the information available to agents, the constraints under which they operate, and the rules of interaction among agents in market and social settings and the sources of variability among agents. These explicit features make these models, like all scientific models, useful vehicles (a) for interpreting empirical evidence using theory; (b) for collating and synthesizing evidence across studies using economic theory; (c) for measuring the welfare effects of policies; (d) for forecasting the welfare and direct effects of previously implemented policies in new environments and the effects of new policies.

These features are absent from the modern treatment effect literature. At the same time, this literature makes fewer statistical assumptions in terms of exogeneity, functional form, exclusion and distributional assumptions than the standard structural estimation literature in econometrics. These are the attractive features of this approach.

In reconciling these two literatures, we reach back to a neglected but important paper by Marschak (1953). Marschak noted that for many questions of policy analysis, it is not necessary to identify fully specified economic models that are invariant to classes of policy modifications. All that may be required for any policy analysis are combinations of subsets of the structural parameters, corresponding to the parameters required to forecast particular policy modifications, which are often much easier to identify (i.e., require fewer and weaker assumptions). Thus in the simultaneous equations system example presented in Section 4.5, policies that only affect X may be forecasted using reduced forms, not knowing the full structure, provided that the reduced forms are invariant to the modifications being considered.[90] Forecasting other policies may only require partial knowledge of the full simultaneous equations system.

We call this principle **Marschak's Maxim** in honor of this insight. The modern statistical treatment effect literature implements Marschak's Maxim where the policies analyzed are the treatments available under a particular policy regime and the goal of policy analysis is restricted to evaluating policies in place (problem P-1) and not in forecasting the effects of new policies or the effects of old policies on new environments. What is often missing from the literature on treatment effects is a clear discussion of the economic question being addressed by the particular treatment effect being identified. When the treatment effect literature does not clearly specify the economic question being addressed, it does not implement Marschak's Maxim.

Population mean treatment parameters are often identified under weaker conditions than are traditionally assumed in structural econometric analysis. Thus to identify the average treatment effect for s and s' we only require $E(Y(s,\omega) \mid X=x) - E(Y(s',\omega) \mid X=x)$. Under (PI-1) and (PI-2), this parameter answers the policy question of determining the average effect on outcomes of moving an agent from s' to s. The parameter

[90] Thus we require that the reduced form Π defined in Section 4.5 does not change when we change the X.

is not designed to evaluate a whole host of other policies. We do not have to know the functional form of the generating g_s functions nor does X have to be exogenous. We do not have to invoke the stronger conditions (PI-3) and (PI-4) about invariance of the choice equations.

However, if we seek to identify $E(Y(s,\omega) \mid X = x, \ D(s,\omega) = 1) - E(Y(s',\omega) \mid X = x, D(s,\omega) = 1)$, we need to invoke versions of (PI-3) and (PI-4) because we condition on a choice. We do not condition on a choice in defining the average treatment effects.

Explicitly formulated economic models or low dimensional economic or statistical models may or may not be structural in the sense defined in this chapter. They may be invariant to some policy modifications but not to others.

Causal models are defined independently of any particular policy manipulation. But if the variations in the arguments of the causal (Marshallian) functions correspond to variations in some policy, causal models as we have defined them, are structural since by definition, causal functions are invariant to variations in the arguments of the functions that generate them.

Treatment effects are causal effects for particular policies that move agents from $s \in \mathcal{S}$ to $s' \in \mathcal{S}$, $s' \neq s$, keeping all other features of the agent and environment the same. These effects are designed to answer policy question P-1.

Invariant, explicitly formulated, economic models are useful for addressing policy problems P-2 and P-3: extrapolation and predicting the effects of new policies, respectively. Invariant low dimensional models are sometimes useful for solving extrapolation problem P-2.

If the goal of an analysis is to predict outcomes, and the environment is stable, then accurate predictions can be made without causal or structural parameters. Consider Haavelmo's analysis of fixing vs. conditioning discussed in Section 4.2. Recall that he analyzed the linear regression model $Y = X\beta + U$ and defined the causal effect of X on Y as the U-constant effect of variations in X. If the goal of an analysis is to predict the effect of X on Y, and if the environment is stable so that the historical data have the same distribution as the data in the forecast sample, least squares projections are optimal predictors under mean square error criteria.[91] We do not need to separate out the causal effect of X on Y, β, from the effect of X on the unobservables operating through $E(U \mid X)$.

Viewed in this light, the treatment effect literature that compares the outcome associated with $s \in \mathcal{S}$ with the outcome associated with $s' \in \mathcal{S}$ seeks to recover a causal effect of s relative to s'. It is a particular causal effect for a particular set of policy interventions. It seeks effects that hold all other factors, observed and unobserved, constant.

Marschak's Maxim urges analysts to formulate the problem being addressed clearly and to use the minimal ingredients required to solve it. The treatment effect literature addresses the problem of comparing treatments under a particular policy regime for a

[91] See, e.g., Goldberger (1964).

particular environment. The original econometric pioneers considered treatments under different policy regimes and with different environments. As analysts ask more difficult questions, it is necessary to specify more features of the models being used to address the questions.

Marschak's Maxim is an application of Occam's Razor to policy evaluation. For certain classes of policy interventions, designed to answer problem P-1, the treatment effect approach may be very powerful and more convincing than explicit economic models which require more assumptions.

Considerable progress has been made in relaxing the parametric structure assumed in the early explicitly economic models [see Matzkin (1994), and Chapter 73 of this Handbook]. As the treatment effect literature is extended to address the more general set of policy forecasting problems entertained in the explicitly economic literature, the distinction between the two approaches will vanish although it is currently very sharp. This chapter, Heckman and Vytlacil (2005) and Heckman (2007) are attempts to bridge this gulf.

Up to this point in the chapter, everything that has been discussed precisely is purely conceptual although we have alluded to empirical problems and problems of identification going from data of various forms to conceptual models. We now discuss the identification problem, which must be solved if causal models are to be empirically operational.

5. Identification problems: Determining models from data

Unobserved counterfactuals are the source of the problems considered in this chapter. For an agent ω in state s, we observe $Y(s, \omega)$ but not $Y(s', \omega)$, $s' \neq s$. A central problem in the literature on causal inference is how to identify counterfactuals and the derived treatment parameters. Unobservables, including missing data, are at the heart of the identification problem for causal inference. As we have seen, counterfactuals play a key role in structural policy analysis.

Different evaluation estimators differ in the amount of knowledge they assume that the analyst has relative to what the agents being studied have when making their program enrollment decisions (or their decisions are made for them as a parent for a child). This distinction is a matter of the quality of the available data. Unless the analyst has access to all of the relevant information that produces the dependence between outcomes and treatment rules (i.e., that produces selection bias), he/she must devise methods to control for the unobserved components of relevant information. We define relevant information precisely in Chapter 71. Loosely speaking, relevant information is the information which, if available to the analyst and conditioned on, would eliminate selection bias.

There may be information known to the agent but not known to the observing analyst that does not give rise to the dependence between outcomes and choices. It is the information that gives rise to the dependence between outcomes and treatment choices that matters for eliminating selection bias, and this is the relevant information.

A priori one might think that the analyst knows a lot less than the agent whose behavior is being analyzed. At issue is whether the analyst knows less *relevant* information, which is not so obvious, if only because the analyst can observe the outcomes of decisions in a way that agents making decisions cannot. This access to *ex post* information can sometimes give the analyst a leg up on the information available to the agent.

Policy forecasting problems P-2 and P-3 raise the additional issue that the support over which treatment parameters and counterfactuals are identified may not correspond to the support that is required to construct a particular policy counterfactual. Common to all scientific models, there is the additional issue of how to select (X, Z), the conditioning variables, and how to deal with them if they are endogenous. Finally, there is the problem of lack of knowledge of functional forms of the models. Different econometric methods solve these problems in different ways. We first present a precise discussion of identification before we turn to a discussion of these issues and how they affect the properties of different evaluation estimators.

5.1. The identification problem

The identification problem asks whether theoretical constructs have any empirical content in a hypothetical population or in real samples. By empirical content, we mean whether the model is uniquely determined by the available data. This formulation considers tasks two and three in Table 1 together, although some analysts like to separate these issues, focusing solely on task two (identification in large samples). The identification problem considers what particular models within a broader class of models are consistent with a given set of data or facts. Specifically, consider a model space M. This is the set of admissible models that are produced by some theory for generating counterfactuals. Elements $m \in M$ are admissible theoretical models.

We may only be interested in some features of a model. For example, we may have a rich model of counterfactuals $\{Y(s, \omega)\}_{s \in \mathcal{S}}$, but we may only be interested in the average treatment effect $E[Y(s, \omega) - Y(s', \omega)]$. Let the objects of interest be $t \in T$, where "t" stands for the target – the goal of the analysis. The target space T may be the whole model space M or something derived from it, a more limited objective.

Define map $g : M \to T$. This maps an element $m \in M$ into an element $t \in T$. In the example in the preceding paragraph, T is the space of all average treatment effects produced by the models of counterfactuals. We assume that g is onto.[92] Associated with each model is an element t derived from the model, which could be the entire model itself. Many models may map into the same t so the inverse map (g^{-1}), mapping T

[92] By this, we mean that for every $t \in T$, there is an element $m \in M$ such that g sends m to t, i.e., the image of M by g is the entire set T. Of course, g may send many elements of M to a single element of T. Note that g as used here is not necessarily the same g as used in Section 4.

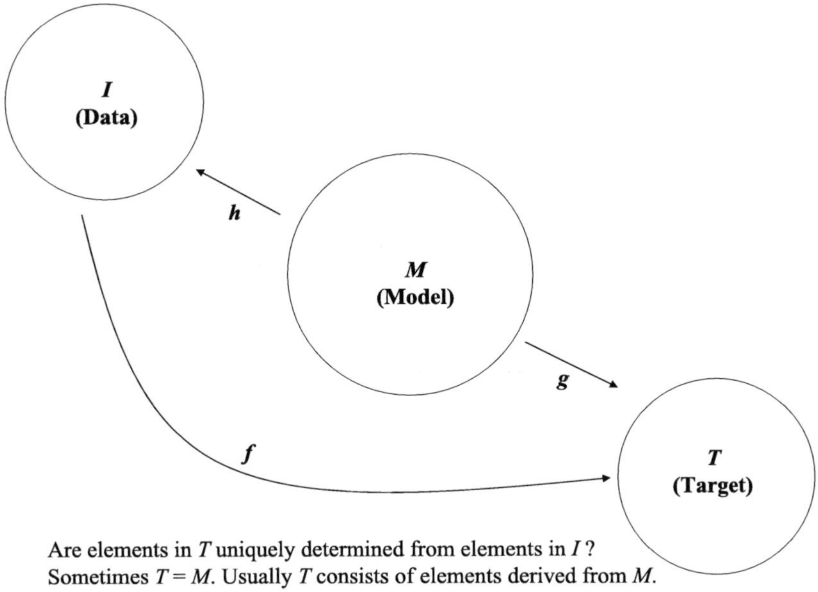

Are elements in T uniquely determined from elements in I?
Sometimes $T = M$. Usually T consists of elements derived from M.

Figure 4. Schematic of model (M), data (I) and target (T) parameter spaces.

to M, may not be well defined. Thus many different models may produce the same average treatment effect.

Let the class of possible information or data be I. Define a map $h : M \to I$. For an element $i \in I$, which is a given set of data, there may be one or more models m consistent with i. If i can only be mapped into a single m, the model is exactly identified.[93] If there are multiple m's, consistent with i, these models are not identified. Thus, in Figure 4, many models (elements of M) may be consistent with the same data (single element of I).

Let $M_h(i)$ be the set of models consistent with i. $M_h(i) = h^{-1}(\{i\}) = \{m \in M: h(m) = i\}$. The data i reject the other models $M \setminus M_h(i)$, but are consistent with all models in $M_h(i)$. If $M_h(i)$ contains more than one element, the data produce set-valued instead of point-valued identification. If $M_h(i) = \emptyset$, the empty set, no model is

[93] Associated with each data set i is a collection of random variables $Q(i)$, which may be a vector. Let $F_Q(q \mid m)$ be the distribution of Q under model m. To establish identification on nonnegligible sets, one needs that, for some true model m^*,

$$\Pr\bigl(\bigl|F_Q(q \mid m^*) - F_Q(q \mid m)\bigr| > \varepsilon\bigr) > 0$$

for some $\varepsilon > 0$ for all $m \neq m^*$. This guarantees that there are observable differences between the data generating process for Q given m and for Q given m^*. We can also define this for $F_Q(q \mid t^*)$ and $F_Q(q \mid t)$. Note that Q is an abstract random variable and not necessarily the specific attributes defined in Section 4.

consistent with the data. By placing restrictions on models, we can sometimes reduce the number of elements in $M_h(i)$ if it has multiple members. Let $RE \subset M$ be a set of restricted models. Thus it is sometimes possible by imposing restrictions to reduce the number of models consistent with the data. Recall that in the two-agent model of social interactions, if $\beta_{12} = 0$ and $\beta_{21} = 0$, we could uniquely identify the remaining parameters under the other conditions maintained in Section 4.5. Thus $RE \cap M_h(i)$ may contain only a single element. Another way to solve this identification problem is to pick another data source $i' \in I$, which may produce more restrictions on the class of admissible models. More information provides more hoops for the model to jump through.

Going after a more limited class of objects such as features of a model $(t \in T)$ rather than the full model $(m \in M)$ is another way to secure unique identification. Let $M_g(t) = g^{-1}(\{t\}) = \{m \in M\colon g(m) = t\}$. Necessary and sufficient conditions for the existence of a unique map $f: I \to T$ with the property $f \circ h = g$ are (a) h must map M *onto* I and (b) for all $i \in I$, there exists $t \in T$ such that $M_h(i) \subseteq M_g(t)$. Condition (b) means that even though one element $i \in I$ may be consistent with many elements in M, so that $M_h(i)$ consists of more than one element, it may be that all elements in $M_h(i)$ are mapped by g into a single element of T. The map f is onto since $g = f \circ h$ and g is onto by assumption. In order for the map f to be one-to-one, it is necessary and sufficient to have equality of $M_h(i)$ and $M_g(t)$ instead of simply inclusion.

If we follow Marschak's Maxim and focus on a smaller target space T, it is possible that g maps the admissible models into a smaller space. Thus the map f described above may produce a single element even if there are multiple models m consistent with the data source i that would be required to answer broader questions. This could arise, for example, if for a given set of data i, we could only estimate the mean μ_1 of Y_1 up to a constant q and the mean μ_2 of Y_2 up to the same constant q. But we could uniquely identify the element $\mu_1 - \mu_2 \in T$.[94] In general, identifying elements of T is easier than identifying elements of M. Thus, in Figure 4, even though many models (elements of M) may be consistent with the same $i \in I$, only one element of T may be consistent with that i. We now turn to empirical causal inference and illustrate the provisional nature of causal inference.

5.2. *The sources of nonidentifiability*

The principle source of identification problems for policy problems P-1–P-3 is the absence of data on outcomes other than the one observed for the agent. Thus if agent ω is observed in state s we observe $Y(s, \omega)$ but not $Y(s', \omega)$, $s' \in \mathcal{S}$, $s \neq s'$. If we had data

[94] Most modern analyses of identification assume that sample sizes are infinite, so that enlarging the sample size is not informative. However, in any applied problem this distinction is not helpful. Having a small sample (e.g., fewer observations than regressors) can produce an identification problem. Our definition of identification addresses task two and task three together if we assume that samples are finite.

on the outcomes for agents in all states in $\mathcal{S}$, we could form *ex post* counterfactuals and solve P-1. We still need to value these counterfactuals (i.e., construct $R(Y(s, \omega))$).

Even with such ideal data, it is necessary to extend $\{Y(s, \omega)\}_{s \in \mathcal{S}}$ and the appropriate valuation functions to new supports to answer policy questions P-2 and P-3. For many econometric estimators, it is necessary to account for the limited supports available in many empirical samples. One can only meaningfully compare comparable agents. A nonparametric approach to estimation guarantees that this condition is satisfied. Respecting empirical support conditions restricts the class of identified parameters, even considering only problem P-1. As we will discuss below, failure of support conditions plagues different estimators and estimation strategies.

Another source of identification problems is the uncertainty regarding the choice of the conditioning variables (the X, W and Z) in any application. This problem is intrinsic to all estimation problems. It affects some estimators more than others, as we note in Chapter 71. For some estimators and for some policy problems, the endogeneity of the regressors is a major concern. We delineate these problems for each estimator and each policy problem. Closely related is the asymmetry in the information available to analysts and the agents they study which we previously discussed. This entails the problem of specifying the information on which agents condition their actions, distinguishing them from the information available to the econometrician and accounting for any information shortfalls. For example, the method of matching makes strong assumptions about the information available to analysts which cannot be verified but which drive the interpretation of the results.

There is also the problem of functional forms. Many traditional approaches to the construction of structural models and econometric counterfactuals make assumptions about the functional forms of outcome equations and choice equations and the distributions of the unobservables. Methods differ in their reliance on these functional forms. Lack of knowledge of the required functional forms is a source of identification problems.

Table 3
Sources of identification problems considered in this chapter

(i)	Absence of data on $Y(s', \omega)$ for $s' \in \mathcal{S} \backslash \{s\}$ where s is the state selected (the evaluation problem).
(ii)	Nonrandom selection of observations on states (the selection problem).
(iii)	Support conditions may fail (outcome distributions for $F(Y_s \mid X = x)$ may be defined on only a limited support of X so $F(X \mid D_s = 1)$ and $F(X \mid D_{s'} = 1)$ have different X supports or limited overlap in their supports).
(iv)	Functional forms of outcome equations and distributions of unobservables may be unknown. To extend some function $Y = G(X)$ to a new support requires functional structure: It cannot be extended outside of sample support by a purely nonparametric procedure.
(v)	Determining the (X, Z, W) conditioning variables.
(vi)	Different information sets for the agent making selection $\mathcal{I}_a$ and the econometrician trying to identify the model $\mathcal{I}_e$ where $\mathcal{I}_a \neq \mathcal{I}_e$.

Table 3 lists the major sources of identification problems. We discuss the sensitivity of alternative evaluation methods to this array of problems in Chapter 71. We next present an identification analysis of our prototypical economic model of choice and outcomes which serves as a benchmark model against which we can formulate the implicit assumptions made in alternative econometric approaches to policy evaluation.

6. Identification of explicit economic models

For the Roy model developed in Section 3, Heckman and Honoré (1990), show that under the conditions they specify it is possible to identify the distribution of treatment outcomes $(Y_1 - Y_0)$ without invoking functional form assumptions. Randomization can only identify the marginal distributions of Y_0 and of Y_1 and not the joint distribution of $(Y_1 - Y_0)$ or the quantiles of $(Y_1 - Y_0)$ [see Heckman (1992)]. Thus, under its assumptions, the Roy model is more powerful than randomization in producing the distributional counterfactuals discussed in Abbring and Heckman (Chapter 72).[95] The role of the choice equation is to motivate and justify the choice of an evaluation method.[96] This is a central feature of the econometric approach that is missing from the statistical and epidemiological literature on treatment effects.

Considerable progress has been made in relaxing the parametric structure assumed in the early structural models. As the treatment effect literature is extended to address the more general set of policy forecasting problems entertained in the structural literature (especially problems P-2 and P-3), the distinction between the two literatures will vanish. This section presents some examples of traditional structural models, how they can be used to construct treatment effects, and how treatment effects can be generated under much weaker conditions.

6.1. *Using parametric assumptions to generate population level treatment parameters*

We now present a brief analysis of identification of the extended Roy model and the generalized Roy model analyzed in Section 3.3. This framework provides a convenient platform from which to summarize the power and limitations of the current literature in structural economics. Matzkin (Chapter 73 of this Handbook) provides a comprehensive discussion of identification. Write a two-sector model with outcomes Y_1, Y_0 under perfect certainty as

$$Y_1 = \mu_1(X, U_1), \tag{6.1a}$$

$$Y_0 = \mu_0(X, U_0) \tag{6.1b}$$

[95] The same analysis applies to matching, which cannot identify the distribution of $(Y_1 - Y_0)$ or derived quantiles.

[96] See Heckman and Robb (1985, 1986).

and costs

$$C = \mu_C(W, U_C). \tag{6.1c}$$

Agents choose sector 1 if $R = Y_1 - Y_0 - C \geqslant 0$. Otherwise they choose sector 0. We have shown in Section 3 how this model can be used to generate the common treatment effects discussed in Section 2. At issue in this section is how to identify the parameters of Equations (6.1a)–(6.1c) from data where only one outcome (Y_1 or Y_0) is observed. Recent advances in microeconometrics allow nonparametric identification of these equations and the distributions of (U_0, U_1, U_C) under conditions we specify below.

First consider identification of the two-outcome generalized Roy model for normal error terms developed in Section 3.3. Suppose that we observe Y_1 when $D = 1$ and Y_0 when $D = 0$. Observed Y may be written in switching regression form as in Quandt (1958, 1972):

$$Y = DY_1 + (1 - D)Y_0.$$

We assume that the analyst observes (Z, X, Y, D), where $Z = (X, W)$. In addition to assumptions (i)–(ii) given in Section 3.3 and Equations (3.4a)–(3.4c), we assume that the model is of full rank.

One traditional approach to econometric identification [see Heckman and Robb (1985, 1986)] is to solve the selection problem for Y_1 and Y_0 and then to use the parameters of the model to solve the evaluation problem. Solutions to the selection problem are developed in Heckman (1976, 1979, 1990), Heckman and Honoré (1990) and are popularized in numerous surveys [see, e.g., Maddala (1983)]. Summarizing known results, assuming $Y_1 = \mu_1(x) + U_1$ and $Y_0 = \mu_0(x) + U_0$, $C = W\varphi + U_C$, and defining $\upsilon = U_1 - U_0 - U_C$, and normalizing $\text{Var}(\upsilon) = 1$,

$$E(Y_1 \mid D = 1,\ X = x,\ Z = z) = x\beta_1 + \text{Cov}(U_1, \upsilon)\lambda(z\gamma),$$
$$E(Y_0 \mid D = 0,\ X = x,\ Z = z) = x\beta_0 + \text{Cov}(U_0, \upsilon)\tilde{\lambda}(z\gamma),$$

where $\lambda(z\gamma) = \varphi(z\gamma)/\Phi(z\gamma)$ and $\tilde{\lambda}(z\gamma) = -\varphi(z\gamma)/\Phi(-z\gamma)$. We can identify γ from a first stage discrete choice analysis (a probit analysis with D as the dependent variable and Z as the regressor) if the Z are of full rank. Under additional rank conditions on the X, we can form $\lambda(z\gamma)$ and $\tilde{\lambda}(z\gamma)$ and use linear regression to recover β_1, $\text{Cov}(U_1, \upsilon)$, β_0, $\text{Cov}(U_0, \upsilon)$ from the conditional means of Y_1 and Y_0. As first proved by Heckman (1976, 1979), we can use the residuals from the regression equations to identify σ_0^2 and σ_1^2. We can also identify the covariances $\sigma_{1\upsilon}$ and $\sigma_{0\upsilon}$ from the coefficients on $\lambda(z\gamma)$ and $\tilde{\lambda}(z\gamma)$ respectively. Without further information, we cannot recover σ_{01} and hence the joint distribution of (Y_0, Y_1). Thus the model is not fully identified, although the marginal distributions are uniquely identified.[97]

[97] Vijverberg (1993) uses a sensitivity or bounding analysis to determine what classes of joint distributions are consistent with the data.

The lack of identification of the joint distribution does not preclude identification of the mean treatment parameters introduced in Sections 2 and 3. Note further that it is possible that there is selection bias for Y_1 ($\text{Cov}(U_1, \upsilon) \neq 0$) and selection bias for Y_0 ($\text{Cov}(U_0, \upsilon) \neq 0$) but no selection on gains $\text{Cov}(U_1 - U_0, \upsilon) = 0$.

Using the analysis of Section 3.3 from the parameters that are identified from selection models, we can identify $\text{ATE}(x)$, $\text{TT}(x, z)$, $\text{MTE}(x)$ from cross section data. Without further information, we cannot identify the joint distribution of the counterfactuals $F(y_1 - y_0 \mid X)$ nor can we determine the proportion of agents who benefit from treatment not accounting for costs $\Pr(Y_1 \geqslant Y_0 \mid Z)$. We *can* identify the proportion of agents who benefit accounting for their costs using choice or revealed preference data:

$$\Pr(Y_1 - Y_0 - C \geqslant 0 \mid Z = z) = \Phi(z\gamma).$$

In the special case of the Roy model, where $\upsilon = U_1 - U_0$, because we can identify the variance of U_1 and U_0, from the coefficients on $\lambda(z\gamma)$ and $\tilde{\lambda}(z\gamma)$, we can identify $\text{Cov}(U_1, U_1 - U_0)$ and $\text{Cov}(U_0, U_1 - U_0)$ and hence we can identify σ_{01}. Thus we can identify the proportion of agents who benefit from treatment, not including costs, because there are no costs and it is the same as $\Phi(z\gamma) = \Pr(Y_1 - Y_0 \geqslant 0 \mid Z = z)$.[98] By using choice data, the Roy model, under its assumptions, produces more information than randomization which only identifies the marginal distributions of Y_0 and Y_1 and not the joint distribution.

Without additional information, one cannot surmount the fundamental evaluation problem that one does not observe both Y_0 and Y_1 for the same agents. The Roy model overcomes this problem using choice data assuming that there are no costs of participation. If it is assumed that $U_C = 0$ but there are observed costs, one can identify γ as before, and identify the covariance σ_{01} because no new random variable enters the cost equation that is not in the outcome equation. This framework is what we call the extended Roy model. For this version of the generalized Roy model one can form all of the distributional treatment effects using the preceding analysis. In general, however, one cannot identify the joint distribution of (Y_1, Y_0) but one can identify the distributions of (Y_1, R) in the notation of Section 3 (or (U_1, υ)) and (Y_0, R) (or (U_0, υ)).

Normality assumptions are traditional and convenient. The linearity, exogeneity, separability and normality assumptions make it possible to solve policy forecasting problems P-1–P-3. By parameterizing the β_i to depend on Q_i as in Equations (3.7a)–(3.7b), it is possible to forecast the demand for new goods. The support problems that plague nonparametric estimators are absent. Heckman, Tobias and Vytlacil (2001, 2003) extend the normal model using alternative distributional assumptions. The normal selection model extends standard normal regression theory intuitions in a natural way. But

98 If we only observe Y_1 or Y_0 but not both in the same sample, we can identify the covariance of (U_1, U_0) provided we normalize a mean (e.g., the mean of the missing Y). Thus if Y_1 is the market wage and Y_0 is the reservation wage, we rarely directly observe Y_0 but we observe Y_1. See Heckman (1974) and Heckman and Honoré (1990).

they are controversial. A huge effort in econometrics in the past 20 years has gone into relaxing these assumptions.[99]

6.2. Two paths toward relaxing distributional, functional form and exogeneity assumptions

At issue in this Handbook is whether the strong exogeneity, linearity and normality assumptions in the conventional literature in econometrics are required to form treatment effects and to evaluate policy. They are not. After this point of agreement, the recent literature on policy evaluation divides. The literature in microeconometric structural estimation focuses on relaxing the linearity, separability, normality and exogeneity conditions invoked in the early literature in order to identify (6.1a)–(6.1c) under much weaker conditions.

Recent advances in econometric theory greatly weaken the distributional and functional form assumptions maintained in the early econometric literature on selection bias. For example, Cosslett (1983), Manski (1988), and Matzkin (1992, 1993, 1994, 2003) relax the distributional assumptions required to identify the discrete choice model. Matzkin (1993) develops multivariate extensions. She surveys this literature in her 1994 Handbook Chapter. Heckman (1980, 1990), Heckman and Robb (1985, 1986), Heckman and Honoré (1990), Ahn and Powell (1993), Heckman and Smith (1998) and Carneiro, Hansen and Heckman (2003) present conditions for nonparametric and semiparametric identification of the selection model. Powell (1994) presents a useful survey for developments up to the early 1990s. Developments by Chen (1999) extend this analysis. Heckman (1990), Heckman and Smith (1998) and Carneiro, Hansen and Heckman (2003) show how to identify all of the mean treatment parameters as well as the distributional treatment parameters. We review the work on estimating distributions of treatment effects in Abbring and Heckman (Chapter 72).

Appendix B presents a formal nonparametric analysis of identification of the prototypical model of choice and outcomes developed in Section 3.1. From this and other explicitly economic models, the mean treatment effects and many distributional treatment effects discussed in Section 2 can be identified. For reasons discussed in the preceding subsection, one cannot form the joint distribution of outcomes across treatment states without some additional information such as the special Roy structure. Abbring and Heckman (Chapter 72) show how restrictions on the dimensionality of the unobservables and extra information can also produce identification of the joint distribution of $Y_1 - Y_0$. Matzkin (Chapter 73) provides a guide to the recent literature on nonparametric identification in explicitly economic models. The goal of this line of work is to

[99] The motivation for this research is largely based on Monte Carlo examples by Goldberger (1983), Arabmazar and Schmidt (1982) and others. In the study of earnings models with truncation and censoring, log normality is a good assumption [see Heckman and Sedlacek (1985)]. In the study of labor supply, it is a very poor assumption [see Killingsworth (1983), and the articles in the special issue of the *Journal of Human Resources* on labor supply and taxation, 1990]. See the evidence summarized in Heckman (2001).

preserve the economic content of the original Roy and generalized Roy models to collate evidence across studies in order to interpret evidence using economics, as well as to forecast the effects of new policies.

The recent literature on treatment effects identifies population level treatment effects under weaker conditions than are invoked in the traditional normal model. It does not aim to recover the structural parameters generating (6.1a)–(6.1c) but rather just certain derived objects, such as the mean treatment effects. These are taken as the invariant structural parameters. The class of modifications considered is the set of treatments in place.

Consider identification of ATE. It is not necessary to assume that X is exogenous if one conditions policy analysis on X and does not seek to identify the effect of changing X. The model of outcomes does not have to be separable in observables and unobservables. We can nonetheless identify ATE under very general conditions.

One transparent way is by randomization, discussed in Chapter 71. If agents of given X are randomized into sectors 1 and 0, and there is compliance with the randomization protocols, we can identify ATE by comparing the mean outcomes of agents randomized into sector 1 with the outcomes of those randomized into sector 0:

$$\mathrm{ATE}(x) = E(Y_1 \mid X) - E(Y_0 \mid X).$$

Matching, discussed in Chapter 71, also identifies ATE without making any assumptions about the distributions of (U_1, U_0, U_C) or the functional forms of the relationships generating outcomes and choices (6.1a)–(6.1c) but assuming that conditioning on X randomizes choices and produces the same data as are generated from an experiment. By focusing on one treatment parameter, in this case ATE, and the questions ATE answers, we can proceed under weaker conditions than were used to develop the selection model although finding a common support for X when $D = 1$ and X when $D = 0$ may be a serious practical issue [see Heckman, Ichimura and Todd (1998)]. In general, matching or randomization do not identify TT or MTE.

ATE answers only one of the many evaluation questions that are potentially interesting to answer. But we can identify ATE under weaker assumptions than are required to identify the full generalized Roy model. Our analysis of ATE is an application of Marschak's Maxim. Doing one thing well has both its advantages and disadvantages. Many of the estimators proposed in the evaluation literature identify some parameters, and not others.

Our strategy in Chapter 71 of this Handbook is to survey the existing literature that relaxes normality assumptions in conducting policy evaluation but that preserves the index structure motivated by economic theory that is at the core of the generalized Roy model and its extensions. The goal is to present a unified analysis of the available models of treatment choice and treatment outcomes, and to unify the analysis of alternative estimation strategies using a nonparametric index model framework. This limits the generality of our survey. At the same time, it links the treatment literature to economic choice theory and so bridges the structural and treatment effect approaches.

Thus, in Chapter 71, we present an economically motivated framework that allows us to integrate the treatment effect literature with the literature on "structural" (economically motivated) econometric methods. We organize the alternative estimators of instrumental variables, matching, regression discontinuity design methods and the like within a common framework developed by Heckman and Vytlacil (1999, 2000, 2005).

Appendix A: The value of precisely formulated economic models in making policy forecasts

Explicitly formulated economic models are useful for three different purposes. First, the derivatives of such functions or finite changes generate the comparative statics *ceteris paribus* variations produced by economic theory. For example, tests of economic theory and measurements of economic parameters (price elasticities, measurements of consumer surplus, etc.) are based on structural equations.

Second, under invariance assumptions, structural equations can be used to forecast the effects of policies evaluated in one population in other populations, provided that the parameters are invariant across populations, and support conditions are satisfied. However, a purely nonparametric structural equation determined on one support cannot be extrapolated to other populations with different supports. Third, Marshallian causal functions and structural equations are one ingredient required to forecast the effect of a new policy, never previously implemented.

The problem of forecasting the effects of a policy evaluated on one population but applied to another population can be formulated in the following way. Let $Y(\omega) = \varphi(X(\omega), U(\omega))$, where $\varphi : \mathcal{D} \to \mathcal{Y}$, $\mathcal{D} \subseteq \mathbb{R}^J$, where $\mathcal{D}$ is the domain of the function, and $\mathcal{Y} \subseteq \mathbb{R}$. φ is a structural equation determining outcome Y, and we assume that it is known only over $\text{Supp}(X(\omega), U(\omega)) = \mathcal{X} \times \mathcal{U}$. $X(\omega)$ and $U(\omega)$ are random input variables. The mean outcome conditional on $X(\omega) = x$ is

$$E_H(Y \mid X = x) = \int_{\mathcal{U}} \varphi(X = x, u)\, \mathrm{d}F_H(u \mid X = x),$$

where $F_H(u \mid X)$ is the distribution of U in the historical data. We seek to forecast the outcome in a target population which may have a different support. The average outcome in the target population (T) is

$$E_T(Y \mid X = x) = \int_{\mathcal{U}^T} \varphi(X = x, u)\, \mathrm{d}F_T(u \mid X = x),$$

where $\mathcal{U}^T$ is the support of U in the target population. Provided that the support of (X, U) is the same in the source and the target populations, from knowledge of F_T it is possible to produce a correct value of $E_T(Y \mid X = x)$ for the target population. Otherwise, it is possible to evaluate this expectation only over the intersection set $\text{Supp}_T(X) \cap \text{Supp}_H(X)$, where $\text{Supp}_A(X)$ is the support of X in the source population. In order to extrapolate over the whole set $\text{Supp}_T(X)$, it is necessary to adopt some form of parametric or functional structure. Additive separability in φ simplifies the extrapolation problem. If φ is additively separable

$$Y = \varphi(X) + U,$$

$\varphi(X)$ applies to all populations for which we can condition on X. However, some structure may have to be imposed to extrapolate from $\text{Supp}_H(X)$ to $\text{Supp}_T(X)$ if $\varphi(X)$ on T is not determined nonparametrically from H.

The problem of forecasting the effect of a new policy, never previously experienced, is similar in character to the policy forecasting problem just discussed. It shares many elements in common with the problem of forecasting the demand for a new good, never previously consumed.[100] Without imposing some structure on this problem, it is impossible to solve. The literature in structural econometrics associated with the work of the Cowles Commission adopts the following five step approach to this problem.

1. Structural functions are determined (e.g., $\varphi(X)$).
2. The new policy is characterized by an invertible mapping from observed random variables to the characteristics associated with the policy: $Q = q(X)$, where Q is the set of characteristics associated with the policy and q, $q : R^J \to R^J$, is a *known* invertible mapping.
3. $X = q^{-1}(Q)$ is solved to associate characteristics that in principle can be observed with the policy. This places the characteristics of the new policy on the same footing as those of the old.
4. It is assumed that, in the historical data, $\text{Supp}(q^{-1}(Q)) \subseteq \text{Supp}(X)$. This ensures that the support of the new characteristics mapped into X space is contained in the support of X. If this condition is not met, some functional structure must be used to forecast the effects of the new policy, to extend it beyond the support of the source population.
5. The forecast effect of the policy on Y is $Y(Q) = \varphi(q^{-1}(Q))$.

The leading example of this approach is Lancaster's method for estimating the demand for a new good [Lancaster (1971)]. New goods are viewed as bundles of old characteristics. McFadden's conditional logit scheme [1974] is based on a similar idea.[101]

Marschak's analysis of the effect of a new commodity tax is another example. Let $P(\omega)$ be the random variable denoting the price facing consumer ω. The tax changes

[100] Quandt and Baumol (1966), Lancaster (1971), Gorman (1980), McFadden (1974) and Domencich and McFadden (1975) consider the problem of forecasting the demand for a new good. Marschak (1953) is the classic reference for evaluating the effect of a new policy. See Heckman (2001) for a survey and synthesis of this literature.

[101] McFadden's stochastic specification is different from Lancaster's specification. See Heckman and Snyder (1997) for a comparison of these two approaches. Lancaster assumes that the $U(\omega)$ are the same for each consumer in all choice settings (they are preference parameters in his setting). McFadden allows for $U(\omega)$ to be different for the same consumer across different choice settings but assumes that the $U(\omega)$ in each choice setting are draws from a common distribution that can be determined from the demand for old goods.

the product price from $P(\omega)$ to $P(\omega)(1+t)$, where t is the tax. With sufficient price variation so that the assumption in Step 4 is satisfied (so the support of the price after tax, $\text{Supp}_{\text{post tax}}(P(\omega)(1+t)) \subseteq \text{Supp}_{\text{pretax}}(P(\omega))$, it is possible to use reduced form demand functions fit on a pretax sample to forecast the effect of a tax never previously put in place. Marschak uses a linear structural equation to solve the problem of limited support. From linearity, determination of the structural equations over a small region determines it everywhere.

Marshallian or structural causal functions are an essential ingredient in constructing such forecasts because they explicitly model the relationship between U and X. The treatment effect approach does not explicitly model this relationship so that treatment parameters cannot be extrapolated in this fashion, unless the dependence of potential outcomes on U and X is specified, and the required support conditions are satisfied. The Rubin (1978)–Holland (1986) model does not specify the required relationships. We discuss a specific way to implement this program in Chapter 71 of this contribution.

Appendix B: Nonparametric identification of counterfactual outcomes for a multinomial discrete choice model with state-contingent outcomes

Let outcomes in s be $Y(s) = \mu_Y(s, X) + U(s)$, $s = 1, \ldots, \bar{S}$, where there are $\bar{S}$ discrete states. Let $R(s) = \mu_R(s, Z) - V(s)$. The $U(s)$ and $V(s)$, $s = 1, \ldots, \bar{S}$, are assumed to be absolutely continuous and variation free as a collection of random variables. Thus the realization of one random variable does not restrict the realizations of the other random variables. State s is selected if

$$s = \text{argmax}_j \{R(j)\}_{j=1}^{\bar{S}}$$

and $Y(s)$ is observed. If s is observed, $D(s) = 1$. Otherwise $D(s) = 0$. $\sum_{s=1}^{\bar{S}} D(s) = 1$.

Define

$$\begin{aligned}
\mu_R^s(Z) &= \big(\mu_R(s, Z) - \mu_R(1, Z), \ldots, \mu_R(s, Z) - \mu_R(\bar{S}, Z)\big),\\
V^s &= \big(V(s) - V(1), \ldots, V(s) - V(\bar{S})\big),\\
\mu_R(Z) &= \big(\mu_R(1, Z), \ldots, \mu_R(\bar{S}, Z)\big),\\
\mu_Y(X) &= \big(\mu_Y(1, X), \ldots, \mu_Y(\bar{S}, X)\big),\\
F_V &= (F_{V(1)}, \ldots, F_{V(\bar{S})}),\\
D(s) &= \mathbf{1}(\mu_R^s(Z) \geqslant V^s).
\end{aligned}$$

Let $F_{U(s),V^s}$ be a candidate joint distribution of $(U(s), V^s)$, $s = 1, \ldots, \bar{S}$, with the true distribution being $F^*_{U(s),V^s}$. The true marginal distribution of V^s is $F^*_{V^s}$. The true marginal distribution of $U(s)$ is $F^*_{U(s)}$. Let $\mu_Y^*(X)$ denote the true value of $\mu_Y(X)$; $\mu_R^*(Z)$ is the true value of $\mu_R(Z)$. Define $\mathcal{M}_Y$ as the space of candidate conditional mean functions for Y: $\mu_Y \in \mathcal{M}_Y$. Define $\mathcal{M}_R$ as the space of candidate conditional mean functions for the discrete indices: $\mu_R \in \mathcal{M}_R$. Let $\mathcal{M} = \mathcal{M}_Y \times \mathcal{M}_R$.

In this notation, $(\mu_Y, \mu_R) \in \mathcal{M}$. Define $\mathcal{H}_V$ as the space of candidate distribution functions for V, $F_V \in \mathcal{H}_V$; $\mathcal{H}_{U,V}$ is the space of candidate distribution functions for $((U(1), V(1)), \ldots, (U(\bar{S}), V(\bar{S})))$, $F_{U,V} \in \mathcal{H}_{U,V}$.

Let $\mathcal{M}_Y^s, \mathcal{M}_R^s$ denote the spaces in which μ_Y^s, μ_R^s reside, $(\mu_Y^s, \mu_R^s) \in \mathcal{M}_Y^s \times \mathcal{M}_R^s$. Let $\mathcal{H}_{U,V}^s \subseteq \mathcal{H}_{U,V}$ denote the space in which candidate distributions $F_{U(s),V^s}$ reside, $F_{U(s),V^s} \in \mathcal{H}_{U,V}^s$. $\mathcal{H}_U^s$ and $\mathcal{H}_V^s$ are defined in a corresponding fashion.

Matzkin (1993) considers identification of polychotomous discrete choice models under the conditions of Theorem 1 below. We extend her analysis to allow for counterfactual outcomes adjoined to each choice. We can identify $\mu_Y(s, X)$, $s = 1, \ldots, \bar{S}$, over the support of X; $\mu_R(s, Z)$, up to scale over the support of Z and the joint distributions of $(U(s), V(s) - V(1), \ldots, V(s) - V(s-1), V(s) - V(s+1), \ldots, V(s) - V(\bar{S}))$ with the contrasts $V(s) - V(\ell)$, $\ell \neq s$, up to a scale that we present below in our discussion of Theorem 1.

THEOREM 1. *Assume*

(i) $\mu_R : \text{Supp}(Z) \to \mathbb{R}^{\bar{S}}$ *is continuous for all* $\mu_R \in \mathcal{M}_R$.

(ii) $(U(s), V^s)$, $s = 1, \ldots, \bar{S}$, *are absolutely continuous random variables so that* $F_{U(s),V^s} \in \mathcal{H}_{U,V}^s$ *is continuous.* $E(U(s)) = 0$.

(iii) $\text{Supp}(V^s) = \mathbb{R}^{\bar{S}-1}$, $s = 1, \ldots, \bar{S}$.

(iv) $(U(s), V^s) \perp\!\!\!\perp (X, Z)$, $s = 1, \ldots, \bar{S}$.

(v) *There exists a* $\widetilde{Z} \subseteq \text{Supp}(Z)$ *such that for all* $\mu_R, \hat{\mu}_R \in \mathcal{M}_R$

 (a) $\mu^1(\widetilde{Z}) = \mathbb{R}^{\bar{S}-1}$.

 (b) $\mu_R^1(z) = \hat{\mu}_R^1(z)$ *for all* $z \in \widetilde{Z}$.

(vi) $\text{Supp}(\mu_R^s(Z), X) = \text{Supp}(\mu_R^s(Z)) \times \text{Supp}(X)$.

(vii) *For all* $\mu_R, \hat{\mu}_R \in \mathcal{M}$ *and* $z \in \text{Supp}(Z)$, $\mu_R(1, z) = \hat{\mu}_R(1, z)$.

Then $\mu_Y^*(s, X)$, $\mu_R^{*,s}(Z)$ *and* $F_{U(s),V^s}^*$, $s = 1, \ldots, \bar{S}$, *are identified.*[102]

PROOF. This theorem is a straightforward extension of Matzkin (1993, Theorem 2). The proof of identifiability of the $\mu_R^{*,s}(Z)$ and $F_{V^s}^*$, $s = 1, \ldots, \bar{S}$, follows directly from her analysis.

Thus, suppose that (F_{V^s}, μ_R^s) are observationally identical to $(F_{V^s}^*, \mu_R^{*,s})$ where both reside in the space $\mathcal{H}_V^s \times \mathcal{M}_R^s$. For all s,

$$F_{V^s}\big(\mu_R^s(z)\big) = F_{V^s}^*\big(\mu_R^{*,s}(z)\big)$$

for all $z \in \text{Supp}(Z)$. For arbitrary $v \in \mathbb{R}^{\bar{S}-1}$, there exists $z_v \in \bar{Z}$ such that $\mu_R^1(z_v) = \mu_R^{1,*}(z_v) = v$ so that

$$F_{V^1}(v) = F_{V^1}\big(\mu_R^1(z_v)\big) = F_{V^1}^*\big(\mu_R^{*,1}(z_v)\big) = F_{V^1}^*(v)$$

[102] Assuming that $\mu_R(s, Z) = Z\gamma_s$, $s = 1, \ldots, \bar{S}$, simplifies the proof greatly and relies on more familiar conditions. See Heckman (1990), Heckman and Smith (1998) or Carneiro, Hansen and Heckman (2003). Matzkin (1993) presents alternative sets of conditions for identifiability of the choice model, all of which apply here.

for $v \in \mathbb{R}^{\bar{S}-1}$. Because V^s is a known linear transformation of V^1, this identifies $F^*_{V^s}$, $s = 1, \ldots, \bar{S}$. Given this distribution, following Matzkin, we can invert the choice probabilities to obtain $\mu_R^{*,s}(z)$, $s = 1, \ldots, \bar{S}$.

Armed with these results, we can find limit set $\mathcal{Z}(x)$, such that

$$\lim_{Z \to \mathcal{Z}(x)} \Pr\bigl(D(s) = 1 \mid Z = z, X = x\bigr) = 1$$

and thus $\lim_{Z \to \mathcal{Z}(x)} E(Y \mid D(s) = 1, Z = z, X = x) = \mu_y^*(s, x) + E(U(s))$. Using $E(U(s)) = 0$, we can identify the $\mu_Y^*(s, X)$ in those limit sets. We can vary $y(s)$ and trace out the marginal distribution of $U(s)$, $s = 1, \ldots, \bar{S}$, since $\lim_{Z \to \mathcal{Z}(x)} \Pr(Y(s) - \mu_y^*(s, x) \leqslant t \mid D(s) = 1, Z = z, X = x) = \Pr[U(s) \leqslant t]$. From the joint distribution of $Y(s)$, $D(s)$ given X, Z, we can identify $F^*_{U(s), V^s}$, $s = 1, \ldots, \bar{S}$, by tracing out different values of $y(s)$, given $X = x$, and $\mu_R^{*,s}(z)$. □

From this model, we can identify the marginal treatment effect [Carneiro, Hansen and Heckman (2003, p. 368, equation (71))] and all pairwise average treatment effects by forming suitable limit sets. We can also identify all pairwise mean treatment on the treated and treatment on the untreated effects.

In the general case, we can identify the densities of $U(s), V(s) - V(1), \ldots, V(s) - V(\bar{S})$, $s = 1, \ldots, \bar{S}$, where $U(s)$ may be a vector and the contrasts are identified. Set $V(\bar{S}) \equiv 0$ (this is only one possible normalization). Then from the choice equation for $\bar{S}$ ($\Pr(D(\bar{S}) = 1 \mid Z = z)$) we can identify the pairwise correlations $\rho_{i,j} = \mathrm{Correl}(V(i), V(j))$, $i, j = 1, \ldots, \bar{S} - 1$. We assume $-1 \leqslant \rho_{i,j} < 1$. If $\rho_{i,j} = 1$ for some i, j, the choice of a normalization is not innocuous. Under our conditions we can identify $\mathrm{Var}(V(s) - V(\ell)) = 2(1 - \rho_{s,\ell})$. This is the scale for contrast s, ℓ. Define $\tau_{s,\ell} = [\mathrm{Var}(V(s) - V(\ell))]^{1/2}$ where positive square roots are used.

Consider constructing the distribution of $Y(\ell)$ given $D(s) = 1, X, Z$. If $\ell \neq s$, this is a counterfactual distribution. From this distribution we can construct, among many possible counterfactual parameters, $E(Y(s) - Y(\ell) \mid D(s) = 1,\ X = x,\ Z = z)$, a treatment on the treated parameter.

To form the distribution of $(U(\ell), \frac{V(s)-V(1)}{\tau_{s,1}}, \ldots, \frac{V(s)-V(\bar{S})}{\tau_{s,\bar{S}}})$ for any $\ell \neq s$ from the objects produced from Theorem 1, we use the normalized versions of $V(s) - V(1), \ldots, V(s) - V(\bar{S})$: $\frac{V(s)-V(1)}{\tau_{s,1}}, \ldots, \frac{V(s)-V(\bar{S})}{\tau_{s,\bar{S}}}$. From the density of $U(\ell)$, $\frac{V(\ell)-V(1)}{\tau_{\ell,1}}, \ldots, \frac{V(\ell)-V(\bar{S})}{\tau_{\ell,\bar{S}}}$ which we identify from Theorem 1, we can transform the contrast variables in the following way.

Define $q(\ell, s) = \frac{V(\ell)-V(s)}{\tau_{\ell,s}}$. From the definitions, $q(s, j) = \frac{V(s)-V(j)}{\tau_{s,j}} = \frac{q(\ell,j)\tau_{\ell,j}-q(\ell,s)\tau_{\ell,s}}{\tau_{s,j}}$, for all $j = 1, 2, \ldots, \bar{S}$. Substitute $\frac{q(\ell,j)\tau_{\ell,j}-q(\ell,s)\tau_{\ell,s}}{\tau_{s,j}}$ for $\frac{V(s)-V(j)}{\tau_{s,j}}$, $j = 1, 2, \ldots, \bar{S}$, $j \neq \ell$, in the density of $(U(\ell), \frac{V(\ell)-V(s)}{\tau_{\ell,s}}, \ldots, \frac{V(\ell)-V(\bar{S})}{\tau_{\ell,\bar{S}}})$ and use the Jacobian of transformation $\prod_{j=1,\ldots,\bar{S},\ j\neq\ell} |\tau_{\ell,j}|$ to obtain the desired density where "$|\ |$" denotes determinant. This produces the desired counterfactual density for all

$s = 1, \ldots, \bar{S}$. Provided that the Jacobians are nonzero (which rules out perfect dependence), we preserve all of the information and can construct the marginal distribution of any $U(\ell)$ for any desired pattern of latent indices. Thus we can construct the desired counterfactuals.

Appendix C: Normal selection model results

The properties of the normal selection model are generated by the properties of a truncated normal model which we now establish. See Heckman and Honoré (1990). Let Z be a standard normal random variable and let $\lambda(d) \overset{\text{def}}{\equiv} E[Z \mid Z \geqslant d]$. For all $d \in (-\infty, \infty)$, we prove the following results:

$$\text{(N-1)}\quad \lambda(d) = \frac{\frac{1}{\sqrt{2\pi}}\exp\{-\frac{d^2}{2}\}}{\Phi(-d)} > \max\{0, d\},$$

$$\text{(N-2)}\quad 0 < \frac{\partial\lambda(d)}{\partial d} = \lambda'(d) = \lambda(d)\big(\lambda(d) - d\big) < 1,$$

$$\text{(N-3)}\quad \frac{\partial^2\lambda(d)}{\partial d^2} > 0,$$

$$\text{(N-4)}\quad 0 < \operatorname{Var}[Z \mid Z \geqslant d] = 1 + \lambda(d)d - [\lambda(d)]^2 < 1,$$

$$\text{(N-5)}\quad \frac{\partial \operatorname{Var}[Z \mid Z \geqslant d]}{\partial d} < 0,$$

$$\text{(N-6)}\quad E\big[\big(Z - \lambda(d)\big)^3 \mid Z \geqslant d\big] = \lambda(d)\big(2[\lambda(d)]^2 - 3d\lambda(d) + d^2 - 1\big) = \frac{\partial^2\lambda(d)}{\partial d^2},$$

$$\text{(N-7)}\quad E[Z \mid Z \geqslant d] \geqslant \operatorname{mode}[Z \mid Z \geqslant d],$$

$$\text{(N-8)}\quad \lim_{d\to-\infty}\lambda(d) = 0, \qquad \lim_{d\to\infty}\lambda(d) = \infty,$$

$$\text{(N-9)}\quad \lim_{d\to-\infty}\frac{\partial\lambda(d)}{\partial d} = 0, \qquad \lim_{d\to\infty}\frac{\partial\lambda(d)}{\partial d} = 1,$$

$$\text{(N-10)}\quad \lim_{d\to-\infty}\operatorname{Var}[Z \mid Z \geqslant d] = 1, \qquad \lim_{d\to\infty}\operatorname{Var}[Z \mid Z \geqslant d] = 0.$$

Results (N-2), (N-4) and (N-5) are implications of log concavity. (N-7) is an implication of symmetry and log concavity. (N-1) and (N-3) are consequences of normality. The left-hand side limits of (N-8) and (N-10) are true for any distribution with zero mean and unit variance. So is the right-hand limit of (N-8) provided that the support of Z is not bounded on the right. The right-hand limits of (N-9) and (N-10) are consequences of normality.

C.1. Proofs of results (N-1) to (N-10)

The moment generating function for a truncated normal distribution with truncation point d is:

$$\mathrm{mgf}(\beta) = e^{\beta/2} \frac{\int_{d-\beta}^{\infty} \frac{1}{\sqrt{2\pi}} \exp(-\frac{1}{2}u^2)\, du}{\int_{d}^{\infty} \frac{1}{\sqrt{2\pi}} \exp(-\frac{1}{2}u^2)\, du}.$$

The equality in (N-1) follows from:

$$\lambda(d) = E[Z \mid Z \geqslant d] = \left. \frac{\partial \,\mathrm{mgf}}{\partial \beta} \right|_{\beta=0}.$$

The inequality is obvious.

By direct calculation, $\lambda'(d) = \lambda(d)(\lambda(d) - d)$. Now note that

$$E\left[Z^2 \mid Z \geqslant d\right] = \left. \frac{\partial^2 \,\mathrm{mgf}}{\partial \beta^2} \right|_{\beta=0} = 1 + \lambda(d)d.$$

Therefore:

$$\mathrm{Var}[Z \mid Z \geqslant d] = 1 - \frac{\partial \lambda(d)}{\partial d}.$$

As $\mathrm{Var}[Z \mid Z \geqslant d] > 0$ and $\lambda(d)(\lambda(d) - d) > 0$ by (N-1), this proves (N-2) and (N-4). To prove (N-3) notice that $\mathrm{Var}[Z \mid Z \geqslant d] = 1 - \frac{\partial \lambda(d)}{\partial d}$, and therefore:

$$\frac{\partial^2 \lambda(d)}{\partial d^2} = -\frac{\partial \,\mathrm{Var}[Z \mid Z \geqslant d]}{\partial d} > 0,$$

where the inequality follows from Proposition 1 in Heckman and Honoré (1990). (N-5) also follows from Proposition 1, whereas (N-6) follows by direct calculation from the expression for $E[(Z - \lambda(d))^3 \mid Z > d]$. (N-7) is trivial. (N-8) is obvious. The first part of (N-9) follows directly from L'Hôpital's rule. (N-2) and (N-3) imply that $\frac{\partial \lambda(d)}{\partial d}$ is increasing and bounded by 1. Therefore $\lim_{d \to \infty} \frac{\partial \lambda(d)}{\partial d}$ exists and does not exceed 1. If $\lim_{d \to \infty} \frac{\partial \lambda(d)}{\partial d} < 1$ then $\lambda(d)$ would eventually be less than d, contradicting (N-1). This proves the second part of (N-9). (N-9) and (N-4) imply (N-10).

References

Abadie, A., Angrist, J.D., Imbens, G. (2002). "Instrumental variables estimates of the effect of subsidized training on the quantiles of trainee earnings". Econometrica 70 (1), 91–117 (January).

Abbring, J.H., Campbell, J.R. (2005). "A firm's first year". Technical Report TI 05-046/3, Tinbergen Institute Discussion Paper, May.

Abbring, J.H., Heckman, J.J. (2007). "Econometric evaluation of social programs, Part III: Distributional treatment effects, dynamic treatment effects, dynamic discrete choice, and general equilibrium policy evaluation". In: Heckman, J.J., Leamer, E. (Eds.), Handbook of Econometrics, vol. 6B. Elsevier. Chapter 72.

Abbring, J.H., Van den Berg, G.J. (2003). "The nonparametric identification of treatment effects in duration models". Econometrica 71 (5), 1491–1517 (September).

Ackerberg, D., Benkard, C.L., Berry, S., Pakes, A. (2007). "Econometric tools for analyzing market outcomes". In: Heckman, J.J., Leamer, E. (Eds.), Handbook of Econometrics, vol. 6A. Elsevier. Chapter 63.

Aguirregabiria, V. (2004). "Pseudo maximum likelihood estimation of structural models involving fixed-point problems". Economics Letters 84 (3), 335–340 (September).

Ahn, H., Powell, J. (1993). "Semiparametric estimation of censored selection models with a nonparametric selection mechanism". Journal of Econometrics 58 (1–2), 3–29 (July).

Amemiya, T. (1985). Advanced Econometrics. Harvard University Press, Cambridge, MA.

Angrist, J.D., Imbens, G.W. (1995). "Two-stage least squares estimation of average causal effects in models with variable treatment intensity". Journal of the American Statistical Association 90 (430), 431–442 (June).

Angrist, J.D., Krueger, A.B. (1999). "Empirical strategies in labor economics". In: Ashenfelter, O., Card, D. (Eds.), Handbook of Labor Economics, vol. 3A. Elsevier, New York, pp. 1277–1366.

Angrist, J.D., Imbens, G.W., Rubin, D. (1996). "Identification of causal effects using instrumental variables". Journal of the American Statistical Association 91 (434), 444–455.

Arabmazar, A., Schmidt, P. (1982). "An investigation of the robustness of the Tobit estimator to non-normality". Econometrica 50 (4), 1055–1063 (July).

Athey, S., Haile, P. (2007). "Nonparametric approaches to auctions". In: Heckman, J.J., Leamer, E. (Eds.), Handbook of Econometrics, vol. 6A. Elsevier, Amsterdam. Chapter 60.

Berk, R., Li, A., Hickman, L.J. (2005). "Statistical difficulties in determining the role of race in capital cases: A re-analysis of data from the state of Maryland". Journal of Quantitative Criminology 21 (4), 365–390 (December).

Björklund, A., Moffitt, R. (1987). "The estimation of wage gains and welfare gains in self-selection". Review of Economics and Statistics 69 (1), 42–49 (February).

Blundell, R., Stoker, T. (2007). "Models of aggregate economic relationships that account for heterogeneity". In: Heckman, J.J., Leamer, E. (Eds.), Handbook of Econometrics, vol. 6A. Elsevier, Amsterdam. Chapter 68.

Blundell, R., Reed, H., Stoker, T. (2003). "Interpreting aggregate wage growth: The role of labor market participation". American Economic Review 93 (4), 1114–1131 (September).

Blundell, R., Costa Dias, M., Meghir, C., Van Reenen, J. (2004). "Evaluating the employment effects of a mandatory job search program". Journal of the European Economic Association 2 (4), 569–606 (June).

Blundell, R., MaCurdy, T., Meghir, C. (2007). "Labor supply models: Unobserved heterogeneity, nonparticipation and dynamics". In: Heckman, J.J., Leamer, E. (Eds.), Handbook of Econometrics, vol. 6A. Elsevier, Amsterdam. Chapter 69.

Boadway, R.W., Bruce, N. (1984). Welfare Economics. B. Blackwell, New York.

Bock, R.D., Jones, L.V. (1968). The Measurement and Prediction of Judgment and Choice. Holden-Day, San Francisco.

Bond, S., Van Reenen, J. (2007). "Microeconometric models of investment and employment". In: Heckman, J.J., Leamer, E. (Eds.), Handbook of Econometrics, vol. 6A. Elsevier, Amsterdam. Chapter 65.

Brock, W.A., Durlauf, S.N. (2001). "Interactions-based models". In: Heckman, J.J., Leamer, E. (Eds.), Handbook of Econometrics, vol. 5. North-Holland, New York, pp. 3463–3568.

Browning, M., Hansen, L.P., Heckman, J.J. (1999). "Micro data and general equilibrium models". In: Taylor, J.B., Woodford, M. (Eds.), Handbook of Macroeconomics, vol. 1A. Elsevier, pp. 543–633. Chapter 8.

Campbell, D.T., Stanley, J.C. (1963). Experimental and Quasi-Experimental Designs for Research. Rand McNally, Chicago. Originally appeared in Gage, N.L. (Ed.), Handbook of Research on Teaching.

Carneiro, P., Hansen, K., Heckman, J.J. (2001). "Removing the veil of ignorance in assessing the distributional impacts of social policies". Swedish Economic Policy Review 8 (2), 273–301 (Fall).

Carneiro, P., Hansen, K., Heckman, J.J. (2003). "Estimating distributions of treatment effects with an application to the returns to schooling and measurement of the effects of uncertainty on college choice". International Economic Review 44 (2), 361–422 (May).

Carrasco, M., Florens, J.-P., Renault, E. (2007). "Linear inverse problems in structural econometrics estimation based on spectral decomposition and regularization". In: Heckman, J.J., Leamer, E. (Eds.), Handbook of Econometrics, vol. 6B. Elsevier, Amsterdam. Chapter 77.

Chan, T.Y., Hamilton, B.H. (2003, July). "Learning, private information and the economic evaluation of randomized experiments". Working paper. Olin School of Business, Washington University, St. Louis.

Chen, S. (1999). "Distribution-free estimation of the random coefficient dummy endogenous variable model". Journal of Econometrics 91 (1), 171–199 (July).

Chen, X. (2007). "Large sample sieve estimation of semi-nonparametric models". In: Heckman, J.J., Leamer, E. (Eds.), Handbook of Econometrics, vol. 6B. Elsevier, Amsterdam. Chapter 76.

Chernozhukov, V., Hansen, C. (2005). "An IV model of quantile treatment effects". Econometrica 73 (1), 245–261 (January).

Cosslett, S.R. (1983). "Distribution-free maximum likelihood estimator of the binary choice model". Econometrica 51 (3), 765–782 (May).

Cox, D.R. (1958). Planning of Experiments. Wiley, New York.

Cunha, F., Heckman, J.J., Navarro, S. (2005). "Separating uncertainty from heterogeneity in life cycle earnings, the 2004 Hicks lecture". Oxford Economic Papers 57 (2), 191–261 (April).

Cunha, F., Heckman, J.J., Navarro, S. (2006). "Counterfactual analysis of inequality and social mobility". In: Morgan, S.L., Grusky, D.B., Fields, G.S. (Eds.), Mobility and Inequality: Frontiers of Research in Sociology and Economics. Stanford University Press, Stanford, CA, pp. 290–348. Chapter 4.

Dahl, G.B. (2002). "Mobility and the return to education: Testing a Roy model with multiple markets". Econometrica 70 (6), 2367–2420 (November).

Dawid, A. (2000). "Causal inference without counterfactuals". Journal of the American Statistical Association 95 (450), 407–424 (June).

Domencich, T., McFadden, D.L. (1975). Urban Travel Demand: A Behavioral Analysis. North-Holland, Amsterdam. Reprinted 1996.

Eckstein, Z., Wolpin, K.I. (1989). "The specification and estimation of dynamic stochastic discrete choice models: A survey". Journal of Human Resources 24 (4), 562–598 (Fall).

Eckstein, Z., Wolpin, K.I. (1999). "Why youths drop out of high school: The impact of preferences, opportunities and abilities". Econometrica 67 (6), 1295–1339 (November).

Fisher, R.A. (1966). The Design of Experiments. Hafner Publishing, New York.

Florens, J.-P., Heckman, J.J. (2003). "Causality and econometrics". Unpublished working paper, University of Chicago, Department of Economics.

Foster, J.E., Sen, A.K. (1997). On Economic Inequality. Oxford University Press, New York.

Geweke, J., Keane, M. (2001). "Computationally intensive methods for integration in econometrics". In: Heckman, J.J., Leamer, E. (Eds.), Handbook of Econometrics, vol. 5. North-Holland, New York, pp. 3463–3568.

Gill, R.D., Robins, J.M. (2001). "Causal inference for complex longitudinal data: The continuous case". The Annals of Statistics 29 (6), 1785–1811 (December).

Goldberger, A.S. (1964). Econometric Theory. Wiley, New York.

Goldberger, A.S. (1983). "Abnormal selection bias". In: Karlin, S., Amemiya, T., Goodman, L.A. (Eds.), Studies in Econometrics, Time Series, and Multivariate Statistics. Academic Press, New York, pp. 67–84.

Gorman, W.M. (1980). "A possible procedure for analysing quality differentials in the egg market". Review of Economic Studies 47 (5), 843–856 (October).

Gronau, R. (1974). "Wage comparisons – a selectivity bias". Journal of Political Economy 82 (6), 1119–1143 (November–December).

Haavelmo, T. (1943). "The statistical implications of a system of simultaneous equations". Econometrica 11 (1), 1–12 (January).

Haavelmo, T. (1944). "The probability approach in econometrics". Econometrica 12 (Suppl.), iii–vi and 1–115.

Hamermesh, D.S. (1993). Labor Demand. Princeton University Press, Princeton, NJ.

Hansen, L.P., Sargent, T.J. (1980). "Formulating and estimating dynamic linear rational expectations models". Journal of Economic Dynamics and Control 2 (1), 7–46 (February).

Harberger, A.C. (1971). "Three basic postulates for applied welfare economics: An interpretive essay". Journal of Economic Literature 9 (3), 785–797 (September).

Harsanyi, J.C. (1955). "Cardinal welfare, individualistic ethics and interpersonal comparisons of utility". Journal of Political Economy 63 (4), 309–321 (August).

Harsanyi, J.C. (1975). "Can the maximin principle serve as a basis for morality? A critique of John Rawls's theory". American Political Science Review 69 (2), 594–606 (June).

Heckman, J.J. (1974). "Shadow prices, market wages and labor supply". Econometrica 42 (4), 679–694 (July).

Heckman, J.J. (1976). "The common structure of statistical models of truncation, sample selection and limited dependent variables and a simple estimator for such models". Annals of Economic and Social Measurement 5 (4), 475–492 (December).

Heckman, J.J. (1978). "Dummy endogenous variables in a simultaneous equation system". Econometrica 46 (4), 931–959 (July).

Heckman, J.J. (1979). "Sample selection bias as a specification error". Econometrica 47 (1), 153–162 (January).

Heckman, J.J. (1980). "Addendum to sample selection bias as a specification error". In: Stromsdorfer, E., Farkas, G. (Eds.), In: Evaluation Studies Review Annual, vol. 5. Sage Publications, Beverly Hills.

Heckman, J.J. (1990). "Varieties of selection bias". American Economic Review 80 (2), 313–318 (May).

Heckman, J.J. (1992). "Randomization and social policy evaluation". In: Manski, C., Garfinkel, I. (Eds.), Evaluating Welfare and Training Programs. Harvard University Press, Cambridge, MA, pp. 201–230.

Heckman, J.J. (2000). "Policies to foster human capital". Research in Economics 54 (1), 3–56 (March). With discussion.

Heckman, J.J. (2001). "Micro, data, heterogeneity and the evaluation of public policy: Nobel lecture". Journal of Political Economy 109 (4), 673–748 (August).

Heckman, J.J. (2005). "The scientific model of causality". Sociological Methodology 35 (1), 1–97 (August).

Heckman, J.J. (2007). Evaluating Economic Policy. Unpublished manuscript. University of Chicago.

Heckman, J.J., Honoré, B.E. (1990). "The empirical content of the Roy model". Econometrica 58 (5), 1121–1149 (September).

Heckman, J.J., MaCurdy, T.E. (1986). "Labor econometrics". In: Griliches, Z., Intriligator, M. (Eds.), Handbook of Econometrics, vol. 3. North-Holland, New York, pp. 1917–1977.

Heckman, J.J., Navarro, S. (2007). "Dynamic discrete choice and dynamic treatment effects". Journal of Econometrics 136 (2), 341–396 (February).

Heckman, J.J., Robb, R. (1985). "Alternative methods for evaluating the impact of interventions". In: Heckman, J.J., Singer, B. (Eds.), Longitudinal Analysis of Labor Market Data, vol. 10. Cambridge University Press, New York, pp. 156–245.

Heckman, J.J., Robb, R. (1986). "Alternative methods for solving the problem of selection bias in evaluating the impact of treatments on outcomes". In: Wainer, H. (Ed.), Drawing Inferences from Self-Selected Samples. Springer-Verlag, New York, pp. 63–107. Reprinted in 2000, Lawrence Erlbaum Associates, Mahwah, NJ.

Heckman, J.J., Sedlacek, G.L. (1985). "Heterogeneity, aggregation and market wage functions: An empirical model of self-selection in the labor market". Journal of Political Economy 93 (6), 1077–1125 (December).

Heckman, J.J., Smith, J.A. (1998). "Evaluating the welfare state". In: Strom, S. (Ed.), Econometrics and Economic Theory in the Twentieth Century: The Ragnar Frisch Centennial Symposium. Cambridge University Press, New York, pp. 241–318.

Heckman, J.J., Snyder, J.M. (1997). "Linear probability models of the demand for attributes with an empirical application to estimating the preferences of legislators". RAND Journal of Economics 28, S142 (Special Issue).

Heckman, J.J., Vytlacil, E.J. (1999). "Local instrumental variables and latent variable models for identifying and bounding treatment effects". Proceedings of the National Academy of Sciences 96, 4730–4734 (April).

Heckman, J.J., Vytlacil, E.J. (2000). "The relationship between treatment parameters within a latent variable framework". Economics Letters 66 (1), 33–39 (January).

Heckman, J.J., Vytlacil, E.J. (2001). "Local instrumental variables". In: Hsiao, C., Morimune, K., Powell, J.L. (Eds.), Nonlinear Statistical Modeling: Proceedings of the Thirteenth International Symposium in Economic Theory and Econometrics: Essays in Honor of Takeshi Amemiya. Cambridge University Press, New York, pp. 1–46.

Heckman, J.J., Vytlacil, E.J. (2005). "Structural equations, treatment effects and econometric policy evaluation". Econometrica 73 (3), 669–738 (May).

Heckman, J.J., Smith, J.A., Clements, N. (1997). "Making the most out of programme evaluations and social experiments: Accounting for heterogeneity in programme impacts". Review of Economic Studies 64 (221), 487–536 (October).

Heckman, J.J., Ichimura, H., Todd, P.E. (1998). "Matching as an econometric evaluation estimator". Review of Economic Studies 65 (223), 261–294 (April).

Heckman, J.J., Lochner, L.J., Taber, C. (1998). "General-equilibrium treatment effects: A study of tuition policy". American Economic Review 88 (2), 381–386 (May).

Heckman, J.J., LaLonde, R.J., Smith, J.A. (1999). "The economics and econometrics of active labor market programs". In: Ashenfelter, O., Card, D. (Eds.), Handbook of Labor Economics, vol. 3A. North-Holland, New York, pp. 1865–2097. Chapter 31.

Heckman, J.J., Hohmann, N., Smith, J., Khoo, M. (2000). "Substitution and dropout bias in social experiments: A study of an influential social experiment". Quarterly Journal of Economics 115 (2), 651–694 (May).

Heckman, J.J., Tobias, J.L., Vytlacil, E.J. (2001). "Four parameters of interest in the evaluation of social programs". Southern Economic Journal 68 (2), 210–223 (October).

Heckman, J.J., Tobias, J.L., Vytlacil, E.J. (2003). "Simple estimators for treatment parameters in a latent variable framework". Review of Economics and Statistics 85 (3), 748–754 (August).

Heckman, J.J., Urzua, S., Vytlacil, E.J. (2006). "Understanding instrumental variables in models with essential heterogeneity". Review of Economics Statistics 88 (3), 389–432.

Hensher, D., Louviere, J., Swait, J. (1999). "Combining sources of preference data". Journal of Econometrics 89 (1–2), 197–221 (March–April).

Hicks, J.R. (1946). Value and Capital: An Inquiry into Some Fundamental Principles of Economic Theory, second ed. Clarendon Press, Oxford.

Holland, P.W. (1986). "Statistics and causal inference". Journal of the American Statistical Association 81 (396), 945–960 (December).

Holland, P.W. (1988). "Causal inference, path analysis and recursive structural equation models". In: Clogg, C., Arminger, G. (Eds.), Sociological Methodology. American Sociological Association, Washington, DC, pp. 449–484.

Hurwicz, L. (1962). "On the structural form of interdependent systems". In: Nagel, E., Suppes, P., Tarski, A. (Eds.), Logic, Methodology and Philosophy of Science. Stanford University Press, pp. 232–239.

Ichimura, H., Todd, P.E. (2007). "Implementing nonparametric and semiparametric estimators". In: Heckman, J.J., Leamer, E. (Eds.), Handbook of Econometrics, vol. 6B. Elsevier, Amsterdam. Chapter 74.

Imbens, G.W., Angrist, J.D. (1994). "Identification and estimation of local average treatment effects". Econometrica 62 (2), 467–475 (March).

Journal of Human Resources (1990, Summer). Special Issue on Taxation and Labor Supply in Industrial Countries, Volume 25.

Katz, D., Gutek, A., Kahn, R., Barton, E. (1975). Bureaucratic Encounters: A Pilot Study in the Evaluation of Government Services. Survey Research Center Institute for Social Research, University of Michigan, Ann Arbor.

Keane, M.P., Wolpin, K.I. (1997). "The career decisions of young men". Journal of Political Economy 105 (3), 473–522 (June).

Killingsworth, M.R. (1983). Labor Supply. Cambridge University Press, Cambridge.

Killingsworth, M.R. (1985). "Substitution and output effects on labor demand: Theory and policy applications". Journal of Human Resources 20 (1), 142–152 (Winter).

Knight, F. (1921). Risk, Uncertainty and Profit. Houghton Mifflin Company, New York.

Koopmans, T.C., Rubin, H., Leipnik, R.B. (1950). "Measuring the equation systems of dynamic economics". In: Koopmans, T.C. (Ed.), Statistical Inference in Dynamic Economic Models. In: Cowles Commission Monograph, vol. 10. John Wiley & Sons, New York, pp. 53–237. Chapter 2.

Lancaster, K.J. (1971). Consumer Demand: A New Approach. Columbia University Press, New York.

Leamer, E.E. (1985). "Vector autoregressions for causal inference?". Carnegie–Rochester Conference Series on Public Policy 22, 255–303 (Spring).

Lechner, M. (2004). "Sequential matching estimation of dynamic causal models". Technical Report 2004, IZA Discussion Paper.

Lee, L.-F. (1978). "Unionism and wage rates: A simultaneous equations model with qualitative and limited dependent variables". International Economic Review 19 (2), 415–433 (June).

Lewis, H.G. (1974). "Comments on selectivity biases in wage comparisons". Journal of Political Economy 82 (6), 1145–1155 (November–December).

Lewis, H.G. (1986). Union Relative Wage Effects: A Survey. University of Chicago Press, Chicago.

Little, I.M., Mirrlees, J.A. (1974). Project Appraisal and Planning for Developing Countries. Basic Books, New York.

Lucas, R.E., Sargent, T.J. (1981). Rational Expectations and Econometric Practice. University of Minnesota Press, Minneapolis.

Maddala, G. (1983). Limited-Dependent and Qualitative Variables in Econometrics. Cambridge University Press, New York.

Magnac, T., Thesmar, D. (2002). "Identifying dynamic discrete decision processes". Econometrica 70 (2), 801–816 (March).

Manski, C.F. (1975). "Maximum score estimation of the stochastic utility model of choice". Journal of Econometrics 3 (3), 205–228 (August).

Manski, C.F. (1988). "Identification of binary response models". Journal of the American Statistical Association 83 (403), 729–738 (September).

Manski, C.F. (2003). Partial Identification of Probability Distributions. Springer-Verlag, New York.

Marschak, J. (1953). "Economic measurements for policy and prediction". In: Hood, W., Koopmans, T. (Eds.), Studies in Econometric Method. Wiley, New York, pp. 1–26.

Marshall, D.A. (1890). Principles of Economics. Macmillan and Company, New York.

Matzkin, R.L. (1992). "Nonparametric and distribution-free estimation of the binary threshold crossing and the binary choice models". Econometrica 60 (2), 239–270 (March).

Matzkin, R.L. (1993). "Nonparametric identification and estimation of polychotomous choice models". Journal of Econometrics 58 (1–2), 137–168 (July).

Matzkin, R.L. (1994). "Restrictions of economic theory in nonparametric methods". In: Engle, R., McFadden, D. (Eds.), Handbook of Econometrics, vol. 4. North-Holland, New York, pp. 2523–2558.

Matzkin, R.L. (2003). "Nonparametric estimation of nonadditive random functions". Econometrica 71 (5), 1339–1375 (September).

Matzkin, R.L. (2004). "Unobserved instruments". Unpublished manuscript. Northwestern University, Department of Economics.

Matzkin, R.L. (2007). "Nonparametric identification". In: Heckman, J.J., Leamer, E. (Eds.), Handbook of Econometrics, vol. 6B. Elsevier Science. Chapter 73.

McFadden, D. (1974). "Conditional logit analysis of qualitative choice behavior". In: Zarembka, P. (Ed.), Frontiers in Econometrics. Academic Press, New York.

McFadden, D. (1981). "Econometric models of probabilistic choice". In: Manski, C., McFadden, D. (Eds.), Structural Analysis of Discrete Data with Econometric Applications. MIT Press, Cambridge, MA.

McFadden, D. (1984). "Econometric analysis of qualitative response models". In: Griliches, Z., Intriligator, M. (Eds.), Handbook of Econometrics, vol. 2. North-Holland, New York, pp. 1396–1457.

McFadden, D. (1985). "Technical problems in social experimentation: Cost versus ease of analysis: Comment". In: Hausman, J.A., Wise, D.A. (Eds.), Social Experimentation, National Bureau of Economic Research Conference Report. University of Chicago Press, Chicago, pp. 214–218.

McFadden, D. (2001). "On selecting regression variables to maximize their significance". In: Hsiao, C., Morimune, K., Powell, J. (Eds.), Nonlinear Statistical Modeling: Proceedings of the Thirteenth International Symposium in Economic Theory and Econometrics: Essays in Honor of Takeshi Amemiya. Cambridge University Press, New York, pp. 259–280.

Miller, R.A. (1984). "Job matching and occupational choice". Journal of Political Economy 92 (6), 1086–1120 (December).

Moulin, H. (1983). The Strategy of Social Choice. North-Holland, New York.

Neyman, J. (1923). "Statistical problems in agricultural experiments". Journal of the Royal Statistical Society II (Suppl. (2)), 107–180.

Osborne, M.J. (2004). An Introduction to Game Theory. Oxford University Press, New York.

Pakes, A. (1986). "Patents as options: Some estimates of the value of holding European patent stocks". Econometrica 54 (4), 755–784 (July).

Pearl, J. (2000). Causality. Cambridge University Press, Cambridge, England.

Persson, T., Tabellini, G.E. (2000). Political Economics: Explaining Economic Policy. MIT Press, Cambridge, MA.

Pitt, M., Rosenzweig, M. (1989). "The selectivity of fertility and the determinants of human capital investments: Parametric and semi-parametric estimates". Living Standards Measurement 119, World Bank.

Powell, J.L. (1994). "Estimation of semiparametric models". In: Engle, R., McFadden, D. (Eds.), Handbook of Econometrics, vol. 4. Elsevier, Amsterdam, pp. 2443–2521.

Quandt, R.E. (1958). "The estimation of the parameters of a linear regression system obeying two separate regimes". Journal of the American Statistical Association 53 (284), 873–880 (December).

Quandt, R.E. (1972). "A new approach to estimating switching regressions". Journal of the American Statistical Association 67 (338), 306–310 (June).

Quandt, R.E. (1974). "A comparison of methods for testing nonnested hypotheses". Review of Economics and Statistics 56 (1), 92–99 (February).

Quandt, R.E., Baumol, W. (1966). "The demand for abstract transport modes: Theory measurement". Journal of Regional Science 6, 13–26.

Quine, W.V.O. (1951). "Main trends in recent philosophy: Two dogmas of empiricism". The Philosophical Review 60 (1), 20–43 (January).

Rawls, J. (1971). "A Theory of Justice". Belknap Press of Harvard University Press, Cambridge, MA.

Reiss, P., Wolak, F. (2007). "Structural econometric modeling: Rationales and examples from industrial organization". In: Heckman, J.J., Leamer, E. (Eds.), Handbook of Econometrics, vol. 6A. Elsevier Science. Chapter 64.

Roy, A. (1951). " Some thoughts on the distribution of earnings". Oxford Economic Papers 3 (2), 135–146 (June).

Rubin, D.B. (1976). "Inference and missing data". Biometrika 63 (3), 581–592 (December).

Rubin, D.B. (1978). "Bayesian inference for causal effects: The role of randomization". Annals of Statistics 6 (1), 34–58 (January).

Rubin, D.B. (1986). "Statistics and causal inference: Comment: Which ifs have causal answers". Journal of the American Statistical Association 81 (396), 961–962.

Rust, J. (1994). "Structural estimation of Markov decision processes". In: Engle, R., McFadden, D. (Eds.), Handbook of Econometrics. North-Holland, New York, pp. 3081–3143.

Ruud, P.A. (1981). "Misspecification in Limited Dependent Variable Models". PhD thesis. Massachusetts Institute of Technology.

Ruud, P.A. (2000). An Introduction to Classical Econometric Theory. Oxford University Press, New York.

Sen, A.K. (1999). "The possibility of social choice". American Economic Review 89 (3), 349–378 (June).

Sims, C.A. (1977). "Exogeneity and causal orderings in macroeconomic models". In: New Methods in Business Cycle Research. Federal Reserve Bank of Minneapolis, Minneapolis, MN, pp. 23–43.

Taber, C.R. (2001). "The rising college premium in the eighties: Return to college or return to unobserved ability?". Review of Economic Studies 68 (3), 665–691 (July).

Tamer, E. (2003). "Incomplete simultaneous discrete response model with multiple equilibria". Review of Economic Studies 70 (1), 147–165 (January).

Thurstone, L.L. (1927). "A law of comparative judgement". Psychological Review 34, 273–286.

Thurstone, L.L. (1959). The Measurement of Values. University of Chicago Press, Chicago.

Tinbergen, J. (1930). "Bestimmung und Deutung von Angebotskurven". Zeitschrift für Nationalökonomie 1 (1), 669–679 (March).

Todd, P.E. (1996). "Essays on empirical methods for evaluating the impact of policy interventions in education and training". PhD dissertation. University of Chicago, Chicago.

Varian, H.R. (1978). Microeconomic Analysis. Norton, New York.

Vickrey, W. (1945). "Measuring marginal utility by reactions to risk". Econometrica 13 (4), 319–333 (October).

Vickrey, W. (1961). "Utility, strategy and social decision rules: Reply". Quarterly Journal of Economics 75 (3), 496–497 (August).

Vijverberg, W.P.M. (1993). "Measuring the unidentified parameter of the extended Roy model of selectivity". Journal of Econometrics 57 (1–3), 69–89 (May–June).

Willis, R.J., Rosen, S. (1979). "Education and self-selection". Journal of Political Economy 87 (5, Part 2), S7–S36 (October).

Wold, H.O.A. (1956). "Causal inference from observational data: A review of end and means". Journal of the Royal Statistical Society. Series A (General) 119 (1), 28–61.

Wooldridge, J.M. (2002). Econometric Analysis of Cross Section and Panel Data. MIT Press, Cambridge, MA.

Chapter 71

ECONOMETRIC EVALUATION OF SOCIAL PROGRAMS, PART II: USING THE MARGINAL TREATMENT EFFECT TO ORGANIZE ALTERNATIVE ECONOMETRIC ESTIMATORS TO EVALUATE SOCIAL PROGRAMS, AND TO FORECAST THEIR EFFECTS IN NEW ENVIRONMENTS*

JAMES J. HECKMAN
The University of Chicago, USA
American Bar Foundation, USA
University College Dublin, Ireland

EDWARD J. VYTLACIL
Columbia University, USA

Contents

* This research was supported by NSF: 97-09-873, 00-99195, and SES-0241858 and NICHD: R01-HD32058-03. We have benefited from comments received from Thierry Magnac and Costas Meghir at the Handbook of Econometrics Conference, December 1998; general comments at the 2001 Chicago Conference; and specific and very helpful comments from Jaap Abbring, Thomas Amorde, Hugo Garduño, Seong Moon, Rodrigo Pinto, Heleno Pioner, Jean-Marc Robin, Peter Saveleyev, G. Adam Savvas, Daniel Schmierer, John Trujillo, Semih Tumen, Sergio Urzua and Jordan Weil. Parts of this document draw on joint work with Sergio Urzua.

Handbook of Econometrics, Volume 6B

DOI: 10.1016/S1573-4412(07)06071-0

Abstract

This chapter uses the marginal treatment effect (MTE) to unify and organize the econometric literature on the evaluation of social programs. The marginal treatment effect is a choice-theoretic parameter that can be interpreted as a willingness to pay parameter for persons at a margin of indifference between participating in an activity or not. All of the conventional treatment parameters as well as the more economically motivated treatment effects can be generated from a baseline marginal treatment effect. All of the estimation methods used in the applied evaluation literature, such as matching, instrumental variables, regression discontinuity methods, selection and control function methods, make assumptions about the marginal treatment effect which we exposit. Models for multiple outcomes are developed. Empirical examples of the leading methods are presented. Methods are presented for bounding treatment effects in partially identified models, when the marginal treatment effect is known only over a limited support. We show how to use the marginal treatment in econometric cost benefit analysis, in defining limits of policy experiments, in constructing the average marginal treatment effect, and in forecasting the effects of programs in new environments.

Keywords

marginal treatment effect, policy evaluation, instrumental variables, forecasting new policies, econometric cost benefit analysis, regression discontinuity, matching, bounds

JEL classification: C10, C13, C50

1. Introduction

This part of our contribution to this Handbook reviews and extends the econometric literature on the evaluation of social policy. We organize our discussion around choice-theoretic models for objective and subjective outcomes of the sort discussed in Chapter 70. Specifically, we organize our discussion of the literature around the concept of the marginal treatment effect (MTE) that was introduced in Chapter 70. Using the marginal treatment effect, we define a variety of treatment effects and show how they can be generated by a single economic functional, the MTE. We then show what various econometric methods assume about the MTE.

In this part, we focus exclusively on microeconomic partial equilibrium evaluation methods, deferring analysis of general equilibrium issues to Abbring and Heckman (Chapter 72). Thus throughout this chapter, except when we discuss randomized evaluation of social programs, we assume that potential outcomes are not affected by interventions but choices among the potential outcomes are affected. Thus, we invoke policy invariance assumptions (PI-3) and (PI-4) of Chapter 70. We also focus primarily on mean responses, leaving analysis of distributions of responses for Abbring and Heckman, Chapter 72.

The plan of this chapter is as follows. In Section 2, we present some basic principles that underlie conventional econometric evaluation estimators. In Section 3, we define the marginal treatment effect in a two potential outcome model that is a semiparametric version of the generalized Roy model. We then show how treatment parameters can be generated as weighted averages of the MTE. We carefully distinguish the definition of parameters from issues of identification. Section 4 considers how instrumental variable methods that supplement the classical instrumental variable assumptions of econometrics can be used to identify treatment parameters. We discuss the crucial role of monotonicity assumptions in the recent IV literature.

They impart an asymmetry to the admissible forms of agent heterogeneity. Outcomes are permitted to be heterogeneous in a general way but responses of choices to external inputs are not. When heterogeneity in choices and outcomes is allowed, the IV enterprise breaks down. Treatment parameters can still be defined but IV does not identify them.

Section 5 extends our analysis to consider regression discontinuity estimators introduced in Campbell (1969) and adapted to modern econometrics in Hahn, Todd and Van der Klaauw (2001). We interpret the regression discontinuity estimator within the MTE framework, as a special type of IV estimator. In Section 6, we show how the output of the IV analysis of Section 4 can be used to extend parameters identified in one population to other populations and to forecast the effects of new programs. These are questions P-2 and P-3 introduced in Chapter 70. Sections 2–5 focus solely on the problem of internal validity, which is the problem defined as P-1. We also develop a cost benefit analysis based on the MTE and we analyze marginal policy changes. In Section 7, we generalize the analysis of instrumental variables to consider models with multiple outcomes. We develop both unordered and ordered choice models linking them to an explicit choice-theoretic literature.

In Section 8, we consider matching as a special case of our framework. Matching applied to estimating conditional means is a version of nonparametric least squares. It assumes that marginal and average returns are the same whereas our general framework allows us to distinguish marginal from average returns and to identify both. Matching is more robust than IV to violations of conventional monotonicity assumptions but the price for this robustness is steep in terms of its economic content. In Section 9, we develop randomization as an instrumental variable. We consider problems with compliance induced by agent self-selection decisions. In Section 10, we consider how to bound the various treatment parameters when models are not identified. Section 11 develops alternative methods for controlling for selection: control functions, replacement functions and proxy variables. Section 12 concludes.

2. The basic principles underlying the identification of the major econometric evaluation estimators

In this section, we review the main principles underlying the major evaluation estimators used in the econometric literature. We assume two potential outcomes (Y_0, Y_1). Models for multiple outcomes are developed in later sections of this chapter. As in Chapter 70, $D = 1$ if Y_1 is observed, and $D = 0$ corresponds to Y_0 being observed. The observed objective outcome is

$$Y = DY_1 + (1 - D)Y_0. \tag{2.1}$$

To briefly recapitulate the lessons of Chapter 70, we distinguish two distinct econometric problems. For simplicity, we focus our discussion on identification of objective outcomes. A parallel analysis can be made for subjective outcomes.

The *evaluation problem* arises because for each person we observe either Y_0 or Y_1 but not both. Thus, in general, it is not possible to identify the individual level treatment effect $Y_1 - Y_0$ for any person. The typical solution to this problem is to reformulate the problem at the population level rather than at the individual level and to identify certain mean outcomes or quantile outcomes or various distributions of outcomes as described in Chapter 70. For example, a common approach is to focus attention on average treatment effects, such as $\text{ATE} = E(Y_1 - Y_0)$.

If treatment is assigned or chosen on the basis of potential outcomes, so

$$(Y_0, Y_1) \not\!\perp\!\!\!\perp D,$$

where $\not\!\perp\!\!\!\perp$ denotes "is not independent" and "$\perp\!\!\!\perp$" denotes independent, we encounter the problem of selection bias. Suppose that we observe people in each treatment state $D = 0$ and $D = 1$. If $Y_j \not\!\perp\!\!\!\perp D$, then the observed Y_j will be selectively different from randomly assigned Y_j, $j = 0, 1$. Thus $E(Y_0 \mid D = 0) \neq E(Y_0)$ and $E(Y_1 \mid D = 1) \neq E(Y_1)$. Using unadjusted data to construct $E(Y_1 - Y_0)$ will produce selection bias:

$$E(Y_1 \mid D = 1) - E(Y_0 \mid D = 0) \neq E(Y_1 - Y_0).$$

The *selection problem* is a key aspect of the problem of evaluating social programs. Many methods have been proposed to solve both problems. This chapter unifies these methods using the concept of the marginal treatment effect (MTE) introduced in Chapter 70 of this Handbook.

The method with the greatest intuitive appeal, which is sometimes called the "gold standard" in evaluation analysis, is the method of random assignment. Nonexperimental methods can be organized by how they attempt to approximate what can be obtained by an ideal random assignment. If treatment is chosen at random with respect to (Y_0, Y_1), or if treatments are randomly assigned and there is full compliance with the treatment assignment,

(R-1) $(Y_0, Y_1) \perp\!\!\!\perp D$.

It is useful to distinguish several cases where (R-1) will be satisfied. The first is that agents (decision makers whose choices are being investigated) pick outcomes that are random with respect to (Y_0, Y_1). Thus agents may not know (Y_0, Y_1) at the time they make their choices to participate in treatment or at least do not act on (Y_0, Y_1), so that $\Pr(D = 1 \mid X, Y_0, Y_1) = \Pr(D = 1 \mid X)$ for all X. Matching assumes a version of (R-1) conditional on matching variables X: $(Y_0, Y_1) \perp\!\!\!\perp D \mid X$.

A second case arises when individuals are randomly assigned to treatment status even if they would choose to self-select into no-treatment status, and they comply with the randomization protocols. Let ξ be randomized assignment status. With full compliance, $\xi = 1$ implies that Y_1 is observed and $\xi = 0$ implies that Y_0 is observed. Then, under randomized assignment,

(R-2) $(Y_0, Y_1) \perp\!\!\!\perp \xi$,

even if in a regime of self-selection, $(Y_0, Y_1) \not\!\perp\!\!\!\perp D$. If randomization is performed conditional on X, we obtain $(Y_0, Y_1) \perp\!\!\!\perp \xi \mid X$.

Let A denote actual treatment status. If the randomization has full compliance among participants, $\xi = 1 \Rightarrow A = 1$; $\xi = 0 \Rightarrow A = 0$. This is entirely consistent with a regime in which a person would choose $D = 1$ in the absence of randomization, but would have no treatment ($A = 0$) if suitably randomized, even though the agent might desire treatment.

If treatment status is chosen by self-selection, $D = 1 \Rightarrow A = 1$ and $D = 0 \Rightarrow A = 0$. If there is imperfect compliance with randomization, $\xi = 1 \not\Rightarrow A = 1$ because of agent choices. In general, $A = \xi D$ so that $A = 1$ only if $\xi = 1$ and $D = 1$. This assumes that persons randomized out of the program cannot participate in it. If treatment status is randomly assigned, either through randomization or randomized self-selection,

(R-3) $(Y_0, Y_1) \perp\!\!\!\perp A$.

This version of randomization can also be defined conditional on X. Under (R-1), (R-2) or (R-3), the average treatment effect (ATE) is the same as the marginal treatment effect and the parameters treatment on the treated (TT) and treatment on the untreated (TUT) as defined in Chapter 70:

$$\text{TT} = \text{MTE} = \text{TUT} = \text{ATE} = E(Y_1 - Y_0) = E(Y_1) - E(Y_0).$$

Observe that even with random assignment of treatment status and full compliance, we cannot, in general, identify the distribution of the treatment effects $(Y_1 - Y_0)$, although we can identify the marginal distributions $F_1(Y_1 \mid A = 1, X = x) = F_1(Y_1 \mid X = x)$ and $F_0(Y_0 \mid A = 0, X = x) = F_0(Y_0 \mid X = x)$. One special assumption, common in the conventional econometrics literature, is that $Y_1 - Y_0 = \Delta(x)$, a constant given x. Since $\Delta(x)$ can be identified from $E(Y_1 \mid A = 1, X = x) - E(Y_0 \mid A = 0, X = x)$ because A is allocated by randomization, the analyst can identify the joint distribution of (Y_0, Y_1).[1] However, this approach assumes that (Y_0, Y_1) have the same distribution up to a parameter Δ (Y_0 and Y_1 are perfectly dependent). One can make other assumptions about the dependence across ranks from perfect positive or negative ranking to independence.[2] In general, the joint distribution of (Y_0, Y_1) or of $(Y_1 - Y_0)$ is not identified unless the analyst can pin down the dependence across (Y_0, Y_1). Thus, even with data from a randomized trial one cannot, without further assumptions, identify the proportion of people who benefit from treatment in the sense of gross gain ($\Pr(Y_1 \geqslant Y_0)$). This problem plagues all evaluation methods. Abbring and Heckman discuss methods for identifying joint distributions of outcomes in Chapter 72.

Assumption (R-1) is very strong. In many cases, it is thought that there is *selection bias* with respect to Y_0, Y_1, so persons who select into status 1 or 0 are selectively different from randomly sampled persons in the population.

The assumption most commonly made to circumvent problems with (R-1) is that even though D is not random with respect to potential outcomes, the analyst has access to control variables X that effectively produce a randomization of D with respect to (Y_0, Y_1) given X. This is the method of matching, which is based on the following conditional independence assumption:

(M-1) $(Y_0, Y_1) \perp\!\!\!\perp D \mid X$.

Conditioning on X randomizes D with respect to (Y_0, Y_1). (M-1) assumes that any selective sampling of (Y_0, Y_1) can be adjusted by conditioning on observed variables. (R-1) and (M-1) are different assumptions and neither implies the other. In a linear equations model, assumption (M-1) that D is independent from (Y_0, Y_1) given X justifies application of least squares on D to eliminate selection bias in mean outcome

[1] Heckman (1992), Heckman, Smith and Clements (1997).

[2] Heckman, Smith and Clements (1997).

parameters. For means, matching is just nonparametric regression.[3] In order to be able to compare X-comparable people, we must assume

(M-2) $0 < \Pr(D = 1 \mid X = x) < 1$.

Assumptions (M-1) and (M-2) justify matching. Assumption (M-2) is required for *any* evaluation estimator that compares treated and untreated persons. It is produced by random assignment if the randomization is conducted for all $X = x$ and there is full compliance.

Observe that from (M-1) and (M-2), it is possible to identify $F_1(Y_1 \mid X = x)$ from the observed data $F_1(Y_1 \mid D = 1, X = x)$ since we observe the left-hand side of

$$\begin{aligned} F_1(Y_1 \mid D = 1, X = x) &= F_1(Y_1 \mid X = x) \\ &= F_1(Y_1 \mid D = 0, X = x). \end{aligned}$$

The first equality is a consequence of conditional independence assumption (M-1). The second equality comes from (M-1) and (M-2). By a similar argument, we observe the left-hand side of

$$\begin{aligned} F_0(Y_0 \mid D = 0, X = x) &= F_0(Y_0 \mid X = x) \\ &= F_0(Y_0 \mid D = 1, X = x), \end{aligned}$$

and the equalities are a consequence of (M-1) and (M-2). Since the pair of outcomes (Y_0, Y_1) is not identified for anyone, as in the case of data from randomized trials, the joint distributions of (Y_0, Y_1) given X or of $Y_1 - Y_0$ given X are not identified without further information.

From the data on Y_1 given X and $D = 1$ and the data on Y_0 given X and $D = 0$, since $E(Y_1 \mid D = 1, X = x) = E(Y_1 \mid X = x) = E(Y_1 \mid D = 0, X = x)$ and $E(Y_0 \mid D = 0, X = x) = E(Y_0 \mid X = x) = E(Y_0 \mid D = 1, X = x)$, we obtain

$$\begin{aligned} E(Y_1 - Y_0 \mid X = x) &= E(Y_1 - Y_0 \mid D = 1, X = x) \\ &= E(Y_1 - Y_0 \mid D = 0, X = x). \end{aligned}$$

Effectively, we have a randomization for the subset of the support of X satisfying (M-2).

At values of X that fail to satisfy (M-2), there is no variation in D given X. We can define the residual variation in D not accounted for by X as

$$\mathcal{E}(x) = D - E(D \mid X = x) = D - \Pr(D = 1 \mid X = x).$$

If the variance of $\mathcal{E}(x)$ is zero, it is not possible to construct contrasts in outcomes by treatment status for those X values and (M-2) is violated. To see the consequences of this violation in a regression setting, use $Y = Y_0 + D(Y_1 - Y_0)$ and take conditional

[3] See the discussion in Section 8. Barnow, Cain and Goldberger (1980) present one application of matching in a regression setting.

expectations, under (M-1), to obtain

$$E(Y \mid X, D) = E(Y_0 \mid X) + D\big[E(Y_1 - Y_0 \mid X)\big].^{4}$$

If $\text{Var}(\mathcal{E}(x)) > 0$ for all x in the support of X, one can use nonparametric least squares to identify $E(Y_1 - Y_0 \mid X = x) = \text{ATE}(x)$ by regressing Y on D and X. The function identified from the coefficient on D is the average treatment effect.[5] If $\text{Var}(\mathcal{E}(x)) = 0$, $\text{ATE}(x)$ is not identified at that x value because there is no variation in D that is not fully explained by X. A special case of matching is linear least squares where we write

$$Y_0 = X\alpha + U, \qquad Y_1 = X\alpha + \beta + U,$$

$U_0 = U_1 = U$ and hence under (M-1),

$$E(Y \mid X, D) = X\alpha + D\beta + E(U \mid X).$$

If D is perfectly predictable by X, we cannot identify β because of a multicollinearity problem. (M-2) rules out perfect collinearity.[6] Matching is a nonparametric version of least squares that does not impose functional form assumptions on outcome equations, and that imposes support condition (M-2). However, matching does not assume exogeneity of X.

Conventional econometric choice models make a distinction between variables that appear in outcome equations (X) and variables that appear in choice equations (Z). The same variables may be in (X) and (Z), but more typically there are some variables not in common. For example, the instrumental variable estimator is based on variables that are not in X but that are in Z. Matching makes no distinction between the X and the Z.[7] It does not rely on exclusion restrictions. The conditioning variables used to achieve conditional independence can in principle be a set of variables Q distinct from the X variables (covariates for outcomes) or the Z variables (covariates for choices). We use X solely to simplify the notation. The key identifying assumption is the assumed existence of a random variable X with the properties satisfying (M-1) and (M-2).

Conditioning on a larger vector (X augmented with additional variables) or a smaller vector (X with some components removed) may or may not produce suitably modified

[4] This follows because $E(Y \mid X, D) = E(Y_0 \mid X, D) + DE(Y_1 - Y_0 \mid X, D)$, but from (M-1), $E(Y_0 \mid X, D) = E(Y_0 \mid X)$ and $E(Y_1 - Y_0 \mid X, D) = E(Y_1 - Y_0 \mid X)$.

[5] Under the conditional independence assumption (M-1), it is also the effect of treatment on the treated $E(Y_1 - Y_0 \mid X, D = 1)$.

[6] Clearly (M-1) and (M-2) are sufficient but not necessary conditions. For the special case of OLS, as a consequence of the assumed linearity in the functional form of the estimating equation, we achieve identification of β if $\text{Cov}(X, U) = 0$, $\text{Cov}(D, U) = 0$ and (D, X) are not perfectly collinear. Observe that (M-1) does not imply that $E(U \mid X) = 0$. Thus, we can identify β but not necessarily α.

[7] Heckman et al. (1998) distinguish X and Z in matching.They consider a case where conditioning on X may lead to failure of (M-1) and (M-2) but conditioning on (X, Z) satisfies a suitably modified version of this condition.

versions of (M-1) and (M-2). Without invoking further assumptions, there is no objective principle for determining what conditioning variables produce (M-1).

Assumption (M-1) is strong. Many economists do not have enough faith in their data to invoke it. Assumption (M-2) is testable and requires no act of faith. To justify (M-1), it is necessary to appeal to the quality of the data.

Using economic theory can help guide the choice of an evaluation estimator. A crucial distinction is the one between the information available to the analyst and the information available to the agent whose outcomes are being studied. Assumptions made about these information sets drive the properties of econometric estimators. Analysts using matching make strong informational assumptions in terms of the data available to them. In fact, all econometric estimators make assumptions about the presence or absence of informational asymmetries, and we exposit them in this chapter.

To analyze the informational assumptions invoked in matching, and other econometric evaluation strategies, it is helpful to introduce five distinct information sets and establish some relationships among them.[8] (1) An information set $\sigma(I_{R^*})$ with an associated random variable that satisfies conditional independence (M-1) is defined as a *relevant* information set; (2) the minimal information set $\sigma(I_R)$ with associated random variable needed to satisfy conditional independence (M-1), the *minimal relevant* information set; (3) the information set $\sigma(I_A)$ available to the agent at the time decisions to participate are made; (4) the information available to the economist, $\sigma(I_{E^*})$; and (5) the information $\sigma(I_E)$ used by the economist in conducting an empirical analysis. We will denote the random variables generated by these sets as I_{R^*}, I_R, I_A, I_{E^*}, and I_E, respectively.[9]

DEFINITION 1. We say that $\sigma(I_{R^*})$ is a *relevant information set* if the information set is generated by the random variable I_{R^*}, possibly vector-valued, and satisfies condition (M-1), so that

$$(Y_0, Y_1) \perp\!\!\!\perp D \mid I_{R^*}.$$

DEFINITION 2. We say that $\sigma(I_R)$ is a *minimal relevant information set* if it is the intersection of all sets $\sigma(I_{R^*})$ and satisfies $(Y_0, Y_1) \perp\!\!\!\perp D \mid I_R$. The associated random variable I_R is a minimum amount of information that guarantees that condition (M-1) is satisfied. There may be no such set.[10]

[8] See the discussion in Barros (1987), Gerfin and Lechner (2002), and Heckman and Navarro (2004).

[9] We start with a primitive probability space (Ω, σ, P) with associated random variables I. We assume minimal σ-algebras and assume that the random variables I are measurable with respect to these σ-algebras. Obviously, strictly monotonic or affine transformations of the I preserve the information and can substitute for the I.

[10] Observe that the intersection of all sets $\sigma(I_{R^*})$ may be empty and hence may not be characterized by a (possibly vector-valued) random variable I_R that guarantees $(Y_0, Y_1) \perp\!\!\!\perp D \mid I_R$. If the information sets that produce conditional independence are nested, then the intersection of all sets $\sigma(I_{R^*})$ producing conditional

If we define a relevant information set as one that produces conditional independence, it may not be unique. If the set $\sigma(I_{R^*})$ satisfies the conditional independence condition, then the set $\sigma(I_{R^*}, Q)$ such that $Q \perp\!\!\!\perp (Y_0, Y_1) \mid I_{R^*}$ would also guarantee conditional independence. For this reason, when possible, it is desirable to use the minimal relevant information set.

DEFINITION 3. The agent's information set, $\sigma(I_A)$, is defined by the information I_A used by the agent when choosing among treatments. Accordingly, we call I_A the *agent's information.*

By the agent we mean the person making the treatment decision, not necessarily the person whose outcomes are being studied (e.g., the agent may be the parent; the person being studied may be a child).

DEFINITION 4. The econometrician's *full information set*, $\sigma(I_{E^*})$, is defined as *all* of the information available to the econometrician, I_{E^*}.

DEFINITION 5. The *econometrician's information set*, $\sigma(I_E)$, is defined by the information *used* by the econometrician when analyzing the agent's choice of treatment, I_E, in conducting an analysis.

For the case where a unique minimal relevant information set exists, only three restrictions are implied by the structure of these sets: $\sigma(I_R) \subseteq \sigma(I_{R^*})$, $\sigma(I_R) \subseteq \sigma(I_A)$, and $\sigma(I_E) \subseteq \sigma(I_{E^*})$.[11] We have already discussed the first restriction. The second restriction requires that the minimal relevant information set must be part of the information the agent uses when deciding which treatment to take or assign. It is the information in $\sigma(I_A)$ that gives rise to the selection problem.

The third restriction requires that the information used by the econometrician must be part of the information that the econometrician observes. Aside from these orderings, the econometrician's information set may be different from the agent's or the relevant information set. The econometrician may know something the agent does not know, for typically he is observing events after the decision is made. At the same time, there may be private information known to the agent but not the econometrician. Assuming a minimal relevant information set exists, matching assumption (M-1) implies that

independence is well defined and has an associated random variable I_R with the required property, although it may not be unique (e.g., strictly monotonic transformations and affine transformations of I_R also preserve the property). In the more general case of nonnested information sets with the required property, it is possible that no uniquely defined minimal relevant set exists. Among collections of nested sets that possess the required property, there is a minimal set defined by intersection but there may be multiple minimal sets corresponding to each collection.

[11] This formulation assumes that the agent makes the treatment decision. The extension to the case where the decision maker and the agent are distinct is straightforward. The requirement $\sigma(I_R) \subseteq \sigma(I_{R^*})$ is satisfied by nested sets.

$\sigma(I_R) \subseteq \sigma(I_E)$, so that the econometrician uses at least the minimal relevant information set, but of course he or she may use more. However, using more information is not guaranteed to produce a model with conditional independence property (M-1) satisfied for the augmented model. Thus an analyst can "overdo" it. We present examples of the consequences of the asymmetry in agent and analyst information sets in Section 8.

The possibility of asymmetry in information between the agent making participation decisions and the observing economist creates the potential for a major identification problem that is ruled out by assumption (M-1). The methods of control functions and instrumental variables estimators (and closely related regression discontinuity design methods) address this problem in different ways. Accounting for this possibility is a more conservative approach to the selection problem than the one taken by advocates of matching. Those advocates assume that they know the X that produces a relevant information set. Heckman and Navarro (2004) show the biases that can result in matching when standard econometric model selection criteria are applied to pick the X that are used to satisfy (M-1) and we summarize their analysis in Section 8. Conditional independence condition (M-1) cannot be tested without maintaining other assumptions.[12] As noted in Chapter 70, choosing the appropriate conditioning variables is a problem that plagues *all* econometric estimators.

The methods of control functions, replacement functions, proxy variables and instrumental variables recognize the possibility of asymmetry in information between the agent being studied and the econometrician and further recognize that even after conditioning on X (variables in the outcome equation) and Z (variables affecting treatment choices, which may include the X), analysts may fail to satisfy conditional independence condition (M-1).[13] These methods postulate the existence of some unobservables θ, which may be vector-valued, with the property that

(U-1) $(Y_0, Y_1) \perp\!\!\!\perp D \mid X, Z, \theta$,

but allow for the possibility that

(U-2) $(Y_0, Y_1) \not\perp\!\!\!\perp D \mid X, Z$.

In the event (U-2) holds, these approaches model the relationship of the unobservable θ with (Y_0, Y_1) and D in various ways. The content in the control function principle is to specify the exact nature of the dependence on the relationship between observables and unobservables in a nontrivial fashion that is consistent with economic theory. We present examples of models that satisfy (U-1) but not (U-2) in Section 8.

12 We discuss the required "exogeneity" conditions in our discussion of matching in Section 8. Thus randomization of assignment of treatment status might be used to test (M-1) but this requires that there be full compliance and that the randomization be valid (no anticipation effects or general equilibrium effects). Abbring and Heckman (Chapter 72) discuss this case.

13 The term and concept of control function is due to Heckman and Robb (1985a, 1985b, 1986a, 1986b). See Blundell and Powell (2003) who call the Heckman–Robb replacement functions control functions. A more recent nomenclature is "control variate". Matzkin (2007) (Chapter 73 in this Handbook) provides a comprehensive discussion of identification principles for these, and other, econometric estimators.

The early literature focused on mean outcomes conditional on covariates [Heckman and Robb (1985a, 1985b, 1986a, 1986b)] and assumes a weaker version of (U-1) based on conditional mean independence rather than full conditional independence. More recent work analyzes distributions of outcomes [e.g., Aakvik, Heckman and Vytlacil (2005), Carneiro, Hansen and Heckman (2003)]. Abbring and Heckman review this work in Chapter 72.

The normal Roy model discussed in Chapter 70 makes distributional assumptions and identifies the joint distribution of outcomes. (Recall the discussion in Section 6.1 of Chapter 70.) A large literature surveyed in Chapter 73 (Matzkin) of this Handbook makes alternative assumptions to satisfy (U-1) in nonparametric settings. Replacement functions [Heckman and Robb (1985a)] are methods that proxy θ. They substitute out for θ using observables.[14] Aakvik, Heckman and Vytlacil (1999, 2005), Carneiro, Hansen and Heckman (2001, 2003), Cunha, Heckman and Navarro (2005), and Cunha, Heckman and Schennach (2006b, 2007) develop methods that integrate out θ from the model assuming $\theta \perp\!\!\!\perp (X, Z)$, or invoking weaker mean independence assumptions, and assuming access to proxy measurements for θ. They also consider methods for estimating the distributions of treatment effects. These methods are discussed in Chapter 72.

The normal selection model discussed in Section 6.1 of Chapter 70 produces partial identification of a generalized Roy model and full identification of a Roy model under separability and normality. It models the conditional expectation of U_0 and U_1 given X, Z, and D. In terms of (U-1), it models the conditional mean dependence of Y_0, Y_1 on D and θ given X and Z. Powell (1994) and Chapter 73 (Matzkin) of this Handbook survey methods for identifying semiparametric versions of these models. Appendix B of Chapter 70 presents a prototypical identification proof for a general selection model that implements (U-1) by estimating the distribution of θ, assuming $\theta \perp\!\!\!\perp (X, Z)$, and invoking support conditions on (X, Z).

Central to both the selection approach and the instrumental variable approach for a model with heterogenous responses is the probability of selection. Let Z denote variables in the choice equation. Fixing Z at different values (denoted z), we define $D(z)$ as an indicator function that is "1" when treatment is selected at the fixed value of z and that is "0" otherwise. In terms of the separable index model introduced in Chapter 70, for a fixed value of z,

$$D(z) = \mathbf{1}\big(\mu_D(z) \geqslant V\big),$$

where $Z \perp\!\!\!\perp V \mid X$. Thus fixing $Z = z$, values of z do not affect the realizations of V for any value of X. An alternative way of representing the independence between Z and V given X, due to Imbens and Angrist (1994), writes that $D(z) \perp\!\!\!\perp Z \mid X$ for all $z \in \mathcal{Z}$,

[14] This is the "control variate" of Blundell and Powell (2003). Heckman and Robb (1985a) and Olley and Pakes (1996) use a similar idea. Chapter 73 (Matzkin) of this Handbook discusses replacement functions.

where $\mathcal{Z}$ is the support of Z. The Imbens–Angrist independence condition for IV is

$$\{D(z)\}_{z\in\mathcal{Z}} \perp\!\!\!\perp Z \mid X.$$

Thus the probabilities that $D(z) = 1$, $z \in \mathcal{Z}$, are independent of Z.

The method of instrumental variables (IV) postulates that

(IV-1) $(Y_0, Y_1, \{D(z)\}_{z\in\mathcal{Z}}) \perp\!\!\!\perp Z \mid X$ *(Independence)*.

One consequence of this assumption is that $E(D \mid Z) = P(Z)$, the propensity score, is random with respect to potential outcomes. Thus $(Y_0, Y_1) \perp\!\!\!\perp P(Z) \mid X$. So are all other functions of Z given X. The method of instrumental variables also assumes that

(IV-2) $E(D \mid X, Z) = P(X, Z)$ *is a nondegenerate function of* Z *given* X (*Rank condition*).

Alternatively, we can write that $\operatorname{Var}(E(D \mid X, Z)) \neq \operatorname{Var}(E(D \mid X))$.

Comparing (IV-1) to (M-1), in the method of instrumental variables, Z is independent of (Y_0, Y_1) given X whereas in matching, D is independent of (Y_0, Y_1) given X. So in (IV-1), Z plays the role of D in matching condition (M-1). Comparing (IV-2) with (M-2), in the method of IV, the choice probability $\Pr(D = 1 \mid X, Z)$ is assumed to vary conditional on X whereas in matching, D varies conditional on X. Unlike the method of control functions, no explicit model of the relationship between D and (Y_0, Y_1) is required in applying IV. We exposit the implicit model of the relationship between D and (Y_0, Y_1) used in instrumental variables in this chapter.

(IV-2) is a rank condition and can be empirically verified. (IV-1) is not testable as it involves assumptions about counterfactuals. In a conventional common coefficient regression model

$$Y = \alpha + \beta D + U,$$

where β is a constant and where we allow for $\operatorname{Cov}(D, U) \neq 0$, (IV-1) and (IV-2) identify β.[15] When β varies in the population and is correlated with D, additional assumptions must be invoked for IV to identify interpretable parameters. We discuss these conditions in Section 4 of this chapter, drawing on and extending the analysis of Heckman and Vytlacil (1999, 2001b, 2005) and Heckman, Urzua and Vytlacil (2006).

Assumptions (IV-1) and (IV-2), with additional assumptions in the case where β varies in the population which we discuss in this chapter, can be used to identify mean treatment parameters. Replacing Y_1 with $\mathbf{1}(Y_1 \leqslant t)$ and Y_0 with $\mathbf{1}(Y_0 \leqslant t)$, where t is a constant, the IV approach allows us to identify marginal distributions $F_1(y_1 \mid X)$ or $F_0(y_0 \mid X)$.

In matching, the variation in D that arises after conditioning on X provides the source of randomness that switches people across treatment status. Nature is assumed to pro-

[15] $\beta = \frac{\operatorname{Cov}(Z,Y)}{\operatorname{Cov}(Z,D)}$.

vide an experimental manipulation conditional on X that replaces the randomization assumed in (R-1)–(R-3). When D is perfectly predictable by X, there is no variation in it conditional on X, and the randomization by nature breaks down. Heuristically, matching assumes a residual $\mathcal{E}(X) = D - E(D \mid X)$ that is nondegenerate and is one manifestation of the randomness that causes persons to switch status.[16]

In the IV method, it is the choice probability $E(D \mid X, Z) = P(X, Z)$ that is random with respect to (Y_0, Y_1), not components of D not predictable by (X, Z). Variation in Z for a fixed X provides the required variation in D that switches treatment status and still produces the required conditional independence:

$$(Y_0, Y_1) \perp\!\!\!\perp P(X, Z) \mid X.$$

Variation in $P(X, Z)$ produces variations in D that switch treatment status. Components of variation in D not predictable by (X, Z) do not produce the required independence. Instead, the predicted component provides the required independence. It is just the opposite in matching. Versions of the method of control functions use measurements to proxy θ in (U-1) and (U-2) and remove spurious dependence that gives rise to selection problems. These are called replacement functions [see Heckman and Robb (1985a)] or control variates [see Blundell and Powell (2003)].

Table 1 summarizes some of the main lessons of this section. We stress that the stated conditions are necessary conditions. There are many versions of the IV and control functions principle and extensions of these ideas which refine these basic postulates more fully and we exposit them in this Handbook. We start with the method of instrumental variables and analyze the general case where responses to treatment are heterogeneous and persons select into treatment status in response to the heterogeneity in treatment response.

Our strategy in this chapter is to anchor all of our analysis around the economic theory of choice as embodied in discrete choice theory and versions of the generalized Roy model developed in Chapter 70. We next show how recent developments allow analysts to define treatment parameters within a well-posed economic framework but without the strong assumptions maintained in the early literature on selection models. To focus our discussion, we first consider the analysis of a prototypical policy evaluation program.

2.1. A prototypical policy evaluation problem

To motivate our discussion in this chapter, consider the following prototypical policy problem. Suppose a policy is proposed for adoption in a country. It has been tried in other countries and we know outcomes there. We also know outcomes in countries

[16] It is heuristically illuminating, but technically incorrect to replace $\mathcal{E}(X)$ with D in (R-1) or ξ in (R-2) or A in (R-3). In general, $\mathcal{E}(X)$ is not independent of X even if it is mean independent.

Table 1
Identifying assumptions under commonly used methods

	Identifying assumptions	Identifies marginal distributions?	Exclusion condition needed?
Random assignment	$(Y_0, Y_1) \perp\!\!\!\perp \xi$, $\xi = 1 \Rightarrow A = 1$, $\xi = 0 \Rightarrow A = 0$ (full compliance). Alternatively, if self-selection is random with respect to outcomes, $(Y_0, Y_1) \perp\!\!\!\perp D$. Assignment can be conditional on X.	Yes	No
Matching	$(Y_0, Y_1) \not\perp\!\!\!\perp D$, but $(Y_0, Y_1) \perp\!\!\!\perp D \mid X$, $0 < \Pr(D = 1 \mid X) < 1$ for all X. So D conditional on X is a nondegenerate random variable.	Yes	No
Control functions and extensions	$(Y_0, Y_1) \not\perp\!\!\!\perp D \mid X, Z$, but $(Y_0, Y_1) \perp\!\!\!\perp D \mid X, Z, \theta$. The method models dependence induced by θ or else proxies θ (replacement function). Version (i). Replacement functions (substitute out θ by observables) [Blundell and Powell (2003), Heckman and Robb (1985a), Olley and Pakes (1996)]. Factor models [Carneiro, Hansen and Heckman (2003)] allow for measurement error in the proxies. Version (ii). Integrate out θ assuming $\theta \perp\!\!\!\perp (X, Z)$ [Aakvik, Heckman and Vytlacil (2005), Carneiro, Hansen and Heckman (2003)]. Version (iii). For separable models for mean response expect out θ conditional on X, Z, D as in standard selection models (control functions in the same sense of Heckman and Robb).	Yes	Yes (for semiparametric models) No (under some parametric assumptions)
IV	$(Y_0, Y_1) \not\perp\!\!\!\perp D \mid X, Z$, but $(Y_1, Y_0) \perp\!\!\!\perp Z \mid X$, $\Pr(D = 1 \mid Z)$ is a nondegenerate function of Z.	Yes	Yes

Notes: (Y_0, Y_1) are potential outcomes that depend on X;

$$D = \begin{cases} 1 & \text{if assigned (or choose) status 1,} \\ 0 & \text{otherwise;} \end{cases}$$

Z are determinants of D, θ is a vector of unobservables. For random assignments, A is a vector of actual treatment status. $A = 1$ if treated; $A = 0$ if not; $\xi = 1$ if a person is randomized to treatment status; $\xi = 0$ otherwise.

where it was not adopted. From the historical record, what can we conclude about the likely effectiveness of the policy in countries that have not implemented it?

To answer questions of this sort, economists build models of counterfactuals. Consider the following model. Let Y_0 be the outcome of a country (e.g., GDP) under a no-policy regime. Y_1 is the outcome if the policy is implemented. $(Y_1 - Y_0)$ is the "treatment effect" of the policy. It may vary among countries. We observe characteristics X of various countries (e.g., level of democracy, level of population literacy, etc.). It is convenient to decompose Y_1 into its mean given X, $\mu_1(X)$, and deviation from mean U_1. We can make a similar decomposition for Y_0:

$$Y_1 = \mu_1(X) + U_1,$$
$$Y_0 = \mu_0(X) + U_0. \tag{2.2}$$

We do not need to assume additive separability but it is convenient and we initially adopt it to simplify the exposition and establish a parallel regression notation that serves to link the statistical literature on treatment effects with the economic literature. We develop more general nonseparable models in later sections of this chapter.

It may happen that controlling for the X, $Y_1 - Y_0$ is the same for all countries. This is the case of homogeneous treatment effects given X. More likely, countries vary in their responses to the policy even after controlling for X.

Figure 1 plots the distribution of $Y_1 - Y_0$ for a benchmark X. It also displays the various treatment parameters introduced in Chapter 70. We use a special form of the generalized Roy model with constant cost C of adopting the policy. This is called the "extended Roy model". We use this model because it is simple and intuitive. (The precise parameterization of the extended Roy model used to generate the figure and the treatment effects is given at the base of Figure 1.) The special case of homogeneity in $Y_1 - Y_0$ arises when the distribution collapses to its mean. It would be ideal if we could estimate the distribution of $Y_1 - Y_0$ given X and there is research that does this. Abbring and Heckman survey methods for doing so in Chapter 72.

More often, economists focus on some mean of the distribution displayed in Figure 1 and use a regression framework to interpret the data. To turn (2.2) into a regression model, it is conventional to use the switching regression framework.[17] Define $D = 1$ if a country adopts a policy; $D = 0$ if it does not. The observed outcome Y is the switching regression model (2.1). Substituting (2.2) into this expression, and keeping all X implicit, we obtain

$$\begin{aligned} Y &= Y_0 + (Y_1 - Y_0)D \\ &= \mu_0 + (\mu_1 - \mu_0 + U_1 - U_0)D + U_0. \end{aligned} \tag{2.3}$$

Using conventional regression notation,

$$Y = \alpha + \beta D + \varepsilon, \tag{2.4}$$

where $\alpha = \mu_0$, $\beta = (Y_1 - Y_0) = \mu_1 - \mu_0 + U_1 - U_0$ and $\varepsilon = U_0$. We will also use the notation that $\eta = U_1 - U_0$, letting $\bar{\beta} = \mu_1 - \mu_0$ and $\beta = \bar{\beta} + \eta$. Throughout this section we use treatment effect and regression notation interchangeably. The coefficient on D is the treatment effect. The case where β is the same for every country is the case conventionally assumed. More elaborate versions assume that β depends on X ($\beta(X)$)

[17] Statisticians sometimes attribute this representation to Rubin (1974, 1978), but it is due to Quandt (1958, 1972). It is implicit in the Roy (1951) model. See our discussion of this basic model of counterfactuals in Chapter 70.

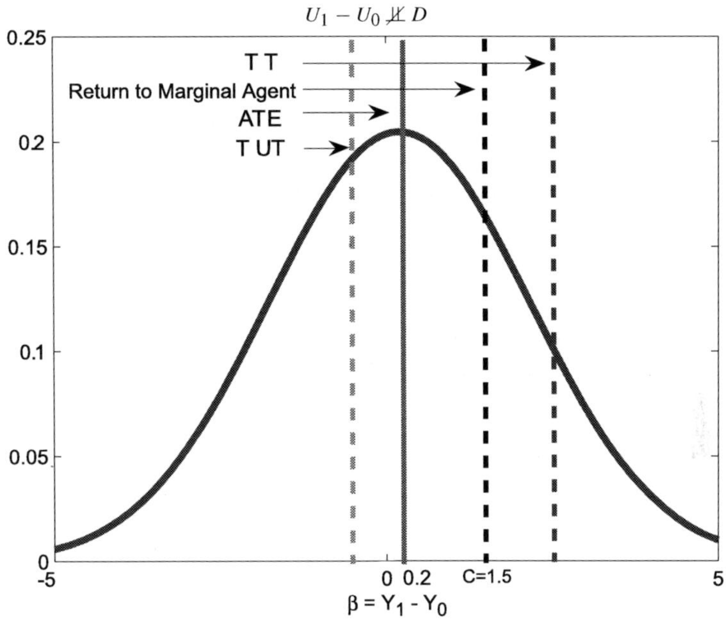

$\text{TT} = 2.666$, $\text{TUT} = -0.632$

Return to marginal agent $= C = 1.5$

$\text{ATE} = \mu_1 - \mu_0 = \bar{\beta} = 0.2$

The model

Outcomes	Choice model
$Y_1 = \mu_1 + U_1 = \alpha + \bar{\beta} + U_1$	$D = \begin{cases} 1 & \text{if } D^* \geqslant 0, \\ 0 & \text{if } D^* < 0 \end{cases}$
$Y_0 = \mu_0 + U_0 = \alpha + U_0$	

General case

$(U_1 - U_0) \not\perp\!\!\!\perp D$

$\text{ATE} \neq \text{TT} \neq \text{TUT}$

The researcher observes (Y, D, C).

$Y = \alpha + \beta D + U_0$ where $\beta = Y_1 - Y_0$.

Parameterization

$$\alpha = 0.67, \quad (U_1, U_0) \sim N(\mathbf{0}, \boldsymbol{\Sigma}), \quad D^* = Y_1 - Y_0 - C$$

$$\bar{\beta} = 0.2, \quad \boldsymbol{\Sigma} = \begin{bmatrix} 1 & -0.9 \\ -0.9 & 1 \end{bmatrix}, \quad C = 1.5$$

Figure 1. Distribution of gains in the Roy economy. *Source*: Heckman, Urzua and Vytlacil (2006).

and estimates interactions of D with X. The case where β varies even after accounting for X is called the “random coefficient” or “heterogenous treatment effect” case. The case where $\eta = U_1 - U_0$ depends on D is the case of essential heterogeneity analyzed by Heckman, Urzua and Vytlacil (2006). This case arises when treatment choices depend at least in part on the idiosyncratic return to treatment. A great deal of attention has been focused on this case in recent decades and we develop the implications of this model in this chapter.

3. An index model of choice and treatment effects: Definitions and unifying principles

We now present the model of treatment effects developed in Heckman and Vytlacil (1999, 2001b, 2005) and Heckman, Urzua and Vytlacil (2006), which relaxes the normality, separability and exogeneity assumptions invoked in the traditional economic selection models. It is rich enough to generate all of the treatment effects displayed in Figure 1 as well as many other policy parameters. It does not require separability. It is a nonparametric generalized Roy model with testable restrictions that can be used to unify the treatment effect literature, identify different treatment effects, link the literature on treatment effects to the literature in structural econometrics and interpret the implicit economic assumptions underlying instrumental variables, regression discontinuity design methods, control functions and matching methods. We follow Heckman and Vytlacil (1999, 2005) and Heckman, Urzua and Vytlacil (2006) in considering binary treatments. We analyze multiple treatments in Section 7. Florens et al. (2002) develop a model with a continuum of treatments and we briefly survey that work at the end of Section 7.

Y is the measured outcome variable. It is produced from the switching regression model (2.1). Outcomes are general nonlinear, nonseparable functions of observables and unobservables:

$$Y_1 = \mu_1(X, U_1), \tag{3.1}$$

$$Y_0 = \mu_0(X, U_0). \tag{3.2}$$

Examples of models that can be written in this form include conventional latent variable models for discrete choice that are generated by a latent variable crossing a threshold: $Y_i = \mathbf{1}(Y_i^* \geqslant 0)$, where $Y_i^* = \mu_i(X) + U_i$, $i = 0, 1$. Notice that in the general case, $\mu_i(X, U_i) - E(Y_i \mid X) \neq U_i$, $i = 0, 1$.

As defined in Chapter 70, the individual treatment effect associated with moving an otherwise identical person from "0" to "1" is $Y_1 - Y_0 = \Delta$ and is defined as the causal effect on Y of a *ceteris paribus* move from "0" to "1". To link this framework to the literature on economic choice models, we characterize the decision rule for program participation by an index model:

$$D^* = \mu_D(Z) - V, \qquad D = 1 \quad \text{if } D^* \geqslant 0, \qquad D = 0 \quad \text{otherwise}, \tag{3.3}$$

where, from the point of view of the econometrician, (Z, X) is observed and (U_0, U_1, V) is unobserved. The random variable V may be a function of (U_0, U_1). For example, in the original Roy model, μ_1 and μ_0 are additively separable in U_1 and U_0, respectively, and $V = -[U_1 - U_0]$. In the original formulations of the generalized Roy model, outcome equations are separable and $V = -[U_1 - U_0 - U_C]$, where U_C arises from the cost function (recall the discussion in Section 3.3 of Chapter 70). Without loss of generality, we define Z so that it includes all of the elements of X as well as any additional variables unique to the choice equation.

We invoke the following assumptions that are weaker than those used in the conventional literature on structural econometrics or the recent literature on semiparametric selection models and at the same time can be used both to define and to identify different treatment parameters.[18] The assumptions are:

(A-1) (U_0, U_1, V) *are independent of* Z *conditional on* X (*Independence*);
(A-2) $\mu_D(Z)$ *is a nondegenerate random variable conditional on* X (*Rank condition*);
(A-3) *the distribution of* V *is continuous*[19];
(A-4) *the values of* $E(|Y_1|)$ *and* $E(|Y_0|)$ *are finite* (*Finite means*);
(A-5) $0 < \Pr(D = 1 \mid X) < 1$.

(A-1) assumes that V is independent of Z given X, and is used below to generate counterfactuals. For the definition of treatment effects, we do not need either (A-1) or (A-2). Our definitions of treatment effects and their unification through MTE do not require any elements of Z that are not elements of X or independence assumptions. However, our analysis of instrumental variables requires that Z contain at least one element not in X. Assumptions (A-1) or (A-2) justify application of instrumental variables methods and nonparametric selection or control function methods. Some parameters in the recent IV literature are defined by an instrument so we make assumptions about instruments up front, noting where they are not needed. Assumption (A-4) is needed to satisfy standard integration conditions. It guarantees that the mean treatment parameters are well defined. Assumption (A-5) is the assumption in the population of both a treatment and a control group for each X. Observe that there are no exogeneity requirements for X. This is in contrast with the assumptions commonly made in the conventional structural literature and the semiparametric selection literature [see, e.g., Powell (1994)].

A counterfactual "no feedback" condition facilitates interpretability so that conditioning on X does not mask the effects of D. Letting X_d denote a value of X if D is set to d, a sufficient condition that rules out feedback from D to X is:

(A-6) *Let* X_0 *denote the counterfactual value of* X *that would be observed if* D *is set to* 0. X_1 *is defined analogously. Assume* $X_d = X$ *for* $d = 0, 1$. (*The* X_D *are invariant to counterfactual manipulations.*)

[18] A much weaker set of conditions is required to define the parameters than is required to identify them. See the discussion in Appendix B. As noted in Section 6, stronger conditions are required for policy forecasting.
[19] Absolutely continuous with respect to Lebesgue measure.

Condition (A-6) is not strictly required to formulate an evaluation model, but it enables an analyst who conditions on X to capture the "total" or "full effect" of D on Y [see Pearl (2000)]. This assumption imposes the requirement that X is an external variable determined outside the model and is not affected by counterfactual manipulations of D. However, the assumption allows for X to be freely correlated with U_1, U_0 and V so it can be endogenous. Until we discuss the problems of external validity and policy forecasting in Section 6, we analyze treatment effects conditional on X, and maintain assumption (A-6).

In this notation, $P(Z)$ is the probability of receiving treatment given Z, or the "propensity score" $P(Z) \equiv \Pr(D = 1 \mid Z) = F_{V|X}(\mu_D(Z))$, where $F_{V|X}(\cdot)$ denotes the distribution of V conditional on X.[20] We sometimes denote $P(Z)$ by P, suppressing the Z argument. We also work with U_D, a uniform random variable ($U_D \sim \text{Unif}[0, 1]$) defined by $U_D = F_{V|X}(V)$.[21] The separability between V and $\mu_D(Z)$ or $D(Z)$ and U_D is conventional. It plays a crucial role in justifying instrumental variable estimators in the general models analyzed in this chapter.

Vytlacil (2002) establishes that assumptions (A-1)–(A-5) for selection model (2.1) and (3.1)–(3.3) are equivalent to the assumptions used to generate the LATE model of Imbens and Angrist (1994) which are developed below in Section 4. Thus the nonparametric selection model for treatment effects developed by Heckman and Vytlacil is implied by the assumptions of the Imbens–Angrist instrumental variable model for treatment effects. Our approach links the IV literature to the literature on economic choice models exposited in Chapter 70. Our latent variable model is a version of the standard sample selection bias model. We weave together two strands of the literature often thought to be distinct [see, e.g., Angrist and Krueger (1999)].

The model of Equations (3.1)–(3.3) and assumptions (A-1)–(A-5) impose two testable restrictions on the distribution of (Y, D, Z, X). First, it imposes an index sufficiency restriction: for any set $\mathcal{A}$ and for $j = 0, 1$,

$$\Pr(Y_j \in \mathcal{A} \mid X, Z, D = j) = \Pr\bigl(Y_j \in \mathcal{A} \bigm| X, P(Z), D = j\bigr).$$

Z (given X) enters the model only through the propensity score $P(Z)$.[22] This restriction has empirical content when Z contains two or more variables not in X. Second, the model also imposes monotonicity in p for $E(YD \mid X = x, P = p)$ and $E(Y(1 - D) \mid$

[20] Throughout this chapter, we will refer to the cumulative distribution function of a random vector A by $F_A(\cdot)$ and to the cumulative distribution function of a random vector A conditional on random vector B by $F_{A|B}(\cdot)$. We will write the cumulative distribution function of A conditional on $B = b$ by $F_{A|B}(\cdot \mid b)$.

[21] This representation is valid whether or not (A-1) is true. However, (A-1) imposes restrictions on counterfactual choices. For example, if a change in government policy changes the distribution of Z by an external manipulation, under (A-1) the model can be used to generate the choice probability from $P(Z)$ evaluated at the new arguments, i.e., the model is invariant with respect to the distribution Z.

[22] The set $\mathcal{A}$ is assumed to be measurable.

$X = x, P = p$). Heckman and Vytlacil (2005, Appendix A) develop this condition further, and show that it is testable.

Even though the model of treatment effects we exposit is not the most general possible model, it has testable implications and hence empirical content. It unites various literatures and produces a nonparametric version of the selection model, and links the treatment literature to economic choice theory. We compare the assumptions used to identify IV with the assumptions used in matching in Section 8.

3.1. Definitions of treatment effects in the two outcome model

As developed in Chapter 70, the difficulty of observing the same individual in both treated and untreated states leads to the use of various population level treatment effects widely used in the biostatistics literature and often applied in economics.[23] The most commonly invoked treatment effect is the average treatment effect (ATE): $\Delta^{\text{ATE}}(x) \equiv E(\Delta \mid X = x)$ where $\Delta = Y_1 - Y_0$. This is the effect of assigning treatment randomly to everyone of type X assuming full compliance, and ignoring general equilibrium effects.[24] The average impact of treatment on persons who actually take the treatment is treatment on the treated (TT): $\Delta^{\text{TT}}(x) \equiv E(\Delta \mid X = x, D = 1)$. This parameter can also be defined conditional on $P(Z)$: $\Delta^{\text{TT}}(x, p) \equiv E(\Delta \mid X = x, P(Z) = p, D = 1)$.[25]

The mean effect of treatment on those for whom $X = x$ and $U_D = u_D$, the marginal treatment effect (MTE), plays a fundamental role in the analysis of this chapter:

$$\Delta^{\text{MTE}}(x, u_D) \equiv E(\Delta \mid X = x, U_D = u_D). \tag{3.4}$$

This parameter is defined independently of any instrument. We separate the definition of parameters from their identification. The MTE is the expected effect of treatment conditional on observed characteristics X and conditional on U_D, the unobservables from the first stage decision rule. For u_D evaluation points close to zero, $\Delta^{\text{MTE}}(x, u_D)$ is the expected effect of treatment on individuals with the value of unobservables that make them most likely to participate in treatment and who would participate even if the mean scale utility $\mu_D(Z)$ is small. If U_D is large, $\mu_D(Z)$ would have to be large to induce people to participate.

One can also interpret $E(\Delta \mid X = x, U_D = u_D)$ as the mean gain in terms of $Y_1 - Y_0$ for persons with observed characteristics X who would be indifferent between treatment or not if they were randomly assigned a value of Z, say z, such that $\mu_D(z) = u_D$. When Y_0 and Y_1 are value outcomes, MTE is a mean willingness-to-pay measure. MTE is a

[23] Heckman, LaLonde and Smith (1999) discuss panel data cases where it is possible to observe both Y_0 and Y_1 for the same person.

[24] See, e.g., Imbens (2004).

[25] These two definitions of treatment on the treated are related by integrating out the conditioning p variable: $\Delta^{\text{TT}}(x) = \int_0^1 \Delta^{\text{TT}}(x, p)\, dF_{P(Z)|X,D}(p \mid x, 1)$ where $F_{P(Z)|X,D}(\cdot \mid x, 1)$ is the distribution of $P(Z)$ given $X = x$ and $D = 1$.

choice-theoretic building block that unites the treatment effect, selection, matching and control function literatures.

A third interpretation is that MTE conditions on X and the residual defined by subtracting the expectation of D^* from D^*: $\tilde{U}_D = D^* - E(D^* \mid Z, X)$. This is a "replacement function" interpretation in the sense of Heckman and Robb (1985a) and Chapter 73 (Matzkin) of this Handbook, or "control function" interpretation in the sense of Blundell and Powell (2003). These three interpretations are equivalent under separability in D^*, i.e., when (3.3) characterizes the choice equation, but lead to three different definitions of MTE when a more general nonseparable model is developed. This point is developed in Section 4.10 where we discuss a general nonseparable model. The additive separability of Equation (3.3) in terms of observables and unobservables plays a crucial role in the justification of instrumental variable methods.

The LATE parameter of Imbens and Angrist (1994) is a version of MTE. We present their full conditions for identification in Section 4. Here we define it in the notation used in this chapter. LATE is defined by an instrument in their analysis. As in Chapter 70, we define LATE independently of any instrument after first presenting the Imbens–Angrist definition. Define $D(z)$ as a counterfactual choice variable, with $D(z) = 1$ if state 1 ($D = 1$) would have been chosen if Z had been set to z, and $D(z) = 0$ otherwise. Let $\mathcal{Z}(x)$ denote the support of the distribution of Z conditional on $X = x$. For any $(z, z') \in \mathcal{Z}(x) \times \mathcal{Z}(x)$ such that $P(z) > P(z')$, LATE is $E(\Delta \mid X = x, D(z) = 1, D(z') = 0) = E(Y_1 - Y_0 \mid X = x, D(z) = 1, D(z') = 0)$, the mean gain to persons who would be induced to switch from $D = 0$ to $D = 1$ if Z were manipulated externally from z' to z. In an example of the returns to education, z' could be the base level of tuition and z a reduced tuition level. Using the latent index model, developed in Chapter 70 and defined in the introduction to this section, Heckman and Vytlacil (1999, 2005) show that LATE can be written as

$$
\begin{aligned}
&E\big(Y_1 - Y_0 \bigm| X = x,\ D(z) = 1,\ D(z') = 0\big) \\
&\quad = E\big(Y_1 - Y_0 \bigm| X = x, u'_D < U_D \leqslant u_D\big) = \Delta^{\mathrm{LATE}}\big(x, u_D, u'_D\big)
\end{aligned}
$$

for $u_D = \Pr(D(z) = 1) = P(z)$, $u'_D = \Pr(D(z') = 1) = P(z')$, where assumption (A-1) implies that $\Pr(D(z) = 1) = \Pr(D = 1 \mid Z = z)$ and $\Pr(D(z') = 1) = \Pr(D = 1 \mid Z = z')$.

Imbens and Angrist define the LATE parameter as the probability limit of an estimator. Their analysis conflates issues of definition of parameters with issues of identification. Our representation of LATE allows us to separate these two conceptually distinct matters and to define the LATE parameter more generally. One can, in principle, evaluate the right-hand side of the preceding equation at any u_D, u'_D points in the unit interval and not only at points in the support of the distribution of the propensity score $P(Z)$ conditional on $X = x$ where it is identified. From assump-

Table 2A
Treatment effects and estimands as weighted averages of the marginal treatment effect

$\text{ATE}(x) = E(Y_1 - Y_0 \mid X = x) = \int_0^1 \Delta^{\text{MTE}}(x, u_D)\, du_D$
$\text{TT}(x) = E(Y_1 - Y_0 \mid X = x, D = 1) = \int_0^1 \Delta^{\text{MTE}}(x, u_D)\omega_{\text{TT}}(x, u_D)\, du_D$
$\text{TUT}(x) = E(Y_1 - Y_0 \mid X = x, D = 0) = \int_0^1 \Delta^{\text{MTE}}(x, u_D)\omega_{\text{TUT}}(x, u_D)\, du_D$
Policy relevant treatment effect: $\text{PRTE}(x) = E(Y_{a'} \mid X = x) - E(Y_a \mid X = x) = \int_0^1 \Delta^{\text{MTE}}(x, u_D)\omega_{\text{PRTE}}(x, u_D)\, du_D$ for two policies a and a' that affect the Z but not the X
$\text{IV}_J(x) = \int_0^1 \Delta^{\text{MTE}}(x, u_D)\omega_{\text{IV}}^J(x, u_D)\, du_D$, given instrument J
$\text{OLS}(x) = \int_0^1 \Delta^{\text{MTE}}(x, u_D)\omega_{\text{OLS}}(x, u_D)\, du_D$

Source: Heckman and Vytlacil (2005).

tions (A-1), (A-3), and (A-4), $\Delta^{\text{LATE}}(x, u_D, u'_D)$ is continuous in u_D and u'_D and $\lim_{u'_D \uparrow u_D} \Delta^{\text{LATE}}(x, u_D, u'_D) = \Delta^{\text{MTE}}(x, u_D)$.[26]

Heckman and Vytlacil (1999) use assumptions (A-1)–(A-5) and the latent index structure to develop the relationship between MTE and the various treatment effect parameters shown in the first three lines of Table 2A. Appendix A presents the formal derivation of the parameters and associated weights and graphically illustrates the relationship between ATE and TT. There we establish that all treatment parameters may be expressed as weighted averages of the MTE:

$$\text{Treatment parameter } (j) = \int_0^1 \Delta^{\text{MTE}}(x, u_D)\, \omega_j(x, u_D)\, du_D,$$

where $\omega_j(x, u_D)$ is the weighting function for the MTE and the integral is defined over the full support of u_D. Except for the OLS weights, the weights in the table all integrate to one, although in some cases the weights for IV may be negative. We analyze how negative weights for IV might arise in Section 4.

In Table 2A, $\Delta^{\text{TT}}(x)$ is shown as a weighted average of Δ^{MTE}:

$$\Delta^{\text{TT}}(x) = \int_0^1 \Delta^{\text{MTE}}(x, u_D)\omega_{\text{TT}}(x, u_D)\, du_D,$$

where

$$\omega_{\text{TT}}(x, u_D) = \frac{1 - F_{P|X}(u_D \mid x)}{\int_0^1 (1 - F_{P|X}(t \mid x))\, dt} = \frac{S_{P|X}(u_D \mid x)}{E(P(Z) \mid X = x)}, \tag{3.5}$$

[26] This follows from Lebesgue's theorem for the derivative of an integral and holds almost everywhere with respect to Lebesgue measure. The ideas of the marginal treatment effect and the limit form of LATE were first introduced in the context of a parametric normal generalized Roy model by Björklund and Moffitt (1987), and were analyzed more generally in Heckman (1997). Angrist, Graddy and Imbens (2000) also define and develop a limit form of LATE.

Table 2B
Weights

$\omega_{\text{ATE}}(x, u_D) = 1$
$\omega_{\text{TT}}(x, u_D) = \left[\int_{u_D}^{1} f_{P\mid X}(p \mid X = x)\, dp\right] \frac{1}{E(P\mid X=x)}$
$\omega_{\text{TUT}}(x, u_D) = \left[\int_{0}^{u_D} f_{P\mid X}(p \mid X = x)\, dp\right] \frac{1}{E((1-P)\mid X=x)}$
$\omega_{\text{PRTE}}(x, u_D) = \left[\frac{F_{P_{a'}\mid X}(u_D\mid x) - F_{P_a\mid X}(u_D\mid x)}{\Delta \overline{P}(x)}\right]$, where
$\Delta \overline{P}(x) = E(P_a \mid X = x) - E(P_{a'} \mid X = x)$
$\omega_{\text{IV}}^{J}(x, u_D) = \left[\int_{u_D}^{1} (J(Z) - E(J(Z) \mid X = x)) f_{J,P\mid X}(j, t \mid X = x)\, dt\, dj\right] \frac{1}{\text{Cov}(J(Z), D\mid X=x)}$
$\omega_{\text{OLS}}(x, u_D) = 1 + \frac{E(U_1\mid X=x, U_D=u_D)\omega_1(x,u_D) - E(U_0\mid X=x, U_D=u_D)\omega_0(x,u_D)}{\Delta^{\text{MTE}}(x,u_D)}$
$\omega_1(x, u_D) = \left[\int_{u_D}^{1} f_{P\mid X}(p \mid X = x)\, dp\right] \frac{1}{E(P\mid X=x)}$
$\omega_0(x, u_D) = \left[\int_{0}^{u_D} f_{P\mid X}(p \mid X = x)\, dp\right] \frac{1}{E((1-P)\mid X=x)}$

Source: Heckman and Vytlacil (2005).

and $S_{P\mid X}(u_D \mid x)$ is $\Pr(P(Z) > u_D \mid X = x)$ and $\omega_{\text{TT}}(x, u_D)$ is a weighted distribution. The parameter $\Delta^{\text{TT}}(x)$ oversamples $\Delta^{\text{MTE}}(x, u_D)$ for those individuals with low values of u_D that make them more likely to participate in the program being evaluated. Treatment on the untreated (TUT) is defined symmetrically with TT and oversamples those least likely to participate. The various weights are displayed in Table 2B. The other weights, treatment effects and estimands shown in this table are discussed later. A central theme of this chapter is that under our assumptions all estimators and estimands can be written as weighted averages of MTE. This allows us to unify the treatment effect literature using a common functional $\Delta^{\text{MTE}}(x, u_D)$.

Observe that if $E(Y_1 - Y_0 \mid X = x, U_D = u_D) = E(Y_1 - Y_0 \mid X = x)$, so $\Delta = Y_1 - Y_0$ is mean independent of U_D given $X = x$, then $\Delta^{\text{MTE}} = \Delta^{\text{ATE}} = \Delta^{\text{TT}} = \Delta^{\text{LATE}}$. Therefore, in cases where there is no heterogeneity in terms of unobservables in MTE (Δ constant conditional on $X = x$) or agents do not act on it so that U_D drops out of the conditioning set, marginal treatment effects are average treatment effects, so that all of the evaluation parameters are the same. Otherwise, they are different. Only in the case where the marginal treatment effect is the average treatment effect will the "effect" of treatment be uniquely defined.

Figure 2A plots weights for a parametric normal generalized Roy model generated from the parameters shown at the base of Figure 2B. This is an instance of the general model developed in Chapter 70, Section 5. The model allows for costs to vary in the population and is more general than the extended Roy model. We discuss the weights for IV depicted in Figure 2B in Section 4 and the weights for OLS in Section 8. A high u_D is associated with higher cost, relative to return, and less likelihood of choosing $D = 1$. The decline of MTE in terms of higher values of u_D means that people with higher u_D

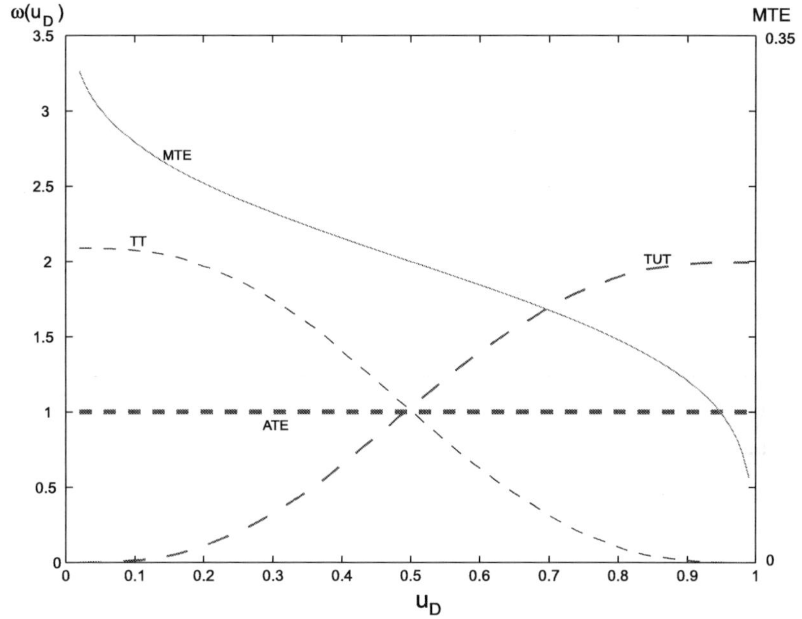

Figure 2A. Weights for the marginal treatment effect for different parameters. *Source*: Heckman and Vytlacil (2005).

have lower gross returns. TT overweights low values of u_D (i.e., it oversamples U_D that make it likely to have $D = 1$). ATE samples U_D uniformly. Treatment on the untreated ($E(Y_1 - Y_0 \mid X = x, D = 0)$), or TUT, oversamples the values of U_D which make it unlikely to have $D = 1$.

Table 3 shows the treatment parameters produced from the different weighting schemes for the model used to generate the weights in Figures 2A and 2B. Given the decline of the MTE in u_D, it is not surprising that TT $>$ ATE $>$ TUT. This is the generalized Roy version of the principle of diminishing returns. Those most likely to self-select into the program benefit the most from it. The difference between TT and ATE is a sorting gain: $E(Y_1 - Y_0 \mid X, D = 1) - E(Y_1 - Y_0 \mid X)$, the average gain experienced by people who sort into treatment compared to what the average person would experience. Purposive selection on the basis of gains should lead to positive sorting gains of the kind found in the table. If there is negative sorting on the gains, then TUT $\geqslant$ ATE $\geqslant$ TT. Later in this chapter, we return to this table to discuss the other numbers in it.

Table 4 reproduced from Heckman (2001) presents evidence on the nonconstancy of the MTE in U_D drawn from a variety of studies of schooling, job training, migration and unionism. Most of the evidence is obtained using parametric normal selection models or variants of such models. With the exception of studies of unionism, a common finding

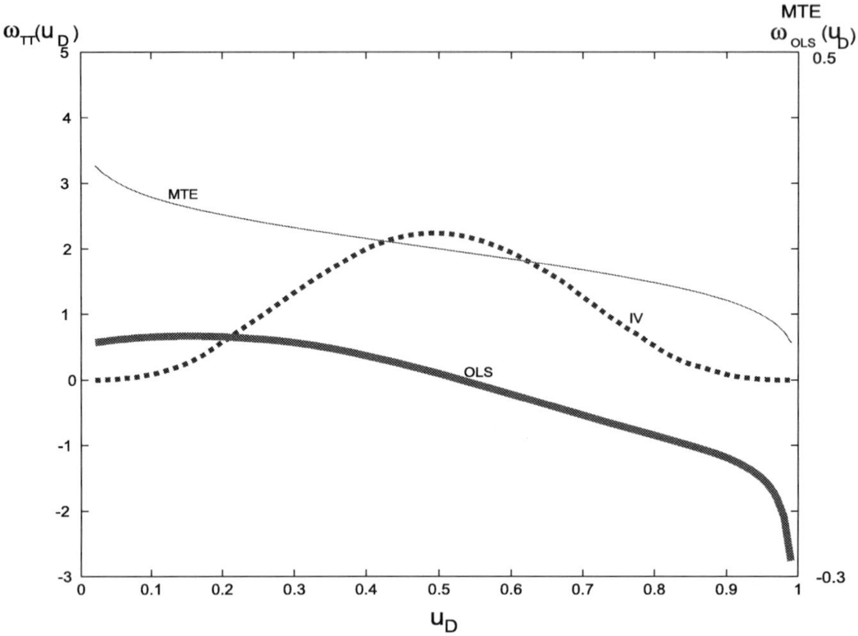

$Y_1 = \alpha + \bar{\beta} + U_1$	$U_1 = \sigma_1 \tau$	$\alpha = 0.67$	$\sigma_1 = 0.012$
$Y_0 = \alpha + U_0$	$U_0 = \sigma_0 \tau$	$\bar{\beta} = 0.2$	$\sigma_0 = -0.050$
$D = 1$ if $Z - V \geqslant 0$	$V = \sigma_V \tau$	$\tau \sim N(0, 1)$	$\sigma_V = -1.000$
	$U_D = \Phi(\frac{V}{\sigma_V \sigma_\tau})$		$Z \sim N(-0.0026, 0.2700)$

Figure 2B. Marginal treatment effect vs. linear instrumental variables and ordinary least squares weights. *Source*: Heckman and Vytlacil (2005).

in the empirical literature is the nonconstancy of MTE given X.[27] The evidence from the literature suggests that different treatment parameters measure different effects, and persons participate in programs based on heterogeneity in responses to the program being studied. The phenomenon of nonconstancy of the MTE that we analyze in this chapter is of substantial empirical interest.

The additively separable latent index model for D [Equation (3.3)] and assumptions (A-1)–(A-5) are far stronger than what is required to define the parameters in terms of the MTE. The representations of treatment effects defined in Table 2A remain valid even if Z is not independent of U_D, if there are no variables in Z that are not also contained in X, or if a more general nonseparable choice model generates D [so $D^* = \mu_D(Z, U_D)$]. An important advantage of our approach over other approaches to the analysis of instrumental variables in the recent literature is that no instrument Z is

[27] However, most of the empirical evidence is based on parametric selection models.

Table 3
Treatment parameters and estimands in the generalized Roy example

Treatment on the treated	0.2353
Treatment on the untreated	0.1574
Average treatment effect	0.2000
Sorting gain[a]	0.0353
Policy relevant treatment effect (PRTE)	0.1549
Selection bias[b]	−0.0628
Linear instrumental variables[c]	0.2013
Ordinary least squares	0.1725

Source: Heckman and Vytlacil (2005).
Note: The model used to create Table 3 is the same as those used to create Figures 2A and 2B. The PRTE is computed using a policy t characterized as follows:

- If $Z > 0$ then $D = 1$ if $Z(1 + t) - V \geqslant 0$.
- If $Z \leqslant t$ then $D = 1$ if $Z - V \geqslant 0$.

For this example t is set equal to 0.2.

[a] $\text{TT} - \text{ATE} = E(Y_1 - Y_0 \mid D = 1) - E(Y_1 - Y_0)$.
[b] $\text{OLS} - \text{TT} = E(Y_0 \mid D = 1) - E(Y_0 \mid D = 0)$.
[c] Using propensity score $P(Z)$ as the instrument.

needed to define the parameters. We separate the tasks of definition and identification of parameters as discussed in Table 1 of Chapter 70, and present an analysis more closely rooted in economics. Appendices A and B define the treatment parameters for both separable (Appendix A) and nonseparable choice equations (Appendix B). We show that the treatment parameters can be defined even if there is no instrument or if instrumental variables methods break down as they do in nonseparable models.

As noted in Chapter 70, the literature on structural econometrics is clear about the basic parameters of interest although it is not always clear about the exact combinations of parameters needed to answer specific policy problems. The literature on treatment effects offers a variety of evaluation parameters. Missing from that literature is an algorithm for defining treatment effects that answer precisely formulated economic policy questions. The MTE provides a framework for developing such an algorithm. In the next section, we present one well defined policy parameter that can be used to generate Benthamite policy evaluations as discussed in Section 5 of Chapter 70.

3.2. *Policy relevant treatment parameters*

The conventional treatment parameters do not always answer economically interesting questions. Their link to cost-benefit analysis and interpretable economic frameworks is sometimes obscure. Each answers a different question. Many investigators estimate a treatment effect and hope that it answers an interesting question. A more promising approach for defining parameters is to postulate a policy question or decision problem

Table 4
Evidence on selection on unobservables and constancy of the MTE for separable models

Study	Method	Finding on the hypothesis of constancy of the MTE
Unionism		
Lee (1978)	Normal selection model (H_0: $\sigma_{1V} = \sigma_{0V}$)	$\sigma_{1V} = \sigma_{0V}$ Do not reject
Farber (1983)	Normal selection model (H_0: $\sigma_{1V} = \sigma_{0V}$)	$\sigma_{1V} = \sigma_{0V}$ Do not reject
Duncan and Leigh (1985)	Normal selection model (H_0: $\sigma_{1V} = \sigma_{0V}$)	$\sigma_{1V} = \sigma_{0V}$ Do not reject
Robinson (1989)	Normal selection model $(\mu_1 - \mu_0)_{\text{IV}} = (\mu_1 - \mu_0)_{\text{normal}}$	$\sigma_{1V} \neq \sigma_{0V}$ Do not reject
Schooling (college vs. high school)		
Willis and Rosen (1979)	Normal selection model (H_0: $\sigma_{1V} = \sigma_{0V}$)	$\sigma_{1V} \neq \sigma_{0V}$ Reject
Heckman, Tobias and Vytlacil (2003)	Normal selection model (H_0: $\sigma_{1V} = \sigma_{0V}$)	$\sigma_{1V} \neq \sigma_{0V}$ Reject
Job training		
Björklund and Moffitt (1987)	Normal selection model (H_0: $\sigma_{1V} = \sigma_{0V}$)	$\sigma_{1V} \neq \sigma_{0V}$ Reject
Heckman et al. (1998; Suppl.)	$E(U_1 - U_0 \mid D = 1, Z, X) = E(U_1 - U_0 \mid D = 1, X)$	Reject selection on unobservables
Sectoral choice		
Heckman and Sedlacek (1990)	Normal selection model (H_0: $\sigma_{1V} = \sigma_{0V}$)	$\sigma_{1V} \neq \sigma_{0V}$ Reject
Migration		
Pessino (1991)	Normal selection model (H_0: $\sigma_{1V} = \sigma_{0V}$)	$\sigma_{1V} \neq \sigma_{0V}$ Reject
Tunali (2000)	H_0: $E(U_1 - U_0 \mid D = 1) = 0$ (estimated using robust selection)	Cannot reject

Source: Heckman (2001).
Notes: $Y = DY_1 + (1 - D)Y_0$
$Y_1 = \mu_1(X) + U_1$
$Y_0 = \mu_0(X) + U_0$
$Z \perp\!\!\!\perp (U_0, U_1)$, $Z \not\perp\!\!\!\perp D$
$D = \mathbf{1}(\mu_D(Z) - V \geqslant 0)$, where $\mu_D(Z) - V$ is the index determining selection into "1" or "0"
Hypothesis: No selection on unobservables (constancy of the MTE)
H_0: $E(U_1 - U_0 \mid D = 1, Z, X)$ does not depend on D where $\text{Cov}(U_1, U_V) = \sigma_{1V}$, $\text{Cov}(U_0, U_V) = \sigma_{0V}$ (in normal model, the null hypothesis is $\sigma_{1V} = \sigma_{0V}$).

of interest and to derive the treatment parameter that answers it. Taking this approach does not in general produce the conventional treatment parameters or the estimands produced from instrumental variables.

Consider a class of policies that affect P, the probability of participation in a program, but do not affect Δ^{MTE}. The policies analyzed in the treatment effect literature that change the Z not in X are more restrictive than the general policies that shift X and Z analyzed in the structural literature. An example from the schooling literature would be policies that change tuition or distance to school but do not directly affect the gross returns to schooling [Card (2001)]. Since we ignore general equilibrium effects in this chapter, the effects on (Y_0, Y_1) from changes in the overall level of education are assumed to be negligible.

Let p and p' denote two potential policies and let D_p and $D_{p'}$ denote the choices that would be made under policies p and p'. When we discuss the policy relevant treatment effect, we use "p" to denote the policy and distinguish it from the realized value of $P(Z)$. Under our assumptions, the policies affect the Z given X, but not the potential outcomes. Let the corresponding decision rules be $D_p = \mathbf{1}[P_p(Z_p) \geqslant U_D]$, $D_{p'} = \mathbf{1}[P_{p'}(Z_{p'}) \geqslant U_D]$, where $P_p(Z_p) = \Pr(D_p = 1 \mid Z_p)$ and $P_{p'}(Z_{p'}) = \Pr(D_{p'} = 1 \mid Z_{p'})$. To simplify the exposition, we will suppress the arguments of these functions and write P_p and $P_{p'}$ for $P_p(Z_p)$ and $P_{p'}(Z_{p'})$. Define $(Y_{0,p}, Y_{1,p}, U_{D,p})$ as (Y_0, Y_1, U_D) under policy p, and define $(Y_{0,p'}, Y_{1,p'}, U_{D,p'})$ correspondingly under policy p'. We assume that Z_p and $Z_{p'}$ are independent of $(Y_{0,p}, Y_{1,p}, U_{D,p})$ and $(Y_{0,p'}, Y_{1,p'}, U_{D,p'})$, respectively, conditional on X_p and $X_{p'}$. Let $Y_p = D_p Y_{1,p} + (1 - D_p) Y_{0,p}$ and $Y_{p'} = D_{p'} Y_{1,p'} + (1 - D_{p'}) Y_{0,p'}$ denote the outcomes that would be observed under policies p and p', respectively.

Δ^{MTE} is policy invariant in the sense of Hurwicz as defined in Chapter 70 if

$E(Y_{1,p} \mid U_{D,p} = u_D, X_p = x)$ and $E(Y_{0,p} \mid U_{D,p} = u_D, X_p = x)$ are invariant to the choice of policy p (Policy invariance for the marginal treatment effect).

Policy invariance can be justified by the strong assumption that the policy being investigated does not change the counterfactual outcomes, covariates, or unobservables, i.e., $(Y_{0,p}, Y_{1,p}, X_p, U_{D,p}) = (Y_{0,p'}, Y_{1,p'}, X_{p'}, U_{D,p'})$. However, Δ^{MTE} is policy invariant if this assumption is relaxed to the weaker assumption that the policy change does not affect the distribution of these variables conditional on X:

(A-7) *The distribution of $(Y_{0,p}, Y_{1,p}, U_{D,p})$ conditional on $X_p = x$ is the same as the distribution of $(Y_{0,p'}, Y_{1,p'}, U_{D,p'})$ conditional on $X_{p'} = x$ (policy invariance for distribution).*

Assumption (A-7) guarantees that manipulations of the distribution of Z do not affect anything in the model except the choice of outcomes. These are specialized versions of (PI-3) and (PI-4) invoked in Chapter 70.

For the widely used Benthamite social welfare criterion $\Upsilon(Y)$, where Υ is a utility function, comparing policies using mean utilities of outcomes and considering the effect for individuals with a given level of $X = x$ we obtain the *policy relevant treatment effect*, PRTE, denoted $\Delta^{\text{PRTE}}(x)$:

$$E(\Upsilon(Y_p) \mid X = x) - E(\Upsilon(Y_{p'}) \mid X = x)$$
$$= \int_0^1 \Delta_\Upsilon^{\text{MTE}}(x, u_D)\{F_{P_{p'}|X}(u_D \mid x) - F_{P_p|X}(u_D \mid x)\}\, du_D, \quad (3.6)$$

where $F_{P_p|X}(\cdot \mid x)$ and $F_{P_{p'}|X}(\cdot \mid x)$ are the distributions of P_p and $P_{p'}$ conditional on $X = x$, respectively, defined for the different policy regimes and $\Delta_\Upsilon^{\text{MTE}}(x, u_D) = E(\Upsilon(Y_{1,p}) - \Upsilon(Y_{0,p}) \mid U_{D,p} = u_D, X_p = x)$.[28,29] The weights in expression (3.6) are derived in Appendix C under the assumption that the policy does not change the joint distribution of outcomes. To simplify the notation, throughout the rest of this chapter when we discuss PRTE, we assume that $\Upsilon(Y) = Y$. Modifications of our analysis for the more general case are straightforward. We also discuss the implications of noninvariance for the definition and interpretation of the PRTE in Appendix C.

Define $\Delta \bar{P}(x) = E(P_p \mid X = x) - E(P_{p'} \mid X = x)$, the change in the proportion of people induced into the program due to the intervention. Assuming $\Delta \bar{P}(x)$ is positive, we may define per person affected weights as

$$\omega_{\text{PRTE}}(x, u_D) = \frac{F_{P_{p'}|X}(u_D \mid x) - F_{P_p|X}(u_D \mid x)}{\Delta \bar{P}(x)}.$$

These weights are displayed in Table 2B. As demonstrated in the next section, in general, conventional IV weights the MTE differently than either the conventional treatment parameters (Δ^{ATE} or Δ^{TT}) or the policy relevant parameter, and so does not recover these parameters.

Instead of hoping that conventional treatment parameters or favorite estimators answer interesting economic questions, the approach developed by Heckman and Vytlacil (1999, 2001a, 2001b, 2005) is to estimate the MTE and weight it by the appropriate weight determined by how the policy changes the distribution of P to construct Δ^{PRTE}. In Heckman and Vytlacil (2005), we also develop an alternative approach that produces a policy weighted instrument to identify Δ^{PRTE} by standard instrumental variables. We elaborate our discussion of policy analysis based in the MTE and develop other policy

[28] We could define policy invariance for Δ^{MTE} in terms of expectations of $\Upsilon(Y_{1,p})$ and $\Upsilon(Y_{0,p})$.

[29] If we assume that the marginal distribution of X_p and $X_{p'}$ are the same as the marginal distribution of a benchmark X, the weights can be integrated against the distribution of X to obtain the total effect of the policy in the population:

$$E(\Upsilon(Y_p)) - E(\Upsilon(Y_{p'}))$$
$$= E_X[E(\Upsilon(Y_p) \mid X) - E(\Upsilon(Y_{p'}) \mid X)]$$
$$= \int \left[\int_0^1 \Delta_\Upsilon^{\text{MTE}}(x, u_D)\{F_{P_{p'}|X}(u_D \mid x) - F_{P_p|X}(u_D \mid x)\}\, du_D\right] dF_X(x).$$

parameters for local and global perturbations of policy in Section 6 after developing the instrumental variable estimator and the related regression discontinuity estimator. The analyses of Sections 4 and 5 give us tools to make specific the discussion of alternative approaches to policy evaluation.

4. Instrumental variables

The method of instrumental variables (IV) is currently the most widely used method in economics for estimating economic models when unobservables are present that violate the matching assumption (M-1).[30] We first present an intuitive exposition of the method and then present a more formal development. We analyze a model with two outcomes. We generalize the analysis to multiple outcomes in Section 7.

Return to the policy adoption example presented at the end of Section 2. The distribution of returns to adoption is depicted in Figure 1. First, consider the method of IV, where β (given X), which is the same as $Y_1 - Y_0$ given X, is the same for every country. This is the familiar case and we develop it first. The model is

$$Y = \alpha + \beta D + \varepsilon, \tag{4.1}$$

where conditioning on X is implicit. A simple least squares regression of Y on D (equivalently a mean difference in outcomes between countries with $D = 1$ and countries with $D = 0$) is possibly subject to a selection bias on Y_0. Countries that adopt the policy may be atypical in terms of their Y_0 $(= \alpha + \varepsilon)$. Thus if countries that would have done well in terms of unobservable ε $(= U_0)$ even in the absence of the policy are the ones that adopt the policy, β estimated from OLS (or its semiparametric version – matching) is upward biased because $\mathrm{Cov}(D, \varepsilon) > 0$.

If there is an instrument Z, with the properties that

$$\mathrm{Cov}(Z, D) \neq 0, \tag{4.2}$$

$$\mathrm{Cov}(Z, \varepsilon) = 0, \tag{4.3}$$

then standard IV identifies β, at least in large samples,

$$\operatorname{plim} \hat{\beta}_{\mathrm{IV}} = \frac{\mathrm{Cov}(Z, Y)}{\mathrm{Cov}(Z, D)} = \beta.\text{[31]}$$

If other instruments exist, each identifies β. Z produces a controlled variation in D relative to ε. Randomization of assignment with full compliance to experimental protocols

[30] More precisely, IV is the most widely used alternative to OLS. OLS is a version of matching that imposes linearity of the functional form of outcome equations and assumes exogeneity of the regressors. See our discussion of matching in Section 8.

[31] The proof is straightforward. Under general conditions [see, e.g., White (1984)],

$$\operatorname{plim} \hat{\beta}_{\mathrm{IV}} = \beta + \frac{\mathrm{Cov}(Z, \varepsilon)}{\mathrm{Cov}(Z, D)} \quad \text{and} \quad \mathrm{Cov}(Z, \varepsilon) = 0,$$

so the second term on the right-hand side vanishes.

is an example of an instrument. From the instrumental variable estimators, we can identify the effect of adopting the policy in any country since all countries respond to the policy in the same way controlling for their X.

If β $(= Y_1 - Y_0)$ varies in the population even after controlling for X, there is a distribution of responses that cannot in general be summarized by a single number. Even if we are interested in the mean of the distribution, a new phenomenon distinct from selection bias might arise. This is a problem of sorting on the gain, which is distinct from sorting on levels. If β varies, even after controlling for X, there may be sorting on the gain ($\mathrm{Cov}(\beta, D) \neq 0$). This is the model of *essential heterogeneity* as defined by Heckman, Urzua and Vytlacil (2006). It is also called a correlated random coefficient model [Heckman and Vytlacil (1998)].

The application of instrumental variables to this case is more problematic. Suppose that we augment the standard instrumental variable assumptions (4.2) and (4.3) by the following assumption:

$$\mathrm{Cov}(Z, \beta) = 0. \tag{4.4}$$

Can we identify the mean of $(Y_1 - Y_0)$ using IV? In general we cannot.[32]

To see why, let $\bar{\beta} = (\mu_1 - \mu_0)$ be the mean treatment effect (the mean of the distribution in Figure 1). $\beta = \bar{\beta} + \eta$, where $U_1 - U_0 = \eta$ and $\bar{\beta} = \mu_1 - \mu_0$ and we keep the conditioning on X implicit. Write Equation (4.1) in terms of these parameters:

$$Y = \alpha + \bar{\beta} D + [\varepsilon + \eta D].$$

The error term of this equation $(\varepsilon + \eta D)$ contains two components. By assumption, Z is uncorrelated with ε and η. But to identify $\bar{\beta}$, we need IV to be uncorrelated with $[\varepsilon + \eta D]$. That requires Z to be uncorrelated with ηD.

If policy adoption is made without knowledge of η $(= U_1 - U_0)$, the idiosyncratic gain to policy adoption after controlling for the observables, then η and D are statistically independent and hence uncorrelated, and IV identifies $\bar{\beta}$.[33] If, however, policy adoption is made with partial or full knowledge of η, IV does not identify $\bar{\beta}$ because $E(\eta D \mid Z) = E(\eta \mid D = 1, Z)\Pr(D = 1 \mid Z)$ and if there is sorting on the unobserved gain η, the first term is not zero. Similar calculations show that IV does not identify the mean gain to the countries that adopt the policy $(E(\beta \mid D = 1))$ and many other summary treatment parameters.[34] Whether η $(= U_1 - U_0)$ is correlated with D depends on the quality of the data available to the empirical economist and cannot be settled

[32] This point was made by Heckman and Robb (1985a, 1986a). See also Heckman (1997).

[33] The proof is straightforward:

$$\operatorname{plim} \hat{\beta}_{\mathrm{IV}} = \bar{\beta} + \frac{\mathrm{Cov}(Z, \varepsilon + \eta D)}{\mathrm{Var}(D, Z)}.$$

But $\mathrm{Cov}(Z, \varepsilon + \eta D) = \mathrm{Cov}(Z, \varepsilon) + \mathrm{Cov}(Z, \eta D)$ and $\mathrm{Cov}(Z, \eta D) = E(Z\eta D) - E(Z)E(\eta D)$, $E(\eta D) = 0$ by the assumed independence. $E(Z\eta D) = E[E(\eta D Z \mid Z)] = E[E(\eta D \mid Z) Z] = 0$ since $E(\eta D \mid Z) = 0$.

[34] See Heckman and Robb (1985a, 1986a), Heckman (1997) or Heckman and Vytlacil (1999).

a priori. The conservative position is to allow for such a correlation. However, this rules out IV as an interesting econometric strategy for identifying any of the familiar mean treatment parameters.

In light of the negative conclusions about IV in the literature preceding their paper, it is remarkable that Imbens and Angrist (1994) establish that under certain conditions, in the model with essential heterogeneity, IV can identify an interpretable parameter. The parameter they identify is a discrete approximation to the marginal gain parameter introduced by Björklund and Moffitt (1987). The Björklund–Moffitt parameter is a version of MTE for a parametric normal selection model. We derive their parameter from a selection model in Section 4.8. Björklund and Moffitt (1987) demonstrate how to use a selection model to identify the marginal gain to persons induced into a treatment status by a marginal change in the cost of treatment. Imbens and Angrist (1994) show how to estimate a discrete approximation to the Björklund–Moffitt parameter using instrumental variables.

Imbens and Angrist (1994) assume the existence of an instrument Z that takes two or more distinct values. This is implicit in (4.2). If Z assumes only one value, the covariance in (4.2) would be zero. Strengthening the covariance conditions of Equations (4.3) and (4.4), they assume (IV-1) and (IV-2) (independence and rank, respectively) and that Z is independent of $\beta = (Y_1 - Y_0)$ and Y_0. Recall that we denote by $D(z)$ the random variable indicating receipt of treatment when Z is set to z. ($D(z) = 1$ if treatment is received; $D(z) = 0$ otherwise.) The Imbens–Angrist independence and rank assumptions are (IV-1) and (IV-2).

They supplement the standard IV assumptions with what they call a "monotonicity" assumption. It is a condition across persons. The assumption maintains that if Z is fixed first at one and then at the other of two distinct values, say $Z = z$ and $Z = z'$, then all persons respond in their choice of D to the change in Z in the same way. In our policy adoption example, this condition states that a movement from z to z', causes all countries to move toward (or against) adoption of the public policy being studied. If some adopt, others do not drop the policy in response to the same change.

More formally, letting $D_i(z)$ be the indicator ($= 1$ if adopted; $= 0$ if not) for adoption of a policy if $Z = z$ for country i, then for any distinct values z and z' Imbens and Angrist (1994) assume:

(IV-3) $D_i(z) \geqslant D_i(z')$ *for all* i, *or* $D_i(z) \leqslant D_i(z')$ *for all* $i = 1, \ldots, I$ (*Monotonicity or uniformity*).

The content in this assumption is not in the order for any person. Rather, the responses have to be uniform across people for a given choice of z and z'. One possibility allowed under (IV-3) is the existence of three values of $z < z' < z''$ such that for all i, $D_i(z) \geqslant D_i(z')$ but $D_i(z') \leqslant D_i(z'')$. The standard usage of the term monotonicity rules out this possibility by requiring that one of the following hold for all i: (a) $z < z'$ componentwise implies $D_i(z) \geqslant D_i(z')$ or (b) $z < z'$ componentwise implies $D_i(z) \leqslant D_i(z')$. Of course, if the $D_i(z)$ are monotonic in Z in the same direction for all i, they are monotonic in the sense of Imbens and Angrist.

For any value of z' in the domain of definition of Z, from (IV-1) and (IV-2) and the definition of $D(z)$, $(Y_0, Y_1, D(z'))$ is independent of Z. For any two values of the instrument $Z = z$ and $Z = z'$, we may write

$$\begin{aligned} &E(Y \mid Z = z) - E(Y \mid Z = z') \\ &\quad = E\big(Y_1 D + Y_0(1 - D) \bigm| Z = z\big) - E\big(Y_1 D + Y_0(1 - D) \bigm| Z = z'\big) \\ &\quad = E\big(Y_0 + D(Y_1 - Y_0) \bigm| Z = z\big) - E\big(Y_0 + D(Y_1 - Y_0) \bigm| Z = z'\big). \end{aligned}$$

From the independence condition (IV-1) and the definition of $D(z)$ and $D(z')$, we may write this expression as $E[(Y_1 - Y_0)(D(z) - D(z'))]$. Using the law of iterated expectations,

$$\begin{aligned} &E(Y \mid Z = z) - E(Y \mid Z = z') \\ &\quad = E\big(Y_1 - Y_0 \bigm| D(z) - D(z') = 1\big) \Pr\big(D(z) - D(z') = 1\big) \\ &\qquad - E\big(Y_1 - Y_0 \bigm| D(z) - D(z') = -1\big) \Pr\big(D(z) - D(z') = -1\big). \end{aligned} \tag{4.5}$$

By the monotonicity condition (IV-3), we eliminate one or the other term in the final expression. Suppose that $\Pr(D(z) - D(z') = -1) = 0$, then

$$\begin{aligned} &E(Y \mid Z = z) - E(Y \mid Z = z') \\ &\quad = E\big(Y_1 - Y_0 \bigm| D(z) - D(z') = 1\big) \Pr\big(D(z) - D(z') = 1\big). \end{aligned}$$

Observe that, by monotonicity, $\Pr(D(z) - D(z') = 1) = \Pr(D = 1 \mid Z = z) - \Pr(D = 1 \mid Z = z')$. For values of z and z' that produce distinct propensity scores $\Pr(D = 1 \mid Z = z)$, using monotonicity once more, we obtain LATE:

$$\begin{aligned} \text{LATE} &= \frac{E(Y \mid Z = z) - E(Y \mid Z = z')}{\Pr(D = 1 \mid Z = z) - \Pr(D = 1 \mid Z = z')} \\ &= E\big(Y_1 - Y_0 \bigm| D(z) - D(z') = 1\big).^{35} \end{aligned} \tag{4.6}$$

This is the mean gain to those induced to switch from "0" to "1" by a change in Z from z' to z.

This is not the mean of $Y_1 - Y_0$ (average treatment effect) unless the Z assume values (z, z') such that $\Pr(D(z) = 1) = 1$ and $\Pr(D(z') = 1) = 0$.[36] It is also not the effect of treatment on the treated $(E(Y_1 - Y_0 \mid D = 1) = E(\beta \mid D = 1))$ unless the analyst has access to one or more values of Z such that $\Pr(D(z) = 1) = 1$.

The LATE parameter is defined by a hypothetical manipulation of instruments. It depends on the particular instrument used.[37] If monotonicity (uniformity) is violated,

[35] $\Pr(D(z) - D(z') = 1) = \Pr(D(z = 1) \wedge D(z' = 0)) = \Pr(D(z) = 1) - \Pr(D(z') = 1)$ from monotonicity.

[36] Such values produce "identification at infinity" or more accurately limit points where $P(z) = 1$ and $P(z') = 0$.

[37] Dependence of the estimands on the choices of IV used to estimate models with essential heterogeneity was first noted in Heckman and Robb (1985a, 1986a).

IV estimates an average response of those induced to switch into the program and those induced to switch out of the program by the change in the instrument because both terms in (4.5) are present.[38]

In an application to wage equations, Card (1999, 2001) interprets the LATE estimator as identifying returns to marginal persons. Heckman (1996) notes that the actual margin of choice selected by the IV estimator is not identified by the instrument. It is unclear as to which segment of the population the return estimated by LATE applies.

If the analyst is interested in knowing the average response $(\bar{\beta})$, the effect of the policy on the outcomes of countries that adopt it $(E(\beta \mid D = 1))$ or the effect of the policy if a particular country adopts it, there is no guarantee that the IV estimator comes any closer to the desired target than the OLS estimator and indeed it may be more biased than OLS. Because different instruments define different parameters, having a wealth of different strong instruments does not improve the precision of the estimate of any particular parameter. This is in stark contrast with the traditional model with $\beta \perp\!\!\!\perp D$. In that case, all valid instruments identify $\bar{\beta}$. The Durbin (1954) – Wu (1973) – Hausman (1978) test for the validity of extra instruments applies to the traditional model. In the more general case with essential heterogeneity, because different instruments estimate different parameters, no clear inference emerges from such specification tests.

When there are more than two distinct values of Z, Imbens and Angrist draw on the analysis of Yitzhaki (1989), which was refined in Yitzhaki (1996) and Yitzhaki and Schechtman (2004), to produce a weighted average of pairwise LATE parameters where the scalars Z are ordered to define the LATE parameter. In this case, IV is a weighted average of LATE parameters with nonnegative weights.[39] Imbens and Angrist generalize this result to the case of vector Z assuming that instruments are monotonic functions of the probability of selection.

Heckman and Vytlacil (1999, 2001b, 2005), Heckman, Urzua and Vytlacil (2006) and Carneiro, Heckman and Vytlacil (2006) generalize the analysis of Imbens and Angrist (1994) in several ways and we report their results in this chapter. Using a choice-theoretic parameter (the marginal treatment effect or MTE) introduced into the literature on selection models by Björklund and Moffitt (1987), they relate the parameters estimated by IV to well formulated choice models. This allows treatment parameters to be defined independent of any values assumed by instruments. It is possible to generate all treatment effects as different weighted averages of the MTE. IV can also be interpreted

[38] Angrist, Imbens and Rubin (1996) consider the case of two way flows for the special case of a scalar instrument when the monotonicity assumption is violated. Their analysis is a version of Yitzhaki's (1989, 1996) analysis, which we summarize in Appendix D. He analyzes the net effect whereas they break the net effect into two components corresponding to the two gross flows that produce the two way flows.

[39] Yitzhaki (1989) shows for a scalar instrument that two stage least squares estimators of Y on $P(Z) = E(D \mid Z)$ identify weighted averages of terms like the second terms in (4.6) with positive weights. See also Yitzhaki (1996) and Yitzhaki and Schechtman (2004). We discuss this work in greater detail in Section 4.3.1, and we derive his weights in Appendix D. The original Yitzhaki (1989) paper is posted at the website of Heckman, Urzua and Vytlacil (2006).

as a weighted average of MTE. Different instruments weight different segments of the MTE differently. Using the nonparametric generalized Roy model, MTE is a limit form of LATE. Using MTE, we overcome a problem that plagues the LATE literature. LATE estimates marginal returns at an unidentified margin (or intervals of margins). We show how to use the MTE to unify diverse instrumental variables estimates and to determine what margins (or intervals of margins) they identify. Instead of reporting a marginal return for unidentified persons, we show how to report marginal returns for all persons identified by their location on the scale of a latent variable that arises from a well defined choice model and is related to the propensity of persons to make the choice being studied. We can interpret the margins of choice identified by various instruments and place diverse instruments on a common interpretive footing.

Heckman and Vytlacil (1999, 2005) establish the central role of the propensity score ($\Pr(D = 1 \mid Z = z) = P(z)$) in both selection and IV models.[40] They show that with vector Z and a scalar instrument $J(Z)$ constructed from vector Z, the weights on LATE and MTE that are implicit in standard IV are not guaranteed to be nonnegative. Thus IV can be negative even though all pairwise LATEs and pointwise MTEs are positive. Thus the treatment effects for any pair of (z, z') can be positive but the IV can be negative. We present examples below. Certain instruments produce positive weights and avoid this particular interpretive problem. Our analysis generalizes the analyses of weights on treatment effects by Yitzhaki and Imbens–Angrist, who analyze a special case where all weights are positive.

We establish the special status of $P(z)$ as an instrument. It always produces non-negative weights for MTE and LATE. It enables analysts to identify MTE or LATE. With knowledge of $P(z)$, and the MTE or LATE, we can decompose any IV estimate into identifiable MTEs (at points) or LATEs (over intervals) and identifiable weights on MTE (or LATE) where the weights can be constructed from data. The ability to decompose IV into interpretable components allows analysts to determine the response to treatment of persons at different levels of unobserved factors that determine treatment status.

We present a simple test for essential heterogeneity (β dependent on D) that allows analysts to determine whether or not they can avoid the complexities of the more general model with heterogeneity in response to treatments. In Section 7, we generalize the analysis of IV in the two-outcome model to a multiple outcome model, analyzing both ordered and unordered choice cases.[41] We also demonstrate the fundamental asymmetry in the recent IV literature for models with heterogeneous outcomes. Responses to treatment are permitted to be heterogeneous in a general way. Responses of choices to instruments are not. When heterogeneity in choice is allowed for in a general way, IV and local IV do not estimate parameters that can be interpreted as weighted averages of MTEs or LATEs. We now turn to an analysis of the two-outcome model.

[40] Rosenbaum and Rubin (1983) establish the control role of the propensity score in matching models.

[41] Angrist and Imbens (1995) consider an ordered choice case with instruments common across all choices. Heckman, Urzua and Vytlacil (2006) consider both common and choice-specific instruments for both ordered and unordered cases.

4.1. IV in choice models

A key contribution of the analysis of Heckman and Vytlacil is to adjoin choice equation (3.3) to the outcome equations (2.1), (3.1) and (3.2). A standard binary threshold cross model for D is $D = \mathbf{1}(D^* \geqslant 0)$, where $\mathbf{1}(\cdot)$ is an indicator ($\mathbf{1}(A) = 1$ if A is true, 0 otherwise). A familiar version of (3.3) sets $\mu_D(Z) = Z\gamma$ and writes

$$D^* = Z\gamma - V, \tag{4.7}$$

where $(V \perp\!\!\!\perp Z) \mid X$. ($V$ is independent of Z given X.) In this notation, the propensity score or choice probability is

$$P(z) = \Pr(D = 1 \mid Z = z) = \Pr(Z\gamma \geqslant V) = F_V(Z\gamma),$$

where F_V is the distribution of V which is assumed to be continuous. In terms of the generalized Roy model where C is the cost of participation in sector 1, $D = \mathbf{1}[Y_1 - Y_0 - C > 0]$. For a separable model in outcomes and in costs,

$$C = \mu_D(W) + U_C,$$

we have $Z = (X, W)$, $\mu_D(Z) = \mu_1(X) - \mu_0(X) - \mu_D(W)$, and $V = -(U_1 - U_0 - U_C)$. In constructing many of our examples, we work with a special version where $U_C = 0$. We call this version the extended Roy model.[42] It is the model used to produce Figure 1. Our analysis, however, applies to more general models, and we also offer examples of generalized Roy models, as we have in Figure 2 and Table 3.

In the case where β (given X) is a constant, under (IV-1) and (IV-2) it is not necessary to specify the choice model to identify β. In a general model with heterogenous responses, the specification of $P(z)$ and its relationship with the instrument play crucial roles. To see this, study the covariance between Z and ηD discussed in the introduction to this section.[43] By the law of iterated expectations, letting $\bar{Z}$ denote the mean of Z,

$$\begin{aligned}
\operatorname{Cov}(Z, \eta D) &= E\big((Z - \bar{Z})D\eta\big) \\
&= E\big((Z - \bar{Z})\eta \bigm| D = 1\big)\Pr(D = 1) \\
&= E\big((Z - \bar{Z})\eta \bigm| Z\gamma > V\big)\Pr(Z\gamma \geqslant V).
\end{aligned}$$

Thus, even if Z and η are independent, they are not independent conditional on $D = \mathbf{1}[Z\gamma \geqslant V]$ if $\eta = (U_1 - U_0)$ is dependent on V (i.e., if the decision maker has partial knowledge of η and acts on it). Selection models allow for this dependence [see Heckman and Robb (1985a, 1986a), Ahn and Powell (1993), and Powell (1994)]. Keeping X implicit, assuming that

$$(U_1, U_0, V) \perp\!\!\!\perp Z \tag{4.8}$$

[42] Recall that the generalized Roy model has $U_C \not\equiv 0$, whereas the extended Roy model sets $U_C = 0$.

[43] Recall that $\eta = U_1 - U_0$.

(alternatively, assuming that $(\varepsilon, \eta) \perp\!\!\!\perp Z$), we obtain

$$\begin{aligned} E(Y \mid D=0, Z=z) &= E(Y_0 \mid D=0, Z=z) \\ &= \alpha + E(U_0 \mid z\gamma < V), \end{aligned}$$

where α and possibly $E(U_0 \mid z\gamma < V)$ depend on X, which can be written as

$$E(Y \mid D=0, Z=z) = \alpha + K_0\big(P(z)\big),$$

where the functional form of K_0 is produced from the distribution of (U_0, V).[44] Focusing on means, the conventional selection approach models the conditional mean dependence between (U_0, U_1) and V.

Similarly,

$$\begin{aligned} E(Y \mid D=1, Z=z) &= E(Y_1 \mid D=1, Z=z) \\ &= \alpha + \bar{\beta} + E(U_1 \mid z\gamma \geqslant V) \\ &= \alpha + \bar{\beta} + K_1\big(P(z)\big), \end{aligned}$$

where α, $\bar{\beta}$ and $K_1(P(z))$ may depend on X. $K_0(P(z))$ and $K_1(P(z))$ are control functions in the sense of Heckman and Robb (1985a, 1986a). The control functions expect out the unobservables θ that give rise to selection bias (see (U-1)). Under standard conditions developed in the literature, analysts can identify $\bar{\beta}$. Powell (1994) discusses semiparametric identification. Because we condition on $Z = z$ (or $P(z)$), correct specification of the Z plays an important role in econometric selection methods. This sensitivity to the full set of instruments in Z appears to be absent from the IV method.

If β is a constant (given X), or if η $(= \beta - \bar{\beta})$ is independent of V, only one instrument from vector Z needs to be used to identify the parameter. Missing or unused instruments play no role in identifying mean responses but may affect the efficiency of the IV estimators. In a model where β is variable and not independent of V, misspecification of Z plays an important role in interpreting what IV estimates analogous to its role in selection models. Misspecification of Z affects both approaches to identification. This is a new phenomenon in models with heterogenous β. We now review results from the recent literature on instrumental variables in the model with essential heterogeneity.

4.2. Instrumental variables and local instrumental variables

In this section, we use Δ^{MTE} defined in Section 3 for a general nonseparable model (3.1)–(3.3) to organize the literature on econometric evaluation estimators. In terms of our simple regression model,

$$\Delta^{\mathrm{MTE}}(x, u_D) = E(\Delta \mid X = x, U_D = u_D)$$

[44] This representation is derived in Heckman (1980), Heckman and Robb (1985a, 1986a), Ahn and Powell (1993) and Powell (1994).

$$= E\big(\beta \mid X = x, V = F_V^{-1}(u_D)\big)$$
$$= \bar{\beta}(x) + E(\eta \mid X = x, V = v),$$

where $v = F_V^{-1}(u_D)$. We assume policy invariance in the sense of Hurwicz for mean parameters (assumption (A-7)). For simplicity, we suppress the a and a' subscripts that indicate specific policies. We focus primarily on instrumental variable estimators and review the method of local instrumental variables. Section 4.1 demonstrated in a simple but familiar case that well established intuitions about instrumental variable identification strategies break down when Δ^{MTE} is nonconstant in u_D given X ($\beta \not\perp\!\!\!\perp D \mid X$). We acquire the probability of selection $P(z)$ as a determinant of the IV covariance relationships.

Two sets of instrumental variable conditions are presented in the current literature for this more general case: those associated with conventional instrumental variable assumptions, which are implied by the assumption of "no selection on heterogenous gains", ($\beta \perp\!\!\!\perp D \mid X$) and those which permit selection on heterogeneous gains. Neither set of assumptions implies the other, nor does either identify the policy relevant treatment effect or other economically interpretable parameters in the general case. Each set of conditions identifies different treatment parameters.

In place of standard instrumental variables methods, Heckman and Vytlacil (1999, 2001b, 2005) advocate a new approach to estimating policy impacts by estimating Δ^{MTE} using local instrumental variables (LIV) to identify all of the treatment parameters from a generator Δ^{MTE} that can be weighted in different ways to answer different policy questions. For certain classes of policy interventions covered by assumption (A-7) and analyzed in Section 6, Δ^{MTE} possesses an invariance property analogous to the invariant parameters of traditional structural econometrics.

4.2.1. *Conditions on the MTE that justify the application of conventional instrumental variables*

In the general case where $\Delta^{\text{MTE}}(x, u_D)$ is nonconstant in u_D ($E(\beta \mid X = x, V = v)$ depends on v), IV does not in general estimate any of the treatment effects defined in Section 3. We consider a scalar instrument $J(Z)$ constructed from Z which may be vector-valued. We sometimes denote $J(Z)$ by J, leaving implicit that J is a function of Z. If Z is a vector, $J(Z)$ can be one coordinate of Z, say Z_1. We develop this particular case in presenting our examples.

The notation is sufficiently general to make $J(Z)$ a general function of Z. The standard conditions $J(Z) \perp\!\!\!\perp (U_0, U_1) \mid X$ and $\text{Cov}(J(Z), D \mid X) \neq 0$ corresponding to (IV-1) and (IV-2), respectively, do not, by themselves, imply that instrumental variables using $J(Z)$ as the instrument will identify conventional or policy relevant treatment effects. When responses to treatment are heterogenous, we must supplement the standard conditions to identify interpretable parameters. To link our analysis to conventional analyses of IV, we continue to invoke familiar-looking representations of additive separability of outcomes in terms of (U_0, U_1) so we invoke (2.2). This is not required. All derivations and results in this subsection hold without assuming additive separability if $\mu_1(x)$ and $\mu_0(x)$ are replaced by $E(Y_1 \mid X = x)$ and $E(Y_0 \mid X = x)$, respectively, and U_1 and U_0 are replaced by $Y_1 - E(Y_1 \mid X)$ and $Y_0 - E(Y_0 \mid X)$, respectively. This highlights the point that all of our analysis of IV is conditional on X and X need not be exogenous with respect to (U_0, U_1) to identify the MTE conditional on X. To simplify the notation, we keep the conditioning on X implicit unless it is useful to break it out separately.

Two distinct sets of instrumental variable conditions in the literature are those due to Heckman and Robb (1985a, 1986a) and Heckman (1997), and those due to Imbens and Angrist (1994) which we previously discussed. We review the conditions of Heckman and Robb (1985a, 1986a) and Heckman (1997) in Appendix L, which is presented in the context of our discussion of matching in Section 8, where we compare IV and matching. In the case where Δ^{MTE} is nonconstant in u_D, standard IV estimates different parameters depending on which assumptions are maintained. We have already shown that when responses to treatment are heterogeneous, and choices are made on the basis of this heterogeneity, standard IV does not identify $\mu_1 - \mu_0 = \bar{\beta}$.

There are two important cases of the variable response model. The first case arises when responses are heterogeneous, but conditional on X, people do not base their participation on these responses. In this case, keeping the conditioning on X implicit,

(C-1) $D \perp\!\!\!\perp \Delta \Rightarrow E(\Delta \mid U_D) = E(\Delta)$, $\Delta^{\text{MTE}}(u_D)$ *is constant in* u_D and $\Delta^{\text{MTE}} = \Delta^{\text{ATE}} = \Delta^{\text{TT}} = \Delta^{\text{LATE}}$, *i.e.*, $E(\beta \mid D = 1) = E(\beta)$, *because* $\beta \perp\!\!\!\perp D$.

In this case, all mean treatment parameters are the same. The second case arises when selection into treatment depends on β:

(C-2) $D \not\perp\!\!\!\perp \Delta$ *and* $E(\Delta \mid U_D) \neq E(\Delta)$ (*i.e.*, $\beta \not\perp\!\!\!\perp D$).

In this case, Δ^{MTE} is nonconstant, and in general, the treatment parameters differ among each other. In this case (IV-1) and (IV-2) for general instruments do not identify $\bar{\beta}$ (as shown in Section 4.1) or $E(\beta \mid D = 1)$.

A sufficient condition that generates (C-1) is the information condition that decisions to participate in the program are not made on the basis of $U_1 - U_0$ $(= \eta)$ (in the notation of Section 4.1):

(I-1) $\Pr(D = 1 \mid Z, U_1 - U_0) = \Pr(D = 1 \mid Z)$
(*i.e.*, $\Pr(D = 1 \mid Z, \beta) = \Pr(D = 1 \mid Z)$).[45]

[45] Given the assumption that $U_1 - U_0$ is independent of Z (given X), (I-1) implies $E(U_1 - U_0 \mid Z, X, D = 1) = E(U_1 - U_0 \mid X)$ so that the weaker mean independence condition is certainly satisfied:

(I-2) $E(U_1 - U_0 \mid Z, X, D = 1) = E(U_1 - U_0 \mid X, D = 1)$,

which is generically necessary and sufficient for linear IV to identify Δ^{TT} and Δ^{ATE}.

Before we investigate what standard instrumental variables estimators identify, we first present the local instrumental variables estimator which directly estimates the MTE. It is a limit form of LATE.

4.2.2. Estimating the MTE using local instrumental variables

Heckman and Vytlacil (1999, 2001b, 2005) develop the local instrumental variable (LIV) estimator to recover Δ^{MTE} pointwise. LIV is the derivative of the conditional expectation of Y with respect to $P(Z) = p$. This is defined as

$$\Delta^{\mathrm{LIV}}(p) \equiv \frac{\partial E(Y \mid P(Z) = p)}{\partial p}. \tag{4.9}$$

It is the population mean response to a policy change embodied in changes in $P(Z)$ analyzed by Björklund and Moffitt (1987). $E(Y \mid P(Z))$ is well defined as a consequence of assumption (A-4), and $E(Y \mid P(Z))$ can be recovered over the support of $P(Z)$.[46] Under our assumptions, LIV identifies MTE at all points of continuity in $P(Z)$ (conditional on X). This expression does not require additive separability of $\mu_1(X, U_1)$ or $\mu_0(X, U_0)$.[47]

Under standard regularity conditions, a variety of nonparametric methods can be used to estimate the derivative of $E(Y \mid P(Z))$ and thus to estimate Δ^{MTE}. With Δ^{MTE} in hand, if the support of the distribution of $P(Z)$ conditional on X is the full unit interval, one can generate all the treatment parameters defined in Section 3 as well as the policy relevant treatment parameter presented in Section 3.2 as weighted versions of Δ^{MTE}. When the support of the distribution of $P(Z)$ conditional on X is not full, it is still possible to identify some parameters. Heckman and Vytlacil (2001b) show that to identify ATE under assumptions (A-1)–(A-5), it is necessary and sufficient that the support of the distribution of $P(Z)$ include 0 and 1. Thus, identification of ATE does not require that the distribution of $P(Z)$ be the full unit interval or that the distribution of $P(Z)$ be continuous. But the support must include $\{0, 1\}$. Sharp bounds on the treatment parameters can be constructed under the same assumptions imposed in this chapter without imposing full support conditions. The resulting bounds are simple and easy to apply

[46] Assumptions (A-1), (A-3) and (A-4) jointly allow one to use Lebesgue's theorem for the derivative of an integral to show that $E(Y \mid P(Z) = p)$ is differentiable in p. Thus we can recover $\frac{\partial}{\partial p} E(Y \mid P(Z) = p)$ for almost all p that are limit points of the support of the distribution of $P(Z)$ (conditional on $X = x$). For example, if the distribution of $P(Z)$ conditional on X has a density with respect to Lebesgue measure, then all points in the support of the distribution of $P(Z)$ are limit points of that support and we can identify $\Delta^{\mathrm{LIV}}(p) = \frac{\partial E(Y|P(Z)=p)}{\partial p}$ for p (almost everywhere).

[47] Note, however, that it does require the assumption of additive separability between U_D and Z in the latent index for selection into treatment. Specifically, for LIV to identify MTE, we require additive separability in the choice equation. See our discussion in Section 4.10.

compared with those presented in the previous literature. We discuss these and other bounds in Section 10.

To establish the relationship between LIV and ordinary IV based on $P(Z)$ and to motivate how LIV identifies Δ^{MTE}, notice that from the definition of Y, the conditional expectation of Y given $P(Z)$ is, recalling that $\Delta = Y_1 - Y_0$,

$$E\big(Y \mid P(Z) = p\big) = E\big(Y_0 \mid P(Z) = p\big) + E\big(\Delta \mid P(Z) = p, D = 1\big)p,$$

where we keep the conditioning on X implicit. Our model and conditional independence assumption (A-1) imply

$$E\big(Y \mid P(Z) = p\big) = E(Y_0) + E(\Delta \mid p \geqslant U_D)p.$$

Applying the IV (Wald) estimator for two different values of $P(Z)$, p and p', for $p \neq p'$, we obtain:

$$\begin{aligned} &\frac{E(Y \mid P(Z) = p) - E(Y \mid P(Z) = p')}{p - p'} \\ &\quad = \Delta^{\text{ATE}} + \frac{E(U_1 - U_0 \mid p \geqslant U_D)p - E(U_1 - U_0 \mid p' \geqslant U_D)p'}{p - p'}, \end{aligned} \tag{4.10}$$

where this particular expression is obtained under the assumption of additive separability in the outcomes.[48,49] Exactly the same equation holds without additive separability if one replaces U_1 and U_0 with $Y_1 - E(Y_1 \mid X)$ and $Y_0 - E(Y_0 \mid X)$.

When $U_1 \equiv U_0$ or $(U_1 - U_0) \perp\!\!\!\perp U_D$ (case (C-1)), IV based on $P(Z)$ estimates Δ^{ATE} because the second term on the right-hand side of the expression (4.10) vanishes. Otherwise, IV estimates a combination of MTE parameters which we analyze further below.

Assuming additive separability of the outcome equations, another representation of $E(Y \mid P(Z) = p)$ reveals the index structure. It writes (keeping the conditioning on X implicit) that

$$\begin{aligned} &E\big(Y \mid P(Z) = p\big) \\ &\quad = E(Y_0) + \Delta^{\text{ATE}} p + \int_0^p E(U_1 - U_0 \mid U_D = u_D)\, du_D. \end{aligned} \tag{4.11}$$

[48] The Wald estimator is IV for two values of the instrument.

[49] Observe that

$$\begin{aligned} E\big(Y \mid P(z) = p\big) &= E\big(Y_0 + D(Y_1 - Y_0) \mid P(z) = p\big) \\ &= \mu_0 + E(Y_1 - Y_0 \mid P(z) = p, D = 1)\Pr(D = 1 \mid Z) \\ &= \mu_0 + (\mu_1 - \mu_0)p + E(U_1 - U_0 \mid p \geqslant U_D)p. \end{aligned}$$

We can differentiate with respect to p and use LIV to identify Δ^{MTE}:

$$\Delta^{\text{MTE}}(p) = \frac{\partial E(Y \mid P(Z) = p)}{\partial p} = \Delta^{\text{ATE}} + E(U_1 - U_0 \mid U_D = p).^{50}$$

Notice that IV estimates Δ^{ATE} when $E(Y \mid P(Z) = p)$ is a linear function of p so the third term on the right-hand side of (4.11) vanishes. Thus a test of the linearity of $E(Y \mid P(Z) = p)$ in p is a test of the validity of linear IV for Δ^{ATE}, i.e., it is a test of whether or not the data are consistent with a correlated random coefficient model ($\beta \not\perp\!\!\!\perp D$). The nonlinearity of $E(Y \mid P(Z) = p)$ in p provides a way to distinguish whether case (C-1) or case (C-2) describes the data. It is also a test of whether or not agents can at least partially anticipate future unobserved (by the econometrician) gains (the $Y_1 - Y_0$ given X) at the time they make their participation decisions. The levels and derivatives of $E(Y \mid P(Z) = p)$ and standard errors can be estimated using a variety of semiparametric methods. Heckman, Urzua and Vytlacil (2006) present an algorithm for estimating Δ^{MTE} using local linear regression.[51]

This analysis generalizes to the nonseparable outcomes case. We use separability in outcomes only to simplify the exposition and link to more traditional models. In particular, exactly the same expression holds with exactly the same derivation for the nonseparable case if we replace U_1 and U_0 with $Y_1 - E(Y_1 \mid X)$ and $Y_0 - E(Y_0 \mid X)$, respectively. This simple test for the absence of general heterogeneity based on linearity of $E(Y \mid Z)$ in $P(Z)$ applies to the case of LATE for any pair of instruments. An equivalent way is to check that all pairwise LATEs are the same over the sample support of Z.[52]

Figure 3A plots two cases of $E(Y \mid P(Z) = p)$ based on the generalized Roy model used to generate the example in Figures 2A and 2B. Recall that in this model, there are unobserved components of cost. When Δ^{MTE} $(= E(\beta \mid X = x, V = v))$ does not depend on u_D (or v) the expectation is a straight line. This is case (C-1). Figure 3B plots the derivatives of the two curves in Figure 3A. When Δ^{MTE} depends on u_D (or v) (case (C-2)), people sort into the program being studied positively on the basis of gains from the program, and one obtains the curved line depicted in Figure 3A.

[50] Making the conditioning on X explicit, we obtain that $E(Y \mid X = x, P(Z) = p) = E(Y_0 \mid X = x) + \Delta^{\text{ATE}}(x)p + \int_0^p E(U_1 - U_0 \mid X = x, U_D = u_D)\,du_D$, with derivative with respect to p given by $\Delta^{\text{MTE}}(x, p)$.

[51] Thus, one can apply any one of the large number of available tests for a parametric null versus a nonparametric alternative [see, e.g., Ellison and Ellison (1999), Zheng (1996)]. With regressors, the null is nonparametric leaving $E(Y \mid X = x, P(Z) = p)$ unspecified except for restrictions on the partial derivatives with respect to p. In this case, the formal test is that of a nonparametric null versus a nonparametric alternative, and a formal test of the null hypothesis can be implemented using the methodology of Chen and Fan (1999).

[52] Note that it is possible that $E(Y \mid Z)$ is linear in $P(Z)$ only over certain intervals of U_D, so there can be local dependence and local independence of (U_0, U_1, U_D).

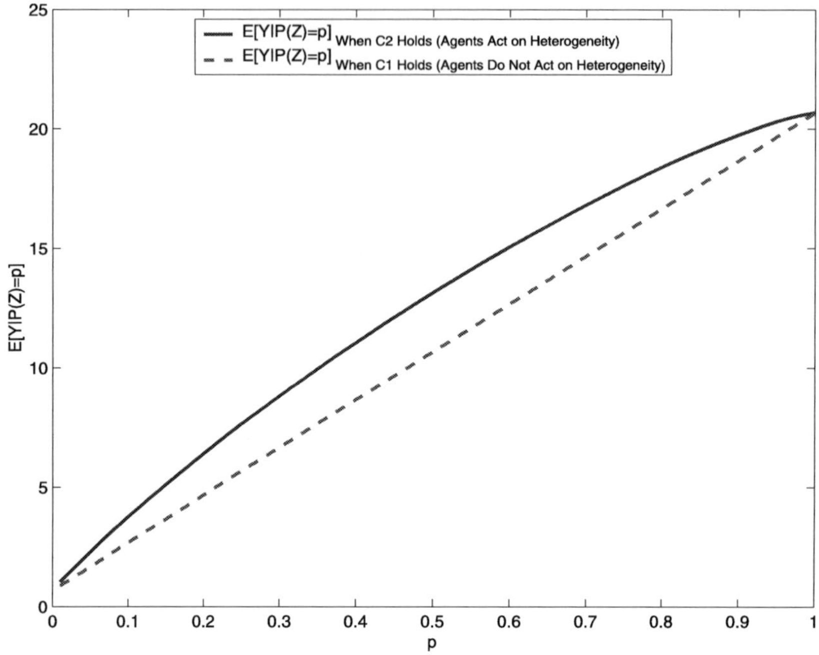

Figure 3A. Plot of the $E(Y \mid P(Z) = p)$. *Source*: Heckman and Vytlacil (2005).

4.3. What does linear IV estimate?

It is instructive to determine what linear IV estimates when Δ^{MTE} is nonconstant and conditions (A-1)–(A-5) hold. We analyze the general nonseparable case. We consider instrumental variables conditional on $X = x$ using a general function of Z as an instrument. We then specialize our result using $P(Z)$ as the instrument. As before, let $J(Z)$ be any function of Z such that $\operatorname{Cov}(J(Z), D) \neq 0$. Define the IV estimator:

$$\beta_{\text{IV}}(J) \equiv \frac{\operatorname{Cov}(J(Z), Y)}{\operatorname{Cov}(J(Z), D)},$$

where to simplify the notation we keep the conditioning on X implicit. Appendix D derives a representation of this expression in terms of weighted averages of the MTE displayed in Table 2B. We exposit this expression in this section.

In Appendix D, we establish that

$$\begin{aligned}
&\operatorname{Cov}\bigl(J(Z), Y\bigr) \\
&\quad = \int_0^1 \Delta^{\text{MTE}}(u_D) E\bigl(J(Z) - E\bigl(J(Z)\bigr) \mid P(Z) \geqslant u_D\bigr) \Pr\bigl(P(Z) \geqslant u_D\bigr)\, du_D.
\end{aligned} \tag{4.12}$$

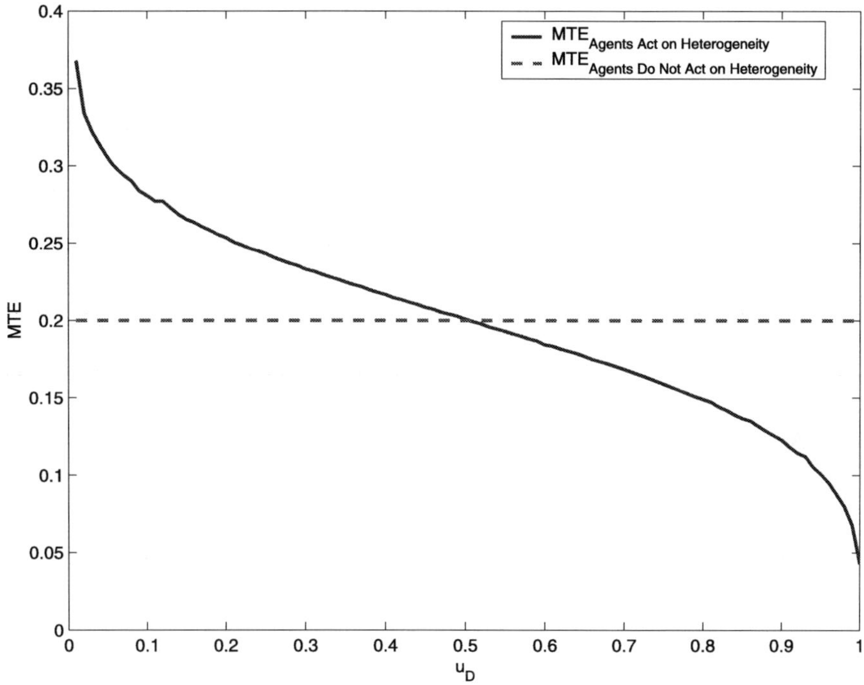

Figure 3B. Plot of the identified marginal treatment effect from Figure 3A (the derivative). *Source*: Heckman and Vytlacil (2005). *Note*: Parameters for the general heterogeneous case are the same as those used in Figures 2A and 2B. For the homogeneous case we impose $U_1 = U_0$ ($\sigma_1 = \sigma_2 = 0.012$).

By the law of iterated expectations, $\mathrm{Cov}(J(Z), D) = \mathrm{Cov}(J(Z), P(Z))$. Thus

$$\beta_{\mathrm{IV}}(J) = \int_0^1 \Delta^{\mathrm{MTE}}(u_D)\omega_{\mathrm{IV}}(u_D \mid J)\, du_D,$$

where

$$\omega_{\mathrm{IV}}(u_D \mid J) = \frac{E(J(Z) - E(J(Z)) \mid P(Z) \geqslant u_D)\Pr(P(Z) \geqslant u_D)}{\mathrm{Cov}(J(Z), P(Z))}, \tag{4.13}$$

assuming the standard rank condition (IV-2) holds: $\mathrm{Cov}(J(Z), P(Z)) \neq 0$. The weights integrate to one,

$$\int_0^1 \omega_{\mathrm{IV}}(u_D \mid J)\, du_D = 1,$$

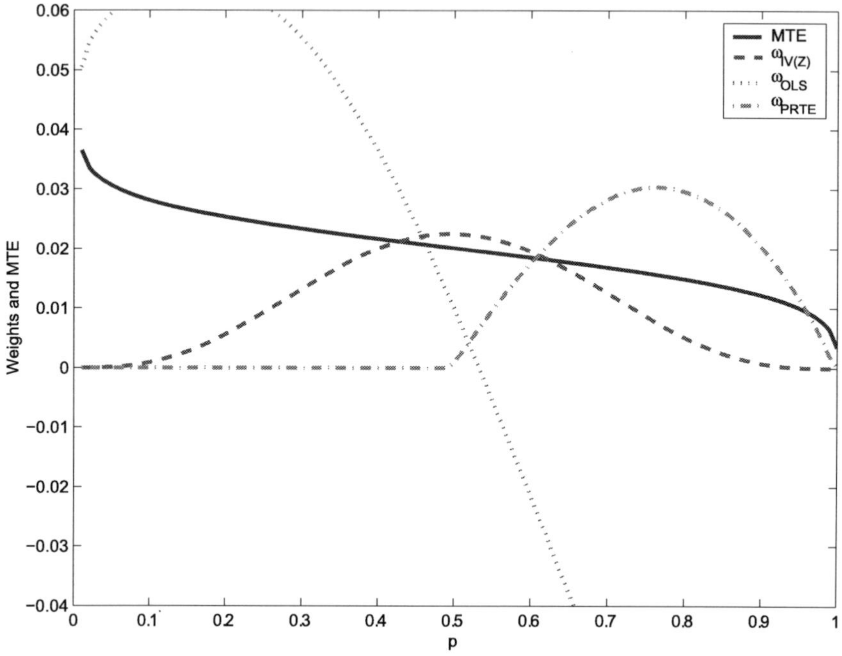

Figure 4A. MTE vs. linear instrumental variables, ordinary least squares, and policy relevant treatment effect weights: when $P(Z)$ is the instrument. The policy is given at the base of Table 3. The model parameters are given at the base of Figure 2. *Source*: Heckman and Vytlacil (2005).

and can be constructed from the data on $P(Z)$, $J(Z)$ and D. Assumptions about the properties of the weights are testable.[53]

We discuss additional properties of the weights for the special case where the propensity score is the instrument $J(Z) = P(Z)$. We then analyze the properties of the weights for a general instrument $J(Z)$. When $J(Z) = P(Z)$, Equation (4.13) specializes to

$$\omega_{\mathrm{IV}}\big(u_D \mid P(Z)\big) = \frac{[E(P(Z) \mid P(Z) \geqslant u_D) - E(P(Z))]\Pr(P(Z) \geqslant u_D)}{\operatorname{Var}(P(Z))}.$$

Figure 4A plots the IV weight for $J(Z) = P(Z)$ and the MTE for our generalized Roy model example developed in Figures 2 and 3 and Table 3. The weights are positive and peak at the mean of P. Figure 4A also plots the OLS weight given in Table 2 and the weight for a policy exercise described below Table 3 and discussed further below.

53 Expressions for IV and OLS as weighted averages of marginal response functions, and the properties and construction of the weights, were first derived by Yitzhaki in 1989 in a paper that was eventually published in 1996 [see Yitzhaki (1996)]. Under monotonicity (IV-3), his expression is a weighted average of MTEs or LATEs. We present Yitzhaki's derivation in Appendix D.

Let p^{Min} and p^{Max} denote the minimum and maximum points in the support of the distribution of $P(Z)$ (conditional on $X = x$). The weights on MTE when $P(Z)$ is the instrument are nonnegative for all evaluation points, are strictly positive for $u_D \in (p^{\text{Min}}, p^{\text{Max}})$ and are zero for $u_D < p^{\text{Min}}$ and for $u_D > p^{\text{Max}}$.[54]

The properties of the weights for general $J(Z)$ depend on the conditional relationship between $J(Z)$ and $P(Z)$. From the general expression for (4.13), it is clear that the IV estimator with $J(Z)$ as an instrument satisfies the following properties:

(i) Two instruments J and J^* weight MTE equally at all values of u_D if and only if they have the same (centered) conditional expectation of J given P, i.e., $E(J \mid P(Z) = p) - E(J) = E(J^* \mid P(Z) = p) - E(J^*)$ for all p in the support of the distribution of $P(Z)$.

(ii) The support of $\omega_{\text{IV}}(u_D \mid J)$ is contained in $[p^{\text{Min}}, p^{\text{Max}}]$ the minimum and maximum value of p in the population (given x). Therefore $\omega_{\text{IV}}(t \mid J) = 0$ for $t < p^{\text{Min}}$ and for $t > p^{\text{Max}}$. Using any instrument other than $P(Z)$ leads to nonzero weights only on a subset of $[p^{\text{Min}}, p^{\text{Max}}]$, and using the propensity score as an instrument leads to nonnegative weights on a larger range of evaluation points than using any other instrument.

(iii) $\omega_{\text{IV}}(u_D \mid J)$ is nonnegative for all u_D if $E(J \mid P(Z) \geqslant p)$ is weakly monotonic in p. Using J as an instrument yields nonnegative weights on Δ^{MTE} if $E(J \mid P(Z) \geqslant p)$ is weakly monotonic in p. This condition is satisfied when $J(Z) = P(Z)$. More generally, if J is a monotonic function of $P(Z)$, then using J as the instrument will lead to nonnegative weights on Δ^{MTE}. There is no guarantee that the weights for a general $J(Z)$ will be nonnegative for all u_D, although the weights integrate to unity and thus must be positive over some range of evaluation points. We produce examples below where the instrument leads to negative weights for some evaluation points. Imbens and Angrist (1994) assume that $J(Z)$ is monotonic in $P(Z)$ and thus produce positive weights. Our analysis is more general.

[54] For u_D evaluation points between p^{Min} and p^{Max}, $u_D \in (p^{\text{Min}}, p^{\text{Max}})$, we have that

$$E\big(P(Z) \mid P(Z) \geqslant u_D\big) > E\big(P(Z)\big) \quad \text{and} \quad \Pr\big(P(Z) \geqslant u_D\big) > 0,$$

so that $\omega_{\text{IV}}(u_D \mid P(Z)) > 0$ for any $u_D \in (p^{\text{Min}}, p^{\text{Max}})$. For $u_D < p^{\text{Min}}$,

$$E\big(P(Z) \mid P(Z) \geqslant u_D\big) = E\big(P(Z)\big).$$

For any $u_D > p^{\text{Max}}$, $\Pr(P(Z) \geqslant u_D) = 0$. Thus, $\omega_{\text{IV}}(u_D \mid P(Z)) = 0$ for any $u_D < p^{\text{Min}}$ and for any $u_D > p^{\text{Max}}$. $\omega_{\text{IV}}(u_D \mid P(Z))$ is strictly positive for $u_D \in (p^{\text{Min}}, p^{\text{Max}})$, and is zero for all $u_D < p^{\text{Min}}$ and all $u_D > p^{\text{Max}}$. Whether the weights are nonzero at the endpoints depends on the distribution of $P(Z)$. However, since the weights are defined for integration with respect to Lebesgue measure, the value taken by the weights at p^{Min} and p^{Max} does not affect the value of the integral.

The propensity score plays a central role in determining the properties of the weights. The IV weighting formula critically depends on the conditional mean dependence between instrument $J(Z)$ and the propensity score.

The interpretation placed on the IV estimand depends on the specification of $P(Z)$ even if only Z_1 (e.g., the first coordinate of Z) is used as the instrument. This drives home the point about the difference between IV in the traditional model and IV in the more general model with heterogeneous responses analyzed in this chapter. In the traditional model, the choice of any valid instrument and the specification of instruments in $P(Z)$ not used to construct a particular IV estimator does not affect the IV estimand. In the more general model, these choices matter. Two economists, using the same $J(Z) = Z_1$, will obtain the same IV point estimate, but the interpretation placed on that estimate will depend on the specification of the Z in $P(Z)$ even if $P(Z)$ is not used as an instrument. The weights can be positive for one instrument and negative for another. We show some examples after developing the properties of the IV weights.

4.3.1. Further properties of the IV weights

Expression (4.13) for the weights does not impose any support conditions on the distribution of $P(Z)$, and thus does not require either that $P(Z)$ be continuous or discrete. To demonstrate this, consider two extreme special cases: (i) when $P(Z)$ is a continuous random variable, and (ii) when $P(Z)$ is a discrete random variable.

To simplify the exposition, initially assume that $J(Z)$ and $P(Z)$ are jointly continuous random variables. This assumption plays no essential role in any of the results of this chapter and we develop the discrete case after developing the continuous case. The weights defined in Equation (4.13) can be written as

$$\omega_{\text{IV}}(u_D) = \frac{\int (j - E(J(Z))) \int_{u_D}^{1} f_{J,P}(j,t)\, dt\, dj}{\operatorname{Cov}(J(Z), D)}, \tag{4.14}$$

where $f_{J,P}$ is the joint density of $J(Z)$ and $P(Z)$ and we implicitly condition on X. The weights can be negative or positive. Observe that $\omega(0) = 0$ and $\omega(1) = 0$. The weights integrate to 1 because as shown in Appendix D,

$$\iint \big(j - E\big(J(Z)\big)\big) \int_{u_D}^{1} f_{J,P}(j,t)\, dt\, dj\, du_D = \operatorname{Cov}\big(J(Z), D\big),$$

so even if the weight is negative over some intervals, it must be positive over other intervals. Observe that when there is one instrument (Z is a scalar), and assumptions (A-1)–(A-5) are satisfied, the weights are always positive provided $J(Z)$ is a monotonic function of the scalar Z. In this case, which is covered by (4.13) but excluded in deriving (4.14), $J(Z)$ and $P(Z)$ have the same distribution and $f_{J,P}(j,t)$ collapses to a univariate distribution. The possibility of negative weights arises when $J(Z)$ is not a monotonic function of $P(Z)$. It also arises when there are two or more instruments, and the analyst computes estimates with only one instrument or a combination of the Z instruments that is not a monotonic function of $P(Z)$ so that $J(Z)$ and $P(Z)$ are not perfectly dependent. If the instrument is $P(Z)$ (so $J(Z) = P(Z)$) then the weights are everywhere nonnegative because from (4.14), $E(P(Z) \mid P(Z) > u_D) - E(P(Z)) \geqslant 0$. In this case, the density of $(P(Z), J(Z))$ collapses to the density of $P(Z)$. For any scalar Z, we can define $J(Z)$ and $P(Z)$ so that they are perfectly dependent, provided that $J(Z)$ and $P(Z)$ are monotonic in Z. Generally, the weight (4.13) is positive if $E(J(Z) \mid P(Z) > u_D)$ is weakly monotonic in u_D. Nonmonotonicity of this expression can produce negative weights.[55]

4.3.2. *Constructing the weights from data*

Observe that the weights can be constructed from data on (J, P, D). Data on $(J(Z), P(Z))$ pairs and $(J(Z), D)$ pairs (for each X value) are all that is required. We can use a smoothed sample frequency to estimate the joint density $f_{J,P}$. Thus, given our maintained assumptions, any property of the weight, including its positivity at any point (x, u_D), can be examined with data. We present examples of this approach below.

As is evident from Tables 2A and 2B and Figures 2A and 2B, the weights on $\Delta^{\text{MTE}}(u_D)$ generating Δ^{IV} are different from the weights on $\Delta^{\text{MTE}}(u_D)$ that generate the average treatment effect which is widely regarded as an important policy parameter [see, e.g., Imbens (2004)] or from the weights associated with the policy relevant treatment parameter which answers well-posed policy questions [Heckman and Vytlacil (2001b, 2005)]. It is not obvious why the weighted average of $\Delta^{\text{MTE}}(u_D)$ produced by IV is of any economic interest. Since the weights can be negative for some values of u_D, $\Delta^{\text{MTE}}(u_D)$ can be positive everywhere in u_D but IV can be negative. Thus, IV may not estimate a treatment effect for any person. We present some examples of IV models with negative weights below. A basic question is why estimate the model with IV at all given the lack of any clear economic interpretation of the IV estimator in the general case.

4.3.3. *Discrete instruments*

The representation (4.13) can be specialized to cover discrete instruments, $J(Z)$. Consider the case where the distribution of $P(Z)$ (conditional on X) is discrete. The support of the distribution of $P(Z)$ contains a finite number of values $p_1 < p_2 < \cdots < p_K$ and the support of the instrument $J(Z)$ is also discrete taking I distinct values where I and K may be distinct. $E(J(Z) \mid P(Z) \geqslant u_D)$ is constant in u_D, for u_D within any $(p_\ell, p_{\ell+1})$ interval, and $\Pr(P(Z) \geqslant u_D)$ is constant in u_D, for u_D within any $(p_\ell, p_{\ell+1})$ interval, and thus $\omega^J_{\text{IV}}(u_D)$ is constant in u_D over any $(p_\ell, p_{\ell+1})$ interval. Let λ_ℓ denote

[55] If it is weakly monotonically increasing, the claim is evident from (4.13). If it is decreasing, the sign of the numerator and the denominator are both negative so the weight is nonnegative.

the weight on LATE for the interval $(\ell, \ell+1)$. In this notation,

$$\begin{aligned}\Delta_J^{\text{IV}} &= \int E(Y_1 - Y_0 \mid U_D = u_D)\omega_{\text{IV}}^J(u_D)\,du_D \\ &= \sum_{\ell=1}^{K-1} \lambda_\ell \int_{p_\ell}^{p_{\ell+1}} E(Y_1 - Y_0 \mid U_D = u_D)\frac{1}{(p_{\ell+1} - p_\ell)}\,du_D \\ &= \sum_{\ell=1}^{K-1} \Delta^{\text{LATE}}(p_\ell, p_{\ell+1})\lambda_\ell. \end{aligned} \tag{4.15}$$

Let j_i be the ith smallest value of the support of $J(Z)$. The discrete version of Equation (4.13) is

$$\lambda_\ell = \frac{\sum_{i=1}^{I}(j_i - E(J(Z)))\sum_{t>\ell}^{K}(f(j_i, p_t))}{\text{Cov}(J(Z), D)}(p_{\ell+1} - p_\ell), \tag{4.16}$$

where f is the probability frequency of (j_i, p_t): the probability that $J(Z) = j_i$ and $P(Z) = p_t$. There is no presumption that high values of $J(Z)$ are associated with high values of $P(Z)$. $J(Z)$ can be one coordinate of Z that may be positively or negatively dependent on $P(Z)$, which depends on the full vector. In the case of scalar Z, as long as $J(Z)$ and $P(Z)$ are monotonic in Z there is perfect dependence between $J(Z)$ and $P(Z)$. In this case, the joint probability density collapses to a univariate density and the weights have to be positive, exactly as in the case for continuous instruments previously discussed. Our expression for the weight on LATE generalizes the expression presented by Imbens and Angrist (1994) who in their analysis of the case of vector Z only consider the case where $J(Z)$ and $P(Z)$ are perfectly dependent because $J(Z)$ is a monotonic function of $P(Z)$.[56] More generally, the weights can be positive or negative for any ℓ but they must sum to 1 over all ℓ.

Monotonicity or uniformity is a property needed with just two values of Z, $Z = z_1$ and $Z = z_2$, to guarantee that IV estimates a treatment effect. With more than two values of Z, we need to weight the LATEs and MTEs. If the instrument $J(Z)$ shifts $P(Z)$ in the same way for everyone, it shifts D in the same way for everyone since $D = \mathbf{1}[P(Z) \geqslant U_D]$ and Z is independent of U_D. If $J(Z)$ is not monotonic in $P(Z)$, it may shift $P(Z)$ in different ways for different people. Negative weights are a tip-off of two-way flows. We present examples below.

4.3.4. *Identifying margins of choice associated with each instrument and unifying diverse instruments within a common framework*

We have just established that different instruments weight the MTE differently. Using $P(Z)$ in the local IV estimator, we can identify the MTE. We can construct the weights

[56] In their case, $I = K$ and $f(j_i, p_t) = 0$, $\forall i \neq t$.

associated with each instrument from the joint distribution of $(J(Z), P(Z))$ given X. By plotting the weights for each instrument, we can determine the margins identified by the different instruments. Using $P(Z)$ as the instrument enables us to extend the support associated with any single instrument, and to determine which segment of the MTE is identified by any particular instrument. As before, we keep conditioning on X implicit.

4.3.5. Yitzhaki's derivation of the weights

An alternative and in some ways more illuminating way to derive the weights used in IV is to follow Yitzhaki (1989, 1996) and Yitzhaki and Schechtman (2004) who prove for a general regression function $E(Y \mid P(Z) = p)$ that a linear regression of Y on P estimates

$$\beta_{Y,P} = \int_0^1 \left[\frac{\partial E(Y \mid P(Z) = p)}{\partial p} \right] \omega(p)\, dp,$$

where

$$\omega(p) = \frac{\int_p^1 (t - E(P))\, dF_P(t)}{\operatorname{Var}(P)},$$

which is exactly the weight (4.13) when P is the instrument. Thus we can interpret (4.13) as the weight on $\frac{\partial E(Y \mid P(Z)=p)}{\partial p}$ when two-stage least squares (2SLS) based on $P(Z)$ is used to estimate the "causal effect" of D on Y. Under uniformity,

$$\left. \frac{\partial E(Y \mid P(Z) = p)}{\partial p} \right|_{p=u_D} = E(Y_1 - Y_0 \mid U_D = u_D) = \Delta^{\text{MTE}}(u_D).$$[57]

Our analysis is more general than that of Yitzhaki (1989) or Imbens and Angrist (1994) because we allow for instruments that are not monotonic functions of $P(Z)$, whereas the Yitzhaki weighting formula only applies to instruments that are monotonic functions of $P(Z)$.[58] The analysis of Yitzhaki (1989) is more general than that of Imbens and Angrist (1994), because he does not impose uniformity (monotonicity). We present some further examples of these weights after discussing the role of $P(Z)$ and the role of monotonicity and uniformity. We present Yitzhaki's Theorem and the relationship of our analysis to Yitzhaki's analysis in Appendices D.1 and D.2.

[57] Yitzhaki's weights are used by Angrist and Imbens (1995) to interpret what 2SLS estimates in the model of Equation (4.1) with heterogeneous β. Yitzhaki (1989) derives the finite sample weights used by Imbens and Angrist. See the refinement in Yitzhaki and Schechtman (2004).

[58] Heckman and Vytlacil (2001b) generalize the Yitzhaki analysis of the IV weights by relaxing separability (monotonicity).

4.4. The central role of the propensity score

Observe that both (4.13) and (4.14) (and their counterparts for LATE (4.15) and (4.16)) contain expressions involving the propensity score $P(Z)$, the probability of selection into treatment. Under our assumptions, it is a monotonic function of the mean utility of treatment, $\mu_D(Z)$. The propensity score plays a central role in selection models as a determinant of control functions in selection models [Heckman and Robb (1985a, 1986a)] as noted in Section 4.1. In matching models, it provides a computationally convenient way to condition on Z [see, e.g., Rosenbaum and Rubin (1983), Heckman and Navarro (2004), and the discussion in Section 8]. For the IV weight to be correctly constructed and interpreted, we need to know the correct model for $P(Z)$, i.e., we need to know exactly which Z determine $P(Z)$. As previously noted, this feature is not required in the traditional model for instrumental variables based on response heterogeneity. In that simpler framework, any instrument will identify $\mu_1(X)-\mu_0(X)$ and the choice of a particular instrument affects efficiency but not identifiability. One can be casual about the choice model in the traditional setup, but not in the model of choice of treatment with essential heterogeneity. Thus, unlike the application of IV to traditional models under condition (C-1), IV applied in the model of essential heterogeneity depends on (a) the choice of the instrument $J(Z)$, (b) its dependence with $P(Z)$, the true propensity score or choice probability, and (c) the specification of the propensity score (i.e., what variables go into Z). Using the propensity score one can identify LIV and LATE and the marginal returns at values of the unobserved U_D. From the MTE identified by $P(Z)$ and the weights that can be constructed from the joint distribution of $(J(Z), P(Z))$ given X, we can identify the segment of the MTE identified by any IV.

4.5. Monotonicity, uniformity and conditional instruments

Monotonicity, or uniformity condition (IV-3), is a condition on a collection of counterfactuals for each person and hence is not testable, since we know only one element of the collection for any person. It rules out general heterogeneous responses to treatment choices in response to changes in vector Z. The recent literature on instrumental variables with heterogeneous responses is thus asymmetric. Outcome equations can be heterogeneous in a general way while choice equations cannot be. If $\mu_D(Z) = Z\gamma$, where γ is a common coefficient shared by everyone, the choice model satisfies the uniformity property. On the other hand, if γ is a random coefficient (i.e., has a nondegenerate distribution) that can take both negative and positive values, and there are two or more variables in Z with nondegenerate γ coefficients, uniformity can be violated. Different people can respond to changes in Z differently, so there can be nonuniformity. The uniformity condition can be violated even when all components of γ are of the same sign if Z is a vector and γ is a nondegenerate random variable.[59]

[59] Thus if $\gamma > 0$ for each component and some components of Z are positive and others are negative, changes from z' to z can increase γZ for some and decrease γZ for others since the γ are different among persons.

Changing one coordinate of Z, holding the other coordinates at different values across people is *not* the experiment that defines monotonicity or uniformity. Changing one component of Z, allowing the other coordinates of Z to vary across people, does not necessarily produce uniform flows toward or against participation in the treatment status. For example, let $\mu_D(z) = \gamma_0 + \gamma_1 z_1 + \gamma_2 z_2 + \gamma_3 z_1 z_2$, where γ_0, γ_1, γ_2 and γ_3 are constants, and consider changing z_1 from a common base state while holding z_2 fixed at different values across people. If $\gamma_3 < 0$, then $\mu_D(z)$ does not necessarily satisfy the uniformity condition. If we move (z_1, z_2) as a pair from the same base values to the same destination values z', uniformity is satisfied even if $\gamma_3 < 0$, although $\mu_D(z)$ is not a monotonic function of z.[60]

Positive weights and uniformity are distinct issues.[61] Under uniformity, and assumptions (A-1)–(A-5), the weights on MTE for any particular instrument may be positive or negative. The weights for MTE using $P(Z)$ must be positive as we have shown so the propensity score has a special status as an instrument. Negative weights associated with the use of $J(Z)$ as an instrument do not necessarily imply failure of uniformity in Z. Even if uniformity is satisfied for Z, it is not necessarily satisfied for $J(Z)$. Condition (IV-3) is an assumption about a vector. Fixing one combination of Z (when J is a function of Z) or one coordinate of Z does not guarantee uniformity in J even if there is uniformity in Z. The flow created by changing one coordinate of Z can be reversed by the flow created by the other components of Z if there is negative dependence among components even if *ceteris paribus* all components of Z affect D in the same direction. We present some examples below.

The issues of positive weights and the existence of one way flows in response to an intervention are conceptually distinct. Even with two values for a scalar Z, flows may be two way [see Equation (4.5)]. If we satisfy (IV-3) for a vector, so uniformity applies, weights for a particular instrument may be negative for certain intervals of U_D (i.e., for some of the LATE parameters).

[60] Associated with $Z = z$ is the counterfactual random variable $D(z)$. Associated with the scalar random variable $J(Z)$ constructed from Z is a counterfactual random variable $D(j(z))$ which is in general different from $D(z)$. The random variable $D(z)$ is constructed from (3.3) using $\mathbf{1}[\mu_D(z) \geqslant V]$. In this expression, V assumes individual specific values which remain fixed as we set different z values. From (A-1), $\Pr(D(z) = 1) = \Pr(D = 1 \mid Z = z)$. The random variable $D(j)$ is defined by the following thought experiment. For each possible realization j of $J(Z)$, define $D(j)$ by setting $D(j) = D(Z(j))$ where $Z(j)$ is a random draw from the distribution of Z conditional on $J(Z) = j$. Set $D(j)$ equal to the choice that would be made given that draw of $Z(j)$. Thus $D(j)$ is a function of $(Z(j), u_D)$. As long as we draw $Z(j)$ randomly (so independent of Z), we have that $(Z(j), U_D) \perp\!\!\!\perp Z$ so $D(j) \perp\!\!\!\perp Z$. There are other possible constructions of the counterfactual $D(j)$ since there are different possible distributions from which Z can be drawn, apart from the actual distribution of Z. The advantage of this construction is that it equates the counterfactual probability that $D(j) = 1$ given $J(Z) = j$ with the population probability. If the Z were uncertain to the agent, this would be a rational expectations assumption. At their website, Heckman, Urzua and Vytlacil (2006) discuss this assumption further.

[61] When they analyze the vector case, Imbens and Angrist (1994) analyze instruments that are monotonic functions of $P(Z)$. Our analysis is more general and recognizes that, in the vector case, IV weights may be negative or positive.

If we condition on $Z_2 = z_2, \ldots, Z_K = z_K$ using Z_1 as an instrument, then a uniform flow condition is satisfied. We call this *conditional uniformity*. By conditioning, we effectively convert the problem back to that of a scalar instrument where the weights must be positive. If uniformity holds for Z_1, fixing the other Z at common values, then one-dimensional LATE/MTE analysis applies. Clearly, the weights have to be defined conditionally.

The concept of conditioning on other instruments to produce positive weights for the selected instrument is a new idea, not yet appreciated in the empirical IV literature and has no counterpart in the traditional IV model. In the conventional model, the choice of a valid instrument affects efficiency but not the definition of the parameters as it does in the more general case.[62]

In summary, nothing in the economics of choice guarantees that if Z is changed from z to z', that people respond in the same direction to the change. See the general expression (4.5). The condition that people respond to choices in the same direction for the same change in Z does not imply that $D(z)$ is monotonic in z for any person in the usual mathematical usage of the term monotonicity. If $D(z)$ is monotonic in the usual usage of this term and responses are in the same direction for all people, then "monotonicity" or better "uniformity" condition (IV-3) would be satisfied.

If responses to a common change of Z are heterogenous in a general way, we obtain (4.5) as the general case. Vytlacil's 2002 Theorem breaks down and IV cannot be expressed in terms of a weighted average of MTE terms. Nonetheless, Yitzhaki's characterization of IV, derived in Appendix D, remains valid and the weights on $\frac{\partial E(Y|P=p)}{\partial p}$ are positive and of the same form as the weights obtained for MTE (or LATE) when the monotonicity condition holds. IV can still be written as a weighted average of LIV terms, even though LIV does not identify the MTE.

4.6. *Treatment effects vs. policy effects*

Even if uniformity condition (IV-3) fails, IV may answer relevant policy questions. By Yitzhaki's analysis, summarized in Section 4.3.5, IV or 2SLS estimates a weighted average of marginal responses which may be pointwise positive or negative. Policies may induce some people to switch into and others to switch out of choices, as is evident from Equation (4.5). These net effects are of interest in many policy analyses. Thus, subsidized housing in a region supported by higher taxes may attract some to migrate to the region and cause others to leave. The net effect from the policy is all that is required to perform cost benefit calculations of the policy on outcomes. If the housing subsidy is the instrument, and the net effect of the subsidy is the parameter of interest, the issue of monotonicity is a red herring. If the subsidy is exogenously imposed, IV estimates the

[62] In the conventional model, with homogenous responses, a linear probability approximation to $P(Z)$ used as an instrument would identify the same parameter as $P(Z)$. In the general model, replacing $P(Z)$ by a linear probability approximation of it (e.g., $E(D \mid Z) = \pi Z = J(Z)$) is not guaranteed to produce positive weights for $\Delta^{\text{MTE}}(x, u_D)$ or $\Delta^{\text{LATE}}(x, u'_D, u_D)$, or to replicate the weights based on the correctly specified $P(Z)$.

net effect of the policy on mean outcomes. Only if the effect of migration on outcomes induced by the subsidy on outcomes is the question of interest, and not the effect of the subsidy, does uniformity emerge as an interesting condition.

4.7. *Some examples of weights in the generalized Roy model and the extended Roy model*

It is useful to develop intuition about the properties of the IV estimator and the structure of the weights for two prototypical choice models. We develop the weights for a generalized Roy model where unobserved cost components are present and an extended Roy model where cost components are observed but there are no unobserved cost components. The extended Roy model is used to generate Figure 1 and was introduced at the end of Section 2.

Table 3 presents the IV estimand for the generalized Roy model used to generate Figures 2A and 2B using $P(Z)$ as the instrument. The model generating $D = \mathbf{1}[Z\gamma \geqslant V]$ is given at the base of Figure 2B (Z is a scalar, γ is 1, V is normal, $U_D = \Phi(\frac{V}{\sigma_V})$). We compare the IV estimand with the policy relevant treatment effect for a policy precisely defined at the base of Table 3. This policy has the structure that if $Z > 0$, persons get a bonus Zt for participation in the program, where $t > 0$. The decision rule for program participation for $Z > 0$ is $D = \mathbf{1}[Z(1+t) \geqslant V]$. People are not forced into participation in the program but are rather induced into it by the bonus. Given the assumed distribution of Z, and the other parameters of the model, we obtain the policy relevant treatment parameter weight $\omega_{\text{PRTE}}(u_D)$ as plotted in Figures 4A–4C (the scales of the ordinates differ across the graphs, but the weight is the same). We use the per capita PRTE and consider three instruments. Table 5 presents estimands for the three instruments shown in the table for the generalized Roy model in three environments.

The first instrument we consider for this example is $P(Z)$, which assumes that there is no policy in place ($t = 0$). It is identified (estimated) on a sample with no policy in place but otherwise the model is the same as the one with the policy in place. The weight on this instrument is plotted in Figure 4A. That figure also displays the OLS weight as well as the MTE that is being weighted to generate the estimate. It also shows the weight used to generate PRTE. The IV weights for $P(Z)$ and the weights for Δ^{PRTE} differ. This is as it should be because Δ^{PRTE} is making a comparison across regimes but the IV in this case makes comparisons within a no policy regime. Given the shape of $\Delta^{\text{MTE}}(u_D)$, it is not surprising that the estimand for IV based on $P(Z)$ is so much above the Δ^{PRTE} which weights a lower-valued segment of $\Delta^{\text{MTE}}(u_D)$ more heavily.[63]

The second instrument we consider exploits the variation induced by the policy in place and fits it on samples where the policy is in place (i.e., the t is the same as that

[63] Heckman and Vytlacil (2005) show how to construct the proper instrument for such policies using a pre-policy sample.

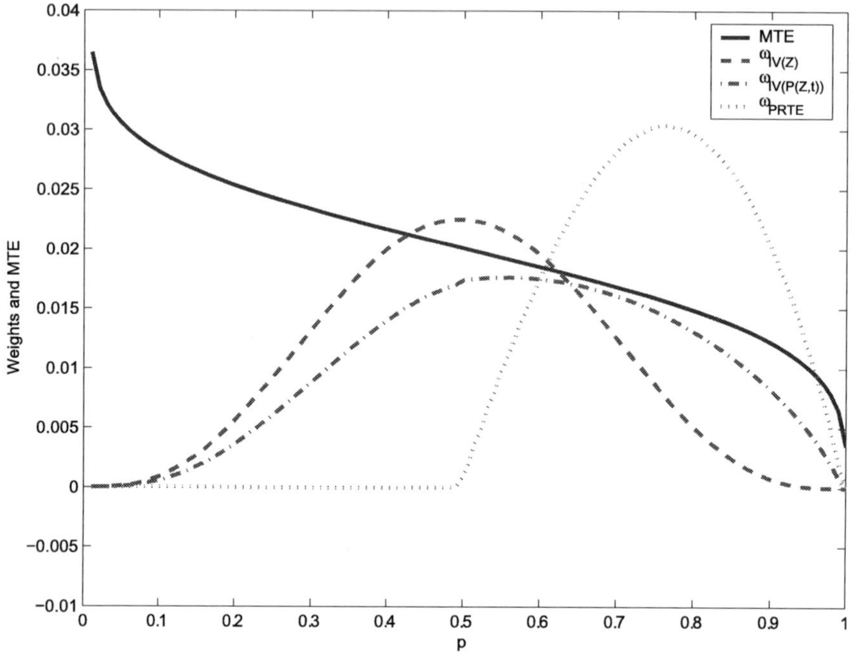

Figure 4B. MTE vs. linear IV with $P(Z(1 + t(\mathbf{1}[Z > 0]))) = \tilde{P}(z, t)$ as an instrument, and policy relevant treatment effect weights for the policy defined at the base of Table 3. The model parameters are given at the base of Figure 2. *Source*: Heckman and Vytlacil (2005).

used to generate the PRTE). On intuitive grounds, this instrument might be thought to work well in identifying the PRTE, but in fact it does not. The instrument is $\tilde{P}(Z, t) = P(Z(1 + t\mathbf{1}[Z > 0]))$ which jumps in value when Z switches from $Z < 0$ to $Z > 0$. This is the choice probability in the regime with the policy in place. Figure 4B plots the weight for this IV along with the weight for $P(Z)$ as an IV and the weight for PRTE (repeated from Figure 4A).[64] While this weight looks a bit more like the weight for Δ^{PRTE} than the previous instrument, it is clearly different.

Figure 4C plots the weight for an ideal instrument for PRTE: a randomization of eligibility. This compares the outcomes in one population where the policy is in place with outcomes in a regime where the policy is not in place. Thus we use an instrument B such that

$$B = \begin{cases} 1 & \text{if a person is eligible to participate in the program,} \\ 0 & \text{otherwise.} \end{cases}$$

Persons for whom $B = 1$, make their participation choices under the policy with a jump in Z, $t\mathbf{1}(Z > 0)$, in their choice sets.[65] If $B = 0$, persons are embargoed from

[64] Remember that the scales are different across the two graphs.

[65] Recall that, in this example, we set $\gamma = 1$.

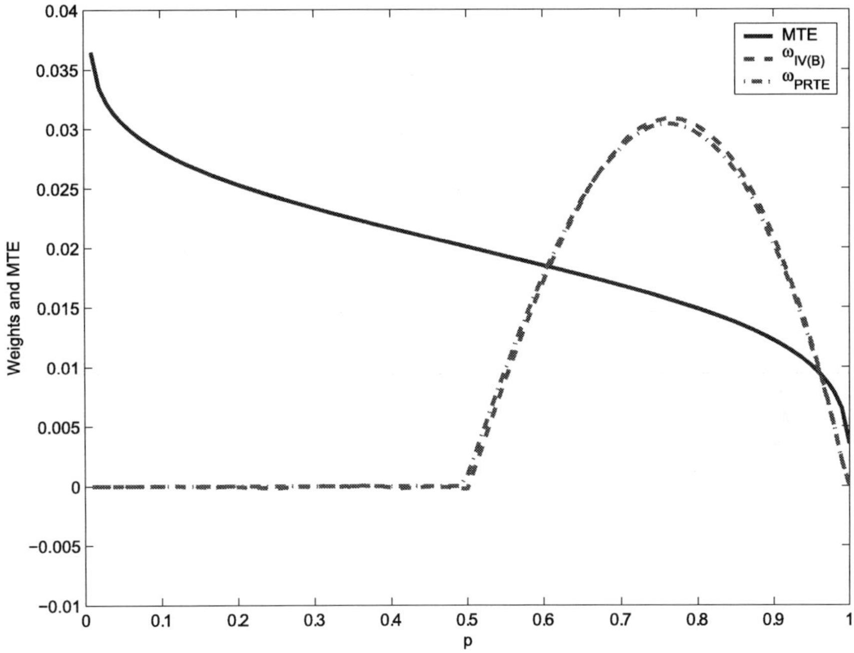

Figure 4C. MTE vs. IV policy and policy relevant treatment effect weights for the policy defined at the base of Table 3. *Source*: Heckman and Vytlacil (2005).

the policy and cannot receive a bonus. The $B = 0$ case is a prepolicy regime. We assume $\Pr[B = 1 \mid Y_0, Y_1, V, Z] = \Pr[B = 1] = 0.5$, so all persons are equally likely to receive or not receive eligibility for the bonus and assignment does not depend on model unobservables in the outcome equation.

The Wald estimator in this case is

$$\frac{E(Y \mid B = 1) - E(Y \mid B = 0)}{\Pr(D = 1 \mid B = 1) - \Pr(D = 1 \mid B = 0)}.$$

Table 5
Linear instrumental variable estimands and the policy relevant treatment effect

Using propensity score $P(Z)$ as the instrument	0.2013
Using propensity score $P(Z(1 + t(\mathbf{1}[Z > 0])))$ as the instrument	0.1859
Using a dummy B as an instrument[a]	0.1549
Policy relevant treatment effect (PRTE)	0.1549

Source: Heckman and Vytlacil (2005).
[a]The dummy B is such that $B = 1$ if an individual belongs to a randomly assigned eligible population, 0 otherwise.

The IV weight for this estimator is a special case of Equation (4.13):

$$\omega_{\text{IV}}(u_D \mid B) = \frac{E(B - E(B) \mid \hat{P}(Z) \geqslant u_D) \Pr(\hat{P}(Z) \geqslant u_D)}{\operatorname{Cov}(B, \hat{P}(Z))},$$

where $\hat{P}(Z) = P(Z(1+t\mathbf{1}[Z > 0]))^B P(Z)^{(1-B)}$. Here, the IV is eligibility for a policy and IV is equivalent to a social experiment that identifies the mean gain per participant who switches to participation in the program. It is to be expected that this IV weight and ω_{PRTE} are identical.

4.7.1. *Further examples within the extended Roy model*

To gain a further understanding of how to construct the weights, and to understand how negative weights can arise, it is useful to return to the policy adoption model presented at the end of Section 2. The only unobservables in this model are in the outcome equations. To simplify the analysis, we use an extended Roy model where the only unobservables are the unmeasured gains.

In this framework, the cost C of adopting the policy is the same across all countries. Countries choose to adopt the policy if $D^* > 0$ where D^* is the net benefit of adoption: $D^* = (Y_1 - Y_0 - C)$ and ATE $= E(\beta) = E(Y_1 - Y_0) = \mu_1 - \mu_0$, while treatment on the treated is $E(\beta \mid D = 1) = E(Y_1 - Y_0 \mid D = 1) = \mu_1 - \mu_0 + E(U_1 - U_0 \mid D = 1)$.

In this setting, the gross return to the country at the margin is C, i.e., $E(Y_1 - Y_0 \mid D^* = 0) = E(Y_1 - Y_0 \mid Y_1 - Y_0 = C) = C$. Recall that Figure 1 presents the standard treatment parameters for the values of the choice parameter presented at the base of the figure. Countries that adopt the policy are above average. In a model where the cost varies (the generalized Roy model with $U_C \neq 0$), and C is negatively correlated with the gain, adopting countries could be below average.[66] We consider cases with discrete instruments and cases with continuous instruments. We first turn to the discrete case.

4.7.2. *Discrete instruments and weights for LATE*

Consider what instrumental variables identify in the model of country policy adoption presented below Figure 5. That figure presents three cases that we analyze in this section. Let cost $C = Z\gamma$ where instrument $Z = (Z_1, Z_2)$. Higher values of Z reduce the probability of adopting the policy if $\gamma \geqslant 0$, component by component.

Consider the "standard" case depicted in Figure 5A. Increasing both components of discrete-valued Z raises costs and hence raises the benefit observed for the country at the margin by eliminating adoption in low return countries. It also reduces the probability that countries adopt the policy. In general a different country is at the margin when different instruments are used.

[66] See, e.g., Heckman (1976a, 1976c) and Willis and Rosen (1979).

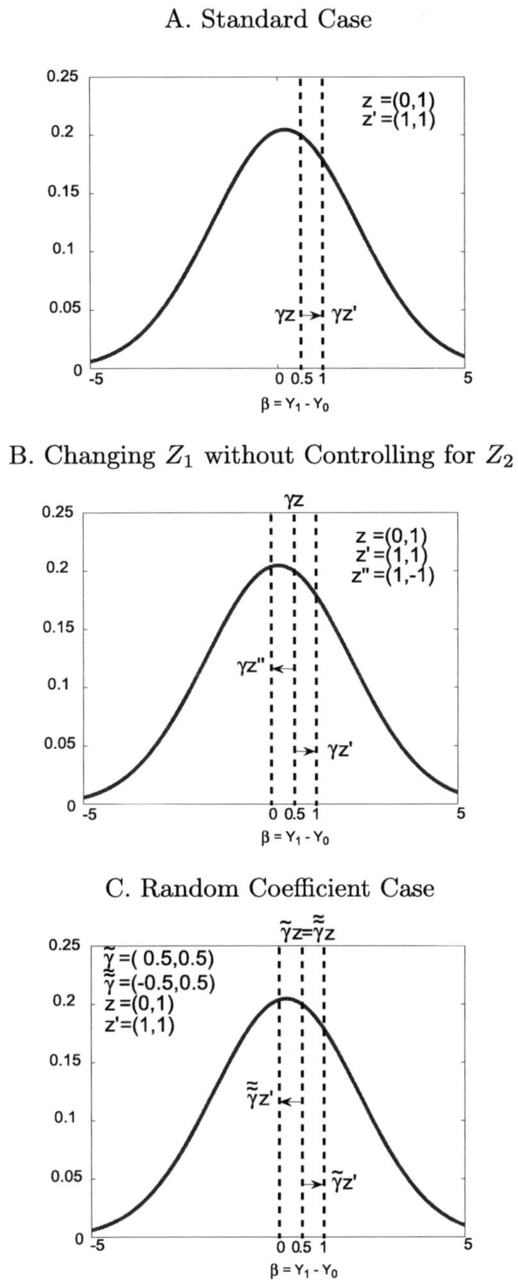

Figure 5. Monotonicity: The extended Roy economy. *Source*: Heckman, Urzua and Vytlacil (2006).

Outcomes	Choice model
$Y_1 = \alpha + \bar{\beta} + U_1$ $Y_0 = \alpha + U_0$	$D = \begin{cases} 1 & \text{if } Y_1 - Y_0 - \gamma Z \geqslant 0, \\ 0 & \text{if } Y_1 - Y_0 - \gamma Z < 0 \end{cases}$ with $\gamma Z = \gamma_1 Z_1 + \gamma_2 Z_2$

Parameterization

$$(U_1, U_0) \sim N(\mathbf{0}, \mathbf{\Sigma}),\ \mathbf{\Sigma} = \begin{bmatrix} 1 & -0.9 \\ -0.9 & 1 \end{bmatrix},\ \alpha = 0.67,\ \bar{\beta} = 0.2,\ \gamma = (0.5, 0.5) \text{ (except in Case C)}$$

$$Z_1 = \{-1, 0, 1\} \text{ and } Z_2 = \{-1, 0, 1\}$$

A. Standard case	B. Changing Z_1 without controlling for Z_2	C. Random coefficient case
$z \to z'$ $z = (0, 1)$ and $z' = (1, 1)$	$z \to z'$ or $z \to z''$ $z = (0, 1)$, $z' = (1, 1)$ and $z'' = (1, -1)$	$z \to z'$ $z = (0, 1)$ and $z' = (1, 1)$ γ is a random vector $\tilde{\gamma} = (0.5, 0.5)$ and $\tilde{\tilde{\gamma}} = (-0.5, 0.5)$ where $\tilde{\gamma}$ and $\tilde{\tilde{\gamma}}$ are two realizations of γ
$D(\gamma z) \geqslant D(\gamma z')$	$D(\gamma z) \geqslant D(\gamma z')$ or $D(\gamma z) < D(\gamma z'')$	$D(\tilde{\tilde{\gamma}} z) \geqslant D(\tilde{\tilde{\gamma}} z')$ and $D(\tilde{\gamma} z) < D(\tilde{\gamma} z')$
For all individuals	Depending on the value of z' or z''	Depending on value of γ

Figure 5. (*Continued*)

Figure 6A plots the weights and Figure 6B plots the components of the weights for the LATE values using $P(Z)$ as an instrument for the distribution of discrete Z values shown at the base of the figure. Figure 6C presents the LATE parameter derived using $P(Z)$ as an instrument. The weights are positive as predicted from Equation (4.5) when $J(Z) = P(Z)$. Thus, the monotonicity condition for the weights in terms of u_D is satisfied. The outcome and choice parameters are the same as those used to generate Figures 1 and 5. The LATE parameters for each interval of P values are presented in a table just below the figures. There are four LATE parameters corresponding to the five distinct values of the propensity score for that value. The LATE parameters exhibit the declining pattern with u_D predicted by the Roy model.

A case producing negative weights is depicted in Figure 5B. In that graph, the same Z is used to generate the choices as is used to generate Figure 1B. However, in this case, the analyst uses Z_1 as the instrument. Z_1 and Z_2 are negatively dependent and $E(Z_1 \mid P(Z) > u_D)$ is not monotonic in u_D. This nonmonotonicity is evident in Figure 7B. It produces the pattern of negative weights shown in Figure 7A. These are associated with two way flows. Increasing Z_1 controlling for Z_2 reduces the probability of country policy adoption. However, we do not condition on Z_2 in constructing this figure. Z_2 is floating. Two way flows are induced by uncontrolled variation in Z_2. For some units, the strength of the associated variation in Z_2 offsets the increase in Z_1 and for other units it does not. Observe that the LATE parameters defined using $P(Z)$ are the same in both examples. They are just weighted differently. We discuss the random coefficient choice model generating Figure 5C in Section 4.10.

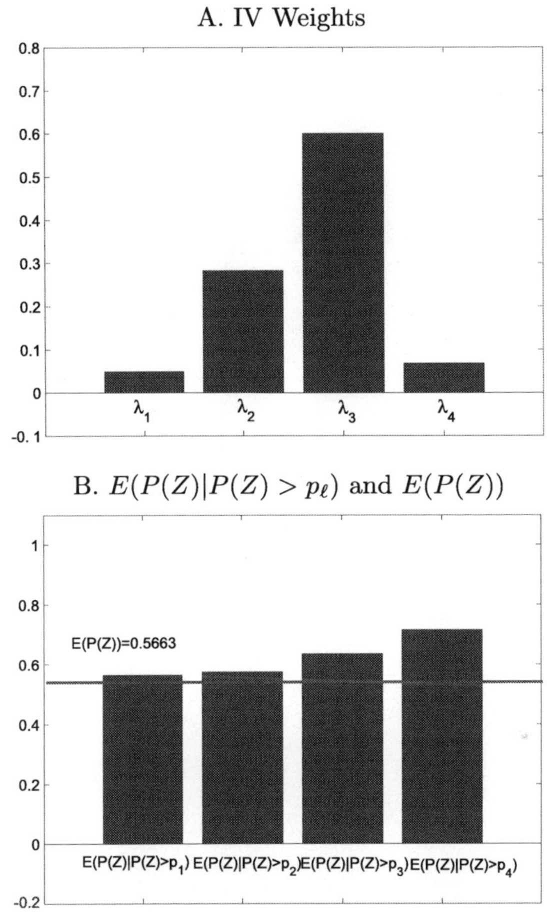

Figure 6. IV weights and its components under discrete instruments when $P(Z)$ is the instrument, the extended Roy economy. *Source*: Heckman, Urzua and Vytlacil (2006).

The IV estimator does not identify ATE, TT or TUT (given at the bottom of Figure 6C). Conditioning on Z_2 produces positive weights. This is illustrated in the weights shown in Table 6 that condition on Z_2 using the same model that generated Figure 6. Conditioning on Z_2 effectively converts the problem back into one with a scalar instrument and the weights are positive for that case.

From Yitzhaki's analysis, for any sample size, a regression of Y on P identifies a weighted average of slopes based on ordered regressors:

$$\frac{E(Y_\ell \mid p_\ell) - E(Y_{\ell-1} \mid p_{\ell-1})}{p_\ell - p_{\ell-1}},$$

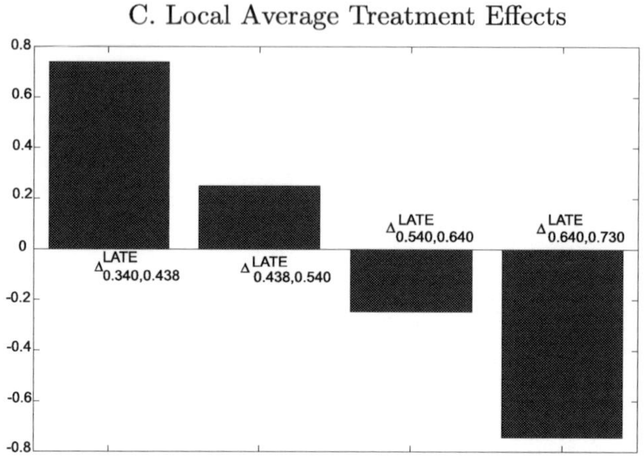

The model is the same as the one presented below Figure 5.

$$\text{ATE} = 0.2,\ \text{TT} = 0.5942,\ \text{TUT} = -0.4823 \text{ and } \Delta^{\text{IV}}_{P(Z)} = \sum_{\ell=1}^{K-1} \Delta^{\text{LATE}}(p_\ell, p_{\ell+1})\lambda_\ell = -0.09$$

$$\begin{aligned}\Delta^{\text{LATE}}(p_\ell, p_{\ell+1}) &= \frac{E(Y \mid P(Z) = p_{\ell+1}) - E(Y \mid P(Z) = p_\ell)}{p_{\ell+1} - p_\ell} \\ &= \frac{\bar{\beta}(p_{\ell+1} - p_\ell) + \sigma_{U_1 - U_0}(\phi(\Phi^{-1}(1 - p_{\ell+1})) - \phi(\Phi^{-1}(1 - p_\ell)))}{p_{\ell+1} - p_\ell}\end{aligned}$$

$$\begin{aligned}\lambda_\ell &= (p_{\ell+1} - p_\ell)\frac{\sum_{i=1}^K (p_i - E(P(Z))) \sum_{t>\ell}^K f(p_i, p_t)}{\text{Cov}(Z_1, D)} \\ &= (p_{\ell+1} - p_\ell)\frac{\sum_{t>\ell}^K (p_t - E(P(Z))) f(p_t)}{\text{Cov}(Z_1, D)}\end{aligned}$$

Joint probability distribution of (Z_1, Z_2) and the propensity score (joint probabilities in ordinary type $(\Pr(Z_1 = z_1, Z_2 = z_2))$; propensity score in italics $(\Pr(D = 1 \mid Z_1 = z_1, Z_2 = z_2))$)

$Z_1 \backslash Z_2$	-1	0	1
-1	0.02	0.02	0.36
	0.7309	*0.6402*	*0.5409*
0	0.3	0.01	0.03
	0.6402	*0.5409*	*0.4388*
1	0.2	0.05	0.01
	0.5409	*0.4388*	*0.3408*

$\text{Cov}(Z_1, Z_2) = -0.5468$

Figure 6. (*Continued*)

where $p_\ell > p_{\ell-1}$ and the weights are the positive Yitzhaki–Imbens–Angrist weights derived in Yitzhaki (1989, 1996) or in Yitzhaki and Schechtman (2004). The weights are positive whether or not monotonicity condition (IV-3) holds. If monotonicity holds, IV is a weighted average of LATEs. Otherwise it is just a weighted average of ordered

Table 6
The conditional instrumental variable estimator ($\Delta^{\text{IV}}_{Z_1|Z_2=z_2}$) and conditional local average treatment effect ($\Delta^{\text{LATE}}(p_\ell, p_{\ell+1} \mid Z_2 = z_2)$) when Z_1 is the instrument (given $Z_2 = z_2$)

The extended Roy economy

	$Z_2 = -1$	$Z_2 = 0$	$Z_2 = 1$
$P(-1, Z_2) = p_3$	0.7309	0.6402	0.5409
$P(0, Z_2) = p_2$	0.6402	0.5409	0.4388
$P(1, Z_2) = p_1$	0.5409	0.4388	0.3408
λ_1	0.8418	0.5384	0.2860
λ_2	0.1582	0.4616	0.7140
$\Delta^{\text{LATE}}(p_1, p_2)$	−0.2475	0.2497	0.7470
$\Delta^{\text{LATE}}(p_2, p_3)$	−0.7448	−0.2475	0.2497
$\Delta^{\text{IV}}_{Z_1\|Z_2=z_2}$	−0.3262	0.0202	0.3920

The model is the same as the one presented below Figure 2.

$$\Delta^{\text{IV}}_{Z_1|Z_2=z_2} = \sum_{\ell=1}^{I-1} \Delta^{\text{LATE}}(p_\ell, p_{\ell+1} \mid Z_2 = z_2)\lambda_{\ell|Z_2=z_2} = \sum_{\ell=1}^{I-1} \Delta^{\text{LATE}}(p_\ell, p_{\ell+1} \mid Z_2 = z_2)\lambda_{\ell|Z_2=z_2}$$

$$\Delta^{\text{LATE}}(p_\ell, p_{\ell+1} \mid Z_2 = z_2) = \frac{E(Y \mid P(Z) = p_{\ell+1}, Z_2 = z_2) - E(Y \mid P(Z) = p_\ell, Z_2 = z_2)}{p_{\ell+1} - p_\ell}$$

$$\lambda_{\ell|Z_2=z_2} = (p_{\ell+1} - p_\ell)\frac{\sum_{i=1}^{I}(z_{1,i} - E(Z_1 \mid Z_2 = z_2))\sum_{t>\ell}^{I} f(z_{1,i}, p_t \mid Z_2 = z_2)}{\text{Cov}(Z_1, D)}$$

$$= (p_{\ell+1} - p_\ell)\frac{\sum_{t>\ell}^{I}(z_{1,t} - E(Z_1 \mid Z_2 = z_2))f(z_{1,t}, p_t \mid Z_2 = z_2)}{\text{Cov}(Z_1, D)}$$

Probability distribution of Z_1 conditional on Z_2 ($\Pr(Z_1 = z_1 \mid Z_2 = z_2)$)

z_1	$\Pr(Z_1 = z_1 \mid Z_2 = -1)$	$\Pr(Z_1 = z_1 \mid Z_2 = 0)$	$\Pr(Z_1 = z_1 \mid Z_2 = 1)$
−1	0.0385	0.25	0.9
0	0.5769	0.125	0.075
1	0.3846	0.625	0.025

Source: Heckman, Urzua and Vytlacil (2006).

(by p_ℓ) estimators consistent with two-way flows. We next discuss continuous instruments.

4.7.3. Continuous instruments

For the case of continuous Z, we present a parallel analysis for the weights associated with the MTE. Figure 8 plots $E(Y \mid P(Z))$ and MTE for the extended Roy models generated by the parameters displayed at the base of the figure. In cases I and II, $\beta \perp\!\!\!\perp D$,

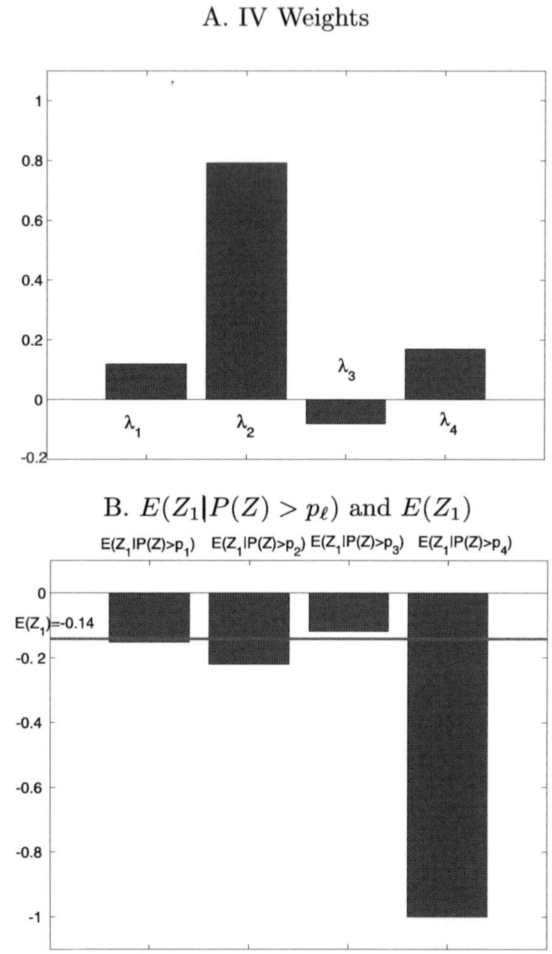

The model is the same as the one presented below Figure 5. The values of the treatment parameters are the same as the ones presented below Figure 6.

Figure 7. IV weights and its components under discrete instruments when Z_1 is the instrument, the extended Roy economy. *Source*: Heckman, Urzua and Vytlacil (2006).

so $\Delta^{\text{MTE}}(u_D)$ is constant in u_D. In case I, this is trivial since β is a constant. In case II, β is random but selection into D does not depend on β. Case III is the model with essential heterogeneity ($\beta \not\perp\!\!\!\perp D$). The graph (Figure 8A) depicts $E(Y \mid P(Z))$ in the three cases. Cases I and II make $E(Y \mid P(Z))$ linear in $P(Z)$. Case III is nonlinear in $P(Z)$. This arises when $\beta \not\perp\!\!\!\perp D$. The derivative of $E(Y \mid P(Z))$ is presented in Figure 8B. It is a constant for cases I and II (flat MTE) but declining in $U_D = P(Z)$ for the case

$$\Delta_{Z_1}^{\mathrm{IV}} = \sum_{\ell=1}^{K-1} \Delta^{\mathrm{LATE}}(p_\ell, p_{\ell+1})\lambda_\ell = 0.1833$$

$$\lambda_\ell = (p_{\ell+1} - p_\ell)\frac{\sum_{i=1}^{I}(z_{1,i} - E(Z_1))\sum_{t>\ell}^{K} f(z_{1,i}, p_t)}{\mathrm{Cov}(Z_1, D)}$$

Joint probability distribution of (Z_1, Z_2) and the propensity score (joint probabilities in ordinary type $(\Pr(Z_1 = z_1, Z_2 = z_2))$; propensity score in italics $(\Pr(D = 1 \mid Z_1 = z_1, Z_2 = z_2))$)

$Z_1 \backslash Z_2$	−1	0	1
−1	0.02	0.02	0.36
	0.7309	*0.6402*	*0.5409*
0	0.3	0.01	0.03
	0.6402	*0.5409*	*0.4388*
1	0.2	0.05	0.01
	0.5409	*0.4388*	*0.3408*

$\mathrm{Cov}(Z_1, Z_2) = -0.5468$

Figure 7. (*Continued*)

with selection on the gain. A simple test for linearity in $P(Z)$ in the outcome equation reveals whether or not the analyst is in cases I and II ($\beta \perp\!\!\!\perp D$) or case III ($\beta \not\perp\!\!\!\perp D$).[67] These cases are the extended Roy counterparts to $E(Y \mid P(Z) = p)$ and MTE shown for the generalized Roy model in Figures 3A and 3B.

MTE gives the mean marginal return for persons who have utility $P(Z) = u_D$. Thus, $P(Z) = u_D$ is the margin of indifference. Those with low u_D values have high returns. Those with high u_D values have low returns. Figure 8 highlights that, in the general case, MTE (and LATE) identify average returns for persons at the margin of indifference at different levels of the mean utility function $(P(Z))$.

Figure 9 plots MTE and LATE for different intervals of u_D using the model generating Figure 8. LATE is the chord of $E(Y \mid P(Z))$ evaluated at different points. The relationship between LATE and MTE is depicted in Figure 9B. LATE is the integral under the MTE curve divided by the difference between the upper and lower limits.

The treatment parameters associated with case III are plotted in Figure 10. The MTE is the same as that presented in Figure 8. ATE has the same value for all p. The effect of treatment on the treated for $P(Z) = p$, $\Delta^{\mathrm{TT}}(p) = E(Y_1 - Y_0 \mid D = 1, P(Z) = p)$ declines in p (equivalently it declines in u_D). Treatment on the untreated given p, $\mathrm{TUT}(p) = \Delta^{\mathrm{TUT}}(p) = E(Y_1 - Y_0 \mid D = 0, P(Z) = p)$ also declines in p,

$$\mathrm{LATE}(p, p') = \frac{\Delta^{\mathrm{TT}}(p')p' - \Delta^{\mathrm{TT}}(p)p}{p' - p}, \quad p' \neq p,$$

$$\mathrm{MTE} = \frac{\partial[\Delta^{\mathrm{TT}}(p)p]}{\partial p}.$$

[67] Recall that we keep the conditioning on X implicit.

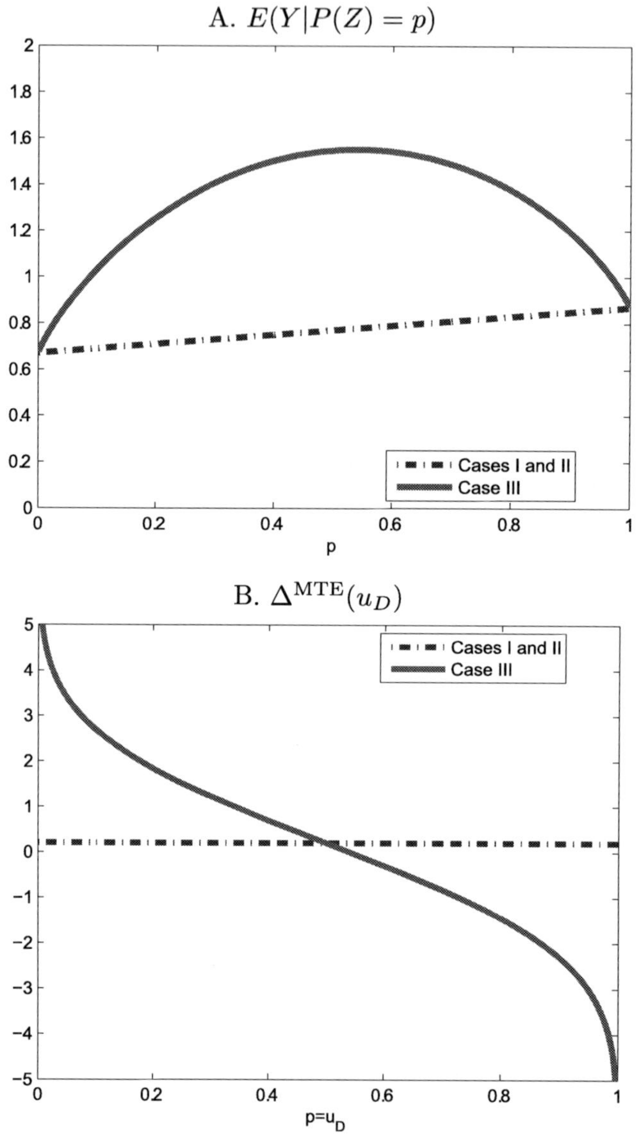

Figure 8. Conditional expectation of Y on $P(Z)$ and the MTE, the extended Roy economy. *Source*: Heckman, Urzua and Vytlacil (2006).

We can generate all of the treatment parameters from $\Delta^{\mathrm{TT}}(p)$.

Matching on $P = p$ (which is equivalent to nonparametric regression given $P = p$) produces a biased estimator of $\mathrm{TT}(p)$. Matching assumes a flat MTE (average return

Outcomes	Choice model
$Y_1 = \alpha + \bar{\beta} + U_1$ $Y_0 = \alpha + U_0$	$D = \begin{cases} 1 & \text{if } D^* \geqslant 0, \\ 0 & \text{if } D^* < 0 \end{cases}$

Case I	Case II	Case III
$U_1 = U_0$	$U_1 - U_0 \perp\!\!\!\perp D$	$U_1 - U_0 \not\perp\!\!\!\perp D$
$\bar{\beta} = \text{ATE} = \text{TT} = \text{TUT} = \text{IV}$	$\bar{\beta} = \text{ATE} = \text{TT} = \text{TUT} = \text{IV}$	$\bar{\beta} = \text{ATE} \neq \text{TT} \neq \text{TUT} \neq \text{IV}$

Parameterization

Cases I, II and III	Cases II and III	Case III
$\alpha = 0.67$	$(U_1, U_0) \sim N(\mathbf{0}, \boldsymbol{\Sigma})$	$D^* = Y_1 - Y_0 - \gamma Z$
$\bar{\beta} = 0.2$	with $\boldsymbol{\Sigma} = \begin{bmatrix} 1 & -0.9 \\ -0.9 & 1 \end{bmatrix}$	$Z \sim N(\boldsymbol{\mu}_Z, \boldsymbol{\Sigma}_Z)$
		$\boldsymbol{\mu}_Z = (2, -2)$ and $\boldsymbol{\Sigma}_Z = \begin{bmatrix} 9 & -2 \\ -2 & 9 \end{bmatrix}$
		$\gamma = (0.5, 0.5)$

Figure 8. (*Continued*)

equals marginal return).[68] Therefore it is systematically biased for $\Delta^{\text{TT}}(p)$ in a model with essential heterogeneity. Making observables alike makes the unobservables dissimilar. Holding p constant across treatment and control groups understates $\text{TT}(p)$ for low values of p and overstates it for high values of p. We develop this point further when we discuss matching in Section 8.

Figure 11 plots the MTE (as a function of u_D where $u_D = F_V(v)$), the weights for ATE, TT and TUT and the IV weights using Z_1 as the instrument for the model used to generate Figure 9. The distribution of the Z is assumed to be normal with generating parameters given at the base of Figure 9. The IV weight for normal Z is always non-negative even if we use only one coordinate of vector Z. This is a consequence of the monotonicity of $E(Z_j \mid P(Z) \geqslant u_D)$ in u_D for any component of vector Z, which is a property of normal selection models.[69]

Panel A of Figure 11 plots the treatment weights derived by Heckman and Vytlacil (1999, 2001b) and the IV weight (4.14), along with the MTE. The ATE = Δ^{ATE} weight is flat ($= 1$). TT oversamples the low u_D agents (those more likely to adopt the policies). TUT oversamples the high u_D agents. The IV weight is positive as it must be when the Z are normally distributed. IV is far from any of the standard treatment parameters. Panel B decomposes the weight into its numerator components $E(Z_1 \mid P(Z) \geqslant u_D)$ and $E(Z_1)$, and the weight itself. The difference $E(Z_1 \mid P(Z) \geqslant u_D) - E(Z_1)$ multiplied by $\Pr(P(Z) \geqslant u_D)$ and normalized by $\text{Cov}(Z_1, D)$ is the weight (see Equation (4.13)). The weight is plotted as the dotted line in Figure 9B.

[68] See Heckman and Vytlacil (2005) and Section 8.

[69] See Heckman and Honoré (1990). In a broad class of models [see, e.g., Heckman, Tobias and Vytlacil (2003)] $E(R \mid S > c)$ is monotonic in c for vector R. The normal model is one member of this family.

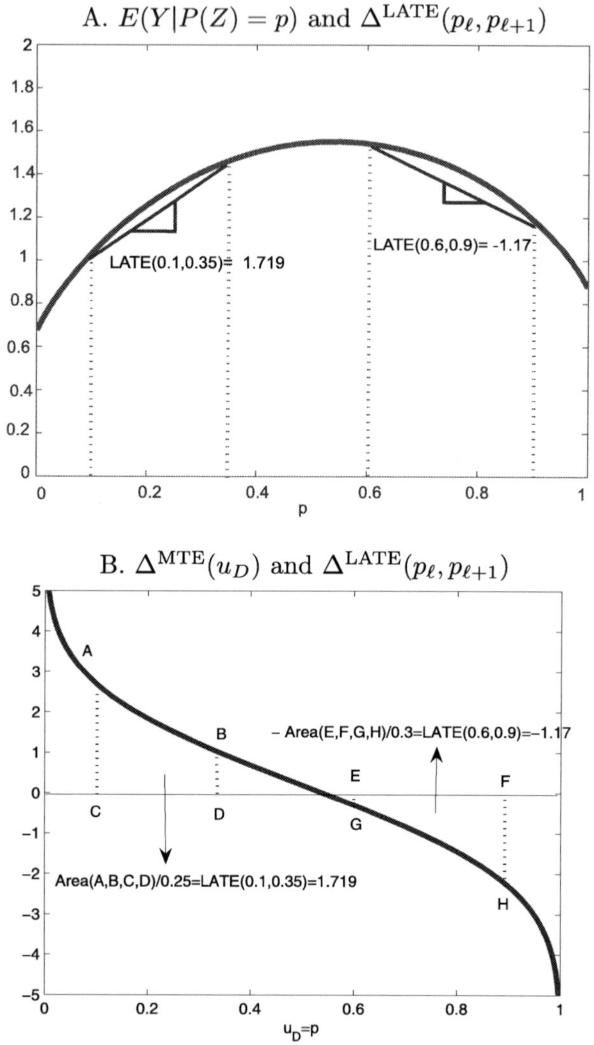

$$\Delta^{\mathrm{LATE}}(p_\ell, p_{\ell+1}) = \frac{E(Y|P(Z)=p_{\ell+1}) - E(Y|P(Z)=p_\ell)}{p_{\ell+1}-p_\ell} = \frac{\int_{p_\ell}^{p_{\ell+1}} \Delta^{\mathrm{MTE}}(u_D)\,du_D}{p_{\ell+1}-p_\ell}$$

$$\Delta^{\mathrm{LATE}}(0.6, 0.9) = -1.17$$

$$\Delta^{\mathrm{LATE}}(0.1, 0.35) = 1.719$$

Outcomes

$$Y_1 = \alpha + \bar{\beta} + U_1$$
$$Y_0 = \alpha + U_0$$

Choice model

$$D = \begin{cases} 1 & \text{if } D^* \geqslant 0, \\ 0 & \text{if } D^* < 0 \end{cases}$$

with $D^* = Y_1 - Y_0 - \gamma Z$

Figure 9. The local average treatment effect, the extended Roy economy. *Source*: Heckman, Urzua and Vytlacil (2006).

Parameterization

$$(U_1, U_0) \sim N(\mathbf{0}, \boldsymbol{\Sigma}) \text{ and } Z \sim N(\boldsymbol{\mu}_Z, \boldsymbol{\Sigma}_Z)$$

$$\boldsymbol{\Sigma} = \begin{bmatrix} 1 & -0.9 \\ -0.9 & 1 \end{bmatrix}, \boldsymbol{\mu}_Z = (2, -2) \text{ and } \boldsymbol{\Sigma}_Z = \begin{bmatrix} 9 & -2 \\ -2 & 9 \end{bmatrix}$$

$$\alpha = 0.67,\ \bar{\beta} = 0.2,\ \gamma = (0.5, 0.5)$$

Figure 9. (*Continued*)

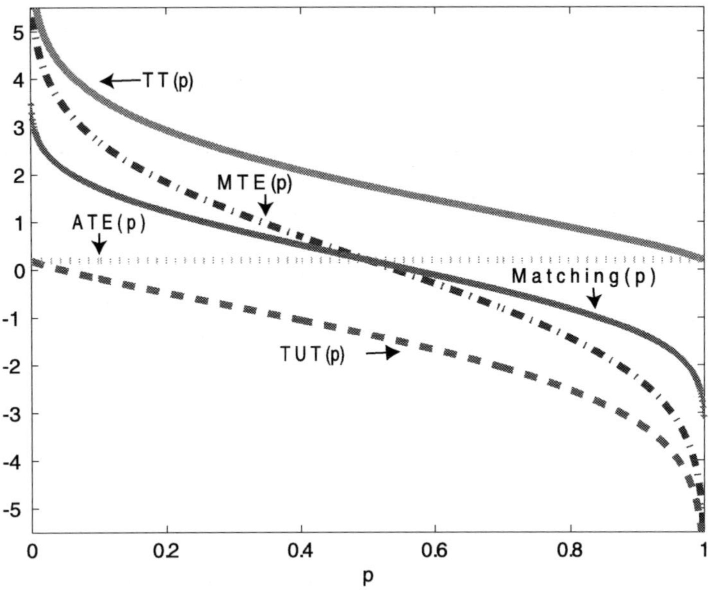

Parameter	Definition	Under assumptions (*)
Marginal treatment effect	$E[Y_1 - Y_0 \mid D^* = 0, P(Z) = p]$	$\bar{\beta} + \sigma_{U_1 - U_0}\Phi^{-1}(1-p)$
Average treatment effect	$E[Y_1 - Y_0 \mid P(Z) = p]$	$\bar{\beta}$
Treatment on the treated	$E[Y_1 - Y_0 \mid D^* \geqslant 0, P(Z) = p]$	$\bar{\beta} + \sigma_{U_1 - U_0}\frac{\phi(\Phi^{-1}(1-p))}{p}$
Treatment on the untreated	$E[Y_1 - Y_0 \mid D^* < 0, P(Z) = p]$	$\bar{\beta} - \sigma_{U_1 - U_0}\frac{\phi(\Phi^{-1}(1-p))}{1-p}$
OLS/Matching on $P(Z)$	$E[Y_1 \mid D^* \geqslant 0, P(Z) = p] - E[Y_0 \mid D^* < 0, P(Z) = p]$	$\bar{\beta} + \left(\frac{\sigma^2_{U_1} - \sigma_{U_1, U_0}}{\sqrt{\sigma_{U_1 - U_0}}}\right)\left(\frac{1-2p}{p(1-p)}\right)\phi(\Phi^{-1}(1-p))$

(*): The model in this case is the same as the one presented below Figure 9.
Note: $\Phi(\cdot)$ and $\phi(\cdot)$ represent the cdf and pdf of a standard normal distribution, respectively. $\Phi^{-1}(\cdot)$ represents the inverse of $\Phi(\cdot)$.

Figure 10. Treatment parameters and OLS/Matching as a function of $P(Z) = p$.
Source: Heckman, Urzua and Vytlacil (2006).

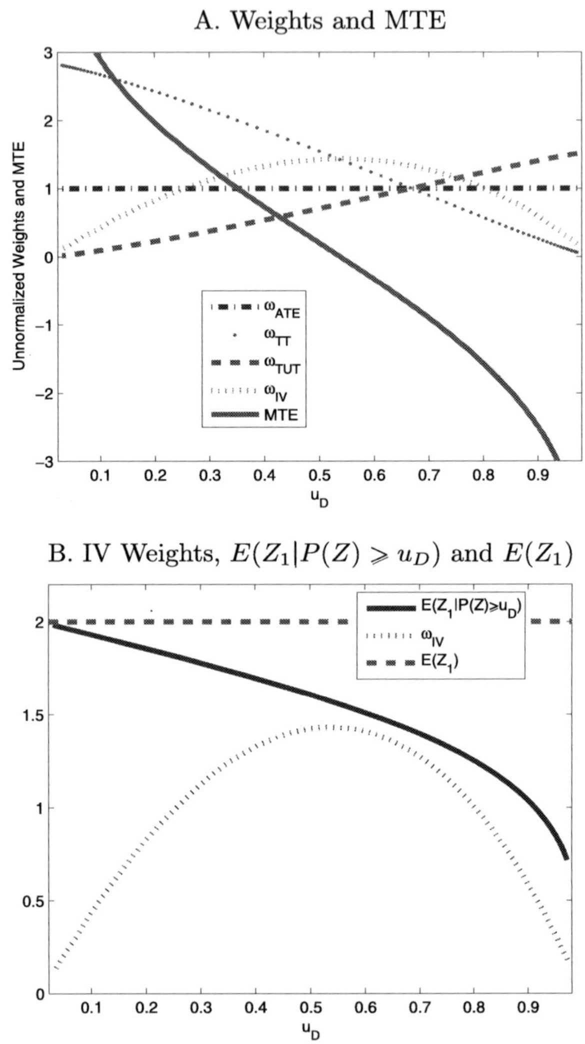

Parameter	Under assumptions (*)
ATE	0.2
TT	1.1878
TUT	−0.9132
IV_{Z_1}	0.0924

(*) The model in this case is the same as the one presented below Figure 9.

Figure 11. Treatment weights, IV weights using Z_1 as the instrument and the MTE. *Source*: Heckman, Urzua and Vytlacil (2004).

Suppose that instead of assuming normality for the regressors, instrument Z is assumed to be a random vector with a distribution function given by a mixture of two normals:

$$Z \sim P_1 N(\kappa_1, \Sigma_1) + P_2 N(\kappa_2, \Sigma_2),$$

where P_1 is the proportion in population 1, P_2 is the proportion in population 2, and $P_1 + P_2 = 1$. This produces a model with continuous instruments, where $E(\tilde{J}(Z) \mid P(Z) \geqslant u_D)$ need not be monotonic in u_D where $\tilde{J}(Z) = J(Z) - E(J(Z))$. Such a data generating process for the instrument could arise from an ecological model in which two different populations are mixed (e.g., rural and urban populations).[70]

Appendix E derives the instrumental variable weights on Δ^{MTE} when Z_1 (the first element of Z) is used as the instrument, i.e., $J(Z) = Z_1$. For simplicity, we assume that there are no X regressors. The probability of selection is generated using $\mu_D(Z) = Z\gamma$. The joint distribution of $(Z_1, Z\gamma)$ is normal within each group.

In our example, the dependence between Z_1 and $Z\gamma$ $(= F_V(Z\gamma) = P(Z))$ is negative in one population and positive in another. Thus in one population, as Z_1 increases $P(Z)$ increases. In the other population, as Z_1 increases $P(Z)$ decreases. If this second population is sufficiently big (P_1 is small) or the negative correlation in the second population is sufficiently big, the weights can become negative because $E(\tilde{J}(Z) \mid P(Z) \geqslant u_D)$ is not monotonic in u_D.

We present examples for a conventional normal outcome selection model generated by the parameters presented at the base of Figure 12. The discrete choice equation is a conventional probit: $\Pr(D = 1 \mid Z = z) = \Phi(\frac{z\gamma}{\sigma_V})$. The outcome equations are linear normal equations. Thus $\Delta^{\mathrm{MTE}}(v) = E(Y_1 - Y_0 \mid V = v)$, is linear in v:

$$E(Y_1 - Y_0 \mid V = v) = \mu_1 - \mu_0 + \frac{\operatorname{Cov}(U_1 - U_0, V)}{\operatorname{Var}(V)} v.$$

At the base of the figure, we define $\bar{\beta} = \mu_1 - \mu_0$ and $\alpha = \mu_0$. The average treatment effects are the same for all different distributions of the Z.

In each of the following examples, we show results for models with vector Z that satisfies (IV-1) and (IV-2) and with $\gamma > 0$ componentwise where γ is the coefficient of Z in the cost equation. We vary the weights and means of the instruments. *Ceteris paribus*, an increase in each component of Z increases $\Pr(D = 1 \mid Z = z)$. Table 7 presents the parameters treatment on the treated $(E(Y_1 - Y_0 \mid D = 1))$, treatment on the untreated $(E(Y_1 - Y_0 \mid D = 0))$, and the average treatment effect $(E(Y_1 - Y_0))$ produced by our model for different distributions of the regressors.

In standard IV analysis, under assumptions (IV-1) and (IV-2) the distribution of Z does not affect the probability limit of the IV estimator. It only affects its sampling distribution. Figure 12A shows three weights corresponding to the perturbations of the variances of the instruments in the second component population Σ_2 and the means

[70] Observe that $E(Z) = P_1\kappa_1 + P_2\kappa_2$.

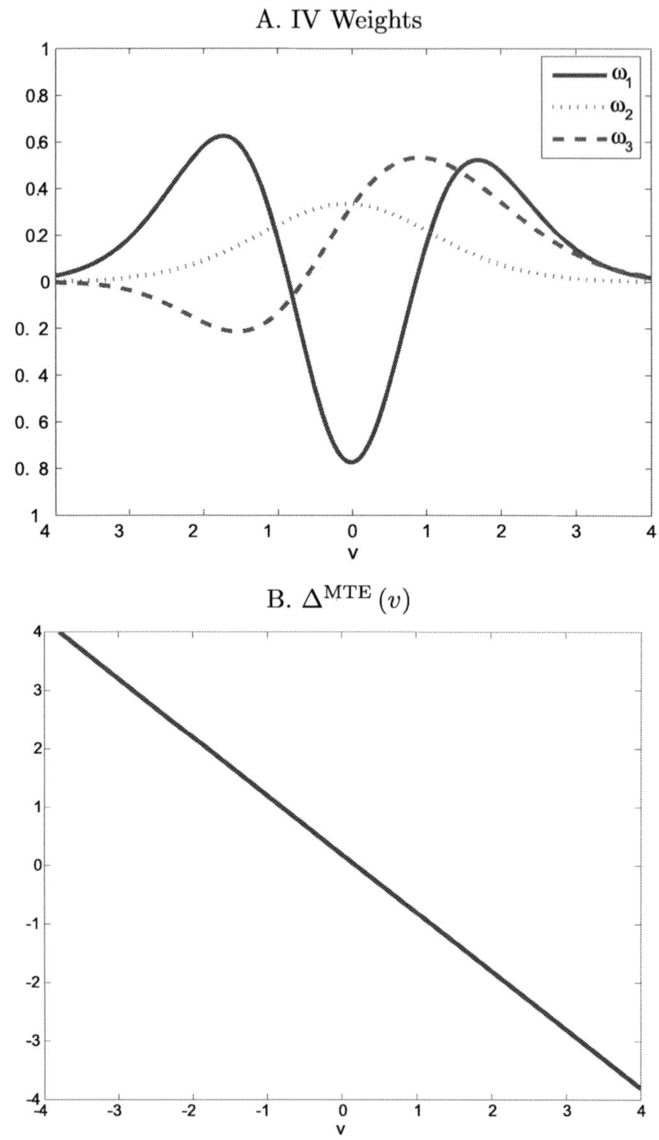

Figure 12. MTE and IV weights using Z_1 as the instrument when $Z = (Z_1, Z_2) \sim p_1 N(\kappa_1, \Sigma_1) + p_2 N(\kappa_2, \Sigma_2)$ for different values of Σ_2.
Source: Heckman, Urzua and Vytlacil (2006).

(κ_1, κ_2) shown at the table at the base of the figure. The Δ_V^{MTE} used in all of our examples are plotted in Figure 12B. The MTE has the familiar shape, reported in Heckman

Outcomes	Choice model
$Y_1 = \alpha + \bar{\beta} + U_1$	$D = \begin{cases} 1 & \text{if } D^* \geqslant 0, \\ 0 & \text{if } D^* < 0 \end{cases}$
$Y_0 = \alpha + U_0$	$D^* = Y_1 - Y_0 - \gamma Z$ and $V = -(U_1 - U_0)$

Parameterization

$$(U_1, U_0) \sim N(\mathbf{0}, \boldsymbol{\Sigma}), \boldsymbol{\Sigma} = \begin{bmatrix} 1 & -0.9 \\ -0.9 & 1 \end{bmatrix}, \alpha = 0.67, \bar{\beta} = 0.2$$

$$Z = (Z_1, Z_2) \sim p_1 N(\kappa_1, \Sigma_1) + p_2 N(\kappa_2, \Sigma_2)$$

$$p_1 = 0.45, p_2 = 0.55; \Sigma_1 = \begin{bmatrix} 1.4 & 0.5 \\ 0.5 & 1.4 \end{bmatrix}$$

$$\mathrm{Cov}(Z_1, \gamma Z) = \gamma \Sigma_1^1 = 0.98; \gamma = (0.2, 1.4)$$

Figure 12. (*Continued*)

Table 7
The IV estimator and $\mathrm{Cov}(Z_2, \gamma Z)$ associated with each value of Σ_2

Weights	Σ_2	κ_1	κ_2	IV	ATE	TT	TUT	$\mathrm{Cov}(Z_2, \gamma Z) = \gamma \Sigma_2^1$
ω_1	$\begin{bmatrix} 0.6 & -0.5 \\ -0.5 & 0.6 \end{bmatrix}$	[0 0]	[0 0]	0.434	0.2	1.401	−1.175	−0.58
ω_2	$\begin{bmatrix} 0.6 & 0.1 \\ 0.1 & 0.6 \end{bmatrix}$	[0 0]	[0 0]	0.078	0.2	1.378	−1.145	0.26
ω_3	$\begin{bmatrix} 0.6 & -0.3 \\ -0.3 & 0.6 \end{bmatrix}$	[0 −1]	[0 1]	−2.261	0.2	1.310	−0.859	−0.30

Source: Heckman, Urzua and Vytlacil (2006).

(2001) and Heckman, Tobias and Vytlacil (2003) that returns are highest for those with values of v that make them more likely to get treatment (i.e., low values of v).

The weights ω_1 and ω_3 plotted in Figure 12A correspond to the case where $E(Z_1 - E(Z_1) \mid P(Z) \geqslant u_D)$ is not monotonic in u_D. In these cases, the sign of the covariance between Z_1 and $Z\gamma$ (i.e., $P(Z)$) is not the same in the two subpopulations. The IV estimates reported in the table at the base of the figure range all over the place even though the parameters of the outcome and choice model are the same.[71]

Different distributions of Z critically affect the probability limit of the IV estimator in the model of essential heterogeneity. The model of outcomes and choices is the same across all of these examples. The MTE and ATE parameters are the same. Only the distribution of the instrument differs. The instrumental variable estimand is sometimes positive and sometimes negative, and oscillates wildly in magnitude depending on the distribution of the instruments. The estimated "effect" is often way off the mark for any

[71] Since TT and TUT depend on the distribution of $P(Z)$, they are not invariant to changes in the distribution of the Z.

desired treatment parameter. These examples show how uniformity in Z does not translate into uniformity in $J(Z)$ (Z_1 in this example). This sensitivity is a phenomenon that does not appear in the conventional homogeneous response model but is a central feature of a model with essential heterogeneity.[72] We now compare selection and IV models.

4.8. Comparing selection and IV models

We now show that local IV identifies the derivatives of a selection model. Making the X explicit, in the standard selection model, U_1 and U_0 are scalar random variables that are additively separable in the outcome equations, $Y_1 = \mu_1(X) + U_1$ and $Y_0 = \mu_0(X) + U_0$. The control function approach conditions on Z and D. As a consequence of index sufficiency, this is equivalent to conditioning on $P(Z)$ and D:

$$E(Y \mid X, D, Z) = \mu_0(X) + \left[\mu_1(X) - \mu_0(X)\right]D + K_1\bigl(P(Z), X\bigr)D + K_0\bigl(P(Z), X\bigr)(1 - D),$$

where the control functions are

$$K_1\bigl(P(Z), X\bigr) = E\bigl(U_1 \mid D = 1, X, P(Z)\bigr),$$
$$K_0\bigl(P(Z), X\bigr) = E\bigl(U_0 \mid D = 0, X, P(Z)\bigr).$$

The IV approach does not condition on D. It works with

$$E(Y \mid X, Z) = \mu_0(X) + \left[\mu_1(X) - \mu_0(X)\right]P(Z) + K_1\bigl(P(Z), X\bigr)P(Z) + K_0\bigl(P(Z), X\bigr)\bigl(1 - P(Z)\bigr), \tag{4.17}$$

the population mean outcome given X, Z.

From index sufficiency, $E(Y \mid X, Z) = E(Y \mid X, P(Z))$. The MTE is the derivative of this expression with respect to $P(Z)$, which we have defined as LIV:

$$\left.\frac{\partial E(Y \mid X, P(Z))}{\partial P(Z)}\right|_{P(Z)=p} = \text{LIV}(X, p) = \text{MTE}(X, p).$$[73]

The distribution of $P(Z)$ and the relationship between $J(Z)$ and $P(Z)$ determine the weight on MTE.[74] Under assumptions (A-1)–(A-5), along with rank and limit conditions [Heckman and Robb (1985a), Heckman (1990)], one can identify $\mu_1(X)$, $\mu_0(X)$, $K_1(P(Z), X)$, and $K_0(P(Z), X)$.

[72] We note parenthetically that if we assume $P_1 = 0$ (or $P_2 = 0$), the weights are positive even if we only use Z_1 as an instrument and Z_1 and Z_2 are negatively correlated. This follows from the monotonicity of $E(R \mid S > c)$ in c for vector R. See Heckman and Honoré (1990). This case is illustrated in Figure 11.

[73] Björklund and Moffitt (1987) analyze this marginal effect for a parametric generalized Roy model.

[74] Because LIV does not condition on D, it discards information. Lost in taking derivatives are the constants in the model that do not interact with $P(Z)$ in Equation (4.17).

The selection (control function) estimator identifies the conditional means

$$E\big(Y_1 \mid X, P(Z), D = 1\big) = \mu_1(X) + K_1\big(X, P(Z)\big) \tag{4.18a}$$

and

$$E\big(Y_0 \mid X, P(Z), D = 0\big) = \mu_0(X) + K_0\big(X, P(Z)\big). \tag{4.18b}$$

These can be identified from nonparametric regressions of Y_1 and Y_0 on X, Z in each population. To decompose these means and separate $\mu_1(X)$ from $K_1(X, P(Z))$ without invoking functional form or curvature assumptions, it is necessary to have an exclusion (a Z not in X).[75] In addition, there must exist a limit set for Z given X such that $K_1(X, P(Z)) = 0$ for Z in that limit set. Otherwise, without functional form or curvature assumptions, it is not possible to disentangle $\mu_1(X)$ from $K_1(X, P(Z))$ which may contain constants and functions of X that do not interact with $P(Z)$ [see Heckman (1990)]. A parallel argument for Y_0 shows that we require a limit set for Z given X such that $K_0(X, P(Z)) = 0$. Selection models operate by identifying the components of (4.18a) and (4.18b) and generating the treatment parameters from these components. Thus they work with levels of the Y.

The local IV method works with derivatives of (4.17) and not levels and cannot directly recover the constant terms in (4.18a) and (4.18b). Using our analysis of LIV but applied to $YD = Y_1D$ and $Y(1-D) = Y_0(1-D)$, it is straightforward to use LIV to estimate the components of the MTE separately. Thus we can identify

$$\mu_1(X) + E(U_1 \mid X, U_D = u_D)$$

and

$$\mu_0(X) + E(U_0 \mid X, U_D = u_D)$$

separately. This corresponds to what is estimated from taking the derivatives of expressions (4.18a) and (4.18b) multiplied by $P(Z)$ and $(1 - P(Z))$, respectively:[76]

$$P(Z)E(Y_1 \mid X, Z, D = 1) = P(Z)\mu_1(X) + P(Z)K_1\big(X, P(Z)\big)$$

and

$$\begin{aligned}&\big(1 - P(Z)\big)E(Y_0 \mid X, Z, D = 0)\\ &\quad = \big(1 - P(Z)\big)\mu_0(X) + \big(1 - P(Z)\big)K_0\big(X, P(Z)\big).\end{aligned}$$

Thus the control function method works with levels, whereas the LIV approach works with slopes of combinations of the same basic functions. Constants that do not depend

[75] See Heckman and Navarro (2007) for use of semiparametric curvature restrictions in identification analysis that do not require functional form assumptions.

[76] Björklund and Moffitt (1987) use the derivative of a selection model in levels to define the marginal treatment effect.

on $P(Z)$ disappear from the estimates of the model. The level parameters are obtained by integration using the formulae in Table 2B.

Misspecification of $P(Z)$ (either its functional form or its arguments) and hence of $K_1(P(Z), X)$ and $K_0(P(Z), X)$, in general, produces biased estimates of the parameters of the model under the control function approach even if semiparametric methods are used to estimate μ_0, μ_1, K_0 and K_1. To implement the method, we need to know all of the arguments of Z. The terms $K_1(P(Z), X)$ and $K_0(P(Z), X)$ can be nonparametrically estimated so it is only necessary to know $P(Z)$ up to a monotonic transformation.[77] The distributions of U_0, U_1 and V do not need to be specified to estimate control function models [see Powell (1994)].

These problems with control function models have their counterparts in IV models. If we use a misspecified $P(Z)$ to identify the MTE or its components, in general, we do not identify MTE or its components. Misspecification of $P(Z)$ plagues both approaches.

One common criticism of selection models is that without invoking functional form assumptions, identification of $\mu_1(X)$ and $\mu_0(X)$ requires that $P(Z) \to 1$ and $P(Z) \to 0$ in limit sets.[78] Identification in limit sets is sometimes called "identification at infinity". In order to identify ATE $= E(Y_1 - Y_0 \mid X)$, IV methods also require that $P(Z) \to 1$ and $P(Z) \to 0$ in limit sets, so an identification at infinity argument is implicit when IV is used to identify this parameter.[79] The LATE parameter avoids this problem by moving the goal posts and redefining the parameter of interest away from a level parameter like ATE or TT to a slope parameter like LATE which differences out the unidentified constants. Alternatively, if we define the parameter of interest to be LATE or MTE, we can use the selection model without invoking identification at infinity.

The IV estimator is model dependent, just like the selection estimator, but in application, the model does not have to be fully specified to obtain Δ^{IV} using Z (or $J(Z)$). However, the distribution of $P(Z)$ and the relationship between $P(Z)$ and $J(Z)$ generates the weights. The interpretation placed on Δ^{IV} in terms of weights on Δ^{MTE} depends crucially on the specification of $P(Z)$. In both control function and IV approaches for the general model of heterogeneous responses, $P(Z)$ plays a central role.

Two economists using the same instrument will obtain the same point estimate using the same data. Their *interpretation* of that estimate will differ depending on how they specify the arguments in $P(Z)$, even if neither uses $P(Z)$ as an instrument. By conditioning on $P(Z)$, the control function approach makes the dependence of estimates on the specification of $P(Z)$ explicit. The IV approach is less explicit and masks the assumptions required to economically interpret the empirical output of an IV estimation. We now turn to some empirical examples of LIV.

[77] See Heckman et al. (1998).

[78] See Imbens and Angrist (1994). Heckman (1990) establishes the identification in the limit argument for ATE in selection models. See Heckman and Navarro (2007) for a generalization to multiple outcome models.

[79] Thus if the support of $P(Z)$ is not full, we cannot identify treatment on the treated or the average treatment effect. We can construct bounds. See Heckman and Vytlacil (1999, 2001a, 2001b).

4.9. *Empirical examples: "The effect" of high school graduation on wages and using IV to estimate "the effect" of the GED*

The previous examples illustrate logical possibilities. This subsection shows that these logical possibilities arise in real data. We analyze two examples: (a) the effect of graduating high school on wages, and (b) the effect of obtaining a GED on wages. We first analyze the effect of graduating high school on wages.

4.9.1. *Empirical example based on LATE: Using IV to estimate* "the effect" *of high school graduation on wages*

We first study the effects of graduating from high school on wages using data from the National Longitudinal Survey of Youth 1979 (NLSY79). This survey gathers information at multiple points in time on the labor market activities for men and women born in the years 1957–1964. We estimate LATE using log hourly wages at age 30 as the outcome measure. Following a large body of research [see Mare (1980)], we use the number of siblings and residence in the south at age 14 as instruments.

Figure 13 plots the weights on LATE using the estimated $P(Z)$. The procedure used to derive the estimates is explained in Heckman, Urzua and Vytlacil (2006). The weights are derived from Equation (4.16). The LATE parameters are both positive and negative. The weights using siblings as an instrument are both positive and negative. The weights using $P(Z)$ as an instrument are positive, as they must be following the analysis of Yitzhaki (1989). The two IV estimates differ from each other because the weights are different. The overall IV estimate is a crude summary of the underlying component LATEs that are both large and positive and large and negative. We next turn to analysis of the GED.

4.9.2. *Effect of the GED on wages*

The GED test is used to certify high school dropouts as high school equivalents. Numerous studies document that the economic return to the GED is low [see Cameron and Heckman (1993), Heckman and LaFontaine (2007)]. It is estimated by the method described in Heckman, Urzua and Vytlacil (2006). In this example, we study the effect of the GED on the wages of recipients compared to wages of dropouts. We use data from the National Longitudinal Survey of Youth 1979 (NLSY79) which gathers information at multiple points in time on the labor market activities for men and women born in the years 1957–1964.

We estimate the MTE for the GED and also consider the IV weights for various instruments for a sample of males at age 25. Figure 14 shows the sample support of $P(Z)$ for both GEDs and high school dropouts. It is not possible to estimate the MTE over its full support. Thus the average treatment effect (ATE) and treatment on the treated (TT) cannot be estimated from these data. The list of Z variables is presented in Table 8 along with IV estimates. The IV estimates fluctuate from positive to negative.

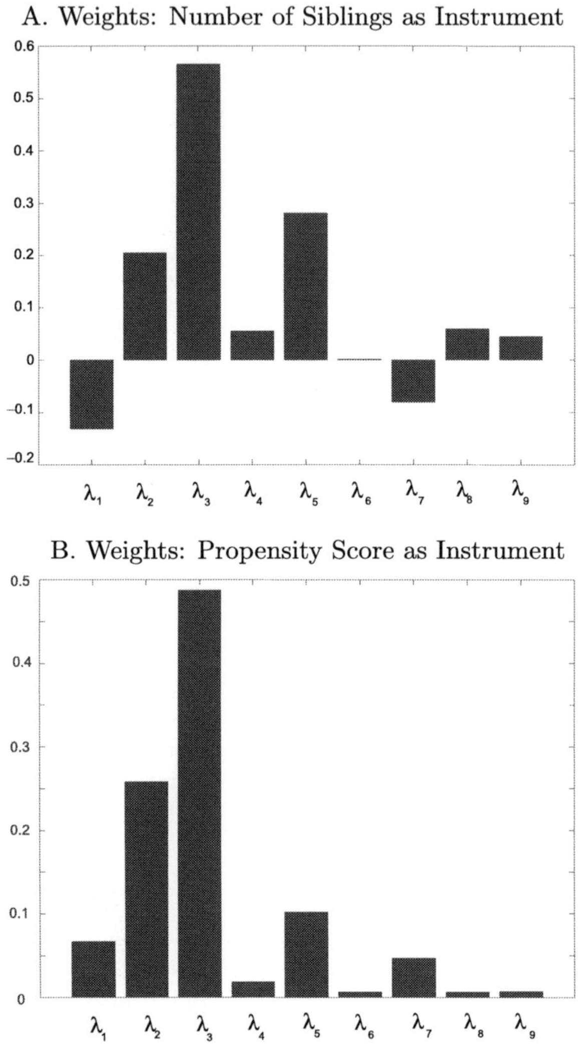

Figure 13. IV weights – the effect of graduating from high school – sample of high school dropouts and high school graduates. *Source*: Heckman, Urzua and Vytlacil (2006).

Using $P(Z)$ as an instrument, the GED effect on log wages is in general negative.[80] For other instruments, the signs and magnitudes vary.

[80] In this example, we use the log of the average nonmissing hourly wages reported between ages 24 and 26. Using the hourly wage reported at age 25 leads to roughly the same results (negative IV weights, and positive and negative IV estimates), but an increase in the standard errors.

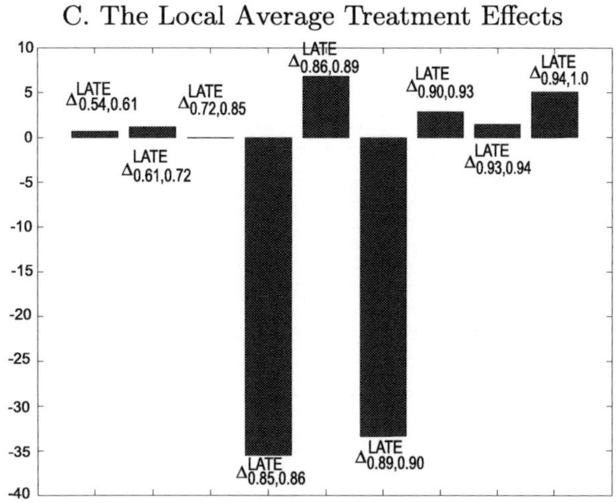

Y = Log per-hour wage at age 30, Z_1 = number of siblings in 1979, Z_2 = mother is a high school graduate

$$D = \begin{cases} 1 & \text{if high school graduate,} \\ 0 & \text{if high school dropout} \end{cases}$$

IV estimates
(bootstrap std. errors in parentheses – 100 replications)

Instrument	Value
Number of siblings in 1979	0.115
	(0.695)
Propensity score	0.316
	(0.110)

Joint probability distribution of (Z_1, Z_2) and the propensity score
(joint probabilities $\Pr(Z_1 = z_1, Z_2 = z_2)$ in ordinary type;
propensity score $\Pr(D = 1 \mid Z_1 = z_1, Z_2 = z_2)$ in italics)

$Z_2 \backslash Z_1$	0	1	2	3	4
0	0.07	0.03	0.47	0.121	0.06
	1.0	*0.54*	*0.86*	*0.72*	*0.61*
1	0.039	0.139	0.165	0.266	0.121
	0.94	*0.89*	*0.90*	*0.85*	*0.93*

$\mathrm{Cov}(Z_1, Z_2) = -0.066$, number of observations = 1,702

Figure 13. (*Continued*)

Figure 15 plots the estimated MTE. Details of the nonparametric estimation procedure used to produce these estimates are shown in an appendix in Heckman, Urzua and Vytlacil (2006). Local linear regression is used to estimate the MTE implementing Equation (4.9). While the standard error band is large, the estimated Δ^{MTE} is in general negative, suggesting a negative marginal treatment effect for most participants. However, we observe that for small values of u_D the point estimates of the marginal effect

Table 8
Instrumental variables estimates[a]: Sample of GED and dropouts – males at age 25[b]

Instruments	IV–MTE
Father's highest grade completed	0.146
	(0.251)
Mother's highest grade completed	−0.052
	(0.179)
Number of siblings	−0.052
	(0.160)
GED cost	−0.053
	(0.156)
Family income in 1979	−0.047
	(0.177)
Dropout's local wage at age 17	−0.013
	(0.218)
High school graduate's local wage at age 17	−0.049
	(0.182)
Dropout's local unemployment rate at age 17	0.443
	(1.051)
High school graduate's local unemployment rate at age 17	−0.563
	(0.577)
Propensity score[c]	−0.058
	(0.164)

Notes:
[a]The IV estimates are computed by taking the weighted sum of the MTE. The standard deviations (in parentheses) are computed using bootstrapping (50 draws).
[b]We excluded the oversample of poor whites and the military sample. The cost of the GED corresponds to the average testing fee per GED battery by state between 1993 and 2000. (*Source*: GED Statistical Report.) Average local wage for dropouts and high school graduates correspond to the average in the place of residence for each group, respectively, and local unemployment rate corresponds to the unemployment rate in the place of residence. Average local wages, local unemployment rates, mother's and father's education refer to the level at age 17.
[c]The propensity score ($P(D = 1 \mid Z = z)$) is computed using as controls the instruments presented in the table, as well as two dummy variables controlling for the place of residence at age 14 (south and urban), and a set of dummy variables controlling for the year of birth (1957–1963).
Source: Heckman, Urzua and Vytlacil (2004).

are positive. This analysis indicates that, for people who are more likely to take the GED exam in terms of their unobservables (i.e., for people at the margin of indifference associated with a small u_D), the marginal effect is in fact positive.

It is instructive to examine the various IV estimates using the one instrument at a time strategy favored by many applied economists who like to do sensitivity analysis.[81]

[81] See, e.g., Card (2001).

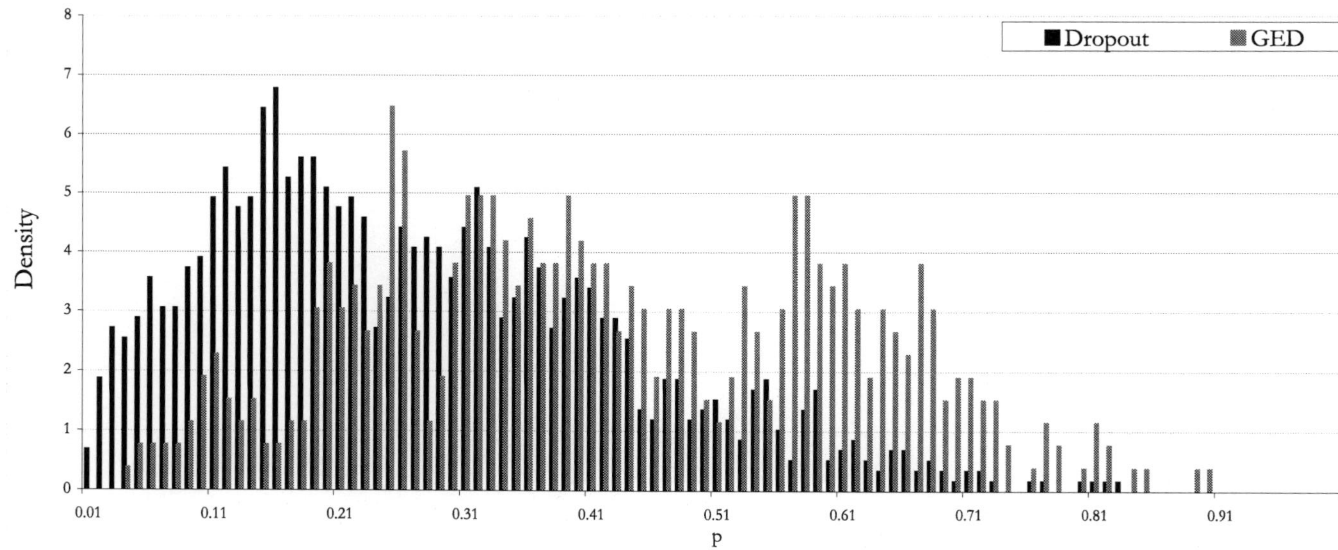

Note: The propensity score ($P(D = 1 \mid Z)$) is computed using as controls (Z): Father's highest grade completed, mother's highest grade completed, number of siblings, GED testing fee by state between 1993 and 2000, family income in 1979, dropout's local wage at age 17, and high school graduate's local unemployment at age 17. We also include two dummy variables controlling for the place of residence at age 14 (south and urban), and a set of dummies controlling for the year of birth (1957–1963).

Figure 14. Frequency of the propensity score by final schooling decision: Dropouts and GEDs, NLSY males at age 25. *Source*: Heckman, Urzua and Vytlacil (2004).

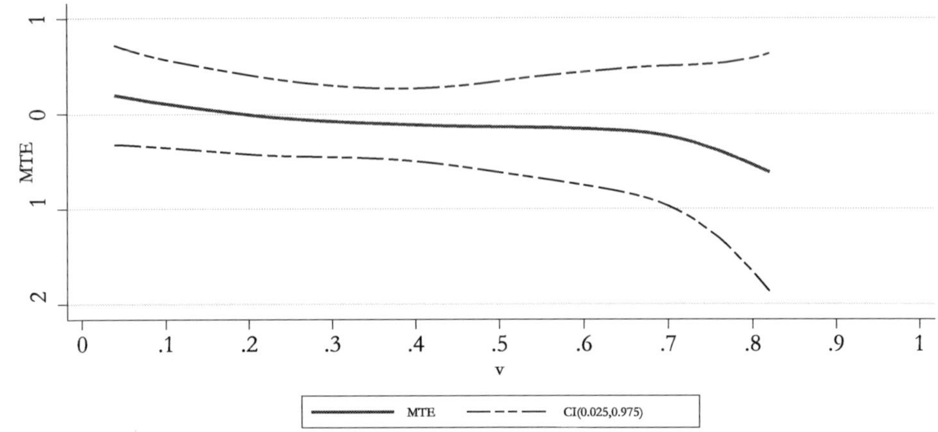

Note: The dependent variable in the outcome equation is the log of the average hourly wage reported between ages 24 and 26. The controls in the outcome equations are tenure, tenure squared, experience, corrected AFQT, black (dummy), Hispanic (dummy), marital status, and years of schooling. Let $D = 0$ denote dropout status and $D = 1$ denote GED status. The model for D (choice model) includes as controls the corrected AFQT, number of siblings, father's education, mother's education, family income at age 17, local GED costs, broken home at age 14, average local wage at age 17 for dropouts and high school graduates, local unemployment rate at age 17 for dropouts and high school graduates, the dummy variables for black and Hispanic, and a set of dummy variables controlling for year of birth. We also include two dummy variables controlling for the place of residence at age 14 (south and urban). The choice model is estimated using a probit model. In computing the MTE, the bandwidths are selected using the "leave one out" cross-validation method. We use biweight kernel functions. The confidence interval is computed from bootstrapping using 50 draws.

Figure 15. MTE of the GED with confidence interval: Dropouts and GEDs, males of the NLSY at the age 25. *Source*: Heckman, Urzua and Vytlacil (2004).

Many of the variables used in the analysis are determined by age 17. Both father's highest grade completed and local unemployment rate among high school dropouts produce positive (if not precisely determined) IV estimates. A negative MTE weighted by negative IV weights produces a positive IV. A naive application of IV could produce the wrong causal inference, i.e., that GED certification raises wages. Our estimates show that our theoretical examples have real world counterparts.[82]

Carneiro, Heckman and Vytlacil (2006) present an extensive empirical analysis of the wage returns to college attendance. They show how to unify and interpret diverse instruments within a common framework using the MTE and the weights derived in Heckman and Vytlacil (1999, 2001a, 2005). They show negative weights on the MTE for commonly used instruments. Basu et al. (2007) use the MTE and the derived weights to identify the ranges of the MTE identified by different instruments in their analysis of the costs of breast cancer. We next discuss the implications of relaxing separability in the choice equations.

[82] We discuss the GED further in Section 7.

4.10. Monotonicity, uniformity, nonseparability, independence and policy invariance: The limits of instrumental variables

The analysis of this section and the entire recent literature on instrumental variables estimators for models with heterogeneous responses (i.e., models with outcomes of the forms (3.1) and (3.2)) relies critically on the assumption that the treatment choice equation has a representation in the additively separable form (3.3). From Vytlacil (2002), we know that under assumptions (A-1)–(A-5), separability is equivalent to the assumption of monotonicity or uniformity, (IV-3).

This uniformity condition imparts an asymmetry to the entire instrumental variable enterprise. Responses are permitted to be heterogeneous in a general way, but choices of treatment are not. In this section, we relax the assumption of additive separability in (3.3). We establish that in the absence of additive separability or uniformity, the entire instrumental variable identification strategy in this section and the entire recent literature collapses. Parameters can be defined as weighted averages of an MTE. MTE and the derived parameters cannot be identified using any instrumental variable strategy. Appendix B presents a comprehensive discussion, which we summarize in this subsection.

One natural benchmark nonseparable model is a random coefficient model of choice $D = \mathbf{1}[Z\gamma \geqslant 0]$, where γ is a random coefficient vector and $\gamma \perp\!\!\!\perp (Z, U_0, U_1)$. If γ is a random coefficient with a nondegenerate distribution and with components that take both positive and negative values, uniformity is clearly violated. However, it can be violated even when all components of γ are of the same sign if Z is a vector.[83]

Relax the additive separability assumption of Equation (3.3) to consider a more general case

$$D^* = \mu_D(Z, V), \tag{4.19a}$$

where $\mu_D(Z, V)$ is not necessarily additively separable in Z and V, and V is not necessarily a scalar.[84] In the random coefficient example, $V = \gamma$ and $\mu_D = z\gamma$.

$$D = \mathbf{1}\big[D^* \geqslant 0\big]. \tag{4.19b}$$

We maintain assumptions (A-1)–(A-5) and (A-7).

In special cases, (4.19a) can be expressed in an additively separable form. For example, if D^* is weakly separable in Z and V, $D^* = \mu_D(\theta(Z), V)$ for any V where $\theta(Z)$ is a scalar function, μ_D is increasing in $\theta(Z)$, and V is a scalar, then we can write (4.19b) in the same form as (3.3):

$$D = \mathbf{1}\big[\theta(Z) \geqslant \tilde{V}\big],$$

[83] Thus, if γ is a vector with positive components, a change from $Z = z$ to $Z = z'$ can produce different effects on choice if γ varies in the population and if components of Z are of different signs.

[84] The additively separable latent index model is more general than it may at first appear. It is shown in Vytlacil (2006a) that a wide class of threshold crossing models without the additive structure on the latent index will have a representation with the additively separable structure on the latent index.

where $\tilde{V} = \mu_D^{-1}(0; V)$ and $\tilde{V} \perp\!\!\!\perp Z \mid X$, and the inverse function is expressed with respect to the first argument [see Vytlacil (2006a)]. Vytlacil (2002) shows that any model that does not satisfy uniformity (or "monotonicity") will not have a representation in this form.[85]

In the additively separable case, the MTE (3.4) has three equivalent interpretations. (i) $U_D = F_V(V)$ is the only unobservable in the first stage decision rule, and MTE is the average effect of treatment given the unobserved characteristics in the decision rule $(V = v)$. (ii) A person with $V = v$ would be indifferent between treatment or not if $P(Z) = u_D$, where $P(Z)$ is a mean scale utility function. Thus, the MTE is the average effect of treatment given that the individual would be indifferent between treatment or not if $P(Z) = u_D$. (iii) One can also view the additively separable form (3.3) as intrinsic in the way we are defining the parameter and interpret the MTE (Equation (3.4)) as an average effect conditional on the additive error term from the first stage choice model. Under all interpretations of the MTE and under the assumptions used in the preceding sections of this chapter, MTE can be identified by LIV; the MTE does not depend on Z and hence it is policy invariant and the MTE integrates up to generate all treatment effects, policy effects and all IV estimands.

The three definitions are not the same in the general nonseparable case (4.19a). Heckman and Vytlacil (2001b) extend MTE in the nonseparable case using interpretation (i). MTE defined this way is policy invariant to changes in Z. Appendix B, which summarizes their work, shows that LIV is a weighted average of the MTE with possibly negative weights and does not identify MTE. If uniformity does not hold, the definition of MTE allows one to integrate MTE to obtain all of the treatment effects, but the instrumental variables estimator breaks down.

Alternatively, one could define MTE based on (ii):

$$\Delta_{\text{ii}}^{\text{MTE}}(z) = E\big(Y_1 - Y_0 \bigm| V \in \{v\colon \mu_D(z, v) = 0\}\big).$$

This is the average treatment effect for individuals who would be indifferent between treatment or not at a given value of z (recall that we keep the conditioning on X implicit). Heckman and Vytlacil (2001b) show that in the nonseparable case LIV does not identify this MTE and that MTE does not change when the distribution of Z changes, provided that the support of MTE does not change.[86] In general, this definition of MTE does not allow one to integrate up MTE to obtain the treatment parameters.

A third possibility is to force the index rule into an additive form by taking $\mu_D^*(Z) = E(\mu_D(Z, V) \mid Z)$, defining $V^* = \mu_D(Z, V) - E(\mu_D(Z, V) \mid Z)$ and define MTE as $E(Y_1 - Y_0 \mid V^* = v^*)$. Note that V^* is not independent of Z, is not policy invariant and is not structural. LIV does not estimate this MTE. With this definition of the MTE it is not possible, in general, to integrate up MTE to obtain the various treatment effects.

[85] In the random coefficient case where $Z = (1, Z_1)$ where Z_1 is a scalar, and $\gamma = (\gamma_0, \gamma_1)$ if $\gamma_1 > 0$ for all realizations, we can write the choice rule in the form of (3.3): $Z_1\gamma_1 \geqslant -\gamma_0 \Rightarrow Z_1 \geqslant -\frac{\gamma_0}{\gamma_1}$ and $\tilde{V} = -\frac{\gamma_0}{\gamma_1}$. This trick does not work in the general case.

[86] If the support of Z changes, then the MTE must be extended to a new support.

For any version of the nonseparable model, except those that can be transformed to separability, index sufficiency fails. To see this, assume that $\mu_D(Z, V)$ is continuous.[87] Define $\Omega(z) = \{v: \mu_D(z, v) \geqslant 0\}$. In the additively separable case, $P(z) \equiv \Pr(D = 1 \mid Z = z) = \Pr(U_D \in \Omega(z))$, $P(z) = P(z') \Leftrightarrow \Omega(z) = \Omega(z')$. This produces index sufficiency. In the more general case of (4.19a), it is possible to have (z, z') such that $P(z) = P(z')$ and $\Omega(z) \neq \Omega(z')$ so index sufficiency does not hold.

4.10.1. Implications of nonseparability

This section develops generalization (i), leaving development of the other interpretations for later research. We focus on an analysis of PRTE, comparing two policies $p, p' \in \mathcal{P}$. Here "p" denotes a policy and not a realization of $P(Z)$ as in the previous sections. This is our convention when we discuss PRTE. The analysis of the other treatment parameters follows by parallel arguments.

For any v in the support of the distribution of V, define $\Omega = \{z: \mu_D(z, v) \geqslant 0\}$. For example, in the random coefficient case, with $V \equiv \gamma$ and $D = \mathbf{1}[Z\gamma \geqslant 0]$, we have $\Omega_g = \{z: zg \geqslant 0\}$, where g is a realization of γ. Define $\mathbf{1}_{\mathcal{A}}(t)$ to be the indicator function for the event $t \in \mathcal{A}$. Then, making the X explicit, Appendix B derives the result that

$$
\begin{aligned}
&E(Y_p) - E(Y_{p'}) \\
&\quad = E\big[E(Y_p \mid X) - E(Y_{p'} \mid X)\big] \\
&\quad = \int \bigg[\int E(\Delta^{\text{MTE}} \mid X = x, V = v) \\
&\qquad \times \big(\Pr[Z_p \in \Omega \mid X = x] - \Pr[Z_{p'} \in \Omega \mid X = x]\big)\, dF_{V|X}(v \mid x) \bigg] dF_X(x).
\end{aligned}
\tag{4.20}
$$

Thus, without additive separability, we can still derive an expression for PRTE and by similar reasoning the other treatment parameters. However, to evaluate the expression requires knowledge of MTE, of $\Pr[Z_p \in \Omega \mid X = x]$ and $\Pr[Z_{p'} \in \Omega \mid X = x]$ for every (v, x) in the support of the distribution of (V, X), and of the distribution of V. In general, if no structure is placed on the μ_D function, one can normalize V to be unit uniform (or a vector of unit uniform random variables) so that $F_{V|X}$ will be known.

However, in this case, the $\Omega = \{z: \mu_D(z, v) \geqslant 0\}$ sets will not in general be identified. If structure is placed on the μ_D function, one might be able to identify the $\Omega = \{z: \mu_D(z, v) \geqslant 0\}$ sets but then one needs to identify the distribution of V (conditional on X). If structure is placed on μ_D, one cannot in general normalize the distribution of V to be unit uniform without undoing the structure being imposed on μ_D.

In particular, consider the random coefficient model $D = \mathbf{1}[Z\gamma \geqslant 0]$ where $V = \gamma$ is a random vector, so that $\Omega_\gamma = \{z: z\gamma \geqslant 0\}$. In this case, if all of the other assumptions

[87] Absolutely continuous with respect to Lebesgue measure.

hold, including $Z \perp\!\!\!\perp \gamma \mid X$, and the policy change does not affect (Y_1, Y_0, X, γ), the PRTE is given by

$$\begin{aligned} E(Y_p) - E(Y_{p'}) &= E\big[E(Y_p \mid X) - E(Y_{p'} \mid X)\big] \\ &= \int\bigg[\int E(\Delta^{\text{MTE}} \mid X = x, \gamma = g)\big(\Pr[Z_p \in \Omega_g \mid X = x] \\ &\qquad - \Pr[Z_{p'} \in \Omega_g \mid X = x]\big)\, dF_{\gamma|X}(g \mid x)\bigg]\, dF_X(x). \end{aligned}$$

Because structure has been placed on the $\mu_D(Z, \gamma)$ function, the sets Ω_γ are known. However, evaluating the function requires knowledge of the distribution of γ which will not in general be identified without further assumptions.[88] Normalizing the distribution of γ to be a vector of unit uniform random variables produces the distribution of γ but eliminates the assumed linear index structure on μ_D and results in Ω_γ sets that are not identified.

Even if the weights are identified, Heckman and Vytlacil (2001b) show that it is not possible to use LIV to identify MTE without additive separability between Z and V in the selection rule index. Appendix F develops this point for the random coefficient model. Without additive separability in the latent index for the selection rule, we can still create an expression for PRTE (and the other treatment parameters) but both the weights and the MTE function are no longer identified using instrumental variables.

One superficially plausible way to avoid these problems would be to define $\tilde{\mu}_D(Z) = E(\mu_D(Z, V) \mid Z)$ and $\tilde{V} = \mu_D(Z, V) - E(\mu_D(Z, V) \mid Z)$, producing the model $D = \mathbf{1}[\tilde{\mu}_D(Z) + \tilde{V} \geqslant 0]$. We keep the conditioning on X implicit. One could redefine MTE using $\tilde{V}$ and proceed as if the true model possessed additive separability between observables and unobservables in the latent index. This is the method pursued in approach (iii).

For two reasons, this approach does not solve the problem of providing an adequate generalization of MTE. First, with this definition, $\tilde{V}$ is a function of (Z, V), and a policy that changes Z will then also change $\tilde{V}$. Thus, policy invariance of the MTE no longer holds. Second, this approach generates a $\tilde{V}$ that is no longer statistically independent of Z so that assumption (A-1) no longer holds when $\tilde{V}$ is substituted for V even when (A-1) is true for V. Lack of independence between observables and unobservables in the latent index both invalidates our expression for PRTE (and the expressions for the other treatment effects) and causes LIV to no longer identify MTE.

The nonseparable model can also restrict the support of $P(Z)$. For example, consider a standard normal random coefficient model with a scalar regressor ($Z = (1, Z_1)$). Assume $\gamma_0 \sim N(0, \sigma_0^2)$, $\gamma_1 \sim N(\bar{\gamma}_1, \sigma_1^2)$, and $\gamma_0 \perp\!\!\!\perp \gamma_1$. Then

$$P(z_1) = \Phi\left(\frac{\bar{\gamma}_1 z_1}{\sqrt{\sigma_0^2 + \sigma_1^2 z_1^2}}\right),$$

[88] See, e.g., Ichimura and Thompson (1998) for conditions for identifying the distribution of γ in a random coefficient discrete choice model when $Z \perp\!\!\!\perp \gamma$.

where Φ is the standard cumulative normal distribution. If the support of z_1 is $\mathbb{R}$, then in the standard additive model, $\sigma_1^2 = 0$ and $P(z_1)$ has support [0, 1]. When $\sigma_1^2 > 0$, the support is strictly within the unit interval.[89] In the special case when $\sigma_0^2 = 0$, the support is one point ($P(z) = \Phi(\frac{\bar{\gamma}_1}{\sigma_1})$). We cannot, in general, identify ATE, TT or any treatment effect requiring the endpoints 0 or 1.

Thus the general models of nonuniformity presented in this section do not satisfy the index sufficiency property, and the support of the treatment effects and estimators is, in general, less than full. The random coefficient model for choice may explain the empirical support problems for $P(Z)$ found in Heckman et al. (1998) and many other evaluation studies.

4.10.2. Implications of dependence

We next consider relaxing the independence assumption (A-1) to allow $Z \not\!\perp\!\!\!\perp V \mid X$ while maintaining the assumption that $Z \perp\!\!\!\perp (Y_0, Y_1) \mid (X, V)$. We maintain the other assumptions, including additive separability between Z and V in the latent index for the selection rule (Equation (3.3)) and the assumption that the policy changes Z but does not change (V, Y_0, Y_1, X). Thus we assume that the policy shift does not change the MTE function (policy invariance). Given these assumptions, we derive in Appendix C the following expression for PRTE in the nonindependent case for policies $p, p' \in \mathcal{P}$:

$$\begin{aligned} &E(Y_p) - E(Y_{p'}) \\ &\quad = E\big[E(Y_p \mid X) - E(Y_{p'} \mid X)\big] \\ &\quad = \int \bigg[\int E(\Delta^{\text{MTE}} \mid X = x, V = v)\big(\Pr[\mu_D(Z_{p'}) < v \mid X = x, V = v] \\ &\qquad - \Pr[\mu_D(Z_p) < v \mid X = x, V = v]\big)\, dF_{V|X}(v \mid x)\bigg] dF_X(x). \end{aligned} \tag{4.21}$$

Notice that "p" denotes a policy and not a realized value of $P(Z)$. Although we can derive an expression for PRTE without requiring independence between Z and V, to evaluate this expression requires knowledge of MTE and of $\Pr[\mu_D(Z_{p'}) < v \mid X = x, V = v]$ and of $\Pr[\mu_D(Z_p) < v \mid X = x, V = v]$ for every (x, v) in the support of the distribution of (X, V). This requirement is stronger than what is needed in the case of independence since the weights no longer depend only on the distribution of $P_p(Z_p)$ and $P_{p'}(Z_{p'})$ conditional on X. To evaluate these weights requires knowledge of the function μ_D and of the joint distribution of (V, Z_p) and $(V, Z_{p'})$ conditional on X, and these will in general not be identified without further assumptions.

Even if the weights are identified, Heckman and Vytlacil (2001b) show that it is not possible to use LIV to identify MTE without independence between Z and V conditional on X. Thus, without conditional independence between Z and V in the latent

[89] The interval is $[\Phi(\frac{-|\bar{\gamma}_1|}{\sigma_1}), \Phi(\frac{|\bar{\gamma}_1|}{\sigma_1})]$.

index for the decision rule, we can still create an expression for PRTE but both the weights and the MTE function are no longer identified without invoking further assumptions.

One superficially appealing way to avoid these problems is to define $\tilde{V} = F_{V|X,Z}(V)$ and $\tilde{\mu}_D(Z) = F_{V|X,Z}(\mu_D(Z))$, so $D = \mathbf{1}[\mu_D(Z) - V \geqslant 0] = \mathbf{1}[\tilde{\mu}_D(Z) - \tilde{V} \geqslant 0]$ with $\tilde{V} \sim \text{Unif}[0, 1]$ conditional on X and Z and so $\tilde{V}$ is independent of X and Z. It might seem that the previous analysis would carry over. However, by defining $\tilde{V} = F_{V|X,Z}(V)$, we have defined $\tilde{V}$ in a way that depends functionally on Z and X, and hence we violate invariance of the MTE with respect to the shifts in the distribution of Z given X.

4.10.3. The limits of instrumental variable estimators

The treatment effect literature focuses on a class of policies that move treatment choices in the same direction for everyone. General instruments do not have universally positive weights on Δ^{MTE}. They are not guaranteed to shift everyone in the same direction. They do not necessarily estimate gross treatment effects. However, the effect of treatment is not always the parameter of policy interest. Thus, in the housing subsidy example developed in Section 4.6, migration is the vehicle through which the policy operates. One might be interested in the effect of migration (the treatment effect) or the effect of the policy (the housing subsidy). These are separate issues unless the policy is the treatment.

Generalizing the MTE to the case of a nonseparable choice equation that violates the monotonicity condition, we can define but cannot identify the policy parameters of interest using ordinary instrumental variables or our extension LIV. If we make the model symmetrically heterogeneous in outcome and choice equations, the method of instrumental variables and our extensions of it break down in terms of estimating economically interpretable parameters. Vytlacil and Yildiz (2006) and Vytlacil, Santos and Shaikh (2005) restore symmetry in the IV analysis of treatment choice and outcome equations by imposing uniformity on both outcome and choice equations. The general case of heterogeneity in both treatment and choice equations is beyond the outer limits of the entire IV literature, although it captures intuitively plausible phenomena. More general structural methods are required.[90]

5. Regression discontinuity estimators and LATE

Campbell (1969) developed the regression discontinuity design which is now widely used. [See an early discussion of this estimator in econometrics by Barnow, Cain and

90 The framework of Carneiro, Hansen and Heckman (2003) can be generalized to allow for random coefficient models in choice equations, and lack of policy invariance in the sense of assumption (A-7). However, a fully semiparametric analysis of treatment and choice equations with random coefficients remains to be developed.

Goldberger (1980).] Hahn, Todd and Van der Klaauw (2001) present an exposition of the regression discontinuity estimator within a LATE framework. This section exposits the regression discontinuity method within our MTE framework.

Suppose assumptions (A-1)–(A-5) hold except that we relax independence assumption (A-1) to assume that $(Y_1 - Y_0, U_D)$ is independent of Z conditional on X. We *do not* impose the condition that Y_0 is independent of Z conditional on X. Relaxing the assumption that Y_0 is independent of Z conditional on X causes the standard LIV estimand to differ from the MTE. We show that the LIV estimand in this case equals MTE plus a bias term that depends on $\frac{\partial}{\partial p}E(Y_0 \mid X = x, P(Z) = p)$. Likewise, we show that the discrete-difference IV formula will no longer correspond to LATE, but will now correspond to LATE plus a bias term.

A regression discontinuity design allows analysts to recover a LATE parameter at a particular value of Z. If $E(Y_0 \mid X = x, Z = z)$ is continuous in z, while $P(z)$ is discontinuous in z at a particular point, then it will be possible to use a regression discontinuity design to recover a LATE parameter. While the regression discontinuity design does have the advantage of allowing Y_0 to depend on Z conditional on X, it only recovers a LATE parameter at a particular value of Z and cannot in general be used to recover either other treatment parameters such as the average treatment effect or the answers to policy questions such as the PRTE. The following discussion is motivated by the analysis of Hahn, Todd and Van der Klaauw (2001).

For simplicity, assume that Z is a scalar random variable. First, consider LIV while relaxing independence assumption (A-1) to assume that $(Y_1 - Y_0, U_D)$ is independent of Z conditional on X but without imposing that Y_0 is independent of Z conditional on X. In order to make the comparison with the regression discontinuity design easier, we will condition on Z instead of $P(Z)$. Using $Y = Y_0 + D(Y_1 - Y_0)$, we obtain

$$\begin{aligned} &E(Y \mid X = x, Z = z) \\ &\quad = E(Y_0 \mid X = x, Z = z) + E\big(D(Y_1 - Y_0) \bigm| X = x, Z = z\big) \\ &\quad = E(Y_0 \mid X = x, Z = z) + \int_0^{P(z)} E(Y_1 - Y_0 \mid X = x, U_D = u_D)\, du_D. \end{aligned}$$

So

$$\begin{aligned} \frac{\frac{\partial}{\partial z}E(Y \mid X = x, Z = z)}{\frac{\partial}{\partial z}P(z)} = {} & \frac{\frac{\partial}{\partial z}E(Y_0 \mid X = x, Z = z)}{\frac{\partial}{\partial z}P(z)} \\ & + E\big(Y_1 - Y_0 \bigm| X = x, U_D = P(z)\big) \end{aligned}$$

where we have assumed that $\frac{\partial}{\partial z}P(z) \neq 0$ and that $E(Y_0 \mid X = x, Z = z)$ is differentiable in z. Notice that under our stronger independence condition (A-1), $\frac{\partial}{\partial z}E(Y_0 \mid X = x, Z = z) = 0$ so that we identify MTE as before. With Y_0 possibly dependent on Z conditional on X, we now get MTE plus the bias term that depends on $\frac{\partial}{\partial z}E(Y_0 \mid X = x, Z = z)$. Likewise, if we consider the discrete change form of IV:

$$\frac{E(Y \mid X=x, Z=z) - E(Y \mid X=x, Z=z')}{P(z)-P(z')} = \underbrace{\frac{E(Y_0 \mid X=x, Z=z) - E(Y_0 \mid X=x, Z=z')}{P(z)-P(z')}}_{\text{Bias for LATE}} + \underbrace{E\big(Y_1 - Y_0 \bigm| X=x, P(z) > U_D > P(z')\big)}_{\text{LATE}}$$

so that we now recover LATE plus a bias term.

Now consider a regression discontinuity design. Suppose that there exists an evaluation point z_0 for Z such that $P(\cdot)$ is discontinuous at z_0, and suppose that $E(Y_0 \mid X=x, Z=z)$ is continuous at z_0. Suppose that $P(\cdot)$ is increasing in a neighborhood of z_0. Let

$$P(z_0-) = \lim_{\epsilon \downarrow 0} P(z_0 - \epsilon),$$
$$P(z_0+) = \lim_{\epsilon \downarrow 0} P(z_0 + \epsilon),$$

and note that the conditions that $P(\cdot)$ is increasing in a neighborhood of z_0 and discontinuous at z_0 imply that $P(z_0+) > P(z_0-)$. Let

$$\mu(x, z_0-) = \lim_{\epsilon \downarrow 0} E(Y \mid X=x, Z=z_0-\epsilon),$$
$$\mu(x, z_0+) = \lim_{\epsilon \downarrow 0} E(Y \mid X=x, Z=z_0+\epsilon),$$

and note that

$$\mu(x, z_0-) = E(Y_0 \mid X=x, Z=z_0) + \int_0^{P(z_0-)} E(Y_1 - Y_0 \mid X=x, U_D=u_D)\,du_D$$

and

$$\mu(x, z_0+) = E(Y_0 \mid X=x, Z=z_0) + \int_0^{P(z_0+)} E(Y_1 - Y_0 \mid X=x, U_D=u_D)\,du_D,$$

where we use the fact that $E(Y_0 \mid X=x, Z=z)$ is continuous at z_0. Thus,

$$\mu(x, z_0+) - \mu(x, z_0-) = \int_{P(z_0-)}^{P(z_0+)} E(Y_1 - Y_0 \mid X=x, U_D=u_D)\,du_D$$
$$\Rightarrow \quad \frac{\mu(x, z_0+) - \mu(x, z_0-)}{P(z_0+) - P(z_0-)} = E\big(Y_1 - Y_0 \bigm| X=x, P(z_0+) \geqslant U_D > P(z_0-)\big)$$

so that we now recover a LATE parameter for a particular point of evaluation. Note that if $P(z)$ is only discontinuous at z_0, then we only identify $E(Y_1 - Y_0 \mid X = x, P(z_0+) \geqslant U_D > P(z_0-))$ and not any LATE or MTE at any other evaluation points. While this discussion assumes that Z is a scalar, it is straightforward to generalize the discussion to allow for Z to be a vector. For more discussion of the regression discontinuity design estimator and an example, see Hahn, Todd and Van der Klaauw (2001).

6. Policy evaluation, out-of-sample policy forecasting, forecasting the effects of new policies and structural models based on the MTE

We have thus far focused on policy problem P-1, the problem of "internal validity". We have shown how to identify a variety of parameters but have not put them to use in evaluating policies. This section discusses policy evaluation and out-of-sample forecasting. We discuss two distinct evaluation and forecasting problems. The first problem uses the MTE to develop a cost benefit analysis. Corresponding to the gross benefit parameters analyzed in Sections 3–4, there is a parallel set of cost parameters that emerge from the economics of the generalized Roy model. This part of our analysis works in the domain of problem P-1 to construct a cost-benefit analysis for programs in place. However, these tools can be extended to new environments using the other results established in this section.

The second topic is the problem of constructing the PRTE in new environments in a more general way. This addresses policy problems P-2 and P-3 and considers large scale changes in policies and forecasts of new policies.

6.1. Econometric cost benefit analysis based on the MTE

This section complements the analysis of Section 3. There we developed gross outcome measures for a generalized Roy model. Here we define a parallel set of treatment parameters for the generalized Roy model corresponding to the average cost of participating in a program. The central feature of the generalized Roy model is that the agent chooses treatment if the benefit exceeds the subjective cost perceived by the agent. This creates a simple relationship between the cost and benefit parameters that can be exploited for identifying or bounding the cost parameters by adapting the results of the previous sections. The main result of this section is that cost parameters in the generalized Roy model can be identified or bounded without direct information on the costs of treatment. Our analysis complements and extends the analysis of Björklund and Moffitt (1987) who first noted this duality.

Assume the outcomes (Y_0, Y_1) are generated by the additively separable system (2.2). Let C denote the individual-specific subjective cost of selecting into treatment. We assume that C is generated by: $C = \mu_C(W) + U_C$, where W is a (possibly vector-valued) observed random variable and U_C is an unobserved random variable. We assume that the agent selects into treatment if the benefit exceeds the cost, using the structure of the generalized Roy model where $D = \mathbf{1}[Y_1 - Y_0 \geqslant C]$ and $C = \mu_C(W) + U_C$, where $\mu_C(W)$ is nondegenerate and integrable; U_C is continuous and $Z = (W, X)$ is independent of (U_C, U_0, U_1).[91]

We do not assume any particular functional form for the functions μ_0, μ_1 and μ_C, and we do not assume that the distribution of U_0, U_1, or U_C is known.[92] Let $V \equiv U_C - (U_1 - U_0)$ and let F_V denote the distribution function of V. As before, we use the convention that U_D is the probability integral transformation of the latent variable generating choices so that $U_D = F_V(V)$. Let $P(z) \equiv \Pr(D = 1 \mid Z = z)$ so that $P(z) = F_V(\mu_1(x) - \mu_0(x) - \mu_C(w))$. For convenience, we will assume that F_V is strictly increasing so that F_V will be invertible, though this assumption is not required. We work with $U_D = F_V(V)$ instead of working directly with V to link our analysis to that in Section 3. In this section we make explicit the conditioning on X, Z, and W because it plays an important role in the analysis.

Corresponding to the treatment parameters defined in Section 2 and Tables 2A and 2B, we can define analogous cost parameters. We define the marginal cost of treatment for a person with characteristics $W = w$ and $U_D = u_D$ as

$$C^{\text{MTE}}(w, u_D) \equiv E(C \mid W = w, U_D = u_D).$$

This is a cost version of the marginal treatment effect. Likewise, we have an analogue average cost:

$$\begin{aligned} C^{\text{ATE}}(w) &\equiv E(C \mid W = w) \\ &= \int_0^1 E(C \mid W = w, U_D = u_D)\, du_D, \end{aligned} \tag{6.1}$$

recalling that $dF_{U_D}(u_D) = du_D$ because U_D is uniform. This is the mean subjective cost of treatment as perceived by the average agent. We next consider

$$\begin{aligned} C^{\text{TT}}\big(w, P(z)\big) &\equiv E\big(C \bigm| W = w, P(Z) = P(z), D = 1\big) \\ &= \frac{1}{P(z)} \int_0^{P(z)} E(C \mid W = w, U_D = u_D)\, du_D. \end{aligned}$$

This is the mean subjective cost of treatment as perceived by the treated with a given value of $P(z)$. Removing the conditioning on $P(z)$,

$$\begin{aligned} C^{\text{TT}}(w) &\equiv E(C \mid W = w, D = 1) \\ &= \int_0^1 E(C \mid W = w, U_D = u_D) g_w(u_D)\, du_D, \end{aligned}$$

[91] We require that U_C be absolutely continuous with respect to Lebesgue measure.

[92] Recall that the original Roy model (1951) assumes that $U_C = 0$, that there are no observed X and W regressors, that $(U_0, U_1) \sim N(0, \Sigma)$ and that only $Y = DY_1 + (1 - D)Y_0$ is observed, but not both components of the sum at the same time.

where $g_w(u_D) = \frac{1-F_{P(Z)|W=w}(u_D)}{\int(1-F_{P(Z)|W=w}(t))\,dt}$ and $F_{P(Z)|W=w}$ denotes the distribution of $P(Z)$ conditional on $W = w$. This is the mean subjective cost of treatment for the treated. Finally, we can derive a LATE version of the cost:

$$C^{\text{LATE}}\big(w, P(z), P(z')\big) \equiv \frac{1}{P(z) - P(z')} \int_{P(z')}^{P(z)} E(C \mid W = w, U_D = u_D)\,du_D.$$

This is the mean subjective cost of switching states for those induced to switch status by a change in the instrument.

The generalized Roy model makes a tight link between the cost of treatment and the benefit of treatment. Thus one might expect a relationship between the gross benefit and cost parameters. We show that the benefit and cost parameters coincide for MTE. This relationship can be used to infer information on the subjective cost of treatment by the use of local instrumental variables.

Define $\Delta^{\text{LIV}}(x, P(z))$ as in Equation (4.9):

$$\Delta^{\text{LIV}}\big(x, P(z)\big) \equiv \frac{\partial E(Y \mid X = x, P(Z) = P(z))}{\partial P(z)}.$$

Under assumptions (A-1)–(A-5), LIV identifies MTE:

$$\Delta^{\text{LIV}}\big(x, P(z)\big) = \Delta^{\text{MTE}}\big(x, P(z)\big).$$

Note that

$$\begin{aligned}\Delta^{\text{MTE}}\big(x, P(z)\big) &= E\big(\Delta \mid X = x, U_D = P(z)\big)\\ &= E\big(\Delta \mid X = x, \Delta(x) = C(w)\big)\\ &= E\big(\Delta(x) \mid \Delta(x) = C(w)\big),\end{aligned} \tag{6.2}$$

where $\Delta(x) = \mu_1(x) - \mu_0(x) + U_1 - U_0$, and $C(w) = \mu_C(w) + U_C$. ($\Delta(x)$ and $C(w)$ are, respectively, the benefit and cost for the agent if the X and W are externally set to x and w without changing (U_1, U_0, U_D) values.) We thus obtain

$$\begin{aligned}E\big(\Delta(x) \mid \Delta(x) = C(w)\big) &= E\big(C(w) \mid \Delta(x) = C(w)\big)\\ &= E\big(C(w) \mid W = w, U_D = P(z)\big)\\ &= C^{\text{MTE}}\big(w, P(z)\big).\end{aligned} \tag{6.3}$$

Thus,

$$\Delta^{\text{LIV}}\big(x, P(z)\big) = \Delta^{\text{MTE}}\big(x, P(z)\big) = C^{\text{MTE}}\big(w, P(z)\big), \tag{6.4}$$

where $\Delta^{\text{LIV}}(w, P(z))$ is $\Delta^{\text{LIV}}(x, P(z))$ defined for the support where $\Delta(x) = C(w)$. The benefit and cost parameters coincide for the MTE parameter because at the margin, the marginal cost should equal the marginal benefit. The benefit to treatment for an agent indifferent between treatment and no treatment is equal to the cost of treatment, and thus the two parameters coincide.

Suppose that one has access to a large sample of (Y, D, X, W) observations. Since $\Delta^{\mathrm{LIV}}(x, P(z)) = \frac{\partial E(Y|X=x, P(Z)=P(z))}{\partial P(z)}$, $\Delta^{\mathrm{LIV}}(x, P(z))$ can be identified for any $(x, P(z))$ in the support of $(X, P(Z))$, and thus the corresponding $\Delta^{\mathrm{MTE}}(x, P(z))$ and $C^{\mathrm{MTE}}(w, P(z))$ parameters can also be identified.[93] One can thus identify the marginal cost parameter without direct information on the cost of treatment by using the structure of the Roy model and by identifying the marginal benefit parameter.

Heckman and Vytlacil (1999) establish conditions under which Δ^{LIV} can be used to identify Δ^{ATE} and Δ^{TT} given large support conditions, and to bound those parameters without large support conditions if the outcome variables are bounded. We review their results on bounds in Section 10. We surveyed their results on identification of Δ^{ATE} and Δ^{TT} in Sections 3 and 4. From (6.1) and (6.4), we can use the same arguments to use C^{MTE} to identify or bound C^{ATE} and C^{TT}. Thus, C^{MTE} can be used to identify $C^{\mathrm{ATE}}(w)$ if the support of $P(Z)$ conditional on $W = w$ is the full unit interval. If the support of $P(Z)$ conditional on $W = w$ is a proper subset of the full unit interval, then C^{MTE} can be used to bound $C^{\mathrm{ATE}}(x)$ if C is bounded. One can thus identify or bound the average cost of treatment or the cost of treatment on the treated without direct information on the cost of treatment.

We next consider what information is available on the underlying benefit functions μ_0 and μ_1 and the underlying cost function $\mu_C(w)$. From the definitions,

$$\begin{aligned}\Delta^{\mathrm{MTE}}\big(x, P(z)\big) &= E\big(\Delta \bigm| X = x, U_D = P(z)\big)\\ &= \mu_1(x) - \mu_0(x) + \Upsilon\big(P(z)\big)\end{aligned} \tag{6.5}$$

with $\Upsilon(P(z)) = E(U_1 - U_0 \mid U_D = P(z))$. Likewise,

$$\begin{aligned}C^{\mathrm{MTE}}\big(w, P(z)\big) &= E\big(C \bigm| W = w, U_D = P(z)\big)\\ &= \mu_C(w) + \Gamma\big(P(z)\big),\end{aligned} \tag{6.6}$$

with $\Gamma(P(z)) = E(U_C \mid U_D = P(z))$. Let $\Delta^{\mathrm{LIV}}(z) = \Delta^{\mathrm{LIV}}(x, P(z))$, and recall from the preceding analysis that $\Delta^{\mathrm{LIV}}(z) = \Delta^{\mathrm{MTE}}(x, P(z)) = C^{\mathrm{MTE}}(w, P(z))$. Consider two points of evaluation (z, z') such that $P(z) = P(z')$. Using Equation (6.4), we obtain

$$\begin{aligned}\Delta^{\mathrm{LIV}}(z) - \Delta^{\mathrm{LIV}}(z') &= \big(\mu_1(x) - \mu_0(x)\big) - \big(\mu_1(x') - \mu_0(x')\big)\\ &= \mu_C(w) - \mu_C(w').\end{aligned}$$

Assuming that X and W each have at least one component not in the other, we can identify $\mu_C(w)$ up to constants within the support of W conditional on $P(Z) = P(z)$ using $\Delta^{\mathrm{LIV}}(z)$. Shifting z while conditioning on $P(z)$ shifts $(\mu_1(x)-\mu_0(x))$ and $\mu_C(w)$ along the line $(\mu_1(x)-\mu_0(x))-\mu_C(w) = F_V^{-1}(p)$. Thus, conditional on $P(z)$, a shift in the benefit, $\mu_1(X)-\mu_0(X)$, is associated with the same shift in the cost, $\mu_C(w)$. For any $p \in (0, 1)$, let $\Omega_p = \{z\colon\ P(z) = p\} = \{(w, x)\colon\ (\mu_1(x)-\mu_0(x))-\mu_C(w) = F_V^{-1}(p)\}$.

[93] Formally, these parameters are identified in the limit points of the set.

As we vary z within the set Ω_p, we trace out changes in $\mu_C(w)$ and $\mu_1(x) - \mu_0(x)$, where the changes in $\mu_C(w)$ equal the changes in $\mu_1(x) - \mu_0(x)$.

For the special case of the generalized Roy model where U_C is degenerate, $\Delta^{\text{LIV}}(z) = \mu_C(w)$. Thus, in the case of a deterministic cost function, LIV identifies $\mu_C(w)$. We plot this case in Figures 5A–5C for the country policy adoption example where the cost C is a constant across all countries.

In the case where U_C is nondegenerate but $U_1 - U_0$ is degenerate, $Y_1 - Y_0 = \mu_1(X) - \mu_0(X)$ ($\beta = \bar{\beta}$ in the context of the model of Section 2), and there is no variation in the gross benefit from participating in the program conditional on X. In that case, $\Delta^{\text{LIV}}(z) = \mu_1(x) - \mu_0(x) = \bar{\beta}$, where we keep the conditioning on X implicit in defining $\Delta^{\text{LIV}}(z)$. Thus, in the case of a deterministic benefit from participation, LIV identifies the benefit function. If U_D and $U_1 - U_0$ are both degenerate, then $\Delta^{\text{LIV}}(z)$ is not well defined.[94]

In summary, the generalized Roy model structure can be exploited to identify cost parameters without direct information on the cost of treatment. The MTE parameter for cost is immediately identified within the proper support, and can be used to identify or bound the average cost of treatment and the cost of treatment on the treated. In addition, the MTE parameter allows one to infer how the cost function shifts in response to a change in observed covariates, and to completely identify the cost function if the cost of treatment is deterministic conditional on observable covariates. Thus we can compute the costs and benefits of alternative programs for various population averages. Heckman and Vytlacil (2007) develop this analysis to consider marginal extensions of the policy relevant treatment effect (PRTE).

6.2. Constructing the PRTE in new environments

In this section, we present conditions for constructing PRTE for new environments and for new programs using historical data for general changes in policies and environments. We consider general changes in the environment and policies and not just the marginal perturbations of the $P(Z)$ considered in the previous section. We address policy problems P-2, forecasting the effects of existing policies to new environments and P-3, forecasting the effects of new policies, never previously implemented.

Let $p \in \mathcal{P}$ denote a policy characterized by random vector Z_p. The usage of "p" in this section is to be distinguished from a realized value of $P(Z)$ as in most other sections in this chapter. Let $e \in \mathcal{E}$ denote an environment characterized by random vector X_e. A history, $\mathcal{H}$, is a collection of policy–environment (p, e) pairs that have been experienced and documented. We assume that the environment is autonomous so

[94] In this case, $E(Y_1 - Y_0 \mid Z = z, D = 0)$ is well defined for $z = (w, x)$ such that $\mu_1(x) - \mu_0(x) \leqslant \mu_C(w)$, in which case $E(Y_1 - Y_0 \mid Z = z, D = 0) = \mu_1(x) - \mu_0(x) \leqslant \mu_C(w)$. Likewise $E(Y_1 - Y_0 \mid Z = z, D = 1)$ is well defined for $z = (w, x)$ such that $\mu_1(x) - \mu_0(x) \geqslant \mu_C(w)$, in which case $E(Y_1 - Y_0 \mid Z = z, D = 1) = \mu_1(x) - \mu_0(x) \geqslant \mu_C(w)$.

the choice of p does not affect X_e. Letting $X_{e,p}$ denote the value of X_e under policy p, autonomy requires that

(A-8) $X_{e,p} = X_e, \; \forall p, e$ (*Autonomy*).

Autonomy is a more general notion than the no-feedback assumption introduced in (A-6). They are the same when the policy is a treatment. General equilibrium feedback effects can cause a failure of autonomy. In this section, we will assume autonomy, in accordance with the partial equilibrium tradition in the treatment effect literature.[95] Autonomy is a version of Hurwicz's policy invariance postulate but for a random variable and not a function.

Evaluating a particular policy p' in environment e' is straightforward if $(p', e') \in \mathcal{H}$. One simply looks at the associated outcomes and treatment effects formed in that policy environment and applies the methods previously discussed to obtain internally valid estimates. The challenge comes in forecasting the impacts of policies (p') in environments (e') for (p', e') not in $\mathcal{H}$.

We show how Δ^{MTE} plays the role of a policy-invariant functional that aids in creating counterfactual states never previously experienced. We focus on the problem of constructing the policy relevant treatment effect Δ^{PRTE} but our discussion applies more generally to the other treatment parameters.

Given the assumptions invoked in Section 3, Δ^{MTE} can be used to evaluate a whole menu of policies characterized by different conditional distributions of $P_{p'}$. In addition, given our assumptions, we can focus on how policy p', which is characterized by $Z_{p'}$, produces the distribution $F_{P_{p'}|X}$ which weights an invariant Δ^{MTE} without having to conduct a new investigation of (Y, X, Z) relationships for each proposed policy.[96]

6.2.1. *Constructing weights for new policies in a common environment*

The problem of constructing Δ^{PRTE} for policy p' (compared to baseline policy $\bar{p}$) in environment e when $(p', e) \notin \mathcal{H}$ entails constructing $E(\Upsilon(Y_{p'}))$. We maintain the assumption that the baseline policy is observed, so $(\bar{p}, e) \in \mathcal{H}$. We also postulate instrumental variable assumptions (A-1)–(A-5), presented in Section 3, and the policy invariance assumption (A-7), presented in Section 3.2 and embedded in assumption (A-8). We use separable choice Equation (3.3) to characterize choices. The policy is assumed not to change the distribution of (Y_0, Y_1, U_D) conditional on X. Under these conditions, Equation (3.6) is a valid expression for PRTE and constructing PRTE only requires identification of Δ^{MTE} and constructing $F_{P_{p'}|X_e}$ from the policy histories $\mathcal{H}_e$, defined as the elements of $\mathcal{H}$ for a particular environment e, $\mathcal{H}_e = \{p\colon\ (p, e) \in \mathcal{H}\}$.

[95] See Heckman, Lochner and Taber (1998) for an example of a nonautonomous treatment model.

[96] Ichimura and Taber (2002) present a discussion of local policy analysis in a more general framework without the MTE structure, using a framework developed by Hurwicz (1962). We review the Hurwicz framework in Chapter 70.

Associated with the policy histories $p \in \mathcal{H}_e$ is a collection of policy variables $\{Z_p: p \in \mathcal{H}_e\}$. Suppose that a new policy p' can be written as $Z_{p'} = T_{p',j}(Z_j)$ for some $j \in \mathcal{H}_e$, where $T_{p',j}$ is a known deterministic transformation and $Z_{p'}$ has the same list of variables as Z_j. Examples of policies that can be characterized in this way are tax and subsidy policies on wages, prices and incomes that affect unit costs (wages or prices) and transfers. Tuition might be shifted upward for everyone by the same amount, or tuition might be shifted according to a nonlinear function of current tuition, parents' income, and other observable characteristics in Z_j.

Constructing $F_{P_{p'}|X_e}$ from data in the policy history entails two distinct steps. From the definitions,

$$\Pr(P_{p'} \leqslant t \mid X_e) = \Pr(\{Z_{p'}: \Pr(D_{p'} = 1 \mid Z_{p'}, X_e) \leqslant t\} \mid X_e).$$

If (i) we know the distribution of $Z_{p'}$, and (ii) we know the function $\Pr(D_{p'} = 1 \mid Z_{p'} = z, X_e = x)$ over the appropriate support, we can then recover the distribution of $P_{p'}$ conditional on X_e. Given that $Z_{p'} = T_{p',j}(Z_j)$ for a known function $T_{p',j}(\cdot)$, step (i) is straightforward since we recover the distribution of $Z_{p'}$ from the distribution of Z_j by using the fact that $\Pr(Z_{p'} \leqslant t \mid X_e) = \Pr(\{Z_j: T_{p',j}(Z_j) \leqslant t\} \mid X_e)$. Alternatively, part of the specification of the policy p' might be the distribution $\Pr(Z_{p'} \leqslant t \mid X_e)$. We now turn to the second step, recovering the function $\Pr(D_{p'} = 1 \mid Z_{p'} = z, X_e = x)$ over the appropriate support.

If $Z_{p'}$ and Z_j contain the same elements though possibly with different distributions, then a natural approach to forecasting the new policy is to postulate that

$$P_j(z) = \Pr(D_j = 1 \mid Z_j = z, X_e) \tag{6.7}$$

$$= \Pr(D_{p'} = 1 \mid Z_{p'} = z, X_e) = P_{p'}(z), \tag{6.8}$$

i.e., that over a common support for Z_j and $Z_{p'}$ the known conditional probability function and the desired conditional probability function agree. Condition (6.7) will hold, for example, if $D_j = \mathbf{1}[\mu_D(Z_j) - V \geqslant 0]$, $D_{p'} = \mathbf{1}[\mu_D(Z_{p'}) - V \geqslant 0]$, $Z_j \perp\!\!\!\perp V \mid X_e$, and $Z_{p'} \perp\!\!\!\perp U_D \mid X_e$, recalling that $U_D = F_{V|X}(V)$. Even if condition (6.7) is satisfied on a common support, the support of Z_j and $Z_{p'}$ may not be the same. If the support of the distribution of $Z_{p'}$ is not contained in the support of the distribution of Z_j, then some form of extrapolation is needed. Alternatively, if we strengthen our assumptions so that (6.7) holds for all $j \in \mathcal{H}_e$, we can identify $P_{p'}(z)$ for all z in $\bigcup_{j \in \mathcal{H}_e} \operatorname{Supp}(Z_j)$. However, there is no guarantee that the support of the distribution of $Z_{p'}$ will be contained in $\bigcup_{j \in \mathcal{H}_e} \operatorname{Supp}(Z_j)$, in which case some form of extrapolation is needed.

If extrapolation is required, one approach is to assume a parametric functional form for $P_j(\cdot)$. Given a parametric functional form, one can use the joint distribution of (D_j, Z_j) to identify the unknown parameters of $P_j(\cdot)$ and then extrapolate the parametric functional form to evaluate $P_j(\cdot)$ for all evaluation points in the support of $Z_{p'}$.

Alternatively, if there is overlap between the support of $Z_{p'}$ and Z_j,[97] so there is some overlap in the historical and policy p' supports of Z, we may use nonparametric methods presented in Matzkin (1994) and extended by her in Chapter 73 (Matzkin) of this Handbook, based on functional restrictions (e.g., homogeneity) to construct the desired probabilities on new supports or to bound them. Under the appropriate conditions, we may use analytic continuation to extend $\Pr(D_j = 1 \mid Z_j = z, X_e = x)$ to a new support for each $X_e = x$ [Rudin (1974)].

The approach just presented is based on the assumption stated in Equation (6.7). That assumption is quite natural when $Z_{p'}$ and Z_j both contain the same elements, say they both contain tuition and parent's income. However, in some cases $Z_{p'}$ might contain additional elements not contained in Z_j. As an example, $Z_{p'}$ might include new user fees while Z_j consists of taxes and subsidies but does not include user fees. In this case, the assumption stated in Equation (6.7) is not expected to hold and is not even well defined if $Z_{p'}$ and Z_j contain a different number of elements.

A more basic approach analyzes a class of policies that operate on constraints, prices and endowments arrayed in vector Q. Given the preferences and technology of the agent, a given $Q = q$, however arrived at, generates the same choices for the agent. Thus a wage tax offset by a wage subsidy of the same amount produces a wage that has the same effect on choices as a no-policy wage. Policy j affects Q (e.g., it affects prices paid, endowments and constraints). Define a map $\Phi_j : Z_j \to Q_j$ which maps a policy j, described by Z_j, into its consequences (Q_j) for the baseline, fixed-dimensional vector Q. A new policy p', characterized by $Z_{p'}$, produces $Q_{p'}$ that is possibly different from Q_j for all previous policies $j \in \mathcal{H}_e$.

To construct the random variable $P_{p'} = \Pr(D_{p'} = 1 \mid Z_{p'}, X_e)$, we postulate that

$$\begin{aligned}\Pr\big(D_j = 1 \bigm| Z_j \in \Phi_j^{-1}(q), X_e = x\big) &= \Pr(D_j = 1 \mid Q_j = q, X_e = x)\\ &= \Pr(D_{p'} = 1 \mid Q_{p'} = q, X_e = x)\\ &= \Pr\big(D_{p'} = 1 \bigm| Z_{p'} \in \Phi_{p'}^{-1}(q), X_e = x\big),\end{aligned}$$

where $\Phi_j^{-1}(q) = \{z\colon \Phi_j(z) = q\}$ and $\Phi_{p'}^{-1}(q) = \{z\colon \Phi_{p'}(z) = q\}$. Given these assumptions, our ability to recover $\Pr(D_{p'} = 1 \mid Z_{p'} = z, X_e = x)$ for all (z, x) in the support of $(Z_{p'}, X_e)$ depends on what Φ_j functions have been historically observed and the richness of the histories of Q_j, $j \in \mathcal{H}_e$. For each $z_{p'}$ evaluation point in the support of the distribution of $Z_{p'}$, there is a corresponding $q = \Phi_{p'}(z_{p'})$ evaluation point in the support of the distribution of $Q_j = \Phi_j(Z_j)$. If, in the policy histories, there is at least one $j \in \mathcal{H}_e$ such that $\Phi_j(z_j) = q$ for a z_j with (z_j, x) in the support of the distribution of (Z_j, X_e), then we can construct the probability of the new policy from data in the policy histories. The methods used to extrapolate $P_{p'}(\cdot)$ over new regions, discussed previously, apply here. If the distribution of $Q_{p'}$ (or $\Phi_{p'}$ and the distribution

[97] If we strengthen condition (6.7) to hold for all $j \in \mathcal{H}_e$, then the condition becomes that $\mathrm{Supp}(Z_{p'}) \cap \bigcup_{j\in\mathcal{H}_e} \mathrm{Supp}(Z_j)$ is not empty.

of $Z_{p'}$) is known as part of the specification of the proposed policy, the distribution of $F_{P_{p'}|X_e}$ can be constructed using the constructed $P_{p'}$. Alternatively, if we can relate $Q_{p'}$ to Q_j by $Q_{p'} = \Psi_{p',j}(Q_j)$ for a known function $\Psi_{p',j}$ or if we can relate $Z_{p'}$ to Z_j by $Z_{p'} = T_{p',j}(Z_j)$ for a known function $T_{p',j}$, and the distributions of Q_j and/or Z_j are known for some $j \in \mathcal{H}_e$, we can apply the method previously discussed to derive $F_{P_{p'}|X_e}$ and hence the policy weights for the new policy.

This approach assumes that a new policy acts on components of Q like a policy in $\mathcal{H}_e$, so it is possible to forecast the effect of a policy with nominally new aspects. The essential idea is to recast the new aspects of policy in terms of old aspects previously measured. Thus in a model of schooling, let $D = \mathbf{1}[Y_1 - Y_0 - B \geqslant 0]$ where $Y_1 - Y_0$ is the discounted gain in earnings from going to school and B is the tuition cost. In this example, a decrease in a unit of cost (B) has the same effect on choice as an increase in return ($Y_1 - Y_0$). Historically, we might only observe variation in $Y_1 - Y_0$ (say tuition has never previously been charged). But B is on the same footing (has the same effect on choice, except for sign) as $Y_1 - Y_0$. The identified historical variation in $Y_1 - Y_0$ can be used to nonparametrically forecast the effect of introducing B, provided that the support of $P_{p'}$ is in the historical support generated by the policy histories in $\mathcal{H}_e$. Otherwise, some functional structure (parametric or semiparametric) must be imposed to solve the support problem for $P_{p'}$. We used this basic principle in constructing our econometric cost benefit analysis in Section 6.1.

As another example, following Marschak (1953), consider the introduction of wage taxes in a world where there has never before been a tax. This example is analyzed in Heckman (2001). Let Z_j be the wage without taxes. We seek to forecast a post-tax net wage $Z_{p'} = (1 - \tau)Z_j + b$ where τ is the tax rate and b is a constant shifter. Thus $Z_{p'}$ is a known linear transformation of policy Z_j. We can construct $Z_{p'}$ from Z_j. We can forecast under (A-1) using $\Pr(D_j = 1 \mid Z_j = z) = \Pr(D_{p'} = 1 \mid Z_{p'} = z)$. This assumes that the response to after tax wages is the same as the response to wages at the after tax level. The issue is whether $P_{p'|X_e}$ lies in the historical support, or whether extrapolation is needed. Nonlinear versions of this example can be constructed.

As a final example, environmental economists use variation in one component of cost (e.g., travel cost) to estimate the effect of a new cost (e.g., a park registration fee). See Smith and Banzhaf (2004). Relating the costs and characteristics of new policies to the costs and characteristics of old policies is a standard, but sometimes controversial, method for forecasting the effects of new policies.

In the context of our model, extrapolation and forecasting are confined to constructing $P_{p'}$ and its distribution. If policy p', characterized by vector $Z_{p'}$, consists of new components that cannot be related to Z_j, $j \in \mathcal{H}_e$, or a base set of characteristics whose variation cannot be identified, the problem is intractable. Then $P_{p'}$ and its distribution cannot be formed using econometric methods applied to historical data.

When it can be applied, our approach allows us to simplify the policy forecasting problem and concentrate our attention on forecasting choice probabilities and their distribution in solving the policy forecasting problem. We can use choice theory and choice data to construct these objects to forecast the impacts of new policies, by relating new policies to previously experienced policies.

6.2.2. *Forecasting the effects of policies in new environments*

When the effects of policy p are forecast for a new environment e' from baseline environment e, and $X_e \neq X_{e'}$, in general both $\Delta^{\text{MTE}}(x, u_D)$ and $F_{P_p|X_e}$ will change. In general, neither object is environment invariant.[98] The new $X_{e'}$ may have a different support than X_e or any other environment in $\mathcal{H}$. In addition, the new $(X_{e'}, U_D)$ stochastic relationship may be different from the historical (X_e, U_D) stochastic relationship. Constructing $F_{P_p|X_{e'}}$ from $F_{P_p|X_e}$ and $F_{Z_p|X_{e'}}$ from $F_{Z_p|X_e}$ can be done using (i) functional form (including semiparametric functional restrictions) or (ii) analytic continuation methods. Notice that the maps $T_{p,j}$ and Φ_p may depend on X_e and so the induced changes in these transformations must also be modeled. There is a parallel discussion for $\Delta^{\text{MTE}}(x, u_D)$. The stochastic dependence between $X_{e'}$ and (U_0, U_1, U_D) may be different from the stochastic dependence between X_e and (U_0, U_1, U_D). We suppress the dependence of U_0 and U_1 on e and p only for convenience of exposition and make it explicit in the next paragraph.

Forecasting new stochastic relationships between $X_{e'}$ and (U_1, U_0, U_D) is a difficult task. Some of the difficulty can be avoided if we invoke the traditional exogeneity assumptions of classical econometrics:

(A-9) $(U_{0,e,p}, U_{1,e,p}, U_{D,e,p}) \perp\!\!\!\perp (X_e, Z_p)\ \forall e, p.$

Under (A-9), we only encounter the support problems for Δ^{MTE} and the distribution of $\Pr(D_p = 1 \mid Z_p, X_e)$ in constructing policy counterfactuals.

Conditions (A-7)–(A-9) are unnecessary if the only goal of the analysis is to establish internal validity, the standard objective of the treatment effect literature. This is problem P-1. Autonomy and exogeneity conditions become important issues if we seek external validity. An important lesson from this analysis is that as we try to make the treatment effect literature do the tasks of structural econometrics (i.e., make out-of-sample forecasts), common assumptions are invoked in the two literatures.

6.2.3. *A comparison of three approaches to policy evaluation*

Table 9 compares the strengths and limitations of the three approaches to policy evaluation that we have discussed in this Handbook chapter and our contribution in Chapter 70: the structural approach, the conventional treatment effect approach, and the approach to treatment effects based on the MTE function developed by Heckman and Vytlacil (1999, 2001b, 2005).

[98] We suppress the dependence of U_D on p for notational convenience.

Table 9
Comparison of alternative approaches to program evaluation

	Structural econometric approach	Treatment effect approach	Approach based on MTE
Interpretability	Well defined economic parameters and welfare comparisons	Link to economics and welfare comparisons obscure	Interpretable in terms of willingness to pay; weighted averages of the MTE answer well-posed economic questions
Range of questions addressed	Answers many counterfactual questions	Focuses on one treatment effect or narrow range of effects	With support conditions, generates all treatment parameters
Extrapolation to new environments	Provides ingredients for extrapolation	Evaluates one program in one environment	Can be partially extrapolated; extrapolates to new policy environments with different distributions of the probability of participation due solely to differences in distributions of Z
Comparability across studies	Policy invariant parameters comparable across studies	Not generally comparable	Partially comparable; comparable across environments with different distributions of the probability of participation due solely to differences in distributions of Z
Key econometric problems	Exogeneity, policy invariance and selection bias	Selection bias	Selection bias: Exogeneity and policy invariance if used for forecasting
Range of policies that can be evaluated	Programs with either partial or universal coverage, depending on variation in data (prices/endowments)	Programs with partial coverage (treatment and control groups)	Programs with partial coverage (treatment and control groups)
Extension to general equilibrium evaluation	Need to link to time series data; parameters compatible with general equilibrium theory	Difficult because link to economics is not precisely specified	Can be linked to nonparametric general equilibrium models under exogeneity and policy invariance

Source: Heckman and Vytlacil (2005).

The approach based on the MTE function and the structural approach share interpretability of parameters. Like the structural approach, it addresses a range of policy evaluation questions. The MTE parameter is less comparable and less easily extrapolated across environments than are structural parameters, unless nonparametric versions of invariance and exogeneity assumptions are made. However, Δ^{MTE} is comparable across populations with different distributions of P (conditional on X_e) and results from one population can be applied to another population under the conditions presented in this section. Analysts can use Δ^{MTE} to forecast a variety of policies. This invariance property is shared with conventional structural parameters. Our framework solves the problem of external validity, which is ignored in the standard treatment effect approach. The price of these advantages of the structural approach is the greater range of econometric problems that must be solved. They are avoided in the conventional treatment approach at the cost of producing parameters that cannot be linked to well-posed economic models and hence do not provide building blocks for an empirically motivated general equilibrium analysis or for investigation of the impacts of new public policies. Δ^{MTE} estimates the preferences of the agents being studied and provides a basis for integration with well posed economic models. If the goal of a study is to examine one policy in place (the problem of internal validity), the stronger assumptions invoked in this section of the chapter, and in structural econometrics, are unnecessary. Even if this is the only goal of the analysis however, our approach allows the analyst to generate all treatment effects and IV estimands from a common parameter and provides a basis for unification of the treatment effect literature.

7. Extension of MTE to the analysis of more than two treatments and associated outcomes

We have thus far analyzed models with two potential outcomes associated with receipt of binary treatments ($D = 0$ or $D = 1$). Focusing on this simple case allows us to develop main ideas. However, models with more than two outcomes are common in empirical work. Angrist and Imbens (1995) analyze an ordered choice model with a single instrument that shifts people across all margins. We generalize their analysis in several ways. We consider vectors of instruments, some of which may affect choices at all margins and some of which affect choices only at certain margins. We then analyze a general unordered choice model.

7.1. Background for our analysis of the ordered choice model

Angrist and Imbens (1995) extend their analysis of LATE to an ordered choice model with outcomes generated by a scalar instrument that can assume multiple values. From their analysis of the effect of schooling on earnings, it is unclear even under a strengthened "monotonicity" condition whether IV estimates the effect of a change of schooling on earnings for a well defined margin of choice.

To summarize their analysis, let $\bar{S}$ be the number of possible outcome states with associated outcomes Y_s and choice indicators D_s, $s = 1, \ldots, \bar{S}$. The s, in their analysis, correspond to different levels of schooling. For any two instrument values $Z = z_i$ and $Z = z_j$ with $z_i > z_j$, we can define associated indicators $\{D_s(z_i)\}_{s=1}^{\bar{S}}$ and $\{D_s(z_j)\}_{s=1}^{\bar{S}}$, where $D_s(z_i) = 1$ if a person assigned instrument value z_i chooses state s. As in the two-outcome model, the instrument Z is assumed to be independent of the potential outcomes $\{Y_s\}_{s=1}^{\bar{S}}$ as well as the associated indicator functions defined by fixing Z at z_i

and z_j. Observed schooling for instrument z_j is $S(z_j) = \sum_{s=1}^{\bar{S}} s D_s(z_j)$. Observed outcomes with this instrument are $Y(z_j) = \sum_{s=1}^{\bar{S}} Y_s D_s(z_j)$.

Angrist and Imbens show that IV (with $Z = z_i$ and $Z = z_j$) applied to S in a two stage least squares regression of Y on S identifies a "causal parameter"

$$\Delta^{\mathrm{IV}} = \sum_{s=2}^{\bar{S}} \{E(Y_s - Y_{s-1} \mid S(z_i) \geqslant s > S(z_j))\} \frac{\Pr(S(z_i) \geqslant s > S(z_j))}{\sum_{s=2}^{\bar{S}} \Pr(S(z_i) \geqslant s > S(z_j))}. \tag{7.1}$$

This "causal parameter" is a weighted average of the gross returns from going from $s-1$ to s for persons induced by the change in the instrument to move from *any* schooling level below s to *any* schooling level s or above. Thus the conditioning set defining the sth component of IV includes people who have schooling below $s-1$ at instrument value $Z = z_j$ and people who have schooling above level s at instrument value $Z = z_i$. In expression (7.1), the average return experienced by some of the people in the conditioning set for each component conditional expectation does not correspond to the average outcome corresponding to the gain in the argument of the expectation. In the case where $\bar{S} = 2$, agents face only two choices and the margin of choice is well defined. Agents in each conditioning set are at different margins of choice. The weights are positive but, as noted by Angrist and Imbens (1995), persons can be counted multiple times in forming the weights. When they generalize their analysis to multiple-valued instruments, they use the Yitzhaki (1989) weights.

Whereas the weights in Equation (7.1) can be constructed empirically using nonparametric discrete choice theory (see, e.g., our analysis in Appendix B of Chapter 70 or the contribution of Matzkin to this Handbook), the terms in braces cannot be identified by any standard IV procedure.[99] We present decompositions with components that are recoverable, whose weights can be estimated from the data and that are economically interpretable.

In this section, we generalize LATE to a multiple outcome case where we can identify agents at different well-defined margins of choice. Specifically, we (1) analyze both ordered and unordered choice models; (2) analyze outcomes associated with choices at various well-defined margins; and (3) develop models with multiple instruments that can affect different margins of choice differently. With our methods, we can define and estimate a variety of economically interpretable parameters. In contrast, the Angrist–Imbens analysis produces a single "causal parameter" (7.1) that does not answer any well-defined policy question such as that posed by the PRTE. We first consider an explicit ordered choice model and decompose the IV into policy-useful (identifiable) components.

[99] It can be identified by a structural model using the methods surveyed in Chapter 72.

7.2. Analysis of an ordered choice model

Ordered choice models arise in many settings. In schooling models, there are multiple grades. One has to complete grade $s-1$ to proceed to grade s. The ordered choice model has been widely used to fit data on schooling transitions [Harmon and Walker (1999), Cameron and Heckman (1998)]. Its nonparametric identifiability has been studied [Carneiro, Hansen and Heckman (2003), Cunha, Heckman and Navarro (2007)]. It can also be used as a duration model for dynamic treatment effects with associated outcomes as in Cunha, Heckman and Navarro (2007). It also represents the "vertical" model of the choice of product quality [Prescott and Visscher (1977), Shaked and Sutton (1982), Bresnahan (1987)].[100]

Our analysis generalizes the analysis for the binary model in a parallel way. Write potential outcomes as

$$Y_s = \mu_s(X, U_s), \quad s = 1, \dots, \bar{S}.$$

The $\bar{S}$ could be different schooling levels or product qualities. We define latent variables $D_S^* = \mu_D(Z) - V$ where

$$D_s = \mathbf{1}\big[C_{s-1}(W_{s-1}) < \mu_D(Z) - V \leqslant C_s(W_s)\big], \quad s = 1, \dots, \bar{S},$$

and the cutoff values satisfy

$$C_{s-1}(W_{s-1}) \leqslant C_s(W_s), \quad C_0(W_0) = -\infty \quad \text{and} \quad C_{\bar{S}}(W_{\bar{S}}) = \infty.$$

The cutoffs used to define the intervals are allowed to depend on observed (by the economist) regressors W_s. In Appendix G we extend the analysis presented in the text to allow the cutoffs to depend on unobserved regressors as well, following structural analysis along these lines by Carneiro, Hansen and Heckman (2003) and Cunha, Heckman and Navarro (2007). Observed outcomes are: $Y = \sum_{s=1}^{\bar{S}} Y_s D_s$. The Z shift the index generally; the W_s affect s-specific transitions. Thus, in a schooling example, Z could include family background variables while W_s could include college tuition or opportunity wages for unskilled labor.[101] Collect the W_s into $W = (W_1, \dots, W_{\bar{S}})$, and the U_s into $U = (U_1, \dots, U_{\bar{S}})$. Larger values of $C_s(W_s)$ make it more likely that $D_s = 1$. The inequality restrictions on the $C_s(W_s)$ functions play a critical role in defining the model and producing its statistical implications.

[100] Cunha, Heckman and Navarro (2007) analyze a dynamic discrete choice setting with sequential revelation of information.

[101] Many of the instruments studied by Harmon and Walker (1999) and Card (2001) are transition-specific. Card's model of schooling is not sufficiently rich to make a distinction between the Z and the W. See Heckman and Navarro (2007) and Cunha, Heckman and Navarro (2007) for more general models of schooling that make these distinctions explicit.

Analogous to the assumptions made for the binary outcome model, we assume

(OC-1) $(U_s, V) \perp\!\!\!\perp (Z, W) \mid X$, $s = 1, \ldots, \bar{S}$ (*Conditional independence of the instruments*);

(OC-2) *$\mu_D(Z)$ is a nondegenerate random variable conditional on X and W* (*Rank condition*);

(OC-3) *the distribution of V is continuous*[102];

(OC-4) $E(|Y_s|) < \infty$, $s = 1, \ldots, \bar{S}$ (*Finite means*);

(OC-5) $0 < \Pr(D_s = 1 \mid X) < 1$ *for* $s = 1, \ldots, \bar{S}$, *for all* X (*In large samples, there are some persons in each treatment state*);

(OC-6) *for* $s = 1, \ldots, \bar{S} - 1$, *the distribution of* $C_s(W_s)$ *conditional on* X, Z *and the other* $C_j(W_j)$, $j = 1, \ldots, \bar{S}$, $j \neq s$, *is nondegenerate and continuous.*[103]

Assumptions (OC-1)–(OC-5) play roles analogous to their counterparts in the two-outcome model, (A-1)–(A-5). (OC-6) is a new condition that is key to identification of the Δ^{MTE} defined below for each transition. It assumes that we can vary the choice sets of agents at different margins of schooling choice without affecting other margins of choice. A necessary condition for (OC-6) to hold is that at least one element of W_s is nondegenerate and continuous conditional on X, Z and $C_j(W_j)$ for $j \neq s$. Intuitively, one needs an instrument (or source of variability) for each transition. The continuity of the regressor allows us to differentiate with respect to $C_s(W_s)$, like we differentiated with respect to $P(Z)$ to estimate the MTE in the analysis of the two-outcome model.

The analysis of Angrist and Imbens (1995) discussed in the introduction to this section makes independence and monotonicity assumptions that generalize their earlier work. They do not consider estimation of transition-specific parameters as we do, or even transition-specific LATE. We present a different decomposition of the IV estimator where each component can be recovered from the data, and where the transition-specific MTEs answer well-defined and economically interpretable policy evaluation questions.[104]

The probability of $D_s = 1$ given X, Z and W is generated by an ordered choice model:

$$\begin{aligned}\Pr(D_s = 1 \mid Z, W, X) &\equiv P_s(Z, W, X)\\ &= \Pr\bigl(C_{s-1}(W_{s-1}) < \mu_D(Z) - V \leqslant C_s(W_s) \bigm| X\bigr).\end{aligned}$$

Analogous to the binary case, we can define $U_D = F_{V|X}(V)$ so $U_D \sim \text{Unif}[0, 1]$ under our assumption that the distribution of V is absolutely continuous with respect to Lebesgue measure. The probability integral transformation used extensively

[102] Absolutely continuous with respect to Lebesgue measure.

[103] Absolutely continuous with respect to Lebesgue measure.

[104] Vytlacil (2006b) shows that their monotonicity and independence conditions imply (and are implied by) a more general version of the ordered choice model with stochastic thresholds, which appears in Heckman, LaLonde and Smith (1999), Carneiro, Hansen and Heckman (2003), and Cunha, Heckman and Navarro (2007), and is analyzed in Appendix G.

in the binary choice model is somewhat less useful for analyzing ordered choices, so we work with both U_D and V in this section of the chapter. Monotonic transformations of V induce monotonic transformations of $\mu_D(Z) - C_s(W_s)$, but one is not free to form arbitrary monotonic transformations of $\mu_D(Z)$ and $C_s(W_s)$ separately. Using the probability integral transformation, the expression for choice s is $D_s = \mathbf{1}[F_{V|X}(\mu_D(Z) - C_{s-1}(W_{s-1})) > U_D \geqslant F_{V|X}(\mu_D(Z) - C_s(W_s))]$. Keeping the conditioning on X implicit, we define $P_s(Z, W) = F_V(\mu_D(Z) - C_{s-1}(W_{s-1})) - F_V(\mu_D(Z) - C_s(W_s))$. It is convenient to work with the probability that $S > s$, $\pi_s(Z, W_s) = F_V(\mu_D(Z) - C_s(W_s)) = \Pr(\sum_{j=s+1}^{\bar{S}} D_j = 1 \mid Z, W_s)$, $\pi_{\bar{S}}(Z, W_{\bar{S}}) = 0$, $\pi_0(Z, W_0) = 1$ and $P_s(Z, W) = \pi_{s-1}(Z, W_{s-1}) - \pi_s(Z, W_s)$.

The transition-specific Δ^{MTE} for the transition from s to $s+1$ is defined in terms of U_D:

$$\Delta^{\text{MTE}}_{s,s+1}(x, u_D) = E(Y_{s+1} - Y_s \mid X = x, U_D = u_D), \quad s = 1, \ldots, \bar{S} - 1.$$

Alternatively, one can condition on V. Analogous to the analysis of the earlier sections of this chapter, when we set $u_D = \pi_s(Z, W_s)$, we obtain the mean return to persons indifferent between s and $s+1$ at mean level of utility $\pi_s(Z, W_s)$.

In this notation, keeping X implicit, the mean outcome Y, conditional on (Z, W), is the sum of the mean outcomes conditional on each state weighted by the probability of being in each state summed over all states:

$$\begin{aligned} E(Y \mid Z, W) &= \sum_{s=1}^{\bar{S}} E(Y_s \mid D_s = 1, Z, W) \Pr(D_s = 1 \mid Z, W) \\ &= \sum_{s=1}^{\bar{S}} \int_{\pi_s(Z,W_s)}^{\pi_{s-1}(Z,W_{s-1})} E(Y_s \mid U_D = u_D)\, du_D, \end{aligned} \tag{7.2}$$

where we use conditional independence assumption (OC-1) to obtain the final expression. Analogous to the result for the binary outcome model, we obtain the index sufficiency restriction $E(Y \mid Z, W) = E(Y \mid \pi(Z, W))$, where $\pi(Z, W) = [\pi_1(Z, W_1), \ldots, \pi_{\bar{S}-1}(Z, W_{\bar{S}-1})]$. The choice probabilities encode all of the influence of (Z, W) on outcomes.

We can identify $\pi_s(z, w_s)$ for (z, w_s) in the support of the distribution of (Z, W_s) from the relationship $\pi_s(z, w_s) = \Pr(\sum_{j=s+1}^{\bar{S}} D_j = 1 \mid Z = z, W_s = w_s)$. Thus $E(Y \mid \pi(Z, W) = \pi)$ is identified for all π in the support of $\pi(Z, W)$. Assumptions (OC-1), (OC-3), and (OC-4) imply that $E(Y \mid \pi(Z, W) = \pi)$ is differentiable in π. So $\frac{\partial}{\partial \pi} E(Y \mid \pi(Z, W) = \pi)$ is well defined.[105] Thus analogous to the result obtained in

[105] For almost all π that are limit points of the support of distribution of $\pi(Z, W)$, we use the Lebesgue theorem for the derivative of an integral. Under assumption (OC-6), all points in the support of the distribution of $\pi(Z, W)$ will be limit points of that support, and we thus have that $\frac{\partial}{\partial \pi} E(Y \mid \pi(Z, W) = \pi)$ is well defined and is identified for (a.e.) π.

the binary case

$$\frac{\partial E(Y \mid \pi(Z, W) = \pi)}{\partial \pi_s} = \Delta^{\text{MTE}}_{s,s+1}(U_D = \pi_s)$$
$$= E(Y_{s+1} - Y_s \mid U_D = \pi_s). \tag{7.3}$$

Equation (7.3) is the basis for identification of the transition-specific MTE from data on (Y, Z, X).

From index sufficiency, we can express (7.2) as

$$\begin{aligned} E\big(Y \mid \pi(Z, W) = \pi\big) &= \sum_{s=1}^{\bar{S}} E(Y_s \mid \pi_s \leqslant U_D < \pi_{s-1})(\pi_{s-1} - \pi_s) \\ &= \sum_{s=1}^{\bar{S}-1} \big[E(Y_{s+1} \mid \pi_{s+1} \leqslant U_D < \pi_s) \\ &\qquad - E(Y_s \mid \pi_s \leqslant U_D < \pi_{s-1})\big]\pi_s \\ &\qquad + E(Y_1 \mid \pi_1 \leqslant U_D < 1) \\ &= \sum_{s=1}^{\bar{S}-1} \big\{m_{s+1}(\pi_{s+1}, \pi_s) - m_s(\pi_s, \pi_{s-1})\big\}\pi_s \\ &\qquad + E(Y_1 \mid \pi_1 \leqslant U_D < 1), \end{aligned} \tag{7.4}$$

where $m_s(\pi_s, \pi_{s-1}) = E[Y_s \mid \pi_s \leqslant U_D < \pi_{s-1}]$. In general, this expression is a nonlinear function of (π_s, π_{s-1}). This model has a testable restriction of index sufficiency in the general case: $E(Y \mid \pi(Z, W) = \pi)$ is a nonlinear function that is additive in functions of (π_s, π_{s-1}) so there are no interactions between π_s and $\pi_{s'}$ if $|s - s'| > 1$, i.e.,

$$\frac{\partial^2 E(Y \mid \pi(Z, W) = \pi)}{\partial \pi_s \partial \pi_{s'}} = 0 \quad \text{if } |s - s'| > 1.$$

Observe that if $U_D \perp\!\!\!\perp U_s$ for $s = 1, \ldots, \bar{S}$,

$$\begin{aligned} E\big(Y \mid \pi(Z, W) = \pi\big) &= \sum_{s=1}^{\bar{S}} E(Y_s)(\pi_{s-1} - \pi_s) \\ &= \sum_{s=1}^{\bar{S}-1} \big[E(Y_{s+1}) - E(Y_s)\big]\pi_s + E(Y_1). \end{aligned}$$

Defining $E(Y_{s+1}) - E(Y_s) = \Delta^{\text{ATE}}_{s,s+1}$, $E(Y \mid \pi(Z, W) = \pi) = \sum_{s=1}^{\bar{S}-1} \Delta^{\text{ATE}}_{s,s+1}\pi_s + E(Y_1)$. Thus, under full independence, we obtain linearity of the conditional mean of Y in the π_s, $s = 1, \ldots, \bar{S}$. This result generalizes the test for the presence of essential heterogeneity presented in Section 4 to the ordered case. We can ignore the complexity induced by the model of essential heterogeneity if $E(Y \mid \pi(Z, W) = \pi)$ is linear in the π_s and can use conventional IV estimators to identify well-defined treatment effects.[106]

7.2.1. The policy relevant treatment effect for the ordered choice model

The policy relevant treatment effect compares the mean outcome under one policy regime p with the mean outcome under policy regime p'. It is defined analogously to the way it is defined in the binary case in Section 3.2 and in Heckman and Vytlacil (2001c, 2005). Policies (p, p') are assumed to induce different distributions of (Z, W), $F^p(Z, W)$. Forming $E_p(Y) = \int E(Y \mid Z = z, W = w)\, dF^p_{Z,W}(z, w)$ for each policy p, the policy relevant treatment effect is $E_{p'}(Y) - E_p(Y)$.

We can represent the PRTE as a weighted average of pairwise MTE:

$$\Delta^{\mathrm{PRTE}}_{p,p'} = E_{p'}(Y) - E_p(Y) = \sum_{s=1}^{\bar{S}-1} \int E(Y_{s+1} - Y_s \mid V = v)\omega_{p,p'}(v)\, dF(v). \tag{7.5}$$

The weights are known functions of the data. See Appendix H for a derivation of the weights and expression (7.5). Using the probability integral transform, we can alternatively express this in terms of $U_D = F_{V|X}(V)$.

7.2.2. What do instruments identify in the ordered choice model?

We now characterize what scalar instrument $J(Z, W)$ identifies. When Y is log earnings, it is common practice to regress Y on S where S is completed years of schooling and call the coefficient on S a rate of return.[107] We seek an expression for the instrumental variables estimator of the effect of S on Y in the ordered choice model:

$$\frac{\mathrm{Cov}(J(Z, W), Y)}{\mathrm{Cov}(J(Z, W), D)}, \tag{7.6}$$

where $S = \sum_{s=1}^{\bar{S}} s D_s$ is the number of years of schooling attainment. We keep the conditioning on X implicit. We now analyze the weights for IV. Their full derivation is presented in Appendix I.

Define $K_s(v) = E(\tilde{J}(Z, W) \mid \mu_D(Z) - C_s(W_s) > v) \Pr(\mu_D(Z) - C_s(W_s) > v)$, where $\tilde{J}(Z, W) = J(Z, W) - E(J(Z, W))$. Thus,

$$\begin{aligned} \Delta^{\mathrm{IV}}_J &= \frac{\mathrm{Cov}(J, Y)}{\mathrm{Cov}(J, S)} \\ &= \sum_{s=1}^{\bar{S}-1} \int E(Y_{s+1} - Y_s \mid V = v)\omega(s, v) f_V(v)\, dv, \end{aligned} \tag{7.7}$$

[106] Notice that if $U_D \not\perp\!\!\!\perp U_s$ for some s, then we obtain an expression with nonlinearities in (π_s, π_{s-1}) in expression (7.4).

[107] Heckman, Lochner and Todd (2006) present conditions under which this economic interpretation is valid.

where

$$\omega(s, v) = \frac{K_s(v)}{\sum_{s=1}^{\bar{S}} s \int [K_{s-1}(v) - K_s(v)] f_V(v)\, dv} = \frac{K_s(v)}{\sum_{s=1}^{\bar{S}-1} \int K_s(v) f_V(v)\, dv},$$

and clearly $\sum_{s=1}^{\bar{S}-1} \int \omega(s, v) f_V(v)\, dv = 1$, $\omega(0, v) = 0$, and $\omega(\bar{S}, v) = 0$. We can rewrite this result in terms of the MTE, expressed in terms of u_D

$$\Delta_{s,s+1}^{\mathrm{MTE}}(u_D) = E(Y_{s+1} - Y_s \mid U_D = u_D)$$

so that

$$\frac{\mathrm{Cov}(J, Y)}{\mathrm{Cov}(J, S)} = \sum_{s=1}^{\bar{S}-1} \int_0^1 \Delta_{s,s+1}^{\mathrm{MTE}}(u_D) \tilde{\omega}(s, u_D)\, du_D,$$

where

$$\tilde{\omega}(s, u_D) = \frac{\tilde{K}_s(u_D)}{\sum_{s=1}^{\bar{S}} s \int_0^1 [\tilde{K}_{s-1}(u_D) - \tilde{K}_s(u_D)]\, du_D} = \frac{\tilde{K}_s(u_D)}{\sum_{s=1}^{\bar{S}-1} \int_0^1 \tilde{K}_s(u_D)\, du_D} \tag{7.8}$$

and

$$\tilde{K}_s(u_D) = E\big(\tilde{J}(Z, W) \bigm| \pi_s(Z, W_s) \geqslant u_D\big) \Pr\big(\pi_s(Z, W_s) \geqslant u_D\big). \tag{7.9}$$

Compare Equations (7.8) and (7.9) for the ordered choice model to Equations (4.13) and (4.14) for the binary choice model. The numerator of the weights for the Δ^{MTE} in the ordered choice model for a particular transition is exactly the numerator of the weights for the binary choice model, substituting $\pi_s(Z, W_s) = \Pr(S > s \mid Z, W_s)$ for $P(Z) = \Pr(D = 1 \mid Z)$. The numerator for the weights for IV in the binary choice model is driven by the connection between the instrument and $P(Z)$. The numerator for the weights for IV in the ordered choice model for a particular transition is driven by the connection between the instrument and $\pi_s(Z, W_s)$. The denominator of the weights is the covariance between the instrument and D (or S) for the binary (or ordered) case, respectively. However, in the binary case the covariance between the instrument and D is completely determined by the covariance between the instrument and $P(Z)$, while in the ordered choice case the covariance with S depends on the relationship between the instrument and the full vector $[\pi_1(Z, W_1), \ldots, \pi_{\bar{S}-1}(Z, W_{\bar{S}-1})]$. Comparing our decomposition of Δ^{IV} to decomposition (7.1), ours corresponds to weighting up marginal outcomes across well-defined and adjacent boundary values experienced by agents having their instruments manipulated whereas the Angrist–Imbens decomposition corresponds to outcomes not experienced by some of the persons whose instruments are being manipulated.

From Equation (7.9), the IV estimator using $J(Z, W)$ as an instrument satisfies the following properties. (a) The numerator of the weights on $\Delta^{\mathrm{MTE}}_{s,s+1}(u_D)$ is nonnegative for all u_D if $E(J(Z, W_s) \mid \pi_s(Z, W_s) \geqslant \pi_s)$ is weakly monotonic in π_s. For example, if $\mathrm{Cov}(\pi_s(Z, W_s), S) > 0$, setting $J(Z, W) = \pi_s(Z, W_s)$ will lead to nonnegative weights on $\Delta^{\mathrm{MTE}}_{s,s+1}(u_D)$, though it may lead to negative weights on other transitions. A second property (b) is that the support of the weights on $\Delta^{\mathrm{MTE}}_{s,s+1}$ using $\pi_s(Z, W_s)$ as the instrument is $(\pi_s^{\mathrm{Min}}, \pi_s^{\mathrm{Max}})$ where π_s^{Min} and π_s^{Max} are the minimum and maximum values in the support of $\pi_s(Z, W_s)$, respectively, and the support of the weights on $\Delta^{\mathrm{MTE}}_{s,s+1}$ using any other instrument is a subset of $(\pi_s^{\mathrm{Min}}, \pi_s^{\mathrm{Max}})$. A third property (c) is that the weights on $\Delta^{\mathrm{MTE}}_{s,s+1}$ implied by using $J(Z, W)$ as an instrument are the same as the weights on $\Delta^{\mathrm{MTE}}_{s,s+1}$ implied by using $E(J(Z, W) \mid \pi_s(Z, W_s))$ as the instrument.

Our analysis generalizes that of Imbens and Angrist (1994) and Angrist and Imbens (1995) by considering multiple instruments and by introducing both transition-specific instruments (W) and general instruments (Z) across all transitions. In general, the method of linear instrumental variables applied to S does not estimate anything that is economically interpretable. It is not guaranteed to estimate a positive number even if the MTE is everywhere positive since the weights can be negative. In contrast, we can use our generalization of LIV presented in Equation (7.3) under conditions (OC-1)–(OC-6) to apply LIV to identify Δ^{MTE} for each transition, which can be used to build up Δ^{PRTE} using weights that can be estimated.

7.2.3. *Some theoretical examples of the weights in the ordered choice model*

Suppose that the distributions of W_s, $s = 1, \ldots, \bar{S}$, are degenerate so that the C_s are constants satisfying $C_1 < \cdots < C_{\bar{S}-1}$. This is the classical ordered choice model. In this case, $\pi_s(Z, W_s) = F_V(\mu_D(Z) - C_s)$ for any $s = 1, \ldots, \bar{S}$. For this special case, using J as an instrument will lead to nonnegative weights on all transitions if $J(Z, W)$ is a monotonic function of $\mu_D(Z)$. For example, note that $\mu_D(Z) - C_s > v$ can be written as $\mu_D(Z) > C_s + F_V^{-1}(u_D)$. Using $\mu_D(Z)$ as the instrument leads to weights on $\Delta^{\mathrm{MTE}}_{s,s+1}(u_D)$ of the form specified above with $\tilde{K}_s(u_D) = [E(\mu_D(Z) \mid \mu_D(Z) > F_V^{-1}(u_D) + C_s) - E(\mu_D(Z))] \Pr(\mu_D(Z) > F_V^{-1}(u_D) + C_s)$. Clearly, these weights will be nonnegative for all points of evaluation and will be strictly positive for any evaluation point u_D such that $1 > \Pr(\mu_D(Z) > F_V^{-1}(u_D) + C_s) > 0$.

Next consider the case where $C_s(W_s) = W_s$, a scalar, for $s = 1, \ldots, \bar{S} - 1$, and where $\mu_D(Z) = 0$. Consider $J(Z, W) = W_s$, a purely transition-specific instrument. In this case, the weight on $\Delta^{\mathrm{MTE}}_{s,s+1}(u_D)$ is of the form given above, with

$$\tilde{K}_s(u_D) = \left[E\left(W_s \mid W_s > F_V^{-1}(u_D)\right) - E(W_s)\right] \Pr\left(W_s > F_V^{-1}(u_D)\right),$$

which will be nonnegative for all evaluation points and strictly positive for any evaluation point such that $1 > \Pr(W_s > F_V^{-1}(u_D)) > 0$.

What are the implied weights on $\Delta^{\text{MTE}}_{s',s'+1}(u_D)$ for $s' \neq s$? First, consider the case where W_s is independent of $W_{s'}$ for $s \neq s'$. This independence of W_s and $W_{s'}$ is not in conflict with the requirement $W_s > W_{s'}$ for $s > s'$ if the supports do not overlap for any $s' \neq s$. In this case, the weight on $\Delta^{\text{MTE}}_{s',s'+1}(u_D)$ for $s' \neq s$ is of the form given above with

$$\tilde{K}_{s'}(u_D) = \big[E\big(W_s \mid W_{s'} > F_V^{-1}(u_D)\big) - E(W_s)\big]\Pr\big(W_{s'} > F_V^{-1}(u_D)\big) = 0.$$

Thus, in this case, the instrument only weights the Δ^{MTE} for the s to $s+1$ transition. Note that this result relies critically on the assumption that W_s is independent of $W_{s'}$ for $s' \neq s$.

Consider another version of this example where $C_s(W_s) = W_s$, $s = 1, \ldots, \bar{S}-1$, with W_s a scalar, but now allow $\mu_D(Z)$ to have a nondegenerate distribution and allow there to be dependence across the W_s. In particular, consider the case where $W = (W_1, \ldots, W_{\bar{S}-1})$ is a continuous random vector with a density given by

$$\frac{\prod_{i=1}^{\bar{S}-1} f_i(w_i)\mathbf{1}[w_1 < w_2 < \cdots < w_{\bar{S}-1}]}{\int \cdots \int [\mathbf{1}[w_1 < w_2 < \cdots < w_{\bar{S}-1}] \prod_{i=1}^{\bar{S}-1} f_i(w_i)]\, dw_1 \cdots dw_{\bar{S}-1}}$$

for some marginal density functions $f_1(w_1), f_2(w_2), \ldots, f_{\bar{S}-1}(w_{\bar{S}-1})$. In this case, using W_j as the instrument, we have

$$\begin{aligned}
\omega(s, v) = {} & \bigg(\int \cdots \int_{-\infty < w_1 < \cdots < w_{\bar{S}-1} < \infty} (w_j - E(w_j))\big(1 - F_{\mu_D(Z)}(w_s + v)\big) \\
& \quad \times f_1(w_1) \cdots f_{\bar{S}-1}(w_{\bar{S}-1})\, dw_1 \cdots dw_{\bar{S}-1}\, f_V(v)\, dv \bigg) \\
& \times \bigg(\sum_{s=1}^{\bar{S}-1} \int \int \cdots \int_{-\infty < w_1 < \cdots < w_{\bar{S}-1} < \infty} (w_j - E(w_j))\big(1 - F_{\mu_D(Z)}(w_s + v)\big) \\
& \quad \times f_1(w_1) \cdots f_{\bar{S}-1}(w_{\bar{S}-1})\, dw_1 \cdots dw_{\bar{S}-1}\, f_V(v)\, dv \bigg)^{-1}.
\end{aligned}$$

In the special case where $\mu_D(Z) \sim \text{Unif}(-K, K)$, with $Z \perp\!\!\!\perp W_s$ for $s = 1, \ldots, \bar{S}-1$, assuming $-K < w_s + v < K$ for all w_s, v in the support of W_s and V, respectively, the numerator is

$$\begin{aligned}
& \int \cdots \int_{-\infty < w_1 < \cdots < w_{\bar{S}-1} < \infty} (w_j - E(w_j)) \\
& \quad \times \frac{(w_s + v + K)}{2K} f_1(w_1) \cdots f_{\bar{S}-1}(w_{\bar{S}-1})\, dw_1 \cdots dw_{\bar{S}-1}\, f_V(v)\, dv
\end{aligned}$$

$$= \frac{1}{2K} \operatorname{Cov}(W_j, W_s \mid W_1 < \cdots < W_{\bar{S}-1}).$$

Observe that when the latent W_j, W_s are independently distributed for all j, s, by Bickel's Theorem (1967), we know that this expression is positive. (This is trivial when $j = s$.) The ordering $W_1 < \cdots < W_{\bar{S}-1}$ implies that W_l is stochastically increasing in W_j for $l < j$ (the lower boundary is shifted to the right). Hence, because of the order on the W implied by the ordered discrete choice model, a positive weighting is produced. This result can be overturned when $F(w)$ has a general structure. The positive dependence induced by the order on the components of W can be reversed by negative dependence in the structure of $F(w)$. We present examples of these phenomena in our discussions in Figures 19 and 20 below.

7.2.4. *Some numerical examples of the IV weights*

Figures 16–18 plot the transition-specific MTEs and the IV weights for the models and distributions of the weights at the base of each of the figures. We consider a three outcome ($\bar{S} = 3$) model with common instruments (Z) and transition-specific (W_s) instruments. The Z and W_s, $s = 1, \ldots, \bar{S}$, are assumed to be independent. The exact specification is given in the notes below Figure 16. In this example, D_s can be interpreted as an indicator of schooling. Y_1 is the potential earnings of the person as a dropout, Y_2 is the potential earnings of the person as a high school graduate, and Y_3 is the potential earnings of the person as a college graduate. There are two transitions: $1 \to 2$ and $2 \to 3$. The IV estimates using Z_1 and W_1 as instruments are reported transition by transition and overall decomposing IV representation (7.7) into its transition-specific components. The IV weights are defined by Equations (7.8) and (7.9). In particular, when the first element of Z, Z_1, is used as the instrument, we can decompose IV^{Z_1} as

$$\begin{aligned}
\mathrm{IV}^{Z_1} &= \sum_{s=1}^{2} \int E(Y_{s+1} - Y_s \mid V = v)\omega^{Z_1}(s, v) f_V(v)\, dv \\
&= \int \Delta_{12}^{\mathrm{MTE}}(v)\omega^{Z_1}(1, v) f_V(v)\, dv + \int \Delta_{23}^{\mathrm{MTE}}(v)\omega^{Z_1}(2, v) f_V(v)\, dv \\
&= \mathrm{IV}_{21}^{Z_1} + \mathrm{IV}_{32}^{Z_1}.
\end{aligned}$$

The same logic applies for the decomposition of IV^P which uses $P(Z)$ as an instrument. These decompositions show in this case that an important component of the total values of IV^Z and IV^{W_1} comes from the $2 \to 3$ transition. The bottom table presents the transition-specific treatment parameters. In Figure 16, the shape of the IV weights for Z_1 and W_1 are nearly identical. The IV estimates reflect this. The bottom table reveals that the IV estimates are far from standard treatment parameters.

In Figure 17, the IV weights for the Z_1 and W_1 are very different. So, correspondingly, are the IV estimates produced from each instrument, which are far off the mark of the standard treatment parameters shown in the bottom of the table. Observe that

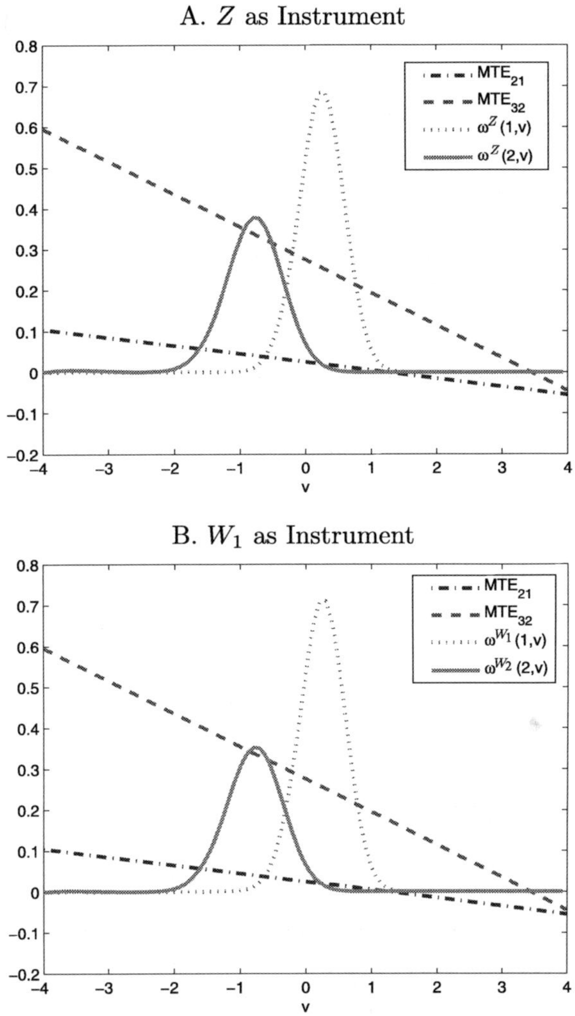

Outcomes	Choice model
$Y_1 = \alpha + \beta_1 + U_1$	$D_s = \mathbf{1}[W_{s-1} < \gamma Z - V \leqslant W_s]$,
$Y_2 = \alpha + \beta_2 + U_2$	$s = 1, 2, 3$
$Y_3 = \alpha + \beta_3 + U_3$	

Figure 16. Treatment parameters and IV – the generalized ordered choice Roy model under normality (Z, W_1). *Source*: Heckman, Urzua and Vytlacil (2004).

the IV weight for W_1 in the second transition is negative for an interval of values. This accounts for the dramatically lower IV estimate based on W_1 as the instrument. Figure 18 shows a different configuration of (Z_1, W_1, W_2). This produces negative weights

Parameterization

$$(U_1, U_2, U_3, V) \sim N(\mathbf{0}, \mathbf{\Sigma}_{UV}), (Z, W_1, W_2) \sim N(\boldsymbol{\mu}_{ZW}, \mathbf{\Sigma}_{ZW}) \text{ and } W_0 = -\infty; W_3 = \infty$$

$$\mathbf{\Sigma}_{UV} = \begin{bmatrix} 1 & 0.16 & 0.2 & -0.3 \\ 0.16 & 0.64 & 0.16 & -0.32 \\ 0.2 & 0.16 & 1 & -0.4 \\ -0.3 & -0.32 & -0.4 & 1 \end{bmatrix}, \ \boldsymbol{\mu}_{ZW} = (-0.6, -1.08, 0.08)$$

$$\text{and } \mathbf{\Sigma}_{ZW} = \begin{bmatrix} 0.1 & 0 & 0 \\ 0 & 0.1 & 0.09 \\ 0 & 0.09 & 0.25 \end{bmatrix}$$

$$\mathrm{Cov}(U_2 - U_1, V) = -0.02, \mathrm{Cov}(U_3 - U_2, V) = -0.08$$

$$\beta_1 = 0; \beta_2 = 0.025; \beta_3 = 0.3; \gamma = 1$$

IV estimates and their components*

Parameter	Value
Δ^{IV_Z}	0.1487
$\Delta_{12}^{\mathrm{IV}_Z}$	*0.0120*
$\Delta_{23}^{\mathrm{IV}_Z}$	*0.1367*
$\Delta^{\mathrm{IV}_{W_1}}$	0.1406
$\Delta_{12}^{\mathrm{IV}_{W_1}}$	*0.0126*
$\Delta_{23}^{\mathrm{IV}_{W_1}}$	*0.1280*

*IV^Z is decomposed as

$$\begin{aligned}\mathrm{IV}^Z =& \int E(Y_2 - Y_1 \mid V = v)\omega^Z(1, v) f_V(v)\,dv \\ &+ \int E(Y_3 - Y_2 \mid V = v)\omega^Z(2, v) f_V(v)\,dv \\ =& \mathrm{IV}_{21}^Z + \mathrm{IV}_{32}^Z.\end{aligned}$$

An analogous decomposition applies to IV^{W_1}.

Treatment parameters and their values

Parameter	Value
$\mathrm{ATE}_{12} = E(Y_2 - Y_1)$	0.025
$\mathrm{ATE}_{23} = E(Y_3 - Y_2)$	0.275
$\mathrm{TT}_{12} = E(Y_2 - Y_1 \mid D_2 = 1)$	0.0282
$\mathrm{TT}_{23} = E(Y_3 - Y_2 \mid D_3 = 1)$	0.1908
$\mathrm{TUT}_{12} = E(Y_2 - Y_1 \mid D_1 = 1)$	0.0060
$\mathrm{TUT}_{23} = E(Y_3 - Y_2 \mid D_2 = 1)$	0.2956

Figure 16. (*Continued*)

for Z_1 for both transitions and a negative weight for W_1 in the second transition. For both instruments, IV is negative even though both MTEs are positive throughout most of their range. IV provides a misleading summary of the underlying marginal treatment effects.

Comparing Figures 16–18, it is important to recall that all are based on the same structural model. All have the same MTE and average treatment effects. But the IV estimates are very different solely as a consequence of the differences in the distributions

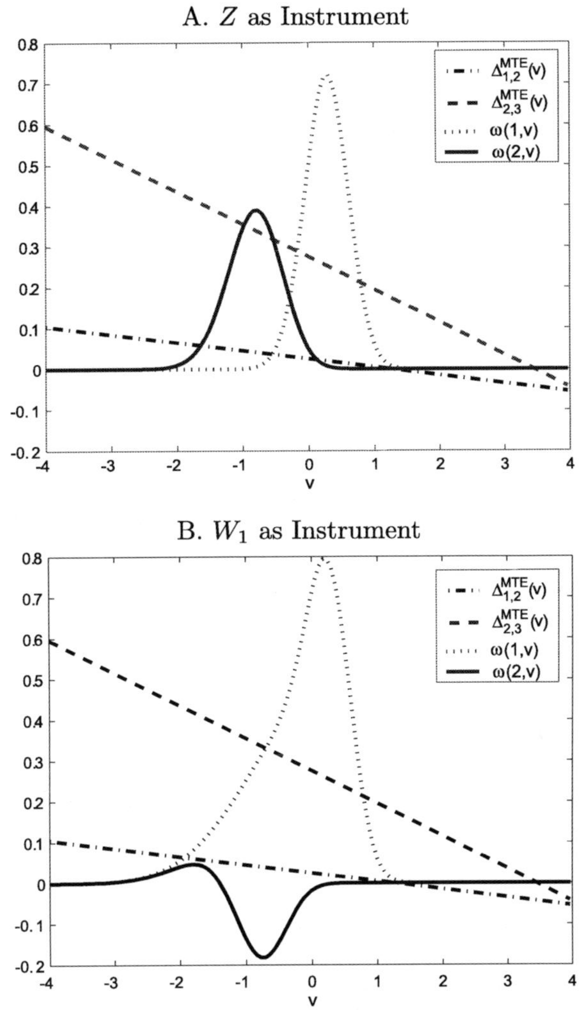

Outcomes	Choice model
$Y_1 = \alpha + \beta_1 + U_1$	$D_s = \mathbf{1}[W_{s-1} < \gamma Z - V \leqslant W_s]$,
$Y_2 = \alpha + \beta_2 + U_2$	$s = 1, 2, 3$
$Y_3 = \alpha + \beta_3 + U_3$	

Figure 17. Treatment parameters and IV – the generalized ordered choice Roy model under normality (Z, W_1), Case I. *Source*: Heckman, Urzua and Vytlacil (2006).

of instruments across the examples. An alternative way to benchmark what IV estimates in the ordered choice model is to compare IV estimates to the PRTE for well-defined policy experiments. We consider two such experiments, corresponding to proportional

Parameterization

$$(U_1, U_2, U_3, V) \sim N(\mathbf{0}, \boldsymbol{\Sigma}_{UV}), (Z, W_1, W_2) \sim N(\boldsymbol{\mu}_{ZW}, \boldsymbol{\Sigma}_{ZW}) \text{ and } W_0 = -\infty; W_3 = \infty$$

$$\boldsymbol{\Sigma}_{UV} = \begin{bmatrix} 1 & 0.16 & 0.2 & -0.3 \\ 0.16 & 0.64 & 0.16 & -0.32 \\ 0.2 & 0.16 & 1 & -0.4 \\ -0.3 & -0.32 & -0.4 & 1 \end{bmatrix}, \boldsymbol{\mu}_{ZW} = (-0.6, -1.08, 0.08)$$

$$\text{and } \boldsymbol{\Sigma}_{ZW} = \begin{bmatrix} 0.1 & 0 & 0 \\ 0 & 0.1 & -0.09 \\ 0 & -0.09 & 0.25 \end{bmatrix}$$

$$\text{Cov}(U_2 - U_1, V) = -0.02, \text{Cov}(U_3 - U_2, V) = -0.08$$
$$\beta_1 = 0; \beta_2 = 0.025; \beta_3 = 0.3; \gamma = 1$$

IV estimates and their components*

Parameter	Value
Δ^{IV_Z}	0.1489
$\Delta_{12}^{\text{IV}_Z}$	*0.0117*
$\Delta_{23}^{\text{IV}_Z}$	*0.1372*
$\Delta^{\text{IV}_{W_1}}$	0.0017
$\Delta_{12}^{\text{IV}_{W_1}}$	*0.0325*
$\Delta_{23}^{\text{IV}_{W_1}}$	*−0.0308*

*Δ^{IV_Z} is decomposed as

$$\begin{aligned}\Delta^{\text{IV}_Z} &= \int E(Y_2 - Y_1 \mid V = v)\omega^Z(1, v) f_V(v)\, dv \\ &\quad + \int E(Y_3 - Y_2 \mid V = v)\omega^Z(2, v) f_V(v)\, dv \\ &= \Delta_{12}^{\text{IV}_Z} + \Delta_{23}^{\text{IV}_Z}.\end{aligned}$$

An analogous decomposition applies to $\Delta^{\text{IV}_{W_1}}$.

Treatment parameters and their values

Parameter	Value
$\text{ATE}_{12} = E(Y_2 - Y_1)$	0.025
$\text{ATE}_{23} = E(Y_3 - Y_2)$	0.275
$\text{TT}_{12} = E(Y_2 - Y_1 \mid D_2 = 1)$	0.0271
$\text{TT}_{23} = E(Y_3 - Y_2 \mid D_3 = 1)$	0.1871
$\text{TUT}_{12} = E(Y_2 - Y_1 \mid D_1 = 1)$	0.0047
$\text{TUT}_{23} = E(Y_3 - Y_2 \mid D_2 = 1)$	0.2854

Figure 17. (*Continued*)

and fixed subsidies for attending different levels of schooling. We use the definition of the PRTE given in Equation (7.5). The baseline model is the one used to generate Figure 17. The weights can be constructed from data and are derived in Appendix H.

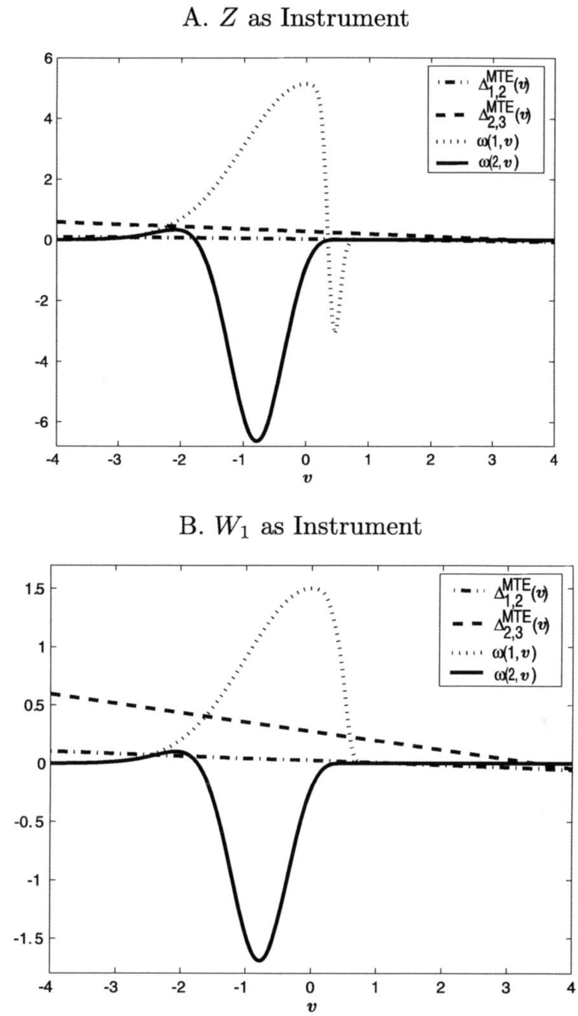

Outcomes	Choice model
$Y_1 = \alpha + \beta_1 + U_1$	$D_s = \mathbf{1}[W_{s-1} < \gamma Z - V \leqslant W_s]$,
$Y_2 = \alpha + \beta_2 + U_2$	$s = 1, 2, 3$
$Y_3 = \alpha + \beta_3 + U_3$	

Figure 18. Treatment parameters and IV – the generalized ordered choice Roy model under normality (Z, W_1), Case II. *Source*: Heckman, Urzua and Vytlacil (2006).

Figure 19 plots the weights for the PRTE for each transition for a policy experiment. We change the economy from the benchmark economy that generates Figure 17 to an economy where W_2 is subsidized by a proportional amount τ. The PRTE weights for

Parameterization

$$(U_1, U_2, U_3, V) \sim N(\mathbf{0}, \boldsymbol{\Sigma}_{UV}), (Z, W_1, W_2) \sim N(\boldsymbol{\mu}_{ZW}, \boldsymbol{\Sigma}_{ZW}) \text{ and } W_0 = -\infty; W_3 = \infty$$

$$\boldsymbol{\Sigma}_{UV} = \begin{bmatrix} 1 & 0.16 & 0.2 & -0.3 \\ 0.16 & 0.64 & 0.16 & -0.32 \\ 0.2 & 0.16 & 1 & -0.4 \\ -0.3 & -0.32 & -0.4 & 1 \end{bmatrix}, \; \boldsymbol{\mu}_{ZW} = (-0.6, -1.08, 0.08)$$

$$\text{and } \boldsymbol{\Sigma}_{ZW} = \begin{bmatrix} 0.1 & 0.092 & -0.036 \\ 0.092 & 0.1 & -0.09 \\ -0.036 & -0.09 & 0.25 \end{bmatrix}$$

$$\text{Cov}(U_2 - U_1, V) = -0.02, \text{Cov}(U_3 - U_2, V) = -0.08$$
$$\beta_1 = 0; \beta_2 = 0.025; \beta_3 = 0.3; \gamma = 1$$

IV estimates and their components*

Parameter	Value
Δ^{IV_Z}	−1.8091
$\Delta_{12}^{\text{IV}_Z}$	*0.2866*
$\Delta_{23}^{\text{IV}_Z}$	*−2.0957*
$\Delta^{\text{IV}_{W_1}}$	−0.4284
$\Delta_{12}^{\text{IV}_{W_1}}$	*0.0909*
$\Delta_{23}^{\text{IV}_{W_1}}$	*−0.5193*

*See the footnote below Figure 16 for details of the decomposition of Δ^{IV_Z} and $\Delta^{\text{IV}_{W_1}}$.

Treatment parameters and their values

Parameter	Value
$\text{ATE}_{12} = E(Y_2 - Y_1)$	0.025
$\text{ATE}_{23} = E(Y_3 - Y_2)$	0.275
$\text{TT}_{12} = E(Y_2 - Y_1 \mid D_2 = 1)$	0.0283
$\text{TT}_{23} = E(Y_3 - Y_2 \mid D_3 = 1)$	0.1754
$\text{TUT}_{12} = E(Y_2 - Y_1 \mid D_1 = 1)$	0.0025
$\text{TUT}_{23} = E(Y_3 - Y_2 \mid D_2 = 1)$	0.2898

Figure 18. (*Continued*)

each transition are negative over certain intervals. The overall PRTE is close to zero and can be decomposed into two components corresponding to a negative component on the second transition. The IV for the benchmark regime (p) and new regime (p') are given in the bottom table. The IV based on Z are far from the PRTE parameter. In general, the IV estimands are far off the mark from the PRTEs.

We next present a comparison between what IV estimates and the PRTE for a policy that consists of changing W_2 to $W_2 - t$ ($t = 1.2$ in the simulations). This can be thought of as a college tuition reduction policy. We compare the weights on PRTE with

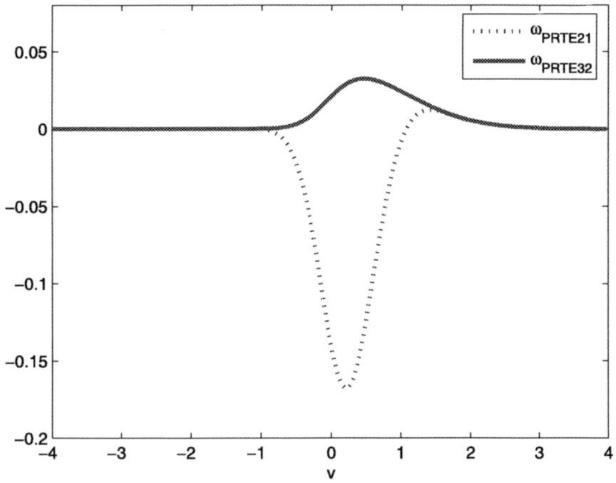

Outcomes	Choice model
$Y_1 = \alpha + \beta_1 + U_1$	$D_s = \mathbf{1}[W_{s-1} < \gamma Z - V \leqslant W_s]$,
$Y_2 = \alpha + \beta_2 + U_2$	$s = 1, 2, 3$
$Y_3 = \alpha + \beta_3 + U_3$	

Parameterization

The benchmark model (regime p) is the same as the one presented below Figure 17.

Under the new regime (regime p') we define $W_1^{p'} = W_1^{p}(1-\tau)$ with $\tau = 0.5$. Thus, under regime p we have

$$\boldsymbol{\mu}_{ZW}^{p'} = (-0.6, -0.54, 0.08) \text{ and } \boldsymbol{\Sigma}_{ZW}^{p} = \begin{bmatrix} 0.1 & 0 & 0 \\ 0 & 0.025 & -0.045 \\ 0 & -0.045 & 0.25 \end{bmatrix}$$

The other parameters remain at the values set under the regime p

PRTE estimates and their components[1]

Parameter	Value
$\text{PRTE}^{p',p}$	0.0076
$\text{PRTE}_{21}^{p',p}$	*−0.0032*
$\text{PRTE}_{32}^{p',p}$	*0.0109*

[1] $\text{PRTE}^{p',p}$ is decomposed as

$$\begin{aligned}\text{PRTE}^{p',p} &= \int E(Y_2 - Y_1 \mid V = v)\omega^{p',p}(1, v) f_V(v)\,dv \\ &\quad + \int E(Y_3 - Y_2 \mid V = v)\omega^{p',p}(2, v) f_V(v)\,dv \\ &= \text{PRTE}_{21}^{p',p} + \text{PRTE}_{32}^{p',p}.\end{aligned}$$

Figure 19. The policy relevant treatment effect weights – the generalized ordered choice Roy model under normality. *Source*: Heckman, Urzua and Vytlacil (2004).

the weights on IV using W_1 (Figure 20) and Z (Figure 21) as instruments. The case using W_2 as an instrument is similar and for the sake of brevity is not discussed. In Figure 20A, we plot the transition-specific MTE for the values of the model presented

IV estimates and treatment parameters under different regimes[2]

Parameter	Regime p	Regime p'
IV^Z	0.1489	0.1521
IV^Z_{12}	*0.0117*	*0.0174*
IV^Z_{23}	*0.1372*	*0.1347*
IV^{W_1}	0.0017	0.0804
$\text{IV}^{W_1}_{12}$	*0.0325*	*0.0358*
$\text{IV}^{W_1}_{23}$	*−0.0308*	*0.0446*
ATE_{12}	0.0250	0.0250
ATE_{23}	0.2750	0.2750
TT_{12}	0.0271	0.0327
TT_{23}	0.1871	0.1789
TUT_{12}	0.0047	0.0103
TUT_{23}	0.2854	0.3067

[2]See footnote below Figure 16 for details of the decompositions of IV^Z and IV^{W_1}.

Figure 19. (*Continued*)

at the base of the table. These are identical to the transition-specific MTE plotted in Figure 21A. Both of the Δ^{MTE} parameters have the typical shape of declining returns for people less likely to make the transition, i.e., those who have a higher $V = v$. Even though the levels are higher for outcomes 2 and 3, the marginal returns are higher for the transition $1 \to 2$. Figure 20B plots the policy weights for the two transitions for a policy that lowers W_2 ("reduces tuition").[108] It also plots the IV weights for the two Δ^{MTE} functions for the case where W_1 is the instrument. The correlation pattern for (W_1, W_2) is positive with specific values given below the figure. The policy studied in Figure 20B shifts 42.8% of the $D_1 = 1$ people into the category $D_3 = 1$ and 92.4% of D_2 people into D_3. In this simulation, the IV weights are positive. The IV weights and Δ^{PRTE} weights are distinctly different and the IV estimate is 0.201 vs. Δ^{PRTE} of 0.166.

When we change the correlation structure between W_1 and W_2 so that they are negatively correlated (Figure 20C), the IV weight for $\Delta^{\text{MTE}}_{2,3}$ becomes *negative* while that for $\Delta^{\text{MTE}}_{1,2}$ remains positive. The contrast in these figures between negative and positive IV weights depends on the correlation structure between W_1 and W_2. The stochastic order $(W_2 > W_1)$ is a force toward positive weights, which can be undone when the dependence induced by the density $(f(w_1, w_2))$ is sufficiently negative. The discord between the IV and Δ^{PRTE} weights is substantial and is reflected in the estimates ($\Delta^{\text{PRTE}} = 0.159$ vs. $\Delta^{\text{IV}} = 0.296$). As Figure 20D illustrates, the weights on Δ^{PRTE} are not guaranteed

[108] Notice that, for clarity, of exposition we change the notation for the weights in Figures 20 and 21 to distinguish IV from PRTE weights.

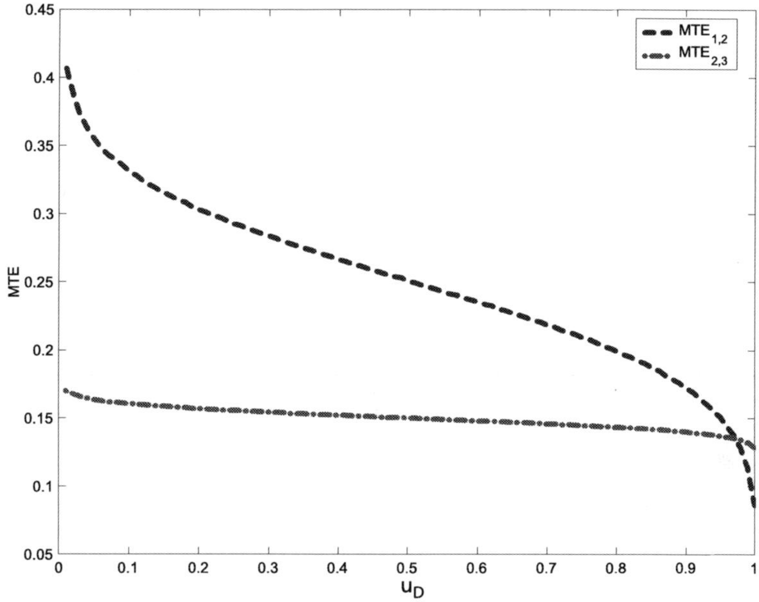

$Y_3 = \alpha + \beta_3 + U_3; D_3 = 1$ if $W_2 < I < \infty$; $U_3 = \sigma_3 \tau$; $\sigma_3 = 0.02, \sigma_2 = 0.012, \sigma_1 = -0.05, \sigma_V = -1$
$Y_2 = \alpha + \beta_2 + U_2; D_2 = 1$ if $W_1 < I \leqslant W_2$; $U_2 = \sigma_2 \tau$; $\alpha = 0.67, \beta_2 = 0.25, \beta_3 = 0.4$
$Y_1 = \alpha + U_1$; $D_1 = 1$ if $-\infty < I \leqslant W_1$; $U_1 = \sigma_1 \tau$; $Z \sim N(-0.0026, 0.27)$ and $Z \perp\!\!\!\perp V$
$I = Z - V$ $V = \sigma_V \tau$; $\tau \sim N(0, 1)$
$U_D = F_V(V)$

Sample size = 1500

Figure 20A. $W_2 - t$ where $t = 1.2$ and W_1 is the instrument: Marginal treatment effects by transition.

to be positive either. Thus neither the IV weights nor the weights on Δ^{PRTE} are guaranteed to be positive or negative and the relationship between the two sets of weights can be quite weak.

Figures 21A–21D present a parallel set of simulations when Z is used as an instrument. Changes in Z shift persons across all transitions whereas W_1 is a transition-specific shifter. Figure 21 reproduces the policy invariant Δ^{MTE} parameters from Figure 20A. Figure 21B shows that the IV weights for $\Delta^{\text{MTE}}_{1,2}$ assume both positive and negative values. The IV weights for $\Delta^{\text{MTE}}_{2,3}$ are positive but not monotonic. In Figure 21C, where there is negative dependence between W_1 and W_2, both sets of IV weights assume both positive and negative values. In the case where $f(w_1, w_2) = f_1(w_1) f_2(w_2)$, the weights on $\Delta^{\text{MTE}}_{1,2}$ for Δ^{PRTE} are negative.

These simulations show a rich variety of shapes and signs for the weights. They illustrate a main point of this chapter – that standard IV methods are not guaranteed to weight marginal treatment effects positively or to produce estimates close to policy rel-

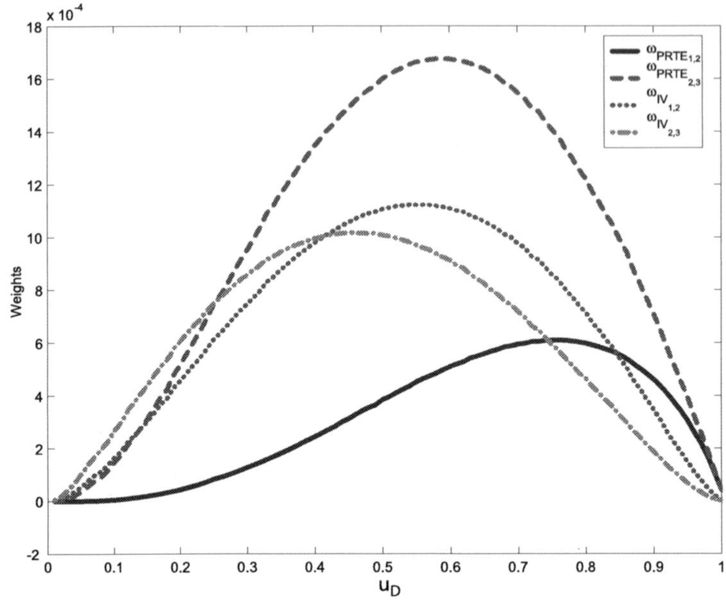

$$(W_1, W_2) \sim N\left(\begin{bmatrix} 0 \\ 0 \end{bmatrix}, \begin{bmatrix} 1 & 0.8 \\ 0.8 & 1 \end{bmatrix}\right)$$

$$\Delta^{\text{PRTE}} = 0.166, \text{IV} = 0.201$$

Proportion induced to change from $D_1 = 1$ to $D_3 = 1 = 42.8\%$

Proportion induced to change from $D_2 = 1$ to $D_3 = 1 = 92.4\%$

Figure 20B. $W_2 - t$ where $t = 1.2$ and W_1 is the instrument: Policy relevant treatment effect vs. instrumental variables weights by transition.

evant treatment effects or even to produce any gross treatment effect. Estimators based on LIV and its extension to the ordered model (7.3) identify Δ^{MTE} for each transition and answer policy relevant questions. We now turn to an analysis of a general unordered model.

7.3. Extension to multiple treatments that are unordered

The previous section analyzes a multiple treatment model where the treatment choice equation is an ordered choice model. In this section, we develop a framework for the analysis of multiple treatments when the choice equation is a nonparametric version of the classical multinomial choice model with no order imposed. Appendix B of Chapter 70, and Chapter 73 (Matzkin) analyze nonparametric and semiparametric identification of discrete choice models. With this framework, treatment effects can be defined as the difference in the counterfactual outcomes that would have been observed if the agent faced different general choice sets, i.e., the ef-

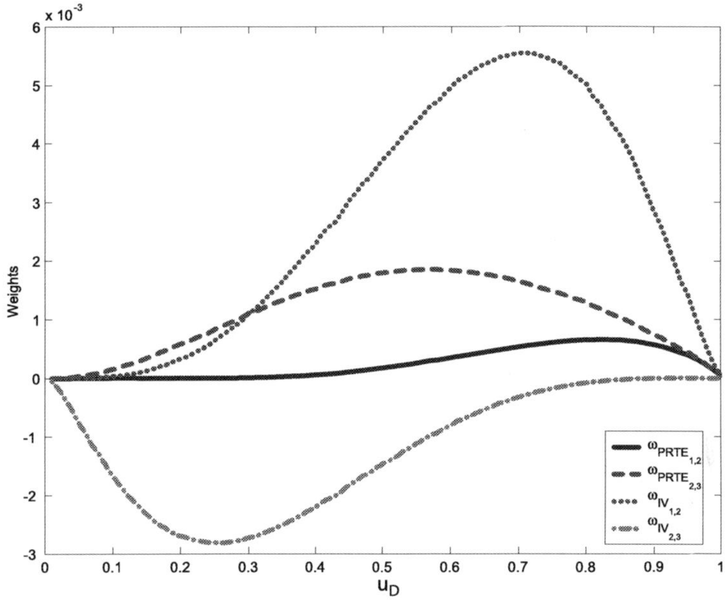

$$(W_1, W_2) \sim N\left(\begin{bmatrix} 0 \\ 0 \end{bmatrix}, \begin{bmatrix} 1 & -0.8 \\ -0.8 & 1 \end{bmatrix}\right)$$

$\Delta^{\text{PRTE}} = 0.159$, IV $= 0.296$

Proportion induced to change from $D_1 = 1$ to $D_3 = 1 = 32.1\%$

Proportion induced to change from $D_2 = 1$ to $D_3 = 1 = 64.7\%$

Figure 20C. $W_2 - t$ where $t = 1.2$ and W_1 is the instrument: Policy relevant treatment effect vs. instrumental variables weights by transition.

fect of the individual being forced to choose from one choice set instead of another. We define treatment parameters for a general multiple treatment problem and present conditions for the application of instrumental variables for identifying a variety of new treatment parameters. Our identification conditions are weaker than the ones used in Appendix B of Chapter 70, which establishes conditions under which it is possible to nonparametrically identify a full multinomial selection model.

Our use of choice theory is a unique aspect of our approach to the analysis of treatment effects. One particularly helpful result we draw on is the representation of the multinomial choices in terms of the choice between a particular choice and the best option among all other choices. This representation is crucial for understanding why LIV allows one to identify the MTE for the effect of one choice versus the best alternative option. The representation was introduced in Domencich and McFadden (1975), and has been used in the analysis of parametric multinomial selection models by Lee (1983)

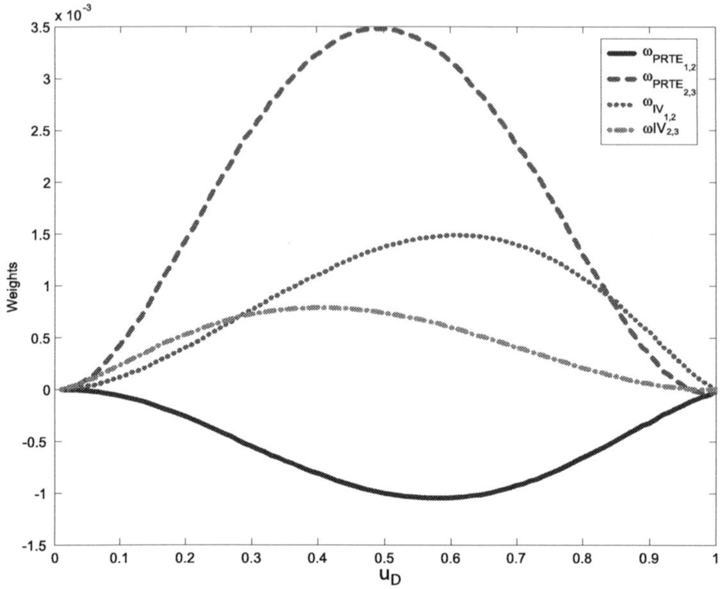

$$(W_1, W_2) \sim N\left(\begin{bmatrix} 0 \\ 0 \end{bmatrix}, \begin{bmatrix} 1 & 0 \\ 0 & 1 \end{bmatrix}\right)$$

$\Delta^{\text{PRTE}} = 0.110$, IV $= 0.210$

Proportion induced to change from $D_1 = 1$ to $D_3 = 1 = 27.5\%$

Proportion induced to change from $D_2 = 1$ to $D_3 = 1 = 76.8\%$

Figure 20D. $W_2 - t$ where $t = 1.2$ and W_1 is the instrument: Policy relevant treatment effect vs. instrumental variables weights by transition.

and Dahl (2002). Unlike those authors, we systematically explore treatment effect heterogeneity, consider nonparametric identification, and examine the application of the LIV methodology to such models.

Our analysis proceeds as follows. We first introduce our nonparametric, multinomial selection model and state our assumptions in Section 7.3.1. In Section 7.3.2, we define treatment effects in a general unordered model as the differences in the counterfactual outcomes that would have been observed if the agent faced different choice sets, i.e., the effects observed if individuals are forced to choose from one choice set instead of another. We also define the corresponding treatment parameters. Treatment effects in this context exhibit a form of treatment effect heterogeneity not present in the binary treatment case. The new form of heterogeneity arises from agents facing different choice sets, which we discuss in Section 7.3.3.

Section 7.3.4 establishes that LIV and the nonparametric Wald-IV estimand produce identification of the MTE/LATE versions of the effect of one choice versus the best alternative option without requiring knowledge of the latent index functions generat-

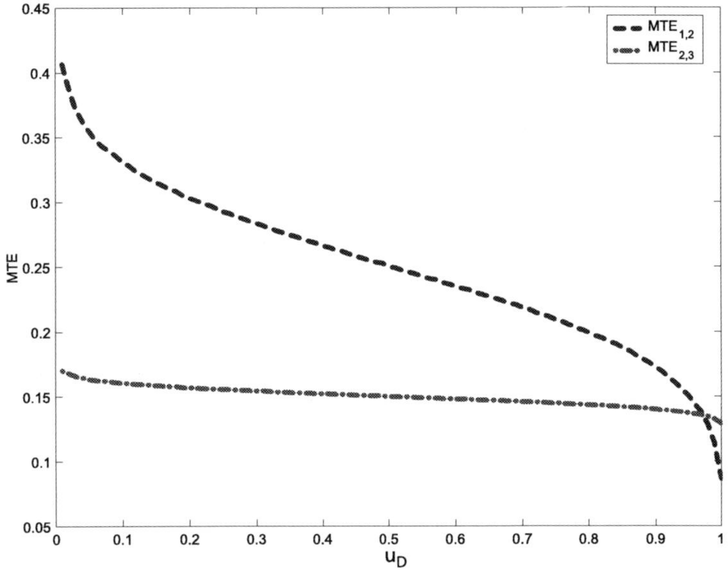

$Y_3 = \alpha + \beta_3 + U_3$; $D_3 = 1$ if $W_2 < I < \infty$; $U_3 = \sigma_3\tau$; $\sigma_3 = 0.02$, $\sigma_2 = 0.012$, $\sigma_1 = -0.05$, $\sigma_V = -1$
$Y_2 = \alpha + \beta_2 + U_2$; $D_2 = 1$ if $W_1 < I \leqslant W_2$; $U_2 = \sigma_2\tau$; $\alpha = 0.67$, $\beta_2 = 0.25$, $\beta_3 = 0.4$
$Y_1 = \alpha + U_1$; $D_1 = 1$ if $-\infty < I \leqslant W_1$; $U_1 = \sigma_1\tau$; $Z \sim N(-0.0026, 0.27)$ and $Z \perp\!\!\!\perp V$
$I = Z - V$ $V = \sigma_V\tau$; $\tau \sim N(0, 1)$
Sample size $= 1500$

Figure 21A. $W_2 - t$ where $t = 1.2$ and Z is the instrument: Marginal treatment effects by transition.

ing choices or large support assumptions. Mean treatment effects comparing one option versus the best alternative are the easiest treatment effects to study using instrumental variable methods because we effectively collapse a multiple outcome model to a series of two-outcome models, picking one outcome relative to the rest. In Section 7.3.5, we consider a more general case and state conditions for identifying the mean effect of the outcome associated with the best option in one choice set to the mean effect of the best option not in that choice set. We show that identification of the corresponding MTE/LATE parameters requires knowledge of the latent index functions of the multinomial choice model. Thus, to identify the parameters by using IV or LIV requires the formulation and estimation of an explicit choice model. In Section 7.3.6, we analyze the identification of treatment parameters corresponding to the mean effect of one specified choice versus another specified choice. Identification of marginal treatment parameters in this case requires the use of identification at infinity arguments relying on large support assumptions, but does not require knowledge of the latent index functions of the multinomial choice problem. This use of large support assumptions is closely related to

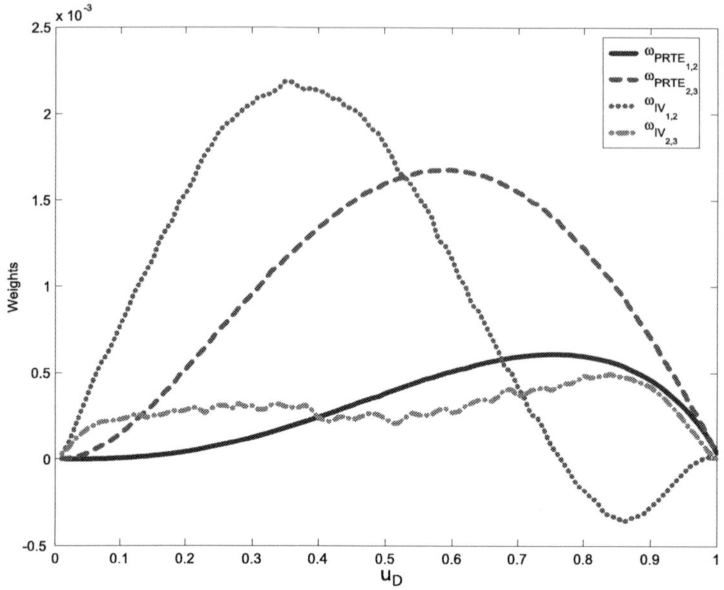

$$(W_1, W_2) \sim N\left(\begin{bmatrix} 0 \\ 0 \end{bmatrix}, \begin{bmatrix} 1 & 0.8 \\ 0.8 & 1 \end{bmatrix}\right)$$

$\Delta^{\text{PRTE}} = 0.166, \text{IV} = 0.247$

Proportion induced to change from $D_1 = 1$ to $D_3 = 1 = 42.8\%$

Proportion induced to change from $D_2 = 1$ to $D_3 = 1 = 92.4\%$

Figure 21B. $W_2 - t$ where $t = 1.2$ and Z is the instrument: Policy relevant treatment effect vs. instrumental variables weights by transition.

the need for large support assumptions to identify the full model developed in Appendix B of Chapter 70 of this Handbook. We summarize our analysis in Section 7.3.7.

7.3.1. Model and assumptions

Consider the following model with multiple choices and multiple outcome states for a general unordered model. Let $\mathcal{J}$ denote the agent's choice set, where $\mathcal{J}$ contains a finite number of elements. The value to the agent of choosing option $j \in \mathcal{J}$ is

$$R_j(Z_j) = \vartheta_j(Z_j) - V_j, \tag{7.10}$$

where Z_j are the agent's observed characteristics that affect the utility from choosing choice j, and V_j is the unobserved shock to the agent's utility from choice j. We will sometimes suppress the argument and write R_j for $R_j(Z_j)$. Let Z denote the random vector containing all unique elements of $\{Z_j\}_{j\in\mathcal{J}}$, i.e., $Z = \bigcup_{j\in\mathcal{J}}\{Z_j\}_{j\in\mathcal{J}}$. We will also sometimes write $R_j(Z)$ for $R_j(Z_j)$, leaving implicit that $R_j(\cdot)$ only depends on

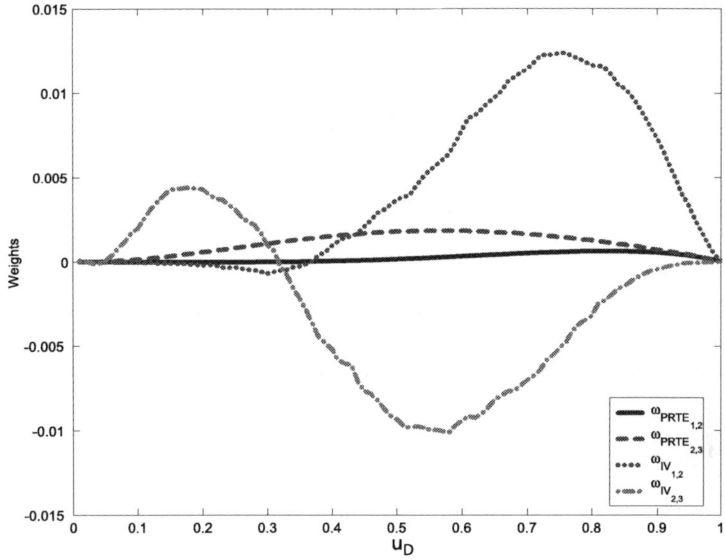

$$(W_1, W_2) \sim N\left(\begin{bmatrix} 0 \\ 0 \end{bmatrix}, \begin{bmatrix} 1 & -0.8 \\ -0.8 & 1 \end{bmatrix}\right)$$

$$\Delta^{\text{PRTE}} = 0.159, \text{IV} = 0.346$$

Proportion induced to change from $D_1 = 1$ to $D_3 = 1 = 32.1\%$

Proportion induced to change from $D_2 = 1$ to $D_3 = 1 = 64.7\%$

Figure 21C. $W_2 - t$ where $t = 1.2$ and Z is the instrument: Policy relevant treatment effect vs. instrumental variables weights by transition.

those elements of Z that are contained in Z_j. Let $D_{\mathcal{J},j}$ be an indicator variable for whether the agent would choose option j if confronted with choice set $\mathcal{J}$[109]:

$$D_{\mathcal{J},j} = \begin{cases} 1 & \text{if } R_j \geqslant R_k,\ \forall k \in \mathcal{J}, \\ 0 & \text{otherwise.} \end{cases}$$

Let $I_{\mathcal{J}}$ denote the choice that would be made by the agent if confronted with choice set $\mathcal{J}$:

$$I_{\mathcal{J}} = j \quad \Longleftrightarrow \quad D_{\mathcal{J},j} = 1.$$

Let $Y_{\mathcal{J}}$ be the outcome variable that would be observed if the agent faced choice set $\mathcal{J}$, determined by

$$Y_{\mathcal{J}} = \sum_{j \in \mathcal{J}} D_{\mathcal{J},j} Y_j,$$

109 We will impose conditions such that ties, $R_j = R_k$ for $j \neq k$, occur with probability zero.

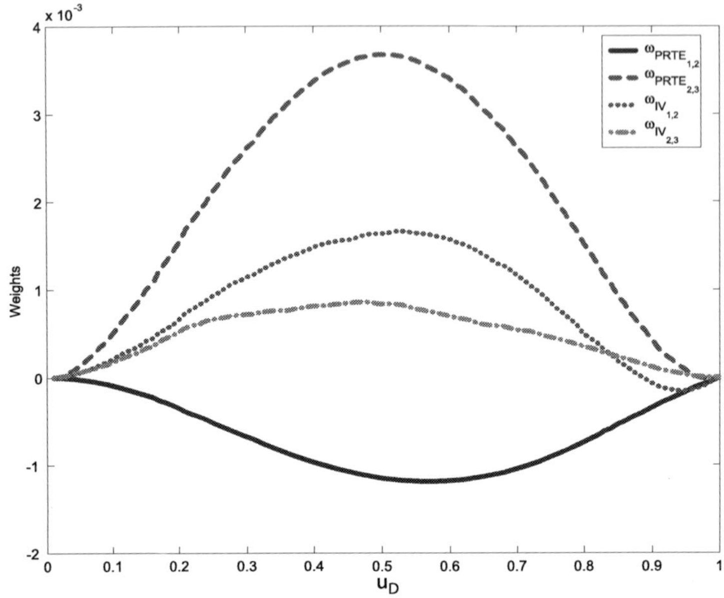

$$(W_1, W_2) \sim N\left(\begin{bmatrix} 0 \\ 0 \end{bmatrix}, \begin{bmatrix} 1 & 0 \\ 0 & 1 \end{bmatrix}\right)$$
$\Delta^{\text{PRTE}} = 0.104$, IV $= 0.215$
Proportion induced to change from $D_1 = 1$ to $D_3 = 1 = 27.3\%$
Proportion induced to change from $D_2 = 1$ to $D_3 = 1 = 69.3\%$

Figure 21D. $W_2 - t$ where $t = 1.2$ and Z is the instrument: Policy relevant treatment effect vs. instrumental variables weights by transition.

where Y_j is the potential outcome, observed only if option j is chosen. Y_j is determined by

$$Y_j = \mu_j(X_j, U_j),$$

where X_j is a vector of the agent's observed characteristics and U_j is an unobserved random vector. Let X denote the random vector containing all unique elements of $\{X_j\}_{j\in\mathcal{J}}$, i.e., $X = \bigcup_{j\in\mathcal{J}}\{X_j\}_{j\in\mathcal{J}}$. $(Z, X, I_{\mathcal{J}}, Y_{\mathcal{J}})$ is assumed to be observed. Define $R_{\mathcal{J}}$ as the maximum obtainable value given choice set $\mathcal{J}$:

$$R_{\mathcal{J}} = \max_{j\in\mathcal{J}}\{R_j\} = \sum_{j\in\mathcal{J}} D_{\mathcal{J},j} R_j.$$

We thus obtain the traditional representation of the decision process that choice j being optimal implies that choice j is better than the "next best" option:

$$I_{\mathcal{J}} = j \quad \Longleftrightarrow \quad R_j \geqslant R_{\mathcal{J}\setminus j}.$$

More generally, a choice from $\mathcal{K}$ being optimal is equivalent to the highest value obtainable from choices in $\mathcal{K}$ being higher than the highest value that can be obtained from choices outside that set,

$$I_{\mathcal{J}} \in \mathcal{K} \quad \Longleftrightarrow \quad R_{\mathcal{K}} \geqslant R_{\mathcal{J}\setminus\mathcal{K}}.$$

As we will show, this simple representation is the key intuition for understanding how nonparametric instrumental variables estimate the effect of a given choice versus the "next best" alternative.

Analogous to our definition of $R_{\mathcal{J}}$, we define $R_{\mathcal{J}}(z)$ to be the maximum obtainable value given choice set $\mathcal{J}$ when instruments are fixed at $Z = z$,

$$R_{\mathcal{J}}(z) = \max_{j\in\mathcal{J}}\left\{R_j(z)\right\}.$$

Thus, for example, a choice from $\mathcal{K}$ is optimal when instruments are fixed at $Z = z$ if $R_{\mathcal{K}}(z) \geqslant R_{\mathcal{J}\setminus\mathcal{K}}(z)$.

We make the following assumptions, which generalize assumptions (A-1)–(A-5) invoked in Heckman and Vytlacil (2001b) and later used in Heckman and Vytlacil (2005), as developed in Section 2. We present the assumptions in a fashion parallel to (A-1)–(A-5) and (OC-1)–(OC-6). For that reason, we present the second assumption, which requires special attention, out of order.

(B-1) $\{(V_j, U_j)\}_{j\in\mathcal{J}}$ *is independent of* Z *conditional on* X.
(B-3) *The distribution of* $(\{V_j\}_{j\in\mathcal{J}})$ *is continuous.*[110]
(B-4) $E(|Y_j|) < \infty$ *for all* $j \in \mathcal{J}$.
(B-5) $\Pr(I_{\mathcal{J}} = j \mid X) > 0$ *for all* $j \in \mathcal{J}$.

Assumption (B-1) and (B-3) imply that $R_j \neq R_k$ w.p.1 for $j \neq k$, so that $\operatorname{argmax}\{R_j\}$ is unique w.p.1. Assumption (B-4) is required for the mean treatment parameters to be well defined. It allows us to integrate to the limit, which will be a crucial step for all identification analysis. Assumption (B-5) requires that at least some individuals participate in each program for all X.

Our definition and analysis of the treatment parameters only require assumptions (B-1) and (B-3)–(B-5). However, we will also impose an exclusion restriction for our identification analysis. Let $Z^{[j]}$ denote the jth components of Z that are in Z_j but not in Z_k, $k \neq j$. Let $Z^{[-j]}$ denote all elements of Z except for the components in $Z^{[j]}$. We work with two alternative assumptions for the exclusion restriction.[111] Consider

[110] Absolutely continuous with respect to Lebesgue measure on $\prod_{j\in\mathcal{J}}\mathbb{R}$.

[111] We work here with exclusion restrictions in part for ease of exposition. By adapting the analysis of Cameron and Heckman (1998) and Heckman and Navarro (2007), one can modify our analysis for the case of no exclusion restrictions if Z contains a sufficient number of continuous variables and there is sufficient variation in the ϑ_k function across k.

(B-2a) *for each* $j \in \mathcal{J}$, *there exists at least one element of* Z, *say* $Z^{[j]}$, *such that* $Z^{[j]}$ *is not an element of* $Z_k, k \neq j$, *and such that the distribution of* $\vartheta_j(Z_j)$ *conditional on* $(X, Z^{[-j]})$ *is nondegenerate,*

or

(B-2b) *for each* $j \in \mathcal{J}$, *there exists at least one element of* Z, *say* $Z^{[j]}$, *such that* $Z^{[j]}$ *is not an element of* $Z_k, k \neq j$, *and such that the distribution of* $\vartheta_j(Z_j)$ *conditional on* $(X, Z^{[-j]})$ *is continuous.*[112]

Assumption (B-2a) imposes the requirement that the analyst be able to independently vary the index for the given value function. This produces variation that affects only the value of the jth value function and causes people to enter or exit sector j. It imposes an exclusion restriction, that for any $j \in \mathcal{J}$, Z contains an element such that (i) it is contained in Z_j; (ii) it is not contained in any Z_k for $k \neq j$ and (iii) $\vartheta_j(\cdot)$ is a nontrivial function of that element conditional on all other regressors. Assumption (B-2b) strengthens (B-2a) by adding a smoothness assumption. A necessary condition for (B-2b) is for the excluded variable to have a density with respect to Lebesgue measure conditional on all other regressors and for $\vartheta_j(\cdot)$ to be a continuous and nontrivial function of the excluded variable.[113] Assumption (B-2a) will be used to identify a generalization of the LATE parameter. Assumption (B-2b) will be used to identify a generalization of the MTE parameter. For certain portions of the analysis, we strengthen (B-2b) to a large support condition, though the large support assumption will not be required for most of our analysis. Assumptions (B-2a) and (B-2b) mirror (A-2) for the binary choice model and are analogous to (OC-2) and (OC-6) in an ordered choice model.

7.3.2. *Definition of treatment effects and treatment parameters*

Treatment effects are defined as the difference in the counterfactual outcomes that would have been observed if the agent faced different choice sets. For any two choice sets, $\mathcal{K}, \mathcal{L} \subset \mathcal{J}$, define

$$\Delta_{\mathcal{K},\mathcal{L}} = Y_{\mathcal{K}} - Y_{\mathcal{L}}.$$

This is the effect of the individual being forced to choose from choice set $\mathcal{K}$ versus choice set $\mathcal{L}$. The conventional treatment effect is defined as the difference in potential outcomes between two specified states,

$$\Delta_{k,l} = Y_k - Y_l,$$

[112] Absolutely continuous with respect to Lebesgue measure.

[113] (B-2b) can be easily relaxed to the weaker assumption that the support of $\vartheta_j(Z_j)$ conditional on $(X, Z^{[-j]})$ contains an open interval, or further weakened to the assumption that the conditional support contains at least one limit point. In these cases, the analysis of this section goes through without change for analysis for points within the open interval or more generally for any limit point.

which is nested within this framework by taking $\mathcal{K} = \{k\}$, $\mathcal{L} = \{l\}$. It is the effect for the individual of having no choice except to choose state l.

$\Delta_{\mathcal{K},\mathcal{L}}$ will be zero for agents who make the same choice when confronted with choice set $\mathcal{K}$ and choice set $\mathcal{L}$. Thus, $I_{\mathcal{K}} = I_{\mathcal{L}}$ implies $\Delta_{\mathcal{K},\mathcal{L}} = 0$, and we have

$$\Delta_{\mathcal{K},\mathcal{L}} = \mathbf{1}(I_{\mathcal{L}} \neq I_{\mathcal{K}})\Delta_{\mathcal{K}\setminus\mathcal{L},\mathcal{L}} \tag{7.11}$$

$$= \mathbf{1}(I_{\mathcal{L}} \neq I_{\mathcal{K}})\left(\sum_{j\in\mathcal{K}\setminus\mathcal{L}} D_{\mathcal{K},j}\Delta_{j,\mathcal{L}}\right). \tag{7.12}$$

Two examples will be of particular importance for our analysis. First, consider choice set $\mathcal{K} = \{k\}$ versus choice set $\mathcal{L} = \mathcal{J} \setminus \{k\}$. In this case, $\Delta_{k,\mathcal{J}\setminus k}$ is the difference between the agent's potential outcome in state k versus the outcome that would have been observed if he or she had not been allowed to choose state k. If $I_{\mathcal{J}} = k$, then $\Delta_{k,\mathcal{J}\setminus k}$ is the difference between the outcome in the agent's preferred state and the outcome in the agent's "next-best" state. Second, consider the set $\mathcal{K} = \mathcal{J}$ versus choice set $\mathcal{L} = \mathcal{J}\setminus\{k\}$. In this case, $\Delta_{\mathcal{J},\mathcal{J}\setminus k}$ is the difference between the agent's best outcome and what his or her outcome would have been if state k had not been available. Note that

$$\Delta_{\mathcal{J},\mathcal{J}\setminus k} = D_{\mathcal{J},k}\Delta_{k,\mathcal{J}\setminus k}.$$

Thus, there is a trivial connection between the two parameters, $\Delta_{\mathcal{J},\mathcal{J}\setminus k}$ and $\Delta_{k,\mathcal{J}\setminus k}$. We will focus on $\Delta_{k,\mathcal{J}\setminus k}$, the effect of being forced to choose option k versus being denied option k. However, one can use Equation (7.11) to use the results for $\Delta_{k,\mathcal{J}\setminus k}$ to obtain results for $\Delta_{\mathcal{J},\mathcal{J}\setminus k}$.

To fix ideas regarding these alternative definitions of treatment effects, consider the following example concerning GED certification. The GED is an exam that certifies that high school dropouts who pass the test are the equivalents of high school graduates.

EXAMPLE (*GED certification*). Consider studying the effect of GED certification on later wages. Consider the case where $\mathcal{J} = \{\{\text{GED}\}, \{\text{HS Degree}\}, \{\text{Permanent Dropout}\}\}$. Let $j = \{\text{GED}\}$, $k = \{\text{HS Degree}\}$, and $l = \{\text{Permanent Dropout}\}$. Suppose one wishes to study the effect of the GED. Then possible definitions of the effect of the GED include:

- $\Delta_{j,k}$ is the individual's outcome if he or she received the GED versus if he or she had graduated from high school;
- $\Delta_{j,l}$ is the individual's outcome if he or she received the GED versus if he or she had been a permanent dropout;
- $\Delta_{j,\mathcal{J}\setminus j}$ is the individual's outcome if he or she had received the GED versus what the outcome would have been if he or she had not had the option of receiving the GED;
- $\Delta_{\mathcal{J},\mathcal{J}\setminus j}$ is the individual's outcome if he or she had the option of receiving the GED versus the outcome if he or she did not have the option of receiving the GED. Notice that $\Delta_{\mathcal{J},\mathcal{J}\setminus j}$ is a version of an option value treatment effect.

We now define treatment parameters for a general unordered model.

Treatment parameters The conventional definition of the average treatment effect (ATE) is

$$\Delta_{k,l}^{\text{ATE}}(x, z) = E(\Delta_{k,l} \mid X = x, Z = z),$$

which immediately generalizes to the class of parameters discussed in this section as

$$\Delta_{\mathcal{K},\mathcal{L}}^{\text{ATE}}(x, z) = E(\Delta_{\mathcal{K},\mathcal{L}} \mid X = x, Z = z).$$

Notice that the treatment parameters now depend on the value of Z. We explain the source of this dependence below. The conventional definition of the treatment on the treated (TT) parameter is

$$\Delta_{k,l}^{\text{TT}}(x, z) = E(\Delta_{k,l} \mid X = x, Z = z, I_{\mathcal{J}} = k),$$

which we generalize to

$$\Delta_{\mathcal{K},\mathcal{L}}^{\text{TT}}(x, z) = E(\Delta_{\mathcal{K},\mathcal{L}} \mid X = x, Z = z, I_{\mathcal{J}} \in \mathcal{K}).$$

We also generalize the marginal treatment effect (MTE) and local average treatment effect (LATE) parameters considered in Heckman and Vytlacil (2001b). We generalize the MTE parameter to be the average effect conditional on being indifferent between the best option among choice set $\mathcal{K}$ versus the best option among choice set $\mathcal{L}$ at some fixed value of the instruments, $Z = z$:

$$\Delta_{\mathcal{K},\mathcal{L}}^{\text{MTE}}(x, z) = E\big(\Delta_{\mathcal{K},\mathcal{L}} \bigm| X = x, Z = z, R_{\mathcal{K}}(z) = R_{\mathcal{L}}(z)\big). \tag{7.13}$$

We generalize the LATE parameter to be the average effect for someone for whom the optimal choice in choice set $\mathcal{K}$ is preferred to the optimal choice in choice set $\mathcal{L}$ at $Z = \tilde{z}$, but who prefers the optimal choice in choice set $\mathcal{L}$ to the optimal choice in choice set $\mathcal{K}$ at $Z = z$:

$$\Delta_{\mathcal{K},\mathcal{L}}^{\text{LATE}}(x, z, \tilde{z}) = E\big(\Delta_{\mathcal{K},\mathcal{L}} \bigm| X = x, Z = z, R_{\mathcal{K}}(\tilde{z}) \geqslant R_{\mathcal{L}}(\tilde{z}), R_{\mathcal{L}}(z) \geqslant R_{\mathcal{K}}(z)\big). \tag{7.14}$$

An important special case of this parameter arises when $z = \tilde{z}$ except for elements that enter the index functions only for choices in $\mathcal{K}$ and not for any choice in $\mathcal{L}$. In that special case, Equation (7.14) simplifies to

$$\Delta_{\mathcal{K},\mathcal{L}}^{\text{LATE}}(x, z, \tilde{z}) = E\big(\Delta_{\mathcal{K},\mathcal{L}} \bigm| X = x, Z = z, R_{\mathcal{K}}(\tilde{z}) \geqslant R_{\mathcal{L}}(z) \geqslant R_{\mathcal{K}}(z)\big),$$

since $R_{\mathcal{L}}(z) = R_{\mathcal{L}}(\tilde{z})$ in this special case.

We have defined each of these parameters as conditional not only on X but also on the "instruments" Z. In general, the parameters depend on the Z evaluation point. For example, $\Delta_{\mathcal{K},\mathcal{L}}^{\text{ATE}}(x, z)$ generally depends on the z evaluation point. To see this, note that $Y_{\mathcal{K}} = \sum_{k \in \mathcal{K}} D_{\mathcal{K},k} Y_k$, and $Y_{\mathcal{L}} = \sum_{l \in \mathcal{L}} D_{\mathcal{L},l} Y_l$. By conditional independence assumption (B-1), $Z \perp\!\!\!\perp \{Y_j\}_{j \in \mathcal{J}} \mid X$, but $D_{\mathcal{K},k}$ and $D_{\mathcal{L},l}$ depend on Z conditional on X and thus $Y_{\mathcal{K}} - Y_{\mathcal{L}}$, in general, is dependent on Z conditional on X.[114] In other words, even though Z is conditionally independent of each individual potential outcome, it is correlated with the indicator for the choice that is optimal within the sets $\mathcal{K}$ and $\mathcal{L}$ and thus is related to $Y_{\mathcal{K}} - Y_{\mathcal{L}}$.

7.3.3. Heterogeneity in treatment effects

Consider heterogeneity in the pairwise treatment effect $\Delta_{j,k}$ (with $(j,k) \in \mathcal{J}$) defined as

$$\Delta_{j,k} = Y_j - Y_k = \mu_j(X_j, U_j) - \mu_k(X_k, U_k),$$

which in general will vary with both observables (X) and unobservables (U_j, U_k). Since we have not assumed that the error terms are additively separable, the treatment effect will in general vary with unobservables even if $U_j = U_k$.

The mean treatment parameters for $\Delta_{j,k}$ will differ if the effect of treatment is heterogeneous and agents base participation decisions, in part, on their idiosyncratic treatment effect. In general, the ATE, TT, and the marginal treatment parameters for $\Delta_{j,k}$ will differ as long as there is dependence between (U_j, U_k) and the decision rule, i.e., if there is dependence between (U_j, U_k) and $(\{V_l\}_{l \in \mathcal{J}})$. If we impose that $(\{V_l\}_{l \in \mathcal{J}})$ is independent of (U_j, U_k), then the treatment effect will still be heterogeneous, but the average treatment effect, average effect of treatment on the treated, and the marginal average treatment effects will all coincide.

The literature on treatment effects often imposes additive separability in outcomes between observables and unobservables. In particular, it is commonly assumed that U_j and U_k are scalar random variables and that $Y_j = \mu_j(X_j) + U_j$, $Y_k = \mu_k(X_k) + U_k$. In that case, a common treatment effect model is produced if the additive error term does not vary with the treatment state: $U_j = U_k$.[115] Thus, in the special case of additive separability, the treatment parameters for $\Delta_{j,k}$ will be the same even if there is dependence between $\{V_l\}_{l \in \mathcal{J}}$ and (U_j, U_k) as long as $U_j = U_k$.[116]

There is an additional source of treatment heterogeneity in the more general case of $\Delta_{\mathcal{K},\mathcal{L}}$ arising from heterogeneity in which states are being compared. Consider, for

[114] An exception is if $\mathcal{K} = \{k\}$, $\mathcal{L} = \{l\}$, i.e., both sets are singletons.

[115] More generally, if U_j, U_k are vector-valued, then additive separability is $Y_j = \mu_{1j}(X_j) + \mu_{2j}(U_j)$, $Y_k = \mu_{1k}(X_k) + \mu_{2k}(U_k)$, and the standard result is that a common treatment effect is produced if $\mu_{2j}(U_j) = \mu_{2k}(U_k)$.

[116] Because the literature often assumes additive separability in outcome equations, questions about the existence of a common treatment effect hinge on whether the additively separable error terms differ by treatment state. If the error terms differ by treatment state, there will be differences in the treatment parameters according to whether the differences in the error terms are stochastically dependent on the participation decision. Aakvik, Heckman and Vytlacil (1999) examine the case where the outcome variable is binary so that an additive separability assumption is not appropriate and Heckman and Vytlacil (2001b, 2005) consider cases without additive separability. Vytlacil, Santos and Shaikh (2005) and Vytlacil and Yildiz (2006) develop the case where $U_j = U_k$, but the model is not additively separable.

example, $\Delta_{j,\mathcal{J}\setminus j}$. We have that

$$\Delta_{j,\mathcal{J}\setminus j} = \sum_{k\in\mathcal{J}\setminus j} D_{\mathcal{J}\setminus j,k}\Delta_{j,k},$$

which will vary over individuals even if each individual has the same $\Delta_{j,k}$ treatment effect. Consider the corresponding ATE and TT parameters:

$$\begin{aligned}
&\Delta^{\mathrm{ATE}}_{j,\mathcal{J}\setminus j}(x,z)\\
&\quad = E(\Delta_{j,\mathcal{J}\setminus j} \mid X = x, Z = z)\\
&\quad = \sum_{k\in\mathcal{J}\setminus j} \Pr(I_{\mathcal{J}\setminus j} = k \mid X = x, Z = z) E(\Delta_{j,k} \mid X = x, Z = z, I_{\mathcal{J}\setminus j} = k)
\end{aligned}$$

and

$$\begin{aligned}
&\Delta^{\mathrm{TT}}_{j,\mathcal{J}\setminus j}(x,z)\\
&\quad = E(\Delta_{j,\mathcal{J}\setminus j} \mid X = x, Z = z, I_{\mathcal{J}} = j)\\
&\quad = \sum_{k\in\mathcal{J}\setminus j} \Pr(I_{\mathcal{J}\setminus j} = k \mid X = x, Z = z, I_{\mathcal{J}} = j)\\
&\qquad\qquad \times E(\Delta_{j,k} \mid X = x, Z = z, I_{\mathcal{J}} = j, I_{\mathcal{J}\setminus j} = k).
\end{aligned}$$

Even in the case where $\{U_j\}_{j\in\mathcal{J}}$ is independent of $\{V_j\}_{j\in\mathcal{J}}$, so that $E(\Delta_{j,k} \mid X = x, Z = z, I_{\mathcal{J}\setminus j} = k) = E(\Delta_{j,k} \mid X = x, Z = z, I_{\mathcal{J}} = j, I_{\mathcal{J}\setminus j} = k)$, it will still in general be the case that $\Delta^{\mathrm{ATE}}_{j,\mathcal{J}\setminus j}(x,z) \neq \Delta^{\mathrm{TT}}_{j,\mathcal{J}\setminus j}(x,z)$ since in general $\Pr(I_{\mathcal{J}\setminus j} = k \mid X = x, Z = z) \neq \Pr(I_{\mathcal{J}\setminus j} = k \mid X = x, Z = z, I_{\mathcal{J}} = j)$. Thus, the ATE and TT parameters will differ in part because they place different weights on the alternative pairwise treatment effects, and thus will differ even in the case where the pairwise (j versus k) treatment effects are common across all individuals.

In summary, $\Delta_{j,k}$ will be heterogeneous depending on the functional form of the $\mu_j(\cdot)$ and $\mu_k(\cdot)$ equations and on the pairwise dependence between the U_j and U_k terms. The $\Delta_{j,k}$ mean treatment parameters will also vary depending on the dependence between $\{V_l\}_{l\in\mathcal{J}}$ and (U_j, U_k). For $\Delta_{j,\mathcal{J}\setminus j}$, there is an additional source of heterogeneity arising from variability in the optimal option in the set $\mathcal{J}\setminus j$. Even if there is no heterogeneity in the pairwise $\Delta_{j,k}$ terms, there will still be heterogeneity in $\Delta_{j,\mathcal{J}\setminus j}$, and heterogeneity in the corresponding mean treatment parameters.

7.3.4. *LIV and nonparametric Wald estimands for one choice vs. the best alternative*

We first consider identification of treatment parameters corresponding to averages of $\Delta_{j,\mathcal{J}\setminus j}$, the effect of choosing option j versus the preferred option in $\mathcal{J}$ if j is not available. We analyze both a discrete change (Wald form for the instrumental variables estimand) and the local instrumental variables (LIV) estimand.[117] Using a concise notation, define $Z^{[j]}$ as the vector of elements in Z_j that do not enter any other choice index, and that $Z^{[-j]}$ is a vector of elements of Z not in $Z^{[j]}$. The $Z^{[j]}$ thus act as shifters attracting people into or out of state j but not affecting the valuations in the arguments of the other choice functions. For this case, we can develop an analysis of IV parallel to that given for the binary case or the ordered choice case if we condition on $Z^{[-j]}$. We obtain monotonicity or uniformity in this model if the movements among states induced by $Z^{[j]}$ are the same for all persons conditional on $Z^{[-j]} = z^{[-j]}$ and $X = x$. For example, *ceteris paribus* if $Z^{[j]} = z^{[j]}$ increases, $R_j(Z_j)$ increases but the $R_k(Z_k)$ are not affected, so the flow is toward state j.

Let $D_{\mathcal{J},j}$ be an indicator variable denoting whether option j is selected:

$$\begin{aligned} D_{\mathcal{J},j} &= \mathbf{1}\Bigl(R_j(Z_j) \geqslant \max_{\ell \neq j}\bigl\{R_\ell(Z_\ell)\bigr\}\Bigr) \\ &= \mathbf{1}\Bigl(\vartheta_j(Z_j) \geqslant V_j + \max_{\ell \neq j}\bigl\{R_\ell(Z_\ell)\bigr\}\Bigr) \\ &= \mathbf{1}\bigl(\vartheta_j(Z_j) \geqslant \tilde{V}_j\bigr), \end{aligned} \tag{7.15}$$

where $\tilde{V}_j = V_j + \max_{\ell \neq j}\{R_\ell(Z_\ell)\}$. Thus we obtain $D_{\mathcal{J},j} = \mathbf{1}(P_j(Z_j) \geqslant U_{D_j})$, where $U_{D_j} = F_{\tilde{V}_J|Z^{[-j]}}(V_j + \max_{\ell \neq j}\{R_\ell(Z_\ell)\} \mid Z^{[-j]} = z^{[-j]})$, where $F_{\tilde{V}_J|Z^{[-j]}}$ is the cdf of $\tilde{V}_j$ given $Z^{[-j]} = z^{[-j]}$. In a format parallel to the binary model, we write

$$Y = D_{\mathcal{J},j}Y_j + (1 - D_{\mathcal{J},j})Y_{\mathcal{J}\setminus j}, \tag{7.16}$$

where $Y_{\mathcal{J}\setminus j}$ is the outcome that would be observed if option j were not available. This case is just a version of the binary case developed in previous sections of the paper. There is one crucial difference, however, and that is that the distributions of the $\tilde{V}_j$ now depend on the excluded $Z = z$. Thus instruments and parameters have to be defined conditionally on $Z = z$. We can define MTE as

$$E\bigl(Y_j - Y_{\mathcal{J}\setminus j} \bigm| X = x, Z = z, \vartheta_j(z_j) - V_j = R_{\mathcal{J}\setminus j}(z)\bigr).$$

We have to condition on $Z = z$ because the choice sets are defined over the max of elements in $\mathcal{J} \setminus j$ (see Equation (7.15)).

We now show that our identification strategies presented in the preceding part of this paper extend naturally to the identification of treatment parameters for $\Delta_{j,\mathcal{J}\setminus j}$. In particular, it is possible to recover LATE and MTE parameters for $\Delta_{j,\mathcal{J}\setminus j}$ by use of discrete change IV methods and local instrumental variable methods, respectively. Averages of the effect of option j versus the next best alternative are the easiest effects to study using instrumental variable methods and are natural generalizations of our two-outcome analysis.

[117] An estimand is the population version of the estimator.

The discrete change instrumental variables estimand will allow us to recover a version of the local average treatment effect (LATE) parameter.[118] Invoke assumption (B-2a). Assume only one excluded variable $Z^{[j]}$ in Z_j. If there are more, pick any one that satisfies (B-2a). Let $Z^{[-j]}$ denote the excluded variable for option j with properties assumed in (B-2a). We let $Z = [Z^{[-j]}, Z^{[j]}]$ and $\tilde{Z} = [\tilde{Z}^{[-j]}, \tilde{Z}^{[j]}]$ be two values where we only manipulate scalar $Z^{[j]}$.

$$\Delta_j^{\text{Wald}}\left(x, z^{[-j]}, z^{[j]}, \tilde{z}^{[j]}\right) = \frac{E(Y \mid X = x, Z = \tilde{z}) - E(Y \mid X = x, Z = z)}{\Pr(D_{\mathcal{J},j} = 1 \mid X = x, Z = \tilde{z}) - \Pr(D_{\mathcal{J},j} = 1 \mid X = x, Z = z)},$$

where for notational convenience we are assuming that $Z^{[j]}$ is the last element of Z. Note that all components of z and $\tilde{z}$ are the same except for the jth component. Without loss of generality, we assume that $\vartheta_j(\tilde{z}) > \vartheta_j(z)$.

If there were no X regressors, and if Z were a scalar, binary random variable, then $\Delta_j^{\text{Wald}}(x, z^{[-j]}, z^{[j]}, \tilde{z}^{[j]})$ would be the probability limit of the Wald form of two-stage least squares regression (2SLS). With X regressors, and with Z a vector possibly including continuous components, it no longer corresponds to a Wald/2SLS, but rather to a nonparametric version of the Wald estimator where the analyst nonparametrically conditions on X and on Z taking one of two specified values.

The local instrumental variables estimator (LIV) estimand introduced in Heckman (1997), and developed further in Heckman and Vytlacil (1999, 2000, 2005) and Florens et al. (2002), will allow us to recover a version of the marginal treatment effect (MTE) parameter. Impose (B-2b), and let $Z^{[j]}$ denote the excluded variable for option j with properties assumed in (B-2b). Because of the index structure, the LIV estimand will be invariant to which particular variable in $Z^{[j]}$ satisfying (B-2b) is used if there is more than one variable with the property assumed in (B-2b). The effects are *not* invariant to variables in $Z^{[-j]}$. Define

$$\Delta_j^{\text{LIV}}(x, z) \equiv \frac{\partial}{\partial z^{[j]}} E(Y \mid X = x, Z = z) \Big/ \frac{\partial}{\partial z^{[j]}} \Pr(D_{\mathcal{J},j} = 1 \mid X = x, Z = z).$$

$\Delta_j^{\text{LIV}}(x, z)$ is thus the limit form of $\Delta_j^{\text{Wald}}(x, z^{[-j]}, z^{[j]}, \tilde{z}^{[j]})$ as $\tilde{z}^{[j]}$ approaches $z^{[j]}$. Given our previous assumptions, one can easily show that this limit exists w.p.1. LIV corresponds to a nonparametric, local version of indirect least squares. It is a function of the distribution of the observable data, and it can be consistently estimated using any nonparametric estimator of the derivative of a conditional expectation.

Given these definitions, we have the following identification theorem.

[118] We are using the Z directly in the following manipulations instead of directly manipulating the $\{\vartheta_l(Z_l)\}_{l\in\mathcal{J}}$ indices. One can modify the following analysis to directly use $\{\vartheta_l(Z_l)\}_{l\in\mathcal{J}}$, with the disadvantage of requiring identification of $\{\vartheta_l(Z_l)\}_{l\in\mathcal{J}}$ (e.g., by an identification at infinity argument) but with the advantage of being able to follow the analysis of Heckman and Navarro (2007) in not requiring an exclusion restriction if Z contains a sufficient number of continuous variables and there is sufficient variation in the ϑ_k functions across k.

THEOREM 6.

1. *Assume* (B-1), (B-3)–(B-5), *and* (B-2a). *Then*

$$\Delta_j^{\mathrm{Wald}}\big(x, z^{[-j]}, z^{[j]}, \tilde{z}^{[j]}\big) = \Delta_{j,\mathcal{J}\setminus j}^{\mathrm{LATE}}(x, z, \tilde{z}),$$

where $\tilde{z} = (z^{[-j]}, \tilde{z}^{[j]})$.

2. *Assume* (B-1), (B-3)–(B-5), *and* (B-2b). *Then*

$$\Delta_j^{\mathrm{LIV}}(x, z) = \Delta_{j,\mathcal{J}\setminus j}^{\mathrm{MTE}}(x, z).$$

PROOF. See Appendix J. □

The intuition underlying the proof is simple. Under (B-1), (B-3)–(B-5), and (B-2a), we can convert the problem of comparing the outcome under j with the outcome under the next best option. This is an IV version of the selection modeling of Dahl (2002).

$\Delta_{j,\mathcal{J}\setminus j}^{\mathrm{LATE}}(x, z, \tilde{z})$ is the average effect of switching to state j from state $I_{\mathcal{J}\setminus j}$ for individuals who would choose $I_{\mathcal{J}\setminus j}$ at $Z = z$ but would choose j at $Z = \tilde{z}$. $\Delta_{j,\mathcal{J}\setminus j}^{\mathrm{MTE}}(x, z)$ is the average effect of switching to state j from state $I_{\mathcal{J}\setminus j}$ (the best option besides state j) for individuals who are indifferent between state j and $I_{\mathcal{J}\setminus j}$ at the given values of the selection indices (at $Z = z$, i.e., at $\{\vartheta_k(Z_k) = \vartheta_k(z_k)\}_{k\in\mathcal{J}}$).

The mean effect of state j versus state $I_{\mathcal{J}\setminus j}$ (the next best option) is a weighted average over $k \in \mathcal{J} \setminus j$ of the effect of state j versus state k, conditional on k being the next best option, weighted by the probability that k is the next best option. For example, for the LATE parameter,

$$\begin{aligned}
&\Delta_{j,\mathcal{J}\setminus j}^{\mathrm{LATE}}(x, z, \tilde{z})\\
&\quad= E\big(\Delta_{j,\mathcal{J}\setminus j} \bigm| X = x, Z = z, R_j(\tilde{z}) \geqslant R_{\mathcal{J}\setminus j}(z) \geqslant R_j(z)\big)\\
&\quad= \sum_{k\in\mathcal{J}\setminus j} \big[\Pr\big(I_{\mathcal{J}\setminus j} = k \bigm| Z \in \{z, \tilde{z}\}, X = x, R_j(\tilde{z}) \geqslant R_{\mathcal{J}\setminus j}(z) \geqslant R_j(z)\big)\\
&\qquad\times E\big(\Delta_{j,k} \bigm| X = x, Z \in \{z, \tilde{z}\}, R_j(\tilde{z}) \geqslant R_{\mathcal{J}\setminus j}(z) \geqslant R_j(z), I_{\mathcal{J}\setminus j} = k\big)\big],
\end{aligned}$$

where we use the result that $R_{\mathcal{J}\setminus j}(z) = R_{\mathcal{J}\setminus j}(\tilde{z})$ since $z = \tilde{z}$ except for one component that only enters the index for the jth option. The higher $\vartheta_k(z_k)$, holding the other indices constant, the larger the weight given to k as the base state. Thus, how heavily each option is weighted in this average depends on the switching probability $\Pr(I_{\mathcal{J}\setminus j} = k \mid Z = z, X = x, R_j(\tilde{z}_j) \geqslant R_k(z_k) \geqslant R_j(z_j))$, which in turn depends on $\{\vartheta_k(z_k)\}_{k\in\mathcal{J}\setminus j}$.

The LIV and Wald estimands depend on the z evaluation point. Alternatively, one can define averaged versions of the LIV and Wald estimands that will recover averaged versions of the MTE and LATE parameters,

$$\begin{aligned}
&\int \Delta_j^{\mathrm{Wald}}\big(x, z^{[-j]}, z^{[j]}, \tilde{z}^{[j]}\big)\, dF_{Z^{[-j]}}\big(z^{[-j]}\big)\\
&\quad= \int \Delta_{j,\mathcal{J}\setminus j}^{\mathrm{LATE}}(x, z, \tilde{z})\, dF_{Z^{[-j]}}\big(z^{[-j]}\big)
\end{aligned}$$

$$= E\big(\Delta_{j,\mathcal{J}\setminus j} \mid X = x, R_j\big(Z^{[-j]}, \tilde{z}^{[j]}\big) \geqslant R_{\mathcal{J}\setminus j}\big(Z^{[-j]}\big) \geqslant R_j\big(Z^{[-j]}, z^{[j]}\big)\big)$$

and

$$\int \Delta_j^{\mathrm{LIV}}(x, z)\, dF_Z(z) = \int \Delta_{j,\mathcal{J}\setminus j}^{\mathrm{MTE}}(x, z)\, dF_Z(z)$$
$$= E\big(\Delta_{j,\mathcal{J}\setminus j} \mid X = x, R_j(Z) = R_{\mathcal{J}\setminus j}(Z)\big).[119]$$

Thus far we have only considered identification of marginal treatment effect parameters, LATE and MTE, and not of the more standard treatment parameters like ATE and TT. However, following Heckman and Vytlacil (1999, 2001b), LATE can approximate ATE or TT arbitrarily well given the appropriate support conditions. Theorem 6 shows that we can use Wald estimands to identify LATE for $\Delta_{j,\mathcal{J}\setminus j}$, and we can thus adapt the analysis of Heckman and Vytlacil (2001b, 2005), as reviewed in Section 4, to identify ATE or TT for $\Delta_{j,\mathcal{J}\setminus j}$. Suppose that $Z^{[j]}$ denotes the excluded variable for option j with properties assumed in (B-2a), and suppose that: (i) the support of the distribution of $Z^{[j]}$ conditional on all other elements of Z is the full real line; (ii) $\vartheta_j(z_j) \to \infty$ as $z^{[j]} \to \infty$, and $\vartheta_j(z_j) \to -\infty$ as $z^{[j]} \to -\infty$. Then $\Delta_{j,\mathcal{J}\setminus j}^{\mathrm{ATE}}(x, z)$ and $\Delta_j^{\mathrm{LATE}}(x, z^{[-j]}, z^{[j]}, \tilde{z}^{[j]})$ are arbitrarily close when evaluated at a sufficiently large value of $\tilde{z}^{[j]}$ and a sufficiently small value of $z^{[j]}$. Following Heckman and Vytlacil (1999), $\Delta_{j,\mathcal{J}\setminus j}^{\mathrm{TT}}(x, z)$ and $\Delta_j^{\mathrm{LATE}}(x, z^{[-j]}, z^{[j]}, \tilde{z}^{[j]})$ are arbitrarily close for sufficiently small $z^{[j]}$. Using Theorem 6, we can use Wald estimands to identify the LATE parameters, and thus can use the Wald estimand to identify the ATE and TT parameters provided that there is sufficient support for the Z. While this discussion has used the Wald estimands, alternatively we could also follow Heckman and Vytlacil (1999), as summarized in Section 3, in expressing ATE and TT as integrated versions of MTE. By Theorem 6, we can use LIV to identify MTE and can thus express ATE and TT as integrated versions of the LIV estimand.

For a general instrument $J(Z^{[j]}, Z^{[-j]})$ constructed from $(Z^{[j]}, Z^{[-j]})$, which we denote as $J^{[j]}$, we can obtain a parallel construction to the characterization of standard IV given in Section 4.3:

$$\Delta_{J^{[j]}}^{\mathrm{IV}} = \int_0^1 \Delta^{\mathrm{MTE}}(x, z, u_{D_j})\, \omega_{\mathrm{IV}}^{J^{[j]}}(u_{D_j})\, du_{D_j}, \tag{7.17}$$

where

$$\omega_{\mathrm{IV}}^{J^{[j]}}(u_{D_j}) = \frac{E[J^{[j]} - E(J^{[j]}) \mid P_j(Z) \geqslant u_{D_j}] \Pr(P_j(Z) \geqslant u_{D_j} \mid Z^{[-j]} = z^{[-j]})}{\mathrm{Cov}(Z^{[j]}, D_{\mathcal{J},j})}, \tag{7.18}$$

[119] We assume that the support of $Z^{[-j]}$ conditional on $Z^{[j]}$ is the same as the support of $Z^{[-j]}$ conditional on $\tilde{Z}^{[j]}$.

where u_{D_j} is defined at the beginning of this subsection and where we keep the conditioning on $X = x$ implicit.

Note that from Theorem 6, we obtain that

$$\frac{\frac{\partial}{\partial z^{[j]}} E[Y \mid X = x, Z = z]}{\frac{\partial P_j(z)}{\partial z^{[j]}}} = \frac{\partial E[Y \mid X = x, Z = z]}{\partial P_j(z)} = E\left[Y_j - Y_{\mathcal{J}\setminus j} \;\middle|\; X = x, Z = z, \vartheta_j(Z_j) - V_j = R_{\mathcal{J}\setminus j}(Z)\right]$$

so LIV identifies MTE and linear IV is a weighted average of LIV with the weights summing to one. These results mirror the results established in the binary case.

In the literature on the effects of schooling ($S = \sum_{j \in \mathcal{J}} j D_{\mathcal{J},j}$) on earnings ($Y_{\mathcal{J}}$), it is conventional to instrument S. The website of Heckman, Urzua and Vytlacil (2006) presents an analysis of this case. For the general unordered case,

$$\Delta^{\mathrm{IV}}_{J^{[j]}} = \frac{\mathrm{Cov}(J^{[j]}, Y_{\mathcal{J}})}{\mathrm{Cov}(J^{[j]}, S)}$$

can be decomposed into economically interpretable components where the weights can be identified but the objects being weighted cannot be identified using local instrumental variables or LATE without making large support assumptions. However, the components can be identified using a structural model.

The trick we have used in this subsection comparing outcomes in j to the next best option converts a general unordered multiple outcome model into a two-outcome setup. This effectively partitions $Y_{\mathcal{J}}$ into two components, as in (7.16). Thus we write

$$Y_{\mathcal{J}} = D_{\mathcal{J},j} Y_j + (1 - D_{\mathcal{J},j}) Y_{\mathcal{J}\setminus j},$$

where

$$Y_{\mathcal{J}\setminus j} = \sum_{\substack{\ell \neq j \\ \ell \in \mathcal{J}}} \frac{D_{\mathcal{J},\ell}}{1 - D_{\mathcal{J},j}} Y_\ell \cdot \mathbf{1}(D_{\mathcal{J},j} \neq 1).$$

In the more general unordered case with three or more choices, to analyze IV estimates of the effect of S on $Y_{\mathcal{J}}$, we must work with $Y_{\mathcal{J}} = \sum_{k \in \mathcal{J}} D_{\mathcal{J},k} Y_k$ and make multiple comparisons across potential outcomes. This requires us to move outside of the LATE/LIV framework, which is inherently based on binary comparisons. We turn to that analysis next.

7.3.5. *Identification: Effect of best option in $\mathcal{K}$ versus best option not in $\mathcal{K}$*

We just presented an analysis of identification for treatment parameters defined as averages of $\Delta_{j,\mathcal{J}\setminus j}$, the effect of choosing option j versus the preferred option in $\mathcal{J}$ if j were not available. We now consider identification of $\Delta_{\mathcal{K},\mathcal{J}\setminus\mathcal{K}}$, the effect of choosing the preferred choice among set $\mathcal{K}$ versus the preferred choice among $\mathcal{J}$ if no option in $\mathcal{K}$ were available. This is an effect where we compare sets of options, and not just a single option compared to the rest.

We first start with an analysis that varies the $\{\vartheta_k(\cdot)\}_{k\in\mathcal{J}}$ indices directly. This analysis would be useful if one first identifies the index function, e.g., through an identification at infinity argument using the analysis in Matzkin (1993), as in Appendix B of Chapter 70 or Chapter 73 (Matzkin) in this Handbook. We then perform an analysis shifting Z directly. We show that it is possible to identify MTE and LATE averages of the $\Delta_{\mathcal{K},\mathcal{J}\setminus\mathcal{K}}$ effect if one has knowledge of the $\{\vartheta_k(\cdot)\}_{k\in\mathcal{J}}$ index functions but is not possible using shifts in Z without knowledge of the index functions. The one exception to this result is the special case already considered, when $\mathcal{K}=k$, i.e., the set only contains one element, in which case it is possible to identify the marginal parameters using shifts in Z directly without knowledge of the index functions.

Let $\vartheta_{\mathcal{J}}(Z)$ denote a random vector stacking the indices,

$$\vartheta_{\mathcal{J}}(Z) = \bigcup_{k\in\mathcal{J}} \{\vartheta_k(Z)\colon k\in\mathcal{J}\}.$$

Let $\vartheta_{\mathcal{J}}$ be a vector denoting a potential evaluation point of $\vartheta_{\mathcal{J}}(Z)$, $\vartheta_{\mathcal{J}}=\{\vartheta_k\colon k\in\mathcal{J}\}$, so that $\vartheta_{\mathcal{J}}(Z)=\vartheta_{\mathcal{J}}$ denotes the event $\{\vartheta_k(Z)=\vartheta_k\colon k\in\mathcal{J}\}$.[120] Let $\vartheta_{\mathcal{J}}+h$ denote $\{\vartheta_k+h\colon k\in\mathcal{J}\}$, where $h\in\mathbb{R}$. We now define a version of the Wald estimand that uses the indices directly as instruments instead of using Z as instruments,

$$\begin{aligned}
&\tilde{\Delta}^{\text{Wald}}_{\mathcal{K}}(x,\vartheta_{\mathcal{J}},h)\\
&\quad\equiv \big[E\big(Y \mid X=x, \vartheta_{\mathcal{K}}(Z)=\vartheta_{\mathcal{K}}+h, \vartheta_{\mathcal{J}\setminus\mathcal{K}}(Z)=\vartheta_{\mathcal{J}\setminus\mathcal{K}}\big)\\
&\qquad - E\big(Y \mid X=x, \vartheta_{\mathcal{J}}(Z)=\vartheta_{\mathcal{J}}\big)\big]\\
&\qquad \times \big[\Pr\big(I_{\mathcal{J}}\in\mathcal{K} \mid X=x, \vartheta_{\mathcal{K}}(Z)=\vartheta_{\mathcal{K}}+h, \vartheta_{\mathcal{J}\setminus\mathcal{K}}(Z)=\vartheta_{\mathcal{J}\setminus\mathcal{K}}\big)\\
&\qquad - \Pr\big(I_{\mathcal{J}}\in\mathcal{K} \mid X=x, \vartheta_{\mathcal{J}}(Z)=\vartheta_{\mathcal{J}}\big)\big]^{-1}.
\end{aligned}$$

$\tilde{\Delta}^{\text{Wald}}_{\mathcal{K}}(x,\vartheta_{\mathcal{J}},h)$ corresponds to the effect of a shift in each index in $\mathcal{K}$ upward by h while holding each index in $\mathcal{J}\setminus\mathcal{K}$ constant. Using indices, we define a version of the LIV estimand using indices $\tilde{\Delta}^{\text{LIV}}_{\mathcal{K}}(x,\vartheta_{\mathcal{J}})$ through a limit expression

$$\tilde{\Delta}^{\text{LIV}}_{\mathcal{K}}(x,\vartheta_{\mathcal{J}}) = \lim_{h\to 0}\tilde{\Delta}^{\text{Wald}}_{\mathcal{K}}(x,\vartheta_{\mathcal{J}},h).$$

Likewise, we define versions of the LATE and MTE parameters that are functions of the ϑ indices instead of functions of z evaluation points,

$$\begin{aligned}
&\tilde{\Delta}^{\text{LATE}}_{\mathcal{K},\mathcal{L}}(x,\vartheta_{\mathcal{J}},h)\\
&\quad = E\big(\Delta_{\mathcal{K},\mathcal{L}} \mid X=x, \vartheta_{\mathcal{J}}(Z)=\vartheta_{\mathcal{J}}, R_{\mathcal{K}}(Z)+h \geqslant R_{\mathcal{L}}(Z) \geqslant R_{\mathcal{K}}(Z)\big),
\end{aligned}$$

[120] Note that in our notation, $R_{\mathcal{J}}=\max\{R_k\}_{k\in\mathcal{J}}$ is a scalar, while $\vartheta_{\mathcal{J}}(Z)=\{\vartheta_k(Z)\colon k\in\mathcal{J}\}$ is a vector.

$$\tilde{\Delta}^{\text{MTE}}_{\mathcal{K},\mathcal{L}}(x, \vartheta_{\mathcal{J}}) = E\big(\Delta_{\mathcal{K},\mathcal{L}} \mid X = x, \vartheta_{\mathcal{J}}(Z) = \vartheta_{\mathcal{J}}, R_{\mathcal{K}}(Z) = R_{\mathcal{L}}(Z)\big).$$

We state the following identification theorem:

THEOREM 7.

1. *Assume* (B-1), (B-3)–(B-5), *and* (B-2a). *Then*

$$\tilde{\Delta}^{\text{Wald}}_{\mathcal{K}}(x, \vartheta_{\mathcal{J}}, h) = \tilde{\Delta}^{\text{LATE}}_{\mathcal{K},\mathcal{J}\setminus\mathcal{K}}(x, \vartheta_{\mathcal{J}}, h).$$

2. *Assume* (B-1), (B-3)–(B-5), *and* (B-2b). *Then*

$$\tilde{\Delta}^{\text{LIV}}_{\mathcal{K}}(x, \vartheta_{\mathcal{J}}) = \tilde{\Delta}^{\text{MTE}}_{\mathcal{K},\mathcal{J}\setminus\mathcal{K}}(x, \vartheta_{\mathcal{J}}).$$

PROOF. Follows with trivial modifications from the proof of Theorem 6. □

Now consider the same analysis shifting Z directly instead of shifting the indices. First consider LATE. If one knew what shifts in Z corresponded to shifting each index in $\mathcal{K}$ upward by the same amount while holding each index in $\mathcal{J} \setminus \mathcal{K}$ constant, then one could immediately follow the preceding analysis to recover $E(\Delta_{\mathcal{K},\mathcal{J}\setminus\mathcal{K}} \mid X = x, \vartheta_{\mathcal{J}}(Z) = \vartheta_{\mathcal{J}}, R_{\mathcal{K}}(Z) + h \geqslant R_{\mathcal{J}\setminus\mathcal{K}}(Z) \geqslant R_{\mathcal{K}}(Z))$. However, unless $\mathcal{K}$ is a singleton, without knowledge of the index functions one does not know what shifts in Z will have this property. One possible approach would be to only shift elements of Z that are elements of Z_j for $j \in \mathcal{K}$ but are excluded from Z_j for $j \in \mathcal{J} \setminus \mathcal{K}$. However, unless the shifts move the indices for choices in $\mathcal{K}$ all by the same amount, the shift in Z will result in movement not only from the set $\mathcal{J} \setminus \mathcal{K}$ to the set $\mathcal{K}$ but also cause movement between choices within $\mathcal{K}$. Thus, one can use shifts in Z to recover a LATE-type parameter for $\Delta_{\mathcal{K},\mathcal{J}\setminus\mathcal{K}}$ only if either (i) the index functions are known, or (ii) $\mathcal{K} = \{k\}$, i.e., the set $\mathcal{K}$ contains only one element. Our analysis establishes a fundamental role for choice theory in recovering the indices needed to perform IV analysis.

Thus far, we have only considered identification of marginal treatment effect parameters for $\Delta_{\mathcal{K},\mathcal{J}\setminus\mathcal{K}}$ and not of the more standard treatment parameters ATE and TT for $\Delta_{\mathcal{K},\mathcal{J}\setminus\mathcal{K}}$. As in the immediately preceding section, we can follow Heckman and Vytlacil (1999) in expressing ATE and TT as integrated versions of MTE or show that ATE and TT can be approximated arbitrarily well by LATE parameters. Given appropriate support conditions, we can again identify MTE over the appropriate range or identify the appropriate LATE parameters and thus identify ATE and TT given the required support conditions.

7.3.6. Identification: Effect of one fixed choice versus another

Consider evaluating the effect of fixed option j versus fixed option k, $\Delta_{j,k}$, i.e., the effect for the individual of having no choice except to choose state j versus no choice except to choose state k. We show that it is possible to identify averages of $\Delta_{j,k}$ if one has sufficient support conditions. These conditions supplement the standard IV conditions developed for the binary case [Heckman, Urzua and Vytlacil (2006)] with the conditions more commonly used in semiparametric estimation. We start by considering the analysis if one knows the ϑ index functions, say from a semiparametric analysis of discrete choice, and then show that knowledge of the ϑ index functions is not necessary.

For notational purposes, for any $j, k \in \mathcal{J}$, define $U_{j,k} = U_j - U_k$, and let $\vartheta_{j,k}(Z) = \vartheta_j(Z_j) - \vartheta_k(Z_k)$. One might try to follow our previous strategy to identify treatment parameters for $\Delta_{j,k}$ if one could shift $\vartheta_j - \vartheta_k = \vartheta_{j,k}$ while holding constant $\{\vartheta_{l,m}\}_{(l,m)\in\mathcal{J}\times\mathcal{J}\setminus\{j,k\}}$, i.e., while holding all other utility contrasts fixed.[121] However, given the structure of the latent variable model determining choices, these are incompatible conditions. To see this, note that $\vartheta_{j,k} = \vartheta_{l,k} - \vartheta_{l,j}$ for any l, and thus $\vartheta_{j,k}$ cannot be shifted while holding $\vartheta_{l,j}$ and $\vartheta_{l,k}$ constant.[122]

To bypass this problem, we develop a limit strategy to make the consequences of shifting $\vartheta_{j,k}$ negligible. Our strategy relies on an identification at infinity argument. For example, consider the case where $\mathcal{J} = \{1, 2, 3\}$, and consider identification of the MTE parameter for option 3 versus option 1. Recall that $D_{\mathcal{J}\setminus 3,l}$ is an indicator variable for whether option l would be chosen if option 3 were not available, so that $D_{\mathcal{J}\setminus 3,l}\Delta_{3,\mathcal{J}\setminus 3} = D_{\mathcal{J}\setminus 3,l}\Delta_{3,l}$. Since 1 and 2 are the only options if 3 is not available, it follows that $\Delta_{3,\mathcal{J}\setminus 3} = D_{\mathcal{J}\setminus 3,1}\Delta_{3,1} + D_{\mathcal{J}\setminus 3,2}\Delta_{3,2}$, and we have that

$$\begin{aligned}
&E\big(\Delta_{3,\mathcal{J}\setminus 3} \bigm| X = x, \vartheta_{\mathcal{J}}(Z) = \vartheta_{\mathcal{J}}, R_3(Z) = R_{\mathcal{J}\setminus 3}(Z)\big) \\
&\quad = E\big(D_{\mathcal{J}\setminus 3,1}\Delta_{3,1} \bigm| X = x, \vartheta_{\mathcal{J}}(Z) = \vartheta_{\mathcal{J}}, R_3(Z) = R_{\mathcal{J}\setminus 3}(Z)\big) \\
&\qquad + E\big(D_{\mathcal{J}\setminus 3,2}\Delta_{3,2} \bigm| X = x, \vartheta_{\mathcal{J}}(Z) = \vartheta_{\mathcal{J}}, R_3(Z) = R_{\mathcal{J}\setminus 3}(Z)\big).
\end{aligned}$$

The smaller ϑ_2 is (holding ϑ_1 and ϑ_3 fixed), the larger the probability that the "next best option" is 1 and not 2. Note that $E(\Delta_{3,1} \mid X = x, \vartheta_{\mathcal{J}}(Z) = \vartheta_{\mathcal{J}}, R_3(Z) = R_1(Z))$ does not depend on the ϑ_2 evaluation point given independence assumption (B-1), so that

$$\begin{aligned}
&E\big(\Delta_{3,1} \bigm| X = x, \vartheta_{\mathcal{J}}(Z) = \vartheta_{\mathcal{J}}, R_3(Z) = R_1(Z)\big) \\
&\quad = E\big(\Delta_{3,1} \bigm| X = x, \vartheta_{\mathcal{J}\setminus 2}(Z) = \vartheta_{\mathcal{J}\setminus 2}, R_3(Z) = R_1(Z)\big).
\end{aligned}$$

121 Alternatively, one can allow $\vartheta_{l,m}(z) \neq \vartheta_{l,m}(z')$ if $\Pr(U_{l,m} \in [\vartheta_{l,m}(z), \vartheta_{l,m}(z')]) = 0$. Such a possibility would be ruled out except "at the limit" by the standard assumption that the support of $U_{l,m}$ is connected. (We discuss this below.) Even without such an assumption, such a possibility occurring simultaneously for all $(l, m) \in \mathcal{J} \times \mathcal{J} \setminus \{j, k\}$ for a particular (z, z') seems extremely implausible, and we will therefore not consider this possibility further.

122 This suggests a nonparametric test of the latent variable model. If there exists (z, z') such that $\Pr(I_{\mathcal{J}} = j \mid Z = z) \neq \Pr(I_{\mathcal{J}} = j \mid Z = z')$, and $\Pr(I_{\mathcal{J}} = k \mid Z = z) \neq \Pr(I_{\mathcal{J}} = k \mid Z = z')$, but $\Pr(I_{\mathcal{J}} = l \mid Z = z) = \Pr(I_{\mathcal{J}} = l \mid Z = z')$ for all $l \in \mathcal{J} \setminus \{j, k\}$, then the latent variable model is rejected. However, shifts in only two indices are possible for sequential models since unexpected innovations in agent information sets will act to shift the current decision without affecting previous decisions. Consider the following sequential model of GED certification. In the first period, the agent chooses to graduate from high school or to dropout of high school. If the agent drops out of high school in the first period, he or she has the option in the second period of attaining GED certification or staying a permanent dropout. An unexpected shock in the second period to the relative value of GED certification versus permanent dropout status will shift the GED/permanent dropout choice without changing the probability of high school graduation.

Thus, by assumptions (B-1) and (B-3) and the Dominated Convergence Theorem, we have that

$$\lim_{\vartheta_2 \to -\infty} E\big(D_{\mathcal{J}\setminus 3,1}\Delta_{3,1} \mid X = x, \vartheta_{\mathcal{J}}(Z) = \vartheta_{\mathcal{J}}, R_3(Z) = R_{\mathcal{J}\setminus 3}(Z)\big)$$
$$= E\big(\Delta_{3,1} \mid X = x, \vartheta_{\mathcal{J}\setminus 2}(Z) = \vartheta_{\mathcal{J}\setminus 2}, R_3(Z) = R_1(Z)\big)$$

while

$$\lim_{\vartheta_2 \to -\infty} E\big(D_{\mathcal{J}\setminus 3,2}\Delta_{3,2} \mid X = x, \vartheta_{\mathcal{J}}(Z) = \vartheta_{\mathcal{J}}, R_3(Z) = R_{\mathcal{J}\setminus 3}(Z)\big) = 0,$$

so that

$$\lim_{\vartheta_2 \to -\infty} E\big(\Delta_{3,\mathcal{J}\setminus 3} \mid X = x, \vartheta_{\mathcal{J}}(Z) = \vartheta_{\mathcal{J}}, R_3(Z) = R_{\mathcal{J}\setminus 3}(Z)\big)$$
$$= E\big(\Delta_{3,1} \mid X = x, \vartheta_{\mathcal{J}\setminus 2}(Z) = \vartheta_{\mathcal{J}\setminus 2}, R_3(Z) = R_1(Z)\big).$$

In other words, as the value of option 2 becomes arbitrarily small, the probability of the "next best option" being 1 becomes arbitrarily close to one. Thus the MTE parameter for option 3 versus the next best option becomes arbitrarily close to the MTE parameter for option 3 versus option 1.

We can identify the MTE parameter for option 3 versus the next best option using the LIV estimand as in Theorem 6, and thus conditioning on ϑ_2 arbitrarily small we have that the LIV estimand is arbitrarily close to the MTE parameter for option 3 versus option 1. This analysis requires the appropriate support conditions in order for the limit operations to be well defined. The following theorem formalizes this idea, and is for the more general case where $\mathcal{J}$ is a general finite set.

THEOREM 8. *Assume* (B-1), (B-3)–(B-5), *and* (B-2b). *Assume that, for any* $t \in \mathbb{R}$,

$$\Pr\big(\vartheta_l(Z_l) \leqslant t \mid \vartheta_j(Z_j), \vartheta_k(Z_k)\big) \geqslant 0 \quad \forall l \in \mathcal{J} \setminus \{j, k\}.$$

Then

$$\lim_{\max_{l \in \mathcal{J}\setminus\{j,k\}}\{\vartheta_l\} \to -\infty} \tilde{\Delta}_j^{\mathrm{LIV}}(x, \vartheta_{\mathcal{J}})$$
$$= E\big(\Delta_{j,k} \mid X = x, \vartheta_{j,k}(Z) = \vartheta_{j,k}, R_j(Z) = R_k(Z)\big)$$

for any

$$x \in \lim_{t \to -\infty} \operatorname{Supp}\Big(X \mid \vartheta_j(Z_j) = \vartheta_j, \vartheta_k(Z_k) = \vartheta_k, \max_{l \in \mathcal{J}\setminus\{j,k\}}\big\{\vartheta_l(Z)\big\} \leqslant t\Big).$$

PROOF. By a trivial modification to the proof of Theorem 6, we have that

$$\tilde{\Delta}_j^{\mathrm{LIV}}(x, \vartheta_{\mathcal{J}}) = E\big(\Delta_{j,\mathcal{J}\setminus j} \mid X = x, \vartheta_{\mathcal{J}}(Z) = \vartheta_{\mathcal{J}}, R_j(Z) = R_{\mathcal{J}\setminus j}(Z)\big).$$

The remainder of the proof follows from an immediate extension of the 3-option case just analyzed. □

Thus, for x values in the appropriate limit support, we can approximate $E(\Delta_{j,k} \mid X = x, \vartheta_{\{j,k\}}(Z) = \vartheta_{\{j,k\}}, R_j(z) = R_k(z))$ arbitrarily well by $\Delta_j^{\text{LIV}}(x, \vartheta_{\mathcal{J}})$ for an arbitrarily small $\max_{l \in \mathcal{J} \setminus \{j,k\}} \{\vartheta_l\}$.

This analysis uses the ϑ index functions directly, but the results can be restated without using the ϑ functions directly. Again consider the three-choice example. The central aspect of the identification strategy is to "zero-out" the second choice by making ϑ_2 arbitrarily small, allowing one to then use the LIV estimand to identify the MTE parameter for the first option versus the third as if the second choice were not an option. If we do not know the ϑ_2 function, we cannot condition on it. However, if we know that ϑ_2 is decreasing in a particular element of Z, say $Z^{[j']}$, where $Z^{[j']}$ does not enter the index function for choices 1 and 3 and where $\vartheta_2(z_2) \to 0$ as $z^{[j']} \to -\infty$, then we can follow the same strategy as if we knew the ϑ_2 index except we condition on $Z^{[j']}$ being small instead of conditioning on ϑ_2 being small. The idea naturally extends to the case of more than three options.

We can follow Heckman and Vytlacil (1999) in following a two-step identification strategy for ATE and TT parameters of $\Delta_{j,k}$. We first identify the appropriate MTE or LATE parameters and then use them to identify ATE and TT given the appropriate support conditions. Notice that the required support conditions are now stronger than those required for the ATE and TT parameters of $\Delta_{j,\mathcal{J}\setminus j}$. For identification of the ATE and TT parameters of $\Delta_{j,\mathcal{J}\setminus j}$, we require a large support assumption only on the jth index. In particular, we require that it be possible to condition on Z values that make ϑ_j arbitrarily small or arbitrarily large while holding the remaining indices fixed. In contrast, for identification of the ATE and TT parameters of $\Delta_{j,k}$, we require a large support assumption on each index. We require that for each index we can condition on Z values that make the index arbitrarily small or arbitrarily large while holding the remaining indices fixed. The reason for this stronger condition is that for identification of $\Delta_{j,k}$ we need to use an identification at infinity strategy on all but the j and k indices to even obtain the marginal parameters. We then need an additional identification at infinity step to use the marginal parameters to recover the ATE and TT parameters.

7.3.7. *Summarizing the results for the unordered model*

We have obtained the following results on the unordered choice model in this section:

- $E(\Delta_{j,\mathcal{J}\setminus j} \mid X = x, Z = z, R_j(z) = R_{\mathcal{J}\setminus j}(z))$ and $E(\Delta_{j,\mathcal{J}\setminus j} \mid X = x, Z = z, R_j(\tilde{z}) \geqslant R_{\mathcal{J}\setminus j}(\tilde{z}) \geqslant R_j(z))$ can be identified without a limit argument.
- $E(\Delta_{j,k} \mid X = x, \{\vartheta_k\}_{k\in\mathcal{J}}, R_j(z) = R_k(z))$ and $E(\Delta_{j,k} \mid X = x, \{\vartheta_k\}_{k\in\mathcal{J}}, R_j(\tilde{z}) \geqslant R_k(\tilde{z}) \geqslant R_j(z))$ can be identified with a limit argument on each index in $\mathcal{J} \setminus \{j,k\}$.
- $\Delta_{j,\mathcal{J}\setminus j}^{\text{ATE}}(x,z)$ and $\Delta_{j,\mathcal{J}\setminus j}^{\text{TT}}(x,z)$ can be identified with a limit argument using the ϑ_j index.
- $\Delta_{j,k}^{\text{ATE}}(x,z)$ and $\Delta_{j,k}^{\text{TT}}(x,z)$ can be identified with a limit argument using each index.

These results establish the central role of choice theory (via $\{\vartheta_k\}_{k\in\mathcal{J}}$) and identification at infinity in using an IV strategy to identify a variety of treatment parameters and their extensions to a general multiple choice model. Our analysis extends the analysis of ordered outcome models developed in the preceding section to a general unordered case. Local instrumental variables identify the marginal treatment effect corresponding to the effect of one option versus the best alternative option without requiring large support assumptions or knowledge of the parameters of the choice model. This result preserves the spirit of the Imbens and Angrist (1994) LATE analysis and the analysis of Heckman and Vytlacil (1999, 2001b, 2005). More generally, LIV can provide identification of the marginal treatment effect corresponding to the effect of choosing between one choice set versus not having that choice set available. However, identification of the more general parameters requires knowledge (identification) of the structural, latent index functions of the multinomial choice model. LIV can also provide identification of the effect of one specified choice versus another, requiring large support assumptions but not knowledge of the latent index functions. In order to identify some treatment parameters, we require identification of the latent index functions generating the multinomial choice model or else having large support assumptions. This connects the LIV analysis in this paper to the more ambitious but demanding identification conditions for the full multinomial selection model developed in Heckman and Navarro (2007), Chapter 73 (Matzkin) of this Handbook, and Appendix B of Chapter 70. We next develop the case of the continuum of outcomes.

7.4. Continuous treatment

Thus far we have considered the case of a treatment variable taking a finite number of values. Now consider the case where the treatment variable D can take a continuum of values. Suppose that

$$Y = \mu(D, X, U),$$
$$D = \vartheta(Z, V),$$

with D a continuous random variable. We do not in general need to restrict U or V to be scalar random variables. We can rewrite this model in potential outcome notation by defining

$$Y_d \equiv \mu_d(X, U) \equiv \mu(d, X, U).$$

For ease of exposition, we will assume that X is exogenous in addition to Z being exogenous, so that $(X, Z) \perp\!\!\!\perp (U, V)$.

We assume that $\mu(d, x, u)$ is continuous in its first argument. Equivalently, we assume that $\{Y_d\}$ is continuous in d for any realization. Implicit in the continuity assumption is an ordering, that two treatments that are close to one another have associated outcomes that are close to one another. The restriction is qualitatively different from any restriction we have considered thus far. In the previous sections, there are no restrictions connecting Y_d to $Y_{d'}$. Equivalently, there are no restrictions connecting $\mu_d(X, U)$ and $\mu_{d'}(X, U)$. In the case of a continuum of treatments, we now tightly link counterfactual values that correspond to treatments that are close to one another.

The literature analyzing continuous endogenous regressors often defines the object of interest not as a treatment effect but instead as the "average structural function" (ASF). Following Blundell and Powell (2004), the ASF is defined as

$$\mu(d, x) = E(Y_d \mid X = x) = \int \mu(d, x, u)\, dF_U(u).$$

In other words, the ASF is defined as the average value of Y that would result from assigning treatment d to all individuals with $X = x$. If D is endogenous, the ASF does not in general equal the conditional expected value of Y in the data, $E(Y_d \mid X = x) \neq E(Y \mid D = d, X = x)$, since $\int \mu(d, x, u)\, dF_U(u) \neq \int \mu(d, x, u)\, dF_{U|X,D}(u \mid x, d)$. This is just a version of the distinction between fixing and conditioning introduced in Haavelmo (1943) and discussed in Chapter 70.

Instead of working with the ASF, we can follow the lead of Florens et al. (2002) and define treatment effect parameters for a continuous treatment. Suppose that $\mu(d, x, u)$ is differentiable in d for any (x, u). We can define the average treatment effect as

$$\Delta_d^{\text{ATE}}(x) = E\left(\frac{\partial}{\partial d} Y_d \;\middle|\; X = x\right) = \int \frac{\partial}{\partial d} \mu(d, x, u)\, dF_U(u),$$

which is the average effect of a marginal increase in the treatment if individuals were randomly assigned treatment level d. Note that in this expression the average treatment effect depends on the base treatment level, d, and for any of the continuum of possible base treatment levels we have a different average treatment effect. The average treatment effect is the derivative of the Blundell and Powell ASF:

$$\Delta_d^{\text{ATE}}(x) = \frac{\partial}{\partial d} \mu(d, x).$$

Florens et al. (2002) define treatment on the treated as

$$\begin{aligned}
\Delta_d^{\text{TT}}(x) &= E\left(\frac{\partial}{\partial d_1} Y_{d_1} \;\middle|\; D = d_2, X = x\right)\Bigg|_{d=d_1=d_2} \\
&= \int \left[\frac{\partial}{\partial d_1} \mu(d_1, x, u)\bigg|_{d=d_1}\right] dF_{U|X,D}(u \mid x, d),
\end{aligned}$$

which is the average effect among those currently choosing treatment level d of an incremental increase in the treatment while leaving their unobservables fixed. Likewise, define the marginal treatment effect as

$$\Delta_d^{\text{MTE}}(x, v) = E\left(\frac{\partial}{\partial d} Y_d \;\middle|\; V = v, X = x\right) = \int \frac{\partial}{\partial d} \mu(d, x, u)\, dF_{U|V}(u \mid v).$$

To illustrate these definitions, suppose D is schooling level measured as a continuous variable, and suppose Y is wages. Then, e.g., Y_{12} would be the potential wage corresponding to receiving exactly 12 years of schooling and $\mu_{12} = E(Y_{12})$ is the average wage if individuals were exogenously assigned exactly 12 years of schooling. Δ_{12}^{ATE} is the average effect on wages of being assigned marginally more than 12 years of schooling versus being assigned exactly 12 years of schooling, and Δ_{12}^{TT} would be the average effect of obtaining marginally more schooling for those who self-select to obtain exactly 12 years of schooling.

One approach to identification of the treatment parameters is to impose more structure on the outcome equation while allowing the treatment selection equation to be unspecified. The nonparametric instrumental variable approach of Darolles, Florens and Renault (2002), Hall and Horowitz (2005), and Newey and Powell (2003) requires that the unobservables in the outcome equation (U) be a scalar random variable and that the outcome be an additive function of the unobservables – Chapter 73 (Matzkin) of this Handbook surveys this literature. Their additivity assumption imposes the restriction of no treatment effect heterogeneity (conditional on X), so that all treatment effect parameters coincide. In exchange for this restriction on the outcome equation, they do not require any structure on the first stage equation so that D does not need to be increasing in V and V is not required to be a scalar random variable. Furthermore, they only require that U be mean independent of (X, Z), not that (U, V) be fully independent of (X, Z).

The additive error term assumption is relaxed by Chernozhukov, Imbens, and Newey (2007), who impose the stronger requirement that the outcome is a strictly increasing function of the error term (i.e., $\mu(x, d, u)$ strictly increasing in u),[123] while strengthening the required independence property to be $(Z, X) \perp\!\!\!\perp U$. The restriction of a scalar error term with the outcome strictly increasing in this error term is again a strong restriction on the forms of treatment effect heterogeneity that are possible in the model.[124] Suppress X for ease of exposition. Under their restriction, if $\mu(d, u) > \mu(d, u')$ at some treatment level d, then $\mu(\tilde{d}, u) > \mu(\tilde{d}, u')$ for all treatment levels $\tilde{d}$. In other words, if individual one has a higher potential outcome at some value of the treatment than a second individual, than that first individual has a higher potential outcome for any value of the treatment than the second individual. Under this restriction, treatment cannot change the rank ordering of outcomes across individuals. These restrictions are in contrast with the Roy model and generalized Roy model, where one individual may have a higher with-treatment potential outcome but a lower without-treatment potential outcome compared to a second individual.

123 More generally, that μ is a weakly separable function of U, so that μ can be rewritten as a function of a scalar aggregator of U.

124 See also Chernozhukov and Hansen (2005), who allow for richer treatment effect heterogeneity but impose a "rank similarity" restriction that requires agents not to act upon their own individual effects. This can be shown to eliminate the general form of heterogeneous responses analyzed by the generalized Roy model. For a discussion of the analysis of Chernozhukov and Hansen (2005), see Chapter 73 (Matzkin) of this Handbook.

In contrast to these approaches, control variate approaches impose more structure on the selection equation, imposing that the unobservables in the treatment selection equation (V) be a scalar random variable,[125] and that the treatment is an additive function of the unobservables or more generally a strictly increasing function of the unobservables. Such approaches thus impose strong restrictions on the heterogeneity in the treatment selection equation. In exchange for these restrictions, such approaches do not require Y to be increasing in U and do not require U to be a scalar random variable. Imbens and Newey (2002) consider identification and estimation of the average structural function in a nonparametric model using the control variate approach, building on the work of Blundell and Powell (2004) and Altonji and Matzkin (2005). Their approach does not impose any further restrictions on the outcome equation, but does require a large support assumption. Another recent contribution to the control function literature is Florens et al. (2006), who restrict Y to be determined by a stochastic polynomial in D but do not require a large support assumption. We now further discuss both approaches.

Imbens and Newey (2002) proceed as follows. They assume that $\vartheta(z, v)$ is strictly monotonic in v. Suppose that $(U, V) \perp\!\!\!\perp (X, Z)$, and without loss of generality normalize V to be unit uniform. Then V is immediately identified (up to the normalization) from $V = F(Y \mid X, Z)$. Given identification of V, they can identify $E(Y \mid D, X, V)$. Their independence assumptions imply that $U \perp\!\!\!\perp D \mid (X, V)$, so that

$$E(Y \mid D = d, X = x, V = v) = E(Y_d \mid X = x, V = v).$$

$E(Y_d \mid X = x, V = v)$ corresponds to the marginal treatment effect except that it is the conditional expectation in level instead of the derivative of the conditional expectation. Then, in parallel to the way Heckman and Vytlacil (1999) integrate up the MTE to recover the ATE, Imbens and Newey integrate up $E(Y_d \mid X = x, V = v)$ to obtain the ASF:

$$\begin{aligned} E(Y_d \mid X = x) &= \int E(Y_d \mid X = x, V = v)\, dF_V(v) \\ &= \int E(Y \mid D = d, X = x, V = v)\, dF_V(v). \end{aligned}$$

Imbens and Newey do not explicitly consider the ATE, TT, or MTE, but we can adapt the Heckman and Vytlacil (1999) weighting analysis summarized in Section 3 to obtain these parameters as a slight modification of the Imbens and Newey analysis. First consider the MTE. We have that

$$\frac{\partial}{\partial d} E(Y \mid D = d, X = x, V = v) = E\left(\frac{\partial}{\partial d} Y_d \,\middle|\, X = x, V = v\right),$$

[125] More generally, that ϑ is a weakly separable function of V, so that ϑ can be rewritten as a function of a scalar aggregator of V.

so that the MTE is identified. Integrating up the MTE we obtain ATE

$$\begin{aligned} E\left(\frac{\partial}{\partial d} Y_d \mid X = x\right) &= \int E\left(\frac{\partial}{\partial d} Y_d \mid X = x, V = v\right) dF_V(v) \\ &= \int \frac{\partial}{\partial d} E(Y \mid D = d, X = x, V = v)\, dF_V(v) \end{aligned}$$

and TT

$$\begin{aligned} &E\left(\frac{\partial}{\partial d_1} Y_{d_1} \mid D = d_2, X = x\right)\Big|_{d=d_1=d_2} \\ &\quad = \int E\left(\frac{\partial}{\partial d} Y_d \mid X = x, V = v\right) dF_{V \mid D=d_2, X}(v \mid x) \\ &\quad = \int \frac{\partial}{\partial d} E(Y \mid D = d, X = x, V = v)\, dF_{V \mid D=d_2, X}(v \mid x). \end{aligned}$$

Note the strong connection between the control variate approach and the LIV/MTE approach of Heckman and Vytlacil (1999). They both proceed by identifying an expectation conditional on the first stage error term, and then integrating that expectation up to obtain the parameter of interest. The primary distinction is that, in the control variate approach with a continuous endogenous treatment, it is possible to assume that the treatment is a strictly increasing function of an error term that is independent of the instruments, to identify this error term, and then to explicitly include the identified first-stage error term as a regressor in the second stage regression for the outcome. In contrast, with a discrete endogenous treatment, it is not possible to characterize the treatment as a strictly increasing function of an error term that is independent of the instruments. It is thus not possible to identify the first-stage error term, and thus not possible to explicitly include an identified first-stage error term in the second stage. The LIV strategy is the approach in the discrete case that by-passes the need to explicitly identify the first stage error term.

In order to be able to integrate $E(Y \mid D = d, X = x, V = v) = E(Y_d \mid X = x, V = v)$ up to obtain the ASF (or to integrate MTE to obtain ATE), it is necessary to evaluate $E(Y \mid D = d, X = x, V = v)$ at all values of v in the support of the distribution of V conditional on X. This is a nontrivial requirement. To show this, suppress X for ease of exposition. One can only evaluate $E(Y \mid D = d, V = v)$ at values of v in the support of the distribution of V conditional on $D = d$, so that the requirement is that the support of the distribution of V conditional on $D = d$ equal the support of the unconditional distribution. This requires, in turn, a large support assumption on an element of Z. For example, suppose that $\vartheta(Z, V) = P(Z) + V$, so that $D = P(Z) + V$. Let $\mathcal{P}$ denote the support of the distribution of $P(Z)$. Then

$$\begin{aligned} \operatorname{Supp}(V \mid D = d) &= \operatorname{Supp}\big(V \mid P(Z) + V = d\big) \\ &= \operatorname{Supp}\big(V \mid V = d - P(Z)\big) = \{d - p \colon p \in \mathcal{P}\}, \end{aligned}$$

where the last equality uses $Z \perp\!\!\!\perp V$. For example, if $\mathcal{P} = [a, b]$, then $\{d - p\colon p \in [a, b]\} = [d - b, d - a]$ which does not depend on d if and only if $a = -\infty$ and $b = \infty$, i.e., if and only if $\mathcal{P} = \mathbb{R}$. For standard models, this requirement in turn necessitates a regressor with unbounded support, analogous to the identification at infinity requirement in selection models shown by Heckman (1990). We have noted the central role played by identification at infinity assumptions in many different settings throughout this Handbook.

Next consider the analysis of Florens et al. (2002). They assume that $(U, V) \perp\!\!\!\perp (X, Z)$. They impose additional structure on the outcome equation, in particular that the outcome equation can be expressed by a finite order stochastic polynomial in the treatment variable:

$$Y = \mu(D, X) + \sum_{j=0}^{K} D^j U_j$$

so that

$$Y_d = \mu_d(X) + \sum_{j=0}^{K} d^j U_j.$$

This specification can be seen as a nonparametric extension of the random coefficient models of Heckman and Vytlacil (1998) and Wooldridge (1997, 2003). As a consequence of the structure on the outcome equation, Florens et al. (2006) are able to identify the ATE without requiring the large support assumption of Imbens and Newey (2002). Instead of a large support assumption, they require measurable separability of D and V conditional on X.

Measurable separability is the requirement that any function of D and X that almost surely equals a function of V and X must be a function of X only. This assumption can be shown to be equivalent to requiring that D not lie in a subset of its support if and only if V lies in a subset of its support (conditional on X). As shown by Florens et al. (2006), measurable separability between D and V follows from the independence assumption $(U, V) \perp\!\!\!\perp (X, Z)$ along with mild regularity conditions. Thus the Florens, Heckman, Meghir, and Vytlacil approach allows for identification of the average treatment effect with continuous endogenous regressors without requiring large support assumptions in exchange for requiring a finite-order, stochastic polynomial assumption on the outcome equation. We next consider the method of matching, which is based on the assumption of conditional independence that is assumed to characterize data structures.

8. Matching

The method of matching assumes selection of treatment based on potential outcomes

$$(Y_0, Y_1) \not\perp\!\!\!\perp D,$$

so $\Pr(D = 1 \mid Y_0, Y_1)$ depends on Y_0, Y_1. It assumes access to variables Q such that conditioning on Q removes the dependence:

(Q-1) $(Y_0, Y_1) \perp\!\!\!\perp D \mid Q$.

Thus,

$$\Pr(D = 1 \mid Q, Y_0, Y_1) = \Pr(D = 1 \mid Q).$$

Comparisons between treated and untreated can be made at all points in the support of Q such that

(Q-2) $0 < \Pr(D = 1 \mid Q) < 1$.

The method does not explicitly model choices of treatment or the subjective evaluations of participants, nor is there any distinction between the variables in the outcome equations (X) and the variables in the choice equations (Z) that is central to the IV method and the method of control functions. In principle, condition (Q-1) can be satisfied using a set of variables Q distinct from all or some of the components of X and Z. The conditioning variables do not have to be exogenous.

From condition (Q-1), we recover the distributions of Y_0 and Y_1 given Q, $\Pr(Y_0 \leqslant y_0 \mid Q = q) = F_0(y_0 \mid Q = q)$ and $\Pr(Y_1 \leqslant y_1 \mid Q = q) = F_1(y_1 \mid Q = q)$ – but not the joint distribution $F(y_0, y_1 \mid Q = q)$, because we do not observe the same persons in the treated and untreated states. This is a standard evaluation problem common to all econometric estimators. Methods for determining which variables belong in Q rely on untested exogeneity assumptions which we discuss in this section.

OLS is a special case of matching that focuses on the identification of certain conditional means. In OLS, linear functional forms are maintained as exact representations or valid approximations. Considering a common coefficient model, OLS writes

(Q-3) $Y = Q\alpha + D\beta + U$,

where α is the treatment effect and

(Q-4) $E(U \mid Q, D) = 0$.

The assumption is made that the variance–covariance matrix of (Q, D) is of full rank:

(Q-5) $\mathrm{Var}(Q, D)$ *full rank*.

Under these conditions, we can identify β even though D and U are dependent: $D \not\perp\!\!\!\perp U$. Controlling for the observable Q eliminates any spurious mean dependence between D and U: $E(U \mid D) \neq 0$ but $E(U \mid D, Q) = 0$. (Q-4) is the linear regression counterpart to (Q-1). (Q-5) is the linear regression counterpart to (Q-2). Failure of (Q-5) would mean that using a nonparametric estimator, we might perfectly predict D given Q, and that $\Pr(D = 1 \mid Q = q) = 1$ or 0.[126]

[126] This condition might be met only at certain values of $Q = q$. For certain parameterizations (e.g., the linear probability model), we may obtain predicted probabilities outside the unit interval.

(Q-5)′ If the goal of the analysis is only to identify β, in place of (Q-4) we can get by with

$$(\text{Q-4})': E(U \mid Q, D) = E(U \mid Q).$$

Assuming $\text{Var}(D \mid Q) > 0$, we can identify β even if we cannot separate αQ from $E(U \mid Q)$.

Matching can be implemented as a nonparametric method. When this is done, the procedure does not require specification of the functional form of the outcome equations. It enforces the requirement that (Q-2) be satisfied by estimating functions pointwise in the support of Q. To link our notation in this section to that in the rest of the chapter, we assume that $Q = (X, Z)$ and that X and Z are the same except where otherwise noted. Thus we invoke assumptions (M-1) and (M-2) presented in Section 2, even though in principle we can use a more general conditioning set.

Assumptions (M-1) and (M-2) introduced in Section 2 or (Q-1) and (Q-2) rule out the possibility that after conditioning on X (or Q), agents possess more information about their choices than econometricians, and that the unobserved information helps to predict the potential outcomes. Put another way, the method allows for potential outcomes to affect choices but only through the observed variables, Q, that predict outcomes. This is the reason why Heckman and Robb (1985a, 1986b) call the method selection on observables.

This section establishes the following points. (1) Matching assumptions (M-1) and (M-2) generically imply a flat MTE in u_D, i.e., they assume that $E(Y_1 - Y_0 \mid X = x, U_D = u_D)$ does not depend on u_D. Thus the unobservables central to the Roy model and its extensions and the unobservables central to the modern IV literature are assumed to be absent once the analyst conditions on X. (M-1) implies that all mean treatment parameters are the same. (2) Even if we weaken (M-1) and (M-2) to mean independence instead of full independence, generically the MTE is flat in u_D under the assumptions of the nonparametric generalized Roy model developed in Section 3, so again all mean treatment parameters are the same. (3) We show that IV and matching make distinct identifying assumptions even though they both invoke conditional independence assumptions. (4) We compare matching with IV and control function (sample selection) methods. Matching assumes that conditioning on observables eliminates the dependence between (Y_0, Y_1) and D. The control function principle models the dependence. (5) We present some examples that demonstrate that if the assumptions of the method of matching are violated, the method can produce substantially biased estimators of the parameters of interest. (6) We show that standard methods for selecting the conditioning variables used in matching assume exogeneity. This is a property shared with many econometric estimators, as noted in Chapter 70, Section 5.2. Violations of the exogeneity assumption can produce biased estimators.

Nonparametric versions of matching embodying (M-2) avoid the problem of making inferences outside the support of the data. This problem is implicit in any application of least squares. Figure 22 shows the support problem that can arise in linear least squares

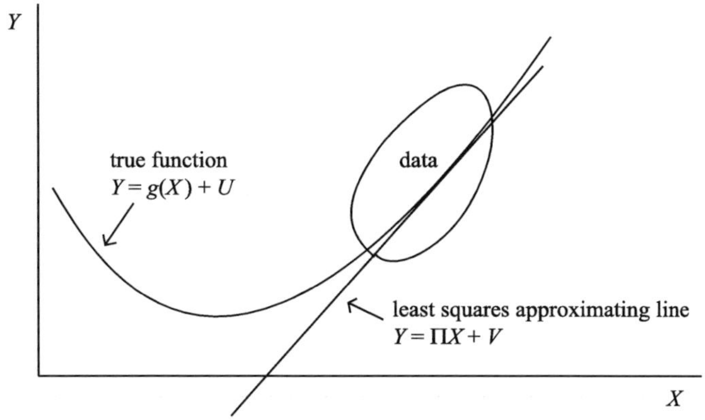

Figure 22. The least squares extrapolation problem avoided by using nonparametric regression or matching.

when the linearity of the regression is used to extrapolate estimates determined in one empirical support to new supports. Careful attention to support problems is a virtue of any nonparametric method, including, but not unique to, nonparametric matching. Heckman et al. (1998) show that the bias from neglecting the problem of limited support can be substantial. See also the discussion in Heckman, LaLonde and Smith (1999).

We now show that matching implies that conditional on X, the marginal return is assumed to be the same as the average return (marginal = average). This is a strong behavioral assumption implicit in statistical conditional independence assumption (M-1). It says that the marginal participant has the same return as the average participant.

8.1. Matching assumption (M-1) implies a flat MTE

An immediate consequence of (M-1) is that the MTE does not depend on U_D. This is so because $(Y_0, Y_1) \perp\!\!\!\perp D \mid X$ implies that $(Y_0, Y_1) \perp\!\!\!\perp U_D \mid X$ and hence that

$$\Delta^{\text{MTE}}(x, u_D) = E(Y_1 - Y_0 \mid X = x, U_D = u_D) = E(Y_1 - Y_0 \mid X = x). \quad (8.1)$$

This, in turn, implies that Δ^{MTE} conditional on X is flat in u_D, so that matching invokes assumption (C-1) invoked in Section 4.2.1. Under our assumptions for the generalized Roy model, it assumes that $E(Y \mid P(Z) = p)$ is linear in p. Thus the method of matching assumes that mean marginal returns and average returns are the same and all mean treatment effects are the same given X. However, one can still distinguish marginal from average effects of the observables (X) using matching. See Carneiro (2002).

It is sometimes said that the matching assumptions are "for free" [see, e.g., Gill and Robins (2001)] because one can always replace unobserved $F_1(Y_1 \mid X = x, D = 0)$ with observed $F_1(Y_1 \mid X = x, D = 1)$ and unobserved $F_0(Y_0 \mid X = x, D = 1)$ with observed $F_0(Y_0 \mid X = x, D = 0)$. Such substitutions do not contradict any observed data.

While the claim is true, it ignores the counterfactual states generated under the matching assumptions. The assumed absence of selection on unobservables is not a "for free" assumption, and produces fundamentally different counterfactual states for the same model under matching and selection assumptions. To explore these issues in depth, consider a nonparametric regression model more general than the linear regression model (Q-3).

Without assumption (M-1), a nonparametric regression of Y on D conditional on X identifies a nonparametric mean difference

$$\begin{aligned}\Delta^{\mathrm{OLS}}(X) &= E(Y_1 \mid X, D = 1) - E(Y_0 \mid X, D = 0)\\ &= E(Y_1 - Y_0 \mid X, D = 1)\\ &\quad + \big\{E(Y_0 \mid X, D = 1) - E(Y_0 \mid X, D = 0)\big\}. \end{aligned} \tag{8.2}$$

The term in braces in the second expression arises from selection on pre-treatment levels of the outcome. OLS identifies the parameter treatment on the treated (the first term in the second line of (8.2)) plus a bias term in braces corresponding to selection on the levels.

The OLS estimator can be represented as a weighted average of Δ^{MTE}. The weight is given in Table 2B where U_1 and U_0 for the OLS model are defined as deviations from conditional expectations, $U_1 = Y_1 - E(Y_1 \mid X)$, $U_0 = Y_0 - E(Y_0 \mid X)$. Unlike the weights for Δ^{TT} and Δ^{ATE}, the OLS weights do not necessarily integrate to one and they are not necessarily nonnegative. Application of IV eliminates the contribution of the second term of Equation (8.2). The weights for the first term are the same as the weights for Δ^{TT} and hence they integrate to one.

The OLS weights for our generalized Roy model example are plotted in Figure 2B. The negative component of the OLS weight leads to a smaller OLS treatment estimate compared to the other treatment effects in Table 3. This table shows the estimated OLS treatment effect for the generalized Roy example. The large negative selection bias in this example is consistent with comparative advantage as emphasized by Roy (1951) and detected empirically by Willis and Rosen (1979) and Cunha, Heckman and Navarro (2005). People who are good in sector 1 (i.e., receive treatment) may be very poor in sector 0 (those who receive no treatment). Hence the bias in OLS for the parameter treatment on the treated may be negative ($E(Y_0 \mid X, D = 1) - E(Y_0 \mid X, D = 0) < 0$). The differences among the policy relevant treatment effects, the conventional treatment effects and the OLS estimand are illustrated in Figure 4A and Table 3 for the generalized Roy model example. As is evident from Table 3, it is not at all clear that the instrumental variable estimator, with instruments that satisfy classical properties, performs better than nonparametric OLS in identifying the policy relevant treatment effect in this example. While IV eliminates the term in braces in (8.2), it reweights the MTE differently from what might be desired for many policy analyses.

If there is no selection on unobserved variables conditional on covariates, $U_D \perp\!\!\!\perp (Y_0, Y_1) \mid X$, then $E(U_1 \mid X, U_D) = E(U_1 \mid X) = 0$ and $E(U_0 \mid X, U_D) = E(U_0 \mid X) = 0$ so that the OLS weights are unity and OLS identifies both ATE and the parameter treatment on the treated (TT), which are the same under this assumption. This condition is an implication of matching condition (M-1). Given the assumed conditional independence in terms of X, we can identify ATE and TT without use of any instrument Z satisfying assumptions (A-1)–(A.2). If there is such a Z, the conditional independence condition implies under (A-1)–(A-5) that $E(Y \mid X, P(Z) = p)$ is linear in p. The conditional independence assumption invoked in the method of matching has come into widespread use for much the same reason that OLS has come into widespread use. It is easy to implement with modern software and makes little demands of the data because it assumes the existence of X variables that satisfy the conditional independence assumptions. The crucial conditional independence assumption is not testable. As we note below, additional assumptions on the X are required to test the validity of the matching assumptions.

If the sole interest is to identify treatment on the treated, Δ^{TT}, it is apparent from representation (8.2) that we can weaken (M-1) to

(M-1)′ $Y_0 \perp\!\!\!\perp D \mid X$.

This is possible because $E(Y_1 \mid X, D = 1)$ is known from data on outcomes of the treated and only need to construct $E(Y_0 \mid X, D = 1)$. In this case, MTE is not restricted to be flat in u_D and all treatment parameters are not the same. A straightforward implication of (M-1)′ in the Roy model, where selection is made solely on the gain, is that persons must sort into treatment status positively in terms of levels of Y_1. We now consider more generally the implications of assuming mean independence of the errors rather than full independence.

8.2. *Matching and MTE using mean independence conditions*

To identify all mean treatment parameters, one can weaken the assumption (M-1) to the condition that Y_0 and Y_1 are mean independent of D conditional on X. However, (Y_0, Y_1) will be mean independent of D conditional on X without U_D being independent of Y_0, Y_1 conditional on X only if fortuitous balancing occurs, with regions of positive dependence of (Y_0, Y_1) on U_D and regions of negative dependence of (Y_0, Y_1) on U_D just exactly offsetting each other. Such a balancing is not generic in the Roy model and in the generalized Roy model.

In particular, assume that $Y_j = \mu_j(X) + U_j$ for $j = 0, 1$ and further assume that $D = \mathbf{1}[Y_1 - Y_0 \geqslant C(Z) + U_C]$. Let $V = U_C - (U_1 - U_0)$. Assume $(U_0, U_1, V) \perp\!\!\!\perp (X, Z)$. Then if $V \perp\!\!\!\perp (U_1 - U_0)$, and U_C has a log concave density, then $E(Y_1 - Y_0 \mid X, V = v)$ is decreasing in v, $\Delta^{\mathrm{TT}}(x) > \Delta^{\mathrm{ATE}}(x)$, and the matching conditions do not hold. If $V \perp\!\!\!\perp (U_1 - U_0)$ but V does not have a log concave density, then it is still the case that $(U_1 - U_0, V)$ is negative quadrant dependent. One can show that $(U_1 - U_0, V)$ being negative quadrant dependent implies that $\Delta^{\mathrm{TT}}(x) > \Delta^{\mathrm{ATE}}(x)$, and thus again that the matching conditions cannot hold. We now develop a more general analysis.

Suppose that we assume selection model (3.3) so that $D = \mathbf{1}[P(Z) \geqslant U_D]$, where Z is independent of (Y_0, Y_1) conditional on X, where $U_D = F_{V|X}(V)$ and

$P(Z) = F_{V|X}(\mu_D(Z))$. Consider the weaker mean independence assumptions in place of assumption (M-1):

(M-3) $E(Y_1 \mid X, D) = E(Y_1 \mid X), E(Y_0 \mid X, D) = E(Y_0 \mid X)$.

This assumption is all that is needed to identify the mean treatment parameters because under it

$$E(Y \mid X = x, Z = z, D = 1) = E(Y_1 \mid X = x, Z = z, D = 1) = E(Y_1 \mid X = x)$$

and

$$E(Y \mid X = x, Z = z, D = 0) = E(Y_0 \mid X = x, Z = z, D = 0) = E(Y_0 \mid X = x).$$

Thus we can identify all the mean treatment parameters over the support that satisfies (M-2).

Recalling that $\Delta = Y_1 - Y_0$, (M-3) implies in terms of U_D that

$$\begin{aligned} &E\big(\Delta \bigm| X = x, Z = z, U_D \leqslant P(z)\big) = E(\Delta \mid X = x) \\ &\iff \quad E\big(\Delta^{\mathrm{MTE}}(X, U_D) \bigm| X = x, U_D \leqslant P(z)\big) = E(\Delta \mid X = x), \end{aligned}$$

and hence

$$\begin{aligned} &E\big(\Delta^{\mathrm{MTE}}(X, U_D) \bigm| X = x, U_D \leqslant P(z)\big) \\ &\quad = E\big(\Delta^{\mathrm{MTE}}(X, U_D) \bigm| X = x, U_D > P(z)\big). \end{aligned}$$

If the support of $P(Z)$ is the full unit interval conditional on $X = x$, then $\Delta^{\mathrm{MTE}}(X, U_D) = E(\Delta \mid X = x)$ for all U_D. If the support of $P(Z)$ is a proper subset of the full unit interval, then generically (M-3) will hold only if $\Delta^{\mathrm{MTE}}(X, U_D) = E(\Delta \mid X = x)$ for all U_D, though positive and negative parts could balance out for any particular value of X.

To see this, note that

$$\begin{aligned} &E_Z\big(E\big(\Delta^{\mathrm{MTE}}(X, U_D) \bigm| X = x, U_D \leqslant P(z)\big) \bigm| X = x, D = 1\big) \\ &\quad = E_Z\big(E\big(\Delta^{\mathrm{MTE}}(X, U_D) \bigm| X = x, U_D > P(z)\big) \bigm| X = x, D = 0\big). \end{aligned}$$

Working with $V = F_{V|X}^{-1}(U_D)$, suppose that $D = \mathbf{1}[\mu_D(Z, V) \geqslant 0]$. Let $\Omega(z) = \{v\colon \mu_D(z, v) \geqslant 0\}$. Then (M-3) implies that

$$E\big(\Delta^{\mathrm{MTE}}(X, V) \bigm| X = x, V \in \Omega(z)\big) = E\big(\Delta^{\mathrm{MTE}}(X, V) \bigm| X = x, V \in \big(\Omega(z)\big)^c\big)$$

so we expect that generically under assumption (M-3) we obtain a flat MTE in terms of $V = F_{V|X}^{-1}(U_D)$. We conduct a parallel analysis for the nonseparable choice model in Appendix K and obtain similar conditions. Matching assumes a flat MTE, i.e., that marginal returns conditional on X and V do not depend on V (alternatively, that marginal returns do not depend on U_D given X).

We already noted in Section 2 that IV and matching invoke very different assumptions. Matching requires no exclusion restrictions whereas IV is based on the existence of exclusion restrictions. Superficially, we can bridge these literatures by invoking matching with an exclusion condition: $(Y_0, Y_1) \not\perp\!\!\!\perp D \mid X$ but $(Y_0, Y_1) \perp\!\!\!\perp D \mid X, Z$. This looks like an IV condition, but it is not.

We explore the relationship between matching with exclusion and IV in Appendix L, and demonstrate a fundamental contradiction between the two identifying conditions. For an additively separable representation of the outcome equations $U_1 = Y_1 - E(Y_1 \mid X)$ and $U_0 = Y_0 - E(Y_0 \mid X)$, we establish that if (U_0, U_1) is mean independent of D conditional on (X, Z), as required by IV, but (U_0, U_1) is not mean independent of D conditional on X alone, then U_0 is dependent on Z conditional on X, contrary to all assumptions used to justify instrumental variables. We next consider how to implement matching.

8.3. Implementing the method of matching

We draw on Heckman et al. (1998) and Heckman, LaLonde and Smith (1999) to describe the mechanics of matching. Todd (2007, 2008) presents a comprehensive treatment of the main issues and a guide to software.

To operationalize the method of matching, we assume two samples: "t" for treatment and "c" for comparison group. Treatment group members have $D = 1$ and control group members have $D = 0$. Unless otherwise noted, we assume that observations are statistically independent within and across groups. Simple matching methods are based on the following idea. For each person i in the treatment group, we find some group of "comparable" persons. The same individual may be in both treated and control groups if that person is treated at one time and untreated at another. We denote outcomes for person i in the treatment group by Y_i^t and we match these outcomes to the outcomes of a subsample of persons in the comparison group to estimate a treatment effect. In principle, we can use a different subsample as a comparison group for each person.

In practice, we can construct matches on the basis of a neighborhood $\xi(X_i)$, where X_i is a vector of characteristics for person i. Neighbors to treated person i are persons in the comparison sample whose characteristics are in neighborhood $\xi(X_i)$. Suppose that there are N_c persons in the comparison sample and N_t in the treatment sample. Thus the persons in the comparison sample who are neighbors to i, are persons j for whom $X_j \in \xi(X_i)$, i.e., the set of persons $\mathcal{A}_i = \{j \mid X_j \in \xi(X_i)\}$. Let $W(i, j)$ be the weight placed on observation j in forming a comparison with observation i and further assume that the weights sum to one, $\sum_{j=1}^{N_c} W(i, j) = 1$, and that $0 \leqslant W(i, j) \leqslant 1$. Form a weighted comparison group mean for person i, given by

$$\bar{Y}_i^c = \sum_{j=1}^{N_c} W(i, j) Y_j^c. \tag{8.3}$$

The estimated treatment effect for person i is $Y_i - \bar{Y}_i^c$. This selects a set of comparison group members associated with i and the mean of their outcomes. Unlike IV or the control function approach, the method of matching identifies counterfactuals for each treated member.

Heckman, Ichimura and Todd (1997) and Heckman, LaLonde and Smith (1999) survey a variety of alternative matching schemes proposed in the literature. Todd (2007, 2008) provides a comprehensive survey. In this chapter, we briefly consider two widely-used methods. The nearest neighbor matching estimator defines $\mathcal{A}_i$ such that only one j is selected so that it is closest to X_i in some metric:

$$\mathcal{A}_i = \left\{ j \mid \min_{j \in \{1,\dots,N_c\}} \|X_i - X_j\| \right\},$$

where "$\| \ \|$" is a metric measuring distance in the X characteristics space. The Mahalanobis metric is one widely used metric for implementing the nearest neighbor matching estimator. This metric defines neighborhoods for i as

$$\| \ \| = (X_i - X_j)' \Sigma_c^{-1} (X_i - X_j),$$

where Σ_c is the covariance matrix in the comparison sample. The weighting scheme for the nearest neighbor matching estimator is

$$W(i, j) = \begin{cases} 1 & \text{if } j \in \mathcal{A}_i, \\ 0 & \text{otherwise.} \end{cases}$$

The nearest neighbor in the metric "$\| \cdot \|$" is used in the match. A version of nearest neighbor matching, called "caliper" matching [Cochran and Rubin (1973)], makes matches to person i only if

$$\|X_i - X_j\| < \varepsilon,$$

where ε is a pre-specified tolerance. Otherwise, person i is bypassed and no match is made to him or her.

Kernel matching uses the entire comparison sample, so that $\mathcal{A}_i = \{1, \dots, N_c\}$, and sets

$$W(i, j) = \frac{K(X_j - X_i)}{\sum_{j=1}^{N_c} K(X_j - X_i)},$$

where K is a kernel.[127] Kernel matching is a smooth method that reuses and weights the comparison group sample observations differently for each person i in the treatment group with a different X_i. Kernel matching can be defined pointwise at each sample point X_i or for broader intervals.

For example, the impact of treatment on the treated can be estimated by forming the mean difference across the i:

$$\hat{\Delta}^{\mathrm{TT}} = \frac{1}{N_t} \sum_{i=1}^{N_t} (Y_i^t - \bar{Y}_i^c) = \frac{1}{N_t} \sum_{i=1}^{N_t} \left(Y_i^t - \sum_{j=1}^{N_c} W(i, j) Y_j^c \right). \tag{8.4}$$

[127] See, e.g., Härdle (1990) or Ichimura and Todd (2007) (Chapter 74 of this Handbook) for a discussion of kernels and choices of bandwidths.

We can define this mean for various subsets of the treatment sample defined in various ways. More efficient estimators weight the observations accounting for the variance [Heckman, Ichimura and Todd (1997, 1998), Heckman (1998), Hirano, Imbens and Ridder (2003), Abadie and Imbens (2006)].[128]

Matching assumes that conditioning on X eliminates selection bias. The method requires no functional form assumptions for outcome equations. If, however, a functional form assumption is maintained, as in the econometric procedure proposed by Barnow, Cain and Goldberger (1980), it is possible to implement the matching assumption using standard regression analysis. Suppose, for example, that Y_0 is linearly related to observables X and an unobservable U_0, so that

$$E(Y_0 \mid X, D = 0) = X\alpha + E(U_0 \mid X, D = 0),$$

and

$$E(U_0 \mid X, D = 0) = E(U_0 \mid X)$$

is linear in X ($E(U \mid X) = \varphi X$). Under these assumptions, controlling for X via linear regression allows one to identify $E(Y_0 \mid X, D = 1)$ from the data on nonparticipants. Under assumption (Q-4)$'$, setting $X = Q$, this approach justifies OLS equation (Q-3) for identifying treatment effects.[129] Such functional form assumptions are not strictly required to implement the method of matching. Moreover, in practice, users of the method of Barnow, Cain and Goldberger (1980) do not impose the common support condition (M-2) for the distribution of X when generating estimates of the treatment effect. The distribution of X may be very different in the treatment group ($D = 1$) and comparison group ($D = 0$) samples, so that comparability is only achieved by imposing linearity in the parameters and extrapolating over different regions.

One advantage of the method of Barnow, Cain and Goldberger (1980) is that it uses data parsimoniously. If the X are high-dimensional, the number of observations in each cell when matching can get very small.

Another solution to this problem that reduces the dimension of the matching problem without imposing arbitrary linearity assumptions is based on the probability of participation or the "propensity score", $P(X) = \Pr(D = 1 \mid X)$. Rosenbaum and Rubin (1983) demonstrate that under assumptions (M-1) and (M-2),

$$(Y_0, Y_1) \perp\!\!\!\perp D \mid P(X) \quad \text{for } X \in \chi_c, \tag{8.5}$$

for some set χ_c, where it is assumed that (M-2) holds in the set. Conditioning either on $P(X)$ or on X produces conditional independence.[130]

[128] Regression-adjusted matching, proposed by Rubin (1979) and clarified in Heckman, Ichimura and Todd (1997, 1998), uses regression-adjusted Y_i, denoted by $\tau(Y_i) = Y_i - X_i\alpha$, in place of Y_i in the preceding calculations. See the cited papers for the econometric details of the procedure.

[129] In Equation (Q-3), this approach shows that α combines the effect of Q on U_0 with the causal effect of Q on Y.

[130] Their analysis is generalized to a multiple treatment setting in Lechner (2001) and Imbens (2003).

Conditioning on $P(X)$ reduces the dimension of the matching problem down to matching on the scalar $P(X)$. The analysis of Rosenbaum and Rubin (1983) assumes that $P(X)$ is known rather than estimated. Heckman, Ichimura and Todd (1998), Hahn (1998), and Hirano, Imbens and Ridder (2003) present the asymptotic distribution theory for the kernel matching estimator in the cases in which $P(X)$ is known and in which it is estimated both parametrically and nonparametrically.

Conditioning on P identifies all treatment parameters but as we have seen, it imposes the assumption of a flat MTE. Marginal returns and average returns are the same. A consequence of (8.5) is that

$$E(Y_1 \mid D = 0, P(X)) = E(Y_1 \mid D = 1, P(X)) = E(Y_1 \mid P(X)),$$
$$E(Y_0 \mid D = 1, P(X)) = E(Y_0 \mid D = 0, P(X)) = E(Y_0 \mid P(X)).$$

Support condition (M-2) has the unattractive feature that if the analyst has too much information about the decision of who takes treatment, so that $P(X) = 1$ or 0, the method breaks down at such values of X because people cannot be compared at a common X. The method of matching assumes that, given X, some unspecified randomization in the economic environment allocates people to treatment. This justifies assumption (Q-5) in the OLS example. The fact that the cases $P(X) = 1$ and $P(X) = 0$ must be eliminated suggests that methods for choosing X based on the fit of the model to data on D are potentially problematic, as we discuss below.

Offsetting these disadvantages, the method of matching with a known conditioning set that produces condition (M-2) does not require separability of outcome or choice equations, exogeneity of conditioning variables, exclusion restrictions, or adoption of specific functional forms of outcome equations. Such features are commonly used in conventional selection (control function) methods and conventional applications of IV although as we have demonstrated in Section 4, recent work in semiparametric estimation relaxes these assumptions. As noted in Section 8.2, the method of matching does not strictly require (M-1). One can get by with weaker mean independence assumptions (M-3) in the place of the stronger conditions (M-1). However, if (M-3) is invoked, the assumption that one can replace X by $P(X)$ does not follow from the analysis of Rosenbaum and Rubin (1983), and is an additional new assumption.

Methods for implementing matching are provided in Heckman et al. (1998) and are discussed extensively in Heckman, LaLonde and Smith (1999). See Todd (1999, 2007, 2008) for software and extensive discussion of the mechanics of matching. We now contrast the identifying assumptions used in the method of control functions with those used in matching.

8.3.1. Comparing matching and control functions approaches

The method of matching eliminates the dependence between (Y_0, Y_1) and D, $(Y_0, Y_1) \not\!\perp\!\!\!\perp D$, by assuming access to conditioning variables X such that (M-1) is satisfied: $(Y_0, Y_1) \perp\!\!\!\perp D \mid X$. By conditioning on observables, one can identify the distributions of Y_0 and Y_1 over the support of X satisfying (M-2).

Other methods model the dependence that gives rise to the spurious relationship and in this way attempt to eliminate it. IV involves exclusion and a different type of conditional independence, $(Y_0, Y_1) \perp\!\!\!\perp Z \mid X$, as well as a rank condition ($\Pr(D = 1 \mid X, Z)$ depends on Z). The instrument Z plays the role of the implicit randomization used in matching by allocating people to treatment status in a way that does not depend on (Y_0, Y_1). We have already established that matching and IV make very different assumptions. Thus, in general, a matching assumption that $(Y_0, Y_1) \perp\!\!\!\perp D \mid X, Z$ neither implies nor is implied by $(Y_0, Y_1) \perp\!\!\!\perp Z \mid X$. One special case where they are equivalent is when treatment status is assigned by randomization with full compliance (letting $\xi = 1$ denote assignment to treatment, $\xi = 1 \Rightarrow A = 1$ and $\xi = 0 \Rightarrow A = 0$) and $Z = \xi$, so that the instrument is the assignment mechanism. $A = 1$ if the person actually receives treatment, and $A = 0$ otherwise.

The method of control functions explicitly models the dependence between (Y_0, Y_1) and D and attempts to eliminate it. Chapter 73 (Matzkin) of this Handbook provides a comprehensive review of these methods. In Section 11, we present a summary of some of the general principles underlying the method of control functions, the method of control variates, replacement functions, and proxy approaches as they apply to the selection problem. All of these methods attempt to eliminate the θ in (U-1) that produces the dependence captured in (U-2).

In this section, we relate matching to the form of the control function introduced in Heckman (1980) and Heckman and Robb (1985a, 1986a). This version was used in our analysis of local instrumental variables (LIV) in Section 4, where we compare LIV with control function approaches and show that LIV and LATE estimate derivatives of the control functions. We analyze conditional means because of their familiarity. Using the fact that $E(\mathbf{1}(Y \leqslant y) \mid X) = F(y \mid X)$, the analysis applies to marginal distributions as well.

Thus we work with conditional expectations of (Y_0, Y_1) given (X, Z, D), where Z is assumed to include at least one variable not in X. Conventional applications of the control function method assume additive separability, which is not required in matching. Strictly speaking, additive separability is not required in the application of control functions either.[131] What is required is a model relating the outcome unobservables to the observables and the unobservables in the choice of treatment equation. Various assumptions give operational content to (U-1) defined in Section 2.

For the additively separable case (2.2), the control function for mean outcomes models the conditional expectations of Y_1 and Y_0 given X, Z, and D as

$$E(Y_1 \mid Z, X, D = 1) = \mu_1(X) + E(U_1 \mid Z, X, D = 1),$$
$$E(Y_0 \mid Z, X, D = 0) = \mu_0(X) + E(U_0 \mid Z, X, D = 0).$$

[131] Examples of nonseparable selection models are found in Cameron and Heckman (1998). See also Altonji and Matzkin (2005) and Chapter 73 (Matzkin) of this Handbook.

In the traditional method of control functions, the analyst models $E(U_1 \mid Z, X, D = 1)$ and $E(U_0 \mid Z, X, D = 0)$. If these functions can be independently varied against $\mu_1(X)$ and $\mu_0(X)$, respectively, one can identify $\mu_1(X)$ and $\mu_0(X)$ up to constant terms.[132] It is not required that X or Z be stochastically independent of U_1 or U_0, although conventional methods often assume this.

Assume that $(U_0, U_1, V) \perp\!\!\!\perp (X, Z)$ and adopt Equation (3.3) as the treatment choice model augmented so that X and Z are determinants of treatment choice, using V as the latent variable that generates D given X, Z: $D = \mathbf{1}(\mu_D(Z) \geqslant 0)$. Let $U_D = F_{V|X}(V)$ and $P(Z) = F_{V|X}(\mu_D(Z))$. In this notation, the control functions are

$$\begin{aligned} E(U_1 \mid Z, D = 1) &= E\big(U_1 \mid \mu_D(Z) \geqslant V\big) \\ &= E\big(U_1 \mid P(Z) \geqslant U_D\big) = K_1\big(P(Z)\big) \quad \text{and} \\ E(U_0 \mid Z, D = 0) &= E\big(U_0 \mid \mu_D(Z) < V\big) \\ &= E\big(U_0 \mid P(Z) < U_D\big) = K_0\big(P(Z)\big), \end{aligned}$$

so the control function only depends on the propensity score $P(Z)$. The key assumption needed to represent the control function solely as a function of $P(Z)$ is

(CF-1) $(U_0, U_1, V) \perp\!\!\!\perp X, Z$.

This assumption is not strictly required but it is traditional and useful in relating LIV and selection models (as in Section 4) and selection models and matching (this section). Under this condition

$$\begin{aligned} E(Y_1 \mid Z, X, D = 1) &= \mu_1(X) + K_1\big(P(Z)\big), \\ E(Y_0 \mid Z, X, D = 0) &= \mu_0(X) + K_0\big(P(Z)\big), \end{aligned}$$

with $\lim_{P\to 1} K_1(P) = 0$ and $\lim_{P\to 0} K_0(P) = 0$. It is assumed that Z can be independently varied for all X, and the limits are obtained by changing Z while holding X fixed.[133] These limit results state that when the values of X, Z are such that the probability of being in a sample ($D = 1$ or $D = 0$, respectively) is 1, there is no selection bias and one can separate out $\mu_1(X)$ from $K_1(P(Z))$ and $\mu_0(X)$ from $K_0(P(Z))$. This is the same identification at infinity condition that is required to identify ATE and TT in IV for models with heterogeneous responses.[134,135]

[132] Heckman and Robb (1985a, 1986a) introduce this general formulation of control functions. The identifiability requires that the members of the pairs $(\mu_1(X), E(U_1 \mid X, Z, D = 1))$ and $(\mu_0(X), E(U_0 \mid X, Z, D = 0))$ be variation-free so that they can be independently varied against each other.

[133] More precisely, we assume that $\text{Supp}(Z \mid X) = \text{Supp}(Z)$ and that limit sets of Z, $\mathbb{Z}_0$, and $\mathbb{Z}_1$ exist so that as $Z \to \mathbb{Z}_0$, $P(Z, X) \to 0$, and as $Z \to \mathbb{Z}_1$, $P(Z, X) \to 1$.

[134] As noted in our discussion in Section 4, we need identification at infinity to obtain ATE and TT. This is a feature of any evaluation model with general heterogeneity.

[135] One can approximate the $K_1(P)$ and $K_0(P)$ terms by polynomials in P [see Heckman (1980), Heckman and Robb (1985a, 1986a), Heckman and Hotz (1989)]. Ahn and Powell (1993) and Powell (1994) develop methods for eliminating $K_1(P(Z))$ and $K_0(P(Z))$ by differencing.

As noted in Section 4, unlike the method of matching based on (M-1), the method of control functions allows the marginal treatment effect to be different from the average treatment effect and from the conditional effect of treatment on the treated. Although conventional practice has been to derive the functional forms of $K_0(P)$ and $K_1(P)$ by making distributional assumptions about (U_0, U_1, V) such as normality or other conventional distributional assumptions, this is not an intrinsic feature of the method and there are many nonnormal and semiparametric versions of this method. See Powell (1994) for a survey.

In its semiparametric implementation, the method of control functions requires an exclusion restriction (a variable in Z not in X) to achieve nonparametric identification.[136] Without any functional form assumptions one cannot rule out a worst case analysis where, for example, if $X = Z$, then $K_1(P(X)) = \tau\mu(X)$ where τ is a scalar. In this situation, there is perfect collinearity between the control function and the conditional mean of the outcome equation, and it is impossible to separately identify either.[137] Even though this case is not generic, it is possible. The method of matching does not require an exclusion restriction, but at the cost of ruling out essential heterogeneity. In the general case, the method of control functions requires that in certain limit sets of Z, $P(Z) = 1$ and $P(Z) = 0$ in order to achieve full nonparametric identification.[138] The conventional method of matching does not invoke such limit set arguments.

All methods of evaluation, including matching and control functions, require that treatment parameters be defined on a common support that is the intersection of the supports of X given $D = 1$ and X given $D = 0$: $\text{Supp}(X \mid D = 1) \cap \text{Supp}(X \mid D = 0)$. This is the requirement for any estimator that seeks to identify treatment effects by comparing samples of treated persons with samples of untreated persons.

In this version of the method of control functions, $P(Z)$ is a conditioning variable used to predict U_1 conditional on D and U_0 conditional on D. In the method of matching, it is used as a conditioning variable to eliminate the stochastic dependence between (U_0, U_1) and D. In the method of LATE or LIV, $P(Z)$ is used as an instrument. In the method of control functions, as conventionally applied, $(U_0, U_1) \perp\!\!\!\perp (X, Z)$, but this assumption is not intrinsic to the method.[139] This assumption plays no role in matching if the correct conditioning set is known.[140] However, as noted below, exogeneity plays a key role in devising algorithms to select the conditioning variables. In addition, as noted in Section 6, exogeneity is helpful in making out-of-sample forecasts. The method of control functions does not require that $(U_0, U_1) \perp\!\!\!\perp D \mid (X, Z)$, which is a central requirement of matching. Equivalently, the method of control functions does not require

$$(U_0, U_1) \perp\!\!\!\perp V \mid (X, Z), \quad \text{or that} \quad (U_0, U_1) \perp\!\!\!\perp V \mid X,$$

[136] No exclusion is required for many common functional forms for the distributions of unobservables.

[137] Clearly $K_1(P(X))$ and $\mu(X)$ cannot be independently varied in this case.

[138] Symmetry of the errors can be used in place of the appeal to limit sets that put $P(Z) = 0$ or $P(Z) = 1$. See Chen (1999).

[139] Relaxing it, however, requires that the analyst model the dependence of the unobservables on the observables and that certain variation-free conditions are satisfied. [See Heckman and Robb (1985a).]

[140] That is, a conditioning set that satisfies (M-1) and (M-2).

whereas matching does and typically equates X and Z. Thus matching assumes access to a richer set of conditioning variables than is assumed in the method of control functions.

The method of control functions allows for outcome unobservables to be dependent on D even after conditioning on (X, Z), and it models this dependence. The method of matching assumes no such D dependence. Thus in this regard, and maintaining all of the assumptions invoked for control functions in this section, matching is a special case of the method of control functions[141] in which under assumptions (M-1) and (M-2),

$$\begin{aligned} &E(U_1 \mid X, D = 1) = E(U_1 \mid X), \\ &E(U_0 \mid X, D = 0) = E(U_0 \mid X). \end{aligned}$$

In the method of control functions, in the case where $(X, Z) \perp\!\!\!\perp (U_0, U_1, V)$, where the Z can include some or all of the elements of X, the conditional expectation of Y given X, Z, D is

$$\begin{aligned} E(Y \mid X, Z, D) &= E(Y_1 \mid X, Z, D = 1)D + E(Y_0 \mid X, Z, D = 0)(1 - D) \\ &= \mu_0(X) + \left[\mu_1(X) - \mu_0(X)\right]D \\ &\quad + E\left(U_1 \mid P(Z), D = 1\right)D + E\left(U_0 \mid P(Z), D = 0\right)(1 - D) \\ &= \mu_0(X) + K_0\left(P(Z)\right) \\ &\quad + \left[\mu_1(X) - \mu_0(X) + K_1\left(P(Z)\right) - K_0\left(P(Z)\right)\right]D. \end{aligned} \tag{8.6}$$

The coefficient on D in the final equation combines $\mu_1(X) - \mu_0(X)$ with $K_1(P(Z)) - K_0(P(Z))$. It does not correspond to any treatment effect. To identify $\mu_1(X) - \mu_0(X)$, one must isolate it from $K_1(P(Z)) - K_0(P(Z))$.

Under assumptions (M-1) and (M-2) of the method of matching, the conditional expectation of Y conditional on $P(X)$ and D is

$$\begin{aligned} E\left(Y \mid P(X), D\right) &= \mu_0\left(P(X)\right) + E\left(U_0 \mid P(X)\right) \\ &\quad + \left[\left(\mu_1\left(P(X)\right) - \mu_0\left(P(X)\right)\right)\right. \\ &\quad \left. + E\left(U_1 \mid P(X)\right) - E\left(U_0 \mid P(X)\right)\right]D. \end{aligned} \tag{8.7}$$

The coefficient on D in this expression is now interpretable and is the average treatment effect. If we assume that $(U_0, U_1) \perp\!\!\!\perp X$, which is not strictly required, we reach a more familiar representation

$$E\left(Y \mid P(X), D\right) = \mu_0\left(P(X)\right) + \left[\mu_1\left(P(X)\right) - \mu_0\left(P(X)\right)\right]D, \tag{8.8}$$

[141] See Aakvik, Heckman and Vytlacil (2005), Carneiro, Hansen and Heckman (2003) and Cunha, Heckman and Navarro (2005) for a generalization of matching that allows for selection on unobservables by imposing a factor structure on the errors and estimating the distribution of the unobserved factors. These methods are discussed in Abbring and Heckman (Chapter 72).

since $E(U_1 \mid P(X)) = E(U_0 \mid P(X)) = 0$. A parallel derivation can be made conditioning on X instead of $P(X)$.

Under the assumptions that justify matching, treatment effects ATE or TT (conditional on $P(X)$) are identified from the coefficient on D in either (8.7) or (8.8). Condition (M-2) guarantees that D is not perfectly predictable by X (or $P(X)$), so the variation in D identifies the treatment parameter.

The coefficient on D in Equation (8.6) for the more general control function model does not correspond to any treatment parameter, whereas the coefficients on D in Equations (8.7) and (8.8) correspond to treatment parameters under the assumptions of the matching model. Under assumption (CF-1), $\mu_1(P(X)) - \mu_0(P(X)) =$ ATE and ATE $=$ TT $=$ MTE, so the method of matching identifies all of the (conditional on $P(X)$) mean treatment parameters.[142]

Under the assumptions justifying matching, when means of Y_1 and Y_0 are the parameters of interest, and X satisfies (M-1) and (M-2), the bias terms vanish. They do not vanish in the more general case considered by the method of control functions. This is the mathematical counterpart of the randomization implicit in matching: conditional on X or $P(X)$, (U_0, U_1) are random with respect to D. The method of control functions allows these error terms to be nonrandom with respect to D and models the dependence. In the absence of functional form assumptions, it requires an exclusion restriction (a variable in Z not in X) to separate out $K_0(P(Z))$ from the coefficient on D. Matching produces identification without exclusion restrictions whereas identification with exclusion restrictions is a central feature of the control function method in the absence of functional form assumptions.

The fact that the control function approach allows for more general dependencies among the unobservables and the conditioning variables than the matching approach allows is implicitly recognized in the work of Rosenbaum (1995) and Robins (1997). Their "sensitivity analyses" for matching when there are unobserved conditioning variables are, in their essence, sensitivity analyses using control functions.[143] Aakvik, Heckman and Vytlacil (2005), Carneiro, Hansen and Heckman (2003) and Cunha, Heckman and Navarro (2005) explicitly model the relationship between matching and selection models using factor structure models, treating the omitted conditioning variables as unobserved factors and estimating their distribution. Abbring and Heckman discuss this work in Chapter 72.

[142] This result also holds even if (CF-1) is not satisfied because $(U_0, U_1) \not\perp\!\!\!\perp X$. In this case, the treatment effects include the term

$$E\big(U_1 \mid P(X)\big) - E\big(U_0 \mid P(X)\big).$$

[143] See also Vijverberg (1993) who does such a sensitivity analysis in a parametric selection model with an unidentified parameter.

8.4. Comparing matching and classical control function methods for a generalized Roy model

Figure 10, developed in connection with our discussion of instrumental variables, shows the contrast between the shape of the MTE and the OLS matching estimand as a function of p for the extended Roy model developed in Section 4. The MTE(p) shows its typical declining shape associated with diminishing returns, and the assumptions justifying matching are violated. Matching attempts to impose a flat MTE(p) and therefore flattens the estimated MTE(p) compared to its true value. It understates marginal returns at low levels of p (associated with unobservables that make it likely to participate in treatment) and overstates marginal returns at high levels of p.

To further illustrate the bias in matching and how the control function eliminates it, we perform sensitivity analyses under different assumptions about the parameters of the underlying selection model. In particular, we assume that the data are generated by the model of Equations (3.1) and (3.2), where $\mu_D(Z) = Z\gamma$, $\mu_0(X) = \mu_0$, $\mu_1(X) = \mu_1$, and

$$(U_0, U_1, V)' \sim N(0, \Sigma),$$
$$\operatorname{corr}(U_j, V) = \rho_{jV},$$
$$\operatorname{Var}(U_j) = \sigma_j^2, \quad j = \{0, 1\}.$$

We assume in this section that $D = \mathbf{1}[\mu_D(Z) + V \geqslant 0]$, in conformity with the examples presented in Heckman and Navarro (2004), from which we draw. This reformulation of choice model (3.3) simply entails a change in the sign of V. We assume that $Z \perp\!\!\!\perp (U_0, U_1, V)$. Using the selection formulae derived in Appendix M, we can write the biases conditional on $P(Z) = p$ using propensity score matching in a generalized Roy model as

$$\text{Bias TT}(Z = z) = \text{Bias TT}\big(P(Z) = p\big) = \sigma_0 \rho_{0V} M(p),$$
$$\text{Bias ATE}(Z = z) = \text{Bias ATE}\big(P(Z) = p\big) = M(p)\big[\sigma_1 \rho_{1V}(1 - p) + \sigma_0 \rho_{0V}\, p\big],$$

where $M(p) = \frac{\phi(\Phi^{-1}(1-p))}{p(1-p)}$, $\phi(\cdot)$ and $\Phi(\cdot)$ are the pdf and cdf of a standard normal random variable and the propensity score $P(z)$ is evaluated at $P(z) = p$. We assume that $\mu_1 = \mu_0$ so that the true average treatment effect is zero.

We simulate the mean bias for TT (Table 10) and ATE (Table 11) for different values of the ρ_{jV} and σ_j. The results in the tables show that, as we let the variances of the outcome equations grow, the value of the mean bias that we obtain can become substantial. With larger correlations between the outcomes and the unobservables generating choices, come larger biases. These tables demonstrate the greater generality of the control function approach, which models the bias rather than assuming it away by conditioning. Even if the correlation between the observables and the unobservables (ρ_{jV}) is small, so that one might think that selection on unobservables is relatively unimportant, we still obtain substantial biases if we do not control for relevant omitted conditioning variables. Only for special values of the parameters do we avoid bias by matching.

Table 10
Mean bias for treatment on the treated

ρ_{0V}	Average bias ($\sigma_0 = 1$)	Average bias ($\sigma_0 = 2$)
−1.00	−1.7920	−3.5839
−0.75	−1.3440	−2.6879
−0.50	−0.8960	−1.7920
−0.25	−0.4480	−0.8960
0.00	0.0000	0.0000
0.25	0.4480	0.8960
0.50	0.8960	1.7920
0.75	1.3440	2.6879
1.00	1.7920	3.5839

Bias TT $= \rho_{0V} * \sigma_0 * M(p)$.

$M(p) = \frac{\phi(\Phi^{-1}(1-p))}{p(1-p)}$.

Source: Heckman and Navarro (2004).

These examples also demonstrate that sensitivity analyses can be conducted for analysis based on control function methods even when they are not fully identified. Vijverberg (1993) provides an example.

8.5. The informational requirements of matching and the bias when they are not satisfied

In this section, we present some examples of when matching "works" and when it breaks down. This section is based on Heckman and Navarro (2004). In particular, we show how matching on some of the relevant information but not all can make the bias using matching worse for standard treatment parameters. These examples also introduce factor models that play a key role in the analysis of Abbring and Heckman in Chapter 72.

Section 2 of this chapter discussed informational asymmetries between the econometrician and the agents whose behavior they are analyzing. The method of matching assumes that the econometrician has access to and uses all of the relevant information in the precise sense defined there. That means that the X that guarantees conditional independence (M-1) is available and is used. The concept of relevant information is a delicate one and it is difficult to find the true conditioning set.

Assume that the economic model generating the data is a generalized Roy model of the form

$$D^* = Z\gamma + V, \quad \text{where}$$
$$Z \perp\!\!\!\perp V \quad \text{and}$$
$$V = \alpha_{V1} f_1 + \alpha_{V2} f_2 + \varepsilon_V,$$

Table 11
Mean bias for average treatment effect

$(\sigma_0 = 1)$									
ρ_{0V}	−1.00	−0.75	−0.50	−0.25	0	0.25	0.50	0.75	1.00
				$\rho_{1V}(\sigma_1 = 1)$					
−1.00	−1.7920	−1.5680	−1.3440	−1.1200	−0.8960	−0.6720	−0.4480	−0.2240	0
−0.75	−1.5680	−1.3440	−1.1200	−0.8960	−0.6720	−0.4480	−0.2240	0	0.2240
−0.50	−1.3440	−1.1200	−0.8960	−0.6720	−0.4480	−0.2240	0	0.2240	0.4480
−0.25	−1.1200	−0.8960	−0.6720	−0.4480	−0.2240	0	0.2240	0.4480	0.6720
0	−0.8960	−0.6720	−0.4480	−0.2240	0	0.2240	0.4480	0.6720	0.8960
0.25	−0.6720	−0.4480	−0.2240	0	0.2240	0.4480	0.6720	0.8960	1.1200
0.50	−0.4480	−0.2240	0	0.2240	0.4480	0.6720	0.8960	1.1200	1.3440
0.75	−0.2240	0	0.2240	0.4480	0.6720	0.8960	1.1200	1.3440	1.5680
1.00	0	0.2240	0.4480	0.6720	0.8960	1.1200	1.3440	1.5680	1.7920
				$\rho_{1V}(\sigma_1 = 2)$					
−1.00	−2.6879	−2.2399	−1.7920	−1.3440	−0.8960	−0.4480	0	0.4480	0.8960
−0.75	−2.4639	−2.0159	−1.5680	−1.1200	−0.6720	−0.2240	0.2240	0.6720	1.1200
−0.50	−2.2399	−1.7920	−1.3440	−0.8960	−0.4480	0	0.4480	0.8960	1.3440
−0.25	−2.0159	−1.5680	−1.1200	−0.6720	−0.2240	0.2240	0.6720	1.1200	1.5680
0	−1.7920	−1.3440	−0.8960	−0.4480	0	0.4480	0.8960	1.3440	1.7920
0.25	−1.5680	−1.1200	−0.6720	−0.2240	0.2240	0.6720	1.1200	1.5680	2.0159
0.50	−1.3440	−0.8960	−0.4480	0	0.4480	0.8960	1.3440	1.7920	2.2399
0.75	−1.1200	−0.6720	−0.2240	0.2240	0.6720	1.1200	1.5680	2.0159	2.4639
1.00	−0.8960	−0.4480	0	0.4480	0.8960	1.3440	1.7920	2.2399	2.6879

BIAS ATE $= \rho_{1V} * \sigma_1 * M_1(p) - \rho_{0V} * \sigma_0 * M_0(p)$.

$M_1(p) = \frac{\phi(\Phi^{-1}(1-p))}{p}$.

$M_0(p) = \frac{-\phi(\Phi^{-1}(1-p))}{(1-p)}$.

Source: Heckman and Navarro (2004).

$$D = \begin{cases} 1 & \text{if } D^* \geqslant 0, \\ 0 & \text{otherwise,} \end{cases}$$

and

$$Y_1 = \mu_1 + U_1, \quad \text{where } U_1 = \alpha_{11} f_1 + \alpha_{12} f_2 + \varepsilon_1,$$
$$Y_0 = \mu_0 + U_0, \quad \text{where } U_0 = \alpha_{01} f_1 + \alpha_{02} f_2 + \varepsilon_0.$$

We remind the reader that contrary to the analysis throughout the rest of this chapter we add V and do not subtract it in the decision equation. This is the familiar representation. By a change in sign in V, we can go back and forth between the specification used in this section and the specification used in other sections of the chapter.

In this specification, $(f_1, f_2, \varepsilon_V, \varepsilon_1, \varepsilon_0)$ are assumed to be mean zero random variables that are mutually independent of each other and Z so that all the correlation among the elements of (U_0, U_1, V) is captured by $f = (f_1, f_2)$. Models that take this form are known as factor models and have been applied in the context of selection models by Aakvik, Heckman and Vytlacil (2005), Carneiro, Hansen and Heckman (2001, 2003), and Hansen, Heckman and Mullen (2004), among others. We keep implicit any dependence on X which may be general.

Generically, the minimal relevant information for this model when the factor loadings are not zero ($\alpha_{ij} \neq 0$) is, for general values of the factor loadings,

$$I_R = \{f_1, f_2\}.$$[144]

Recall that we assume independence between Z and all error terms. If the econometrician has access to I_R and uses it, (M-1) is satisfied conditional on I_R. Note that I_R plays the role of θ in (U-1). In the case where the economist knows I_R, the economist's information set $\sigma(I_E)$ contains the relevant information ($\sigma(I_E) \supseteq \sigma(I_R)$).

The agent's information set may include different variables. If we assume that $\varepsilon_0, \varepsilon_1$ are shocks to outcomes not known to the agent at the time treatment decisions are made, but the agent knows all other aspects of the model, the agent's information is

$$I_A = \{f_1, f_2, Z, \varepsilon_V\}.$$

Under perfect certainty, the agent's information set includes ε_1 and ε_0:

$$I_A = \{f_1, f_2, Z, \varepsilon_V, \varepsilon_1, \varepsilon_0\}.$$

In either case, all of the information available to the agent is not required to satisfy conditional independence (M-1). All three information sets guarantee conditional independence, but only the first is minimal relevant.

In the notation of Section 2, the observing economist may know some variables not in I_A, I_{R^*} or I_R but may not know all of the variables in I_R. In the following subsections, we study what happens when the matching assumption that $\sigma(I_E) \supseteq \sigma(I_R)$ does not hold. That is, we analyze what happens to the bias from matching as the amount of information used by the econometrician is changed. In order to get closed form expressions for the biases of the treatment parameters, we make the additional assumption that

$$(f_1, f_2, \varepsilon_V, \varepsilon_1, \varepsilon_0) \sim N(0, \Sigma),$$

where Σ is a matrix with $(\sigma^2_{f_1}, \sigma^2_{f_2}, \sigma^2_{\varepsilon_V}, \sigma^2_{\varepsilon_1}, \sigma^2_{\varepsilon_0})$ on the diagonal and zero in all the nondiagonal elements. This assumption links matching models to conventional normal selection models of the sort developed in Chapter 70 and further analyzed in Section 2 of this chapter. However, the examples based on this specification illustrate more general principles. We now analyze various commonly encountered cases.

[144] Notice that for a fixed set of α_{ij}, the minimal information set is $(\alpha_{11} - \alpha_{01})f_1 + (\alpha_{12} - \alpha_{02})f_2$, which captures the dependence between D and (Y_0, Y_1).

8.5.1. The economist uses the minimal relevant information: $\sigma(I_R) \subseteq \sigma(I_E)$

We begin by analyzing the case in which the information used by the economist is $I_E = \{Z, f_1, f_2\}$, so that the econometrician has access to a relevant information set and it is larger than the minimal relevant information set. In this case, it is straightforward to show that matching identifies all of the mean treatment parameters with no bias. The matching estimator has population mean

$$\begin{aligned}
&E(Y_1 \mid D = 1, I_E) - E(Y_0 \mid D = 0, I_E) \\
&\quad = \mu_1 - \mu_0 + (\alpha_{11} - \alpha_{01}) f_1 + (\alpha_{12} - \alpha_{02}) f_2,
\end{aligned}$$

and all of the mean treatment parameters collapse to this same expression since, conditional on knowing f_1 and f_2, there is no selection because $(\varepsilon_0, \varepsilon_1) \perp\!\!\!\perp V$. Recall that for arbitrary choices of $\alpha_{11}, \alpha_{01}, \alpha_{12}$, and α_{02}, $I_R = \{f_1, f_2\}$ and the economist needs less information to achieve (M-1) than is contained in I_E.

In this case, the analysis of Rosenbaum and Rubin (1983) tells us that knowledge of (Z, f_1, f_2) and knowledge of $P(Z, f_1, f_2)$ are equally useful in identifying all of the treatment parameters conditional on P. If we write the propensity score as

$$\begin{aligned}
P(I_E) &= \Pr\left(\frac{\varepsilon_V}{\sigma_{\varepsilon_V}} > \frac{-Z\gamma - \alpha_{V1} f_1 - \alpha_{V2} f_2}{\sigma_{\varepsilon_V}}\right) \\
&= 1 - \Phi\left(\frac{-Z\gamma - \alpha_{V1} f_1 - \alpha_{V2} f_2}{\sigma_{\varepsilon_V}}\right) = p,
\end{aligned}$$

the event ($D^* \lesseqgtr 0$, given $f = \tilde{f}$ and $Z = z$) can be written as $\frac{\varepsilon_V}{\sigma_{\varepsilon_V}} \lesseqgtr \Phi^{-1}(1 - P(z, \tilde{f}))$, where Φ is the cdf of a standard normal random variable and $f = (f_1, f_2)$. We abuse notation slightly by using z as the realized fixed value of Z and $\tilde{f}$ as the realized value of f. The population matching condition (M-1) implies that

$$\begin{aligned}
&E\big(Y_1 \bigm| D = 1, P(I_E) = P(z, \tilde{f})\big) - E\big(Y_0 \bigm| D = 0, P(I_E) = P(z, \tilde{f})\big) \\
&\quad = \mu_1 - \mu_0 + E\big(U_1 \bigm| D = 1, P(I_E) = P(z, \tilde{f})\big) \\
&\qquad - E\big(U_0 \bigm| D = 0, P(I_E) = P(z, \tilde{f})\big) \\
&\quad = \mu_1 - \mu_0 + E\left(U_1 \,\middle|\, \frac{\varepsilon_V}{\sigma_{\varepsilon_V}} > \Phi^{-1}\big(1 - P(z, \tilde{f})\big)\right) \\
&\qquad - E\left(U_0 \,\middle|\, \frac{\varepsilon_V}{\sigma_{\varepsilon_V}} \leqslant \Phi^{-1}\big(1 - P(z, \tilde{f})\big)\right) \\
&\quad = \mu_1 - \mu_0.
\end{aligned}$$

This expression is equal to all of the treatment parameters discussed in this chapter, since

$$E\left(U_1 \,\middle|\, \frac{\varepsilon_V}{\sigma_{\varepsilon_V}} > \Phi^{-1}\big(1 - P(z, \tilde{f})\big)\right) = \frac{\operatorname{Cov}(U_1, \varepsilon_V)}{\sigma_{\varepsilon_V}} M_1\big(P(z, \tilde{f})\big)$$

and

$$E\left(U_0 \;\middle|\; \frac{\varepsilon_V}{\sigma_{\varepsilon_V}} \leqslant \Phi^{-1}\big(1 - P(z, \tilde{f})\big)\right) = \frac{\operatorname{Cov}(U_0, \varepsilon_V)}{\sigma_{\varepsilon_V}} M_0\big(P(z, \tilde{f})\big),$$

where

$$M_1\big(P(z, \tilde{f})\big) = \frac{\phi(\Phi^{-1}(1 - P(z, \tilde{f})))}{P(z, \tilde{f})},$$

$$M_0\big(P(z, \tilde{f})\big) = -\frac{\phi(\Phi^{-1}(1 - P(z, \tilde{f})))}{1 - P(z, \tilde{f})},$$

where ϕ is the density of a standard normal random variable. As a consequence of the assumptions about mutual independence of the errors

$$\operatorname{Cov}(U_i, \varepsilon_V) = \operatorname{Cov}(\alpha_{i1} f_1 + \alpha_{i2} f_2 + \varepsilon_i, \varepsilon_V) = 0, \quad i = 0, 1.$$

In the context of the generalized Roy model, the case considered in this subsection is the one matching is designed to solve. Even though a selection model generates the data, the fact that the information used by the econometrician includes the minimal relevant information makes matching a correct solution to the selection problem. We can estimate the treatment parameters with no bias since, as a consequence of our assumptions, $(U_0, U_1) \perp\!\!\!\perp D \mid (f, Z)$, which is exactly what matching requires. The minimal relevant information set is even smaller. For arbitrary factor loadings, we only need to know (f_1, f_2) to secure conditional independence. We can define the propensity score solely in terms of f_1 and f_2, and the Rosenbaum–Rubin result still goes through. Our analysis in this section focuses on treatment parameters conditional on particular values of $P(Z, f) = P(z, \tilde{f})$, i.e., for fixed values of p, but we could condition more finely. Conditioning on $P(z, \tilde{f})$ defines the treatment parameters more coarsely. We can use either fine or coarse conditioning to construct the unconditional treatment effects.

In this example, using more information than what is in the relevant information set (i.e., using Z) is harmless. But this is not generally true. If $Z \not\perp\!\!\!\perp (U_0, U_1, V)$, adding Z to the conditioning set can violate conditional independence assumption (M-1):

$$(Y_0, Y_1) \perp\!\!\!\perp D \mid (f_1, f_2),$$

but

$$(Y_0, Y_1) \not\perp\!\!\!\perp D \mid (f_1, f_2, Z).$$

Adding extra variables can destroy the crucial conditional independence property of matching. We present an example of this point below. We first consider a case where $Z \perp\!\!\!\perp (U_0, U_1, V)$ but the analyst conditions on Z and not (f_1, f_2). In this case, there is selection on the unobservables that are not conditioned on.

8.5.2. *The economist does not use all of the minimal relevant information*

Next, suppose that the information used by the econometrician is

$$I_E = \{Z\},$$

and there is selection on the unobservable (to the analyst) f_1 and f_2, i.e., the factor loadings α_{ij} are all nonzero. Recall that we assume that Z and the f are independent. In this case, the event $(D^* \lesseqgtr 0, Z = z)$ is characterized by

$$\frac{\alpha_{V1} f_1 + \alpha_{V2} f_2 + \varepsilon_V}{\sqrt{\alpha_{V1}^2 \sigma_{f_1}^2 + \alpha_{V2}^2 \sigma_{f_2}^2 + \sigma_{\varepsilon_V}^2}} \lesseqgtr \Phi^{-1}\big(1 - P(z)\big).$$

Using the analysis presented in Appendix M, the bias for the different treatment parameters is given by

$$\text{Bias TT}(Z = z) = \text{Bias TT}\big(P(Z) = P(z)\big) = \eta_0 M\big(P(z)\big), \tag{8.9}$$

where $M(P(z)) = M_1(P(z)) - M_0(P(z))$.

$$\begin{aligned}\text{Bias ATE}(Z = z) &= \text{Bias ATE}\big(P(Z) = P(z)\big) \\ &= M\big(P(z)\big)\big\{\eta_1\big[1 - P(z)\big] + \eta_0 P(z)\big\},\end{aligned} \tag{8.10}$$

where

$$\eta_1 = \frac{\alpha_{V1}\alpha_{11}\sigma_{f_1}^2 + \alpha_{V2}\alpha_{12}\sigma_{f_2}^2}{\sqrt{\alpha_{V1}^2 \sigma_{f_1}^2 + \alpha_{V2}^2 \sigma_{f_2}^2 + \sigma_{\varepsilon_V}^2}},$$

$$\eta_0 = \frac{\alpha_{V1}\alpha_{01}\sigma_{f_1}^2 + \alpha_{V2}\alpha_{02}\sigma_{f_2}^2}{\sqrt{\alpha_{V1}^2 \sigma_{f_1}^2 + \alpha_{V2}^2 \sigma_{f_2}^2 + \sigma_{\varepsilon_V}^2}}.$$

It is not surprising that matching on sets of variables that exclude the relevant conditioning variables produces bias for the conditional (on $P(z)$) treatment parameters. The advantage of working with a closed form expression for the bias is that it allows us to answer questions about the *magnitude* of this bias under different assumptions about the information available to the analyst, and to present some simple examples. We next use expressions (8.9) and (8.10) as benchmarks against which to compare the relative size of the bias when we enlarge the econometrician's information set beyond Z.

8.5.3. *Adding information to the econometrician's information set I_E: Using some but not all the information from the minimal relevant information set I_R*

Suppose that the econometrician uses more information but not all of the information in the minimal relevant information set. He still reports values of the parameters conditional on specific p values but now the model for p has different conditioning variables.

For example, the data set assumed in the preceding section might be augmented or else the econometrician decides to use information previously available. In particular, assume that the econometrician's information set is

$$I'_E = \{Z, f_2\},$$

and that he uses this information set. Under Conditions 1 and 2 presented below, the biases for the treatment parameters conditional on values of $P = p$ are reduced in absolute value relative to their values in Section 8.5.2 by changing the conditioning set in this way. But these conditions are not generally satisfied, so that adding extra information does not necessarily reduce bias and may actually increase it. To show how this happens in our model, we define expressions comparable to η_1 and η_0 for this case:

$$\eta'_1 = \frac{\alpha_{V1}\alpha_{11}\sigma^2_{f_1}}{\sqrt{\alpha^2_{V1}\sigma^2_{f_1} + \sigma^2_{\varepsilon_V}}},$$

$$\eta'_0 = \frac{\alpha_{V1}\alpha_{01}\sigma^2_{f_1}}{\sqrt{\alpha^2_{V1}\sigma^2_{f_1} + \sigma^2_{\varepsilon_V}}}.$$

We compare the biases under the two cases using formulae (8.9)–(8.10), suitably modified, but keeping p fixed at a specific value even though this implies different conditioning sets in terms of $(z, \tilde{f})$.

CONDITION 1. *The bias produced by using matching to estimate* TT *is smaller in absolute value for any given p when the new information set $\sigma(I'_E)$ is used if*

$$|\eta_0| > |\eta'_0|.$$

There is a similar result for ATE:

CONDITION 2. *The bias produced by using matching to estimate* ATE *is smaller in absolute value for any given p when the new information set $\sigma(I'_E)$ is used if*

$$|\eta_1(1-p) + \eta_0 p| > |\eta'_1(1-p) + \eta'_0 p|.$$

PROOF OF CONDITIONS 1 AND 2. These conditions are a direct consequence of formulae (8.9) and (8.10), modified to allow for the different covariance structure produced by the information structure assumed in this section (replacing η_0 with η'_0, η_1 with η'_1). □

It is important to notice that we condition on the same value of p in deriving these expressions although the variables in P are different across different specifications of the model. Propensity-score matching defines them conditional on $P = p$, so we are being faithful to that method.

These conditions do not always hold. In general, whether or not the bias will be reduced by adding additional conditioning variables depends on the relative importance of the additional information in both the outcome equations and on the signs of the terms inside the absolute value.

Consider whether Condition 1 is satisfied in general. Assume $\eta_0 > 0$ for all α_{02}, α_{V2}. Then $\eta_0 > \eta_0'$ if

$$\eta_0 = \frac{\alpha_{V1}\alpha_{01}\sigma_{f_1}^2 + (\alpha_{V2}^2)(\frac{\alpha_{02}}{\alpha_{V2}})\sigma_{f_2}^2}{\sqrt{\alpha_{V1}^2\sigma_{f_1}^2 + \alpha_{V2}^2\sigma_{f_2}^2 + \sigma_{\varepsilon_V}^2}} > \frac{\alpha_{V1}\alpha_{11}\sigma_{f_1}^2}{\sqrt{\alpha_{V1}^2\sigma_{f_1}^2 + \sigma_{\varepsilon_V}^2}} = \eta_0'.$$

When $\frac{\alpha_{02}}{\alpha_{V2}} = 0$, clearly $\eta_0 < \eta_0'$. Adding information to the conditioning set increases bias. We can vary $(\frac{\alpha_{02}}{\alpha_{V2}})$ holding all of the other parameters constant and hence can make the left-hand side arbitrarily large.[145] As α_{02} increases, there is some critical value α_{02}^* beyond which $\eta_0 > \eta_0'$. If we assumed that $\eta_0 < 0$, however, the opposite conclusion would hold, and the conditions for reduction in bias would be harder to meet, as the relative importance of the new information is increased. Similar expressions can be derived for ATE and MTE, in which the direction of the effect depends on the signs of the terms in the absolute value.

Figures 23A and 23B illustrate the point that adding some but not all information from the minimal relevant set might increase the point-wise bias and the unconditional or average bias for ATE and TT, respectively.[146] Values of the parameters of the model are presented at the base of the figures. In these figures, we compare conditioning on $P(z)$, which in general is not guaranteed to eliminate bias, with conditioning on $P(z)$ and f_2 but not f_1. Adding f_2 to the conditioning increases bias.

The fact that the point-wise (and overall) bias might increase when adding some but not all information from I_R is a feature that is not shared by the method of control functions. Because the method of control functions models the stochastic dependence of the unobservables in the outcome equations on the observables, changing the variables observed by the econometrician to include f_2 does not generate bias. It only changes the control function used. That is, by adding f_2 we change the control function from

$$K_1\big(P(Z) = P(z)\big) = \eta_1 M_1\big(P(z)\big),$$
$$K_0\big(P(Z) = P(z)\big) = \eta_0 M_0\big(P(z)\big)$$

to

$$K_1'\big(P(Z, f_2) = P(z, \tilde{f}_2)\big) = \eta_1' M_1\big(P(z, \tilde{f}_2)\big),$$

145 A direct computation shows that

$$\frac{\partial\eta_0}{\partial(\frac{\alpha_{02}}{\alpha_{V2}})} = \frac{\alpha_{V2}^2\sigma_{f_2}^2}{\sqrt{\alpha_{V1}^2\sigma_{f_1}^2 + \alpha_{V2}^2\sigma_{f_2}^2 + \sigma_{\varepsilon_V}^2}} > 0.$$

146 Heckman and Navarro (2004) show comparable plots for MTE.

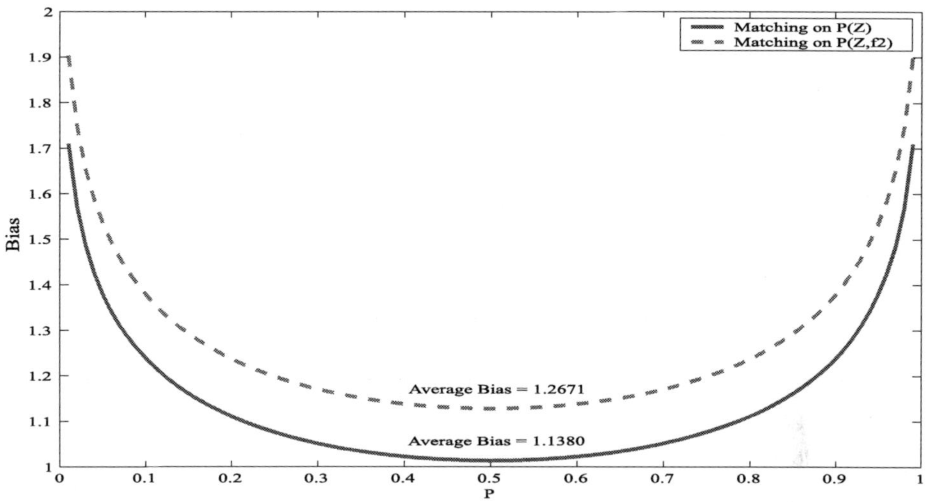

Figure 23A. Bias for treatment on the treated. *Source*: Heckman and Navarro (2004).

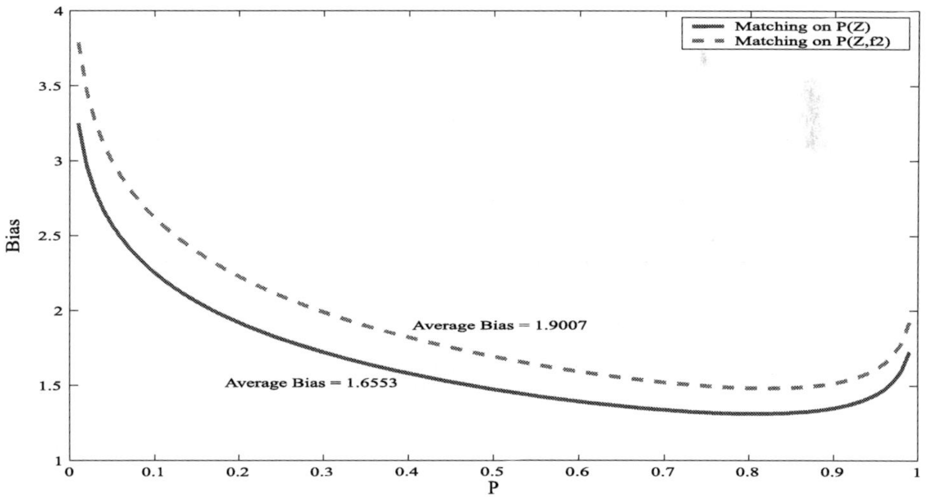

Note: Using proxy $\tilde{Z}$ for f_2 increases the bias. Correlation $(\tilde{Z}, f_2) = 0.5$.

Model:

$V = Z + f_1 + f_2 + \varepsilon_V$;	$Y_1 = 2f_1 + 0.1f_2 + \varepsilon_1$;	$Y_0 = f_1 + 0.1f_2 + \varepsilon_0$
$\varepsilon_V \sim N(0, 1)$;	$\varepsilon_1 \sim N(0, 1)$;	$\varepsilon_0 \sim N(0, 1)$
$f_1 \sim N(0, 1)$;	$f_2 \sim N(0, 1)$	

Figure 23B. Bias for average treatment effect. *Source*: Heckman and Navarro (2004).

$$K_0'\big(P(Z, f_2) = P(z, \tilde{f}_2)\big) = \eta_0' M_0\big(P(z, \tilde{f}_2)\big)$$

but do not generate any bias in using the control function estimator. This is a major advantage of this method.

It controls for the bias of the omitted conditioning variables by modeling it. Of course, if the model for the bias term is not valid, neither is the correction for the bias. Semiparametric selection estimators are designed to protect the analyst against model misspecification. [See, e.g., Powell (1994).] Matching evades this problem by assuming that the analyst always knows the correct conditioning variables and that they satisfy (M-1). In actual empirical settings, agents rarely know the relevant information set. Instead they use proxies.

8.5.4. *Adding information to the econometrician's information set: Using proxies for the relevant information*

Suppose that instead of knowing some part of the minimal relevant information set, such as f_2, the analyst has access to a proxy for it.[147] In particular, assume that he has access to a variable $\tilde{Z}$ that is correlated with f_2 but that is not the full minimal relevant information set. That is, define the econometrician's information to be

$$\tilde{I}_E = \{Z, \tilde{Z}\},$$

and suppose that he uses it so $I_E = \tilde{I}_E$. In order to obtain closed-form expressions for the biases we assume that

$$\tilde{Z} \sim N\big(0, \sigma_{\tilde{Z}}^2\big),$$
$$\operatorname{corr}(\tilde{Z}, f_2) = \rho, \quad \text{and} \quad \tilde{Z} \perp\!\!\!\perp (\varepsilon_0, \varepsilon_1, \varepsilon_V, f_1).$$

We define expressions comparable to η and η':

$$\tilde{\eta}_1 = \frac{\alpha_{11}\alpha_{V1}\sigma_{f_1}^2 + \alpha_{12}\alpha_{V2}(1-\rho^2)\sigma_{f_2}^2}{\sqrt{\alpha_{V1}^2\sigma_{f_1}^2 + \alpha_{V2}^2\sigma_{f_2}^2(1-\rho^2) + \sigma_{\varepsilon_V}^2}},$$

$$\tilde{\eta}_0 = \frac{\alpha_{01}\alpha_{V1}\sigma_{f_1}^2 + \alpha_{02}\alpha_{V2}(1-\rho^2)\sigma_{f_2}^2}{\sqrt{\alpha_{V1}^2\sigma_{f_1}^2 + \alpha_{V2}^2\sigma_{f_2}^2(1-\rho^2) + \sigma_{\varepsilon_V}^2}}.$$

By substituting for I_E' by $\tilde{I}_E$ and η_j' by $\tilde{\eta}_j$ ($j = 0, 1$) in Conditions 1 and 2 of Section 8.5.3, we can obtain results for the bias in this case. Whether $\tilde{I}_E$ will be bias-reducing depends on how well it spans I_R and on the signs of the terms in the absolute values in those conditions in Section 8.5.3.

[147] For example, the returns-to-schooling literature often uses different test scores, like AFQT or IQ, to proxy for missing ability variables. We discuss these proxy, replacement function, methods in Section 11. See also Abbring and Heckman (Chapter 72).

In this case, however, there is another parameter to consider: the correlation ρ between $\tilde{Z}$ and f_2, ρ. If $|\rho| = 1$ we are back to the case of $\tilde{I}_E = I'_E$ because $\tilde{Z}$ is a perfect proxy for f_2. If $\rho = 0$, we are essentially back to the case analyzed in Section 8.5.3. Because we know that the bias at a particular value of p might either increase or decrease when f_2 is used as a conditioning variable but f_1 is not, we know that it is not possible to determine whether the bias increases or decreases as we change the correlation between f_2 and $\tilde{Z}$. That is, we know that going from $\rho = 0$ to $|\rho| = 1$ might change the bias in any direction. Use of a better proxy in this correlational sense may produce a *more* biased estimate.

From the analysis of Section 8.5.3, it is straightforward to derive conditions under which the bias generated when the econometrician's information is $\tilde{I}_E$ is smaller than when it is I'_E. That is, it can be the case that knowing *the proxy* variable $\tilde{Z}$ is *better* than knowing the actual variable f_2. Returning to the analysis of treatment on the treated as an example (i.e., Condition 1), the bias in absolute value (at a fixed value of p) is reduced when $\tilde{Z}$ is used instead of f_2 if

$$\left| \frac{\alpha_{01}\alpha_{V1}\sigma_{f_1}^2 + \alpha_{02}\alpha_{V2}(1-\rho^2)\sigma_{f_2}^2}{\sqrt{\alpha_{V1}^2\sigma_{f_1}^2 + \alpha_{V2}^2\sigma_{f_2}^2(1-\rho^2) + \sigma_{\varepsilon V}^2}} \right| < \left| \frac{\alpha_{01}\alpha_{V1}\sigma_{f_1}^2}{\sqrt{\alpha_{V1}^2\sigma_{f_1}^2 + \sigma_{\varepsilon V}^2}} \right|.$$

Figures 24A and 24B, use the same true model as used in the previous section to illustrate the two points being made here. Namely, *using* a *proxy* for an unobserved relevant variable *might increase the bias*. On the other hand, it *might* be *better* in terms of bias to use a *proxy* than to use the actual variable, f_2. However, as Figures 25A and 25B show, by changing α_{02} from 0.1 to 1, using a proxy might increase the bias versus using the actual variable f_2. Notice that the bias need not be universally negative or positive but depends on p.

The point of these examples is that matching makes very knife-edge assumptions. If the analyst gets the right conditioning set, (M-1) is satisfied and there is no bias. But determining the correct information set is not a trivial task, as we note in Section 8.5.6. Having good proxies in the standard usage of that term can create substantial bias in estimating treatment effects. Half a loaf may be worse than none.

8.5.5. *The case of a discrete outcome variable*

Heckman and Navarro (2004) construct parallel examples for cases including discrete dependent variables. In particular, they consider nonnormal, nonseparable equations for odds ratios and probabilities. The proposition that matching identifies the correct treatment parameter if the econometrician's information set includes all the minimal relevant information is true more generally, provided that any additional extraneous information used is exogenous in a sense to be defined precisely in the next section.

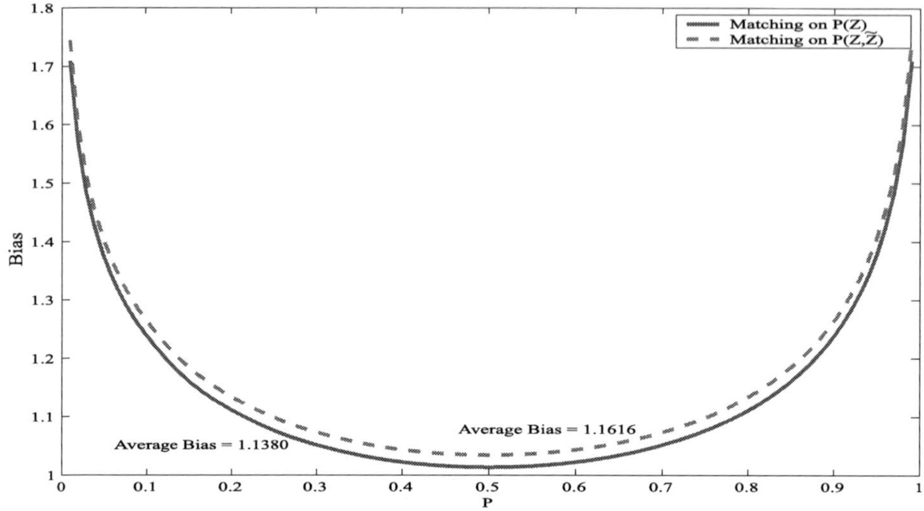

Figure 24A. Bias for treatment on the treated. *Source*: Heckman and Navarro (2004).

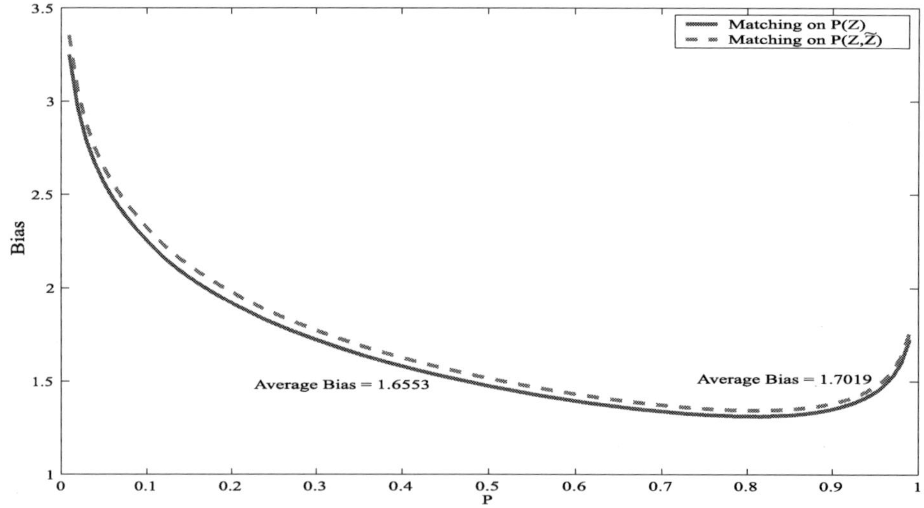

Note: Using proxy $\tilde{Z}$ for f_2 increases the bias. Correlation $(\tilde{Z}, f_2) = 0.5$.

Model:

$V = Z + f_1 + f_2 + \varepsilon_V$; $\varepsilon_V \sim N(0, 1)$; $f_1 \sim N(0, 1)$;

$Y_1 = 2f_1 + 0.1f_2 + \varepsilon_1$; $\varepsilon_1 \sim N(0, 1)$; $f_2 \sim N(0, 1)$

$Y_0 = f_1 + 0.1f_2 + \varepsilon_0$; $\varepsilon_0 \sim N(0, 1)$

Figure 24B. Bias for average treatment effect. *Source*: Heckman and Navarro (2004).

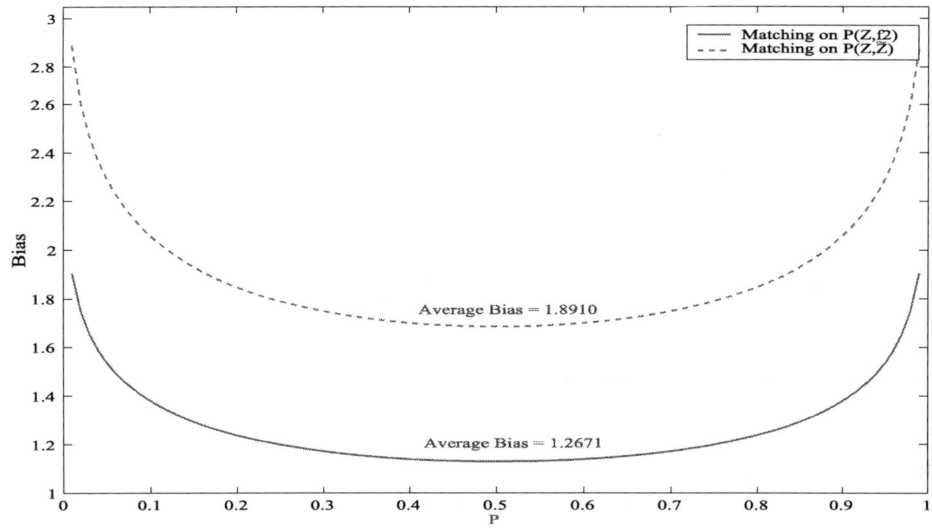

Figure 25A. Bias for treatment on the treated. *Source*: Heckman and Navarro (2004).

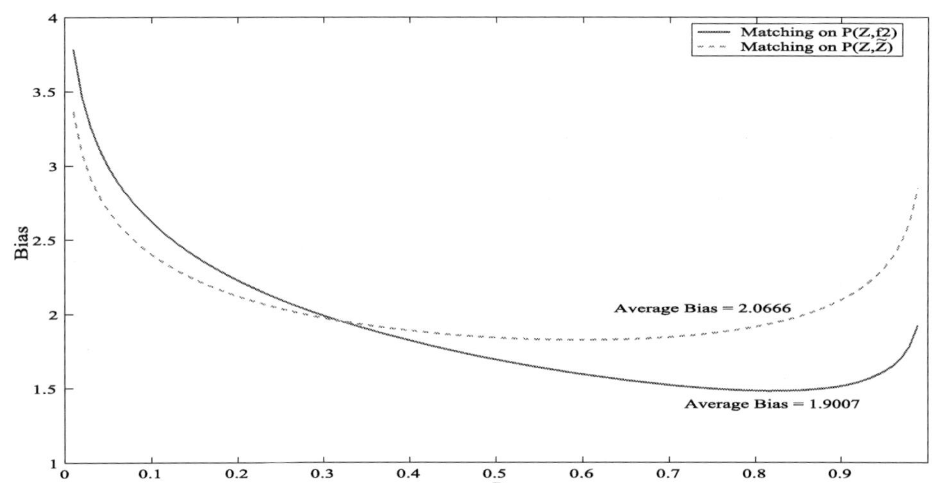

Note: Using proxy $\tilde{Z}$ for f_2 increases the bias. Correlation $(\tilde{Z}, f_2) = 0.5$.

Model:

$V = Z + f_1 + f_2 + \varepsilon_V$; $Y_1 = 2f_1 + 0.1f_2 + \varepsilon_1$; $Y_0 = f_1 + f_2 + \varepsilon_0$

$\varepsilon_V \sim N(0, 1)$; $\varepsilon_1 \sim N(0, 1)$; $\varepsilon_0 \sim N(0, 1)$

$f_1 \sim N(0, 1)$; $f_2 \sim N(0, 1)$

Figure 25B. Bias for average treatment effect. *Source*: Heckman and Navarro (2004).

8.5.6. On the use of model selection criteria to choose matching variables

We have already shown by way of example that adding more variables from a minimal relevant information set, but not all variables in it, may increase bias. By a parallel argument, adding additional variables to the relevant conditioning set may make the bias worse. Although we have used our prototypical Roy model as our point of departure, the point is more general.

There is no rigorous rule for choosing the conditioning variables that produce (M-1). Adding variables that are statistically significant in the treatment choice equation is not guaranteed to select a set of conditioning variables that satisfies condition (M-1). This is demonstrated by the analysis of Section 8.5.3 that shows that adding f_2 when it determines D may increase bias at any selected value of p.

The existing literature [e.g., Heckman et al. (1998)] proposes criteria based on selecting a set of conditioning variables based on a goodness of fit criterion (λ), where a higher λ means a better fit in the equation predicting D. The intuition behind such criteria is that by using some measure of goodness of fit as a guiding principle one is using information relevant to the decision process. In the example of Section 8.5.3, using f_2 improves goodness of fit of the model for D, but increases bias for the parameters. In general, such a rule is deficient if f_1 is not known or is not used.

An implicit assumption underlying such procedures is that the added conditioning variables $\mathcal{X}$ are exogenous in the following sense:

(E-1) $(Y_0, Y_1) \perp\!\!\!\perp D \mid I_{\text{int}}, \mathcal{X}$,

where I_{int} is interpreted as the variables initially used as conditioning variables before $\mathcal{X}$ is added. Failure of exogeneity is a failure of (M-1) for the augmented conditioning set, and matching estimators based on the augmented information set $(I_{\text{int}}, \mathcal{X})$ are biased when the condition is not satisfied.

Exogeneity assumption (E-1) is not usually invoked in the matching literature, which largely focuses on problem P-1, evaluating a program in place, rather than extrapolating to new environments (P-2). Indeed, the robustness of matching to such exogeneity assumptions is trumpeted as one of the virtues of the method. In this section, we show some examples that illustrate the general point that standard model selection criteria fail to produce correctly specified conditioning sets unless some version of exogeneity condition (E-1) is satisfied.

In the literature, the use of model selection criteria is justified in two different ways. Sometimes it is claimed that they provide a *relative* guide. Sets of variables with better goodness of fit in predicting D (a higher λ in the notation of Table 12) are alleged to be better than sets of variables with lower λ in the sense that they generate lower biases. However, we have already shown that this is not true. We know that enlarging the analyst's information from $I_{\text{int}} = \{Z\}$ to $I'_{\text{int}} = \{Z, f_2\}$ will improve fit since f_2 is also in I_A and I_R. But, going from I_{int} to I'_{int} might increase the bias. So it is not true that combinations of variables that increase some measure of fit λ necessarily reduce the bias. Table 12 illustrates this point using our normal example. Going from row 1 to

Table 12

Variables in probit	Goodness of fit statistics λ		Average bias	
	Correct in-sample prediction rate	Pseudo-R^2	TT	ATE
Z	66.88%	0.1284	1.1380	1.6553
Z, f_2	75.02%	0.2791	1.2671	1.9007
Z, f_1, f_2	83.45%	0.4844	0.0000	0.0000
Z, S_1	77.38%	0.3282	0.9612	1.3981
Z, S_2	92.25%	0.7498	0.9997	1.4541

Model: $V = Z + f_1 + f_2 + \varepsilon_V$; $\varepsilon_V \sim N(0, 1)$; $Y_1 = 2f_1 + 0.1f_2 + \varepsilon_1$; $\varepsilon_1 \sim N(0, 1)$; $Y_0 = f_1 + 0.1f_2 + \varepsilon_0$; $\varepsilon_0 \sim N(0, 1)$; $S_1 = V + U_1$; $U_1 \sim N(0, 4)$; $S_2 = V + U_2$; $U_2 \sim N(0, 0.25)$; $f_1 \sim N(0, 1)$; $f_2 \sim N(0, 1)$.

row 2 (adding f_2) improves goodness of fit and increases the unconditional or overall bias for all three treatment parameters, because (E-1) is violated.

The following rule of thumb argument is sometimes invoked as an absolute standard against which to compare alternative models. In versions of the argument, the analyst asserts that there is a combination of variables I'' that satisfy (M-1) and hence produces zero bias and a value of $\lambda = \lambda''$ larger than that of any other I. In our examples, conditioning on $\{Z, f_1, f_2\}$ generates zero bias. We can exclude Z and still obtain zero bias. Because Z is a determinant of D, this shows immediately that the best fitting model does not necessarily identify the minimal relevant information set. In this example including Z is innocuous because there is still zero bias and the added conditioning variables satisfy (E-1) where $I_{\text{int}} = (f_1, f_2)$. In general, such a rule is not innocuous if Z is not exogenous. If goodness of fit is used as a rule to choose variables on which to match, there is no guarantee it produces a desirable conditioning set. If we include in the conditioning set variables $\mathcal{X}$ that violate (E-1), they may improve the fit of predicted probabilities but worsen the bias.

Heckman and Navarro (2004) produce a series of examples that have the following feature. Variables S (shown at the base of Table 12) are added to the information set that improve the prediction of D but are correlated with (U_0, U_1). Their particular examples use imperfect proxies (S_1, S_2) for (f_1, f_2). The point is more general. The S variables fail exogeneity and produce greater bias for TT and ATE but they improve the prediction of D as measured by the correct in-sample prediction rate and the pseudo-R^2. See the bottom two rows of Table 12.

We next turn to the method of randomization, which is frequently held up to be an ideal approach for evaluating social programs. Randomization attempts to use a random assignment to achieve the conditional independence assumed in matching.

9. Randomized evaluations

This section analyzes randomized social experiments as tools for evaluating social programs. In the introduction to this chapter, we discussed an ideal randomization where treatment status is randomly assigned. In this section, we discuss actual social experiments, where self-selection decisions often intrude on the randomization decisions of experimenters.

Two cases have been made for the application of social experimentation. One case is a classical argument in experimental design. Inducing variation in regressors increases precision of estimates and the power of tests. The other case focuses on solving endogeneity and self-selection problems. Randomization is an instrumental variable.[148] The two cases are mutually compatible, but involve different emphases.

Both cases can be motivated within a linear regression model for outcome Y with treatment indicator D and covariates X:

$$Y = X\alpha + D\beta + U, \tag{9.1}$$

where U is an unobservable. β may be the same for all observations (conditional on X) as in the common coefficient setup, or it may be a variable coefficient of the type extensively discussed in this chapter. D (and the X) may be statistically dependent on U. We also entertain the possibility that when β is random it is dependent on D, as in the generalized Roy model.

Both cases for social experimentation seek to secure identification of some parameters of (9.1) or parameters that can be generated from (9.1). Analysts advocating the first case for experimentation typically assume a common coefficient model for α and β. They address the problem that variation in (X, D) may be insufficient to identify or precisely estimate (α, β). Manipulating (X, D) through randomization, or more generally, through controlled variation, can secure identification. It is typically assumed that (X, D) is independent of U or at least mean independent. This is the traditional case analyzed in a large literature on experimental design in statistics.[149]

Good examples in economics of experimentation designed to increase the variation in the regressors are studies by Conlisk (1973), Conlisk and Watts (1969), and Aigner (1979a, 1979b, 1985). The papers by Conlisk show how experimental manipulation can solve a multicollinearity problem. In analyzing the effects of taxes on labor supply, it is necessary to isolate the effect of wages (the substitution effect) from the effect of pure asset income (the income effect) on labor supply. In observational data, empirical measures of wages and asset income are highly intercorrelated. In addition, asset income is often poorly measured. By experimentally assigning these variables as in the negative income tax experiments, it is possible to identify both income and substitution effects in labor supply equations [see Cain and Watts (1973)]. Aigner (1979b) shows how variation in the prices paid for electricity across the day can identify price effects that cannot be identified in regimes with uniform prices across all hours of the day.[150]

Random assignment is not essential to this approach. Any regressor assignment rule based on variables Q that are stochastically independent of U will suffice, although the

[148] See Heckman (1996).

[149] See, e.g., Silvey (1970).

[150] Zellner and Rossi (1987) present a comprehensive discussion of this literature.

efficiency of the estimates will depend on the choice of Q and care must be taken to avoid inducing multicollinearity by the choice of an assignment rule.

The second case for social experiments and the one that receives the most attention in applied work in economics and in this chapter focuses on the dependence between (X, D) and U that invalidates least squares as an estimator of the causal effect of X and D on Y. This is the problem of least squares bias raised by Haavelmo (1943) and extensively discussed in Chapter 70. In the second case, experimental variation in (X, D) is sought to make it "exogenous" or "external" to U. A popular argument in favor of experiments is that they produce simple, transparent estimates of the effects of the programs being evaluated in the presence of such biases. A quotation from Banerjee (2006) is apt:

> *The beauty of randomized evaluations is that the results are what they are: we compare the outcome in the treatment [group] with the outcome in the control group, see whether they are different, and if so by how much. Interpreting quasi-experiments sometimes requires statistical legerdemain, which makes them less attractive ...*

This argument assumes that interesting evaluation questions can be answered by the marginal distributions produced from experiments. It also assumes that no economic model is needed to interpret evidence, contrary to a main theme of this chapter.

Randomization is an instrument. As such, it shares all of the assets and liabilities of IV already discussed. In particular, randomization applied to a correlated random coefficient (or a model of essential heterogeneity) raises the same issues about the multiplicity of parameters identified by different randomizations as were discussed there in connection with the multiplicity of parameters identified by different instruments.

The two popular arguments for social experimentation are closely related. Exogenous variation in (X, D) can, if judiciously administered, solve collinearity, precision, and endogeneity problems. Applying the terminology of Chapter 70 to the analysis of model (9.1), randomization can identify a model that can solve all three policy evaluation problems: P-1, the problem of internal validity; P-2, the problem of extrapolation to new environments (by virtue of the linearity of (9.1)); and P-3, the problem of forecasting new policies that can be described by identifiable functions of (X, D) and any external variables.

As noted in the concluding section of Chapter 70, the modern literature tends to reject functional form assumptions such as those embodied in Equation (9.1). It has evolved towards a more focused attempt to solve problem P-1 to protect against endogeneity of D with respect to U. Sometimes the parameter being identified is not clearly specified. When it is, this focus implements Marschak's Maxim of doing one thing well, as discussed in Chapter 70.

Common to the literature on IV estimation, proponents of randomization often ignore the consequences of heterogeneity in β and dependence of β on D – the problem of essential heterogeneity. Our discussion in the previous sections applies with full force to randomization as an instrument. Only if the randomization (instrument) corresponds exactly to the policy that is sought to be evaluated will the IV (randomization) identify the parameters of economic interest.[151] This section considers the case for randomization as an instrumental variable to solve endogeneity problems.

9.1. *Randomization as an instrumental variable*

The argument justifying randomization as an instrument assumes that randomization (or more generally the treatment assignment rule) does not alter subjective or objective potential outcomes. This is covered by assumption (PI-3) presented in Chapter 70. We also maintain absence of general equilibrium effects (PI-4) throughout this section. We discuss violations of (PI-3) when we discuss randomization bias.[152,153]

To be explicit about particular randomization mechanisms, we return to our touchstone generalized Roy model. Potential outcomes are (Y_0, Y_1) and cost of participation is C. Assume perfect certainty in the absence of randomization. Under self-selection, the treatment choice is governed by

$$D = \mathbf{1}(Y_1 - Y_0 - C \geqslant 0).$$

This model of program participation abstracts from the important practical feature of many social programs that multiple agents contribute to decisions about program participation. We consider a more general framework in Section 9.5. We assume additive separability between the observables (X, W) and the unobservables (U_0, U_1, U_C) for convenience:

$$\begin{aligned}
&Y_1 = \mu_1(X) + U_1, \qquad Y_0 = \mu_0(X) + U_0,\\
&C = \mu_C(W) + U_C, \qquad V = U_1 - U_0 - U_C,\\
&\mu_I(X, W) = \mu_1(X) - \mu_0(X) - \mu_C(W), \qquad Z = (X, W).
\end{aligned}$$

Only some components of X and/or W may be randomized. Randomization can be performed unconditionally or conditional on strata, Q, where the strata may or may not include components of (X, W) that are not randomized. Specifically, it can be performed conditional on X, just as in our analysis of IV. Parameters can be defined conditional on X.[154] Examples of treatments randomly assigned include the tax/benefit plans of the negative income tax programs; the price of electricity over the course of the day; variable tolls and bonuses; textbooks to pupils; reducing class size. Under invariance condition (PI-3), the functions $\mu_0(X)$, $\mu_1(X)$, $\mu_C(W)$ (and hence $\mu_I(X, W)$) are

[151] The exchange between Banerjee (2006) and Deaton (2006) raises this point.

[152] We maintain the absence of general equilibrium or spill over effects, assumption (PI-2). Such effects are discussed in Abbring and Heckman (Chapter 72).

[153] For evaluation of distributional and mean parameters, assumption (PI-3) can be weakened as in our invocation of policy invariance for the MTE to say that randomization does not alter the distributions of outcomes or certain means or conditional means (recall assumption (A-7)).

[154] In Equation (9.1), if X is endogenous and we randomize treatment D conditional on X with respect to U, we cannot identify α, but we can identify β.

invariant to such modifications. The intervention is assumed to change the arguments of functions without shifting the functions themselves. Thus for the intervention of randomization, the functions are assumed to be structural in the sense of Hurwicz (1962). The distributions of (U_0, U_1, U_C) conditional on X, and hence the distribution of V conditional on X, are also invariant. Under full compliance, the manipulated Z are the same as the Z facing the agent. We formalize this assumption:

(R-4) *The Z assigned agent ω conditional on X are the Z realized and acted on by the agent conditional on X.*[155]

In terms of the generalized Roy model, this assumption states that the Z assigned ω given X is the W that appears in the cost function and the derived decision rule.

Some randomizations alter the environments facing agents in a more fundamental way by introducing new random variables into the model instead of modifying the variables that would be present in a pre-experimental environment. Comparisons of these randomizations involve an implicit dynamics, better exposited using the dynamic models presented in Abbring and Heckman (Chapter 72). For simplicity and to present some main ideas, we initially invoke an implicit dynamics suitable to the generalized Roy model. We develop a more explicit dynamic model of randomized evaluation in Section 9.5.

The most commonly used randomizations restrict eligibility either in advance of agent decisions about participation in a program or after agent decisions are made, but before actual participation begins. Unlike statistical discussions of randomization, we build agent choice front and center into our analysis. Agents choose and experimenters can only manipulate choice sets.

Let $\xi = 1$ if an agent is eligible to participate in the program; $\xi = 0$ otherwise. $\tilde{\xi} = \{0, 1\}$ is the set of possible values of ξ. Let D indicate participation under ordinary conditions. In the absence of randomization, D is an indicator of whether the agent actually participates in the program. Let actual participation be A. By construction, under invariance condition (PI-3) presented in Chapter 70,

$$A = D\xi. \tag{9.2}$$

This assumes that eligibility is strictly enforced.

There is a distinction between desired participation by the agent (D) and actual participation (A). This distinction is conceptually distinct from the *ex-ante*, *ex-post* distinction. At all stages of the application and enrollment process, agents may be perfectly informed about their value of ξ and desire to participate (D), but may not be allowed to participate. On the other hand, the agent may be surprised by ξ after applying to the program. In this case, there is revelation of information and there is a distinction between *ex ante* expectations and *ex post* realizations. Our analysis covers both cases.

We consider two types of randomization of eligibility.

[155] Assumptions (R-1)–(R-3) are presented in Section 2.

RANDOMIZATION OF TYPE 1. *A random mechanism (possibly conditional on* (X, Z)*) is used to determine* ξ*. The probability of eligibility is* $\Pr(\xi = 1 \mid X, Z)$.

For this type of randomization, in the context of the generalized Roy model, it is assumed that

(e-1a) $\xi \perp\!\!\!\perp (U_0, U_1, U_C) \mid X, Z$ *(Randomization of eligibility)*

and

(e-1b) $\Pr(A = 1 \mid X, Z, \xi)$ *depends on* ξ.

This randomization affects the eligibility of the agent for the program but because agents still self-select, there is no assurance that eligible agents will participate in the program. This condition does not impose exogeneity on X, Z.[156] Thus Z can fail as an instrument but ξ remains a valid instrument. Alternatively, (e-1a) and (e-1b) may be formulated according to the notation of Imbens and Angrist (1994). Define $A(z, e)$ to be the value of A when we set $Z = z$ and $\xi = e$. Define $\mathcal{Z}$ as the set of admissible Z and $\widetilde{\xi}$ as the set of admissible ξ. In this notation, we may rewrite assumptions (e-1a) and (e-1b) as

(e-1a)′ $\xi \perp\!\!\!\perp (Y_0, Y_1, \{A(z, e)\}_{(z,e) \in \mathcal{Z} \times \widetilde{\xi}}) \mid X, Z$

and

(e-1b)′ $\Pr(A = 1 \mid X, Z, \xi)$ *depends on* ξ.[157]

A second type of randomization conditions on individuals manifesting a desire to participate through their decision to apply to the program. This type of randomization is widely used.

RANDOMIZATION OF TYPE 2. *Eligibility may be a function of* D *(conditionally on some or all components of* X, Z, Q *or unconditionally). It is common to deny entry into programs among people who applied and were accepted into the program* $(D = 1)$ *so the probability of eligibility is* $\Pr(\xi = 1 \mid X, Z, Q, D = 1)$. *This assumes* (PI-3) *stated in Chapter* 70.

For this type of randomization of eligibility, it is assumed that

(e-2a) $\xi \perp\!\!\!\perp (U_0, U_1) \mid X, Z, Q, D = 1$

and

[156] In place of the randomization, one might assign treatment on the basis of external variables Q including variables in addition to X and Z. Care must be taken to avoid inducing collinearity problems. Random assignment is simpler. It produces through randomization the independent variation assumed in matching.

[157] When ξ is deterministic, (e-1a)′ is trivially satisfied.

(e-2b) $\Pr(A = 1 \mid X, Z, D = 1, \xi = 1) = 1; \Pr(A = 1 \mid X, Z, D = 1, \xi = 0) = 0.$

Agent failure to comply with the eligibility rules or protocols of experiments can lead to violations of (e-1) and/or (e-2).

An equivalent way to formulate (e-2a) and (e-2b) uses the Imbens–Angrist notation for IV:

(e-2a)′ $\xi \perp\!\!\!\perp (Y_0, Y_1) \mid X, Z, Q, D = 1$

and

(e-2b)′ $\Pr(A = 1 \mid X, Z, D = 1, \xi = 1) = 1; \Pr(A = 1 \mid X, Z, D = 1, \xi = 0) = 0.$

Both randomizations are instruments as defined in Section 4. Under the stated conditions, both satisfy (IV-1) and (IV-2), suitably redefined for eligibility randomizations, replacing D by A.

A variety of conditioning variables is permitted by these definitions. Thus, (e-1) and (e-2) allow for the possibility that the conventional instruments Z fail (IV-1) and (IV-2), but nonetheless the randomization generates a valid instrument ξ. The simplest randomizations do not condition on any variables.[158] We next consider what these instruments identify.

9.2. *What does randomization identify?*[159]

Under invariance assumption (PI-3) and under one set of randomization assumptions just presented, IV is an instrument that identifies some treatment effect for an ongoing program. The question is: which treatment effect? Following our discussion of IV with essential heterogeneity presented in Section 4, different randomizations (or instruments) identify different parameters unless there is a common coefficient model ($Y_1 - Y_0 = \beta(X)$ is the same for everyone given X) or unless there is no dependence between the treatment effect ($Y_1 - Y_0$) and the indicator D of the agents' desire to participate in the treatment. In these two special cases, all mean treatment parameters are the same. Using IV, we can identify the marginal distributions $F_0(y_0 \mid X)$ and $F_1(y_1 \mid X)$.[160]

In a model with essential heterogeneity, the instruments generated by randomization can identify parameters that are far from the parameters of economic interest. Randomization of components of W (or Z given X) under (R-4) and conditions (IV-1) and (IV-2) from Section 2 produces instruments with the same problems and possibilities as analyzed in our discussion of instrumental variables. Using W as an instrument may lead to negative weights on the underlying LATEs or MTEs.[161] Thus, unless we condi-

[158] We do not discuss optimal randomized experiments and the best choice of a randomization mechanism.

[159] This subsection is based on Heckman (1992).

[160] We can also identify $F_0(y_0 \mid X, Z)$ and $F_1(y_1 \mid X, Z)$ if Z does not satisfy the conditions required for it to be an instrument but experimental variation provides new instruments.

[161] In the special case where randomization of some components of W makes them fully independent of the other components of W, under monotonicity for the randomized component irrespective of the values of the other components, the IV weights must be nonnegative.

tion on the other instruments, the IV defined by randomization can be negative even if all of the underlying treatment effects or LATEs and MTEs generating choice behavior are positive. The weighted average of the MTE generated by the instrument may be far from the policy relevant treatment effect.

Under (PI-3) and (e-1), or equivalently (e-1)′, the first type of eligibility randomization identifies $\Pr(D = 1 \mid X, Z)$ (the choice probability) and hence relative subjective evaluations, and the marginal outcome distributions $F_0(y_0 \mid X, D = 0)$ and $F_1(y_1 \mid X, D = 1)$ for the eligible population ($\xi = 1$). Agents made eligible for the program self-select as usual. For those deemed ineligible ($\xi = 0$), under our assumptions, we would identify the distribution of Y_0, which can be partitioned into components for those who would have participated in the program had it not been for the randomization and components for those who would not have participated if offered the opportunity to do so:

$$\begin{aligned} F_0(y_0 \mid X) = {} & F_0(y_0 \mid X, D = 0) \Pr(D = 0 \mid X) \\ & + F_0(y_0 \mid X, D = 1) \Pr(D = 1 \mid X). \end{aligned}$$

Since we know $F_0(y_0 \mid X, D = 0)$ and $\Pr(D = 1 \mid X)$ from the eligible population, we can identify $F_0(y_0 \mid X, D = 1)$. This is the new piece of information produced by the randomization compared to what can be obtained from standard observational data. In particular, we can identify the parameter TT, $E(Y_1 - Y_0 \mid X, D = 1)$, but without further assumptions, we cannot identify the other treatment parameters ATE ($= E(Y_1 - Y_0 \mid X)$) or the joint distributions $F(y_0, y_1 \mid X)$ or $F(y_0, y_1 \mid X, D = 1)$.

To show that ξ is a valid instrument for A, form the Wald estimand,

$$\mathrm{IV}_{(\text{e-1})} = \frac{E(Y \mid \xi = 1, Z, X) - E(Y \mid \xi = 0, Z, X)}{\Pr(A = 1 \mid \xi = 1, Z, X) - \Pr(A = 1 \mid \xi = 0, Z, X)}. \tag{9.3}$$

Under invariance assumption (PI-3), $\Pr(D = 1 \mid Z, X)$ is the same in the presence or absence of randomization.[162] Assuming full compliance so that agents randomized to ineligibility do not show up in the program,

$$\Pr(A = 1 \mid \xi = 0, Z, X) = 0,$$

and

$$\begin{aligned} E(Y \mid \xi = 0, Z, X) &= E(Y_0 \mid Z, X) \\ &= E(Y_0 \mid D = 1, X, Z) \Pr(D = 1 \mid X, Z) \\ &\quad + E(Y_0 \mid D = 0, X, Z) \Pr(D = 0 \mid X, Z). \end{aligned}$$

If Z also satisfies the requirement (IV-1) that it is an instrument, then $E(Y_0 \mid Z, X) = E(Y_0 \mid X)$. Under (e-1) or (e-1)′ we do not have to assume that Z is a valid instrument.[163] Using (e-1) and assumption (PI-3), the first term in the numerator of (9.3) can

[162] $\Pr(D = 1 \mid Z, X, \xi = 0) = \Pr(D = 1 \mid Z, X, \xi = 1)$.

[163] If Z fails to be an instrument, absorb Z into X.

be written as

$$E(Y \mid \xi = 1, Z, X) = E(Y_1 \mid D = 1, Z, X) \Pr(D = 1 \mid Z, X) + E(Y_0 \mid D = 0, Z, X) \Pr(D = 0 \mid Z, X).$$

Substituting this expression into the numerator of Equation (9.3) and collecting terms, $\mathrm{IV}_{(\text{e-1})}$ identifies the parameter treatment on the treated:

$$\mathrm{IV}_{(\text{e-1})} = E(Y_1 - Y_0 \mid D = 1, Z, X).$$

It does not identify the other mean treatment effects, such as LATE or the average treatment effect ATE, unless the common coefficient model governs the data or $(Y_1 - Y_0)$ is mean independent of D. Using the result that $F(y \mid X) = E(\mathbf{1}(Y \leqslant y) \mid X)$, $\mathrm{IV}_{(\text{e-1})}$ also identifies $F_0(y_0 \mid X, D = 1)$, since we can compute conditional means of $\mathbf{1}(Y \leqslant y)$ for all y. The distribution $F_1(y_1 \mid X, D = 1)$ can be identified from observational data. Thus we can identify the outcome distributions for Y_0 and for Y_1 separately, conditional on $D = 1, X, Z$, but without additional assumptions we cannot identify the joint distribution of outcomes or the other treatment parameters.

Randomization not conditional on (X, Z) ($\xi \perp\!\!\!\perp (X, Z)$) creates an instrument ξ that satisfies the monotonicity or uniformity conditions. If the randomization is performed on (X, Z) strata, then the IV must be used conditional on the strata variables to ensure monotonicity is satisfied.

The second type of eligibility randomization proceeds conditionally on $D = 1$. Accordingly, data generated from such experiments do not identify choice probabilities ($\Pr(D = 1 \mid X, Z)$) and hence do not identify the subjective evaluations of agents [Heckman (1992), Moffitt (1992)]. Under (PI-3) and (e-2) (or equivalent conditions (e-2)$'$) randomization identifies $F_0(y_0 \mid D = 1, X, Z)$ from the data on the randomized-out participants. This conditional distribution cannot be constructed from ordinary observational data unless additional assumptions are invoked. From the data for the eligible ($\xi = 1$) population, we identify $F_1(y_1 \mid D = 1, X, Z)$.

The Wald estimator for mean outcomes in this case is

$$\mathrm{IV}_{(\text{e-2})} = \frac{E(Y \mid D = 1, \xi = 1, X, Z) - E(Y \mid D = 1, \xi = 0, X, Z)}{\Pr(A = 1 \mid D = 1, \xi = 1, X, Z) - \Pr(A = 1 \mid D = 1, \xi = 0, X, Z)}.$$

Under (e-2)/(e-2)$'$,

$$\Pr(A = 1 \mid D = 1, \xi = 1, X, Z) = 1,$$
$$\Pr(A = 1 \mid D = 1, \xi = 0, X, Z) = 0,$$
$$E(Y \mid A = 0, D = 1, \xi = 0, X, Z) = E(Y_0 \mid D = 1, X, Z) \quad \text{and}$$
$$E(Y \mid A = 1, D = 1, \xi = 1, X, Z) = E(Y_1 \mid D = 1, X, Z).$$

Thus,

$$\mathrm{IV}_{(\text{e-2})} = E(Y_1 - Y_0 \mid D = 1, X, Z).$$

In the general model with essential heterogeneity, randomized trials with full compliance that do not disturb the activity being evaluated answer a limited set of questions, and do not in general identify the policy relevant treatment effect (PRTE). Randomizations have to be carefully chosen to make sure that they answer interesting economic questions. Their analysis has to be supplemented with the methods previously analyzed to answer the full range of policy questions addressed there.

Thus far we have assumed that the randomizations do not violate the invariance assumption (PI-3). Yet many randomizations alter the environment they are studying and inject what may be unwelcome sources of uncertainty into agent decision making. We now examine the consequences of violations of invariance.

9.3. *Randomization bias*

If randomization alters the program being evaluated, the outcomes of a randomized trial may bear little resemblance to the outcomes generated by an ongoing version of the program that has not been subject to randomization. In this case, assumption (PI-3) is violated. Such violations are termed "Hawthorne effects" and are called "randomization bias" in the economics literature.[164] The process of randomization may affect objective outcomes, subjective outcomes or both.

Even if (PI-3) is violated, randomization may still be a valid instrument for the altered program. Although the program studied may be changed, under the assumptions made in Section 9.2, randomization can produce "internally valid" treatment effects for the altered program. Thus randomization can answer policy question P-1 for a program changed by randomization, but not for the program as it would operate in the absence of randomization.

As noted repeatedly, a distinctive feature of the econometric approach to social program evaluation is its emphasis on choice and agent subjective evaluations of programs. This feature accounts for the distinction between the statistician's invariance assumption (PI-1) and the economist's invariance assumption (PI-3). (These are presented in Chapter 70.) It is instructive to consider the case where assumption (PI-1) is valid but assumption (PI-3) is not. This case might arise when randomization alters risk-averse agent decision behavior but has no effects on potential outcomes. Thus the $R(s, \omega)$ are affected, but not the $Y(s, \omega)$.

In this case, the parameter $\text{ATE}(X) = E(Y_1 - Y_0 \mid X)$ is the same in the ongoing program as in the population generated by the randomized trial. However, treatment parameters conditional on choices such as

$$\text{TT}(X) = E(Y_1 - Y_0 \mid X, D = 1),$$
$$\text{TUT}(X) = E(Y_1 - Y_0 \mid X, D = 0)$$

[164] See Campbell and Stanley (1963) for a discussion of Hawthorne effects and evidence of their prevalence in educational interventions. See Heckman (1992) for a discussion of randomization bias in economics.

are not, in general, invariant. If the subjective valuations are altered, so are the parameters based on choices produced by the subjective valuations. Different random variables generate the conditioning sets in the randomized and nonrandomized regimes and, in general, they will have a different dependence structure with the outcomes $Y(s,\omega)$. This arises because randomization alters the composition of participants in the conditioning set that defines the treatment parameter.

This analysis applies with full force to LATE. LATE based on $P(Z)$ for two distinct values of Z ($Z = z$ and $Z = z'$) is $E(Y_1 - Y_0 \mid X, P(z') \leqslant U_D \leqslant P(z))$. In the randomized trial, violation of (PI-3) because of lack of invariance of $R(s,\omega)$ changes U_D and the values of $P(Z)$ for the same $Z = z$. In general, this alters LATE.[165]

The case where (PI-1) holds, but (PI-3) does not, generates invariant conditional (on choice) parameters if there is no treatment effect heterogeneity or if there is such heterogeneity that is independent of D. These are the familiar conditions: (a) $Y_1 - Y_0$ is the same for all people with the same $X = x$ or (b) $Y_1 - Y_0$ is (mean) independent of D given $X = x$. In these cases, the MTE is flat in U_D.

In general, in a model with essential heterogeneity, even if the Rubin invariance conditions (PI-1) and (PI-2) are satisfied, but conditions (PI-3) and (PI-4) are not, treatment parameters defined conditional on choices are not invariant to the choice of randomization.[166] This insight shows the gain in clarity in interpreting what experiments identify from adopting a choice-theoretic, econometric approach to the evaluation of social programs, as opposed to the conventional approach adopted by statisticians. We now show another advantage of the economic approach in an analysis of noncompliance and its implications for interpreting experimental evidence.

9.4. Compliance

The statistical treatment effect literature extensively analyzes the problem of noncompliance.[167] Persons assigned to a treatment may not accept it. In the notation of Equation (9.3), let $\xi = 1$ if a person is assigned to treatment, $\xi = 0$ otherwise. Compliance is said to be perfect when $\xi = 1 \Rightarrow A = 1$ and $\xi = 0 \Rightarrow A = 0$. In the presence of self-selection by agents, these conditions do not, in general, hold. People assigned to treatment may not comply ($\xi = 1$ but $D = 0$). This is also called the "dropout" problem [Mallar, Kerachsky and Thorton (1980), Bloom (1984)]. In its formulation of this problem, the literature assumes that outcomes are measured for each participant but that outcomes realized are not always those intended by the randomizers.[168] In addition,

[165] Technically, for identifying MTE or LATE, we can get by with weaker conditions than (PI-3) and (PI-4). All we need is invariance of the conditional mean of $Y_1 - Y_0$ with respect to U_D. Recall our discussion of policy invariance surrounding our discussion of assumption (A-7).

[166] Rubin combines (PI-1) and (PI-2) in his "SUTVA" condition.

[167] See, e.g., Bloom (1984), Manski (1996), and Hotz, Mullin and Sanders (1997).

[168] The problem of missing data is called the attrition problem. Thus we assume no attrition from the database, but we allow for the possibility that people assigned to a treatment do not receive it.

people denied treatment may find substitutes for the treatment outside of the program. This is the problem of substitution bias. Since self-selection is an integral part of choice models, noncompliance, as the term is used by the statisticians, is a feature of most social experiments.

The econometric approach builds in the possibility of self-selection as an integral part of model specification. As emphasized in the econometric literature since the work of Gronau (1974), Heckman (1974a, 1974b, 1976b), and McFadden (1974), agent decisions to participate are informative about their subjective evaluations of the program. In the dynamic setting discussed in Section 3 of Chapter 72 of this Handbook, agent decisions to attrite from a program are informative about their update of information about the program [Heckman and Smith (1998), Chan and Hamilton (2006), Smith, Whalley and Wilcox (2006) and Heckman and Navarro (2007)]. Noncompliance is a source of information about subjective evaluations of programs.

Noncompliance is a problem if the goal of the social experiment is to estimate $\mathrm{ATE}(X) = E(Y_1 - Y_0 \mid X)$ without using the econometric methods previously discussed. We established in Section 9.3 that in the presence of self-selection, in a general case with essential heterogeneity, experiments under assumptions (PI-3) and (PI-4) and (e-1) or (e-2) identify $E(Y_1 - Y_0 \mid X, D = 1)$ instead of $\mathrm{ATE}(X)$.

Concerns about noncompliance often arise from adoption of the Neyman–Cox–Rubin "causal model" discussed in Chapter 70, Section 4.4. Experiments are conceived as tools for direct allocation of agricultural treatments. For that reason, that literature elevates ATE to pre-eminence as the parameter of interest because it is thought that this parameter can be produced by experiments. In social experiments, it is rare that the experimenter can force anyone to do anything. As the old adage goes, "you can lead a horse to water but you cannot make it drink". Agent choice behavior intervenes. Thus it is no accident that if they are not compromised, the two randomizations most commonly implemented directly identify parameters conditional on choices.[169]

There is a more general version of the noncompliance problem which requires a dynamic formulation. Agents are assigned to treatment ($\xi = 1$) and some accept ($D = 1$) but drop out of the program at a later stage. We need to modify the formulation in this section to cover this case. We now turn to that modification.

9.5. The dynamics of dropout and program participation

Actual programs are more dynamic in character than the stylized program just analyzed. Multiple actors are involved, such as the agents being studied and the groups administering the programs. People apply, are accepted, enroll, and complete the program. A fully dynamic analysis, along the lines of the models developed by Abbring

[169] Randomizations of treatment to entire geographically segmented regions can produce ATE assuming homogeneity in background conditions across regions. This is the logic behind the Progressa experiment [see Behrman, Sengupta and Todd (2005)].

and Heckman in Chapter 72, analyzes each of these decisions, accounting for the updating of agent and program administrators' information.[170] This section briefly discusses some new issues that arise in a more dynamic formulation of the dropout problem. Heckman (1992), Heckman, Smith and Taber (1998), Hotz, Mullin and Sanders (1997), and Manski (1996, 2003) discuss these issues in greater depth.

In this subsection, we analyze the effects of dropouts on inferences from social experiments and assume no attrition. Our analysis of this case is of interest both in its own right and as a demonstration of the power of our approach.

Consider a stylized multiple stage program. In stage "0", the agent (possibly in conjunction with program officials) decides to participate or not to participate in the program. This is an enrollment phase prior to treatment. Let $D_0 = 1$ denote that the agent does not choose to participate. $D_0 = 0$ denotes that the agent participates and receives some treatment among J possible program levels beyond the no treatment state. The outcome associated with state "0" is Y_0. This assumes that acts of inquiry about a program or registration in it have no effect on outcomes.[171] One could disaggregate stage "0" into recruitment, application, and acceptance stages, but for expositional simplicity we collapse these into one stage.

If the J possible treatment stages are ordered, say, by the intensity of treatment, then "1" is the least amount of treatment and "J" is the greatest amount. A more general model would allow people to transit to stage j but not complete it. The J distinct stages can be interpreted quite generally. If a person no longer participates in the program after stage j, $j = 1, \dots, J$, we set indicator $D_j = 1$. The person is assumed to receive stage j treatment. $D_J = 1$ corresponds to completion of the program in all J stages of its treatment phase. Note that, by construction, $\sum_{j=0}^{J} D_j = 1$. The sequential updating model developed by Abbring and Heckman in Chapter 72 can be used to formalize these decisions and their associated outcomes. We can also use the simple multinomial choice model developed and analyzed in Appendix B of Chapter 70.

Let $\{D_j(z)\}_{z \in \mathcal{Z}}$ be the set of potential treatment choices for choice j associated with setting $Z = z$. For each $Z = z$, $\sum_{j=0}^{J} D_j(z) = 1$. Using the methods exposited in Abbring and Heckman (Chapter 72), we could update the information sets at each stage. We keep this updating implicit. Different components of Z may determine different choice indicators. Array the collections of choice indicators evaluated at each $Z = z$ into a vector

$$D(z) = \left(\left\{D_1(z)\right\}_{z \in \mathcal{Z}}, \dots, \left\{D_J(z)\right\}_{z \in \mathcal{Z}}\right).$$

The potential outcomes associated with each of the $J + 1$ states are

$$Y_j = \mu_j(X, U_j), \quad j = 0, \dots, J.$$

[170] Heckman and Smith (1999) analyze the determinants of program participation for a job training program.

[171] Merely being interested in a program, such as an HIV treatment program, may signal information that affects certain outcomes prior to receiving any treatment. We ignore these effects, but can easily accommodate them by making application a stage of the program.

Y_0 is the no treatment state, and the Y_j, $j \geqslant 1$, correspond to outcomes associated with dropping out at various stages of the program. In the absence of randomization, the observed Y is

$$Y = \sum_{j=0}^{J} D_j Y_j,$$

the Roy–Quandt switching regime model. Let $\tilde{Y} = (Y_0, \ldots, Y_J)$ denote the vector of potential outcomes associated with all phases of the program. Through selection, the Y_j for persons with $D_j = 1$ may be different from the Y_j for persons with $D_j = 0$.

Appendix B of Chapter 70 gives conditions under which the distributions of the Y_j and the subjective evaluations R_j, $j = 0, \ldots, J$, that generate choices D_j are identified. Using the tools for multiple outcome models developed in Section 7, we can use IV and our extensions of IV to identify the treatment parameters discussed there.

In this subsection, we consider what randomizations at various stages identify. We assume that the randomizations do not disturb the program. Thus we invoke assumption (PI-3). Recall that we also assume absence of general equilibrium effects (PI-4). Let $\xi_j = 1$ denote whether the person is eligible to move beyond stage j. $\xi_j = 0$ means the person is randomized out of the program after completing stage j. A randomization at stage j with $\xi_j = 1$ means the person is allowed to continue on to stage $j + 1$, although the agent may still choose not to. We set $\xi_J \equiv 1$ to simplify the notation. The ξ_j are ordered in a natural way: $\xi_j = 1$ only if $\xi_\ell = 1$, $\ell = 0, \ldots, j - 1$. Array the ξ_j into a vector ξ and denote its support by $\tilde{\xi}$.

Because of agent self-selection, a person who does not choose to participate at stage j cannot be forced to do so. For a person who would choose k ($D_k = 1$) in a nonexperimental environment, Y_k is observed if $\prod_{\ell=0}^{k-1} \xi_\ell = 1$. Otherwise, if $\xi_{k-1} = 0$ but, say, $\prod_{\ell=0}^{k'-1} \xi_\ell = 1$ and $\prod_{\ell=0}^{k'} \xi_\ell = 0$ for $k' < k$, we observe $Y_{k'}$ for the agent. From an experiment with randomization administered at different stages, we observe

$$Y = \sum_{j=0}^{J} D_j \left(\sum_{k=0}^{j} \left(\prod_{\ell=0}^{k-1} \xi_\ell \right) (1 - \xi_k) Y_k \right).$$

To understand this formula, consider a program with three stages ($J = 3$) after the initial participation stage. For a person who would like to complete the program ($D_3 = 1$), but is stopped by randomization after stage 2, we observe Y_2 instead of Y_3. If the person is randomized out after stage 1, we observe Y_1 instead of Y_3.[172]

[172] A more descriptively accurate but notationally cumbersome framework would disaggregate the participation decision and would also recognize that enrolling in a program stage is different from completing it. Thus, let $D_{\mathrm{R}} = 1$ if a person is recruited, $D_{\mathrm{R}} = 0$ if not; $D_{\mathrm{A}} = 1$ if a person applies, $D_{\mathrm{A}} = 0$ if not; $D_{\mathrm{Acc}} = 1$ if a person is accepted, $D_{\mathrm{Acc}} = 0$ if not; $D_{1\mathrm{e}} = 1$ if a person enrolls in stage 1, $D_{1\mathrm{e}} = 0$ if not; $D_{1\mathrm{c}} = 1$ if a person completes stage 1, $D_{1\mathrm{c}} = 0$ if not; and so forth up to $D_{J\mathrm{e}} = 1$ or 0; $D_{J\mathrm{c}} = 1$ or 0. Associated with completing stage ℓ but no later stage is Y_ℓ, $\ell \in \{\mathrm{R}, \mathrm{A}, \mathrm{Acc}, 1\mathrm{e}, 1\mathrm{c}, \ldots, J\mathrm{e}, J\mathrm{c}\}$. Information can be revealed

Let A_k be the indicator that we observe the agent with a stage k outcome. This can happen if a person would have chosen to stop at stage k ($D_k = 1$) and survives randomization through k ($\prod_{\ell=0}^{k-1} \xi_\ell = 1$), or if a person would have chosen to stop at a stage later than k but was thwarted from doing so by the randomization and settles for the best attainable state given the constraint imposed by the randomization. We can express A_k as

$$A_k = D_k \prod_{\ell=0}^{k-1} \xi_\ell + \sum_{j \geqslant k} D_j \left(\prod_{\ell=0}^{k-1} \xi_\ell \right)(1 - \xi_k), \quad k = 1, \ldots, J.$$

If a person who chooses $D_k = 1$ survives all stages of randomization through $k - 1$ and hence is allowed to transit to k, we observe Y_k for that person. For persons who would choose $D_j = 1$, $j > k$, but get randomized out at k, i.e., $(\prod_{\ell=0}^{k-1} \xi_\ell)(1 - \xi_k) = 1$, we also observe Y_k.[173]

We now state the conditions under which sequential randomizations are instrumental variables for the A_j. Let $A_i(z, e_i)$ be the value of A_i when $Z = z$ and $\xi_i = e_i$. Array the A_i, $i = 1, \ldots, J$, into a vector

$$A(z, e) = \big(A_1(z, e_1), A_2(z, e_2), \ldots, A_J(z, e_J)\big).$$

A variety of randomization mechanisms are possible in which randomization depends on the information known to the randomizer at each stage of the program.

IV conditions for ξ are satisfied under the following sequential randomization assumptions. They parallel the sequential randomization conditions developed in the dynamic models analyzed by Abbring and Heckman (Chapter 72) of our contribution:

(e-3a) $\xi_i \perp\!\!\!\perp (\tilde{Y}, \{A(z, e)\}_{(z,e) \in \mathcal{Z} \times \tilde{\xi}}) \mid X, Z, D_\ell = 1$ *for* $\ell < i$, $\prod_{\ell=0}^{i-1} \xi_\ell = 1)$, *for* $i = 1, \ldots, J$,[174]

and

(e-3b) $\Pr(A_i = 1 \mid X, Z, D_\ell = 1$ for $\ell < i, \xi_i, \prod_{\ell=0}^{i-1} \xi_\ell = 1)$ *depends on* ξ_i, *for* $i = 1, \ldots, J$.

at stage ℓ. Observed Y is

$$Y = \sum_{\ell \in \{\mathrm{R}, \mathrm{A}, \mathrm{Acc}, 1e, 1c, \ldots, Je, Jc\}} D_\ell Y_\ell.$$

Randomization can be administered at any stage. We write $\xi_\ell = 0$ if $\prod_{j=1}^{\ell-1} \xi_j = 1$ and a person is randomized out at stage ℓ.

173 Assumption (PI-3) is crucial in justifying this formula. If randomization alters agent choice behavior, persons who would choose j but get randomized out at k, $k < j$, might change their valuations and decision rule (i.e., there may be randomization bias).

174 The special case where $\xi_J \equiv 1$ satisfies (e-3a), because in that case ξ_i is a constant.

These expressions assume that the components of $\tilde{Y} = (Y_0, \dots, Y_J)$ that are realized are known to the randomizer after the dropout decision is made, and thus cannot enter the conditioning set for the sequential randomizations.

To fix ideas, consider a randomization of eligibility ξ_0, setting $\xi_1 = \cdots = \xi_J = 1$. This is a randomization that makes people eligible for participation at all stages of the program. We investigate what this randomization identifies, assuming invariance conditions (PI-3) and (PI-4) hold. For those declared eligible,

$$E(Y \mid \xi_0 = 1) = \sum_{j=0}^{J} E(Y_j \mid D_j = 1) \Pr(D_j = 1). \tag{9.4}$$

For those declared ineligible,

$$E(Y \mid \xi_0 = 0) = \sum_{j=0}^{J} E(Y_0 \mid D_j = 1) \Pr(D_j = 1), \tag{9.5}$$

since agents cannot participate in any stage of the program and are all in the state "0" with outcome Y_0. From observed choice behavior, we can identify each of the components of (9.4). We observe $\Pr(D_j = 1)$ from observed choices of treatment, and we observe $E(Y_j \mid D_j = 1)$ from observed outcomes for each treatment choice. Except for the choice probabilities ($\Pr(D_j = 1)$, $j = 0, \dots, J$) and $E(Y_0 \mid D_0 = 1)$, we cannot identify individual components of (9.5) for $J > 1$. When $J = 1$, we can identify all of the components of (9.5). The individual components of (9.5) cannot, without further assumptions, be identified by the experiment, although the sum can be. Comparing the treatment group with the control group, we obtain the "intention to treat" parameter with respect to the randomization of ξ_0 alone, setting $\xi_1 = \cdots = \xi_J = 1$ for anyone for whom $\xi_0 = 1$,

$$E(Y \mid \xi_0 = 1) - E(Y \mid \xi_0 = 0) = \sum_{j=1}^{J} E(Y_j - Y_0 \mid D_j = 1) \Pr(D_j = 1). \tag{9.6}$$

For $J > 1$, this simple experimental estimator does not identify the effect of full participation in the program for those who participate ($E(Y_J - Y_0 \mid D_J = 1)$) unless additional assumptions are invoked, such as the assumption that partial participation has the same mean effect as full participation for persons who drop out at the early stages, i.e., $E(Y_j - Y_0 \mid D_j = 1) = E(Y_J - Y_0 \mid D_j = 1)$ for all j. This assumption might be appropriate if just getting into the program is all that matters – a pure signaling effect.

A second set of conditions for identification of this parameter is that $E(Y_j - Y_0 \mid D_j = 1) = 0$ for all $j < J$. Under those conditions, if we divide the mean difference by $\Pr(D_J = 1)$, we obtain the "Bloom" estimator [Mallar, Kerachsky and Thorton (1980), Bloom (1984)]

$$\mathrm{IV}_{\mathrm{Bloom}} = \frac{E(Y \mid \xi_0 = 1) - E(Y \mid \xi_0 = 0)}{\Pr(D_J = 1)},$$

assuming $\Pr(D_J = 1) \neq 0$. This is an IV estimator using ξ_0 as the instrument for A_J. In general, the mean difference between the treated and the controlled identifies only the composite term shown in (9.6). In this case, the simple randomization estimator identifies a not-so-simple or easily interpreted parameter.

More generally, if we randomize persons out after completing stage k ($[\prod_{\ell=0}^{k-1} \xi_\ell](1 - \xi_k) = 1$) and for another group establish full eligibility at all stages ($\prod_{\ell=0}^{J} \xi_\ell = 1$), we obtain

$$E\left[Y \,\middle|\, \prod_{\ell=0}^{J} \xi_\ell = 1\right] - E\left[Y \,\middle|\, \left(\prod_{\ell=0}^{k-1} \xi_\ell\right)(1 - \xi_k) = 1\right] = \sum_{j=k}^{J} E(Y_j - Y_k \mid D_j = 1) \Pr(D_j = 1),$$

and hence, since we know $E(Y_k \mid D_k = 1)$ and $\Pr(D_k = 1)$ from observational data, we can identify the combination of parameters

$$\sum_{j=k+1}^{J} E(Y_k \mid D_j = 1) \Pr(D_j = 1), \tag{9.7}$$

for each randomization that stops persons from advancing beyond level k, $k = 0, \ldots, J - 1$.

Observe that a randomization of eligibility that prevents people from going to stage $J - 1$ but not to stage J ($[\prod_{\ell=0}^{J-2} \xi_\ell](1 - \xi_{J-1}) = 1$) identifies $E(Y_J - Y_{J-1} \mid D_J = 1)$:

$$E(Y \mid \xi_0 = 1, \ldots, \xi_{J-2} = 1, \xi_{J-1} = 0) = \left[\sum_{j=0}^{J-1} E(Y_j \mid D_j = 1) \Pr(D_j = 1)\right] + E(Y_{J-1} \mid D_J = 1) \Pr(D_J = 1).$$

Thus,

$$E(Y \mid \xi_0 = 1, \ldots, \xi_J = 1) - E(Y \mid \xi_0 = 1, \ldots, \xi_{J-1} = 1, \xi_J = 0) = E(Y_J - Y_{J-1} \mid D_J = 1) \Pr(D_J = 1).$$

Since $\Pr(D_J = 1)$ is observed from choice data, as is $E(Y_J \mid D_J = 1)$, we can identify $E(Y_{J-1} \mid D_J = 1)$ from the experiment.

In the general case under assumptions (PI-3) and (PI-4), a randomization that prevents agents from moving beyond stage ℓ ($\xi_0 = 1, \ldots, \xi_{\ell-1} = 1, \xi_\ell = 0$) directly identifies

$$E(Y \mid \xi_0 = 1, \ldots, \xi_{\ell-1} = 1, \xi_\ell = 0) = \underbrace{\sum_{j=0}^{\ell} E(Y_j \mid D_j = 1) \Pr(D_j = 1)}_{\text{all components known from observational data}}$$

$$+ \underbrace{\sum_{j=\ell+1}^{J} E(Y_\ell \mid D_j = 1) \Pr(D_j = 1)}_{\text{sum and probability weights known, but not individual } E(Y_\ell \mid D_j = 1)}.$$

All of the components of the first set of terms on the right-hand side are known from observational data. The probabilities in the second set of terms are known, but the individual conditional expectations $E(Y_\ell \mid D_j = 1)$, $j = \ell + 1, \ldots, J$, are not known without further assumptions.

Randomization at stage ℓ is an IV. To show this, decompose the observed outcome Y into components associated with each value of A_j, the indicator associated with observing a stage j outcome:

$$Y = \sum_{j=0}^{J} A_j Y_j.$$

We can interpret ξ_ℓ as an instrument for A_ℓ. Keeping the conditioning on X, Z implicit, we obtain

$$\begin{aligned} \mathrm{IV}_{\xi_\ell} &= \frac{E[Y \mid \xi_\ell = 0] - E[Y \mid \xi_\ell = 1]}{\Pr(A_\ell = 1 \mid \xi_\ell = 0) - \Pr(A_\ell = 1 \mid \xi_\ell = 1)} \\ &= \frac{\sum_{j=\ell+1}^{J} E[Y_\ell - Y_j \mid D_j = 1] \Pr(D_j = 1)}{\sum_{j=\ell+1}^{J} \Pr(D_j = 1)}, \quad \ell = 0, \ldots, J - 1. \end{aligned}$$

By the preceding analysis, we know the numerator term but not the individual components. We know the denominator from choices measured in observational data and invariance assumption (PI-3). The IV formalism is less helpful in the general case.

Table 13 summarizes the parameters or combinations of parameters that can be identified from randomizations performed at different stages. It presents the array of factual and counterfactual conditional mean outcomes $E(Y_j \mid D_\ell = 1)$, $j = 0, \ldots, J$ and $\ell = 0, \ldots, J$. The conditional mean outcomes obtained from observational data are on the diagonal of the table ($E(Y_j \mid D_j = 1)$, $j = 0, \ldots, J$). Because of choices of agents, experiments do not directly identify the elements in the table that are above the diagonal. Under assumptions (PI-3) and (PI-4), experiments described at the base of the table identify the *combinations* of the parameters below the diagonal. Recall that if $\xi_\ell = 0$, the agent cannot advance beyond stage ℓ.[175] If we randomly deny eligibility to move to J ($\xi_{J-1} = 0$), we point identify $E(Y_{J-1} \mid D_J = 1)$, as well as the parameters that can be obtained from observational data. In general, we can only identify the combinations of parameters shown at the base of the table. Following Balke and Pearl (1997), Manski (1989, 1990, 1996, 2003), and Robins (1989), we can use the identified combinations

[175] This definition of ξ_ℓ assumes that $\xi_0 = \cdots = \xi_{\ell-1} = 1$.

Table 13
Parameters and combinations of parameters that can be identified by different randomizations

Choice probabilities (known)	Choice	Outcome						
		Y_0	Y_1	$\cdots$	Y_j	$\cdots$	Y_{J-1}	Y_J
$\Pr(D_0 = 1)$	D_0	$E(Y_0 \mid D_0 = 1)$	$E(Y_1 \mid D_0 = 1)$	$\cdots$	$E(Y_j \mid D_0 = 1)$	$\cdots$	$E(Y_{J-1} \mid D_0 = 1)$	$E(Y_J \mid D_0 = 1)$
$\Pr(D_1 = 1)$	D_1	$E(Y_0 \mid D_1 = 1)$	$E(Y_1 \mid D_1 = 1)$	$\cdots$	$E(Y_j \mid D_1 = 1)$	$\cdots$	$E(Y_{J-1} \mid D_1 = 1)$	$E(Y_J \mid D_1 = 1)$
$\Pr(D_2 = 1)$	D_2	$E(Y_0 \mid D_2 = 1)$	$E(Y_1 \mid D_2 = 1)$	$\cdots$	$E(Y_j \mid D_2 = 1)$	$\cdots$	$E(Y_{J-1} \mid D_2 = 1)$	$E(Y_J \mid D_2 = 1)$
$\vdots$	$\vdots$	$\vdots$	$\vdots$		$\vdots$		$\vdots$	$\vdots$
$\Pr(D_j = 1)$	D_j	$E(Y_0 \mid D_j = 1)$	$E(Y_1 \mid D_j = 1)$	$\cdots$	$E(Y_j \mid D_j = 1)$	$\cdots$	$E(Y_{J-1} \mid D_j = 1)$	$E(Y_J \mid D_j = 1)$
$\vdots$	$\vdots$	$\vdots$	$\vdots$		$\vdots$		$\vdots$	$\vdots$
$\Pr(D_{J-1} = 1)$	D_{J-1}	$E(Y_0 \mid D_{J-1} = 1)$	$E(Y_1 \mid D_{J-1} = 1)$	$\cdots$	$E(Y_j \mid D_{J-1} = 1)$	$\cdots$	$E(Y_{J-1} \mid D_{J-1} = 1)$	$E(Y_J \mid D_{J-1} = 1)$
$\Pr(D_J = 1)$	D_J	$E(Y_0 \mid D_J = 1)$	$E(Y_1 \mid D_J = 1)$	$\cdots$	$E(Y_j \mid D_J = 1)$	$\cdots$	$E(Y_{J-1} \mid D_J = 1)$	$E(Y_J \mid D_J = 1)$
Randomization		$\xi_0 = 0$	$\xi_1 = 0$	$\cdots$	$\xi_j = 0$	$\cdots$	$\xi_{J-1} = 0$	$\xi_J = 0$
New identified combinations of parameters		$\sum_{\ell=1}^{J}\{E(Y_0 \mid D_\ell = 1) \times \Pr(D_\ell = 1)\}$	$\sum_{\ell=2}^{J}\{E(Y_1 \mid D_\ell = 1) \times \Pr(D_\ell = 1)\}$	$\cdots$	$\sum_{\ell=j+1}^{J}\{E(Y_j \mid D_\ell = 1) \times \Pr(D_\ell = 1)\}$	$\cdots$	$E(Y_{J-1} \mid D_J = 1)$	

from different randomizations to bound the admissible values of counterfactuals below the diagonal of Table 13.

Heckman, Smith and Taber (1998) present a test for a strengthened version of the identifying assumptions made by Bloom.[176] They perform a sensitivity analysis to analyze departures from the assumption that dropouts have the same outcomes as nonparticipants. Hotz, Mullin and Sanders (1997) apply the Manski bounds in carefully executed empirical examples and show the difficulties involved in using the Bloom estimator in experiments with multiple outcomes. We next turn to some evidence on the importance of randomization bias.

9.6. *Evidence on randomization bias*

Violations of assumption (PI-3) in the general case with essential heterogeneity affect the interpretation of the outputs of social experiments. They are manifestations of a more general problem termed "Hawthorne effects" that arise from observing any population [see Campbell and Stanley (1963), Cook and Campbell (1979)]. How important is this theoretical possibility in practice? Surprisingly, very little is known about the answer to this question for the social experiments conducted in economics. This is so because randomized social experimentation has usually only been implemented on "pilot projects" or "demonstration projects" designed to evaluate new programs never previously estimated. Disruption by randomization cannot be confirmed or denied using data from these experiments. In one ongoing program evaluated by randomization by the Manpower Demonstration Research Corporation (MDRC), participation was compulsory for the target population [Doolittle and Traeger (1990)]. Hence randomization did not affect applicant pools or assessments of applicant eligibility by program administrators.

There is some information on the importance of randomization, although it is indirect. In the 1980s, the US Department of Labor financed a large-scale experimental evaluation of the ongoing, large-scale manpower training program authorized under the Job Training Partnership Act (JTPA). A study by Doolittle and Traeger (1990) gives some indirect information from which it is possible to determine whether randomization bias was present in an ongoing program.[177] Job training in the United States is organized through geographically decentralized centers. These centers receive incentive payments for placing unemployed persons and persons on welfare in "high-paying" jobs. The participation of centers in the experiment was not compulsory. Funds were set aside to compensate job centers for the administrative costs of participating in the experiment. The funds set aside range from 5 percent to 10 percent of the total operating costs of the centers.

In attempting to enroll geographically dispersed sites, MDRC experienced a training center refusal rate in excess of 90 percent. The reasons for refusal to participate are

[176] They show how to test Bloom's identifying assumption when it is made for distributions rather than just means.

[177] Hotz (1992) summarizes and extends their discussion.

Table 14
Percentage of local JTPA agencies citing specific concerns about participating in the experiment

Concern	Percentage of training centers citing the concern
1. Ethical and public relations implications of:	
a. Random assignment in social programs	61.8
b. Denial of services to controls	54.4
2. Potential negative effect of creation of a control group on achievement of client recruitment goals	47.8
3. Potential negative impact on performance standards	25.4
4. Implementation of the study when service providers do intake	21.1
5. Objections of service providers to the study	17.5
6. Potential staff administrative burden	16.2
7. Possible lack of support by elected officials	15.8
8. Legality of random assignment and possible grievances	14.5
9. Procedures for providing controls with referrals to other services	14.0
10. Special recruitment problems for out-of-school youth	10.5
Sample size: 228	

Notes: Concerns noted by fewer than 5 percent of the training centers are not listed. Percentages add up to more than 100.0 because training centers could raise more than one concern.
Source: Based on responses of 228 local JTPA agencies contacted about possible participation in the National JTPA Study.
Source: Heckman (1992), based on Doolittle and Traeger (1990).

given in Table 14. (The reasons stated there are not mutually exclusive.) Leading the list are ethical and public relations objections to randomization. Major fears (items 2 and 3) were expressed about the effects of randomization on the quality of applicant pool, which would impede the profitability of the training centers. By randomizing, the centers had to widen the available pool of persons deemed eligible, and there was great concern about the effects of this widening on applicant quality – precisely the behavior ruled out by assumptions (PI-3) and (PI-4). In attempting to entice centers to participate, MDRC had to reduce the randomized rejection probability from $\frac{1}{2}$ to as low as $\frac{1}{6}$ for certain centers. The resulting reduction in the size of the control group impairs the power of statistical tests designed to test the null hypothesis of no program effect. Compensation for participation was expanded sevenfold in order to get any centers to participate in the experiment. The MDRC analysts conclude:

> *Implementing a complex random assignment research design in an ongoing program providing a variety of services does inevitably change its operation in some ways. The most likely difference arising from a random assignment field study of program impacts is a change in the mix of clients served. Expanded recruitment efforts, needed to generate the control group, draw in additional applicants who are not identical to the people previously served. A second likely change is that the*

> *treatment categories may somewhat restrict program staff's flexibility to change service recommendations* [Doolittle and Traeger (1990), p. 121].

These authors go on to note that

> *Some [training centers] because of severe recruitment problems or up-front services cannot implement the type of random assignment model needed to answer the various impact questions without major changes in procedures* [Doolittle and Traeger (1990), p. 123].

This indirect evidence is hardly decisive even about the JTPA experiment, much less all experiments. Training centers may offer these arguments only as a means of avoiding administrative scrutiny, and there may be no "real" effect of randomization. During the JTPA experiment conducted at Corpus Christi, Texas, center administrators successfully petitioned the government of Texas for a waiver of its performance standards on the ground that the experiment disrupted center operations. Self-selection likely guarantees that participant sites are the least likely sites to suffer disruption. Such a selective participation in the experiment calls into question the validity of experimental estimates as a statement about the JTPA system as a whole, as it clearly poses a threat to external validity – problem P-2 as defined in Chapter 70. Torp et al. (1993) report similar problems in a randomized evaluation of a job training program in Norway.

Kramer and Shapiro (1984) note that subjects in drug trials were less likely to participate in randomized trials than in nonexperimental studies. They discuss one study of drugs administered to children afflicted with a disease. The study had two components. The nonexperimental phase of the study had a 4 percent refusal rate, while 34 percent of a subsample of the same parents refused to participate in a randomized subtrial, although the treatments were equally nonthreatening.

These authors cite further evidence suggesting that refusal to participate in randomization schemes is selective. In a study of treatment of adults with cirrhosis, no effect of the treatment was found for participants in a randomized trial. But the death rates for those randomized out of the treatment were substantially lower than among those individuals who refused to participate in the experiment, despite the fact that both groups were administered the same alternative treatment. Part of any convincing identification strategy by randomization requires that the agent document the absence of randomization bias. We next consider some evidence on the importance of dropping out and noncompliance with experimental protocols.

9.7. Evidence on dropping out and substitution bias

Dropouts are a feature of all social programs. Randomization may raise dropout rates, but the evidence for such effects is weak.[178] In addition, most social programs have good substitutes, so that the estimated effect of a program as typically estimated has to be

[178] See Heckman, LaLonde and Smith (1999).

defined relative to the full range of substitute activities in which nonparticipants engage. Experiments exacerbate this problem by creating a pool of persons who attempt to take training who then flock to substitute programs when they are placed in an experimental control group ($\xi = 0$ in the simple randomization analyzed in Sections 9.1–9.4).

Table 15 [reproduced from Heckman et al. (2000)] demonstrates the practical importance of both dropout and substitution bias in experimental evaluations. It reports the rates of treatment group dropout and control group substitution from a variety of social experiments. It reveals that the fraction of treatment group members receiving program services is often less than 0.7, and sometimes less than 0.5. Furthermore, the observed characteristics of the treatment group members who drop out often differ from those who remain and receive the program services.[179] With regard to substitution bias, Table 15 shows that as many as 40% of the controls in some experiments received substitute services elsewhere. In a simple one treatment experiment with full compliance ($\xi = 1 \Rightarrow A = 1$ and $\xi = 0 \Rightarrow A = 0$), all individuals assigned to the treatment group receive the treatment and there is no control group substitution, so that the difference between the fraction of treatments and controls that receive the treatment equals 1.0. In practice, this difference is often well below 1.0. Randomization reduced and delayed receipt of training in the experimental control group but by no means eliminated it. Many of the treatment group members received no treatment.

The extent of both substitution and dropout depends on the characteristics of the treatment being evaluated and the local program environment. In the NSW study, where the treatment was relatively unique and of high enough quality to be clearly perceived as valuable by participants, dropout and substitution rates were low enough to approximate the ideal case. In contrast, for the NJS and for other programs that provide low cost services widely available from other sources, substitution and dropout rates are high. In the NJS, the substitution problem is accentuated by the fact that the program relied on outside vendors to provide most of its training. Many of these vendors, such as community colleges, provided the same training to the general public, often with subsidies from other government programs such as Pell Grants. In addition, in order to help in recruiting sites to participate in the NJS, evaluators allowed them to provide control group members with a list of alternative training providers in the community. Of the 16 sites in the NJS, 14 took advantage of this opportunity to alert control group members to substitute training opportunities.

There are counterpart findings in the application of randomized clinical trials. For example, Palca (1989) notes that AIDS patients denied potentially life-saving drugs took steps to undo random assignment. Patients had the pills they were taking tested to see if they were getting a placebo or an unsatisfactory treatment, and were likely to drop out of the experiment in either case or to seek more effective medication, or both. In the MDRC experiment, in some sites qualified trainees found alternative avenues for securing exactly the same training presented by the same subcontractors by using other

[179] For the NSW shown in this table, see LaLonde (1984). For the NJS data, see Smith (1992).

Table 15
Fraction of experimental treatment and control groups receiving services in experimental evaluations of employment and training programs

Study	Authors/time period	Target group(s)	Fraction of treatments receiving services	Fraction of controls receiving services
1. NSW	Hollister et al. (1984) (9 months after RA)	Long-term AFDC women	0.95	0.11
		Ex-addicts	NA	0.03
		17–20 year old high school dropouts	NA	0.04
2. SWIM	Friedlander and Hamilton (1993) (Time period not reported)	AFDC women: applicants and recipients		
		a. Job search assistance	0.54	0.01
		b. Work experience	0.21	0.01
		c. Classroom training/OJT	0.39	0.21
		d. Any activity	0.69	0.30
		AFDC-U unemployed fathers		
		a. Job search assistance	0.60	0.01
		b. Work experience	0.21	0.01
		c. Classroom training/OJT	0.34	0.22
		d. Any activity	0.70	0.23
3. JOBSTART	Cave et al. (1993) (12 months after RA)	Youth high school dropouts		
		Classroom training/OJT	0.90	0.26
4. Project Independence	Kemple et al. (1995) (24 months after RA)	AFDC women: applicants and recipients		
		a. Job search assistance	0.43	0.19
		b. Classroom training/OJT	0.42	0.31
		c. Any activity	0.64	0.40
5. New chance	Quint et al. (1994) (18 months after RA)	Teenage single mothers		
		Any education services	0.82	0.48
		Any training services	0.26	0.15
		Any education or training	0.87	0.55
6. National JTPA Study	Heckman and Smith (1998) (18 months after RA)	Self-reported from survey data		
		Adult males	0.38	0.24
		Adult females	0.51	0.33
		Male youth	0.50	0.32
		Female youth	0.81	0.42
	Combined Administrative Survey Data			
		Adult males	0.74	0.25
		Adult females	0.78	0.34
		Male youth	0.81	0.34
		Female youth	0.81	0.42

(*Continued on next page*)

Table 15
(*Continued*)

Notes: RA = random assignment. H.S. = high school. AFDC = Aid to Families with Dependent Children. OJT=On the Job Training.
Service receipt includes any employment and training services. The services received by the controls in the NSW study are CETA and WIN jobs. For the Long Term AFDC Women, this measure also includes regular public sector employment during the period.
Sources for data: Maynard and Brown (1980), p. 169, Table A14; Masters and Maynard (1981), p. 148, Table A.15; Friedlander and Hamilton (1993), p. 22, Table 3.1; Cave et al. (1993), p. 95, Table 4.1; Quint et al. (1994), p. 110, Table 4.9; and Kemple et al. (1995), p. 58, Table 3.5; Heckman and Smith (1998) and calculations by the authors.
Source: Heckman, LaLonde and Smith (1999) and Heckman et al. (2000).

methods of financial support. Heckman, LaLonde and Smith (1999) discuss a variety of other problems that sometimes plague social experiments.

Our discussion up to this point has focused on point identification of parameters over the empirical supports. A large and emerging literature produces bounds on the parameters and distributions when point identification is not possible. We now consider bounds on the parameters within the framework of economic models of choice and the MTE.

10. Bounding and sensitivity analysis

Thus far we have assumed full support conditions and have presented conditions for identification over those supports. We now consider partial identification in the context of the MTE framework. We return to the two-outcome model to develop the basic approach in a simpler setting.

The central evaluation problem is that we observe the distribution of $(Y, D, X, Z) = (DY_1+(1-D)Y_0, D, X, Z)$, but do not observe the distribution of all of the components that comprise it (Y_1, Y_0, D, X, Z). Let η denote a distribution for (Y_1, Y_0, D, X, Z), and let it be known that η belongs to the class $\mathcal{H} \subset \mathcal{F}$, where $\mathcal{F}$ is the space of all probability distributions on (Y_1, Y_0, D, X, Z). Let P_η denote the resulting distribution of $(DY_1 + (1 - D)Y_0, D, X, Z)$ if η is the distribution for (Y_1, Y_0, D, X, Z). Let η^0 and P_{η^0} denote the corresponding true distributions. Knowledge of the distribution of $(DY_1+(1-D)Y_0, D, X, Z)$ allows us to infer that η lies in the set $\{\eta \in \mathcal{H}\colon P_\eta = P_{\eta^0}\}$. All elements of $\{\eta \in \mathcal{H}\colon P_\eta = P_{\eta^0}\}$ are consistent with the true distribution of the observed data.

Let $\mathcal{H}^0 = \{\eta \in \mathcal{H}\colon P_\eta = P_{\eta^0}\}$. Let E_η denote expectation with respect to the measure η, i.e., $E_\eta(A) = \int A\, d\eta$, so that $E(A) = E_{\eta^0}(A)$. Consider inference for ATE, $E(Y_1 - Y_0)$. Knowledge of the distribution of the observed variables allows us to infer that

$$E(Y_1 - Y_0) \in \left\{E_\eta(Y_1 - Y_0)\colon \eta \in \mathcal{H}^0\right\}.$$

The identification analyses of the previous sections proceed by imposing sufficient restrictions on $\mathcal{H}$ such that $\{E_\eta(Y_1 - Y_0)\colon \eta \in \mathcal{H}^0\}$ contains only one element and thus $E(Y_1 - Y_0)$ is point identified. Bounding analysis proceeds by finding a set $\mathcal{B}$ such that $\mathcal{B} \supseteq \{E_\eta(Y_1 - Y_0)\colon \eta \in \mathcal{H}^0\}$.[180] One goal of bounding analysis is to construct $\mathcal{B}$ such that $\mathcal{B} = \{E_\eta(Y_1 - Y_0)\colon \eta \in \mathcal{H}^0\}$ in which case the bounds are said to be *sharp*. If the bounds are sharp, then the bounds exploit all information and no smaller bounds can be constructed without imposing additional structure. In contrast, if $\{E_\eta(Y_1 - Y_0)\colon \eta \in \mathcal{H}^0\}$ is a proper subset of $\mathcal{B}$, then smaller bounds can be constructed. In every example we consider, the set $\{E_\eta(Y_1 - Y_0)\colon \eta \in \mathcal{H}^0\}$ is a closed interval, so that $\{E_\eta(Y_1 - Y_0)\colon \eta \in \mathcal{H}^0\} = [\inf_{\eta\in\mathcal{H}^0} E_\eta(Y_1 - Y_0), \sup_{\eta\in\mathcal{H}^0} E_\eta(Y_1 - Y_0)]$.

Sensitivity analysis is a commonly used procedure. It varies the parameters fixed in a model and determines the sensitivity of estimates to the perturbations of the parameter. Sensitivity analysis is formally equivalent to bounding. In particular, in sensitivity analysis, one parameterizes η and then constructs bounds based on letting the parameters vary over some set.[181] Parameterize η as $\eta(\theta)$ for some parameter vector $\theta \in \Theta$, and let θ^0 be the "true" parameter value so that $\eta^0 = \eta(\theta^0)$. θ is typically finite-dimensional, though it need not be. Let $\Theta^0 = \{\theta \in \Theta\colon P_{\eta(\theta)} = P_{\eta(\theta^0)}\}$. If θ is point identified given the observed variables, then Θ^0 will contain only one element, but if not all parameters are identified given the observed data then Θ will contain more than one element. Consider

$$\left\{E_{\eta(\theta)}(Y_1 - Y_0)\colon \theta \in \Theta^0\right\}.$$

This can trivially be seen as a special case of bounding analysis by taking $\mathcal{H} = \{\eta(\theta)\colon \theta \in \Theta\}$ and $\mathcal{H}^0 = \{\eta(\theta)\colon \theta \in \Theta^0\}$. Likewise, by taking a proper parameterization, any bounding analysis can be seen as a special case of sensitivity analysis.

We consider bounds on ATE. The corresponding bounds on treatment on the treated follow with trivial modifications.[182] We focus on bounds that exploit instrumental variable type assumptions or latent index assumptions, and we do not attempt to survey the entire literature on bounds.[183] We begin by describing the bounds that only assume that the outcome variables are bounded. We then consider imposing additional assumptions. We consider imposing the assumption of comparative advantage in the decision

[180] Examples of bounding analysis include Balke and Pearl (1997), Heckman, Smith and Clements (1997), Manski (1989, 1990, 1997, 2003) and Robins (1989).

[181] Examples of sensitivity analysis include Glynn, Laird and Rubin (1986), Smith and Welch (1986), and Rosenbaum (1995).

[182] We do not consider bounds on the joint distribution of (Y_1, Y_0). Identification of the joint distribution of (Y_1, Y_0) is substantially more difficult than identification of the ATE or treatment on the treated (TT). For example, even a perfect randomized experiment does not point identify the joint distribution of (Y_1, Y_0) without further assumptions. See Heckman and Smith (1993), Heckman, Smith and Clements (1997), and Heckman, LaLonde and Smith (1999) for an analysis of this problem.

[183] Surveys of the bounding approach include Manski (1995, 2003). Heckman, LaLonde and Smith (1999) includes an alternative survey of the bounding approach.

rule, then consider instead imposing an instrumental variables type assumption, and conclude by considering the combination of comparative advantage and instrumental variables assumptions. We examine the relative power of these alternative assumptions to narrow the very wide bounds that result from only imposing that the outcome variables are bounded.

10.1. Outcome is bounded

We first consider bounds on $E(Y_1 - Y_0)$ that only assume that the outcomes be bounded. We consider this case as a point of contrast for the later bounds that exploit instrumental variable conditions, and also for the pedagogical purpose of showing the bounding methodology in a simple context. We impose that the outcomes are bounded with probability 1.

ASSUMPTION B *(Outcome is Bounded).* For $j = 0, 1$,

$$\Pr(y^l \leqslant Y_j \leqslant y^u) = 1.$$[184]

In our notation, this corresponds to

$$\mathcal{H} = \{\eta \in \mathcal{F}\colon \eta[y^l \leqslant Y_1 \leqslant y^u] = 1, \eta[y^l \leqslant Y_0 \leqslant y^u] = 1\}.$$

For example, if Y is an indicator variable, then the bounds are $y^l = 0$ and $y^u = 1$.

Following Manski (1989) and Robins (1989), use the law of iterated expectations to obtain

$$E(Y_1) = \Pr[D = 1]E(Y_1 \mid D = 1) + (1 - \Pr[D = 1])E(Y_1 \mid D = 0),$$
$$E(Y_0) = \Pr[D = 1]E(Y_0 \mid D = 1) + (1 - \Pr[D = 1])E(Y_0 \mid D = 0).$$

$\Pr[D = 1]$, $E(Y_1 \mid D = 1)$, and $E(Y_0 \mid D = 0)$ are identified, while $E(Y_0 \mid D = 1)$ and $E(Y_1 \mid D = 0)$ are bounded by y^l and y^u, so that

$$\begin{aligned}
&\Pr[D = 1]E(Y_1 \mid D = 1) + (1 - \Pr[D = 1])y^l \\
&\quad \leqslant E(Y_1) \leqslant \Pr[D = 1]E(Y_1 \mid D = 1) + (1 - \Pr[D = 1])y^u, \\
&\Pr[D = 1]y^l + (1 - \Pr[D = 1])E(Y_0 \mid D = 0) \\
&\quad \leqslant E(Y_0) \leqslant \Pr[D = 1]y^u + (1 - \Pr[D = 1])E(Y_0 \mid D = 0)
\end{aligned}$$

[184] We assume that Y_1 and Y_0 have the same bounds for ease of exposition. The modifications required to analyze the more general case are straightforward.

and thus

$$\mathcal{B} = [B^L, B^U],$$

with

$$\begin{aligned} B^L &= \left(\Pr[D=1]E(Y \mid D=1) + \left(1-\Pr[D=1]\right)y^l\right) \\ &\quad - \left(\Pr[D=1]y^u + \left(1-\Pr[D=1]\right)E(Y \mid D=0)\right), \\ B^U &= \left(\Pr[D=1]E(Y \mid D=1) + \left(1-\Pr[D=1]\right)y^u\right) \\ &\quad - \left(\Pr[D=1]y^l + \left(1-\Pr[D=1]\right)E(Y \mid D=0)\right) \end{aligned}$$

with the width of these bounds given by

$$B^U - B^L = y^u - y^l.$$

For example, if $Y = 0, 1$, then the width of the bounds equals 1, $B^U - B^L = 1$.

These bounds are sharp. To show this, for any $M \in [B^L, B^U]$, one can trivially construct a distribution η of (Y_0, Y_1, D) which is consistent with the observed data, consistent with the restriction that the outcomes are bounded, and for which $E_\eta(Y_1 - Y_0) = M$, thus showing that $M \in [B^L, B^U]$. Since this is true for any $M \in [B^L, B^U]$, it follows that $[B^L, B^U] \subseteq \{E_\eta(Y_1 - Y_0)\colon \eta \in \mathcal{H}_0\}$. Since we have already shown that $[B^L, B^U]$ are valid bounds, $[B^L, B^U] \supseteq \{E_\eta(Y_1 - Y_0)\colon \eta \in \mathcal{H}_0\}$, we conclude that $[B^L, B^U] = \{E_\eta(Y_1 - Y_0)\colon \eta \in \mathcal{H}_0\}$ and thus that the bounds are sharp. This illustrates a common technique towards the construction of sharp bounds: in a first step, construct a natural set of bounds, and in a second step, use a proof by construction to show that the bounds are sharp.

Note the following features of these bounds. First, as noted by Manski (1990), these bounds always include zero. Thus, bounds that only exploit that the outcomes are bounded can never reject the null of zero average treatment effect. The bounds themselves depend on the data, but the width of the bounds, $B^U - B^L = y^u - y^l$, is completely driven by the assumed bounds on Y_1, Y_0. For example, if Y_1 and Y_0 are binary, the width of the bounds is always 1.

10.2. Latent index model: Roy model

The bounds that only impose that the outcomes are bounded are typically very wide, never provide point identification, and can never reject the null of zero average treatment effect. This lack of identifying power raises the question of whether one can impose additional structure to narrow the bounds. The central issue with bounding analysis is to explore the trade-off between assumptions and width of the resulting bounds. In this section, we discuss bounds that follow from maintaining Assumption B, that the outcomes are bounded, but also add the assumption of a Roy model for selection into treatment.[185] Such an assumption substantially narrows the width of the bounds compared to only imposing that the outcomes themselves are bounded, but does not provide point identification.

Again impose Assumption B: the outcomes are bounded. In addition, assume a model of comparative advantage, in particular,

ASSUMPTION RM *(Roy Model).*

$$D = \mathbf{1}[Y_1 \geqslant Y_0]. \tag{10.1}$$

Restriction RM imposes a special case of a latent index model, $D = \mathbf{1}[Y^* \geqslant 0]$ with $Y^* = Y_1 - Y_0$. Using the assumption of a Roy model while maintaining the assumption that the outcomes are bounded, we can narrow the bounds compared to the case where we only imposed that the outcomes are bounded. Peterson (1976) constructs the sharp bounds for the competing risks model, which is formally equivalent to a Roy model. Manski (1995) constructs the same bounds for the Roy model.

Following Peterson (1976) and Manski (1995), we have that

$$\begin{aligned} E[Y_1 \mid D = 1] &= E[Y_1 \mid Y_0 \leqslant Y_1] \\ &\geqslant E[Y_0 \mid Y_0 \leqslant Y_1] \\ &= E[Y_0 \mid D = 1] \end{aligned}$$

and by a parallel argument, $E[Y_0 \mid D = 0] \geqslant E[Y_1 \mid D = 0]$. We thus have upper bounds on $E(Y_0 \mid D = 1)$ and $E(Y_1 \mid D = 0)$. The lower bounds on $E[Y_0 \mid D = 1]$ and $E[Y_1 \mid D = 0]$ are the same as for the bounds that only imposed that the outcomes are bounded. We then have

$$E(Y_1 - Y_0) \in \mathcal{B} \equiv \left[B^L, B^U\right],$$

with

$$\begin{aligned} B^L &= \left(\Pr[D = 1]E(Y \mid D = 1) + \left(1 - \Pr[D = 1]\right)y^l\right) \\ &\quad - \left(\Pr[D = 1]E(Y \mid D = 1) + \left(1 - \Pr[D = 1]\right)E(Y \mid D = 0)\right), \\ B^U &= \left(\Pr[D = 1]E(Y \mid D = 1) + \left(1 - \Pr[D = 1]\right)E(Y \mid D = 0)\right) \\ &\quad - \left(\Pr[D = 1]y^l + \left(1 - \Pr[D = 1]\right)E(Y \mid D = 0)\right), \end{aligned}$$

[185] In contrast to the comparative advantage Roy model, one could instead impose an absolute advantage model as in the bounding analysis of Smith and Welch (1986). They assume that those with $D = 1$ have an absolute advantage over those with $D = 0$ in terms of their Y_1 outcomes: $\frac{1}{2}E(Y_1 \mid D = 1) \leqslant E(Y_1 \mid D = 0) \leqslant E(Y_1 \mid D = 1)$, and use this assumption to bound $E(Y_1)$. In their application, Y_1 is the wage and D is an indicator variable for working, so that there is not a well defined Y_0 variable. However, if one were to adapt their idea of absolute advantage to the treatment effect literature, one could assume, e.g., that $E(Y_0 \mid D = 0) \leqslant E(Y_0 \mid D = 1) \leqslant \frac{3}{2}E(Y_0 \mid D = 0)$ with the bounds on ATE following immediately from these assumptions.

and we can rewrite these bounds as

$$B^L = \big(1 - \Pr[D = 1]\big)\big(y^l - E(Y \mid D = 0)\big),$$
$$B^U = \Pr[D = 1]\big(E(Y \mid D = 1) - y^l\big),$$

with the width of the bounds given by

$$B^U - B^L = E(Y) - y^l.$$

For example, if $Y = 0, 1$, then the width of the bounds is given by $B^U - B^L = \Pr(Y = 1)$. Following an argument similar to that presented in the previous section, one can show that these bounds are sharp.

Note the following features of these bounds. First, the bounds do not involve y^u, and actually the same bounds will hold if we were to weaken the maintained assumption that $\Pr[y^l \leqslant Y_j \leqslant y^u] = 1$ for $j = 0, 1$, to instead only require that $\Pr[y^l \leqslant Y_j] = 1$. The width of the bounds imposing comparative advantage are $E(Y) - y^l$, so that the bounds will never provide point identification (as long as $E(Y) > y^l$). For example, if Y is binary, the width of the bounds is $\Pr[Y = 1]$, the bounds will not provide point identification unless all individuals have $Y = 0$. However, the bounds will always improve upon the bounds that impose only that the outcome is bounded – imposing comparative advantage shrinks the width of the bounds from $y^u - y^l$ to $E(Y) - y^l$, thus shrinking the bounds by an amount equal to $y^u - E(Y)$. For example, if Y is binary, then imposing the bounds shrinks the width of the bounds from 1 to $\Pr[Y = 1]$. Finally, note that the bounds will always include zero, so that imposing comparative advantage does not by itself allow one to ever reject the null of zero average treatment effect.

10.3. Bounds that exploit an instrument

The previous section considered bounds that exploit knowledge of the selection process, in particular that selection is determined by a Roy model. An alternative way to narrow the bounds over simply imposing that the outcome is bounded is to assume access to an instrument. We now discuss bounds with various types of instrumental variables assumptions. We begin with the Manski (1990) analysis for bounds that exploit a mean-independence condition, then consider the Balke and Pearl (1997) analysis for bounds that exploit a full statistical independence condition, and finally conclude with a discussion of Heckman and Vytlacil (1999) who combine an instrumental variable assumption with a nonparametric selection model.

10.3.1. Instrumental variables: Mean independence condition

Again impose Assumption B so that the outcomes are bounded. In addition, following Manski (1990), impose a mean-independence assumption:

ASSUMPTION IV.

$$E(Y_1 \mid Z = z) = E(Y_1),$$
$$E(Y_0 \mid Z = z) = E(Y_0)$$

for $z \in \mathcal{Z}$ where $\mathcal{Z}$ denotes the support of the distribution of Z.

For any $z \in \mathcal{Z}$, following the exact same series of steps as for the bounds that only imposed Assumption B, we have that

$$E(DY \mid Z = z) + \big(1 - P(z)\big)y^l \leqslant E(Y_1 \mid Z = z) \leqslant E(DY \mid Z = z) + \big(1 - P(z)\big)y^u.$$

By the IV assumption, we have $E(Y_1 \mid Z = z) = E(Y_1)$. Since these bounds hold for any $z \in \mathcal{Z}$, we have

$$\sup_{z\in\mathcal{Z}}\big\{E(DY \mid Z = z) + \big(1 - P(z)\big)y^l\big\} \leqslant E(Y_1) \leqslant \inf_{z\in\mathcal{Z}}\big\{E(DY \mid Z = z) + \big(1 - P(z)\big)y^u\big\}.$$

Applying the same analysis for $E(Y_0)$, we have

$$E(Y_1 - Y_0) \in \mathcal{B} = \big[B^L, B^U\big],$$

with

$$\begin{aligned} B^L &= \sup_{z\in\mathcal{Z}}\big\{E(DY \mid Z = z) + \big(1 - P(z)\big)y^l\big\} \\ &\quad - \inf_{z\in\mathcal{Z}}\big\{E\big((1 - D)Y \bigm| Z = z\big) + P(z)y^u\big\}, \\ B^U &= \inf_{z\in\mathcal{Z}}\big\{E(DY \mid Z = z) + \big(1 - P(z)\big)y^u\big\} \\ &\quad - \sup_{z\in\mathcal{Z}}\big\{E\big((1 - D)Y \bigm| Z = z\big) + P(z)y^l\big\}. \end{aligned}$$

As discussed by Manski (1994), these bounds are sharp under the mean-independence condition.[186] As noted by Manski (1990), these bounds do not necessarily include zero, so that it may be possible to use the bounds to test the null of zero average treatment effect. Let $p^u = \sup_{z\in\mathcal{Z}} \Pr[D = 1 \mid Z = z]$, $p^l = \inf_{z\in\mathcal{Z}} \Pr[D = 1 \mid Z = z]$. A trivial modification to Corollaries 1 and 2 of Proposition 6 of Manski (1994) shows that

(1) $p^u \geqslant \frac{1}{2}$ and $p^l \geqslant \frac{1}{2}$ is a necessary condition for $B^L = B^U$, i.e., for point identification from the mean independence condition.

[186] See Manski and Pepper (2000) for extensions of these bounds.

(2) If Y_1, Y_0 are independent of D, then the width of the IV-bounds is $((1 - p^u) + p^l)(y^u - y^l)$. Thus, if Y_1, Y_0 are independent of D, the bounds will collapse to point identification if and only if $p^u = 1$, $p^l = 0$.

Note that it is neither necessary nor sufficient for $P(z)$ to be a nontrivial function of z for these bounds to improve upon the bounds that only imposed that the outcome is bounded. Likewise, comparing these bounds to the comparative advantage bounds shows that neither set of bounds will in general be narrower than the other. Finally, note that these bounds are relatively complicated, and to evaluate the bounds and the width of the bounds requires use of $P(z)$, $E(YD \mid Z = z)$, and $E(Y(1 - D) \mid Z = z)$ for all $z \in \mathcal{Z}$.

10.3.2. Instrumental variables: Statistical independence condition

While Manski constructs sharp bounds for mean-independence conditions, Balke and Pearl (1997) construct sharp bounds for the statistical independence condition for the case where Y and Z are binary. Balke and Pearl impose the same independence condition as the Imbens and Angrist (1994) LATE independence condition. In particular, let D_0, D_1 denote the counterfactual choices that would have been made had Z been set exogenously to 0 and 1, respectively, and impose the following assumption.

ASSUMPTION IV-BP.

$$(Y_0, Y_1, D_0, D_1) \perp\!\!\!\perp Z.$$

Note that this strengthens the Manski conditions not only in imposing that potential outcomes are statistically independent of Z instead of mean-independent of Z, but also imposing that the counterfactual choices are independent of Z.

For the case of Z and Y binary, Balke and Pearl manage to transform the problem of constructing sharp bounds into a linear programming problem. Assuming that the identified set is a closed interval, the sharp bounds are by definition $[B^L, B^U]$ with

$$B^L = \inf_{\eta \in \mathcal{H}^0} E_\eta(Y_1 - Y_0),$$
$$B^U = \sup_{\eta \in \mathcal{H}^0} E_\eta(Y_1 - Y_0).$$

In general, the constrained set of distributions, $\eta \in \mathcal{H}^0$, may be high-dimensional and nonconvex. Using the assumption that Z and Y are binary, they transform the problem into the minimization of a linear function over a finite-dimensional vector space subject to a set of linear constraints. The resulting bounds are somewhat complex. For some distributions of the observed data, they will coincide with the Manski mean-independence bounds, but for other distributions of the observed data they will be narrower than the Manski mean-independence bounds. Thus, imposing statistical independence does narrow the bounds over the mean independence bounds.

It is not immediately clear how to generalize the Balke and Pearl analysis to distributions with continuous Z or Y, or how to construct sharp bounds under the statistical independence condition for Z or Y continuous. The appropriate generalization of Balke and Pearl's analysis to a more general setting remains an open question.

10.3.3. Instrumental variables: Nonparametric selection model/LATE conditions

We started with the mean independence version of the instrumental variables condition, and then discussed strengthening the instrumental variables condition to full independence in the special case where Y and Z are binary. The result of shifting from mean independence to full independence is to sometimes reduce the width of the resulting bounds but also to have an even more complicated form for the bounds. We now consider further strengthening the instrumental variables either by imposing a nonparametric selection model for the first stage as in Heckman and Vytlacil (1999) or by imposing instrumental variable conditions of the form considered by Imbens and Angrist (1994). The sharp bounds corresponding to these strengthened versions of instrumental variables do not reduce the bounds compared to imposing a weaker form of the instrumental variables assumption but produces a much simpler form for the bounds.

Let $D(z)$ denote the counterfactual choices that would have been made had Z been set exogenously to z. Consider the LATE independence, rank, and monotonicity conditions (IV-1), (IV-2), (IV-3), respectively, of Imbens and Angrist (1994) presented in Sections 2 and 4.

Note that the LATE monotonicity assumption (IV-3) strengthens assumption [IV-BP]. The LATE independence assumption (IV-1) is exactly the same as assumption [IV-BP] except that the assumption is stated here without requiring Z to be binary. In their context of binary Z and Y, Balke and Pearl discuss the LATE monotonicity condition and show that the LATE monotonicity condition imposes constraints on the observed data which imply that the Balke and Pearl (1997) bounds and the Manski mean-independence bounds will coincide.[187]

Consider the nonparametric selection model of Heckman and Vytlacil (1999):

NONPARAMETRIC SELECTION MODEL S. $D = \mathbf{1}[\mu(Z) \geqslant U]$ and $Z \perp\!\!\!\perp (Y_0, Y_1, U)$. This is a consequence of Equations (3.3) and assumptions (A-1)–(A-5) presented in Section 4.

From Vytlacil (2002), we have that the Imbens and Angrist conditions (IV-1)–(IV-3) are equivalent to imposing a nonparametric selection model of the form S. Thus, the bounds derived under one set of assumptions will be valid under the alternative set of assumptions, and bounds that are sharp under one set will be sharp under the alternative

[187] Robins (1989) constructs the same bounds under the LATE condition for the case of Z and Y binary, though he does not prove that the bounds are sharp.

set of assumptions. This equivalence implies that the Balke and Pearl result also holds for the selection model: if Z and Y are binary, then the sharp bounds under the nonparametric selection model coincide with the sharp bounds under mean independence IV.

We now consider the more general case where neither Z nor Y need be binary. Heckman and Vytlacil (1999) derived bounds on the average treatment effect under the assumptions that the outcomes are generated from a bounded outcome nonparametric selection model for treatment without requiring that Z or Y be binary or any other restrictions on the support of the distributions of Z and Y beyond the assumption that the outcomes are bounded (Assumption B). In particular, they derived the following bounds on the average treatment effect:

$$B^L \leqslant E(Y_1 - Y_0) \leqslant B^U,$$

with

$$\begin{aligned}
B^U &= E\big(DY \mid P(Z) = p^u\big) + \big(1 - p^u\big)y^u \\
&\quad - E\big((1 - D)Y \mid P(Z) = p^l\big) - p^l y^l, \\
B^L &= E\big(DY \mid P(Z) = p^u\big) + \big(1 - p^u\big)y^l - E\big((1 - D)Y \mid P(Z) = p^l\big) - p^l y^u.
\end{aligned}$$

Note that these bounds do not necessarily include zero. The width of the bounds is

$$B^U - B^L = \big((1 - p^u) + p^l\big)\big(y^u - y^l\big).$$

For example, if Y is binary then the width of the bounds is simply $B^U - B^L = ((1 - p^u) + p^l)$. Trivially, $p^u = 1$ and $p^l = 0$ is necessary and sufficient for the bounds to collapse to point identification, with the width of the bounds linearly related to the distance between p^u and 1 and the distance between p^l and 0. Note that it is necessary and sufficient for $P(z)$ to be a nontrivial function of z for these bounds to improve upon the bounds that only imposed that the outcomes are bounded. Evaluating the width of the bounds only requires p^u, p^l. The only additional information required to evaluate the bounds themselves is $E(DY \mid P(Z) = p^u)$ and $E((1 - D)Y \mid P(Z) = p^l)$.

Heckman and Vytlacil (2001a) analyze how these bounds compare to the Manski (1990) mean independence bounds, and analyze whether these bounds are sharp. They show that the selection model imposes restrictions on the observed data such that the Manski (1990) mean independence bounds collapse to the simpler Heckman and Vytlacil (2001a) bounds. In particular, given assumption S, they show that

$$\begin{aligned}
&\inf_{z \in \mathcal{Z}}\big\{E(DY \mid Z = z) + \big(1 - P(z)\big)y^u\big\} = E\big(DY \mid P(Z) = p^u\big) + \big(1 - p^u\big)y^u, \\
&\sup_{z \in \mathcal{Z}}\big\{E\big((1 - D)Y \mid Z = z\big) + P(z)y^l\big\} = E\big((1 - D)Y \mid P(Z) = p^l\big) - p^l y^l
\end{aligned}$$

and thus the Manski (1990) upper bound collapses to the Heckman and Vytlacil (1999) upper bound under assumption S. The parallel result holds for the lower bounds. Furthermore, Heckman and Vytlacil (2001a) establish that the Heckman and Vytlacil (1999) bounds are sharp given Assumptions B and S. Thus, somewhat surprisingly, imposing the stronger assumption of the existence of an instrument in a nonparametric selection model does not narrow the bounds compared to the case of imposing only the weaker assumption of mean independence, but does impose structure on the data which substantially simplifies the form of the mean-independence bounds. By the Vytlacil (2002) equivalence result, the same conclusion holds for the LATE assumptions – imposing the LATE assumptions does not narrow the bounds compared to only imposing the weaker assumption of mean independence, but does impose restrictions on the data that substantially simplify the form of the bounds. Vytlacil, Santos and Shaikh (2005) extend these bounds.

10.4. Combining comparative advantage and instrumental variables

We have thus far examined bounds that impose a comparative advantage model, and bounds that exploit an instrumental variables assumption. In general, neither restriction has more identifying power than the other. We now consider combining both types of assumptions.

Assume $D = \mathbf{1}[Y_1 - Y_0 \geqslant C(Z)]$, with Z observed and $Z \perp\!\!\!\perp (Y_0, Y_1)$. This is a Roy model with a cost $C(Z)$ of treatment, with the cost of treatment a function of an "instrument" Z. For ease of exposition, assume that Z is a continuous scalar random variable and that (Y_0, Y_1) are continuous random variables.[188] Also for ease of exposition, assume that $\mathcal{Z}$ (the support of the distribution Z) is compact and that $C(\cdot)$ is a continuous function. These assumptions are only imposed for ease of exposition.

The model is a special case of the nonparametric selection model considered by Heckman and Vytlacil (2001a), but with more structure that we can now exploit. Begin by following steps similar to Heckman and Vytlacil (2001a). Using the fact that $D = \mathbf{1}[Y_1 - Y_0 \geqslant C(Z)]$ and that $Z \perp\!\!\!\perp (Y_0, Y_1)$, we have

$$P(Z) = 1 - F_{Y_1 - Y_0}\big(C(Z)\big),$$

where $F_{Y_1 - Y_0}$ is the distribution function of $Y_1 - Y_0$. Given our assumptions, we have that there will exist z^u and z^l such that

$$\begin{aligned}
&C\big(z^u\big) = \sup\big\{C(z)\colon z \in \mathcal{Z}\big\},\\
&P\big(z^u\big) = 1 - F_{Y_1 - Y_0}\big(C\big(z^u\big)\big) = \inf\big\{P(Z)\colon z \in \mathcal{Z}\big\},\\
&C\big(z^l\big) = \inf\big\{C(z)\colon z \in \mathcal{Z}\big\},\\
&P\big(z^l\big) = 1 - F_{Y_1 - Y_0}\big(C\big(z^l\big)\big) = \sup\big\{P(Z)\colon z \in \mathcal{Z}\big\}.
\end{aligned}$$

In other words, $Z = z^u$ is associated with the highest possible cost of treatment and thus the lowest possible conditional probability of $D = 1$, while $Z = z^l$ is associated with the lowest possible cost of treatment and thus the highest possible conditional

188 More formally, impose that the distribution of Z has a density with respect to Lebesgue measure on $\mathbb{R}$, and assume that (Y_1, Y_0) has a density with respect to Lebesgue measure on $\mathbb{R}^2$.

probability of $D = 1$. Since $P(\cdot)$ for $z \in \mathcal{Z}$ is identified, we have that z^u and z^l are identified.

Consider identification of $C(z)$. Using the model and the independence assumptions, we have

$$\begin{aligned}
&\frac{\partial}{\partial z} E(Y \mid Z = z) \\
&\quad = \frac{\partial}{\partial z} E(YD \mid Z = z) + \frac{\partial}{\partial z} E\bigl(Y(1 - D) \bigm| Z = z\bigr) \\
&\quad = \frac{\partial}{\partial z} \int_{C(z)}^{\infty} E(Y_1 \mid Y_1 - Y_0 = t)\, dF_{Y_1 - Y_0}(t) \\
&\qquad + \frac{\partial}{\partial z} \int_{-\infty}^{C(z)} E(Y_0 \mid Y_1 - Y_0 = t)\, dF_{Y_1 - Y_0}(t) \\
&\quad = -\bigl[E\bigl(Y_1 \bigm| Y_1 - Y_0 = C(z)\bigr) - E\bigl(Y_0 \bigm| Y_1 - Y_0 = C(z)\bigr)\bigr] f_{Y_1 - Y_0}\bigl(C(z)\bigr) C'(z) \\
&\quad = -C(z) C'(z) f_{Y_1 - Y_0}\bigl(C(z)\bigr)
\end{aligned}$$

and

$$\begin{aligned}
\frac{\partial}{\partial z} P(z) &= \frac{\partial}{\partial z} \int_{C(z)}^{\infty} dF_{Y_1 - Y_0}(t) \\
&= -C'(z) f_{Y_1 - Y_0}\bigl(C(z)\bigr)
\end{aligned}$$

and thus

$$\left[\frac{\partial}{\partial z} E(Y \mid Z = z) \Big/ \frac{\partial}{\partial z} P(z)\right] = C(z)$$

for any $z \in \mathcal{Z}$ such that $\frac{\partial}{\partial z} P(z) \neq 0$, i.e., for any $z \in \mathcal{Z}$ such that $C'(z) \neq 0$ and $F_{Y_1 - Y_0}(C(z)) \neq 0$. We thus conclude that $C(z)$ is identified for $z \in \mathcal{Z}$.

Our goal is to identify $E(Y_1 - Y_0)$. For any $z \in \mathcal{Z}$, we have by the law of iterated expectations that

$$\begin{aligned}
E(Y_j) &= \int E(Y_j \mid Y_1 - Y_0 = t)\, dF_{Y_1 - Y_0}(t) \\
&= \int_{-\infty}^{C(z)} E(Y_j \mid Y_1 - Y_0 = t)\, dF_{Y_1 - Y_0}(t) \\
&\quad + \int_{C(z)}^{\infty} E(Y_j \mid Y_1 - Y_0 = t)\, dF_{Y_1 - Y_0}(t)
\end{aligned}$$

for $j = 0, 1$. Using the model for D and the assumption that $Z \perp\!\!\!\perp (Y_0, Y_1)$, we have

$$\int_{C(z)}^{\infty} E(Y_1 \mid Y_1 - Y_0 = t)\, dF_{Y_1 - Y_0}(t) = E(DY \mid Z = z), \tag{10.2}$$

$$\int_{-\infty}^{C(z)} E(Y_0 \mid Y_1 - Y_0 = t)\, dF_{Y_1 - Y_0}(t) = E\bigl((1 - D)Y \bigm| Z = z\bigr). \tag{10.3}$$

We identify the right-hand sides of these equations for any $z \in \mathcal{Z}$, and thus identify the left-hand sides for any $z \in \mathcal{Z}$. In particular, consider evaluating Equation (10.2) at $z = z^l$ and Equation (10.3) at $z = z^u$. Then, to bound $E(Y_1 - Y_0)$, we need to bound $\int_{-\infty}^{C(z^l)} E(Y_1 \mid Y_1 - Y_0 = t)\, dF_{Y_1 - Y_0}(t)$ and $\int_{C(z^u)}^{\infty} E(Y_0 \mid Y_1 - Y_0 = t)\, dF_{Y_1 - Y_0}(t)$.

We have

$$\begin{aligned}
&\int_{-\infty}^{C(z^l)} E(Y_1 \mid Y_1 - Y_0 = t)\, dF_{Y_1 - Y_0}(t) \\
&\quad = \bigl(1 - P(z^l)\bigr) E\bigl[Y_1 \mid Z = z^l, Y_1 \leqslant Y_0 + C(z^l)\bigr] \\
&\quad \leqslant \bigl(1 - P(z^l)\bigr) E\bigl[Y_0 + C(z^l) \mid Z = z^l, Y_1 \leqslant Y_0 + C(z^l)\bigr] \\
&\quad = E\bigl[(1 - D)Y \mid Z = z^l\bigr] + \bigl(1 - P(z^l)\bigr) C(z^l) \\
&\quad = E\bigl[(1 - D)Y \mid Z = z^l\bigr] - \left[\frac{\partial}{\partial z} E(Y \mid Z = z) \Big/ \frac{\partial}{\partial z} \ln\bigl(1 - P(z)\bigr)\right]\Bigg|_{z = z^l},
\end{aligned}$$

where the inequality arises from the conditioning $Y_1 \leqslant Y_0 + C(z^l)$. The final expression follows from our derivation of $C(z)$. Since $\Pr[y^l \leqslant Y_1 \leqslant y^u] = 1$ by assumption, we have

$$\begin{aligned}
&\bigl(1 - P(z^l)\bigr) y^l \\
&\quad \leqslant \int_{-\infty}^{C(z^l)} E(Y_1 \mid Y_1 - Y_0 = t)\, dF_{Y_1 - Y_0}(t) \\
&\quad \leqslant E\bigl[(1 - D)Y \mid Z = z^l\bigr] - \left[\frac{\partial}{\partial z} E(Y \mid Z = z) \Big/ \frac{\partial}{\partial z} \ln\bigl(1 - P(z)\bigr)\right]\Bigg|_{z = z^l}.
\end{aligned}$$

By a parallel argument, we have

$$\begin{aligned}
P(z^u) y^l &\leqslant \int_{C(z^u)}^{\infty} E(Y_0 \mid Y_1 - Y_0 = t)\, dF_{Y_1 - Y_0}(t) \\
&\leqslant E\bigl[DY \mid Z = z^u\bigr] + \left[\frac{\partial}{\partial z} E(Y \mid Z = z) \Big/ \frac{\partial}{\partial z} \ln P(z)\right]\Bigg|_{z = z^u}.
\end{aligned}$$

We thus have the bounds

$$B^L \leqslant E(Y_1 - Y_0) \leqslant B^U,$$

with

$$\begin{aligned}
B^U = {} & E\bigl(Y \mid Z = z^l\bigr) \\
& - \left[\frac{\partial}{\partial z} E(Y \mid Z = z) \Big/ \frac{\partial}{\partial z} \ln\bigl(1 - P(z)\bigr)\right]\Bigg|_{z = z^l} \\
& - E\bigl((1 - D)Y \mid Z = z^u\bigr) - P(z^u) y^l,
\end{aligned}$$

$$B^L = E(DY \mid Z = z^l) + [1 - P(z^l)]y^l - E(Y \mid Z = z^u)$$
$$- \left[\frac{\partial}{\partial z} E(Y \mid Z = z) \Big/ \frac{\partial}{\partial z} \ln P(z)\right]\bigg|_{z=z^u}.$$

The last two terms in B^U come from the lower bound for $E(Y_0)$ and the first two terms come from the upper bound for $E(Y_1)$ just derived. The terms for B^L are decomposed in an analogous fashion, reversing the roles of the upper and lower bounds for $E(Y_1)$ and $E(Y_0)$. These bounds improve over the bounds that only impose a nonparametric selection model (Assumption S) without imposing the Roy model structure. We next consider some alternative approaches to the solution of selection and hence evaluation problems developed in the literature using replacement functions, proxy functions, and other conditions.

11. Control functions, replacement functions, and proxy variables

This chapter analyzes the main tools used to evaluate social programs in the presence of selection bias in observational data. Yet many other tools have not been analyzed. We briefly summarize these approaches. Chapter 73 (Matzkin) of this Handbook establishes conditions under which some of the methods we discuss produce identification of econometric models. Abbring and Heckman (Chapter 72) use some of these tools.

The methods of replacement functions and proxy variables all start from characterizations (U-1) and (U-2) which we repeat for convenience:

(U-1) $(Y_0, Y_1) \perp\!\!\!\perp D \mid X, Z, \theta$,

but

(U-2) $(Y_0, Y_1) \not\perp\!\!\!\perp D \mid X, Z$,

where θ is not observed by the analyst and (Y_0, Y_1) are not observed directly but Y is observed as are the X, Z:

$$Y = DY_1 + (1 - D)Y_0.$$

Missing variables θ produce selection bias which creates a problem with using observational data to evaluate social programs. From (U-1), if we condition on θ, we would satisfy the condition (M-1) for matching, and hence could identify the parameters and distributions that can be identified if the conditions required for matching are satisfied.

The most direct approach to controlling for θ is to assume access to a function $\tau(X, Z, Q)$ that perfectly proxies θ:

$$\theta = \tau(X, Z, Q). \tag{11.1}$$

This approach based on a perfect proxy is called the *method of replacement functions* by Heckman and Robb (1985a). In (U-1), we can substitute for θ in terms of observables

(X, Z, Q). Then

$$(Y_0, Y_1) \perp\!\!\!\perp D \mid X, Z, Q.$$

We can condition nonparametrically on (X, Z, Q) and do not have to know the exact functional form of τ, although knowledge of τ might reduce the dimensionality of the matching problem, θ can be a vector and τ can be a vector of functions. This method has been used in the economics of education for decades [see the references in Heckman and Robb (1985a)]. If θ is ability and τ is a test score, it is sometimes assumed that the test score is a perfect proxy (or replacement function) for θ and τ is entered into the regressions of earnings on schooling to escape the problem of ability bias, typically assuming a linear relationship between τ and θ.[189] Heckman and Robb (1985a) discuss the literature that uses replacement functions in this way. Olley and Pakes (1996) apply this method and consider nonparametric identification of the τ function. Chapter 73 (Matzkin) of this Handbook provides a rigorous proof of identification for this approach in a general nonparametric setting.

The method of replacement functions assumes that (11.1) is a perfect proxy. In many applications, this assumption is far too strong. More often, we measure θ with error. This produces a factor model or measurement error model [Aigner et al. (1984)]. Chapter 73 (Matzkin) of this Handbook surveys this method. We can represent the factor model in a general way by a system of equations:

$$Y_j = g_j(X, Z, Q, \theta, \varepsilon_j), \quad j = 1, \ldots, J. \tag{11.2}$$

A linear factor model separable in the unobservables writes

$$Y_j = g_j(X, Z, Q) + \lambda_j \theta + \varepsilon_j, \quad j = 1, \ldots, J, \tag{11.3}$$

where

$$(X, Z, Q) \perp\!\!\!\perp (\theta, \varepsilon_j), \quad \varepsilon_j \perp\!\!\!\perp \theta, \quad j = 1, \ldots, J, \tag{11.4}$$

and the ε_j are mutually independent. Observe that under (11.2) and (11.3), Y_j controlling for X, Z, Q only imperfectly proxies θ because of the presence of ε_j. The θ are called factors, λ_j factor loadings and the ε_j "uniquenesses" [see, e.g., Aigner et al. (1984)].

A large literature, partially reviewed in Abbring and Heckman (Chapter 72), Section 1, and in Chapter 73 (Matzkin) of this Handbook, shows how to establish identification of econometric models under factor structure assumptions. Cunha, Heckman

[189] Thus if $\tau = \alpha_0 + \alpha_1 X + \alpha_2 Q + \alpha_3 Z + \theta$, we can write

$$\theta = \tau - \alpha_0 - \alpha_1 X - \alpha_2 Q - \alpha_3 Z,$$

and use this as the proxy function. Controlling for τ, X, Q, Z controls for θ. Notice that we do not need to know the coefficients $(\alpha_0, \alpha_1, \alpha_2, \alpha_3)$ to implement the method. We can condition on X, Q, Z.

and Matzkin (2003), Schennach (2004) and Hu and Schennach (2006) establish identification in nonlinear models of the form (11.2).[190] The key to identification is multiple, but imperfect (because of ε_j), measurements on θ from the Y_j, $j = 1, \ldots, J$, and X, Z, Q, and possibly other measurement systems that depend on θ. Carneiro, Hansen and Heckman (2003), Cunha, Heckman and Navarro (2005, 2006) and Cunha and Heckman (2008, 2007) apply and develop these methods. Under assumption (11.4), they show how to nonparametrically identify the econometric model and the distributions of the unobservables $F_\theta(\theta)$ and $F_{\varepsilon_j}(\varepsilon_j)$. In the context of classical simultaneous equations models, identification is secured by using covariance restrictions across equations exploiting the low dimensionality of vector θ compared to the high-dimensional vector of (imperfect) measurements on it. The recent literature [Cunha, Heckman and Matzkin (2003), Hu and Schennach (2006), Cunha, Heckman and Schennach (2006b)] extends the linear model to a nonlinear setting.

The recent econometric literature applies in special cases the idea of the *control function principle* introduced in Heckman and Robb (1985a). This principle, versions of which can be traced back to Telser (1964), partitions θ in (U-1) into two or more components, $\theta = (\theta_1, \theta_2)$, where only one component of θ is the source of bias. Thus it is assumed that (U-1) is true, and (U-1)$'$ is also true:

$$\text{(U-1)}' \quad (Y_0, Y_1) \perp\!\!\!\perp D \mid X, Z, \theta_1,$$

and (U-2) holds. For example, in the normal selection model analyzed in Chapter 70, Section 9, we broke U_1, the error term associated with Y_1, into two components:

$$U_1 = E(U_1 \mid V) + \varepsilon,$$

where V plays the role of θ_1 and arises from the choice equation. Under normality, ε is independent of $E(U_1 \mid V)$. Further,

$$E(U_1 \mid V) = \frac{\operatorname{Cov}(U_1, V)}{\operatorname{Var}(V)} V, \tag{11.5}$$

assuming $E(U_1) = 0$ and $E(V) = 0$. In that section, we show how to construct a control function in the context of the choice model

$$D = \mathbf{1}\big[\mu_D(Z) \geqslant V\big].$$

Controlling for V controls for the component of θ_1 in (U-1)$'$ that gives rise to the spurious dependence. The Blundell and Powell (2003, 2004) application of the control function principle assumes functional form (11.5) but assumes that V can be perfectly proxied by a first stage equation. Thus they use a replacement function in their first stage. Their method does not work when one can only condition on D rather than on

190 Cunha, Heckman and Schennach (2007, 2006b) apply and extend this approach to a dynamic factor setting where the θ_t are time-dependent.

$D^* = \mu_D(Z) - V$.[191] In the sample selection model, it is not necessary to use V. As developed in Chapter 70 and reviewed in Sections 4.8 and 8.3.1 of this chapter, under additive separability for the outcome equation for Y_1, we can write

$$E(Y_1 \mid X, Z, D = 1) = \mu_1(X) + \underbrace{E\big(U_1 \bigm| \mu_D(Z) \geqslant V\big)}_{\text{control function}}$$

so we "expect out" rather than solve out the effect of the component of V on U_1 and thus control for selection bias under our maintained assumptions. In terms of the propensity score, under the conditions specified in Chapter 70, we may write the preceding expression in terms of $P(Z)$:

$$E(Y_1 \mid X, Z, D = 1) = \mu_1(X) + K_1\big(P(Z)\big),$$

where $K_1(P(Z)) = E(U_1 \mid X, Z, D = 1)$. It is not necessary to know V or be able to estimate it. The Blundell and Powell (2003, 2004) application of the control function principle assumes that the analyst can condition on and estimate V.

The Blundell–Powell method and the method of Imbens and Newey (2002) build heavily on (11.5) and implicitly make strong distributional and functional form assumptions that are not intrinsic to the method of control functions. As just noted, their method uses a replacement function to obtain $E(U_1 \mid V)$ in the first step of their procedures. The general control function method does not require a replacement function approach. The literature has begun to distinguish between the more general control function approach and the *control variate* approach that uses a first stage replacement function.

Matzkin (2003) develops the method of unobservable instruments which is a version of the replacement function approach applied to nonlinear models. Her unobservable instruments play the role of covariance restrictions used to identify classical simultaneous equations models [see Fisher (1966)]. Her approach is distinct from and therefore complementary with linear factor models. Instead of assuming $(X, Z, Q) \perp\!\!\!\perp (\theta, \varepsilon_j)$, she assumes in a two equation system that $(\theta, \varepsilon_1) \perp\!\!\!\perp Y_2 \mid Y_1, X, Z$. See the discussion in Chapter 73 (Matzkin) of this Handbook.

We have not discussed panel data methods in this chapter. The most commonly used panel data method is difference-in-differences as discussed in Heckman and Robb (1985a), Blundell, Duncan and Meghir (1998), Heckman, LaLonde and Smith (1999), and Bertrand, Duflo and Mullainathan (2004), to cite only a few key papers. Most of the estimators we have discussed can be adapted to a panel data setting. Heckman et al. (1998) develop difference-in-differences matching estimators. Abadie (2002) extends this work.[192] Separability between errors and observables is a key feature of the panel data approach in its standard application. Altonji and Matzkin (2005) and Matzkin (2003) present analyses of nonseparable panel data methods.

[191] Imbens and Newey (2002) extend their approach. See the discussion in Chapter 73 (Matzkin) of this Handbook.

[192] There is related work by Athey and Imbens (2006).

12. Summary

This chapter summarizes the main methods used to identify mean treatment effect parameters under semiparametric and nonparametric assumptions. We have used the marginal treatment effect as the unifying parameter to straddle a diverse econometric literature summarized in Table 1 of this chapter. For each estimator, we establish what it identifies, the economic content of the estimand and the identifying assumptions of the method.

Appendix A: Relationships among parameters using the index structure

Given the index structure, a simple relationship exists among the parameters. It is immediate from the definitions $D = \mathbf{1}(U_D \leqslant P(z))$ and $\Delta = Y_1 - Y_0$ that

$$\Delta^{\mathrm{TT}}\big(x, P(z)\big) = E\big(\Delta \mid X = x, U_D \leqslant P(z)\big). \tag{A.1}$$

Next consider $\Delta^{\mathrm{LATE}}(x, P(z), P(z'))$. Note that

$$\begin{aligned} &E\big(Y \mid X = x, P(Z) = P(z)\big) \\ &\quad = P(z)\big[E\big(Y_1 \mid X = x, P(Z) = P(z), D = 1\big)\big] \\ &\qquad + \big(1 - P(z)\big)\big[E\big(Y_0 \mid X = x, P(Z) = P(z), D = 0\big)\big] \\ &\quad = \int_0^{P(z)} E(Y_1 \mid X = x, U_D = u_D)\, du_D \\ &\qquad + \int_{P(z)}^1 E(Y_0 \mid X = x, U_D = u_D)\, du_D, \end{aligned}$$

so that

$$\begin{aligned} &E\big(Y \mid X = x, P(Z) = P(z)\big) - E\big(Y \mid X = x, P(Z) = P(z')\big) \\ &\quad = \int_{P(z')}^{P(z)} E(Y_1 \mid X = x, U_D = u_D)\, du_D \\ &\qquad - \int_{P(z')}^{P(z)} E(Y_0 \mid X = x, U_D = u_D)\, du_D, \end{aligned}$$

and thus

$$\Delta^{\mathrm{LATE}}\big(x, P(z), P(z')\big) = E\big(\Delta \mid X = x, P(z') \leqslant U_D \leqslant P(z)\big).$$

Notice that this expression could be taken as an alternative definition of LATE. Note that, in this expression, we could replace $P(z)$ and $P(z')$ with u_D and u'_D. No instrument needs to be available to define LATE.

We can rewrite these relationships in succinct form in the following way:

$$\Delta^{\mathrm{MTE}}(x, u_D) = E(\Delta \mid X = x, U_D = u_D),$$

$$\Delta^{\text{ATE}}(x) = \int_0^1 E(\Delta \mid X = x, U_D = u_D)\, du_D,$$

$$P(z)\big[\Delta^{\text{TT}}\big(x, P(z)\big)\big] = \int_0^{P(z)} E(\Delta \mid X = x, U_D = u_D)\, du_D,$$

$$\big(P(z) - P(z')\big)\big[\Delta^{\text{LATE}}\big(x, P(z), P(z')\big)\big] = \int_{P(z')}^{P(z)} E(\Delta \mid X = x, U_D = u_D)\, du_D. \tag{A.2}$$

We stress that everywhere in these expressions we can replace $P(z)$ with u_D and $P(z')$ with u'_D. Each parameter is an average value of MTE, $E(\Delta \mid X = x, U_D = u_D)$, but for values of U_D lying in different intervals and with different weighting functions. MTE defines the treatment effect more finely than do LATE, ATE, or TT. The relationship between MTE and LATE or TT conditional on $P(z)$ is analogous to the relationship between a probability density function and a cumulative distribution function. The probability density function and the cumulative distribution function represent the same information, but for some purposes the density function is more easily interpreted. Likewise, knowledge of TT for all $P(z)$ evaluation points is equivalent to knowledge of the MTE for all u_D evaluation points, so it is not the case that knowledge of one provides more information than knowledge of the other. However, in many choice-theoretic contexts it is often easier to interpret MTE than the TT or LATE parameters. It has the interpretation as a measure of willingness to pay on the part of people on a specified margin of participation in the program.

$\Delta^{\text{MTE}}(x, u_D)$ is the average effect for people who are just indifferent between participation in the program ($D = 1$) or not ($D = 0$) if the instrument is externally set so that $P(Z) = u_D$. For values of u_D close to zero, $\Delta^{\text{MTE}}(x, u_D)$ is the average effect for individuals with unobservable characteristics that make them the most inclined to participate in the program ($D = 1$), and for values of u_D close to one it is the average treatment effect for individuals with unobserved (by the econometrician) characteristics that make them the least inclined to participate. ATE integrates $\Delta^{\text{MTE}}(x, u_D)$ over the entire support of U_D (from $u_D = 0$ to $u_D = 1$). It is the average effect for an individual chosen at random from the entire population. $\Delta^{\text{TT}}(x, P(z))$ is the average treatment effect for persons who chose to participate at the given value of $P(Z) = P(z)$; it integrates $\Delta^{\text{MTE}}(x, u_D)$ up to $u_D = P(z)$. As a result, it is primarily determined by the MTE parameter for individuals whose unobserved characteristics make them the most inclined to participate in the program. LATE is the average treatment effect for someone who would not participate if $P(Z) \leqslant P(z')$ and would participate if $P(Z) \geqslant P(z)$. The parameter $\Delta^{\text{LATE}}(x, P(z), P(z'))$ integrates $\Delta^{\text{MTE}}(x, u_D)$ from $u_D = P(z')$ to $u_D = P(z)$.

Using the third expression in Equation (A.2) to substitute into Equation (A.1), we obtain an alternative expression for the TT parameter as a weighted average of MTE parameters:

$$\Delta^{\mathrm{TT}}(x) = \int_0^1 \frac{1}{p}\left[\int_0^p E(\Delta \mid X = x, U_D = u_D)\, du_D\right] dF_{P(Z)|X,D}(p|x, D = 1).$$

Using Bayes' rule, it follows that

$$dF_{P(Z)|X,D}(p \mid x, 1) = \frac{\Pr(D = 1 \mid X = x, P(Z) = p)}{\Pr(D = 1 \mid X = x)}\, dF_{P(Z)|X}(p|x).$$

Since $\Pr(D = 1 \mid X = x, P(Z) = p) = p$, it follows that

$$\Delta^{\mathrm{TT}}(x) = \frac{1}{\Pr(D = 1 \mid X = x)} \times \int_0^1 \left(\int_0^p E(\Delta \mid X = x, U_D = u_D)\, du_D\right) dF_{P(Z)|X}(p|x). \qquad \text{(A.3)}$$

Note further that since $\Pr(D = 1 \mid X = x) = E(P(Z) \mid X = x) = \int_0^1 (1 - F_{P(Z)|X}(t|x))\, dt$, we can reinterpret (A.3) as a weighted average of local IV parameters where the weighting is similar to that obtained from a length-biased, size-biased, or P-biased sample:

$$\begin{aligned}
\Delta^{\mathrm{TT}}(x) &= \frac{1}{\Pr(D = 1 \mid X = x)} \\
&\quad \times \int_0^1 \left(\int_0^1 \mathbf{1}(u_D \leqslant p) E(\Delta \mid X = x, U_D = u_D)\, du_D\right) dF_{P(Z)|X}(p|x) \\
&= \frac{1}{\int (1 - F_{P(Z)|X}(t|x))\, dt} \\
&\quad \times \int_0^1 \left(\int_0^1 E(\Delta \mid X = x, U_D = u_D) \mathbf{1}(u_D \leqslant p)\, dF_{P(Z)|X}(p|x)\right) du_D \\
&= \int_0^1 E(\Delta \mid X = x, U_D = u_D) \left(\frac{1 - F_{P(Z)|X}(u_D|x)}{\int (1 - F_{P(Z)|X}(t|x))\, dt}\right) du_D \\
&= \int_0^1 E(\Delta \mid X = x, U_D = u_D) g_x(u_D)\, du_D,
\end{aligned}$$

where

$$g_x(u_D) = \frac{1 - F_{P(Z)|X}(u_D|x)}{\int (1 - F_{P(Z)|X}(t|x))\, dt}.$$

Thus $g_x(u_D)$ is a *weighted distribution* [Rao (1985)]. Since $g_x(u_D)$ is a nonincreasing function of u_D, we have that drawings from $g_x(u_D)$ oversample persons with low values of U_D, i.e., values of unobserved characteristics that make them the most likely to

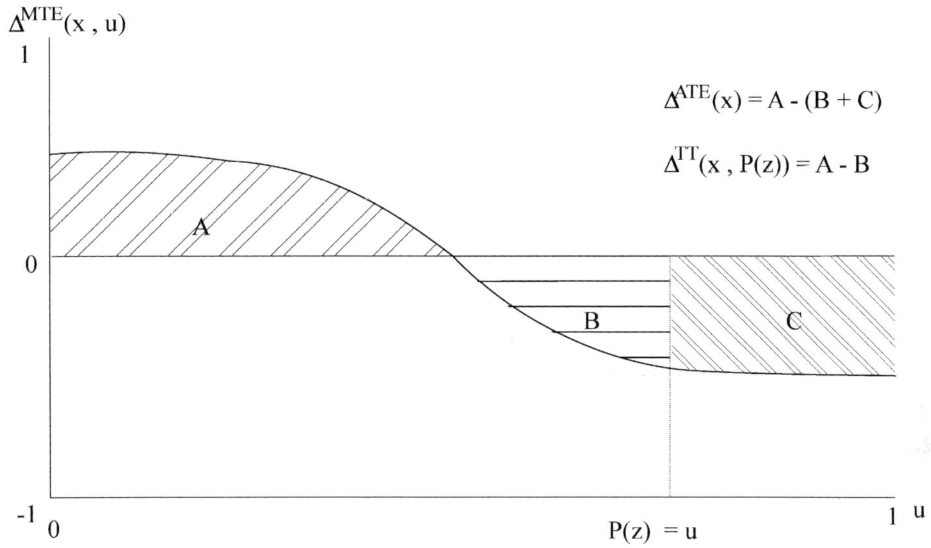

Figure A.1. MTE integrates to ATE and TT under full support (for dichotomous outcome). *Source*: Heckman and Vytlacil (2000).

participate in the program no matter what their value of $P(Z)$. Since

$$\Delta^{\text{MTE}}(x, u_D) = E(\Delta \mid X = x, U_D = u_D)$$

it follows that

$$\Delta^{\text{TT}}(x) = \int_0^1 \Delta^{\text{MTE}}(x, u_D) g_x(u_D)\, du_D.$$

The TT parameter is thus a weighted version of MTE, where $\Delta^{\text{MTE}}(x, u_D)$ is given the largest weight for low u_D values and is given zero weight for $u_D \geqslant p_x^{\max}$, where $p_x^{\max}$ is the maximum value in the support of $P(Z)$ conditional on $X = x$.

Figure A.1 graphs the relationship between $\Delta^{\text{MTE}}(u_D)$, Δ^{ATE} and $\Delta^{\text{TT}}(P(z))$, assuming that the gains are the greatest for those with the lowest U_D values and that the gains decline as U_D increases. The curve is the MTE parameter as a function of u_D, and is drawn for the special case where the outcome variable is binary so that MTE parameter is bounded between -1 and 1. The ATE parameter averages $\Delta^{\text{MTE}}(u_D)$ over the full unit interval (i.e., is the area under A minus the area under B and C in the figure). $\Delta^{\text{TT}}(P(z))$ averages $\Delta^{\text{MTE}}(u_D)$ up to the point $P(z)$ (is the area under A minus the area under B in the figure). Because $\Delta^{\text{MTE}}(u_D)$ is assumed to be declining in u_D, the TT parameter for any given $P(z)$ evaluation point is larger then the ATE parameter.

Equation (A.2) relates each of the other parameters to the MTE parameter. One can also relate each of the other parameters to the LATE parameter. This relationship turns out to be useful later on in this chapter when we encounter conditions where LATE can be identified but MTE cannot. MTE is the limit form of LATE:

$$\Delta^{\text{MTE}}(x, p) = \lim_{p' \to p} \Delta^{\text{LATE}}(x, p, p').$$

Direct relationships between LATE and the other parameters are easily derived. The relationship between LATE and ATE is immediate:

$$\Delta^{\text{ATE}}(x) = \Delta^{\text{LATE}}(x, 0, 1).$$

Using Bayes' rule, the relationship between LATE and TT is

$$\Delta^{\text{TT}}(x) = \int_0^1 \Delta^{\text{LATE}}(x, 0, p) \frac{p}{\Pr(D = 1 \mid X = x)} \, dF_{P(Z)|X}(p|x). \tag{A.4}$$

Appendix B: Relaxing additive separability and independence

There are two central assumptions that underlie the latent index representation used in this chapter: that V is independent of Z, and that V and Z are additively separable in the index.[193] The latent index model with these two restrictions implies the independence and monotonicity assumptions of Imbens and Angrist (1994) and the latent index model implied by those assumptions implies a latent index model with a representation that satisfies both the independence and the monotonicity assumptions. In this appendix, we consider the sensitivity of the analysis presented in the text to relaxation of either of these assumptions.

First, consider allowing V and Z to be nonseparable in the treatment index:

$$D^* = \mu_D(Z, V),$$

$$D = \begin{cases} 1 & \text{if } D^* \geqslant 0, \\ 0 & \text{otherwise,} \end{cases}$$

while maintaining the assumption that Z is independent of (V, U_1, U_0). We do not impose any restrictions on the cross partials of μ_D. The monotonicity condition of Imbens and Angrist (1994) is that for any (z, z') pair, $\mu_D(z, v) \geqslant \mu_D(z', v)$ for all v, or $\mu_D(z, v) \leqslant \mu_D(z', v)$ for all v.[194] Vytlacil (2002) shows that monotonicity always implies one representation of μ_D as $\mu_D(z, v) = \mu_D(z) + v$. We now reconsider the analysis in the text without imposing the monotonicity condition by considering the latent index model without additive separability. Since we have imposed no structure on the $\mu_D(z, v)$ index, one can easily show that this model is equivalent to imposing the independence condition of Imbens and Angrist (1994) without imposing their

[193] Recall that $U_D = F_{V|X}(V)$.

[194] Note that the monotonicity condition is a restriction across v. For a given fixed v, it will always trivially have to be the case that either $\mu_D(z, v) \geqslant \mu_D(z', v)$ or $\mu_D(z, v) \leqslant \mu_D(z', v)$.

monotonicity condition. A random coefficient discrete choice model with $\mu_D = Z\gamma + \varepsilon$ where γ and ε are random, and γ can assume positive or negative values is an example of this case, i.e., $V = (\gamma, \varepsilon)$.

We impose the regularity condition that, for any $z \in \mathrm{Supp}(Z)$, $\mu_D(z, V)$ is absolutely continuous with respect to Lebesgue measure.[195] Let

$$\Omega(z) = \{v\colon \mu_D(z, v) \geqslant 0\},$$

so that

$$P(z) \equiv \Pr(D = 1 \mid Z = z) = \Pr\bigl(V \in \Omega(z)\bigr).$$

Under additive separability, $P(z) = P(z') \Leftrightarrow \Omega(z) = \Omega(z')$. This equivalence enables us to define the parameters in terms of the $P(z)$ index instead of the full z vector. In the more general case without additive separability, it is possible to have (z, z') such that $P(z) = P(z')$ and $\Omega(z) \neq \Omega(z')$. We present a random coefficient choice model example of this case in Section 4.10.1 in the text. In this case, we can no longer replace $Z = z$ with $P(Z) = P(z)$ in the conditioning sets.

Define, using $\Delta = Y_1 - Y_0$,

$$\Delta^{\mathrm{MTE}}(x, v) = E(\Delta \mid X = x, V = v).$$

For ATE, we obtain the same expression as before:

$$\Delta^{\mathrm{ATE}}(x) = \int_{-\infty}^{\infty} E(\Delta \mid X = x, V = v)\, dF_{V|X}(v).$$

For TT, we obtain a similar but slightly more complicated expression:

$$\begin{aligned}\Delta^{\mathrm{TT}}(x, z) &\equiv E(\Delta \mid X = x, Z = z, D = 1)\\ &= E\bigl(\Delta \bigm| X = x, V \in \Omega(z)\bigr)\\ &= \frac{1}{P(z)} \int_{\Omega(z)} E(\Delta \mid X = x, V = v)\, dF_{V|X}(v).\end{aligned}$$

Because it is no longer the case that we can define the parameter solely in terms of $P(z)$ instead of z, it is possible to have (z, z') such that $P(z) = P(z')$ but $\Delta^{\mathrm{TT}}(x, z) \neq \Delta^{\mathrm{TT}}(x, z')$.

Following the same derivation as used in the text for the TT parameter not conditional on Z,

$$\begin{aligned}&\Delta^{\mathrm{TT}}(x)\\ &\quad\equiv E(\Delta \mid X = x, D = 1)\\ &\quad= \int E(\Delta \mid X = x, Z = z, D = 1)\, dF_{Z|X,D}(z|x, 1)\end{aligned}$$

[195] We impose this condition to ensure that $\Pr(\mu_D(z, V) = 0) = 0$ for any $z \in \mathrm{Supp}(Z)$.

$$
\begin{aligned}
&= \frac{1}{\Pr(D=1 \mid X=x)} \\
&\quad \times \int \left[\int_{-\infty}^{\infty} \mathbf{1}\left[v \in \Omega(z)\right] E(\Delta \mid X=x, V=v)\, dF_{V|X}(v) \right] dF_{Z|X}(z|x) \\
&= \frac{1}{\Pr(D=1 \mid X=x)} \\
&\quad \times \int_{-\infty}^{\infty} \left[\int \mathbf{1}\left[v \in \Omega(z)\right] E(\Delta \mid X=x, V=v)\, dF_{Z|X}(z|x) \right] dF_{V|X}(v) \\
&= \int_{-\infty}^{\infty} E(\Delta \mid X=x, V=v) g_x(v)\, dv,
\end{aligned}
$$

where

$$
g_x(v) = \frac{\int \mathbf{1}[v \in \Omega(z)]\, dF_{Z|X}(z|x)}{\Pr(D=1 \mid X=x)} = \frac{\Pr(D=1 \mid V=v, X=x)}{\Pr(D=1 \mid X=x)}.
$$

Thus the definitions of the parameters and the relationships among them that are developed in the main text of this chapter generalize in a straightforward way to the nonseparable case. Separability allows us to define the parameters in terms of $P(z)$ instead of z and allows for slightly simpler expressions, but is not crucial for the definition of parameters or the relationship among them.

Separability is, however, crucial to the form of LATE when we allow V and Z to be additively nonseparable in the treatment index. For simplicity, we will keep the conditioning on X implicit. Define the following sets

$$
\begin{aligned}
A(z,z') &= \left\{v\colon \mu_D(z,v) \geqslant 0, \mu_D(z',v) \geqslant 0\right\}, \\
B(z,z') &= \left\{v\colon \mu_D(z,v) \geqslant 0, \mu_D(z',v) < 0\right\}, \\
C(z,z') &= \left\{v\colon \mu_D(z,v) < 0, \mu_D(z',v) < 0\right\}, \\
D(z,z') &= \left\{v\colon \mu_D(z,v) < 0, \mu_D(z',v) \geqslant 0\right\}.
\end{aligned}
$$

Monotonicity implies that either $B(z,z')$ or $D(z,z')$ is empty. Suppressing the z, z' arguments, we have

$$
\begin{aligned}
E(Y \mid Z=z) &= \Pr(A \cup B) E(Y_1 \mid A \cup B) + \Pr(C \cup D) E(Y_0 \mid C \cup D), \\
E(Y \mid Z=z') &= \Pr(A \cup D) E(Y_1 \mid A \cup D) + \Pr(B \cup C) E(Y_0 \mid B \cup C)
\end{aligned}
$$

so that

$$
\begin{aligned}
&\frac{E(Y \mid Z=z) - E(Y \mid Z=z')}{\Pr(D=1 \mid Z=z) - \Pr(D=1 \mid Z=z')} \\
&\quad = \frac{E(Y \mid Z=z) - E(Y \mid Z=z')}{\Pr(A \cup B) - \Pr(A \cup D)}
\end{aligned}
$$

$$= \frac{\Pr(B)E(Y_1 - Y_0 \mid B) - \Pr(D)E(Y_1 - Y_0 \mid D)}{\Pr(B) - \Pr(D)}$$
$$= w_B E(\Delta \mid B) - w_D E(\Delta \mid D)$$

with

$$w_B = \frac{\Pr(B \mid B \cup D)}{\Pr(B \mid B \cup D) - \Pr(D \mid B \cup D)},$$
$$w_D = \frac{\Pr(D \mid B \cup D)}{\Pr(B \mid B \cup D) - \Pr(D \mid B \cup D)}.$$

Under monotonicity, either $\Pr(B) = 0$ and LATE identifies $E(\Delta \mid D)$ or $\Pr(D) = 0$ and LATE identifies $E(\Delta \mid B)$. Without monotonicity, the IV estimator used as the sample analogue to LATE converges to the above weighted difference in the two terms, and the relationship between LATE and the other treatment parameters presented in the text no longer holds.

Consider what would happen if we could condition on a given v. For $v \in A \cup C$, the denominator is zero and the parameter is not well defined. For $v \in B$, the parameter is $E(\Delta \mid V = v)$, for $v \in D$, the parameter is $E(\Delta \mid V = v)$. If we could restrict conditioning to $v \in B$ (or $v \in D$), we would obtain monotonicity within the restricted sample.

Now consider LIV. For simplicity, assume z is a scalar. Assume $\mu_D(z, v)$ is continuously differentiable in (z, v), with $\mu^j(z, v)$ denoting the partial derivative with respect to the jth argument. Assume that $\mu_D(Z, V)$ is absolutely continuous with respect to Lebesgue measure. Fix some evaluation point, z_0. One can show that there may be at most a countable number of v points such that $\mu_D(z_0, v) = 0$. Let $j \in \mathcal{J} = \{1, \ldots, L\}$ index the set of v evaluation points such that $\mu_D(z_0, v) = 0$, where L may be infinity, and thus write: $\mu_D(z_0, v_j) = 0$ for all $j \in \mathcal{J}$. (Both the number of such evaluation points and the evaluation points themselves depend on the evaluation point, z_0, but we suppress this dependence for notational convenience.) Assume that there exists $\{B_k\}_{k\in\mathcal{J}}, \sum_{k\in\mathcal{J}} B_k < \infty$ such that $|\frac{\mu^1(z,v_k)}{\mu^2(z,v_k)}| \leqslant B_k$ for $k \in \mathcal{J}$ and all z in some neighborhood of z_0. One can show that

$$\frac{\partial}{\partial z}\big[E(Y \mid Z = z)\big]\Big|_{z=z_0} = \sum_{k=1}^{L} \frac{\mu^1(z_0, v_k)}{|\mu^2(z_0, v_k)|} E(\Delta \mid V = v_k)$$

and

$$\frac{\partial}{\partial z}\big[\Pr(D = 1 \mid Z = z)\big]\Big|_{z=z_0} = \sum_{k=1}^{L} \frac{\mu^1(z_0, v_k)}{|\mu^2(z_0, v_k)|}.$$

LIV is the ratio of these two terms, and does not in general equal the MTE. Thus, the relationship between LIV and MTE breaks down in the nonseparable case.

As an example, take the case where L is finite and $\frac{\mu^1(z_0,v_k)}{|\mu^2(z_0,v_k)|}$ does not vary with k. For this case,

$$\begin{aligned}\Delta^{\text{LIV}}(z_0) = {} & \Pr\big(\mu^1(z_0,V) > 0 \bigm| \mu(z_0,V)=0\big) \\ & \cdot E\big(\Delta \bigm| \mu_D(z_0,V)=0, \mu^1(z_0,V) > 0\big) \\ & - \Pr\big(\mu^1(z_0,V) < 0 \bigm| \mu(z_0,V)=0\big) \\ & \cdot E\big(\Delta \bigm| \mu_D(z_0,V)=0, \mu^1(z_0,V) < 0\big).\end{aligned}$$

Thus, while the definition of the parameters and the relationship among them does not depend crucially on the additive separability assumption, the connection between the LATE or LIV estimators and the underlying parameters crucially depends on the additive separability assumption.

Next consider the assumption that V and Z are separable in the treatment index while allowing them to be stochastically dependent:

$$D^* = \mu_D(Z) - V,$$

$$D = \begin{cases} 1 & \text{if } D^* \geqslant 0, \\ 0 & \text{otherwise,} \end{cases}$$

with Z independent of (U_0, U_1), but allowing Z and V to be stochastically dependent. The analysis of Vytlacil (2002) can be easily adapted to show that the latent index model with separability but without imposing independence is equivalent to imposing the monotonicity assumption of Imbens and Angrist without imposing their independence assumption.[196]

We have

$$\Omega(z) = \{v\colon \mu_D(z) \geqslant v\}$$

and

$$P(z) \equiv \Pr(D=1 \mid Z=z) = \Pr\big(V \in \Omega(z) \bigm| Z=z\big).$$

Note that $\Omega(z) = \Omega(z') \Rightarrow \mu_D(z) = \mu_D(z')$, but $\Omega(z) = \Omega(z')$ does not imply $P(z) = P(z')$ since the distribution of V conditional on $Z = z$ need not equal the distribution of V conditional on $Z = z'$. Likewise, $P(z) = P(z')$ does not imply $\Omega(z) = \Omega(z')$. As occurred in the nonseparable case, we can no longer replace $Z = z$ with $P(Z) = P(z)$ in the conditioning sets.[197]

[196] To show that the monotonicity assumption implies a separable latent index model, one can follow the proofs of Vytlacil (2002) with the sole modification of replacing $P(z) = \Pr(D = 1 \mid Z = z)$ with $\Pr(D(z) = 1)$, where $D(z)$ is the indicator variable for whether the agent would have received treatment if Z had been externally set to z.

[197] However, we again have equivalence between the alternative conditioning sets if we assume index sufficiency, i.e., that $F_{V|Z}(v|z) = F_{V|P(Z)}(v|P(z))$.

Consider the definition of the parameters and the relationship among them. The definition of MTE and ATE in no way involves Z, nor does the relationship between them, so that both their definition and their relationship remains unchanged by allowing Z and V to be dependent. Now consider the TT parameter where now we make the dependence of X explicit:

$$\begin{aligned}\Delta^{\mathrm{TT}}(x,z) &= E\big(\Delta \mid X=x, Z=z, V \leqslant \mu_D(z)\big)\\ &= \frac{1}{P(z)}\int_{-\infty}^{\mu_D(z)} E(\Delta \mid X=x, V=v)\,dF_{V\mid Z,X}(v\mid z,x)\\ &= \frac{1}{P(z)}\int_{-\infty}^{\mu_D(z)} E(\Delta \mid X=x, V=v)\frac{f_{Z\mid V,X}(z\mid v,x)}{f_{Z\mid X}(z\mid x)}\,dF_{V\mid X}(v\mid x),\end{aligned}$$

where $f_{Z|X}$ and $f_{Z|V,X}$ denote the densities corresponding to $F_{Z|X}$ and $F_{Z|V,X}$ with respect to the appropriate dominating measure. We thus obtain

$$\begin{aligned}\Delta^{\mathrm{TT}}(x) &= E\big(\Delta \mid X=x, V \leqslant \mu_D(Z)\big)\\ &= \frac{1}{\Pr(D=1\mid X=x)}\int\bigg[\int_{-\infty}^{\mu_D(z)} E(\Delta \mid X=x, V=v)\\ &\qquad \times \frac{f_{Z\mid U,X}(z\mid v,x)}{f_{Z\mid X}(z\mid x)}\,dF_{V\mid X}(v\mid x)\bigg]\,dF_{Z\mid X}(z\mid x)\\ &= \frac{1}{\Pr(D=1\mid X=x)}\int_{-\infty}^{\infty}\bigg[\int \mathbf{1}\big[v\leqslant \mu_D(z)\big]E(\Delta \mid X=x, V=v)\\ &\qquad \times \frac{f_{Z\mid U,X}(z\mid v,x)}{f_{Z\mid X}(z\mid x)}\,dF_{Z\mid X}(z\mid x)\bigg]\,dF_{V\mid X}(v\mid x)\\ &= \frac{1}{\Pr(D=1\mid X=x)}\\ &\quad\times \int_{-\infty}^{\infty}\bigg[\int \mathbf{1}\big[v\leqslant \mu_D(z)\big]\\ &\qquad \times E(\Delta \mid X=x, V=v)\,dF_{Z\mid V,X}(z\mid v,x)\bigg]\,dF_{V\mid X}(v\mid x)\\ &= \int_{-\infty}^{\infty} E(\Delta \mid X=x, V=v)g_x(v)\,dv,\end{aligned}$$

where

$$g_x(v) = \frac{\Pr(D=1\mid V=v, X=x)}{\Pr(D=1\mid X=x)}.$$

Thus the definitions of parameters and the relationships among the parameters that are developed in the text generalize naturally to the case where Z and V are stochastically dependent. Independence (combined with the additive separability assumption) allows us to define the parameters in terms of $P(z)$ instead of z and allows for slightly simpler expressions, but is not crucial for the definition of parameters or the relationship among them.

We next investigate LATE when we allow V and Z to be stochastically dependent. We have

$$\begin{aligned}
&E(Y \mid X=x, Z=z) \\
&\quad = P(z)\big[E(Y_1 \mid X=x, Z=z, D=1)\big] \\
&\qquad + \big(1-P(z)\big)\big[E(Y_0 \mid X=x, Z=z, D=0)\big] \\
&\quad = \int_{-\infty}^{\mu_D(z)} E(Y_1 \mid X=x, V=v)\, dF_{V|X,Z}(v|x,z) \\
&\qquad + \int_{\mu_D(z)}^{\infty} E(Y_0 \mid X=x, V=v)\, dF_{V|X,Z}(v|x,z).
\end{aligned}$$

For simplicity, take the case where $\mu_D(z) > \mu_D(z')$. Then

$$\begin{aligned}
&E(Y \mid X=x, Z=z) - E(Y \mid X=x, Z=z') \\
&\quad = \left[\int_{\mu_D(z')}^{\mu_D(z)} E(Y_1 \mid X=x, V=v)\, dF_{V|X,Z}(v|x,z)\right. \\
&\qquad \left. - \int_{\mu_D(z')}^{\mu_D(z)} E(Y_0 \mid X=x, V=v)\, dF_{V|X,Z}(v|x,z')\right] \\
&\qquad + \int_{-\infty}^{\mu_D(z')} E(Y_1 \mid X=x, V=v)\big(dF_{V|X,Z}(v|x,z) - dF_{V|X,Z}(v|x,z')\big) \\
&\qquad + \int_{\mu_D(z)}^{\infty} E(Y_0 \mid X=x, V=v)\big(dF_{V|X,Z}(v|x,z) - dF_{V|X,Z}(v|x,z')\big)
\end{aligned}$$

and thus

$$\begin{aligned}
&\Delta^{\mathrm{LATE}}(x, z, z') \\
&\quad = \delta_0(z) E\big(Y_1 \bigm| X=x, Z=z, \mu_D(z') \leqslant V \leqslant \mu_D(z)\big) \\
&\qquad - \delta_0(z') E\big(Y_0 \bigm| X=x, Z=z', \mu_D(z') \leqslant V \leqslant \mu_D(z)\big) \\
&\qquad + \big[\delta_1(z) E\big(Y_1 \bigm| X=x, Z=z, V \leqslant \mu_D(z')\big) \\
&\qquad - \delta_1(z') E\big(Y_1 \mid X=x, Z=z', V \leqslant \mu_D(z')\big)\big] \\
&\qquad + \big[\delta_2(z) E\big(Y_0 \bigm| X=x, Z=z, V > \mu_D(z)\big) \\
&\qquad - \delta_2(z') E\big(Y_0 \bigm| X=x, Z=z', V > \mu_D(z)\big)\big],
\end{aligned}$$

with

$$\delta_0(t) = \frac{\Pr(\mu_D(z') \leqslant V \leqslant \mu_D(z) \mid Z=t)}{\Pr(V \leqslant \mu_D(z) \mid Z=z, X=x) - \Pr(V \leqslant \mu_D(z') \mid Z=z', X=x)},$$

$$\delta_1(t) = \frac{\Pr(V \leqslant \mu_D(z') \mid Z=t)}{\Pr(V \leqslant \mu_D(z) \mid Z=z, X=x) - \Pr(V \leqslant \mu_D(z') \mid Z=z', X=x)},$$

$$\delta_2(t) = \frac{\Pr(V > \mu_D(z) \mid Z = t)}{\Pr(V \leqslant \mu_D(z) \mid Z = z, X = x) - \Pr(V \leqslant \mu_D(z') \mid Z = z', X = x)}.$$

Note that $\delta_0(z) = \delta_0(z') = 1$ and the two terms in brackets are zero in the case where Z and V are independent. In the more general case, δ_0 may be bigger or smaller than 1, and the terms in brackets are of unknown sign. In general, LATE may be negative even when Δ is positive for all individuals.

Now consider LIV. For simplicity, take the case where Z is a continuous scalar r.v. Let $f_{V|Z}(v|z)$ denote the density of V conditional on $Z = z$, and assume that this density is differentiable in z. Then we obtain

$$\begin{aligned}
&\frac{\partial E(Y \mid X = x, Z = z)}{\partial z} \\
&\quad = E\big(\Delta \mid X = x, V = \mu_D(z)\big)\mu_D'(z) f_{V|Z,X}\big(v \mid x, \mu_D(z)\big) \\
&\qquad + \left[\int_{-\infty}^{\mu_D(z)} E(Y_1 \mid X = x, V = v)\frac{\partial f_{V|Z,X}(v|z,x)}{\partial z}\,dv\right. \\
&\qquad + \left.\int_{\mu_D(z)}^{\infty} E(Y_0 \mid X = x, V = v)\frac{\partial f_{V|Z,X}(v|z,x)}{\partial z}\,dv\right],
\end{aligned}$$

and

$$\begin{aligned}
\frac{\partial \Pr(D = 1 \mid Z = z)}{\partial z} &= f_{V|Z,X}\big(v \mid x, \mu_D(z)\big)\mu_D'(z) \\
&\quad + \int_{-\infty}^{\mu_D(z)} \frac{\partial f_{V|Z,X}(v|z,x)}{\partial z}\,dv.
\end{aligned}$$

LIV is the ratio of the two terms. Thus, without the independence condition, the relationship between LIV and the MTE breaks down.

PROOF OF EQUATION (4.20).

$$\begin{aligned}
&E(Y_p \mid X) \\
&\quad = \int E(Y_p \mid X, V = v, Z_p = z)\,dF_{V,Z_p|X}(v,z) \\
&\quad = \int \big(\mathbf{1}_\Omega(z)E(Y_1 \mid X, V = v, Z_p = z) \\
&\qquad + \mathbf{1}_{\Omega^c}(z)E(Y_0 \mid X, V = v, Z_p = z)\big)\,dF_{V,Z_p|X}(v,z) \\
&\quad = \int \big(\mathbf{1}_\Omega(z)E(Y_1 \mid X, V = v) + \mathbf{1}_{\Omega^c}(z)E(Y_0 \mid X, V = v)\big)\,dF_{V,Z_p|X}(v,z) \\
&\quad = \int\left[\int \big(\mathbf{1}_\Omega(z)E(Y_1 \mid X, V = v)\right. \\
&\qquad \left. + \mathbf{1}_{\Omega^c}(z)E(Y_0 \mid X, V = v)\big)\,dF_{Z_p|X}(z)\right] dF_{V|X}(v)
\end{aligned}$$

$$= \int \big[\Pr[Z_p \in \Omega \mid X] E(Y_1 \mid X, V = v) + \big(1 - \Pr[Z_p \in \Omega(z) \mid X]\big) E(Y_0 \mid X, V = v)\big]\, dF_{V|X}(v),$$

where $\Omega^c(z)$ denotes the complement of $\Omega(z)$ and where the first equality follows from the law of iterated expectations; the second equality follows by plugging in our threshold crossing model for D; the third equality follows from independence $Z \perp\!\!\!\perp (Y_1, Y_0, V) \mid X$; the fourth and fifth equalities follow by an application of Fubini's Theorem and a rearrangement of terms. Fubini's Theorem may be applied by assumption (A-4). Thus comparing policy p to policy p', we obtain (4.20):

$$\begin{aligned} &E(Y_p \mid X) - E(Y_{p'} \mid X) \\ &\quad = \int E(\Delta \mid X, V = v)\big(\Pr[Z_p \in \Omega \mid X] - \Pr[Z_{p'} \in \Omega \mid X]\big)\, dF_{V|X}(v). \end{aligned}$$

□

PROOF OF EQUATION (4.21).

$$\begin{aligned} &E(Y_p \mid X) \\ &\quad = \int E(Y_p \mid X, V = v, Z_p = z)\, dF_{V,Z_p|X}(v, z) \\ &\quad = \int \big[\mathbf{1}_{[-\infty,\mu_D(z)]}(v) E(Y_1 \mid X, Z = z, V = v) \\ &\qquad + \mathbf{1}_{(\mu_D(z),\infty]}(v) E(Y_0 \mid X, Z = z, V = v)\big]\, dF_{V,Z_p|X}(v, z) \\ &\quad = \int \big[\mathbf{1}_{[-\infty,\mu_D(z)]}(v) E(Y_1 \mid X, V = v) \\ &\qquad + \mathbf{1}_{(\mu_D(z),\infty]}(v) E(Y_0 \mid X, V = v)\big]\, dF_{V,Z_p|X}(v, z) \\ &\quad = \int \bigg[\int \big(\mathbf{1}_{[-\infty,\mu_D(z)]}(v) E(Y_1 \mid X, V = v) \\ &\qquad + \mathbf{1}_{(\mu_D(z),\infty]}(v) E(Y_0 \mid X, V = v)\big)\, dF_{Z_p|V}(z|v)\bigg]\, dF_{V|X}(v) \\ &\quad = \int \big[\big(1 - \Pr\big[\mu_D(Z_p) < v \bigm| V = v\big]\big) E(Y_1 \mid X, V = v) \\ &\qquad + \Pr\big[\mu_D(Z_p) < v \bigm| V = v\big] E(Y_0 \mid X, V = v)\big]\, dF_{V|X}(v), \end{aligned}$$

where the first equality follows from the law of iterated expectations; the second equality follows by plugging in our model for D; the third equality follows from independence $Z \perp\!\!\!\perp (Y_1, Y_0) \mid X, V$; the fourth equality follows by an application of Fubini's Theorem; and the final equality follows immediately. Thus comparing policy p to policy p', we obtain (4.21) in the text. □

Appendix C: Derivation of PRTE and implications of noninvariance for PRTE

PROOF OF EQUATION (3.6). To simplify the notation, assume that $\Upsilon(Y) = Y$. Modifications required for the more general case are obvious. Define $\mathbf{1}_{\mathcal{P}}(t)$ to be the indicator function for the event $t \in \mathcal{P}$. Then

$$\begin{aligned}
&E(Y_p \mid X) \\
&= \int_0^1 E\big(Y_p \mid X, P_p(Z_p) = t\big)\, dF_{P_p|X}(t) \\
&= \int_0^1 \Bigg[\int_0^1 \big[\mathbf{1}_{[0,t]}(u_D) E(Y_{1,p} \mid X, U_D = u_D) \\
&\qquad + \mathbf{1}_{(t,1]}(u_D) E(Y_{0,p} \mid X, U_D = u_D)\big]\, du_D \Bigg] dF_{P_p|X}(t) \\
&= \int_0^1 \Bigg[\int_0^1 \big[\mathbf{1}_{[u_D,1]}(t) E(Y_{1,p} \mid X, U_D = u_D) \\
&\qquad + \mathbf{1}_{(0,u_D]}(t) E(Y_{0,p} \mid X, U_D = u_D)\big]\, dF_{P_p|X}(t) \Bigg] du_D \\
&= \int_0^1 \big[\big(1 - F_{P_p|X}(u_D)\big) E(Y_{1,p} \mid X, U_D = u_D) \\
&\qquad + F_{P_p|X}(u_D) E(Y_{0,p} \mid X, U_D = u_D)\big]\, du_D.
\end{aligned}$$ [198]

This derivation involves changing the order of integration. Note that from (A-4),

$$\begin{aligned}
&E\big|\mathbf{1}_{[0,t]}(u_D) E(Y_{1,p} \mid X, U_D = u_D) \\
&\qquad + \mathbf{1}_{(t,1]}(u_D) E(Y_{0,p} \mid X, U_D = u_D)\big| \leqslant E\big(|Y_1| + |Y_0|\big) < \infty,
\end{aligned}$$

so the change in the order of integration is valid by Fubini's Theorem. Comparing policy p to policy p',

$$\begin{aligned}
&E(Y_p \mid X) - E(Y_{p'} \mid X) \\
&= \int_0^1 E(\Delta \mid X, U_D = u_D)\big(F_{P_{p'}|X}(u_D) - F_{P_p|X}(u_D)\big)\, du_D,
\end{aligned}$$

which gives the required weights. (Recall $\Delta = Y_1 - Y_0$ and from (A-7) we can drop the p, p' subscripts on outcomes and errors.) □

[198] Recall that p denotes the policy in this section and t is a value assumed by $P(Z)$.

RELAXING A-7 *(Implications of noninvariance for PRTE).* Suppose that all of the assumptions invoked up through Section 3.2 are satisfied, including additive separability in the latent index choice equation (3.3) (equivalently, the monotonicity or uniformity condition). Impose the normalization that the distribution of U_D is unit uniform ($U_D = F_{V|X}(V \mid X)$). Suppose however, contrary to (A-7), that the distribution of (Y_1, Y_0, U_D, X) is different under the two regimes p and p'. Thus, let $(Y_{1,p}, Y_{0,p}, U_{D,p}, X_p)$ and $(Y_{1,p'}, Y_{0,p'}, U_{D,p'}, X_{p'})$ denote the random vectors under regimes p and p', respectively. Following the same analysis as used to derive Equation (3.6), the PRTE conditional on X is given by

$$
\begin{aligned}
&E(Y_p \mid X_p = x) - E(Y_{p'} \mid X_{p'} = x) \\
&\quad = \int_0^1 E(Y_{1,p} - Y_{0,p} \mid X_p = x, U_{D,p} = u) \\
&\qquad \times \left[F_{P_{p'}|X_{p'}}(u|x) - F_{P_p|X_p}(u|x)\right] du \qquad \text{(I)} \\
&\qquad + \int_0^1 \left[E(Y_{0,p} \mid X_p = x, U_{D,p} = u) - E(Y_{0,p'} \mid X_{p'} = x, U_{D,p'} = u)\right] du \qquad \text{(II)} \\
&\qquad + \int_0^1 \big[\big(1 - F_{P_{p'}|X_{p'}}(u|x)\big)\big(E(Y_{1,p} - Y_{0,p} \mid X_p = x, U_{D,p} = u) \\
&\qquad - E(Y_{1,p'} - Y_{0,p'} \mid X_{p'} = x, U_{D,p'} = u)\big)\big] du. \qquad \text{(III)}
\end{aligned}
$$

Thus, when the policy affects the distribution of (Y_1, Y_0, U_D, X), the PRTE is given by the sum of three terms: (I) the value of PRTE if the policy did not affect (Y_1, Y_0, X, U_D); (II) the weighted effect of the policy change on $E(Y_0 \mid X, U_D)$; and (III) the weighted effect of the policy change on MTE. Evaluating the PRTE requires knowledge of the MTE function in both regimes, knowledge of $E(Y_0 \mid X = x, U_D = u)$ in both regimes, as well as knowledge of the distribution of $P(Z)$ in both regimes. Note, however, that if we assume that the distribution of $(Y_{1,p}, Y_{0,p}, U_{D,p})$ conditional on $X_p = x$ equals the distribution of $(Y_{1,p'}, Y_{0,p'}, U_{D,p'})$ conditional on $X_{p'} = x$, then $E(Y_{1,p} \mid U_{D,p} = u, X_p = x) = E(Y_{1,p'} \mid U_{D,p'} = u, X_{p'} = x)$, $E(Y_{0,p} \mid U_{D,p} = u, X_p = x) = E(Y_{0,p'} \mid U_{D,p'} = u, X_{p'} = x)$, and thus the last two terms vanish and the expression for PRTE simplifies to the expression of Equation (3.6).

Appendix D: Deriving the IV weights on MTE

We consider instrumental variables conditional on $X = x$ using a general function of Z as an instrument. To simplify the notation, we keep the conditioning on X implicit. Let $J(Z)$ be any function of Z such that $\operatorname{Cov}(J(Z), D) \neq 0$. Consider the population analogue of the IV estimator,

$$
\frac{\operatorname{Cov}(J(Z), Y)}{\operatorname{Cov}(J(Z), D)}.
$$

First consider the numerator of this expression,

$$\begin{aligned}\operatorname{Cov}(J(Z), Y) &= E([J(Z) - E(J(Z))]Y)\\ &= E((J(Z) - E(J(Z)))(Y_0 + D(Y_1 - Y_0)))\\ &= E((J(Z) - E(J(Z)))D(Y_1 - Y_0)),\end{aligned}$$

where the second equality comes from substituting in the definition of Y and the third equality follows from conditional independence assumption (A-1). Define $\tilde{J}(Z) \equiv J(Z) - E(J(Z))$. Then

$$\begin{aligned}&\operatorname{Cov}(J(Z), Y)\\ &\quad = E(\tilde{J}(Z)\mathbf{1}[U_D \leqslant P(Z)](Y_1 - Y_0))\\ &\quad = E(\tilde{J}(Z)\mathbf{1}[U_D \leqslant P(Z)]E(Y_1 - Y_0 \mid Z, U_D))\\ &\quad = E(\tilde{J}(Z)\mathbf{1}[U_D \leqslant P(Z)]E(Y_1 - Y_0 \mid U_D))\\ &\quad = E_{U_D}(E_Z[\tilde{J}(Z)\mathbf{1}[U_D \leqslant P(Z)] \mid U_D]E(Y_1 - Y_0 \mid U_D))\\ &\quad = \int_0^1 \{E(\tilde{J}(Z) \mid P(Z) \geqslant u_D)\Pr(P(Z) \geqslant u_D)E(Y_1 - Y_0 \mid U_D = u_D)\}\, du_D\\ &\quad = \int_0^1 \Delta^{\mathrm{MTE}}(x, u_D)E(\tilde{J}(Z) \mid P(Z) \geqslant u_D)\Pr(P(Z) \geqslant u_D)\, du_D,\end{aligned}$$

where the first equality follows from plugging in the model for D; the second equality follows from the law of iterated expectations with the inside expectation conditional on (Z, U_D); the third equality follows from conditional independence assumption (A-1); the fourth equality follows from Fubini's Theorem and the law of iterated expectations with the inside expectation conditional on $(U_D = u_D)$ (and implicitly on X); this allows to reverse the order of integration in a multiple integral; the fifth equality follows from the normalization that U_D is distributed unit uniform conditional on X; and the final equality follows from plugging in the definition of Δ^{MTE}. Next consider the denominator of the IV estimand. Observe that by iterated expectations

$$\operatorname{Cov}(J(Z), D) = \operatorname{Cov}(J(Z), P(Z)).$$

Thus, the population analogue of the IV estimator is given by

$$\int_0^1 \Delta^{\mathrm{MTE}}(u_D)\omega(u_D)\, du_D, \tag{D.1}$$

where

$$\omega(u_D) = \frac{E(\tilde{J}(Z) \mid P(Z) \geqslant u_D)\Pr(P(Z) \geqslant u_D)}{\operatorname{Cov}(J(Z), P(Z))}, \tag{D.2}$$

where by assumption $\operatorname{Cov}(J(Z), P(Z)) \neq 0$.

If $J(Z)$ and $P(Z)$ are continuous random variables, then an interpretation of the weight can be derived from (D.2) by noting that

$$\int (j - E(J(Z))) \int_{u_D}^{1} f_{P,J}(t, j)\, dt\, dj$$
$$= \int (j - E(J(Z))) f_J(j) \int_{u_D}^{1} f_{P|J}(t \mid J(Z) = j)\, dt\, dj.$$

Write

$$\int_{u_D}^{1} f_{P|J}(t \mid J(Z) = j)\, dt = 1 - F_{P|J}(u_D \mid J(Z) = j)$$
$$= S_{P|J}(u_D \mid J(Z) = j),$$

where $S_{P|J}(u_D \mid J(Z) = j)$ is the probability of $(P(Z) \geqslant u_D)$ given $J(Z) = j$ (and implicitly $X = x$). Likewise, $\Pr[P(Z) > U_D \mid J(Z)] = S_{P|J}(U_D \mid J(Z))$. Using these results, we may write the weight as

$$\omega(u_D) = \frac{\operatorname{Cov}(J(Z), S_{P|J}(u_D \mid J(Z)))}{\operatorname{Cov}(J(Z), S_{P|J}(U_D \mid J(Z)))}.$$

For fixed u_D and x evaluation points, $S_{P|J}(u_D \mid J(Z))$ is a function of the random variable $J(Z)$. The numerator of the preceding expression is the covariance between $J(Z)$ and the probability that the random variable $P(Z)$ is greater than the evaluation point u_D conditional on $J(Z)$.

$S_{P|J}(U_D \mid J(Z))$ is a function of the random variables U_D and $J(Z)$. The denominator of the above expression is the covariance between $J(Z)$ and the probability that the random variable $P(Z)$ is greater than the random variable U_D conditional on $J(Z)$. Thus, it is clear that if the covariance between $J(Z)$ and the conditional probability that $(P(Z) > u_D)$ given $J(Z)$ is positive for all u_D, then the weights are positive. The conditioning is trivially satisfied if $J(Z) = P(Z)$, so the weights are positive and IV estimates a gross treatment effect. If the $J(Z)$ and $P(Z)$ are discrete-valued, we obtain expressions and (4.15) and (4.16) in the text.

D.1. Yitzhaki's Theorem and the IV weights [Yitzhaki (1989)]

THEOREM. *Assume (Y, X) i.i.d., $E(|Y|) < \infty$, $E(|X|) < \infty$, $g(X) = E(Y \mid X)$, $g'(X)$ exists and $E(|g'(x)|) < \infty$. Let $\mu_Y = E(Y)$ and $\mu_X = E(X)$. Then,*

$$\frac{\operatorname{Cov}(Y, X)}{\operatorname{Var}(X)} = \int_{-\infty}^{\infty} g'(t)\omega(t)\, dt,$$

where

$$\omega(t) = \frac{1}{\operatorname{Var}(X)} \int_{t}^{\infty} (x - \mu_X) f_X(x)\, dx$$

$$= \frac{1}{\mathrm{Var}(X)} E(X - \mu_X \mid X > t)\Pr(X > t).$$

PROOF.

$$\begin{aligned}\mathrm{Cov}(Y, X) &= \mathrm{Cov}\big(E(Y \mid X), X\big) = \mathrm{Cov}\big(g(X), X\big) \\ &= \int_{-\infty}^{\infty} g(t)(t - \mu_X)\, f_X(t)\, dt.\end{aligned}$$

Integration by parts implies that

$$\begin{aligned}&= g(t) \int_{-\infty}^{t} (x - \mu_X) f_X(x)\, dx \bigg|_{-\infty}^{\infty} \\ &\quad - \int_{-\infty}^{\infty} g'(t) \int_{-\infty}^{t} (x - \mu_X)\, f_X(x)\, dx\, dt \\ &= \int_{-\infty}^{\infty} g'(t) \int_{t}^{\infty} (x - \mu_X)\, f_X(x)\, dx\, dt,\end{aligned}$$

since $E(X - \mu_X) = 0$ and the first term in the first expression vanishes.

Therefore,

$$\mathrm{Cov}(Y, X) = \int_{-\infty}^{\infty} g'(t) E(X - \mu_X \mid X > t)\Pr(X > t)\, dt,$$

so

$$\omega(t) = \frac{1}{\mathrm{Var}(X)} E(X - \mu_X \mid X > t)\Pr(X > t).$$

□

Notice that:

(i) The weights are nonnegative ($\omega(t) \geqslant 0$).
(ii) They integrate to one (use an integration by parts formula).
(iii) $\omega(t) \to 0$ when $t \to -\infty$, and $\omega(t) \to 0$ when $t \to \infty$.

We get the formula in the text when we use $P(Z)$, with a suitably defined domain, in place of X. We apply Yitzhaki's result to the treatment effect model:

$$Y = \alpha + \beta D + \varepsilon,$$

$$\begin{aligned}E\big(Y \mid P(Z)\big) &= \alpha + E\big(\beta \mid D = 1, P(Z)\big)P(Z) \\ &= \alpha + E\big(\beta \mid P(Z) > u_D, P(Z)\big)P(Z) \\ &= g\big(P(Z)\big).\end{aligned}$$

By the law of iterated expectations, we eliminate the conditioning on $D = 0$. Using our previous results for OLS,

$$\text{IV} = \frac{\text{Cov}(Y, P(Z))}{\text{Cov}(D, P(Z))} = \int g'(t)\omega(t)\,dt,$$

$$g'(t) = \frac{\partial[E(\beta \mid D = 1, P(Z))]P(Z)}{\partial P(Z)}\bigg|_{P(Z)=t},$$

$$\omega(t) = \frac{\int_t^1 [\varphi - E(P(Z))] f_P(\varphi)\,d\varphi}{\text{Cov}(P(Z), D)}.$$

Under (A-1) to (A-5) and separability, $g'(t) = \Delta^{\text{MTE}}(t)$ but $g'(t) = \text{LIV}$, for $P(Z)$ as an instrument.

D.2. Relationship of our weights to the Yitzhaki weights[199]

Under our assumptions the Yitzhaki weights and ours are equivalent. Using (4.12),

$$\begin{aligned}\text{Cov}\big(J(Z), Y\big) &= E(Y \cdot \tilde{J}) = E\big(E(Y \mid Z) \cdot \tilde{J}(Z)\big) \\ &= E\big(E\big(Y \mid P(Z)\big) \cdot \tilde{J}(Z)\big) = E\big(g\big(P(Z)\big) \cdot \tilde{J}(Z)\big).\end{aligned}$$

The third equality follows from index sufficiency and $\tilde{J} = J(Z) - E(J(Z) \mid P(Z) \geqslant u_D)$, where $E(Y \mid P(Z)) = g(P(Z))$. Writing out the expectation and assuming that $J(Z)$ and $P(Z)$ are continuous random variables with joint density $f_{P,J}$ and that $J(Z)$ has support $[\underline{J}, \bar{J}]$,

$$\begin{aligned}\text{Cov}\big(J(Z), Y\big) &= \int_0^1 \int_{\underline{J}}^{\bar{J}} g(u_D)\tilde{j} f_{P,J}(u_D, j)\,dj\,du_D \\ &= \int_0^1 g(u_D) \int_{\underline{J}}^{\bar{J}} \tilde{j} f_{P,J}(u_D, j)\,dj\,du_D.\end{aligned}$$

Using an integration by parts argument as in Yitzhaki (1989) and as summarized in Heckman, Urzua and Vytlacil (2006), we obtain

$$\begin{aligned}\text{Cov}\big(J(Z), Y\big) &= g(u_D) \int_0^{u_D} \int_{\underline{J}}^{\bar{J}} \tilde{j} f_{P,J}(p, j)\,dj\,dp\bigg|_0^1 \\ &\quad - \int_0^1 g'(u_D) \int_0^{u_D} \int_{\underline{J}}^{\bar{J}} \tilde{j} f_{P,J}(p, j)\,dj\,dp\,du_D \\ &= \int_0^1 g'(u_D) \int_{u_D}^1 \int_{\underline{J}}^{\bar{J}} \tilde{j} f_{P,J}(p, j)\,dj\,dp\,du_D\end{aligned}$$

[199] We thank Benjamin Moll for the derivation presented in this subsection.

$$= \int_0^1 g'(u_D) E\big(\tilde{J}(Z) \mid P(Z) \geqslant u_D\big) \Pr\big(P(Z) \geqslant u_D\big)\, du_D,$$

which is then exactly the expression given in (4.12), where

$$g'(u_D) = \frac{\partial E(Y \mid P(Z) = p)}{\partial P(Z)}\bigg|_{p=u_D} = \Delta^{\mathrm{MTE}}(u_D).$$

Appendix E: Derivation of the weights for the mixture of normals example

Writing E_1 as the expectation for group 1, letting μ_1 be the mean of Z for population 1 and μ_{11} be the mean of the first component of Z,

$$\begin{aligned}
&E_1(Z_1 \mid \gamma' Z > v) \\
&\quad = \mu_{11} + \frac{\gamma' \Sigma_1^1}{\gamma' \Sigma_1 \gamma} E_1(Z_1 - \mu_1 \mid \gamma' Z > v) \\
&\quad = \mu_{11} + \frac{\gamma' \Sigma_1^1}{(\gamma' \Sigma_1 \gamma)^{1/2}} E_1\left(\frac{\gamma'(Z - \mu_1)}{(\gamma' \Sigma_1 \gamma)^{1/2}} \;\Big|\; \frac{\gamma'(Z - \mu_1)}{(\gamma' \Sigma_1 \gamma)^{1/2}} > \frac{(v - \gamma' \mu_1)}{(\gamma' \Sigma_1 \gamma)^{1/2}}\right) \\
&\quad = \mu_{11} + \frac{\gamma' \Sigma_1^1}{(\gamma' \Sigma_1 \gamma)^{1/2}} \lambda\left(\frac{(v - \gamma' \mu_1)}{(\gamma' \Sigma_1 \gamma)^{1/2}}\right),
\end{aligned}$$

where

$$\lambda(c) = \frac{1}{\sqrt{2\pi}} \frac{e^{-c^2/2}}{\Phi(-c)},$$

where $\Phi(\cdot)$ is the unit normal cumulative distribution function.

By the same logic, in the second group:

$$E_2(Z_1 \mid \gamma' Z > v) = \mu_{21} + \frac{\gamma' \Sigma_2^1}{(\gamma' \Sigma_2 \gamma)^{1/2}} \lambda\left(\frac{(v - \gamma' \mu_2)}{(\gamma' \Sigma_2 \gamma)^{1/2}}\right).$$

Therefore for the overall population we obtain

$$\begin{aligned}
&E\big(Z_1 - E(Z_1) \mid \gamma' Z > v\big) \Pr(\gamma' Z > v) \\
&\quad = (P_1 \mu_{11} + P_2 \mu_{21}) \Pr(\gamma' Z > v) \\
&\qquad + \frac{P_1 \gamma \Sigma_1^1}{(\gamma' \Sigma_1 \gamma)^{1/2} \sqrt{2\pi}} \exp\left[-\frac{1}{2}\left(\frac{v - \gamma' \mu_1}{(\gamma' \Sigma_1 \gamma)^{1/2}}\right)^2\right] \\
&\qquad + \frac{P_2 \gamma \Sigma_2^1}{(\gamma' \Sigma_2 \gamma)^{1/2} \sqrt{2\pi}} \exp\left[-\frac{1}{2}\left(\frac{v - \gamma' \mu_2}{(\gamma' \Sigma_2 \gamma)^{1/2}}\right)^2\right] \\
&\qquad - (P_1 \mu_{11} + P_2 \mu_{21}) \Pr(\gamma' Z > v) \\
&\quad = \frac{P_1 \gamma \Sigma_1^1}{(\gamma' \Sigma_1 \gamma)^{1/2} \sqrt{2\pi}} \exp\left[-\frac{1}{2}\left(\frac{v - \gamma' \mu_1}{(\gamma' \Sigma_1 \gamma)^{1/2}}\right)^2\right]
\end{aligned}$$

$$+\frac{P_2\gamma\Sigma_2^1}{(\gamma'\Sigma_2\gamma)^{1/2}\sqrt{2\pi}}\exp\left[-\frac{1}{2}\left(\frac{v-\gamma'\mu_2}{(\gamma'\Sigma_2\gamma)^{1/2}}\right)^2\right].$$

We need $\mathrm{Cov}(D, Z_1)$. To obtain it, observe that

$$D = \mathbf{1}[\gamma' Z - V > 0],$$
$$E(Z_1 D) = E\big(Z_1 \mathbf{1}(\gamma' Z - V \geqslant 0)\big).$$

Let E_1 denote the expectation for group 1, and let E_2 denote the expectation for group 2.

$$\begin{aligned}
E(Z_1 D) &= \left\{P_1\left[\mu_{11} + \frac{\gamma'\Sigma_1^1}{\gamma'\Sigma_1\gamma+\sigma_V^2}E_1(Z_1-\mu_{11}\mid\gamma'Z-V\geqslant 0)\right]\right.\\
&\quad\left. + P_2\left[\mu_{21} + \frac{\gamma'\Sigma_2^1}{\gamma'\Sigma_2\gamma+\sigma_V^2}E_2(Z_1-\mu_{21}\mid\gamma'Z-V\geqslant 0)\right]\right\}\\
&\quad \times \Pr\big[(\gamma'Z-V)>0\big]\\
&= (P_1\mu_{11}+P_2\mu_{21})\Pr(\gamma'Z-V\geqslant 0)\\
&\quad + \frac{P_1\gamma'\Sigma_1^1}{(\gamma'\Sigma_1\gamma+\sigma_V^2)^{1/2}\sqrt{2\pi}}\exp\left[-\left(\frac{-\gamma'\mu_1}{(\gamma'\Sigma_1\gamma+\sigma_V^2)^{1/2}}\right)^2\right]\\
&\quad + \frac{P_2\gamma'\Sigma_2^1}{(\gamma'\Sigma_2\gamma+\sigma_V^2)^{1/2}\sqrt{2\pi}}\exp\left[-\left(\frac{-\gamma'\mu_2}{(\gamma'\Sigma_2\gamma+\sigma_V^2)^{1/2}}\right)^2\right].
\end{aligned}$$

Because

$$E(D)E(Z_1) = \Pr(\gamma'Z - V \geqslant 0)(P_1\mu_{11} + P_2\mu_{21})$$

and

$$\mathrm{Cov}(D, Z_1) = E(Z_1 D) - E(Z_1)E(D)$$

$$\begin{aligned}
\therefore\quad \mathrm{Cov}(D, Z_1) &= \frac{P_1\gamma'\Sigma_1^1}{(\gamma'\Sigma_1\gamma+\sigma_V^2)^{1/2}\sqrt{2\pi}}\exp\left[-\left(\frac{-\gamma'\mu_1}{(\gamma'\Sigma_1\gamma+\sigma_V^2)^{1/2}}\right)^2\right]\\
&\quad + \frac{P_2\gamma'\Sigma_2^1}{(\gamma'\Sigma_2\gamma+\sigma_V^2)^{1/2}\sqrt{2\pi}}\exp\left[-\left(\frac{-\gamma'\mu_2}{(\gamma'\Sigma_2\gamma+\sigma_V^2)^{1/2}}\right)^2\right].
\end{aligned}$$

Thus the IV weights for this set-up are

$$\begin{aligned}
\tilde{\omega}_{\mathrm{IV}}(v) &= \left\{\left[\frac{P_1\gamma'\Sigma_1^1}{(\gamma'\Sigma_1\gamma)^{1/2}}\exp\left[-\frac{1}{2}\left(\frac{v-\gamma'\mu_1}{(\gamma'\Sigma_1\gamma)^{1/2}}\right)^2\right]\right.\right.\\
&\quad\left.\left. + \frac{P_2\gamma'\Sigma_2^1}{(\gamma'\Sigma_2\gamma)^{1/2}}\exp\left[-\frac{1}{2}\left(\frac{v-\gamma'\mu_2}{(\gamma'\Sigma_2\gamma)^{1/2}}\right)^2\right]\right]f_V(v)\right\}
\end{aligned}$$

$$\times \left\{ \frac{P_1 \gamma' \Sigma_1^1}{(\gamma' \Sigma_1 \gamma + \sigma_V^2)^{1/2}} \exp\left[-\left(\frac{-\gamma' \mu_1}{(\gamma' \Sigma_1 \gamma + \sigma_V^2)^{1/2}} \right)^2 \right] + \frac{P_2 \gamma' \Sigma_2^1}{(\gamma' \Sigma_2 \gamma + \sigma_V^2)^{1/2}} \exp\left[-\left(\frac{-\gamma' \mu_2}{(\gamma' \Sigma_2 \gamma + \sigma_V^2)^{1/2}} \right)^2 \right] \right\}^{-1},$$

where σ_V^2 represents the variance of V. Clearly, $\tilde{\omega}_{\mathrm{IV}}(-\infty) = 0$, $\tilde{\omega}_{\mathrm{IV}}(\infty) = 0$ and the weights integrate to one over the support of $V = (-\infty, \infty)$. Observe that the weights must be positive if $P_2 = 0$. Thus the structure of the covariances of the instrument with the choice index $\gamma' Z$ is a key determinant of the positivity of the weights for any instrument. It has nothing to do with the *ceteris paribus* effect of Z_1 on $\gamma' Z$ or $P(Z)$ in the general case.

A necessary condition for $\omega_{\mathrm{IV}} < 0$ over some values of v is that $\operatorname{sign}(\gamma' \Sigma_1^1) = -\operatorname{sign}(\gamma' \Sigma_2^1)$, i.e., that the covariance between Z_1 and $\gamma' Z$ be of opposite signs in the two subpopulations so Z_1 and $P(Z)$ have different relationships in the two component populations. Without loss of generality, assume that $\gamma' \Sigma_1^1 > 0$. If it equals zero, we fail the rank condition in the first population and we are back to a one subpopulation model with positive weights. The numerator of the expression for $\omega_{\mathrm{IV}}(v)$ switches signs if for some values of v,

$$\frac{P_1 \gamma' \Sigma_1^1}{(\gamma' \Sigma_1 \gamma)^{1/2}} \exp\left[-\frac{1}{2} \left(\frac{v - \gamma' \mu_1}{(\gamma' \Sigma_1 \gamma)^{1/2}} \right)^2 \right] < -\frac{P_2 \gamma' \Sigma_2^1}{(\gamma' \Sigma_2 \gamma)^{1/2}} \exp\left[-\frac{1}{2} \left(\frac{v - \gamma' \mu_2}{(\gamma' \Sigma_2 \gamma)^{1/2}} \right)^2 \right],$$

while for other values the inequality is reversed. (Observe that the denominator is a constant.) Rewriting and taking logarithms, we obtain under the assumption that $\operatorname{sign}(\gamma' \Sigma_1^1) = -\operatorname{sign}(\gamma' \Sigma_2^1)$, the following expression:

$$\frac{1}{2} \left[\frac{(v - \gamma' \mu_2)^2}{\gamma' \Sigma_2 \gamma} - \frac{(v - \gamma' \mu_1)^2}{\gamma' \Sigma_1 \gamma} \right] < \ln\left(\frac{1 - P_1}{P_1} \right) + \ln\left[\frac{-\gamma' \Sigma_2^1}{\gamma' \Sigma_1^1} \right] + \ln\left[\frac{\gamma' \Sigma_1 \gamma}{\gamma' \Sigma_2 \gamma} \right],$$

where we assume $0 < P_1 < 1$. Observe that $\frac{1-P_1}{P_1}$ can be made as large or as small a non-negative number as we like by varying P_1. Varying (μ_1, μ_2) does not affect the right-hand side. For $\mu_1 = \mu_2 = 0$, the inequality becomes

$$\frac{1}{2} v^2 \left[\frac{1}{\gamma' \Sigma_2 \gamma} - \frac{1}{\gamma' \Sigma_1 \gamma} \right] < \ln\left(\frac{1 - P_1}{P_1} \right) + \ln\left[\frac{-\gamma' \Sigma_2^1}{\gamma' \Sigma_1^1} \right] + \ln\left[\frac{\gamma' \Sigma_1 \gamma}{\gamma' \Sigma_2 \gamma} \right].$$

Suppose that $\gamma' \Sigma_2 \gamma < \gamma' \Sigma_1 \gamma$. Then the left-hand side is positive except when $v = 0$. For any fixed γ, Σ_1, Σ_2 we can find a value of P_1 sufficiently small so that right-hand side of the equation is positive and for any such value of P_1 there will be a v sufficiently small for the inequality to be satisfied. There is also a value of v that reverses the inequality.

The inequality is satisfied for some $v^* \geqslant 0$. But with v arbitrarily large, the inequality can be reversed so that the weight will switch signs at some value of v. The key necessary condition is that $\mathrm{Cov}(Z_1, \gamma' Z)$ be of opposite signs in the two subpopulations. Using Z_1 as an IV, but not conditioning or controlling for the other components of Z, produces sometimes negative and sometimes positive movements in the components of $Z_2, \dots, Z_k$ which can offset the *ceteris paribus* ($Z_2 = z_2, \dots, Z_k = z_k$) movements of Z_1.

Appendix F: Local instrumental variables for the random coefficient model

Consider the model:

$$D = \mathbf{1}[Z\gamma \geqslant 0],$$

where γ is a random variable. For ease of exposition, we leave implicit the conditioning on X covariates. Assume that $(Y_0, Y_1, \gamma) \perp\!\!\!\perp Z$. Assume that γ has a density that is absolutely continuous with respect to Lebesgue measure on $\mathbb{R}^K$. We have

$$E(Y \mid Z = z) = E(DY_1 \mid Z = z) + E\big((1 - D)Y_0 \bigm| Z = z\big).$$

To simplify the exposition, consider the first term, $E(DY_1 \mid Z = z)$. In this proof, let $Z^{[K]}$ denote the Kth element of Z and $Z^{[-K]}$ denote all other elements of Z, and write $Z = (Z^{[-K]}, Z^{[K]})$. Using the model, the independence assumption, and the law of iterated expectations, we have

$$\begin{aligned} E(DY \mid Z = z) &= E\big(\mathbf{1}[z\gamma \geqslant 0]Y_1\big) = E\big(\mathbf{1}[z\gamma \geqslant 0]E(Y_1 \mid \gamma)\big) \\ &= E\big(\mathbf{1}\big\{z^{[K]}\gamma^{[K]} \geqslant -z^{[-K]}\gamma^{[-K]}\big\}\, E(Y_1 \mid \gamma)\big), \end{aligned}$$

where the final outer expectation is over γ. Consider taking the derivative with respect to the Kth element of Z assumed to be continuous. Partition z, γ, and g as $z = (z^{[-K]}, z^{[K]})$, $\gamma = (\gamma^{[-K]}, \gamma^{[K]})$, and $g = (g^{[-K]}, g^{[K]})$, where z is a realization of Z and g is a realization of γ. For simplicity, suppose that the Kth element of z is positive, $z^{[K]} > 0$. We obtain

$$\begin{aligned} E(DY \mid Z = z) &= E\big[E\big(\mathbf{1}\big\{z^{[K]}\gamma^{[K]} \geqslant -z^{[-K]}\gamma^{[-K]}\big\}E(Y_1 \mid \gamma) \bigm| \gamma^{[-K]}\big)\big] \\ &= E\left[E\left(\mathbf{1}\left\{\gamma^{[K]} \geqslant \frac{-z^{[-K]}\gamma^{[-K]}}{z^{[K]}}\right\}E(Y_1 \mid \gamma) \Bigm| \gamma^{[-K]}\right)\right], \end{aligned}$$

where the inside expectation is over $\gamma^{[K]}$ conditional on $\gamma^{[-K]}$, i.e., is over the Kth element of γ conditional on all other components of γ. Computing the derivative with respect to $z^{[K]}$, we obtain

$$\frac{\partial}{\partial z^{[K]}} E(DY \mid Z = z) = \int E\big(Y_1 \mid \gamma = M\big(g^{[-K]}\big)\big)\tilde{w}\big(g^{[-K]}\big)\, dg^{[-K]},$$

where

$$M\left(g^{[-K]}\right) = \left(\left(g^{[-K]}\right)', \frac{-z^{[-K]}g^{[-K]}}{z^{[K]}}\right)' \quad \text{and}$$

$$\tilde{w}\left(g^{[-K]}\right) = \frac{z^{[-K]}g^{[-K]}}{(z^{[K]})^2} f\left(g^{[-K]}, \frac{-z^{[-K]}g^{[-K]}}{z^{[K]}}\right),$$

with $f(\cdot)$ the density of γ (with respect to Lebesgue measure), and where for notational simplicity we suppress the dependence of the function $M(\cdot)$ and the weights $\tilde{w}(\cdot)$ on the z evaluation point. In this expression, we are averaging over $E(Y_1 \mid \gamma = g)$, but only over g evaluation points such that $zg = 0$. In particular, the expression averages over the $K-1$ space of $g^{[-K]}$, while for each potential realization of $g^{[-K]}$ it is filling in the value of $g^{[K]}$ such that $z^{[K]}g^{[K]} = -z^{[-K]}g^{[-K]}$ so that $z^{[K]}g^{[K]} + z^{[-K]}g^{[-K]} = 0$. Note that the weights $\tilde{w}(g^{[-K]})$ will be zero for any $g^{[-K]}$ such that $f(g^{[-K]}, \frac{-z^{[-K]}g^{[-K]}}{z^{[K]}}) = 0$, i.e., the weights will be zero for any $g^{[-K]}$ such that there does not exist $g^{[K]}$ in the conditional support of $\gamma^{[K]}$ with $z^{[K]}g^{[K]} = -z^{[-K]}g^{[-K]}$.

Following the same logic for $E((1-D)Y_0 \mid Z = z)$, we obtain

$$\frac{\partial}{\partial z^{[K]}} E((1-D)Y \mid Z = z) = -\int E\left(Y_0 \mid \gamma = M\left(g^{[-K]}\right)\right)\tilde{w}\left(g^{[-K]}\right) dg^{[-K]}$$

and likewise have

$$\frac{\partial}{\partial z^{[K]}} \Pr(D = 1 \mid Z = z) = \int \tilde{w}\left(g^{[-K]}\right) dg^{[-K]}$$

so that

$$\frac{\frac{\partial}{\partial z^{[K]}} E(Y \mid Z = z)}{\frac{\partial}{\partial z^{[K]}} \Pr(D = 1 \mid Z = z)} = \int E\left(Y_1 - Y_0 \mid \gamma = M\left(g^{[-K]}\right)\right) w\left(g^{[-K]}\right) dg^{[-K]},$$

where

$$w\left(g^{[-K]}\right) = \tilde{w}\left(g^{[-K]}\right) \Big/ \int \tilde{w}\left(g^{[-K]}\right) dg^{[-K]}.$$

Now consider the question of whether this expression will have both positive and negative weights. Recall that $\tilde{w}(g^{[-K]}) = \frac{z^{[-K]}g^{[-K]}}{(z^{[K]})^2} f(g^{[-K]}, \frac{-z^{[-K]}g^{[-K]}}{z^{[K]}})$. Thus,

$$\tilde{w}\left(g^{[-K]}\right) \geqslant 0 \quad \text{if } z^{[-K]}g^{[-K]} > 0, \qquad \tilde{w}\left(g^{[-K]}\right) \leqslant 0 \quad \text{if } z^{[-K]}g^{[-K]} < 0,$$

and will be nonzero if $z^{[-K]}g^{[-K]} \neq 0$ and there exists $g^{[K]}$ in the conditional support of $\gamma^{[K]}$ with $z^{[K]}g^{[K]} = z^{[-K]}g^{[-K]}$, i.e., with $zg = 0$. We thus have that there will be both positive and negative weights on the MTE if there exist values of g in the support of γ with both $z^{[-K]}g^{[-K]} > 0$ and $zg = 0$, and there exist other values of g in the support of γ with $z^{[-K]}g^{[-K]} < 0$ and $zg = 0$.

Appendix G: Generalized ordered choice model with stochastic thresholds

The ordered choice model presented in the text with parameterized, but nonstochastic, thresholds is analyzed in Cameron and Heckman (1998) who establish its nonparametric identifiability under the conditions they specify. Treating the W_s (or components of it) as unobservables, we obtain the generalized ordered choice model analyzed in Carneiro, Hansen and Heckman (2003) and Cunha, Heckman and Navarro (2007). In this appendix, we present the main properties of this more general model.

The thresholds are now written as $Q_s + C_s(W_s)$ in place of $C_s(W_s)$, where Q_s is a random variable. In addition to the order on the $C_s(W_s)$ in the text, we impose the order $Q_s + C_s(W_s) \geqslant Q_{s-1} + C_{s-1}(W_{s-1})$, $s = 2, \ldots, \bar{S} - 1$. We impose the requirement that $Q_{\bar{S}} = \infty$ and $Q_0 = -\infty$. The latent index D_s^* is as defined in the text, but now

$$\begin{aligned} D_s &= \mathbf{1}\big[C_{s-1}(W_{s-1}) + Q_{s-1} < \mu_D(Z) - V \leqslant C_s(W_s) + Q_s\big] \\ &= \mathbf{1}\big[l_{s-1}(Z, W_{s-1}) - Q_{s-1} > V \geqslant l_s(Z, W_s) - Q_s\big], \end{aligned}$$

where $l_s = \mu_D(Z) - C_s(W_s)$. Using the fact that $l_s(Z, W_s) - Q_s < l_{s-1}(Z, W_{s-1}) - Q_{s-1}$, we obtain

$$\begin{aligned} &\mathbf{1}\big[l_{s-1}(Z, W_{s-1}) - Q_{s-1} > V \geqslant l_s(Z, W_s) - Q_s\big] \\ &\quad = \mathbf{1}\big[V + Q_{s-1} < l_{s-1}(Z, W_{s-1})\big] - \mathbf{1}\big[V + Q_s \leqslant l_s(Z, W_s)\big]. \end{aligned}$$

The nonparametric identifiability of this choice model is established in Carneiro, Hansen and Heckman (2003) and Cunha, Heckman and Navarro (2007). We retain assumptions (OC-2)–(OC-6), but alter (OC-1) to

(OC-1)′ $(Q_s, U_s, V) \perp\!\!\!\perp (Z, W) \mid X$, $s = 1, \ldots, \bar{S}$.

Vytlacil (2006b) shows that this model with no transition specific instruments (with W_s degenerate for each s) implies and is implied by the independence and monotonicity conditions of Angrist and Imbens (1995) for an ordered model. Define $Q = (Q_1, \ldots, Q_{\bar{S}})$. Redefine $\pi_s(Z, W_s) = F_{V+Q_s}(\mu_D(Z) + C_s(W_s))$ and define $\pi(Z, W) = [\pi_1(Z, W_1), \ldots, \pi_{\bar{S}-1}(Z, W_{\bar{S}-1})]$. Redefine $U_{D,s} = F_{V+Q_s}(V + Q_s)$. We have that

$$\begin{aligned} &E(Y \mid Z, W) \\ &\quad = E\left(\sum_{s=1}^{\bar{S}} \mathbf{1}\big[l_{s-1}(Z, W_{s-1}) - Q_{s-1} > V \geqslant l_s(Z, W_s) - Q_s\big] Y_s \;\Big|\; Z, W\right) \\ &\quad = \sum_{s=1}^{\bar{S}} \Big(E\big(\mathbf{1}\big[V + Q_{s-1} < l_{s-1}(Z, W_{s-1})\big] Y_s \mid Z, W\big) \\ &\qquad - E\big(\mathbf{1}\big[V + Q_s \leqslant l_s(Z, W_s)\big] Y_s \mid Z, W\big)\Big) \end{aligned}$$

$$= \sum_{s=1}^{\bar{S}} \left(\int_{-\infty}^{l_{s-1}(Z,W_{s-1})} E(Y_s \mid V + Q_{s-1} = t)\, dF_{V+Q_{s-1}}(t) \right.$$

$$\left. - \int_{-\infty}^{l_s(Z,W_s)} E(Y_s \mid V + Q_s = t)\, dF_{V+Q_s}(t) \right)$$

$$= \sum_{s=1}^{\bar{S}} \left(\int_{0}^{\pi_{s-1}(Z,W_{s-1})} E(Y_s \mid U_{D,s-1} = t)\, dt \right.$$

$$\left. - \int_{0}^{\pi_s(Z,W_s)} E(Y_s \mid U_{D,s} = t)\, dt \right).$$

We thus have the index sufficiency restriction that $E(Y \mid Z, W) = E(Y \mid \pi(Z, W))$, and in the general case $\frac{\partial}{\partial \pi_s} E(Y \mid \pi(Z, W) = \pi) = E(Y_{s+1} - Y_s \mid U_{D,s} = \pi_s)$. Also, notice that we have the restriction that $\frac{\partial^2}{\partial \pi_s \partial \pi_{s'}} E(Y \mid \pi(Z, W) = \pi) = 0$ if $|s - s'| > 1$. Under full independence between U_s and $V + Q_s$, $s = 1, \ldots, \bar{S}$, we can test full independence for the more general choice model by testing for linearity of $E(Y \mid \pi(Z, W) = \pi)$ in π.

Define

$$\Delta^{\text{MTE}}_{s+1,s}(x, u) = E(Y_{s+1} - Y_s \mid X = x, U_{D,s} = u),$$

so that our result above can be rewritten as

$$\frac{\partial}{\partial \pi_s} E\big(Y \mid \pi(Z, W) = \pi\big) = \Delta^{\text{MTE}}_{s+1,s}(x, \pi_s).$$

Since $\pi_s(Z, W_s)$ can be nonparametrically identified from

$$\pi_s(Z, W_s) = \Pr\left(\sum_{j=s+1}^{\bar{S}} D_j = 1 \;\middle|\; Z, W_s \right),$$

we have identification of MTE for all evaluation points within the appropriate support.

The policy relevant treatment effect is defined analogously. H_s^p is defined as the cumulative distribution function of $\mu_D(Z) - C_s(W_s)$. We have that

$$E_p(Y_p)$$

$$= E_p\big(E(Y \mid V, Q, Z, W)\big)$$

$$= E_p\left(\sum_{s=1}^{\bar{S}} \mathbf{1}\big[l_{s-1}(Z, W_{s-1}) - Q_{s-1} > V \geqslant l_s(Z, W_s) - Q_s\big] \right.$$

$$\left. \times E(Y_s \mid V, Q, Z, W) \right)$$

$$= E_p\left(\sum_{s=1}^{\bar{S}} \mathbf{1}\big[l_{s-1}(Z, W_{s-1}) - Q_{s-1} > V \geqslant l_s(Z, W_s) - Q_s\big] E(Y_s \mid V, Q)\right)$$

$$= \sum_{s=1}^{\bar{S}} E_p\big(E(Y_s \mid V, Q)\big\{H_s^p(V + Q_s) - H_{s-1}^p(V + Q_{s-1})\big\}\big)$$

$$= \sum_{s=1}^{\bar{S}} \int \big(E(Y_s \mid V = v, Q = q)\big\{H_s^p(v + q_s) - H_{s-1}^p(v + q_{s-1})\big\}\big)\, dF_{V,Q}(v, q)$$

$$= \sum_{s=1}^{\bar{S}} \left(\int E(Y_s \mid V + Q_s = t) H_s^p(t)\, dF_{V+Q_s}(t) - \int E(Y_s \mid V + Q_{s-1} = t) H_{s-1}^p(t)\, dF_{V+Q_{s-1}}(t)\right),$$

where V, Q_s enter additively, and

$$\Delta_{p,p'}^{\text{PRTE}} = E_{p'}(Y) - E_p(Y) = \sum_{s=1}^{\bar{S}-1} \int \big(E(Y_{s+1} - Y_s \mid V + Q_s = t)\big\{H_s^p(t) - H_s^{p'}(t)\big\}\big)\, dF_{V+Q_s}(t).$$

Alternatively, we can express this result in terms of MTE,

$$E_p(Y_p) = \sum_{s=1}^{\bar{S}} \left(\int E(Y_s \mid U_{D,s} = t) \tilde{H}_s^p(t)\, dt - \int E(Y_s \mid U_{D,s-1} = t) \tilde{H}_{s-1}^p(t)\, dt\right)$$

so that

$$\Delta_{p,p'}^{\text{PRTE}} = E_{p'}(Y) - E_p(Y) = \sum_{s=1}^{\bar{S}-1} \int \big(E(Y_{s+1} - Y_s \mid U_{D,s} = t)\big\{\tilde{H}_s^p(t) - \tilde{H}_s^{p'}(t)\big\}\big)\, dt,$$

where $\tilde{H}_s^p$ is the cumulative distribution function of the random variable $F_{U_{D,s}}(\mu_D(Z) - C_s(W_s))$.

Appendix H: Derivation of PRTE weights for the ordered choice model

To derive the $\omega_{p,p'}$ weights used in expression (7.5), let $l_s(Z, W_s) = \mu_D(Z) - C_s(W_s)$, and let $H_s^p(\cdot)$ denote the cumulative distribution function of $l_s(Z, W_s)$ under regime p,

$H_s^p(t) = \int \mathbf{1}[\mu_D(z) - C_s(w_s) \leqslant t]\, dF_{Z,W}^p(z, w)$. Because $C_0(W_0) = -\infty$ and $C_{\bar{S}}(W_{\bar{S}}) = \infty$, $l_0(Z, W_0) = \infty$ and $l_{\bar{S}}(Z, W_{\bar{S}}) = -\infty$, $H_0^p(t) = 0$ and $H_{\bar{S}}^p(t) = 1$ for any policy p and for all evaluation points. Since $l_{s-1}(Z, W_{s-1})$ is always larger than $l_s(Z, W_s)$, we obtain

$$\begin{aligned}
&\mathbf{1}\big[l_s(Z, W_s) \leqslant V < l_{s-1}(Z, W_{s-1})\big] \\
&\quad = \mathbf{1}\big[V < l_{s-1}(Z, W_{s-1})\big] - \mathbf{1}\big[V \leqslant l_s(Z, W_s)\big],
\end{aligned}$$

so that under assumption (OC-1),

$$E_p\big(\mathbf{1}\big[l_s(Z, W_s) \leqslant V < l_{s-1}(Z, W_{s-1})\big] \mid V\big) = H_s^p(V) - H_{s-1}^p(V).$$

Collecting these results we obtain

$$\begin{aligned}
E_p(Y) &= E_p\big[E(Y \mid V, Z, W)\big] \\
&= \sum_{s=1}^{\bar{S}} \int \big[E(Y_s \mid V = v)\big\{H_s^p(v) - H_{s-1}^p(v)\big\}\big] f_V(v)\, dv.^{200}
\end{aligned}$$

Comparing two policies under p and p', the policy relevant treatment effect is $\Delta_{p,p'}^{\text{PRTE}} = E_{p'}(Y) - E_p(Y) = \sum_{s=1}^{\bar{S}-1} \int E(Y_{s+1} - Y_s \mid V = v)[H_s^p(v) - H_s^{p'}(v)] f_V(v)\, dv$. Alternatively, we can express this in terms of Δ^{MTE}: $\Delta_{p,p'}^{\text{PRTE}} = \sum_{s=1}^{\bar{S}-1} \int \Delta_{s,s+1}^{\text{MTE}}(u)[\tilde{H}_s^p(u) - \tilde{H}_s^{p'}(u)]\, du$ where $\tilde{H}_s^p(t)$ is the cumulative distribution function of $F_V(\mu_D(Z) - C_s(W_s))$ under policy p, $\tilde{H}_s^p(t) = \int \mathbf{1}[F_V(\mu_D(z) - C_s(w_s)) \leqslant t]\, dF_{Z,W_s}^p(z, w_s)$.

Appendix I: Derivation of the weights for IV in the ordered choice model

We first derive $\text{Cov}(J(Z, W), Y)$. Its derivation is typical of the other terms needed to form (7.6) in the text. Defining $\tilde{J}(Z, W) = J(Z, W) - E(J(Z, W))$, we obtain, since $\text{Cov}(J(Z, W), Y) = E(\tilde{J}(Z, W)Y)$,

[200] The full derivation is $E_p(Y) = E_p[E(Y|V, Z, W)] = E_p[\sum_{s=1}^{\bar{S}} \mathbf{1}[l_s(Z, W_s) \leqslant V < l_{s-1}(Z, W_{s-1})] \times E(Y_s|V, Z, W)] = \sum_{s=1}^{\bar{S}} E_p[\mathbf{1}[l_s(Z, W_s) \leqslant V < l_{s-1}(Z, W_{s-1})] E(Y_s|V)] = \sum_{s=1}^{\bar{S}} E_p[E(Y_s|V) \times \{H_s^p(V) - H_{s-1}^p(V)\}] = \sum_{s=1}^{\bar{S}} \int [E(Y_s|V = v)\{H_s^p(v) - H_{s-1}^p(v)\}] f_V(v)\, dv$. The first equality is from the law of iterated expectations; the second equality comes from the definition of Y; the third equality follows from linearity of expectations and independence assumption (OC-1); the fourth equality applies the law of iterated expectations; and the final equality rewrites the expectation explicitly as an integral over the distribution of V. Recalling that $H_0^p(v) = 0$ and $H_{\bar{S}}^p(v) = 1$, we may rewrite this result as $E_p(Y) = \sum_{s=1}^{\bar{S}-1} \int E(Y_s - Y_{s+1} \mid V = v) H_s^p(v) f_V(v)\, dv + \int E(Y_{\bar{S}} \mid V = v) f_V(v)\, dv$, where the last term is $E(Y_{\bar{S}})$.

$$\begin{aligned}
&E(\tilde{J}(Z,W)Y) \\
&\quad = E\left[\tilde{J}(Z,W)\sum_{s=1}^{\bar{S}} \mathbf{1}[l_s(Z,W_s) \leqslant V < l_{s-1}(Z,W_{s-1})] E(Y_s \mid V,Z,W)\right] \\
&\quad = \sum_{s=1}^{\bar{S}} E[\tilde{J}(Z,W)\mathbf{1}[l_s(Z,W_s) \leqslant V < l_{s-1}(Z,W_{s-1})] E(Y_s \mid V)],
\end{aligned}$$

where the first equality comes from the definition of Y and the law of iterated expectations, and the second equality follows from linearity of expectations and independence assumption (OC-1). Let $H_s(\cdot)$ equal $H_s^p(\cdot)$ for p equal to the policy that characterizes the observed data, i.e., $H_s(\cdot)$ is the cumulative distribution function of $l_s(Z,W_s)$,

$$H_s^p(t) = \Pr(l_s(Z,W_s) \leqslant t) = \Pr(\mu_D(Z) - C_s(W_s) \leqslant t).$$

Using the law of iterated expectations, we obtain

$$\begin{aligned}
E(\tilde{J}(Z,W)Y) &= \sum_{s=1}^{\bar{S}} E[E(\tilde{J}(Z,W)\{\mathbf{1}[V < l_{s-1}(Z,W_{s-1})] \\
&\qquad - \mathbf{1}[V \leqslant l_s(Z,W_s)]\} \mid V) E(Y_s \mid V)] \\
&= \sum_{s=1}^{\bar{S}} \int [E(Y_s \mid V=v)\{K_{s-1}(v) - K_s(v)\}] f_V(v)\, dv \\
&= \sum_{s=1}^{\bar{S}-1} \int [E(Y_{s+1} - Y_s \mid V=v) K_s(v)] f_V(v)\, dv,
\end{aligned}$$

where $K_s(v) = E(\tilde{J}(Z,W) \mid l_s(Z,W_s) > v)(1 - H_s(v))$ and we use the fact that $K_{\bar{S}}(v) = K_0(v) = 0$. Now consider the denominator of the IV estimand,

$$\begin{aligned}
&E(S\tilde{J}(Z,W)) \\
&\quad = E\left[\tilde{J}(Z,W)\sum_{s=1}^{\bar{S}} s\mathbf{1}[l_s(Z,W_s) \leqslant V < l_{s-1}(Z,W_{s-1})]\right] \\
&\quad = \sum_{s=1}^{\bar{S}} sE[\tilde{J}(Z,W)\mathbf{1}[l_s(Z,W_s) \leqslant V < l_{s-1}(Z,W_{s-1})]] \\
&\quad = \sum_{s=1}^{\bar{S}} sE_V[E(\tilde{J}(Z,W)\{\mathbf{1}[V < l_{s-1}(Z,W_{s-1})] - \mathbf{1}[V \leqslant l_s(Z,W_s)]\} \mid V)] \\
&\quad = \sum_{s=1}^{\bar{S}} s\int [K_{s-1}(v) - K_s(v)] f_V(v)\, dv = \sum_{s=1}^{\bar{S}-1} \int K_s(v) f_V(v)\, dv.
\end{aligned}$$

Collecting results, we obtain an expression for the IV estimand (7.6):

$$\frac{\text{Cov}(J, Y)}{\text{Cov}(J, S)} = \sum_{s=1}^{\bar{S}-1} \int E(Y_{s+1} - Y_s \mid V = v)\omega(s, v) f_V(v)\, dv,$$

where

$$\omega(s, v) = \frac{K_s(v)}{\sum_{s=1}^{\bar{S}} s \int [K_{s-1}(v) - K_s(v)] f_V(v)\, dv} = \frac{K_s(v)}{\sum_{s=1}^{\bar{S}-1} \int K_s(v) f_V(v)\, dv}$$

and clearly

$$\sum_{s=1}^{\bar{S}-1} \int \omega(s, v) f_V(v)\, dv = 1, \quad \omega(0, v) = 0, \quad \text{and} \quad \omega(\bar{S}, v) = 0.$$

Appendix J: Proof of Theorem 6

We now prove Theorem 6.

PROOF. The basic idea is that we can bring the model back to a two choice set up of j versus the "next best" option. We prove the result for the second assertion, that $\Delta_j^{\text{LIV}}(x, z)$ recovers the marginal treatment effect parameter. The first assertion, that $\Delta_j^{\text{Wald}}(x, z^{[-j]}, z^{[j]}, \tilde{z}^{[j]})$ recovers a LATE parameter, follows from a trivial modification to the same proof strategy. Recall that $R_{\mathcal{J}\setminus j}(z) = \max_{i \in \mathcal{J}\setminus j}\{R_i(z)\}$ and that $I_{\mathcal{J}\setminus j} = \operatorname{argmax}_{i \in \mathcal{J}\setminus j}(R_i(Z))$. We may write $Y = Y_{I_{\mathcal{J}\setminus j}} + D_{\mathcal{J},j}(Y_j - Y_{I_{\mathcal{J}\setminus j}})$. We have

$$\begin{aligned}
&\Pr(D_{\mathcal{J},j} = 1 \mid X = x, Z = z) \\
&\quad = \Pr\big(R_j(z_j) \geqslant R_{\mathcal{J}\setminus j}(z) \bigm| X = x, Z = z\big) \\
&\quad = \Pr\big(\vartheta_j(z_j) \geqslant R_{\mathcal{J}\setminus j}(z) + V_j \bigm| X = x, Z = z\big).
\end{aligned}$$

Using independence assumption (B-1), $R_{\mathcal{J}\setminus j}(z) - V_j$ is independent of Z conditional on X, so that

$$\Pr(D_{\mathcal{J},j} = 1 \mid X = x, Z = z) = \Pr\big(\vartheta_j(z_j) \geqslant R_{\mathcal{J}\setminus j}(z) + V_j \bigm| X = x\big).$$

$\vartheta_k(\cdot)$ does not depend on $z^{[j]}$ for $k \neq j$ by assumption (B-2b), and thus $R_{\mathcal{J}\setminus j}(z)$ does not depend on $z^{[j]}$, and we will therefore (with an abuse of notation) write $R_{\mathcal{J}\setminus j}(z^{[-j]})$ for $R_{\mathcal{J}\setminus j}(z)$. Write $F_{X|Z^{[-j]}}(\cdot; X = x, Z^{[-j]} = z^{[-j]})$ for the distribution function of $R_{\mathcal{J}\setminus j}(z^{[-j]}) + V_j$ conditional on $X = x$. Then

$$\Pr(D_{\mathcal{J},j} = 1 \mid X = x, Z = z) = F\big(\vartheta_j(z_j); x, z^{[-j]}\big),$$

and

$$\begin{aligned}
&\frac{\partial}{\partial z^{[j]}} \Pr(D_{\mathcal{J},j} = 1 \mid X = x, Z = z) \\
&\quad = \left[\frac{\partial}{\partial z^{[j]}} \vartheta_j(z_j)\right] f_{X|Z^{[-j]}}\big(\vartheta_j(z_j); X = x, Z^{[-j]} = z^{[-j]}\big),
\end{aligned}$$

where $f_{X|Z^{[-j]}}(\cdot; X = x, Z^{[-j]} = z^{[-j]})$ is the density of $R_{\mathcal{J}\backslash j}(z^{[-j]}) - V_j$ conditional on $X = x$. Consider

$$\begin{aligned}
E(Y \mid X = x, Z = z) = {} & E(Y_{I_{\mathcal{J}\backslash j}} \mid X = x, Z = z) \\
& + E\big(D_{\mathcal{J},j}(Y_j - Y_{I_{\mathcal{J}\backslash j}}) \bigm| X = x, Z = z\big).
\end{aligned}$$

As a consequence of (B-1), (B-3)–(B-5), and (B-2b), we have that $E(Y_{I_{\mathcal{J}\backslash j}} \mid X = x, Z = z)$ does not depend on $z^{[j]}$. Using the assumptions and the law of iterated expectations, we may write

$$\begin{aligned}
&E\big(D_{\mathcal{J},j}(Y_j - Y_{I_{\mathcal{J}\backslash j}}) \bigm| X = x, Z = z\big) \\
&\quad = \int_{-\infty}^{\vartheta_j(z)} E\big(Y_j - Y_{I_{\mathcal{J}\backslash j}} \bigm| X = x, Z = z, R_{\mathcal{J}\backslash j}(z^{[-j]}) + V_j = t\big) \\
&\qquad \times f_{X|Z^{[-j]}}\big(t; X = x, Z^{[-j]} = z^{[-j]}\big)\, dt \\
&\quad = \int_{-\infty}^{\vartheta_j(z)} E\big(Y_j - Y_{I_{\mathcal{J}\backslash j}} \bigm| X = x, Z^{[-j]} = z^{[-j]}, R_{\mathcal{J}\backslash j}(z^{[-j]}) + V_j = t\big) \\
&\qquad \times f_{X|Z^{[-j]}}\big(t; X = x, Z^{[-j]} = z^{[-j]}\big)\, dt.
\end{aligned}$$

Thus,

$$\begin{aligned}
&\frac{\partial}{\partial z^{[j]}} E(Y \mid X = x, Z = z) \\
&\quad = E\big(Y_j - Y_{I_{\mathcal{J}\backslash j}} \bigm| X = x, Z^{[-j]} = z^{[-j]}, R_j(z) = R_{\mathcal{J}\backslash j}(z)\big) \\
&\qquad \times \left[\frac{\partial}{\partial z^{[j]}} \vartheta_j(z_j)\right] f_{X|Z^{[-j]}}\big(\vartheta_j(z_j) \mid X = x, Z^{[-j]} = z^{[-j]}\big).
\end{aligned}$$

Combining results, we have

$$\begin{aligned}
&\frac{\partial}{\partial z^{[j]}} E(Y \mid X = x, Z = z) \Big/ \frac{\partial}{\partial z^{[j]}} \Pr(D_{\mathcal{J},j} = 1 \mid X = x, Z = z) \\
&\quad = E\big(Y_j - Y_{I_{\mathcal{J}\backslash j}} \bigm| X = x, Z^{[-j]} = z^{[-j]}, R_j(z) = R_{\mathcal{J}\backslash j}(z)\big).
\end{aligned}$$

Finally, noting that

$$\begin{aligned}
&E\big(Y_j - Y_{I_{\mathcal{J}\backslash j}} \bigm| X = x, Z^{[-j]} = z^{[-j]}, R_j(z) = R_{\mathcal{J}\backslash j}(z)\big) \\
&\quad = E\big(Y_j - Y_{I_{\mathcal{J}\backslash j}} \bigm| X = x, Z = z, R_j(z) = R_{\mathcal{J}\backslash j}(z)\big)
\end{aligned}$$

provides the stated result. The proof for the LATE result follows from the parallel argument using discrete changes in the instrument. □

Appendix K: Flat MTE within a general nonseparable matching framework

The result in the text that conditional mean independence of Y_0 and Y_1 in terms of D given X implies a flat MTE holds in a more general nonseparable model. We establish this claim and also establish some additional restrictions implied by an IV assumption.

Assume a nonseparable selection model, $D = \mathbf{1}[\mu_D(X, Z, V) \geqslant 0]$, with Z independent of (Y_0, Y_1, V) conditional on X. Let $\Omega(x, z) = \{v\colon \mu_D(x, z, v) \geqslant 0\}$. Let $\Omega(x, z)^c$ denote the complement of $\Omega(x, z)$. Consider the mean independence assumption

(M-3) $E(Y_1 \mid X, D) = E(Y_1 \mid X), E(Y_0 \mid X, D) = E(Y_0 \mid X)$.

(M-3) implies that for $\Delta = Y_1 - Y_0$

$$E\big(\Delta \bigm| X = x, V \in \Omega(X, Z)\big) = E\big(\Delta \bigm| X = x, V \in \Omega(X, Z)^c\big),$$

where c here denotes "complement". Thus,

$$\begin{aligned} &E_{Z|X}\big(E\big(\Delta^{\text{MTE}}(x, V) \bigm| X = x, V \in \Omega(x, Z)\big) \bigm| X = x\big) \\ &\quad = E_{Z|X}\big(E\big(\Delta^{\text{MTE}}(x, V) \bigm| X = x, V \in \Omega(x, Z)^c\big) \bigm| X = x\big) \end{aligned}$$

for all x in the support of X. (We assume $0 < \Pr(D = 1 \mid X) < 1$.) This establishes that the MTE is flat.

Now suppose that (M-3) holds, but suppose that there is an instrument Z such that

(M-3)′ $E(Y_1 \mid X, Z, D) \neq E(Y_1 \mid X), E(Y_0 \mid X, Z, D) \neq E(Y_0 \mid X)$.

(*Note*: $E(Y_j \mid X, Z) = E(Y_j \mid X)$ by assumption.) In this case, (M-3) implies that

$$\begin{aligned} &E_{Z|X}\big(E\big(\Delta^{\text{MTE}}(X, V) \bigm| X = x, V \in \Omega(x, Z)\big) \bigm| X = x\big) \\ &\quad = E_{Z|X}\big(E\big(\Delta^{\text{MTE}}(X, V) \bigm| X = x, V \in \big(\Omega(x, Z)\big)^c\big) \bigm| X = x\big), \end{aligned}$$

but (M-3)′ implies that there exists z in the support of Z conditional on X such that

$$E\big(\Delta^{\text{MTE}}(X, V) \bigm| X = x, V \in \Omega(x, z)\big) \neq E\big(\Delta^{\text{MTE}}(X, V) \bigm| X = x\big)$$

and

$$E\big(\Delta^{\text{MTE}}(X, V) \bigm| X = x, V \in \Omega(x, z)^c\big) \neq E\big(\Delta^{\text{MTE}}(X, V) \bigm| X = x\big)$$

so that $\Delta^{\text{MTE}}(X, V)$ is not constant in V. Note that, if $E(Y_1 \mid X, Z = z, D = 1) \neq E(Y_1 \mid X, Z = z', D = 1)$ for any z, z' evaluation points in the support of Z conditional on X, then $E(Y_1 \mid X, Z, D) \neq E(Y_1 \mid X)$. Thus, (M-3)′ is testable, given the maintained assumption that Z is a proper exclusion restriction. Note that (M-3)′ implies (M-3), so it is a stronger condition.

Now assume

(M-1)′ $E(Y_1 \mid X, Z, D) = E(Y_1 \mid X),\ E(Y_0 \mid X, Z, D) = E(Y_0 \mid X)$.

In this case, we get a stronger restriction on MTE than is produced from (M-3). We obtain

$$E(\Delta^{\mathrm{MTE}}(X, V) \mid X = x, V \in \Omega(x, z)) = E(\Delta^{\mathrm{MTE}}(X, V) \mid X = x)$$

and

$$E(\Delta^{\mathrm{MTE}}(X, V) \mid X = x, V \in \Omega(x, z)^c) = E(\Delta^{\mathrm{MTE}}(X, V) \mid X = x)$$

for all (x, z) in the proper support. Again, the MTE is not flat.

Appendix L: The relationship between exclusion conditions in IV and exclusion conditions in matching

We now investigate the relationship between IV and matching identification conditions. They are very distinct. We analyze mean treatment parameters. We define (U_0, U_1) by $U_0 = Y_0 - E(Y_0 \mid X)$ and $U_1 = Y_1 - E(Y_1 \mid X)$. We consider standard IV as a form of matching where matching does not hold conditional on X but does hold conditional on (X, Z), where Z is the instrument. Consider the following two matching conditions based on an exclusion restriction Z:

(M-4) *(U_0, U_1) are mean independent of D conditional on (X, Z). ($E(U_0|X, Z, D) = E(U_0 \mid X, Z)$ and $E(U_1 \mid X, Z, D) = E(U_1 \mid X, Z)$.)*
(M-5) *(U_0, U_1) are not mean independent of D conditional on X. ($E(U_0 \mid X, D) \neq E(U_0 \mid X)$ and $E(U_1 \mid X, D) \neq E(U_1 \mid X)$.)*

(M-4) says that the matching conditions hold conditional on (X, Z). However, (M-5) says that the matching conditions do not hold if one only conditions on X. By the definitions of U_0, U_1, these conditions are equivalent to stating that Y_0, Y_1 are mean independent of D conditional on (X, Z) but not mean independent of D conditional on X. These look like instrumental variable conditions. We now consider whether these assumptions are compatible with standard IV conditions as used by Heckman and Robb (1985a, 1986a) and Heckman (1997) to use IV to identify treatment parameters when responses are heterogenous (the model of essential heterogeneity). For ATE, they show that standard IV identifies ATE if:

(ATE-1) *U_0 is mean independent of Z conditional on X.*
(ATE-2) *$D(U_1 - U_0)$ is mean independent of Z conditional on X.*[201]

[201] When $Y = Y_0 + D(Y_1 - Y_0)$, assuming separability so that $Y_0 = \mu_0(X) + U_0$, $Y_1 = \mu_1(X) + U_1$, and $Y = \mu_0(X) + D(\mu_1(X) - \mu_0(X) + U_1 - U_0) + U_0$, identification of ATE by IV requires the rank condition (IV-2) plus $E(U_0 + D(U_1 - U_0) \mid X, Z) = E(U_0 + D(U_1 - U_0) \mid X)$, which is implied by (ATE-1) and (ATE-2).

They show that standard IV identifies TT if:

(TT-1) *U_0 is mean independent of Z conditional on X.*
(TT-2) *$U_1 - U_0$ is mean independent of Z conditional on $D = 1$ and on X.*[202]

The conventional assumption in means is that

(IV-1)′ *(U_0, U_1) are mean independent of Z conditional on X.*
(IV-2) *Rank condition* (IV-2) *is still required*: $\Pr(D = 1 \mid Z, X)$ *is a nondegenerate function of Z.*

Condition (IV-1)′ is a commonly invoked instrumental variable condition, even though Heckman and Robb (1986a) and Heckman (1997) show it is neither necessary nor sufficient to identify ATE or TT by linear IV. In Section 4, we used the stronger condition (IV-1): $(U_0, U_1) \perp\!\!\!\perp Z \mid X$ along with the rank conditions. Clearly, (IV-1) implies (IV-1)′.

We now show that assumptions (M-4) and (M-5) are inconsistent with any of the sets of IV assumptions. In particular, we show that assuming (M-4) and that U_0 is mean independent of Z conditional on X jointly imply that U_0 is mean independent of D conditional on X. If (M-4) and (M-5) hold, then Z cannot satisfy condition (IV-1)′ (or stronger condition (IV-1)), (ATE-1) or (TT-1). Thus matching based on an exclusion restriction and IV are distinct conditions. We show this by establishing a series of claims.

CLAIM 1. *Conditions* (M-4) *and* (IV-1)′ *jointly imply U_0 is mean independent of D conditional on X. Thus,* (M-4) *and* [(IV-1)′ *or* (ATE-1) *or* (TT-1)] *jointly imply that* (M-5) *cannot hold.*

PROOF. Assume (M-4) and (IV-1)′. We have

$$E(U_0 \mid D, X, Z) = E(U_0 \mid X, Z)$$
$$= E(U_0 \mid X),$$

[202] In the separable model,

$$Y = \mu_0(X) + D\big(\overbrace{\mu_1(X) - \mu_0(X) + E(U_1 - U_0 \mid X, D = 1)}^{\Delta^{\mathrm{TT}}(X)}\big) + U_0 + D\big(U_1 - U_0 - E(U_1 - U_0 \mid X, D = 1)\big).$$

Identification requires that

$$E\big(U_0 + D\big(U_1 - U_0 - E(U_1 - U_0 \mid X, D = 1)\big) \bigm| X, Z\big) = E\big(U_0 + D\big(U_1 - U_0 - E(U_1 - U_0 \mid X, D = 1)\big) \bigm| X\big),$$

which is implied by (TT-1) and (TT-2).

where the first equality follows from (M-4) and the second equality follows from (IV-1)$'$. Thus,

$$\begin{aligned} E(U_0 \mid D, X) &= E_Z\big[E(U_0 \mid D, X, Z) \bigm| D, X\big] \\ &= E_Z\big[E(U_0 \mid X) \bigm| D, X\big] \\ &= E(U_0 \mid X). \end{aligned}$$

□

Thus (M-4) and (M-5) are inconsistent with any of the sets of IV assumptions that we have considered. However, this analysis raises the question of whether it is still possible to invoke (M-5) and the assumption that U_1 is not mean independent of D conditional on X. The following results show that it is not possible.

CLAIM 2. (M-4) *and* (IV-1)$'$ *imply* U_1 *is mean independent of* D *conditional on* X.

PROOF. Follows with trivial modification from the proof to Claim 1. □

A similar claim can be shown for (TT-1) and (TT-2).

CLAIM 3. (M-4) *and* (TT-1), (TT-2) *imply* U_1 *is mean independent of* D *conditional on* X.

PROOF. Assume (M-4) and (TT-1), (TT-2). We have

(N-1) $E(U_0 \mid X, Z, D) = E(U_0 \mid X, Z) = E(U_0 \mid X)$,

where the first equality follows from (M-4) and the second equality follows from (TT-1). Using the result from the proof of Claim 1, we obtain

(N-2) $E(U_0 \mid X, Z, D) = E(U_0 \mid X, D)$.

By (TT-2), we have

$$\begin{aligned} &E(U_1 \mid X, Z, D = 1) - E(U_1 \mid X, D = 1) \\ &\quad = E(U_0 \mid X, Z, D = 1) - E(U_0 \mid X, D = 1). \end{aligned}$$

By equation (N-2), the right-hand side of the preceding expression is zero, and we thus have

(N-3) $E(U_1 \mid X, Z, D = 1) = E(U_1 \mid X, D = 1)$.

By (M-4), we have

(N-4) $E(U_1 \mid X, Z, D = 1) = E(U_1 \mid X, Z)$.

Combining equations (N-3) and (N-4), we obtain

$$E(U_1 \mid X, Z) = E(U_1 \mid X, D = 1).$$

Integrating both sides of this expression against the distribution of Z conditional on X, we obtain

$$E(U_1 \mid X) = E(U_1 \mid X, D = 1).$$

□

It is straightforward to show that (M-4) and (ATE-1), (ATE-2) jointly imply that U_1 is mean independent of D conditional on X.

In summary, (U_0, U_1) mean independent of D conditional on (X, Z) but not conditional on X implies that U_0 is dependent on Z conditional on X in contradiction to all of the assumptions used to justify instrumental variables. Thus (U_0, U_1) mean independent of D conditional on (X, Z) but not conditional on X implies that none of the three sets of IV conditions will hold. In addition, if we weaken these conditions to only consider U_1, so that we assume that U_1 is mean independent of D conditional on (X, Z) but not conditional on X, we obtain that U_1 is dependent on Z conditional on X. We have shown that this implies that (IV-1) does not hold, and implies that (TT-1), (TT-2) will not hold. A similar line of argument shows that (ATE-1), (ATE-2) will not hold. Thus, the exclusion conditioning in matching is not the same as the exclusion conditioning in IV.

Appendix M: Selection formulae for the matching examples

Consider a generalized Roy model of the form $Y_1 = \mu_1 + U_1$; $Y_0 = \mu_0 + U_0$; $D^* = \mu_D(Z) + V$; $D = 1$ if $D^* \geqslant 0$, $= 0$ otherwise; and $Y = DY_1 + (1 - D)Y_0$, where

$$(U_0, U_1, V)' \sim N(0, \Sigma), \qquad \mathrm{Var}(U_i) = \sigma_i^2, \quad i = 0, 1,$$
$$\mathrm{Var}(V) = \sigma_V^2, \qquad \mathrm{Cov}(U_1, U_0) = \sigma_{10},$$
$$\mathrm{Cov}(U_1, V) = \sigma_{1V}, \qquad \mathrm{Cov}(U_0, V) = \sigma_{0V}.$$

Assume $Z \perp\!\!\!\perp (U_0, U_1, V)$. Let $\phi(\cdot)$ and $\Phi(\cdot)$ be the pdf and the cdf of a standard normal random variable. Then, the propensity score for this model for $Z = z$ is given by

$$\Pr(D^* > 0 \mid Z = z) = \Pr\bigl(V > -\mu_D(z)\bigr) = P(z) = \Phi\left(\frac{\mu_D(z)}{\sigma_V}\right).$$

Thus $\frac{\mu_D(z)}{\sigma_V} = \Phi^{-1}(P(z))$, and

$$\frac{-\mu_D(z)}{\sigma_V} = \Phi^{-1}\bigl(1 - P(z)\bigr).$$

The event $(V \lesseqgtr 0, Z = z)$ can be written as $\frac{V}{\sigma_V} \lesseqgtr -\frac{\mu_D(z)}{\sigma_V} \Leftrightarrow \frac{V}{\sigma_V} \lesseqgtr \Phi^{-1}(1 - P(z))$. We can write the conditional expectations required to get the biases for the treatment parameters as a function of $P(z) = p$. For U_1:

$$\begin{aligned} E(U_1 \mid D^* \geqslant 0, Z = z) &= \frac{\sigma_{1V}}{\sigma_V} E\left(\frac{V}{\sigma_V} \,\Big|\, \frac{V}{\sigma_V} \geqslant \frac{-\mu_D(z)}{\sigma_V}\right) \\ &= \frac{\sigma_{1V}}{\sigma_V} E\left(\frac{V}{\sigma_V} \,\Big|\, \frac{V}{\sigma_V} \geqslant \Phi^{-1}\big(1 - P(z)\big)\right) \\ &= \eta_1 M_1\big(P(z)\big), \end{aligned}$$

where

$$\eta_1 = \frac{\sigma_{1V}}{\sigma_V}.$$

Similarly for U_0

$$\begin{aligned} E(U_0 \mid D^* > 0, Z = z) &= \eta_0 M_1\big(P(z)\big), \\ E(U_0 \mid D^* < 0, Z = z) &= \eta_0 M_0\big(P(z)\big), \end{aligned}$$

where $\eta_0 = \frac{\sigma_{0V}}{\sigma_V}$ and

$$M_1(P(z)) = \frac{\phi(\Phi^{-1}(1 - P(z)))}{P(z)} \quad \text{and} \quad M_0(P(z)) = -\frac{\phi(\Phi^{-1}(1 - P(z)))}{1 - P(z)}$$

are inverse Mills ratio terms.

Substituting these into the expressions for the biases for the treatment parameters conditional on z we obtain

$$\begin{aligned} \text{Bias TT}\big(P(z)\big) &= \eta_0 M_1\big(P(z)\big) - \eta_0 M_0\big(P(z)\big) \\ &= \eta_0 M\big(P(z)\big), \\ \text{Bias ATE}\big(P(z)\big) &= \eta_1 M_1\big(P(z)\big) - \eta_0 M_0\big(P(z)\big) \\ &= M\big(P(z)\big)\big(\eta_1\big(1 - P(z)\big) + \eta_0 P(z)\big). \end{aligned}$$

References

Aakvik, A., Heckman, J.J., Vytlacil, E.J. (1999). "Training effects on employment when the training effects are heterogeneous: An application to Norwegian vocational rehabilitation programs". University of Bergen Working Paper 0599; and University of Chicago.

Aakvik, A., Heckman, J.J., Vytlacil, E.J. (2005). "Estimating treatment effects for discrete outcomes when responses to treatment vary: An application to Norwegian vocational rehabilitation programs". Journal of Econometrics 125 (1–2), 15–51.

Abadie, A. (2002). "Bootstrap tests of distributional treatment effects in instrumental variable models". Journal of the American Statistical Association 97 (457), 284–292 (March).

Abadie, A., Imbens, G.W. (2006). "Large sample properties of matching estimators for average treatment effects". Econometrica 74 (1), 235–267 (January).

Ahn, H., Powell, J. (1993). "Semiparametric estimation of censored selection models with a nonparametric selection mechanism". Journal of Econometrics 58 (1–2), 3–29 (July).

Aigner, D.J. (1979a). "A brief introduction to the methodology of optimal experimental design". Journal of Econometrics 11 (1), 7–26.

Aigner, D.J. (1979b). "Sample design for electricity pricing experiments: Anticipated precision for a time-of-day pricing experiment". Journal of Econometrics 11 (1), 195–205 (September).

Aigner, D.J. (1985). "The residential electricity time-of-use pricing experiments: What have we learned?". In: Hausman, J.A., Wise, D.A. (Eds.), Social Experimentation. University of Chicago Press, Chicago, pp. 11–41.

Aigner, D.J., Hsiao, C., Kapteyn, A., Wansbeek, T. (1984). "Latent variable models in econometrics". In: Griliches, Z., Intriligator, M.D. (Eds.), Handbook of Econometrics, vol. 2. Elsevier, pp. 1321–1393 (Chapter 23).

Altonji, J.G., Matzkin, R.L. (2005). "Cross section and panel data estimators for nonseparable models with endogenous regressors". Econometrica 73 (4), 1053–1102 (July).

Angrist, J.D., Imbens, G.W. (1995). "Two-stage least squares estimation of average causal effects in models with variable treatment intensity". Journal of the American Statistical Association 90 (430), 431–442 (June).

Angrist, J.D., Krueger, A.B. (1999). "Empirical strategies in labor economics". In: Ashenfelter, O., Card, D. (Eds.), Handbook of Labor Economics, vol. 3A. North-Holland, New York, pp. 1277–1366.

Angrist, J.D., Graddy, K., Imbens, G. (2000). "The interpretation of instrumental variables estimators in simultaneous equations models with an application to the demand for fish". Review of Economic Studies 67 (3), 499–527 (July).

Angrist, J.D., Imbens, G.W., Rubin, D. (1996). "Identification of causal effects using instrumental variables". Journal of the American Statistical Association 91 (434), 444–455.

Athey, S., Imbens, G.W. (2006). "Identification and inference in nonlinear difference-in-differences models". Econometrica 74 (2), 431–497 (March).

Balke, A., Pearl, J. (1997). "Bounds on treatment effects from studies with imperfect compliance". Journal of the American Statistical Association 92 (439), 1171–1176 (September).

Banerjee, A.V. (2006). "Making aid work: How to fight global poverty – Effectively". Boston Review 31 (4) (July/August).

Barnow, B.S., Cain, G.G., Goldberger, A.S. (1980). "Issues in the analysis of selectivity bias". In: Stromsdorfer, E., Farkas, G. (Eds.), Evaluation Studies, vol. 5. Sage Publications, Beverly Hills, CA, pp. 42–59.

Barros, R.P. (1987). "Two essays on the nonparametric estimation of economic models with selectivity using choice-based samples". PhD thesis. University of Chicago.

Basu, A., Heckman, J.J., Navarro-Lozano, S., Urzua, S. (2007). "Use of instrumental variables in the presence of heterogeneity and self-selection: An application to treatments in breast cancer patients". Health Economics 16 (11), 1133–1157 (October).

Behrman, J.R., Sengupta, P., Todd, P. (2005). "Progressing through PROGRESA: An impact assessment of a school subsidy experiment in rural Mexico". Economic Development and Cultural Change 54 (1), 237–275 (October).

Bertrand, M., Duflo, E., Mullainathan, S. (2004). "How much should we trust differences-in-differences estimates?". Quarterly Journal of Economics 119 (1), 249–275 (February).

Bickel, P.J. (1967). "Some contributions to the theory of order statistics". In: LeCam, L., Neyman, J. (Eds.), Proceedings of the Fifth Berkeley Symposium on Mathematical Statistics and Probability. University of California Press, Berkeley, CA, pp. 575–591.

Björklund, A., Moffitt, R. (1987). "The estimation of wage gains and welfare gains in self-selection". Review of Economics and Statistics 69 (1), 42–49 (February).

Bloom, H.S. (1984). "Accounting for no-shows in experimental evaluation designs". Evaluation Review 82 (2), 225–246.

Blundell, R., Powell, J. (2003). "Endogeneity in nonparametric and semiparametric regression models". In: Dewatripont, L.P.H.M., Turnovsky, S.J. (Eds.), Advances in Economics and Econometrics: Theory and Applications, Eighth World Congress, vol. 2. Cambridge Univ. Press, Cambridge, UK.

Blundell, R., Powell, J. (2004). "Endogeneity in semiparametric binary response models". Review of Economic Studies 71 (3), 655–679 (July).

Blundell, R., Duncan, A., Meghir, C. (1998). "Estimating labor supply responses using tax reforms". Econometrica 66 (4), 827–861 (July).

Bresnahan, T.F. (1987). "Competition and collusion in the American automobile industry: The 1955 price war". Journal of Industrial Economics 35 (4), 457–482 (June).

Cain, G.G., Watts, H.W. (1973). Income Maintenance and Labor Supply: Econometric Studies. Academic Press, New York.

Cameron, S.V., Heckman, J.J. (1993). "The nonequivalence of high school equivalents". Journal of Labor Economics 11 (1, Part 1), 1–47 (January).

Cameron, S.V., Heckman, J.J. (1998). "Life cycle schooling and dynamic selection bias: Models and evidence for five cohorts of American males". Journal of Political Economy 106 (2), 262–333 (April).

Campbell, D.T. (1969). "Reforms as experiments". American Psychologist 24 (4), 409–429. Reprinted in: Struening, E.L., Guttentag, M. (Eds.), Handbook of Evaluation Research, vols. 1, 2. Sage Publication, Beverly Hills, CA, 1975, pp. 71–99 (vol. 1).

Campbell, D.T., Stanley, J.C. (1963). Experimental and Quasi-Experimental Designs for Research. Rand McNally, Chicago (originally appeared in Gage, N.L. (Ed.), Handbook of Research on Teaching).

Card, D. (1999). "The causal effect of education on earnings". In: Ashenfelter, O., Card, D. (Eds.), Handbook of Labor Economics, vol. 5. North-Holland, New York, pp. 1801–1863.

Card, D. (2001). "Estimating the return to schooling: Progress on some persistent econometric problems". Econometrica 69 (5), 1127–1160 (September).

Carneiro, P. (2002). "Heterogeneity in the returns to schooling: Implications for policy evaluation". PhD thesis. University of Chicago.

Carneiro, P., Hansen, K., Heckman, J.J. (2001). "Removing the veil of ignorance in assessing the distributional impacts of social policies". Swedish Economic Policy Review 8 (2), 273–301 (Fall).

Carneiro, P., Hansen, K., Heckman, J.J. (2003). "Estimating distributions of treatment effects with an application to the returns to schooling and measurement of the effects of uncertainty on college choice". International Economic Review 44 (2), 361–422 (May). 2001 Lawrence R. Klein Lecture.

Carneiro, P., Heckman, J.J., Vytlacil, E.J. (2006). "Estimating marginal and average returns to education". American Economic Review. Submitted for publication.

Cave, G., Bos, H., Doolittle, F., Toussaint, C. (1993). "JOBSTART: Final report on a program for school dropouts". Technical report, MDRC.

Chan, T.Y., Hamilton, B.H. (2006). "Learning, private information and the economic evaluation of randomized experiments". Journal of Political Economy 114 (6), 997–1040 (December).

Chen, S. (1999). "Distribution-free estimation of the random coefficient dummy endogenous variable model". Journal of Econometrics 91 (1), 171–199 (July).

Chen, X., Fan, Y. (1999). "Consistent hypothesis testing in semiparametric and nonparametric models for econometric time series". Journal of Econometrics 91 (2), 373–401 (August).

Chernozhukov, V., Hansen, C. (2005). "An IV model of quantile treatment effects". Econometrica 73 (1), 245–261 (January).

Chernozhukov, V., Imbens, G.W., Newey, W.K. (2007). "Nonparametric identification and estimation of nonseparable models". Journal of Econometrics 139 (1), 1–3 (July).

Cochran, W.G., Rubin, D.B. (1973). "Controlling bias in observational studies: A review". Sankyha Ser. A 35 (Part 4), 417–446.

Conlisk, J. (1973). "Choice of response functional form in designing subsidy experiments". Econometrica 41 (4), 643–656 (July).

Conlisk, J., Watts, H. (1969). "A model for optimizing experimental designs for estimating response surfaces". American Statistical Association Proceedings Social Statistics Section, 150–156.

Cook, T.D., Campbell, D.T. (1979). Quasi-Experimentation: Design and Analysis Issues for Field Settings. Rand McNally College Publishing Company, Chicago.

Cunha, F., Heckman, J.J. (2007). "Identifying and estimating the distributions of *Ex Post* and *Ex Ante* returns to schooling: A survey of recent developments". Labour Economics 14 (6), 870–893 (December).

Cunha, F., Heckman, J.J. (2008). "A new framework for the analysis of inequality". Macroeconomic Dynamics. Submitted for publication.
Cunha, F., Heckman, J.J., Matzkin, R. (2003). "Nonseparable factor analysis". Unpublished manuscript. Department of Economics, University of Chicago.
Cunha, F., Heckman, J.J., Navarro, S. (2005). "Separating uncertainty from heterogeneity in life cycle earnings". Oxford Economic Papers 57 (2), 191–261 (April). The 2004 Hicks lecture.
Cunha, F., Heckman, J.J., Navarro, S. (2006). "Counterfactual analysis of inequality and social mobility". In: Morgan, S.L., Grusky, D.B., Fields, G.S. (Eds.), Mobility and Inequality: Frontiers of Research in Sociology and Economics. Stanford Univ. Press, Stanford, CA, pp. 290–348 (Chapter 4).
Cunha, F., Heckman, J.J., Navarro, S. (2007). "The identification and economic content of ordered choice models with stochastic cutoffs". International Economic Review. In press, November.
Cunha, F., Heckman, J.J., Schennach, S.M. (2007). "Estimating the technology of cognitive and noncognitive skill formation". Unpublished manuscript, University of Chicago, Department of Economics. Presented at the Yale Conference on Macro and Labor Economics, May 5–7, 2006. Econometrica. Submitted for publication.
Cunha, F., Heckman, J.J., Schennach, S.M. (2006b). "Nonlinear factor analysis". Unpublished manuscript. Department of Economics, University of Chicago.
Dahl, G.B. (2002). "Mobility and the return to education: Testing a Roy model with multiple markets". Econometrica 70 (6), 2367–2420 (November).
Darolles, S., Florens, J.-P., Renault, E. (2002). "Nonparametric instrumental regression". Working Paper 05-2002. Centre interuniversitaire de recherche en économie quantitative, CIREQ.
Deaton, A. (2006). "Evidence-based aid must not become the latest in a long string of development fads". Boston Review 31 (4) (July/August).
Domencich, T., McFadden, D.L. (1975). Urban Travel Demand: A Behavioral Analysis. North-Holland, Amsterdam. Reprinted 1996.
Doolittle, F.C., Traeger, L. (1990). Implementing the National JTPA Study. Manpower Demonstration Research Corporation, New York.
Duncan, G.M., Leigh, D.E. (1985). "The endogeneity of union status: An empirical test". Journal of Labor Economics 3 (3), 385–402 (July).
Durbin, J. (1954). "Errors in variables". Review of the International Statistical Institute 22, 23–32.
Ellison, G., Ellison, S.F. (1999). "A simple framework for nonparametric specification testing". Journal of Econometrics 96, 1–23 (May).
Farber, H.S. (1983). "Worker preferences for union representation". In: Reid, J. (Ed.), Research in Labor Economics, Volume Supplement 2: New Approaches to Labor Unions. JAI Press, Greenwich, CT.
Fisher, R.A. (1966). The Design of Experiments. Hafner Publishing, New York.
Florens, J.-P., Heckman, J.J., Meghir, C., Vytlacil, E.J. (2002). "Instrumental variables, local instrumental variables and control functions". Technical Report CWP15/02, CEMMAP. Econometrica. Submitted for publication.
Florens, J.-P., Heckman, J.J., Meghir, C., Vytlacil, E.J. (2006). "Control functions for nonparametric models without large support". Unpublished manuscript. University of Chicago.
Friedlander, D., Hamilton, G. (1993). "The Saturation Work Initiative Model in San Diego: A Five-Year Follow-Up Study". Manpower Demonstration Research Corporation, New York.
Gerfin, M., Lechner, M. (2002). "A microeconomic evaluation of the active labor market policy in Switzerland". Economic Journal 112 (482), 854–893 (October).
Gill, R.D., Robins, J.M. (2001). "Causal inference for complex longitudinal data: The continuous case". The Annals of Statistics 29 (6), 1785–1811 (December).
Glynn, R.J., Laird, N.M., Rubin, D.B. (1986). "Selection modeling versus mixture modeling with nonignorable nonresponse". In: Wainer, H. (Ed.), Drawing Inferences from Self-Selected Samples. Springer-Verlag, New York, pp. 115–142. Reprinted in: Lawrence Erlbaum Associates, Mahwah, NJ, 2000.
Gronau, R. (1974). "Wage comparisons – A selectivity bias". Journal of Political Economy 82 (6), 1119–1143 (November–December).

Haavelmo, T. (1943). "The statistical implications of a system of simultaneous equations". Econometrica 11 (1), 1–12 (January).

Hahn, J. (1998). "On the role of the propensity score in efficient semiparametric estimation of average treatment effects". Econometrica 66 (2), 315–331 (March).

Hahn, J., Todd, P.E., Van der Klaauw, W. (2001). "Identification and estimation of treatment effects with a regression-discontinuity design". Econometrica 69 (1), 201–209 (January).

Hall, P., Horowitz, J. (2005). "Nonparametric methods for inference in the presence of instrumental variables". Annals of Statistics 33 (6), 2904–2929 (September).

Hansen, K.T., Heckman, J.J., Mullen, K.J. (2004). "The effect of schooling and ability on achievement test scores". Journal of Econometrics 121 (1–2), 39–98 (July–August).

Härdle, W. (1990). Applied Nonparametric Regression. Cambridge Univ. Press, New York.

Harmon, C., Walker, I. (1999). "The marginal and average returns to schooling in the UK". European Economic Review 43 (4–6), 879–887 (April).

Hausman, J.A. (1978). "Specification tests in econometrics". Econometrica 46 (6), 1251–1272 (November).

Heckman, J.J. (1974a). "Effects of child-care programs on women's work effort". Journal of Political Economy 82 (2), S136–S163. Reprinted in: Schultz, T.W. (Ed.), Economics of the Family: Marriage, Children and Human Capital. University of Chicago Press, 1974 (March/April).

Heckman, J.J. (1974b). "Shadow prices, market wages, and labor supply". Econometrica 42 (4), 679–694 (July).

Heckman, J.J. (1976a). "The common structure of statistical models of truncation, sample selection and limited dependent variables and a simple estimator for such models". Annals of Economic and Social Measurement 5 (4), 475–492 (December).

Heckman, J.J. (1976b). "A life-cycle model of earnings, learning, and consumption". Journal of Political Economy 84 (4, Part 2), S11–S44 (August). Journal Special Issue: Essays in Labor Economics in Honor of H. Gregg Lewis.

Heckman, J.J. (1976c). "Simultaneous equation models with both continuous and discrete endogenous variables with and without structural shift in the equations". In: Goldfeld, S., Quandt, R. (Eds.), Studies in Nonlinear Estimation. Ballinger Publishing Company, Cambridge, MA, pp. 235–272.

Heckman, J.J. (1980). "Addendum to sample selection bias as a specification error". In: Stromsdorfer, E., Farkas, G. (Eds.), Evaluation Studies Review Annual, vol. 5. Sage Publications, Beverly Hills, CA.

Heckman, J.J. (1990). "Varieties of selection bias". American Economic Review 80 (2), 313–318 (May).

Heckman, J.J. (1992). "Randomization and social policy evaluation". In: Manski, C., Garfinkel, I. (Eds.), Evaluating Welfare and Training Programs. Harvard Univ. Press, Cambridge, MA, pp. 201–230.

Heckman, J.J. (1996). "Randomization as an instrumental variable". Review of Economics and Statistics 78 (2), 336–340 (May).

Heckman, J.J. (1997). "Instrumental variables: A study of implicit behavioral assumptions used in making program evaluations". Journal of Human Resources 32 (3), 441–462 (Summer). Addendum published in: Juornal of Human Resources 33 (1) (1998) (Winter).

Heckman, J.J. (1998). "The effects of government policies on human capital investment, unemployment and earnings inequality". In: Third Public GAAC Symposium: Labor Markets in the USA and Germany, vol. 5. German–American Academic Council Foundation, Bonn, Germany.

Heckman, J.J. (2001). "Micro data, heterogeneity, and the evaluation of public policy: Nobel lecture". Journal of Political Economy 109 (4), 673–748 (August).

Heckman, J.J., Honoré, B.E. (1990). "The empirical content of the Roy model". Econometrica 58 (5), 1121–1149 (September).

Heckman, J.J., Hotz, V.J. (1989). "Choosing among alternative nonexperimental methods for estimating the impact of social programs: The case of Manpower Training". Journal of the American Statistical Association 84 (408), 862–874 (December). Rejoinder also published in: Journal of the American Statistical Association 84 (408) (1989) (December).

Heckman, J.J., LaFontaine, P. (2007). America's Dropout Problem: The GED and the Importance of Social and Emotional Skills. University of Chicago Press, Chicago. Submitted for publication.

Heckman, J.J., Navarro, S. (2004). "Using matching, instrumental variables, and control functions to estimate economic choice models". Review of Economics and Statistics 86 (1), 30–57 (February).

Heckman, J.J., Navarro, S. (2007). "Dynamic discrete choice and dynamic treatment effects". Journal of Econometrics 136 (2), 341–396 (February).

Heckman, J.J., Robb, R. (1985a). "Alternative methods for evaluating the impact of interventions". In: Heckman, J., Singer, B. (Eds.), Longitudinal Analysis of Labor Market Data, vol. 10. Cambridge Univ. Press, New York, pp. 156–245.

Heckman, J.J., Robb, R. (1985b). "Alternative methods for evaluating the impact of interventions: An overview". Journal of Econometrics 30 (1–2), 239–267 (October–November).

Heckman, J.J., Robb, R. (1986a). "Alternative methods for solving the problem of selection bias in evaluating the impact of treatments on outcomes". In: Wainer, H. (Ed.), Drawing Inferences from Self-Selected Samples. Springer-Verlag, New York, pp. 63–107. Reprinted in: Lawrence Erlbaum Associates, Mahwah, NJ, 2000.

Heckman, J.J., Robb, R. (1986b). "Postscript: A rejoinder to Tukey". In: Wainer, H. (Ed.), Drawing Inferences from Self-Selected Samples. Springer-Verlag, New York, pp. 111–114. Reprinted in: Lawrence Erlbaum Associates, Mahwah, NJ, 2000.

Heckman, J.J., Sedlacek, G.L. (1990). "Self-selection and the distribution of hourly wages". Journal of Labor Economics 8 (1, Part 2), S329–S363. Essays in Honor of Albert Rees.

Heckman, J.J., Smith, J.A. (1993). "Assessing the case for randomized evaluation of social programs". In: Jensen, K., Madsen, P. (Eds.), Measuring Labour Market Measures: Evaluating the Effects of Active Labour Market Policy Initiatives, Proceedings from the Danish Presidency Conference "Effects and Measuring of Effects of Labour Market Policy Initiatives". Denmark Ministry of Labour, Copenhagen, pp. 35–95.

Heckman, J.J., Smith, J.A. (1998). "Evaluating the welfare state". In: Strom, S. (Ed.), Econometrics and Economic Theory in the Twentieth Century: The Ragnar Frisch Centennial Symposium. Cambridge Univ. Press, New York, pp. 241–318.

Heckman, J.J., Smith, J.A. (1999). "The pre-programme earnings dip and the determinants of participation in a social programme. Implications for simple programme evaluation strategies". Economic Journal 109 (457), 313–348 (July). Winner of the Royal Economic Society Prize, 1999.

Heckman, J.J., Vytlacil, E.J. (1998). "Instrumental variables methods for the correlated random coefficient model: Estimating the average rate of return to schooling when the return is correlated with schooling". Journal of Human Resources 33 (4), 974–987 (Fall).

Heckman, J.J., Vytlacil, E.J. (1999). "Local instrumental variables and latent variable models for identifying and bounding treatment effects". Proceedings of the National Academy of Sciences 96, 4730–4734 (April).

Heckman, J.J., Vytlacil, E.J. (2000). "The relationship between treatment parameters within a latent variable framework". Economics Letters 66 (1), 33–39 (January).

Heckman, J.J., Vytlacil, E.J. (2001a). "Instrumental variables, selection models, and tight bounds on the average treatment effect". In: Lechner, M., Pfeiffer, F. (Eds.), Econometric Evaluation of Labour Market Policies. Center for European Economic Research, New York, pp. 1–15.

Heckman, J.J., Vytlacil, E.J. (2001b). "Local instrumental variables". In: Hsiao, C., Morimune, K., Powell, J.L. (Eds.), Nonlinear Statistical Modeling: Proceedings of the Thirteenth International Symposium in Economic Theory and Econometrics. Essays in Honor of Takeshi Amemiya. Cambridge Univ. Press, New York, pp. 1–46.

Heckman, J.J., Vytlacil, E.J. (2001c). "Policy-relevant treatment effects". American Economic Review 91 (2), 107–111 (May).

Heckman, J.J., Vytlacil, E.J. (2005). "Structural equations, treatment effects and econometric policy evaluation". Econometrica 73 (3), 669–738 (May).

Heckman, J.J., Vytlacil, E.J. (2007). "Evaluating marginal policy changes and the average effect of treatment for individuals at the margin". Columbia University, Department of Economics. Unpublished manuscript.

Heckman, J.J., Ichimura, H., Todd, P.E. (1997). "Matching as an econometric evaluation estimator: Evidence from evaluating a job training programme". Review of Economic Studies 64 (4), 605–654 (October).

Heckman, J.J., Ichimura, H., Todd, P.E. (1998). "Matching as an econometric evaluation estimator". Review of Economic Studies 65 (223), 261–294 (April).
Heckman, J.J., LaLonde, R.J., Smith, J.A. (1999). "The economics and econometrics of active labor market programs". In: Ashenfelter, O., Card, D. (Eds.), Handbook of Labor Economics, vol. 3A. North-Holland, New York, pp. 1865–2097 (Chapter 31).
Heckman, J.J., Lochner, L.J., Taber, C. (1998). "General-equilibrium treatment effects: A study of tuition policy". American Economic Review 88 (2), 381–386 (May).
Heckman, J.J., Lochner, L.J., Todd, P.E. (2006). "Earnings equations and rates of return: The Mincer equation and beyond". In: Hanushek, E.A., Welch, F. (Eds.), Handbook of the Economics of Education. North-Holland, Amsterdam, pp. 307–458.
Heckman, J.J., Smith, J.A., Clements, N. (1997). "Making the most out of programme evaluations and social experiments: Accounting for heterogeneity in programme impacts". Review of Economic Studies 64 (221), 487–536 (October).
Heckman, J.J., Smith, J.A., Taber, C. (1998). "Accounting for dropouts in evaluations of social programs". Review of Economics and Statistics 80 (1), 1–14 (February).
Heckman, J.J., Tobias, J.L., Vytlacil, E.J. (2003). "Simple estimators for treatment parameters in a latent variable framework". Review of Economics and Statistics 85 (3), 748–754 (August).
Heckman, J.J., Urzua, S., Vytlacil, E.J. (2004). "Understanding instrumental variables in models with essential heterogeneity: Unpublished results". Unpublished manuscript. Department of Economics, University of Chicago.
Heckman, J.J., Urzua, S., Vytlacil, E.J. (2006). "Understanding instrumental variables in models with essential heterogeneity". Review of Economics and Statistics 88 (3), 389–432.
Heckman, J.J., Ichimura, H., Smith, J., Todd, P.E. (1998). "Characterizing selection bias using experimental data". Econometrica 66 (5), 1017–1098 (September).
Heckman, J.J., Hohmann, N., Smith, J., Khoo, M. (2000). "Substitution and dropout bias in social experiments: A study of an influential social experiment". Quarterly Journal of Economics 115 (2), 651–694 (May).
Hirano, K., Imbens, G.W., Ridder, G. (2003). "Efficient estimation of average treatment effects using the estimated propensity score". Econometrica 71 (4), 1161–1189 (July).
Hollister, R.G., Kemper, P., Maynard, R.A. (1984). The National Supported Work Demonstration. University of Wisconsin Press, Madison, WI.
Hotz, V.J. (1992). "Designing an evaluation of the Job Training Partnership Act". In: Manski, C., Garfinkel, I. (Eds.), Evaluating Welfare and Training Programs. Harvard Univ. Press, Cambridge, MA, pp. 76–114.
Hotz, V.J., Mullin, C.H., Sanders, S.G. (1997). "Bounding causal effects using data from a contaminated natural experiment: Analysing the effects of teenage childbearing". Review of Economic Studies 64 (4), 575–603 (October).
Hu, Y., Schennach, S.M. (2006). "Identification and estimation of nonclassical nonlinear errors-in-variables models with continuous distributions". Working Paper. University of Chicago.
Hurwicz, L. (1962). "On the structural form of interdependent systems". In: Nagel, E., Suppes, P., Tarski, A. (Eds.), Logic, Methodology and Philosophy of Science. Stanford Univ. Press, pp. 232–239.
Ichimura, H., Taber, C. (2002). "Semiparametric reduced-form estimation of tuition subsidies". American Economic Review 92 (2), 286–292 (May).
Ichimura, H., Thompson, T.S. (1998). "Maximum likelihood estimation of a binary choice model with random coefficients of unknown distribution". Journal of Econometrics 86 (2), 269–295 (October).
Ichimura, H., Todd, P.E. (2007). "Implementing nonparametric and semiparametric estimators". In: Heckman, J., Leamer, E. (Eds.), Handbook of Econometrics, vol. 6B. Elsevier, Amsterdam.
Imbens, G.W. (2003). "Sensitivity to exogeneity assumptions in program evaluation". American Economic Review 93 (2), 126–132 (May).
Imbens, G.W. (2004). "Nonparametric estimation of average treatment effects under exogeneity: A review". Review of Economics and Statistics 86 (1), 4–29 (February).
Imbens, G.W., Angrist, J.D. (1994). "Identification and estimation of local average treatment effects". Econometrica 62 (2), 467–475 (March).

Imbens, G.W., Newey, W.K. (2002). "Identification and estimation of triangular simultaneous equations models without additivity". Technical Working Paper 285. National Bureau of Economic Research.
Kramer, M.S., Shapiro, S.H. (1984). "Scientific challenges in the application of randomized trials". JAMA: The Journal of the American Medical Association 252 (19), 2739–2745 (November).
Kemple, J.J., Friedlander, D., Fellerath, V. (1995). "Florida's Project Independence: Benefits, Costs, and Two-Year Impacts of Florida's JOBS Program". Manpower Demonstration Research Corporation, New York.
LaLonde, R.J. (1984). "Evaluating the econometric evaluations of training programs with experimental data". Technical Report 183. Industrial Relations Section, Department of Economics, Princeton University.
Lechner, M. (2001). "Identification and estimation of causal effects of multiple treatments under the conditional independence assumption". In: Lechner, M., Pfeiffer, F. (Eds.), Econometric Evaluations of Active Labor Market Policies in Europe. Physica/Springer, Heidelberg.
Lee, L.-F. (1978). "Unionism and wage rates: A simultaneous equations model with qualitative and limited dependent variables". International Economic Review 19 (2), 415–433 (June).
Lee, L.-F. (1983). "Generalized econometric models with selectivity". Econometrica 51 (2), 507–512 (March).
Mallar, C., Kerachsky, S., Thorton, C. (1980). "The short-term economic impact of the Job Corps program". In: Stromsdorfer, E., Farkas, G. (Eds.), Evaluation Studies Review Annual, vol. 5. Sage Publications.
Manski, C.F. (1989). "Anatomy of the selection problem". Journal of Human Resources 24 (3), 343–360 (Summer).
Manski, C.F. (1990). "Nonparametric bounds on treatment effects". American Economic Review 80 (2), 319–323 (May).
Manski, C.F. (1994). "The selection problem". In: Sims, C. (Ed.), Advances in Econometrics: Sixth World Congress. Cambridge Univ. Press, New York, pp. 143–170.
Manski, C.F. (1995). Identification Problems in the Social Sciences. Harvard Univ. Press, Cambridge, MA.
Manski, C.F. (1996). "Learning about treatment effects from experiments with random assignment of treatments". Journal of Human Resources 31 (4), 709–733 (Autumn).
Manski, C.F. (1997). "Monotone treatment response". Econometrica 65 (6), 1311–1334 (November).
Manski, C.F. (2003). Partial Identification of Probability Distributions. Springer-Verlag, New York.
Manski, C.F., Pepper, J.V. (2000). "Monotone instrumental variables: With an application to the returns to schooling". Econometrica 68 (4), 997–1010 (July).
Mare, R.D. (1980). "Social background and school continuation decisions". Journal of the American Statistical Association 75 (370), 295–305 (June).
Marschak, J. (1953). "Economic measurements for policy and prediction". In: Hood, W., Koopmans, T. (Eds.), Studies in Econometric Method. Wiley, New York, pp. 1–26.
Masters, S.H., Maynard, R.A. (1981). The Impact of Supported Work on Long-Term Recipients of AFDC Benefits. Manpower Demonstration Research Corporation, New York.
Matzkin, R.L. (1993). "Nonparametric identification and estimation of polychotomous choice models". Journal of Econometrics 58 (1–2), 137–168 (July).
Matzkin, R.L. (1994). "Restrictions of economic theory in nonparametric methods". In: Engle, R., McFadden, D. (Eds.), Handbook of Econometrics, vol. 4. North-Holland, New York, pp. 2523–2558.
Matzkin, R.L. (2003). "Nonparametric estimation of nonadditive random functions". Econometrica 71 (5), 1339–1375 (September).
Matzkin, R.L. (2007). "Nonparametric identification". In: Heckman, J., Leamer, E. (Eds.), Handbook of Econometrics, vol. 6B. Elsevier, Amsterdam.
Maynard, R., Brown, R.S. (1980). The Impact of Supported Work on Young School Dropouts. Manpower Demonstration Research Corporation, New York.
McFadden, D. (1974). "Conditional logit analysis of qualitative choice behavior". In: Zarembka, P. (Ed.), Frontiers in Econometrics. Academic Press, New York.
Moffitt, R. (1992). "Evaluation methods for program entry effects". In: Manski, C., Garfinkel, I. (Eds.), Evaluating Welfare and Training Programs. Harvard Univ. Press, Cambridge, MA, pp. 231–252.
Newey, W.K., Powell, J.L. (2003). "Instrumental variable estimation of nonparametric models". Econometrica 71 (5), 1565–1578 (September).

Olley, G.S., Pakes, A. (1996). "The dynamics of productivity in the telecommunications equipment industry". Econometrica 64 (6), 1263–1297 (November).

Palca, J. (1989). "AIDS drug trials enter new age". Science, New Series 246 (4926), 19–21 (October 6).

Pearl, J. (2000). Causality. Cambridge Univ. Press, Cambridge, England.

Pessino, C. (1991). "Sequential migration theory and evidence from Peru". Journal of Development Economics 36 (1), 55–87 (July).

Peterson, A.V. (1976). "Bounds for a joint distribution function with fixed sub-distribution functions: Application to competing risks". Proceedings of the National Academy of Sciences 73 (1), 11–13 (January).

Powell, J.L. (1994). "Estimation of semiparametric models". In: Engle, R., McFadden, D. (Eds.), Handbook of Econometrics, vol. 4. Elsevier, Amsterdam, pp. 2443–2521.

Prescott, E.C., Visscher, M. (1977). "Sequential location among firms with foresight". Bell Journal of Economics 8 (2), 378–893 (Autumn).

Quandt, R.E. (1958). "The estimation of the parameters of a linear regression system obeying two separate regimes". Journal of the American Statistical Association 53 (284), 873–880 (December).

Quandt, R.E. (1972). "A new approach to estimating switching regressions". Journal of the American Statistical Association 67 (338), 306–310 (June).

Quint, J.C., Polit, D.F., Bos, H., Cave, G. (1994). New Chance Interim Findings on a Comprehensive Program for Disadvantaged Young Mothers and Their Children. Manpower Demonstration Research Corporation, New York.

Rao, C.R. (1985). "Weighted distributions". In: Atkinson, A., Fienberg, S. (Eds.), A Celebration of Statistics: The ISI Centenary Volume. Springer-Verlag, New York.

Robins, J.M. (1989). "The analysis of randomized and non-randomized AIDS treatment trials using a new approach to causal inference in longitudinal studies". In: Sechrest, L., Freeman, H., Mulley, A. (Eds.), Health Services Research Methodology: A Focus on AIDS. United States Department of Health and Human Services, National Center for Health Services Research and Health Care Technology Assessment, Rockville, MD, pp. 113–159.

Robins, J.M. (1997). "Causal inference from complex longitudinal data". In: Berkane, M. (Ed.), Latent Variable Modeling and Applications to Causality. In: Lecture Notes in Statistics. Springer-Verlag, New York, pp. 69–117.

Robinson, C. (1989). "The joint determination of union status and union wage effects: Some tests of alternative models". Journal of Political Economy 97 (3), 639–667.

Rosenbaum, P.R. (1995). Observational Studies. Springer-Verlag, New York.

Rosenbaum, P.R., Rubin, D.B. (1983). "The central role of the propensity score in observational studies for causal effects". Biometrika 70 (1), 41–55 (April).

Roy, A. (1951). "Some thoughts on the distribution of earnings". Oxford Economic Papers 3 (2), 135–146 (June).

Rubin, D.B. (1974). "Estimating causal effects of treatments in randomized and nonrandomized studies". Journal of Educational Psychology 66 (5), 688–701 (October).

Rubin, D.B. (1978). "Bayesian inference for causal effects: The role of randomization". Annals of Statistics 6 (1), 34–58 (January).

Rubin, D.B. (1979). "Using multivariate matched sampling and regression adjustment to control bias in observational studies". Journal of the American Statistical Association 74 (366), 318–328 (June).

Rudin, W. (1974). Real and Complex Analysis, second ed. McGraw–Hill, New York.

Schennach, S.M. (2004). "Estimation of nonlinear models with measurement error". Econometrica 72 (1), 33–75 (January).

Shaked, A., Sutton, J. (1982). "Relaxing price competition through product differentiation". Review of Economic Studies 49 (1), 3–13 (January).

Silvey, S.D. (1970). Statistical Inference. Penguin, Harmondsworth.

Smith, J.A. (1992). "The JTPA selection process: A descriptive analysis". Unpublished working paper. Department of Economics, University of Chicago.

Smith, V.K., Banzhaf, H.S. (2004). "A diagrammatic exposition of weak complementarity and the Willig condition". American Journal of Agricultural Economics 86 (2), 455–466 (May).

Smith, J.P., Welch, F.R. (1986). Closing the Gap: Forty Years of Economic Progress for Blacks. RAND Corporation, Santa Monica, CA.

Smith, J., Whalley, A., Wilcox, N. (2006). "Are program participants good evaluators?" Unpublished manuscript. Department of Economics, University of Michigan.

Telser, L.G. (1964). "Iterative estimation of a set of linear regression equations". Journal of the American Statistical Association 59 (307), 845–862 (September).

Todd, P.E. (1999). "A practical guide to implementing matching estimators". Unpublished manuscript. Department of Economics, University of Pennsylvania. Prepared for the IADB meeting in Santiago, Chile. (October).

Todd, P.E. (2007). "Evaluating social programs with endogenous program placement and selection of the treated". In: Handbook of Development Economics. Elsevier, Amsterdam. In press.

Todd, P.E. (2008). "Matching estimators". In: Durlauf, S., Blume, L.E. (Eds.), The New Palgrave Dictionary of Economics. Palgrave Macmillan, New York. In press.

Torp, H., Raaum, O., Hernæs, E., Goldstein, H. (1993). "The first Norwegian experiment". In: Burtless, G. (Ed.), Measuring Labour Market Measures: Evaluating the Effects of Active Labour Market Policy Initiatives, Proceedings from the Danish Presidency Conference "Effects and Measuring of Effects of Labour Market Policy Initiatives". Kolding, May 1993. Denmark Ministry of Labour, Copenhagen.

Tunali, I. (2000). "Rationality of migration". International Economic Review 41 (4), 893–920 (November).

Vijverberg, W.P.M. (1993). "Measuring the unidentified parameter of the extended Roy model of selectivity". Journal of Econometrics 57 (1–3), 69–89 (May–June).

Vytlacil, E.J. (2002). "Independence, monotonicity, and latent index models: An equivalence result". Econometrica 70 (1), 331–341 (January).

Vytlacil, E.J. (2006a). "A note on additive separability and latent index models of binary choice: Representation results". Oxford Bulletin of Economics and Statistics 68 (4), 515–518 (August).

Vytlacil, E.J. (2006b). "Ordered discrete choice selection models: Equivalence, nonequivalence, and representation results". Review of Economics and Statistics 88 (3), 578–581 (August).

Vytlacil, E.J., Yildiz, N. (2006). "Dummy endogenous variables in weakly separable models". Unpublished manuscript. Department of Economics, Columbia University.

Vytlacil, E.J., Santos, A., Shaikh, A.M. (2005). "Limited dependent variable models and bounds on treatment effects: A nonparametric analysis". Unpublished manuscript. Department of Economics, Columbia University.

White, H. (1984). Asymptotic Theory for Econometricians. Academic Press, Orlando, FL.

Willis, R.J., Rosen, S. (1979). "Education and self-selection". Journal of Political Economy 87 (5, Part 2), S7–S36 (October).

Wooldridge, J.M. (1997). "On two stage least squares estimation of the average treatment effect in a random coefficient model". Economics Letters 56 (2), 129–133 (October).

Wooldridge, J.M. (2003). "Further results on instrumental variables estimation of average treatment effects in the correlated random coefficient model". Economics Letters 79 (2), 185–191 (May).

Wu, D. (1973). "Alternative tests of independence between stochastic regressors and disturbances". Econometrica 41 (4), 733–750 (July).

Yitzhaki, S. (1989). "On using linear regression in welfare economics". Working Paper 217. Department of Economics, Hebrew University.

Yitzhaki, S. (1996). "On using linear regressions in welfare economics". Journal of Business and Economic Statistics 14 (4), 478–486 (October).

Yitzhaki, S., Schechtman, E. (2004). "The Gini Instrumental Variable, or the "double instrumental variable" estimator". Metron 62 (3), 287–313.

Zellner, A., Rossi, P.E. (1987). "Evaluating the methodology of social experiments". In: Munnell, A.H. (Ed.), Lessons from the Income Maintenance Experiments: Proceedings of a Conference Held at Melvin Village. New Hampshire, September, 1986. In: Federal Reserve Bank of Boston Conference Series, vol. 30. Brookings Institution, Washington, DC, pp. 131–157.

Zheng, J.X. (1996). "A consistent test of functional form via nonparametric estimation techniques". Journal of Econometrics 75, 263–289 (December).

Chapter 72

ECONOMETRIC EVALUATION OF SOCIAL PROGRAMS, PART III: DISTRIBUTIONAL TREATMENT EFFECTS, DYNAMIC TREATMENT EFFECTS, DYNAMIC DISCRETE CHOICE, AND GENERAL EQUILIBRIUM POLICY EVALUATION*

JAAP H. ABBRING

Vrije Universiteit Amsterdam, The Netherlands

Tinbergen Institute, The Netherlands

JAMES J. HECKMAN

The University of Chicago, USA

American Bar Foundation, USA

University College Dublin, Ireland

Contents

* This research was supported by NSF: 9709873, 0099195, and SES-0241858 and NICHD: R01-HD32058, and the American Bar Foundation. The views expressed in this chapter are those of the authors and not necessarily those of funders listed here. We have benefited from discussions with Thomas Amorde, Flavio Cunha, and Sergio Urzua, and detailed proofreading by Seong Moon, Rodrigo Pinto, Peter Savelyev, G. Adam Savvas, John Trujillo, Semih Tumen, and Jordan Weil. Section 2 of this chapter is based, in part, on joint work with Flavio Cunha and Salvador Navarro.

Handbook of Econometrics, Volume 6B

DOI: 10.1016/S1573-4412(07)06072-2

Abstract

This chapter develops three topics. (1) Identification of the distributions of treatment effects and the distributions of agent subjective evaluations of treatment effects. Methods for identifying *ex ante* and *ex post* distributions are presented and empirical examples are given. (2) Identification of dynamic treatment effects. The relationship between the statistical literature on dynamic causal inference based on sequential-randomization and the dynamic discrete-choice literature is exposited. The value of well posed economic choice models for decision making under uncertainty in analyzing and interpreting dynamic intervention studies is developed. A survey of the dynamic discrete-choice literature is presented. (3) The key ideas and papers in the recent literature on general equilibrium evaluations of social programs are summarized.

Keywords

distributions of treatment effects, dynamic treatment effects, dynamic discrete choice, general equilibrium policy evaluation

JEL classification: C10, C23, C41, C50

1. Introduction

Part I of this Handbook contribution by Heckman and Vytlacil (Chapter 70) presents a general framework for policy evaluation. Three distinct policy problems are analyzed: P-1 (Internal Validity)—evaluating the effects of a policy in place; P-2 (External Validity)—forecasting the effect of a policy in place in a new environment, and P-3—forecasting the effect of new policies never previously implemented. Among other topics, Part I considers the analysis of distributions of treatment effects and distinguishes private (subjective) valuations of programs from objective valuations. It also discusses the dynamic revelation of information and the uncertainty facing agents. It makes a distinction between *ex ante* expectations of subjective and objective treatment effects and *ex post* realizations of subjective and objective treatment effects. It presents a framework for defining the option value of participating in social programs. The analysis there is largely microeconomic in focus and does not consider the full general equilibrium impacts of policies.

Part II by Heckman and Vytlacil (Chapter 71) focuses primarily on methods for conducting *ex post* evaluations of policies in place (problem P-1), organizing our discussion around the marginal treatment effect (MTE). Mean treatment effect parameters receive the most attention. The methods exposited there can be used to identify marginal impact distributions for Y_0 and Y_1 separately. We show how to use the marginal treatment effect to solve problems P-2 and P-3 in constructing *ex post* evaluations but we do not consider general equilibrium policy analysis.

This chapter presents methods that implement the most innovative aspects of Part I. It is organized in three sections. The first section analyzes methods for the identification of distributions of treatment effects ($Y_1 - Y_0$) and not just the distribution of marginal outcome distributions (or their means) for Y_0 and Y_1 separately. We first analyze *ex post* realized distributions. A different way to say this is that we initially ignore uncertainty. We then present methods for identifying *ex ante* distributions of treatment effects and the information that agents act on when they make their treatment choices prior to the realization of outcomes. Agent *ex ante* expectations are one form of subjective valuation. We present empirical examples based on the research of Carneiro, Hansen and Heckman (2001, 2003), Cunha, Heckman and Navarro (2005, 2006) and Cunha and Heckman (2007b, 2007c, 2008). This part of the chapter helps move the evaluation literature out of statistics and into economics. It presents methods for developing subjective and objective distributions of outcomes.

In the second portion of this contribution, we build on the analysis in the first portion to consider dynamic treatment effects, where sequential revelation of information plays a prominent role. We consider dynamic matching models introduced by Robins (1997), Gill and Robins (2001) and Lok (2007), and applied in economics by Lechner and Miquel (2002) and Fitzenberger, Osikominu and Völter (2006). We then consider more economically motivated models based on continuous-time duration analysis [see Abbring and Van den Berg (2003b)] and dynamic generalizations of the Roy model [Heckman and Navarro (2007)]. We consider identification of mean treatment effects and joint distributions of both objective and subjective outcomes. In the third section of the paper, we briefly consider general equilibrium policy evaluation for distributions of outcomes. We now turn to identification of the distributions of treatment effects.

2. Identifying distributions of treatment effects

The fundamental problem of policy evaluation is that we cannot observe agents in more than one possible state. Chapter 71 focused on various methods for identifying mean outcomes and marginal distributions. Methods useful for identifying means apply in a straightforward way to identification of quantiles of marginal distributions as well as the full marginal distributions. In a two potential outcome world, we can identify $\Pr(Y_1 \leqslant y \mid X) = E(\mathbf{1}[Y_1 \leqslant y] \mid X)$ and $\Pr(Y_0 \leqslant y \mid X) = E(\mathbf{1}[Y_0 \leqslant y] \mid X)$ using the variety of methods summarized in that chapter. One can compare outcomes at one quantile of Y_1 with outcomes at a quantile of Y_0. See, e.g., Heckman, Smith and Clements (1997) or Abadie, Angrist and Imbens (2002). However, these methods do not in general identify the quantiles of the distribution of $Y_1 - Y_0$.

The research reported here is based on work by Aakvik, Heckman and Vytlacil (2005), Heckman and Smith (1998), Heckman, Smith and Clements (1997), Carneiro, Hansen and Heckman (2001, 2003), Cunha, Heckman and Navarro (2005, 2006), and Cunha and Heckman (2007b, 2007c, 2008). It moves beyond means as descriptions of policy outcomes and considers joint counterfactual distributions of outcomes (for example, $F(y_1, y_0)$, gains, $F(y_1 - y_0)$ or outcomes for participants $F(y_1, y_0 \mid D = 1)$). These are the *ex post* distributions realized after treatment is received. We also analyze *ex ante* distributions, inferring the information available to agents when they make their choices. From knowledge of the *ex post* joint distributions of counterfactual outcomes, it is possible to determine the proportion of people who benefit or lose from treatment, and hence *ex post* regret, the origin and destination outcomes of those who change status because of treatment and the amount of gain (or loss) from various policies targeted to persons at different deciles of an initial pre-policy income distribution.[1] Using the joint distribution of counterfactuals, it is possible to develop a more nuanced understanding of the distributional impacts of public policies, and to move beyond comparisons of aggregate distributions induced by different policies to consider how people in different portions of an initial distribution are affected by public policy.

Except in special cases, which we discuss in this portion of the chapter, the methods discussed in Chapter 71 do not solve the fundamental problem of identifying the distribution of treatment effects, i.e., constructing the joint distribution of (Y_0, Y_1) and of the treatment effects $Y_1 - Y_0$. This part of the Handbook reviews methods for constructing or bounding these distributions. We now state precisely the problem analyzed in this section.

[1] It is also possible to generate all mean, median or other quantile gains to treatment, to identify all pairwise treatment effects in a multi-outcome setting, and to determine how much of the variability in returns across persons comes from variability in the distributions of the outcome selected and how much comes from variability in distributions for alternative opportunities.

2.1. The problem

Consider a two-outcome model. The methods surveyed apply in a straightforward way to models with more than two outcomes, as we demonstrate after analyzing the two-outcome case. For expositional convenience, we focus on scalar outcomes unless explicitly stated otherwise. We do not usually observe (Y_0, Y_1) as a pair, but rather only one coordinate and that subject to a selection bias. Thus the problem of recovering joint distributions from cross-section data has two aspects. The first is the selection problem. From data on outcomes, $F_1(y_1 \mid D = 1, X)$, $F_0(y_0 \mid D = 0, X)$, under what conditions can one recover $F_1(y_1 \mid X)$ and $F_0(y_0 \mid X)$, respectively? The second problem is how to construct the joint distribution of $F(y_0, y_1 \mid X)$ from the two marginal distributions. We assume in this section that one of the methods for dealing with the selection problem discussed in Chapters 70 and 71 has been applied and the analyst knows $\Pr(Y_0 \leqslant y_0 \mid X) = F_0(y_0 \mid X)$ and $\Pr(Y_1 \leqslant y_1 \mid X) = F_1(y_1 \mid X)$. The problem is to construct $\Pr(Y_0 \leqslant y_0, Y_1 \leqslant y_1 \mid X) = F(y_0, y_1 \mid X)$. A related problem is how to construct the joint distribution of (Y_0, Y_1, D): $F(y_0, y_1, d \mid X)$. We also consider methods for bounding joint distributions. But first we answer the question, "Why bother"?

2.2. Why bother identifying joint distributions?

Given the intrinsic difficulty in identifying joint distributions of counterfactual outcomes, it is natural to ask, "why not settle for the marginals $F_0(y_0 \mid X)$ and $F_1(y_1 \mid X)$?" The methods surveyed in Chapter 71 afford identification of the marginal distributions. Any method that can identify means or quantiles of distributions can be modified to identify marginal distributions since $E[\mathbf{1}(Y_j \leqslant y_j) \mid X] = F_j(y_j \mid X)$, $j = 0, 1$.[2]

The literature on the measurement of economic inequality as surveyed by Foster and Sen (1997) focuses on marginal distributions across different policy states. Invoking the anonymity postulate, it does not keep track of individual fortunes across different policy states. It does not decompose overall outcomes in each policy state, $Y = DY_1 + (1 - D)Y_0$, into their component parts Y_1, Y_0, attributable to treatment, and D due to choice or assignment mechanisms. Thus, in comparing policies p and $p' \in \mathcal{P}$, it compares the marginal distributions of

$$Y^p = D^p Y_1^p + (1 - D^p) Y_0^p,$$

where D^p is the treatment choice indicator under policy p, and

$$Y^{p'} = D^{p'} Y_1^{p'} + (1 - D^{p'}) Y_0^{p'}$$

without seeking information on the subjective valuations of the policy change or the components of the treatment distributions under each policy (Y_0^p and Y_1^p; $Y_0^{p'}$ and $Y_1^{p'}$).

[2] Quantile methods [Chesher (2003), Koenker and Xiao (2002), Koenker (2005)] and many of the methods surveyed in Chapter 73 (Matzkin) of this Handbook also recover these marginal distributions under appropriate assumptions.

It compares $F_{Y^p}(y^p \mid X)$ and $F_{Y^{p'}}(y^{p'} \mid X)$ in making comparisons of welfare and does not worry about the component distributions, subjective valuations of agents, or any issues of self-selection.

Distinguishing the contributions of the component outcome distributions $F_0(y_0)$ and $F_1(y_1)$ and the choice mechanisms is essential for understanding the channels through which different policies operate [Carneiro, Hansen and Heckman (2001, 2003), and Cunha and Heckman (2008)]. Throughout this section, we assume policy invariance for outcomes, (PI-1) and (PI-2), in the notation of Chapter 70, unless otherwise noted.

Heckman, Smith and Clements (1997) and Heckman (1998) apply the concepts of first and second order stochastic dominance used in the conventional inequality measurement literature to compare outcome distributions across treatment states within a policy regime.[3] The same methods can be used to compare treatment outcome distributions across policy states.[4]

Some economists appeal to classical welfare economics and classical decision theory to argue that marginal distributions of treatment outcomes are all that is required to implement the criteria used by these approaches. The argument is that under expected utility maximization with information set $\mathcal{I}$, the agent should be assigned to (choose) treatment 1 if

$$E\big(\Upsilon(Y_1) - \Upsilon(Y_0) \mid \mathcal{I}\big) \geqslant 0,$$

where Υ is the preference function and $\mathcal{I}$ is the appropriate information set (that of the social planner or the agent). To compute this expectation it is only necessary to know $F_1(y_1 \mid \mathcal{I})$ and $F_0(y_0 \mid \mathcal{I})$, and not the full joint distribution $F(y_0, y_1 \mid \mathcal{I})$. For many other criteria used in classical decision theory, marginal distributions are all that is required.

As noted in Section 2.5 of Chapter 70, if one seeks to know the proportion of people who benefit in terms of income from the program in gross terms ($\Pr(Y_1 \geqslant Y_0 \mid \mathcal{I})$), one needs to know the joint distribution of (Y_0, Y_1) given the appropriate information set. Thus if one seeks to determine the proportion of agents who benefit from 1 compared to 0, it is necessary to determine the joint distribution of (Y_0, Y_1) unless information set $\mathcal{I}$ is known to the econometrician and the agent uses the Roy model to make choices. For the Roy model,

$$D = \mathbf{1}[Y_1 \geqslant Y_0],$$

the probability of selecting treatment given the econometrician's information set $\mathcal{I}_E$ is

$$\Pr(D = 1 \mid \mathcal{I}_E) = \Pr(Y_1 \geqslant Y_0 \mid \mathcal{I}_E).$$

[3] Abadie (2002) develops standard errors for this method and presents additional references.

[4] Under the conventional microeconometric partial equilibrium approach to policy evaluation surveyed in Chapter 70, the marginal distributions of (Y_0, Y_1) are invariant to the choice of the policy regime. This assumption is relaxed in our analysis of general equilibrium effects in Section 4.

If there are no direct costs of participation, and agents participate in the program based on self-selection under perfect certainty, and $\mathcal{I}_E$ is both the econometrician's and the agent's information set, then data on choices identify this proportion without need for any further econometric analysis. See the discussion in Section 2.6 below. More generally, agents may use the generalized Roy model presented in Chapter 70, or some other model, to make decisions, but the analyst seeks to know the proportion who gain *ex post*, conditioning on a different information set. Individual choice data will not reveal this probability if (a) agents do not use a Roy model formulated in *ex post* outcomes, (b) they use a more general decision rule, or (c) the information set of the agent is different from that of the econometrician. In these cases, further econometric analysis is required to identify $\Pr(Y_1 \geqslant Y_0 \mid \mathcal{I})$ for any particular information set.

Clearly the joint distribution of (Y_0, Y_1) given $\mathcal{I}$ is required to compute the gain in gross outcomes in general terms. In analyzing the option values of social programs and the distribution of returns to schooling (e.g., $(Y_1 - Y_0)$), in identifying dynamic discrete-choice models (reviewed in Section 3), and in determining *ex post* regret, knowledge of the full joint distribution of outcomes is required.

Section 2.10 presents examples of the richer, more nuanced, approach to policy evaluation that is possible when the analyst has access to the joint distribution of outcomes across counterfactual states. We show how the tools presented in this section allow economists to move beyond the limitations of the anonymity postulate to consider who benefits and who loses from policy reforms. We present estimates of the proportion of people who have *ex post* regret about their schooling choices and estimates of the *ex ante* and *ex post* distributions of returns to schooling ($\frac{Y_1 - Y_0}{Y_0}$) which inherently require knowledge of the joint distribution of outcomes across states. We now turn to methods for identifying or bounding joint distributions.

2.3. Solutions

There are two basic approaches in the literature to solving the problem of identifying $F(y_0, y_1 \mid X)$: (A) solutions that postulate assumptions about dependence between Y_0 and Y_1 and (B) solutions based on information from agent participation rules and additional data on choice. Recently developed methods build on these two basic approaches and combine choice theory with supplementary data and assumptions about the structure of dependence among model unobservables. We survey all of these methods. In addition to methods for exact identification, Fréchet bounds can be placed on the joint distributions from knowledge of the marginals [see, e.g., Heckman and Smith (1993, 1995), Heckman, Smith and Clements (1997), Manski (1997)]. We first consider these bounds.

2.4. Bounds from classical probability inequalities

The problem of bounding an unknown joint distribution from known marginal distributions is a classical problem in mathematical statistics. Hoeffding (1940) and Fréchet

(1951) demonstrate that the joint distribution is bounded by two functions of the marginal distributions. Their inequalities state that

$$\max\left[F_0(y_0 \mid X) + F_1(y_1 \mid X) - 1, 0\right] \leqslant F(y_0, y_1 \mid X) \leqslant \min\left[F_0(y_0 \mid X), F_1(y_1 \mid X)\right].$$ [5]

To simplify the notation, we keep conditioning on X implicit in the remainder of this section. Rüschendorf (1981) establishes that these bounds are tight.[6] Mardia (1970) establishes that both the lower bound and the upper bound are proper probability distributions. At the upper bound, $Y_1 = F_1^{-1}(F_0(Y_0))$ is a non-decreasing deterministic function of Y_0. At the lower bound, Y_1 is a non-increasing deterministic function of Y_0: $Y_1 = F_1^{-1}(1 - F_0(Y_0))$.

By a theorem of Cambanis, Simons and Stout (1976), if $k(y_1, y_0)$ is superadditive (or subadditive), then extreme values of $E(k(Y_1, Y_0))$ are obtained from the upper and lower bounding distributions.[7,8] Since $k(y_1, y_0) = (y_1 - E(Y_1))(y_0 - E(Y_0))$ is superadditive, the maximum attainable product-moment correlation $r_{Y_0 Y_1}$ is obtained from the upper bound distribution while the minimum attainable product moment correlation is obtained at the lower bound distribution. Let $\Delta = Y_1 - Y_0$. It is possible to bound $\mathrm{Var}(\Delta) = (\mathrm{Var}(Y_1) + \mathrm{Var}(Y_0) - 2r_{Y_0 Y_1}[\mathrm{Var}(Y_1)\,\mathrm{Var}(Y_0)]^{1/2})$ with the minimum obtained from the Fréchet–Hoeffding upper bound.[9] Checking whether the lower bound of $\mathrm{Var}(\Delta)$ is statistically significantly different from zero provides a test of whether or not the data are consistent with the common effect model. For example, if $Y_1 - Y_0 = \beta$, a constant, $\mathrm{Var}(\Delta) = 0$.

Tchen (1980) establishes that Kendall's τ and Spearman's ρ also attain their extreme values at the bounding distributions. The upper and lower bounding distributions produce the cases of perfect positive dependence and perfect negative dependence, respectively. Often the bounds on the quantiles of the Δ distribution obtained from the Fréchet–Hoeffding bounds are very wide.[10] Table 1 presents the range of values of $r_{Y_0 Y_1}$,

[5] King (1997) applies these inequalities to solve the problem of ecological correlation. These inequalities are used in the missing data literature for contingency tables [see, e.g., Bishop, Fienberg and Holland (1975)].

[6] An upper bound is "tight" if it is the smallest possible upper bound. A lower bound is tight if it is the largest lower bound.

[7] k is assumed to be Borel-measurable and right-continuous. k is strictly superadditive if $y_1 > y_1'$ and $y_0 > y_0'$ imply that $k(y_1, y_0) + k(y_1', y_0') > k(y_1, y_0') + k(y_1', y_0)$. k is strictly subadditive if the final inequality is reversed.

[8] An interesting application of the analysis of Cambanis, Simons and Stout (1976) is to the assignment problem studied by Koopmans and Beckmann (1957) and Becker (1974). If total output of a match $k(y_0, y_1)$ is superadditive, as it is in the Cobb–Douglas model ($k(y_0, y_1) = y_0 y_1$), then the optimal sorting rule is obtained by the upper bound of the Fréchet distribution.

[9] Note that the maximum value of $r_{Y_0 Y_1}$ is obtained at the upper bound and that all other components of the variance of Δ are obtained from the marginal distributions. Thus the minimum variance of Δ is obtained from the Fréchet–Hoeffding upper bound distribution.

[10] See the examples in Heckman and Smith (1993).

Table 1
Characteristics of the distribution of impacts on earnings in the 18 months after random assignment at the Fréchet–Hoeffding bounds (National JTPA Study 18 month impact sample: adult females)

Statistic	From lower bound distribution	From upper bound distribution
Impact standard deviation	14968.76	674.50
	(211.08)	(137.53)
Outcome correlation	−0.760	0.998
	(0.013)	(0.001)
Spearman's ρ	−0.9776	0.9867
	(0.0016)	(0.0013)

Notes: 1. These estimates were obtained using the empirical c.d.f.s calculated at 100 dollar earnings intervals rather than using the percentiles of the two c.d.f.s.
2. Bootstrap standard errors in parentheses.
Source: Heckman, Smith and Clements (1997).

Spearman's ρ and $[\text{Var}(\Delta)]^{1/2}$ for the Job Training Partnership Act (JTPA) data analyzed in Heckman, Smith and Clements (1997).[11] The ranges are rather wide, but it is interesting to observe that the bounds rule out the common effect model, as $\text{Var}(\Delta)$ is bounded away from zero.

The Fréchet–Hoeffding bounds apply to all joint distributions.[12] The outcome variables may be discrete, continuous or both discrete and continuous. It is fruitful to consider the bounds for this model with binary outcomes to establish the variability in the distribution of impacts for a discrete variable such as employment. For specificity, we analyze the employment data from the JTPA experiment reported in Heckman, Smith and Clements (1997). The data are multinomial.[13] Let (E, E) denote the event "employed with treatment" and "employed without treatment" and let (E, N) be the event "employed with treatment, not employed without treatment." Similarly, (N, E) and (N, N) refer respectively to cases where a person would not be employed if treated but would be employed if not treated, and where a person would not be employed in either case. The probabilities associated with these events are P_{EE}, P_{EN}, P_{NE} and P_{NN}, respectively. This model can be written in the form of a contingency table. The columns refer to employment and nonemployment in the untreated state. The rows refer to employment and nonemployment in the treated state.

[11] Heckman, Smith and Clements (1997) discuss the properties of the estimates of the standard errors reported in Table 1. JTPA was a job training program in place in the US in the 1980s and 1990s.
[12] Formulae for multivariate bounds are given in Tchen (1980) and Rüschendorf (1981).
[13] The following formulation owes a lot to the missing cell literature in contingency table analysis. See, e.g., Bishop, Fienberg and Holland (1975).

Untreated

		E	N	
Treated	E	P_{EE}	P_{EN}	$P_{E\cdot}$
	N	P_{NE}	P_{NN}	$P_{N\cdot}$
		$P_{\cdot E}$	$P_{\cdot N}$	

If we observed the same person in both the treated and untreated states, we could fill in the table and estimate the full distribution. With experimental data or data corrected for selection using the methods discussed in Chapter 71, one can estimate the marginals of the table parameters:

$$P_{E\cdot} = P_{EE} + P_{EN} \quad \text{(employment proportion among the treated),} \tag{2.1a}$$

$$P_{\cdot E} = P_{EE} + P_{NE} \quad \text{(employment proportion among the untreated).} \tag{2.1b}$$

The treatment effect is usually defined as

$$\Delta = P_{EN} - P_{NE}. \tag{2.2}$$

This is the proportion of people who would switch from being nonemployed to being employed as a result of treatment minus the proportion of persons who would switch from being employed to not being employed as a result of treatment. Using (2.1a) and (2.1b), we obtain the treatment effect as

$$\Delta = P_{E\cdot} - P_{\cdot E}, \tag{2.3}$$

so that Δ is identified by subtracting the proportion employed in the control group ($\hat{P}_{\cdot E}$) from the proportion employed in the treatment group ($\hat{P}_{E\cdot}$).

If we wish to decompose Δ into its two components, experimental data or selection-corrected data do not in general give an exact answer. In terms of the contingency table presented above, we know the row and column marginals but not the individual elements in the table. The case in the 2×2 table corresponding to the common effect model for continuous outcomes restricts the effect of the program on employment to be always positive or always negative, so that either P_{EN} or $P_{NE} = 0$, respectively. Under such assumptions, the model is fully identified. This is analogous to the continuous case in which the common effect assumption, or more generally, an assumption of perfect positive dependence, identifies the joint distribution of outcomes.

More generally, the Fréchet–Hoeffding bounds restrict the range of admissible values for the cell probabilities. Their application in this case produces:

$$\max[P_{E\cdot} + P_{\cdot E} - 1, 0] \leqslant P_{EE} \leqslant \min[P_{E\cdot}, P_{\cdot E}],$$

$$\max[P_{E\cdot} - P_{\cdot E}, 0] \leqslant P_{EN} \leqslant \min[P_{E\cdot}, 1 - P_{\cdot E}],$$

$$\max[-P_{E\cdot} + P_{\cdot E}, 0] \leqslant P_{NE} \leqslant \min[1 - P_{E\cdot}, P_{\cdot E}],$$

$$\max[1 - P_{E\cdot} - P_{\cdot E}, 0] \leqslant P_{NN} \leqslant \min[1 - P_{E\cdot}, 1 - P_{\cdot E}].$$

Table 2
Fraction employed in the 16th, 17th or 18th month after random assignment and Fréchet–Hoeffding bounds on the probabilities P_{NE} and P_{EN} (National JTPA study 18 month impact sample: adult females)

Parameter	Estimate
Fraction employed in the treatment group	0.64 (0.01)
Fraction employed in the control group	0.61 (0.01)
Bounds on P_{EN}	[0.03, 0.39] (0.01), (0.01)
Bounds on P_{NE}	[0.00, 0.36] (0.00), (0.01)

Notes: 1. Employment percentages are based on self-reported employment in months 16, 17 and 18 after random assignment. A person is coded as employed if the sum of their self-reported earnings over these three months is positive.
2. P_{ij} is the probability of having employment status i in the treated state and employment status j in the untreated state, where i and j take on the values E for employed and N for not employed. The Fréchet–Hoeffding bounds are given in the text.
3. Standard errors are discussed in Heckman, Smith and Clements (1997).
Source: Heckman, Smith and Clements (1997).

Table 2, taken from the analysis of Heckman, Smith and Clements (1997), presents the Fréchet–Hoeffding bounds for P_{NE} and P_{EN} from the national JTPA experiment—the source of data for Table 1. The outcome variable is whether or not a person is employed in the 16th, 17th or 18th month after random assignment. The bounds are very wide. Even without taking into account sampling error, the experimental evidence for adult females is consistent with a value of P_{NE} ranging from 0.00 to 0.36. The range for P_{EN} is equally large. Thus as many as 39% and as few as 3% of adult females may have had their employment status improved by participating in the training program. As many as 36% and as few as 0% may have had their employment status harmed by participating in the program. From (2.2), we know that the net difference $P_{EN} - P_{NE} = \Delta$, so that high values of P_{EN} are associated with high values of P_{NE}. As few as 25% $[(0.64 - 0.39) \times 100\%]$ and as many as 61% of the women would have worked whether or not they entered the program ($P_{EE} \in [0.25, 0.61]$).

From the evidence presented in Table 2, one cannot distinguish two different stories. The first story is that the JTPA program benefits many people by facilitating their employment but it also harms many people who would have worked if they had not participated in the program. The second story is that the program benefits and harms few people.[14] Heckman, Smith and Clements (1997) and Manski (1997, 2003) develop these bounds further. We next consider methods to point identify the joint distributions of outcomes. All entail using some auxiliary information.

2.5. Solutions based on dependence assumptions

A variety of approaches solve the problem of identifying the joint distribution of potential outcomes by making dependence assumptions connecting Y_0 and Y_1. We review some of the major approaches.

2.5.1. Solutions based on conditional independence or matching

An approach based on matching postulates access to variables Q that have the property that conditional on Q, $F_0(y_0 \mid D = 0, X, Q) = F_0(y_0 \mid X, Q)$ and $F_1(y_1 \mid D = 1, X, Q) = F_1(y_1 \mid X, Q)$. As discussed in Section 9 of Chapter 71, matching assumes that conditional on observed variables, Q, there is no selection problem: $(Y_0 \perp\!\!\!\perp D \mid X, Q)$ and $(Y_1 \perp\!\!\!\perp D \mid X, Q)$. If it is further assumed that all of the dependence between (Y_0, Y_1) given X comes through Q, it follows that

$$F(y_1, y_0 \mid X, Q) = F_1(y_1 \mid X, Q) F_0(y_0 \mid X, Q).$$

Using these results, it is possible to identify the joint distribution $F(y_0, y_1 \mid X)$ because

$$F(y_0, y_1 \mid X) = \int F_0(y_0 \mid X, Q) F_1(y_1 \mid X, Q)\, d\mu(Q \mid X),$$

where $\mu(Q \mid X)$ is the conditional distribution of Q given X. Under the assumption that we observe X and Q, this conditional distribution can be constructed from data. We obtain $F_0(y_0 \mid X, Q)$, $F_1(y_1 \mid X, Q)$ by matching. Thus we can construct the right-hand side of the preceding expression. As noted in Chapter 71, matching makes the strong assumption that conditional on (Q, X) the marginal return to treatment is the same as the average return, although returns may differ by the level of Q and X.

2.5.2. The common coefficient approach

The traditional approach in economics to identifying joint distributions is to assume that the joint distribution $F(y_0, y_1 \mid X)$ is a degenerate, one dimensional distribution. Conditional on X, Y_0 and Y_1 are assumed to be deterministically related:

$$Y_1 - Y_0 = \Delta, \tag{2.4}$$

[14] Heckman, Smith and Clements (1997) show that conditioning on other background variables does not reduce the intrinsic uncertainty in the data. Thus in both the discrete and continuous cases, the data from the JTPA experiment are consistent with a wide variety of impact distributions.

where Δ is a constant given X. It is the difference in means between Y_1 and Y_0 for the selection corrected distribution.[15] This approach assumes that treatment has the same effect on everyone (with the same X), and that the effect is Δ. Because (2.4) implies a perfect ranking across quantiles of the outcome distributions Y_0 and Y_1, Δ can be identified from the difference in the quantiles between Y_0 and Y_1 for any quantile. Even if the means do not exist, one can still identify Δ. From knowledge of $F_0(y_0 \mid X)$ and $F_1(y_1 \mid X)$, one can identify the means and quantiles. Hence one can identify Δ.

2.5.3. More general dependence assumptions

Heckman, Smith and Clements (1997) and Heckman and Smith (1998) relax the common coefficient assumption by postulating perfect ranking in the positions of individuals in the $F_1(y_1 \mid X)$ and $F_0(y_0 \mid X)$ distributions. The best in one distribution is the best in the other. Assuming continuous and strictly increasing marginal distributions, they postulate that quantiles are perfectly ranked so $Y_1 = F_1^{-1}(F_0(Y_0))$. This is the tight upper bound of the Fréchet bounds. An alternative assumption is that people are perfectly inversely ranked so the best in one distribution is the worst in the other:

$$Y_1 = F_1^{-1}\bigl(1 - F_0(Y_0)\bigr).$$

This is the tight Fréchet lower bound.

One can associate quantiles across the marginal distributions more generally. Heckman, Smith and Clements (1997) use Markov transition kernels that stochastically map quantiles of one distribution into quantiles of another. They define a pair of Markov kernels $M(y_1, y_0 \mid X)$ and $\tilde{M}(y_0, y_1 \mid X)$ with the property that they map marginals into marginals:

$$F_1(y_1 \mid X) = \int M(y_1, y_0 \mid X)\, dF_0(y_0 \mid X),$$

$$F_0(y_0 \mid X) = \int \tilde{M}(y_0, y_1 \mid X)\, dF_1(y_1 \mid X).$$

Allowing these kernels to be degenerate produces a variety of deterministic transformations, including the two previously presented, as special cases of a general mapping. Different $(M, \tilde{M})$ pairs produce different joint distributions. These transformations supply the missing information needed to construct the joint distributions.[16]

[15] Δ may be a function of X.

[16] For given marginal distributions F_0 and F_1, we cannot independently pick M and $\tilde{M}$. Consistency requires that

$$\int_{-\infty}^{y_0} M(y_1, y \mid X)\, dF_0(y \mid X) = \int_{-\infty}^{y_1} \tilde{M}(y_0, y \mid X)\, dF_1(y \mid X),$$

for all y_0, y_1.

A perfect ranking (or perfect inverse ranking) assumption generalizes the perfect ranking, constant-shift assumptions implicit in the conventional literature. It allows analysts to apply conditional quantile methods to estimate the distributions of gains.[17] However, it imposes a strong and arbitrary dependence across distributions. Lehmann and D'Abrera (1975), Robins (1989, 1997), Koenker and Xiao (2002), and many others maintain this assumption under the rubric of "rank invariance" in order to identify the distribution of treatment effects.

Table 3 shows the percentiles of the earnings impact distribution ($F_{\Delta}(y_1 - y_0)$) for females in the National JTPA experiment under various assumptions about dependence

Table 3
Percentiles of the impact distribution as ranking across distributions (τ) varies based on random samples of 50 permutations with each value of τ (National JTPA study 18 month impact sample: adult females)

Measure of rank correlation τ	Minimum	5th percentile	25th percentile	50th percentile	75th percentile	95th percentile	Maximum
1.00	0.00	0.00	572.00	864.00	966.00	2003.00	18550.00
	(703.64)	(47.50)	(232.90)	(269.26)	(305.74)	(543.03)	(5280.67)
0.95	−14504.00	0.00	125.50	616.00	867.00	1415.50	48543.50
	(1150.01)	(360.18)	(124.60)	(280.19)	(272.60)	(391.51)	(8836.49)
0.90	−18817.00	−1168.00	0.00	487.00	876.50	2319.50	49262.00
	(1454.74)	(577.84)	(29.00)	(265.71)	(282.77)	(410.27)	(6227.38)
0.70	−25255.00	−8089.50	−136.00	236.50	982.50	12158.50	55169.50
	(1279.50)	(818.25)	(260.00)	(227.38)	(255.78)	(614.45)	(5819.28)
0.50	−28641.50	−12037.00	−1635.50	0.00	1362.50	16530.00	58472.00
	(1149.22)	(650.31)	(314.39)	(83.16)	(249.29)	(329.44)	(5538.14)
0.30	−32621.00	−14855.50	−3172.50	0.00	4215.50	16889.00	54381.00
	(1843.48)	(548.48)	(304.62)	(37.96)	(244.67)	(423.05)	(5592.86)
0.00	−44175.00	−18098.50	−6043.00	0.00	7388.50	19413.25	60599.00
	(2372.05)	(630.73)	(300.47)	(163.17)	(263.25)	(423.63)	(5401.02)
−0.30	−48606.00	−20566.00	−8918.50	779.50	9735.50	21093.25	65675.00
	(1281.80)	(545.99)	(286.92)	(268.02)	(300.59)	(462.13)	(5381.91)
−0.50	−48606.00	−21348.00	−9757.50	859.00	10550.50	22268.00	67156.00
	(1059.06)	(632.55)	(351.55)	(315.37)	(255.28)	(435.78)	(5309.90)
−0.70	−48606.00	−22350.00	−10625.00	581.50	11804.50	23351.00	67156.00
	(1059.06)	(550.00)	(371.38)	(309.84)	(246.58)	(520.93)	(5309.90)
−0.90	−48606.00	−22350.00	−11381.00	580.00	12545.00	23351.00	67156.00
	(1059.06)	(547.17)	(403.30)	(346.12)	(251.07)	(341.41)	(5309.90)
−0.95	−48606.00	−22350.00	−11559.00	580.00	12682.00	23351.00	67156.00
	(1059.06)	(547.17)	(404.67)	(366.37)	(255.97)	(341.41)	(5309.90)
−1.00	−48606.00	−22350.00	−11755.00	580.00	12791.00	23351.00	67156.00
	(1059.06)	(547.17)	(411.83)	(389.51)	(253.18)	(341.41)	(5309.90)

(*continued on next page*)

[17] See, e.g., Heckman, Smith and Clements (1997).

Table 3
(*continued*)

Notes: 1. This table shows selected percentiles of the empirical distribution of $Y_1 - Y_0$ under different assumptions about the dependence of Y_1 and Y_0. The empirical distribution of $Y_1 - Y_0$ for each indicated value of Kendall's rank correlation τ is constructed by pairing the percentiles of the empirical distributions of Y_0 and Y_1 in a way consistent with the value of τ. There are $J!$ ways of pairing the $J = 100$ percentiles of both marginal distributions, each corresponding to lining up the Y_0 percentiles to one of the $J!$ permutations of the Y_1 percentiles. First, consider the two extreme cases, $\tau = 1$ and $\tau = -1$. If the percentiles of Y_0 are assigned to the corresponding percentile of Y_1, then the rank correlation τ between the percentiles among the resulting J pairs equals 1. The difference between the percentile of Y_1 and the associated percentile of Y_0 in each pair is the impact for that pair. Taken together, the J pairs' impacts form the distribution of impacts for $\tau = 1$. It is the minimum, maximum and percentiles of this impact distribution that are reported in the first row of the table. If the percentile comparisons are based on pairing the biggest in one distribution with the smallest in the other distribution, then $\tau = -1$. Computations for $\tau = -1$ are reported in the table's last row.
Intermediate values of τ are obtained by considering pairings of percentiles with a specified number of inversions in the ranks. An inversion is said to arise if, among two pairs of quantiles, a lower Y_0 quantile is matched with a higher Y_1 quantile. For a given pairing of percentiles (permutation of the Y_1 percentiles) the total number of inversions is

$$\eta = \sum_j \sum_{i<j} h_{ij}, \quad h_{ij} = \begin{cases} 1, & Y_1^{(i)} > Y_1^{(j)}, \\ 0 \end{cases}$$

where $Y_1^{(j)}$ is the percentile of Y_1 associated with the jth percentile of Y_0. The value of η ranges from 0 (corresponding to perfect positive rank correlation) to $\frac{1}{2}J(J-1)$ (perfect negative rank correlation). Kendall's rank correlation measure τ is

$$\tau = 1 - \frac{4\eta}{J(J-1)}, \quad \text{where } \tau \in [-1, 1].$$

There are multiple pairings of percentiles consistent with each intermediate value of τ (number of inversions η), unlike in the cases of $\tau = 1$ and $\tau = -1$. Therefore, for intermediate values of τ the table reports the mean of the indicated parameters of the impact distribution over a random sample of 50 pairings having the indicated value of τ.
2. Bootstrap standard errors in parentheses.
Source: Heckman, Smith and Clements (1997).

between Y_1 and Y_0. The experiment identified $F_1(y_1)$ and $F_0(y_0)$ separately. The table reports selected percentiles of the estimated impact distributions for different assumed levels of dependence, τ (Kendall's rank correlation). As shown in the first footnote to the table, $\tau = 1$ corresponds to the Fréchet upper bound. $\tau = -1$ corresponds to the Fréchet lower bound. Since without further information in hand, the joint distribution is not identified, the data are consistent with all values of τ and so each row of the table is a possible outcome distribution. Notice that the medians (50th percentile) are reasonable, but many percentiles are not. Heckman, Smith and Clements (1997) suggest that prior information about plausible outcomes, possibly formalized by a Bayesian analysis, can be used to pick reasonable values of τ. We next consider alternative deconvolution assumptions that can be used to point identify the joint distributions.

2.5.4. Constructing distributions from assuming independence of the gain from the base

An alternative assumption about the dependence across outcomes is that $Y_1 = Y_0 + \Delta$, where Δ, the treatment effect, is a random variable stochastically independent of Y_0 given X, i.e.,

(CON-1) $Y_0 \perp\!\!\!\perp \Delta \mid X$.

This assumption states that the gain from participating in the program is independent of the base Y_0. If we assume

(M-1) $(Y_0, Y_1) \perp\!\!\!\perp D \mid X$,

and (CON-1), we can identify $F(y_0, y_1 \mid X)$ from the cross-section outcome distributions of participants and nonparticipants and estimate the joint distribution by using deconvolution.[18] Methods for using this information are presented in Appendix A.

Horowitz and Markatou (1996) develop the asymptotic properties of convolution estimators with regression building on the work of Stefanski and Carroll (1991). Heckman, Smith and Clements (1997) and Heckman and Smith (1998) use deconvolution to analyze the distribution of gains from the JTPA data. Neither (CON-1) nor (M-1) is an attractive assumption from the point of view of economic choice models. (M-1) implies that marginal entrants into a social program have the same return as average participants. The assumption (CON-1) is not a prediction of general choice models.

2.5.5. Random coefficient regression approaches

In a regression setting in which means and variances are assumed to capture all of the relevant information about the distributions of outcomes and treatment effects, the convolution approach discussed in the preceding section is equivalent to the traditional normal random coefficient model. Letting

$$Y_1 = \mu_1(X) + U_1, \quad E(U_1 \mid X) = 0,$$
$$Y_0 = \mu_0(X) + U_0, \quad E(U_0 \mid X) = 0,$$

this version of the model may be written as

$$Y = \mu_0(X) + \underbrace{\left(\mu_1(X) - \mu_0(X) + U_1 - U_0\right)}_{\beta(X)} D + U_0$$

[18] Barros (1987) uses this assumption in the context of an analysis of selection bias.

$$= \mu_0(X) + \big(\mu_1(X) - \mu_0(X)\big)D + (U_1 - U_0)D + U_0$$
$$= \mu_0(X) + \bar{\beta}(X)D + \upsilon D + U_0, \tag{2.5}$$

where in the notation of Chapter 71, $\beta(X)$ is the treatment effect $(= \Delta)$, $\bar{\beta}(X) = \mu_1(X) - \mu_0(X)$, and $\upsilon = U_1 - U_0$. From (M-1), $(U_0, U_1) \perp\!\!\!\perp D \mid X$.

Nonparametric regression methods may be used to recover $\mu_0(X)$ and $\mu_1(X) - \mu_0(X)$ or one may use ordinary parametric regression methods if one assumes that $\mu_1(X) = X\beta_1$ and $\mu_0(X) = X\beta_0$. Equation (2.5) is a components-of-variance model and a test of (CON-1) given (M-1) is that

$$\begin{aligned}\operatorname{Var}(Y \mid D = 1, X) &= \operatorname{Var}(Y_0 + \Delta \mid D = 1, X)\\ &= \operatorname{Var}(Y_0 \mid X) + \operatorname{Var}(\Delta \mid X)\\ &\geqslant \operatorname{Var}(Y \mid D = 0, X) = \operatorname{Var}(Y_0 \mid X).\end{aligned}$$

Under standard conditions, each component of variance is identified and estimable from the residuals obtained from the nonparametric regression of Y on D and X. Thus one can jointly test a prediction of (CON-1) and (M-1) by checking these inequalities.

2.6. *Information from revealed preference*

An alternative approach, rooted more deeply in economics, uses information on agent choices to recover the joint population distribution of potential outcomes.[19] Unlike the method of matching or the methods based on particular assumptions about dependence between Y_0 and Y_1, the method based on revealed preference capitalizes on a close relationship between (Y_0, Y_1) and decisions about program participation. Participation includes voluntary entry into a program or attrition from it.

The prototypical framework is the Roy (1951) model extensively utilized in Chapters 70 and 71. In that setup, as previously noted in Section 2.2,

$$D = \mathbf{1}[Y_1 \geqslant Y_0]. \tag{2.6}$$

If we postulate that the outcome equations can be written in a separable form, so that

$$\begin{aligned} Y_1 &= \mu_1(X) + U_1, \quad & E(U_1 \mid X) = 0,\\ Y_0 &= \mu_0(X) + U_0, \quad & E(U_0 \mid X) = 0,\end{aligned}$$

then $\Pr(D = 1 \mid X) = \Pr(Y_1 - Y_0 \geqslant 0 \mid X) = \Pr(U_1 - U_0 \geqslant -(\mu_1(X) - \mu_0(X)))$. Heckman and Honoré (1990) demonstrate that if $X \perp\!\!\!\perp (U_0, U_1)$, $\operatorname{Var}(U_0) < \infty$ and $\operatorname{Var}(U_1) < \infty$, and (U_0, U_1) are normal, the full model $F(y_0, y_1, D \mid X)$ is identified even if we only observe Y_0 or Y_1 for any person and there are no regressors and

[19] Heckman (1974a, 1974b) demonstrates how access to censored samples on hours of work, wages for workers, and employment choices identifies the joint distribution of the value of nonmarket time and potential market wages under a normality assumption. Heckman and Honoré (1990) consider nonparametric versions of this model without labor supply.

no exclusion restrictions. If instead of assuming normality, it is assumed that the support of $(\mu_0(X), \mu_1(X))$ contains the support of (U_0, U_1), $(\mu_0(X), \mu_1(X))$ and the joint distribution of (U_0, U_1) are nonparametrically identified up to location normalizations. The proof of this theorem due to Heckman and Honoré (1990) is a special case of the general theorem proved in Appendix B of Chapter 70.

A crucial feature of the Roy model is that the decision to participate in the program is made solely in terms of potential outcomes. No new unobserved variables enter the model that do not also appear in the outcome equations (Y_0, Y_1). We could augment decision rule (2.6) to be $D = \mathbf{1}[Y_1 - Y_0 - \mu_C(Z) \geqslant 0]$, where $\mu_C(Z)$ is the cost of participation in the program and Z is observed, and still preserve the identifiability of the Roy model. Provided that we measure Z and condition on it, and provided that $(U_0, U_1) \perp\!\!\!\perp (X, Z)$, the model remains nonparametrically identified. The crucial property of the identification result is that no new unobservable enters the model through the participation equation. However, if we add components of cost based on observables, subjective valuations of gain $(Y_1 - Y_0 - \mu_C(Z))$ no longer equal "objective" measures $(Y_1 - Y_0)$. This is the distinction between the generalized Roy model and the extended Roy model extensively discussed in Chapter 71.

In the case of the Roy model, information about who participates in the program also informs the analyst about the distribution of the value of the program to participants $F_\Delta(y_1 - y_0 \mid Y_1 \geqslant Y_0, X)$. Thus, we acquire the distribution of implicit values of the program for participants. In the Roy model, "objective" and "subjective" outcomes coincide and agent's choices are informative on the outcome not chosen.

For more general decision rules with additional sources of unobservables apart from those arising from (Y_0, Y_1), it is not generally possible to identify $F(y_0, y_1)$ from information on (Y, D, X, Z) without invoking additional assumptions. For the generalized Roy model,

$$D = \mathbf{1}[Y_1 - Y_0 - C \geqslant 0],$$

where, for example,

$$C = \mu_C(Z) + U_C.$$

Let $U_I = U_1 - U_0 - U_C$, $I = Y_1 - Y_0 - C$ and $\mu_I(X, Z) = \mu_1(X) - \mu_0(X) - \mu_C(Z)$. Define $P(X, Z) = \Pr(D = 1 \mid X, Z)$. If U_C is not perfectly predicted by (U_0, U_1), then we cannot, in general, estimate the joint distribution of (Y_0, Y_1, C) given (X, Z) or the distribution of (U_0, U_1, U_C) from data on Y, D, X and Z.

However, under the conditions in Appendix B of Chapter 70, we can identify up to an unknown scale for I, $F_{Y_0,I}(y_0, i \mid X, Z)$ and $F_{Y_1,I}(y_1, i \mid X, Z)$.[20] The following intuition motivates the conditions under which $F_{Y_0,I}(y_0, i \mid X, Z)$ is identified. A parallel argument holds for $F_{Y_1,I}(y_1, i \mid X, Z)$. First, under the conditions given in Cosslett (1983), Manski (1988), Matzkin (1992) and Appendix B of Chapter 70, we can identify

[20] In our application of that theorem, there are only two choices so $\bar{S} = 2$ in the notation of that theorem.

$\frac{\mu_I(X,Z)}{\sigma_{U_I}}$ from $\Pr(D = 1 \mid X, Z) = \Pr(\mu_I(X, Z) + U_I \geqslant 0 \mid X, Z)$. $\sigma^2_{U_I}$ is the variance of U_I. We can also identify the distribution of $\frac{U_I}{\sigma_{U_I}}$. Second, from this information and $F_0(y_0 \mid D = 0, X, Z) = \Pr(Y_0 \leqslant y_0 \mid \mu_I(X, Z) + U_I < 0, X, Z)$, we can form

$$F_0(y_0 \mid D = 0, X, Z) \Pr(D = 0 \mid X, Z) = \Pr(Y_0 \leqslant y_0, I < 0 \mid X, Z).$$

The left-hand side of this expression is known (we observe Y_0 when $D = 0$ and we know the probability that $D = 0$ given X, Z). The right-hand side can be written as

$$\Pr\left(Y_0 \leqslant y_0, \frac{U_I}{\sigma_{U_I}} < -\frac{\mu_I(X, Z)}{\sigma_{U_I}} \;\middle|\; X, Z\right).$$

In particular if $\mu_I(X, Z)$ can be made arbitrarily small ($\mu_I(X, Z) \to -\infty$), for a given X, we can recover the marginal distribution Y_0 from which we can recover $\mu_0(X)$, and hence the distribution of U_0.

From the definition of Y_0, $U_0 = Y_0 - \mu_0(X)$. We may write the preceding probability as

$$\Pr\left(U_0 \leqslant y_0 - \mu_0(X), \frac{U_I}{\sigma_{U_I}} < \frac{-\mu_I(X, Z)}{\sigma_{U_I}} \;\middle|\; X, Z\right).$$

Note that the X and Z can be varied and y_0 is a number. Thus, by varying the known y_0 and $\frac{\mu_I(X,Z)}{\sigma_{U_I}}$, we can trace out the joint distribution of $(U_0, \frac{U_I}{\sigma_{U_I}})$. Thus we can recover the joint distribution of

$$(Y_0, I) = \left(\mu_0(X) + U_0, \frac{\mu_I(X, Z) + U_I}{\sigma_{U_I}}\right).$$

Notice the three key ingredients required to recover the joint distribution:

(a) The independence between (U_0, U_I) and (X, Z).

(b) The assumption that we can make $\frac{\mu_I(X,Z)}{\sigma_{U_I}}$ arbitrarily small for a given X (so we get the marginal distribution of Y_0 and hence $\mu_0(X)$). As noted in Chapter 71, this type of identification-at-infinity assumption plays a key role in the entire selection and evaluation literature for identifying many important evaluation parameters, such as the average treatment effect and treatment on the treated.

(c) The assumption that $\frac{\mu_I(X,Z)}{\sigma_{U_I}}$ can be varied independently of $\mu_0(X)$. This enables us to trace out the joint distribution of $(U_0, \frac{U_I}{\sigma_{U_I}})$.[21]

[21] Another way to see how identification works is to note that from Cosslett (1983), Manski (1988), Matzkin (1992) and ingredients (a) and (b), we can express

$$F_0(y_0 \mid D = 0, X, Z) \Pr(D = 0 \mid X, Z)$$

as a function of $\mu_0(X)$ and $\frac{\mu_I(X,Z)}{\sigma_{U_I}}$. The dependence on X and Z operating only through the indices $\mu_0(X)$ and $\frac{\mu_I(X,Z)}{\sigma_{U_I}}$ is called index sufficiency. Varying the $\mu_0(X)$ and $\frac{\mu_I(X,Z)}{\sigma_{U_I}}$ traces out the distribution of $(U_0, \frac{U_I}{\sigma_{U_I}})$.

A parallel argument establishes identification of the distribution of (Y_1, I) given X and Z.

Identification of the Roy model follows from this analysis. Recall that the model assumes that $U_I = U_1 - U_0$ so $\sigma^2_{U_I} = \mathrm{Var}(U_1 - U_0)$. From the distributions of (Y_0, I) and (Y_1, I), given X and Z, we can recover the joint distributions of $(U_0, \frac{U_1-U_0}{\sigma_{U_I}})$ and $(U_1, \frac{U_1-U_0}{\sigma_{U_I}})$ and hence the joint distribution of (U_0, U_1). We can recover the joint distribution of $U_1 - U_0$ even if $\mu_I(X, Z) \neq \mu_1(X) - \mu_0(X)$ as long as $U_C \equiv 0$.

2.7. *Using additional information*

We have established that data from social experiments or observational data corrected for selection do not in general identify joint distributions of potential outcomes. In the special case of the Roy model, choice data supplemented with outcome data will identify the joint distribution. But this result is fragile. For more general choice criteria, we cannot without further assumptions identify the joint distribution of potential outcomes. Recent approaches build on these results to supplement choice models with dependence assumptions to identify the joint distribution of (U_0, U_1).

Aakvik, Heckman and Vytlacil (2005), Carneiro, Hansen and Heckman (2001, 2003), Cunha, Heckman and Navarro (2005, 2006), and Cunha and Heckman (2007b, 2008) use factor models to capture the dependence across the unobservables (U_0, U_1, U_I) and to supplement the information used in order to construct the joint distribution of counterfactuals. Their approach is a version of the proxy/replacement function approach developed in Heckman and Robb (1985, 1986) that is discussed in Section 10 of Chapter 71 and in Chapter 73 (Matzkin) of this Handbook. It extends factor models developed by Jöreskog and Goldberger (1975) and Jöreskog (1977) to restrict the dependence among the (U_0, U_1, U_I). A low dimensional set of random variables generates the dependence across the outcome unobservables. Such dimension reduction coupled with the use of choice data and additional measurements that proxy or replace the factors can provide enough information to identify the joint distributions of (Y_0, Y_1) and (Y_0, Y_1, D).

The factor models are built around a conditional-independence assumption. Conditional on the factors, outcomes and choice equations are independent. Thus the factor models have a close affinity with matching except that they do not assume that the analyst observes the factors and must instead integrate them out and identify their distribution.

To demonstrate how this approach works, assume separability between observables and unobservables:

$$Y_1 = \mu_1(X) + U_1,$$
$$Y_0 = \mu_0(X) + U_0.$$

Denote I as the latent variable generating treatment choices:

$$I = \mu_I(Z) + U_I,$$

$$D = \mathbf{1}[I \geqslant 0].$$

Allow any X to be in Z so the notation is general.

To understand this approach, it is convenient but not essential to assume that (U_0, U_1, U_I) is normally distributed with mean zero and covariance matrix Σ. Normality plays no essential role in the analysis of this section. The key role is played by the factor structure assumption introduced below. Assume access to data on (Y, D, X, Z). We can identify $F_0(y_0 \mid D = 0, X, Z)$, $F_1(y_1 \mid D = 1, X, Z)$ and $\Pr(D = 1 \mid X, Z)$. Under certain conditions presented in Appendix B, Chapter 70 and the preceding section, we can identify the distributions of $(U_0, \frac{U_I}{\sigma_{U_I}})$ and $(U_1, \frac{U_I}{\sigma_{U_I}})$ nonparametrically. We can sometimes identify the scale on U_I.

To restrict the dependence across the unobservables, we adopt a factor structure model for the U_0, U_1, U_I. Other restrictions across the unobservables are possible. Models for a single factor are extensively developed by Jöreskog and Goldberger (1975). Aakvik, Heckman and Vytlacil (2005) and Carneiro, Hansen and Heckman (2001, 2003) extend their analysis to generate distributions of counterfactuals.

Initially assume a one-factor model where θ is a scalar factor (say unmeasured ability) that generates dependence across the unobservables assumed to be independent of (X, Z):

$$\begin{aligned}
U_0 &= \alpha_0\theta + \varepsilon_0,\\
U_1 &= \alpha_1\theta + \varepsilon_1,\\
U_I &= \alpha_{U_I}\theta + \varepsilon_{U_I},\\
\theta &\perp\!\!\!\perp (\varepsilon_0, \varepsilon_1, \varepsilon_{U_I}), \qquad (\varepsilon_0, \varepsilon_1, \varepsilon_{U_I}) \text{ are mutually independent.}
\end{aligned}$$

We discuss methods for multiple factors in the next section. Assume that $E(U_0) = 0$, $E(U_1) = 0$ and $E(U_I) = 0$. In addition, $E(\theta) = 0$. Thus $E(\varepsilon_0) = 0$, $E(\varepsilon_1) = 0$ and $E(\varepsilon_{U_I}) = 0$. To set the scale of the unobserved factor, normalize one "loading" (coefficient on θ) to 1. Note that all the dependence in the unobservables across equations arises from θ.

From the joint distributions of $(U_0, \frac{U_I}{\sigma_{U_I}})$ and $(U_1, \frac{U_I}{\sigma_{U_I}})$ we can identify

$$\begin{aligned}
\operatorname{Cov}\left(U_0, \frac{U_I}{\sigma_{U_I}}\right) &= \frac{\alpha_0\alpha_{U_I}}{\sigma_{U_I}}\sigma_\theta^2,\\
\operatorname{Cov}\left(U_1, \frac{U_I}{\sigma_{U_I}}\right) &= \frac{\alpha_1\alpha_{U_I}}{\sigma_{U_I}}\sigma_\theta^2,
\end{aligned}$$

assuming that the covariances on the left-hand side exist. From the ratio of the second covariance to the first we obtain $\frac{\alpha_1}{\alpha_0}$. Thus we obtain the sign of the dependence between U_0, U_1 because

$$\operatorname{Cov}(U_0, U_1) = \alpha_0\alpha_1\sigma_\theta^2.$$

From the ratio, we obtain α_1 if we normalize $\alpha_0 = 1$. Without further information, we cannot identify the variance of U_I, $\sigma_{U_I}^2$. We normalize it to 1. (Alternatively, we could normalize the variance of ε_{U_I} to 1.) Below, we present a condition that sets the scale of U_I.

With additional information, one can identify the full joint distribution of (U_0, U_1, U_I) and hence can construct the joint distribution of potential outcomes. In this section, we show this by a series of examples for a normal model. In a normal model, the joint distribution of (Y_0, Y_1) is determined (given X) if one can identify the variances of Y_0 and Y_1 and their covariance. We then show that normality plays no essential role in this analysis. We first consider what can be identified from access to a proxy M for θ (e.g., a test score).

2.7.1. Some examples

EXAMPLE 1 *(Access to a single proxy measure (e.g., a test score)).* Assume access to data on Y_0 given $D = 0$, X, Z; to data on Y_1 given $D = 1$, X, Z; and to data on D given X, Z. Suppose that the analyst also has access to a proxy for θ. Denote the proxy measure by M. In a schooling example, it could be a test score:

$$M = \mu_M(X) + U_M,$$

where

$$U_M = \alpha_M\theta + \varepsilon_M,$$

so

$$M = \mu_M(X) + \alpha_M\theta + \varepsilon_M,$$

where ε_M is independent of ε_0, ε_1, ε_{U_I} and θ, as well as (X, Z) ($\varepsilon_M \perp\!\!\!\perp (\varepsilon_0, \varepsilon_1, \varepsilon_{U_I}, \theta, X, Z)$). We can identify the mean $\mu_M(X)$ from observations on M and X. From this additional information, we acquire three additional covariance terms, conditional on X, Z, where we keep the conditioning implicit and define I as normalized by σ_{U_I}:

$$\begin{aligned}
\operatorname{Cov}(Y_1, M) &= \alpha_1\alpha_M\sigma_\theta^2, \\
\operatorname{Cov}(Y_0, M) &= \alpha_0\alpha_M\sigma_\theta^2, \\
\operatorname{Cov}(I, M) &= \frac{\alpha_{U_I}}{\sigma_{U_I}}\alpha_M\sigma_\theta^2.
\end{aligned}$$ [22]

Suppose that we normalize the loading on the proxy (or test score) to one ($\alpha_M = 1$). It is no longer necessary to normalize $\alpha_0 = 1$ as in the preceding section. From the ratio of the covariance of Y_1 with I with the covariance of I with M, we obtain the right-hand

[22] Conditioning on X, Z, we can remove the dependence of Y_1, Y_0, M and I on these variables and effectively work with the residuals $Y_0 - \mu_0(X) = U_0$, $Y_1 - \mu_1(X) = U_1$, $M - \mu_M(X) = U_M$, $I - \mu_I(Z) = U_I$, where we keep the scale on I implicit.

side of

$$\frac{\text{Cov}(Y_1, I)}{\text{Cov}(I, M)} = \frac{\alpha_1 \alpha_{U_I} \sigma_\theta^2}{\alpha_{U_I} \alpha_M \sigma_\theta^2} = \alpha_1,$$

because $\alpha_M = 1$ (normalization). From the discussion in the preceding section where no proxy is assumed, we obtain α_0 since

$$\frac{\text{Cov}(Y_1, I)}{\text{Cov}(Y_0, I)} = \frac{\alpha_1 \alpha_{U_I} \sigma_\theta^2}{\alpha_0 \alpha_{U_I} \sigma_\theta^2} = \frac{\alpha_1}{\alpha_0}.$$

From knowledge of α_1 and α_0 and the normalization for α_M, we obtain σ_θ^2 from $\text{Cov}(Y_1, M)$ or $\text{Cov}(Y_0, M)$. We obtain α_{U_I} (up to scale σ_{U_I}) from $\text{Cov}(I, M) = \frac{\alpha_{U_I} \alpha_M \sigma_\theta^2}{\sigma_{U_I}}$ since we know α_M $(= 1)$ and σ_θ^2. The model is overidentified. We can identify the scale of σ_{U_I} by a standard argument from the discrete-choice literature. We review this argument below.

Observe that if we write out the decision rule in terms of costs, we can characterize the latent variable determining choices as:

$$I = Y_1 - Y_0 - C,$$

where $C = \mu_C(Z) + U_C$ and $U_C = \alpha_C \theta + \varepsilon_C$, where ε_C is independent of θ and the other ε's. $E(U_C) = 0$ and U_C is independent of (X, Z). Then, $U_I = U_1 - U_0 - U_C$ and

$$\begin{aligned}
\alpha_{U_I} &= \alpha_1 - \alpha_0 - \alpha_C, \\
\varepsilon_{U_I} &= \varepsilon_1 - \varepsilon_0 - \varepsilon_C, \\
\text{Var}(\varepsilon_{U_I}) &= \text{Var}(\varepsilon_1) + \text{Var}(\varepsilon_0) + \text{Var}(\varepsilon_C).
\end{aligned}$$

Identification of α_0, α_1 and α_{U_I} implies identification of α_C. Identification of the variance of ε_{U_I} implies identification of the variance of ε_C since the variances of ε_1 and ε_0 are known.

Observe further that the scale σ_{U_I} is identified if there are variables in X but not in Z [see Heckman (1976, 1979), Heckman and Robb (1985, 1986), Willis and Rosen (1979)].[23] From the variance of M given X, we obtain $\text{Var}(\varepsilon_M)$ since we know $\text{Var}(M)$ (conditional on X) and we know $\alpha_M^2 \sigma_\theta^2$:

$$\text{Var}(M) - \alpha_M^2 \sigma_\theta^2 = \sigma_{\varepsilon_M}^2.$$

(Recall that we keep the conditioning on X implicit.) By similar reasoning, it is possible to identify $\text{Var}(\varepsilon_0)$, $\text{Var}(\varepsilon_1)$ and the fraction of $\text{Var}(U_I)$ due to ε_{U_I}. We can thus

[23] The easiest case to understand is one where $\mu_C(Z) = Z\gamma$, $\mu_1(X) = X\beta_1$, $\mu_0(X) = X\beta_0$ and $\mu_I(Z, X) = X(\beta_1 - \beta_0) - Z\gamma$. We identify the coefficients of the index $\mu_I(Z, X)$ up to scale σ_{U_I}, but we know $\beta_1 - \beta_0$ from the earnings functions. Thus if one X is not in Z and its associated coefficient is not zero, we can identify σ_{U_I}. See, e.g., Heckman (1976).

construct the joint distribution of (Y_0, Y_1, C) and hence the joint distribution of (Y_0, Y_1) since we identified $\mu_C(Z)$ and all of the factor loadings. Thus we can identify the objective outcome distribution for (Y_0, Y_1) and the subjective distribution for C as well as their joint distribution (Y_0, Y_1, C).

We have assumed normality because it is convenient to do so. Carneiro, Hansen and Heckman (2003), Cunha, Heckman and Navarro (2005, 2006) and Cunha and Heckman (2008) show that it is possible to nonparametrically identify the distributions of θ, ε_0, ε_1, ε_{U_I} and ε_M so our results do not hinge on arbitrary distributional assumptions as we establish in the next section.

We next show by way of example that choice data are not strictly required to secure identification of the joint distributions of counterfactuals. It is the extra information joined with the factor restriction on the dependence that allows us to identify the joint distribution of outcomes.

EXAMPLE 2 *(Identification without choice data).* This example builds on Example 1. Let M be two dimensional so $M = (M_1, M_2)$, and M_1, M_2 are indicators that depend on θ and assume that they are both observed. In place of I from choice theory as in the preceding section, we can work with a second indicator of θ, i.e., a second measurement M_2. Suppose that either by limit operations ($P(X, Z) \to 0$ or $P(X, Z) \to 1$ along certain sequences in its support) or some randomization we observe triplets (Y_0, M_1, M_2), (Y_1, M_1, M_2) but not Y_0 and Y_1 together. We can still identify the joint distribution of (Y_0, Y_1).

Example 1 applies to this case with only trivial modifications. We can identify all of the variances and covariances of the factor model as well as the factor loadings up to one normalization. Thus we can identify the joint distribution of (Y_0, Y_1). Since the (M_1, M_2) are assumed to be observed and their scale is known, we can identify the variances of M_1 and M_2 directly. In this example, we do not need to use any of the apparatus of discrete-choice theory except to govern the limit operations that control for selection.

There are other ways to construct the joint distributions that do not require a proxy M that may be extended to the model. Access to panel data on earnings affords identification. One way, that motivates our analysis of *ex ante* vs. *ex post* returns developed later, is given next.

EXAMPLE 3 *(Two (or more) periods of panel data on outcomes).* Suppose that for each person we have two periods of outcome data in one counterfactual state or the other. Thus we observe $(Y_{0,1}, Y_{0,2})$ or $(Y_{1,1}, Y_{1,2})$ but never both pairs of vectors together for the same person. We also observe choices. We assume that $Y_{j,t} = \mu_{j,t}(X) + U_{j,t}$, $j = 0, 1$, $t = 1, 2$, and write

$$U_{1,t} = \alpha_{1,t}\theta + \varepsilon_{1,t} \quad \text{and} \quad U_{0,t} = \alpha_{0,t}\theta + \varepsilon_{0,t}$$

to obtain

$$Y_{1,t} = \mu_{1,t}(X) + \alpha_{1,t}\theta + \varepsilon_{1,t}, \quad t = 1, 2,$$

$$Y_{0,t} = \mu_{0,t}(X) + \alpha_{0,t}\theta + \varepsilon_{0,t}, \quad t = 1, 2.$$

In the context of a schooling choice model as analyzed by Carneiro, Hansen and Heckman (2001, 2003) and Cunha, Heckman and Navarro (2005, 2006), if we assume that the interest rate is zero and that agents maximize the present value of their income, the index generating choices is

$$I = (Y_{1,2} + Y_{1,1}) - (Y_{0,2} + Y_{0,1}) - C,$$
$$D = \mathbf{1}[I \geqslant 0],$$

where C was defined previously, and

$$I = \mu_{1,1}(X) + \mu_{1,2}(X) - \mu_{0,1}(X) - \mu_{0,2}(X) - \mu_C(Z) + U_{1,1} + U_{1,2} - U_{0,1} - U_{0,2} - U_C.$$

We assume no proxy—just two periods of panel data. The multiple periods of earnings serve as the proxy.

Under normality, application of the standard normal selection model allows us to identify $\mu_{1,t}(X)$ for $t = 1, 2$; $\mu_{0,t}(X)$ for $t = 1, 2$ and $\mu_{1,1}(X) + \mu_{1,2}(X) - \mu_{0,1}(X) - \mu_{0,2}(X) - \mu_C(Z)$, the latter up to a scalar σ_{U_I} where

$$U_I = U_{1,1} + U_{1,2} - U_{0,1} - U_{0,2} - U_C.$$

Following our discussion of Example 1, we can recover the scale σ_{U_I} if there are variables in X that are not in Z such that $(\mu_{1,1}(X) + \mu_{1,2}(X) - (\mu_{0,1}(X) + \mu_{0,2}(X)))$ can be varied independently from $\mu_C(Z)$. To simplify the analysis, we assume that this condition holds.[24]

From normality, we can recover the joint distributions of $(I, Y_{1,1}, Y_{1,2})$ and $(I, Y_{0,1}, Y_{0,2})$ but not directly the joint distribution of $(I, Y_{1,1}, Y_{1,2}, Y_{0,1}, Y_{0,2})$. Thus, conditioning on X and Z, we can recover the joint distribution of $(U_I, U_{0,1}, U_{0,2})$ and $(U_I, U_{1,1}, U_{1,2})$ but apparently not that of $(U_I, U_{0,1}, U_{0,2}, U_{1,1}, U_{1,2})$. However, under our factor structure assumptions, this joint distribution can be recovered as we next show.

From the available data, we can identify the following covariances:

$$\begin{aligned}
\mathrm{Cov}(U_I, U_{1,2}) &= (\alpha_{1,2} + \alpha_{1,1} - \alpha_{0,2} - \alpha_{0,1} - \alpha_C)\alpha_{1,2}\sigma_\theta^2, \\
\mathrm{Cov}(U_I, U_{1,1}) &= (\alpha_{1,2} + \alpha_{1,1} - \alpha_{0,2} - \alpha_{0,1} - \alpha_C)\alpha_{1,1}\sigma_\theta^2, \\
\mathrm{Cov}(U_I, U_{0,1}) &= (\alpha_{1,2} + \alpha_{1,1} - \alpha_{0,2} - \alpha_{0,1} - \alpha_C)\alpha_{0,1}\sigma_\theta^2, \\
\mathrm{Cov}(U_I, U_{0,2}) &= (\alpha_{1,2} + \alpha_{1,1} - \alpha_{0,2} - \alpha_{0,1} - \alpha_C)\alpha_{0,2}\sigma_\theta^2, \\
\mathrm{Cov}(U_{1,1}, U_{1,2}) &= \alpha_{1,1}\alpha_{1,2}\sigma_\theta^2, \\
\mathrm{Cov}(U_{0,1}, U_{0,2}) &= \alpha_{0,1}\alpha_{0,2}\sigma_\theta^2.
\end{aligned}$$

[24] If not, then $\mu_C(Z)$, $\sigma^2_{\varepsilon C}$ and α_C are only identified up to normalizations.

If we normalize $\alpha_{0,1} = 1$ (recall that one normalization is needed to set the scale of θ), we can form the ratios

$$\frac{\operatorname{Cov}(U_I, U_{1,2})}{\operatorname{Cov}(U_I, U_{0,1})} = \alpha_{1,2}, \qquad \frac{\operatorname{Cov}(U_I, U_{1,1})}{\operatorname{Cov}(U_I, U_{0,1})} = \alpha_{1,1},$$

$$\frac{\operatorname{Cov}(U_I, U_{0,2})}{\operatorname{Cov}(U_I, U_{0,1})} = \alpha_{0,2}.$$

From these coefficients and the remaining covariances, using $\operatorname{Cov}(U_{1,1}, U_{1,2})$ and/or $\operatorname{Cov}(U_{0,1}, U_{0,2})$, we identify σ_θ^2. Thus if the factor loadings are nonzero, we can identify σ_θ^2 from two relationships, both of which are identified:

$$\frac{\operatorname{Cov}(U_{1,1}, U_{1,2})}{\alpha_{1,1}\alpha_{1,2}} = \sigma_\theta^2$$

and

$$\frac{\operatorname{Cov}(U_{0,1}, U_{0,2})}{\alpha_{0,1}\alpha_{0,2}} = \sigma_\theta^2.$$

Since we know $\alpha_{1,1}\alpha_{2,2}$ and $\alpha_{0,1}\alpha_{0,2}$, we can recover σ_θ^2 from $\operatorname{Cov}(U_{1,1}, U_{1,2})$ and $\operatorname{Cov}(U_{0,1}, U_{0,2})$. We can also recover α_C since we know σ_θ^2, $\alpha_{1,2}+\alpha_{1,1}-\alpha_{0,2}-\alpha_{0,1}-\alpha_C$, and $\alpha_{1,1}, \alpha_{1,2}, \alpha_{0,1}, \alpha_{0,2}$. We can form (conditional on X)

$$\operatorname{Cov}(Y_{1,1}, Y_{0,1}) = \alpha_{1,1}\alpha_{0,1}\sigma_\theta^2; \quad \operatorname{Cov}(Y_{1,2}, Y_{0,1}) = \alpha_{1,2}\alpha_{0,1}\sigma_\theta^2;$$

$$\operatorname{Cov}(Y_{1,1}, Y_{0,2}) = \alpha_{1,1}\alpha_{0,2}\sigma_\theta^2 \quad \text{and} \quad \operatorname{Cov}(Y_{1,2}, Y_{0,2}) = \alpha_{1,2}\alpha_{0,2}\sigma_\theta^2.$$

We can identify $\mu_C(Z)$ from the schooling choice equation since we know $\mu_{0,1}(X)$, $\mu_{0,2}(X)$, $\mu_{1,1}(X)$, $\mu_{1,2}(X)$ and we have assumed that there are some Z not in X so that σ_{U_I} is identified. Thus we can identify the joint distribution of $(Y_{0,1}, Y_{0,2}, Y_{1,1}, Y_{1,2}, C)$.

These examples extend to nonnormal and nonparametric models. The key idea to constructing joint distributions of counterfactuals using the analysis of Cunha and Heckman (2008) and Cunha, Heckman and Navarro (2005, 2006) is *not* the factor structure for unobservables although it is convenient. The crucial idea is the assumption that a low dimensional set of random variables generates the dependence across outcomes. Other low dimensional representations such as the ARMA model or the dynamic factor structure model [see Sargent and Sims (1977)] can also be used. Cunha and Heckman (2007a) and Cunha, Heckman and Schennach (2007) extend factor models to more general frameworks where the θ evolve over time as in state space models. The factor structure model presented in this section is easy to exposit and has been used to estimate joint distributions of counterfactuals. We present some examples in a later subsection. That subsection reviews recent work that generalizes the analysis of this section to derive *ex ante* and *ex post* outcome distributions, and measure the fundamental uncertainty facing agents in the labor market. With these methods it is possible to compute the distributions of both *ex ante* and *ex post* returns to treatments. Before presenting a more general analysis, we relate factor models to matching models.

2.7.2. Relationship to matching

If the analyst knew θ and could condition on it, the analyst would obtain the conditional-independence assumption of matching, (M-1), in Chapter 71:

(U-1) $(Y_0, Y_1) \perp\!\!\!\perp D \mid X, Z, \theta$.

This is also the general control function assumption (U-1) in Chapter 71.

The approach developed by Aakvik, Heckman and Vytlacil (2005), Carneiro, Hansen and Heckman (2001, 2003), Cunha, Heckman and Navarro (2005, 2006), and Cunha and Heckman (2007b, 2007c, 2008) extends matching and treats θ as an unobservable. It uses proxies for θ and identifies the distribution of θ under the following assumption:

(U-2) $\theta \perp\!\!\!\perp X, Z$.

Thus the factor approach is a version of matching on unobservables, where the unobserved match variables are integrated out.

2.7.3. Nonparametric extensions

The analysis of the generalized Roy model developed in Appendix B of Chapter 70 establishes conditions under which it is possible to nonparametrically identify the joint distribution of (Y_0, I, M) given X, Z and the joint distribution of (Y_1, I, M) given X, Z, where we also allow the functions determining M to be nonparametrically determined.[25] These conditions can be extended to provide identification of the distributions of (Y_0, I, M) and (Y_1, I, M) where M is observed for all persons treated or not whereas Y_0 and Y_1 are observed only if $D = 0$ or $D = 1$, respectively. The identification conditions are also easily extended to account for vector Y_0 and Y_1 (e.g., $Y_0 = (Y_{0,1}, Y_{0,2})$ and $Y_1 = (Y_{1,1}, Y_{1,2})$) as our third example in Section 2.7.1 reveals. We present a general theorem for the identification of state-contingent outcomes free of selection bias in the next section and in Appendix B of this chapter. With the state-contingent distributions nonparametrically identified, we can apply factor analysis to identify the factor loadings because we identify the required covariances as a by-product of our nonparametric analysis.

With the α_j (or $\alpha_{i,j}$) in hand, we can nonparametrically identify the distribution of θ and the ε_j (or $\varepsilon_{i,j}$) for the different models assuming mutual independence between θ and all of the components of ε_j (or $\varepsilon_{i,j}$) using Kotlarski's Theorem [Kotlarski (1967), Prakasa-Rao (1992)]. That theorem states that, for any pair of random variables T_1, T_2 generated by a common random variable θ, we can nonparametrically identify the distribution of θ and the associated components of errors: ε_1 and ε_2. Stated precisely:

[25] Recall that, depending on the assumptions discussed in Section 2.7.1, the scale of I may, or may not, be identified.

THEOREM 1. *If*

$$T_1 = \theta + \varepsilon_1$$

and

$$T_2 = \theta + \varepsilon_2$$

and $(\theta, \varepsilon_1, \varepsilon_2)$ *are mutually independent, the means of all three generating random variables are finite and are normalized to* $E(\varepsilon_1) = E(\varepsilon_2) = 0$, *and the random variables possess nonvanishing* (a.e.) *characteristic functions, then the densities of* $(\theta, \varepsilon_1, \varepsilon_2)$, $g_\theta(\theta)$, $g_1(\varepsilon_1)$, $g_2(\varepsilon_2)$, *respectively, are identified.*

PROOF. See Kotlarski (1967). See also Prakasa-Rao (1992). □

Applied to our context, consider the first two equations of a vector of indicators M which are stochastically dependent only through θ. We write

$$M_1 = \lambda_1\theta + \varepsilon_1, \quad \text{where } \lambda_1 = 1,$$
$$M_2 = \lambda_2\theta + \varepsilon_2, \quad \text{where } \lambda_2 \neq 0.$$

By the preceding analysis, we can identify λ_2 (subject to a normalization $\lambda_1 = 1$) from factor models. Thus we can rewrite these equations as

$$M_1 = \theta + \varepsilon_1,$$
$$\frac{M_2}{\lambda_2} = \theta + \varepsilon_2^*,$$

where $\varepsilon_2^* = \varepsilon_2/\lambda_2$. Applying Kotlarski's Theorem, we can nonparametrically identify the densities $g_\theta(\theta)$, $g_1(\varepsilon_1)$ and $g_2(\varepsilon_2^*)$. Since we know λ_2, we can nonparametrically identify $g_2(\varepsilon_2)$. Schennach (2004), Hu and Schennach (2006), and Cunha, Heckman and Schennach (2007) weaken many of the strong independence conditions to mean independence assumptions. Carneiro, Hansen and Heckman (2003) extend the analysis of this section to the case of vector θ.

2.8. General models

The analysis of Carneiro, Hansen and Heckman (2003), Cunha, Heckman and Navarro (2005, 2006) and Cunha and Heckman (2007c, 2008) generalizes the analysis of the preceding sections to consider vectors of outcomes (Y_0 and Y_1), vectors of measurements (M) and more general choice equations. We summarize that work here. This analysis feeds directly into our analysis of dynamic treatment effects and dynamic discrete choice presented in Section 3.

Our analysis has three components: (1) Identifying the choice of treatment equation and hence evaluation of treatments as perceived by agents; (2) Identifying the joint distributions of outcomes and measurements in each treatment state s, $s = 1, \ldots, \bar{S}$, where $\bar{S}$ is the number of treatment states; and (3) Identifying the joint distribution of outcomes across treatment states. Only the third step requires a factor structure. Step 1 is conventional nonparametric discrete-choice analysis. Step 2 solves the selection problem using nonparametric methods. Step 3 solves the evaluation problem using factor models.

Conditions for nonparametric identification of discrete-choice models are presented in Matzkin (1992, 1993, 1994) and in her contribution to this Handbook (Chapter 73). Appendix B of Chapter 70 presents a nonparametric proof of identification of choice equations as part of a nonparametric analysis of choice and outcome equations for a general static discrete-choice model. Carneiro, Hansen and Heckman (2003) present a parallel analysis for an ordered choice model.[26] Heckman and Navarro (2007) present an identification analysis that is used in this section and in Section 3. We now establish an extension of the theorem proved in Appendix B of Chapter 70 to account for vectors of outcomes and for associated vectors of measurements. This provides a solution to the selection problem.

2.8.1. Steps 1 and 2: Solving the selection problem within each treatment state

Associated with each treatment s, $s = 1, \ldots, \bar{S}$, is a vector of outcomes of length $\bar{A}$,

$$Y\big(s, X, U(s)\big) = \big(Y\big(1, s, X, U(1, s)\big), \ldots, Y\big(a, s, X, U(a, s)\big), \ldots, Y\big(\bar{A}, s, X, U(\bar{A}, s)\big)\big).$$

They depend on observables X and unobservables $U(s) = (U(1, s), \ldots, U(a, s), \ldots, U(\bar{A}, s))$, where the observability distinction is made from the point of view of the econometrician. The X may also have a- and s-specific subvectors, but for the sake of notational simplicity we do not make this explicit. We can make the list of outcomes s-dependent, but only at the cost of notational complexity. Elements of $Y(s, X, U(s))$ are outcomes associated with receiving treatment s. They are factual outcomes if treatment s is actually selected, which we denote by $D(s) = 1$. Outcomes corresponding to treatments s' that are not selected—we denote this by $D(s') = 0$—are counterfactuals. The outcome variables are not necessarily what the agent thinks will happen when he or she chooses treatment s, but rather what actually happens. The treatments s may be associated with stages that are not necessarily identical with real time events, although this framework can be used in our analysis of dynamic choices evolving in real time that is presented in Section 3.

Henceforth, whenever we have random variables with multiple arguments $R_0(s, Q_0, \ldots)$ or $R_1(a, s, Q_0, \ldots)$ where the argument list begins with treatment state s or both age a and state s (perhaps followed by other arguments $Q_0, \ldots$), we will make use of several condensed notations: (a) dropping the first argument as we collect the

[26] Cunha, Heckman and Navarro (2007) present a nonparametric identification analysis of the ordered choice model. They also establish that it imposes the absence of option values.

components into vectors $R_0(Q_0, \ldots)$ or $R_1(s, Q_0, \ldots)$ of length $\bar{S}$ or $\bar{A}$, respectively, and (b) going further in the case of R_1, dropping the s argument as we collect the vectors $R_1(s, Q_0, \ldots)$ into a single $\bar{S} \times \bar{A}$ array $R_1(Q_0, \ldots)$, but also (c) suppressing one or more of the other arguments and writing $R_1(a, s)$ or $R_1(a, s, Q_0)$ instead of $R_1(a, s, Q_0, Q_1, \ldots)$, etc. This notation is sufficiently rich to represent the life cycle of outcomes for persons who receive treatment s. We use this notation in the remainder of this section and in Section 3.

Following Carneiro, Hansen and Heckman (2003), the variables in $Y(a, s, X, U(a, s))$ may include discrete, continuous or mixed discrete-continuous components. For the discrete or mixed discrete-continuous cases, we assume that latent continuous variables cross thresholds to generate the discrete components. Durations can be generated by latent index models associated with each outcome crossing thresholds analogous to the model we develop in Section 3 below, in the discussion surrounding Equation (3.11). In this framework, we can model the effect of attaining s years of schooling on durations of unemployment or durations of employment.

We decompose $Y(a, s)$ into continuous and discrete components:

$$Y(a, s) = \begin{bmatrix} Y_c(a, s) \\ Y_d(a, s) \end{bmatrix}.$$

Associated with the jth component of $Y_d(a, s)$, $Y_{d,j}(a, s)$ is a latent variable $Y^*_{d,j}(a, s)$. We define

$$Y_{d,j}(a, s) = \mathbf{1}\big(Y^*_{d,j}(a, s) \geqslant 0\big).$$[27]

From standard results in the discrete-choice literature, without additional information, we can only know $Y^*_{d,j}(a, s)$ up to scale.

We assume an additively separable model for the continuous variables and latent continuous indices. Making the X explicit, we write

$$\begin{aligned} Y_c(a, s, X) &= \mu_c(a, s, X) + U_c(a, s), \\ Y^*_d(a, s, X) &= \mu_d(a, s, X) - U_d(a, s), \\ &1 \leqslant s \leqslant \bar{S},\ 1 \leqslant a \leqslant \bar{A}. \end{aligned}$$

We array the $Y_c(a, s, X)$ into a matrix $Y_c(s, X)$ and the $Y^*_d(a, s, X)$ into a matrix $Y^*_d(s, X)$. We decompose these vectors into components corresponding to the means $\mu_c(s, X)$, $\mu_d(s, X)$ and the unobservables $U_c(s)$, $U_d(s)$. Thus

$$\begin{aligned} Y_c(s, X) &= \mu_c(s, X) + U_c(s), \\ Y^*_d(s, X) &= \mu_d(s, X) - U_d(s). \end{aligned}$$

[27] Extensions to nonbinary discrete outcomes are straightforward. Thus we could entertain, at greater notational cost, a multinomial outcome model at each age a for each counterfactual state.

$Y_d^*(s, X)$ generates $Y_d(s, X)$. Using our condensed notation, we write

$$Y_c(X) = \mu_c(X) + U_c,$$
$$Y_d^*(X) = \mu_d(X) - U_d.$$

Following Carneiro, Hansen and Heckman (2003), Cunha, Heckman and Navarro (2005, 2006) and Cunha and Heckman (2007b, 2007c, 2008), we may also have a system of measurements with both discrete and continuous components. The measurements are not s-indexed. They are the same for each treatment state.[28] We write the equations for the measurements in an additively separable form, in a fashion comparable to those of the outcomes. The equations for the continuous measurements and latent indices producing discrete measurements are

$$M_c(a, X) = \mu_{c,M}(a, X) + U_{c,M}(a),$$
$$M_d^*(a, X) = \mu_{d,M}(a, X) - U_{d,M}(a),$$

where the discrete variable corresponding to the jth index in $M_d^*(a, X)$ is

$$M_{d,j}(a, X) = \mathbf{1}\big(M_{d,j}^*(a, X) \geqslant 0\big).$$

The measurements play the role of indicators unaffected by the process being studied. We array $M_c(a, X)$ and $M_d^*(a, X)$ into matrices $M_c(X)$ and $M_d^*(X)$. We array $\mu_{c,M}(a, X)$, $\mu_{d,M}(a, X)$ into matrices $\mu_{c,M}(X)$ and $\mu_{d,M}(X)$. We array the corresponding unobservables into $U_{c,M}$ and $U_{d,M}$. In this notation,

$$M_c(X) = \mu_{c,M}(X) + U_{c,M},$$
$$M_d^*(X) = \mu_{d,M}(X) - U_{d,M}.$$

In the notation of Appendix B of Chapter 70, write the utility valuation of treatment state s as

$$R(s, Z) = \mu_R(s, Z) - V(s), \quad s = 1, \ldots, \bar{S}.$$

Collect $R(s, Z)$, $s = 1, \ldots, \bar{S}$, into a vector

$$R(Z) = \big(R(1, Z), \ldots, R(\bar{S}, Z)\big).$$

Collect $\mu_R(s, Z)$, $s = 1, \ldots, \bar{S}$, into a vector

$$\mu_R(Z) = \big(\mu_R(1, Z), \ldots, \mu_R(\bar{S}, Z)\big).$$

Collect $V(s)$, $s = 1, \ldots, \bar{S}$, into a vector

$$V = \big(V(1), \ldots, V(\bar{S})\big).$$

[28] Thus measurements are not causally affected by treatment. Measurements that are causally affected by treatment can be included in the model as outcomes using the analysis of Hansen, Heckman and Mullen (2004).

$D(s) = 1$ (state s is selected) if

$$s = \underset{j=1,\ldots,\bar{S}}{\operatorname{argmax}}\{R(j, Z)\}.$$

Otherwise $D(s) = 0$.

$$\sum_{j=1}^{\bar{S}} D(j) = 1.$$

Define

$$V^s = \left(V(s) - V(1), \ldots, V(s) - V(\bar{S})\right),$$
$$\mu_R^s(Z) = \left(\mu_R(s, Z) - \mu_R(1, Z), \ldots, \mu_R(s, Z) - \mu_R(\bar{S}, Z)\right), \quad s = 1, \ldots, \bar{S}.$$

These contrast vectors are standard in discrete-choice theory, where utilities in treatment state s are compared with utilities in other treatment states. We assume that we have access to a large i.i.d. sample from the distribution of $(Y_c, Y_d, M_c, M_d, \{D(s)\}_{s=1}^{\bar{S}})$.[29]

We now state a basic theorem that solves the selection problem (Step 2) for the general model of this section. We draw on the work of Matzkin (1992, 1993, 1994) and Chapter 73 of this Handbook to provide a general characterization of nonparametric functions and their identifiability. We define the Matzkin class of functions in Appendix B and use it in the next proof. They include all of the familiar linear-in-parameters functional forms for discrete choice as well as a variety of other classes of functions that can be identified under conditions specified in her papers.

THEOREM 2. *The joint distribution of* $(U_c(s), U_d(s), U_{c,M}, U_{d,M}, V^s)$ *is identified along with the functions* $(\mu_c(s, X), \mu_d(s, X), \mu_{c,M}(X), \mu_{d,M}(X), \mu_R^s(Z))$ *(the components of* $\mu_d(s, X)$ *and* $\mu_{d,M}(X)$ *over the supports admitted by the supports of the errors) if, for* $s = 1, \ldots, \bar{S}$,

(i) $E[U_c(s)] = E[U_{c,M}] = 0$. $(U_c(s), U_d(s), U_{c,M}, U_{d,M}, V^s)$ *are continuous random variables with support* $(\underline{U}_c(s), \overline{U}_c(s)) \times (\underline{U}_d(s), \overline{U}_d(s)) \times (\underline{U}_{c,M}, \overline{U}_{c,M}) \times (\underline{U}_{d,M}, \overline{U}_{d,M}) \times \mathbb{R}^{s-1}$. *These conditions are assumed to apply within each component of each subvector. The joint system is thus variation free for each component with respect to every other component.*

(ii) $(U_c(s), U_d(s), U_{c,M}, U_{d,M}, V^s) \perp\!\!\!\perp (X, Z)$.

(iii) $\operatorname{Supp}(\mu_R^s(Z), X) = \operatorname{Supp}(\mu_R^s(Z)) \times \operatorname{Supp}(X)$.

(iv) $\operatorname{Supp}(\mu_d(s, X), \mu_{d,M}(X)) \supseteq \operatorname{Supp}(U_d(s), U_{d,M})$.

(v) $\mu_c(s, X)$, $\mu_{c,M}(X)$ *and* $\mu_R(Z)$ *are continuous functions. The components of the* $\mu_d(s, X)$ *and* $\mu_{d,M}(X)$ *belong to the Matzkin class of functions given in Appendix* B. $\mu_R^1(z)$ *is known for* $z \in \widetilde{\mathcal{Z}}$ *with* $\widetilde{\mathcal{Z}} \subseteq \operatorname{Supp}(Z)$ *such that* $\{\mu_R^1(z); z \in \widetilde{\mathcal{Z}}\} = \mathbb{R}^{\bar{S}-1}$. $\mu_R(1, Z)$ *is known.*

[29] We can allow for dependence across individuals by invoking appropriate limit laws for dependent random variables.

PROOF. See Appendix B.[30] □

This proof presents conditions for producing a selection-bias free joint distribution of $(Y_c(s, X),\ Y_d(s, X),\ M_c(X),\ M_d(X),\ V^s)$, $s = 1, \ldots, \bar{S}$ conditionally on X which are the inputs for our factor analysis to which we now turn.

2.8.2. Step 3: Constructing counterfactual distributions using factor models

The analysis of the preceding section presented conditions under which subjective relative evaluations of treatment outcomes from choice functions and objective outcome distributions in state s, $s = 1, \ldots, \bar{S}$, can be identified. Missing is an analysis of identification of joint outcome distributions. In this subsection, we generalize the analysis of Section 2.7 to present conditions under which joint distributions can be identified in a multifactor setting.

Theorem 2 gives conditions under which the distributions of $(U_c(s), U_d(s), U_{c,M}, U_{d,M}, V^s)$, $s = 1, \ldots, \bar{S}$, are identified. If we factor analyze these errors, we can identify the joint distributions of these vectors across treatment states. We write in the case of vector θ,

$$\begin{aligned} U_c(s) &= \alpha'_{c,s}\theta + \varepsilon_c(s), \\ U_d(s) &= \alpha'_{d,s}\theta + \varepsilon_d(s), \\ U_{c,M} &= \alpha'_{c,M}\theta + \varepsilon_{c,M}, \\ U_{d,M} &= \alpha'_{d,M}\theta + \varepsilon_{d,M}, \\ V^s &= \alpha'_{V^s}\theta + \varepsilon_V(s), \end{aligned} \tag{2.7}$$

or more compactly, using the notation

$$\begin{aligned} U(s) &= \big(U_c(s), U_d(s), U_{c,M}, U_{d,M}, V^s\big), \\ \varepsilon(s) &= \big(\varepsilon_c(s), \varepsilon_d(s), \varepsilon_{c,M}, \varepsilon_{d,M}, \varepsilon_V(s)\big), \end{aligned}$$

we may write the preceding system as a system of equations:

$$U(s) = \Lambda(s)\theta + \varepsilon(s), \quad s = 1, \ldots, \bar{S}, \tag{2.8}$$

where the components of $\varepsilon = (\varepsilon(1), \ldots, \varepsilon(\bar{S}))$ are mutually independent and $\varepsilon \perp\!\!\!\perp \theta$. The factor loadings may differ across treatment states. All of the dependence among outcomes and measurements and the choice indicators $\{D(s)\}_{s=1}^{\bar{S}}$ is generated by dependence on common factors θ. The outcome, choice, and measurement equations all contribute to the $U(s)$ and are a source of information on the distribution of θ.

The same principles guide identifiability in this system of equations as in the one-factor models analyzed in Section 2.7. With enough measurements, outcomes and

[30] Matzkin (1993) presents alternative sets of conditions for identifiability of the choice model.

choices relative to the dimensionality of θ, it is possible to identify the joint distribution of outcomes across counterfactual states.

Identification problems in factor analysis were first clearly stated by Anderson and Rubin (1956). If, for example, there are $L(s)$ components of $U(s)$ and θ is $K \times 1$, $\varepsilon(s)$ is $L(s) \times 1$ and $\Lambda(s)$ is $L(s) \times K$. Even if the θ_i, $i = 1, \ldots, K$, are mutually independent, the model of Equation (2.8) is underidentified. To see this, note that $\mathrm{Cov}(U(s)) = \Lambda(s)\Sigma_\theta \Lambda'(s) + D_{\varepsilon(s)}$, where Σ_θ is a matrix of the variances of the factors, assumed to be diagonal in this example, $D_{\varepsilon(s)}$ is a diagonal matrix of the variances of the uniquenesses.[31] We have identified $\mathrm{Cov}(U(s))$, the discrete components up to scale, but we do not directly observe θ or $\varepsilon(s)$. Any orthogonal transformation applied to $\Lambda(s)$ is consistent with the same $\mathrm{Cov}(U(s))$.

Without restrictions on $\Lambda(s)$, and on the dependence structure among the components of θ, identification of the model is not possible. Conventional factor-analytic models make assumptions to identify parameters. The diagonals of $\mathrm{Cov}(U(s))$ combine elements of $D_{\varepsilon(s)}$ with parameters from the rest of the model. Once those other parameters are determined, the diagonals identify $D_{\varepsilon(s)}$. Accordingly, one can only rely on the $L(s)(L(s)-1)/2$ non-diagonal elements to identify the K variances (assuming $\theta_i \perp\!\!\!\perp \theta_j$, $\forall i \neq j$), and the $L(s) \times K$ factor loadings. Since the scale of each θ_i is arbitrary, one factor loading devoted to each factor must be normalized to set the scale. Typically the normalization is unity. Accordingly, we require as a necessary condition for identification of the variances and parameters of (2.8) for a given s

$$\underbrace{\frac{L(s)(L(s)-1)}{2}}_{\substack{\text{Number of off-diagonal}\\ \text{covariance elements}}} \geqslant \underbrace{\big((L(s) \times K) - K\big)}_{\text{Number of unrestricted } \Lambda} + \underbrace{K.}_{\text{Variances of } \theta}$$
$$\iff \quad L(s) \geqslant 2K + 1. \tag{2.9}$$

Anderson and Rubin (1956), Chamberlain (1975), Carneiro, Hansen and Heckman (2003), Hansen, Heckman and Mullen (2004), Cunha, Heckman and Navarro (2005) and Cunha, Heckman and Schennach (2007) present alternative normalizations and identification assumptions for models with multiple factors. Carneiro, Hansen and Heckman (2003) and Cunha, Heckman and Schennach (2006, 2007) use information from higher moments to identify the model.[32] Many of the identifying assumptions in various empirical literatures such as the literature on earnings dynamics are motivated by appeals to empirical conventions and to economic theory [see, e.g., Cunha and Heckman (2007b, 2007c, 2008)]. Case-specific analyses are necessary to provide economically interpretable identifying assumptions. Access to measurements facilitates this task.

[31] The uniquenesses are the $\varepsilon(s)$ in Equation (2.8).

[32] See also Bonhomme and Robin (2004). Note that restrictions across the s-systems facilitate identification.

2.9. Distinguishing ex ante from ex post returns

The analysis of the preceding sections presents tools for estimating joint distributions of outcomes and subjective valuations of outcomes across counterfactual states. It is silent about the information that agents possess about expected returns at the time they make their program participation decisions. Uncertainty and the dynamics of information revelation are not systematically incorporated in the current literature on treatment effects. As noted in Chapter 70 of this Handbook, anticipated (*ex ante*) returns may differ from realized (*ex post*) returns and understanding these differences is important for computing the welfare gains to program participation, the regret that agents may experience about participating or not participating in a program, and the option value of social programs. In addition, subjective evaluations are not a part of the literature on statistical treatment effects.

In a medical trial [see, e.g., Chan and Hamilton (2006)], the patient will not only value the medical treatment but he/she will also consider the medical benefits or costs (pain and suffering) connected with the treatment. Agents may be pleasantly or unpleasantly surprised by arrival of information during a course of therapy, and this information revision will affect choices of future treatment. Knowing agent preferences and perceptions is helpful in determining compliance and patient welfare. In an analysis of job training programs, agents may be disappointed, *ex post* about the treatment they have received [Heckman and Smith (1998)].

Empirical analyses of the "returns to education" that have extensively used *IV* methods focus exclusively on the *ex post* returns to education rather than the *ex ante* returns that motivate agent schooling decisions. As Hicks (1946, p. 179) puts it,

> "Ex post *calculations of capital accumulation have their place in economic and statistical* history*; they are a useful measuring-rod for economic progress; but they are of no use to theoretical economists who are trying to find out how the system works, because they have no significance for conduct*."

This section presents some recent results on the identification of agent information sets and *ex ante* and *ex post* distributions of outcomes. It builds on and synthesizes work by Carneiro, Hansen and Heckman (2001, 2003), Cunha, Heckman and Navarro (2005, 2006) and Cunha and Heckman (2007b, 2007c, 2008).

To motivate the main ideas underlying this approach, consider the problem of estimating the return to an activity. It could be schooling or the installation of a new technology. The problem can be cast as a prototypical generalized Roy model with two sectors and solutions to it apply to many related problems. Let D denote different choices. $D = 0$ denotes choice of sector 0 and $D = 1$ denotes choice of sector 1. In a schooling example this could represent high school ($D = 0$) and college ($D = 1$). Each person chooses to be in one or the other sector but cannot be in both. Let the two potential outcomes be represented by the pair (Y_0, Y_1), only one of which is observed by the analyst for any agent. Denote by C the direct cost of choosing sector 1. In a schooling example these would include tuition and nonpecuniary costs of attending college expressed in monetary values.

Y_1 is the *ex post* present value of making the choice 1, discounted over horizon $\bar{T}$ for a person choosing at a fixed age, assumed for convenience to be one,

$$Y_1 = \sum_{t=1}^{\bar{T}} \frac{Y_{1,t}}{(1+r)^{t-1}},$$

and Y_0 is the *ex post* present value of making the choice 0 at age one,

$$Y_0 = \sum_{t=1}^{\bar{T}} \frac{Y_{0,t}}{(1+r)^{t-1}},$$

where r is the one-period risk-free interest rate. Y_1 and Y_0 can be constructed from time series of *ex post* potential outcome streams in the two states: $(Y_{0,1}, \ldots, Y_{0,\bar{T}})$ and $(Y_{1,1}, \ldots, Y_{1,\bar{T}})$. A practical problem is that we only observe one or the other of these streams for any person. This is the fundamental program evaluation problem. In addition, we observe these streams selectively, i.e., for those who chose $D = 0$ or $D = 1$, respectively.

The variables Y_1, Y_0, and C are *ex post* realizations of returns and costs, respectively. At the time agents make their choices, these random variables may only be partially known to the agent. Using the information set notation introduced in Section 2.6 of Chapter 70, let $\mathcal{I}_A$ denote the information set of an agent at the time the choice is made, which is time period $t = 1$ in our notation. Under a complete markets assumption with all risks diversifiable (so that there is risk-neutral pricing) or under a perfect foresight model with unrestricted borrowing or lending but full repayment, the decision rule governing sectoral choices at decision time 1 is

$$D = \begin{cases} 1, & \text{if } E(Y_1 - Y_0 - C \mid \mathcal{I}_A) \geqslant 0, \\ 0, & \text{otherwise.}^{33} \end{cases} \tag{2.10}$$

Under perfect foresight, the postulated information set would include Y_1, Y_0, and C. Under either model of information, the decision rule is simple: one chooses sector 1 if the expected gains from doing so are greater than or equal to the expected costs. Thus under either set of assumptions, a separation theorem governs choices. Agents maximize expected wealth independently of their consumption decisions over time.[34]

[33] If there are aggregate sources of risk, full insurance would require a linear utility function.

[34] The decision rule is more complicated in the absence of full risk diversifiability and depends on the curvature of utility functions, the availability of markets to spread risk, and possibilities for storage. [See Heckman, Lochner and Todd (2006) for a more extensive discussion.] In these more realistic economic settings, the components of earnings and costs required to forecast the gain to the choice depend on higher moments than the mean. In this section, we use a model with a simple market setting to motivate the identification analysis of a more general environment analyzed elsewhere [Carneiro, Hansen and Heckman (2003)].

Suppose that we seek to determine $\mathcal{I}_A$. This is a difficult task. Typically we can only partially identify $\mathcal{I}_A$ and generate a list of candidate variables that belong to the information set. We can usually only estimate the distributions of the unobservables in $\mathcal{I}_A$ (from the standpoint of the econometrician) and not individual realizations of the unobservables.

Cunha, Heckman and Navarro (2005, 2006) and Cunha and Heckman (2007b, 2007c) exploit covariances between choices and realized outcomes that arise under different information structures to test which information structure characterizes the data, building on the analysis of Carneiro, Hansen and Heckman (2003). To see how the method works, we simplify the exposition to a two-choice framework. In Section 3 of this contribution, we extend this analysis to multiple choices in a dynamic setting.

Suppose, contrary to what is possible, that the analyst observes Y_0, Y_1, and C for each person. Such information would come from an ideal data set in which the evaluation problem is solved and we could observe two different lifetime outcome streams for the same person as well as the costs they pay for choosing sector 1. From such information, we could construct $Y_1 - Y_0 - C$. If we knew the information set $\mathcal{I}_A$ of the agent that governs choices, we could also construct $E(Y_1 - Y_0 - C \mid \mathcal{I}_A)$. Under the correct model of expectations, we could form the residual

$$\zeta_{\mathcal{I}_A} = (Y_1 - Y_0 - C) - E(Y_1 - Y_0 - C \mid \mathcal{I}_A),$$

and from the *ex ante* choice decision, we could determine whether D depends on $\zeta_{\mathcal{I}_A}$. It should not if we have specified $\mathcal{I}_A$ correctly.

A test for correct specification of candidate information set $\widetilde{\mathcal{I}}_A$ for an agent is a test of whether D depends on $\zeta_{\widetilde{\mathcal{I}}_A}$, where

$$\zeta_{\widetilde{\mathcal{I}}_A} = (Y_1 - Y_0 - C) - E(Y_1 - Y_0 - C \mid \widetilde{\mathcal{I}}_A).$$

More precisely, the information set is valid if $D \perp\!\!\!\perp \zeta_{\widetilde{\mathcal{I}}_A} \mid \widetilde{\mathcal{I}}_A$. A test of misspecification of $\widetilde{\mathcal{I}}_A$ is a test of whether the coefficient of $\zeta_{\widetilde{\mathcal{I}}_A}$ in the choice equation is statistically significantly different from zero.

More generally, $\widetilde{\mathcal{I}}_A$ is the correct information set if $\zeta_{\widetilde{\mathcal{I}}_A}$ does not help to predict schooling. One can search among candidate information sets $\widetilde{\mathcal{I}}_A$ to determine which ones satisfy the requirement that the generated $\zeta_{\widetilde{\mathcal{I}}_A}$ does not predict D and what components of $Y_1 - Y_0 - C$ (and $Y_1 - Y_0$) are predictable at the age schooling decisions are made for the specified information set. This procedure is motivated by a Sims (1972) version of a Wiener–Granger causality test. There may be several information sets that satisfy this property.[35] For a properly specified $\widetilde{\mathcal{I}}_A$, $\zeta_{\widetilde{\mathcal{I}}_A}$ should not cause (predict) schooling choices. The components of $\zeta_{\widetilde{\mathcal{I}}_A}$ that are unpredictable are intrinsic components of uncertainty at the date the choice represented by D is made.

[35] Thus different combinations of variables may contain the same information. The issue of the existence of a smallest information set is a technical one concerning a minimum σ-algebra that satisfies the conditions used to define $\mathcal{I}_A$.

It is difficult to determine the exact content of $\mathcal{I}_A$ known to each agent. If we could, we would perfectly predict D given our decision rule. More realistically, we might find variables that proxy $\mathcal{I}_A$ or their distribution. This strategy is pursued in Cunha, Heckman and Navarro (2005, 2006) for a two-choice model, and is generalized by Cunha and Heckman (2007b) and Heckman and Navarro (2007). We now present an example of this approach. We consider identification of information sets as well as identification of the psychic costs of treatment.

2.9.1. *An approach based on factor structures*

Consider the following model for $\bar{T}$ periods. Write outcomes in each counterfactual state as

$$
\begin{aligned}
Y_{0,t} &= \mu_{0,t}(X_t) + U_{0,t}, \\
Y_{1,t} &= \mu_{1,t}(X_t) + U_{1,t}, \quad t = 1, \ldots, \bar{T}.
\end{aligned}
$$

We let costs of picking sector 1 be defined as

$$C = \mu_C(Z) + U_C.$$

Assume that the horizon of the agent ends at period $\bar{T}$.

Suppose that there exists a vector of mutually independent factors

$$\theta = (\theta_1, \theta_2, \ldots, \theta_K).$$

Under the factor assumption, the error term in outcomes in period t for an agent can be represented in the following manner:

$$
\begin{aligned}
U_{0,t} &= \alpha_{0,t}\theta + \varepsilon_{0,t}, \\
U_{1,t} &= \alpha_{1,t}\theta + \varepsilon_{1,t},
\end{aligned}
$$

where $\alpha_{0,t}$ and $\alpha_{1,t}$ are now $1 \times K$ vectors and θ is a $K \times 1$ vector. The $\varepsilon_{0,t}$, $\varepsilon_{1,t}$, and θ are mutually independent. We can also decompose the cost function C in a similar fashion:

$$C = \mu_C(Z) + \alpha_C\theta + \varepsilon_C.$$

All of the statistical dependence across potential outcomes and costs is generated by θ, X, and Z. Thus, if we could match on θ (as well as X and Z), we could use matching to infer the distribution of counterfactuals and capture all of the dependence across the counterfactual states through θ. Carneiro, Hansen and Heckman (2001, 2003), Cunha, Heckman and Navarro (2005, 2006) and Cunha and Heckman (2007b, 2007c, 2008) allow for the possibility that not all of the required elements of θ are observed.

The parameters α_C and $\alpha_{s,t}$, for $s = 0, 1$, and $t = 1, \ldots, \bar{T}$ are the factor loadings. ε_C is independent of the θ and the other ε components. In this notation, the choice equation can be written as:

$$D^* = E\left(\sum_{t=1}^{\bar{T}} \frac{(\mu_{1,t}(X_t) + \alpha_{1,t}\theta + \varepsilon_{1,t}) - (\mu_{0,t}(X_t) + \alpha_{0,t}\theta + \varepsilon_{0,t})}{(1+r)^{t-1}} - \left(\mu_C(Z) + \alpha_C\theta + \varepsilon_C\right) \,\middle|\, \mathcal{I}_A \right),$$

$$D = 1 \quad \text{if } D^* \geqslant 0; \qquad D = 0 \quad \text{otherwise.} \tag{2.11}$$

The first term in the summation inside the parentheses is discounted outcomes in state 1 minus discounted outcomes in state 0. The second term in the expression is the cost.

Equation (2.11) entails counterfactual comparisons. Even if the outcomes associated with one choice are observed over the horizon using panel data, the outcomes in the counterfactual state are not. After the choice is made, some components of the X_t, the θ, and the ε_t may be revealed (e.g., unemployment rates, macroshocks) to both the observing economist and the agent, although different components may be revealed to each and at different times.

Examining alternative information sets, one can determine which ones produce models for outcomes that fit the data best in terms of producing a model that predicts date $t = 1$ choices and at the same time passes the test for misspecification of predicted earnings and costs described in the previous subsection. Some components of the error terms of the outcome equations may be known or not known at the date schooling choices are made. The unforecastable components are intrinsic uncertainty. The forecastable information is called heterogeneity.[36]

To formally characterize an empirical procedure to test for and measure the importance of uncertainty, it is useful to introduce some additional notation. Let $\odot$ denote the Hadamard product, $a \odot b = (a_1 b_1, \ldots, a_L b_L)$, for vectors a and b of length L. This is a componentwise multiplication of vectors to produce a vector. Let κ_{X_t}, $t = 1, \ldots, \bar{T}$, κ_Z, κ_θ, κ_{ε_t}, κ_{ε_C}, denote coefficient vectors associated with the X_t, $t = 1, \ldots, \bar{T}$, the Z, the θ, the $\varepsilon_{1,t} - \varepsilon_{0,t}$, and the ε_C, respectively. For a proposed information set $\widetilde{\mathcal{I}}_A$ which may or may not be the true information set on which agents act, define the proposed choice index $\tilde{D}^*$ in the following way. For simplicity write $\mu_{1,t}(X_t) = X_t\beta_{1,t}$, $\mu_{0,t}(X_t) = X_t\beta_{0,t}$, and $\mu_C(Z) = Z\gamma$. Then

$$\tilde{D}^* = \sum_{t=1}^{\bar{T}} \frac{E(X_t \mid \widetilde{\mathcal{I}}_A)}{(1+r)^{t-1}}(\beta_{1,t} - \beta_{0,t}) + \sum_{t=1}^{\bar{T}} \frac{[X_t - E(X_t \mid \widetilde{\mathcal{I}}_A)]}{(1+r)^{t-1}}(\beta_{1,t} - \beta_{0,t}) \odot \kappa_{X_t} + \left[\sum_{t=1}^{\bar{T}} \frac{(\alpha_{1,t} - \alpha_{0,t})}{(1+r)^{t-1}} - \alpha_C \right] E(\theta \mid \widetilde{\mathcal{I}}_A)$$

[36] The term 'heterogeneity' is somewhat unfortunate. This term includes trends common across all people (e.g., macrotrends). The real distinction they are making is between components of realized outcomes forecastable by agents at the time they make their choices vs. components that are not forecastable.

$$
\begin{aligned}
&+\left\{\left[\sum_{t=1}^{\bar{T}}\frac{(\alpha_{1,t}-\alpha_{0,t})}{(1+r)^{t-1}}-\alpha_C\right]\odot\kappa_\theta\right\}\left[\theta-E(\theta\mid\widetilde{\mathcal{I}}_A)\right]\\
&+\sum_{t=1}^{\bar{T}}\frac{E(\varepsilon_{1,t}-\varepsilon_{0,t}\mid\widetilde{\mathcal{I}}_A)}{(1+r)^{t-1}}+\sum_{t=1}^{\bar{T}}\frac{[(\varepsilon_{1,t}-\varepsilon_{0,t})-E(\varepsilon_{1,t}-\varepsilon_{0,t}\mid\widetilde{\mathcal{I}}_A)]}{(1+r)^{t-1}}\kappa_{\varepsilon_t}\\
&-E(Z\mid\widetilde{\mathcal{I}}_A)\gamma-\left[Z-E(Z\mid\widetilde{\mathcal{I}}_A)\right]\gamma\odot\kappa_Z-E(\varepsilon_C\mid\widetilde{\mathcal{I}}_A)\\
&-\left[\varepsilon_C-E(\varepsilon_C\mid\widetilde{\mathcal{I}}_A)\right]\kappa_{\varepsilon_C}.
\end{aligned}
\tag{2.12}
$$

Fit a choice model based on the proposed information set. Estimate the parameters of the model including the κ parameters. The κ parameters will be estimated to be nonzero in a choice equation if a proposed information set is not the actual information set used by agents. This particular decomposition for $\tilde{D}^*$ assumes that agents know the β, the γ, and the α.[37] If this assumption is not correct, the presence of additional unforecastable components due to unknown coefficients affects the interpretation of the estimates. A test of no misspecification of information set $\widetilde{\mathcal{I}}_A$ is a joint test of the hypothesis that the κ are all zero. That is, when $\widetilde{\mathcal{I}}_A = \mathcal{I}_A$ then the proposed choice index $\tilde{D}^* = D^*$. In a model with a correctly specified information set, the components associated with zero κ_j are the unforecastable elements or the elements which, even if known to the agent, are not acted on in making schooling choices.

To illustrate the method of Cunha, Heckman and Navarro (2005), assume that the X_t, the Z, the ε_C, the $\beta_{1,t}$, $\beta_{0,t}$, the $\alpha_{1,t}$, $\alpha_{0,t}$, and α_C are known to the agent at the time decisions about D are being made, and that the $\varepsilon_{j,t}$ are unknown, and that the agents set them at their mean values of zero. We can infer which components of the θ are known and acted on in making decisions if we postulate that some components of θ are known perfectly at date $t = 1$ while others are not known at all, and their forecast values have mean zero given $\mathcal{I}_A$.

If there is an element of the vector θ, say θ_2 (factor 2), that has nonzero loadings (coefficients) in the choice equation and a nonzero loading on one or more potential future outcomes, then one can say that at the time the choice is made, the agent knows the unobservable captured by factor 2 that affects future outcomes. If θ_2 does not enter the choice equation but explains future outcomes, then θ_2 is unknown (not predictable by the agent) at the age decisions are made. An alternative interpretation is that the second component of

$$\left[\sum_{t=1}^{\bar{T}}\frac{(\alpha_{1,t}-\alpha_{0,t})}{(1+r)^{t-1}}-\alpha_C\right]$$

is zero, i.e., that even if the component is known, it is not acted on. Analysts can only test for what the agent knows and acts on.

[37] Cunha, Heckman and Navarro (2005) and Cunha and Heckman (2007b) relax this assumption.

One plausible scenario is that ε_C is known to the agent, since costs are assumed to be incurred up front, but that the future $\varepsilon_{1,t}$ and $\varepsilon_{0,t}$ are not and have mean zero. If there are components of the $\varepsilon_{j,t}$ that are predictable at age $t = 1$, they will induce additional dependence between D and future outcomes that will pick up additional factors beyond those initially specified. The procedure can be generalized to consider all components of the outcome equations. Using this procedure, the analyst can test the predictive power of each subset of the possible information set at the date the decision is being made. The approach allows the analyst to determine which components of θ and $\{\varepsilon_{0,t}, \varepsilon_{1,t}\}_{t=1}^{\bar{T}}$ are known and acted on at the time decisions are made.

Statistical decompositions do not tell us which components of error variance are known at the time agents make their decisions. A model of expectations and choices is needed. If some of the components of $\{\varepsilon_{0,t}, \varepsilon_{1,t}\}_{t=1}^{\bar{T}}$ are known to the agent at the date decisions are made and enter decision equation (2.11), then additional dependence between D and future $Y_1 - Y_0$ due to the $\{\varepsilon_{0,t}, \varepsilon_{1,t}\}_{t=1}^{\bar{T}}$, beyond that due to θ, would be estimated. Our version of the Sims test can in principle detect these components.

It is helpful to contrast the dependence between D and future $Y_{0,t}$, $Y_{1,t}$ arising from θ and the dependence between D and the $\{\varepsilon_{0,t}, \varepsilon_{1,t}\}_{t=1}^{\bar{T}}$. Some of the θ in the *ex post* outcomes equation may not appear in the choice equation. Under other information sets, some additional dependence between D and $\{\varepsilon_{0,t}, \varepsilon_{1,t}\}_{t=1}^{\bar{T}}$ may arise. The contrast between the sources generating realized outcomes and the sources generating dependence between D and realized outcomes is the essential idea in inferring the information in the agent's information set when decisions are being made. The method can be generalized to deal with nonlinear preferences and imperfect market environments.[38] We next show how to operationalize this method and identify psychic costs and agent information sets. This econometric analysis is followed by some empirical applications of this methodology.

2.9.2. *Operationalizing the method*

In order to see how to operationalize the method, we draw on the work of Cunha and Heckman (2007b). Assume normality to simplify the analysis. The normality assumption plays no essential role in the analysis and is relaxed below. Our empirical examples in fact show the estimated models to be highly nonnormal.

The key idea underlying this approach is to have more measurement, outcome and choice equations than components in θ. These are the necessary conditions for identification encapsulated in inequality (2.9). Here we assume that we have multiple periods of data on outcomes associated with each treatment state s, $s = 1, \dots, \bar{S}$, as well as measurement equations. We assume a two-factor example and show how to test

[38] See Carneiro, Hansen and Heckman (2003), Cunha and Heckman (2007c) and the survey in Heckman, Lochner and Todd (2006).

whether factors that predict post-treatment earnings appear in the choice equation. For specificity, one can think of the choice as schooling (high school vs. college), and the outcomes as earnings.

2.9.3. The estimation of the components in the information set

We show how we can determine the unobservable components of the information set $\mathcal{I}_A$ of the agent at the time of the choice by exploring the convenient structure provided by the factor models. Assume that X, Z, ε_C, and the factor loadings and parameters of cost equations and outcome equations are in the information set $\mathcal{I}_A$. We can test for what is in agent's decision sets using the Sims test described in Section 2.9.1. To conserve on notation, we define factor loadings on each factor in (2.12) using the condensed expression

$$\alpha_{k,D} = \sum_{t=1}^{\bar{T}} \left(\frac{1}{1+r}\right)^{t-1} (\alpha_{k,1,t} - \alpha_{k,0,t}) - \alpha_{k,C} \quad \text{for } k = 1, \ldots, K. \tag{2.13}$$

Suppose that for a two-factor ($K = 2$) model, θ_1 and θ_2 are in the agent's information set $\mathcal{I}_A$ but $\varepsilon_{s,t}$ is not. If the null hypothesis that θ_1 and θ_2 are in $\mathcal{I}_A$ is true, we may write the choice index D^* as:

$$D^* = \mu_D(X, Z) + \alpha_{1,D}\theta_1 + \alpha_{2,D}\theta_2 + \varepsilon_C. \tag{2.14}$$

The choice index is written in terms of structural parameters using (2.10). From our analysis of Step 2, we can identify $\mu_D(X, Z)$ and $\beta_{s,t}$ for all s and t. Given observations on X and Z, we can obtain from data on outcomes, (Y, X, D, Z), the covariance between the terms $D^* - \mu_D(X, Z)$ and $Y_{1,1} - X\beta_{1,1}$. Under the null hypothesis that θ_1 and θ_2 are both in the agents' information sets, this covariance is equal to

$$\operatorname{Cov}\big(D^* - \mu_D(X, Z), Y_{1,1} - \mu_{1,1}(X)\big) = \alpha_{1,D}\alpha_{1,1,1}\sigma_{\theta_1}^2 + \alpha_{2,D}\alpha_{2,1,1}\sigma_{\theta_2}^2. \tag{2.15}$$

We seek to test the null that θ_1 and θ_2 are in $\mathcal{I}_A$ against alternative hypotheses. To fix ideas, consider the alternative assumption that θ_1 is in $\mathcal{I}_A$ but θ_2 is not, and maintain that $E[\theta_2 \mid \mathcal{I}_A] = 0$. If the alternative is valid, the choice index (2.14) may be written as

$$D^* = \mu_D(X, Z) + \alpha_{1,D}\theta_1 + \varepsilon_C. \tag{2.16}$$

In this case, the covariance between the terms $D^* - \mu_D(X, Z)$ and $Y_{1,1} - \mu_{1,1}(X)$ satisfies

$$\operatorname{Cov}\big(D^* - \mu_D(X, Z), Y_{1,1} - \mu_{1,1}(X)\big) = \alpha_{1,D}\alpha_{1,1,1}\sigma_{\theta_1}^2, \tag{2.17}$$

and the difference between the choice generated by the null and the alternative hypotheses is the term $\alpha_{2,D}\alpha_{2,1,1}\sigma_{\theta_2}^2$ that appears in (2.15) but not in (2.17). This insight allows us to redefine the Sims test by generating parameters κ_{θ_1} and κ_{θ_2} to satisfy:

$$\operatorname{Cov}\big(D^* - \mu_D(X,Z), Y_{1,1} - \mu_{1,1}(X)\big) - \kappa_{\theta_1}\alpha_{1,D}\alpha_{1,1,1}\sigma^2_{\theta_1} - \kappa_{\theta_2}\alpha_{2,D}\alpha_{2,1,1}\sigma^2_{\theta_2} = 0.$$

It is easy to see how we can rewrite the test in terms of κ_{θ_1} and κ_{θ_2}. We conclude that agents know and act on the information contained in factors 1 and 2, so that θ_1 and θ_2 are in $\mathcal{I}_A$, if we reject both $\kappa_{\theta_1} = 0$ and $\kappa_{\theta_2} = 0$. Parallel tests can be conducted for other components of realized earnings.

It remains to be shown that we can actually identify all of the parameters of the model, in particular, the function $\mu_D(X, Z)$, the parameters β and α in the test and earnings equations, the distribution of the factors, F_θ, as well as the distribution of idiosyncratic components F_ε in the measurement, outcomes and cost equations.

We start by analyzing the measurement equations which in the context of a schooling choice problem could be test score equations. We assume that the measurement equations only depend on θ_1 and not the other factors. In an analysis of college choices, test scores are typically available for all agents before their decisions are made, and they proxy ability. By assumption, there is no selection bias in observations on the measurement equations. We can identify the mean outcome equations $\mu_{M,n}(X)$, $n = 1, \dots, N$, where N is the number of measurements.

Given knowledge of these parameters, we can construct differences $M_n - \mu_{M,n}(X)$ and compute the covariances, as in the case of three measurements:

$$\operatorname{Cov}\big(M_1 - \mu_{M,1}(X), M_2 - \mu_{M,2}(X)\big) = \alpha_1^M \alpha_2^M \sigma^2_{\theta_1}, \tag{2.18}$$

$$\operatorname{Cov}\big(M_1 - \mu_{M,1}(X), M_3 - \mu_{M,3}(X)\big) = \alpha_1^M \alpha_3^M \sigma^2_{\theta_1}, \tag{2.19}$$

$$\operatorname{Cov}\big(M_2 - \mu_{M,2}(X), M_3 - \mu_{M,3}(X)\big) = \alpha_2^M \alpha_3^M \sigma^2_{\theta_1}. \tag{2.20}$$

The left-hand sides of (2.18), (2.19), and (2.20) can be computed from sample moments. The right-hand sides of (2.18), (2.19), and (2.20) are implications of the factor model, assuming measurements are dependent only through θ_1. We need to normalize one of the factor loadings. Let $\alpha_1^M = 1$. If we take the ratio of (2.20) to (2.18), we identify α_3^M. Analogously, the ratio of (2.20) to (2.19) allows us to recover α_2^M. Given the normalization of $\alpha_1^M = 1$ and identification of α_2^M, we recover $\sigma^2_{\theta_1}$ from (2.18). Finally, we can identify the variance of ε_k^M from the variance of $M_k - \mu_{M,k}$. Because the factor θ_1 and uniquenesses ε_k are independently normally distributed random variables, we have identified their distribution. Normality plays no crucial role here. Our analysis in Section 2.7.3 shows how this analysis can be made fully nonparametric under the conditions of Theorem 1.

2.9.4. Outcome and choice equations

Establishing the identification of the joint distribution of outcomes requires more work because of the evaluation problem. We only observe one stream of outcomes for each agent, corresponding to outcomes associated with treatment D. It is at this stage of the analysis that focusing the discussion on normally distributed factors and uniquenesses becomes helpful for understanding how identification can be secured. We can use the closed-form solutions developed in the traditional econometric literature to reduce the identification problem to the identification of a few parameters. However, the analysis does not require normality.

All of the dependence among $U_{0,t}$, $U_{1,t}$, and U_C is captured through the factors θ_1 and θ_2. To establish identification most transparently, assume that they are normally distributed with the following mean and covariance matrix:

$$\begin{pmatrix} \theta_1 \\ \theta_2 \end{pmatrix} \sim N\left(\begin{pmatrix} 0 \\ 0 \end{pmatrix}, \begin{bmatrix} \sigma_{\theta_1}^2 & 0 \\ 0 & \sigma_{\theta_2}^2 \end{bmatrix} \right).$$

Because of the loadings $\alpha_{1,s,t}$, $\alpha_{2,s,t}$, $\alpha_{1,C}$, and $\alpha_{2,C}$ the factors θ can affect $U_{0,t}$, $U_{1,t}$, and U_C differently. By adopting the factor structure representation, we are not imposing, for example, perfect ranking in the sense that the best in the distribution of earnings in sector s at period t is the best (or the worst) in the distribution of earnings in sector s' at period t' as in the models of rank invariance surveyed in Section 2.5. The joint distribution of the earnings $Y_{0,t}$, $Y_{1,t}$ conditional on X is:

$$\begin{aligned} &\begin{bmatrix} Y_{0,t} \\ Y_{1,t} \end{bmatrix} \Big| X \\ &\sim N\left(\begin{bmatrix} \mu_{0,t}(X) \\ \mu_{1,t}(X) \end{bmatrix}, \begin{bmatrix} \alpha_{1,0,t}^2 \sigma_{\theta_1}^2 + \alpha_{2,0,t}^2 \sigma_{\theta_2}^2 + \sigma_{\varepsilon_{0,t}}^2 & \alpha_{1,0,t}\alpha_{1,1,t}\sigma_{\theta_1}^2 + \alpha_{2,0,t}\alpha_{2,1,t}\sigma_{\theta_2}^2 \\ \alpha_{1,0,t}\alpha_{1,1,t}\sigma_{\theta_1}^2 + \alpha_{2,0,t}\alpha_{2,1,t}\sigma_{\theta_2}^2 & \alpha_{1,1,t}^2 \sigma_{\theta_1}^2 + \alpha_{2,1,t}^2 \sigma_{\theta_2}^2 + \sigma_{\varepsilon_{1,t}}^2 \end{bmatrix} \right). \end{aligned} \tag{2.21}$$

The joint distribution of $\begin{bmatrix} Y_{0,t} \\ Y_{1,t} \end{bmatrix}$ and $\begin{bmatrix} Y_{0,t'} \\ Y_{1,t'} \end{bmatrix}$ is fully determined by the means of each vector, the variance matrix of each vector, and the covariance matrix

$$\begin{aligned} &\operatorname{Cov}\left(\begin{bmatrix} Y_{0,t} \\ Y_{1,t} \end{bmatrix}, \begin{bmatrix} Y_{0,t'} \\ Y_{1,t'} \end{bmatrix} \Big| X \right) \\ &= \begin{bmatrix} \alpha_{1,0,t}\alpha_{1,0,t'}\sigma_{\theta_1}^2 + \alpha_{2,0,t}\alpha_{2,0,t'}\sigma_{\theta_2}^2 & \alpha_{1,0,t}\alpha_{1,1,t'}\sigma_{\theta_1}^2 + \alpha_{2,0,t}\alpha_{2,1,t'}\sigma_{\theta_2}^2 \\ \alpha_{1,0,t}\alpha_{1,1,t'}\sigma_{\theta_1}^2 + \alpha_{2,0,t}\alpha_{2,1,t'}\sigma_{\theta_2}^2 & \alpha_{1,1,t}\alpha_{1,1,t'}\sigma_{\theta_1}^2 + \alpha_{2,1,t}\alpha_{2,1,t'}\sigma_{\theta_2}^2 \end{bmatrix}, \end{aligned} \tag{2.22}$$

for all $t \neq t'$. If we determine the means and the covariances across all of the t, t' under a normality assumption, we fully specify the joint distributions of $(Y_{0,1}, \ldots, Y_{0,\bar{T}}, Y_{1,1}, \ldots, Y_{1,\bar{T}})$ and $(Y_{0,1}, \ldots, Y_{0,\bar{T}}, Y_{1,1}, \ldots, Y_{1,\bar{T}}, D^*)$. As a result, identification of the joint distributions reduces to the identification of the functions $\mu_{0,t}(X)$, $\mu_{1,t}(X)$, $\alpha_{k,s,t}$, $\alpha_{k,D}$, $\sigma_{\varepsilon_{s,t}}$, σ_{ε_C} (possibly up to scale) and $\sigma_{\theta_j}^2$ for $s = 0, 1$; $t = 1, \ldots, \bar{T}$ and $j = 1, 2$, and $k = 1, 2$. This also entails identification of the distributions of θ_1 and θ_2 as well as the parameters associated with the choice equation. Using the methods discussed in Sections 2.7 and 2.8, we can relax the normality assumption. The factor structure is essential to model the dependence across observations. The factors can be nonnormal. We now show an example of how to secure identification.

From the observed data and the factor structure it follows that

$$E(Y_{1,t} \mid X, Z, D = 1) = \mu_{1,t}(X) + \alpha_{1,1,t} E[\theta_1 \mid X, Z, D = 1] + \alpha_{2,1,t} E[\theta_2 \mid X, Z, D = 1] + E[\varepsilon_{1,t} \mid X, Z, D = 1]. \tag{2.23}$$

The event $D = 1$ is the event $D^* = E(\sum_{t=1}^{\bar{T}} (\frac{1}{1+r})^{t-1}(Y_{1,t} - Y_{0,t}) - C \mid \mathcal{I}_A) \geqslant 0$. For simplicity, assume that r is known by the analyst. It can be identified along with the other parameters.[39]

It is important to distinguish the role played by the factors θ from the role played by the uniquenesses $\varepsilon_{s,t}$. We assume in this example that the $\varepsilon_{s,t}$ are unknown to the agent at the time choices are made. If not, those components would fail the Sims test for their exclusion from the choice equation, and would be in agent information sets. By definition, the terms that affect the covariance between future outcomes and choices are what is in the information set at the time choices are made. Under our assumptions and initial specification of the information set,

$$E\left(\sum_{t=1}^{\bar{T}} \left(\frac{1}{1+r} \right)^{t-1} (Y_{1,t} - Y_{0,t}) - C \,\middle|\, \mathcal{I}_A \right) = \mu_D(X, Z) + \alpha_{1,D}\theta_1 + \alpha_{2,D}\theta_2 - \varepsilon_C.$$

Let V_D be the linear combination of the three independent normal random variables in the decision rule:

$$V_D = \alpha_{1,D}\theta_1 + \alpha_{2,D}\theta_2 - \varepsilon_C.$$

Then, $V_D \sim N(0, \sigma_{V_D}^2)$, with $\sigma_{V_D}^2 = \alpha_{1,D}^2\sigma_{\theta_1}^2 + \alpha_{2,D}^2\sigma_{\theta_2}^2 + \sigma_{\varepsilon_c}^2$ and

$$D = 1 \quad \Leftrightarrow \quad V_D \geqslant -\mu_D(X, Z). \tag{2.24}$$

We now use standard normal sample selection arguments to establish identifiability. If we use representation (2.24) in place of $D = 1$ in Equation (2.23) and use the fact that $\varepsilon_{s,t}$ is independent of X, Z, and V_D, it follows that

$$E(Y_{1,t} \mid X, Z, D = 1) = \mu_{1,t}(X) + \alpha_{1,1,t} E\big[\theta_1 \mid X, Z, V_D \geqslant -\mu_D(X, Z)\big] + \alpha_{2,1,t} E\big[\theta_2 \mid X, Z, V_D \geqslant -\mu_D(X, Z)\big]. \tag{2.25}$$

Second, because θ_1, θ_2 and V_D are normal random variables, we can use the projection property for normal random variables to break θ_j into statistically independent components predictable by V_D and components that are not predictable:

$$\theta_j = \frac{\mathrm{Cov}(\theta_j, V_D)}{\mathrm{Var}(V_D)} V_D + \nu_j \quad \text{for } j = 1, 2, \tag{2.26}$$

[39] See the discussion and references in Section 3.

where ν_j is a mean zero, normal random variable independent of V_D. Because $\text{Cov}(\theta_1, V_D) = \sigma^2_{\theta_1}\alpha_{1,D}$ and $\text{Cov}(\theta_2, V_D) = \sigma^2_{\theta_2}\alpha_{2,D}$, it follows that:

$$E\big[\theta_1 \mid X, Z, V_D \geqslant -\mu_D(X, Z)\big] = \frac{\sigma^2_{\theta_1}\alpha_{1,D}}{\sigma^2_{V_D}} E\big[V_D \mid X, Z, V_D \geqslant -\mu_D(X, Z)\big],$$

$$E\big[\theta_2 \mid X, Z, V_D \geqslant -\mu_D(X, Z)\big] = \frac{\sigma^2_{\theta_2}\alpha_{2,D}}{\sigma^2_{V_D}} E\big[V_D \mid X, Z, V_D \geqslant -\mu_D(X, Z)\big].$$

From the standard normal selection formulae presented in Appendix C of Chapter 70,

$$E\big(Y_{1,t} \mid X, Z, V_D \geqslant -\mu_D(X, Z)\big) = \mu_{1,t}(X) + \pi_{1,t}\frac{\phi\big(\frac{\mu_D(X,Z)}{\sigma_{V_D}}\big)}{\Phi\big(\frac{\mu_D(X,Z)}{\sigma_{V_D}}\big)}, \tag{2.27}$$

where ϕ is the density, Φ is the cdf of the unit normal, and

$$\pi_{1,t} = \frac{\text{Cov}(U_{1,t}, V_D)}{(\text{Var}(V_D))^{\frac{1}{2}}} = \frac{\alpha_{1,D}\,\alpha_{1,1,t}\,\sigma^2_{\theta_1} + \alpha_{2,D}\,\alpha_{2,1,t}\,\sigma^2_{\theta_2}}{\sigma_{V_D}}.$$

Following the same steps, we can derive a similar expression for mean observed earnings in sector "0":

$$E\big(Y_{0,t} \mid X, Z, V_D < -\mu_D(X, Z)\big) = \mu_{0,t}(X) - \pi_{0,t}\frac{\phi\big(\frac{\mu_D(X,Z)}{\sigma_{V_D}}\big)}{\Phi\big(-\frac{\mu_D(X,Z)}{\sigma_{V_D}}\big)}.\text{[40]} \tag{2.28}$$

Standard arguments show that we can identify $\mu_{0,t}(X)$, $\mu_{1,t}(X)$, $\pi_{0,t}$, and $\pi_{1,t}$. Given identification of $\beta_{s,t}$ for all s and t, we can construct the differences $Y_{s,t} - \mu_{s,t}(X)$ and compute the covariances:

$$\text{Cov}\big(M_1 - \mu_{M,1}(X), Y_{0,t} - \mu_{0,t}(X)\big) = \alpha_{1,0,t}\sigma^2_{\theta_1}, \tag{2.29}$$

$$\text{Cov}\big(M_1 - \mu_{M,1}(X), Y_{1,t} - \mu_{1,t}(X)\big) = \alpha_{1,1,t}\sigma^2_{\theta_1}. \tag{2.30}$$

The left-hand sides of (2.29) and (2.30) are identified from sample moments. The right-hand sides are implied by the factor model and the assumption that the measurements depend only on factor 1. We determined $\sigma^2_{\theta_1}$ from the analysis of the test scores. From Equations (2.29) and (2.30) we can recover $\alpha_{1,0,t}$ and $\alpha_{1,1,t}$ for all t. Note that we can also identify the $\frac{\alpha_{1,C}}{\sigma_{V_D}}$ by computing the covariance:

$$\text{Cov}\left(M_1 - \mu_{M,1}(X), \frac{D^* - \mu_D(X, Z)}{\sigma_{V_D}}\right)$$
$$= \frac{\sum_{t=1}^{\bar{T}}(\frac{1}{1+r})^{t-1}(\alpha_{1,1,t} - \alpha_{1,0,t}) - \alpha_{1,C}}{\sigma_{V_D}}\sigma^2_{\theta_1}. \tag{2.31}$$

[40] $\pi_{0,t} = (\alpha_{1,D}\alpha_{1,0,t}\sigma^2_{\theta_1} + \alpha_{2,D}\alpha_{2,0,t}\sigma^2_{\theta_2})/\sigma_{V_D}$.

Using (2.29) and (2.30), we can identify $\alpha_{1,1,t}$ and $\alpha_{1,0,t}$ for all t. The only remaining term to be identified is the ratio $\frac{\alpha_{1,C}}{\sigma_{V_D}}$, which we can obtain from the covariance equation (2.31).

With enough panel data on outcomes, we can also identify the parameters related to factor θ_2, such as $\alpha_{2,s,t}$ and $\sigma^2_{\theta_2}$. To see this, first normalize $\alpha_{2,0,1} = 1$ and compute the covariances:

$$\operatorname{Cov}\big(Y_{0,1} - \mu_{0,1}(X), Y_{0,2} - \mu_{0,2}(X)\big) - \alpha_{1,0,1}\alpha_{1,0,2}\sigma^2_{\theta_1} = \alpha_{2,0,2}\sigma^2_{\theta_2}, \tag{2.32}$$

$$\begin{aligned}
&\operatorname{Cov}\left(Y_{0,1} - \mu_{0,1}(X), \frac{D^* - \mu_D(X,Z)}{\sigma_{V_D}}\right) \\
&\quad - \frac{\alpha_{1,0,1}\sigma^2_{\theta_1}\sum_{t=1}^{\bar{T}}((\frac{1}{1+r})^{t-1}(\alpha_{1,1,t} - \alpha_{1,0,t}) - \alpha_{1,C})}{\sigma_{V_D}} \\
&\quad = \frac{\sigma^2_{\theta_2}\sum_{t=1}^{\bar{T}}((\frac{1}{1+r})^{t-1}(\alpha_{2,1,t} - \alpha_{2,0,t}) - \alpha_{2,C})}{\sigma_{V_D}},
\end{aligned} \tag{2.33}$$

$$\begin{aligned}
&\operatorname{Cov}\left(Y_{0,2} - \mu_{0,2}(X), \frac{D^* - \mu_D(X,Z)}{\sigma_{V_D}}\right) \\
&\quad - \frac{\alpha_{1,0,2}\sigma^2_{\theta_1}\sum_{t=1}^{\bar{T}}((\frac{1}{1+r})^{t-1}(\alpha_{1,1,t} - \alpha_{1,0,t}) - \alpha_{1,C})}{\sigma_{V_D}} \\
&\quad = \frac{\alpha_{2,0,2}\sigma^2_{\theta_2}\sum_{t=1}^{\bar{T}}((\frac{1}{1+r})^{t-1}(\alpha_{2,1,t} - \alpha_{2,0,t}) - \alpha_{2,C})}{\sigma_{V_D}}.
\end{aligned} \tag{2.34}$$

The left-hand sides of (2.32), (2.33), and (2.34) are identified from sample moments. If we compute the ratio of (2.34) to (2.33) we can recover $\alpha_{2,0,2}$. From (2.32), we can recover $\sigma^2_{\theta_2}$. From the covariances from the earnings associated with $s = 1$,

$$\operatorname{Cov}\big(Y_{1,1} - \mu_{1,1}(X), Y_{1,2} - \mu_{1,2}(X)\big) - \alpha_{1,1,1}\alpha_{1,1,2}\sigma^2_{\theta_1} = \alpha_{2,1,1}\alpha_{2,1,2}\sigma^2_{\theta_2}, \tag{2.35}$$

$$\begin{aligned}
&\operatorname{Cov}\left(Y_{1,1} - \mu_{1,1}(X), \frac{D^* - \mu_D(X,Z)}{\sigma_{V_D}}\right) \\
&\quad - \frac{\alpha_{1,1,1}\sigma^2_{\theta_1}\sum_{t=1}^{\bar{T}}((\frac{1}{1+r})^{t-1}(\alpha_{1,1,t} - \alpha_{1,0,t}) - \alpha_{1,C})}{\sigma_{V_D}} \\
&\quad = \frac{\alpha_{2,1,1}\sigma^2_{\theta_2}\sum_{t=1}^{\bar{T}}((\frac{1}{1+r})^{t-1}(\alpha_{2,1,t} - \alpha_{2,0,t}) - \alpha_{2,C})}{\sigma_{V_D}},
\end{aligned} \tag{2.36}$$

$$\begin{aligned}
&\operatorname{Cov}\left(Y_{1,2}-\mu_{1,2}(X), \frac{D^*-\mu_D(X,Z)}{\sigma_{V_D}}\right) \\
&\quad - \frac{\alpha_{1,1,2}\sigma^2_{\theta_1}\sum_{t=1}^{\bar{T}}((\frac{1}{1+r})^{t-1}(\alpha_{1,1,t}-\alpha_{1,0,t})-\alpha_{1,C})}{\sigma_{V_D}} \\
&= \frac{\alpha_{2,1,2}\sigma^2_{\theta_2}\sum_{t=1}^{\bar{T}}((\frac{1}{1+r})^{t-1}(\alpha_{2,1,t}-\alpha_{2,0,t})-\alpha_{2,C})}{\sigma_{V_D}}.
\end{aligned} \tag{2.37}$$

Taking the ratios of (2.37) to (2.35) and (2.36) to (2.35) and assuming nonzero denominators, we obtain $\alpha_{2,1,2}$ and $\alpha_{2,1,1}$ respectively. Finally, we use the information in $\operatorname{Var}(Y_{0,t} \mid X, Z, D = 0)$ and $\operatorname{Var}(Y_{1,t} \mid X, Z, D = 1)$ to compute $\sigma^2_{\varepsilon_{0,t}}$ and $\sigma^2_{\varepsilon_{1,t}}$, respectively. Thus we can identify all of the elements that characterize the joint distribution as specified in (2.21) and can construct the counterfactual joint distributions. Using the factor loadings identified within each treatment group, we can form the covariance (2.22) and identify the joint distribution of $(Y_{0,1}, \ldots, Y_{0,\bar{T}}, Y_{1,1}, \ldots, Y_{1,\bar{T}})$, and, in a similar fashion, the joint distribution of $(Y_{0,1}, \ldots, Y_{0,\bar{T}}, Y_{1,1}, \ldots, Y_{1,\bar{T}}, D^*)$.

Our use of normality in this example is merely for expositional convenience. As established in Section 2.7.3 and in Section 2.8, all we require is the factor structure assumption (2.6). We can nonparametrically identify all means and distributions of unobservables as a consequence of Theorem 2. The covariances are a by-product of a general nonparametric identification analysis. We next consider two applications of the method. In the context of an analysis of college choice and earnings, they show examples of how to use panel data to identify agent information sets, regret, intrinsic uncertainty and *ex ante* and *ex post* distributions, and the psychic costs facing agents at the time they make their schooling decisions.

2.10. Two empirical studies

This subsection presents two applications of the factor methodology exposited in this section. We draw on work by Cunha and Heckman (2007b, 2008). The computational algorithms used to compute the estimates are described in Carneiro, Hansen and Heckman (2003), Cunha, Heckman and Navarro (2005, 2006) and Cunha and Heckman (2007b, 2008). Geweke and Keane (2001) present relevant background on the Bayesian computational methods used to produce the estimates reported here.

Using data from the National Longitudinal Sample of Youth (NLSY79) on lifetime earnings, ability and college choices for white males, Cunha and Heckman (2007b) estimate a six-factor model ($K = 6$). The θ are assumed to be mutually independent. Agents are assumed to know ε_C, the coefficients of the factors and the regression coefficients, but not the ε's in the earnings equation. They can update their expectation of θ after choices are made, as in the normal model presented in the preceding section. The θ are estimated as mixtures of normals and there is strong evidence that most of the components are nonnormal. Using the Sims testing procedure described in Section 2.9, Cunha and Heckman conclude that three factors $(\theta_1, \theta_2, \theta_3)$ are in agents' information sets at the age college going decisions are made.

Table 4
Ex ante conditional distributions for the NLSY79 (college earnings Y_1 conditional on high school earnings Y_0)

High school	College									
	1	2	3	4	5	6	7	8	9	10
1	0.2995	0.1685	0.1114	0.0789	0.0570	0.0413	0.0393	0.0431	0.0471	0.1137
2	0.2273	0.2119	0.1597	0.1271	0.0907	0.0678	0.0450	0.0288	0.0180	0.0236
3	0.1532	0.1840	0.1656	0.1472	0.1146	0.0914	0.0642	0.0434	0.0230	0.0132
4	0.1110	0.1368	0.1492	0.1474	0.1418	0.1184	0.0882	0.0588	0.0334	0.0148
5	0.0748	0.1100	0.1244	0.1413	0.1459	0.1403	0.1172	0.0836	0.0462	0.0162
6	0.0494	0.0866	0.1146	0.1204	0.1371	0.1399	0.1283	0.1242	0.0736	0.0258
7	0.0306	0.0582	0.0904	0.1094	0.1264	0.1436	0.1506	0.1430	0.1064	0.0414
8	0.0236	0.0348	0.0531	0.0769	0.0989	0.1252	0.1638	0.1799	0.1676	0.0761
9	0.0264	0.0262	0.0316	0.0459	0.0651	0.0929	0.1308	0.1784	0.2431	0.1594
10	0.0457	0.0182	0.0214	0.0216	0.0321	0.0446	0.0772	0.1176	0.2291	0.3925

Notes: $\Pr(d_i < Y_1 < d_{i+1} \mid d_j < Y_0 < d_{j+1}, \mathcal{I})$ where d_i is the ith decile of the college lifetime *ex ante* earnings distribution and d_j is the jth decile of the high school *ex ante* lifetime earnings distribution. The agent fixes unknown θ at their means. The information set includes $\{\theta_1, \theta_2, \theta_3\}$. Correlation $(Y_1, Y_0) = 0.1666$.
Source: Cunha and Heckman (2007b).

Table 4 presents the estimated *ex ante* conditional distributions of the college earnings conditional on high school earnings in the overall population. They show a mild positive correlation that is far from the perfect dependence across potential outcomes assumed by the rank invariance approaches discussed in Section 2.5. Table 5 shows the *ex post* joint distribution of college earnings after all components of θ and the ε are realized.[41] The dependence across potential outcomes in the *ex post* distribution is stronger than that in the *ex ante* distribution.

Table 6 documents that there are substantial unpredictable components in college Y_1, high school Y_0 and the returns $(Y_1 - Y_0)$ distributions after conditioning on X, Z at the time agents make their schooling decisions. Figures 1–3 plot the distributions of total residual and unforecastable components of $Y_1 - Y_0$, Y_1 and Y_0, respectively, where forecasts are measured from the date college decisions are made (age 17). There are substantial components of uncertainty that are distinct from variability observed in the data. *Ex post*, many agents regret their choices (see Table 7). Only 3.1% of those who attend college regret that decision, while 7.5% of those who do not proceed beyond high school regret not attending college.[42]

[41] It assumes that, *ex post*, agents perfectly observe all potential outcome streams. More realistically, agents would only know one stream or the other.

[42] This calculation is for a stationary environment and ignores the secular growth in the mean earning gap between college and high school graduates that is documented by Katz and Autor (1999). Accounting for the growth in this gap substantially reduces the regret of those going to college and raises the regret of those who stopped at high school.

Table 5

Ex post conditional distributions for the NLSY79 (college earnings Y_1 conditional on high school earnings Y_0)

High school	College									
	1	2	3	4	5	6	7	8	9	10
1	0.2118	0.1614	0.1188	0.0932	0.0782	0.0654	0.0532	0.0554	0.0651	0.0974
2	0.1684	0.1777	0.1557	0.1213	0.1038	0.0862	0.0640	0.0516	0.0417	0.0296
3	0.1374	0.1676	0.1464	0.1390	0.1244	0.0954	0.0754	0.0577	0.0333	0.0234
4	0.1080	0.1336	0.1433	0.1378	0.1213	0.1115	0.0980	0.0746	0.0475	0.0243
5	0.0787	0.1105	0.1232	0.1335	0.1345	0.1291	0.1144	0.0862	0.0614	0.0286
6	0.0656	0.1028	0.1149	0.1201	0.1276	0.1330	0.1250	0.0998	0.0823	0.0288
7	0.0548	0.0779	0.0842	0.1097	0.1196	0.1224	0.1410	0.1331	0.1132	0.0441
8	0.0428	0.0507	0.0741	0.0880	0.0994	0.1224	0.1410	0.1585	0.1539	0.0693
9	0.0416	0.0436	0.0474	0.0577	0.0803	0.1001	0.1277	0.1728	0.1939	0.1348
10	0.0386	0.0204	0.0269	0.0292	0.0339	0.0520	0.0704	0.1155	0.1945	0.4186

Notes: $\Pr(d_i < Y_1 < d_{i+1} \mid d_j < Y_0 < d_{j+1}, \mathcal{I})$ where d_i is the ith decile of the college lifetime *ex post* earnings distribution and d_j is the jth decile of the high school *ex post* lifetime earnings distribution. Individual fixes unknown θ at their means. The information set includes $\{\theta_1, \theta_2, \theta_3, \theta_4, \theta_5, \theta_6\}$. Correlation $(Y_1, Y_0) = 0.2842$.

Source: Cunha and Heckman (2007b).

Table 6

Uncertainty at age 17 about future returns

	College	High school	Returns
Total residual variance*	709.7487	507.2910	906.0066
Variance of unforecastable components*	372.3509	272.3596	432.8733

Source: Cunha and Heckman (2007b).

*After conditioning on X, Z.

Table 7

Percentage that regret schooling choices

Percentage of high school graduates who regret not graduating from college	0.0749
Percentage of college graduates who regret graduating from college	0.0311

Notes: *Ex post* people know their "luck" components (i.e., the uncertain $\varepsilon_{s,t}$ for each schooling group s for all ages t on their earnings equations) when making their schooling decisions. These calculations are for a stationary environment and ignore the growth in the mean of college distribution experienced in recent decades.

Source: Cunha and Heckman (2007b).

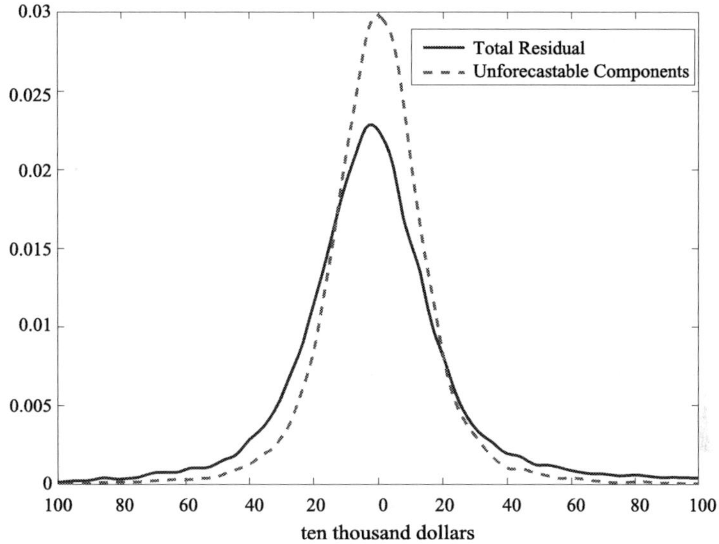

Figure 1. The densities of total residual vs. unforecastable components. Returns to college vs. high school (NLSY79). In this figure, we plot the density of the total residual (the solid curve) against the density of unforecastable components (the dashed curve) for the present value of returns to college from ages 22 to 41. The present value of returns to college is calculated using a 5% interest rate.
Source: Cunha and Heckman (2007b).

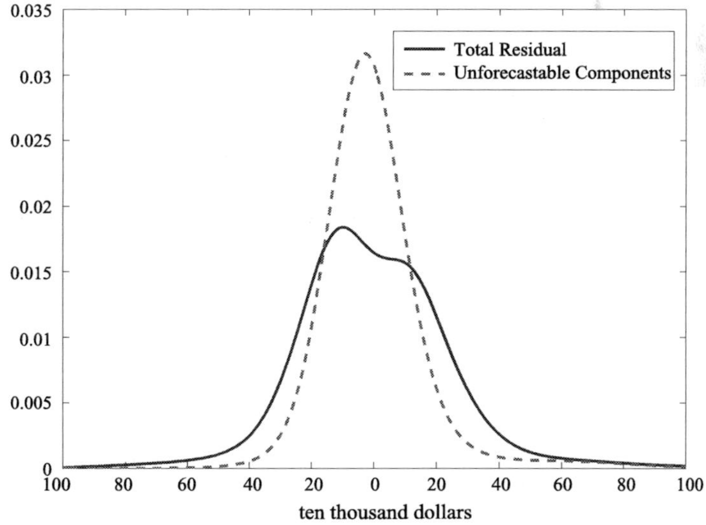

Figure 2. The densities of total residual vs. unforecastable components in present value of high school earnings. In this figure, we plot the density of the total residual (the solid curve) against the density of unforecastable components (the dashed curve) for the present value of high school earnings from ages 22 to 41. The present value of earnings is calculated using a 5% interest rate. *Source*: Cunha and Heckman (2007b).

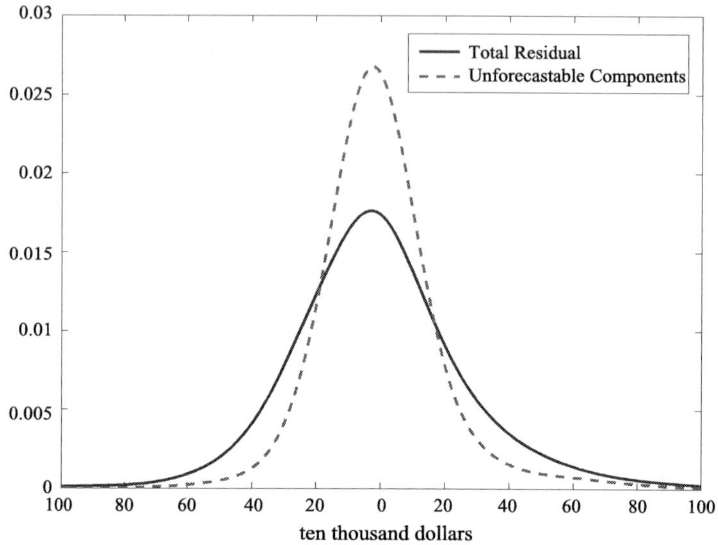

Figure 3. The densities of total residual vs. unforecastable components in present value of college earnings. In this figure, we plot the density of the total residual (the solid curve) against the density of unforecastable components (the dashed curve) for the present value of college earnings from ages 22 to 41. The present value of earnings is calculated using a 5% interest rate. *Source*: Cunha and Heckman (2007b).

Selection on the first three factors is illustrated in Figures 4–6. Factor one is associated with ability as measured by a test score (θ_1 in the examples of the previous sections). The factors sort on the basis of schooling choices. Cunha and Heckman (2007b) show that accounting for nonnormality of the factors is empirically important.

Table 8 presents the selection-corrected mean rates of return to 4 years of college. It is close to 10% for college goers, 8.25% for those who choose to stop their education at high school and 8.75% for those who are at the margin of indifference between attending high school and going to college. Matching assumption (M-1), which requires that average returns equal marginal returns, is not supported by these estimates. For further details on these estimates, see Cunha and Heckman (2007b).

To show the possibilities for a more nuanced approach to policy evaluation that is possible, we draw on a second, earlier, paper by Cunha and Heckman (2008). While this research is superceded by the richer empirical analysis in Cunha and Heckman (2007b), it illustrates the potential of the method exposited in this chapter.[43] They estimate a

[43] Cunha and Heckman (2007b) use many more periods of panel data, have many more measurements and estimate a six-factor model. Cunha and Heckman (2008) use many fewer periods, have a lower dimension $L(s)$ in the notation of condition (2.9) and determine that $K = 2$ fits the data they analyze.

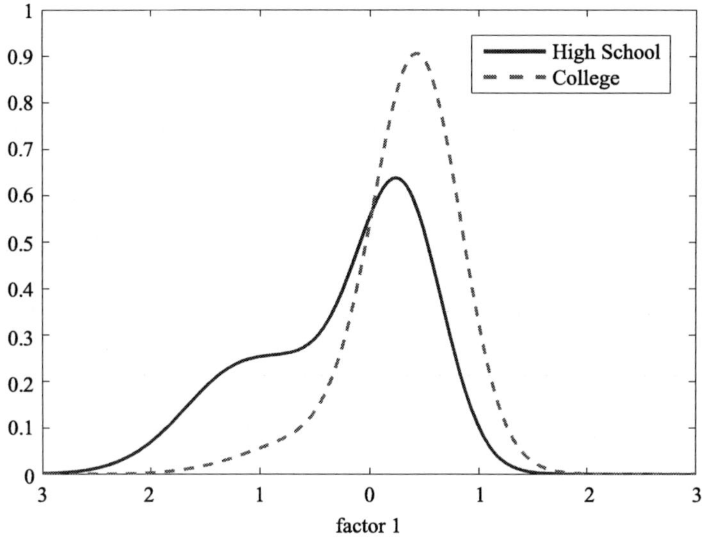

Figure 4. Densities of factor 1 by schooling level (NLSY79). The solid line plots the density of the factor for high school graduates. The dashed line plots the density of the factor for college graduates. *Source*: Cunha and Heckman (2007b).

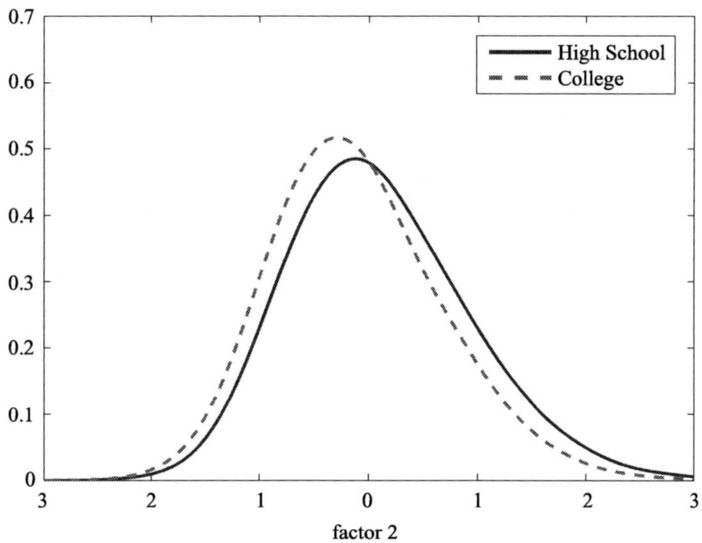

Figure 5. Densities of factor 2 by schooling level (NLSY79). The solid line plots the density of the factor for high school graduates. The dashed line plots the density of the factor for college graduates. *Source*: Cunha and Heckman (2007b).

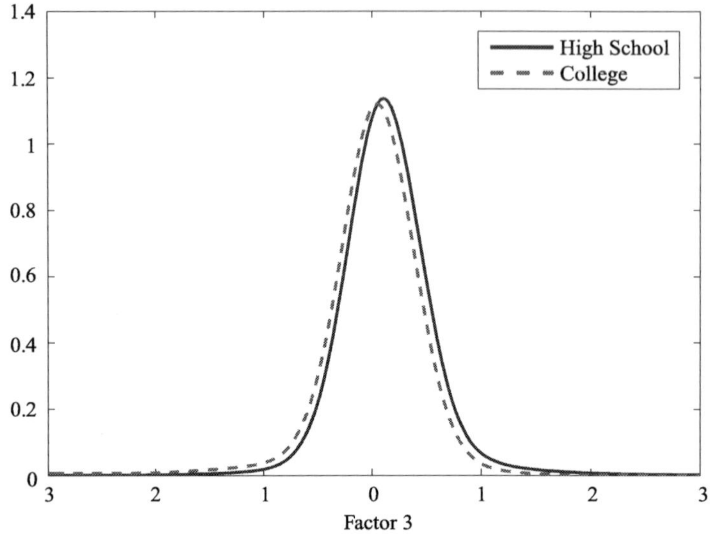

Figure 6. Densities of factor 3 by schooling level (NLSY79). The solid line plots the density of the factor for high school graduates. The dashed line plots the density of the factor for college graduates. *Source*: Cunha and Heckman (2007b).

Table 8
Mean rates of return to college by schooling group (NLSY79)

Schooling group	Mean returns	Standard error
High school graduates	0.3095	0.0113
College graduates	0.3994	0.0129
Individuals at the margin	0.3511	0.0535

Source: Cunha and Heckman (2007b).

two-factor model. Figures 7 and 8 plot the densities of the present value of earnings and the associated counterfactual distribution for college graduates ($D = 1$, Figure 7) and high school graduates ($D = 0$, Figure 8). Gross rates of return ($\frac{Y_1 - Y_0}{Y_0}$) are plotted in Figure 9 for both high school and college graduates.

The overlap in the factual and counterfactual distributions for each schooling level is substantial. The returns to college for high school graduates are substantial. One reason why such large monetary returns to college are not realized is shown in Figure 10 which plots the psychic costs (C) of attending college. Confirming earlier findings by Carneiro, Hansen and Heckman (2003) and Cunha, Heckman and Navarro (2005), there are substantial psychic costs of attending school for the high school graduates (see Figure 10).

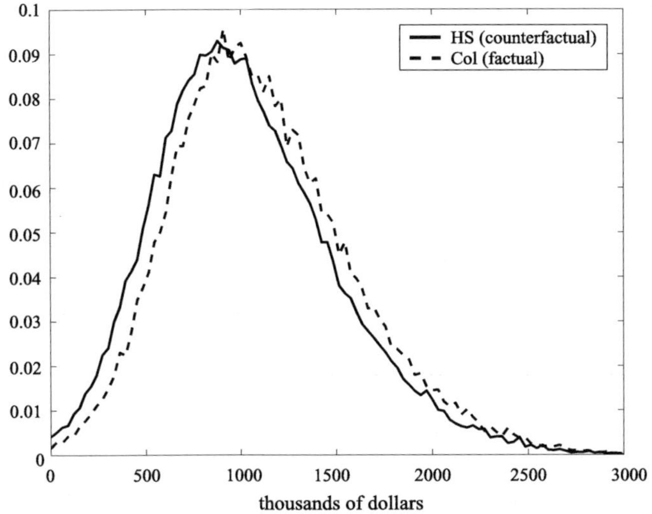

Figure 7. Density of present value of earnings in the college sector. Let Y_1 denote present value of earnings (discounted at a 3% interest rate) in the college sector. Let $f_1(y_1)$ denote its density function. The dashed line plots the predicted Y_1 density conditioned on choosing college, that is, $f_1(y_1 \mid D = 1)$, while the solid line shows the counterfactual density function of Y_0 for those agents that are actually college graduates, that is, $f_0(y_0 \mid D = 1)$. *Source*: Cunha and Heckman (2008).

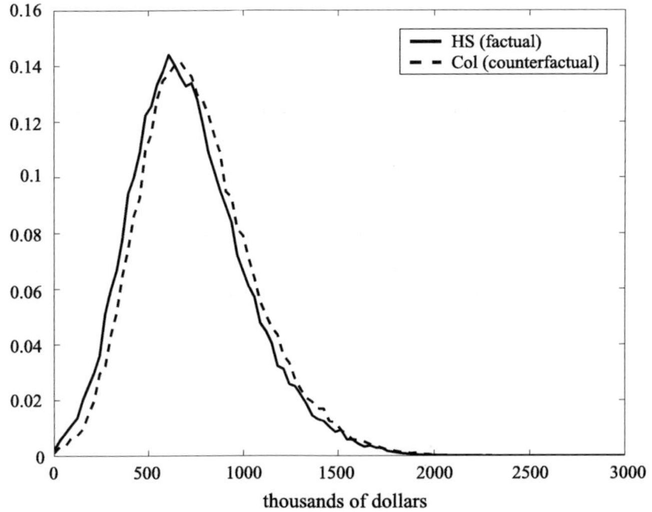

Figure 8. Density of present value of earnings in the high school sector. Let Y_0 denote present value of earnings (discounted at a 3% interest rate) in the high school sector. Let $f_0(y_0)$ denote its density function. The solid curve plots the predicted Y_0 density conditioned on choosing high school, that is, $f_0(y_0 \mid D = 0)$, while the dashed line shows the counterfactual density function of Y_1 for those agents that are high-school graduates, that is, $f_1(y_1 \mid D = 0)$. *Source*: Cunha and Heckman (2008).

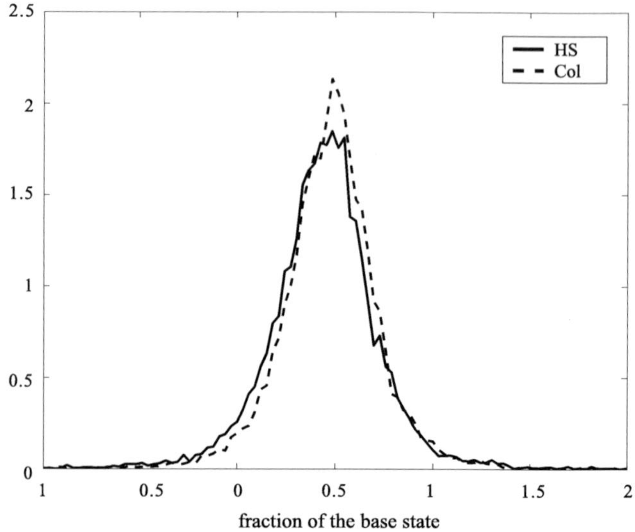

Figure 9. Density of *ex post* returns to college by schooling level chosen. Let Y_0, Y_1 denote the present value of earnings in high school and college sectors, respectively. Define *ex post* returns to college as the ratio $R = (Y_1 - Y_0)/Y_0$. Let $f(r)$ denote the density function of random variable R. The solid line is the density of *ex post* returns to college for high school graduates, that is, $f(r \mid D = 0)$. The dashed line is the density of *ex post* returns to college for college graduates, that is, $f(r \mid D = 1)$. *Source*: Cunha and Heckman (2008).

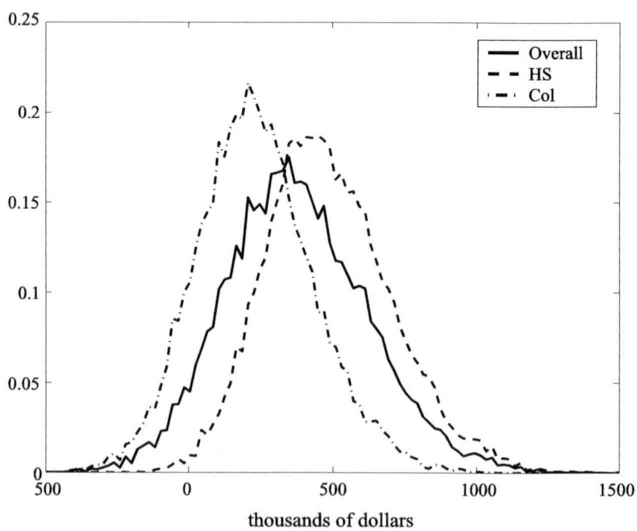

Figure 10. Density of monetary value of psychic cost both overall and by schooling level. In this figure we plot the monetary value of psychic costs, which we denote by C. It is defined as: $C = Z\gamma + \theta_1\alpha_{1,C} + \theta_2\alpha_{2,C} + \varepsilon_C$. The contribution of ability to the costs of attending college, in monetary value, is $\theta_1\alpha_{1,C}$. *Source*: Cunha and Heckman (2008).

A comparison of Figures 9 and 10 is revealing. There are small differences in objective returns to college between those who go to college and those who do not. However, the subjective returns (inclusive of psychic costs) are substantially different. This evidence of large subjective costs highlights the value of the econometric approach to the evaluation of social programs, and the importance of the distinction between objective and subjective outcomes in interpreting choices and outcomes.

As an example of the power of these methods to evaluate the consequences of policy on income inequality, Cunha and Heckman (2008) analyze a cross-subsidized tuition policy indexed by family income level. The traditional approach to policy evaluation compares overall income distributions before and after a policy change is implemented. Although this approach can be justified by certain axiomatic approaches [see, e.g., Foster and Sen (1997), and Cowell (2000)], it does not present a very accurate summary of the true distributional consequences of policies.

Cunha and Heckman (2008) construct joint distributions of outcomes within policy regimes (treatment and no treatment or schooling and no schooling) and joint distributions of outcomes ($Y = DY_1 + (1 - D)Y_0$) across policy regimes. The policy they analyze is as follows. A prospective student whose family income at age 17 is below the mean is allowed to attend college free of charge. The policy is self financing within each schooling cohort. To pay for this policy, persons attending college with family income above the mean pay a tuition charge equal to the amount required to cover the costs of the students from lower income families as well as their own.

Total tuition raised covers the cost Q of educating each student. Thus if there are N_P poor students and N_R rich students, total costs are $(N_P + N_R)Q$. For the proposed policy, the poor pay nothing. So each rich person is charged a tuition

$$T = Q\left(1 + \frac{N_P}{N_R}\right).$$

To determine T, notice that there is a unique tuition level T such that

$$T = Q\left(1 + \frac{N_P(T)}{N_R(T)}\right),$$

with $N_P(T)$ and $N_R(T)$ the numbers of poor and rich people attending college if the rich pay a fee T. They iterate to find the unique self-financing T. Notice that $N_P(T)$, the number of poor people who attend college when tuition is zero, is the same for all values of T ($N_P(T) = N_P(0)$ for all T). N_R is sensitive to the tuition level charged.

Figure 11 shows that the marginal distributions of overall income in both the pre-policy state and the post-policy state are essentially identical. Under the standard anonymity postulate used to evaluate income distributions [see Foster and Sen (1997), and Cowell (2000)], we would judge these two situations as equally good using Lorenz measures or second order stochastic dominance. Cunha and Heckman (2008) move beyond anonymity and analyze the effect that the policy has on what Fields (2003) calls "positional" mobility.

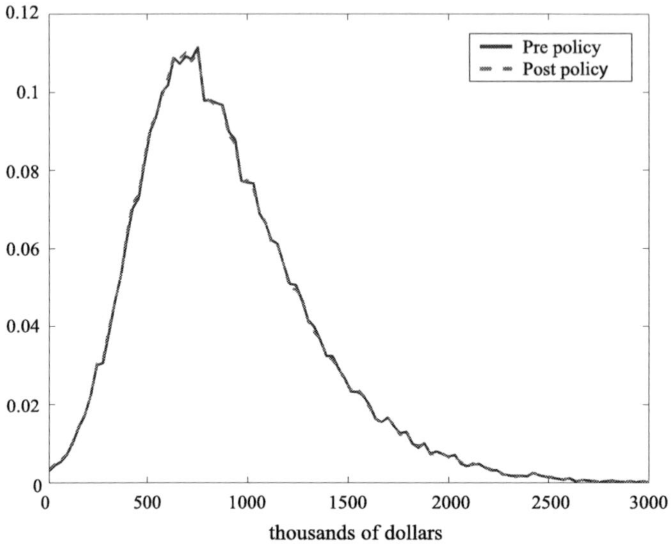

Figure 11. Density of present value of lifetime earnings before and after implementing cross-subsidy policy. Let Y^A, Y^B denote the observed present value of earnings pre and post policy, respectively. Define $f(y^A)$, $g(y^B)$ as the marginal densities of present value of earnings pre and post policy. In this figure, we plot $f(y^A)$, $g(y^B)$. *Source*: Cunha and Heckman (2007a).

Panel 1 of Table 9 presents this analysis by describing how the 9.2% of the people who are affected by the policy move between deciles of the distribution of income. These statistics describe movements from one income distribution in the initial regime to another income distribution associated with the new regime. The policy affects more people at the top deciles than at the lower deciles. Around half of the people affected who start at the first decile remain at the first decile. People in the middle deciles are spread both up and down and a large proportion of people in the upper deciles is moved into a lower position (only sixteen percent of those starting on the top decile (the first) remain there after the policy is implemented). Moving beyond the anonymity postulate (which instructs us to examine only marginal distributions), we learn much more about the effects of the policy on different groups by looking at joint distributions.

Thus far, we have focused on constructing and interpreting the joint distribution of outcomes across the two policy regimes. If outcomes under both regimes are observed, these comparisons could be made using panel data. No use of econometric analysis would be necessary. However, the methods discussed by Cunha and Heckman (2007b) will apply if either or both policy regimes are unobserved but are proposed. Taking advantage of the fact that we can identify not only joint distributions of earnings over policy regimes but also over counterfactual states within regimes we can learn a great

Table 9
Mobility of people affected by cross-subsidizing tuition

Fraction by decile of origin	Deciles of origin	Probability of moving to a different decile of the lifetime earnings distribution 1	2	3	4	5	6	7	8	9	10
Panel 1											
Overall. Fraction of total population who switch schooling levels: 0.0923											
0.0730	1	0.5680	0.2052	0.1245	0.0647	0.0288	0.0076	0.0012	0.0000	0.0000	0.0000
0.0869	2	0.2079	0.1712	0.1715	0.1690	0.1585	0.0870	0.0322	0.0025	0.0002	0.0000
0.0957	3	0.1148	0.1489	0.0935	0.1137	0.1573	0.1888	0.1387	0.0409	0.0034	0.0000
0.1001	4	0.0619	0.1557	0.0910	0.0534	0.0764	0.1615	0.2084	0.1557	0.0360	0.0000
0.1035	5	0.0296	0.1495	0.1387	0.0630	0.0304	0.0571	0.1411	0.2456	0.1396	0.0055
0.1053	6	0.0066	0.0959	0.1726	0.1471	0.0520	0.0142	0.0415	0.1671	0.2605	0.0425
0.1087	7	0.0006	0.0336	0.1411	0.1956	0.1269	0.0420	0.0082	0.0348	0.2346	0.1827
0.1092	8	0.0000	0.0046	0.0519	0.1765	0.2211	0.1495	0.0388	0.0034	0.0513	0.3029
0.1104	9	0.0000	0.0000	0.0055	0.0421	0.1570	0.2733	0.2302	0.0447	0.0014	0.2459
0.1071	10	0.0000	0.0000	0.0000	0.0002	0.0041	0.0517	0.2082	0.3242	0.2490	0.1626
Panel 2											
High school. Fraction of total population who switch from high school to college due to the policy: 0.0450											
0.1014	1	0.4049	0.2618	0.1817	0.0958	0.0427	0.0112	0.0018	0.0000	0.0000	0.0000
0.1282	2	0.0382	0.1220	0.2176	0.2325	0.2200	0.1210	0.0448	0.0035	0.0003	0.0000
0.1372	3	0.0023	0.0188	0.0692	0.1536	0.2244	0.2701	0.1984	0.0584	0.0049	0.0000
0.1370	4	0.0000	0.0016	0.0088	0.0368	0.1116	0.2417	0.3123	0.2332	0.0540	0.0000
0.1288	5	0.0000	0.0000	0.0007	0.0052	0.0277	0.0903	0.2324	0.4047	0.2300	0.0090
0.1125	6	0.0000	0.0000	0.0000	0.0004	0.0024	0.0151	0.0792	0.3209	0.5004	0.0816
0.1019	7	0.0000	0.0000	0.0000	0.0000	0.0000	0.0009	0.0101	0.0761	0.5133	0.3997
0.0798	8	0.0000	0.0000	0.0000	0.0000	0.0000	0.0000	0.0000	0.0067	0.1440	0.8493
0.0559	9	0.0000	0.0000	0.0000	0.0000	0.0000	0.0000	0.0000	0.0000	0.0032	0.9968
0.0173	10	0.0000	0.0000	0.0000	0.0000	0.0000	0.0000	0.0000	0.0000	0.0000	1.0000
Panel 3											
College. Fraction of total population who switch from college to high school due to the policy: 0.0473											
0.0460	1	0.9066	0.0878	0.0056	0.0000	0.0000	0.0000	0.0000	0.0000	0.0000	0.0000
0.0477	2	0.6423	0.2972	0.0534	0.0062	0.0009	0.0000	0.0000	0.0000	0.0000	0.0000
0.0562	3	0.3763	0.4510	0.1501	0.0211	0.0015	0.0000	0.0000	0.0000	0.0000	0.0000
0.0649	4	0.1860	0.4648	0.2559	0.0868	0.0059	0.0007	0.0000	0.0000	0.0000	0.0000
0.0794	5	0.0753	0.3801	0.3518	0.1522	0.0347	0.0059	0.0000	0.0000	0.0000	0.0000
0.0985	6	0.0138	0.2001	0.3602	0.3064	0.1059	0.0133	0.0004	0.0000	0.0000	0.0000
0.1152	7	0.0011	0.0618	0.2598	0.3603	0.2337	0.0766	0.0066	0.0000	0.0000	0.0000
0.1371	8	0.0000	0.0071	0.0807	0.2744	0.3436	0.2323	0.0603	0.0015	0.0000	0.0000
0.1623	9	0.0000	0.0000	0.0073	0.0559	0.2084	0.3628	0.3056	0.0593	0.0008	0.0000
0.1926	10	0.0000	0.0000	0.0000	0.0002	0.0044	0.0561	0.2260	0.3519	0.2702	0.0911

Notes: Cross subsidy consists in making tuition zero for people with family income below average and making the budget balance by raising tuition for college students with family income above the average. For example, we read from the first panel row 1, column 1 that 7.3% of the people who switch schooling levels come from the lowest decile. Out of those, 56.8% are still in the first decile after the policy while 2.88% jump to the fifth decile. Panel 2 has the same interpretation but it only looks at people who switch from high school to college while panel 3 looks at individuals who switch from college to high school.
Source: Cunha and Heckman (2008).

Table 10
Mobility of people affected by cross-subsidizing tuition (extracted from Table 9)

Fraction of the total population who switch schooling levels: 0.0923
Pre-policy choice

	Fraction of high school graduates	
	Do not switch	Become college graduates
High school	0.9197	0.0803
	Fraction of college graduates	
	Do not switch	Become high school graduates
College	0.8923	0.1077

Note: Cross subsidy consists of making tuition zero for people with family income below average and making the budget balance by raising tuition for college students with family income above the average.
Source: Cunha and Heckman (2008).

deal more about the effects of this policy, whether or not policy regimes are observed.[44] In this way, one solves problems P-1, P-2, and P-3 stated in Chapter 70.

Panels 2 and 3 of Table 9 reveal that not only 9.2% of the population is affected by the policy, but that actually about half of them moved from high school into college (4.5% of the population) and half moved from college into high school (4.7% percent of the population). This translates into saying that, of those affected by the policy, 92% of the high school graduates stay in high school in the post-policy regime while only 89% of college graduates stay put. (See Table 10.) Thus the policy is slightly biased against college attendance. We can form the joint distributions of lifetime earnings by initial schooling level. Figure 12 breaks out some of the evidence implicit in Table 9. Panels 2 and 3 of Table 9 show that the policy affects very few high school graduates at the top end of the income distribution (only 1.7% of those affected come from the 10th percentile) and a lot of college graduates in the same situation (19% of college graduates affected come from the top decile). We can also see that the policy tends to move high school graduates up in the income distribution and moves college graduates down.

As another example of the generality of our method and the new insight into income mobility induced by policy that it provides, we can determine where people come from and where they end up at in the counterfactual distributions of earnings. Table 11 shows where in the pre-policy distribution of high school earnings persons induced to go to college come from and where in the post-policy distribution of college earnings they go to. Most people stay in their decile or move to closely adjacent ones. Given that some people benefit from the policy while others lose, it is not clear whether society as a

[44] It is implausible that analysts would have panel data on policy regimes where under one regime a person goes to school and under another he does not.

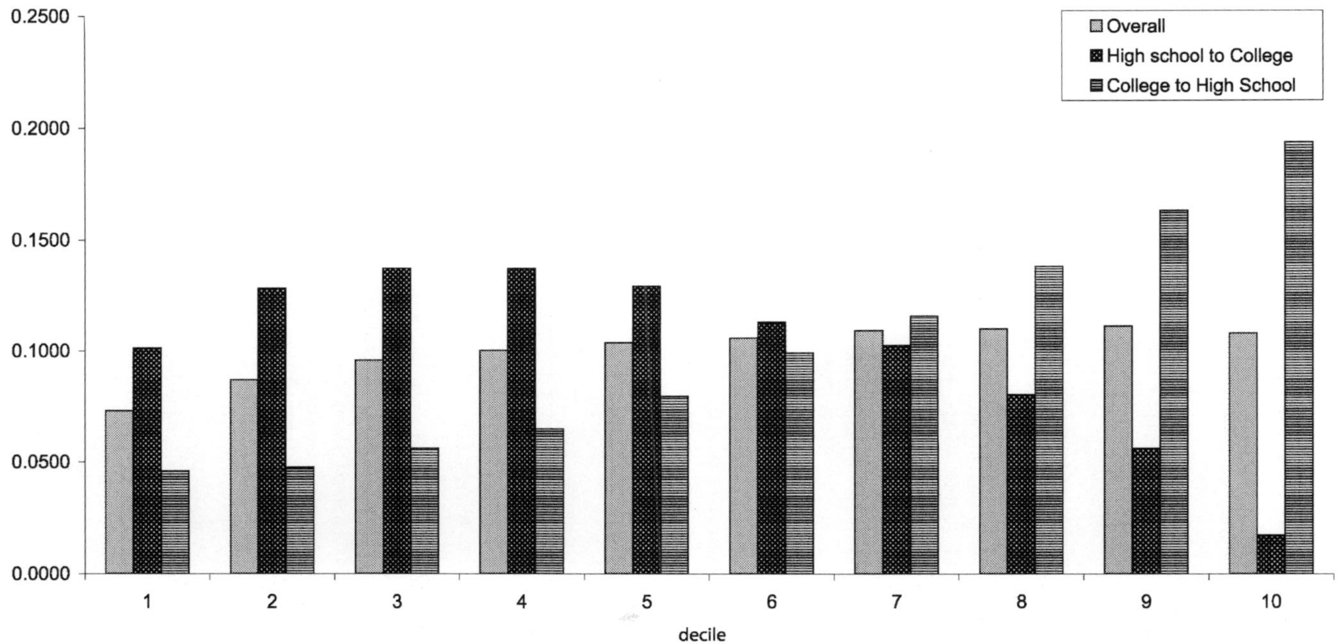

Figure 12. Fraction of people who switch schooling levels when tuition is cross subsidized by decile of origin from the lifetime earnings distribution. Cross subsidy consists in making tuition zero for people with family income below average and making the budget balance by raising tuition for college students with family income above the average. *Source*: Cunha and Heckman (2008).

Table 11

Mobility of people affected by cross-subsidizing tuition across counterfactual distributions

Panel 1

High school. Fraction of total population who switch from high school to college due to the policy: 0.0450

Fraction by decile of origin in the pre-policy high school distribution	Deciles of origin	Probability of moving to a different decile of the post-policy college lifetime earnings distribution									
		1	2	3	4	5	6	7	8	9	10
0.0668	1	0.8563	0.1272	0.0145	0.0021	0.0000	0.0000	0.0000	0.0000	0.0000	0.0000
0.0813	2	0.4046	0.4112	0.1491	0.0296	0.0055	0.0000	0.0000	0.0000	0.0000	0.0000
0.0910	3	0.1488	0.3544	0.3059	0.1419	0.0445	0.0039	0.0005	0.0000	0.0000	0.0000
0.1000	4	0.0401	0.2343	0.3096	0.2490	0.1234	0.0379	0.0053	0.0004	0.0000	0.0000
0.1049	5	0.0089	0.0713	0.2081	0.3053	0.2348	0.1282	0.0365	0.0068	0.0000	0.0000
0.1060	6	0.0004	0.0202	0.0950	0.2155	0.2761	0.2416	0.1273	0.0239	0.0000	0.0000
0.1064	7	0.0000	0.0033	0.0243	0.0896	0.1888	0.3026	0.2662	0.1155	0.0096	0.0000
0.1118	8	0.0000	0.0004	0.0016	0.0159	0.0630	0.1690	0.3220	0.3228	0.1024	0.0028
0.1140	9	0.0000	0.0000	0.0000	0.0016	0.0043	0.0293	0.1227	0.3271	0.4568	0.0582
0.1176	10	0.0000	0.0000	0.0000	0.0000	0.0000	0.0000	0.0027	0.0333	0.2626	0.7014

Panel 2

College. Fraction of total population who switch from college to high school due to the policy: 0.0473

Fraction by decile of origin in the pre-policy college distribution	Deciles of origin	Probability of moving to a different decile of the post-policy high school lifetime earnings distribution									
		1	2	3	4	5	6	7	8	9	10
0.1098	1	0.5505	0.2962	0.1141	0.0318	0.0062	0.0012	0.0000	0.0000	0.0000	0.0000
0.1059	2	0.1076	0.3257	0.2937	0.1789	0.0716	0.0204	0.0016	0.0004	0.0000	0.0000
0.1039	3	0.0180	0.1473	0.2776	0.2657	0.1833	0.0857	0.0200	0.0024	0.0000	0.0000
0.1016	4	0.0004	0.0355	0.1535	0.2349	0.2866	0.1890	0.0847	0.0150	0.0004	0.0000
0.1016	5	0.0000	0.0050	0.0467	0.1503	0.2654	0.2705	0.1903	0.0668	0.0050	0.0000
0.0983	6	0.0000	0.0000	0.0091	0.0513	0.1678	0.2683	0.2972	0.1786	0.0276	0.0000
0.0980	7	0.0000	0.0000	0.0000	0.0087	0.0463	0.1609	0.3071	0.3387	0.1362	0.0022
0.0956	8	0.0000	0.0000	0.0000	0.0004	0.0044	0.0430	0.1560	0.4020	0.3617	0.0324
0.0967	9	0.0000	0.0000	0.0000	0.0000	0.0000	0.0009	0.0127	0.1337	0.5355	0.3173
0.0885	10	0.0000	0.0000	0.0000	0.0000	0.0000	0.0000	0.0000	0.0034	0.0915	0.9051

Notes: Cross subsidy consists in making tuition zero for people with family income below average and making the budget balance by raising tuition for college students with family income above the average. For example, we read from the first panel row 1, column 1 that 6.68% of the people who switch from high school to college come from the lowest decile of the pre-policy high school distribution. Out of those, 85.63% are still in the first decile of the post-policy college earnings distribution after the policy is implemented while 1.45% "jump" to the third decile. Panel 2 has the same interpretation but it only looks at people who switch from college to high school.

Source: Cunha and Heckman (2008).

Table 12
Voting outcome of proposing cross-subsidizing tuition

Fraction of the total population who switch schooling levels: 0.0923	
Average pre-policy lifetime earnings*	920.55
Average post-policy lifetime earnings*	905.96
Fraction of the population who vote	
Yes	0.0716
No	0.6152
Indifferent	0.3132

Note: Cross subsidy consists of making tuition zero for people with family income below average and making the budget balance by raising tuition for college students with family income above the average.
Source: Cunha and Heckman (2008).
*In thousands of dollars.

whole values this policy positively or not. An advantage of examining the joint distribution of outcomes is that it allows us to calculate the effect that the policy has on welfare. An individual's relative utility is not only given by earnings but also by the monetary value of psychic costs. We can predict how people would vote if the policy analyzed in this section were proposed. Table 12 shows the result of such an exercise. The policy lowers the mean earnings for people affected by it. Most people not indifferent to the policy would vote against it.

We next turn to the development of models for the timing of treatment choice. The models that distinguish *ex ante* from *ex post* outcomes discussed in this section of the chapter have an implicit dynamics. Agents make decisions under one information set. That information set is revised in light of subsequent flows of information. The outcomes realized after the choice is made will differ in general from the outcomes that are anticipated. However, in this section, choices are one shot. While this framework advances models that ignore uncertainty, it does not capture the rich dynamics that comes from updating information in real time. We next consider models that analyze the choice of the timing of treatment and the consequences of the choices. Analyses of decisions about the timing of dropping out of school, the timing of initiating or terminating a medical treatment, when to end a period of unemployment, and the consequences of such decisions raise new issues to which we now turn.

3. Dynamic models[45]

We now develop econometric and statistical models for the choice of timing of treatment and the consequences of alternative treatment times on subjective and objective

[45] This section draws in part on Abbring and Heckman (2008) and the papers they cite.

outcomes. The analysis presented in this section extends the analysis of multiple treatments and treatment choices presented in Chapter 71 by explicitly considering dynamics and information updating. We first develop some main ideas in a framework with general dynamic treatments. We subsequently focus on the choice of the timing of a single treatment which may have very different consequences when implemented in different periods. The same treatments administered at different times can be thought of as different treatments. Thus, dropping out of school at grade 11 may have different consequences than dropping out at grade 10. Starting chemotherapy eight months after diagnosis of the onset of cancer may have different consequences than chemotherapy starting after one month. There is a close affinity between econometric models for discrete choice and models for the analysis of the choice of treatment times which is developed in this section.

The plan of this section is as follows. Section 3.1 briefly reviews the policy evaluation problem extensively discussed by Heckman and Vytlacil in Chapter 70 and discusses the treatment-effects approach to policy evaluation. It establishes the notation used in the rest of this section. Section 3.2 reviews an approach to the analysis of dynamic treatment effects developed in statistics based on a sequential randomization assumption that is popular in biostatistics [Robins (1997), Gill and Robins (2001), Lok (2007)] and has been applied in economics [see Fitzenberger, Osikominu and Völter (2006) and Lechner and Miquel (2002)]. This is a dynamic version of matching. We relate the assumptions justifying this approach to the assumptions underlying the econometric dynamic discrete-choice literature based on Rust's (1987) conditional-independence condition which, as discussed in Section 3.4.5 below, is frequently invoked in the structural econometrics literature. We note the limitations of the dynamic matching treatment-effects approach in accounting for dynamic information accumulation. In Sections 3.3 and 3.4, we discuss two econometric approaches for the analysis of treatment times that allow for nontrivial dynamic selection on unobservables. Section 3.3 discusses the continuous-time event-history approach to policy evaluation developed by Abbring and Van den Berg (2003b, 2005) and Abbring (2008). Section 3.4 introduces an approach that builds on and extends the discrete-time dynamic discrete-choice literature. Like the analysis of Abbring and Van den Berg, it does not rely on the conditional-independence assumptions used in dynamic matching. This part of our survey is based on the work of Heckman and Navarro (2007). The approach exposited in this section generalizes the factor model approach exposited in Section 2 to a dynamic setting. The two complementary approaches surveyed in this section span the existing econometric literature on dynamic treatment effects.

3.1. Policy evaluation and treatment effects

3.1.1. The evaluation problem

We review the evaluation problem discussed in Chapter 70 using a succinct notation employed in the analysis of this section. Let Ω be the set of agent types. It is the sample space of a probability space $(\Omega, \mathcal{I}, \mathbb{P})$, and all choices and outcomes are random variables defined on this probability space. Each agent type $\omega \in \Omega$ represents a single agent in a particular state of nature. We could distinguish variation between agents from within-agent randomness by taking $\Omega = J \times \tilde{\Omega}$, with J the set of agents and $\tilde{\Omega}$ the set of possible states of nature. However, we do not make this distinction explicit in this section, and often simply refer to agents instead of agent types.[46]

Consider a policy that targets the allocation of each agent in Ω to a single treatment from a set $\mathcal{S}$. In the most basic binary version, $\mathcal{S} = \{0, 1\}$, where "1" represents "treatment", such as a training program, and "0" some baseline, "control" program. Alternatively, $\mathcal{S}$ could take a continuum of values, e.g., $\mathbb{R}_+ = [0, \infty)$, representing, e.g., unemployment benefit levels, or duration of time in a program.

A policy $p = (a, \tau) \in \mathcal{A} \times \mathcal{T} = \mathcal{P}$ consists of a planner's rule $a : \Omega \to \mathcal{B}$ for allocating constraints and incentives to agents, and a rule $\tau : \Omega \times \mathcal{A} \to \mathcal{S}$ that generates agent treatment choices for a given constraint allocation a. This framework allows agent ω's treatment choice to depend both on the constraint assignment mechanism a—in particular, the distribution of the constraints in the population—and on the constraints $a(\omega) \in \mathcal{B}$ assigned to agent ω.[47]

The randomness in the planner's constraint assignment a may reflect heterogeneity of agents as observed by the planner, but it may also be due to explicit randomization. For example, consider profiling on background characteristics of potential participants in the assignment a to treatment eligibility. If the planner observes some background characteristics on individuals in the population of interest, she could choose eligibility status to be a deterministic function of those characteristics and, possibly, some other random variable under her control by randomization. This includes the special case in which the planner randomizes persons into eligibility. We denote the information set generated by the variables observed by the planner when she assigns constraints, including those generated through deliberate randomization, by $\mathcal{I}_P$.[48] The planner's information set $\mathcal{I}_P$ determines how precisely she can target agents ω when assigning constraints. The variables in the information set fully determine the constraints assignment a.

Subsequent to the planner's constraints assignment a, each agent ω chooses treatment $\tau(\omega, a)$. We assume that agents know the constraint assignment mechanism a in place. However, agents do not directly observe their types ω, but only observe realizations $I_A(\omega)$ of some random variables I_A. For given $a \in \mathcal{A}$, agent ω's treatment

[46] For example, we could have $\Omega = [0, 1]$ indexing the population of agents, with $\mathbb{P}$ being Lebesgue measure on $[0, 1]$. Alternatively, we could take $\Omega = [0, 1] \times \tilde{\Omega}$ and have $[0, 1]$ represent the population of agents and $\tilde{\Omega}$ states of nature.

[47] In Chapter 70, the dependence of agent ω's treatment choice τ on the constraints $a(\omega)$ was made explicit by defining τ on $\Omega \times \mathcal{A} \times \mathcal{B}$, and subsequently restricting τ to $\{(\omega, a, b) \in \Omega \times \mathcal{A} \times \mathcal{B}\colon a(\omega) = b\}$. Because the constraints $b = a(\omega)$ assigned are already encoded in a and ω, we can drop the constraints b from τ assigned without loss of generality. In the dynamic context of this chapter, this convention simplifies the discussion of dynamic information accumulation.

[48] Formally, $\mathcal{I}_P$ is a sub-σ-algebra of $\mathcal{I}$ and a is assumed to be $\mathcal{I}_P$-measurable.

choice $\tau(\omega, a)$ can only depend on ω through his observations $I_A(\omega)$. Typically, $I_A(\omega)$ includes the variables used by the planner in determining $a(\omega)$, so that agents know the constraints that they are facing. Other components of $I_A(\omega)$ may be determinants of preferences and outcomes. Variation in $I_A(\omega)$ across ω may thus reflect preference heterogeneity, heterogeneity in the assigned constraints, and heterogeneity in outcome predictors. We use $\mathcal{I}_A$ to denote the information set generated by I_A.[49] An agent's information set $\mathcal{I}_A$ determines how precisely the agent can tailor his treatment choice to his type ω. For expositional convenience, we assume that agents know more when choosing treatment than what the planner knows when assigning constraints, so that $\mathcal{I}_A \supseteq \mathcal{I}_P$. One consequence is that agents observe the constraints $a(\omega)$ assigned to them, as previously discussed. In turn, the econometrician may not have access to all of the information that is used by the agents when they choose treatment.[50] In this case, $\mathcal{I}_A \nsubseteq \mathcal{I}_E$, where $\mathcal{I}_E$ denotes the econometrician's information set.

We define $s_p(\omega)$ as the treatment selected by agent ω under policy p. With $p = (a, \tau)$, we have that $s_p(\omega) = \tau(\omega, a)$. The random variable $s_p : \Omega \to \mathcal{S}$ represents the allocation of agents to treatments implied by policy p.[51] Randomness in this allocation reflects both heterogeneity in the planner's assignment of constraints and the agent's heterogeneous responses to this assignment. One extreme case arises if the planner assigns agents to treatment groups and agents perfectly comply, so that $\mathcal{B} = \mathcal{S}$ and $s_p(\omega) = \tau(\omega, a) = a(\omega)$ for all $\omega \in \Omega$. In this case, all variation of s_p is due to heterogeneity in the constraints $a(\omega)$ across agents ω. At the other extreme, agents do not respond at all to the incentives assigned by mechanisms in $\mathcal{A}$, and $\tau(a, \omega) = \tau(a', \omega)$ for all $a, a' \in \mathcal{A}$ and $\omega \in \Omega$. In general, there are policies that have a nontrivial (that is, nondegenerate) constraint assignment a, where at least some agents respond to the assigned constraints a in their treatment choice, $\tau(a, \omega) \neq \tau(a', \omega)$ for some $a, a' \in \mathcal{A}$ and $\omega \in \Omega$.

We seek to evaluate a policy p in terms of some outcome Y_p, for example, earnings. For each $p \in \mathcal{P}$, Y_p is a random variable defined on the population Ω. We index outcomes by a policy subscript in order to simplify the notation. To avoid notational confusion, we will not use treatment subscripts in this section. The evaluation can focus

[49] Formally, $\mathcal{I}_A$ is a sub-σ-algebra of $\mathcal{I}$ – the σ-algebra generated by I_A – and $\omega \in \Omega \mapsto \tau(\omega, a) \in \mathcal{S}$ should be $\mathcal{I}_A$-measurable for all $a \in \mathcal{A}$. The possibility that different agents have different information sets is allowed for because a distinction between agents and states of nature is implicit. As suggested in the introduction to this section, we can make it explicit by distinguishing a set J of agents and a set $\tilde{\Omega}$ of states of nature and writing $\Omega = J \times \tilde{\Omega}$. For expositional convenience, let J be finite. We can model that agents observe their identity j by assuming that the random variable J_A on Ω that reveals their identity, that is $J_A(j, \tilde{\omega}) = j$, is in their information set $\mathcal{I}_A$. If agents, in addition, observe some other random variable V on Ω, then the information set $\mathcal{I}_A$ generated by (J_A, V) can be interpreted as providing each agent $j \in J$ with perfect information about his identity j and with the agent-j-specific information about the state of nature $\tilde{\omega}$ encoded in the random variable $\tilde{\omega} \mapsto V(j, \tilde{\omega})$ on $\tilde{\Omega}$.

[50] See the discussion by Heckman and Vytlacil in Chapter 71, Sections 2 and 9, of their contribution to this Handbook.

[51] Formally, $\{s_p\}_{p \in \mathcal{A} \times \mathcal{T}}$ is a stochastic process indexed by p.

on objective outcomes Y_p, on the subjective valuation $R(Y_p)$ of Y_p by the planner or the agents, or on both types of outcomes. The evaluation can be performed relative to a variety of information sets reflecting different actors (the agent, the planner and the econometrician) and the arrival of information in different time periods. Thus, the randomness of Y_p may represent both (*ex ante*) heterogeneity among agents known to the planner when constraints are assigned (that is, variables in $\mathcal{I}_P$) and/or heterogeneity known to the agents when they choose treatment (that is, information in $\mathcal{I}_A$), as well as (*ex post*) shocks that are not foreseen by the policy maker or by the agents. An information-feasible (*ex ante*) policy evaluation by the planner would be based on some criterion using the distribution of Y_p conditional on $\mathcal{I}_P$. The econometrician can assist the planner in computing this evaluation if the planner shares her *ex ante* information and $\mathcal{I}_P \subseteq \mathcal{I}_E$. We discussed *ex ante* and *ex post* evaluations in Section 2 in the context of a one shot model. It is also discussed in Chapter 70 of this Handbook. In this section, we discuss information revelation and *ex ante* and *ex post* evaluations in a dynamic setting.

Suppose that we have data on outcomes Y_{p_0} under policy p_0 with corresponding treatment assignment s_{p_0}. Consider an intervention that changes the policy from the actual p_0 to some counterfactual p' with associated treatments $s_{p'}$ and outcomes $Y_{p'}$. This could involve a change in the planner's constraint assignment from a_0 to a' for given $\tau_0 = \tau'$, a change in the agent choice rule from τ_0 to τ' for given $a_0 = a'$, or both.

The policy evaluation problem involves contrasting $Y_{p'}$ and Y_{p_0} or functions of these outcomes. For example, if the outcome of interest is mean earnings, we might be interested in some weighted average of $E[Y_{p'} - Y_{p_0} \mid \mathcal{I}_P]$, such as $E[Y_{p'} - Y_{p_0}]$. The special case where $\mathcal{S} = \{0, 1\}$ and $s_{p'} = a' = 0$ generates the effect of abolishing the program.[52] Implementing such a policy requires that the planner be able to induce all agents into the control group by assigning constraints $a' = 0$. In particular, as discussed in Chapter 71, Section 10, this assumes that there are no substitute programs available to agents that are outside the planner's control.

For notational convenience, write $S = s_{p_0}$ for treatment assignment under the actual policy p_0 in place. Cross-sectional microdata typically provide a random sample from the joint distribution of (Y_{p_0}, S).[53] Clearly, without further assumptions, such data do not identify the effects of the policy shift from p_0 to p'. This identification problem becomes even more difficult if we do not seek to compare the counterfactual policy p' with the actual policy p_0, but rather with another counterfactual policy p'' that also has never been observed. A leading example is the binary case in which $0 < \Pr(S = 1) < 1$, but we seek to know the effects of $s_{p'} = 0$ (universal nonparticipation) and $s_{p''} = 1$ (universal treatment), where neither policy has ever been observed in place. As we have

[52] Such a widespread policy would likely have general equilibrium effects. In this section, we will abstract from these by invoking invariance assumptions (PI-1)–(PI-4) discussed in Chapter 70. Section 4 discusses general equilibrium effects.

[53] Notice that a random sample of outcomes under a policy may entail nonrandom selection of treatments as individual agents select individual treatments given τ and the constraints they face assigned by a.

stressed repeatedly in Chapters 70 and 71 of this Handbook, determining the average treatment effect (ATE) is often a difficult task.

The standard microeconometric approach to the policy evaluation problem assumes that the (subjective and objective) outcomes for any individual agent are the same across all policy regimes for any particular treatment assigned to the individual [see, e.g., Heckman, LaLonde and Smith (1999)]. The invariance assumptions (PI-1)–(PI-4) that justify this practice are presented in Chapter 70. They simplify the task of evaluating policy p to determining (i) the assignment s_p of treatments under policy p and (ii) treatment effects for individual outcomes. Even within this simplified framework, there are still two difficult, and distinct, problems in identifying treatment effects on individual outcomes:

(A) *The Evaluation Problem*: *that we observe an agent in one treatment state and seek to determine that agent's outcomes in another state*; *and*

(B) *The Selection Problem: that the distributions of outcomes for the agents we observe in a given treatment state are not the marginal population distributions that would be observed if agents were randomly assigned to the state.*

The assignment mechanism s_p of treatments under counterfactual policies p is straightforward in the case where the planner assigns agents to treatment groups and agents fully comply, so that $s_p = a$. More generally, an explicit model of agent treatment choices is needed to derive s_p for counterfactual policies p. An explicit model of agent treatment choices can also be helpful in addressing the selection problem, and in identifying agent subjective valuations of outcomes. We now formalize the notation for the treatment-effect approach that we will use in this section.

3.1.2. *The treatment-effect approach*

For each agent $\omega \in \Omega$, let $y(s, X(\omega), U(\omega))$ be the potential outcome when the agent is assigned to treatment $s \in \mathcal{S}$. Here, X and U are covariates that are not causally affected by the treatment or the outcomes.[54,55] In the language of Kalbfleisch and Prentice (1980) and Leamer (1985), we say that such covariates are "external" to the causal model. X is observed by the econometrician (that is, in $\mathcal{I}_E$) and U is not.

Recall that s_p is the assignment of agents to treatments under policy p. For all policies p that we consider, the outcome Y_p is linked to the potential outcomes by the

[54] This is the "no feedback" condition (A-6) presented in Chapter 71. The condition requires that X and U are the same fixing $S = s$ for all s. See Haavelmo (1943), Pearl (2000), or the discussion in Chapter 70.

[55] Note that this framework is rich enough to capture the case in which potential outcomes depend on treatment-specific unobservables as in Sections 2 and 3.4, because these can be simply stacked in U and subsequently selected by y. For example, in the case where $\mathcal{S} = \{0, 1\}$ we can write $y(s, X, (U_0, U_1)) = sy_1(X, U_1) + (1 - s)y_0(X, U_0)$ for some y_0 and y_1. A specification without treatment-dependent unobservables is more tractable in the case of continuous treatments in Section 3.2 and, in particular, continuous treatment times in Section 3.3.

consistency condition $Y_p = y(s_p, X, U)$. This condition follows from the invariance assumptions presented in Chapter 70. It embodies the assumption that an agent's outcome only depends on the treatment assigned to the agent and not separately on the mechanism used to assign treatments. This excludes (strategic) interactions between agents and equilibrium effects of the policy.[56] It ensures that we can specify individual outcomes y from participating in programs in $\mathcal{S}$ independently of the policy p and treatment assignment s_p. Economists say that y is autonomous, or structurally invariant with respect to the policy environment [see Frisch (1938), Hurwicz (1962), and our discussion of structure and invariance in Chapter 70].[57] With this notation in hand, we now turn to the dynamic policy evaluation problem.

3.1.3. Dynamic policy evaluation

Interventions often have consequences that span over many periods. Policy interventions at different points in time can be expected to affect not only current outcomes, but also outcomes at other points in time. The same policy implemented at different time periods may have different consequences. Moreover, policy assignment rules often have nontrivial dynamics. The assignment of programs at any point in time can be contingent on the available data on past program participation, intermediate outcomes and covariates.

The dynamic policy evaluation problem can be formalized in a fashion similar to the way we formalized the static problem in Chapter 70 and in Section 3.1.1. In this subsection, we analyze a discrete-time finite-horizon model. We consider continuous-time models in Section 3.3. The possible treatment assignment times are $1, \ldots, \bar{T}$. We do not restrict the set $\mathcal{S}$ of treatments. We allow the same treatment to be assigned on multiple occasions. In general, the set of available treatments at each time t may depend on time t and on the history of treatments, outcomes, and covariates. For expositional convenience, we will only make this explicit in Sections 3.3 and 3.4, where we focus on the timing of a single treatment.

We define a dynamic policy $p = (a, \tau) \in \mathcal{A} \times \mathcal{T} = \mathcal{P}$ as a dynamic constraint assignment rule $a = \{a_t\}_{t=1}^{\bar{T}}$ with a dynamic treatment choice rule $\tau = \{\tau_t\}_{t=1}^{\bar{T}}$. At each time t, the planner assigns constraints $a_t(\omega)$ to each agent $\omega \in \Omega$, using information in the time-t policy-p information set $\mathcal{I}_P(t, p) \subseteq \mathcal{I}$. The planner's information set $\mathcal{I}_P(t, p)$ could be based on covariates and random variables under the planner's control, as well as past choices and realized outcomes. We denote the sequence of planner's information sets by $\mathcal{I}_P(p) = \{\mathcal{I}_P(t, p)\}_{t=1}^{\bar{T}}$. We assume that the planner does not

[56] See Pearl (2000), Heckman (2005), or the discussion in Chapter 70.

[57] See also Aldrich (1989) and Hendry and Morgan (1995). Rubin's (1986) stable-unit-treatment-value assumption is a version of the classical invariance assumptions of econometrics [see Abbring (2003), for discussion of this point, and the discussion in Chapter 70].

forget any information she once had, so that her information improves over time and $\mathcal{I}_P(t, p) \subseteq \mathcal{I}_P(t + 1, p)$ for all t.[58]

Each agent ω chooses treatment $\tau_t(\omega, a)$ given their information about ω at time t under policy p and given the constraint assignment mechanism $a \in \mathcal{A}$ in place. We assume that agents know the constraint assignment mechanism a in place. At time t, under policy p, agents infer their information about their type ω from random variables $I_A(t, p)$ that may include preference components and determinants of constraints and future outcomes. $\mathcal{I}_A(t, p)$ denotes the time-t policy-p information set generated by $I_A(t, p)$ and $\mathcal{I}_A(p) = \{\mathcal{I}_A(t, p)\}_{t=1}^{\bar{T}}$. We assume that agents are increasingly informed as time goes by, so that $\mathcal{I}_A(t, p) \subseteq \mathcal{I}_A(t + 1, p)$.[59] For expositional convenience, we also assume that agents know more than the planner at each time t, so that $\mathcal{I}_P(t, p) \subseteq \mathcal{I}_A(t, p)$.[60] Because all determinants of past and current constraints are in the planner's information set $\mathcal{I}_P(t, p)$, this implies that agents observe $(a_1(\omega), \ldots, a_t(\omega))$ at time t. Usually, they do not observe all determinants of their future constraints $(a_{t+1}(\omega), \ldots, a_{\bar{T}}(\omega))$.[61] Thus, the treatment choices of the agents may be contingent on past and current constraints, their preferences, and on their predictions of future outcomes and constraints given their information $\mathcal{I}_A(t, p)$ and given the constraint assignment mechanism a in place.

Extending the notation for the static case, we denote the assignment of agents to treatment τ_t at time t implied by a policy p by the random variable $s_p(t)$ defined so that $s_p(\omega, t) = \tau_t(\omega, a)$. We use the shorthand s_p^t for the vector $(s_p(1), \ldots, s_p(t))$ of treatments assigned up to and including time t under policy p, and write $s_p = s_p^{\bar{T}}$. The assumptions made so far about the arrival of information imply that treatment assignment $s_p(t)$ can only depend on the information $\mathcal{I}_A(t, p)$ available to agents at time t.[62]

Because past outcomes typically depend on the policy p, the planner's information $\mathcal{I}_P(p)$ and the agents' information $\mathcal{I}_A(p)$ will generally depend on p as well. In the treatment-effect framework that we develop in the next section, at each time t different policies may have selected different elements in the set of potential outcomes in the past. The different elements reveal different aspects of the unobservables underlying past and future outcomes. We will make assumptions that limit the dependence of information sets on policies in the context of the treatment-effects approach developed in the next section.

Objective outcomes associated with policies p are expressed as a vector of time-specific outcomes $Y_p = (Y_p(1), \ldots, Y_p(\bar{T}))$. The components of this vector may

[58] Formally, the information $\mathcal{I}_P(p)$ that accumulates for the planner under policy p is a filtration in $\mathcal{I}$, and a is a stochastic process that is adapted to $\mathcal{I}_P(p)$.

[59] Formally, the information $\mathcal{I}_A(p)$ that accumulates for the agents is a filtration in $\mathcal{I}$.

[60] If agents are strictly better informed, and $\mathcal{I}_P(t, p) \subset \mathcal{I}_A(t, p)$, it is unlikely that the planner catches up and learns the agent's information with a delay (e.g., $\mathcal{I}_A(t, p) \subseteq \mathcal{I}_P(t + 1, p)$) unless agent's choices and outcomes reveal all their private information.

[61] Formally, $a_1, \ldots, a_t$ are $\mathcal{I}_A(t, p)$-measurable, but $a_{t+1}, \ldots, a_{\bar{T}}$ are not.

[62] Formally, $\{s_p(t)\}_{t=1}^{\bar{T}}$ is a stochastic process that is adapted to $\mathcal{I}_A(p)$.

also be vectors. We denote the outcomes from time 1 to time t under policy p by $Y_p^t = (Y_p(1), \ldots, Y_p(t))$. We analyze both subjective and objective evaluations of policies in Section 3.4, where we consider more explicit economic models. Analogous to our analysis of the static case, we cannot learn about the outcomes $Y_{p'}$ that would arise under a counterfactual policy p' from data on outcomes Y_{p_0} and treatments $s_{p_0} = S$ under a policy $p_0 \neq p'$ without imposing further structure on the problem.[63] We follow the approach exposited for the static case and assume policy invariance of individual outcomes under a given treatment. These are the invariance assumptions (PI-1)–(PI-4) presented in Chapter 70. They reduce the evaluation of a dynamic policy p to identifying (i) the dynamic assignment s_p of treatments under policy p and (ii) the dynamic treatment effects on individual outcomes. We focus our discussion on the fundamental evaluation problem and the selection problem that haunt inference about treatment effects. In the remainder of the section, we review alternative approaches to identifying dynamic treatment effects, and some approaches to modeling dynamic treatment choice. We first analyze methods recently developed in statistics.

3.2. Dynamic treatment effects and sequential randomization

In a series of papers, Robins extends the static Neyman–Rubin model based on selection on observables discussed in Chapter 71 to a dynamic setting [see, e.g., Robins (1997), and the references therein]. He does not consider agent choice or subjective evaluations. Here, we review his extension, discuss its relationship to dynamic choice models in econometrics, and assess its merits as a framework for economic policy analysis. We follow the exposition of Gill and Robins (2001), but add some additional structure to their basic framework to exposit the connection of their approach to the dynamic approach pursued in econometrics.

3.2.1. Dynamic treatment effects

3.2.1.1. Dynamic treatment and dynamic outcomes To simplify the exposition, suppose that $\mathcal{S}$ is a finite discrete set.[64] Recall that, at each time t and for given p, treatment assignment $s_p(t)$ is a random variable that only depends on the agent's information $\mathcal{I}_A(t, p)$, which includes personal knowledge of preferences and determinants of constraints and outcomes. To make this dependence explicit, suppose that external covariates Z, observed by the econometrician (that is, variables in $\mathcal{I}_E$), and unobserved external covariates V_1 that affect treatment assignment are revealed to the agents at time 1. Then, at the start of each period $t \geqslant 2$, past outcomes $Y_p(t-1)$ corresponding

[63] If outcomes under different policy regimes are informative about the same technology and preferences, for example, then the analyst and the agent could learn about the ingredients that produce counterfactual outcomes in all outcome states.

[64] All of the results presented in this subsection extend to the case of continuous treatments. We will give references to the appropriate literature in subsequent footnotes.

to the outcomes realized under treatment assignment s_p and external unobserved covariates V_t enter the agent's information set.[65] In this notation, $\mathcal{I}_A(1, p)$ is the information $\sigma(Z, V_1)$ conveyed to the agent by (Z, V_1) and, for $t \geqslant 2$, $\mathcal{I}_A(t, p) = \sigma(Y_p^{t-1}, Z, V^t)$, with $V^t = (V_1, \dots, V_t)$. In the notation of the previous subsection, $I_A(1, p) = (Z, V_1)$ and, for $t \geqslant 2$, $I_A(t, p) = (Y_p^{t-1}, Z, V^t)$. Among the elements of $I_A(t, p)$ are the determinants of the constraints faced by the agent up to t, which may or may not be observed by the econometrician.

We attach *ex post* potential outcomes $Y(t, s) = y_t(s, X, U_t)$, $t = 1, \dots, \bar{T}$, to each treatment sequence $s = (s(1), \dots, s(\bar{T}))$. Here, X is a vector of observed (by the econometrician) external covariates and U_t, $t = 1, \dots, \bar{T}$, are vectors of unobserved external covariates. Some components of X and U_t may be in agent information sets. We denote $Y^t(s) = (Y(1, s), \dots, Y(t, s))$, $Y(s) = Y^{\bar{T}}(s)$, and $U = (U_1, \dots, U_{\bar{T}})$. As in the static case, potential outcomes y are assumed to be invariant across policies p, which ensures that $Y_p(t) = y_t(s_p, X, U_t)$. In the remainder of this section, we keep the dependence of outcomes on observed covariates X implicit and suppress all conditioning on X.

We assume no causal dependence of outcomes on future treatment:[66]

(NA) *For all* $t \geqslant 1$, $Y(t, s) = Y(t, s')$ *for all* s, s' *such that* $s^t = (s')^t$,

where $s^t = (s(1), \dots, s(t))$ and $(s')^t = (s'(1), \dots, s'(t))$. Abbring and Van den Berg (2003b) and Abbring (2003) define this as a "no-anticipation" condition. It requires that outcomes at time t (and before) be the same across policies that allocate the same treatment up to and including t, even if they allocate different treatments after t. In the structural econometric models discussed in Sections 3.2.2 and 3.4 below, this condition is trivially satisfied if all state variables relevant to outcomes at time t are included as inputs in the outcome equations $Y(t, s) = y_t(s, U_t)$, $t = 1, \dots, \bar{T}$.

Because Z and V_1 are assumed to be externally determined, and therefore not affected by the policy p, the initial agent information set $\mathcal{I}_A(1, p) = \sigma(Z, V_1)$ does not depend on p. Agent ω has the same initial data $(Z(\omega), V_1(\omega))$ about his type ω under all policies p. Thus, $\mathcal{I}_A(1, p) = \mathcal{I}_A(1, p')$ is a natural benchmark information set for an *ex ante* comparison of outcomes at time 1 among different policies. For $t \geqslant 2$, (NA) implies that actual outcomes up to time $t - 1$ are equal between policies p and p', $Y_p^{t-1} = Y_{p'}^{t-1}$, if the treatment histories coincide up to time $t - 1$ so that $s_p^{t-1} = s_{p'}^{t-1}$. Together with the assumption that Z and V^t are externally determined, it follows that agents have the same time-t information set structure about ω under policies p and p',

[65] Note that any observed covariates that are dynamically revealed to the agents can be subsumed in the outcomes.

[66] For statistical inference from data on the distribution of (Y_{p_0}, S, Z), these equalities only need to hold on events $\{\omega \in \Omega\colon S^t(\omega) = s^t\}$, $t \geqslant 1$, respectively.

$\mathcal{I}_A(t,p) = \sigma(Y_p^{t-1}, Z, V^t) = \sigma(Y_{p'}^{t-1}, Z, V^t) = \mathcal{I}_A(t,p')$, if $s_p^{t-1} = s_{p'}^{t-1}$.[67,68] In this context, $\mathcal{I}_A(t,p) = \mathcal{I}_A(t,p')$ is a natural information set for an *ex ante* comparison of outcomes from time t onwards between any two policies p and p' such that $s_p^{t-1} = s_{p'}^{t-1}$.

With this structure on the agent information sets in hand, it is instructive to review the separate roles in determining treatment choice of information about ω and knowledge about the constraint assignment rule a. First, agent ω's time-t treatment choice $s_p(\omega,t) = \tau_t(\omega,a)$ may depend on distributional properties of a, for example the share of agents assigned to particular treatment sequences, and on the past and current constraints $(a_1(\omega),\ldots,a_t(\omega))$ that were actually assigned to them. We have assumed both to be known to the agent. Both may differ between policies, even if the agent information about ω is fixed across the policies. Second, agent ω's time-t treatment choice may depend on agent ω's predictions of future constraints and outcomes. A forward-looking agent ω will use observations of his covariates $Z(\omega)$ and $V^t(\omega)$ and past outcomes $Y_p^{t-1}(\omega)$ to infer his type ω and subsequently predict future external determinants $(U_t(\omega),\ldots,U_{\bar{T}}(\omega))$ of his outcomes and $(V_{t+1}(\omega),\ldots,V_{\bar{T}}(\omega))$ of his constraints and treatments. In turn, this information updating allows agent ω to predict his future potential outcomes $(Y(t,s,\omega),\ldots,Y(\bar{T},s,\omega))$ and, for a given policy regime p, his future constraints $(a_{t+1}(\omega),\ldots,a_{\bar{T}}(\omega))$, treatments $(s_p(t+1,\omega),\ldots,s_p(\bar{T},\omega))$, and realized outcomes $(Y_p(t,\omega),\ldots,Y_p(\bar{T},\omega))$. Under different policies, the agent may gather different information on his type ω and therefore come up with different predictions of the external determinants of his future potential outcomes and constraints. In addition, even if the agent has the same time-t predictions of the external determinants of future constraints and potential outcomes, he may translate these into different predictions of future constraints and outcomes under different policies.

Assumption (NA) requires that current potential outcomes are not affected by future treatment. Justifying this assumption requires specification of agent information about future treatment and agent behavior in response to that information. Such an interpretation requires that we formalize how information accumulates for agents across treatment sequences s and s' such that $s^t = (s')^t$ and $(s_{t+1},\ldots,s_{\bar{T}}) \neq (s'_{t+1},\ldots,s'_{\bar{T}})$. To this end, consider policies p and p' such that $s_p = s$ and $s_{p'} = s'$. These policies produce the same treatment assignment up to time t, but are different in the future. We have previously shown that, even though the time-t agent information about ω is the

[67] If $s_p^{t-1}(\omega) = s_{p'}^{t-1}(\omega)$ only holds for ω in some subset $\Omega_{t-1} \subset \Omega$ of agents, then $Y_p^{t-1}(\omega) = Y_{p'}^{t-1}(\omega)$ only for $\omega \in \Omega_{t-1}$, and information coincides between p and p' only for agents in Ω_{t-1}. Formally, let Ω_{t-1} be the set $\{\omega \in \Omega\colon s_p^{t-1}(\omega) = s_{p'}^{t-1}(\omega)\}$ of agents that share the same treatment up to and including time $t-1$. Then, Ω_{t-1} is in the agent's information set under both policies, $\Omega_{t-1} \in \mathcal{I}_A(t,p) \cap \mathcal{I}_A(t,p')$. Moreover, the partitioning of Ω_{t-1} implied by $\mathcal{I}_A(t,p)$ and $\mathcal{I}_A(t,p')$ is the same. To see this, note that the collections of all sets in, respectively, $\mathcal{I}_A(t,p)$ and $\mathcal{I}_A(t,p')$ that are weakly included in Ω_{t-1} are identical σ-algebras on Ω_{t-1}.

[68] Notice that the realizations of the random variables $Y_{p'}^{t-1}$, Z, V^t may differ among agents.

same under both policies, $\mathcal{I}_A(t, p) = \mathcal{I}_A(t, p')$, agents may have different predictions of future constraints, treatments and outcomes because the policies may differ in the future and agents know this. The policy-invariance conditions (PI-1)–(PI-4) of Chapter 70 ensure that time-t potential outcomes are nevertheless the same under each policy. This requires that potential outcomes be determined externally, and are not affected by agent actions in response to different predictions of future constraints, treatments and outcomes.

In general, different policies in $\mathcal{P}$ will produce different predictions of future constraints, treatment and outcomes. In the dynamic treatment-effects framework, this may affect outcomes indirectly through agent treatment choices. If potential outcomes are directly affected by agent's forward-looking decisions, then the invariance conditions (PI-1)–(PI-4) of Chapter 70 underlying the treatment-effects framework will be violated. Section 3.2.3 illustrates this issue, and the no-anticipation condition, with some examples.

3.2.1.2. Identification of treatment effects Suppose that the econometrician has data that allows her to estimate the joint distribution of (Y_{p_0}, S, Z) of outcomes, treatments and covariates under some policy p_0, where again $S = s_{p_0}$. These data are not enough to identify dynamic treatment effects.

To secure identification, Gill and Robins (2001) invoke a dynamic version of the matching assumption (conditional independence) which relies on sequential randomization:[69]

(M-2) *For all treatment sequences s and all t,*

$$S(t) \perp\!\!\!\perp \big(Y(t, s), \ldots, Y(\bar{T}, s)\big) \mid \big(Y_{p_0}^{t-1}, S^{t-1} = s^{t-1}, Z\big),$$

where the conditioning set $(Y_{p_0}^0, S^0 = s^0, Z)$ for $t = 1$ should be simply stated as Z.

Equivalently,

$$S(t) \perp\!\!\!\perp (U_t, \ldots, U_{\bar{T}}) \mid \big(Y_{p_0}^{t-1}, S^{t-1}, Z\big)$$

for all t without further restricting the data. Sequential randomization allows the $Y_{p_0}(t)$ to be "dynamic confounders"—variables that are affected by past treatment and that affect future treatment assignment.

The sequence of conditioning information sets appearing in the sequential randomization assumption, $\mathcal{I}_E(1) = \sigma(Z)$ and, for $t \geqslant 2$, $\mathcal{I}_E(t) = \sigma(Y_{p_0}^{t-1}, S^{t-1}, Z)$, is a filtration $\mathcal{I}_E$ of the econometrician's information set $\sigma(Y_{p_0}, S, Z)$. Note that $\mathcal{I}_E(t) \subseteq \mathcal{I}_A(t, p_0)$ for each t. If treatment assignment is based on strictly more information than $\mathcal{I}_E$, so

[69] Formally, we need to restrict attention to sequences s in the support of S. Throughout this section, we will assume this and related support conditions hold.

that agents know strictly more than the econometrician and act on their superior information, (M-2) is likely to fail if that extra information also affects outcomes. This point is made in a static setting in Chapter 71.

Together with the no-anticipation condition (NA), which is a condition on outcomes and distinct from (M-2), the dynamic potential-outcome model set up so far is a natural dynamic extension of the Neyman–Rubin model for a static (stratified) randomized experiment.

Under assumption (M-2) that the actual treatment assignment S is sequentially randomized, we can sequentially identify the causal effects of treatment from the distribution of the data (Y_{p_0}, S, Z) and construct the distribution of the potential outcomes $Y(s)$ for any treatment sequence s in the support of S.

Consider the case in which all variables are discrete. No-anticipation condition (NA) ensures that potential outcomes for a treatment sequence s equal actual (under policy p_0) outcomes up to time $t-1$ for agents with treatment history s^{t-1} up to time $t-1$. Formally, $Y^{t-1}(s) = Y_{p_0}^{t-1}$ on the set $\{S^{t-1} = s^{t-1}\}$. Using this, sequential randomization assumption (M-2) can be rephrased in terms of potential outcomes: for all s and t,

$$S(t) \perp\!\!\!\perp \big(Y(t,s), \ldots, Y(\bar{T}, s)\big) \mid \big(Y^{t-1}(s), S^{t-1} = s^{t-1}, Z\big).$$

In turn, this implies that, for all s and t,

$$\begin{aligned}
&\Pr\big(Y(t,s) = y(t) \mid Y^{t-1}(s) = y^{t-1}, S^t = s^t, Z\big) \\
&\quad = \Pr\big(Y(t,s) = y(t) \mid Y^{t-1}(s) = y^{t-1}, Z\big),
\end{aligned} \tag{3.1}$$

where $y^{t-1} = (y(1), \ldots, y(t-1))$ and $y = y^{\bar{T}}$. From Bayes' rule and (3.1), it follows that

$$\begin{aligned}
&\Pr\big(Y(s) = y \mid Z\big) \\
&\quad = \Pr\big(Y(1,s) = y(1) \mid Z\big) \prod_{t=2}^{\bar{T}} \Pr\big(Y(t,s) = y(t) \mid Y^{t-1}(s) = y^{t-1}, Z\big) \\
&\quad = \Pr\big(Y(1,s) = y(1) \mid S(1) = s(1), Z\big) \\
&\qquad \times \prod_{t=2}^{\bar{T}} \Pr\big(Y(t,s) = y(t) \mid Y^{t-1}(s) = y^{t-1}, S^t = s^t, Z\big).
\end{aligned}$$

Invoking (NA), in particular $Y(t,s) = Y_{p_0}(t)$ and $Y^{t-1}(s) = Y_{p_0}^{t-1}$ on $\{S^t = s^t\}$, produces

$$\begin{aligned}
&\Pr\big(Y(s) = y \mid Z\big) \\
&\quad = \Pr\big(Y_{p_0}(1) = y(1) \mid S(1) = s(1), Z\big) \\
&\qquad \times \prod_{t=2}^{\bar{T}} \Pr\big(Y_{p_0}(t) = y(t) \mid Y_{p_0}^{t-1} = y^{t-1}, S^t = s^t, Z\big).
\end{aligned} \tag{3.2}$$

This is a version of Robins' (1997) "g-computation formula".[70,71] We can sequentially identify each component on the left-hand side of the first expression, and hence identify the counterfactual distributions. This establishes identification of the distribution of $Y(s)$ by expressing it in terms of objects that can be identified from data. Identification is exact (or "tight") in the sense that the identifying assumptions, no anticipation and sequential randomization, do not restrict the factual data and are therefore not testable [Gill and Robins (2001, Section 6)].[72]

EXAMPLE 4. Consider a two-period ($\bar{T} = 2$) version of the model in which agents take either "treatment" (1) or "control" (0) in each period. Then, $S(1)$ and $S(2)$ have values in $\mathcal{S} = \{0, 1\}$. The potential outcomes in period t are $Y(t, (0, 0))$, $Y(t, (0, 1))$, $Y(t, (1, 0))$ and $Y(t, (1, 1))$. For example, $Y(2, (0, 0))$ is the outcome in period 2 in the case that the agent is assigned to the control group in each of the two periods. Using Bayes' rule, it follows that

$$\begin{aligned}&\Pr\bigl(Y(s) = y \mid Z\bigr)\\&\quad = \Pr\bigl(Y(1, s) = y(1) \mid Z\bigr) \Pr\bigl(Y(2, s) = y(2) \mid Y(1, s) = y(1), Z\bigr).\end{aligned} \tag{3.3}$$

The g-computation approach to constructing $\Pr(Y(s) = y \mid Z)$ from data replaces the two probabilities in the right-hand side with probabilities of the observed (by the econometrician) variables (Y_{p_0}, S, Z). First, note that $\Pr(Y(1, s) = y(1) \mid Z) = \Pr(Y(1, s) = y(1) \mid S(1) = s(1), Z)$ by (M-2). Moreover, (NA) ensures that potential outcomes in period 1 do not depend on the treatment status in period 2, so that

$$\Pr\bigl(Y(1, s) = y(1) \mid Z\bigr) = \Pr\bigl(Y_{p_0} = y(1) \mid S(1) = s(1), Z\bigr).$$

[70] Gill and Robins (2001) present versions of (NA) and (M-2) for the case with more general distributions of treatments, and prove a version of the g-computation formula for the general case. For a random vector X and a function f that is integrable with respect to the distribution of X, let $\int_{x \in A} f(x) \Pr(X \in dx) = E[f(X)\mathbf{1}(X \in A)]$. Then,

$$\begin{aligned}\Pr\bigl(Y(s) \in A \mid Z\bigr) = \int_{y \in A} & \Pr\bigl(Y_{p_0}(\bar{T}) \in dy(\bar{T}) \mid Y_{p_0}^{\bar{T}-1} = y^{\bar{T}-1}, S^{\bar{T}} = s^{\bar{T}}, Z\bigr)\\ & \vdots\\ & \times \Pr\bigl(Y_{p_0}(2) \in dy(2) \mid Y_{p_0}(1) = y(1), S^2 = s^2, Z\bigr)\\ & \times \Pr\bigl(Y_{p_0}(1) \in dy(1) \mid S(1) = s(1), Z\bigr),\end{aligned}$$

where A is a set of $Y(s)$. The right-hand side of this expression is almost surely unique under regularity conditions presented by Gill and Robins (2001).

[71] An interesting special case arises if the outcomes are survival indicators, that is if $Y_{p_0}(t) = 1$ if the agent survives up to and including time t and $Y_{p_0}(t) = 0$ otherwise, $t \geqslant 1$. Then, no anticipation (NA) requires that treatment after death does not affect survival, and the g-computation formula simplifies considerably [Abbring (2003)].

[72] Gill and Robins' (2001) analysis only involves causal inference on a final outcome (i.e., our $Y(s, \bar{T})$) and does not invoke the no-anticipation condition. However, their proof directly applies to the case studied in this chapter.

Similarly, subsequently invoking (NA) and (M-2), then (M-2), and then (NA), gives

$$\begin{aligned}
&\Pr\big(Y(2,s)=y(2)\mid Y(1,s)=y(1),Z\big)\\
&\quad=\Pr\big(Y(2,s)=y(2)\mid Y_{p_0}(1),S(1)=s(1),Z\big)\quad\big(\text{by (NA) and (M-2)}\big)\\
&\quad=\Pr\big(Y(2,s)=y(2)\mid Y_{p_0}(1),S=s,Z\big)\quad\big(\text{by (M-2)}\big)\\
&\quad=\Pr\big(Y_{p_0}(2)=y(2)\mid Y_{p_0}(1),S=s,Z\big).\quad\big(\text{by (NA)}\big)
\end{aligned}$$

Substituting these equations into the right-hand side of (3.3) gives the g-computation formula,

$$\begin{aligned}
\Pr\big(Y(s)=y\mid Z\big)=&\Pr\big(Y_{p_0}(1)=y(1)\mid S(1)=s(1),Z\big)\\
&\times\Pr\big(Y_{p_0}(2)=y(2)\mid Y_{p_0}(1)=y(1),S=s,Z\big).
\end{aligned}$$

Note that the right-hand side does not generally reduce to $\Pr(Y_{p_0}=y\mid S=s,Z)$. This would require the stronger, static matching condition $S \perp\!\!\!\perp Y(s)\mid Z$, which we have not assumed here.

Matching on pre-treatment covariates is a special case of the g-computation approach. Suppose that the entire treatment path is assigned independently of potential outcomes given pre-treatment covariates Z or, more precisely, $S \perp\!\!\!\perp Y(s)\mid Z$ for all s. This implies sequential randomization (M-2), and directly gives identification of the distributions of $Y(s)\mid Z$ and $Y(s)$. The matching assumption imposes no restriction on the data since $Y(s)$ is only observed if $S=s$. The no-anticipation condition (NA) is not required for identification in this special case because no conditioning on S^t is required. Matching on pre-treatment covariates is equivalent to matching in a static model. The distribution of $Y(s)\mid Z$ is identified without (NA), and assuming it to be true would impose testable restrictions on the data. In particular, it would imply that treatment assignment cannot be dependent on past outcomes given Z. The static matching assumption is not likely to hold in applications where treatment is dynamically assigned based on information on intermediate outcomes. This motivates an analysis based on the more subtle sequential randomization assumption. An alternative approach, developed in Section 3.4, is to explicitly model and identify the evolution of the unobservables.

Gill and Robins claim that their sequential randomization and no-anticipation assumptions are "neutral", "for free", or "harmless". As we will argue later, from an economic perspective, some of the model assumptions, notably the no-anticipation assumption, can be interpreted as substantial behavioral/informational assumptions. For example, Heckman and Vytlacil (2005, and Chapter 70 of this Handbook) and Heckman and Navarro (2004) show how matching imposes the condition that marginal and average returns are equal. Because of these strong assumptions, econometricians sometimes phrase their "neutrality" result more negatively as a nonidentification result [Abbring and Van den Berg (2003b)], since it is possible that (M-2) and/or (NA) may not hold.

3.2.2. Policy evaluation and dynamic discrete-choice analysis

3.2.2.1. The effects of policies Consider a counterfactual policy p' such that the corresponding allocation of treatments $s_{p'}$ satisfies sequential randomization, as in (M-2):

(M-3) *For all treatment sequences s and all t,*

$$s_{p'}(t) \perp\!\!\!\perp \big(Y(t,s),\ldots,Y(\bar{T},s)\big) \mid \big(Y_{p'}^{t-1}, s_{p'}^{t-1} = s^{t-1}, Z\big).$$

The treatment assignment rule $s_{p'}$ is equivalent to what Gill and Robins (2001) call a "randomized plan". The outcome distribution under such a rule cannot be constructed by integrating the distributions of $\{Y(s)\}$ with respect to the distribution of $s_{p'}$, because there may be feedback from intermediate outcomes into treatment assignment. Instead, under the assumptions of the previous subsection and a support condition, we can use a version of the g-computation formula for randomized plans given by Gill and Robins to compute the distribution of outcomes under the policy p':[73]

$$\begin{aligned}\Pr(Y_{p'} = y \mid Z) = \sum_{s\in\mathcal{S}} &\Pr\big(Y_{p_0}(1) = y(1) \mid S(1) = s(1), Z\big)\\ &\times \Pr\big(s_{p'}(1) = s(1) \mid Z\big)\\ &\times \prod_{t=2}^{\bar{T}}\big[\Pr\big(Y_{p_0}(t) = y(t) \mid Y_{p_0}^{t-1} = y^{t-1}, S^t = s^t, Z\big)\\ &\times \Pr\big(s_{p'}(t) = s(t) \mid Y_{p'}^{t-1} = y^{t-1}, s_{p'}^{t-1}(1) = s^{t-1}, Z\big)\big]. \quad (3.4)\end{aligned}$$

[73] The corresponding formula for the case with general treatment distributions is

$$\begin{aligned}\Pr(Y_{p'} \in A \mid Z) = \int_{y\in A}\int_{s\in\mathcal{S}} &\Pr\big(Y_{p_0}(\bar{T}) \in dy(\bar{T}) \mid Y_{p_0}^{\bar{T}-1} = y^{\bar{T}-1}, S^{\bar{T}} = s^{\bar{T}}, Z\big)\\ &\times \Pr\big(s_{p'}(\bar{T}) \in ds(\bar{T}) \mid Y_{p'}^{\bar{T}-1} = y^{\bar{T}-1}, s_{p'}^{\bar{T}-1} = s^{\bar{T}-1}, Z\big)\\ &\vdots\\ &\times \Pr\big(Y_{p_0}(2) \in dy(2) \mid Y_{p_0}(1) = y(1), S(1) = s(1), Z\big)\\ &\times \Pr\big(s_{p'}(2) \in ds(2) \mid Y_{p'}(1) = y(1), s_{p'}(1) = s(1), Z\big)\\ &\times \Pr\big(Y_{p_0}(1) \in dy(1) \mid S(1) = s(1), Z\big)\Pr\big(s_{p'}(1) \in ds(1) \mid Z\big).\end{aligned}$$

The support condition on $s_{p'}$ requires that, for each t, the distribution of $s_{p'}(t) \mid (Y_{p'}^{t-1} = y^{t-1}, s_{p'}^{t-1} = s^{t-1}, Z = z)$ is absolutely continuous with respect to the distribution of $S(t) \mid (Y_{p_0}^{t-1} = y^{t-1}, S^{t-1} = s^{t-1}, Z = z)$ for almost all (y^{t-1}, s^{t-1}, z) from the distribution of $(Y_{p_0}^{t-1}, S^{t-1}, Z)$.

In the special case of static matching on Z, so that $s_{p'} \perp\!\!\!\perp U \mid Z$, this simplifies to integrating the distribution of $Y_{p_0} \mid (S = s, Z)$ over the distribution of $s_{p'} \mid Z$:[74]

$$\Pr(Y_{p'} = y \mid Z) = \sum_{s \in \mathcal{S}} \Pr(Y_{p_0} = y \mid S = s, Z) \Pr(s_{p'} = s \mid Z).$$

3.2.2.2. Policy choice and optimal policies We now consider the problem of choosing a policy p that is optimal according to some criterion. This problem is both of normative interest and of descriptive interest if actual policies are chosen to be optimal. We could, for example, study the optimal assignment a' of constraints and incentives to agents. Alternatively, we could assume that agents pick τ to maximize their utilities, and use the methods discussed in this section to model τ.

Under the policy invariance assumptions that underlie the treatment-effects approach, p only affects outcomes through its implied treatment allocation s_p. Thus, the problem of choosing an optimal policy boils down to choosing an optimal treatment allocation s_p under informational and other constraints specific to the problem at hand. For example, suppose that the planner and the agents have the same information, $\mathcal{I}_P(p) = \mathcal{I}_A(p)$, the planner assigns eligibility to a program by a, and agents fully comply, so that $\mathcal{B} = \mathcal{S}$ and $s_p = a$. Then, s_p can be any rule from $\mathcal{A}$ and is adapted to $\mathcal{I}_P(p) = \mathcal{I}_A(p)$.

For expositional convenience, we consider the optimal choice of a treatment assignment s_p adapted to the agent's information $\mathcal{I}_A(p)$ constructed earlier. We will use the word "agents" to refer to the decision maker in this problem, even though it can also apply to the planner's decision problem. An econometric approach to this problem is to estimate explicit dynamic choice models with explicit choice-outcome relationships. One emphasis in the literature is on Markovian discrete-choice models that satisfy Rust's (1987) conditional-independence assumption [see Rust (1994)]. Other assumptions are made in the literature and we exposit them in Section 3.4.

Here, we explore the use of Rust's (1987) model as a model of treatment choice in a dynamic treatment-effects setting. In particular, we make explicit the additional structure that Rust's model, and in particular his conditional-independence assumption, imposes on Robins' dynamic potential-outcomes model. We follow Rust (1987) and focus on a finite treatment (control) space $\mathcal{S}$. In the notation of our model, payoffs are determined by the outcomes Y_p, treatment choices s_p, the "cost shocks" V, and the covariates Z. Rust (1987) assumes that $\{Y_p(t-1), V_t, Z\}$ is a controlled first-order Markov process, with initial condition $Y_p(0) \equiv 0$ and control s_p.[75] As before, V_t and Z

[74] In the general case this condition becomes

$$\Pr(Y_{p'} \in A \mid Z) = \int_{s \in \mathcal{S}} \Pr(Y_{p_0} \in A \mid S = s, Z) \Pr(s_{p'} \in ds \mid Z).$$

[75] Rust (1987) assumes an infinite-horizon, stationary environment. Here, we present a finite-horizon version to facilitate a comparison with the dynamic potential-outcomes model and to link up with the analysis in Section 3.4.

are not causally affected by choices, but $Y_p(t)$ may causally depend on current and past choices. The agents choose a treatment assignment rule s_p that maximizes

$$E\left[\sum_{t=1}^{\bar{T}} \Upsilon_t\{Y_p(t-1), V_t, s_p(t), Z\} + \Upsilon_{\bar{T}+1}\{Y_p(\bar{T}), Z\} \,\middle|\, \mathcal{I}_A(1)\right], \tag{3.5}$$

for some (net and discounted) utility functions Υ_t and $\mathcal{I}_A(1) = \mathcal{I}_A(1, p)$, which is independent of p. $\Upsilon_{\bar{T}+1}\{Y_p(\bar{T}), Z\}$ is the terminal value. Under standard regularity conditions on the utility functions, we can solve backward for the optimal policy s_p. Because of Rust's Markov assumption, s_p has a Markovian structure,

$$s_p(t) \perp\!\!\!\perp \left(Y_p^{t-2}, V^{t-1}\right) \mid \left[Y_p(t-1), V_t, Z\right],$$

for $t = 2, \dots, \bar{T}$, and $\{Y_p(t-1), V_t, Z\}$ is a first-order Markov process. Note that Z enters the model as an observed (by the econometrician) factor that shifts net utility. A key assumption embodied in the specification of (3.5) is time-separability of utility. Rust (1987), in addition, imposes separability between observed and unobserved state variables. This assumption plays no essential role in expositing the core ideas in Rust, and we will not make it here.

Rust's (1987) conditional-independence assumption imposes two key restrictions on the decision problem. It is instructive to consider these restrictions in isolation from Rust's Markov restriction. We make the model's causal structure explicit using the potential-outcomes notation. Note that the model has a recursive causal structure—the payoff-relevant state is controlled by current and past choices only—and satisfies no-anticipation condition (NA). Setting $Y(0, s) \equiv 0$ for specificity, and ignoring the Markov restriction, Rust's conditional-independence assumption requires, in addition to the assumption that there are no direct causal effects of choices on V, that

$$Y(s, t) \perp\!\!\!\perp V^t \mid \left[Y^{t-1}(s), Z\right], \tag{3.6}$$

$$V_{t+1} \perp\!\!\!\perp V^t \mid \left[Y^t(s), Z\right] \tag{3.7}$$

for all s and t. As noted by Rust (1987, p. 1011) condition (3.6) ensures that the observed (by the econometrician) controlled state evolves independently of the unobserved payoff-relevant variables. It is equivalent to [Florens and Mouchart (1982)][76]

(M-4) $[Y(s, t), \dots, Y(s, \bar{T})] \perp\!\!\!\perp V^t \mid [Y^{t-1}(s), Z]$ *for all* t *and* s.

In turn, (M-4) implies (M-2) and is equivalent to the assumption that (M-3) holds for all $s_{p'}$.[77]

[76] Note that (3.6) is a Granger (1969) noncausality condition stating that, for all s and conditional on Z, V does not cause $Y(s)$.

[77] If V has redundant components, that is components that do not nontrivially enter any assignment rule s_p, (M-4) imposes more structure, but structure that is irrelevant to the decision problem and its empirical analysis.

Condition (3.7) excludes serial dependence of the unobserved payoff-relevant variables conditional on past outcomes. In contrast, Robins' g-computation framework allows for such serial dependence, provided that sequential randomization holds if serial dependence is present. For example, if $V \perp\!\!\!\perp U \mid Z$, then (M-2) and its variants hold without further assumptions on the time series structure of V_t.

The first-order Markov assumption imposes additional restrictions on potential outcomes. These restrictions are twofold. First, potential outcomes follow a first-order Markov process. Second, $s(t)$ only directly affects the Markov transition from $Y(t, s)$ to $Y(t+1, s)$. This strengthens the no-anticipation assumption presented in Section 3.2.1.1. The Markov assumption also requires that V_{t+1} only depends on $Y(s, t)$, and not on $Y^{t-1}(s)$, given $Y(s, t)$.

In applications, we may assume that actual treatment assignment S solves the Markovian decision problem. Together with specifications of Υ_t, this further restricts the dynamic choice-outcome model. Alternatively, one could make other assumptions on S and use (3.5) to define and find an optimal, and typically counterfactual, assignment rule $s_{p'}$.

Our analysis shows that the substantial econometric literature on the structural empirical analysis of Markovian decision problems under conditional independence can be applied to policy evaluation under sequential randomization. Conversely, methods developed for potential-outcomes models with sequential randomization can be applied to learn about aspects of dynamic discrete-choice models. Murphy (2003) develops methods to estimate an optimal treatment assignment rule using Robins' dynamic potential-outcomes model with sequential randomization (M-3).

3.2.3. The information structure of policies

One concern about methods for policy evaluation based on the potential-outcomes model is that potential outcomes are sometimes reduced form representations of dynamic models of agent's choices. A policy maker choosing optimal policies typically faces a population of agents who act on the available information, and their actions in turn affect potential outcomes. For example, in terms of the model of Section 3.2.2, a policy may change financial incentives—the $b \in \mathcal{B}$ assigned through a could enter the net utilities Υ_t—and leave it to the agents to control outcomes by choosing treatment. In econometric policy evaluation, it is therefore important to carefully model the information $\mathcal{I}_A$ that accumulates to the agents in different program states and under different policies, separately from the policy maker's information $\mathcal{I}_P$.

This can be contrasted with common practice in biostatistics. Statistical analyses of the effects of drugs on health are usually concerned with the physician's (planner's) information and decision problem. Gill and Robins' (2001) sequential randomization assumption, for example, is often justified by the assumption that physicians base their treatment decisions on observable (by the analyst) information only. This literature, however, often ignores the possibility that many variables known to the physician may not be known to the observing statistician and that the agents being given drugs alter the protocols.

Potential outcomes will often depend on the agent's information. Failure to correctly model the information will often lead to violation of (NA) and failure of invariance. Potential outcomes may therefore not be valid inputs in a policy evaluation study. A naive specification of potential outcomes would only index treatments by actual participation in, e.g., job search assistance or training programs. Such a naive specification is incomplete in the context of economies inhabited by forward-looking agents who make choices that affect outcomes. In specifying potential outcomes, we should not only consider the effects of actual program participation, but also the effects of the information available to agents about the program and policy. We now illustrate this point.

EXAMPLE 5. Black et al. (2003) analyze the effect of compulsory training and employment services provided to unemployment insurance (UI) claimants in Kentucky on the exit rate from UI and earnings. In the program they study, letters are sent out to notify agents some time ahead whether they are selected to participate in the program. This information is recorded in a database and available to them. They can analyze the letter as part of a program that consists of information provision and subsequent participation in training. The main empirical finding of their paper is that the threat of future mandatory training conveyed by the letters is more effective in increasing the UI exit rate than training itself.

The data used by Black et al. (2003) are atypical of many economic data sets, because the data collectors carefully record the information provided to agents. This allows Black et al. to analyze the effects of the provision of information along with the effects of actual program participation. In many econometric applications, the information on the program under study is less rich. Data sets may provide information on actual participation in training programs and some background information on how the program is administered. Typically, however, the data do not record all of the letters sent to agents and do not record every phone conversation between administrators and agents. Then, the econometrician needs to make assumptions on how this information accumulates for agents. In many applications, knowledge of specific institutional mechanisms of assignment can be used to justify specific informational assumptions.

EXAMPLE 6. Abbring, Van den Berg and Van Ours (2005) analyze the effect of punitive benefits reductions, or sanctions, on Dutch UI on re-employment rates. In the Netherlands, UI claimants have to comply with certain rules concerning search behavior and registration. If a claimant violates these rules, a sanction may be applied. A sanction is a punitive reduction in benefits for some period of time and may be accompanied by increased levels of monitoring by the UI agency.[78] Abbring, Van den Berg and Van

[78] See Grubb (2000) for a review of sanction systems in the OECD.

Ours (2005) use administrative data and know the re-employment duration, the duration at which a sanction is imposed if a sanction is imposed, and some background characteristics for each UI case.

Without prior knowledge of the Dutch UI system, an analyst might make a variety of informational assumptions. One extreme is that UI claimants know at the start of their UI spells that their benefits will be reduced at some specific duration if they are still claiming UI at that duration. This results in a UI system with entitlement periods that are tailored to individual claimants and that are set and revealed at the start of the UI spells. In this case, claimants will change their labor-market behavior from the start of their UI spell in response to the future benefits reduction [e.g., Mortensen (1977)]. At another extreme, claimants receive no prior signals of impending sanctions and there are no anticipatory effects of actual benefits reductions. However, agents may still be aware of the properties of the sanctions process and to some extent this will affect their behavior. Abbring, Van den Berg and Van Ours (2005) analyze a search model with these features. Abbring and Van den Berg (2003b) provide a structural example where the data cannot distinguish between these two informational assumptions. We discuss this example further in Section 3.3.1. Abbring, Van den Berg and Van Ours (2005) use institutional background information to argue in favor of the second informational assumption as the one that characterizes their data.

If data on information provision are not available and simplifying assumptions on the program's information structure cannot be justified, the analyst needs to model the information that accumulates to agents as an unobserved determinant of outcomes. This is the approach followed, and further discussed, in Section 3.4.

The information determining outcomes typically includes aspects of the policy. In Example 5, the letter announcing future training will be interpreted differently in different policy environments. If agents are forward looking, the letter will be more informative under a policy that specifies a strong relation between the letter and mandatory training in the population than under a policy that allocates letters and training independently. In Example 6, the policy is a monitoring regime. Potential outcomes are UI durations under different sanction times. A change in monitoring policy changes the value of unemployment. In a job-search model with forward looking agents, agents will respond by changing their search effort and reservation wage, and UI duration outcomes will change. In either example, potential outcomes are not invariant to variation in the policy. In the terminology of Hurwicz (1962), the policy is not "structural" with regard to potential outcomes and violates invariance assumptions (PI-1)–(PI-4) presented in Chapter 70. One must control for the effects of agents' information.

3.2.4. Selection on unobservables

In econometric program evaluations, (sequentially) randomized assignment is unlikely to hold. We illustrate this in the models developed in Section 3.4. Observational data are characterized by a lot of heterogeneity among agents, as documented by the empirical examples in Section 2 and in Heckman, LaLonde and Smith (1999). This heterogeneity is unlikely to be fully captured by the observed variables in most data sets. In a dynamic context, such unmeasured heterogeneity leads to violations of the assumptions of Gill and Robins (2001) and Rust (1987) that choices represent a sequential randomization. This is true even if the unmeasured variables only affect the availability of slots in programs but not outcomes directly. If agents are rational, forward-looking and observe at least some of the unmeasured variables that the econometrician does not, they will typically respond to these variables through their choice of treatment and through their investment behavior. In this case, the sequential randomization condition fails.

For the same reason, identification based on instrumental variables is relatively hard to justify in dynamic models [Hansen and Sargent (1980), Rosenzweig and Wolpin (2000), Abbring and Van den Berg (2005)]. If the candidate instruments only vary across persons but not over time for the same person, then they are not likely to be valid instruments because they affect expectations and future choices and may affect current potential outcomes. Instead of using instrumental variables that vary only across persons, we require instruments based on unanticipated person-specific shocks that affect treatment choices but not outcomes at each point in time. In the context of continuously assigned treatments, the implied data requirements seem onerous. To achieve identification, Abbring and Van den Berg (2003b) focus on regressor variation rather than exclusion restrictions in a sufficiently smooth model of continuous-time treatment effects. We discuss their analysis in Section 3.3. Heckman and Navarro (2007) show that curvature conditions, not exclusion restrictions, that result in the same variables having different effects on choices and outcomes in different periods, are motivated by economic theory and can be exploited to identify dynamic treatment effects in discrete time without literally excluding any variables. We discuss their analysis in Section 3.4. We now consider a formulation of the analysis in continuous time.

3.3. The event-history approach to policy analysis

The discrete-time models just discussed in Section 3.2 have an obvious limitation. Time is continuous and many events are best described by a continuous-time model. There is a rich field of continuous-time event-history analysis that has been adapted to conduct policy evaluation analysis.[79] For example, the effects of training and counseling on unemployment durations and job stability have been analyzed by applying event-history methods to data on individual labor-market and training histories [Ridder (1986), Card and Sullivan (1988), Gritz (1993), Ham and LaLonde (1996), Eberwein, Ham and LaLonde (1997), Bonnal, Fougère and Sérandon (1997)]. Similarly, the moral hazard effects of unemployment insurance have been studied by analyzing the effects of time-varying benefits on labor-market transitions [e.g., Meyer (1990), Abbring, Van den Berg

[79] Abbring and Van den Berg (2004) discuss the relation between the event-history approach to program evaluation and more standard latent-variable and panel-data methods, with a focus on identification issues.

and Van Ours (2005), Van den Berg, Van der Klaauw and Van Ours (2004)]. In fields like epidemiology, the use of event-history models to analyze treatment effects is widespread [see, e.g., Andersen et al. (1993), Keiding (1999)].

The event-history approach to program evaluation is firmly rooted in the econometric literature on state dependence (lagged dependent variables) and heterogeneity [Heckman and Borjas (1980), and Heckman (1981a)]. Event-history models along the lines of Heckman and Singer (1984, 1986) are used to jointly model transitions into programs and transitions into outcome states. Causal effects of programs are modelled as the dependence of individual transition rates on the individual history of program participation. Dynamic selection effects are modelled by allowing for dependent unobserved heterogeneity in both the program and outcome transition rates.

Without restrictions on the class of models considered, true state dependence and dynamic selection effects cannot be distinguished.[80] Any history dependence of current transition rates can be explained both as true state dependence and as the result of unobserved heterogeneity that simultaneously affects the history and current transitions. This is a dynamic manifestation of the problem of drawing causal inference from observational data. In applied work, researchers avoid this problem by imposing additional structure. A typical, simple, example is a mixed semi-Markov model in which the causal effects are restricted to program participation in the previous spell [e.g., Bonnal, Fougère and Sérandon (1997), see Section 3.3.2]. There is a substantial literature on the identifiability of state-dependence effects and heterogeneity in duration and event-history models that exploit such additional structure [see Heckman and Taber (1994), and Van den Berg (2001), for reviews]. Here, we provide discussion of some canonical cases.

3.3.1. Treatment effects in duration models

3.3.1.1. Dynamically assigned binary treatments and duration outcomes We first consider the simplest case of mutual dependence of events in continuous time, involving only two binary events. This case is sufficiently rich to capture the effect of a dynamically assigned binary treatment on a duration outcome. Binary events in continuous time can be fully characterized by the time at which they occur and a structural model for their joint determination is a simultaneous-equations model for durations. We develop such a model along the lines of Abbring and Van den Berg (2003b). This model is an extension, with general marginal distributions and general causal and spurious dependence of the durations, of Freund's (1961) bivariate exponential model.

Consider two continuously-distributed random durations Y and S. We refer to one of the durations, S, as the time to treatment and to the other duration, Y, as the outcome duration. Such an asymmetry arises naturally in many applications. For example, in Abbring, Van den Berg and Van Ours's (2005) study of unemployment insurance, the

[80] See Heckman and Singer (1986).

treatment is a punitive benefits reduction (sanction) and the outcome re-employment. The re-employment process continues after imposition of a sanction, but the sanctions process is terminated by re-employment. The current exposition, however, is symmetric and unifies both cases. It applies to both the asymmetric setup of the sanctions example and to applications in which both events may causally affect the other event.

Let $Y(s)$ be the potential outcome duration that would prevail if the treatment time is externally set to s. Similarly, let $S(y)$ be the potential treatment time resulting from setting the outcome duration to y. We assume that *ex ante* heterogeneity across agents is fully captured by observed covariates X and unobserved covariates V, assumed to be external and temporally invariant. Treatment causally affects the outcome duration through its hazard rate. We denote the hazard rate of $Y(s)$ at time t for an agent with characteristics (X, V) by $\theta_Y(t \mid s, X, V)$. Similarly, outcomes affect the treatment times through its hazard $\theta_S(t \mid y, X, V)$. Causal effects on hazard rates are produced by recursive economic models driven by point processes, such as search models. We provide an example below, and further discussion in Section 3.3.3.

Without loss of generality, we partition V into (V_S, V_Y) and assume that $\theta_Y(t \mid s, X, V) = \theta_Y(t \mid s, X, V_Y)$ and $\theta_S(t \mid y, X, V) = \theta_S(t \mid y, X, V_S)$. Intuitively, V_S and V_Y are the unobservables affecting, respectively, treatment and outcome, and the joint distribution of (V_S, V_Y) is unrestricted. In particular, V_S and V_Y may have elements in common.

The corresponding integrated hazard rates are defined by $\Theta_Y(t \mid s, X, V_Y) = \int_0^t \theta_Y(u \mid s, X, V_Y)\,du$ and $\Theta_S(t \mid y, X, V_S) = \int_0^t \theta_S(u \mid y, X, V_S)\,du$. For expositional convenience, we assume that these integrated hazards are strictly increasing in t. We also assume that they diverge to ∞ as $t \to \infty$, so that the duration distributions are non-defective.[81] Then, $\Theta_Y(Y(s) \mid s, X, V_Y)$ and $\Theta_S(S(y) \mid y, X, V_S)$ are unit exponential for all $y, s \in \mathbb{R}_+$.[82] This implies the following model of potential outcomes and treatments,[83]

$$Y(s) = y(s, X, V_Y, \varepsilon_Y) \quad \text{and} \quad S(y) = s(y, X, V_S, \varepsilon_S),$$

for some unit exponential random variables ε_Y and ε_S that are independent of (X, V), $y = \Theta_Y^{-1}$, and $s = \Theta_S^{-1}$.

[81] Abbring and Van den Berg (2003b) allow for defective distributions, which often have structural interpretations. For example, some women never have children and some workers will never leave a job. See Abbring (2002) for discussion.

[82] Let $T \mid X$ be distributed with density $f(t \mid X)$, non-defective cumulative distribution function $F(t \mid X)$, and hazard rate $\theta(t \mid X) = f(t \mid X)/[1 - F(t \mid X)]$. Then, $\int_0^T \theta(t \mid X)\,dt = -\ln[1 - F(T \mid X)]$ is a unit exponential random variable that is independent of X.

[83] The causal hazard model only implies that the distributions of ε_Y and ε_S are invariant across assigned treatments and outcomes, respectively; their realizations may not be. This is sufficient for the variation of $y(s, X, V_Y, \varepsilon_Y)$ with s and of $s(y, X, V_S, \varepsilon_S)$ with y to have a causal interpretation. The further restriction that the random variables ε_Y and ε_S are invariant is made for simplicity, and is empirically innocuous. See Abbring and Van den Berg (2003b) for details and Freedman (2004) for discussion.

The exponential errors ε_Y and ε_S embody the *ex post* shocks that are inherent to the individual hazard processes, that is the randomness in the transition process after conditioning on covariates X and V and survival. We assume that $\varepsilon_Y \perp\!\!\!\perp \varepsilon_S$, so that $\{Y(s)\}$ and $\{S(y)\}$ are only dependent through the observed and unobserved covariates (X, V). This conditional-independence assumption is weaker than the conditional-independence assumption underlying the analysis of Section 3.2 and used in matching, because it allows for conditioning on the invariant unobservables V. It shares this feature with the discrete-time models developed in Section 3.4 and is a version of matching on unobserved variables discussed in Section 2.

We assume a version of the no-anticipation condition of Section 3.2.1: for all $t \in \mathbb{R}_+$,

$$\theta_Y(t \mid s, X, V_Y) = \theta_Y(t \mid s', X, V_Y) \quad \text{and} \quad \theta_S(t \mid y, X, V_S) = \theta_S(t \mid y', X, V_S)$$

for all $s, s', y, y' \in [t, \infty)$. This excludes effects of anticipation of the treatment on the outcome. Similarly, there can be no anticipation effects of future outcomes on the treatment hazard.

EXAMPLE 7. Consider a standard search model describing the job search behavior of an unemployed individual [e.g., Mortensen (1986)] with characteristics (X, V). Job offers arrive at a rate $\lambda > 0$ and are random draws from a given distribution F. Both λ and F may depend on (X, V), but for notational simplicity we suppress all explicit representations of conditioning on (X, V) throughout this example. An offer is either accepted or rejected. A rejected offer cannot be recalled at a later time. The individual initially receives a constant flow of unemployment-insurance benefits. However, the individual faces the risk of a sanction—a permanent reduction of his benefits to some lower, constant level—at some point during his unemployment spell. During the unemployment spell, sanctions arrive independently of the job-offer process at a constant rate $\mu > 0$. The individual cannot foresee the exact time a sanction is imposed, but he knows the distribution of these times.[84] The individual chooses a job-acceptance rule as to maximize his expected discounted lifetime income. Under standard conditions, this is a reservation-wage rule: at time t, the individual accepts each wage of $\underline{w}(t)$ or higher. The corresponding re-employment hazard rate is $\lambda(1 - F(\underline{w}(t)))$. Apart from the sanction, which is not foreseen and arrives at a constant rate during the unemployment spell, the model is stationary. This implies that the reservation wage is constant, say equal to $\underline{w}_0$, up to and including time s, jumps to some lower level $\underline{w}_1 < \underline{w}_0$ at time s and stays constant at $\underline{w}_1$ for the remainder of the unemployment spell if benefits would be reduced at time s.

The model is a version of the simultaneous-equations model for durations. To see this, let Y be the re-employment duration and S the sanction time. The potential-outcome

[84] This is a rudimentary version of the search model with punitive benefits reductions, or sanctions, of Abbring, Van den Berg and Van Ours (2005). The main difference is that in the present version of the model the sanctions process cannot be controlled by the agent.

hazards are

$$\theta_Y(t \mid s) = \begin{cases} \lambda_0 & \text{if } 0 \leqslant t \leqslant s, \\ \lambda_1 & \text{if } t > s, \end{cases}$$

where $\lambda_0 = \lambda[1 - F(\underline{w}_0)]$ and $\lambda_1 = \lambda[1 - F(\underline{w}_1)]$, and clearly $\lambda_1 \geqslant \lambda_0$. Similarly, the potential-treatment time hazards are $\theta_S(t \mid y) = \mu$ if $0 \leqslant t \leqslant y$, and 0 otherwise. Note that the no-anticipation condition follows naturally from the recursive structure of the economic decision problem in this case in which we have properly accounted for all relevant components of agent information sets. Furthermore, the assumed independence of the job offer and sanction processes at the individual level for given (X, V) implies that $\varepsilon_Y \perp\!\!\!\perp \varepsilon_S$.

The actual outcome and treatment are related to the potential outcomes and treatments by $S = S(Y)$ and $Y = Y(S)$. The no-anticipation assumption ensures that this system has a unique solution (Y, S) by imposing a recursive structure on the underlying transition processes. Without anticipation effects, current treatment and outcome hazards only depend on past outcome and treatment events, and the transition processes evolve recursively [Abbring and Van den Berg (2003b)]. Together with a distribution $G(\cdot \mid X)$ of $V \mid X$, this gives a nonparametric structural model of the distribution of $(Y, S) \mid X$ that embodies general simultaneous causal dependence of Y and S, dependence of (Y, X) on observed covariates X, and general dependence of the unobserved errors V_Y and V_S.

There are two reasons for imposing further restrictions on this model. First, it is not identified from data on (Y, S, X). Take a version of the model with selection on unobservables ($V_Y \not\!\perp\!\!\!\perp V_S \mid X$) and consider the distribution of $(Y, S) \mid X$ generated by this version of the model. Then, there exists an alternative version of the model that satisfies both no-anticipation and $V_Y \perp\!\!\!\perp V_S \mid X$, and that generates the same distribution of $(Y, S) \mid X$ [Abbring and Van den Berg (2003b, Proposition 1)]. In other words, for each version of the model with selection on unobservables and anticipation effects, there is an observationally-equivalent model version that satisfies no-anticipation and conditional randomization. This is a version of the nonidentification result discussed in Section 3.2.1.

Second, even if we ensure nonparametric identification by assuming no-anticipation and conditional randomization, we cannot learn about the agent-level causal effects embodied in y and s without imposing even further restrictions. At best, under regularity conditions we can identify $\theta_Y(t \mid s, X) = E[\theta_Y(t \mid s, X, V_Y) \mid X, Y(s) \geqslant t]$ and $\theta_S(t \mid y, X) = E[\theta_S(t \mid y, X, V_S) \mid X, S(y) \geqslant t]$ from standard hazard regressions [e.g., Andersen et al. (1993), Fleming and Harrington (1991)]. Thus we can identify the distributions of $Y(s) \mid X$ and $S(y) \mid X$, and therefore solve the selection problem if we are only interested in these distributions. However, if we are also interested in the causal effects on the corresponding hazard rates for given X, V, we face an additional dynamic selection problem. The hazards of the identified distributions of $Y(s) \mid X$ and $S(y) \mid X$ only condition on observed covariates X, and not on unobserved covariates V, and are confounded with dynamic selection effects [Heckman and Borjas (1980), Heckman and Singer (1986), Meyer (1996), Abbring and Van den Berg (2005)]. For example, the difference between $\theta_Y(t \mid s, X)$ and $\theta_Y(t \mid s', X)$ does not only reflect agent-level differences between $\theta_Y(t \mid s, X, V_Y)$ and $\theta_Y(t \mid s', X, V_Y)$, but also differences in the subpopulations of survivors $\{X, Y(s) \geqslant t\}$ and $\{X, Y(s') \geqslant t\}$ on which the hazards are computed.

In the next two subsections, we discuss what can be learned about treatment effects in duration models under additional model restrictions. We take the no-anticipation assumption as fundamental. As explained in Section 3.2, this requires that we measure and include in our model all relevant information needed to define potential outcomes. However, we relax the randomization assumption. We first consider Abbring and Van den Berg's (2003b) analysis of identification without exclusion restrictions. They argue that these results are useful, because exclusion restrictions are hard to justify in an inherently dynamic setting with forward-looking agents. Abbring and Van den Berg (2005) further clarify this issue by studying inference for treatment effects in duration models using a social experiment. We discuss what can be learned from such experiments at the end of this section.

3.3.1.2. Identifiability without exclusion restrictions Abbring and Van den Berg consider an extension of the multivariate Mixed Proportional Hazard (MPH) model [Lancaster (1979)] in which the hazard rates of $Y(s) \mid (X, V)$ and $S(y) \mid (X, V)$ are given by

$$\theta_Y(t \mid s, X, V) = \begin{cases} \lambda_Y(t)\phi_Y(X)V_Y & \text{if } t \leqslant s, \\ \lambda_Y(t)\phi_Y(X)\delta_Y(t, s, X)V_Y & \text{if } t > s \end{cases} \quad \text{and} \tag{3.8}$$

$$\theta_S(t \mid y, X, V) = \begin{cases} \lambda_S(t)\phi_S(X)V_S & \text{if } t \leqslant y, \\ \lambda_S(t)\phi_S(X)\delta_S(t, y, X)V_S & \text{if } t > y, \end{cases} \tag{3.9}$$

respectively, and $V = (V_Y, V_S)$ is distributed independently of X. The baseline hazards $\lambda_Y : \mathbb{R}_+ \to (0, \infty)$ and $\lambda_S : \mathbb{R}_+ \to (0, \infty)$ capture duration dependence of the individual transition rates. The integrated hazards are $\Lambda_Y(t) = \int_0^t \lambda_Y(\tau)\, d\tau < \infty$ and $\Lambda_S(t) = \int_0^t \lambda_S(\tau)\, d\tau < \infty$ for all $t \in \mathbb{R}_+$. The regressor functions $\phi_Y : \mathcal{X} \to (0, \infty)$ and $\phi_S : \mathcal{X} \to (0, \infty)$ are assumed to be continuous, with $\mathcal{X} \subset \mathbb{R}^q$ the support of X. In empirical work, these functions are frequently specified as $\phi_Y(x) = \exp(x'\beta_Y)$ and $\phi_S(x) = \exp(x'\beta_S)$ for some parameter vectors β_Y and β_S. We will not make such parametric assumptions. Note that the fact that both regressor functions are defined on the same domain $\mathcal{X}$ is not restrictive, because each function ϕ_Y and ϕ_S can "select" certain elements of X by being trivial functions of the other elements. In the parametric example, the vector β_Y would only have nonzero elements for those regressors that matter to the outcome hazard. The functions δ_Y and δ_S capture the causal effects. Note that $\delta_Y(t, s, X)$ only enters $\theta_Y(t \mid s, X, V)$ at durations $t > s$, so that the model satisfies no anticipation of treatment. Similarly, it satisfies no anticipation of outcomes and has a recursive causal structure as required by the no-anticipation assumption. If $\delta_Y = 1$, treatment is ineffective; if δ_Y is larger than 1, it stochastically reduces the remaining outcome duration.

Note that this model allows δ_Y and δ_S to depend on elapsed duration t, past endogenous events, and the observed covariates X, but not on V. Abbring and Van den Berg also consider an alternative model that allows δ_Y and δ_S to depend on unobservables in a general way, but not on past endogenous events.

Abbring and Van den Berg show that these models are nonparametrically identified from single-spell data under the conditions for the identification of competing risks models based on the multivariate MPH model given by Abbring and Van den Berg (2003a). Among other conditions are the requirements that there is some independent local variation of the regressor effects in both hazard rates and a finite-mean restriction on V, and are standard in the analysis of multivariate MPH models. With multiple-spell data, most of these assumptions, and the MPH structure, can be relaxed [Abbring and Van den Berg (2003b)].

The models can be parameterized in a flexible way and estimated by maximum likelihood. Typical parameterizations involve linear-index structures for the regressor and causal effects, a discrete distribution G, and piecewise-constant baseline hazards λ_S and λ_Y. Abbring and Van den Berg (2003c) develop a simple graphical method for inference on the sign of $\ln(\delta_Y)$ in the absence of regressors. Abbring, Van den Berg and Van Ours (2005) present an empirical application.

3.3.1.3. Inference based on instrumental variables The concerns expressed in Section 3.2.4 about the validity of exclusion restrictions in dynamic settings carry over to event-history models.

EXAMPLE 8. A good illustration of this point is offered by the analysis of Eberwein, Ham and LaLonde (1997), who study the effects of a training program on labor-market transitions. Their data are particularly nice, as potential participants are randomized into treatment and control groups at some baseline point in time. This allows them to estimate the effect of intention to treat (with training) on subsequent labor-market transitions. This is directly relevant to policy evaluation in the case that the policy involves changing training enrollment through offers of treatment which may or may not be accepted by agents.

However, Eberwein et al. are also interested in the effect of actual participation in the training program on post-program labor-market transitions. This is a distinct problem, because compliance with the intention-to-treat protocol is imperfect. Some agents in the control group are able to enroll in substitute programs, and some agents in the treatment group choose never to enroll in a program at all. Moreover, actual enrollment does not take place at the baseline time, but is dispersed over time. Those in the treatment group are more likely to enroll earlier. This fact, coupled with the initial randomization, suggests that the intention-to-treat indicator might be used as an instrument for identifying the effect of program participation on employment and unemployment spells.

The dynamic nature of enrollment into the training program, and the event-history focus of the analysis complicate matters considerably. Standard instrumental-variables methods cannot be directly applied. Instead, Eberwein et al. use a parametric duration model for pre- and post-program outcomes that excludes the intention-to-treat indicator from directly determining outcomes. They specify a duration model for training enrollment that includes an intention-to-treat indicator as an explanatory variable, and specify a model for labor-market transitions that excludes the intention-to-treat indicator and imposes a no-anticipation condition on the effect of actual training participation on labor-market transitions. Such a model is consistent with an environment in which agents cannot perfectly foresee the actual training time they will be assigned and in which they do not respond to information about this time revealed by their assignment to an intention-to-treat group. This is a strong assumption. In a search model with forward-looking agents, for example, such information would typically affect the *ex ante* values of unemployment and employment. Then, it would affect the labor-market transitions before actual training enrollment through changes in search efforts and reservation wages, unless these are both assumed to be exogenous. An assumption of perfect foresight on the part of the agents being studied only complicates matters further.

Abbring and Van den Berg (2005) study what can be learned about dynamically assigned programs from social experiments if the intention-to-treat instrument cannot be excluded from the outcome equation. They develop bounds, tests for unobserved heterogeneity, and point-identification results that extend those discussed in this section.[85]

3.3.2. Treatment effects in more general event-history models

It is instructive to place the causal duration models developed in Section 3.3.1 in the more general setting of event-history models with state dependence and heterogeneity. We do this following Abbring's (2008) analysis of the mixed semi-Markov model.

3.3.2.1. The mixed semi-Markov event-history model The model is formulated in a fashion analogous to the frameworks of Heckman and Singer (1986). The point of departure is a continuous-time stochastic process assuming values in a finite set $\mathcal{S}$ at each point in time. We will interpret realizations of this process as agents' event histories of transitions between states in the state space $\mathcal{S}$.

Suppose that event histories start at real-valued random times T_0 in an $\mathcal{S}$-valued random state S_0, and that subsequent transitions occur at random times $T_1, T_2, \ldots$ such that $T_0 < T_1 < T_2 < \cdots$. Let S_l be the random destination state of the transition at T_l. Taking the sample paths of the event-history process to be right-continuous, we have that S_l is the state occupied in the interval $[T_l, T_{l+1})$.

[85] In the special case that a static treatment, or treatment plan, is assigned at the start of the spell, standard instrumental-variables methods may be applied. See Abbring and Van den Berg (2005).

Suppose that heterogeneity among agents is captured by vectors of time-constant observed covariates X and unobserved covariates V.[86] In this case, state dependence in the event-history process for given individual characteristics X, V has a causal interpretation.[87] We structure such state dependence by assuming that the event-history process conditional on X, V is a time-homogeneous semi-Markov process. Conditional on X, V the length of a spell in a state and the destination state of the transition ending that spell depend only on the past through the current state. In our notation, $(\Delta T_l, S_l) \perp\!\!\!\perp \{(T_i, S_i),\ i = 0, \dots, l-1\} \mid S_{l-1}, X, V$, where $\Delta T_l = T_l - T_{l-1}$ is the length of spell l. Also, the distribution of $(\Delta T_l, S_l) \mid S_{l-1}, X, V$ does not depend on l. Note that, conditional on $X, V, \{S_l,\ l \geqslant 0\}$ is a time-homogeneous Markov chain under these assumptions.

Nontrivial dynamic selection effects arise because V is not observed. The event-history process conditional on observed covariates X only is a mixed semi-Markov process. If V affects the initial state S_0, or transitions from there, subpopulations of agents in different states at some time t typically have different distributions of the unobserved characteristics V. Therefore, a comparison of the subsequent transitions in two such subpopulations does not only reflect state dependence, but also sorting of agents with different unobserved characteristics into the different states they occupy at time t.

We model $\{(\Delta T_l, S_l),\ l \geqslant 1\} \mid T_0, S_0, X, V$ as a repeated competing risks model. Due to the mixed semi-Markov assumption, the latent durations corresponding to transitions into the possible destination states in the lth spell only depend on the past through the current state S_{l-1}, conditional on X, V. This implies that we can fully specify the repeated competing risks model by specifying a set of origin-destination-specific latent durations, with corresponding transition rates. Let T^l_{jk} denote the latent duration corresponding to the transition from state j to state k in spell l. We explicitly allow for the possibility that transitions between certain (ordered) pairs of states may be impossible. To this end, define the correspondence $\mathcal{Q}: \mathcal{S} \to \sigma(\mathcal{S})$ assigning to each $s \in \mathcal{S}$ the set of all destination states to which transitions are made from s with positive probability.[88] Here, $\sigma(\mathcal{S})$ is the set of all subsets of $\mathcal{S}$ (the "power set" of $\mathcal{S}$). Then, the length of spell l is given by $\Delta T_l = \min_{s \in \mathcal{Q}(S_{l-1})} T^l_{S_{l-1}s}$, and the destination state by $S_l = \arg\min_{s \in \mathcal{Q}(S_{l-1})} T^l_{S_{l-1}s}$.

We take the latent durations to be mutually independent, jointly independent from T_0, S_0, and identically distributed across spells l, all conditional on X, V. This reflects

86 We restrict attention to time-invariant observed covariates for expositional convenience. The analysis can easily be adapted to more general time-varying external covariates. Restricting attention to time-constant regressors is a worst-case scenario for identification. External time variation in observed covariates aids identification [Heckman and Taber (1994)].

87 We could make this explicit by extending the potential-outcomes model of Section 3.3.1 to the general event-history setup. However, this would add a lot of complexity, but little extra insight.

88 Throughout this section, we assume that $\mathcal{Q}$ is known. It is important to note, however, that $\mathcal{Q}$ can actually be identified trivially in all cases considered.

both the mixed semi-Markov assumption and the additional assumption that all dependence between the latent durations corresponding to the competing risks in a given spell l is captured by the observed regressors X and the unobservables V. This is a standard assumption in econometric duration analysis, which, with the semi-Markov assumption, allows us to characterize the distribution of $\{(\Delta T_l, S_l),\ l \geqslant 1\} \mid T_0, S_0, X, V$ by specifying origin-destination-specific hazards $\theta_{jk}(t \mid X, V)$ for the marginal distributions of $T_{jk}^l \mid X, V$.

We assume that the hazards $\theta_{jk}(t \mid X, V)$ are of the mixed proportional hazard (MPH) type:[89]

$$\theta_{jk}(t \mid X, V) = \begin{cases} \lambda_{jk}(t)\phi_{jk}(X)V_{jk} & \text{if } k \in \mathcal{Q}(j), \\ 0 & \text{otherwise.} \end{cases} \tag{3.10}$$

The baseline hazards $\lambda_{jk} : \mathbb{R}_+ \to (0, \infty)$ have integrated hazards $\Lambda_{jk}(t) = \int_0^t \lambda_{jk}(\tau)\, d\tau < \infty$ for all $t \in \mathbb{R}_+$. The regressor functions $\phi_{jk} : \mathcal{X} \to (0, \infty)$ are assumed to be continuous. Finally, the $(0, \infty)$-valued random variable V_{jk} is the scalar component of V that affects the transition from state j to state k. Note that we allow for general dependence between the components of V. This way, we can capture, for example, that agents with lower re-employment rates have higher training enrollment rates.

This model fully characterizes the distribution of the transitions $\{(\Delta T_l, S_l),\ l \geqslant 1\}$ conditional on the initial conditions T_0, S_0 and the agents' characteristics X, V. A complete model of the event histories $\{(T_l, S_l),\ l \geqslant 0\}$ conditional on X, V would in addition require a specification of the initial conditions T_0, S_0 for given X, V. It is important to stress here that T_0, S_0 are the initial conditions of the event-history process itself, and should not be confused with the initial conditions in a particular sample (which we will discuss below). In empirical work, interest in the dependence between start times T_0 and characteristics X, V is often limited to the observation that the distribution of agent's characteristics may vary over cohorts indexed by T_0. The choice of initial state S_0 may in general be of some interest, but is often trivial. For example, we could model labor-market histories from the calendar time T_0 at which agents turn 15 onwards. In an economy with perfect compliance to a mandatory schooling up to age 15, the initial state S_0 would be "(mandatory) schooling" for all. Therefore, we will not consider a model of the event history's initial conditions, but instead focus on the conditional model of subsequent transition histories.

Because of the semi-Markov assumption, the distribution of $\{(\Delta T_l, S_l),\ l \geqslant 1\} \mid T_0, S_0, X, V$ only depends on S_0, and not T_0. Thus, T_0 only affects observed event histories through cohort effects on the distribution of unobserved characteristics V. The initial state S_0, on the other hand, may both have causal effects on subsequent transitions and be informative on the distribution of V. For expositional clarity, we assume

[89] Proportionality can be relaxed if we have data on sufficiently long event-histories. See Honoré (1993) and Abbring and Van den Berg (2003a, 2003b) for related arguments for various multi-spell duration models.

that $V \perp\!\!\!\perp (T_0, S_0, X)$. This is true, for example, if all agents start in the same state, so that S_0 is degenerate, and V is independent of the start date T_0 and the observed covariates X.

An econometric model for transition histories conditional on the observed covariates X can be derived from the model of $\{(\Delta T_l, S_l),\ l \geqslant 1\} \mid S_0, X, V$ by integrating out V. The exact way this should be done depends on the sampling scheme used. Here, we focus on sampling from the population of event-histories. We assume that we observe the covariates X, the initial state S_0, and the first L transitions from there. Then, we can model these transitions for given S_0, X by integrating the conditional model over the distribution of V.

Abbring (2008) discusses more complex, and arguably more realistic, sampling schemes. For example, when studying labor-market histories we may randomly sample from the stock of the unemployed at a particular point in time. Because the unobserved component V affects the probability of being unemployed at the sampling date, the distribution of $V \mid X$ in the stock sample does not equal its population distribution. This is again a dynamic version of the selection problem. Moreover, in this case we typically do not observe an agent's entire labor-market history from T_0 onwards. Instead, we may have data on the time spent in unemployment at the sampling date and on labor-market transitions for some period after the sampling date. This "initial conditions problem" complicates matters further [Heckman (1981b)].

In the next two subsections, we first discuss some examples of applications of the model and then review a basic identification result for the simple sampling scheme above.

3.3.2.2. Applications to program evaluation Several empirical papers study the effect of a single treatment on some outcome duration or set of transitions. Two approaches can be distinguished. In the first approach, the outcome and treatment processes are explicitly and separately specified. The second approach distinguishes treatment as one state within a single event-history model with state dependence.

The first approach is used in a variety of papers in labor economics. Eberwein, Ham and LaLonde (1997) specify a model for labor-market transitions in which the transition intensities between various labor-market states (not including treatment) depend on whether someone has been assigned to a training program in the past or not. Abbring, Van den Berg and Van Ours (2005) and Van den Berg, Van der Klaauw and Van Ours (2004) specify a model for re-employment durations in which the re-employment hazard depends on whether a punitive benefits reduction has been imposed in the past. Similarly, Van den Berg, Holm and Van Ours (2002) analyze the duration up to transition into medical trainee positions and the effect of an intermediate transition into a medical assistant position (a "stepping-stone job") on this duration. In all of these papers, the outcome model is complemented with a hazard model for treatment choice.

These models fit into the framework of Section 3.3.1 or a multi-state extension thereof. We can rephrase the class of models discussed in Section 3.3.1 in terms of a simple event-history model with state dependence as follows. Distinguish three states, untreated (O), treated (P) and the exit state of interest (E), so that $\mathcal{S} = \{O, P, E\}$. All subjects start in O, so that $S_0 = O$. Obviously, we do not want to allow for all possible transitions between these three states. Instead, we restrict the correspondence $\mathcal{Q}$ representing the possible transitions as follows:

$$\mathcal{Q}(s) = \begin{cases} \{P, E\} & s = O, \\ \{E\} \quad \text{if} & s = P, \\ \emptyset & s = E. \end{cases}$$

State dependence of the transition rates into E captures treatment effects in the sense of Section 3.3.1. Not all models in Abbring and Van den Berg (2003b) are included in the semi-Markov setup discussed here. In particular, in this paper we do not allow the transition rate from P to E to depend on the duration spent in O. This extension with "lagged duration dependence" [Heckman and Borjas (1980)] would be required to capture one variant of their model.

The model for transitions from "untreated" (O) is a competing risks model, with program enrollment (transition to P) and employment (E) competing to end the untreated spell. If the unobservable factor V_{OE} that determines transitions to employment and the unobservable factor V_{OP} affecting program enrollment are dependent, then program enrollment is selective in the sense that the initial distribution of V_{OE}—and also typically that of V_{PE}—among those who enroll at a given point in time does not equal its distribution among survivors in O up to that time.[90]

The second approach is used by Gritz (1993) and Bonnal, Fougère and Sérandon (1997), among others. Consider the following simplified setup. Suppose workers are either employed (E), unemployed (O), or engaged in a training program (P). We can now specify a transition process among these three labor-market states in which a causal effect of training on unemployment and employment durations is modeled as dependence of the various transition rates on the past occurrence of a training program in the labor-market history. Bonnal, Fougère and Sérandon (1997) only have limited information on agents' labor-market histories before the sample period. Partly to avoid difficult initial conditions problems, they restrict attention to "first order lagged occurrence dependence" [Heckman and Borjas (1980)] by assuming that transition rates only depend on the current and previous state occupied. Such a model is not directly covered by the semi-Markov model, but with a simple augmentation of the state space it can be covered. In particular, we have to include lagged states in the state space on which the transition process is defined. Because there is no lagged state in the event-history's first spell, initial states should be defined separately. So, instead of just distinguishing states in $\mathcal{S}^* = \{E, O, P\}$, we distinguish augmented states in $\mathcal{S} = \{(s, s') \in (\mathcal{S}^* \cup \{I\}) \times \mathcal{S}^*\colon s \neq s'\}$. Then, (I, s), $s \in \mathcal{S}^*$, denote the initial states, and $(s, s') \in \mathcal{S}$ the augmented state of an agent who is currently in s' and came from $s \neq s'$. In order to preserve the interpretation of the model as a model of lagged

[90] Note that, in addition, the survivors in O themselves are a selected subpopulation. Because V affects survival in O, the distribution of V among survivors in O is not equal to its population distribution.

occurrence dependence, we have to exclude certain transitions by specifying

$$\mathcal{Q}(s, s') = \{(s', s''),\ s'' \in \mathcal{S}^* \setminus \{s'\}\}.$$

This excludes transitions to augmented states that are labeled with a lagged state different from the origin state. Also, it ensures that agents never return to an initial state. For example, from the augmented state (O, P)—previously unemployed and currently enrolled in a program—only transitions to augmented states (P, s'')—previously enrolled in a program and currently in s''—are possible. Moreover, it is not possible to be currently employed and transiting to initially unemployed, (I, O). Rather, an employed person who loses her job would transit to (E, O)—currently unemployed and previously employed.

The effects of, for example, training are now modeled as simple state-dependence effects. For example, the effect of training on the transition rate from unemployment to employment is simply the contrast between the individual transition rate from (E, O) to (O, E) and the transition rate from (P, O) to (O, E). Dynamic selection into the augmented states (E, O) and (P, O), as specified by the transition model, confounds the empirical analysis of these training effects. Note that due to the fact that we have restricted attention to first-order lagged occurrence dependence, there are no longer-run effects of training on transition rates from unemployment to employment.

3.3.2.3. Identification without exclusion restrictions In this section, we sketch a basic identification result for the following sampling scheme. Suppose that the economist randomly samples from the population of event-histories, and that we observe the first $\bar{L}$ transitions (including destinations) for each sampled event-history, with the possibility that $\bar{L} = \infty$.[91] Thus, we observe a random sample of $\{(T_l, S_l),\ l \in \{0, 1, \dots, \bar{L}\}\}$, and X.

First note that we can only identify the determinants of θ_{jk} for transitions (j, k) that occur with positive probability among the first $\bar{L}$ transitions. Moreover, without further restrictions, we can only identify the joint distribution of a vector of unobservables corresponding to (part of) a sequence of transitions that can be observed among the first $\bar{L}$ transitions.

With this qualification, identification can be proved by extending Abbring and Van den Berg's (2003a) analysis of the MPH competing risks model to the present setting. This analysis assumes that transition rates have an MPH functional form. Identification again requires specific moments of V to be finite, and independent local variation in the regressor effects.

3.3.3. A structural perspective

Without further restrictions, the causal duration model of Section 3.3.1 is versatile. It can be generated as the reduced form of a wide variety of continuous-time economic

[91] Note that this assumes away econometric initial conditions problems of the type previously discussed.

models driven by point processes. Leading examples are sequential job-search models in which job-offer arrival rates, and other model parameters, depend on agent characteristics (X, V) and policy interventions [see, e.g., Mortensen (1986), and Example 7].

The MPH restriction on this model, however, is hard to justify from economic theory. In particular, nonstationary job-search models often imply interactions between duration and covariate effects; the MPH model only results under strong assumptions [Heckman and Singer (1986), Van den Berg (2001)]. Similarly, an MPH structure is hard to generate from models in which agents learn about their individual value of the model's structural parameters, that is about (X, V), through Bayesian updating.

An alternative class of continuous-time models, not discussed in this chapter, specifies durations as the first time some Gaussian or more general process crosses a threshold. Such models are closely related to a variety of dynamic economic models. They have attracted recent attention in statistics [see, e.g., Aalen and Gjessing (2004)]. Abbring (2007) analyzes identifiability of "mixed hitting-time models", continuous-time threshold-crossing models in which the parameters depend on observed and unobserved covariates, and discusses their link with optimizing models in economics. This is a relatively new area of research, and a full development is beyond the scope of this paper. It extends to a continuous-time framework the dynamic threshold-crossing model developed in Heckman (1981a, 1981b) that is used in the next subsection of this chapter.

We now discuss a complementary discrete-time approach where it is possible to make many important economic distinctions that are difficult to make in the setting of continuous-time models and to avoid some difficult measure-theoretic problems. In the structural version, it is possible to specify precisely agent information sets in a fashion that is not possible in conventional duration models.

3.4. Dynamic discrete choice and dynamic treatment effects

Heckman and Navarro (2007) and Cunha, Heckman and Navarro (2007) present econometric models for analyzing time to treatment and the consequences of the choice of a particular treatment time. Treatment may be a medical intervention, stopping schooling, opening a store, conducting an advertising campaign at a given date or renewing a patent. Associated with each treatment time, there can be multiple outcomes. They can include a vector of health status indicators and biomarkers; lifetime employment and earnings consequences of stopping at a particular grade of schooling; the sales revenue and profit generated from opening a store at a certain time; the revenues generated and market penetration gained from an advertising campaign; or the value of exercising an option at a given time. Heckman and Navarro (2007) unite and contribute to the literatures on dynamic discrete choice and dynamic treatment effects. For both classes of models, they present semiparametric identification analyses. We summarize their work in this section. It is a natural extension of the framework for counterfactual analysis of multiple treatments developed in Section 2 to a dynamic setting. It is formulated in discrete time, which facilitates the specification of richer unobserved and observed covariate processes than those entertained in the continuous-time framework of Abbring and Van den Berg (2003b).

Heckman and Navarro extend the literature on treatment effects to model choices of treatment times and the consequences of choice and link the literature on treatment effects to the literature on precisely formulated structural dynamic discrete-choice models generated from index models crossing thresholds. They show the value of precisely formulated economic models in extracting the information sets of agents, in providing model identification, in generating the standard treatment effects and in enforcing the nonanticipating behavior condition (NA) discussed in Section 3.2.1.[92]

They establish the semiparametric identifiability of a class of dynamic discrete-choice models for stopping times and associated outcomes in which agents sequentially update the information on which they act. They also establish identifiability of a new class of reduced form duration models that generalize conventional discrete-time duration models to produce frameworks with much richer time series properties for unobservables and general time-varying observables and patterns of duration dependence than conventional duration models. Their analysis of identification of these generalized models requires richer variation driven by observables than is needed in the analysis of the more restrictive conventional models. However, it does not require conventional period-by-period exclusion restrictions, which are often difficult to justify. Instead, they rely on curvature restrictions across the index functions generating the durations that can be motivated by dynamic economic theory.[93] Their methods can be applied to a variety of outcome measures including durations.

The key to their ability to identify structural models is that they supplement information on stopping times or time to treatment with additional information on measured consequences of choices of time to treatment as well as measurements. The dynamic discrete-choice literature surveyed in Rust (1994) and Magnac and Thesmar (2002) focuses on discrete-choice processes with general preferences and state vector evolution equations, typically Markovian in nature. Rust's (1994) paper contains negative results on nonparametric identification of discrete-choice processes. Magnac and Thesmar (2002) present some positive results on nonparametric identification if certain parameters or distributions of unobservables are assumed to be known. Heckman and Navarro (2007) produce positive results on nonparametric identification of a class of dynamic discrete-choice models based on expected income maximization developed in labor economics by Flinn and Heckman (1982), Keane and Wolpin (1997) and Eckstein and Wolpin (1999). These frameworks are dynamic versions of the Roy model. Heckman and Navarro (2007) show how use of cross-equation restrictions joined with data on supplementary measurement systems can undo Rust's nonidentification result. We exposit

[92] Aakvik, Heckman and Vytlacil (2005), Heckman, Tobias and Vytlacil (2001, 2003), Carneiro, Hansen and Heckman (2001, 2003) and Heckman and Vytlacil (2005) show how standard treatment effects can be generated from structural models.

[93] See Heckman and Honoré (1989) for examples of such an identification strategy in duration models. See also Cameron and Heckman (1998).

their work and the related literature in this section. With their structural framework, they can distinguish objective outcomes from subjective outcomes (valuations by the decision maker) in a dynamic setting. Applying their analysis to health economics, they can identify the causal effects on health of a medical treatment as well as the associated subjective pain and suffering of a treatment regime for the patient.[94] Attrition decisions also convey information about agent preferences about treatment.[95]

They do not rely on the assumption of conditional independence of unobservables with outcomes, given observables, that is used throughout much of the dynamic discrete-choice literature and the dynamic treatment literature surveyed in Section 3.2.[96] As noted in Section 3.1, sequential conditional-independence assumptions underlie recent work on reduced form dynamic treatment effects.[97] The semiparametric analysis of Heckman and Navarro (2007) based on factors generalizes matching to a dynamic setting. In their paper, some of the variables that would produce conditional independence and would justify matching if they were observed, are treated as unobserved match variables. They are integrated out and their distributions are identified.[98] They consider two classes of models. We review both.

3.4.1. Semiparametric duration models and counterfactuals

Heckman and Navarro (2007), henceforth HN, develop a semiparametric index model for dynamic discrete choices that extends conventional discrete time duration analysis. They separate out duration dependence from heterogeneity in a semiparametric framework more general than conventional discrete-time duration models. They produce a new class of reduced form models for dynamic treatment effects by adjoining time-to-treatment outcomes to the duration model. This analysis builds on Heckman (1981a, 1981b, 1981c).

Their models are based on a latent variable for choice at time s,

$$I(s) = \Psi\big(s, Z(s)\big) - \eta(s),$$

where the $Z(s)$ are observables and $\eta(s)$ are unobservables from the point of view of the econometrician. Treatments at different times may have different outcome consequences which they model after analyzing the time to treatment equation. Define $D(s)$ as an indicator of receipt of treatment at date s. Treatment is taken the first time $I(s)$

94 See Chan and Hamilton (2006) for a structural dynamic empirical analysis of this problem.

95 See Heckman and Smith (1998). Use of participation data to infer preferences about outcomes is developed in Heckman (1974b).

96 See, e.g., Rust (1987), Manski (1993), Hotz and Miller (1993) and the papers cited in Rust (1994).

97 See, e.g., Gill and Robins (2001) and Lechner and Miquel (2002).

98 For estimates based on this idea see Carneiro, Hansen and Heckman (2003), Aakvik, Heckman and Vytlacil (2005), Cunha and Heckman (2007b, 2008), Cunha, Heckman and Navarro (2005, 2006), and Heckman and Navarro (2005).

becomes positive. Thus,

$$D(s) = \mathbf{1}\big[I(s) \geqslant 0,\ I(s-1) < 0,\ \ldots,\ I(1) < 0\big],$$

where the indicator function $\mathbf{1}[\cdot]$ takes the value of 1 if the term inside the braces is true.[99] They derive conditions for identifying a model with general forms of duration dependence in the time to treatment equation using a large sample from the distribution of (D, Z).

3.4.1.1. Single spell duration model Individuals are assumed to start spells in a given (exogenously determined) state and to exit the state at the beginning of time period S.[100] S is thus a random variable representing total completed spell length. Let $D(s) = 1$ if the individual exits at time s, $S = s$, and $D(s) = 0$ otherwise. In an analysis of drug treatments, S is the discrete-time period in the course of an illness at the beginning of which the drug is administered. Let $\bar{S}$ ($< \infty$) be the upper limit on the time the agent being studied can be at risk for a treatment. It is possible in this example that $D(1) = 0, \ldots, D(\bar{S}) = 0$, so that a patient never receives treatment. In a schooling example, "treatment" is not schooling, but rather dropping out of schooling.[101] In this case, $\bar{S}$ is an upper limit to the number of years of schooling, and $D(\bar{S}) = 1$ if $D(1) = 0$, $\ldots, D(\bar{S} - 1) = 0$.

The duration model can be specified recursively in terms of the threshold-crossing behavior of the sequence of underlying latent indices $I(s)$. Recall that $I(s) = \Psi(s, Z(s)) - \eta(s)$, with $Z(s)$ being the regressors that are observed by the analyst. The $Z(s)$ can include expectations of future outcomes given current information in the case of models with forward-looking behavior. For a given stopping time s, let $D^s = (D(1), \ldots, D(s))$ and designate by $d(s)$ and d^s values that $D(s)$ and D^s assume. Thus, $d(s)$ can be zero or one and d^s is a sequence of s zeros or a sequence containing $s - 1$ zeros and a single one. Denote a sequence of all zeros by (0), regardless of its length. Then,

$$D(1) = \mathbf{1}\big[I(1) \geqslant 0\big] \quad \text{and}$$

$$D(s) = \begin{cases} \mathbf{1}[I(s) \geqslant 0] & \text{if } D^{s-1} = (0), \\ 0 & \text{otherwise,} \end{cases} \qquad s = 2, \ldots, \bar{S}. \tag{3.11}$$

For $s = 2, \ldots, \bar{S}$, the indicator $\mathbf{1}[I(s) \geqslant 0]$ is observed if and only if the agent is still at risk of treatment, $D^{s-1} = (0)$. To identify period s parameters from period s outcomes, one must condition on all past outcomes and control for any selection effects.

99 This framework captures the essential feature of any stopping time model. For example, in a search model with one wage offer per period, $I(s)$ is the gap between market wages and reservation wages at time s. See, e.g., Flinn and Heckman (1982). This framework can also approximate the explicit dynamic discrete-choice model analyzed in Section 3.4.2.

100 Thus we abstract from the initial conditions problem discussed in Heckman (1981b).

101 In the drug treatment example, S may designate the time a treatment regime is completed.

Let $Z = (Z(1), \ldots, Z(\bar{S}))$, and let $\eta = (\eta(1), \ldots, \eta(\bar{S}))$.[102] Assume that Z is statistically independent of η. Heckman and Navarro (2007) assume that $\Psi(s, Z(s)) = Z(s)\gamma_s$. We deal with a more general case. $\Psi(Z) = (\Psi(1, Z(1)), \ldots, \Psi(\bar{S}, Z(\bar{S})))$. We let Ψ denote the abstract parameter. Depending on the values assumed by $\Psi(s, Z(s))$, one can generate very general forms of duration dependence that depend on the values assumed by the $Z(s)$. HN allow for period-specific effects of regressors on the latent indices generating choices.

This model is the reduced form of a general dynamic discrete-choice model. Like many reduced form models, the link to choice theory is not clearly specified. It is not a conventional multinomial choice model in a static (perfect certainty) setting with associated outcomes.

3.4.1.2. Identification of duration models with general error structures and duration dependence Heckman and Navarro (2007) establish semiparametric identification of the model of Equation (3.11) assuming access to a large sample of i.i.d. (D, Z) observations. Let $Z^s = (Z(1), \ldots, Z(s))$. Data on (D, Z) directly identify the conditional probability $\Pr(D(s) = d(s) \mid Z^s, D^{s-1} = (0))$ a.e. $F_{Z^s|D^{s-1}=(0)}$ where $F_{Z^s|D^{s-1}=(0)}$ is the distribution of Z^s conditional on previous choices $D^{s-1} = (0)$. Assume that $(\Psi, F_\eta) \in \Phi \times \mathcal{H}$, where F_η is the distribution of η and $\Phi \times \mathcal{H}$ is the parameter space. The goal is to establish conditions under which knowledge of $\Pr(D(s) = d(s) \mid Z, D^{s-1} = (0))$ a.e. $F_{Z|D^{s-1}=(0)}$ allows the analyst to identify a unique element of $\Phi \times \mathcal{H}$. They use a limit strategy that allows them to recover the parameters by conditioning on large values of the indices of the preceding choices. This identification strategy is widely used in the analysis of discrete choice.[103]

They establish sufficient conditions for the identification of model (3.11). We prove the following more general result:

THEOREM 3. *For the model defined by Equation* (3.11), *assume the following conditions*:

(i) $\eta \perp\!\!\!\perp Z$.

(ii) η *is an absolutely continuous random variable on* $\mathbb{R}^{\bar{S}}$ *with support* $\prod_{s=1}^{\bar{S}}(\underline{\eta}(s), \bar{\eta}(s))$, *where* $-\infty \leqslant \underline{\eta}(s) < \bar{\eta}(s) \leqslant +\infty$ *for all* $s = 1, \ldots, \bar{S}$.

(iii) *The* $\Psi(s, Z(s))$ *are members of the Matzkin class of functions defined in Appendix* B.1, $s = 1, \ldots, \bar{S}$.

[102] A special case of the general model arises when $\eta(s)$ has a factor model representation as analyzed in Section 2. We will use such a representation when we adjoin outcomes to treatment times later in this section.

[103] See, e.g., Manski (1988), Heckman (1990), Heckman and Honoré (1989, 1990), Matzkin (1992, 1993), Taber (2000), and Carneiro, Hansen and Heckman (2003). A version of the strategy of this proof was first used in psychology where agent choice sets are eliminated by experimenter manipulation. The limit set argument effectively uses regressors to reduce the choice set confronting agents. See Falmagne (1985) for a discussion of models of choice in psychology.

(iv) $\mathrm{Supp}(\Psi^{s-1}(Z), Z(s)) = \mathrm{Supp}(\Psi^{s-1}(Z)) \times \mathrm{Supp}(Z(s))$, $s = 2, \ldots, \bar{S}$.
(v) $\mathrm{Supp}(\Psi(Z)) \supseteq \mathrm{Supp}(\eta)$.

Then F_η and $\Psi(Z)$ are identified, where the $\Psi(s, Z(s))$, $s = 1, \ldots, \bar{S}$, are identified over the relevant support admitted by (ii).

PROOF. We sketch the proof for $\bar{S} = 2$. The result for general $\bar{S}$ follows by a recursive application of this argument. Consider the following three probabilities.

$$\text{(a)}\quad \Pr\bigl(D(1) = 1 \mid Z = z\bigr) = \int_{\underline{\eta}(1)}^{\Psi(1,z(1))} f_{\eta(1)}(u)\, du.$$

$$\text{(b)}\quad \Pr\bigl(D(2) = 1, D(1) = 0 \mid Z = z\bigr)$$
$$= \int_{\underline{\eta}(2)}^{\Psi(2,z(2))} \int_{\Psi(1,z(1))}^{\bar{\eta}(1)} f_{\eta(1),\eta(2)}(u_1, u_2)\, du_1\, du_2.$$

$$\text{(c)}\quad \Pr\bigl(D(2) = 0, D(1) = 0 \mid Z = z\bigr)$$
$$= \int_{\Psi(2,z(2))}^{\bar{\eta}(2)} \int_{\Psi(1,z(1))}^{\bar{\eta}(1)} f_{\eta(1),\eta(2)}(u_1, u_2)\, du_1\, du_2.$$

The left-hand sides are observed from data on those who stop in period 1 (a); those who stop in period 2 (b); and those who terminate in the "0" state in period 2 (c). From Matzkin (1992), under our conditions on the class of functions Φ, which are stronger than hers, we can identify $\Psi(1, z(1))$ and $F_{\eta(1)}$ from (a). Using (b), we can fix $z(2)$ and vary $\Psi(1, z(1))$. From (iv) and (v) there exists a limit set $\tilde{\mathcal{Z}}_1$, possibly dependent on $z(2)$, such that $\lim_{z(1)\to\tilde{\mathcal{Z}}_1} \Psi(1, z(1)) = \underline{\eta}(1)$. Thus we can construct

$$\Pr\bigl(D(2) = 0 \mid Z = z\bigr) = \int_{\Psi(2,z(2))}^{\bar{\eta}(2)} f_{\eta(2)}(u_2)\, du_2$$

and identify $\Psi(2, z(2))$ and $F_{\eta(2)}(\eta(2))$. Using the $\Psi(1, z(1))$, $\Psi(2, z(2))$, one can trace out the joint distribution $F_{\eta(1),\eta(2)}$ over its support. Under the Matzkin conditions, identification is achieved on a nonnegligible set. The proof generalizes in a straightforward way to general $\bar{S}$. □

Observe that if the $\eta(s)$ are bounded by finite upper and lower limits, we can only determine the $\Psi(s, Z(s))$ over the limits so defined. Consider the first step of the proof. Under the Matzkin conditions, $F_{\eta(1)}$ is known. From assumption (ii) we can determine

$$\Psi\bigl(1, z(1)\bigr) = F_{\eta(1)}^{-1}\bigl(\Pr\bigl(D(1) = 1 \mid Z = z\bigr)\bigr),$$

but only over the support $(\underline{\eta}(1), \bar{\eta}(1))$. If the support of $\eta(1)$ is $\mathbb{R}$, we determine $\Psi(1, z(1))$ for all $z(1)$. Heckman and Navarro (2007) analyze the special case $\Psi(s, Z(s)) = Z(s)\gamma_s$ and invoke sequential rank conditions to identify γ_s, even over limited supports. They also establish that the limit sets are nonnegligible in this case so that standard definitions of identifiability [see, e.g., Matzkin (1992)] will be satisfied.[104] Construction of the limit set $\widetilde{Z}_s$, $s = 1, \ldots, \bar{S}$, depends on the functional form specified for the $\Psi(s, z(s))$. For the linear-in-parameters case $\Psi(s, z(s)) = Z(s)\gamma_s$, they are obtained by letting arguments get big or small. Matzkin (1992) shows how to establish the limit sets for functions in her family of functions.

A version of Theorem 3 with $\Psi(s, Z(s)) = Z_s\gamma_s$ that allows dependence between Z and η^s except for one component can be proved using the analysis of Lewbel (2000) and Honoré and Lewbel (2002).[105]

The assumptions of Theorem 3 will be satisfied if there are transition-specific exclusion restrictions for Z with the required properties. As noted in Section 3.3, in models with many periods, this may be a demanding requirement. Very often, the Z variables are time invariant and so cannot be used as exclusion restrictions. Corollary 1 in HN, for the special case $\Psi(s, Z(s)) = Z(s)\gamma_s$, tells us that the HN version of the model can be identified even if there are no conventional exclusion restrictions and the $Z(s)$ are the *same* across all time periods if sufficient structure is placed on how the γ_s vary with s. Variations in the values of γ_s across time periods arise naturally in finite-horizon dynamic discrete-choice models where a shrinking horizon produces different effects of the same variable in different periods. For example, in Wolpin's (1987) analysis of a search model, the value function depends on time and the derived decision rules weight the same invariant characteristics differently in different periods. In a schooling model, parental background and resources may affect education continuation decisions differently at different stages of the schooling decision. The model generating equation (3.11) can be semiparametrically identified without transition-specific exclusions if the duration dependence is sufficiently general. For a proof, see Corollary 1 in Heckman and Navarro (2007).

The conditions of Theorem 3 are somewhat similar to the conditions on the regressor effects needed for identification of the continuous-time event-history models in Section 3.3. One difference is that the present analysis requires independent variation of the regressor effects over the support of the distribution of the unobservables generating outcomes. The continuous-time analysis based on the functional form of the mixed proportional hazard model (MPH) as analyzed by Abbring and Van den Berg (2003a) only requires local independent variation.

Theorem 3 and Corollary 1 in HN have important consequences. The $\Psi(s, Z(s))$, $s = 1, \ldots, \bar{S}$, can be interpreted as duration dependence parameters that are modified by the $Z(s)$ and that vary across the spell in a more general way than is permitted in

[104] Heckman and Navarro (2007) prove their theorem for a model where $D(s) = \mathbf{1}[I(s) \leqslant 0]$ if $D^{s-1} = (0)$, $s = 2, \ldots, \bar{S}$. Our formulation of their result is consistent with the notation in this chapter.

[105] HN discuss a version of such an extension at their website. Lewbel's conditions are very strong. To account for general forms of dependence between Z and η^s requires modeling the exact form of the dependence. Nonparametric solutions to this problem remain an open question in the literature on dynamic discrete choice. One solution is to assume functional forms for the error terms, but in general, this is not enough to identify the model without further restrictions imposed. See Heckman and Honoré (1990).

mixed proportional hazards (MPH), generalized accelerated failure time (GAFT) models or standard discrete-time hazard models.[106] Duration dependence in conventional specifications of duration models is usually generated by variation in model intercepts. The regressors are allowed to interact with the duration dependence parameters. In the specifications justified by Theorem 3, the "heterogeneity" distribution F_η is identified for a general model. No special "permanent-transitory" structure is required for the unobservables although that specification is traditional in duration analysis. Their explicit treatment of the stochastic structure of the duration model is what allows HN to link in a general way the unobservables generating the duration model to the unobservables generating the outcome equations that are introduced in the next section. Such an explicit link is not currently available in the literature on continuous-time duration models for treatment effects surveyed in Section 3.3, and is useful for modelling selection effects in outcomes across different treatment times. Their outcomes can be both discrete and continuous and are not restricted to be durations.

Under conditions given in Corollary 1 of HN, no period-specific exclusion conditions are required on the Z. Hansen and Sargent (1980) and Abbring and Van den Berg (2003b) note that period-specific exclusions are not natural in reduced form duration models designed to approximate forward-looking life cycle models. Agents make current decisions in light of their forecasts of future constraints and opportunities, and if they forecast some components well, and they affect current decisions, then they are in $Z(s)$ in period s. Corollary 1 in HN establishes identification without such exclusions. HN adjoin a system of counterfactual outcomes to their model of time to treatment to produce a model for dynamic counterfactuals. We summarize that work next.

3.4.1.3. Reduced form dynamic treatment effects This section reviews a reduced form approach to generating dynamic counterfactuals developed by HN. They apply and extend the analysis of Carneiro, Hansen and Heckman (2003) and Cunha, Heckman and Navarro (2005, 2006) to generate *ex post* potential outcomes and their relationship with the time to treatment indices $I(s)$ analyzed in the preceding subsection. With reduced form models, it is difficult to impose restrictions from economic theory or to make distinctions between *ex ante* and *ex post* outcomes. In the structural model developed below, these and other distinctions can be made easily.

The reduced form model's specification closely follows the exposition of Section 2.8.1. Associated with each treatment s, $s = 1, \ldots, \bar{S}$, is a vector of $\bar{T}$ outcomes,

$$\begin{aligned} &Y\big(s, X, U(s)\big) \\ &\quad = \big(Y\big(1, s, X, U(1, s)\big), \ldots, Y\big(t, s, X, U(t, s)\big), \ldots, Y\big(\bar{T}, s, X, U(\bar{T}, s)\big)\big). \end{aligned}$$

In this section, treatment time s is synonymous with treatment state s in Section 2. Outcomes depend on covariates X and $U(s) = (U(1, s), \ldots, U(t, s), \ldots, U(\bar{T}, s))$

[106] See Ridder (1990) for a discussion of these models.

that are, respectively, observable and unobservable by the econometrician. Elements of $Y(s, X, U(s))$ are outcomes associated with stopping or receiving treatment at the beginning of period s. They are factual outcomes if treatment s is actually selected ($S = s$ and $D(s) = 1$). Outcomes corresponding to treatments s' that are not selected ($D(s') = 0$) are counterfactuals. The outcomes associated with each treatment may be different, and indeed the treatments administered at different times may be different.

The components $Y(t, s, X, U(t, s))$ of the vector $Y(s, X, U(s))$ can be interpreted as the outcomes revealed at age t, $t = 1, \ldots, \bar{T}$, and may themselves be vectors. The reduced form approach presented in this section is not sufficiently rich to capture the notion that agents revise their anticipations of components of $Y(s, X, U(s))$, $s = 1, \ldots, \bar{S}$, as they acquire information over time. This notion is systematically developed using the structural model discussed below in Section 3.4.2.

The treatment "times" may be stages that are not necessarily connected with real times. Thus s may be a schooling level. The correspondence between stages and times is exact if each stage takes one period to complete. Our notation is more flexible, and time and periods can be defined more generally. Our notation in this section accommodates both cases.

In this section of the chapter, we use the condensed notation introduced in Section 2.8.1. This notation is sufficiently rich to represent the life cycle of outcomes for persons who receive treatment at s. Thus, in a schooling example, the components of this vector may include life cycle earnings, employment, and the like associated with a person with characteristics X, $U(s)$, $s = 1, \ldots, \bar{S}$, who completes s years of schooling and then forever ceases schooling. It could include earnings while in school at some level for persons who will eventually attain further schooling as well as post-school earnings.

We measure age and treatment time on the same time scale, with origin 1, and let $\bar{T} \geqslant \bar{S}$. Then, the $Y(t, s, X, U(t, s))$ for $t < s$ are outcomes realized while the person is in school at age t (s is the time the person will leave school; t is the current age) and before "treatment" (stopping schooling) has occurred. When $t \geqslant s$, these are post-school outcomes for treatment with s years of schooling. In this case, $t - s$ is years of post-school experience. In the case of a drug trial, the $Y(t, s, X, U(t, s))$ for $t < s$ are measurements observed before the drug is taken at s and if $t \geqslant s$, they are the post-treatment measurements.

Following Carneiro, Hansen and Heckman (2003) and our analysis in Section 2, the variables in $Y(t, s, X, U(t, s))$ may include discrete, continuous or mixed discrete-continuous components. For the discrete or mixed discrete-continuous cases, HN assume that latent continuous variables cross thresholds to generate the discrete components. Durations can be generated by latent index models associated with each outcome crossing thresholds analogous to the model presented in Equation (3.11). In this framework, for example, we can model the effect of attaining s years of schooling on durations of unemployment or durations of employment.

The reduced form analysis in this section does not impose restrictions on the temporal (age) structure of outcomes across treatment times in constructing outcomes and specifying identifying assumptions. Each treatment time can have its own age path of outcomes pre and post treatment. Outcomes prior to treatment and outcomes after treatment are treated symmetrically and both may be different for different treatment times. In particular, HN can allow earnings at age t for people who receive treatment at some future time s' to differ from earnings at age t for people who receive treatment at some future time s'', $\min(s', s'') > t$ even after controlling for U and X.

This generality is in contrast with the analyses of Robins (1997) and Gill and Robins (2001) discussed in Section 3.2 and the analysis of Abbring and Van den Berg (2003b) discussed in Section 3.3. These analyses require exclusion of such anticipation effects to secure identification, because their models attribute dependence of treatment on past outcomes to selection effects. The sequential randomization assumption (M-2) underlying the work of Gill and Robins allows treatment decisions $S(t)$ at time t to depend on past outcomes $Y_{p_0}^{t-1}$ in a general way. Therefore, without additional restrictions, it is not possible to also identify *causal* (anticipatory) effects of treatment $S(t)$ on $Y_{p_0}^{t-1}$. The no-anticipation condition (NA) excludes such effects and secures identification in their framework.[107] It is essential for applying the conditional-independence assumptions in deriving the g-computation formula.

HN's very different approach to identification allows them to incorporate anticipation effects. As in their analysis of the duration model, they assume that there is an exogenous source of independent variation of treatment decisions, independent of past outcomes. Any variation in current outcomes with variation in future treatment decisions induced by this exogenous source cannot be due to selection effects (since they explicitly control for the unobservables) and is interpreted as anticipatory effects of treatment in their framework. However, their structural analysis naturally excludes such effects (see Section 3.4.2 below). Therefore, a natural interpretation of the ability of HN to identify anticipatory effects is that they have overidentifying restrictions that allow them to test their model and, if necessary, relax their assumptions.

In a model with uncertainty, agents act on and value *ex ante* outcomes. The model developed below in Section 3.4.2 distinguishes *ex ante* from *ex post* outcomes. The

[107] The role of the no-anticipation assumption in Abbring and Van den Berg (2003b) is similar. However, their main analysis assumes an asymmetric treatment-outcome setup in which treatment is not observed if it takes place after the outcome transition. In that case, the treatment time is censored at the outcome time. In this asymmetric setup, anticipatory effects of treatment on outcomes cannot be identified because the econometrician cannot observe variation of outcome transitions with future treatment times. This point may appear to be unrelated to the present discussion, but it is not. As was pointed out by Abbring and Van den Berg (2003b), and in Section 3.3, the asymmetric Abbring and Van den Berg (2003b) model can be extended to a fully symmetric bivariate duration model in which treatment hazards may be causally affected by the past occurrence of an outcome event just like outcomes may be affected by past treatment events. This model could be used to analyze data in which both treatment and outcome times are fully observed. In this symmetric setup, any dependence in the data of the time-to-treatment hazard on past outcome events is interpreted as an effect of outcomes on future treatment decisions, and not an anticipatory effect of treatment on past outcomes. If one does not restrict the effects of outcomes on future treatment, without further restrictions, the data on treatments occurring after the outcome event carry no information on anticipatory effects of treatment on outcomes and they face an identification problem similar to that in the asymmetric case.

model developed in this section cannot because, within it, it is difficult to specify the information sets on which agents act or the mechanism by which agents forecast and act on $Y(s, X, U(s))$ when they are making choices.

One justification for not making an *ex ante–ex post* distinction is that the agents being modeled operate under perfect foresight even though econometricians do not observe all of the information available to the agents. In this framework, the $U(s)$, $s = 1, \ldots, \bar{S}$, are an ingredient of the econometric model that accounts for the asymmetry of information between the agent and the econometrician studying the agent.

Without imposing assumptions about the functional structure of the outcome equations, it is not possible to nonparametrically identify counterfactual outcome states $Y(s, X, U(s))$ that have never been observed. Thus, in a schooling example, HN assume that analysts observe life cycle outcomes for some persons for each stopping time (level of final grade completion) and our notation reflects this.[108] However, analysts do not observe $Y(s, X, U(s))$ for all s for anyone. A person can have only one stopping time (one completed schooling level). This observational limitation creates the "fundamental problem of causal inference".[109]

In addition to this problem, there is the standard selection problem that the $Y(s, X, U(s))$ are only observed for persons who stop at s and not for a random sample of the population. The selected distribution may not accurately characterize the population distribution of $Y(s, X, U(s))$ for persons selected at random. Note also that without further structure, we can only identify treatment responses within a given policy environment. In another policy environment, where the rules governing selection into treatment and/or the outcomes from treatment may be different, the same time to treatment may be associated with entirely different responses.[110] We now turn to the HN analysis of identification of outcome and treatment time distributions.

3.4.1.4. Identification of outcome and treatment time distributions We assume access to a large i.i.d. sample from the distribution of $(S, Y(S, X, U(S)), X, Z)$, where S is the stopping time, X are the variables determining outcomes and Z are the variables determining choices. We also know $\Pr(S = s \mid Z = z)$ for $s = 1, \ldots, \bar{S}$, from the data. For expositional convenience, we first consider the case of scalar outcomes $Y(S, X, U(S))$. An analysis for vector $Y(S, X, U(S))$ is presented in HN and is discussed below.

Consider the analysis of continuous outcomes. HN analyze more general cases. Their results extend the analyses of Heckman and Honoré (1990), Heckman (1990) and Carneiro, Hansen and Heckman (2003) by considering choices generated by a stopping

[108] In practice, analysts can only observe a portion of the life cycle after treatment. See the discussion on pooling data across samples in Cunha, Heckman and Navarro (2005) to replace missing life cycle data.

[109] See Holland (1986) or Gill and Robins (2001).

[110] This is the problem of general equilibrium effects, and leads to violation of the policy invariance conditions. See Heckman, Lochner and Taber (1998a), Heckman, LaLonde and Smith (1999) or Abbring and Van den Berg (2003b) for discussion of this problem.

time model. To simplify the notation in this section, assume that the scalar outcome associated with stopping at time s can be written as $Y(s) = \mu(s, X) + U(s)$, where $Y(s)$ is shorthand for $Y(s, X, U(s))$. $Y(s)$ is observed only if $D(s) = 1$ where the $D(s)$ are generated by the model analyzed in Theorem 3. Write $I(s) = \Psi(s, Z(s)) - \eta(s)$. Assume that the $\Psi(s, Z(s))$ belong to the Matzkin class of functions described in Appendix B. We use the condensed representations I, $\Psi(Z)$, η, Y, $\mu(X)$ and U as described in Section 2.8.1, and in the previous subsection.

Heckman and Navarro permit general stochastic dependence within the components of U, within the components of η and across the two vectors. They assume that (X, Z) are independent of (U, η). Each component of (U, η) has a zero mean. The joint distribution of (U, η) is assumed to be absolutely continuous.

With "sufficient variation" in the components of $\Psi(Z)$, one can identify $\mu(s, X)$, $[\Psi(1, Z(1)), \ldots, \Psi(s, Z(s))]$ and the joint distribution of $U(s)$ and η^s. This enables the analyst to identify average treatment effects across all stopping times, since one can extract $E(Y(s) - Y(s') \mid X = x)$ from the marginal distributions of $Y(s)$, $s = 1, \ldots, \bar{S}$.

THEOREM 4. *Write* $\Psi^s(Z) = (\Psi(1, Z(1), \ldots, \Psi(s, Z(s)))$. *Assume in addition to the conditions in Theorem* 3 *that*

(i) $E[U(s)] = 0$. *$(U(s), \eta^s)$ are continuous random variables with support* $\mathrm{Supp}(U(s)) \times \mathrm{Supp}(\eta^s)$ *with upper and lower limits* $(\overline{U}(s), \bar{\eta}^s)$ *and* $(\underline{U}(s), \underline{\eta}^s)$, *respectively,* $s = 1, \ldots, \bar{S}$. *These conditions hold for each component of each subvector. The joint system is thus variation free for each component with respect to every other component.*

(ii) $(U(s), \eta^s) \perp\!\!\!\perp (X, Z)$, $s = 1, \ldots, \bar{S}$ *(independence).*

(iii) $\mu(s, X)$ *is a continuous function,* $s = 1, \ldots, \bar{S}$.

(iv) $\mathrm{Supp}(\Psi(Z), X) = \mathrm{Supp}(\Psi(Z)) \times \mathrm{Supp}(X)$.

Then one can identify $\mu(s, X)$, $\Psi^s(Z)$ $F_{\eta^s, U(s)}$, $s = 1, \ldots, \bar{S}$, *where* $\Psi(Z)$ *is identified over the support admitted by condition* (ii) *of Theorem* 3.

PROOF. See Appendix C. □

Appendix D, which extends Heckman and Navarro (2007), states and proves the more general Theorem D.1 for vector outcomes and both discrete and continuous variables that is parallel to the proof of Theorem 2 for the static model.

Theorem 4 does not identify the joint distribution of $Y(1), \ldots, Y(\bar{S})$ because analysts observe only one of these outcomes for any person. Observe that exclusion restrictions in the arguments of the choice of treatment equation are not required to identify the counterfactuals. What is required is independent variation of arguments which might be achieved by exclusion conditions but can be obtained by other functional restrictions (see HN, Corollary 1, for example). One can identify the $\mu(s, X)$ (up to constants) without the limit set argument. Thus one can identify certain features of the model without using the limit set argument. See HN.

The proof of Theorem 4 in Appendix C covers the case of vector $Y(s, X, U(s))$ where each component is a continuous random variable. The analysis in Appendix D allows for age-specific outcomes $Y(t, s, X, U(t, s))$, $t = 1, \ldots, \bar{T}$, where Y can be a vector of outcomes. In particular, HN can identify age-specific earnings flows associated with multiple sources of income.

As a by-product of Theorem 4, one can construct various counterfactual distributions of $Y(s)$ for agents with index crossing histories such that $D(s) = 0$ (that is, for whom $Y(s)$ is not observed). Define $B(s) = \mathbf{1}[I(s) \geqslant 0]$, $B^s = (B(1), \ldots, B(s))$, and let b^s denote a vector of possible values of B^s. $D(s)$ was defined as $B(s)$ if $B^{s-1} = (0)$ and 0 otherwise. Theorem 4 gives conditions under which the counterfactual distribution of $Y(s)$ for those with $D(s') = 1$, $s' \neq s$, can be constructed. More generally, it can be used to construct

$$\Pr\bigl(Y(s) \leqslant y(s) \mid B^{s'} = b^{s'}, X = x, Z = z\bigr)$$

for all of the $2^{s'}$ possible sequences $b^{s'}$ of $B^{s'}$ outcomes up to $s' \leqslant s$. If $b^{s'}$ equals a sequence of $s' - 1$ zeros followed by a one, then $B^{s'} = b^{s'}$ corresponds to $D(s') = 1$. The event $B^{s'} = (0)$ corresponds to $D^{s'} = (0)$, i.e., $S > s'$. For all other sequences $b^{s'}$, $B^{s'} = b^{s'}$ defines a subpopulation of the agents with $D(s'') = 1$ for some $s'' < s'$ and multiple index crossings. For example, $B^{s'} = (0, 1, 0)$ corresponds to $D(2) = 1$ and $I(3) < 0$. This defines a subpopulation that takes treatment at time 2, but that would not take treatment at time 3 if it would not have taken treatment at time 2.[111] It is tempting to interpret such sequences with multiple crossings as corresponding to multiple entry into and exit from treatment. However, this is inconsistent with the stopping time model (3.11), and would require extension of the model to deal with recurrent treatment. Whether a threshold-crossing model corresponds to a structural model of treatment choice is yet another issue, which is taken up in the next section and is also addressed in Cunha, Heckman and Navarro (2007).

The counterfactuals that are identified by fixing different $D(s') = 1$ for different treatment times s' in the general model of HN have an asymmetric aspect. HN can generate $Y(s)$ distributions for persons who are treated at s or before. Without further structure, they cannot generate the distributions of these random variables for people who receive treatment at times after s.

The source of this asymmetry is the generality of duration model (3.11). At each stopping time s, HN acquire a new random variable $\eta(s)$ which can have arbitrary dependence with $Y(s)$ and $Y(s')$ for all s and s'. From Theorem 4, HN can identify the dependence between $\eta(s')$ and $Y(s)$ if $s' \leqslant s$. They cannot identify the dependence between $\eta(s')$ and $Y(s)$ for $s' > s$ without imposing further structure on the unobservables.[112] Thus one can identify the distribution of college outcomes for high school graduates who do not go on to college and can compare these to outcomes for high

[111] Cunha, Heckman and Navarro (2007) develop an ordered choice model with stochastic thresholds.

[112] One possible structure is a factor model which is applied to this problem in the next section.

school graduates, so they can identify the parameter "treatment on the untreated." However, one cannot identify the distribution of high school outcomes for college graduates (and hence treatment on the treated parameters) without imposing further structure.[113] Since one can identify the marginal distributions under the conditions of Theorem 4, one can identify pairwise average treatment effects for all s, s'.

It is interesting to contrast the model identified by Theorem 4 with a conventional static multinomial discrete-choice model with an associated system of counterfactuals, as presented in Appendix B of Chapter 70 and analyzed in Section 2 of this chapter. Using standard tools, it is possible to establish semiparametric identification of the conventional static model of discrete choice joined with counterfactuals and to identify all of the standard mean counterfactuals. For that model there is a fixed set of unobservables governing all choices of states. Thus the analyst does not acquire new unobservables associated with each stopping time as occurs in a dynamic model. Selection effects for $Y(s)$ depend on the unobservables up to s but not later innovations. Selection effects in a static discrete-choice model depend on a fixed set of unobservables for all outcomes. With suitable normalizations, HN identify the joint distributions of choices and associated outcomes without the difficulties, just noted, that appear in the reduced form dynamic model. HN develop models for discrete outcomes including duration models.

3.4.1.5. Using factor models to identify joint distributions of counterfactuals From Theorem 4 and its generalizations reported in HN, one can identify joint distributions of outcomes for each treatment time s and the index generating treatment times. One cannot identify the joint distributions of outcomes across treatment times. Moreover, as just discussed, one cannot, in general, identify treatment on the treated parameters.

As reviewed in Section 2, Aakvik, Heckman and Vytlacil (2005) and Carneiro, Hansen and Heckman (2003) show how to use factor models to identify the joint distributions across treatment times and recover the standard treatment parameters. HN use their approach to identify the joint distribution of $Y = (Y(1), \dots, Y(\bar{S}))$.

The basic idea underlying this approach is to use joint distributions for outcomes measured at each treatment time s along with the choice index to construct the joint distribution of outcomes across treatment choices. To illustrate how to implement this intuition, suppose that we augment Theorem 4 by appealing to Theorem 2 in Carneiro, Hansen and Heckman (2003) or the extension of Theorem 4 proved in Appendix D to identify the joint distribution of the vector of outcomes at each stopping time along with $I^s = (I(1), \dots, I(s))$ for each s. For each s, we may write

$$Y\bigl(t, s, X, U(t,s)\bigr) = \mu(t, s, X) + U(t, s), \quad t = 1, \dots, \bar{T},$$
$$I(s) = \Psi\bigl(s, Z(s)\bigr) - \eta(s).$$

[113] In the schooling example, one can identify treatment on the treated for the final category $\bar{S}$ since $D^{\bar{S}-1} = (0)$ implies $D(\bar{S}) = 1$. Thus at stage $\bar{S} - 1$, one can identify the distribution of $Y(\bar{S} - 1)$ for persons for whom $D(0) = 0, \dots, D(\bar{S} - 1) = 0, D(\bar{S}) = 1$. Hence, if college is the terminal state, and high school the state preceding college, one can identify the distribution of high school outcomes for college graduates.

The scale of $\Psi(s, Z(s))$ is determined from the Matzkin (1994) conditions presented in Appendix B. If we specify the Matzkin functions only up to scale, we determine the functions up to scale and make a normalization. From Theorem 4, we can identify the joint distribution of $(\eta(1), \ldots, \eta(s), U(1, s), \ldots, U(\bar{T}, s))$.

To review these concepts and their application to the model discussed in this section, suppose that we adopt a one-factor model where θ is the factor. It has mean zero. The errors can be represented by

$$\eta(s) = \varphi_s \theta + \varepsilon_{\eta(s)},$$
$$U(t, s) = \alpha_{t,s} \theta + \varepsilon_{t,s}, \quad t = 1, \ldots, \bar{T}, \ s = 1, \ldots, \bar{S}.$$

The θ are independent of all of the $\varepsilon_{\eta(s)}$, $\varepsilon_{t,s}$ and the ε's are mutually independent mean zero disturbances. The φ_s and $\alpha_{t,s}$ are factor loadings. Since θ is an unobservable, its scale is unknown. One can set the scale of θ by normalizing one-factor loading, say $\alpha_{\bar{T},\bar{S}} = 1$. From the joint distribution of $(\eta^s, U(s))$, one can identify σ_θ^2, $\alpha_{t,s}$, φ_s, $t = 1, \ldots, \bar{T}$, for $s = 1, \ldots, \bar{S}$, using the same argument as presented in Section 2.8. A sufficient condition is $\bar{T} \geqslant 3$, but this ignores possible additional information from cross-system restrictions. From this information, one can form for $t \neq t'$ or $s \neq s''$ or both,

$$\operatorname{Cov}\big(U(t, s), U(t', s'')\big) = \alpha_{t,s} \alpha_{t',s''} \sigma_\theta^2,$$

even though the analyst does not observe outcomes for the same person at two different stopping times. In fact, one can construct the joint distribution of $(U, \eta) = (U(1), \ldots, U(\bar{S}), \eta)$. From this joint distribution, one can recover the standard mean treatment effects as well as the joint distributions of the potential outcomes. One can determine the percentage of participants at treatment time s who benefit from participation compared to what their outcomes would be at other treatment times. One can perform a parallel analysis for models for discrete outcomes and durations. The analysis can be generalized to multiple factors in precisely the same way as described in Section 2.8. Conventional factor analysis assumes that the unobservables are normally distributed. Carneiro, Hansen and Heckman (2003) establish nonparametric identifiability of the θ's and the ε's and their analysis of nonparametric identifiability applies here.

Theorem 4, strictly applied, actually produces only one scalar outcome along with one or more choices for each stopping time, although the proof of the extended Theorem 4 in Appendix D is for a vector-outcome model with both discrete and continuous outcomes.[114] If vector outcomes are not available, access to a measurement system M that assumes the same values for each stopping time can substitute for the need for vector outcomes for Y. Let M_j be the jth component of this measurement system. Write

$$M_j = \mu_{j,M}(X) + U_{j,M}, \quad j = 1, \ldots, J,$$

where $U_{j,M}$ are mean zero and independent of X.

[114] HN analyze the vector-outcome case.

Suppose that the $U_{j,M}$ have a one-factor structure so $U_{j,M} = \alpha_{j,M}\theta + \varepsilon_{j,M}$, $j = 1, \ldots, J$, where the $\varepsilon_{j,M}$ are mean zero, mutually independent random variables, independent of the θ. Adjoining these measurements to the one outcome measure $Y(s)$ can substitute for the measurements of $Y(t, s)$ used in the previous example. In an analysis of schooling, the M_j can be test scores that depend on ability θ. Ability is assumed to affect outcomes $Y(s)$ and the choice of treatment times indices.

To extend a point made in Section 2 to the framework for dynamic treatment effects, the factor models implement a matching on unobservables assumption, $\{Y(s)\}_{s=1}^{\bar{S}} \perp\!\!\!\perp S \mid X, Z, \theta$. HN allow for the θ to be unobserved variables and present conditions under which their distributions can be identified.

3.4.1.6. Summary of the reduced form model A limitation of the reduced form approach pursued in this section is that, because the underlying model of choice is not clearly specified, it is not possible without further structure to form, or even define, the marginal treatment effect analyzed in Heckman and Vytlacil (1999, 2001, 2005, and Chapters 70 and 71 in this Handbook) or Heckman, Urzua and Vytlacil (2006). The absence of well defined choice equations is problematic for the models analyzed thus far in this section of our chapter, although it is typical of many statistical treatment effect analyses.[115] In this framework, it is not possible to distinguish objective outcomes from subjective evaluations of outcomes, and to distinguish *ex ante* from *ex post* outcomes. Another limitation of this analysis is its strong reliance on large support conditions on the regressors coupled with independence assumptions. Independence can be relaxed following Lewbel (2000) and Honoré and Lewbel (2002). The large support assumption plays a fundamental role here and throughout the entire evaluation literature.

HN develop an explicit economic model for dynamic treatment effects that allows analysts to make these and other distinctions. They extend the analysis presented in this subsection to a more precisely formulated economic model. They explicitly allow for agent updating of information sets. A well posed economic model enables economists to evaluate policies in one environment and accurately project them to new environments as well as to accurately forecast new policies never previously experienced. We now turn to an analysis of a more fully articulated structural econometric model.

3.4.2. *A sequential structural model with option values*

This section analyzes the identifiability of a structural sequential optimal stopping time model. HN use ingredients assembled in the previous sections to build an economically interpretable framework for analyzing dynamic treatment effects. For specificity, Heckman and Navarro focus on a schooling model with associated earnings outcomes

[115] Heckman (2005) and the analysis of Chapters 70 and 71 point out that one distinctive feature of the economic approach to program evaluation is the use of choice theory to define parameters and evaluate alternative estimators.

that is motivated by the research of Keane and Wolpin (1997) and Eckstein and Wolpin (1999). They explicitly model costs and build a dynamic version of a Roy model. We briefly survey the literature on dynamic discrete choice in Section 3.4.5 below.

In the model of this section, it is possible to interpret the literature on dynamic treatment effects within the context of an economic model; to allow for earnings while in school as well as grade-specific tuition costs; to separately identify returns and costs; to distinguish private evaluations from "objective" *ex ante* and *ex post* outcomes and to identify persons at various margins of choice. In the context of medical economics, HN consider how to identify the pain and suffering associated with a treatment as well as the distribution of benefits from the intervention. They also model how anticipations about potential future outcomes associated with various choices evolve over the life cycle as sequential treatment choices are made.

In contrast to the analysis of Section 3.4.1, the identification proof for their dynamic choice model works in reverse starting from the last period and sequentially proceeding backward. This approach is required by the forward-looking nature of dynamic choice analysis and makes an interesting contrast with the analysis of identification for the reduced form models which proceeds forward from initial period values.

HN use limit set arguments to identify the parameters of outcome and measurement systems for each stopping time $s = 1, \ldots, \bar{S}$, including means and joint distributions of unobservables. These systems are identified without invoking any special assumptions about the structure of model unobservables. When they invoke factor structure assumptions for the unobservables, they identify the factor loadings associated with the measurements (as defined in Section 3.4.1) and outcomes. They also nonparametrically identify the distributions of the factors and the distributions of the innovations to the factors. With the joint distributions of outcomes and measurements in hand for each treatment time, HN can identify cost (and preference) information from choice equations that depend on outcomes and costs (preferences). HN can also identify joint distributions of outcomes across stopping times. Thus they can identify the proportion of people who benefit from treatment. Their analysis generalizes the one shot decision models of Cunha and Heckman (2007b, 2008), Cunha, Heckman and Navarro (2005, 2006) to a sequential setting.

All agents start with one year of schooling at age 1 and then sequentially choose, at each subsequent age, whether to continue for another year in school. New information arrives at each age. One of the benefits of staying in school is the arrival of new information about returns. Each year of schooling takes one year of age to complete. There is no grade repetition. Once persons leave school, they never return.[116] As a consequence, an agent's schooling level equals her age up to the time $S \leqslant \bar{S}$ she leaves school. After that, ageing continues up to age $\bar{T} \geqslant \bar{S}$, but schooling does not. We again denote

[116] It would be better to derive such stopping behavior as a feature of a more general model with possible recurrence of states. Cunha, Heckman and Navarro (2007) develop general conditions under which it is optimal to stop and never return.

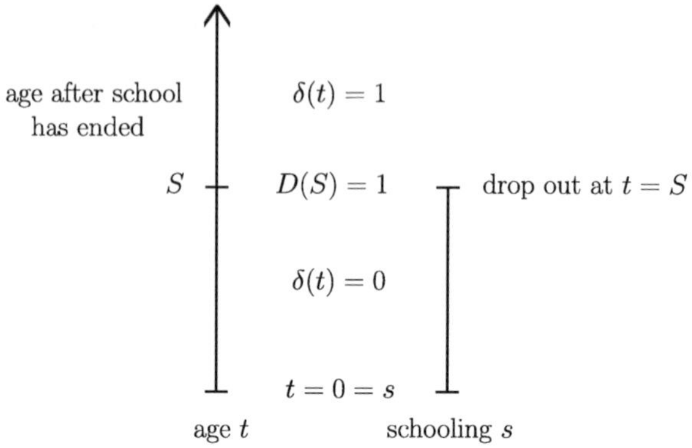

Figure 13. Evolution of grades and age.

$D(s) = \mathbf{1}(S = s)$ for all $s \in \{1, \dots, \bar{S}\}$. Let $\delta(t) = 1$ if a person has left school at or before age t; $\delta(t) = 0$ if a person is still in school. Figure 13 shows the evolution of age and grades, and clarifies the notation used in this section.

A person's earnings at age t depend on her *current* schooling level s and whether she has left school on or before age t ($\delta(t) = 1$) or not ($\delta(t) = 0$). Thus,

$$Y\big(t, s, \delta(t), X\big) = \mu\big(t, s, \delta(t), X\big) + U\big(t, s, \delta(t)\big). \tag{3.12}$$

Note that $Y(t, s, 0, X)$ is only meaningfully defined if $s = t$, in which case it denotes the earnings of a person as a student at age and schooling level s. More precisely, $Y(s, s, 0, X)$ denotes the earnings of an individual with characteristics X who is still enrolled in school at age and schooling level s and goes on to complete at least $s + 1$ years of schooling. The fact that earnings in school depend only on the current schooling level, and not on the final schooling level obtained, reflects the no-anticipation condition (NA). $U(t, s, \delta(t))$ is a mean zero shock that is unobserved by the econometrician but may, or may not, be observed by the agent. $Y(t, s, 1, X)$ is meaningfully defined only if $s \leqslant t$, in which case it denotes the earnings at age t of an agent who has decided to stop schooling at s.

The direct cost of remaining enrolled in school at age and schooling level s is

$$C\big(s, X, Z(s)\big) = \Phi\big(s, X, Z(s)\big) + W(s)$$

where X and $Z(s)$ are vectors of observed characteristics (from the point of view of the econometrician) that affect costs at schooling level s, and $W(s)$ are mean zero shocks that are unobserved by the econometrician that may or may not be observed by the agent. Costs are paid in the period before schooling is undertaken. The agent is assumed to know the costs of making schooling decisions at each transition. The agent is also assumed to know the X and $Z = (Z(1), \ldots, Z(\bar{S}-1))$ from age 1.[117]

The optimal schooling decision involves comparisons of the value of continuing in school for another year and the value of leaving school forever at each age and schooling level $s \in \{1, \ldots, \bar{S}-1\}$. We can solve for these values, and the optimal schooling decision, by backward recursion.

The agent's expected reward of stopping schooling forever at level and age s (i.e., receiving treatment s) is given by the expected present value of her remaining lifetime earnings:

$$R(s, I_s) = E\left(\sum_{j=0}^{\bar{T}-s} \left(\frac{1}{1+r}\right)^j Y(s+j, s, 1, X) \,\middle|\, I_s \right), \tag{3.13}$$

where I_s are the state variables generating the age-s-specific information set $\mathcal{I}_s$.[118] They include the schooling level attained at age s, the covariates X and Z, as well as all other variables known to the agent and used in forecasting future variables. Assume a fixed, nonstochastic, interest rate r.[119] The continuation value at age and schooling level s given information I_s is denoted by $K(s, I_s)$.

At $\bar{S}-1$, when an individual decides whether to stop or continue on to $\bar{S}$, the expected reward from remaining enrolled and continuing to $\bar{S}$ (i.e., the continuation value) is the earnings while in school less costs plus the expected discounted future return that arises from completing $\bar{S}$ years of schooling:

$$\begin{aligned} K(\bar{S}-1, I_{\bar{S}-1}) = {} & Y(\bar{S}-1, \bar{S}-1, 0, X) - C\big(\bar{S}-1, X, Z(\bar{S}-1)\big) \\ & + \frac{1}{1+r} E\big(R(\bar{S}, I_{\bar{S}}) \mid I_{\bar{S}-1}\big) \end{aligned}$$

where $C(\bar{S}-1, X, Z(\bar{S}-1))$ is the direct cost of schooling for the transition to $\bar{S}$. This expression embodies the assumption that each year of school takes one year of age. $I_{\bar{S}-1}$ incorporates all of the information known to the agent.

The value of being in school just before deciding on continuation at age and schooling level $\bar{S}-1$ is the larger of the two expected rewards that arise from stopping at $\bar{S}-1$ or continuing one more period to $\bar{S}$:

$$V(\bar{S}-1, I_{\bar{S}-1}) = \max\big\{R(\bar{S}-1, I_{\bar{S}-1}), K(\bar{S}-1, I_{\bar{S}-1})\big\}.$$

More generally, at age and schooling level s this value is

[117] These assumptions can be relaxed and are made for convenience. See Carneiro, Hansen and Heckman (2003), Cunha, Heckman and Navarro (2005) and Cunha and Heckman (2007b) for a discussion of selecting variables in the agent's information set.

[118] We only consider the agent's information set here, and drop the subscript A for notational convenience.

[119] This assumption is relaxed in HN who present conditions under which r can be identified.

$$
\begin{aligned}
V(s, I_s) &= \max\{R(s, I_s), K(s, I_s)\} \\
&= \max\left\{R(s, I_s), \begin{pmatrix} Y(s, s, 0, X) - C(s, X, Z(s)) \\ + \frac{1}{1+r} E(V(s+1, I_{s+1}) \mid I_s) \end{pmatrix}\right\}.
\end{aligned}
$$ [120]

Following the exposition of the reduced form decision rule in Section 3.4.1, define the decision rule in terms of a first passage of the "index" $R(s, I_s) - K(s, I_s)$,

$$
\begin{aligned}
D(s) = \mathbf{1}\big[&R(s, I_s) - K(s, I_s) \geqslant 0,\ R(s-1, I_{s-1}) - K(s-1, I_{s-1}) < 0, \ldots, \\
&R(1, I_1) - K(1, I_1) < 0\big].
\end{aligned}
$$

An individual stops at the schooling level at the first age where this index becomes positive. From data on stopping times, one can nonparametrically identify the conditional probability of stopping at s,

$$
\Pr(S = s \mid X, Z) = \Pr\left(\begin{matrix} R(s, I_s) - K(s, I_s) \geqslant 0, \\ R(s-1, I_{s-1}) - K(s-1, I_{s-1}) < 0, \ldots, \\ R(1, I_1) - K(1, I_1) < 0 \end{matrix} \;\middle|\; X, Z\right).
$$

HN use factor structure models based on the θ introduced in Section 3.4.1 to define the information updating structure. Agents learn about different components of θ as they evolve through life. The HN assumptions allow for the possibility that agents may know some or all the elements of θ at a given age t regardless of whether or not they determine earnings at or before age t. Once known, they are not forgotten. As agents accumulate information, they revise their forecasts of their future earnings prospects at subsequent stages of the decision process. This affects their decision rules and subsequent choices. Thus HN allow for learning which can affect both pre-treatment outcomes and post-treatment outcomes.[121,122] All dynamic discrete choice models make some assumptions

[120] This model allows no recall and is clearly a simplification of a more general model of schooling with option values. Instead of imposing the requirement that once a student drops out the student never returns, it would be useful to derive this property as a feature of the economic environment and the characteristics of individuals. Cunha, Heckman and Navarro (2007) develop such conditions. In a more general model, different persons could drop out and return to school at different times as information sets are revised. This would create further option value beyond the option value developed in the text that arises from the possibility that persons who attain a given schooling level can attend the next schooling level in any future period. Implicit in this analysis of option values is the additional assumption that persons must work at the highest level of education for which they are trained. An alternative model allows individuals to work each period at the highest wage across all levels of schooling that they have attained. Such a model may be too extreme because it ignores the costs of switching jobs, especially at the higher educational levels where there may be a lot of job-specific human capital for each schooling level. A model with these additional features is presented in Heckman, Urzua and Yates (2007).

[121] This type of learning about unobservables can be captured by HN's reduced form model, but not by Abbring and Van den Berg's (2003b) single-spell mixed proportional hazards model. Their model does not allow for time-varying unobservables. Abbring and Van den Berg develop a multiple-spell model that allows for time-varying unobservables. Moreover, their nonparametric discussion of (NA) and randomization does not exclude the sequential revelation to the agent of a general finite number of unobserved factors although they do not systematically develop such a model.

[122] It is fruitful to distinguish models with exogenous arrival of information (so that information arrives at each age t independent of any actions taken by the agent) from information that arrives as a result of choices

about the updating of information and any rigorous identification analysis of this class of models must test among competing specifications of information updating.

Variables unknown to the agent are integrated out by the agent in forming expectations over future outcomes. Variables known to the agent are treated as constants by the agents. They are integrated out by the econometrician to control for heterogeneity. These are separate operations except for special cases. In general, the econometrician knows less than what the agent knows. The econometrician seeks to identify the distributions of the variables in the agent information sets that are used by the agents to form their expectations as well as the distributions of variables known to the agent and treated as certain quantities by the agent but not known by the econometrician. Determining which elements belong in the agent's information set can be done using the methods exposited in Cunha, Heckman and Navarro (2005) and Cunha and Heckman (2007b) who consider testing what components of X, Z, ε as well as θ are in the agent's information set (see Section 2). We briefly discuss this issue at the end of the next section.[123] HN establish semiparametric identification of the model assuming a given information structure. Determining the appropriate information structure facing the agent and its evolution is an essential aspect of identifying any dynamic discrete-choice model.

Observe that agents with the same information variables I_t at age t have the same expectations of future returns, and the same continuation and stopping values. They make the same investment choices. Persons with the same *ex ante* reward, state and preference variables have the same *ex ante* distributions of stopping times. *Ex post*, stopping times may differ among agents with identical *ex ante* information. Controlling for I_t, future realizations of stopping times do not affect past rewards. This rules out the problem that the future can cause the past, which may happen in HN's reduced form model. It enforces the (NA) condition of Abbring and Van den Berg. Failure to accurately model I_t produces failure of (NA).

HN establish semiparametric identification of their model without period-by-period exclusion restrictions. Their analysis extends Theorems 3 and 4 to an explicit choice-theoretic setting. They use limit set arguments to identify the joint distributions of earnings (for each treatment time s across t) and any associated measurements that do not depend on the stopping time chosen. For each stopping time, they construct the means of earnings outcomes at each age and of the measurements and the joint distributions of the unobservables for earnings and measurements. Factor analyzing the joint distributions of the unobservables, under conditions specified in Carneiro, Hansen and Heckman (2003), they identify the factor loadings, and nonparametrically identify the distributions of the factors and the independent components of the error terms in the earnings and measurement equations. Armed with this knowledge, they use choice data

by the agent. The HN model is in the first class. The models of Miller (1984) or Pakes (1986) are in the second class. See our discussion in Section 3.4.5.

[123] The HN model of learning is clearly very barebones. Information arrives exogenously across ages. In the factor model, all agents who advance to a stage get information about additional factors at that stage of their life cycles but the realizations of the factors may differ across persons.

to identify the distribution of the components of the cost functions that are not directly observed. They construct the joint distributions of outcomes across stopping times. They also present conditions under which the interest rate r is identified.

In their model, analysts can distinguish period by period *ex ante* expected returns from *ex post* realizations by applying the analysis of Cunha, Heckman and Navarro (2005). See the survey in Heckman, Lochner and Todd (2006) for a discussion of this approach or recall our analysis in Section 2. Because they link choices to outcomes through the factor structure assumption, they can also distinguish *ex ante* preference or cost parameters from their *ex post* realizations. *Ex ante*, agents may not know some components of θ. *Ex post*, they do. All of the information about future rewards and returns is embodied in the information set $\mathcal{I}_t$. Unless the time of treatment is known with perfect certainty, it cannot cause outcomes prior to its realization.

The analysis of HN is predicated on specification of the agent's information sets. This information set should be carefully distinguished from that of the econometrician. Cunha, Heckman and Navarro (2005) present methods for determining which components of future outcomes are in the information sets of agents at each age, $\mathcal{I}_t$. If there are components unknown to the agent at age t, under rational expectations, agents form their value functions used to make schooling choices by integrating out the unknown components using the distributions of the variables in their information sets. Components that are known to the agent are treated as constants by the individual in forming the value function but as unknown variables by the econometrician and their distribution is estimated. The true information set of the agent is determined from the set of possible specifications of the information sets of agents by picking the specification that best fits the data on choices and outcomes penalizing for parameter estimation. If neither the agent nor the econometrician knows a variable, the econometrician identifies the determinants of the distribution of the unknown variables that is used by the agent to form expectations. If the agent knows some variables, but the econometrician does not, the econometrician seeks to identify the distribution of the variables, but the agent treats the variables as known constants.

HN can identify all of the treatment parameters including pairwise ATE, the marginal treatment effect (MTE) for each transition (obtained by finding mean outcomes for individuals indifferent between transitions), all of the treatment on the treated and treatment on the untreated parameters and the population distribution of treatment effects by applying the analysis of Carneiro, Hansen and Heckman (2003) and Cunha, Heckman and Navarro (2005) to this model. Their analysis can be generalized to cover the case where there are vectors of contemporaneous outcome measures for different stopping times. See HN for proofs and details.[124]

[124] The same limitations regarding independence assumptions between the regressors and errors discussed in the analysis of reduced forms apply to the structural model.

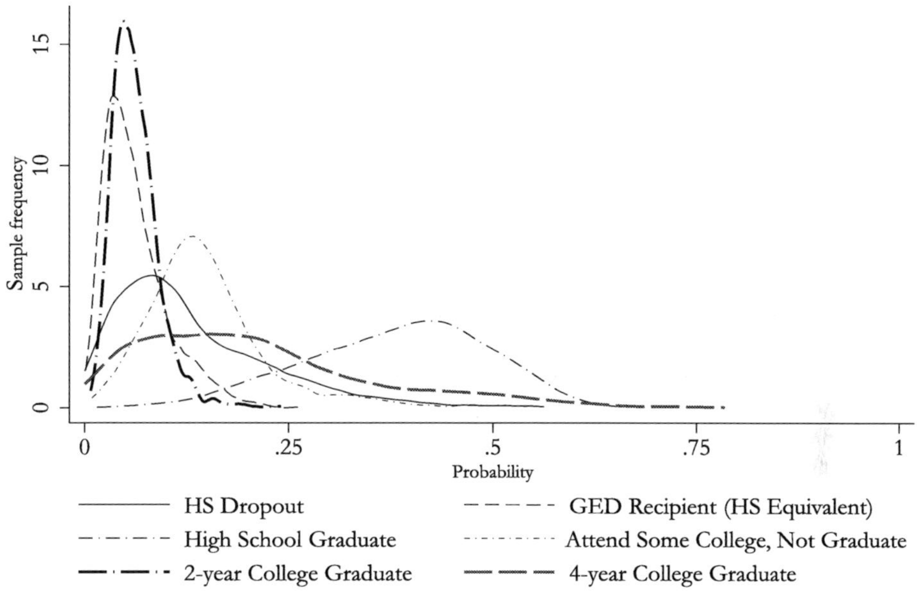

Figure 14. Sample distribution of schooling attainment probabilities for males from the National Longitudinal Survey of Youth. *Source*: Heckman, Stixrud and Urzua (2006).

3.4.3. *Identification at infinity*

Heckman and Navarro (2007), and many other researchers, rely on identification at infinity to obtain their main identification results. As noted in Chapter 71, identification at infinity is required to identify the average treatment effect (ATE) using IV and control function methods and in the reduced form discrete-time models developed in the previous subsections. While this approach is controversial, it is also testable. In any sample, one can plot the distributions of the probability of each state (exit time) to determine if the identification conditions are satisfied in any sample. Figure 14, taken from Heckman, Stixrud and Urzua (2006), shows such plots for a six-state static schooling model that they estimate. To identify the marginal outcome distributions for each state, the support of the state probabilities should be the full unit interval. The identification at infinity condition is clearly not satisfied in their data.[125] Only the empirical distribution of the state probability of graduating from a four year college comes even close to covering the full unit interval. Thus, their empirical results rely on parametric assumptions, and ATE and the marginal distributions of outcomes are nonparametrically nonidentified in their data without invoking additional structure.

[125] One can always argue that they are satisfied in an infinite sample that has not yet been realized. That statement has no empirical content.

3.4.4. Comparing reduced form and structural models

The reduced form model analyzed in Section 3.4.1 is typical of many reduced form statistical approaches within which it is difficult to make important conceptual distinctions. Because agent choice equations are not modeled explicitly, it is hard to use such frameworks to formally analyze the decision makers' expectations, costs of treatment, the arrival of information, the content of agent information sets and the consequences of the arrival of information for decisions regarding time to treatment as well as outcomes. Key behavioral assumptions are buried in statistical assumptions. It is difficult to distinguish *ex post* from *ex ante* valuations of outcomes in the reduced form models. Cunha, Heckman and Navarro (2005), Carneiro, Hansen and Heckman (2003) and Cunha and Heckman (2007b, 2008) present analyses that distinguish *ex ante* anticipations from *ex post* realizations.[126] In reduced form models, it is difficult to make the distinction between private evaluations and preferences (e.g., "costs" as defined in this section) from objective outcomes (the Y variables).

Statistical and reduced form econometric approaches to analyzing dynamic counterfactuals appeal to uncertainty to motivate the stochastic structure of models. They do not explicitly characterize how agents respond to uncertainty or make treatment choices based on the arrival of new information [see Robins (1989, 1997), Lok (2007), Gill and Robins (2001), Abbring and Van den Berg (2003b), and Van der Laan and Robins (2003)]. The structural approach surveyed in Section 3.4.2 and developed by HN allows for a clear treatment of the arrival of information, agent expectations, and the effects of new information on choice and its consequences. In an environment of imperfect certainty about the future, it rules out the possibility of the future causing the past once the effects of agent information are controlled for.

The structural model developed by HN allows agents to learn about new factors (components of θ) as they proceed sequentially through their life cycles. It also allows agents to learn about other components of the model [see Cunha, Heckman and Navarro (2005)]. Agent anticipations of when they will stop and the consequences of alternative stopping times can be sequentially revised. Agent anticipated payoffs and stopping times are sequentially revised as new information becomes available. The mechanism by which agents revise their anticipations is modeled and identified. See Cunha, Heckman and Navarro (2005, 2006), Cunha and Heckman (2007b, 2008) and the discussion in Section 2 for further discussion of these issues and Heckman, Lochner and Todd (2006) for a partial survey of recent developments in the literature.

The clearest interpretation of the models in the statistical literature on dynamic treatment effects is as *ex post* selection-corrected analyses of distributions of events that have occurred. In a model of perfect certainty, where *ex post* and *ex ante* choices and outcomes are identical, the reduced form approach can be interpreted as approximating clearly specified choice models. In a more general analysis with information arrival and

[126] See the summary of this literature in Heckman, Lochner and Todd (2006).

agent updating of information sets, the nature of the approximation is less clear cut. Thus the current reduced form literature is unclear as to which agent decision-making processes and information arrival assumptions justify the conditional sequential randomization assumptions widely used in the dynamic treatment effect literature [see, e.g., Gill and Robins (2001), Lechner and Miquel (2002), Lok (2007), Robins (1989, 1997), Van der Laan and Robins (2003)]. Section 3.2.2 provides some insight by highlighting the connection to the conditional-independence assumption often employed in the structural dynamic discrete-choice literature [see Rust (1987), and the survey in Rust (1994)]. Reduced form approaches are not clear about the source of the unobservables and their relationship with conditioning variables. It would be a valuable exercise to exhibit which structural models are approximated by various reduced form models. In the structural analysis, this specification emerges as part of the analysis, as our discussion of the stochastic properties of the unobservables presented in the preceding section makes clear.

The HN analysis of both structural and reduced form models relies heavily on limit set arguments. They solve the selection problem in limit sets. The dynamic matching models of Gill and Robins (2001) and Lok (2007) solve the selection problem by invoking recursive conditional-independence assumptions. In the context of the models of HN, they assume that the econometrician knows the θ or can eliminate the effect of θ on estimates of the model by conditioning on a suitable set of variables. The HN analysis entertains the possibility that analysts know substantially less than the agents they study. It allows for some of the variables that would make matching valid to be unobservable. As we have noted in early subsections, versions of recursive conditional-independence assumptions are also used in the dynamic discrete-choice literature [see the survey in Rust (1994)]. The HN factor models allow analysts to construct the joint distribution of outcomes across stopping times. This feature is missing from the statistical treatment effect literature.

Both HN's structural and reduced form models of treatment choice are stopping time models. Neither model allows for multiple entry into and exit from treatment, even though agents in these models would like to reverse their treatment decisions for some realizations of their index if this was not too costly (or, in the case of the reduced form model, if the index thresholds for returning would not be too low).[127] Cunha, Heckman and Navarro (2007) derive conditions on structural stopping models from a more basic model that entertains the possibility of return from dropout states but which nonetheless exhibits the stopping time property. The HN identification strategy relies on the nonrecurrent nature of treatment. Their identification strategy of using limit sets can be applied to a recurrent model provided that analysts confine attention to subsets of (X, Z) such that in those subsets the probability of recurrence is zero.

[127] Recall that treatment occurs if the index turns positive. If there are costs to reversing this decision, agents would only reverse their decision if the index falls below some negative threshold. The stopping time assumption is equivalent to the assumption that the costs of reversal are prohibitively large, or that the corresponding threshold is at the lower end of the support of the index.

3.4.5. A short survey of dynamic discrete-choice models

Table 13 presents a brief summary of the models used to analyze dynamic discrete choices. Rust (1994) presents a widely cited nonparametric nonidentification theorem for dynamic discrete-choice models. It is important to note the restrictive nature of his negative results. He analyzes a recurrent-state infinite-horizon model in a stationary environment. He does not use any exclusion restrictions or cross outcome-choice restrictions. He uses a general utility function. He places no restrictions on period-specific utility functions such as concavity or linearity nor does he specify restrictions connecting preferences and outcomes. One can break Rust's nonidentification result with additional information.

Magnac and Thesmar (2002) present an extended comment on Rust's analysis including positive results for identification when the econometrician knows the distributions of unobservables, assumes that unobservables enter period-specific utility functions in an additively separable way and is willing to specify functional forms of utility functions or other ingredients of the model, as do Pakes (1986), Keane and Wolpin (1997), Eckstein and Wolpin (1999), and Hotz and Miller (1988, 1993). Magnac and Thesmar (2002) also consider the case where one state (choice) is absorbing [as do Hotz and Miller (1993)] and where the value functions are known at the terminal age ($\bar{T}$) [as do Keane and Wolpin (1997) and Belzil and Hansen (2002)]. In HN, each treatment time is an absorbing state. In a separate analysis, Magnac and Thesmar consider the case where unobservables from the point of view of the econometrician are correlated over time (or age t) and choices (s) under the assumption that the distribution of the unobservables is known. They also consider the case where exclusion restrictions are available. Throughout their analysis, they maintain that the distribution of the unobservables is known both by the agent and the econometrician.

HN provide a semiparametric identification of a finite-horizon finite-state model with an absorbing state with semiparametric specifications of reward and cost functions.[128] Given that rewards are in value units, the scale of their utility function is fixed. Choices are not invariant to arbitrary affine transformations so that one source of nonidentifiability in Rust's analysis is eliminated. They can identify the error distributions nonparametrically given their factor structure. They do not have to assume either the functional form of the unobservables or knowledge of the entire distribution of unobservables.

HN present a fully specified structural model of choices and outcomes motivated by, but not identical to, the analyses of Keane and Wolpin (1994, 1997) and Eckstein and Wolpin (1999). In their setups, outcome and cost functions are parametrically specified. Their states are recurrent while those of HN are absorbing. In their model, once an agent drops out of school, the agent does not return. In the Keane–Wolpin model, an

[128] Although their main theorems are for additively separable reward and cost functions, it appears that additive separability can be relaxed using the analysis of Matzkin (2003).

Table 13
Comparisons among papers in the literature on dynamic discrete-choice models

	Use outcomes along with discrete choices?	Finite or infinite horizon	Recurrent states	Stationary environment	Temporal correlation of unobserved shocks	Information updating	Nonparametric or parametric identification	Terminal value assumed to be known	Cross-equation restrictions?[1]
Flinn and Heckman (1982)	Yes (wages)	Infinite	Yes	Yes	Temporal independence given heterogeneity	Arrival of independent shocks	Nonparametric	No	Yes
Miller (1984)	Yes (wages)	Infinite	Yes	Yes	Bayesian normal learning induces dependence	Bayesian learning, arrival of independent shocks	Parametric	No	Yes
Pakes (1986)	No (use cost data to identify discrete choice)	Finite	No	No	AR-1 dependence on unobservables	Arrival of independent shocks	Parametric[2]	Yes	No
Wolpin (1984)	No	Finite	Yes	No	Temporal independence	Temporal independence	Parametric	Yes	No
Wolpin (1987)	Yes	Finite	No	No	Independent shocks	Arrival of independent shocks	Parametric	No	Yes
Wolpin (1992)	Yes (wages)	Finite	Yes	No	Renewal process for shocks; job-specific shocks independent across jobs	Arrival of independent shocks (from new jobs)	Parametric	Yes	Yes
Rust (1987)	Yes[3]	Infinite	Yes	Yes	Shocks conditionally independent given state variables	Arrival of independent shocks	Parametric	No	No
Hotz and Miller (1993)	No	Infinite	Yes	Yes	Shocks conditionally independent given state variables	Synthetic cohort assumption	Parametric	Yes	No

(continued on next page)

Table 13
(continued)

	Use outcomes along with discrete choices?	Finite or infinite horizon	Recurrent states	Stationary environment	Temporal correlation of unobserved shocks	Information updating	Nonparametric or parametric identification	Terminal value assumed to be known	Cross-equation restrictions?[1]
Manski (1993)	No	Infinite	Yes	Yes	Shocks conditionally independent given state variables	Synthetic cohort assumption	Nonparametric	No	No
Keane and Wolpin (1997)	Yes	Finite	Yes	No	Shocks temporally independent given initial condition	Shocks temporally independent	Parametric	Yes	Yes
Taber (2000)	No	Finite (2 periods)	No	No	General dependence	General dependence	Nonparametric	No	No
Magnac and Thesmar (2002)	Yes[3]	Both finite and infinite	Yes	Yes	Conditional independence given state variables in main case	Conditional dependence	Conditional nonparametric	No	No
Heckman and Navarro (2007)	Yes	Finite	No	No	General dependence (updating)	Serially correlated updating of states	Nonparametric	No	Yes

[1]Cross equation means restrictions used between outcome and choice equations.

[2]Pakes and Simpson (1989) sketch a nonparametric proof of this model.

[3]There is an associated state vector equation which can be interpreted as an outcome equation.

agent who drops out can return. Keane and Wolpin do not establish identification of their model whereas HN establish semiparametric identification of their model. They analyze models with more general times series processes for unobservables. In both the HN and Keane–Wolpin frameworks, agents learn about unobservables. In the Keane–Wolpin framework, such learning is about temporally independent shocks that do not affect agent expectations about returns relevant to possible future choices. The information just affects the opportunity costs of current choices. In the HN framework, learning affects agent expectations about future returns as well as opportunity costs.

The HN model extends previous work by Carneiro, Hansen and Heckman (2003) and Cunha and Heckman (2007b, 2008), Cunha, Heckman and Navarro (2006, 2005) by considering explicit multiperiod dynamic models with information updating. They consider one-shot decision models with information updating and associated outcomes.

Their analysis is related to that of Taber (2000). Like Cameron and Heckman (1998), both HN and Taber use identification-in-the-limit arguments.[129] Taber considers identification of a two period model with a general utility function whereas in Section 3.4.2, we discuss how HN consider identification of a specific form of the utility function (an earnings function) for a multiperiod maximization problem. As in HN, Taber allows for the sequential arrival of information. His analysis is based on conventional exclusion restrictions, but the analysis of HN is not. They use outcome data in conjunction with the discrete dynamic choice data to exploit cross-equation restrictions, whereas Taber does not.

The HN treatment of serially correlated unobservables is more general than any discussion that appears in the current dynamic discrete choice and dynamic treatment effect literature. They do not invoke the strong sequential conditional-independence assumptions used in the dynamic treatment effect literature in statistics [Gill and Robins (2001), Lechner and Miquel (2002), Lok (2007), Robins (1989, 1997)], nor the closely related conditional temporal independence of unobserved state variables given observed state variables invoked by Rust (1987), Hotz and Miller (1988, 1993), Manski (1993) and Magnac and Thesmar (2002) (in the first part of their paper) or the independence assumptions invoked by Wolpin (1984).[130] HN allow for more general time series dependence in the unobservables than is entertained by Pakes (1986), Keane and Wolpin (1997) or Eckstein and Wolpin (1999).[131]

[129] Pakes and Simpson (1989) sketch a proof of identification of a model of the option values of patents that is based on limit sets for an option model.

[130] Manski (1993) and Hotz and Miller (1993) use a synthetic cohort effect approach that assumes that young agents will follow the transitions of contemporaneous older agents in making their life cycle decisions. The synthetic cohort approach has been widely used in labor economics at least since Mincer (1974). Manski and Hotz and Miller exclude any temporally dependent unobservables from their models. See Ghez and Becker (1975), MaCurdy (1981) and Mincer (1974) for applications of the synthetic cohort approach. For empirical evidence against the assumption that the earnings of older workers are a reliable guide to the earnings of younger workers in models of earnings and schooling choices for recent cohorts of workers, see Heckman, Lochner and Todd (2006).

[131] Rust (1994) provides a clear statement of the stochastic assumptions underlying the dynamic discrete-choice literature up to the date of his survey.

Like Miller (1984) and Pakes (1986), HN explicitly model, identify and estimate agent learning that affects expected future returns.[132] Pakes and Miller assume functional forms for the distributions of the error process and for the serial correlation pattern about information updating and time series dependence. The HN analysis of the unobservables is nonparametric and they estimate, rather than impose, the stochastic structure of the information updating process.

Virtually all papers in the literature, including the HN analysis, invoke rational expectations. An exception is the analysis of Manski (1993) who replaces rational expectations with a synthetic cohort assumption that choices and outcomes of one group can be observed (and acted on) by a younger group. This assumption is more plausible in stationary environments and excludes any temporal dependence in unobservables. In recent work, Manski (2004) advocates use of elicited expectations as an alternative to the synthetic cohort approach.

While HN use rational expectations, they estimate, rather than impose the structure of agent information sets. Miller (1984), Pakes (1986), Keane and Wolpin (1997), and Eckstein and Wolpin (1999) assume that they know the law governing the evolution of agent information up to unknown parameters.[133] Following the procedure presented in Cunha and Heckman (2007b, 2008), Cunha, Heckman and Navarro (2005, 2006) and Navarro (2005), HN can test for which factors (θ) appear in agent information sets at different stages of the life cycle and they identify the distributions of the unobservables nonparametrically.

The HN analysis of dynamic treatment effects is comparable, in some aspects, to the recent continuous-time event-history approach of Abbring and Van den Berg (2003b) previously analyzed. Those authors build a continuous time model of counterfactuals for outcomes that are durations. They model treatment assignment times using a continuous-time duration model.

The HN analysis is in discrete time and builds on previous work by Heckman (1981a, 1981c) on heterogeneity and state dependence that identifies the causal effect of employment (or unemployment) on future employment (or unemployment).[134] They model time to treatment and associated vectors of outcome equations that may be discrete, continuous or mixed discrete-continuous. In a discrete-time setting, they are able to generate a variety of distributions of counterfactuals and economically motivated parameters. They allow for heterogeneity in responses to treatment that has a general time series structure.

As noted in Section 3.4.4, Abbring and Van den Berg (2003b) do not identify explicit agent information sets as HN do in their paper and as is done in Cunha, Heckman

[132] As previously noted, the previous literature assumes learning only about current costs.

[133] They specify *a priori* particular processes of information arrival as well as which components of the unobservables agents know and act on, and which components they do not.

[134] Heckman and Borjas (1980) investigate these issues in a continuous-time duration model. See also Heckman and MaCurdy (1980).

and Navarro (2005), and they do not model learning about future rewards. Their outcomes are restricted to be continuous-time durations. The HN framework is formulated in discrete time, which facilitates the specification of richer unobserved and observed covariate processes than those entertained in the continuous-time framework of Abbring and Van den Berg (2003b). It is straightforward to attach a vector of treatment outcomes in the HN model that includes continuous outcomes, discrete outcomes and durations expressed as binary strings.[135] At a practical level, the approach often can produce very fine-grained descriptions of continuous-time phenomena by using models with many finite periods. Clearly a synthesis of the event-history approach with the HN approach would be highly desirable. That would entail taking continuous-time limits of the discrete-time models. It is a task that awaits completion.

Flinn and Heckman (1982) utilize information on stopping times and associated wages to derive cross-equation restrictions to partially identify an equilibrium job search model for a stationary economic environment where agents have an infinite horizon. They establish that the model is nonparametrically nonidentified. Their analysis shows that use of outcome data in conjunction with data on stopping times is not sufficient to secure nonparametric identification of a dynamic discrete-choice model, even when the reward function is linear in outcomes unlike the reward functions in Rust (1987) and Magnac and Thesmar (2002). Parametric restrictions can break their nonidentification result. Abbring and Campbell (2005) exploit such restrictions, together with cross-equation restrictions on stopping times and noisy outcome measures, to prove identification of an infinite-horizon model of firm survival and growth with entrepreneurial learning. Alternatively, nonstationarity arising from finite horizons can break their nonidentification result [see Wolpin (1987)]. The HN analysis exploits the finite-horizon backward-induction structure of our model in conjunction with outcome data to secure identification and does not rely on arbitrary period by period exclusion restrictions. They substantially depart from the assumptions maintained in Rust's nonidentification theorem (1994). They achieve identification by using cross-equation restrictions, linearity of preferences and additional measurements, and exploiting the structure of their finite-horizon nonrecurrent model. Nonstationarity of regressors greatly facilitates identification by producing both exclusion and curvature restrictions which can substitute for standard exclusion restrictions.

3.5. Summary of the state of the art in analyzing dynamic treatment effects

This section has surveyed new methods for analyzing the dynamic effects of treatment. We have compared and contrasted the statistical dynamic treatment approach based on sequential conditional-independence assumptions that generalize matching to a dynamic panel setting to approaches developed in econometrics. We compared and

[135] Abbring (2008) considers nonparametric identification of mixed semi-Markov event-history models that extends his work with Van den Berg. See Section 3.3.

contrasted a continuous-time event-history approach developed by Abbring and Van den Berg (2003b) to discrete time reduced form and structural models developed by Heckman and Navarro (2007), and Cunha, Heckman and Navarro (2005).

4. Accounting for general equilibrium, social interactions, and spillover effects

The treatment-control paradigm motivates the modern treatment effect literature. Outcomes of persons who are "treated" are compared to outcomes of those who are not. The "untreated" are assumed to be completely unaffected by who else gets treatment. This assumption is embodied in invariance assumptions (PI-2) and (PI-4) in Chapter 70. In the "Rubin" model, (PI-2) is one component of his "SUTVA" assumption.[136]

In any social setting, this assumption is very strong, and many economists have built models to account for various versions of social interactions and their consequences for policy evaluation. The literature on general equilibrium policy analysis is vast and the details of particular approaches are difficult to synthesize in a concise way. In this section, we make a few general points and offer some examples where accounting for general equilibrium effects has substantial consequences for the evaluation of public policy. Note that there are also cases where accounting for general equilibrium has little effect on policy evaluations. One cannot say that a full-fledged empirical general equilibrium analysis is an essential component of every evaluation. However, ignoring general equilibrium and social interactions can be perilous.

It is fruitful to distinguish interactions of agents through market mechanisms, captured by the literature on general equilibrium analysis, from social interactions. Social interactions are a type of direct externality in which the actions of one agent directly affect the actions (preferences, constraints, technology) of other agents.[137] The former type of interaction is captured by general equilibrium models. The second type of interaction is captured in the recent social interactions literature. Within the class of equilibrium models where agents interact through markets, there is a full spectrum of possible interactions from partial equilibrium models where agent interactions in some markets are modeled, to full fledged general equilibrium models where all interactions are modeled.

The social interactions literature is explicitly microeconomic in character, since it focuses on the effects of individuals (or groups) on other individuals. The traditional general equilibrium literature is macroeconomic in its focus and deals with aggregates. A more recent version moves beyond the representative consumer paradigm and considers heterogeneity and the impact of policy on individuals. We first turn to versions of the empirical general equilibrium literature.

[136] Recall the discussion in Chapter 70, Section 4.4.

[137] This distinction is captured in neoclassical general equilibrium models by the contrast between pecuniary and nonpecuniary externalities.

4.1. General equilibrium policy evaluation

There is a large literature on empirical general equilibrium models applied to trade, public finance, finance, macroeconomics, energy policy, industrial organization, and labor economics. The essays in Kehoe, Srinivasan and Whalley (2005) present a rich collection of empirical general equilibrium models and references to a large body of related work. Much of the traditional general equilibrium analysis analyzes representative models using aggregate data.

Lewis (1963) is an early study of the partial equilibrium spillover effects of unionism on the wages of nonunion workers.[138] Leading examples of empirical general equilibrium studies based on the representative consumer paradigm are Auerbach and Kotlikoff (1987), Hansen and Sargent (1980), Huggett (1993), Jorgenson and Slesnick (1997), Jorgenson and Yun (1990), Kehoe, Srinivasan and Whalley (2005), Krusell and Smith (1998), Kydland and Prescott (1982), Shoven and Whalley (1977). There are many other important studies and this list is intended to be illustrative, and not exhaustive. Jorgenson and Slesnick (1997) give precise conditions for aggregation of microdata into macro aggregates that can be used to identify clearly defined economic parameters and policy criteria.

These models provide specific frameworks for analyzing policy interventions. Their specificity is a source of controversy because so many components of the social system need to be accounted for, and so often there is little professional consensus on these components and their empirical importance. Being explicit has its virtues and stimulates research promoting improved understanding of mechanisms and parameters. However, rhetorically, this clarity can be counterproductive. By sweeping implicit assumptions under the rug, the treatment effect literature appears to some to offer a universality and generality that is absent from the general equilibrium approach, in which mechanisms of causation and agent interaction are more clearly specified.

There is a large and often controversial literature about the sources of parameter estimates for the representative agent models. The "calibration vs. estimation debate" concerns the best way to secure parameters for these models [see Kydland and Prescott (1996), Hansen and Heckman (1996), and Sims (1996)]. Dawkins, Srinivasan and Whalley (2001) present a useful guide to this literature. Browning, Hansen and Heckman (1999) discuss the sources of the estimates for a variety of prototypical general equilibrium frameworks. In this section, we discuss the smaller body of literature that links general equilibrium models to microdata to evaluate public policy.

4.2. General equilibrium approaches based on microdata

A recent example of general equilibrium analysis applied to policy problems is the study of Heckman, Lochner and Taber (1998a, 1998b, 1998c), who consider the evaluation of

[138] He does not consider the effect of unionism on product prices or other factor markets besides the labor market.

tuition subsidy programs in a general equilibrium model of human capital accumulation with both schooling and on the job training, and with heterogeneous skills in which prices are flexible. We first discuss their model and then turn to other frameworks. Their model is an overlapping generations empirical general equilibrium model with heterogeneous agents across and within generations which generalizes the analysis of Auerbach and Kotlikoff (1987) by introducing human capital and by synthesizing micro- and macrodata analysis.

The standard microeconomic evaluation of tuition policy on schooling choices estimates the response of college enrollment to tuition variation using geographically dispersed cross-sections of individuals facing different tuition rates. These estimates are then used to determine how subsidies to tuition will raise college enrollment. The impact of tuition policies on earnings are evaluated using a schooling–earnings relationship fit on pre-intervention data and do not account for the enrollment effects of the taxes raised to finance the tuition subsidy. Kane (1994), Dynarski (2000), and Cameron and Heckman (1998, 2001) exemplify this approach. This approach is neither partial equilibrium or general equilibrium in character. It entirely ignores market interactions.

The danger in this widely used practice is that what is true for policies affecting a small number of individuals, as studied by social experiments or as studied in the microeconomic "treatment effect" literature, may not be true for policies that affect the economy at large. A national tuition-reduction policy may stimulate substantial college enrollment and will also likely reduce skill prices. However, agents who account for these changes will not enroll in school at the levels calculated from conventional procedures which ignore the impact of the induced enrollment on skill prices. As a result, standard policy evaluation practices are likely to be misleading about the effects of tuition policy on schooling attainment and wage inequality. The empirical question is to determine the extent to which this is true. Heckman, Lochner and Taber (1998a, 1998b, 1998c) show that conventional practices in the educational evaluation literature lead to estimates of enrollment responses that are ten times larger than the long-run general equilibrium effects, which account for the effect of policy on all factor markets. They improve on current practice in the "treatment effects" literature by considering both the gross benefits of the program and the tax costs of financing the policy as borne by different groups.

Evaluating the general equilibrium effects of a national tuition policy requires more information than the tuition-enrollment parameter that is the centerpiece of the micro policy analyses, which ignore any equilibrium effects. Policy proposals of all sorts typically extrapolate well outside the range of known experience and ignore the effects of induced changes in skill quantities on skill prices. To improve on current practice, Heckman, Lochner and Taber (1998a) use microdata to identify an empirically estimated rational expectations, perfect foresight overlapping-generations general equilibrium framework for the pricing of heterogeneous skills and the adjustment of capital. It is based on an empirically grounded theory of the supply of schooling and post-school human capital, where different schooling levels represent different skills. Individuals differ in their learning ability and in initial endowments of human capital.

Household saving behavior generates the aggregate capital stock, and output is produced by combining the stocks of different types of human capital with physical capital. Factor markets are competitive, and it is assumed that wages are set in flexible, competitive markets. Their model explains the pattern of rising wage inequality experienced in the United States in the past 30 years. They apply their framework to evaluate tuition policies that attempt to increase college enrollment.

They present two reasons why the "treatment effect" framework that ignores the general equilibrium effects of tuition policy is inadequate. First, the conventional treatment parameters depend on who in the economy is "treated" and who is not. Second, these parameters do not measure the full impact of the program. For example, increasing tuition subsidies may increase the earnings of uneducated individuals who do not take advantage of the subsidy. They become more scarce after the policy is implemented. The highly educated are taxed to pay for the subsidy, and depending on how taxes are collected this may affect their investment behavior. In addition, more competitors for educated workers enter the market as a result of the policy, and their earnings are depressed. Conventional methods ignore the effect of the policy on nonparticipants operating through changes in equilibrium skill prices and on taxes. In order to account for these effects, it is necessary to conduct a general equilibrium analysis.

The analysis of Heckman, Lochner and Taber (1998a, 1998b, 1998c) has important implications for the widely-used difference-in-differences estimator. If the tuition subsidy changes the aggregate skill prices, the decisions of nonparticipants will be affected. The "no treatment" benchmark group is affected by the policy and the difference-in-differences estimator does not identify the effect of the policy for anyone compared to a no treatment state.

Using their estimated model, Heckman, Lochner and Taber (1998c) simulate the effects of a revenue-neutral $500 increase in college tuition subsidy on top of existing programs that is financed by a proportional tax, on enrollment in college and wage inequality. They start from a baseline economy that describes the US in the mid-1980s and that produces wage growth profiles and schooling enrollment and capital stock data that match micro- and macroevidence. The microeconomic treatment effect literature predicts an increase in college attendance of 5.3 percent. This analysis holds college and high school wage rates fixed. This is the standard approach in the microeconomic "treatment effect" literature.

When the policy is evaluated in a general equilibrium setting, the estimated effect falls to 0.46 percent. Because the college–high school wage ratio falls as more individuals attend college, the returns to college are less than when the wage ratio is held fixed. Rational agents understand this effect of the tuition policy on skill prices and adjust their college-going behavior accordingly. Policy analysis of the type offered in the "treatment effect" literature ignores equilibrium price adjustment and the responses of rational agents to the policies being evaluated. Their analysis shows substantial attenuation of the effects of tuition policy on capital and on the stocks of the different skills in their model compared to a treatment effect model. They show that their results are robust to a variety of specifications of the economic model.

Table 14
Simulated effects of $5000 tuition subsidy on different groups. Steady state changes in present value of lifetime wealth (in thousands of US dollars)

Group (proportion)[1]	After-tax earnings using base tax (1)	After-tax earnings (2)	After-tax earnings net of tuition (3)	Utility[2] (4)
High School–High School (0.528)	9.512	−0.024	−0.024	−0.024
High School–College (0.025)	−4.231	−13.446	1.529	1.411
College–High School (0.003)	−46.711	57.139	−53.019	−0.879
College–College (0.444)	−7.654	−18.204	0.420	0.420

[1]The groups correspond to each possible counterfactual. For example, the "High School–High School" group consists of individuals who would not attend college in either steady state, and the "High School–College" group would not attend college in the first steady state, but would in the second, etc.
[2]Column (1) reports the after-tax present value of earnings in thousands of 1995 US dollars discounted using the after-tax interest rate where the tax rate used for the second steady state is the base tax rate. Column (2) adds the effect of taxes, column (3) adds the effect of tuition subsidies and column (4) includes the nonpecuniary costs of college in dollar terms.
Source: Heckman, Lochner and Taber (1998b).

They also analyze short run effects. When they simulate the model with rational expectations, the short-run college enrollment effects in response to the tuition policy are also very small, as agents anticipate the effects of the policy on skill prices and calculate that there is little gain from attending college at higher rates. Under myopic expectations, the short-run enrollment effects are much closer to the estimated treatment effects. With learning on the part of agents, but not perfect foresight, there is still a substantial gap between treatment and general equilibrium estimates. The sensitivity of policy estimates to model specification is a source of concern and a stimulus to research. The treatment effect literature ignores these issues.

Heckman, Lochner and Taber (1998a, 1998b, 1998c) also consider the impact of a policy change on discounted earnings and utility and decompose the total effects into benefits and costs, including tax costs for each group. Table 14 compares outcomes in two steady states: (a) the benchmark steady state and (b) the steady state associated with the new tuition policy.[139] The row "High School–High School" reports the change in a variety of outcome measures for those persons who would be in high school under either the benchmark or new policy regime; the "High School–College" row reports the change in the same measures for high school students in the benchmark state who are induced to attend college by the new policy; the "College–High School" outcomes refer

[139] Given that the estimated schooling response to a $500 subsidy is small, Heckman, Lochner and Taber instead use a $5000 subsidy for the purpose of exploring general equilibrium effects on earnings. Current college tuition subsidy levels are this high or higher at many colleges in the US.

to those persons in college in the benchmark economy who only attend high school after the policy; and so forth. Because agents choose sectors, there is spillover from one sector to another.

By the measure of the present value of earnings, some of those induced to change are worse off. Contrary to the monotonicity assumption built into the LATE parameter discussed in Chapters 70 and 71, and defined in this context as the effect of the tuition subsidy on the earnings of those induced by it to go to college, Heckman, Lochner and Taber find that the tuition policy produces a two-way flow. Some people who would have attended college in the benchmark regime no longer do so. The rest of society is also affected by the policy—again, contrary to the implicit assumption built into LATE that only those who change status are affected by the policy. People who would have gone to college without the policy and continue to do so after the policy are financially worse off for two reasons: (a) the price of their skill is depressed and (b) they must pay higher taxes to finance the policy. However, they now receive a tuition subsidy and for this reason, on net, they are better off both financially and in terms of utility. Those who abstain from attending college in both steady states are worse off. They pay higher taxes, and do not get the benefits of a college education. Those induced to attend college by the policy are better off in terms of utility. Note that neither category of non-changers is a natural benchmark for a difference-in-differences estimator. The movement in their wages before and after the policy is due to the policy and cannot be attributed to a benchmark "trend" that is independent of the policy.

Table 15 presents the impact of a \$5000 tuition policy on the log earnings of individuals with ten years of work experience for different definitions of treatment effects. The treatment effect version given in the first column holds skill prices constant at initial steady state values. The general equilibrium version given in the second column allows prices to adjust when college enrollment varies. Consider four parameters initially defined in a partial equilibrium context. The *average treatment effect* is defined for a randomly selected person in the population in the benchmark economy and asks how that person would gain in wages by moving from high school to college. The parameter *treatment on the treated* is defined as the average gain over their non-college alternative of those who attend college in the benchmark state. The parameter *treatment on the untreated* is defined as the average gain over their college wage received by individuals who did not attend college in the benchmark state. The *marginal treatment effect* is defined for individuals who are indifferent between going to college or not. This parameter is a limit version of the LATE parameter under the assumptions presented in Chapter 71. Column (2) presents the general equilibrium version of *treatment on the treated.* It compares the earnings of college graduates in the benchmark economy with what they would earn if no one went to college.[140] The treatment on the

[140] In the empirical general equilibrium model of Heckman, Lochner and Taber (1998a, 1998b, 1998c), the Inada conditions for college and high school are not satisfied for the aggregate production function and the marginal product of each skill group when none of it is utilized is a bounded number. If the Inada conditions were satisfied, this counterfactual and the counterfactual treatment on the untreated would not be defined.

Table 15
Treatment effect parameters: treatment effect and general equilibrium difference in log earnings, college graduates vs. high school graduates at 10 years of work experience

Parameter	Prices fixed[1] (1)	Prices vary[2] (2)	Fraction of sample[3] (3)
Average treatment effect (ATE)	0.281	1.801	100%
Treatment on treated (TT)	0.294	3.364	44.7%
Treatment on untreated (TUT)	0.270	−1.225	55.3%
Marginal treatment effect (MTE)	0.259	0.259	–
LATE[4] \$5000 subsidy:			
Partial equilibrium	0.255	–	23.6%
GE (H.S. to College) (LATE)	0.253	0.227	2.48%
GE (College to H.S.) (LATER)	0.393	0.365	0.34%
GE net (TLATE)	–	0.244	2.82%
LATE[4] \$500 subsidy:			
Partial equilibrium	0.254	–	2.37%
GE (H.S. to College) (LATE)	0.250	0.247	0.24%
GE (College to H.S.) (LATER)	0.393	0.390	0.03%
GE net (TLATE)	–	0.264	0.27%

[1] In column (1), prices are held constant at their initial steady state levels when wage differences are calculated.
[2] In column (2), we allow prices to adjust in response to the change in schooling proportions when calculating wage differences.
[3] For each row, column (3) presents the fraction of the sample over which the parameter is defined.
[4] The LATE group gives the effect on earnings for persons who would be induced to attend college by a tuition change. In the case of GE, LATE measures the effect on individuals induced to attend college when skill prices adjust in response to quantity movements among skill groups. The treatment effect LATE measures the effect of the policy on those induced to attend college when skill prices are held at the benchmark level.
Source: Heckman, Lochner and Taber (1998b).

untreated parameter is defined analogously by comparing what high school graduates in the benchmark economy would earn if everyone in the population were forced to go to college. The *average treatment effect* compares the average earnings in a world in which everyone attends college versus the earnings in a world in which nobody attends college. Such dramatic policy shifts produce large estimated effects. In contrast, the general equilibrium marginal treatment effect parameter considers the gain to attending college for people on the margin of indifference between attending college and only attending high school. In this case, as long as the mass of people in the indifference set is negligible, the standard treatment effect and general equilibrium parameters are the same.

The final set of parameters considered by Heckman, Lochner and Taber (1998b) are versions of the LATE parameter. This parameter depends on the particular intervention being studied and its magnitude. The standard version of LATE is defined on the outcomes of individuals induced to attend college, assuming that skill prices do not change.

The general equilibrium version is defined for the individuals induced to attend college when prices adjust in response to the policy. In this general equilibrium model, the two LATE parameters are quite close to each other and are also close to the marginal treatment effect.[141] General equilibrium effects change the group over which the parameter is defined compared to the standard treatment effect case. For a $5000 subsidy, there are substantial price effects and the standard treatment effect parameter differs substantially from the general equilibrium version.

Heckman, Lochner and Taber (1998a, 1998b, 1998c) also present standard treatment effect and general equilibrium estimates for two extensions of the LATE concept: LATER (the effect of the policy on those induced to attend only high school rather than go to college)—Reverse LATE—and TLATE (the effect of the policy on all of those induced to change whichever direction they flow). LATER is larger than LATE, indicating that those induced to drop out of college have larger gains from dropping out than those induced to enter college have from entering. TLATE is a weighted average of LATE and LATER with weights given by the relative proportion of people who switch in each direction.

The general equilibrium impacts of tuition on college enrollment are an order of magnitude smaller than those reported in the literature on microeconometric treatment effects. The assumptions used to justify the LATE parameter in a microeconomic setting do not carry over to a general equilibrium framework. Policy changes, in general, induce two-way flows and violate the monotonicity—or one-way flow—assumption of LATE. Heckman, Lochner and Taber (1998b) extend the LATE concept to allow for the two-way flows induced by the policies. They present a more comprehensive approach to program evaluation by considering both the tax and benefit consequences of the program being evaluated and placing the analysis in a market setting. Their analysis demonstrates the possibilities of the general equilibrium approach and the limitations of the microeconomic "treatment effect" approach to policy evaluation.

4.2.1. Subsequent research

Subsequent research by Blundell et al. (2004), Duflo (2004), Lee (2005), and Lee and Wolpin (2006) estimate—or estimate and calibrate—general equilibrium models for the effects of policies on labor markets. Lee (2005) assumes that occupational groups are perfect substitutes and that people can costlessly switch between skill categories. These assumptions neutralize any general equilibrium effects. They are relaxed and shown to be inconsistent with data from US labor markets in Lee and Wolpin (2006).

Lee and Wolpin (2006) assume adaptive expectations rather than rational expectations. Heckman, Lochner and Taber (1998a) establish the sensitivity of the policy evaluations to specifications of expectations. Duflo (2004) demonstrates the importance

[141] The latter is a consequence of the discrete-choice framework for schooling choices analyzed in the Heckman, Lochner and Taber (1998b) model. See Chapter 71.

of general equilibrium effects on wages for the evaluation of a large scale schooling program in Indonesia. However, accounting for general equilibrium does not affect her estimates of the rate of return of schooling.

4.2.2. Equilibrium search approaches

Equilibrium search models are another framework for studying market level interactions among agents. Search theory as developed by Mortensen and Pissarides (1994) and Pissarides (2000) has begun to be tested on microdata [see Van den Berg (1999)]. It accounts for direct and indirect effects without imposing full equilibrium price adjustment. Some versions of search theory allow for wage flexibility through a bargaining mechanism while other approaches assume rigid wages. Search theory produces an explicit theory of unemployment. Davidson and Woodbury (1993) consider direct and indirect effects of a bonus scheme to encourage unemployed workers to find jobs more quickly using a Mortensen–Pissarides (1994) search model in which prices are fixed. Their model is one of displacement with fixed prices.

More recent studies of equilibrium search models in which wages are set through bargaining that have been used for policy analysis include papers by Lise, Seitz and Smith (2005a, 2005b) and Albrecht, Van den Berg and Vroman (2005). Lise, Seitz and Smith (2005a) present a careful synthesis of experimental and nonexperimental data combining estimation and calibration. They provide evidence on labor-market feedback effects associated with job subsidy schemes. In their analysis, accounting for general equilibrium feedback reverses the cost–benefit evaluations of a job subsidy program in Canada. Albrecht, Van den Berg and Vroman (2005) demonstrate important equilibrium effects of an adult education program on employment and job vacancies, showing a skill bias of the programs.

4.3. Analyses of displacement

Newly trained workers from a job training program may displace previously trained workers if wages are inflexible, as they are in many European countries. For some training programs in Europe, substantial displacement effects have been estimated [Organization for Economic Cooperation and Development (1993), Calmfors (1994)]. If wages are flexible, the arrival of new trained workers to the market tends to lower the wages of previously trained workers but does not displace any worker.

Even if the effect of treatment on the treated is positive, nonparticipants may be worse off as a result of the program compared to what they would have experienced in a no program state. Nonparticipants who are good substitutes for the new trainees are especially adversely affected. Complementary factors benefit. These spillover effects can have important consequences for the interpretation of traditional evaluation parameters. The benchmark "no treatment" state is affected by the program and invariance assumption (PI-2) presented in Chapter 70 is violated.

To demonstrate these possibilities in a dramatic way, consider the effect of a wage subsidy for employment in a labor market for low-skill workers. Assume that firms act to minimize their costs of employment. Wage subsidies operate by taking nonemployed persons and subsidizing their employment at firms. Firms who employ the workers receive the wage subsidy.

Many active labor-market policies have a substantial wage-subsidy component. Suppose that the reason for nonemployment of low-skill workers is that minimum wages are set too high. This is the traditional justification for wage subsidies.[142] If the number of subsidized workers is less than the number of workers employed at the minimum wage, a wage subsidy financed from lump sum taxes has no effect on total employment in the low wage sector because the price of labor for the marginal worker hired by firms is the minimum wage. It is the same before and after the subsidy program is put in place. Thus the marginal worker is unsubsidized both before and after the subsidy program is put in place.

The effects of the program are dramatic on the individuals who participate in it. Persons previously nonemployed become employed as firms seek workers who carry a wage subsidy. Many previously-employed workers become nonemployed as their employment is not subsidized. There are no effects of the wage subsidy program on GDP unless the taxes raised to finance the program have real effects on output. Yet there is substantial redistribution of employment. Focusing solely on the effects of the program on subsidized workers greatly overstates its beneficial impact on the economy at large.

In order to estimate the impact of the program on the overall economy, it is necessary to look at outcomes for both participants and nonparticipants. Only if the benefits accruing to previously-nonemployed participants are adopted as the appropriate evaluation criterion would the effect of treatment on the treated be a parameter of interest. Information on both participants and nonparticipants affected by the program is required to estimate the net gain in earnings and employment resulting from the program.

In the case of a wage subsidy, comparing the earnings and employment of subsidized participants during their subsidized period to their earnings and employment in the pre-subsidized period can be a very misleading estimator of the total impact of the program. So is a cross-section comparison of participants and nonparticipants. In the example of a subsidy in the presence of a minimum wage, the before–after estimate of the gain exceeds the cross-section estimate unless the subsidy is extended to a group of nonemployed workers as large as the number employed at the minimum wage. For subsidy coverage levels below this amount, some proportion of the unsubsidized employment is paid the minimum wage. Under these circumstances, commonly-used evaluation estimators produce seriously misleading estimates of program impacts.

The following example clarifies and extends these points to examine the effect of displacement on conventional estimators. Let N be the number of participants in the low-wage labor market. Let N_E be the number of persons employed at the minimum

[142] See, e.g., Johnson (1979), or Johnson and Layard (1986).

wage M and let N_S be the number of persons subsidized. Subsidization operates solely on persons who would otherwise have been nonemployed and had no earnings. Assume $N_E > N_S$. Therefore, the subsidy has no effect on total employment in the market, because the marginal cost of labor to a firm is still the minimum wage. Workers with the subsidy are worth more to the firm by the amount of the subsidy S. Firms would be willing to pay up to $S + M$ per subsidized worker to attract them.

The estimated wage gain using a before–after comparison for subsidized participants is:

$$\textit{Before–After}: \quad \underbrace{(S + M)}_{\text{after}} - \underbrace{(0)}_{\text{before}} = S + M,$$

because all subsidized persons earn a zero wage prior to the subsidy. For them, the program is an unmixed blessing. The estimated wage gain using cross-section comparisons of participants and nonparticipants is:

$$\textit{Cross-Section}: \quad \underbrace{S + M}_{\text{participant's wage}} - \underbrace{M}_{\substack{\text{nonparticipant's} \\ \text{wage}}} \times \left(\frac{N_E - N_S}{N - N_S}\right)$$

$$= S + M \underbrace{\left(\frac{N - N_E}{N - N_S}\right)}_{(<1)} < S + M.$$

Since $N_E > N_S$, the before–after estimator is larger than the cross-section estimator. The widely used difference-in-differences estimator compares the before–after outcome measure for participants to the before–after outcome measure for nonparticipants:

$$\textit{Difference-in-Differences}: \quad (S + M - 0) - M\left(\frac{N_E - N_S}{N - N_S} - \frac{N_E}{N - N_S}\right)$$

$$= S + M\left(\frac{N}{N - N_S}\right) > S + M.$$

The gain estimated from the difference-in-differences estimator exceeds the gain estimated from the before–after estimator which in turn exceeds the gain estimated from the cross-section estimator. The "no treatment" benchmark in the difference-in-differences model is contaminated by treatment. The estimate of employment creation obtained from the three estimators is obtained by setting $M = 1$ and $S = 0$ in the previous expressions. This converts those expressions into estimates of employment gains for the different groups used in their definition.

None of these estimators produces a correct assessment of wage or employment gain for the economy at large. Focusing only on direct participants causes analysts to lose sight of overall program impacts. Only an aggregate analysis of the economy as a whole, or random samples of the entire economy, would produce the correct assessment that no wage increase or job creation is produced by the program. The problem of indirect effects poses a major challenge to conventional micro methods used in evaluation research that focus on direct impacts instead of total impacts, and demonstrates the need for program evaluations to utilize market-wide data and general equilibrium methods.

Calmfors (1994) presents a comprehensive review of the issues that arise in evaluating active labor-market programs and an exhaustive list of references on theoretical and empirical work on this topic. He distinguishes a number of indirect effects including *displacement effects* (jobs created by one program at the expense of other jobs), *deadweight effects* (subsidizing hiring that would have occurred in the absence of the program), *substitution effects* (jobs created for a certain category of workers replace jobs for other categories because relative wage costs have changed) and *tax effects* (the effects of taxation required to finance the programs on the behavior of everyone in society). A central conclusion of this literature is that the estimates of program impact from the microeconomic treatment effect literature provide incomplete information about the full impacts of active labor-market programs. The effect of a program on participants may be a poor approximation to the total effect of the program, as our simple example has shown. Blundell et al. (2004) present evidence on substitution and displacement for an English active labor-market program.

4.4. Social interactions

There is a growing empirical literature on social interactions. Brock and Durlauf (2001) and Durlauf and Fafchamps (2005) present comprehensive surveys of the methods and evidence from this emerging field. Instead of being market mediated, as in search and general equilibrium models, the social interactions considered in this literature are at the individual or group level which can include family interactions through transfers. Linkages through family and other social interactions undermine the sharp treatment-control separation assumed in the microeconomic treatment effect literature.

A recent paper by Angelucci and De Giorgi (2006) illustrates this possibility. They analyze the effect of the Progressa program in Mexico on both treated and untreated families. Progressa paid families to send their children to school. They present evidence that noneligible families received transfers from the eligible families and altered their saving and consumption behavior. Thus, through the transfer mechanism, the "untreated" receive treatment. However, they show no general equilibrium effects of the program on the product and labor markets that they study.

4.5. Summary of general equilibrium approaches

Many policies affect both "treatment" groups and indirectly affect "control" groups through market and social interactions. Reliance on microeconomic treatment effect approaches to evaluate such policies can produce potentially misleading estimates. The analysis of Heckman, Lochner and Taber (1998a) and the later work by Albrecht, Van den Berg and Vroman (2005), Blundell et al. (2004), Duflo (2004), Angelucci and De

Giorgi (2006), Lee (2005), Lise, Seitz and Smith (2005a, 2005b), and Lee and Wolpin (2006) indicate that ignoring indirect effects can produce misleading policy evaluations.

The cost of this enhanced knowledge is the difficulty in assembling all of the behavioral parameters required to conduct a general equilibrium evaluation. From a long run standpoint, these costs are worth incurring. Once a solid knowledge base is put in place, a more trustworthy framework for policy evaluation will be available, one that will offer an economically-justified framework for accumulating evidence across studies and will motivate empirical research by microeconomists to provide better empirical foundations for general equilibrium policy analyses.

5. Summary

This chapter extends the traditional static *ex post* literature on mean treatment effects to consider the identification of distributions of treatment effects, the identification of *ex ante* and *ex post* distributions of treatment effects, the measurement of uncertainty facing agents and the analysis of subjective valuations of programs. We also survey methods for identifying dynamic treatment effects with information updating by agents, using both explicitly formulated economic models and less explicit approaches. We discuss general equilibrium policy evaluation and evaluation of models with social interactions.

Appendix A: Deconvolution

To see how to use (CON-1) and (M-1) to identify $F(y_0, y_1 \mid X)$, note that

$$Y = Y_0 + D\Delta.$$

From $F_Y(y \mid X, D = 0)$, we identify $F_0(y_0 \mid X)$ as a consequence of matching assumption (M-1). From $F_Y(y \mid X, D = 1)$ we identify $F_1(y_1 \mid X) = F_{Y_0+\Delta}(y_0 + \Delta \mid X)$. If Y_0 and Y_1 have densities, then, as a consequence of (CON-1) and (M-1), the densities satisfy

$$f_1(y_1 \mid X) = f_\Delta(\Delta \mid X) * f_0(y_0 \mid X)$$

where "$*$" denotes convolution. The characteristic functions of Y_0, Y_1 and Δ are related in the following way:

$$E\left(e^{i\ell Y_1} \mid X\right) = E\left(e^{i\ell\Delta} \mid X\right)E\left(e^{i\ell Y_0} \mid X\right).$$

Since we can identify $F_1(y_1 \mid X)$, we know its characteristic function. By a similar argument, we can recover $E(e^{i\ell Y_0} \mid X)$. Thus, from

$$E\left(e^{i\ell\Delta} \mid X\right) = \frac{E(e^{i\ell Y_1} \mid X)}{E(e^{i\ell Y_0} \mid X)},$$

and by the inversion theorem,[143] we can recover the density $f_\Delta(\Delta \mid X)$. We know the joint density

$$f_{\Delta,Y_0}(\Delta, y_0 \mid X) = f_\Delta(\Delta \mid X) f_0(y_0 \mid X).$$

From the definition of Δ, we obtain

$$f_\Delta(y_1 - y_0 \mid X) f_0(y_0 \mid X) = f(y_1, y_0 \mid X).$$

Thus we can recover the full joint distribution of outcomes and the distribution of gains.

Under assumption (M-1), assumption (CON-1) is testable. The ratio of two characteristic functions is not necessarily a characteristic function. If it is not, the estimated density f_Δ recovered from the ratio of the characteristic functions need not be positive and the estimated variance of Δ can be negative.[144]

Appendix B: Matzkin conditions and proof of Theorem 2

We prove Theorem 2. We first present a review of the conditions Matzkin (1992) imposes for identification of nonparametric discrete choice models which are used in this proof.

B.1. The Matzkin conditions

Consider a binary choice model, $D = \mathbf{1}[\varphi(Z) > V]$, where Z is observed and V is unobserved. Let φ^* denote the true φ and let F_V^* denote the true cdf of V. Let $\mathcal{Z} \subseteq \mathbb{R}^K$ denote the support of Z. Let $\mathcal{H}$ denote the set of monotone increasing functions from $\mathbb{R}$ into $[0, 1]$. Assume:

(i) $\varphi \in \Phi$, where Φ is a set of real valued, continuous functions defined over $\mathcal{Z}$, which is also assumed to be the domain of definition of φ, and the true function is $\varphi^* \in \Phi$. There exists a subset $\widetilde{\mathcal{Z}} \subseteq \mathcal{Z}$ such that (a) for all $\varphi, \varphi' \in \Phi$, and all $z \in \widetilde{\mathcal{Z}}$, $\varphi(z) = \varphi'(z)$, and (b) for all $\varphi \in \Phi$ and all t in the range space of $\varphi^*(z)$ for $z \in \mathcal{Z}$, there exists a $\tilde{z} \in \widetilde{\mathcal{Z}}$ such that $\varphi(\tilde{z}) = t$. In addition, φ^* is strictly increasing in the Kth coordinate of Z.

(ii) $Z \perp\!\!\!\perp V$.

(iii) The Kth component of Z possesses a Lebesgue density conditional on the other components of Z.

[143] See, e.g., Kendall and Stuart (1977).

[144] For the ratio of characteristic functions, $r(\ell)$, to be a characteristic function, it must satisfy the requirement that $r(0) = 1$, that $r(\ell)$ is continuous in ℓ and $r(\ell)$ is nonnegative definite. This identifying assumption can be tested using the procedures developed in Heckman, Robb and Walker (1990).

(iv) F_V^* is strictly increasing on the support of $\varphi^*(Z)$. Matzkin (1992) notes that if one assumes that V is absolutely continuous, and the other conditions hold, one can relax the condition that φ^* is strictly increasing in one coordinate (listed in (i)) and the requirement in (iii).

Then (φ^*, F_V^*) is identified within $\Phi \times \mathcal{H}$, where F_V^* is identified on the support of $\varphi^*(Z)$.

Matzkin establishes identifiability for the following alternative representations of functional forms that satisfy condition (i) for exact identification for $\varphi(Z)$.

1. $\varphi(Z) = Z\gamma$, $\|\gamma\| = 1$ or $\gamma_1 = 1$.
2. $\varphi(z)$ is homogeneous of degree one and attains a given value α at $z = z^*$ (e.g., cost functions).
3. The $\varphi(Z)$ are least concave functions that attain common values at two points in their domain.
4. The $\varphi(Z)$ are additively separable functions:
   (a) Functions additively separable into a continuous monotone increasing function and a continuous monotone increasing function which is concave and homogeneous of degree one;
   (b) Functions additively separable into the value of one variable and a continuous, monotone increasing function of the remaining variables;
   (c) A set of functions additively separable in each argument [see Matzkin (1992, Example 5, p. 255)].

We now prove Theorem 2.

B.2. *Proof of Theorem 2*

PROOF. Proof of the identifiability of the joint distribution of V^s and $\mu_R^s(Z)$ follows from Matzkin (1993), Theorem 2. See also the proof presented in Chapter 70 (Appendix B) of this Handbook. We condition on the event $D(s) = 1$. From the data on $Y_c(s, X)$, $Y_d(s, X)$, $M_c(X)$, $M_d(X)$ for $D(s) = 1$, and the treatment selection probabilities, we can construct the left-hand side of the following equation:

$$\Pr\left(\begin{matrix} Y_c(s,X) \leqslant y_c, \mu_d(s,X) \leqslant U_d(s), \\ M_c(X) \leqslant m_c, \mu_{d,M}(X) \leqslant U_{d,M} \end{matrix} \,\middle|\, D(s) = 1, X = x, Z = z\right)$$
$$\times \Pr\big(D(s) = 1 \mid X = x, Z = z\big)$$
$$= \int_{\underline{U}_c(s)}^{y_c - \mu_c(s,x)} \int_{\mu_d(s,x)}^{\overline{U}_d(s)} \int_{\underline{U}_{c,M}}^{m_c - \mu_{c,M}(x)} \int_{\mu_{d,M}(x)}^{\overline{U}_{d,M}} \int_{\underline{V}^s(1)}^{\mu_R(s,z) - \mu_R(1,z)} \cdots$$
$$\int_{\underline{V}^s(\bar{S})}^{\mu_R(s,z) - \mu_R(\bar{S},z)} f_{U_c(s), U_d(s), U_{c,M}, U_{d,M}, V^s}\big(u_c(s), u_d(s), u_{c,M}, u_{d,M},$$
$$v(s) - v(1), v(s) - v(\bar{S})\big)$$

$$\cdot\, d\big(v(s) - v(\bar{S})\big) \cdots d\big(v(s) - v(1)\big)\, du_{d,M}\, du_{c,M}\, du_d(s)\, du_c(s). \tag{B.1}$$

Parallel expressions can be derived for the other possible values of $M_d(X)$ and $Y_d(s, X)$. We obtain the selection-bias free distribution of $Y_c(s, X), Y_d(s, X), M_c(X), M_d(X)$ given X, $\Pr(Y_c(s, X) \leqslant y_c, Y_d(s, X) = y_d, M_c(X) \leqslant m_c, M_d(X) = m_d \mid X)$, from $\Pr(Y_c(s, X) \leqslant y_c, Y_d(s, X) = y_d, M_c(X) \leqslant m_c, D(s) = 1 \mid X, Z = z)$ for $z \to \mathcal{Z}_s$, a limit set, possibly dependent on X, such that $\lim_{z \to \mathcal{Z}_s} \Pr(D(s) = 1 \mid X, Z = z) = 1$. This produces the $\mu_c(s, X)$, $\mu_{c,M}(X)$ directly and the $\mu_d(s, X)$, $\mu_{d,M}(X)$ using the analysis of Matzkin (1992, 1993, 1994) for the class of Matzkin functions defined in Appendix B.1. Varying the $y_c - \mu_c(s, X)$, $\mu_d(s, X)$, $m_c - \mu_{c,M}(X)$, $\mu_{d,M}(X)$, $\mu_R^s(Z)$, under the conditions of the theorem we can trace out the joint distribution of $(U_c(s), U_d(s), U_{c,M}, U_{d,M}, V^s)$ for each $s = 1, \ldots, \bar{S}$. □

As a consequence of (ii), we can identify $\mu_c(s, X)$, $\mu_{c,M}(X)$ directly from the means of the limit outcome distributions. We can thus identify all pairwise average treatment effects

$$E\big(Y_c(s, X) \mid X = x\big) - E\big(Y_c(s', X) \mid X = x\big)$$

for all s, s' and any other linear functionals derived from the distributions of the continuous variables defined at s and s'. Identification of the means and distributions of the latent variables giving rise to the discrete outcomes is more subtle, but standard [see Carneiro, Hansen and Heckman (2003)]. With one continuous regressor among the X, one can identify the marginal distributions of the $U_d(s)$ and the $U_{d,M}$. To identify the joint distributions of $U_d(s)$ and $U_{d,M}$ one must use condition (iv) component by component.

Thus for system s, suppose that there are $N_{d,s}$ discrete outcome components with associated means $\mu_{d,j}(s, X)$ and error terms $U_{d,j}(s)$, $j = 1, \ldots, N_{d,s}$. As a consequence of condition (iv) of this theorem, $\mathrm{Supp}(\mu_d(s, X)) \supseteq \mathrm{Supp}(U_d(s))$. We thus can trace out the joint distribution of $U_d(s)$ and identify it (up to scale if we specify the Matzkin class only up to scale). By a parallel argument for the measurements, we can identify the joint distribution of $U_{d,M}$. Let $N_{d,M}$ be the number of discrete measurements. From condition (iv), we obtain $\mathrm{Supp}(\mu_{d,M}(X)) \supseteq \mathrm{Supp}(U_{d,M})$. Under these conditions, we can trace out the joint distribution of $U_{d,M}$ and identify it (up to scale for Matzkin class of functions specified up to scale) within the limit sets. In the general case, we can vary each limit of the integral in (B.1) and similar integrals for the other possible values of the discrete measurements and outcomes independently and trace out the full joint distribution of $(U_c(s), U_d(s), U_{c,M}, U_{d,M}, V^s)$. For further discussion, see the analysis in Carneiro, Hansen and Heckman (2003, Theorem 3).

Appendix C: Proof of Theorem 4

PROOF. From Theorem 3, we obtain identifiability of $\Psi^s(Z)$ and the joint distribution of η^s. From the data on $Y(s, X)$, for $D(s) = 1$, and from the time to treatment probabilities, we can construct the left-hand side of the following equation:

$$\begin{aligned}
&\Pr\bigl(Y(s, X) \leqslant y \mid D(s) = 1, X = x, Z = z\bigr) \\
&\quad \times \Pr\bigl(D(s) = 1 \mid X = x, Z = z\bigr) \\
&\quad = \int_{\underline{U}(s)}^{y-\mu(s,x)} \int_{\underline{\eta}(s)}^{\Psi(s,z(s))} \int_{\Psi(s-1,z(s-1))}^{\bar{\eta}(s-1)} \cdots \\
&\quad \int_{\Psi(1,z(1))}^{\bar{\eta}(1)} f_{U(s),\eta^s}\bigl(u(s), \eta(1), \ldots, \eta(s)\bigr)\, d\eta(1) \cdots d\eta(s)\, du(s). \qquad \text{(C.1)}
\end{aligned}$$

Under assumption (iv), for all $x \in \operatorname{Supp}(X)$, we can vary the $\Psi(j, Z(j))$, $j = 1, \ldots, s$, and obtain a limit set $\mathcal{Z}_s$, possibly dependent on X, such that $\lim_{z \to \mathcal{Z}_s} \Pr(D(s) = 1 \mid X = x, Z = z) = 1$. We can identify the joint distribution of $Y(s, X)$, free of selection bias in this limit set for all $s = 1, \ldots, \bar{S}$. We know the limit sets given the functional forms in Matzkin (1992, 1993, 1994) with the leading case being $\Psi(s, Z(s)) = Z(s)\gamma_s$. From the analysis of Theorem 3, we achieve identifiability on nonnegligible sets.

As a consequence of (ii), we can identify $\mu(s, X)$ directly from the means of the limit outcome distributions. We can thus identify all pairwise average treatment effects $E(Y(s, X) \mid X = x) - E(Y(s', X) \mid X = x)$ for all s, s' and any other linear functionals derived from the distributions of the continuous variables defined at s and s'.

In the general case, we can vary each limit of the integral in (C.1) independently and trace out the full joint distribution of $(U(s), \eta(1), \ldots, \eta(s))$. For further discussion, see the analysis in Carneiro, Hansen and Heckman (2003, Theorem 3). Note the close parallel to the proof of Theorem 2. The key difference between the two proofs is the choice equation. In Theorem 2, the choice of treatment equation is a conventional multivariate discrete-choice model. In Theorem 3, it is the reduced form dynamic model extensively analyzed in Heckman and Navarro (2007). □

Appendix D: Proof of a more general version of Theorem 4

This appendix states and proves a more general version of Theorem 4. Use $Y(t, s)$ as shorthand for $Y(t, s, X, U(t, s))$. Ignore (for notational simplicity) the mixed discrete-continuous outcome case. One can build that case from the continuous and discrete cases and for the sake of brevity we do not analyze it here. We also do not analyze duration outcomes although it is straightforward to do so. Decompose $Y(t, s)$ into discrete and continuous components:

$$Y(t, s) = \begin{bmatrix} Y_c(t, s) \\ Y_d(t, s) \end{bmatrix}.$$

Associated with the jth component of $Y_d(t,s)$, $Y_{d,j}(t,s)$, is a latent variable $Y^*_{d,j}(t,s)$. Define, as in Theorem 2,

$$Y_{d,j}(t,s) = \mathbf{1}\big(Y^*_{d,j}(t,s) \geqslant 0\big).$$[145]

From standard results in the discrete-choice literature, without additional information, one can only identify $Y^*_{d,j}(t,s)$ up to scale.

Assume an additively separable model for the continuous variables and latent continuous indices. Making the X explicit, we obtain

$$\begin{aligned} Y_c(t,s,X) &= \mu_c(t,s,X) + U_c(t,s), \\ Y^*_d(t,s,X) &= \mu_d(t,s,X) - U_d(t,s), \\ &1 \leqslant s \leqslant \bar{S},\ 1 \leqslant t \leqslant \bar{T}. \end{aligned}$$

Array the $Y_c(t,s,X)$ into a matrix $Y_c(s,X)$ and the $Y^*_d(t,s,X)$ into a matrix $Y^*_d(s,X)$. Decompose these vectors into components corresponding to the means $\mu_c(s,X)$, $\mu_d(s,X)$ and the unobservables $U_c(s)$, $U_d(s)$. Thus

$$\begin{aligned} Y_c(s,X) &= \mu_c(s,X) + U_c(s), \\ Y^*_d(s,X) &= \mu_d(s,X) - U_d(s). \end{aligned}$$

$Y^*_d(s,X)$ generates $Y_d(s,X)$. To simplify the notation, make use of the condensed forms $Y_c(X)$, $Y^*_d(X)$, $\mu_c(X)$, $\mu_d(X)$, U_c and U_d as described in the text. In this notation,

$$\begin{aligned} Y_c(X) &= \mu_c(X) + U_c, \\ Y^*_d(X) &= \mu_d(X) - U_d. \end{aligned}$$

Following Carneiro, Hansen and Heckman (2003) and Cunha and Heckman (2007b, 2008), Cunha, Heckman and Navarro (2005, 2006), one may also have a system of measurements with both discrete and continuous components. The measurements are not s-indexed. They are the same for each stopping time. Write the equations for the measurements in an additively separable form, in a fashion comparable to those of the outcomes. The equations for the continuous measurements and latent indices producing discrete measurements are

$$\begin{aligned} M_c(t,X) &= \mu_{c,M}(t,X) + U_{c,M}(t), \\ M^*_d(t,X) &= \mu_{d,M}(t,X) - U_{d,M}(t), \end{aligned}$$

where the discrete variable corresponding to the jth index in $M^*_d(t,X)$ is

$$M_{d,j}(t,X) = \mathbf{1}\big(M^*_{d,j}(t,X) \geqslant 0\big).$$

145 Extensions to nonbinary discrete outcomes are straightforward. Thus one could entertain, at greater notational cost, a multinomial outcome model at each age t for each counterfactual state, building on the analysis of Appendix B in Chapter 70.

The measurements play the role of indicators unaffected by the process being studied. We array $M_c(t, X)$ and $M_d^*(t, X)$ into matrices $M_c(X)$ and $M_d^*(X)$. We array $\mu_{c,M}(t, X)$, $\mu_{d,M}(t, X)$ into matrices $\mu_{c,M}(X)$ and $\mu_{d,M}(X)$. We array the corresponding unobservables into $U_{c,M}$ and $U_{d,M}$. Thus we write

$$M_c(X) = \mu_{c,M}(X) + U_{c,M},$$
$$M_d^*(X) = \mu_{d,M}(X) - U_{d,M}.$$

We use the notation of Section 3.4.1 to write $I(s) = \Psi(s, Z(s)) - \eta(s)$ and collect $I(s)$, $\Psi(s, Z(s))$ and $\eta(s)$ into vectors I, $\Psi(Z)$, η. We define $\eta^s = (\eta(1), \ldots, \eta(s))$ and $\Psi^s(Z) = (\Psi(1, Z(1)), \ldots, \Psi(s, Z(s)))$. Using this notation, we extend the analysis of Carneiro, Hansen and Heckman (2003) to identify our model assuming that we have a large i.i.d. sample from the distribution of (Y_c, Y_d, M_c, M_d, I).

THEOREM D.1. *Assuming the conditions of Theorem 3 hold, for $s = 1, \ldots, \bar{S}$, the joint distribution of $(U_c(s), U_d(s), U_{c,M}, U_{d,M}, \eta^s)$ is identified along with the mean functions $(\mu_c(s, X), \mu_d(s, X), \mu_{c,M}(X), \mu_{d,M}(X), \Psi^s(Z))$ (the components of $\mu_d(s, X)$ and $\mu_{d,M}(X)$ over the supports admitted by the supports of the errors) if*

(i) $E[U_c(s)] = E[U_{c,M}] = 0$. *$(U_c(s), U_d(s), U_{c,M}, U_{d,M}, \eta^s)$ are continuous random variables with support*: $\mathrm{Supp}(U_c(s)) \times \mathrm{Supp}(U_d(s)) \times \mathrm{Supp}(U_{c,M}) \times \mathrm{Supp}(U_{d,M}) \times \mathrm{Supp}(\eta^s)$ *with upper and lower limits $(\overline{U}_c(s), \overline{U}_d(s), \overline{U}_{c,M}, \overline{U}_{d,M}, \bar{\eta}^s)$ and $(\underline{U}_c(s), \underline{U}_d(s), \underline{U}_{c,M}, \underline{U}_{d,M}, \underline{\eta}^s)$ respectively. These conditions are assumed to apply within each component of each subvector. The joint system is thus variation free for each component with respect to every other component.*

(ii) $(U_c(s), U_d(s), U_{c,M}, U_{d,M}, \eta^s) \perp\!\!\!\perp (X, Z)$.

(iii) $\mathrm{Supp}(\Psi(Z), X) = \mathrm{Supp}(\Psi(Z)) \times \mathrm{Supp}(X)$.

(iv) $\mathrm{Supp}(\mu_d(s, X), \mu_{d,M}(X)) \supseteq \mathrm{Supp}(U_d(s), U_{d,M})$.

(v) *$\mu_c(s, X)$ and $\mu_{c,M}(X)$ are continuous functions. The components of the $\mu_d(s, X)$ and $\mu_{d,M}(X)$ satisfy the Matzkin conditions developed in Appendix* B.1.

PROOF. We use the proof of Theorem 3 to identify $\Psi^s(Z)$ and the distributions of η^s, $s = 1, \ldots, \bar{S}$. From the data on $Y_c(s, X)$, $Y_d(s, X)$, $M_c(X)$, $M_d(X)$ for $D(s) = 1$, and from the time to treatment probabilities, we can construct the left-hand side of the following equation:

$$\Pr\left(\begin{matrix} Y_c(s, X) \leqslant y_c, \mu_d(s, X) \leqslant U_d(s), \\ M_c(X) \leqslant m_c, \mu_{d,M}(X) \leqslant U_{d,M} \end{matrix} \;\middle|\; D(s) = 1, X = x, Z = z \right)$$
$$\times \Pr\bigl(D(s) = 1 \mid X = x, Z = z\bigr)$$

$$= \int_{\underline{U}_c(s)}^{y_c-\mu_c(s,x)} \int_{\mu_d(s,x)}^{\overline{U}_d(s)} \int_{\underline{U}_{c,M}}^{m_c-\mu_{c,M}(x)} \int_{\mu_{d,M}(x)}^{\overline{U}_{d,M}} \int_{\underline{\eta}(s)}^{\Psi(s,z(s))} \int_{\Psi(s-1,z(s-1))}^{\bar{\eta}(s-1)} \cdots$$

$$\int_{\Psi(1,z(1))}^{\bar{\eta}(1)} f_{U_c(s),U_d(s),U_{c,M},U_{d,M},\eta^s}\big(u_c(s), u_d(s), u_{c,M}, u_{d,M}, \eta(1), \ldots, \eta(s)\big)$$

$$\cdot\, d\eta(1) \cdots d\eta(s)\, du_{d,M}\, du_{c,M}\, du_d(s)\, du_c(s). \tag{D.1}$$

We can construct distributions for the other configurations of conditioning events defining the discrete dependent variables (i.e., $\mu_d(s, X) > U_d(s)$, $\mu_{d,M}(X) > U_{d,M}$; $\mu_d(s, X) > U_d(s)$, $\mu_{d,M}(X) < U_{d,M}$; $\mu_d(s, X) \leqslant U_d(s)$, $\mu_{d,M}(X) > U_{d,M}$).

Under assumption (iii), for all $x \in \operatorname{Supp}(X)$, we can vary the $\Psi(j, z(j))$, $j = 1, \ldots, s$, and obtain a limit set $\mathcal{Z}_s$, possibly dependent on X, such that $\lim_{z\to\mathcal{Z}_s} \Pr(D(s) = 1 \mid X = x, Z = z) = 1$. We can use (D.1) and parallel distributions for the other configurations for the discrete dependent variables to identify the joint distribution of $Y_c(s, X)$, $Y_d(s, X)$, $M_c(X)$, $M_d(X)$ free of selection bias for all $s = 1, \ldots, \bar{S}$ in these limit sets. We identify the parameters of $Y_d(s, X)$, $s = 1, \ldots, \bar{S}$, and $M_d(X)$. We know the limit sets given the functional forms for the $\Psi(s, Z(s))$, $s = 1, \ldots, \bar{S}$, presented in B.1 or in Matzkin (1992, 1993, 1994).

As a consequence of (ii), we can identify $\mu_c(s, X)$, $\mu_{c,M}(X)$ directly from the means of the limit outcome distributions. We can thus identify all pairwise average treatment effects

$$E\big(Y_c(s, X) \mid X = x\big) - E\big(Y_c(s', X) \mid X = x\big)$$

for all s, s' and any other linear functionals derived from the distributions of the continuous variables defined at s and s'. Identification of the means and distributions of the latent variables giving rise to the discrete outcomes is more subtle. The required argument is standard. With one continuous regressor among the X, one can identify the marginal distributions of the $U_d(s)$ and the $U_{d,M}$ (up to scale if the Matzkin functions are only specified up to scale). To identify the joint distributions of $U_d(s)$ and $U_{d,M}$, one can invoke (iv).

Thus for system s, suppose that there are $N_{d,s}$ discrete outcome components with associated means $\mu_{d,j}(s, X)$ and error terms $U_{d,j}(s)$, $j = 1, \ldots, N_{d,s}$. As a consequence of condition (iv) of this theorem, $\operatorname{Supp}(\mu_d(s, X)) \supseteq \operatorname{Supp}(U_d(s))$. We thus can trace out the joint distribution of $U_d(s)$ and identify it (up to scale if we specify the Matzkin class only up to scale). By a parallel argument for the measurements, we can identify the joint distribution of $U_{d,M}$. Let $N_{d,M}$ be the number of discrete measurements. From condition (iv), we obtain $\operatorname{Supp}(\mu_{d,M}(X)) \supseteq \operatorname{Supp}(U_{d,M})$. Under these conditions, we can trace out the joint distribution of $U_{d,M}$ and identify it (up to scale for the Matzkin class of functions specified up to scale) within the limit sets. From assumption (v), we obtain identification on nonnegligible sets.

We can vary each limit of the integral in (D.1) independently and trace out the full joint distribution of $(U_c(s), U_d(s), U_{c,M}, U_{d,M}, \eta(1), \ldots, \eta(s))$ using the parameters determined from the marginals. For further discussion, see the analysis in Carneiro,

Hansen and Heckman (2003, Theorem 3). We obtain identifiability on nonnegligible sets by combining the conditions in Theorem 3 with those in condition (v).

□

References

Aakvik, A., Heckman, J.J., Vytlacil, E.J. (2005). "Estimating treatment effects for discrete outcomes when responses to treatment vary: An application to Norwegian vocational rehabilitation programs". Journal of Econometrics 125 (1–2), 15–51.

Aalen, O.O., Gjessing, H.K. (2004). "Survival models based on the Ornstein–Uhlenbeck process". Lifetime Data Analysis 10 (4), 407–423 (December).

Abadie, A. (2002). "Bootstrap tests of distributional treatment effects in instrumental variable models". Journal of the American Statistical Association 97 (457), 284–292 (March).

Abadie, A., Angrist, J.D., Imbens, G. (2002). "Instrumental variables estimates of the effect of subsidized training on the quantiles of trainee earnings". Econometrica 70 (1), 91–117 (January).

Abbring, J.H. (2002). "Stayers versus defecting movers: A note on the identification of defective duration models". Economics Letters 74 (3), 327–331 (February).

Abbring, J.H. (2003). "Dynamic econometric program evaluation". Discussion Paper 804. IZA, Bonn. Paper prepared for the H. Theil Memorial Conference, Amsterdam, 16–18 August 2002.

Abbring, J.H. (2007). "Mixed hitting-time models". Discussion Paper 2007-057/3. Tinbergen Institute, Amsterdam.

Abbring, J.H. (2008). "The event-history approach to program evaluation". In: Millimet, D., Smith, J., Vytlacil, E. (Eds.), Modeling and Evaluating Treatment Effects in Econometrics. In: Advances in Econometrics, vol. 21. Elsevier Science, Oxford (forthcoming).

Abbring, J.H., Campbell, J.R. (2005). "A firm's first year". Discussion Paper 2005-046/3. Tinbergen Institute, Amsterdam (May).

Abbring, J.H., Heckman, J.J. (2008). "Dynamic policy analysis". In: Mátyás, L., Sevestre, P. (Eds.), The Econometrics of Panel Data, third ed. Kluwer, Dordrecht (forthcoming).

Abbring, J.H., Van den Berg, G.J. (2003a). "The identifiability of the mixed proportional hazards competing risks model". Journal of the Royal Statistical Society, Series B 65 (3), 701–710 (September).

Abbring, J.H., Van den Berg, G.J. (2003b). "The nonparametric identification of treatment effects in duration models". Econometrica 71 (5), 1491–1517 (September).

Abbring, J.H., Van den Berg, G.J. (2003c). "A simple procedure for inference on treatment effects in duration models". Discussion paper 810. IZA, Bonn.

Abbring, J.H., Van den Berg, G.J. (2004). "Analyzing the effect of dynamically assigned treatments using duration models, binary treatment models and panel data models". Empirical Economics 29 (1), 5–20 (January).

Abbring, J.H., Van den Berg, G.J. (2005). "Social experiments and instrumental variables with duration outcomes". Discussion Paper 2005-047/3. Tinbergen Institute, Amsterdam.

Abbring, J.H., Van den Berg, G.J., Van Ours, J.C. (2005). "The effect of unemployment insurance sanctions on the transition rate from unemployment to employment". Economic Journal 115 (505), 602–630 (July).

Albrecht, J., Van den Berg, G.J., Vroman, S. (2005). "The knowledge lift: The Swedish adult education program that aimed to eliminate low worker skill levels". Discussion Paper 1503. Institute for the Study of Labor (IZA), Bonn (February).

Aldrich, J. (1989). "Autonomy". Oxford Economic Papers 41 (1), 15–34 (January).

Andersen, P.K., Borgan, Ø., Gill, R., Keiding, N. (1993). Statistical Models Based on Counting Processes. Springer-Verlag, New York.

Anderson, T., Rubin, H. (1956). "Statistical inference in factor analysis". In: Neyman, J. (Ed.), Proceedings of the Third Berkeley Symposium on Mathematical Statistics and Probability, 5. University of California Press, Berkeley, pp. 111–150.

Angelucci, M., De Giorgi, G. (2006). "Indirect effects of an aid program: The case of Progresa and consumption". Discussion Paper 1955. Institute for the Study of Labor (IZA) (January).
Auerbach, A.J., Kotlikoff, L.J. (1987). Dynamic Fiscal Policy. Cambridge University Press, Cambridge, New York.
Barros, R.P. (1987). "Two essays on the nonparametric estimation of economic models with selectivity using choice-based samples". PhD thesis. University of Chicago.
Becker, G.S. (1974). "A theory of marriage: Part II". Journal of Political Economy 82 (2, Part 2: Marriage, Family Human Capital and Fertility), S11–S26 (March).
Belzil, C., Hansen, J. (2002). "Unobserved ability and the return to schooling". Econometrica 70 (5), 2075–2091 (September).
Bishop, Y.M., Fienberg, S.E., Holland, P.W. (1975). Discrete Multivariate Analysis: Theory and Practice. The MIT Press, Cambridge, Massachusetts.
Black, D.A., Smith, J.A., Berger, M.C., Noel, B.J. (2003). "Is the threat of reemployment services more effective than the services themselves? Evidence from random assignment in the UI system". American Economic Review 93 (4), 1313–1327 (September).
Blundell, R., Costa Dias, M., Meghir, C., Van Reenen, J. (2004). "Evaluating the employment effects of a mandatory job search program". Journal of the European Economic Association 2 (4), 569–606 (June).
Bonhomme, S., Robin, J.-M. (2004). "Nonparametric identification and estimation of independent factor models". Unpublished working paper. Sorbonne, Paris.
Bonnal, L., Fougère, D., Sérandon, A. (1997). "Evaluating the impact of French employment policies on individual labour market histories". Review of Economic Studies 64 (4), 683–713 (October).
Brock, W.A., Durlauf, S.N. (2001). "Interactions-based models". In: Heckman, J.J., Leamer, E. (Eds.), Handbook of Econometrics, vol. 5. North-Holland, New York, pp. 3463–3568.
Browning, M., Hansen, L.P., Heckman, J.J. (1999). "Micro data and general equilibrium models". In: Taylor, J.B., Woodford, M. (Eds.), Handbook of Macroeconomics, vol. 1A. Elsevier, pp. 543–633, Chapter 8 (December).
Calmfors, L. (1994). "Active labour market policy and unemployment – a framework for the analysis of crucial design features". OECD Economic Studies 22, 7–47 (Spring).
Cambanis, S., Simons, G., Stout, W. (1976). "Inequalities for $e(k(x, y))$ when the marginals are fixed". Zeitschrift für Wahrscheinlichkeitstheorie und verwandte Gebiete 36, 285–294.
Cameron, S.V., Heckman, J.J. (1998). "Life cycle schooling and dynamic selection bias: Models and evidence for five cohorts of American males". Journal of Political Economy 106 (2), 262–333 (April).
Cameron, S.V., Heckman, J.J. (2001). "The dynamics of educational attainment for black, Hispanic and white males". Journal of Political Economy 109 (3), 455–499 (June).
Card, D., Sullivan, D.G. (1988). "Measuring the effect of subsidized training programs on movements in and out of employment". Econometrica 56 (3), 497–530 (May).
Carneiro, P., Hansen, K., Heckman, J.J. (2001). "Removing the veil of ignorance in assessing the distributional impacts of social policies". Swedish Economic Policy Review 8 (2), 273–301 (Fall).
Carneiro, P., Hansen, K., Heckman, J.J. (2003). "Estimating distributions of treatment effects with an application to the returns to schooling and measurement of the effects of uncertainty on college choice". 2001 Lawrence R. Klein Lecture. International Economic Review 44 (2), 361–422 (May).
Chamberlain, G. (1975). "Unobservables in econometric models". PhD thesis. Harvard University.
Chan, T.Y., Hamilton, B.H. (2006). "Learning, private information and the economic evaluation of randomized experiments". Journal of Political Economy 114 (6), 997–1040.
Chesher, A. (2003). "Identification in nonseparable models". Econometrica 71 (5), 1405–1441 (September).
Cosslett, S.R. (1983). "Distribution-free maximum likelihood estimator of the binary choice model". Econometrica 51 (3), 765–782 (May).
Cowell, F.A. (2000). "Measurement of inequality". In: Atkinson, A., Bourguignon, F. (Eds.), Handbook of Income Distribution, vol. 1. North-Holland, New York, pp. 87–166.
Cunha, F., Heckman, J.J. (2007a). "Formulating, identifying and estimating the technology of cognitive and noncognitive skill formation". Unpublished manuscript. University of Chicago, Department of Economics. Journal of Human Resources (forthcoming).

Cunha, F., Heckman, J.J. (2007b). "The evolution of earnings risk in the US economy". Presented at the 9th World Congress of the Econometric Society, London.

Cunha, F., Heckman, J.J. (2007c). "Identifying and estimating the distributions of *ex post* and *ex ante* returns to schooling: A survey of recent developments". Labour Economics (forthcoming).

Cunha, F., Heckman, J.J. (2008). "A framework for the analysis of inequality". Macroeconomic Dynamics (forthcoming).

Cunha, F., Heckman, J.J., Navarro, S. (2005). "Separating uncertainty from heterogeneity in life cycle earnings, the 2004 Hicks lecture". Oxford Economic Papers 57 (2), 191–261 (April).

Cunha, F., Heckman, J.J., Navarro, S. (2006). "Counterfactual analysis of inequality and social mobility". In: Morgan, S.L., Grusky, D.B., Fields, G.S. (Eds.), Mobility and Inequality: Frontiers of Research in Sociology and Economics. Stanford University Press, Stanford, CA, pp. 290–348 (Chapter 4).

Cunha, F., Heckman, J.J., Navarro, S. (2007). "The identification and economic content of ordered choice models with stochastic cutoffs". International Economic Review (forthcoming, November).

Cunha, F., Heckman, J.J., Schennach, S.M. (2006). "Nonlinear factor analysis". Unpublished manuscript. University of Chicago, Department of Economics.

Cunha, F., Heckman, J.J., Schennach, S.M. (2007). "Estimating the technology of cognitive and noncognitive skill formation". Unpublished manuscript. University of Chicago, Department of Economics. Presented at the Yale Conference on Macro and Labor Economics, May 5–7, 2006. Econometrica (under revision).

Davidson, C., Woodbury, S.A. (1993). "The displacement effect of reemployment bonus programs". Journal of Labor Economics 11 (4), 575–605 (October).

Dawkins, C., Srinivasan, T.N., Whalley, J. (2001). "Calibration". In: Heckman, J.J., Leamer, E. (Eds.), Handbook of Econometrics. In: Handbooks in Economics, vol. 5. Elsevier Science, New York, pp. 3653–3703.

Duflo, E. (2004). "The medium run effects of educational expansion: Evidence from a large school construction program in Indonesia". Journal of Development Economics 74 (1), 163–197 (June, special issue).

Durlauf, S., Fafchamps, M. (2005). "Social capital". In: Durlauf, S., Aghion, P. (Eds.), Handbook of Growth Economics. In: Handbooks in Economics, vol. 1B. Elsevier, pp. 1639–1699.

Dynarski, S.M. (2000). "Hope for whom? Financial aid for the middle class and its impact on college attendance". National Tax Journal 53 (3, Part 2), 629–661 (September).

Eberwein, C., Ham, J.C., LaLonde, R.J. (1997). "The impact of being offered and receiving classroom training on the employment histories of disadvantaged women: Evidence from experimental data". Review of Economic Studies 64 (4), 655–682 (October).

Eckstein, Z., Wolpin, K.I. (1999). "Why youths drop out of high school: The impact of preferences, opportunities and abilities". Econometrica 67 (6), 1295–1339 (November).

Falmagne, J.-C. (1985). Elements of Psychophysical Theory. Oxford Psychology Series. Oxford University Press, New York.

Fields, G.S. (2003). "Economic and social mobility really are multifaceted". Paper presented at the Conference on Frontiers in Social and Economic Mobility. Cornell University, Ithaca, New York (March).

Fitzenberger, B., Osikominu, A., Völter, R. (2006). "Get training or wait? Long-run employment effects of training programs for the unemployed in West Germany". Technical Report 2121. IZA (Institute for the Study of Labor) (May).

Fleming, T.R., Harrington, D.P. (1991). Counting Processes and Survival Analysis. Wiley, New York.

Flinn, C., Heckman, J.J. (1982). "New methods for analyzing structural models of labor force dynamics". Journal of Econometrics 18 (1), 115–168 (January).

Florens, J.-P., Mouchart, M. (1982). "A note on noncausality". Econometrica 50 (3), 583–591 (May).

Foster, J.E., Sen, A.K. (1997). On Economic Inequality. Oxford University Press, New York.

Fréchet, M. (1951). "Sur les tableaux de corrélation dont les marges sont données". Annales de l'Université de Lyon A Series 3 14, 53–77.

Freedman, D.A. (2004). "On specifying graphical models for causation and the identification problem". Evaluation Review 28 (4), 267–293 (August).

Freund, J.E. (1961). "A bivariate extension of the exponential distribution". Journal of the American Statistical Association 56 (296), 971–977 (December).

Frisch, R. (1938). "Autonomy of economic relations". Paper given at League of Nations. Reprinted in: Hendry, D.F., Morgan, M.S. (Eds.), The Foundations of Econometric Analysis. Cambridge University Press, 1995.

Geweke, J., Keane, M. (2001). "Computationally intensive methods for integration in econometrics". In: Heckman, J.J., Leamer, E. (Eds.), Handbook of Econometrics, vol. 5. North-Holland, New York, pp. 3463–3568.

Ghez, G.R., Becker, G.S. (1975). The Allocation of Time and Goods over the Life Cycle. National Bureau of Economic Research, New York.

Gill, R.D., Robins, J.M. (2001). "Causal inference for complex longitudinal data: The continuous case". The Annals of Statistics 29 (6), 1785–1811 (December).

Granger, C.W.J. (1969). "Investigating causal relations by econometric models and cross-spectral methods". Econometrica 37 (3), 424–438 (August).

Gritz, R.M. (1993). "The impact of training on the frequency and duration of employment". Journal of Econometrics 57 (1–3), 21–51 (May–June).

Grubb, D. (2000). "Eligibility criteria for unemployment benefits". In: Special Issue: Making Work Pay. OECD Economic Studies 31, 147–184. OECD.

Haavelmo, T. (1943). "The statistical implications of a system of simultaneous equations". Econometrica 11 (1), 1–12 (January).

Ham, J.C., LaLonde, R.J. (1996). "The effect of sample selection and initial conditions in duration models: Evidence from experimental data on training". Econometrica 64 (1), 175–205 (January).

Hansen, K.T., Heckman, J.J., Mullen, K.J. (2004). "The effect of schooling and ability on achievement test scores". Journal of Econometrics 121 (1–2), 39–98 (July–August).

Hansen, L.P., Heckman, J.J. (1996). "The empirical foundations of calibration". Journal of Economic Perspectives 10 (1), 87–104 (Winter).

Hansen, L.P., Sargent, T.J. (1980). "Formulating and estimating dynamic linear rational expectations models". Journal of Economic Dynamics and Control 2 (1), 7–46 (February).

Heckman, J.J. (1974a). "Effects of child-care programs on women's work effort". Journal of Political Economy 82 (2), S136–S163 (March/April). Reprinted in: Schultz, T.W. (Ed.), Economics of the Family: Marriage, Children and Human Capital. University of Chicago Press, 1974.

Heckman, J.J. (1974b). "Shadow prices, market wages and labor supply". Econometrica 42 (4), 679–694 (July).

Heckman, J.J. (1976). "A life-cycle model of earnings, learning, and consumption". In: Journal Special Issue: Essays in Labor Economics in Honor of H. Gregg Lewis. Journal of Political Economy 84 (4, Part 2), S11–S44 (August).

Heckman, J.J. (1979). "Sample selection bias as a specification error". Econometrica 47 (1), 153–162 (January).

Heckman, J.J. (1981a). "Heterogeneity and state dependence". In: Rosen, S. (Ed.), Studies in Labor Markets, National Bureau of Economic Research. University of Chicago Press, pp. 91–139.

Heckman, J.J. (1981b). "The incidental parameters problem and the problem of initial conditions in estimating a discrete time-discrete data stochastic process and some Monte Carlo evidence". In: Manski, C., McFadden, D. (Eds.), Structural Analysis of Discrete Data with Econometric Applications. MIT Press, Cambridge, MA, pp. 179–185.

Heckman, J.J. (1981c). "Statistical models for discrete panel data". In: Manski, C., McFadden, D. (Eds.), Structural Analysis of Discrete Data with Econometric Applications. MIT Press, Cambridge, MA, pp. 114–178.

Heckman, J.J. (1990). "Varieties of selection bias". American Economic Review 80 (2), 313–318 (May).

Heckman, J.J. (1998). "The effects of government policies on human capital investment, unemployment and earnings inequality". In: Third Public GAAC Symposium: Labor Markets in the USA and Germany, vol. 5. German–American Academic Council Foundation, Bonn, Germany.

Heckman, J.J. (2005). "The scientific model of causality". Sociological Methodology 35 (1), 1–97 (August).

Heckman, J.J., Borjas, G.J. (1980). "Does unemployment cause future unemployment? Definitions, questions and answers from a continuous time model of heterogeneity and state dependence". In: Special Issue on Unemployment. Economica 47 (187), 247–283 (August).

Heckman, J.J., Honoré, B.E. (1989). "The identifiability of the competing risks model". Biometrika 76 (2), 325–330 (June).

Heckman, J.J., Honoré, B.E. (1990). "The empirical content of the Roy model". Econometrica 58 (5), 1121–1149 (September).

Heckman, J.J., LaLonde, R.J., Smith, J.A. (1999). "The economics and econometrics of active labor market programs". In: Ashenfelter, O., Card, D. (Eds.), Handbook of Labor Economics, vol. 3A. North-Holland, New York, pp. 1865–2097 (Chapter 31).

Heckman, J.J., Lochner, L.J., Taber, C. (1998a). "Explaining rising wage inequality: Explorations with a dynamic general equilibrium model of labor earnings with heterogeneous agents". Review of Economic Dynamics 1 (1), 1–58 (January).

Heckman, J.J., Lochner, L.J., Taber, C. (1998b). "General-equilibrium treatment effects: A study of tuition policy". American Economic Review 88 (2), 381–386 (May).

Heckman, J.J., Lochner, L.J., Taber, C. (1998c). "Tax policy and human-capital formation". American Economic Review 88 (2), 293–297 (May).

Heckman, J.J., Lochner, L.J., Todd, P.E. (2006). "Earnings equations and rates of return: The Mincer equation and beyond". In: Hanushek, E.A., Welch, F. (Eds.), Handbook of the Economics of Education. North-Holland, Amsterdam, pp. 307–458.

Heckman, J.J., MaCurdy, T.E. (1980). "A life cycle model of female labour supply". Review of Economic Studies 47 (1), 47–74 (January).

Heckman, J.J., Navarro, S. (2004). "Using matching, instrumental variables and control functions to estimate economic choice models". Review of Economics and Statistics 86 (1), 30–57 (February).

Heckman, J.J., Navarro, S. (2005). "Empirical estimates of option values of education and information sets in a dynamic sequential choice model". Unpublished manuscript. University of Chicago, Department of Economics.

Heckman, J.J., Navarro, S. (2007). "Dynamic discrete choice and dynamic treatment effects". Journal of Econometrics 136 (2), 341–396 (February).

Heckman, J.J., Robb, R. (1985). "Alternative methods for evaluating the impact of interventions". In: Heckman, J., Singer, B. (Eds.), Longitudinal Analysis of Labor Market Data, vol. 10. Cambridge University Press, New York, pp. 156–245.

Heckman, J.J., Robb, R. (1986). "Alternative methods for solving the problem of selection bias in evaluating the impact of treatments on outcomes". In: Wainer, H. (Ed.), Drawing Inferences from Self-Selected Samples. Springer-Verlag, New York, pp. 63–107. Reprinted in: Lawrence Erlbaum Associates, Mahwah, NJ, 2000.

Heckman, J.J., Robb, R., Walker, J.R. (1990). "Testing the mixture of exponentials hypothesis and estimating the mixing distribution by the method of moments". Journal of the American Statistical Association 85 (410), 582–589 (June).

Heckman, J.J., Singer, B.S. (1984). "Econometric duration analysis". Journal of Econometrics 24 (1–2), 63–132 (January–February).

Heckman, J.J., Singer, B.S. (1986). "Econometric analysis of longitudinal data". In: Griliches, Z., Intriligator, M.D. (Eds.), Handbook of Econometrics, vol. 3. North-Holland, pp. 1690–1763 (Chapter 29).

Heckman, J.J., Smith, J.A. (1993). "Assessing the case for randomized evaluation of social programs". In: Jensen, K., Madsen, P. (Eds.), Measuring Labour Market Measures: Evaluating the Effects of Active Labour Market Policy Initiatives. Proceedings from the Danish Presidency Conference "Effects and Measuring of Effects of Labour Market Policy Initiatives". Denmark Ministry of Labour, Copenhagen, pp. 35–95.

Heckman, J.J., Smith, J.A. (1995). "Assessing the case for social experiments". Journal of Economic Perspectives 9 (2), 85–110 (Spring).

Heckman, J.J., Smith, J.A. (1998). "Evaluating the welfare state". In: Strom, S. (Ed.), Econometrics and Economic Theory in the Twentieth Century: The Ragnar Frisch Centennial Symposium. Cambridge University Press, New York, pp. 241–318.
Heckman, J.J., Smith, J.A., Clements, N. (1997). "Making the most out of programme evaluations and social experiments: Accounting for heterogeneity in programme impacts". Review of Economic Studies 64 (221), 487–536 (October).
Heckman, J.J., Stixrud, J., Urzua, S. (2006). "The effects of cognitive and noncognitive abilities on labor market outcomes and social behavior". Journal of Labor Economics 24 (3), 411–482 (July).
Heckman, J.J., Taber, C. (1994). "Econometric mixture models and more general models for unobservables in duration analysis". Statistical Methods in Medical Research 3 (3), 279–299.
Heckman, J.J., Tobias, J.L., Vytlacil, E.J. (2001). "Four parameters of interest in the evaluation of social programs". Southern Economic Journal 68 (2), 210–223 (October).
Heckman, J.J., Tobias, J.L., Vytlacil, E.J. (2003). "Simple estimators for treatment parameters in a latent variable framework". Review of Economics and Statistics 85 (3), 748–754 (August).
Heckman, J.J., Urzua, S., Vytlacil, E.J. (2006). "Understanding instrumental variables in models with essential heterogeneity". Review of Economics and Statistics 88 (3), 389–432.
Heckman, J.J., Urzua, S., Yates, G. (2007). "The identification and estimation of option values in a model with recurrent states". Unpublished manuscript. University of Chicago, Department of Economics.
Heckman, J.J., Vytlacil, E.J. (1999). "Local instrumental variables and latent variable models for identifying and bounding treatment effects". Proceedings of the National Academy of Sciences 96, 4730–4734 (April).
Heckman, J.J., Vytlacil, E.J. (2001). "Causal parameters, treatment effects and randomization". Unpublished manuscript. University of Chicago, Department of Economics.
Heckman, J.J., Vytlacil, E.J. (2005). "Structural equations, treatment effects and econometric policy evaluation". Econometrica 73 (3), 669–738 (May).
Heckman, J.J., Vytlacil, E.J. (2007a). "Econometric evaluation of social programs, Part I: Causal models, structural models and econometric policy evaluation". In: Heckman, J., Leamer, E. (Eds.), Handbook of Econometrics, vol. 6B. Elsevier, Amsterdam (Chapter 70 in this Handbook).
Heckman, J.J., Vytlacil, E.J. (2007b). "Econometric evaluation of social programs, Part II: Using the marginal treatment effect to organize alternative economic estimators to evaluate social programs, and to forecast their effects in new environments". In: Heckman, J., Leamer, E. (Eds.), Handbook of Econometrics, vol. 6B. Elsevier, Amsterdam (Chapter 71 in this Handbook).
Hendry, D.F., Morgan, M.S. (1995). The Foundations of Econometric Analysis. Cambridge University Press, New York.
Hicks, J.R. (1946). Value and Capital: An Inquiry into Some Fundamental Principles of Economic Theory, second ed. Clarendon Press, Oxford.
Hoeffding, W. (1940). "Masstabinvariante korrelationtheorie". Schriften des Mathematischen Instituts und des Instituts für Angewandte Mathematik und Universität Berlin 5, 197–233.
Holland, P.W. (1986). "Statistics and causal inference". Journal of the American Statistical Association 81 (396), 945–960 (December).
Honoré, B.E. (1993). "Identification results for duration models with multiple spells". Review of Economic Studies 60 (1), 241–246 (January).
Honoré, B.E., Lewbel, A. (2002). "Semiparametric binary choice panel data models without strictly exogenous regressors". Econometrica 70 (5), 2053–2063 (September).
Horowitz, J.L., Markatou, M. (1996). "Semiparametric estimation of regression models for panel data". Review of Economic Studies 63 (1), 145–168 (January).
Hotz, V.J., Miller, R.A. (1988). "An empirical analysis of life cycle fertility and female labor supply". Econometrica 56 (1), 91–118 (January).
Hotz, V.J., Miller, R.A. (1993). "Conditional choice probabilities and the estimation of dynamic models". Review of Economic Studies 60 (3), 497–529 (July).
Hu, Y., Schennach, S.M. (2006). "Identification and estimation of nonclassical nonlinear errors-in-variables models with continuous distributions". Working Paper. University of Chicago.

Huggett, M. (1993). "The risk-free rate in heterogeneous-agent incomplete-insurance economies". Journal of Economic Dynamics and Control 17 (5–6), 953–969 (September–November).

Hurwicz, L. (1962). "On the structural form of interdependent systems". In: Nagel, E., Suppes, P., Tarski, A. (Eds.), Logic, Methodology and Philosophy of Science. Stanford University Press, pp. 232–239.

Johnson, G.E. (1979). "The labor market displacement effect in the analysis of the net impact of manpower training programs". In: Bloch, F. (Ed.), Evaluating Manpower Training Programs: Revisions of Papers Originally Presented at the Conference on Evaluating Manpower Training Programs, Princeton University, May 1976. JAI Press, Greenwich, CT.

Johnson, G.E., Layard, R. (1986). "The natural rate of unemployment: Explanation and policy". In: Ashenfelter, O., Layard, R. (Eds.), Handbook of Labor Economics, vol. 2. North-Holland, New York, pp. 921–999.

Jöreskog, K.G. (1977). "Structural equations models in the social sciences: Specification, estimation and testing". In: Krishnaiah, P. (Ed.), Applications of Statistics. North-Holland, New York, pp. 265–287.

Jöreskog, K.G., Goldberger, A.S. (1975). "Estimation of a model with multiple indicators and multiple causes of a single latent variable". Journal of the American Statistical Association 70 (351), 631–639 (September).

Jorgenson, D.W., Slesnick, D.T. (1997). "General equilibrium analysis of economic policy". In: Jorgenson, D.W. (Ed.), Measuring Social Welfare. In: Welfare, vol. 2. MIT Press, Cambridge, MA, pp. 165–218.

Jorgenson, D.W., Yun, K.-Y. (1990). "Tax reform and U.S. economic growth". Journal of Political Economy 98 (5), 151–193 (October).

Kalbfleisch, J.D., Prentice, R.L. (1980). The Statistical Analysis of Failure Time Data. Wiley, New York.

Kane, T.J. (1994). "College entry by blacks since 1970: The role of college costs, family background and the returns to education". Journal of Political Economy 102 (5), 878–911 (October).

Katz, L.F., Autor, D.H. (1999). "Changes in the wage structure and earnings inequality". In: Ashenfelter, O., Card, D. (Eds.), Handbook of Labor Economics, vol. 3. North-Holland, New York, pp. 1463–1555 (Chapter 25).

Keane, M.P., Wolpin, K.I. (1994). "The solution and estimation of discrete choice dynamic programming models by simulation and interpolation: Monte Carlo evidence". The Review of Economics and Statistics 76 (4), 648–672 (November).

Keane, M.P., Wolpin, K.I. (1997). "The career decisions of young men". Journal of Political Economy 105 (3), 473–522 (June).

Kehoe, T.J., Srinivasan, T.N., Whalley, J. (2005). Frontiers in Applied General Equilibrium Modeling. Cambridge University Press, New York.

Keiding, N. (1999). "Event history analysis and inference from observational epidemiology". Statistics in Medicine 18 (17–18), 2353–2363 (September).

Kendall, M.G., Stuart, A. (1977). The Advanced Theory of Statistics, vol. 1, fourth ed. C. Griffen, London.

King, G. (1997). A Solution to the Ecological Inference Problem: Reconstructing Individual Behavior from Aggregate Data. Princeton University Press, Princeton, NJ.

Koenker, R. (2005). Quantile Regression. Cambridge University Press, New York.

Koenker, R., Xiao, Z. (2002). "Inference on the quantile regression process". Econometrica 70 (4), 1583–1612 (July).

Koopmans, T.C., Beckmann, M. (1957). "Assignment problems and the location of economic activities". Econometrica 25 (1), 53–76 (January).

Kotlarski, I.I. (1967). "On characterizing the gamma and normal distribution". Pacific Journal of Mathematics 20, 69–76.

Krusell, P., Smith, A.A. (1998). "Income and wealth heterogeneity in the macroeconomy". Journal of Political Economy 106 (5), 867–896 (October).

Kydland, F.E., Prescott, E.C. (1982). "Time to build and aggregate fluctuations". Econometrica 50 (6), 1345–1370 (November).

Kydland, F.E., Prescott, E.C. (1996). "The computational experiment: An econometric tool". Journal of Economic Perspectives 10 (1), 69–85 (Winter).

Lancaster, T. (1979). "Econometric methods for the duration of unemployment". Econometrica 47 (4), 939–956 (July).

Leamer, E.E. (1985). "Vector autoregressions for causal inference?". Carnegie–Rochester Conference Series on Public Policy 22, 255–303 (Spring).

Lechner, M., Miquel, R. (2002). "Identification of effects of dynamic treatments by sequential conditional independence assumptions". Discussion paper. University of St. Gallen, Department of Economics.

Lee, D. (2005). "An estimable dynamic general equilibrium model of work, schooling, and occupational choice". International Economic Review 46 (1), 1–34 (February).

Lee, D., Wolpin, K.I. (2006). "Intersectoral labor mobility and the growth of the service sector". Econometrica 74 (1), 1–40 (January).

Lehmann, E.L., D'Abrera, H.J.M. (1975). Nonparametrics: Statistical Methods Based on Ranks. Holden–Day, San Francisco.

Lewbel, A. (2000). "Semiparametric qualitative response model estimation with unknown heteroscedasticity or instrumental variables". Journal of Econometrics 97 (1), 145–177 (July).

Lewis, H.G. (1963). Unionism and Relative Wages in the United States: An Empirical Inquiry. University of Chicago Press, Chicago.

Lise, J., Seitz, S., Smith, J. (2005a). "Equilibrium policy experiments and the evaluation of social programs", Working Paper 1076. Queen's University, Department of Economics, Kingston, Ontario.

Lise, J., Seitz, S., Smith, J. (2005b). "Evaluating search and matching models using experimental data". Working Paper 1074. Queen's University, Department of Economics, Kingston, Ontario.

Lok, J.J. (2007). "Statistical modelling of causal effects in continuous time". Annals of Statistics (forthcoming).

MaCurdy, T.E. (1981). "An empirical model of labor supply in a life-cycle setting". Journal of Political Economy 89 (6), 1059–1085 (December).

Magnac, T., Thesmar, D. (2002). "Identifying dynamic discrete decision processes". Econometrica 70 (2), 801–816 (March).

Manski, C.F. (1988). "Identification of binary response models". Journal of the American Statistical Association 83 (403), 729–738 (September).

Manski, C.F. (1993). "Dynamic choice in social settings: Learning from the experiences of others". Journal of Econometrics 58 (1–2), 121–136 (July).

Manski, C.F. (1997). "The mixing problem in programme evaluation". Review of Economic Studies 64 (4), 537–553 (October).

Manski, C.F. (2003). Partial Identification of Probability Distributions. Springer-Verlag, New York.

Manski, C.F. (2004). "Measuring expectations". Econometrica 72 (5), 1329–1376 (September).

Mardia, K.V. (1970). Families of Bivariate Distributions. Griffin, London.

Matzkin, R.L. (1992). "Nonparametric and distribution-free estimation of the binary threshold crossing and the binary choice models". Econometrica 60 (2), 239–270 (March).

Matzkin, R.L. (1993). "Nonparametric identification and estimation of polychotomous choice models". Journal of Econometrics 58 (1–2), 137–168 (July).

Matzkin, R.L. (1994). "Restrictions of economic theory in nonparametric methods". In: Engle, R., McFadden, D. (Eds.), Handbook of Econometrics, vol. 4. North-Holland, New York, pp. 2523–2558.

Matzkin, R.L. (2003). "Nonparametric estimation of nonadditive random functions". Econometrica 71 (5), 1339–1375 (September).

Matzkin, R.L. (2007). "Nonparametric identification". In: Heckman, J.J., Leamer, E. (Eds.), Handbook of Econometrics, vol. 6B. Elsevier, Amsterdam (Chapter 73 in this Handbook).

Meyer, B.D. (1990). "Unemployment insurance and unemployment spells". Econometrica 58 (4), 757–782. (July).

Meyer, B.D. (1996). "What have we learned from the Illinois reemployment bonus experiment?". Journal of Labor Economics 14 (1), 26–51 (January).

Miller, R.A. (1984). "Job matching and occupational choice". Journal of Political Economy 92 (6), 1086–1120 (December).

Mincer, J. (1974). Schooling, Experience and Earnings. Columbia University Press for National Bureau of Economic Research, New York.

Mortensen, D.T. (1977). "Unemployment insurance and job search decisions". Industrial and Labor Relations Review 30 (4), 505–517 (July).

Mortensen, D.T. (1986). "Job search and labor market analysis". In: Ashenfelter, O., Card, D. (Eds.), Handbook of Labor Economics. In: Handbooks in Economics, vol. 2. Elsevier Science, New York, pp. 849–919.

Mortensen, D.T., Pissarides, C.A. (1994). "Job creation and job destruction in the theory of unemployment". Review of Economic Studies 61 (3), 397–415 (July).

Murphy, S.A. (2003). "Optimal dynamic treatment regimes". Journal of the Royal Statistical Society, Series B 65 (2), 331–366 (May).

Navarro, S. (2005). "Understanding schooling: Using observed choices to infer agent's information in a dynamic model of schooling choice when consumption allocation is subject to borrowing constraints". PhD Dissertation. University of Chicago, Chicago, IL.

Organization for Economic Cooperation and Development (1993). "Active labour market policies: Assessing macroeconomic and microeconomic effects". In: Employment Outlook. OECD, Paris, pp. 39–67.

Pakes, A. (1986). "Patents as options: Some estimates of the value of holding European patent stocks". Econometrica 54 (4), 755–784 (July).

Pakes, A., Simpson, M. (1989). "Patent renewal data". Brookings Papers on Economic Activity, 331–401 (special issue).

Pearl, J. (2000). Causality. Cambridge University Press, Cambridge, England.

Pissarides, C.A. (2000). Equilibrium Unemployment Theory. MIT Press, Cambridge, MA.

Prakasa-Rao, B.L.S. (1992). Identifiability in Stochastic Models: Characterization of Probability Distributions. Probability and Mathematical Statistics. Academic Press, Boston.

Ridder, G. (1986). "An event history approach to the evaluation of training, recruitment and employment programmes". Journal of Applied Econometrics 1 (2), 109–126 (April).

Ridder, G. (1990). "The non-parametric identification of generalized accelerated failure-time models". Review of Economic Studies 57 (2), 167–181 (April).

Robins, J.M. (1989). "The analysis of randomized and non-randomized aids treatment trials using a new approach to causal inference in longitudinal studies". In: Sechrest, L., Freeman, H., Mulley, A. (Eds.), Health Services Research Methodology: A Focus on AIDS. U.S. Department of Health and Human Services, National Center for Health Services Research and Health Care Technology Assessment, Rockville, MD, pp. 113–159.

Robins, J.M. (1997). "Causal inference from complex longitudinal data". In: Berkane, M. (Ed.), Latent Variable Modeling and Applications to Causality. In: Lecture Notes in Statistics. Springer-Verlag, New York, pp. 69–117.

Rosenzweig, M.R., Wolpin, K.I. (2000). "Natural "natural experiments" in economics". Journal of Economic Literature 38 (4), 827–874 (December).

Roy, A. (1951). "Some thoughts on the distribution of earnings". Oxford Economic Papers 3 (2), 135–146 (June).

Rubin, D.B. (1986). "Statistics and causal inference: Comment: Which ifs have causal answers". Journal of the American Statistical Association 81 (396), 961–962.

Rüschendorf, L. (1981). "Sharpness of Fréchet bounds". Zeitschrift für Wahrscheinlichkeitstheorie und verwandte Gebiete 41, 293–302.

Rust, J. (1987). "Optimal replacement of GMC bus engines: An empirical model of Harold Zurcher". Econometrica 55 (5), 999–1033 (September).

Rust, J. (1994). "Structural estimation of Markov decision processes". In: Engle, R., McFadden, D. (Eds.), Handbook of Econometrics. North-Holland, New York, pp. 3081–3143.

Sargent, T.J., Sims, C.A. (1977). "Business cycle modeling without much a priori economic theory". In: New Methods in Business Cycle Research: Proceedings from a Conference. Federal Reserve Bank of Minneapolis, Minneapolis.

Schennach, S.M. (2004). "Estimation of nonlinear models with measurement error". Econometrica 72 (1), 33–75 (January).

Shoven, J.B., Whalley, J. (1977). "Equal yield tax alternatives: General equilibrium computational techniques". Journal of Public Economics 8 (2), 211–224 (October).

Sims, C.A. (1972). “Money, income and causality”. American Economic Review 62 (4), 540–552 (September).

Sims, C.A. (1996). “Macroeconomics and methodology”. Journal of Economic Perspectives 10 (1), 105–120.

Stefanski, L.A., Carroll, R.J. (1991). “Deconvolution-based score tests in measurement error models”. The Annals of Statistics 19 (1), 249–259 (March).

Taber, C.R. (2000). “Semiparametric identification and heterogeneity in discrete choice dynamic programming models”. Journal of Econometrics 96 (2), 201–229 (June).

Tchen, A.H. (1980). “Inequalities for distributions with given marginals”. Annals of Probability 8 (4), 814–827 (August).

Van den Berg, G.J. (1999). “Empirical inference with equilibrium search models of the labour market”. Economic Journal 109 (456), F283–F306 (June).

Van den Berg, G.J. (2001). “Duration models: Specification, identification and multiple durations”. In: Heckman, J.J., Leamer, E. (Eds.), Handbook of Econometrics. In: Handbooks in Economics, vol. 5. North-Holland, New York, pp. 3381–3460.

Van den Berg, G.J., Holm, A., Van Ours, J.C. (2002). “Do stepping-stone jobs exist? Early career paths in the medical profession”. Journal of Population Economics 15 (4), 647–665 (November).

Van den Berg, G.J., Van der Klaauw, B., Van Ours, J.C. (2004). “Punitive sanctions and the transition rate from welfare to work”. Journal of Labor Economics 22 (1), 211–241 (January).

Van der Laan, M.J., Robins, J.M. (2003). Unified Methods for Censored Longitudinal Data and Causality. Springer-Verlag, New York.

Willis, R.J., Rosen, S. (1979). “Education and self-selection”. Journal of Political Economy 87 (5, Part 2), S7–S36 (October).

Wolpin, K.I. (1984). “An estimable dynamic stochastic model of fertility and child mortality”. Journal of Political Economy 92 (5), 852–874 (October).

Wolpin, K.I. (1987). “Estimating a structural search model: The transition from school to work”. Econometrica 55 (4), 801–817 (July).

Wolpin, K.I. (1992). “The determinants of black–white differences in early employment careers: Search, layoffs, quits, and endogenous wage growth”. Journal of Political Economy 100 (3), 535–560.

PART 19

RECENT ADVANCES IN ECONOMETRIC METHODS

Chapter 73

NONPARAMETRIC IDENTIFICATION*

ROSA L. MATZKIN

Department of Economics, University of California – Los Angeles, USA
e-mail: matzkin@econ.ucla.edu

Contents

* The support of NSF through grants SES 0551272, BCS 0433990, and SES 0241858 is gratefully acknowledged. I have greatly benefitted from the input of James Heckman and from the comments and suggestions of Daniel McFadden, Whitney Newey, Susanne Schennach, Viktor Soubbotine, graduate students at Northwestern and at California Institute of Technology that used this manuscript as lecture notes in graduate econometrics courses, and participants at the econometrics workshop at the University of Chicago (May 2006). This chapter was written while the author was Professor of Economics at Northwestern University and, partly, while she was Visiting Professor of Economics at the Division of the Humanities and Social Sciences, California Institute of Technology, whose warm hospitality is gratefully acknowledged.

Handbook of Econometrics, Volume 6B

DOI: 10.1016/S1573-4412(07)06073-4

Abstract

When one wants to estimate a model without specifying the functions and distributions parametrically, or when one wants to analyze the identification of a model independently of any particular parametric specification, it is useful to perform a nonparametric analysis of identification. This chapter presents some of the recent results on the identification of nonparametric econometric models. It considers identification in models that are additive in unobservable random terms and in models that are nonadditive in unobservable random terms. Single equation models as well as models with a system of equations are studied. Among the latter, special attention is given to structural models whose reduced forms are triangular in the unobservable random terms, and to simultaneous equations, where the reduced forms are functions of all the unobservable variables in the system.

The chapter first presents some general identification results for single-equation models that are additive in unobservable random terms, single-equation models that are nonadditive in unobservable random terms, single-equation models that possess and index structure, simultaneous equations nonadditive in unobservable random terms, and discrete choice models. Then, particular ways of achieving identification are considered. These include making use of conditional independence restrictions, marginal independence restrictions, shape restrictions on functions, shape restrictions on distributions, and restrictions in both functions and distributions. The objective is to provide insight into some of the recent techniques that have been developed recently, rather than on presenting a complete survey of the literature.

Keywords

identification, nonparametric models, simultaneous equations, nonadditive models, nonseparable models

JEL classification: C01, C14, C2, C3

1. Introduction

This chapter presents some of the recent results on the identification of nonparametric econometric models, concentrating on nonadditive models. It complements many current existent surveys that cover nonparametric identification, such as the books by Horowitz (1998), Pagan and Ullah (1999), and Yatchew (2003), articles in recent volumes of this Handbook by Härdle and Linton (1994), Matzkin (1994), Powell (1994), and van den Berg (2001), recent survey articles on semiparametric and nonparametric identification, such as Blundell and Powell (2003), Florens (2003), and Chesher (2007), and other chapters in this volume, such as the ones by X. Chen, Heckman and Vytlacil, and Ridder and Moffit. The objective of this chapter is to provide insight into some recent techniques that have been developed to identify nonparametric models, rather than on presenting a complete survey of the literature. As a consequence, many very important related works have been left out of the presentation and the references.

When estimating an element in a model, it is necessary to determine first the identification of such an element. The study of identification in parametric econometric models dates back to the works by Workings (1925, 1927), Tinbergen (1930), Frisch (1934, 1938), Haavelmo (1943, 1944), Koopmans (1949), Hurwicz (1950), Koopmans and Reiersol (1950), Koopmans, Rubin and Leipnik (1950), Wald (1950), Fisher (1959, 1961, 1965, 1966), Wegge (1965), Rothenberg (1971), and Bowden (1973). [See Hausman (1983) and Hsiao (1983) in Volume 1 of this Handbook, for early review articles.]

Lately, the analysis of identification in econometric models has been developing in several directions. One of these directions is the econometric analysis of systems of equations that require few or no parametric assumptions on the functions and distributions in the system. All the recent review articles mentioned above treat this topic. Imposing parametric specifications for functions and distributions had been the standard procedure in a world where large data sets were rarely available and computers could not easily handle estimation methods that require complicated computational algorithms. In such a world, estimating models with only a few parameters was part of the standard procedure. As computers processing power became faster and cheaper and the availability to deal with large data sets increased, it became possible to consider estimation of increasingly complicated functions, with increasing numbers of parameters. This, in turn, drove attention to the analysis of identification of functions and distributions that do not necessarily belong to parametric families. The emphasis was originally on estimation of probability densities and conditional expectations, but, later, more complicated models were considered. Rather than asking whether some parameters were identified, the question of interest became whether a function or distribution was identified within a general set of functions or distributions. Establishing such a nonparametric identification was recognized as an important first step in the econometric analysis of even parametric models.

Establishing that a function or distribution is nonparametrically identified within a set of nonparametric functions or distributions implies its identification within any subset of the set of nonparametric functions. In particular, if the subset is defined as the set of functions that satisfy a parametric structure, such as being linear or quadratic, then identification within these subsets is implied by identification within the larger set of nonparametric functions that include linear, quadratic, and possibly many other parametric specifications. If, on the other hand, one does not know whether the function is nonparametrically identified but one can establish its identification when a particular specification is imposed on the function, then it is not clear how robust any estimation results would be. When a function is nonparametrically identified, one can develop tests for different parametric structures, by comparing the results obtained from a nonparametric estimator for the function with those obtained from specific parametric estimators [Wooldridge (1992), Hong and White (1995), and Fan and Li (1996) are examples of such tests]. When a function is nonparametrically identified, one can allow the function to possess local behavior that would not be possible under some parametric specifications. [See, for example, the examples in Härdle (1991).] When a model or a function within a model is not identified nonparametrically, one can consider imposing sequentially stronger sets of restrictions in the model, up to the point where identification is achieved. This provides a method for analyzing the trade-off between imposing restrictions and achieving identification. [See, for example, Matzkin (1994) for such an analysis.] This chapter will present several of the developments in the nonparametric identification in economic models.

Another area of active research, specially in recent years, was in the development of econometric models that were specified with properties closer to those of models studied in economic theory. The analysis of identification in the past, which concentrated on models that were linear in variables and parameters and additive in unobservable random terms, contrasted strongly with the standard practice in economic theory, where functions were only specified to possess some properties, such as continuity or monotonicity. On those times, economic theorists would work on models involving very general functions and distributions. Econometricians, on the other side, would work on models with well specified and typically quite restrictive functional forms and distributions. Even though the main goals of both groups were in many instances very similar, the solutions as well as the languages used in each of them were very different. The picture is drastically different nowadays. The development of nonparametric techniques for the estimation and testing of economic models has been shortening the distance between those roads to the point where now some econometric models are specified with no more restrictions than those that a theorist would impose.

The advances that have decreased the distance between economic theory and econometrics have not concentrated only on the relaxation of parametric structures. Lately, there has also been an increasing effort to relax the way in which the unobservable random terms are treated. A practice that has been and still is commonly used when specifying an econometric model proceeds by first using economic theory to specify a relationship between a vector of observable explanatory variables and a vector of dependent variables, and then adding unobservable random variables to the relationships, as an after-thought. The seminal works by Heckman (1974), McFadden (1974), Heckman and Willis (1977), and Lancaster (1979) have shown that one can analyze econometric models where the unobservable random terms have important economic interpretations. They may represent, for example, heterogeneity parameters in utility functions, productivity shocks in production functions, or utility values for unobserved product attributes. When interpreting the unobservables in this way, it is rarely the case that they enter in additive ways into the models of interest. Several recent papers have considered the identification and estimation of nonparametric models with nonadditive random terms. Some of these will be reviewed in this chapter.

Ideally, one would like to be able to identify all the unknown functions and distributions in a model without imposing more restrictions than those implied by the theory of the model. Restrictions derived from optimization, such as concavity and linear homogeneity, or equilibrium conditions, have been shown to be useful to identify functions in models that had been thought in the past to be identified only under very restrictive parametric assumptions. [See the survey chapter by Matzkin (1994) in Volume 4 of this Handbook for several such examples.] Nevertheless, in some cases, the identification of all functions and distributions in a model that imposes so few restrictions might not be possible. In such cases, one may consider several options. One may try to determine what can be identified without imposing any more restrictions on the model. One may impose some additional restrictions on some of the functions or distributions, to achieve identification. Or, one may consider enlarging the model, by augmenting the set of observable variables that can provide information about the functions or distributions of interest in the model. In this chapter we discuss some of the recent related techniques that have been developed.

While restrictions implied by economic theory may, in some cases, aid in achieving identification, in some other cases, they may also hinder identification. This occurs when restrictions such as agent's optimization and equilibrium conditions generate interrelationships among observable variables, X, and unobservable variables, ε, that affect a common observable outcome variable, Y. In such cases, the joint distribution of (Y, X) does not provide enough information to recover the causal effect of X on Y, since changes in X do not leave the value of ε fixed. A typical example of this is when Y denotes quantity demanded for a product, X denotes the price of the product, and ε is an unobservable demand shifter. If the price that will make firms produce a certain quantity increases with quantity, this change in ε will generate an increment in the price X. Hence, the observable effect of a change in price in demanded quantity would not correspond to the effect of changing the value of price when the value ε stays constant. Another typical example arises when analyzing the effect of years of education on wages. An unobservable variable, such as ability, affects wages but also years of education. When an individual chooses years of education to maximize the discounted stream of future income, he takes ability into account because it influences the productivity of education. [See, for example, Card (2001).] As a result of this connection between ability and years of education, the distribution of ability, given years of education, changes with the years of education. In this chapter, we will review some of the methods that have been developed to identify causal effects in these situations.

The outline of the chapter is as follows. In the next section, we describe several econometric models. In Section 3, we analyze, in general terms, identification in those models. In Section 4 we discuss some particular techniques that have been used to achieve identification. Section 5 concludes.

2. The econometric model

2.1. *From the economic model to the econometric model*

The description of an economic model typically starts out by describing the economic agents involved, their objective functions, their information, and the interactions among the agents. When an econometrician tries to fit an economic model to the available data, he first needs to determine which of the variables in the model are observable and which are unobservable. Another important division of the variables in the model is between the variables that are determined outside of the model and those that are determined inside the model. The variables in the latter set are functions of the variables in the former set. In economic models, they are typically determined either by the choice of some agents or by the interaction among several agents. We will denote by X the vector of variables that are determined outside the model and are observable, and by ε the vector of variables that are determined outside the model and are unobservable. X and ε are also called the observable and unobservable explanatory, or exogenous, variables. We will denote the number of coordinates of X by K and the number of coordinates of ε by L. The vectors of observable and unobservable variables that are determined within the model will be denoted, respectively, by Y and Υ. These are observable and unobservable outcome variables. We will denote the number of coordinates in the vector of observable variables, Y, determined within the model, by G, and the number of coordinates in the vector of unobservable variables, Υ, determined within the model by G^{Υ}. Following the standard terminology, we will say that Y and Υ are vectors of, respectively, observable and unobservable endogenous variables. The description of an economic model contains, as well as a list of variables, a list of functions and distributions. Some of these functions and distributions are primitive, in the sense that they are determined outside the model. Some are derived within the model. Let $\underline{h}$ denote the list of all primitive functions and let $\underline{F}$ denote the list of all primitive distributions. We will describe the interrelation between the primitive functions and distributions and the observable and unobservable variables by a known vector function υ and an equation

$$\upsilon(Y, \Upsilon, X, \varepsilon;\ \underline{h}, \underline{F}) = 0.$$

This equation can be used to derive the joint distribution of the vector of observable variables, (Y, X), as a function of the primitives of the model, $(\underline{h}, \underline{F})$.

To provide an example, consider a model of consumer demand for a consumption good and a composite good. Let I denote the income that the consumer can spend on these two goods. Let the price of the composite good be 1 and let p denote the price of the consumption good. Let y and z denote the quantities chosen by the consumer of, respectively, the consumption good and the composite good. Suppose that the economic model specifies that the individual has preferences over bundles (y, z), and chooses the one that maximizes those preferences over the set of all bundles that cost no more than I. Suppose, further, that the consumer preferences can be represented by a strictly increasing, strictly concave, twice differentiable utility function, U, on (y, z), and that such a utility function is different for different individuals in a population. In particular, assume that the utility function depends on observable socioeconomic characteristics of the individual, such as age and marital status, denoted by w, and on unobservable tastes for (y, z), denoted by ε. Then, for an individual with characteristics w and ε, and with observable income I, the observed choice (y, z) is defined as

$$(y, z) = \arg\max_{(\tilde{y},\tilde{z})} \bigl\{U(\tilde{y}, \tilde{z}, w, \varepsilon) \bigm| p\tilde{y} + \tilde{z} \leqslant I\bigr\}.$$

Since the monotonicity of U with respect to $(\tilde{y}, \tilde{z})$ implies that all the available income will be used, this is equivalent to

$$y = \arg\max_{\tilde{y}} \bigl\{U(\tilde{y}, I - p\tilde{y}, w, \varepsilon)\bigr\},$$
$$z = I - py.$$

The differentiability, strict concavity, and strict monotonicity of U imply then that y satisfies

$$U_{\tilde{y}}(y, I - py, w, \varepsilon) - pU_{\tilde{z}}(y, I - py, w, \varepsilon) = 0.$$

In this model, the income, I, the vector of socioeconomic variables, w, and the price p are observable variables determined outside the system. The unobservable taste, ε, is also determined outside the system. The chosen quantity, y, of the commodity is observed and determined within the system. The utility function $U(\cdot,\cdot,\cdot,\cdot)$ is an unknown primitive function; and the distribution of (p, I, w, ε) is an unknown primitive distribution function. Given any particular utility function U, satisfying the differentiability, monotonicity and concavity restrictions imposed above, and given any distribution for (p, I, w, ε), one can use the above equation to derive the joint distribution of the vector of observable variables, (Y, p, I, w). This is derived from the equation

$$\begin{aligned} v(Y, X, \varepsilon) &= v(Y, p, I, w, \varepsilon) \\ &= U_y(Y, I - pY, w, \varepsilon) - U_z(Y, I - pY, w, \varepsilon)p \\ &= 0. \end{aligned}$$

Under our assumptions, the value of Y that satisfies this equation, for given values of (p, I, w, ε), is unique. Let m denote the function that assigns the optimal value of Y to (p, I, w, ε). Then, the demand function $m(p, I, w, \varepsilon)$ satisfies the first order conditions

$$\begin{aligned} &U_y\bigl(m(p, I, w, \varepsilon), I - pm(p, I, \varepsilon), w, \varepsilon\bigr) \\ &\quad - U_z\bigl(m(p, I, w, \varepsilon), I - pm(p, I, \varepsilon), w, \varepsilon\bigr)p = 0. \end{aligned}$$

The demand model

$$Y = m(p, I, w, \varepsilon)$$

is the *reduced form* model. The reduced form model maps the observable and unobservable explanatory variables into the observable endogenous variables, without necessarily specifying behavioral and equilibrium conditions from which the mapping might have been derived. The reduced form model suffices to analyze many situations where this underlying structure does not change. For example, as will be discussed in more detail below, when m is strictly increasing in ε and ε is distributed independently of (p, I, w), the reduced model above suffices to analyze the causal effect of (p, I, w) on Y. This is the effect on demand from changing the value of (p, I, w), leaving the value of ε unchanged.

The analysis of counterfactuals, on the other hand, would typically require knowledge of the primitive function U. Suppose, for example, that we were interested in predicting the behavior of a consumer that possesses preferences as in the model above, when the price of the consumption good depends on the quantity chosen, instead of being a fixed value, p, as considered above. Denote the price function as $s(y)$. To predict the choice of the consumer with utility function $U(\tilde{y}, \tilde{z}, w, \varepsilon)$ when his set of affordable consumption bundles is

$$\{(\tilde{y}, \tilde{z}) \mid s(\tilde{y})\tilde{y} + \tilde{z} = I\}$$

we would need to know the function $U(\tilde{y}, \tilde{z}, w, \varepsilon)$ to calculate the new optimal values

$$(y, z) = \arg\max_{(\tilde{y}, \tilde{z})} \{U(\tilde{y}, \tilde{z}, w, \varepsilon) \mid s(\tilde{y})\tilde{y} + \tilde{z} = I\}.$$

This would require analyzing the *structural model* of utility maximization described earlier. The structural model uses behavioral and/or equilibrium conditions, to define a mapping between the primitive functions and distributions, on one side, and the distribution of the observable variables, on the other. Path diagrams [Pearl (2000)] are often very useful to clarify the role of each variable and the ordering of the variables in terms of cause and effect. Support conditions, which may allow one to identify only the local behavior of some functions should also be taken into consideration. In the analysis in this chapter, unless explicitly stated otherwise, it will be assumed that the support conditions necessary to obtain the results are always satisfied.

2.1.1. Dependence between ε and X

In many cases, a model is not completely specified. Some of the unobservable explanatory variables in the model are themselves functions of observable variables, in a way that is not described within the model. Consider, for example, the utility maximization model described in the previous subsection. In that model, the income of the consumer, I, was assumed to be determined outside of the model. The unobservable ε was assumed to denote taste for consumption. In many cases, one could think of income as being partially determined by ε. Individuals with a larger taste for consumption will typically make lifetime decisions, such as the choice of profession, that would generate higher incomes. In particular, if we let $\tilde{r}$ denote a function and let δ denote additional variables, which are determined outside the system and which affect income I, we could specify that $I = \tilde{r}(\varepsilon, \delta)$. If this latter relationship were added to the specification of the model, then, in the augmented model, the variables determined within the system would be (Y, Z, I), and those determined outside the system would be (p, ε, δ). Suppose that we wanted to infer the causal effect of income I on demand Y. This is the effect on Y of changing I, when the value of (p, w, ε) stays fixed. If I is a function of ε, the total effect will be different from this partial effect. A similar example occurs when variables are determined jointly. Haavelmo (1943, 1944) argued that in these cases a joint probability distribution is needed to analyze the data.

2.2. *Definition of an econometric model*

Following up on the model described in the beginning of Section 2, we define an *econometric model* by a specification of variables that are observed and variables that are unobserved, variables that are determined within the model and variables that are determined outside of the model, functional relationships among all the variables, and restrictions on the functions and distributions. We will denote by S the set of all vectors of functions and distributions that satisfy the restrictions imposed by the model. We assume that for any element $\zeta \in S$, we can derive the distribution, $F_{Y,X}(\cdot;\ \zeta)$, of the observable vector of variables that is generated by S. The observable distribution, $F_{Y,X}$, corresponds to the true value ζ^* of ζ.

For example, in the consumer demand model described above, ε and (p, I, w) are, respectively, the vectors of unobservable and observable explanatory variables and Y is the vector of observable endogenous variables. The elements of S are pairs $\zeta = (U, F_{\varepsilon,p,I,w})$, such that for all (w, ε), $U(\cdot, \cdot, w, \varepsilon) : R^2 \to R$ is strictly increasing, strictly concave, and twice differentiable, and $F_{\varepsilon,p,I,w}$ is a distribution function. Given $\zeta = (U, F_{\varepsilon,p,I,w})$ and $X = (p, I, w)$, the distribution of Y given X is calculated by the distribution of ε given (p, I, w) and the function U, using the first order conditions. Note that since X is observable, the marginal distribution of X, F_X, can be assumed to be known. Hence, one of the restrictions that $F_{\varepsilon,p,I,w}$ would be required to satisfy is that the marginal distribution of (p, I, w) coincides with $F_{p,I,w}$.

2.2.1. *Examples*

We next describe several models, whose identification will be discussed in Sections 3 and 4. We denote random variables with capital letters and their realizations with lower case letters.

2.2.1.1. Additive models In additive models, the unobservable variables that are determined outside the model affect the values of the variables that are determined within the model in an additive way. A standard example of such a model is where Y denotes an observable dependent variable, X denotes a vector of observable explanatory variables, ε denotes an unobservable explanatory variable, and the functional relationship between these variables is given by

$$Y = X\beta + \varepsilon$$

for some β. Allowing X to influence Y in a nonlinear, possibly unknown way, while leaving the influence of ε additive, will also give rise to an additive model. In this latter case

$$Y = g(X) + \varepsilon$$

for some function g. Typical restrictions that are imposed on such a model are that g is continuous and that the distribution of ε given X has support R. Typically, one would like to add the restriction that the distribution of (X, ε) is such that for all x in some set, the conditional expectation of ε given $X = x$ is 0. In such a case $g(x)$ denotes the conditional expectation of Y given $X = x$, which is an object of interest when forecasting the value of Y conditional on $X = x$, under a squared-error loss function. In other situations, one may want to add the restriction that the conditional median, or other quantile of ε, given $X = x$ is 0. Many methods exist to estimate conditional means and conditional quantiles nonparametrically. Prakasa-Rao (1983), Härdle and Linton (1994), Pagan and Ullah (1999), Matzkin (1994), Koenker (2005), and X. Chen (2007), among others, survey parts of this literature.

2.2.1.2. Nonadditive models When the unobservable random terms in an economic model have important interpretations such as being variables representing tastes of consumers, or productivity shocks in production functions, it is rarely the case that these unobservable random terms influence the dependent variables in the model in an additive way. Nonadditive models allow the unobservable variables that are determined outside the model to affect the values of the variables that are determined within the model in nonadditive ways.

For a simple example, let Y denote an observable dependent variable, X denote a vector of observable explanatory variables, and ε denote an unobservable explanatory variable. We can specify the functional relationship between these variables as

$$Y = m(X, \varepsilon)$$

for some function $m : R^K \times R \to R$. We may impose the restrictions that the function m is strictly increasing in ε, for all values of X, and that the distribution, $F_{\varepsilon,X}$, of (X, ε) is strictly increasing over R^{K+1}. We may add the restriction that m is differentiable, or that X and ε are distributed independently of each other. When the latter restriction is imposed, we will call such a model an *independent nonadditive model*. An example of such a model could be when X denotes hours of work of an individual, ε denotes the ability of the individual to perform some task, and Y is output of the individual. Conditional on working the same quantity x of hours of work, output is higher when ability is higher.

Nonparametric models of this type were studied in Roehrig (1988), Olley and Pakes (1996), Brown and Matzkin (1998), Matzkin (1999, 2003), Altonji and Ichimura (2000),

Altonji and Matzkin (2001), and Imbens and Newey (2003), among others. When the distribution of ε is specified to be $U(0,1)$ and m is strictly increasing in ε, the function m can be interpreted as a nonparametric conditional quantile function. See Chaudhuri (1991) and Chaudhuri, Doksum and Samarov (1997), for nonparametric estimation, as well as the references in Koenker (2005).

The additive model described in Section 2.2.1.1 can be interpreted as a different representation of the nonadditive model. One can always express the model: $Y = m(X, \varepsilon)$ as $Y = g(X) + \eta$, where for each x, $g(x) = E(Y|X = x)$. In such a case, the value of the additive unobservable η has, by construction, conditional expectation equal 0, given $X = x$. The distribution of η given $X = x$ can be derived from the function m and the distribution of ε given $X = x$, since by its definition, $\eta = Y - E(Y|X = x) = m(X, \varepsilon) - g(x)$.

2.2.1.3. Triangular nonadditive model When m and ε are multivalued, a particular nonadditive model is the *triangular nonadditive model*. In this model, there are G endogenous (outcome) variables, $Y_1, \ldots, Y_G$, and G unobservable variables, $\varepsilon_1, \ldots, \varepsilon_G$. Given a vector of explanatory variables, $X \in R^K$, the value of each Y_g is determined recursively from $X, Y_1, \ldots, Y_{g-1}$, and ε_g:

$$\begin{aligned}
Y_1 &= m_1(X, \varepsilon_1), \\
Y_2 &= m_2(X, Y_1, \varepsilon_2), \\
Y_3 &= m_3(X, Y_1, Y_2, \varepsilon_3), \\
&\vdots \\
Y_G &= m_G(X, Y_1, Y_2, \ldots, Y_{G-1}, \varepsilon_G).
\end{aligned}$$

This is a nonparametric nonadditive version of the triangular system in linear simultaneous equations [see Hausman (1983)], where for some lower triangular, $G \times G$ matrix A and some $G \times K$ matrix B,

$$\varepsilon = AY + BX$$

where ε is the $G \times 1$ vector $(\varepsilon_1, \ldots, \varepsilon_G)'$, Y is the $G \times 1$ vector $(Y_1, \ldots, Y_G)'$, and X is the $K \times 1$ vector $(X_1, \ldots, X_K)'$.

Nonparametric identification in the nonparametric, nonadditive model has been studied recently by Chesher (2003) and Imbens and Newey (2003), among others. The latter considers also nonparametric estimation. [Ma and Koenker (2006) compare the approaches of those two papers. See also Matzkin (2004).] A typical example [see Imbens and Newey (2003) and Chesher (2003)] is the model where Y_2 denotes lifetime discounted income, Y_1 denotes years of education, X is a variable denoting the cost of education, ε_1 is (unobserved) ability, and ε_2 is another unobservable variable that affects income. In this example, X is an argument of the function m_1 but not of the function m_2. Many panel data models, where the unobservables incorporate fixed effects, fall into this structure.

By recursively substituting the endogenous variables, in the above system of the equations, one can obtain the system of reduced form equations, where each endogenous variable is solely determined by observable and unobservable exogenous variables. This system has the form

$$
\begin{aligned}
Y_1 &= h_1(X, \varepsilon_1),\\
Y_2 &= h_2(X, \varepsilon_1, \varepsilon_2),\\
Y_3 &= h_3(X, \varepsilon_1, \varepsilon_2, \varepsilon_3),\\
&\vdots\\
Y_G &= h_G(X, \varepsilon_1, \varepsilon_2, \ldots, \varepsilon_G)
\end{aligned}
$$

where

$$
\begin{aligned}
h_1(X, \varepsilon_1) &= m_1(X, \varepsilon_1),\\
h_2(X, \varepsilon_1, \varepsilon_2) &= m_2(X, Y_1, \varepsilon_1, \varepsilon_2) = m_2(X, h_1(X, \varepsilon_1), \varepsilon_1, \varepsilon_2),
\end{aligned}
$$

and so on. As can be seen from above, the reduced form of this model, which represents the G-dimensional vector of outcomes $Y_1, \ldots, Y_G$ as G functions of the vector of observable explanatory variables, X, and the vector of G unobservable variables $\varepsilon_1, \ldots, \varepsilon_G$, is triangular in $(\varepsilon_1, \ldots, \varepsilon_G)$, in the sense that for each g, Y_g does not depend on $\varepsilon_{g+1}, \ldots, \varepsilon_G$.

2.2.1.4. Nonadditive index models In many situations in economics, we might be interested in analyzing the effect that some vector of variables X has on a variable, Y, when the model establishing such a relationship between X and Y is either very complicated or only vaguely known. If we could determine that the effect of X on Y is weakly separable from the other variables, then we might be able to identify features of the aggregator, or "index" function, $h(X)$, even though we might not be able to infer all the functions and distributions in the model.

A simple example of a nonadditive index model is where Y denotes an observable dependent variable, X denotes a vector of observable explanatory variables, and ε denotes an unobservable explanatory variable. The functional relationship between these variables is specified as

$$Y = m\big(h(X), \varepsilon\big)$$

where $m : R^2 \to R$ and $h : R^K \to R$. We may impose the restrictions that m is increasing in each coordinate and h is continuous.

Stoker (1986), Han (1987), Powell, Stock and Stoker (1989), Ichimura (1993), Horowitz (1996), Horowitz and Härdle (1996), Abrevaya (2000), and Das (2001) have considered semiparametric estimation of single index linear models, where the function h is specified as a linear-in-parameters function. Ichimura and Lee (1991) considered identification and estimation of semiparametric, multiple linear index models. Matzkin

(1991b) considered estimation of a nonparametric h. Matzkin and Newey (1993), Horowitz (2001), and Lewbel and Linton (2007) considered estimation of h and the distribution of ε nonparametrically. Heckman and Vytlacil (1999, 2000), and Vytlacil and Yildiz (2004), among others, consider identification of average effects. Chesher (2005) considers local identification when X is endogenous and ε is vector-valued.

If we impose the restriction that X and ε are independently distributed, we will call it the *independent nonadditive index model*. Consider, for example, a duration model, with a proportional hazard function, $\lambda(t, x, \nu)$, given by

$$\lambda(t, x, \nu) = s\big(t, h(x)\big)e^{\nu}$$

where x denotes the value of observable characteristics, X, ν denotes the value of an unobservable characteristic, and t denotes the time, Y, at which the hazard is evaluated. Suppose that r is an unknown positive function over R_{+}, h is an unknown function over the support of X, and ν is distributed independently of X. Such a model could describe a situation where Y denotes the length of time that it takes an individual with observable characteristics, X, and unobservable characteristic, ν, to find employment. When the probability-density of finding employment at time t conditional on not having found employment yet is given by the above specification for the hazard function, the model that describes the relation between Y and X is

$$Y = m\big(h(X), \eta + \nu\big)$$

where η possesses an extreme value distribution, independent of (X, ν). Moreover, m is strictly decreasing in $\eta + \nu$.

Semiparametric and nonparametric identification of duration models, as well as corresponding estimation methods, were studied by Elbers and Ridder (1982), Heckman (1991), Heckman and Singer (1984a, 1984b), Barros and Honoré (1988), Honoré (1990), Ridder (1990), Horowitz (1999), van den Berg (2001), and Abbring and van den Berg (2003). [See also the chapters on this topic in Lancaster (1990).]

2.2.1.5. Nonadditive simultaneous equations models In many economic models the values of the dependent variables are determined simultaneously. A standard example is the model of demand and supply. Let m^d denote an aggregate demand function, which determines the aggregate quantity demanded of a product, Q^d, as a function of the price of the product, p, the income level of the consumers, I, and an unobservable variable ε^d. Let m^s denote the aggregate supply function, which determines the aggregate supplied output, Q^s, as a function of the price of the product, P, input prices, W, and an unobservable variable, ε^s. In equilibrium, $Q^d = Q^s$. The model can then be described as

$$Q^d = m^d\big(P, I, \varepsilon^d\big),$$
$$Q^s = m^s\big(P, W, \varepsilon^s\big),$$
$$Q^d = Q^s$$

where the last equation denotes the equilibrium conditions that aggregate demand equals aggregate supply. In this model, the equilibrium quantity, $Q = Q^d = Q^s$, and the equilibrium price are determined simultaneously. In most multidimensional optimization problems, such as those faced by a consumer maximizing a utility function or by a multiproduct firm maximizing profits, the optimal choices are also determined simultaneously.

The analysis of simultaneous equations models is typically more complicated than that of many other models because the unobservables that affect any one of the endogenous variables affect, through the simultaneity, also the other endogenous variables. This was made clear for linear models by Haavelmo (1943), who showed that least squares was not the correct method to estimate models with endogenous variables. Suppose, for example, that in the demand and supply example described above, m^d is strictly increasing in ε^d and m^s is strictly decreasing in ε^s. Then, the system can be expressed as

$$\varepsilon^d = r^d(Q, P, I),$$
$$\varepsilon^s = r^s(Q, P, W)$$

where r^d is the inverse function of m^d with respect to ε^d and r^s is the inverse function of m^s with respect to ε^s. Assuming that, for any value of the vector of exogenous variables, $(I, W, \varepsilon^d, \varepsilon^s)$, this system of structural equations possesses a unique solution for (P, Q), one can derive the reduced form system of the model, which can be expressed as

$$Q = h^1(I, W, \varepsilon^d, \varepsilon^s),$$
$$P = h^2(I, W, \varepsilon^d, \varepsilon^s).$$

When the structural equations in the simultaneous equations model above are linear in the variables, as in the standard linear models for simultaneous equations, the reduced form equations turn out to be linear in the unobservables. In such a case, to each reduced form equation there corresponds a unique unobservable random term, which enters the equation in an additive way. The value of each such unobservable is a function of ε^d, ε^s and of the coefficients that appear in r^d and r^s. Identification in linear simultaneous equations can be analyzed using the results in Koopmans (1949), Koopmans, Rubin and Leipnik (1950), and Fisher (1966), among others. [See Hausman (1983) and Hsiao (1983) for surveys of that literature.]

We will consider below the nonadditive simultaneous equations model described by

$$\varepsilon = r(Y, X)$$

where $Y \in R^G$ denote a vector of observable dependent variables, $X \in R^K$ denote a vector of observable explanatory variables, and $\varepsilon \in R^L$ denote a vector of unobservable explanatory variables. The function $r : R^G \times R^K \to R^L$ specifies the relationship between these vectors. In our analysis of this model, we will impose the restriction that r is differentiable and is such that for all values of (X, ε), there is a unique Y satisfying the above equation. We will also impose the restriction that X and ε are independently distributed with support $R^K \times R^G$ and that r is such that for each x, the density of Y given $X = x$ has support R^G.

The identification of nonparametric simultaneous equations satisfying these properties was first analyzed by Roehrig (1988), following a technique developed by B. Brown (1983) for parametric, nonlinear in variables, simultaneous equations models. Recently, Benkard and Berry (2004) showed that Roehrig's conditions may not guarantee identification. Matzkin (2005b) proposed a different set of conditions. Manski (1983) proposed a closest empirical distribution method for estimation of a semiparametric version of these models, which did not require a parametric specification for the density of ε. Brown and Matzkin (1998) developed a nonparametric closest empirical distribution method, which did not require either the distribution of ε or the function r to be parametric. A seminonparametric maximum likelihood method, such as that developed in Gallant and Nychka (1987), or a semiparametric maximum likelihood method, as in Ai (1997) could also be used to estimate identified models.

When a structural function is additive in the unobservable random term, estimation can proceed using the nonparametric instrumental variable methods of Newey and Powell (1989, 2003), Ai and Chen (2003), Darolles, Florens and Renault (2000), and Hall and Horowitz (2005). When it is nonadditive, the methods of Chernozhukov and Hansen (2005), or Chernozhukov, Imbens and Newey (2007) could be used.

2.2.1.6. Discrete choice models Discrete choice models are models typically used to describe the situation where an individual has a finite number, $1, \ldots, G$, of alternatives to choose from. The individual has preferences defined over those alternatives and chooses one that maximizes those preferences. It is assumed that the preference of the individual for each alternative can be represented by a function, V_g, which depends on observable and unobserved characteristics of the individual and of the alternative. Let S denote a vector of observable socioeconomic characteristics of a typical individual. Let Z_g denote a vector of observable characteristics of alternative g. Let ε denote a vector of unobservable variables. It is typically assumed that $\varepsilon \in R^J$ where $J \geqslant G$. For each g, let $Y_g^* = V_g(S, Z_g, \varepsilon)$, and let $Y_g = 1$ if the individual chooses alternative g and $Y_g = 0$ otherwise. Assume that the functions $V_1, \ldots, V_G$ and the distribution of ε are such that there is zero probability that for some $g \neq k$, $V_g(S, Z_g, \varepsilon) = V_k(S, Z_k, \varepsilon)$. In this model, the vector of unobserved endogenous variables is $Y^* = (Y_1^*, \ldots, Y_G^*)$, and the vector of observable endogenous variables is $Y = (Y_1, \ldots, Y_G)$ where, for each g,

$$Y_g = \begin{cases} 1 & \text{if } V_g(S, Z_g, \varepsilon) > V_k(S, Z_k, \varepsilon) \text{ for all } k \neq g, \\ 0 & \text{otherwise.} \end{cases}$$

The vector of observable explanatory variables is $X = (S, Z_1, \ldots, Z_G)$. The conditional probability of Y given X is given by

$$\Pr(Y_g = 1|X) = \Pr\left(\left\{\varepsilon \mid V_g(S, Z_g, \varepsilon) > V_k(S, Z_k, \varepsilon) \text{ for all } k \equiv j\right\}\right).$$

Discrete choice models were originally developed by McFadden (1974) under the linear additive specification that for all g

$$V_g(S, Z_g, \varepsilon) = \alpha_g + \gamma_g S + \beta_g Z_g + \varepsilon_g$$

and $\varepsilon = (\varepsilon_1, \ldots, \varepsilon_G)$. Initially, McFadden (1974) specified a parametric distributions for ε. Subsequent work by Manski (1975, 1985), Cosslett (1983), Powell, Stock and Stoker (1989), Horowitz (1992), Ichimura (1993), and Klein and Spady (1993), among others, developed methods that did not require a parametric specification for ε. Matzkin (1991a) considered identification when the distribution of $\varepsilon = (\varepsilon_1, \ldots, \varepsilon_G)$ is specified parametrically and for each g

$$V_g(S, Z_g, \varepsilon) = v_g(S, Z_g) + \varepsilon_g$$

for some unknown functions v_g. Matzkin (1992, 1993) extended these results to the case where both the distribution of $(\varepsilon_1, \ldots, \varepsilon_G)$ and the functions $v_1, \ldots, v_G$ are nonparametric.

3. Identification

3.1. Definition of identification

Following the description of an econometric model in Section 2, we denote the set of all vectors of functions and distributions that satisfy the restrictions imposed by a model by S. We denote any element in S by ζ, and we denote the element of S corresponding to the vector of true functions and distributions by ζ^*. For any element ζ in S, we will denote by $F_{Y,X}(\cdot, \cdot; \zeta)$ the distribution of the observable variables generated by ζ. The distribution of the observable variables generated by ζ^* will be denoted by $F_{Y,X}(\cdot, \cdot; \zeta^*)$ or simply by $F_{Y,X}$.

The analysis of identification deals with the mapping between the distribution of the observable variables and the underlying elements in the model. Given a model, with an associated vector of functions and distributions, ζ^*, and a set S of vectors of functions and distributions satisfying the same restrictions that ζ^* is assumed to satisfy, we can ask what elements of ζ^* are uniquely determined from $F_{Y,X}$. More generally, we may ask what features of ζ^* can be uniquely recovered from $F_{Y,X}$. By a *feature* of ζ, we mean any function $\Psi : S \to \Omega$. This could be an element of ζ, or a property such as, for example, the sign of the derivative of a particular function in ζ. We will let $\psi^* = \Psi(\zeta^*)$; ψ^* then denotes the true value of the feature of ζ^*. Elements in the range, $\Psi(S)$, of Ψ will be denoted by ψ. Given $\psi \in \Psi(S)$, we define $\Gamma_{Y,X}(\psi, S)$ to be the set of all probability distributions of (Y, X) that are consistent with ψ and S. Formally,

$$\Gamma_{Y,X}(\psi, S) = \{ F_{Y,X}(\cdot, \cdot; \zeta) \mid \zeta \in S \text{ and } \Psi(\zeta) = \psi \}.$$

In other words, $\Gamma_{Y,X}(\psi, S)$ is the set of all distributions of (Y, X) that are generated by some vector of functions and distributions in S and whose value of the element that we want to infer is ψ.

In the model of consumer demand, ψ^* may denote, for example, the utility function U^*, the expected demand of a socioeconomic group at a particular budget

$E[m^*(p, I, w, \varepsilon)|p, I, w]$, or the expected infinitesimal effect in the demand of a change in price, $E[\partial m^*(p, I, w, \varepsilon)/\partial p|p, I, w]$.

A key concept when analyzing identification is the one of observational equivalence. Two values $\psi, \psi' \in \Omega$ are observationally equivalent if there exist at least two vectors, $\zeta, \zeta' \in S$ with $\Psi(\zeta) = \psi$, $\Psi(\zeta') = \psi'$, and $F_{Y,X}(\cdot, \cdot; \zeta) = F_{Y,X}(\cdot, \cdot; \zeta')$:

DEFINITION 3.1. $\psi, \psi' \in \Omega$ are *observationally equivalent* in the model S if

$$[\Gamma_{Y,X}(\psi, S) \cap \Gamma_{Y,X}(\psi', S)] \neq \emptyset.$$

The feature ψ^* is identified if there is no $\psi \in \Omega$ such that $\psi \neq \psi^*$ and ψ is observationally equivalent to ψ^*:

DEFINITION 3.2. $\psi^* \in \Omega$ is *identified in model S* if for any $\psi \in \Omega$ such that $\psi \neq \psi^*$

$$[\Gamma_{Y,X}(\psi, S) \cap \Gamma_{Y,X}(\psi^*, S)] = \emptyset.$$

The following characterization is often used to prove identification when it is easy to show that ψ^* can be recovered uniquely from any distribution in $\Gamma_{Y,X}(\psi^*, S)$ in particular models:

DEFINITION 3.3. $\psi^* \in \Omega$ is *identified in model S* if for any $\psi \in \Omega$

$$([\Gamma_{Y,X}(\psi, S) \cap \Gamma_{Y,X}(\psi^*, S)] \neq \emptyset) \quad \Rightarrow \quad [\psi = \psi^*].$$

3.2. *Identification in additive models*

Consider the model

$$Y = g^*(X) + \varepsilon$$

where Y denotes an observable dependent variable, $X \in R^K$ denotes a vector of observable explanatory variables, ε denotes an unobservable explanatory variable, and $g^* : R^K \to R$ is an unknown, continuous function. Suppose that we were interested in the value $g^*(\bar{x})$ of the function g^* at a particular value $\bar{x}$ of X. For any distribution $\widetilde{F}_{\varepsilon,X}$ of (ε, X), let $E[\varepsilon|X = x; \widetilde{F}_{\varepsilon,X}]$ denote the expectation of ε conditional on $X = x$, calculated using $\widetilde{F}_{\varepsilon,X}$, and let $\tilde{f}_X$ denote the probability density of the marginal distribution $\widetilde{F}_X$. Let $S = \{(\tilde{g}, \widetilde{F}_{\varepsilon,X}) \mid \tilde{g} : R^K \to R$ is continuous and $\widetilde{F}_{\varepsilon,X}$ is a distribution on R^{K+1} such that (i) $\tilde{f}_X(\bar{x}) > 0$ and $\tilde{f}_X$ is continuous at $\bar{x}$, (ii) $E[\varepsilon|X = \bar{x}; \widetilde{F}_{\varepsilon,X}] = 0$ and $E[\varepsilon|X = x; \widetilde{F}_{\varepsilon,X}]$ is continuous in x at $\bar{x}\}$. Let Ω denote the set of all possible values that $\psi^* = g^*(\bar{x})$ can attain. Then,

(3.a) $\psi^* = g^*(\bar{x})$ *is identified.*

PROOF OF (3.a). Let $E[Y|X = x; \tilde{g}, \widetilde{F}_{\varepsilon,X}]$ denote the conditional expectation of Y given $X = x$, for the distribution generated by $(\tilde{g}, \widetilde{F}_{\varepsilon,X})$. Suppose that $(g^*, F'_{\varepsilon,X}), (\tilde{g}, \widetilde{F}_{\varepsilon,X}) \in S$ and $\tilde{g}(\bar{x}) \neq g^*(\bar{x})$. Then, since

$$E[Y|X = \bar{x}; \tilde{g}, \widetilde{F}_{\varepsilon,X}] = \tilde{g}(\bar{x}) + E[\varepsilon|X = \bar{x}; \widetilde{F}_{\varepsilon,X}] = \tilde{g}(\bar{x}),$$
$$E\left[Y\middle|X = \bar{x}; g^*, F'_{\varepsilon,X}\right] = g^*(\bar{x}) + E\left[\varepsilon\middle|X = \bar{x}; F'_{\varepsilon,X}\right] = g^*(\bar{x})$$

and both functions are continuous at $\bar{x}$, it follows by the properties of $F'_{\varepsilon,X}$ and $\widetilde{F}_{\varepsilon,X}$ that

$$F_{Y,X}\left(\cdot; g^*, F'_{\varepsilon,X}\right) \neq F_{Y,X}(\cdot; \tilde{g}, \widetilde{F}_{\varepsilon,X}).$$

Hence, ψ^* is identified. □

When g^* is identified, we can also identify $F^*_{\varepsilon,X}$. Assume for simplicity that the marginal distribution F_X has an everywhere positive density. Let $S = \{(\tilde{g}, \widetilde{F}_{\varepsilon,X}) \mid \tilde{g} : R^K \to R$ is continuous and $\widetilde{F}_{\varepsilon,X}$ is a distribution that has support R^{K+1} and is such that $E[\varepsilon|X = x; \widetilde{F}_{\varepsilon,X}]$ is continuous in x and it equals 0 at all values of $x\}$. Let Ω denote the set of all possible pairs of functions $\psi = (g, F_{\varepsilon,X})$. Then,

(3.b) $\psi^* = \left(g^*, F^*_{\varepsilon,X}\right)$ *is identified.*

PROOF OF (3.b). Using the same arguments as in the proof of (3.a), we can show that, for any x, $g^*(x)$ is identified. To show that $F^*_{\varepsilon,X}$ is identified, note that

$$\begin{aligned} F_{Y|X=x}(y) &= \Pr(Y \leqslant y|X = x) \\ &= \Pr\left(g^*(X) + \varepsilon \leqslant y\middle|X = x\right) \\ &= \Pr\left(\varepsilon \leqslant y - g^*(x)\middle|X = x\right) \\ &= F^*_{\varepsilon|X=x}\left(y - g^*(x)\right). \end{aligned}$$

Since the marginal density, f^*_X, of X is identified, it follows that $F^*_{\varepsilon,X}(x, e)$ is identified. □

The linear model is, of course, the most well-known case of an additive model. In this case, for all x,

$$g^*(x) = \alpha^* + \beta^* x$$

for some $\alpha^* \in R$, $\beta^* \in R^K$. To identify $\psi^* = (\alpha^*, \beta^*)$ within the set of all vectors $(\alpha, \beta) \in R^{1+K}$, one needs a rank condition in addition to the location normalization. Suppose that for $K + 1$ vectors $x^{(1)}, \ldots, x^{(K+1)}$, $g^*(x^{(k)})$ is identified and the rank of the $(K + 1) \times (K + 1)$ matrix whose kth row is $(1, x^{(k)})$ is $K + 1$. Then, the system of $K + 1$ linear equations

$$\alpha^* + \beta^* x^{(k)} = g^*\left(x^{(k)}\right), \quad k = 1, \ldots, K + 1,$$

has a unique solution. Hence, (α^*, β^*) is identified. □

3.3. Identification in nonadditive models

Since the nonadditive model is more general than the additive model, it would not be surprising to find out that stronger conditions are necessary for the identification of the function m^* and distribution $F^*_{\varepsilon,X}$ in the model where Y is an observable dependent variable, X is a vector of observable explanatory variables, ε is an unobservable random term explanatory variable, and

$$Y = m^*(X, \varepsilon).$$

In fact, Matzkin (2003, Lemma 1) establishes that even when m^* is assumed to be strictly increasing in ε and ε is distributed independently of X, one cannot identify m^*. Assume that F_X is known. Let Ξ denote the support of X, which will be assumed to be R^K. We will assume that F^*_ε has support R and that ε is distributed independently of X. Hence, we can characterize the model by pairs (m, F_ε).

THEOREM 3.1. *[See Matzkin (2003).] Let* $S = \{(\tilde{m}, \widetilde{F}_\varepsilon) \mid \tilde{m} : \Xi \times R \to R$ *is continuous on* $\Xi \times R$ *and strictly increasing in its last coordinate and* $\widetilde{F}_\varepsilon$ *is continuous and strictly increasing on* $R\}$. *Let* $\Psi : S \to \Omega$ *denote the first coordinate of* $\zeta = (m, F_\varepsilon) \in S$. *Then,* $m, \tilde{m} \in \Omega$ *are observationally equivalent iff for some continuous and strictly increasing function* $s : R \to R$ *and all* $x \in \Xi$, $\varepsilon \in R$

$$\tilde{m}\big(x, s(\varepsilon)\big) = m(x, \varepsilon).$$

PROOF. Suppose $m, \tilde{m} \in \Omega$ are observationally equivalent. Then, there exist continuous and strictly increasing $F_\varepsilon, \widetilde{F}_\varepsilon$ such that for all $x \in \Xi$, $y \in R$

$$F_{Y|X=x}\big(y;\ (m, F_\varepsilon)\big) = F_{Y|X=x}\big(y;\ (\tilde{m}, \widetilde{F}_\varepsilon)\big).$$

Let $r(x, \cdot)$ and $\tilde{r}(x, \cdot)$ denote, respectively, the inverses of $m(x, \cdot)$ and $\tilde{m}(x, \cdot)$. Since for all y, x

$$F_{Y|X=x}\big(y;\ (m, F_\varepsilon)\big) = \Pr\big(Y \leqslant y | X = x;\ (m, F_\varepsilon)\big) = F_\varepsilon\big(r(y, x)\big)$$

and

$$F_{Y|X=x}\big(y;\ (\tilde{m}, \widetilde{F}_\varepsilon)\big) = \Pr\big(Y \leqslant y | X = x;\ (\tilde{m}, \widetilde{F}_\varepsilon)\big) = \widetilde{F}_\varepsilon\big(\tilde{r}(y, x)\big)$$

it follows that for all y, x

$$F_\varepsilon\big(r(y, x)\big) = \widetilde{F}_\varepsilon\big(\tilde{r}(y, x)\big).$$

Since $F_\varepsilon, \widetilde{F}_\varepsilon$ are strictly increasing and continuous, the function $s(t) = \widetilde{F}_\varepsilon^{-1}(F_\varepsilon(t))$ is strictly increasing and continuous and $\tilde{r}(y, x) = s(r(y, x))$. Let $y = m(x, \varepsilon)$. Since $\tilde{r}$ is the inverse of $\tilde{m}$

$$y = \tilde{m}\big(x, \tilde{r}(y, x)\big) = \tilde{m}\big(x, s\big(r(y, x)\big)\big) = \tilde{m}\big(x, s(\varepsilon)\big).$$

Hence,

$$m(x, \varepsilon) = \tilde{m}\big(x, s(\varepsilon)\big).$$

Conversely, suppose that m and $\tilde{m}$ are such that for a strictly increasing and continuous function s, all x and ε

$$m(x, \varepsilon) = \tilde{m}\big(x, s(\varepsilon)\big).$$

Let F_ε denote any continuous and strictly increasing distribution on R. Let $\tilde{\varepsilon} = s(\varepsilon)$ and let $\widetilde{F}_\varepsilon$ denote the distribution of $\tilde{\varepsilon}$, which is derived from s and F_ε. Let r and $\tilde{r}$ denote respectively the inverse functions of m with respect to ε and of $\tilde{m}$ with respect to $\tilde{\varepsilon}$. Then, for all y, x

$$F_{Y|X=x}\big(y;\ (m, F_\varepsilon)\big) = \Pr\big(Y \leqslant y\big|X = x;\ (m, F_\varepsilon)\big) = F_\varepsilon\big(r(y, x)\big)$$

and

$$F_{Y|X=x}\big(y;\ (\tilde{m}, \widetilde{F}_\varepsilon)\big) = \Pr\big(Y \leqslant y\big|X = x;\ (\tilde{m}, \widetilde{F}_\varepsilon)\big) = \widetilde{F}_\varepsilon\big(\tilde{r}(y, x)\big).$$

Hence, m and $\tilde{m}$ are observationally equivalent. □

An implication of the above result is that to identify m^*, one must restrict m^* to belong to a set of functions such that for any two different continuous functions in the set, their corresponding inverse functions are not continuous, strictly increasing transformations of each other. Suppose, for example, that we impose the normalization that for some $\bar{x}$ for which $f_X(\bar{x}) > 0$, where f_X, the marginal probability density of X, is continuous at $\bar{x}$, and for all ε, all $m \in \Omega$ satisfy

$$m(\bar{x}, \varepsilon) = \varepsilon.$$

Then, all the inverse functions, r, must satisfy

$$r(\varepsilon, \bar{x}) = \varepsilon.$$

Suppose $r, \tilde{r}$ are any two such functions and for a strictly increasing s, and all ε, x

$$\tilde{r}(\varepsilon, x) = s\big(r(\varepsilon, x)\big).$$

Then, letting $x = \bar{x}$, it follows that for any t

$$t = \tilde{r}(t, \bar{x}) = s\big(r(t, \bar{x})\big) = s(t).$$

Hence, s is the identity function.

Clearly, if m^* is identified, so is F_ε^*, since for all e and any x

$$\begin{aligned} F_\varepsilon^*(e) &= \Pr(\varepsilon \leqslant e) = \Pr(\varepsilon \leqslant e|X = x) \\ &= \Pr\big(m^*(X, \varepsilon) \leqslant m^*(x, e)\big|X = x\big) = F_{Y|X=x}\big(m^*(x, e)\big). \end{aligned}$$

In this expression, the first equality follows by the definition of F_ε^*, the second by the independence between ε and X, the third by the strict monotonicity of m^* in its last coordinate, and the last equality follows by the definition of Y and that of $F_{Y|X}$.

It is also clear that if F_ε^* is specified, then m^* is identified, since from the above equation it follows that

$$m^*(x, e) = F_{Y|X=x}^{-1}\big(F_\varepsilon^*(e)\big).$$

Imbens and Newey (2003) and Blundell and Powell (2003), for example, use a normalization that amounts to specifying ε to be $U(0, 1)$.

3.3.1. *Identification of derivatives*

Rather than normalizing the set of functions, as above, we may ask what features can be identified without normalizations. It turns out that derivatives and discrete changes are identified. For the first result, let $\bar{x}$ and $\bar{y}$ denote particular values of, respectively, X and Y. Let $\bar{\varepsilon}$ denote the value of ε at which $\bar{y} = m^*(\bar{x}, \bar{\varepsilon})$. Assume that ε and X have differentiable densities, strictly positive at $\bar{\varepsilon}$ and $\bar{x}$, and that m^* is differentiable at $(\bar{x}, \bar{\varepsilon})$. Let Ω denote the set of all values that $\partial m^*(\bar{x}, \bar{\varepsilon})/\partial x$ may attain. Then,

(3.c) $\psi^* = \partial m^*(\bar{x}, \bar{\varepsilon})/\partial x$ *is identified.*

PROOF OF (3.c). We follow closely Matzkin (1999) and Chesher (2003). By independence between X and ε and the strict monotonicity of m,

$$\begin{aligned} F_\varepsilon^*(\bar{\varepsilon}) &= F_{\varepsilon|X=\bar{x}}^*(\bar{\varepsilon}) \\ &= \Pr(\varepsilon \leqslant \bar{\varepsilon}|X = \bar{x}) \\ &= \Pr\big(m^*(X, \varepsilon) \leqslant m^*(\bar{x}, \bar{\varepsilon})\big|X = \bar{x}\big) \\ &= \Pr\big(Y \leqslant m^*(\bar{x}, \bar{\varepsilon})\big|X = \bar{x}\big) \\ &= F_{Y|X=\bar{x}}\big(m^*(\bar{x}, \bar{\varepsilon})\big). \end{aligned}$$

Taking derivatives with respect to x, on both sides, we get that

$$\begin{aligned} 0 = {} & \frac{\partial F_{Y|X=\bar{x}}(t)}{\partial x}\bigg|_{t=m^*(\bar{x},\bar{\varepsilon})} \\ & + \frac{\partial F_{Y|X=\bar{x}}(t)}{\partial t}\bigg|_{t=m^*(\bar{x},\bar{\varepsilon})} \frac{\partial m^*(\bar{x}, \bar{\varepsilon})}{\partial x}. \end{aligned}$$

Hence, the derivative

$$\frac{\partial m^*(\bar{x}, \bar{\varepsilon})}{\partial x} = -\left[\frac{\partial F_{Y|X=\bar{x}}(\bar{y})}{\partial y}\right]^{-1} \frac{\partial F_{Y|X=\bar{x}}(\bar{y})}{\partial x}$$

is uniquely derived from the distribution $F_{Y,X}$ of the observable variables. □

3.3.2. Identification of finite changes

Finite changes can also be identified. Fix again the value of (Y, X) at $(\bar{y}, \bar{x})$, and let again $\bar{\varepsilon}$ be such that $\bar{y} = m^*(\bar{x}, \bar{\varepsilon})$. We are interested in the value of $y' - \bar{y}$ where $y' = m^*(x', \bar{\varepsilon})$. This is the causal effect on Y of changing the value of X from $\bar{x}$ to x', while leaving the value of the unobservable variable, ε, unchanged. Assume that the probability density f_X^* has a continuous extension and is strictly positive at $\bar{x}$ and x', and that the density of ε is strictly positive at $\bar{\varepsilon}$. Let Ω denote the set of all values that $y' - \bar{y}$ may attain. Then,

(3.d) $\psi^* = m^*(x', \bar{\varepsilon}) - m^*(\bar{x}, \bar{\varepsilon})$ *is identified.*

PROOF OF (3.d). The independence between X and ε and the strict monotonicity of m imply that

$$F_\varepsilon(\bar{\varepsilon}) = F_{Y|X=\bar{x}}\big(m^*(\bar{x}, \bar{\varepsilon})\big)$$

and, similarly, that

$$F_\varepsilon(\bar{\varepsilon}) = F_{Y|X=x'}\big(m^*(x', \bar{\varepsilon})\big).$$

The strict monotonicity of $F_{Y|X=x'}$ then implies that

$$\begin{aligned} y' - \bar{y} &= m^*(x', \varepsilon^*) - \bar{y} \\ &= F^{-1}_{Y|X=x'}\big(F_\varepsilon(\varepsilon^*)\big) - \bar{y} \\ &= F^{-1}_{Y|X=x'}\big(F_{Y|X=\bar{x}}\big(m^*(\bar{x}, \bar{\varepsilon})\big)\big) - \bar{y} \\ &= F^{-1}_{Y|X=x'}\big(F_{Y|X=\bar{x}}(\bar{y})\big) - \bar{y}. \end{aligned}$$

Hence, the change in the value of Y when X is changed from $\bar{x}$ to x' is identified. □

3.3.3. Identification in triangular systems

In a model with a nonadditive, unobserved efficiency variable, Olley and Pakes (1996) used the strict monotonicity between investment and the unobserved index variable, conditional on observable age and capital stock of the firm, to express the unobserved efficiency index in terms of the observables age, capital stock, and investment. In a similar spirit, Chesher (2003) derived expressions for unobserved variables from conditional distributions, and used them to derive expressions for the derivatives of functions in a triangular system of equations with nonadditive random terms. Chesher used a local independence assumption. We will analyze here a special case of Chesher's model where the independence restrictions are stronger.

To provide an example, suppose that the model of consumer demand is

$$Y = m(p, I, \varepsilon, \eta)$$

where ε and η are unobservable variables and m is strictly increasing in η. Suppose that I is determined by ε and an observable variable Z, according to a function $\tilde{r}$, strictly increasing in ε:

$$I = \tilde{r}(Z, \varepsilon).$$

Assume that Z is distributed independently of (ε, η). For simplicity, assume full support for all variables and differentiability for all functions. Then,

$$\text{(3.e)} \quad \frac{\partial m(p, I, \varepsilon, \eta)}{\partial I} \quad \textit{can be identified.}$$

PROOF OF (3.e). Letting r denote the inverse of $\tilde{r}$ with respect to ε and substituting in the demand function, we have that

$$Y = m\big(p, I, r(Z, I), \eta\big).$$

Let

$$v(p, I, Z, \eta) = m\big(p, I, r(Z, I), \eta\big).$$

Note that

$$\frac{\partial v(p, I, Z, \eta)}{\partial I} = \frac{\partial m(p, I, r(Z, I), \eta)}{\partial I} + \frac{\partial m(p, I, r(Z, I), \eta)}{\partial \varepsilon} \frac{\partial r(Z, I)}{\partial I}$$

and

$$\frac{\partial v(p, I, Z, \eta)}{\partial Z} = \frac{\partial m(p, I, r(Z, I), \eta)}{\partial \varepsilon} \frac{\partial r(Z, I)}{\partial Z}.$$

Hence,

$$\left.\frac{\partial m(p, I, \varepsilon, \eta)}{\partial I}\right|_{\varepsilon = r(Z,I)} = \frac{\partial v(p, I, Z, \eta)}{\partial I} - \frac{\partial v(p, I, Z, \eta)}{\partial Z} \left[\frac{\frac{\partial r(Z,I)}{\partial I}}{\frac{\partial r(Z,I)}{\partial Z}} \right].$$

This implies that, if we know the functions v and r, we can identify the derivative of m with respect to I, at particular values of ε and δ. But, the models

$$I = \tilde{r}(Z, \varepsilon)$$

and

$$Y = v(p, I, Z, \eta)$$

are just the independent nonadditive model, when ε and Z are independently distributed, (p, I, Z) and η are also independently distributed, and when v and $\tilde{r}$ are strictly increasing, respectively, in η and ε. Hence, the derivatives of $\tilde{r}$ and of v are identified from the distribution of, respectively, (I, Z) and (Y, p, I, Z). In particular, using the results in the previous section, it immediately follows that

$$\frac{\partial v(p, I, Z, \eta)}{\partial I} = -\left[\frac{\partial F_{Y|I,Z}(y^*)}{\partial y} \right]^{-1} \frac{\partial F_{Y|I,Z}(y^*)}{\partial I}$$

and

$$\frac{\partial v(p, I, Z, \eta)}{\partial Z} = -\left[\frac{\partial F_{Y|I,Z}(y^*)}{\partial y}\right]^{-1} \frac{\partial F_{Y|I,Z}(y^*)}{\partial Z}$$

at y^* such that $y^* = m(I, Z, \eta)$. Differentiating the expression

$$F_\varepsilon\big(r(Z, I)\big) = F_{I|Z}(I)$$

which can be shown to be equivalent to the expression

$$F_\varepsilon(\varepsilon) = F_{I|Z}\big(\tilde{r}(Z, \varepsilon)\big)$$

we get, similarly, that

$$\frac{\partial r(Z, I)}{\partial I} = -\left[\frac{\partial F_\varepsilon(\varepsilon)}{\partial \varepsilon}\bigg|_{\varepsilon = r(Z,I)}\right]^{-1} \frac{\partial F_{I|Z}(I)}{\partial I}$$

and

$$\frac{\partial r(Z, I)}{\partial Z} = -\left[\frac{\partial F_\varepsilon(\varepsilon)}{\partial \varepsilon}\bigg|_{\varepsilon = r(Z,I)}\right]^{-1} \frac{\partial F_{I|Z}(I)}{\partial Z}.$$

Hence,

$$\frac{\partial m(p, I, \varepsilon, \eta)}{\partial I} = \left[\frac{\partial F_{Y|I,Z}(y^*)}{\partial y}\right]^{-1} \left[\frac{\partial F_{Y|I,Z}(y^*)}{\partial Z}\left[\frac{\frac{\partial F_{I|Z}(I)}{\partial I}}{\frac{\partial F_{I|Z}(I)}{\partial Z}}\right] - \frac{\partial F_{Y|I,Z}(y^*)}{\partial I}\right]$$

at $\varepsilon = r(I, Z)$ and $y^* = m(p, I, \varepsilon, \eta)$.

Hence, using the variable Z we can identify the derivative of m with respect to I, leaving the value of ε fixed. □

3.4. Identification in nonadditive index models

Consider the model

$$Y = m^*\big(h^*(X), \varepsilon\big)$$

where Y denotes an observable dependent variable, ε denotes an unobservable explanatory variable whose support is R, X denotes a vector of observable explanatory variables that possesses support $\Xi = R^K$, X is such that the last coordinate, X_K, of X possesses an everywhere positive density conditional on the other coordinates of X, ε is distributed independently of X, $m^* : R^2 \to R$ is increasing in each coordinate, nonconstant, and satisfies that for all t, t',

$$t < t' \quad \Rightarrow \quad \text{there exists } \varepsilon \text{ such that } m^*(t, \varepsilon) < m^*(t', \varepsilon)$$

and $h^* : \Xi \to R$ is continuous on Ξ and strictly increasing in its last coordinate. Assume that F_X is known. The model, S, is then characterized by the set of all triplets

$\zeta = (\tilde{h}, \widetilde{F}_\varepsilon, \tilde{m})$ such that $\tilde{h}$, $\widetilde{F}_\varepsilon$, and $\tilde{m}$ satisfy the assumptions that, respectively, h^*, F_ε^*, and m^* are assumed to satisfy. Let Ω denote the set composed of all first coordinates, $\tilde{h}$, of $(\tilde{h}, \widetilde{F}_\varepsilon, \tilde{m}) \in S$. Let $\circ$ denote the composition of two functions, so that $(g \circ \tilde{h})(t) = g(\tilde{h}(t))$. The following theorem was stated in Matzkin (1994). Its proof is a modification of the identification result in Han (1987) for semiparametric index models.

THEOREM 3.2. *In the model described above, two functions $h, \tilde{h} \in \Omega$ are observationally equivalent if and only if there exists a continuous, strictly increasing function $g : R \to R$ such that $\tilde{h} = g \circ h$.*

PROOF. Suppose that for all x, $\tilde{h}(x) = g(h(x))$. Then, letting $\tilde{m}(t, e) = m(g^{-1}(t), e)$, it follows that for all x, e

$$\begin{aligned} \tilde{m}(\tilde{h}(x), e) &= m(g^{-1}(g(h(x))), e) \\ &= m(h(x), e). \end{aligned}$$

Hence, for any distribution, F_ε, $F_{Y,X}(\cdot, \cdot;\, h, F_\varepsilon, m) = F_{Y,X}(\cdot, \cdot;\, \tilde{h}, F_\varepsilon, \tilde{m})$. It follows that h and $\tilde{h}$ are observationally equivalent.

On the other hand, suppose that there exists no strictly increasing, continuous g such that $\tilde{h} = g \circ h$, then, there must exist $x', x'' \in \Xi$ such that

$$h(x') < h(x'') \quad \text{and} \quad \tilde{h}(x') > \tilde{h}(x'').$$

By the properties of any $\tilde{m}$, m, specified by the model, this implies that there exist ε, $\tilde{\varepsilon}$ such that

$$m(h(x'), \varepsilon) < m(h(x''), \varepsilon) \quad \text{and} \quad \tilde{m}(\tilde{h}(x'), \tilde{\varepsilon}) > \tilde{m}(\tilde{h}(x''), \tilde{\varepsilon}).$$

Let F_ε, $\widetilde{F}_\varepsilon$ be any distributions that have support R. By independence between X and ε, the full support of ε, and the monotonicity of m and $\tilde{m}$, this implies that

$$\begin{aligned} &\Pr\{(e', e'') | (\tilde{m}(\tilde{h}(x'), e') > \tilde{m}(\tilde{h}(x''), e''))\} \\ &\quad > \Pr\{(e', e'') | (\tilde{m}(\tilde{h}(x'), e') < \tilde{m}(\tilde{h}(x''), e''))\} \end{aligned}$$

while

$$\begin{aligned} &\Pr\{(e', e'') | (m(h(x'), e') > m(h(x''), e''))\} \\ &\quad < \Pr\{(e', e'') | (m(h(x'), e') < m(h(x''), e''))\}. \end{aligned}$$

Hence, either

$$\begin{aligned} &\Pr\{(e', e'') | (\tilde{m}(\tilde{h}(x'), e') < \tilde{m}(\tilde{h}(x''), e''))\} \\ &\quad \neq \Pr\{(e', e'') | (m(h(x'), e') < m(h(x''), e''))\} \end{aligned}$$

or

$$\Pr\{(e',e'')|(\tilde{m}(\tilde{h}(x'),e') > \tilde{m}(\tilde{h}(x''),e''))\}$$
$$\neq \Pr\{(e',e'')|(m(h(x'),e') > m(h(x''),e''))\}.$$

Let $F_{Y,X}(\cdot;\,\tilde{h},\widetilde{F}_\varepsilon,\tilde{m})$ and $F_{Y,X}(\cdot;\,h,F_\varepsilon,m)$ denote the distributions generated by, respectively, $(\tilde{h},\widetilde{F}_\varepsilon,\tilde{m})$ and (h,F_ε,m). Let Y' and Y'' denote the random variables that have, respectively, distributions $F_{Y|X=x'}$ and $F_{Y|X=x''}$. If any of the two inequalities above are satisfied, the probability of the event $Y' > Y''$ calculated using $F_{Y|X=x'}(\cdot,\cdot;\,\tilde{m},\tilde{h},\widetilde{F}_\varepsilon)$ and $F_{Y|X=x''}(\cdot,\cdot;\,\tilde{m},\tilde{h},\widetilde{F}_\varepsilon)$ will be different from the probability of the same event calculated using $F_{Y|X=x'}(\cdot,\cdot;\,m,h,F_\varepsilon)$ and $F_{Y|X=x''}(\cdot,\cdot;\,m,h,F_\varepsilon)$. By continuity of the functions, and the support conditions of X, this will still hold for all $\tilde{x}'$ and $\tilde{x}''$ in neighborhoods, respectively, of x' and x'', which have positive probability. Hence, $F_{Y,X}(\cdot,\cdot;\,\tilde{m},\tilde{h},\widetilde{F}_\varepsilon) \neq F_{Y|X}(\cdot,\cdot;\,m,h,F_\varepsilon)$. It follows that h and $\tilde{h}$ are not observationally equivalent. □

This result implies that if one restricts h^* to belong to a set of functions such that no two functions in the set are strictly increasing transformations of each other, then in that set h^* is identified. Matzkin (1994) describes several such sets of functions. [See also Section 4.4.]

3.5. *Identification in simultaneous equations models*

Consider the simultaneous equations model, described in Section 2.2.1.5, where $Y \in R^G$ denotes a vector of observable dependent variables, $X \in R^K$ denotes a vector of observable explanatory variables, $\varepsilon \in R^L$ denotes a vector of unobservable explanatory variables, and the relationship between these vectors is specified by a function $r^*: R^G \times R^K \to R^L$ such that

$$\varepsilon = r^*(Y,X).$$

The set S consisted of vectors of twice differentiable functions $r: R^G \times R^K \to R^G$ and twice differentiable, strictly increasing distributions $F_{\varepsilon,X}: R^G \times R^K \to R$ such that (i) for all $F_{\varepsilon,X}$, ε and X are distributed independently of each other, (ii) for all r and all y,x, $|\partial r(y,x)/\partial y| > 0$, (iii) for all r and all x,ε, there exists a unique value of y such that $\varepsilon = r(y,x)$, and (iv) for all r, all $F_{\varepsilon,X}$, and all x, the distribution of Y given $X=x$, induced by r and $F_{\varepsilon|X=x}$ has support R^G.

For any $(r,F_{\varepsilon,X}) \in S$, condition (iii) implies that there exists a function h such that for all ε, X,

$$Y = h(X,\varepsilon).$$

This is the reduced form system of the structural equations system determined by r. We will let h^* denote the reduced form function determined by r^*.

A special case of this model is the linear system of simultaneous equations, where for some invertible, $G \times G$ matrix A and some $G \times K$ matrix B,

$$\varepsilon = AY + BX.$$

Premultiplication by $(A)^{-1}$ yields the reduced form system

$$Y = \Pi X + \nu$$

where $\Pi = -(A)^{-1}B$ and $\nu = (A)^{-1}\varepsilon$. The identification of the true values, A^*, B^*, of the matrices A and B, and the distribution of ε has been the object of study in the works by Koopmans (1949), Koopmans, Rubin and Leipnik (1950), and Fisher (1966), among others, and it is treated in most econometrics textbooks. The chapters by Hausman (1983) and Hsiao (1983) present the main known results. Assume that $E(\varepsilon) = 0$, and $\text{Var}(\varepsilon) = \Sigma^*$, an unknown matrix. Let W denote the variance of ν. Π and W can be identified from the distribution of the observable variables (Y, X). The identification of any element of (A^*, B^*, Σ^*) is achieved when it can be uniquely recovered from Π and $\text{Var}(\nu)$. A priori restrictions on A^*, B^*, and Σ^* are typically used to determine the existence of a unique solution for any element of (A^*, B^*, Σ^*). [See Fisher (1966).]

In an analogous way, one can obtain necessary and sufficient conditions to uniquely recover r^* and F^*_ε from the distribution of the observable variables (Y, X), when the system of structural equations is nonparametric. The question of identification is whether we can uniquely recover the density f^*_ε and the function r^* from the conditional densities $f_{Y|X=x}$.

Following the definition of observational equivalence, we can state that two functions $r, \tilde{r}$ satisfying the assumptions of the model are observationally equivalent iff there exist $f_\varepsilon, \tilde{f}_\varepsilon$ such that $(f_\varepsilon, r), (\tilde{f}_\varepsilon, \tilde{r}) \in S$ and for all y, x

$$f_{\tilde{\varepsilon}}\big(\tilde{r}(y, x)\big)\left|\frac{\partial \tilde{r}(y, x)}{\partial y}\right| = f_\varepsilon\big(r(y, x)\big)\left|\frac{\partial r(y, x)}{\partial y}\right|. \tag{3.5.1}$$

The function $\tilde{r}$ can be expressed as a transformation of (ε, x). To see this, define

$$g(\varepsilon, x) = \tilde{r}\big(h(x, \varepsilon), x\big).$$

Since

$$\left|\frac{\partial g(\varepsilon, x)}{\partial \varepsilon}\right| = \left|\frac{\partial \tilde{r}(h(x, \varepsilon), x)}{\partial y}\right|\left|\frac{\partial h(x, \varepsilon)}{\partial \varepsilon}\right|$$

it follows that $|\partial g(\varepsilon, x)/\partial \varepsilon| > 0$. Let $\tilde{\varepsilon} = \tilde{r}(y, x)$. Since, conditional on x, h is invertible in ε and $\tilde{r}$ is invertible in y, it follows that g is invertible in ε. Substituting in (3.5.1), we get that $(\tilde{r}, f_{\tilde{\varepsilon}}) \in S$ is observationally equivalent to $(r, f_\varepsilon) \in S$ iff for all ε, x

$$f_{\tilde{\varepsilon}}\big(g(\varepsilon, x)\big)\left|\frac{\partial g(\varepsilon, x)}{\partial \varepsilon}\right| = f_\varepsilon(\varepsilon).$$

The following theorem provides conditions guaranteeing that a transformation g of ε does not generate an observable equivalent pair $(\tilde{r}, f_{\tilde{\varepsilon}}) \in S$ of a pair $(r, f_\varepsilon) \in S$.

THEOREM 3.3. *[See Matzkin (2005b).] Let $(r, f_\varepsilon) \in S$. Let $g(\varepsilon, x)$ be such that $\tilde{r}(y, x) = g(r(y, x), x)$ and $\tilde{\varepsilon} = g(\varepsilon, x)$ are such that $(\tilde{r}, f_{\tilde{\varepsilon}}) \in S$, where $f_{\tilde{\varepsilon}}$ denotes the marginal density of $\tilde{\varepsilon}$, If for some ε, x, the rank of the matrix*

$$\begin{pmatrix} (\frac{\partial g(\varepsilon,x)}{\partial \varepsilon})' & \frac{\partial \log f_{\tilde{\varepsilon}}(u)}{\partial \varepsilon} - \frac{\partial \log |\frac{\partial g(\varepsilon,x)}{\partial \varepsilon}|}{\partial \varepsilon} \\ (\frac{\partial g(\varepsilon,x)}{\partial x})' & -\frac{\partial \log |\frac{\partial g(\varepsilon,x)}{\partial \varepsilon}|}{\partial x} \end{pmatrix}$$

is strictly larger than G, then, $(\tilde{r}, f_{\tilde{\varepsilon}})$ is not observationally equivalent to (r, f_ε).

Alternatively, we can express an identification theorem for the function r^*.

THEOREM 3.4. *[See Matzkin (2005b).] Let $M \times \Gamma$ denote the set of pairs $(r, f_\varepsilon) \in S$. The function r^* is identified in M if $r^* \in M$ and for all $f_\varepsilon \in \Gamma$ and all $\tilde{r}, r \in M$ such that $\tilde{r} \neq r$, there exist y, x such that the rank of the matrix*

$$\begin{pmatrix} (\frac{\partial \tilde{r}(y,x)}{\partial y})' & \Delta_y(y, x; \partial r, \partial^2 r, \partial \tilde{r}, \partial^2 \tilde{r}) - \frac{\partial \log(f_\varepsilon(r(y,x)))}{\partial \varepsilon} \frac{\partial r(y,x)}{\partial y} \\ (\frac{\partial \tilde{r}(y,x)}{\partial x})' & \Delta_x(y, x; \partial r, \partial^2 r, \partial \tilde{r}, \partial^2 \tilde{r}) - \frac{\partial \log(f_\varepsilon(r(y,x)))}{\partial \varepsilon} \frac{\partial r(y,x)}{\partial x} \end{pmatrix}$$

is strictly larger than G, where

$$\Delta_y\big(y, x; \partial r, \partial^2 r, \partial \tilde{r}, \partial^2 \tilde{r}\big) = \frac{\partial}{\partial y} \log\left|\frac{\partial r(y, x)}{\partial y}\right| - \frac{\partial}{\partial y} \log\left|\frac{\partial \tilde{r}(y, x)}{\partial y}\right|,$$

$$\Delta_x\big(y, x; \partial r, \partial^2 r, \partial \tilde{r}, \partial^2 \tilde{r}\big) = \frac{\partial}{\partial x} \log\left|\frac{\partial r(y, x)}{\partial y}\right| - \frac{\partial}{\partial x} \log\left|\frac{\partial \tilde{r}(y, x)}{\partial y}\right|.$$

EXAMPLE 3.1. As a very simple example, consider the simultaneous equations model, analyzed in Matzkin (2007c), where for some unknown function, g^*, and some parameter values β^*, γ^*,

$$y_1 = g^*(y_2) + \varepsilon_1,$$
$$y_2 = \beta^* y_1 + \gamma^* x + \varepsilon_2.$$

Assume that $(\varepsilon_1, \varepsilon_2)$ has an everywhere positive, differentiable density $f^*_{\varepsilon_1,\varepsilon_2}$ such that for two, not necessarily known a priori, values $(\bar{\varepsilon}_1, \bar{\varepsilon}_2)$ and $(\varepsilon_1'', \varepsilon_2'')$,

$$\frac{\partial \log f^*_{\varepsilon_1,\varepsilon_2}(\bar{\varepsilon}_1, \bar{\varepsilon}_2)}{\partial \varepsilon_1} \neq \frac{\partial \log f^*_{\varepsilon_1,\varepsilon_2}(\varepsilon_1'', \varepsilon_2'')}{\partial \varepsilon_1}$$

and

$$\frac{\partial \log f^*_{\varepsilon_1,\varepsilon_2}(\bar{\varepsilon}_1, \bar{\varepsilon}_2)}{\partial \varepsilon_2} = \frac{\partial \log f^*_{\varepsilon_1,\varepsilon_2}(\varepsilon_1'', \varepsilon_2'')}{\partial \varepsilon_2} = 0.$$

The observable exogenous variable x is assumed to be distributed independently of $(\varepsilon_1, \varepsilon_2)$ and to possess support R. In this model

$$\varepsilon_1 = r_1^*(y_1, y_2, x) = y_1 - g^*(y_2),$$
$$\varepsilon_2 = r_2^*(y_1, y_2, x) = -\beta^* y_1 + y_2 - \gamma^* x.$$

The Jacobian determinant is

$$\left|\begin{pmatrix} 1 & -\frac{\partial g^*(y_2)}{\partial y_2} \\ -\beta^* & 1 \end{pmatrix}\right| = 1 - \beta^* \frac{\partial g^*(y_2)}{\partial y_2}$$

which will be positive as long as $1 > \beta^* \partial g^*(y_2)/\partial y_2$. Since the first element in the diagonal is positive, it follows by Gale and Nikaido (1965) that the function r^* is globally invertible if the condition $1 > \beta^* \partial g^*(y_2)/\partial y_2$ holds for every y_2. Let $r, \tilde{r}$ be any two differentiable functions satisfying this condition and the other properties assumed about r^*. Suppose that at some y_2, either $\partial \tilde{g}(y_2)/\partial y_2 \neq \partial g(y_2)/\partial y_2$ or $\partial \log(\tilde{g}(y_2))/\partial y_2 \neq \partial \log(g(y_2))/\partial y_2$. Assume also that $\gamma \neq 0$ and $\tilde{\gamma} \neq 0$. Let $f_{\varepsilon_1,\varepsilon_2}$ denote any density satisfying the same properties that $f^*_{\varepsilon_1,\varepsilon_2}$ is assumed to satisfy. Denote by $(\varepsilon_1, \varepsilon_2)$ and $(\varepsilon_1', \varepsilon_2')$ the two points such that

$$\frac{\partial \log f_{\varepsilon_1,\varepsilon_2}(\varepsilon_1, \varepsilon_2)}{\partial \varepsilon_1} \neq \frac{\partial \log f_{\varepsilon_1,\varepsilon_2}(\varepsilon_1', \varepsilon_2')}{\partial \varepsilon_1}$$

and

$$\frac{\partial \log f_{\varepsilon_1,\varepsilon_2}(\varepsilon_1, \varepsilon_2)}{\partial \varepsilon_2} = \frac{\partial \log f_{\varepsilon_1,\varepsilon_2}(\varepsilon_1', \varepsilon_2')}{\partial \varepsilon_2} = 0.$$

Define

$$\begin{aligned} a_1(y_1, y_2, x) &= \frac{\partial \log f_{\varepsilon_1,\varepsilon_2}(y_1 - g(y_2), -\beta y_1 + y_2 - \gamma x)}{\partial \varepsilon_1} \\ &\quad - \beta^* \frac{\partial \log f_{\varepsilon_1,\varepsilon_2}(y_1 - g(y_2), -\beta y_1 + y_2 - \gamma x)}{\partial \varepsilon_2}, \\ a_2(y_1, y_2, x) &= \left(\frac{\partial \log \tilde{g}(y_2)}{\partial y_2} - \frac{\partial \log g(y_2)}{\partial y_2}\right) \\ &\quad + \left(\frac{\partial g(y_2)}{\partial y_2}\right)\left(\frac{\partial \log f_{\varepsilon_1,\varepsilon_2}(y_1 - g(y_2), -\beta y_1 + y_2 - \gamma x)}{\partial \varepsilon_1}\right) \\ &\quad - \frac{\partial \log f_{\varepsilon_1,\varepsilon_2}(y_1 - g(y_2), -\beta y_1 + y_2 - \gamma x)}{\partial \varepsilon_2} \end{aligned}$$

and

$$a_3(y_1, y_2, x) = -\gamma \frac{\partial \log f_{\varepsilon_1,\varepsilon_2}(y_1 - g(y_2), -\beta y_1 + y_2 - \gamma x)}{\partial \varepsilon_2}.$$

By Theorem 3.4, r and $\tilde{r}$ will not be observationally equivalent if for all $f_{\varepsilon_1,\varepsilon_2}$ there exists (y_1, x) such that the rank of the matrix

$$A = \begin{pmatrix} 1 & -\tilde{\beta} & a_1(y_1, y_2, x) \\ -\frac{\partial \tilde{g}(y_2)}{\partial y_2} & 1 & a_2(y_1, y_2, x) \\ 0 & -\tilde{\gamma} & a_3(y_1, y_2, x) \end{pmatrix}$$

is 3. Let

$$a_1'(y_1, y_2, x) = (\tilde{\beta} - \beta)\frac{\partial \log f_{\varepsilon_1,\varepsilon_2}(y_1 - g(y_2), -\beta y_1 + y_2 - \gamma x)}{\partial \varepsilon_2},$$

$$\begin{aligned} a_2'(y_1, y_2, x) &\\ &= \left(\frac{\partial \log \tilde{g}(y_2)}{\partial y_2} - \frac{\partial \log g(y_2)}{\partial y_2}\right) \\ &\quad + \left(\frac{\partial \tilde{g}(y_2)}{\partial y_2} - \frac{\partial g(y_2)}{\partial y_2}\right)\left(\frac{\partial \log f_{\varepsilon_1,\varepsilon_2}(y_1 - g(y_2), -\beta y_1 + y_2 - \gamma x)}{\partial \varepsilon_1}\right) \end{aligned}$$

and

$$a_3'(y_1, y_2, x) = -\gamma\frac{\partial \log f_{\varepsilon_1,\varepsilon_2}(y_1 - g(y_2), -\beta y_1 + y_2 - \gamma x)}{\partial \varepsilon_2}.$$

Multiplying the first column of A by $-\partial \log f_{\varepsilon_1,\varepsilon_2}(y_1 - g(y_2), -\beta y_1 + y_2 - \gamma x)/\partial \varepsilon_1$ and adding it to the third column, and multiplying the second column by $-\partial \log f_{\varepsilon_1,\varepsilon_2}(y_1 - g(y_2), -\beta y_1 + y_2 - \gamma x)/\partial \varepsilon_2$ and adding it to the third column, we obtain the matrix

$$\begin{pmatrix} 1 & -\tilde{\beta} & a_1'(y_1, y_2, x) \\ -\frac{\partial \tilde{g}(y_2)}{\partial y_2} & 1 & a_2'(y_1, y_2, x) \\ 0 & -\tilde{\gamma} & a_3'(y_1, y_2, x) \end{pmatrix}$$

which has the same rank as A. By assumption, either

$$\left(\frac{\partial \log \tilde{g}(y_2)}{\partial y_2} - \frac{\partial \log g(y_2)}{\partial y_2}\right) + \left(\frac{\partial \tilde{g}(y_2)}{\partial y_2} - \frac{\partial g(y_2)}{\partial y_2}\right)\left(\frac{\partial \log f_{\varepsilon_1,\varepsilon_2}(\varepsilon_1, \varepsilon_2)}{\partial \varepsilon_1}\right) \neq 0$$

or

$$\left(\frac{\partial \log \tilde{g}(y_2)}{\partial y_2} - \frac{\partial \log g(y_2)}{\partial y_2}\right) + \left(\frac{\partial \tilde{g}(y_2)}{\partial y_2} - \frac{\partial g(y_2)}{\partial y_2}\right)\left(\frac{\partial \log f_{\varepsilon_1,\varepsilon_2}(\varepsilon_1', \varepsilon_2')}{\partial \varepsilon_1}\right) \neq 0.$$

Suppose the latter. Let $y_1 = g(y_2) + \varepsilon_1'$ and let $x = (-\beta y_1 + y_2 - \varepsilon_2')/\gamma$. It then follows that

$$\frac{\partial \log f_{\varepsilon_1,\varepsilon_2}(y_1 - g(y_2), -\beta y_1 + y_2 - \gamma x)}{\partial \varepsilon_2} = 0.$$

At such y_1, x, the above matrix becomes the rank 3 matrix

$$\begin{pmatrix} 1 & -\tilde{\beta} & 0 \\ -\frac{\partial \tilde{g}(y_2)}{\partial y_2} & 1 & a_2'(y_1, y_2, x) \\ 0 & -\tilde{\gamma} & 0 \end{pmatrix}.$$

Hence, derivatives of g^* and of the log of g^* are identified.

EXAMPLE 3.2. A similar example provides sufficient conditions for the identification of a utility function and its distribution, in a multidimensional version of the utility maximization problem described in Section 2. Let the utility function U^* for products $1, \dots, G+1$, for a consumer with unobservable tastes $\varepsilon_1, \dots, \varepsilon_G$, be specified as

$$U^*(y_1, \dots, y_{G+1}, \varepsilon_1, \dots, \varepsilon_G) = v^*(y_1, \dots, y_G) + \sum_{g=1}^{G} \varepsilon_g y_g + y_{G+1}$$

where v^* is a strictly monotone, strictly concave, twice differentiable function and where $\varepsilon = (\varepsilon_1, \dots, \varepsilon_G)$ is distributed independently of (p, I) with a differentiable density that has known convex support. [This utility specification was studied in Brown and Calsamiglia (2004) in their development of tests for utility maximization; it is a slight modification of the specification used in Brown and Matzkin (1998) to analyze the identification of a distribution of utility functions from the distribution of demand.] Normalize the price of the $(G+1)$th commodity to equal 1. Maximization of U^* with respect to $(y_1, \dots, y_{G+1})$ subject to the budget constraint $\sum_{g=1}^{G} p_g y_g + y_{G=1} = I$ yields the first order conditions

$$\varepsilon_g = p_g - \partial v^*(y_1, \dots, y_G)/\partial y_g, \quad g = 1, \dots, G,$$

$$y_{G+1} = I - \sum_{g=1}^{G} p_g y_g.$$

Let $Dv^*(y)$ and $D^2 v^*(y)$ denote, respectively, the gradient and Hessian of v^* at $y = (y_1, \dots, y_G)$. The first set of G equations represent a system of simultaneous equations with observable endogenous variables $(y_1, \dots, y_G)$ and observable exogenous variables $(p_1, \dots, p_G)$. The strict concavity of v^* guaranties that for any $(p_1, \dots, p_G)$ and $(\varepsilon_1, \dots, \varepsilon_G)$, a unique solution for $(y_1, \dots, y_G)$ exists. Let W denote the set of functions v satisfying the same restrictions that v^* is assumed to satisfy. Let $\bar{\varepsilon}$ denote a given value of the vector ε. Let Γ denote the set of all densities f_ε of ε such that (i) f_ε is differentiable, (ii) $f_\varepsilon(\varepsilon) > 0$ on a neighborhood of radius δ around $\bar{\varepsilon}$, (iii) for all ε in the support of f_ε, $\partial \log(f_\varepsilon(\varepsilon))\partial\varepsilon = 0$ iff $\varepsilon = \bar{\varepsilon}$, (iv) for all g, there exist two distinct values, ε' and ε'', in the δ-neighborhood of $\bar{\varepsilon}$ such that $f_\varepsilon(\varepsilon'), f_\varepsilon(\varepsilon'') > 0$, $0 \neq \partial \log(f_\varepsilon(\varepsilon'))/\partial\varepsilon_g \neq \partial \log(f_\varepsilon(\varepsilon''))/\partial\varepsilon_g \neq 0$, and for $j \neq g$, $\partial \log(f_\varepsilon(\varepsilon'))/\partial\varepsilon_j = \partial \log(f_\varepsilon(\varepsilon''))/\partial\varepsilon_j = 0$. Suppose that W and the support of p is such for all y, for all $v \in W$, there exists a set of prices, Q, such that the density of p is uniformly bounded away from zero on Q and the range of $Dv(y) - p$, when considered as a function of p over Q, is the δ neighborhood of $\bar{\varepsilon}$. Then, if $v, \tilde{v}$ belong to W and $D\tilde{v} \neq Dv$, there exist, for all $f_\varepsilon \in \Gamma$, values y, p such that the rank of the corresponding matrix in Theorem 3.4 is larger than G. [See Matzkin (2007a).]

3.6. *Identification in discrete choice models*

Consider the discrete choice model described in Section 2.2.1.6, where a typical individual has to choose between $G+1$ alternatives. Let $V_g(s, z_g, \omega)$ denote the utility for alternative g, where s denotes a vector of observable characteristics of the consumer, z_g denotes a vector of observable attributes of alternative g, and ω is an unobservable random vector. The vector of observable dependent variables is $y = (y_1, \ldots, y_{G+1})$ defined by

$$y_g = \begin{cases} 1 & \text{if } V_g(s, z_g, \omega) > V_k(s, z_g, \omega) \text{ for all } k \neq g, \\ 0 & \text{otherwise.} \end{cases}$$

Let z denote the vector $(z_1, \ldots, z_{G+1})$. The conditional choice probability, for each $g = 1, \ldots, G+1$ is

$$\Pr(\{y_g = 1|s, z\}) = \Pr(\{\omega \mid V_g(s, z_g, \omega) > V_k(s, z_k, \omega) \text{ for all } k \neq g\}).$$

Since the choice probabilities of each alternative depend only on the differences between the utilities of the alternatives, only those differences can be identified. Hence, for simplicity, we may specify $V_{G+1}(s, z_{G+1}, \omega)$ equal to 0 for all (s, z_{G+1}, ω). Then,

$$\Pr(\{y_{G+1} = 1|s, z\}) = \Pr(\{\omega \mid 0 > V_k(s, z_k, \omega) \text{ for all } k \neq G+1\}).$$

[We assume that the probability of ties is zero.]

3.6.1. Subutilities additive in the unobservables

The simplest case to analyze is when $\omega = (\omega_1, \ldots, \omega_G)$, each V_g depends only on one coordinate, ω_g of ω, and ω_g is additive:

$$V_g(s, z_g, \omega) = v_g(s, z_g) + \omega_g$$

where v_g is a nonparametric function. [Matzkin (1991a) studies identification in this model when the distribution of ω is specified parametrically. Matzkin (1992, 1993, 1994) extends some of those results for the case of nonparametric distributions.] Under the additivity assumption:

$$\Pr(\{y_{G+1} = 1|s, z\}) = F_{\omega_1,\ldots,\omega_G}(-v_1(s, z_1), \ldots, -v_G(s, z_G))$$

where $F_{\omega_1,\ldots,\omega_G}$ is the unknown distribution of $(\omega_1, \ldots, \omega_G)$. This is of the form of a multiple index model, and it could therefore be analyzed using techniques for those models.

Assume, for example, that each of the z_g vectors includes a coordinate $z_g^{(1)}$ which is such that

$$v_g(s, z_g^{(1)}, z_g^{(2)}) = z_g^{(1)} + m_g(s, z_g^{(2)})$$

where $z_g = (z_g^{(1)}, z_g^{(2)})$ and m_g is a nonparametric function. Then,

$$\Pr(\{y_{G+1} = 1|s, z\}) = F_{\omega_1,\ldots,\omega_G}(-z_1^{(1)} - m_1(s, z_1^{(2)}), \ldots, -z_G^{(1)} - m_G(s, z_G^{(2)})).$$

Assume that $(\omega_1, \ldots, \omega_G)$ is distributed independently of $(s, z_1, \ldots, z_G)$. Let $(\bar{s}, \bar{z}^{(2)}) = (\bar{s}, \bar{z}_1^{(2)}, \ldots, \bar{z}_G^{(2)})$ denote a particular value of $(s, z^{(2)})$. Assume that

$z^{(1)} = (z_1^{(1)}, \ldots, z_G^{(1)}) \in R^G$ possesses an everywhere positive density on R^G, conditional on $(\bar{s}, \bar{z}^{(2)}) = (\bar{s}, \bar{z}_1^{(2)}, \ldots, \bar{z}_G^{(2)})$. Let $\alpha_g \in R$ and specify that for $g = 1, \ldots, G$

$$m_g(\bar{s}, \bar{z}_g^{(2)}) = \alpha_g.$$

Then,

$$\Pr(\{y_{G+1} = 1 | \bar{s}, z^{(1)}, \bar{z}^{(2)}\}) = F_{\omega_1,\ldots,\omega_G}(-z_g^{(1)} - \alpha_g, \ldots, -z_g^{(1)} - \alpha_G),$$

which shows that $F_{\omega_1,\ldots,\omega_G}$ can be recovered from the choice probabilities, evaluated at appropriate values of $(s, z^{(1)}, z^{(2)})$.

In an influential paper, Lewbel (2000) shows that the requirement that $(\omega_1, \ldots, \omega_G)$ be independent of (s, z) is not needed for identification of $F_{\omega_1,\ldots,\omega_G}$. It suffices that $(\omega_1, \ldots, \omega_G)$ be independent of $z^{(1)}$ conditional on $(s, z^{(2)})$, in addition to the large support condition on $z^{(1)}$. Since the work of Lewbel (2000), the vector $z^{(1)}$ has been called a "special regressor". Its identification force has been extended to many models other than discrete choice models.

3.6.2. *Subutilities nonadditive in the unobservables*

Applying Lewbel's special regressor technique, one can analyze models with nonadditive unobservables, as described in Matzkin (2005b). Suppose that each V_g is specified as

$$V_g(s, z_g^{(1)}, z_g^{(2)}, \omega) = z_g^{(1)} + v_g(s, z_g^{(2)}, \omega)$$

where v_g is a nonparametric function. Assume that ω is distributed independently of (s, z). Define Υ_g for each g by

$$\Upsilon_g = v_g(s, z_g^{(2)}, \omega).$$

Since ω is distributed independently of (s, z), $(\Upsilon_1, \ldots, \Upsilon_G)$ is distributed independently of $z^{(1)}$, conditional on $(s, z^{(2)})$. Hence, using the arguments in Lewbel (2000), one can recover the distribution of $(\Upsilon_1, \ldots, \Upsilon_G)$ given $(s, z^{(2)})$. From this distribution, one can identify the functions $v_1, \ldots, v_G$ and the distribution of $(\omega_1, \ldots, \omega_G)$ in the system

$$\begin{aligned}
\Upsilon_1 &= v_1(s, z_1^{(2)}, \omega_1, \ldots, \omega_G), \\
\Upsilon_2 &= v_2(s, z_2^{(2)}, \omega_1, \ldots, \omega_G), \\
&\vdots \\
\Upsilon_G &= v_G(s, z_G^{(2)}, \omega_1, \ldots, \omega_G)
\end{aligned}$$

using the results in Matzkin (2005a, 2005b). In particular, assume that, given $(s, z^{(2)})$, the system of functions $(v_1, \ldots, v_G)$ is invertible in ω. Then, it can be equivalently expressed as

$$\omega = r(\Upsilon, s, z^{(2)})$$

where ω is the vector $(\omega_1, \ldots, \omega_G)'$ and $\Upsilon = (\Upsilon_1, \ldots, \Upsilon_G)$. This has the same structure as considered in the previous sections. [See Matzkin (2007a) for more detail.] Unobservable vectors of dimension larger than G can be dealt with making use of additional functional restrictions and conditional independence assumptions. [See the Appendix in Matzkin (2003).]

4. Ways of achieving identification

When a feature of interest is not identified, one may proceed in different ways to achieve identification. One may augment the model, incorporating more observable variables. One may impose further restrictions on either the functions, or the distributions, or both. The analysis of observational equivalence together with economic theory can often be used to determine appropriate restrictions. In this section, we describe examples of some of the techniques that have been developed, following one or more of these approaches. The emphasis will be in showing how one can recover particular features, once objects such as conditional distributions and conditional expectations are identified.

4.1. Conditional independence

A common situation encountered in econometric models is where the unobservable variables affecting the value of an outcome variable are not distributed independently of the observed explanatory variables. Without additional information, identifying the causal effect of the observable explanatory variables on the outcome variable is typically not possible in such a situation. Usually, the additional information involves variables and restrictions guaranteeing some exogenous variation on the value of the explanatory variable. The leading procedures to achieve this are based on conditional independence methods and instrumental variable methods. In the first set of procedures, independence between the unobservable and observable explanatory variables in a model is achieved after conditioning on some event, some function, or some value of an external variable or function. The second set of procedures usually derives identification from an independence condition between the unobservable and an external variable (an instrument) or function. In this subsection, we will deal with conditional independence. In Section 4.2, we will deal with instrumental variables.

4.1.1. Identification of functions and distributions in a nonadditive model using conditional independence

Consider the nonadditive model

$$Y_1 = m_1(X, \varepsilon_1)$$

where ε and X are not independently distributed and m is strictly increasing in ε. A standard example [see Chesher (2003) and Imbens and Newey (2003)] is where Y_1 denotes earnings, X denotes years of education, and ε denotes the effect of unobservable explanatory variables, which includes unobserved ability. Since X is determined as a function of ε, these variables are not independently distributed. Suppose, however, that some variable W is available, such that for some function m_2 and some ε_2,

$$X = m_2(W, \varepsilon_2).$$

Denoting X by Y_2, the system of the two above equations is a triangular system. Imbens and Newey (2003) developed identification results for this system when W is observable and independent of $(\varepsilon_1, \varepsilon_2)$. Chesher (2003) considered local independence conditions for identification of local derivatives. Matzkin (2004) studied identification when ε_1 and ε_2 are independent, conditional on either a particular value or all possible values of W. [A footnote in Chesher (2003) also discusses independence restrictions on the unobservables as a source of identification.] When W is independent of $(\varepsilon_1, \varepsilon_2)$, independence between ε_1 and X can be determined conditional on the unobservable ε_2. When ε_1 and ε_2 are independent conditional on W, independence between ε_1 and X can be determined conditional on the observable W. The following theorem, in Matzkin (2004), provides insight into the sources of identification.

THEOREM 4.1 *(Equivalence Theorem). [See Matzkin (2004).] Consider the model* $Y_1 = m_1(X, \varepsilon_1)$. *Suppose that* m_1 *is strictly increasing in* ε_1, *and that for all values* w *of* W, *the conditional distribution,* $F_{X,\varepsilon|W=w}$, *of* (X, ε) *given* $W = w$ *is strictly increasing. Then, the following statements are equivalent*:

(i) *There exists a strictly increasing function* $m_2(W, \cdot)$ *and an unobservable random term* ε_2 *such that*

$$X = m_2(W, \varepsilon_2) \quad \text{and}$$
$$\varepsilon_2 \text{ is independent of } (W, \varepsilon_1).$$

(ii) *There exists a strictly increasing function* $r(W, \cdot)$ *and an unobservable random term* δ *such that*

$$\varepsilon_1 = r(W, \delta),$$
$$\delta \text{ is independent of } (X, W).$$

(iii) ε_1 *is independent of* X, *conditional on* W.

Consider the nonadditive model

$$Y_1 = m_1(X, \varepsilon_1).$$

To be able to identify m_1, we need to observe independent variation in each coordinate of m. The theorem considers three different representations of the model:

$$\begin{aligned} Y &= m_1\big(m_2(W, \varepsilon_2), \varepsilon_1\big) \\ &= m_1\big(m_2(W, \varepsilon_2), r(W, \delta)\big) \\ &= m_1\big(X, r(W, \delta)\big). \end{aligned}$$

From the first expression, it follows that if ε_1 and ε_2 are independent conditional on at least one value $\bar{w}$ of W, then we will be able to observe events where, conditional on W, each coordinate of m_1 achieves values independently of the other coordinates of m_1. From the third expression, it follows that if δ is independent of X conditional on at least one value $\bar{w}$ of W, then, again each coordinate of m_1 will achieve values independently of the other coordinates of m_1, when conditioning on at least one value of W. The second expression provides the same result, when we can establish that δ and ε_2 are independent, conditional on at least one value $\bar{w}$ of W. The equivalence theorem above states that as long as we show that the conditions for one of these representations are satisfied, then the conditions for the other representations also hold. The above theorem also holds when W is unobservable, ε_2 is observable, and ε_2 is distributed independently of (ε_1, W). In such a case, that (i) implies (iii) is shown in Imbens and Newey (2003) as follows: The restriction that ε_2 is independent of (W, ε_1) implies that, conditional on W, ε_2 and ε_1 are independent. Since conditional on W, X is a function of ε_2, and ε_2 is independent of ε_1, if follows that conditional on W, X is independent of ε_1.

The local condition, that conditional on $W = \bar{w}$, ε_1 and ε_2 are independent, can be shown to imply, under some additional assumptions, that m_1 and the distribution of (X, ε_1) can both be identified, up to a normalization on the distribution of ε_1 given $W = \bar{w}$. In particular, Matzkin (2004) shows that if m_1 is strictly increasing in ε_1, $F_{\varepsilon_1, X|W=\bar{w}}$ is strictly increasing in (ε_1, X), for each x, $F_{\varepsilon_1|(X,W)=(x,\bar{w})}$ is strictly increasing in ε_1, and if there exists a function m_2 and an unobservable ε_2 such that $X = m_2(W, \varepsilon_2)$, m_2 is strictly increasing in ε_2 when $W = \bar{w}$, and ε_1 is independent of ε_1 conditional on $W = \bar{w}$, then for all x, e

$$\text{(4.a)}\quad m(x,e) = F^{-1}_{Y|(X,W)=(x,\bar{w})}\big(F_{\varepsilon_1|W=\bar{w}}(e)\big) \quad \text{and}$$

$$F_{\varepsilon_1|X=x}(e) = F_{Y|X=x}\Big(F^{-1}_{Y|(X,W)=(x,\bar{w})}\big(F_{\varepsilon_1|W=\bar{w}}(e)\big)\Big).$$

Matzkin (2004) describes several examples where economic theory implies the conditional exogeneity of the unobservable ε_2, for particular variables W.

PROOF OF (4.a). Let x be given and let e_2 denote the value of ε_2 such that $x = m_2(\bar{w}, e_2)$. By conditional independence and strict monotonicity

$$\begin{aligned}\Pr(\varepsilon_1 \leqslant e|W=\bar{w}) &= \Pr(\varepsilon_1 \leqslant e|\varepsilon_2 = e_2,\ W=\bar{w}) \\ &= \Pr\big(m_1(X,\varepsilon_1) \leqslant m_1(x,e)\big|X = m_1(\bar{w}, e_2),\ W=\bar{w}\big) \\ &= F_{Y_1|X=x,\ W=\bar{w}}\big(m_1(x,e)\big).\end{aligned}$$

Hence,

$$m_1(x,e) = F^{-1}_{Y_1|X=x,\ W=\bar{w}}\big(F_{\varepsilon_1|W=\bar{w}}(e)\big).$$

Since

$$F_{\varepsilon_1|X=x} = F_{Y|X=x}\big(m_1(x,e)\big)$$

it follows that

$$F_{\varepsilon_1|X=x} = F_{Y|X=x}\big(F^{-1}_{Y_1|X=x,\, W=\bar{w}}\big(F_{\varepsilon_1|W=\bar{w}}(e)\big)\big). \qquad \square$$

As with the case where X and ε_1 are independently distributed, identification of derivatives of m_1 with respect to X does not require additional normalizations. Altonji and Matzkin (2001) present the following result [see also Altonji and Ichimura (2000)].

4.1.2. *Identification of average derivatives in a nonadditive model using conditional independence*

Consider the nonseparable model

$$Y = m(X, \varepsilon_1, \ldots, \varepsilon_J)$$

where no particular assumptions are made regarding monotonicity of m. Let $\varepsilon = (\varepsilon_1, \ldots, \varepsilon_J)$. Assume that m and the density $f_{\varepsilon|X}$ are differentiable with respect to X in a neighborhood of a value x of X, that $f_{\varepsilon|X}$ is everywhere positive in ε and the marginal density f_X is strictly positive on a neighborhood of x. Assuming that the integral and all the terms inside the integral exist, suppose that we wanted to recover the average derivative

$$\beta(x) = \int \frac{\partial m(x, \varepsilon)}{\partial x} f_{\varepsilon|X=x}(e)\, de$$

using a conditioning vector of variables W. Altonji and Matzkin (2001, 2005) show that if ε is independent of X conditional on W, then

(4.b) *$\beta(x)$ can be recovered from the distribution of the observable variables.*

PROOF OF (4.b). Since for all e, x, w,

$$f_{\varepsilon|W=w,\, X=x}(e) = f_{\varepsilon|W=w}(e)$$

one has that

$$\frac{\partial f_{\varepsilon|W=w, X=x}(e)}{\partial x} = 0.$$

Let $E[Y|W = w,\ X = x]$ denote the conditional expectation of Y given $(W = w,\ X = x)$. Then,

$$\begin{aligned}
&\int \frac{\partial E[Y|W = w,\ X = x]}{\partial x} f_{W|X=x}(w)\, dw \\
&\quad = \int \frac{\partial}{\partial x} \int m(x, \varepsilon) f_{\varepsilon|W=w,\, X=x}(\varepsilon) \frac{f_{W,X}(w, x)}{f_X(x)}\, dw \\
&\quad = \int \left[\frac{\partial}{\partial x} \int m(x, \varepsilon) f_{\varepsilon|W=w,\, X=x}(\varepsilon)\, d\varepsilon\right] \frac{f_{W,X}(w, x)}{f_X(x)}\, dw
\end{aligned}$$

$$
\begin{aligned}
&= \int \left[\int \frac{\partial m(x,\varepsilon)}{\partial x} f_{\varepsilon|W=w,\,X=x}(\varepsilon)\, d\varepsilon \right.\\
&\quad \left. + \int m(x,\varepsilon) \frac{\partial f_{\varepsilon|W=w,\,X=x}(\varepsilon)}{\partial x}\, d\varepsilon \right] \frac{f_{W,X}(w,x)}{f_X(x)}\, dw \\
&= \int \left[\int \frac{\partial m(x,\varepsilon)}{\partial x} f_{\varepsilon|W=w,\,X=x}(\varepsilon)\, d\varepsilon \right] \frac{f_{W,X}(w,x)}{f_X(x)}\, dw \\
&= \int \int \frac{\partial m(x,\varepsilon)}{\partial x} \frac{f_{\varepsilon,W,X}(\varepsilon,w,x)}{f_{W,X}(w,x)} \frac{f_{W,X}(w,x)}{f_X(x)}\, d\varepsilon\, dw \\
&= \int \int \frac{\partial m(x,\varepsilon)}{\partial x} \frac{f_{\varepsilon,W,X}(\varepsilon,w,x)}{f_X(x)}\, dw\, d\varepsilon \\
&= \int \frac{\partial m(x,\varepsilon)}{\partial x} \frac{f_{\varepsilon,X}(\varepsilon,x)}{f_X(x)}\, d\varepsilon \\
&= \int \frac{\partial m(x,\varepsilon)}{\partial x} f_{\varepsilon|X=x}(\varepsilon)\, d\varepsilon \\
&= \beta(x).
\end{aligned}
$$

Since $E[Y|W = w, X = x]$ and $f_{W|X}$ can be recovered from the distribution of (Y, W, X), $\beta(x)$ can also be recovered from it. □

Many other functions, average derivatives, and other functions can be derived and shown to be identified in the nonadditive model $Y_1 = m_1(X, \varepsilon_1)$. Blundell and Powell (2003) consider identification and estimation of the "average structural function", defined for $X = x$ as

$$G(x) = \int m_1(x, \varepsilon_1) f_{\varepsilon_1}(e)\, de.$$

Blundell and Powell (2003) assumed the existence of a random vector

$$\nu = v(y, x, w)$$

which is identified and estimable, and it is such that the distribution of ε_1 conditional on (X, W) is the same as the distribution of ε_1 conditional on (X, ν), which is the same as the distribution of ε_1 conditional on ν. The average structural function is then obtained from the distribution of (Y, X, ν) as

$$G(x) = \int E(Y|X, \nu) f_\nu(\nu)\, d\nu.$$

This follows because

$$
\begin{aligned}
G(x) &= \int m_1(x, \varepsilon_1) f_{\varepsilon_1}(e)\, de \\
&= \int \left[\int m_1(x, \varepsilon_1) f_{\varepsilon_1|\nu}(e)\, de \right] f_\nu(\nu)\, d\nu \\
&= \int \left[E(Y|X, \nu) \right] f_\nu(\nu)\, d\nu.
\end{aligned}
$$

Imbens and Newey (2003) consider identification of the "quantile structural function", defined for $\tau \in (0, 1)$ and all x as

$$m_1\big(x, q_{\varepsilon_1}(\tau)\big)$$

where $q_{\varepsilon_1}(\tau)$ is the τ-quantile of the distribution of ε_1. Letting ν be such that ε_1 is independent of X conditional on ν, they obtain the following expression for the inverse $m_1^{-1}(x, y)$ of m_1 with respect to $q_{\varepsilon_1}(\tau)$:

$$\begin{aligned} m_1^{-1}(x, y) &= \Pr\big(m_1\big(x, q_{\varepsilon_1}(\tau)\big) \leqslant y\big) \\ &= \int \Pr(Y \leqslant y|\nu) f_\nu(\nu)\, d\nu \\ &= \int \Pr(Y \leqslant y|X = x, \nu) f_\nu(\nu)\, d\nu. \end{aligned}$$

For the average derivative, Imbens and Newey (2003) use the fact that, under conditional independence

$$\begin{aligned} \delta &= E\left[\frac{\partial m_1(x, \varepsilon_1)}{\partial x}\right] \\ &= E\left[\int \frac{\partial m_1(x, \varepsilon_1)}{\partial x} f_{\varepsilon_1|X=x,\nu}(\varepsilon_1)\, d\varepsilon_1\right] \\ &= E\left[\int \frac{\partial m_1(x, \varepsilon_1)}{\partial x} f_{\varepsilon_1|X=x,\nu}(\varepsilon_1)\, d\varepsilon_1\right] \\ &= E\left[\frac{\partial}{\partial x} E(Y|X = x, \nu)\right]. \end{aligned}$$

4.2. *Marginal independence*

In many situations, such as in models with simultaneity, establishing conditional independence between the unobservable and observable explanatory variables that determine the value of an outcome variable may require undesirable strong assumptions [see Blundell and Matzkin (2007)]. A variable that is independent of the unobservable variables, and not independent of the observable variables may be used in such and other situations. In the model

$$Y = m(X, \varepsilon)$$

where X is not distributed independently of ε, an instrument is a variable, Z, that is distributed independently of ε and is not distributed independently of X.

4.2.1. *Instrumental variables in nonadditive models*

Chernozhukov and Hansen (2005), Chernozhukov, Imbens and Newey (2007), and Matzkin (2004, 2005b) consider identification of nonadditive models using instruments.

Chernozhukov, Imbens and Newey (2007)'s model is

$$Y = m(X, Z_1, \varepsilon)$$

where X is a vector of observable variables that is not distributed independently of ε, m is strictly increasing in ε, $Z = (Z_1, Z_2)$ is an observable vector that is distributed independently of ε, and the density of ε is everywhere positive. Since the distribution of ε and m are not jointly identified, one may normalize the marginal distribution of ε to be $U(0, 1)$. Independence between ε and Z imply that for each $\tau \in (0, 1)$

$$\begin{aligned}\tau &= E\big[1(\varepsilon < \tau)\big] = E\big[1(\varepsilon < \tau)\big|Z\big]\\ &= E\big[E\big[1(\varepsilon < \tau)\big|W, Z\big]\big|Z\big]\\ &= E\big[E\big[1\big(m(W, \varepsilon) < m(W, \tau)\big)\big|W, Z\big]\big|Z\big]\\ &= E\big[1\big(Y < m(W, \tau)\big)\big|Z\big].\end{aligned}$$

Define $\rho(Y, W, \tau, m) = 1(Y < m(W, \tau)) - \tau$. Then, the above defines a conditional moment restriction

$$E\big[\rho(Y, W, \tau, m)\big|Z\big] = 0.$$

The following theorem provides sufficient conditions for local identification, in the sense of Rothenberg (1971), of $\rho(Y, W, \tau, m)$.

THEOREM 4.2. *[See Chernozhukov, Imbens and Newey (2007).] Suppose that Y is continuously distributed conditional on X and Z with density $f(y|x, z)$, and that there exists $C > 0$ such that*

$$\big|f(y|x, z) - f(\tilde{y}|x, z)\big| \leqslant C|y - \tilde{y}|$$

and for $D(V) = f(m(W, \tau)|W, Z)$, $E[D(V)\Delta(V)|Z] = 0$ implies $\Delta(V) = 0$ then $m(W, \tau)$ is locally identified.

In simultaneous equations, of the type considered in previous sections, an observed or identified exogenous variable that is excluded from one equation may be used as an instrument for that equation. Consider, for example, the simultaneous equation model

$$\begin{aligned}Y_1 &= m_1(Y_2, \varepsilon_1),\\ Y_2 &= m_2(Y_1, X, \varepsilon_2)\end{aligned}$$

where X is distributed independently of $(\varepsilon_1, \varepsilon_2)$. Matzkin (2007b) establishes restrictions on the functions m_1 and m_2 and on the distribution of $(\varepsilon_1, \varepsilon_2, X)$ under which

$$\left[\frac{\partial r_1(y_1, y_2)}{\partial y_2}\right]^{-1}\left[\frac{\partial r_1(y_1, y_2)}{\partial y_1}\right]$$

can be expressed as a function of the values of $f_{Y_1,Y_2,X}$ at $(Y_1, Y_2) = (y_1, y_2)$ and particular values of X.

4.2.2. Unobservable instruments

Matzkin (2004) considers the use of *unobservable* instruments to identify nonadditive models. These are variables that are known to be distributed independently of unobservable random terms in an equation of interest, but are themselves unobservable. This is in the spirit of Fisher (1966), who developed an extensive set of conditions on the unobservables in linear systems of simultaneous equations that provide identification. The method is also related to the one in Hausman and Taylor (1983). Matzkin (2004) considers the model

$$Y_1 = m(Y_2, X, \varepsilon)$$

with m strictly increasing in ε and ε distributed independently of X. She assumes that a second equation,

$$Y_2 = g(Y_1, \eta)$$

is identified, and that the unobservables η and ε are independently distributed. The identification of the function g in general will require imposing additional restrictions. If, for example, g were specified to be a linear function and one assumed that $E[\eta|X] = 0$, then identification of g would follow by standard results. If g were nonparametric and additive in η, then, under the assumption that $E[\eta|X] = 0$ one could identify it using the methods in Newey and Powell (1989, 2003), Darolles, Florens and Renault (2000), or Hall and Horowitz (2005). Suppose that g is identified. Matzkin (2004) proposes a pointwise direct identification of the function m. The argument proceeds by using η to estimate the reduced form equations

$$Y_1 = r_1(X, \eta, \varepsilon),$$
$$Y_2 = r_2(X, \eta, \varepsilon).$$

Under the assumption that ε is independent of (X, η), these equations are identified using the arguments in 3.3. These equations are next used to identify m. To see this, suppose that we wanted to identify the value of m at a particular value (y_2, x, e). Let η^* denote the value of η that solves the equation

$$y_2 = r_2(x, \eta^*, e).$$

Let $y_1^* = r_1(x, \eta^*, e)$. If then follows by the definition of m and of the functions r_1 and r_2 that

$$\begin{aligned} m(y_2, x, e) &= m\big(r_2(x, \eta^*, e), x, e\big) \\ &= r_1(x, \eta^*, e) \\ &= y_1^*. \end{aligned}$$

Hence, one can recover the function m.

4.2.3. Instrumental variables in additive models

In additive models, the requirement that $Z = (Z_1, Z_2)$ be independent of ε_1 may be weakened to a conditional mean independence. Newey and Powell (1989, 2003), Darolles, Florens and Renault (2000), Ai and Chen (2003), and Hall and Horowitz (2005) considered the model

$$Y = m(X, Z_1) + \varepsilon$$

where $E[\varepsilon|X] \neq 0$. They assumed the existence of an instrument, Z, satisfying

$$E[\varepsilon|Z_1, Z_2] = 0.$$

Using the definition of ε, this yields the equation

$$\begin{aligned} E[Y|Z_1 = z_1,\ Z_2 = z_2] &= E\big[m(X, z_1)\big|Z_1 = z_1,\ Z_2 = z_2\big] \\ &= \int m(x, z_1) f_{X|Z_1=z_1,\, Z_2=z_2}(x)\, dx. \end{aligned}$$

Since the "reduced form" $E[Y|Z_1, Z_2]$ is identified from the distribution of (Y, Z_1, Z_2) and $f_{X|Z_1=z_1,\, Z_2=z_2}(x)$ is identified from the distribution of (X, Z), the only unknown in the above integral equation is $m(x, z_1)$. Newey and Powell (2003) provided conditions characterizing the identification of the function m solely from the above integral equation.

THEOREM 4.3. *[See Newey and Powell (2003).] Suppose that* $Y = m(X, Z_1) + \varepsilon$ *and* $E[\varepsilon|Z_1, Z_2] = 0$. *Then, m is identified if and only if for all functions* $\delta(x, z_1)$ *with finite expectation,* $E[\delta(x, z_1)|Z = z] = 0$ *implies that* $\delta(x, z_1) = 0$.

Das (2004) and Newey and Powell (2003) considered identification of this model when the endogenous variables are discrete. To state the result presented in Newey and Powell (2003), assume that both X and Z_2 are discrete. Denote the support of X and Z_2 by, respectively, $\{x_1, \ldots, x_S\}$ and $\{z_{21}, \ldots, z_{2T}\}$. Let $P(z_1)$ denote the $S \times T$ matrix whose ijth element is $\Pr(X = x_i|Z_1 = z_1,\ Z_2 = z_{2j})$.

THEOREM 4.4. *[See Newey and Powell (2003).] Suppose that* $Y = m(X, Z_1) + \varepsilon$, $E[\varepsilon|Z_1, Z_2] = 0$, *and X and* Z_2 *have finite support. Then,* $m(x, z_1)$ *is identified if and only if* $\Pr[\text{rank}(P(z_1)) = s] = 1$.

4.2.4. Instrumental variables in additive models with measurement error

A common situation where an observable explanatory variable is not independent of the unobserved explanatory variable is when the observed explanatory variable is an imperfect measurement of the true explanatory variable, which is unobserved. For this situation, Schennach (2007) established identification of an additive model using instrumental variables. She considered the model

$$Y = m(X^*) + \varepsilon,$$
$$X = X^* + \eta_X,$$
$$X^* = r(Z) + \eta_Z$$

where the nonparametric function m is the object of interest, X^* is unobservable, Z, X, and Y are observable, $E(\varepsilon|Z, \eta_Z) = E(\eta_X|Z, \eta_Z, \varepsilon) = E(\eta_Z) = 0$, and η_Z and Z are independently distributed. Since, in this model,

$$X = r(Z) + \eta_X + \eta_Z$$

and $E(\eta_X + \eta_Z|Z) = 0$, the function r is identified from the joint distribution of (X, Z). The model implies the two moment conditions

$$E(Y|Z = z) = \int m\big(r(Z) + \eta_Z\big)\, dF(\eta_Z),$$

$$E(YX|Z = z) = \int \big(r(Z) + \eta_Z\big) m\big(r(Z) + \eta_z\big)\, dF(\eta_Z).$$

[These moment conditions were used in Newey (2001) to deal with a parametric version of the model with measurement error.] Using the representation of these in terms of characteristic functions, Schennach (2007) shows that m and the distribution of X^* are identified.

4.3. *Shape restrictions on distributions*

Particular shapes or some local conditions on the distributions can often be used to provide identification. We provide two examples.

4.3.1. *Exchangeability restrictions in the nonadditive model*

Altonji and Matzkin (2005) considered the model

$$Y = m(X, \varepsilon)$$

where ε is not distributed independently of X, but for some observable variable Z, it is the case that for all x there exists values $z(x)$, $z(x, \bar{x})$ of Z such that for all e

$$F_{\varepsilon|X=x,\, Z=z(x)}(e) = F_{\varepsilon|X=\bar{x},\, Z=z(x,\bar{x})}(e).$$

Their leading example is where X denotes the value of a variable for one member of a group, Z denotes the value of the same variable for another member of the same group, and ε, which incorporates the unobservable group effect, is such that its distribution is exchangeable in X and Z, so that for all values t, t' and all e

$$F_{\varepsilon|X=t,\, Z=t'}(e) = F_{\varepsilon|X=t',\, Z=t}(e).$$

In such a case, $z(x) = \bar{x}$ and $z(x, \bar{x}) = x$. Assume that for all x, z, $F_{\varepsilon|X=x,\, Z=z}$ is strictly increasing. As with the case where ε is assumed to be independent of X, a normalization is needed either on the function m or on the distribution. Assume that $m(\bar{x}, \varepsilon) = \varepsilon$.

Under these assumptions

(4.c) *m and $F_{\varepsilon|X=x}$ can be recovered from* $(F_{Y|X=x,\,Z=z(x)}, F_{Y|X=\bar{x},\,Z=z(x,\bar{x})})$.

PROOF OF (4.c). Let x and e be given. By the strict monotonicity of m in ε, $F_{\varepsilon|X=x,\,Z=z(x)}(e) = F_{\varepsilon|X=\bar{x},\,Z=z(x,\bar{x})}(e)$ implies that

$$F_{Y|X=x,\,Z=z(x)}\big(m(x,e)\big) = F_{Y|X=\bar{x},\,Z=z(x,\bar{x})}\big(m(\bar{x},e)\big).$$

Hence, since $m(\bar{x}, e)$, it follows that

$$m(x,e) = F^{-1}_{Y|X=x,\,Z=z(x)}\big(F_{Y|X=\bar{x},\,Z=z(x,\bar{x})}(e)\big).$$

Next, since the strict monotonicity of m in ε implies that for all x and e

$$F_{\varepsilon|X=x}(e) = F_{Y|X=x}\big(m(x,e)\big)$$

it follows that

$$F_{\varepsilon|X=x}(e) = F_{Y|X=x}\big(F^{-1}_{Y|X=x,\,Z=z(x)}\big(F_{Y|X=\bar{x},\,Z=z(x,\bar{x})}(e)\big)\big).$$ □

Rather than imposing a normalization, one may ask what can be identified without imposing any normalization. Suppose that the exchangeability condition considered in Altonji and Matzkin (2005) is satisfied. Let m, e be given and let $y^* = m(x,e)$. Then,

$$m(\bar{x},e) = F^{-1}_{Y|X=\bar{x},\,Z=x}\big(F_{Y|X=x,\,Z=\bar{x}}(y^*)\big)$$

and for any x'

$$\begin{aligned} m(x',e) &= F^{-1}_{Y|X=x',\,Z=\bar{x}}\big(F_{Y|X=\bar{x},\,Z=x'}\big(m(\bar{x},e)\big)\big) \\ &= F^{-1}_{Y|X=x',\,Z=\bar{x}}\big(F_{Y|X=\bar{x},\,Z=x'}\big(F^{-1}_{Y|X=\bar{x},\,Z=x}\big(F_{Y|X=x,\,Z=\bar{x}}(y^*)\big)\big)\big). \end{aligned}$$

Hence, the effect of changing X from x to x' is

$$\begin{aligned} &m(x',e) - m(x,e) \\ &\quad = F^{-1}_{Y|X=x',\,Z=\bar{x}}\big(F_{Y|X=\bar{x},\,Z=x'}\big(F^{-1}_{Y|X=\bar{x},\,Z=x}\big(F_{Y|X=x,\,Z=\bar{x}}(y^*)\big)\big)\big) - y^*. \end{aligned}$$

4.3.2. Local independence restrictions in the nonadditive model

Chesher (2003) used a local insensitivity assumption to achieve local identification of the partial derivatives of structural functions in a triangular system of equations. To demonstrate a simple version of this restriction, consider a nonadditive model, specified as

$$Y = m^*(X,\varepsilon)$$

where m is strictly increasing in ε. Suppose that we were interested in inferring the partial derivative of m with respect to X. Following arguments analogous to those used in Section 3.3, one can show that for any x, ε

$$F_{Y|X=x}\big(m^*(x,\varepsilon)\big) = F^*_{\varepsilon|X=x}(\varepsilon).$$

Assuming that all the functions are differentiable, we get that

$$\frac{\partial m^*(\bar{x},\bar{\varepsilon})}{\partial x} = \frac{\partial F_{Y|X=\bar{x}}(t)}{\partial t}\bigg|_{t=m^*(\bar{x},\bar{\varepsilon})}\left[\frac{\partial F_{Y|X=\bar{x}}(t)}{\partial x}\bigg|_{t=m^*(\bar{x},\bar{\varepsilon})} - \frac{\partial F^*_{\varepsilon|X=\bar{x}}(\bar{\varepsilon})}{\partial x}\right].$$

The local insensitivity assumption can be stated as the restriction that at $X = \bar{x}$ and $\varepsilon = \varepsilon$

$$\frac{\partial F^*_{\varepsilon|X=\bar{x}}(\bar{\varepsilon})}{\partial x} = 0.$$

Assume that the value of $m^*(\bar{x},\bar{\varepsilon})$ is known. It then follows that the derivative of m^* with respect to x, evaluated at $(\bar{x},\bar{\varepsilon})$, can be identified.

4.4. *Shape restrictions on functions*

One of the main parts in the specification of an econometric model is the set of restrictions on the functions and distributions of the model. We concentrate here on shape restrictions. These may prove useful when a specification is such that a particular feature of interest is not identified. In such a situation, one may consider tightening the set of restrictions by considering particular shapes. The analysis of observational equivalence can often be used to determine the search for restrictions that, when added to the model, help to determine identification. Economic theory can be used to choose among the possible restrictions. We provide some examples.

4.4.1. *Homogeneity restrictions*

Homogeneous functions are often encountered in economic models. Profit and cost functions of firms in perfectly competitive environments are homogeneous of degree one. Production functions are often homogeneous. Given the ubiquity of this type of functions, it is worthwhile considering how this restriction can aid in identifying features of a model. We provide some examples.

4.4.1.1. Independent nonadditive model Consider the independent nonadditive model, described in Section 2.2.1.2, where $Y = m^*(X,\varepsilon)$, m^* is strictly increasing in ε, and ε and X are independently distributed. Suppose that we are interested in identifying m^*. The analysis of identification in Section 3.3 showed that one can partition the set, Ω, of possible functions m, into classes such that for any two functions, m and $\tilde{m}$ in a class, there exists a strictly increasing $g: R \to R$ such that for all x, ε

$$\tilde{m}\big(x, g(\varepsilon)\big) = m(x,\varepsilon).$$

Functions within each such class are observationally equivalent, while functions from different classes are not. This suggests, then, that any restriction on the set of functions m, which guarantees that for any two different functions in the restricted set, no such g exists, will be sufficient to guarantee identification of m^* within that set.

Suppose that the function m^* is the profit function of a firm in a perfectly competitive environment, and suppose that (x, ε) is the vector of prices, assumed to possess support R_+^{K+1}. Economic theory implies that m^* is continuous and homogenous of degree one in $(x, \varepsilon) \in R_+^{K+1}$. Let $(\bar{x}, \bar{\varepsilon})$ denote a specified value of (x, ε) and let $\alpha > 0$ denote a specified number. Let Ω denote the set of all functions m that are continuous and homogeneous of degree one and satisfy $m(\bar{x}, \bar{\varepsilon}) = \alpha$. Then,

(4.d) *if* $m, \tilde{m} \in \Omega$ *and for some strictly increasing* $g : R_+ \to R_+$

$$\tilde{m}\big(x, g(\varepsilon)\big) = m(x, \varepsilon)$$

it must be that for all $\varepsilon \in R_+$,

$$g(\varepsilon) = \varepsilon.$$

PROOF OF (4.d). [See Matzkin (2003).] Substituting $x = \bar{x}$ and $\varepsilon = \bar{\varepsilon}$, and using the homogeneity of degree one assumption and the assumption that $\tilde{m}(\bar{x}, \bar{\varepsilon}) = m(\bar{x}, \bar{\varepsilon}) = \alpha$, we get that for all $\lambda > 0$

$$\tilde{m}\big(\lambda\bar{x}, g(\lambda\bar{\varepsilon})\big) = m(\lambda\bar{x}, \lambda\bar{\varepsilon}) = \lambda\alpha = \tilde{m}(\lambda\bar{x}, \lambda\bar{\varepsilon}).$$

Since $\tilde{m}$ is strictly increasing in its last coordinate

$$\tilde{m}\big(\lambda\bar{x}, g(\lambda\bar{\varepsilon})\big) = \tilde{m}(\lambda\bar{x}, \lambda\bar{\varepsilon}) \quad \text{implies that} \quad g(\lambda\bar{\varepsilon}) = \lambda\bar{\varepsilon}.$$

Since this holds for every $\lambda > 0$, the result follows. □

The implication of this result is that in the independent nonadditive model, if we restrict the set to which m^* belongs to be such that all functions, m, in that set are continuous, homogenous of degree one, and satisfy $m(\bar{x}, \bar{\varepsilon}) = \alpha$, then m^* will be identified in that set.

4.4.1.2. Independent index model Consider the independent index model, 2.2.1.4, where $Y = m^*(h^*(X), \varepsilon)$, and ε and X are independently distributed. The analysis of identification in Section 3.4 showed that one can partition the set, Ω, of possible functions h into classes such that for any two functions, h and $\tilde{h}$, in a class, there exists a strictly increasing $g : R \to R$ such that for all x

$$\tilde{h}(x) = g\big(h(x)\big).$$

Functions within each such class are observationally equivalent, while functions from different classes are not. Hence, any restriction which guarantees that any two function in the restricted set cannot be strictly increasing transformations of each other will suffice to guarantee identification of h^* within that set.

Let Ω denote the set of all functions $h : X \to R$ that satisfy the restrictions in the independent index model described in 2.2.1.4 and, in addition, are homogeneous of degree one and satisfy $h(\bar{x}) = \alpha$. Assume $h^* \in \Omega$. Then,

(4.e) *h^* is identified in Ω.*

PROOF OF (4.e). [See Matzkin (1991b, 1994).] Let $h \in \Omega$. Suppose that h is observationally equivalent to h^*. Then, by the theorem in Section 3.4, there is some strictly increasing $g : R \to R$, such that

$$h(x) = g\big(h^*(x)\big).$$

Since both $h, h^* \in \Omega$, for all λ

$$\lambda = \left(\frac{\lambda}{\alpha}\right)\alpha = \left(\frac{\lambda}{\alpha}\right)h(\bar{x}) = h\left(\left(\frac{\lambda}{\alpha}\right)\bar{x}\right) = g\left(h^*\left(\left(\frac{\lambda}{\alpha}\right)\bar{x}\right)\right).$$

The second equality follows by the definition of Ω, the third by the homogeneity of degree one of h, the fourth because for all x, $h(x) = g(h^*(x))$. By the homogeneity of degree one of h^* and the specification that $h^*(\bar{x}) = \alpha$, it follows that

$$g\left(\left(\frac{\lambda}{\alpha}\right)h^*(\bar{x})\right) = g\left(\left(\frac{\lambda}{\alpha}\right)\alpha\right) = g(\lambda).$$

Hence, for all λ, $g(\lambda) = \lambda$. Since for all x, $h(x) = g(h^*(x))$, this implies that $h = h^*$. Hence, the only function in Ω that is observationally equivalent to h^* is h^*. □

4.4.1.3. Discrete choice model Consider the discrete choice model described in Section 2.2.1.6 with additive unobservables and with the normalization that $V_J(s, z_J, \omega) = 0$. Then

$$\Pr(y_J = 0|s,\ x_1, \ldots, x_J) = F^*_{\varepsilon_1,\ldots,\varepsilon_{J-1}}\big(V_1^*(s, x_1), \ldots, V^*_{J-1}(s, x_{J-1})\big).$$

From the above analysis it is clear that homogeneity restrictions in each of the V_j^* functions can be used to identify $F^*_{\varepsilon_1,\ldots,\varepsilon_{J-1}}$. To see this, suppose that the functions $V_1^*, \ldots, V^*_{J-1}$ are such that for some $\bar{s}$, and each j, there exist $\bar{x}_j$ and α_j such that for all s and all λ such that $\lambda\bar{x}_j \in X$, $V_j^*(\bar{s}, \bar{x}_j) = a_j$ and $V_j^*(\bar{s}, \lambda\bar{x}_j) = \lambda a_j$. Then, for any $(t_1, \ldots, t_{J-1})$,

$$\begin{aligned}
&F^*_{\varepsilon_1,\ldots,\varepsilon_{J-1}}(t_1, \ldots, t_{J-1})\\
&\quad = F^*_{\varepsilon_1,\ldots,\varepsilon_{J-1}}\left(\left(\frac{t_1}{\alpha_1}\right)\alpha_1, \ldots, \left(\frac{t_{J-1}}{\alpha_{J-1}}\right)\alpha_{J-1}\right)\\
&\quad = F^*_{\varepsilon_1,\ldots,\varepsilon_{J-1}}\left(\left(\frac{t_1}{\alpha_1}\right)V_1^*(\bar{s}, \bar{x}_1), \ldots, \left(\frac{t_{J-1}}{\alpha_{J-1}}\right)V^*_{J-1}(\bar{s}, \bar{x}_{J-1})\right)\\
&\quad = F^*_{\varepsilon_1,\ldots,\varepsilon_{J-1}}\left(V_1^*\left(\bar{s}, \left(\frac{t_1}{\alpha_1}\right)\bar{x}_1\right), \ldots, V^*_{J-1}\left(\bar{s}, \left(\frac{t_{J-1}}{\alpha_{J-1}}\right)\bar{x}_{J-1}\right)\right)\\
&\quad = \Pr\left(y_J = 0\middle|\bar{s}, x_1 = \left(\frac{t_1}{\alpha_1}\right)\bar{x}_1, \ldots, x_{J-1} = \left(\frac{t_{J-1}}{\alpha_{J-1}}\right)\bar{x}_{J-1}\right).
\end{aligned}$$

Hence, $F^*_{\varepsilon_1,\dots,\varepsilon_{J-1}}(t_1,\dots,t_{J-1})$ can be recovered from $\Pr(y_J = 0|\bar{s}, x_1 = (\frac{t_1}{\alpha_1})\bar{x}_1,\dots, x_{J-1} = (\frac{t_{J-1}}{\alpha_{J-1}})\bar{x}_{J-1})$ as long as this conditional probability is identified. When $F^*_{\varepsilon_1,\dots,\varepsilon_{J-1}}$ is identified, one can recover each V^*_g function as in Matzkin (1991a). [See Matzkin and Newey (1993) and Lewbel and Linton (2007) for the use of homogeneity restrictions when $J = 2$.]

4.4.2. *Additivity restrictions*

As with homogeneous functions, additive functions also appear often in economic models. Aggregate demand is the sum of individual demands; cost functions are sums of fixed cost and variable cost functions; total income is the sum of income from work and income from other sources. We describe below two particular examples where additivity can be used to identify nonparametric functions.

4.4.2.1. Additivity in conditional expectations Consider an additive model, where for unknown functions m_1^* and m_2^*,

$$E\bigl(Y\big|X = (x_1, x_2)\bigr) = m_1^*(x_1) + m_2^*(x_2).$$

Following the arguments in Linton and Nielsen (1995), one can show that

(4.f) *m_1^* and m_2^* can be recovered, up to at an additive constant, from $E\bigl(Y|X = (x_1, x_2)\bigr)$.*

PROOF OF (4.f). Note that

$$\int E\bigl(Y\big|X = (x_1, x_2)\bigr) f(x_2)\,dx_2 = \int \bigl(m_1^*(x_1) + m_2^*(x_2)\bigr) f(x_2)\,dx_2$$
$$= m_1^*(x_1) + \int m_2^*(x_2) f(x_2)\,dx_2.$$

Hence, once one specifies a value for $\int m_2^*(x_2) f(x_2)\,dx_2$, one can obtain $m_1^*(x_1)$ for all x_1. For each x_2, the value of $m^*(x_2)$ can then be obtained by

$$\begin{aligned} m^*(x_2) &= E\bigl(Y\big|X = (x_1, x_2)\bigr) - m^*(x_1) \\ &= E\bigl(Y\big|X = (x_1, x_2)\bigr) \\ &\quad - \int E\bigl(Y\big|X = (x_1, x_2)\bigr) f(x_2)\,dx_2 + \int m_2^*(x_2) f(x_2)\,dx_2 \end{aligned}$$

which depends on the same constant $\int m_2^*(x_2) f(x_2)\,dx_2$. □

4.4.2.2. Additivity in a known function When a nonparametric function can only be identified up to a strictly increasing transformation, a scale as well as a location normalization will be necessary. An often convenient way of imposing these is to assume that the nonparametric function is linearly additive in one of the coordinates, the coefficient of that coordinate is known, and the value of the subfunction of the other coordinates is specified at one point. In other words, partition X into subvectors $X_1, \ldots, X_J$, so that $X_1 \in R$, and $X = (X_1, \ldots, X_J) \in R^K$. Suppose that for functions $h_2^*, \ldots, h_J^*$,

$$h^*(X) = X_1 + \sum_{j=2}^{J} h_j^*(X_j)$$

and that for some value $(\bar{x}_2, \ldots, \bar{x}_J)$ of $(X_2, \ldots, X_J)$, the value of $\sum_{j=2}^{J} h_j^*(\bar{x}_j)$ is specified, then,

(4.g) *if $h^*, \bar{h}$ are two functions satisfying these restrictions, $h^*, \bar{h}$ cannot be strictly increasing transformations of each other.*

PROOF OF (4.g). Let $g : R \to R$ be a strictly increasing function. Suppose that for all X, $h^*(X) = g(\tilde{h}(X))$. Then, letting $X = (x_1, \bar{x}_2, \ldots, \bar{x}_J)$, it follows that for all x_1, $g(x_1 + \sum_{j=2}^{J} \tilde{h}_j(\bar{x}_j)) = x_1 + \sum_{j=2}^{J} h_j^*(\bar{x}_j)$. Since $\sum_{j=2}^{J} \tilde{h}_j(\bar{x}_j) = \sum_{j=2}^{J} h_j^*(\bar{x}_j)$, it follows that g must be the identity function. □

This result can be used in the nonadditive model, the nonadditive index model, and discrete choice models, using arguments similar to the ones used for the homogeneity of degree one case.

4.5. Restrictions on functions and distributions

Often, a combination of restrictions on functions and distributions is used. We provide some examples below.

4.5.1. Control functions

A control function is a function of observable variables such that conditioning on its value purges any statistical dependence that may exist between the observable and unobservable explanatory variables in an original model. The *control function* approach was fully developed, and analyzed for parametric selection models, in Heckman and Robb (1985). The method is commonly used for identification of models where the explanatory observable variables, X, and the explanatory unobserved variables, ε, are not independently distributed. In this method, the unobservable, ε, is modeled as a function of observed or identified variables, W, which have independent variation from the endogenous explanatory variables, X. We provide an example.

4.5.1.1. A control function in an additive model Newey, Powell and Vella (1999) considered identification and estimation of the model

$$Y = m(X, Z_1) + \varepsilon$$

with the additional equation

$$X = \pi(Z) + u$$

and the restrictions

$$E[\varepsilon|u, Z] = E[\varepsilon|u] \quad \text{and} \quad E[u|Z] = 0$$

where Z_1 is a subvector of Z. [See also Ng and Pinkse (1995) and Pinkse (2000).] Since, in this model, $E[\varepsilon|u] = E[\varepsilon|u, Z] = E[\varepsilon|u, X, Z]$, u can be used as a control function to identify m. Since $E[u|Z] = 0$, the function π can be recovered from the joint distribution of (X, Z). Hence, $u = X - \pi(Z)$ can also be recovered. Moreover, the structure of the model implies that for some g

$$\begin{aligned} E[Y|X, Z] &= m(X, Z_1) + E[\varepsilon|u] \\ &= m(X, Z_1) + g\big(X - \pi(Z)\big). \end{aligned}$$

The following identification result is established in Newey, Powell and Vella (1999):

THEOREM 4.5. *[See Newey, Powell and Vella (1999).] Suppose that $m(x, z_1)$, $g(u)$, and $\pi(Z)$ are differentiable, the boundary of the support of (Z, u) has zero probability, and with probability one,* $\operatorname{rank}(\partial\pi(Z_1, Z_2)/\partial Z_2) = d_X$, *where d_X denotes the dimension of X. Then, $m(X, Z_1)$ is identified (up to constant).*

As noted in Newey, Powell and Vella (1999), one can use the additive structure to derive the derivatives of the functions m directly. Let $h(X, Z_1, Z_2) = E[Y|X, Z_1, Z_2]$. Then, since

$$h(X, Z_1, Z_2) = m(X, Z_1) + g\big(X - \pi(Z)\big)$$

it follows that

$$\frac{\partial h(X, Z_1, Z_2)}{\partial X} = \frac{\partial m(X, Z_1)}{\partial X} + \left.\frac{\partial g(u)}{\partial u}\right|_{u=X-\pi(Z)},$$

$$\frac{\partial h(X, Z_1, Z_2)}{\partial Z_1} = \frac{\partial m(X, Z_1)}{\partial Z_1} - \left(\frac{\partial \pi(Z_1, Z_2)}{\partial Z_1}\right)' \left.\frac{\partial g(u)}{\partial u}\right|_{u=X-\pi(Z)},$$

$$\frac{\partial h(X, Z_1, Z_2)}{\partial Z_2} = -\left(\frac{\partial \pi(Z_1, Z_2)}{\partial Z_2}\right)' \left.\frac{\partial g(u)}{\partial u}\right|_{u=X-\pi(Z)}.$$

Assume that $\operatorname{rank}(\partial\pi(Z_1, Z_2)/\partial Z_2) = d_X$. Define

$$D(Z) = \left[\left(\frac{\partial \pi(Z_1, Z_2)}{\partial Z_2}\right)\left(\frac{\partial \pi(Z_1, Z_2)}{\partial Z_2}\right)'\right]^{-1}\left(\frac{\partial \pi(Z_1, Z_2)}{\partial Z_2}\right).$$

Then, multiplying $\partial h(X, Z_1, Z_2)/\partial Z_2$ by $D(Z)$ and solving gives

$$\frac{\partial m(X, Z_1)}{\partial X} = \frac{\partial h(X, Z_1, Z_2)}{\partial X} - D(Z)\frac{\partial h(X, Z_1, Z_2)}{\partial Z_2},$$

$$\frac{\partial m(X, Z_1)}{\partial Z_1} = \frac{\partial h(X, Z_1, Z_2)}{\partial Z_1} + \left(\frac{\partial \pi(Z_1, Z_2)}{\partial Z_1}\right)' D(Z) \frac{\partial h(X, Z_1, Z_2)}{\partial Z_2}.$$

The above gives identification of m up to an additive constant. An additional restriction is necessary to identify such a constant. Suppose, for example, that $E[\varepsilon] = 0$. Then, as shown in Newey, Powell and Vella (1999), for any function $\tau(u)$ such that $\int \tau(u)\, du = 1$,

$$\begin{aligned}
&\int E[Y|X, Z_1, u]\tau(u)\, du - E\left[\int E[Y|X, Z_1, u]\tau(u)\, du\right] + E[Y] \\
&\quad = m(X, Z_1) - E\big[m(X, Z_1)\big] + E[Y] \\
&\quad = m(X, Z_1).
\end{aligned}$$

Hence, the constant of m is identified.

4.5.2. *Linear factor models*

When the unobservable vector ε in a model is driven by factors that are common to some equations, one might want to use a factor model. Factor models were introduced into economics by Jöreskog and Goldberger (1972), Goldberger (1972), Chamberlain and Griliches (1975), and Chamberlain (1977a, 1977b). [See Aigner et al. (1984) for an in-depth review and analysis.] The standard situation analyzed in factor models is the one where there are L measurements on K mutually independent factors arrayed in a vector θ. Let G denote the vector of measurements. Then, the model is specified as

$$G = \mu + \Lambda\theta + \delta$$

where G is $L \times 1$, θ is independent of δ, μ is an $L \times 1$ vector of means, which may depend on a vector of observable variables X, θ is $K \times 1$, δ is $L \times 1$, and Λ is $L \times K$, the coordinates of $\delta = (\delta_1, \ldots, \delta_L)$ are assumed to be mutually independent, as well as the coordinates of $\theta = (\theta_1, \ldots, \theta_K)$, and δ and θ are assumed to be independent. Anderson and Rubin (1956) discuss the identification problem in factor models. More recently, Carneiro, Hansen and Heckman (2003) have shown that factor models can be identified when the matrix Λ has a particular structure. Bonhomme and Robin (2006) analyze identification using the third and fourth moments of the distributions of the measurements.

Carneiro, Hansen and Heckman (2003) consider a system of L measurements on K factors,

$$\begin{aligned}
M_1 &= m_1(X) + \beta_{11}\theta_1 + \cdots + \beta_{1K}\theta_K + \delta_1, \\
M_2 &= m_2(X) + \beta_{21}\theta_1 + \cdots + \beta_{2K}\theta_K + \delta_2, \\
&\vdots \\
M_L &= m_L(X) + \beta_{L1}\theta_1 + \cdots + \beta_{LK}\theta_K + \delta_2
\end{aligned}$$

where $\delta = (\delta_1, \dots, \delta_L)$, $E(\delta) = 0$, and where $\theta = (\theta_1, \dots, \theta_K)$ is distributed independently of δ. A special case that they consider is one where there are two or more measurements devoted exclusively to factor θ_1, and at least three measurements that are generated by factor θ_1, two of more further measurements that are devoted only to factors θ_1 and θ_2, with at least three measurements on θ_2, and so fourth, in blocks of at least two. Order G under this assumption so that

$$\Lambda = \begin{pmatrix} 1 & 0 & \cdot & 0 & \cdots & 0 \\ \lambda_{21} & 1 & \cdot & 0 & \cdots & 0 \\ \lambda_{31} & \lambda_{32} & 1 & 0 & \cdots & 0 \\ \lambda_{41} & \lambda_{42} & \lambda_{43} & 0 & \cdots & 0 \\ \cdots & \cdots & \cdots & 0 & \cdots & 0 \\ \lambda_{L1} & \lambda_{L2} & \lambda_{L3} & \cdots & \cdots & \lambda_{LK} \end{pmatrix}.$$

Assuming nonzero covariances,

$$\operatorname{Cov}(g_j, g_l) = \lambda_{j1}\lambda_{l1}\sigma^2_{\theta_1}, \quad l = 1, 2, \ j = 1, \dots, L, \ j \neq l,$$

where $G = (g_1, \dots, g_L)$. In particular,

$$\operatorname{Cov}(g_1, g_l) = \lambda_{l1}\sigma^2_{\theta_1},$$
$$\operatorname{Cov}(g_2, g_l) = \lambda_{l1}\lambda_{21}\sigma^2_{\theta_1}.$$

Hence, assuming that $\lambda_{l1} \neq 0$, one obtains

$$\lambda_{21} = \frac{\operatorname{Cov}(g_2, g_l)}{\operatorname{Cov}(g_1, g_l)}.$$

It follows that from $\operatorname{Cov}(g_1, g_l) = \lambda_{21}\sigma^2_{\theta_1}$, one can obtain $\sigma^2_{\theta_1}$, and hence λ_{l1}, $l = 1, \dots, L$. One can then proceed to the next set of two measurements and identify

$$\operatorname{Cov}(g_l, g_j) = \lambda_{l1}\lambda_{j1}\sigma^2_{\theta_1} + \lambda_{l2}\lambda_{j2}\sigma^2_{\theta_2}, \quad l = 3, 4, \ j \geqslant 3, \ j \neq l.$$

Since we can know the first term on the right-hand side by the previous arguments, we can proceed using $\operatorname{Cov}(g_l, g_j) - \lambda_{l1}\lambda_{j1}\sigma^2_{\theta_1}$ and identify the λ_{j2}, $j = 1, \dots, L$, using similar arguments. Proceeding in this fashion, one can identify Λ and the variance of θ, Σ_θ, subject to diagonal normalizations. Knowing Λ and Σ_θ, one can identify the variance, D_δ, of δ. Next, using the mutual independence of the factors θ_i ($i = 1, \dots, K$), one can identify the densities of each θ_i.

To provide a simple case, developed in Carneiro, Hansen and Heckman (2003), suppose that

$$G_1 = \lambda_{11}\theta_1 + \delta_1,$$
$$G_2 = \lambda_{21}\theta_1 + \delta_2$$

where $\lambda_{11} = 1$ and $\lambda_{21} \neq 0$. Subject to the normalization that $\lambda_{11} = 1$, λ_{21} is identified. Thus, one can write these equations as

$$G_1 = \theta_1 + \delta_1,$$
$$\frac{G_2}{\lambda_{21}} = \theta_1 + \left(\frac{\delta_2}{\lambda_{21}}\right)$$

where θ_1, δ_1, and (δ_2/λ_{21}) are mutually independent. By Kotlarski (1967), one can nonparametrically identify the densities of θ_1, δ_1, and (δ_2/λ_{21}). The next equations in the system

$$G_3 = \lambda_{31}\theta_1 + \theta_2 + \delta_3,$$
$$G_4 = \lambda_{41}\theta_1 + \lambda_{42}\theta_2 + \delta_4$$

can be written as

$$G_3 - \lambda_{31}\theta_1 = \theta_2 + \delta_3,$$
$$\frac{G_4 - \lambda_{41}\theta_1}{\lambda_{42}} = \theta_2 + \left(\frac{\delta_4}{\lambda_{42}}\right)$$

where θ_2, δ_3, and (δ_4/λ_{42}) are mutually independent. Again, one can apply Kotlarski's theorem. Proceeding in this fashion, all the densities are identified. From the knowledge about the densities of θ_i and the factor loadings, one can apply standard deconvolution methods to nonparametrically identify the δ terms in the model.

Cunha, Heckman and Matzkin (2004) extend this analysis to factor models of the type

$$Y_t = m_t(X, \beta_t\theta + \delta_t), \quad t = 1, \ldots, T,$$

where m_t is strictly increasing in it last argument. Assuming that $(\theta, \delta_1, \ldots, \delta_T)$ is distributed independently of X and that at some specified value $\bar{x}_t$ of X,

$$m_t(\bar{x}_t, \beta_t\theta + \delta_t) = \beta_t\theta + \delta_t$$

one can recover the distribution of $\eta_t = \beta_t\theta + \varepsilon_t$, and the function m_t, since, by previous arguments

$$F_{\eta_t}(\eta_t) = F_{Y_t|X_t=\bar{x}_t}(\eta_t) \quad \text{and} \quad m_t(x_t, \eta_t) = F^{-1}_{Y_t|X_t=x_t}\left(F_{Y_t|X_t=\bar{x}_t}(\eta_t)\right).$$

Let r_t denote the inverse of m_t with respect to η_t. Then, given y_t, x_t

$$\eta_t = r_t(x_t, y_t) = F^{-1}_{Y_t|X_t=\bar{x}_t}\left(F_{Y_t|X_t=x_t}(y_t)\right).$$

We can then analyze the identification of the factor model, as in Carneiro, Hansen and Heckman (2003), from the system

$$\eta_t = \beta_t\theta + \varepsilon_t$$

where η_t is interpreted as a measurement on θ. One could also allow X to depend on η_t, using Matzkin (2004). Suppose that there exists Z_t such that η_t is independent of X_t

conditional on Z_t. Then, one can obtain identification of m_t and η_t. One way of guaranteeing that this condition is satisfied is by assuming that there exists an unobservable ϕ_t and a function v_t, such that

$$X_t = v_t(Z_t, \phi_t)$$

and ϕ_t is independent of (θ, δ_t) conditional on Z_t.

4.5.3. *Index models with fixed effects*

Abrevaya (2000) established the identification of the coefficients of a linear index model for panel data models with two observations. Abrevaya's model was

$$Y_{it} = D \circ G(\beta X_{it}, \varepsilon_i, \eta_{it}), \quad i = 1, \dots, N, \ t = 1, 2,$$

where for each ε_i, the function G is strictly increasing in βX_{it} and η_{it}. The function D is assumed to be monotone increasing and nonconstant, (η_{i1}, η_{i2}) is independent of $(X_{i1}, X_{i2}, \varepsilon_i)$ and has support R^2, and one of the coordinates of $X_{it} \in R^K$ is continuously distributed with support R, conditional on the other coordinates. The model is then like the one studied in Han (1987) with the added fixed effect ε_i. In the same way that Matzkin (1991b) modified the arguments in Han (1987) to show the identification of a nonparametric index function, one can modify Abrevaya's arguments to establish the identification of the nonparametric function h^* in the model

$$Y_{it} = D \circ G\big(h^*(X_{it}), \varepsilon_i, \eta_{it}\big), \quad i = 1, \dots, N, \ t = 1, 2.$$

Assume that the function G is strictly increasing in its first and third arguments; the function D is monotone increasing and nonconstant; (η_{i1}, η_{i2}) is independent of $(X_{i1}, X_{i2}, \varepsilon_i)$; conditional on ε_i, (X_{i1}, η_{i1}) is independent of (X_{i2}, η_{i2}); and (X_{i1}, X_{i2}) has support R^{2K}. Let h^* belong to a set of continuous, homogeneous of degree one functions, $h : R^K \to R$, that are strictly increasing in the last coordinate, and satisfy $h(\bar{x}) = \alpha$. Then, within this set,

(4.h) *h^* is identified.*

PROOF OF (4.h). Suppose that h belongs to the set of continuous, homogeneous of degree one functions, that are strictly increasing in the last coordinate, and satisfy $h(\bar{x}) = \alpha$, and that $h \neq h^*$. Then, following the arguments in Matzkin (1991b), one can show that there exist neighborhoods N_1 and N_2 such that for all $x_1'' \in N_1$ and $x_2'' \in N_2$,

$$h^*(x_1'') > h^*(x_2'') \quad \text{and} \quad h(x_1'') < h(x_2'').$$

For each ε_i, the model is as the one considered in Matzkin (1991b). Hence, by analogous arguments, it follows by independence that, conditional on ε_i, since$h^*(x_1'') > h^*(x_2'')$

$$\Pr\big[Y_{it} > Y_{is} \big| X_{it} = x_1'', \ X_{is} = x_2'', \ \varepsilon_i; \ h^*\big]$$

$$= \Pr\{(\eta_{it}, \eta_{is}) | D \circ G(h^*(x_1''), \varepsilon_i, \eta_{it}) > D \circ G(h^*(x_2''), \varepsilon_i, \eta_{is})\}$$
$$< \Pr\{(\eta_{it}, \eta_{is}) | D \circ G(h^*(x_1''), \varepsilon_i, \eta_{it}) < D \circ G(h^*(x_2''), \varepsilon_i, \eta_{is})\}$$
$$= \Pr[Y_{it} > Y_{is} | X_{it} = x_1'', X_{is} = x_2'', \varepsilon_i; h^*]$$

and, since $h(x_1'') < h(x_2'')$,

$$\Pr[Y_{it} > Y_{is} | X_{it} = x_1'', X_{is} = x_2'', \varepsilon_i; h]$$
$$= \Pr\{(\eta_{it}, \eta_{is}) | D \circ G(h(x_1''), \varepsilon_i, \eta_{it}) > D \circ G(h(x_2''), \varepsilon_i, \eta_{is})\}$$
$$> \Pr\{(\eta_{it}, \eta_{is}) | D \circ G(h(x_1''), \varepsilon_i, \eta_{it}) < D \circ G(h(x_2''), \varepsilon_i, \eta_{is})\}$$
$$= \Pr[Y_{it} > Y_{is} | X_{it} = x_1'', X_{is} = x_2'', \varepsilon_i; h].$$

Integrating over any two possible distributions for ε_i conditional on (x_1'', x_2''), we get

$$\Pr[Y_{it} > Y_{is} | X_{it} = x_1'', X_{is} = x_2''; h^*] < \Pr[Y_{it} > Y_{is} | X_{it} = x_1'', X_{is} = x_2''; h^*]$$

and

$$\Pr[Y_{it} > Y_{is} | X_{it} = x_1'', X_{is} = x_2''; h] > \Pr[Y_{it} > Y_{is} | X_{it} = x_1'', X_{is} = x_2''; h].$$

Hence, the distribution of the observable variables is different under h than under h^*. It follows that h^* is identified. □

Chesher (2005) considers a model with many unobservables.

4.5.4. *Single equation models with multivariate unobservables*

Matzkin (2003) considers the model

$$Y = m(X, \varepsilon_1, \ldots, \varepsilon_K)$$

where $(\varepsilon_1, \ldots, \varepsilon_K)$ is independent of X and $\varepsilon_1, \ldots, \varepsilon_K$ are mutually independent. Suppose that X can be partitioned into $(X_1, \ldots, X_K)$ such that for some known r and unknown functions $m_1, \ldots, m_K$,

$$Y = r(m_1(X_1, \varepsilon_1), m_2(X_2, \varepsilon_2), \ldots, m_K(X_K, \varepsilon_K)).$$

Suppose that r is strictly increasing in each coordinate and that for each k, there exist for all coordinates j different from k, values $x_j^{(k)}$ such that, when $x = (x_1^{(k)}, \ldots, x_{k-1}^{(k)}, x_k, x_{k+1}^{(k)}, \ldots, x_K^{(k)})$ the conditional distribution $F_{Y|X=x}$ of Y given $X = (x_1^{(k)}, \ldots, x_K^{(k)})$ is strictly increasing and identified, and for all $j \neq k$,

$$m_j(x_j^{(k)}, \varepsilon_j) = \alpha_j$$

for a specified value α_j. Then, for all x_k and ε_k

$$F_{Y|X=(x_1^{(k)},\ldots,x_{k-1}^{(k)},x_k,x_{k+1}^{(k)},\ldots,x_K^{(k)})}\big(r\big(\alpha_1,\ldots,\alpha_{k-1},m_k(x_k,\varepsilon_k),\alpha_{k+1},\ldots,\alpha_K\big)\big)$$
$$= F_{\varepsilon_k}(\varepsilon_k).$$

In this expression, all functions and values are known except for $m_k(x_k, \varepsilon_k)$ and $F_{\varepsilon_k}(\varepsilon_k)$. A normalization on either of these, as described in Section 3.3, or a restriction on m_k, as described in Section 4.1.1, can be used to identify m_k and F_{ε_k}. A similar argument can be used to show that under analogous conditions, all the functions m_k and all the marginal distributions F_{ε_k} can be identified. Since $\varepsilon_1, \ldots, \varepsilon_K$ are assumed to be mutually independent, the identification of the marginal distributions of each of the ε_k implies the identification of $F_{\varepsilon_1,\ldots,\varepsilon_K}$. To provide an example, suppose that

$$Y = \sum_{k=1}^{K} m_k(x_k, \varepsilon_k)$$

where for each k, all ε_k, and for specified values $\alpha_1, \ldots, \alpha_K$, $\tilde{x}_k$ and $\bar{x}_k$, $m_k(\tilde{x}_k, \varepsilon_k) = \alpha_k$ and $m_k(\bar{x}_k, \varepsilon_k) = \varepsilon_k$. Then, letting $x^* = (\tilde{x}_1^{(k)}, \ldots, \tilde{x}_{k-1}^{(k)}, \bar{x}_k, \tilde{x}_{k+1}^{(k)}, \ldots, \tilde{x}_K^{(k)})$, $x^{**} = (\tilde{x}_1^{(k)}, \ldots, \tilde{x}_{k-1}^{(k)}, x_k, \tilde{x}_{k+1}^{(k)}, \ldots, \tilde{x}_K^{(k)})$

$$m_k(x_k, \varepsilon_k) = F^{-1}_{Y|X=x^{**}}\left(F_{Y|X=x^*}\left(\varepsilon_k - \sum_{j=1,\, j\neq k}^{K} \alpha_j\right)\right) - \sum_{j=1,\, j\neq k}^{K} \alpha_j.$$

Note that the linear random coefficients model, where $Y = \sum_{k=1}^{K} \beta_k x_k$, for unobservable, mutually independent $\beta_1, \ldots, \beta_K$, is an example of a model that satisfies the above restrictions. In this case, $\tilde{x}_k = 0$ and $\bar{x}_k = 1$.

5. Conclusions

This chapter has attempted to provide some insight into some of the results that have been developed recently for nonparametric models, with emphasis on those with nonadditive unobservable random terms. We first presented some general identification results about nonparametric models with additive unobservables, nonadditive unobservables, index models, simultaneous equations models, and discrete choice models. Next, we discussed some techniques that have been used to achieve identification, such as imposing additional restrictions on the functions and/or distributions in the models, or augmenting the data.

References

Abbring, J.H., van den Berg, G.J. (2003). "The nonparametric identification of treatment effects in duration models". Econometrica 71, 1491–1517.

Abrevaya, J.A. (2000). "Rank estimation of a generalized fixed-effects regression model". Journal of Econometrics 95, 1–23.
Ai, C. (1997). "A semiparametric maximum likelihood estimator". Econometrica 65, 933–963.
Ai, C., Chen, X. (2003). "Efficient estimation of models with conditional moments restrictions containing unknown functions". Econometrica 71, 1795–1843.
Aigner, D.J., Hsiao, C., Kapteyn, A., Wansbeek, T. (1984). "Latent variable models in econometrics". In: Griliches, Z., Intriligator, M.D. (Eds.), Handbook of Econometrics, vol. 2. North-Holland, Amsterdam.
Altonji, J.G., Ichimura, H. (2000). "Estimating derivatives in nonseparable models with limited dependent variables". Mimeo. Revision of 1996 working paper.
Altonji, J.G., Matzkin, R.L. (2001). "Panel data estimators for nonseparable models with endogenous regressors". NBER Working Paper T0267. Revision of 1997 working paper.
Altonji, J.G., Matzkin, R.L. (2005). "Cross section and panel data estimators for nonseparable models with endogenous regressors". Econometrica 73 (3), 1053–1102.
Anderson, T.W., Rubin, H. (1956). "Statistical inference in factor analysis". In: Neyman, J. (Ed.), Proceedings of Third Berkeley Symposium on Mathematical Statistics and Probability, vol. 5. University of California Press, pp. 111–150.
Barros, R., Honoré, B. (1988). "Identification of duration models with unobserved heterogeneity". Working paper. Northwestern University.
Benkard, C.L., Berry, S. (2004). "On the nonparametric identification of nonlinear simultaneous equations models: Comment on B. Brown (1983) and Roehrig (1988)". Cowles Foundation Discussion Paper #1482.
Blundell, R., Matzkin, R.L. (2007). "Conditions for the existence of control functions in nonseparable simultaneous equations models". Mimeo. Northwestern University.
Blundell, R., Powell, J.L. (2003). "Endogeneity in nonparametric and semiparametric regression models". In: Dewatripont, M., Hansen, L.P., Turnovsky, S.J. (Eds.), Advances in Economics and Econometrics, Theory and Applications, Eighth World Congress, vol. II. Cambridge Univ. Press, Cambridge, UK.
Bonhomme, S., Robin, J.-M. (2006). "Using high-order moments to estimate linear independent factor models". Mimeo, UCL.
Bowden, R. (1973). "The theory of parametric identification". Econometrica 41, 1069–1074.
Brown, B.W. (1983). "The identification problem in systems nonlinear in the variables". Econometrica 51, 175–196.
Brown, D.J., Calsamiglia, C. (2004). The strong law of demand. CFDP # 1399, Yale University.
Brown, D.J., Matzkin, R.L. (1998). "Estimation of nonparametric functions in simultaneous equations models, with an application to consumer demand". Cowles Foundation Discussion Paper #1175.
Card, D. (2001). "Estimating the return to schooling: Progress on some persistent econometric problems". Econometrica 69, 1127–1160.
Carneiro, P., Hansen, K.T., Heckman, J.J. (2003). "Estimating distributions of counterfactuals with an application to the returns to schooling and measurement of the effects of uncertainty on college choice". International Economic Review.
Chamberlain, G. (1977a). "Education, income, and ability revisited". Journal of Econometrics 5 (2), 241–257.
Chamberlain, G. (1977b). "An instrumental variable interpretation of identification in variance components and MIMIC models". In: Taubman, P. (Ed.), Kinometrics: Determinants of Socio-Economic Success Within and Between Families. North-Holland, Amsterdam.
Chamberlain, G., Griliches, Z. (1975). "Unobservables with a variance-component structure: Ability, schooling, and the economic success of brothers". International Economic Review 16 (2), 422–449.
Chaudhuri, P. (1991). "Nonparametric estimation of regression quantiles and their local Badahur representation". Annals of Statistics 19, 760–777.
Chaudhuri, P., Doksum, K., Samarov, A. (1997). "On average derivatives quantile regression". Annals of Statistics 25, 715–744.
Chen, X. (2007). "Large sample sieve estimation of semi-nonparametric models". In: Heckman, J.J., Leamer, E. (Eds.), In: Handbook of Econometrics, vol. 6B. Elsevier (Chapter 76).
Chernozhukov, V., Hansen, C. (2005). "An IV model of quantile treatment effects". Econometrica 73, 245–261.

Chernozhukov, V., Imbens, G., Newey, W. (2007). "Instrumental variable estimation of nonseparable models". Journal of Econometrics 139 (1), 4–14.
Chesher, A. (2003). "Identification in nonseparable models". Econometrica 71 (5).
Chesher, A. (2005). "Identification with excess heterogeneity". Mimeo. CEMMAP.
Chesher, A. (2007). "Identification of nonadditive structural functions". In: Blundell, R., Newey, W.K., Persson, T. (Eds.), Advances in Economics and Econometrics: Theory and Applications, Ninth World Congress, Vol. III. Cambridge University Press, New York.
Cosslett, S.R. (1983). "Distribution-free maximum likelihood estimator of the binary choice model". Econometrica 51 (3), 765–782.
Cunha, F., Heckman, J.J., Matzkin, R.L. (2004). "Identification of factors in nonadditive models". Mimeo.
Darolles, S., Florens, J.P., Renault, E. (2000). "Nonparametric instrumental regression". Mimeo. IDEI, Toulouse.
Das, M. (2001). "Monotone comparative statics and estimation of behavioral parameters". Mimeo. Columbia University.
Das, M. (2004). "Instrumental variables estimators of nonparametric models with discrete endogenous regressors". Journal of Econometrics 124, 335–361.
Elbers, C., Ridder, G. (1982). "True and spurious duration dependence: The identificability of the proportional Hazard model". Review of Economic Studies 49, 403–409.
Fan, Y., Li, Q. (1996). "Consistent model specification tests: Omitted variables and semiparametric functional forms". Econometrica 64 (4).
Fisher, F.M. (1959). "Generalization of the rank and order conditions for identifiability". Econometrica 27 (3), 431–447.
Fisher, F.M. (1961). "Identifiability criteria in nonlinear systems". Econometrica 29, 574–590.
Fisher, F.M. (1965). "Identifiability criteria in nonlinear systems: A further note". Econometrica 33, 197–205.
Fisher, F.M. (1966). The Identification Problem in Econometrics. McGraw–Hill, New York.
Florens, J.P. (2003). "Inverse problems and structural econometrics: The example of instrumental variables". In: Dewatripont, M., Hansen, L.P., Turnovsky, S. (Eds.), Advances in Economics and Econometrics, Theory and Applications, vol. II. Cambridge Univ. Press, Cambridge.
Frisch, R.A.K. (1934). "Statistical confluence analysis by means of complete regression systems". Publication No. 5. Universitets Okonomiske Institutt, Oslo.
Frisch, R.A.K. (1938). "Statistical versus theoretical relations in economic macrodynamics". Memorandum prepared for a conference in Cambridge, England, July 18–20, 1938, to discuss drafts of Tinbergen's League of Nations publications.
Gale, D., Nikaido, H. (1965). "The Jacobian matrix and global univalence of mappings". Math. Annalen 159, 81–93.
Gallant, A.R., Nychka, D.W. (1987). "Seminonparametric maximum likelihood estimation". Econometrica 55, 363–390.
Goldberger, A.S. (1972). "Structural equation methods in the social sciences". Econometrica 40, 979–1001.
Haavelmo, T. (1943). "The statistical implications of a system of simultaneous equations". Econometrica 11 (1), 1–12.
Haavelmo, T. (1944). "The probability approach in econometrics". Econometrica 12 (Suppl.) (July).
Hall, P., Horowitz, J.L. (2005). "Nonparametric methods for inference in the presence of instrumental variables". Annals of Statistics 33, 2904–2929.
Han, A.K. (1987). "Nonparametric analysis of a generalized regression model: The maximum rank correlation estimation". Journal of Econometrics 35, 303–316.
Härdle, W. (1991). Applied Nonparametric Regression. Cambridge Univ. Press, Cambridge.
Härdle, W., Linton, O. (1994). "Applied nonparametric methods". In: Engel, R.F., McFadden, D.F. (Eds.), Handbook of Econometrics, vol. 4. Elsevier, Amsterdam (Chapter 38).
Hausman, J.A. (1983). "Specification and estimation of simultaneous equation models". In: Griliches, Z., Intriligator, M.D. (Eds.), Handbook of Econometrics, vol. I.
Hausman, J.A., Taylor, W.E. (1983). "Identification in linear simultaneous equations models with covariance restrictions: An instrumental variables interpretation". Econometrica 51 (5), 1527–1550.

Heckman, J.J. (1974). "Shadow prices, market wages, and labor supply". Econometrica 42, 679–693.

Heckman, J.J. (1991). "Identifying the hand of past: Distinguishing state dependence from heterogeneity". In: Papers and Proceedings of the Hundred and Third Annual Meeting of the American Economic Association. American Economic Review 81 (2), 75–79.

Heckman, J.J., Robb, R. (1985). "Alternative methods for evaluating the impact of interventions". In: Heckman, J.J., Singer, B. (Eds.), Longitudinal Analysis of Labor Market Data. In: Econometric Society Monograph, vol. 10. Cambridge Univ. Press, Cambridge, UK.

Heckman, J.J., Singer, B. (1984a). "The identifiability of the proportional hazard model". Review of Economic Studies 51, 231–243.

Heckman, J.J., Singer, B. (1984b). "A method of minimizing the impact of distributional assumptions in econometric models for duration data". Econometrica 52, 271–320.

Heckman, J.J., Vytlacil, E.J. (1999). "Local instrumental variables and latent variable models for identifying and bounding treatment effects". Proceedings of the National Academy of Science 96.

Heckman, J.J., Vytlacil, E.J. (2000). "Structural equations, treatment effects and econometric policy evaluation". Mimeo. University of Chicago.

Heckman, J.J., Willis, R. (1977). "A beta-logistic model for the analysis of sequential labor force participation by married women". Journal of Political Economy.

Hong, Y., White, H. (1995). "Consistent specification testing via nonparametric series regression". Econometrica 63 (5), 1133–1159.

Honoré, B.E. (1990). "Simple estimation of a duration model with unobserved heterogeneity". Econometrica 58, 453–473.

Horowitz, J.L. (1992). "A smoothed maximum score estimator for the binary response model". Econometrica 60, 505–531.

Horowitz, J.L. (1996). "Semiparametric estimation of a regression model with an unknown transformation of the dependent variable". Econometrica 64, 103–137.

Horowitz, J.L. (1998). Semiparametric Methods in Econometrics. Springer-Verlag, New York.

Horowitz, J.L. (1999). "Semiparametric estimation of a proportional hazard model with unobserved heterogeneity". Econometrica.

Horowitz, J.L. (2001). "Nonparametric estimation of a generalized additive model with an unknown link function". Econometrica.

Horowitz, J.L., Härdle, W. (1996). "Direct semiparametric estimation of single index models with discrete covariates". Journal of the American Statistical Association 91, 1632–1640.

Hsiao, C. (1983). "Identification". In: Griliches, Z., Intriligator, M.D. (Eds.), Handbook of Econometrics, vol. 1. North-Holland Publishing Company.

Hurwicz, L. (1950). "Generalization of the concept of identification". In: Statistical Inference in Dynamic Economic Models. In: Cowles Commission Monograph, vol. 10. John Wiley, New York.

Ichimura, H. (1993). "Semiparametric least squares (SLS) and weighted SLS estimation of single-index models". Journal of Econometrics 58, 71–120.

Ichimura, H., Lee, L.-F. (1991). "Semiparametric least squares estimation of multiple index models: Single equation estimation". In: Barnett, W.A., Powell, J., Tauchen, G. (Eds.), Nonparametric and Semiparametric Methods in Econometrics and Statistics. Cambridge Univ. Press, Cambridge (Chapter 1).

Imbens, G.W., Newey, W.K. (2003). "Identification and estimation of triangular simultaneous equations models without additivity". Mimeo. MIT.

Jöreskog, K.G., Goldberger, A.S. (1972). "Factor analysis by generalized least squares". Psychometrika 37, 243–265.

Klein, R.W., Spady, R.H. (1993). "An efficient semiparametric estimator for binary response models". Econometrica 61, 387–421.

Koenker, R.W. (2005). Quantile Regression. Econometric Society Monograph Series. Cambridge Univ. Press, Cambridge.

Koopmans, T.C. (1949). "Identification problems in economic model construction". Econometrica 17 (2), 125–144.

Koopmans, T.C., Reiersol, O. (1950). "The identification of structural characteristics". Annals of Mathematical Statistics 21, 165–181.

Koopmans, T.C., Rubin, A., Leipnik, R.B. (1950). "Measuring the equation system of dynamic economics". In: Statistical Inference in Dynamic Equilibrium Models. In: Cowles Commission Monograph, vol. 10. John Wiley, New York.

Kotlarski, I. (1967). "On characterizing the Gamma and normal distribution". Pacific Journal of Mathematics 20, 69–76.

Lancaster, T. (1979). "Econometric methods for the analysis of unemployment". Econometrica 47, 939–956.

Lancaster, T. (1990). The Econometrics of Transition Data. Econometric Society Monograph, vol. 17. Cambridge Univ. Press.

Lewbel, A. (2000). "Semiparametric qualitative response model estimation with unknown heteroskedasticity and instrumental variables". Journal of Econometrics 97, 145–177.

Lewbel, A., Linton, O.B. (2007). "Nonparametric matching and efficient estimators of homothetically separable functions". Econometrica 75 (4), 1209–1227.

Linton, O.B., Nielsen, J.P. (1995). "A kernel method of estimating structured nonparametric regression based on marginal integration". Biometrika 82, 93–100.

Ma, L., Koenker, R.W. (2006). "Quantile regression methods for recursive structural equation models". Journal of Econometrics 134 (2), 471–506.

Manski, C.F. (1975). "Maximum score estimation of the stochastic utility model of choice". Journal of Econometrics 3, 205–228.

Manski, C.F. (1983). "Closest empirical distribution estimation". Econometrica 51 (2), 305–320.

Manski, C.F. (1985). "Semiparametric analysis of discrete response: Asymptotic properties of the maximum score estimator". Journal of Econometrics 27, 313–334.

Matzkin, R.L. (1991a). "Semiparametric estimation of monotone and concave utility functions for polychotomous choice models". Econometrica 59, 1315–1327.

Matzkin, R.L. (1991b). "A nonparametric maximum rank correlation estimator". In: Barnett, W., Powell, J., Tauchen, G. (Eds.), Nonparametric and Semiparametric Methods in Econometrics and Statistics. Cambridge Univ. Press, Cambridge.

Matzkin, R.L. (1992). "Nonparametric and distribution-free estimation of the binary threshold crossing and the binary choice models". Econometrica 60, 239–270.

Matzkin, R.L. (1993). "Nonparametric identification and estimation of polychotomous choice models". Journal of Econometrics 58, 137–168.

Matzkin, R.L. (1994). "Restrictions of economic theory in nonparametric methods". In: Engel, R.F., McFadden, D.L. (Eds.), Handbook of Econometrics, vol. IV. Elsevier, Amsterdam (Chapter 42).

Matzkin, R.L. (1999). "Nonparametric estimation of nonadditive random functions". Mimeo. Northwestern University.

Matzkin, R.L. (2003). "Nonparametric estimation of nonadditive random functions". Econometrica 71, 1339–1375.

Matzkin, R.L. (2004). "Unobservable instruments". Mimeo, Northwestern University.

Matzkin, R.L. (2005a). "Identification of consumers' preferences when individuals' choices are unobservable". Economic Theory 26 (2), 423–443.

Matzkin, R.L. (2005b). "Identification in nonparametric simultaneous equations models". Mimeo. Northwestern University.

Matzkin, R.L. (2007a). "Heterogenous choice". In: Blundell, R., Newey, W.K., Persson, T. (Eds.), Advances in Economics and Econometrics: Theory and Applications, Ninth World Congress, Vol. III. Cambridge University Press, New York.

Matzkin, R.L. (2007b). "Estimation of nonparametric simultaneous equations models". Mimeo. Northwestern University.

Matzkin, R.L. (2007c). "Identification in nonparametric simultaneous equations models". Mimeo. Northwestern University. Revision of 2005 working paper.

Matzkin, R.L., Newey, W.K. (1993). "Kernel estimation of nonparametric limited dependent variable models". Working paper. Northwestern University.

McFadden, D. (1974). "Conditional logit analysis of qualitative choice behavior". In: Zarembka, P. (Ed.), Frontiers in Econometrics. Academic Press, New York, pp. 105–142.
Ng, S., Pinkse, J. (1995). "Nonparametric-two-step estimation of unknown regression functions when the regressors and the regression error are not independent". Cahiers de recherche 9551. Universite de Montreal, Departement de sciences economiques.
Newey, W.K. (2001). "Flexible simulated moment estimation of nonlinear error-in-variables models". Review of Economics and Statistics 83, 616–627.
Newey, W., Powell, J. (1989). "Instrumental variables estimation of nonparametric models". Mimeo.
Newey, W. Powell, J. (2003). "Instrumental variables estimation of nonparametric models". Econometrica.
Newey, W.K., Powell, J.L., Vella, F. (1999). "Nonparametric estimation of triangular simultaneous equations models". Econometrica 67, 565–603.
Olley, G.S., Pakes, A. (1996). "The dynamics of productivity in the telecommunications equipment industry". Econometrica 64 (6), 1263–1297.
Pagan, A., Ullah, A. (1999). Nonparametric Econometrics. Cambridge Univ. Press, Cambridge, UK.
Pearl, J. (2000). Causality: Models, Reasoning, and Inference. Cambridge Univ. Press, New York.
Pinkse, J. (2000). "Nonparametric two-step regression estimation when regressors and errors are dependent". Canadian Journal of Statistics 28 (2), 289–300.
Powell, J.L. (1994). "Estimation of semiparametric models". In: Engel, R.F., McFadden, D.L. (Eds.), Handbook of Econometrics, vol. IV. Elsevier, Amsterdam (Chapter 41).
Powell, J.L., Stock, J.H., Stoker, T.M. (1989). "Semiparametric estimation of index coefficients". Econometrica 51, 1403–1430.
Prakasa-Rao, B.L.S. (1983). Nonparametric Functional Estimation. Academic Press.
Ridder, G. (1990). "The nonparametric identification of generalized accelerated failure-time models". Review of Economic Studies 57, 167–182.
Roehrig, C.S. (1988). "Conditions for identification in nonparametric and parametric models". Econometrica 56 (2), 433–447.
Rothenberg, T.J. (1971). "Identification in parametric models". Econometrica 39, 577–592.
Schennach, S. (2007). "Instrumental variable estimation of nonlinear errors-in-variables model". Econometrica 75 (1), 201–239.
Stoker, T.M. (1986). "Consistent estimation of scaled coefficients". Econometrica 54, 1461–1481.
Tinbergen, J. (1930). "Bestimmung und Deutung von Angebotskurven: Ein Beispiel". Zeitschrift für Nationalökonomie 70, 331–342.
van den Berg, G. (2001). "Duration models: Specification, identification, and multiple durations". In: Heckman, J., Leamer, E. (Eds.), Handbook of Econometrics, vol. 5.
Vytlacil, E., Yildiz, N. (2004). "Dummy endogenous variables in weakly separable models". Mimeo. Department of Economics, Stanford University.
Wald, A. (1950). "Note on identification of economic relations". In: Statistical Inference in Dynamic Economic Models. In: Cowles Commission Monograph, vol. 10. John Wiley, New York.
Wegge, L.L. (1965). "Identifiability criteria for a system of equations as a whole". The Australian Journal of Statistics 7, 67–77.
Wooldridge, J.M. (1992). "A test for functional form against nonparametric alternatives". Econometric Theory 8, 452–475.
Working, E.J. (1927). "What do statistical 'demand curves' show?". Quarterly Journal of Economics 41, 212–235.
Working, H. (1925). "The statistical determination of demand curves". Quarterly Journal of Economics 39, 503–543.
Yatchew, A. (2003). Semiparametric Regression for the Applied Econometrician. Cambridge Univ. Press, Cambridge, UK.

Chapter 74

IMPLEMENTING NONPARAMETRIC AND SEMIPARAMETRIC ESTIMATORS*

HIDEHIKO ICHIMURA

Graduate School of Economics, University of Tokyo, Tokyo, Japan
e-mail: ichimura@e.u-tokyo.ac.uk

PETRA E. TODD

Department of Economics, University of Pennsylvania, Philadelphia, PA, USA
e-mail: ptodd@econ.upenn.edu

Contents

* This research was supported by NSF grant #SBR-9730688, ESRC grant RES-000-23-0797, and JSPS grant 18330040. We thank Yoichi Arai, James Heckman, Whitney Newey, and Susanne Schennach for helpful comments. We also thank Jennifer Boober for detailed editorial comments.

Handbook of Econometrics, Volume 6B

DOI: 10.1016/S1573-4412(07)06074-6

Abstract

This chapter reviews recent advances in nonparametric and semiparametric estimation, with an emphasis on applicability to empirical research and on resolving issues that arise in implementation. It considers techniques for estimating densities, conditional mean functions, derivatives of functions and conditional quantiles in a flexible way that imposes minimal functional form assumptions.

The chapter begins by illustrating how flexible modeling methods have been applied in empirical research, drawing on recent examples of applications from labor economics, consumer demand estimation and treatment effects models. Then, key concepts in semiparametric and nonparametric modeling are introduced that do not have counterparts in parametric modeling, such as the so-called curse of dimensionality, the notion of models with an infinite number of parameters, the criteria used to define optimal convergence rates, and "dimension-free" estimators. After defining these new concepts, a large literature on nonparametric estimation is reviewed and a unifying framework presented for thinking about how different approaches relate to one another. Local polynomial estimators are discussed in detail and their distribution theory is developed. The chapter then shows how nonparametric estimators form the building blocks for many semiparametric estimators, such as estimators for average derivatives, index models, partially linear models, and additively separable models. Semiparametric methods offer a middle ground between fully nonparametric and parametric approaches. Their main advantage is that they typically achieve faster rates of convergence than fully nonparametric approaches. In many cases, they converge at the parametric rate.

The second part of the chapter considers in detail two issues that are central with regard to implementing flexible modeling methods: how to select the values of smoothing parameters in an optimal way and how to implement "trimming" procedures. It also reviews newly developed techniques for deriving the distribution theory of semiparametric estimators. The chapter concludes with an overview of approximation methods that speed up the computation of nonparametric estimates and make flexible estimation feasible even in very large size samples.

Keywords

flexible modeling, nonparametric estimation, semiparametric estimation, local polynomial estimators, smoothing parameter choice, convergence rates, asymptotic distribution theory, additively separable models, index models, average derivative estimator, maximum score estimator, least absolute deviations estimator, semiparametric least squares estimator, trimming, binning algorithms

JEL classification: C1, C13, C14, C52

1. Introduction

In the last two decades significant progress has been made in the study of nonparametric and semiparametric models. This chapter describes recent advances with special emphasis on their applicability to empirical research and on issues that arise in implementation. As the coverage of the chapter is broad, our discussion provides only an overview. It covers mostly cross sectional analysis emphasizing methods which have rigorous theoretical justifications, albeit in most cases only in first order asymptotic forms from frequentists' view point.[1] Nevertheless, we hope the chapter captures the basic motivations and ideas behind the developments and serves as a guide to using the methods appropriately. We begin by briefly summarizing the nature of recent progress, implications for empirical research, and some implementation issues.

1.1. The nature of recent progress

A major motivation for work on flexible models is the desire to avoid masking important features of the data by use of parametric models.[2] Recent progress has provided many new ways of modeling and estimating different aspects of a conditional probability distribution. For example, there are now a number of alternatives to linear regression model for modeling and estimating the conditional mean function as well as methods available for examining other features of distributions, such as conditional quantiles. Another area of advance has been in the study of models with limited dependent variables. In the early eighties, the standard approach with such models was to specify the error distribution parametrically and employ parametric maximum likelihood (ML) estimation. Recent research has shown that parametric specification of the error term is often unnecessary for consistent estimation of slope parameters. Models with simultaneity problems can also now be analyzed under weaker functional form assumptions. In these contexts and in others, model specification is beginning to be made more flexible. These developments enable empirical work to be carried out under fewer restrictions than was deemed possible twenty years ago.

Another important motivation for research on flexible models is the pursuit of a classical theme in econometrics: the study of the trade-off between efficiency and allowing for less restrictive models. We often wish to identify a parameter within the broadest class of models possible, but broadening a class sometimes comes at the expense of less efficient estimation. Recent research has clarified the trade-offs in terms of convergence rates and attainable efficiency bounds between specifying more or less restrictive models.

[1] For developments in studying panel data, see Arellano and Honoré (2001).

[2] See McFadden (1985). For brevity, we refer to nonparametric and semiparametric models as flexible models.

1.2. Benefits of flexible modeling approaches for empirical research

From an empirical perspective, the primary benefit of recent work in flexible modeling is a provision of new estimation methods with a better understanding of the efficiency loss associated with different modeling approaches. Another benefit is that the departure from the traditional linear modeling framework decreases the tendency to focus on the conditional mean function as the sole object of interest. Using flexible models provides a natural way of considering other aspects of the probability distribution that may be of interest, such as conditional quantiles.[3] Research on limited dependent variable models has shown that quantile restrictions provide sharper restrictions than conditional mean restrictions for identifying model parameters.[4]

When we construct an econometric model of a dependent variable, either explicitly or implicitly, we model the form of a conditional distribution function. Sometimes the conditional distribution function is the parameter of interest, but more often we are interested in particular aspects of it, such as the conditional mean function, conditional quantile function, or derivatives of these functions, as we will see in the next section. When data on the dependent variable given some conditioning variables are directly observed for a random sample of the population, then the nonparametric methods discussed later in this chapter can be directly applied. However, often the application is not straightforward, because the conditional distribution that is observed differs from the conditional distribution in a random population. This can arise in variety of modeling situations, such as with limited dependent variable models, with models with measurement error, and with simultaneity. For example, a demand function can be represented as a conditional distribution of demand given price, but the distribution of the observed quantity-price data may differ from the conceptual conditional distribution we wish to study, because the supply side can affect the observed quantity and price as well.

When the conditional distribution of interest differs from the conditional distribution that can be measured directly from the data, there are two different approaches taken in the literature. One is to search for a source of variation in the data that can be used to identify the conceptual distribution of interest. This may require using data generated from a randomized experiment or from a so-called "natural experiment".[5] When variation of this sort is available in the data, the methods described in this chapter can often be directly applied. An alternative approach is to explicitly model the relationship between the observed distribution and the conceptual distribution of interest and then try to identify some aspects of the distribution of interest from the observed distribution. Much work has been done towards extending nonparametric methods to account for limited dependent variables, sample selectivity, and simultaneity. Section 2.2.3 provides some examples of applications of semiparametric selection models.

[3] See e.g. Buchinsky (1995, 1998), Chamberlain (1995), Buchinsky and Hahn (1998).

[4] Powell (1984), Manski (1985), Chamberlain (1986a), and Cosslett (1987).

[5] See Rosenzweig and Wolpin (2000) for a discussion of the use of natural experiments in economics.

An additional benefit of using flexible models is that they allow for a more direct connection between the parameters of interest and the identification restrictions being exploited in estimation. For example, consider the linear regression model with the conditional mean restriction $E(y|x) = x'\beta_0$. Here β_0 represents a vector that defines the conditional mean function and also a vector that defines the derivative of the conditional mean function. Generally, in a restricted framework conceptually different parameters may coincide and there can be a discrepancy between the parameter of interest and the source of variation in the data used to estimate the parameter. Using flexible models makes more transparent the source of variation in the data that should be used to estimate the parameter of interest. For example, it is natural to estimate β_0 by ordinary least squares when it represents a vector defining the conditional mean function and to estimate it by an average derivative estimator, when it represents a vector defining the derivative of the conditional mean function. Average derivative estimators are discussed below in Section 5. Actual implementation may require using a more restricted model for the curse of dimensionality problem we will discuss, however.

Finally, flexible models provide a systematic way of addressing concerns about model specification. First, they require fewer modeling assumptions, which directly eliminates the need for some specification testing. Second, they provide a formal framework for conducting the specification search. In parametric models, searches often proceed piecemeal, leaving the selection of which models to examine and the order in which to examine them up to the researcher. The route by which a particular model is chosen is often not made explicit, which makes it difficult to obtain general results about the properties of the estimators. Another difficulty is that there is no formal language for effectively communicating the domain of search, and the description of the domain is usually left up to the researcher's conscious effort. With nonparametric estimators, the class of models for which the estimation is valid is *a priori* specified, so that the domain is clear and the process by which a particular model is chosen is more transparent.

Careful researchers have always been aware of potential drawbacks of parametric models and have guarded against misspecification by examining the sensitivity of empirical results to alternative specifications and using imaginative ways of checking model restrictions.[6] The recent progress in flexible modeling makes it easier for researchers to address concerns about model specification and also to assess the variability of estimation procedures. The progress represents an important step towards replacing what has been characterized as the difficult art of model specification with a simpler, more systematic approach.

1.3. Implementation issues

So far we have emphasized the benefits of using flexible models. To fully realize these benefits, however, there are still some questions that need to be resolved regarding how

[6] Various formal specification tests and model selection rules have been developed. See for example Davidson and MacKinnon (1982), Hansen (1982), Hausman (1978), Newey (1985, 1987), Tauchen (1985), White (1980), and Wu (1974).

to choose a model and an estimation method that is well suited to a particular application and how to implement the chosen estimation method.

A key consideration in using a flexible model is that greater flexibility often comes at a cost of a slower convergence rate. Thus, understanding the trade-off between flexibility and efficiency is important to choosing an appropriate estimation strategy. A barrier to implementing the new estimators is how to choose from a bewildering array of available estimators. A first impression from studying nonparametric literature is the richness in the variety of methods. In this chapter, we attempt to pick up some common threads among different methods, to highlight differences and commonalities, and to discuss how each method has been theoretically justified.

Another consideration is that there is a degree of arbitrariness in many of the available estimation procedures that takes the form of unspecified parameters. The arbitrariness is not problematic for certain theoretical questions of interest, such as the question of whether a particular level of convergence rate is achievable. But the arbitrariness poses a problem when we implement the method, because different ways of specifying these parameters can greatly affect the estimates. For example, parameter estimates or asymptotic variance estimates can be highly sensitive to the choice of smoothing parameters or to different ways of trimming the data.[7] One focus of this chapter is on how to choose the values of these unspecified parameters.

A third problem we address is how to assess the variability of nonparametric and semiparametric estimators. In many empirical applications, the model used and methods applied deviate in some respects from the prototypical models and methods studied in the theoretic literature. Hence, it is important for researchers to be able to modify theories according to their needs and to derive the properties of modified versions of the estimators. For models and estimators based on moment conditions with finite dimensional parameters, Hansen (1982) and Pakes and Pollard (1989) provide results that are sufficiently general to accommodate many different kinds of modifications. For semiparametric models, some progress has also been made along similar lines. See Andrews (1994), and Newey and McFadden (1994), Ai and Chen (2003) and Chen, Linton and Van Keilegom (2003), and Ichimura and Lee (2006) and Chen (2007) in this volume (Chapter 76).

Finally, another obstacle in applying flexible estimators is that they can be computationally intensive, particularly for large data sets. Because of slower rates of convergence, the methods are ideally suited for larger data sets. Yet it is precisely when sample sizes are large, say on the order of 100,000, when the computational burden of these methods can make them impractical. We discuss approximation methods that speed up estimation and provide great gains in speed, making it feasible to analyze even very large samples.

[7] "Trimming" is the practice of excluding a fraction of observations in local nonparametric estimation. Trimming is required when the density of the data is low at these observations and a nonparametric estimate would be unreliable. See Section 6.

1.4. Overview of chapter

In Section 2, we illustrate through examples drawn from different empirical literatures how flexible estimation methods have been used as an alternative or as a supplement to more traditional estimation approaches. Section 3 describes some concepts in semiparametric and nonparametric modeling and makes precise how new developments in the literature broaden the kinds of models and parameters of interest that can be considered in empirical research.

Section 4 discusses nonparametric estimation of densities, conditional mean functions, and derivatives of functions. Although fully nonparametric analysis are not often practical because of slow rates of convergence, we begin with nonparametric estimators because they serve as building blocks for many semiparametric estimators. We discuss how apparently different estimators are in some ways closely related and present a unifying framework for thinking about nonparametric density and conditional mean estimators.

Section 5 considers estimation of the same parameters of interest (densities, conditional mean functions, and derivatives of functions) using semiparametric modeling methods that overcome the problem of slow-convergence of fully nonparametric estimators. We describe a variety of semiparametric approaches to estimating densities and conditional mean functions. Although there are many estimators proposed for a variety of semiparametric and nonparametric models in the literature, we only discuss a subset of them. The models we cover are additively separable models, index models, and partially linear models as well as nonparametric models.

Section 6 focuses on the question of how to choose smoothing parameters and trimming methods in implementing nonparametric and semiparametric models. The problem of choosing the values of these unspecified parameters is similar to a model selection problem in a parametric context. For each estimator, we summarize existing research on how to choose the values of these parameters and describe the evidence on the effectiveness of various smoothing parameter selection methods, some of which comes from our own Monte Carlo studies.

Section 7 discusses how to assess the variability of different estimation procedures. Section 8 examines the problem of how to compute local nonparametric estimates in large samples. We describe binning algorithms that speed up computation through accurate approximation of nonparametric densities and conditional mean functions.

Section 9 concludes with a discussion of other issues left for future research.

1.5. Related literature

There are many useful surveys in the literature to which we will at times refer in this chapter. For an excellent introduction to nonparametric literature in book form we recommend Silverman (1986) and Fan and Gijbels (1996). Surveys by Blundell and Duncan (1998), Härdle and Linton (1994), and Yatchew (1998) cover nonparametric methods compactly. Useful surveys for semiparametric models are given by Arellano and Honoré (2001), Delgado and Robinson (1992), Linton (1995b), Matzkin (1994), Newey and McFadden (1994), Powell (1994), and Robinson (1988).

Books by Bierens (1985), Härdle (1990), Prakasa-Rao (1983), and Scott (1992) cover nonparametric density or regression function estimation methods. Books by Horowitz (1998), Lee (1996), Pagan and Ullah (1999), Stoker (1991), Ullah and Vinod (1993), and Yatchew (2003) cover both nonparametric and semiparametric methods. Deaton (1996) describes how nonparametric and semiparametric models are used in substantively important applications related to household behavior and policy analysis in developing countries.

Efficiency issues are dealt with concisely by Newey (1990, 1994a) and in detail by Bickel et al. (1993). Most of the probabilistic techniques are explained by van der Vaart (1998) and van der Vaart and Wellner (1996).

2. Applications of flexible modeling approaches in economics

We first illustrate through several examples how flexible models have been used in empirical work, either as an alternative to more traditional estimation approaches or as a supplement to them. The examples are drawn from the literatures on estimating consumer demand functions, estimating the determinants of worker earnings, correcting for sample selection bias, and evaluating the effects of social programs. Our examples are chosen to highlight different kinds of parameters that may be of interest in empirical studies, such as densities, conditional mean and quantile functions and averages of the functions.

2.1. Density estimation

In many empirical studies, researchers are interested in analyzing the distribution of some random variable. Nonparametric density estimators provide a straightforward way of estimating densities. One nonparametric estimator that has already gained widespread use is the histogram estimator, which estimates the density by the fraction of observations falling within a specified bin divided by the bin width. In Section 4, we discuss how the histogram relates to other nonparametric density estimators and how to optimally choose the bin width. We also present alternatives to the histogram estimator that have superior properties, such as the Nadaraya–Watson kernel density estimator for particular choices of kernel functions, which can be viewed as a generalized version of the histogram estimator.

An innovative empirical application of nonparametric density estimation methods is given by DiNardo, Fortin and Lemiex (1996), which investigates the effects of institutional and labor market factors on changes in the US wage distribution over time. DiNardo, Fortin and Lemiex (1996) write the overall wage density at time t, $f_w(w|t)$, in terms of the conditional wage densities, where conditioning is on a set of labor market or institutional factors, z, whose effects on earnings they analyze:

$$f_w(w|t) = \int_Z f_w(w|z,t) f_z(z|t)\,dz.$$

In their study, z includes variables indicating union status, industrial sector, and whether the wage falls above or below the minimum wage. Counter-factual wage densities are then constructed by replacing $f_z(z|t)$ by a different hypothetical conditional density, $g_z(z|t)$, for the purpose of inferring the effect of changes in elements of z on the wage distribution.

A traditional parametric approach to simulating wage distributions would specify a parametric functional form for the w and z distributions, in which case inference would only be valid within the class of models specified. The approach taken in DiNardo, Fortin and Lemiex (1996) is to estimate the densities nonparametrically, using a nonparametric kernel density estimator that will be discussed in Section 4 of this chapter. Using a flexible modeling approach makes inference valid for a broader class of models and avoids the need to search for an appropriate parametric model specification for $f_w(w|z,t)$ and $f_z(z|t)$.

2.2. *Conditional mean and conditional quantile function estimation*

2.2.1. *Earnings function estimation*

In addition to studying the shape of the earnings distribution, economists are often interested in examining how changes in individual characteristics, such as education or years of labor market experience, affect some aspect of the distribution, such as the mean. An earnings specification that is widely used in empirical labor research is that of Mincer (1974), which writes log earnings as a linear function of years of schooling (s) and as a quadratic in years of work experience (exp) and other control variables (z):

$$\ln y = \alpha_0 + \rho s + \beta_1 \exp + \beta_2 \exp^2 + z'\gamma + \varepsilon.$$

This simple parametric specification captures several empirical regularities, such as concavity of log earnings-age and experience profiles and steeper profiles for persons with more years of education.[8] However, Mincer's model was derived under some strong assumptions, so it is of interest to also consider more general specifications of the earnings equation such as

$$\ln y = g(s, \exp, z) + \varepsilon,$$

where g is a function that is continuous in the continuous variable (experience). Usually the g function is interpreted as the conditional mean function. In Heckman, Lochner and Todd (in press), nonparametric regression methods are applied to estimate the above

[8] See Willis (1986) for a discussion of the use of the Mincer model in labor economics.

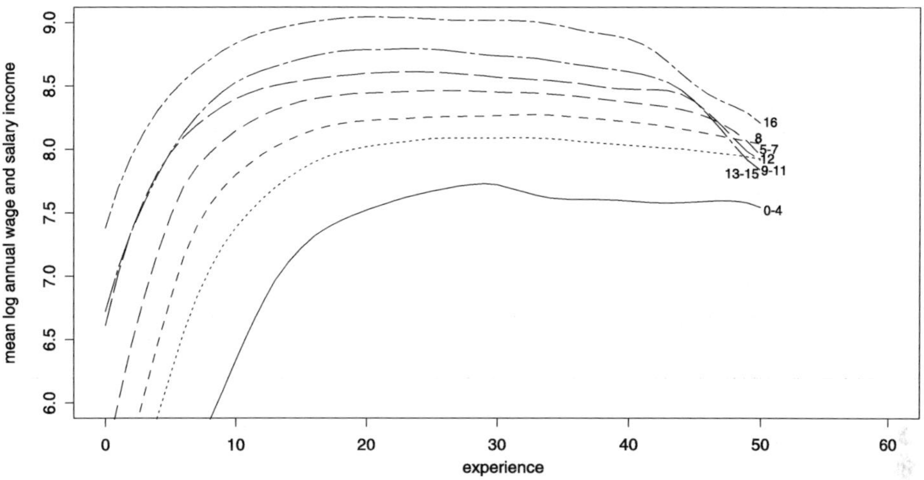

Figure 1. Earnings–experience profiles by education level estimated nonparametrically by a local linear regression estimator.

equation and to examine the empirical support for the parametric Mincer model. Their study finds substantial support for the parametric specification in decennial Census data from 1940–1960 but not in more recent decades.[9] Figure 1 shows the nonparametrically estimated log earnings–experience relationship for alternative schooling classes for adult males from the 1960 US decennial census [the same data analyzed by Mincer (1974)]. Nonparametric estimation was performed using local linear regression methods that are described in Section 4 of this chapter.

One can also interpret the g function to be the conditional quantile function, in which case the nonparametric or semiparametric quantile estimation methods [Koenker and Basset (1978) and Koenker (2005)] can be applied. For example, Buchinsky (1994) applies semiparametric conditional quantile estimation methods to study changes in the US Wage Structure from 1963–1987, using data from the Current Population Survey. He estimates a model of the form:

$$Y = X\beta_\theta + u_\theta,$$

where β_θ is a parameter that characterizes the conditional quantile. The model is estimated under the restriction that the θth conditional quantile of Y given $X = x$ is $x'\beta_\theta$.

The estimation yields a time series of the estimated returns to education and experience at different quantiles of the earnings distribution. Buchinsky (1994) finds that the

[9] Data from the 1940, 1950, 1960 show support for the model, but data from 1970, 1980 and 1990 show important deviations from the model, which Heckman, Lochner and Todd (in press) attribute in part to changing skill prices over recent decades, which violates an assumption of the traditional Mincer model.

mean returns to education and experience and the returns at different quantiles generally follow similar patterns. Analysis of the spreads of the distributions reveals large changes in the 0.75–0.25 spread and that changes in inequality come mainly from longer tails at both ends of the wage distribution.

2.2.2. *Analysis of consumer demand*

Several recent studies in consumer demand analysis have made use of flexible estimation techniques in estimating Engel curves, which relate a consumer's budget share or expenditure on a good to total expenditure or income. Economic theory does not place strong restrictions on functional forms for Engel curves, so earlier research addressed the question of model specification mainly by adopting flexible parametric functional forms. Recent research by Banks, Blundell and Lewbel (1997), Blundell and Duncan (1998), Deaton and Paxson (1998), Härdle, Hildenbrand and Jerison (1991), Schmalensee and Stoker (1999), and Blundell, Browning and Crawford (2003) consider nonparametric and semiparametric estimation of Engel curves. The basic modeling framework is

$$y = g(x, z) + u,$$

where y is the budget share of a good, x is total expenditure or income, and z represents other household or individual characteristics included as conditioning variables. Typically $g(x, z)$ is assumed to be the conditional mean function of y given x and z so that $E(u|x, z) = 0$.

The traditional approach to estimating conditional mean functions specifies the functional form of g up to some finite number of parameters. In consumer demand analysis, the Engel curve function is often assumed to be linear or quadratic in $\ln x$ and z and the coefficients on the conditioning variables are estimated by ordinary least squares (OLS). A nonparametric estimation approach places no restrictions on the $g(x, z)$ relationship other than assuming that the $g(\cdot)$ function lies within a class of smooth functions (such as the class of twice continuously differentiable functions).

As discussed in Section 3, with a large number of regressors fully nonparametric estimators converge at a rate that is too slow to be practical in conventional size samples. Semiparametric modeling approaches provide a more practical alternative. These methods achieve a faster rate of convergence by allowing some aspects of the $g(x, z)$ relationship to be flexible while imposing some parametric restrictions. For example, the approach taken in Banks, Blundell and Lewbel (1997), Blundell and Duncan (1998), and Deaton and Paxon (1998) is to model the budget–share–log-income relationship nonparametrically under the parametric restriction that other z covariates enter in a linear, additively separable way. This yields a *partially linear model*[10]:

$$y = g(x) + z\gamma + u.$$

[10] Schmalensee and Stoker (1999) adopt a similar but slightly more general specification.

Engle et al. (1986) considered electricity demand, x corresponds to the temperature and z captures household characteristics. In this application, the parameter of interest was $g(x)$, how the electricity demand peaked as temperature varied. When z are discrete variables, assuming that they enter in a linear fashion imposes only the assumption of additive separability.[11] Analogous to the Mincer example, the partially linear model may also be regarded as a conditional quantile function. Blundell, Chen and Kristensen (2003) have considered the consumer demand model allowing for endogeneity of income variable.

A variety of semiparametric estimators that allow for flexibility in different model components have been proposed in the econometrics and statistics literatures. Several classes of estimators will be discussed in Section 5 of this chapter.

2.2.3. *Analysis of sample selection*

A leading area of application of flexible estimation methods in economics is to the sample selection problem. In fact, several estimators for the partially linear model were developed with the sample selection model in mind.[12] In the sample selection problem, an outcome is observed for a nonrandom subsample of the population and the goal is to draw inferences that are valid for the full population. For example, in the analysis of labor supply the outcome equation corresponds to the market wage, observed only for workers, and the selection equation corresponds to the decision to participate in the labor force. The wage model takes the form

$$w = w(x, \theta_1) + u$$

where x denotes individual characteristics, w is observed if the wage exceeds the individual's reservation wage, w_r, which is the minimum wage the individual would be willing to accept.

Under sample selection, the above model leads to the wage model of the form:

$$w = w(x, \theta_1) + \varphi(x, z) + u$$

where $\varphi(x, z) = E(u|w > w_r, x)$ is the so-called *control function* that needs to be estimated along with parameter θ_1.[13] Clearly, in the above equation the functions $w(x, \theta_1)$ and $\varphi(x, z)$ could not be nonparametrically separately identified without some additional restrictions. Section 5 of this chapter considers alternative estimators for the sample selection model under different kinds of restrictions.

[11] In more recent work, Ai, Blundell and Chen (2000) consider the consumer demand model of the form

$$y = g(x + z\gamma) + z\gamma + u$$

and show that including the term $z\gamma$ both in the $g(\cdot)$ function and in the linear term is necessary to make the Engel curve consistent with a consumer demand system.

[12] The sample selection model is developed by Gronau (1973a, 1973b), Heckman (1976), and Lewis (1974).

[13] See Heckman (1980).

There have been numerous applications of the partially linear sample selection model. For example, Newey, Powell and Walker (1990) and Buchinsky (1998) apply the model to study female labor force participation. Stern (1996) uses it to study labor force participation among disabled workers. Olley and Pakes (1996) use the partially linear model to control for nonrandom firm exit decisions in a study of productivity in the telecommunications industry. Some additional applications are discussed in Section 5.

2.3. *Averages of functions: Evaluating effects of treatments*

A common problem that arises in economics as well as many other fields is that of determining the impact of some intervention or treatment on some measured outcome variables. For example, one may be interested in estimating the effect of a job training program on earnings or employment outcomes.[14] In evaluating social programs, the average effect of the program for people participating in it (known as the mean impact of treatment on the treated) is a key parameter of interest on which many studies focus.

Let (y_1, y_0) denote the outcomes for an individual in two hypothetical states of the world corresponding to with and without receiving treatment. Let d be an indicator variable that takes the value 1 if treatment is received and 0 otherwise. The outcome observed for each individual can be written as $y = dy_1 + (1-d)y_0$. The mean effect of the program for program participants with characteristic z is given by $E(y_1 - y_0|d = 1, z)$. The average of this parameter for the treated $(d = 1)$ population is $E(y_1 - y_0|d = 1)$.

Clearly the first parameter is more informative than the second. However, as discussed in detail in the next section and in Section 6, the conditional on z parameter can be estimated nonparametrically less accurately than the second parameter can be estimated nonparametrically.

A variety of estimators have been put forth in the literature to estimate $E(y_1 - y_0|D = 1)$. One class of estimators are so-called matching estimators, which impute no-treatment outcomes for treated persons by matching each treated person to one or more observably similar untreated persons. Heckman, Ichimura and Todd (1997, 1998a, 1998b) develop nonparametric matching estimators that use local polynomial regression methods to construct matched outcomes. Local polynomial regression estimators are discussed in Section 4. The application of these estimators in program evaluation settings is considered in this handbook in the preceding chapters by Abbring and Heckman (2007) and by Heckman and Vytlacil (2007a, 2007b). Other applications include Stock (1991) and Ichimura and Taber (2000).

3. Convergence rates, asymptotic bias, and the curse of dimensionality

A key motivation for developing flexible models is to achieve a closer match between the functional form restrictions suggested by economic theory, which are typically

[14] See, e.g., Ashenfelter (1978), Bassi (1984), Ashenfelter and Card (1985), Fraker and Maynard (1987), Heckman and Hotz (1989), Heckman and Smith (1995), Heckman et al. (1998), and Heckman, Ichimura and Todd (1997, 1998b), and Smith and Todd (2001, 2005).

weak, and the functional forms used in empirical work. To study aspects of the conditional distribution functions, such as the conditional mean function and the conditional quantile function, the linear in parameter model is traditionally used. Let the conditioning finite dimensional random vector be X, and a *known* finite dimensional vector-valued function evaluated at $X = x$ be $r(x)$. Then the linear in parameter model specifies the conditional mean function or the conditional quantile function of a dependent random variable Y by $r(x)'\theta$ for some *unknown finite dimensional vector* θ. For example $x = (x_1, x_2)'$ and $r(x) = (1, x_1, x_1^2, x_2, x_2^2, x_1 \cdot x_2)'$. The ordinary least squares (OLS) estimator estimates the conditional mean function and the quantile regression estimator estimates the conditional quantile function. Alternatively, the most flexible model would specify $\theta(x)$ for some *unknown function* $\theta(\cdot)$. The unknown function itself or its derivative could be the parameter of interest.

The specification of parametric models involves two difficulties: which variables to include in the model and what functional form to use. Although nonparametric methods do not resolve the first difficulty, they do resolve the second. Thus if $\theta(\cdot)$ could be estimated with the same accuracy as that for the finite dimensional case, then there would be no reason to consider a finite dimensional parameter model. Unfortunately, that is not the case.

Recall that under very general regularity conditions, including the random sampling, most of the familiar estimators – the OLS estimator, the generalized method of moment (GMM) estimator, and the maximum likelihood (ML) estimator – have the property that $n^{1/2}(\hat{\beta} - \beta)$ converges in distribution to the mean zero random vector with some finite variance–covariance matrix as the sample size n goes to infinity, where $\hat{\beta}$ denotes the estimator and β the target parameter. This implies not only that $\hat{\beta} - \beta$ converges to 0 in probability, but that the difference is bounded with arbitrarily high probability (i.e. stochastically bounded) even when it is blown up by the increasing sequence $n^{1/2}$. In this case, we say that the difference converges to 0 with rate $n^{-1/2}$, that the estimator is $n^{1/2}$-consistent and that its convergence rate is $n^{-1/2}$. More generally, if an estimator has the property that $r_n(\hat{\beta} - \beta)$ is stochastically bounded, then the estimator is said to be r_n-consistent or to have convergence rate is $1/r_n$. If $r_n/n^{1/2}$ converges to zero, then the r_n-consistent estimator converges to β slower than the $n^{1/2}$-consistent estimator does. When two estimators of the same parameter have different convergence rates, the one that approaches to the target faster is generally more desirable asymptotically.[15]

As discussed, there are estimators of the regression coefficient θ, such as the OLS estimator, that converge with rate $n^{-1/2}$, so that $r(x)'\theta$ can be estimated with the same rate. But in the context of estimating the conditional mean function, Stone (1980, 1982) showed that any estimator of the regression function $\theta(\cdot)$ converges slower than $n^{-1/2}$.

To state Stone's results, we need to clarify two complications that arise because the target parameter is a function rather than a point in a finite dimensional space $\mathbb{R}^d$ for

[15] Note that this is an asymptotic statement and the finite sample performance may be different. Clearly, it would also be desirable to have a better understanding about the sample size at which one estimator dominates the other.

some positive integer d. First, we need to define what we mean by an estimator to converge to a function. If we consider a function at a point, then the convergence rate can be considered in the same way discussed above. If we want to consider a convergence of an estimator of a regression function as a whole to the target regression function, then we need to define a measure of distance between two functions. There are different ways we can define the distance between the functions and the discussion about the convergence rate will generally depend on the distance measure used. Typically a norm is used to define the distance.

To define a few examples of the norms used, let $k = (k_1, \ldots, k_d)$ where k_j is a nonnegative integer for each $j = 1, \ldots, d$, and define $D^k\theta(x) = \partial^{k_1+\cdots+k_d}\theta(x)/\partial x_1^{k_1}\cdots\partial x_d^{k_d}$. Leading examples of the norms used are the L_q-norm for $1 \leqslant q < \infty$ ($\|\cdot\|_q$), the sup-norm ($\|\cdot\|_\infty$), and more generally the Sobolev norm ($\|\cdot\|_{\alpha,q}$ or $\|\cdot\|_{\alpha,\infty}$):

$$\left[\sum_{0\leqslant k_1+\cdots+k_d\leqslant\alpha}\int_{\mathcal{X}}\left|D^k\left(\hat{\theta}_n(x)-\theta(x)\right)\right|^q \mathrm{d}\mu(x)\right]^{1/q} \quad \text{or}$$

$$\max_{0\leqslant k_1+\cdots+k_d\leqslant\alpha}\ \sup_{x\in\mathcal{X}}\left|D^k\left(\hat{\theta}_n(x)-\theta(x)\right)\right|.$$

Note that $\|\cdot\|_{0,q} = \|\cdot\|_q$ and $\|\cdot\|_{0,\infty} = \|\cdot\|_\infty$.[16]

Once a norm is defined, then consistency and hence the rate of convergence concept can be defined using one of the three standard consistency concepts, convergence in probability, convergence almost surely, and the qth order moment convergence by how fast the distance between the estimator and the target function converges to 0.[17]

Which norm is more appropriate will depend on how the estimator is going to be used. For example if a function value at a point or its derivative is of interest, then L^q-norm is not useful because there are many functions close to a function in L^q-sense, which does not determine the value at that point, and the derivative values may be rather different. For these type of applications, the sup-norm may be used.

For any two norms, $\|\cdot\|_1$ and $\|\cdot\|_2$ in a finite dimensional space Θ there exist positive constants C_H and C_L such that for any θ and $\theta' \in \Theta$,

$$C_L\|\theta-\theta'\|_1 \leqslant \|\theta-\theta'\|_2 \leqslant C_H\|\theta-\theta'\|_1.$$

Hence, consistency using one norm implies consistency using another norm on the same space. For infinite dimensional spaces, this is no longer the case without any restriction on the class of functions under consideration. Thus we need to be more explicit about which norm is used to define consistency.[18]

[16] Clearly we need to restrict the class of functions so that the objects are well defined.

[17] More generally one can define a metric on a relevant space of functions, but that generality may not be useful as we typically want the distance between $\hat{m}(x)$ and $m(x)$ and that between $\hat{m}(x)+c(x)$ and $m(x)+c(x)$ for any $c(x)$ to be the same.

[18] One might wonder if a point-wise consistency concept can be regarded as a consistency concept using a metric or a norm. Whether this is possible will depend on what the domain of $m(x)$ is and what the set of functions is. Without any restriction this is not possible.

Next we need to define the class of functions under consideration. When the target parameter is a point in $\mathbb{R}^d$, the class to which the parameter belongs is well defined. When the target parameter is a function, however, we need to be more specific about the class of functions to which the target belongs.

Stone specified a set of differentiable functions restricting the highest order derivative to be Hölder continuous. Let $\lfloor p \rfloor$ denote the maximum integer that is strictly smaller than p and $\Theta_{p,C}$ be a class of functions which are $\lfloor p \rfloor$-times continuously differentiable with their $\lfloor p \rfloor$th derivative being Hölder continuous with exponent $0 < \gamma \leqslant 1$: denoting $p = \lfloor p \rfloor + \gamma$

$$\Theta_{p,C} = \left\{ f;\ \max_{k_1+\cdots+k_d=\lfloor p \rfloor} \left| D^k f(x) - D^k f(x') \right| \leqslant C \cdot \|x - x'\|^\gamma \right\}$$

for some positive C.

Denote the distribution of the dependent variable Y conditional on X by $h(y|x,t)\phi(\mathrm{d}y)$, where ϕ is a measure on $\mathbb{R}$ and t is an unknown real-valued parameter in an open interval J, and t is the mean of Y given X so that

$$\int y h(y|x,t)\phi(\mathrm{d}y) = t \quad \text{for } x \in \mathbb{R}^d \text{ and } t \in J.$$

By the construction, t varies with x according to $t = \theta(x)$, where $\theta(x) \in \Theta$.

Stone (1980, 1982) considers a model with some regularity conditions which imply: (1) t does not shift the support of h or some aspects of the conditional distribution other than the mean, (2) the effect of a change in t on the log-density is smooth (3) h is bounded away from 0 at relevant points and for the global case (4) h has at most an exponential tail and (5) the region defining the L^q-norm is compact.

For the model which satisfies the regularity conditions, Stone shows that the optimal convergence rate for estimating the mth order derivative of $\theta(\cdot)$ point-wise or with L^q-norm for any q with $0 < q < \infty$ depends on the dimension of the number of continuous conditioning variables d and the smoothness p $(p > m)$ of $\theta(\cdot)$. Let $r = (p - m)/(2p + d)$. In particular he shows that the optimal rate of convergence is n^{-r}. For the sup-norm, he shows that the optimal rate is $(\log n/n)^r$. Note that $r < 1/2$ so that Stone's results imply that the optimal rate for estimating a regression function within a very general class of functions specified by $\Theta_{p,C}$ is slower than $n^{-1/2}$. Stone also shows that an analogous result holds for the estimation of Lebesgue densities.

If we specify a different class of functions in place of $\Theta_{p,C}$, then the optimality result may change. For example, the neural network literature considers a class of functions Θ_C representable by an inverse Fourier transform formula with finite absolute first moment:

$$\Theta_C = \left\{ \theta;\ \theta(x) = \int e^{i\omega\cdot x} \tilde{F}(\mathrm{d}\omega) \quad \text{for some complex measure } \tilde{F} \text{ with} \right.$$
$$\left. \int_{\mathbb{R}^d} |\omega| \left| \mathrm{d}\tilde{F}(\omega) \right| \mathrm{d}\omega \leqslant C \right\}.$$

See, for example, Barron (1993). For this class of functions, Chen and White (1999) construct an estimator which converges in mean square with rate

$$(n/\ln n)^{-(1+2/(d+1))/[4(1+1/(d+1))]}.$$

Whether this is the best rate for Θ_C is an open question. This rate is better than the Stone's optimal rate when $p < d/2 + d/(d+1)$. This implies that not all functions which are less smooth than $d/2 + d/(d+1)$ is in Θ_C. Let $[s]$ denote the largest integer which is less or equal to s. Barron (1993) has shown that if the partial derivatives of $\theta(x)$ of order $[d/2]+2$ are continuous on $\mathbb{R}^d$, then those functions can be considered to be in Θ_C.[19]

That the optimal rate may be slower than the regular $n^{-1/2}$-rate may be intuitive. Consider estimating the conditional mean function $\theta(x) = E(y|x)$ at a point x. If X has a probability mass at x, then we can use data whose corresponding X equals x and construct the conditional mean function estimator at point x. However, if X has continuous distribution and if we do not wish to presume any particular functional form in the conditional mean function, all we can make use of are data that lie close to x. Let it be an ε-neighborhood of x. In general we will have sample size of order $n\varepsilon^d$ if the underlying density is bounded away from 0 and finite. This implies that the variance of the sample mean will decrease with rate $1/(n\varepsilon^d)$ under i.i.d. sampling.[20] If we are to construct a consistent estimator for a large set of functions, we will have to make ε smaller as sample size increases, because without making ε smaller we will not be able to guarantee the estimator to be consistent for a broad class of functions specified in the set. This consideration separates nonparametric estimators from more restricted estimation. That ε converges to zero implies that the variance will decrease with rate slower than n^{-1} which in turn implies the estimator to converge at rate slower than the $n^{-1/2}$-rate.

This intuition can be used to gain more insight to the formula obtained by Stone. As we discussed, the variance of an estimator of the mean in an ε-neighborhood is of order $(n\varepsilon^d)^{-1}$. On the other hand, if $\theta(\cdot)$ has smoothness p, then a parametric assumption of polynomial of order $\lfloor p \rfloor$ in the neighborhood will result in the bias of order ε^p if we are to consider all functions in set $\Theta_{p,C}$. Thus the mean square error to the first order is, for some constants C_1 and C_2

$$\frac{C_1}{n\varepsilon^d} + C_2 \cdot \varepsilon^{2p}.$$

Minimizing this expression over ε yields $r = p/(2p+d)$. If the target function is the mth order derivative of $\theta(x)$, note that the bias changes to something of order ε^{p-m}. The variance also changes because the target changes to the difference of means divided by

[19] It will be useful to clarify the relationship between $\Theta_{p,C}$ and Θ_C more completely.

[20] An uncritical assertion we take for granted is that the mean of y whose corresponding regressors are in the neighborhood is the best estimator of the $\theta(x_0)$.

something of order ε^m.[21] Because the number of observations is still of order $n\varepsilon^d$, the mean square error expression changes to

$$\frac{C_1}{n\varepsilon^{d-2m}} + C_2 \cdot \varepsilon^{2(p-m)}.$$

Minimizing this expression with respect to ε yields $r = (p-m)/(2p+d)$.

The result means that if we can only restrict ourselves to conditional functions with a certain degree of smoothness, then we can estimate the function with a slower rate than the $n^{-1/2}$-rate which depends on three factors: the number of continuous regressors, underlying smoothness of the target function, and the order of the derivative of the target function itself. The result is in sharp contrast to the situation where we obtain the convergence rate $n^{-1/2}$ regardless of these factors in estimating regression function or its derivatives under random sampling.

The above analysis makes clear the reason the convergence rate for the nonparametric case is slower than for the parametric case. It is because we need to make ε converge to zero to reduce the potential bias for a broad class of functions and the number of data points in the shrinking ε-neighborhood grows slower than the sample size. The sample size within an ε-neighborhood also grows more slowly when the dimension is high. When the underlying function is smooth, ε can be shrunk less rapidly to reduce the potential bias. The fact that the standard error decreases with the square root of the relevant sample size (sample size within ε-neighborhood) does not change.

In the above discussion, we observed that the extent to which the small neighborhood approximates the underlying function depends on the smoothness of the function itself. Also, the function is only an approximation and thus there is an approximation error even in the neighborhood, which distinguishes nonparametric or semiparametric approach from the parametric approach. For example, consider estimating a one-dimensional regression function. One flexible estimator that could be used is a nonparametric power series expansion estimator (described in Section 5), which estimates the regression function by a finite power series. For the estimator to be consistent, the order of the polynomials must increase with the sample size to cover all potential models. But for any finite sample size, the number of polynomial terms used is fixed so that superficially the estimator appears to be the same as a standard regression problem. The key distinction between whether we have a parametric or a nonparametric model in mind is whether the estimator is considered to have a negligible bias relative to the rate of convergence or not. If we regard the estimator only as an approximation to the true regression function, then the model is nonparametric and there is a bias that needs to be taken into account in conducting inference which results in slower convergence rate. Admitting the possibility of misspecification leads us to use a more conservative

[21] For example

$$\lim_{\epsilon \to 0} \frac{f(x+\epsilon) - 2f(x) + f(x-\epsilon)}{\epsilon^2} = f''(x).$$

standard error as the convergence rate is slower than the standard $n^{-1/2}$ rate and the form of variance will be different as well.

The dependence of the convergence rate on the dimension in particular is often referred to as *the curse of dimensionality*, which limits our ability to examine conditional mean functions or Lebesgue densities in a completely flexible way. This limitation of fully flexible models has motivated the development of semiparametric modeling methods, which offer a middle ground between fully parametric and fully nonparametric approaches. For a clarifying discussion of the definition of semiparametric models we refer the readers to Powell (1994, Section 1.2). Note that the discussion so far concentrated on the estimation of the conditional mean function but results would be analogous for the estimation of the conditional quantile function.

Interestingly, not all nonparametric estimation of functions face the curse of dimensionality. A leading example is the cumulative distribution function. As it can be expressed as the mean of a random variable defined using an indicator function, the finite dimensional cumulative distribution can be estimated with $n^{-1/2}$-rate nonparametrically. We will briefly discuss a necessary condition for the $n^{1/2}$-consistent estimability of the parameter under consideration in the next subsection as a part of the discussion of how the curse of dimensionality has been addressed in the literature.

3.1. *Semiparametric approaches*

The curse of dimensionality has been addressed using one of the following three approaches: by restricting the class of considered models, by changing the target parameter, and by changing the stochastic assumption maintained. We shall see that all three approaches can be understood within a single framework, but first we will discuss each of the concrete approaches in turn.

3.1.1. *Using semiparametric models*

The first approach is to impose some restrictions on the underlying models. Leading semiparametric models of the conditional functions are the additive separable model, the partially linear model, and the single and the multiple index models. These models provide ways to strike a balance between the flexibility and the curse of dimensionality.

The additive separable model is

$$\theta(x) = \phi_1(x_1) + \cdots + \phi_k(x_k),$$

where ϕ_j $(j = 1, \ldots, k)$ are unknown functions and x_j are sub-vectors of x with different dimension.

For the additive model for the conditional mean function, Linton and Nielsen (1995), Linton (1997), and Huang (1998) constructed an estimator of $\phi_j(x_j)$ which converges with the rate that depends only on the number of continuous regressors and smoothness of $\phi_j(\cdot)$. Thus the convergence rate for estimating $\theta(x)$ is driven by the maximum number of continuous regressors in $\{\phi_j(\cdot)\}$ assuming the same degree of smoothness for each of the component functions. For the conditional quantile function, Horowitz and Lee (2005) have constructed an estimator with analogous properties.

The partially linear model is

$$\theta(x) = r(x_0)'\beta + \phi(x_1),$$

where $r(\cdot)$ is a known function, $\phi(\cdot)$ is an unknown function and x_0 and x_1 are subvectors of x. Robinson (1988) shows that when $\theta(x)$ is the conditional mean function, β can be estimated with $n^{-1/2}$-rate regardless of the number of regressors in x_1 and constructs an estimator of ϕ which performs as if β were known. Thus the convergence rate for estimating $\theta(x)$ is driven by the number of continuous regressors in x_1 and smoothness of $\phi(\cdot)$.

The multiple index model is

$$\theta(x) = r_0(x_0)'\beta_0(\theta) + \phi\big(r_1(x_1)'\beta_1(\theta), \ldots, r_k(x_k)'\beta_k(\theta)\big),$$

where r_j $(j = 0, 1, \ldots, k)$ are known functions and $\phi(\cdot)$ is an unknown function. Note that the multiple index model reduces to the partially linear model when $\beta_j(\theta)$ $(j = 1, \ldots, k)$ are known. Ichimura (1993) constructed an estimator of β_1 in a single-index model without β_0. Using the same idea, Ichimura and Lee (1991) show that θ can be estimated with $n^{-1/2}$-rate regardless of the dimension of unknown function ϕ. It is straightforward to show that the estimation of ϕ can be done as if $\beta_j(\theta)$ for $j = 0, \ldots, k$ are known. For the single index model, Blundell and Powell (2003) develop a method to allow for an endogenous regressor and Ichimura and Lee (2006) study the asymptotic property of Ichimura's estimator under general misspecification. Ichimura and Lee (2006) also examine the single index model under a quantile restriction, rather than the conditional mean restriction and shows that results analogous to the conditional mean restriction case hold.

We will discuss these models and accompanying estimation methods in some detail in Section 5. The advantage of using these models is clear. Because the parameters are estimated without being subject to the curse of dimensionality and because these models typically include the linear in parameter specification as a special case, they permit examining the conditional mean and quantile functions under less stringent conditions than previously thought possible.

There are at least two limitations in using semiparametric models. First, we do not know which of these three or an alternative semiparametric model to use. Second, there could be a discrepancy between the parameter we want to estimate and the variation we would use to estimate the parameter. As Powell (1994) has emphasized, the defining characteristic of a semiparametric model is that there are different ways to express the same parameters. For example, consider the partially linear model with $r(x_0) = x_0$ and assume that x_0 and x_1 do not have a common variable and that all relevant moments are finite. In this case, β is the partial derivative of $\theta(x)$ with respect to x_0. When $\theta(x) = E(y|x)$, β is also a solution to minimizing $E[\mathrm{Var}(y - x_0'b|x_1)]$ with respect to b and at the same time β is a solution (corresponding to b) to minimizing $E[(y - x_0'b - f(x_1))^2]$

with respect to b and a measurable function f.[22] Thus one can estimate β using any of the sample counterpart of these observations. Depending on how the estimator is going to be used, we may want to use different estimation methods but using a semiparametric model tends to mask this distinction. The second limitation can be overcome by carefully choosing the appropriate estimation method, but the first limitation seems harder to resolve at this point.

3.1.2. Changing the parameter

The second approach to addressing the curse of dimensionality is to shift the focus of estimation to an aspect of $\theta(\cdot)$ rather than $\theta(\cdot)$ itself. This approach does not restrict the class of functions we consider to a parametric or a semiparametric model. For example Schweder (1975), Ahmad (1976), Hasminskii and Ibragimov (1979) studied estimation of $\int \theta(x)^2 \, dx$ where $\theta(x)$ is a Lebesgue density of a random variable. This object is of interest in studying rank estimation of a location parameter and also studying optimal density estimation. The parameter can be estimated at the $n^{-1/2}$-rate and thus the curse of dimensionality can be avoided.

Stoker (1986) considers average derivative of the form $\int \{\partial\theta(x)/\partial x\} w(x) \, dx$ where $w(x)$ is a given weight function. Even though $\partial\theta(x)/\partial x$ itself cannot be estimated point-wise at the $n^{-1/2}$-rate, Powell, Stock and Stoker (1989) and Robinson (1989) showed that this type of parameter can be estimated with $n^{-1/2}$-rate regardless of the dimension of x. By changing the weighting function $w(x)$ appropriately, the average derivative parameter can inform us about different aspects of $\partial\theta(x)/\partial x$. Altonji and Ichimura (1998) have studied average derivative estimation when dependent data are observed with censoring. We will discuss average derivative method in some detail in Section 5.

As previously discussed, DiNardo, Fortin and Lemiex (1996) study a density $f(x)$ via conditional density $\theta(x, z)$ and the marginal distribution of z, $F_z(z)$:

$$f(x) = \int_Z \theta(x, z) \, dF_z(z).$$

They study various hypothetical wage densities by replacing $F_z(z)$ with hypothetical marginal distributions. In their application z consists of discrete variables. Thus both $f(x)$ and $\theta(x, z)$ are estimated with the same rate. But if z contains a continuous variable, then this is an example in which integration improves the rate of convergence. This is also the case for Heckman et al. (1998). In their work $\theta(\cdot)$ is the conditional mean function and $F_z(z)$ is replaced by a distribution which is estimated.

[22] The latter two problems lead to the same solution for b even in a nonparametric setup.

3.1.3. Specifying different stochastic assumptions within a semiparametric model

Even when the model is restricted to a semiparametric model which has a finite dimensional parameter, such as β in the partially linear regression model, it is not always possible to estimate the finite dimensional parameter with the standard $n^{-1/2}$-rate. The role that different stochastic assumptions can play in this regard is clarified in the context of the censored regression model by Powell (1984) and Chamberlain (1986a) and Cosslett (1987). An illustration of the results requires us to fully specify the probability model.

A probability model is specified by a class of conditional or unconditional distribution of a random variable z, say $\mathcal{F}$. To distinguish conditional and unconditional models, we write $z = (y, x)$ where x represents conditioning variables. Let $\mathcal{F}_x$ denote a conditional probability model. Sometimes $\mathcal{F}$ is specified indirectly as a known mapping, say h, from another parameter space Θ into a space of distributions, $\mathcal{F} = \{f\colon f(z) = h(z; \theta), \theta \in \Theta\}$. This is the conventional way the standard parametric model specifies $\mathcal{F}$. When the indirect specification of a probability model can be accomplished based on a finite dimensional space Θ in some 'smooth' way, the model is called a parametric model.[23]

Consider, for example, the censored linear regression model censored from below at 0, with only an intercept term. In this case the model of the distribution of y is

$$\mathcal{F} = \left\{f;\ f(y) = h(y-\mu)^{1\{y>0\}}\left[\int_{-\infty}^{-\mu} h(s)\,\mathrm{d}s\right]^{1\{y=0\}},\ h \in \Gamma\right\},$$

where Γ is a class of densities with certain stochastic properties. The parameter space is $\Theta = \mathbb{R} \times \Gamma$. In the econometric literature in the past it was common to treat the parameter space as $\mathbb{R}$ leaving the nonparametric component Γ implicit. Specifying the probability model completely turned out to be an important step towards understanding the convergence rate and efficiency bound of a semiparametric estimator.

As an illustration consider estimating μ semiparametrically under two alternative stochastic restrictions on Γ under random sampling. One model restricts that h has mean 0 and the other model restricts that h has median 0. We will argue that the first stochastic assumption will not allow us to estimate μ with $n^{-1/2}$ rate but the second assumption will.

To see this, suppose h is known. Then under random sampling, the most efficient estimator is the ML estimator and its asymptotic variance in this case is 1 over

$$\frac{h^2(-\mu)}{H(-\mu)} + \int_{-\mu}^{\infty} \frac{[h'(s)]^2}{h^2(s)} h(s)\,\mathrm{d}s,$$

[23] Without a smoothness restriction on the mapping from the finite dimensional parameter space to the space of probability distributions, the definition of the parametric model is not meaningful. Without smoothness one can 'encode' an infinite dimensional space into a finite dimensional space.

where $H(t) = \int_{-\infty}^{t} h(s)\,\mathrm{d}s$. Note that the first term can be made arbitrarily small under both models. Under the model with mean 0 restriction, the second term can be made arbitrarily small also because only a small probability needs to be on $[-\mu, \infty)$ to satisfy the mean 0 restriction. However, with the median restriction, when $\mu > 0$, and $H(-\mu) < 1$, for example, the second term is strictly positive. To see this, note that the second term divided by $1 - H(-\mu)$ corresponds to the inverse of the asymptotic variance of the ML estimator of the mean when the random variable under consideration is supported on $[-\mu, \infty)$. Since we know that the mean can be estimated with rate $n^{-1/2}$ when the variance is restricted to be finite, the infimum of the second term cannot be 0. Thus with the restrictions on Γ, the infimum over Γ of the second term should be strictly positive so that the asymptotic variance is bounded above. Thus whether the conditional mean or the conditional median, or more generally the conditional quantile is restricted to zero makes a fundamental difference.

We intuitively argued that the bound on the asymptotic variance of any estimator of μ could be obtained by considering the worst case among Γ after computing the smallest asymptotic variance of a possible estimator of μ given a particular function in Γ. This is the approach of Stein (1956) further developed by various researchers. The work is summarized in Bickel et al. (1993). Newey (1990) provides a useful survey of the literature as do van der Vaart and Wellner (1996) and van der Vaart (1998). It has been shown that the bound thus computed provides a lower bound of the asymptotic variance of the $n^{1/2}$-consistent "regular" estimators where regularity is defined to exclude super-efficient estimators as well as estimators that use an unknown aspect of the probability model under consideration. When the bound is infinite, then there is no $n^{1/2}$-consistent estimator. A finite bound does not imply that $n^{1/2}$-consistent estimator exists, because it may not be achievable. See Ritov and Bickel (1990) for examples. On the other hand, when there is a regular estimator that achieves the bound, then it is reasonable to call the estimator efficient.[24] For the example considered above, the estimator considered by Powell (1984) gives an example that achieves the $n^{1/2}$-consistency and Newey and Powell (1990) constructs an asymptotically efficient estimator for the model.

To some extent, these developments partly solve the specification search problem that was described in the introduction. For the censored regression model, for example, the specification search for the error distribution has become completely redundant as the slope parameters can be estimated at the parametric rate without specifying a functional form for the error distribution. However, search problems still remain for the specification of the systematic component of the model. For the average derivative example, the specification search problem reduces to that of fully nonparametric models: the main difficulty being which variables to use and not which functional form to adopt.

[24] For an alternative formulation of an efficiency concept that does not restrict estimators to the regular estimators, see van der Vaart (1998, Chapter 8).

In a parametric setting, specification search often makes it difficult to assess the variability of the resulting estimator. In contrast, there are now large classes of semiparametric and nonparametric models for which at least asymptotic assessment of the variability of estimators is possible. Not only has consistency been proved for many estimators, but the explicit form of the asymptotic bias and variance has also been obtained.

4. Nonparametric estimation methods

While the above discussion of the curse of dimensionality may leave one with an impression that nonparametric methods are useful only for a low dimensional cases, they are nonetheless important to study, if only because they form the building blocks of many semiparametric estimators.

Roughly speaking, there are two types of nonparametric estimation methods: local and global. These two approaches reflect two different ways to reduce the problem of estimating a function into estimation of real numbers. Local approaches consider a real valued function $h(x)$ at a single point $x = x_0$. The problem of estimating a function becomes estimating a real number $h(x_0)$. If we are interested in evaluating the function in the neighborhood of the point x_0, we can approximate the function by $h(x_0)$ or, if $h(x)$ is continuously differentiable at x_0, then a better approximation might be $h(x_0) + h'(x_0)(x - x_0)$. Thus, the problem of estimating a function at a point may be thought of as estimating two real numbers $h(x_0)$ and $h'(x_0)$, making use of observations in the neighborhood. Either way, if we want to estimate the function over a wider range of x values, the same, point-wise problem can be solved at the different points of evaluation.

Global approaches introduce a coordinate system in a space of functions, which reduces the problem of estimating a function into that of estimating a set of real numbers. Recall that any element v in a d-dimensional vector space can be uniquely expressed using a system of independent vectors $\{b_j\}_{j=1}^{d}$ as $v = \sum_{j=1}^{d} \theta_j \cdot b_j$, where one can think of $\{b_j\}_{j=1}^{d}$ as a system of coordinates and $(\theta_1, \ldots, \theta_d)'$ as the representation of v using the coordinate system. Likewise, using an appropriate set of linearly independent functions $\{\phi_j(x)\}_{j=1}^{\infty}$ as coordinates any square integrable real valued function can be uniquely expressed by a set of coefficients. That is, given an appropriate set of linearly independent functions $\{\phi_j(x)\}_{j=1}^{\infty}$, any square integrable function $h(x)$ has unique coefficients $\{\theta_j\}_{j=1}^{\infty}$ such that

$$h(x) = \sum_{j=1}^{\infty} \theta_j \cdot \phi_j(x).$$

One can think of $\{\phi_j(x)\}_{j=1}^{\infty}$ as a system of coordinates and $(\theta_1, \theta_2, \ldots)'$ as the representation of $h(x)$ using the coordinate system. This observation allows us to translate the problem of estimating a function into a problem of estimating a sequence of real numbers $\{\theta_j\}_{j=1}^{\infty}$.

Well-known bases are polynomial series and Fourier series. These bases are infinitely differentiable everywhere. Other well-known bases are polynomial spline bases and wavelet bases. One-dimensional linear spline bases are: for a given knot locations t_j, $j = 1, \ldots, J$,

$$1, x, (x - t_j)1\{x \geqslant t_j\},$$

quadratic spline bases are:

$$1, x, x^2, (x - t_j)^2 1\{x \geqslant t_j\},$$

and cubic spline bases are:

$$1, x, x^2, x^3, (x - t_j)^3 1\{x \geqslant t_j\}.$$

By making the knot locations denser, a larger class of functions can be approximated. A function represented by a linear combination of the linear spline bases is continuous, that represented by the quadratic spline is continuously differentiable, and that represented by the cubic spline is twice continuously differentiable. Higher dimensional functions can be approximated by an appropriate Tensor product of the one-dimensional bases. Polynomial spline bases have an unpleasant feature that imposing higher order of smoothness requires more parameters.

Wavelet bases are generated by a single function ϕ and written as

$$2^{k/2}\phi(2^k x - \ell)$$

where k is a nonnegative integer and ℓ is any integer and ϕ satisfies certain conditions so that $\{2^{k/2}\phi(2^k x - \ell)\}_\ell$ is an orthonormal family in L^2-space. Now many functions ϕ, including an infinitely differentiable function, are known to define the orthonormal bases. Since these functions themselves can be infinitely differentiable and yet can approximate any function in L^2-space, the bases are useful to examine functions without a known degree of smoothness. See Fan and Gijbels (1996) for a concise discussion of the wavelet analysis. For a fuller discussion see Chui (1992) and Daubechies (1992).

Below, we illustrate both local and global approaches to density and conditional mean function estimation. We emphasize commonalities among estimation approaches that on the surface may appear very different. While we believe it is useful to understand the local and global nonparametric approaches, we shall see that even that distinction is not as clear cut as it seems at first.

4.1. *How do we estimate densities?*

As with parametric estimation, nonparametric estimation of a density can be carried out using either likelihood based estimation or a moment based estimation. Here we classify various density estimators, using the maximum likelihood vs method of moment classification in addition to the local vs global classification.

4.1.1. Moment based estimators

If there were a standard function $\delta_x(s)$, such that for any continuous function f

$$\int_{-\infty}^{+\infty} \delta_x(s) f(s)\,\mathrm{d}s = f(x),$$

then by regarding f as the Lebesgue density function of a random variable X, this equality can be used as the moment condition

$$E\{\delta_x(X)\} = f(x)$$

to estimate the density. Unfortunately, it is well known that such function $\delta_x(s)$, called the Dirac-delta function, does not exist as a standard function.[25] However, it can be expressed as a limit of a class of standard functions indexed by a positive real number h, say $\delta_x(s, h)$.[26] For example

$$\delta_x(s, h) = \frac{1}{h} K\left(\frac{x - s}{h}\right)$$

where $\int_{-\infty}^{+\infty} K(u)\,\mathrm{d}u = 1$ satisfies the requirement for a continuous Lebesgue density $f(x)$ if $\lim_{|u|\to\infty} |u|K(u) = 0$.

Method-of-moment estimation based on this specification for $\delta_x(s, h)$ leads to the so-called kernel density estimator of Rosenblatt (1956). See also Parzen (1962):

$$\hat{f}_h(x) = n^{-1} \sum_{i=1}^{n} K_h(x - x_i),$$

where $K_h(s) = h^{-1} K(s/h)$. When the function $K(\cdot)$ is a density function, the estimator itself is a density function. Smoothness on estimated density function can be imposed by choosing a smooth function $K(\cdot)$. See Silverman (1986) for a very useful discussion of the estimator.[27]

Implementing this estimator requires specifying the function $K(\cdot)$, referred to as the kernel function, and the parameter h, which is called the *window-width, bandwidth*, or *smoothing parameter*.

When a symmetric kernel function with a finite variance is used, a calculation using the change of variables formula and the Taylor's series expansion under the assumption that the density is twice continuously differentiable shows that the highest order of the point-wise mean square error of the kernel density estimator is

$$\left(h^2/2 \int u^2 K(u)\,\mathrm{d}s f''(x)\right)^2 + \frac{1}{nh} \int K^2(u)\,\mathrm{d}u f(x).$$

[25] See for example, Zemanian (1965, p. 10).

[26] See Walter and Blum (1979).

[27] Härdle and Linton (1994) summarize the asymptotic properties of this estimator in Chapter 38. See also Scott (1992).

The bandwidth that minimizes the leading terms of the mean squared error is

$$h^* = \left[\frac{\int K^2(u)\,\mathrm{d}u f(x)}{(\int u^2 K(u)\,\mathrm{d}s)^2[f''(x)]^2}\right]^{1/5} n^{-1/5}.$$

The optimal bandwidth is larger when the density is high, because then the variance is higher; the optimal bandwidth is larger when the second derivative is small, because then the bias is smaller so that wider bandwidth can be tolerated. Because the optimal bandwidth involves the unknown density itself and its second derivative, it is not feasible. However, there is a large literature that we review in Section 6 that studies methods that use the data to come close to the optimal bandwidth.

With the optimal bandwidth, the highest order of the mean square error is

$$\frac{5}{4}\left(\int K^2(u)\,\mathrm{d}u\right)^{4/5}\left(\int u^2 K(u)\,\mathrm{d}u\right)^{2/5} f^{4/5}(x)\left[\left(f''(x)\right)^2\right]^{1/5} n^{-4/5}.$$

This shows three things: first, the convergence rate of the kernel density estimator is $n^{-4/5}$, which corresponds to the optimal rate Stone obtained for the estimation of one-dimensional twice continuously differentiable densities. Second, regardless of the unknowns, the optimal kernel function can be chosen by minimizing

$$\left(\int K^2(u)\,\mathrm{d}u\right)\left(\int u^2 K(u)\,\mathrm{d}u\right)^{1/2},$$

under the restriction that the kernel function is symmetric and the second moment is finite and normalized to 1, Epanechnikov (1969) showed that the optimal kernel function is

$$K(u) = \frac{3}{4\cdot 5^{3/2}}\left(5-u^2\right)1\left\{u^2 \leqslant 5\right\}.$$

This kernel function is usually referred to as the Epanechnikov kernel.[28] The envelope theorem implies that a slight deviation from the optimal kernel function would not affect the asymptotic mean square error very much. In fact, Epanechnikov showed numerically that the efficiency loss by using commonly used kernel functions such as the normal kernel is about 5% and that by the uniform kernel is about 7%. This observation lead subsequent researches to concentrate more on how to choose the bandwidth sequence. Note that the Epanechnikov kernel is not differentiable at the edges of its support. If we impose three times continuous differentiability via the quartic kernel function, sometimes called the biweight kernel,

$$K(u) = \frac{15}{16\cdot 7^{5/2}}\left(7-u^2\right)^2 1\left\{u^2 \leqslant 7\right\},$$

the efficiency loss to the first order is less than 1%.[29]

[28] Sometimes the support is normalized between −1 and 1 rather than the variance being normalized to 1. However, this normalization will make the comparison to the kernel function with unbounded support difficult.

[29] See, for example, Scott (1992, Table 6.2).

The *histogram estimator* can be viewed as a kernel density estimator which uses a uniform kernel function $K_h(s) = 1(|s| < h)/2$. Although the simplicity of the histogram is appealing and it can be interpreted as an estimator of the cell probability divided by twice the bandwidth for each finite observation, it has two disadvantages; one is that density estimates generated by a histogram are discontinuous at bin endpoints, and the other is that there is about 7% efficiency loss discussed above. Figure 2 compares the density of earnings estimated by a histogram to that estimated using a kernel density estimator.

Another density estimator which can be viewed as a kernel density estimator is the nearest neighbor estimator. The estimator is based on the equality $\int_{x_0-R_n}^{x_0+R_n} f(s)\,\mathrm{d}s =$

Figure 2. Comparison of earnings density estimated by a histogram and by a kernel density estimator.

$\Pr\{|X - x_0| \leqslant R_n\}$, where f is the Lebesgue density of random variable X. Because the left-hand side is approximately $2R_n f(x_0)$ and the right-hand side can be estimated by the fraction of observations which fall within the R_n distance from x_0, by using the distance R_n to the nearest k_n observations from x_0, the density at $x = x_0$ can be estimated by equating $2R_n f(x_0)$ and k_n/n; i.e. by $k_n/(2R_n n)$. This can be written as

$$n^{-1} \sum_{i=1}^{n} K_{R_n}(x - x_i)$$

where the kernel function is the uniform kernel function.[30] Thus the nearest neighbor estimator can be viewed as a histogram estimator for a particular way of choosing the bandwidth. Note that the way bandwidth is selected does not consider the second derivative of the density at the point of estimation, so when the density is twice continuously differentiable the nearest neighbor estimator cannot be optimal.

The estimators discussed so far are all local estimators. We next show that method of moment based global estimators can be viewed also as a local estimator. As discussed earlier, let $\{\phi_j(x)\}_{j=1}^{\infty}$ be an orthonormal basis in the space of square integrable functions and consider the class of Lebesgue densities in the same space. Then one can write

$$f(x) = \sum_{j=1}^{\infty} c_j \phi_j(x)$$

for some sequence $\{c_j\}_{j=1}^{\infty}$. The coefficients can be computed by

$$\int f(x)\phi_k(x)\,\mathrm{d}x = \sum_{j=1}^{\infty} c_j \int \phi_j(x)\phi_k(x)\,\mathrm{d}x = c_k,$$

where the last equality follows from the orthonormality of $\{\phi_j(x)\}_{j=1}^{\infty}$.

Thus a global method to estimate the Lebesgue density in L_2 is to use the first J elements of the series just discussed and estimating c_j by the sample average of $\phi_j(X)$ where X has the Lebesgue density $f(x)$. In this case the estimator of c_j is $\hat{c}_j = n^{-1} \sum_{i=1}^{n} \phi_j(x_i)$ so that the estimator of $f(x)$ is

$$\hat{f}(x) = \frac{1}{n} \sum_{i=1}^{n} \sum_{j=1}^{J} \phi_j(x_i)\phi_j(x).$$

This results in another example of $\delta_x(s, h)$. Denoting the number of series used by $J = 1/h$:

$$\delta_x(s, h) = \sum_{j=1}^{1/h} \phi_j(s)\phi_j(x).$$

[30] See Moore and Yackel (1977a, 1977b).

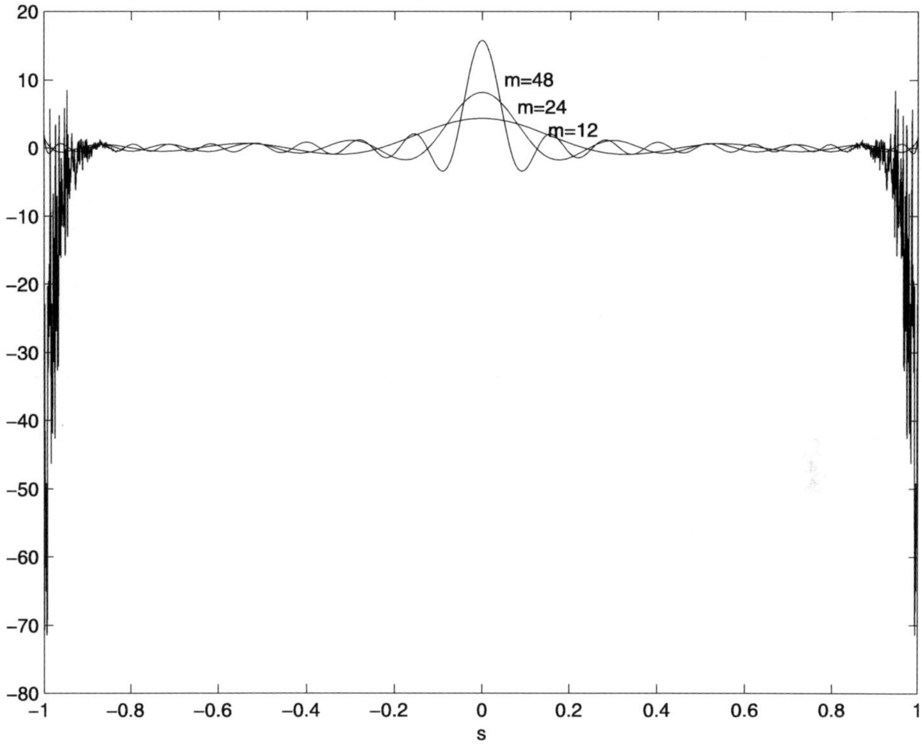

Figure 3. Implicit kernel function for the Fourier series density estimator.

This form of an approximation to the delta function is known as a reproducing kernel. See Weinert (1982), Saitoh (1989), Wahba (1990), and Berlinet and Thomas-Agnan (2003). For example, when we consider densities supported on $[-\pi, \pi]$ and 0 at the boundaries, we can use $1/(2\pi), \cos(x)/\pi, \sin(x)/\pi, \cos(2x)/\pi, \sin(2x)/\pi, \ldots$ as the orthonormal bases. In this case one can show that $\delta_x(s, 1/J)$ is the Dirichlet kernel:

$$\delta_x(s, 1/J) = \frac{1}{2\pi} \frac{\sin \frac{2J+1}{2}(s-x)}{\sin \frac{s-x}{2}}.$$

Figure 3 plots this function.

We are not advocating using the series estimator as discussed above. In fact this simple version of the implementation has been shown to have undesirable features that have been improved. For a discussion see Scott (1992).

A notable difference between the kernel density and series expansion estimators is that kernel functions that correspond to orthogonal expansion methods have support independent from the number of terms in the expansion, whereas standard kernel functions have a support that depends on the bandwidth choice if the kernel function is supported on a finite interval.

For the general series estimators, the highest order of the bias and the variance have not been characterized although the rate of convergence have been characterized. For the wavelet based bases, however, the highest order of the bias and the variance are computed by Hall and Patil (1995). See also Huang (1999) and Ochiai and Naito (2003).

We have seen that moment based density estimators can be regarded as reflecting different ways to approximate the delta function. A single parameter h in the approximation $\delta_x(s,h)$ is used to construct a model of densities. If $\int \delta_x(s,h)\,\mathrm{d}x = 1$ and $\delta_x(s) \geqslant 0$, then an estimator itself is a valid density. As discussed, Epanechnikov (1969) argued that among the kernel density estimators, the choice of bandwidth is more important than the choice of kernel function. For the same reason, the above discussion may indicate that among method-of-moment based methods the more important issue is how to choose the smoothing parameter rather than which method of moment estimator to use. This remains to be seen.

4.1.2. Likelihood-based approaches

Another natural way of estimating densities is a maximum likelihood (ML) approach; however, a straightforward application of the likelihood method fails in nonparametric density estimation. To see why consider the ML estimator

$$\max_{f\in\mathcal{F}} \sum_{i=1}^{n} \log f(x_i)$$

where $\mathcal{F}$ is an *a priori* specified class of densities. If $\mathcal{F}$ is not restricted, then for each n one can choose an f with spikes at x_i and yet f can be a density. Thus the likelihood can be made as high as desired regardless of the underlying density and the method leads to an inconsistent estimator.

Many modifications have been proposed to resolve this failure by restricting $\mathcal{F}$ in some way.[31] Imposing smoothness alone does not correct the situation. To see this, first observe that the likelihood value is only affected by values of $f(x)$ on the data points $x_1,\ldots,x_n$. As one can construct a polynomial function that passes through any given finite points that are a subset of the graph of $\log f(x)$, the likelihood value can be made arbitrarily large. Stronger restrictions are needed.

As discussed below, some restrictions are needed regardless of whether one takes a global or a local approach. The global method, such as that of Stone et al. (1997), restricts the rate at which more complex functions are included in $\mathcal{F}$ as the sample size increases. The local method attempts to approximate the density locally holding the complexity of the functions fixed. The approach taken by Hjort and Jones (1996) and Loader (1996) is to approximate a density locally by a parametric density.

[31] See Prakasa-Rao (1983), Silverman (1982b), and Scott (1992).

Global likelihood estimation The global likelihood-based approach restricts the rate at which complex functions are included in $\mathcal{F}$ as the sample size increases. Here, we describe a density estimation implementation of Stone's extended linear modeling, as exposited in Stone et al. (1997). Their starting point is to observe that the log-density function can be written in the form

$$l(h, X) = h(X) - \log \int_{\mathcal{X}} \exp h(x)\,\mathrm{d}x$$

for any function $h(x) \in H$, where H is a linear space of real-valued functions on $\mathcal{X}$. The second term on the right-hand side ensures that $\exp[l(h, X)]$ is a proper density.

Stone et al. (1997) define the estimator of the log-density as the maximizer of the log-likelihood function

$$\sum_{i=1}^{n} h(X_i) - n \log \int_{\mathcal{X}} \exp\bigl[h(x)\bigr]\,\mathrm{d}x$$

over h in a finite dimensional linear subset of H, denoted G. With no restriction on H to a smaller subset G, the problem pointed out earlier in relation to inconsistency of the unrestricted ML estimator also arises here. By choosing h to have spikes at observation points we can make $\sum_{i=1}^{n} h(X_i)$ as large as we wish, while keeping the contribution to $n \log \int_{\mathcal{X}} \exp[h(x)]\,\mathrm{d}x$ small. Also, for any constant value C, $h(x)$ and $h(x) + C$ give rise to the same log-likelihood value so we need a normalization. Stone et al. (1997) use the normalization $E[h(X)] = 0$, which guarantees a unique optimizer in G since the log likelihood function is strictly concave. The implementation of the method depends crucially on how G is chosen. The choice of G represents the finite dimensional model used to approximate the unknown density. In their formulation of d-dimensional functions, the first stage is the additive separable model. The second stage includes two-dimensional function etc. In this way, the additive separable model could be embedded in a series of less restrictive models.

Local likelihood estimation Loader (1996) and Hjort and Jones (1996) propose a localized likelihood based estimator. The local likelihood is defined as

$$\mathcal{L}(f, x) = \sum_{i=1}^{n} K_h(x - X_i) \log f(X_i) - n \int_{\mathcal{X}} K_h(x - X_i) f(u)\,\mathrm{d}u.$$

Because the data are localized through the use of kernel weighting, we need only to approximate the log-density locally. Loader considers polynomial approximation of the log density, which is equivalent to using exponential models. Hjort and Jones consider approximation by general parametric models. If we do not restrict the class of models to a small subset like the ones considered in these papers, then the optimization problem does not have a well-defined solution.

To gain insight into the form of the above objective function, we show that one can view the objective function as an approximation to a likelihood for observing data only in an area within h of point x. When the density is f, the likelihood contribution if the data falls within the interval is $f(X_i)$ but if not, then it also contributes by computing the probability of not observing in the interval. Thus we can write the likelihood as

$$\sum_{i=1}^{n} I_i \log f(X_i) + (1 - I_i) \log\left(1 - \int_{\mathcal{X}} I\{|x-u| \leqslant h\} f(u)\, du\right).$$

Using the approximation $\log(1 - \int_{\mathcal{X}} I\{|x-u| \leqslant h\} f(u)\, du) \approx -\int_{\mathcal{X}} I\{|x-u| \leqslant h\} f(u)\, du$ gives

$$\sum_{i=1}^{n} I_i \log f(X_i) - n \int_{\mathcal{X}} I\{|x-u| \leqslant h\} f(u)\, du$$
$$- \sum_{i=1}^{n} I_i \int_{\mathcal{X}} I\{|x-u| \leqslant h\} f(u)\, du,$$

where the leading two terms are of higher order. Approximating the indicator function by the kernel function $K_h(x - X_i)$ gives the objective function

$$\sum_{i=1}^{n} K_h(x - X_i) \log f(X_i) - n \int_{\mathcal{X}} K_h(x-u) f(u)\, du,$$

which is the objective function studied by Loader (1996) and Hjort and Jones (1996).[32]

We have grouped density estimation methods into moment-based and likelihood-based methods. Recent developments in empirical likelihood literature suggest a link between the method of moment estimators and likelihood estimators, which still needs to be clarified in this context.

4.2. *How do we estimate conditional mean functions?*

As with density estimation, there are both local and global approaches to estimating the conditional mean function. Because the conditional mean function does not characterize the conditional distribution, most of the methods analyzed extensively in the literature are based on the method-of-moments approach rather than the likelihood approach. Let $\mathcal{M}$ denote a class of functions in which the conditional mean function $m(x) = E(Y|X = x)$ lies. We can characterize the conditional mean function in two ways: as the solution to

$$\inf_{g(\cdot)\in\mathcal{M}} E\{[Y - g(X)]^2\}$$

[32] The local likelihood estimator is available as a supplement to the Splus statistical software package. In Section 6, we present some Monte Carlo results on the performance of these estimators.

or as the solution to

$$\inf_{g(\cdot)\in\mathcal{M}} E\{(Y-g(X))^2 | X=x\}.$$

The global method is based on the first characterization and the local method on the second. Analogous to the ML-based density estimation, both global and local approaches to estimating conditional mean functions require that the space $\mathcal{M}$ be restricted to avoid over-fitting.

Below we discuss nonparametric estimators of the conditional mean function. Estimators of the conditional quantile function can be constructed by replacing the quadratic loss function with that of Koenker and Bassett (1978). Also, see Tsybakov (1982), Härdle and Gasser (1984), and Chaudhuri (1991a, 1991b).

The global approach As described earlier, the global approach to nonparametric estimation constructs a sequence of parametric models M_n such that approximation error of $m(\cdot)$ by an element of M_n eventually goes down to zero as $n \to \infty$. A well-known sequence is a sequence of polynomial functions, a sequence of spline functions,[33] or a sequence of wavelets as discussed above. All sequences specify for each n some set of functions $\{\phi_{nj}(x)\}_{j=1}^{J_n}$, and use them to define the sequence of models by

$$M_n = \{f;\ f(x) = \theta_1\phi_{n1}(x) + \cdots + \theta_{J_n}\phi_{nJ_n}(x) \text{ for some } \theta_1, \ldots, \theta_{J_n} \in \mathbb{R}\}.$$

Then, for each n the global estimator can be defined as $\hat{m}(x, J_n) = \hat{\theta}_1\phi_{n1}(x) + \cdots + \hat{\theta}_{J_n}\phi_{nJ_n}(x)$, where $\hat{\theta}_1, \ldots, \hat{\theta}_{J_n}$ are obtained by the least squares minimization problem of the following objective function:

$$\sum_{i=1}^{n} [y_i - (\theta_1\phi_{n1}(x_i) + \cdots + \theta_{J_n}\phi_{nJ_n}(x_i))]^2.$$

As discussed before, for more than 1 regressor cases, appropriate Tensor products of a one-dimensional bases are used to construct the base functions.

Different global methods can be viewed as different combinations of decisions about how the class $\mathcal{M}$ is restricted and how the data are used in choosing the class $\mathcal{M}$. Clearly the properties of this estimator crucially depends on how we choose the base functions $\{\phi_{nj}(x)\}_{j=1}^{J_n}$ and J_n. Typically the order in which different base functions are brought in is given and the literature discusses how to choose J_n using a model selection criterion. For example when the polynomial series are used base functions are ordered in terms of the degree of polynomials. In the wavelet literature, there is an attempt to endogenize the choice of the bases themselves so as to estimate the degree of smoothness.

Global approaches can be a convenient way of imposing global properties of underlying functions such as monotonicity, concavity, and additive separability. It is also easy

[33] See Schoenberg (1964) and also Eubank (1999) and Green and Silverman (1994).

to restrict a class of functions so that any function in the class goes through a certain point.

For global estimation methods, there has been less progress in analyzing the form of the first order bias in comparison to local methods. Although the rate of convergence is known, the exact expression for the highest order term is known only for limited cases. See Newey (1997) for the convergence rate results and see Zhou, Shen and Wolfe (1998) and Huang (2003) for some results about the first order bias computations.

The local approach Let $f(y, x)$ and $f(x)$ denote the joint density of (Y, X) and the marginal density of X, respectively. Using the Dirac-delta function, $\delta_x(s)$, as used previously in setting up the moment condition for the density estimation (Section 4.1), we can write

$$\begin{aligned}\iint [y - g(s)]^2 f(y, s)\delta_x(s)\,\mathrm{d}s\,\mathrm{d}y &= \int [y - g(x)]^2 f(y, x)\,\mathrm{d}y \\ &= E\{(Y - g(X))^2 | X = x\} f(x).\end{aligned}$$

As the last term is proportional to $E\{(Y - g(X))^2|X = x\}$, the solution to the infimum problem is the same if $f(x) > 0$. Following the same logic as for the density estimation case, one can construct a sample analog objective function using some approximation to the Dirac-delta function.

If we do not restrict the class of functions ($\mathcal{M}$) over which infimum is taken, then the optimization problem does not have a well-defined solution. Different local estimation methods can be viewed as different combinations of decisions about (1) how to approximate the Dirac-delta function (2) how to restrict the class $\mathcal{M}$ and (3) how to use the data in choosing the approximation and the class $\mathcal{M}$.

For example, if we approximate the Dirac-delta function by

$$\frac{1}{h} K\left(\frac{x - s}{h}\right)$$

as we did in the density estimation case, and restrict $\mathcal{M}$ to the class of constant functions, the left-hand side of the above expression has the sample analog:

$$\frac{1}{n}\sum_{i=1}^{n}(y_i - \beta)^2 K_h(x_i - x).$$

Minimizing this with respect to β we get the kernel regression estimator[34]:

$$\hat{m}_K(x) = \frac{\sum_{i=1}^{n} y_i K_h(x_i - x)}{\sum_{i=1}^{n} K_h(x_i - x)},$$

[34] See Nadaraya (1964) and Watson (1964) and Härdle (1990).

whenever the denominator is not zero. Writing

$$w_{ni}^{K}(x) = \frac{K_h(x_i - x)}{\sum_{i=1}^{n} K_h(x_i - x)}$$

we see that $\hat{m}_K(x) = \sum_{i=1}^{n} y_i w_{ni}^{K}(x)$ and $\sum_{i=1}^{n} w_{ni}^{K}(x) = 1$.

If function $K(s)$ takes the form $1(|s| \leqslant 1)$ where $|s|$ denotes a norm of s and the smoothing parameter h is chosen to be the distance between x and the kth closest observation in $\{x_i\}_{i=1}^{n}$, then the estimator is the kth-nearest neighbor estimator.

For the same Dirac-delta approximation, when $\mathcal{M}$ is replaced by a class of a finite dimensional polynomial function, we get the local polynomial regression estimator of $E(Y|X = x)$ at $x = x_0$.[35] It is defined as the solution corresponding to $\beta^{(0)}$ of the following minimization problem:

$$\min_{\beta^{(0)},\beta^{(1)},\dots,\beta^{(p)}} \frac{1}{n}\sum_{i=1}^{n}\Bigg[y_i - \beta^{(0)} - \sum_{\nu=1}^{p} \sum_{j_1+\cdots+j_d=\nu} \frac{1}{j_1!\cdots j_d!}\beta_{\nu,j_1,\dots,j_d}(x_{i1} - x_{01})^{j_1}\cdots(x_{id} - x_{0d})^{j_d}\Bigg]^2 \times K_h(x_i - x_0),$$

where for $\nu = 1, \dots, p$ the length of vector $\beta^{(\nu)}$ is $(\nu + d - 1)!/((d-1)!\nu!)$ and its elements are denoted by $\beta_{\nu,j_1,\dots,j_d}$ where $j_1 + \cdots + j_d = \nu$ and $j_1, \dots, j_d$ are nonnegative integers. For concreteness and for later purpose we order $j = (j_1, \dots, j_d)$ lexicographically putting highest order to the first element, the next to the second element, etc.

To gain an understanding of the objective function, observe that

$$Y = m(X) + \epsilon = m(x_0) + \big[m(X) - m(x_0)\big] + \epsilon.$$

Consider the one-dimensional case and assume that $K(\cdot)$ is a symmetric, unimodal density function supported on the interval $[-1, 1]$. In that case, observations whose $X = x_i$ are close to x_0 receive more weight than others and if an observation's $X = x_i$ is more than h apart from x_0, it receives 0 weight. If function $m(\cdot)$ is continuous at $X = x_0$, then the approximation error $[m(X) - m(x_0)]$ is not very big so long as we restrict attention to observations whose x_i is close to x_0. Thus ignoring the approximation error, minimizing the objective function for the kernel regression estimator is justified.

To motivate the objective function of the higher order polynomial estimator, consider a one-dimensional case and let $m^{(\nu)}(x)$ denote the νth order derivative of function $m(\cdot)$. Observe that

[35] See Stone (1977) and Fan and Gijbels (1996, pp. 105–106).

$$\begin{aligned}
Y &= m(X) + \epsilon \\
&= m(x_0) + m^{(1)}(x_0)(X - x_0) + \cdots + m^{(p)}(x_0)(X - x_0)^p/p! \\
&\quad + \left\{m(X) - \left[m(x_0) + m^{(1)}(x_0)(X - x_0) + \cdots + m^{(p)}(x_0)(X - x_0)^p/p!\right]\right\} \\
&\quad + \epsilon,
\end{aligned}$$

where $\{m(X) - [m(x_0) + m^{(1)}(x_0)(X - x_0) + \cdots + m^{(p)}(x_0)(X - x_0)^p/p!]\}$ constitutes the approximation error. The objective function is the weighted least squares objective function ignoring the approximation error where the observations whose x_i are closer to x_0 receive higher weights. Clearly, the solution corresponding to the constant term is the estimator of the conditional mean function evaluated at x_0 and the solution corresponding to the coefficient of $(x_i - x_0)^\nu/\nu!$ is the estimator of the νth order derivative of the conditional mean function evaluated at x_0. For higher dimensional problems, we interpret $m^{(\nu)}(x_0)$, as a vector of partial derivatives of order ν and $(X - x_0)^{(\nu)}/\nu!$ as a vector of elements $(X_1 - x_{01})^{j_1} \cdots (X_d - x_{0d})^{j_d}/(j_1! \cdots j_d!)$, where $j_1 + \cdots + j_d = \nu$. For concreteness, we assume both are ordered in the lexicographical way as above.

Fan (1992) clarifies the theoretical reasons why we may prefer to use the local polynomial regression estimator with $p \geqslant 1$ instead of the kernel regression estimator $(p = 0)$. The advantage is the ability of the estimator to control the bias in *finite sample*. As we have seen above, in finite sample the kernel regression estimator ignores $[m(X) - m(x_0)]$, which is of order h in the neighborhood of x_0 when the underlying function is twice differentiable with bounded second derivative. If the local linear estimator is used, then under the same condition, the approximation error ignored is of order h^2 in the neighborhood of x_0. If pth order polynomial is used and the underlying function is at least r-times differentiable with bounded rth derivative where $r \geqslant p + 1$, the approximation error is of order h^{p+1} in *finite sample*. This leads to practical and theoretical advantages.

For the kernel regression estimator evaluated at the interior point of the support of regressors, when the underlying function is twice differentiable and the second derivative is bounded, the first order asymptotic analysis shows that the asymptotic bias is of order h^2, which is the same order with the local linear estimator. However, note that this is an asymptotic result and applicable to interior points. For the local linear estimator, the bias is of order h^2 in finite sample whenever the estimator is well defined. For the local polynomial regression estimator of order p, so long as the estimator is defined and the underlying function is sufficiently smooth, the bias is of order h^{p+1} in finite sample. This is the practical advantage.

When a nonparametric estimator is used to construct a semiparametric estimator and the asymptotic properties of the resulting semiparametric estimator is examined, as we shall see later, typically the uniform convergence needs to be established with a certain convergence rate. Since the same convergence rate can be achieved without the boundary consideration, the theoretical development simplifies. This is the theoretical advantage.

We clarify above points in some detail as the results will be useful to understand the asymptotic results discussed below and the bandwidth selection methods discussed later. Let $j = (j_1, \ldots, j_d)$ and denote $|j| = j_1 + \cdots + j_d$. Also let $\beta = (\beta^{(0)}, \beta^{(1)'}, \ldots, \beta^{(p)'})'$, $N_u = (u + d - 1)!/((d - 1)!u!)$, $N = \sum_{u=0}^{p} N_u$, and $X^{(u)}$ be an $n \times N_u$ matrix with the ith row being $(x_i - x_0)^j/j!$ for $|j| = u$, interpreted as specified above, ι_n be the vector of n ones, $X = (\iota_n X^{(1)} \cdots X^{(p)})$ (an $n \times N$ matrix), $y = (y_1, \ldots, y_n)'$ and W be an $n \times n$ diagonal matrix with ith diagonal element being $K_h(x_i - x_0)$.

With these notations, the local polynomial objective function can be written as

$$(y - X\beta)'W(y - X\beta)$$

so that the local polynomial estimator is, when it exists, $\hat{\beta} = (X'WX)^{-1}X'Wy$. The local polynomial estimator of the conditional mean function is the first element of $\hat{\beta}$ so that it can be written as $\sum_{i=1}^{n} w_{ni}^{L}(x_0)y_i$ where

$$\big(w_{n1}^{L}(x_0), \ldots, w_{nn}^{L}(x_0)\big) = e_N'(X'WX)^{-1}X'W,$$

where e_N is a vector of length N with first element being one and the rest of the elements are zero. Observe that

$$\big(w_{n1}^{L}(x_0), \ldots, w_{nn}^{L}(x_0)\big)X = e_N'(X'WX)^{-1}X'WX = e_N' I_N.$$

Reading off the row, we observe that $\sum_{i=1}^{n} w_{ni}^{L}(x_0) = 1$, $\sum_{i=1}^{n} w_{ni}^{L}(x_0)(x_i - x_0) = 0$, and generally $\sum_{i=1}^{n} w_{ni}^{L}(x_0)(x_i - x_0)^{(j)}/j! = 0$ for any j with $1 \leqslant |j| \leqslant p$. As we shall see below, these orthogonality properties of the weight function are key to controlling bias in finite sample.

The weights for the kernel regression estimator satisfy $\sum_{i=1}^{n} w_{ni}^{K}(x_0) = 1$, but satisfy

$$\sum_{i=1}^{n} w_{ni}^{K}(x_0)(x_i - x_0) \to 0$$

only asymptotically when x_0 is at the interior point of the support of x_i. The latter does not hold asymptotically if x_0 is on the boundary of the support of x_i.

One might think that the limitation of the kernel regression estimator at the boundary points is not so important practically, because there are many more interior points than boundary points. However, two points need to be taken into account. First, the comparable performance of the kernel regression estimator in interior points is obtained asymptotically, not in the finite sample as for the local polynomial estimator. Second, in finite sample, it is entirely plausible that the data are unevenly distributed, so that there are many more data points lying on one side of the point of evaluation (x_0) than the other. This is even more likely to occur in higher dimensions. In these cases, the asymptotic properties of the kernel regression estimator may not capture well the finite sample behavior. In some sense, in finite sample, there are likely many points at which the boundary behavior of the estimator may better represent its performance.

To see these points more clearly, define $\epsilon = (\epsilon_1, \ldots, \epsilon_n)'$, $\beta_0^{(\nu)} = m^{(\nu)}(x_0)$ for $\nu = 0, \ldots, p$ and β_0 to be the vector of length N constructed by stacking these sub-vectors.

We can write

$$y = X\beta_0 + r + \epsilon$$

where $r = (r_1, \dots, r_n)' = m - X\beta_0$ with $m = (m(x_1), \dots, m(x_n))'$. Thus

$$\hat{\beta} = \beta_0 + (X'WX)^{-1}X'Wr + (X'WX)^{-1}X'W\epsilon.$$

The second term on the right-hand side is the bias term and the third, the variance term. We examine the bias and the variance terms in turn.

Bias Let H be the diagonal matrix with N_u diagonal elements of $1/h^u$ for $u = 0, \dots, p$, in this order. Then

$$\begin{aligned}\hat{\beta}^{(0)} &= \beta_0^{(0)} + e_N' H(HX'WXH)^{-1}HX'Wr + e_N' H(HX'WXH)^{-1}HX'W\epsilon \\ &= \beta_0^{(0)} + e_N'(HX'WXH)^{-1}HX'Wr + e_N'(HX'WXH)^{-1}HX'W\epsilon.\end{aligned}$$

One can show that $HX'WXH/(nh^d)$ converges in probability to an invertible matrix, under general conditions specified later. To see this, note that the typical element of the matrix is, for vectors of nonnegative integers j and j',

$$\frac{1}{nh^d}\sum_{i=1}^{n}\big((x_i - x_0)/h\big)^{(j)}\big((x_i - x_0)/h\big)^{(j')}K\big((x_i - x_0)/h\big)/(j!j'!).$$

Applying the Taylor series expansion we obtain

$$r_i = m^{(p+1)}(\bar{x}_i)(x_i - x_0)^{(p+1)}/(p+1)!,$$

where $m^{(p+1)}(\bar{x}_i)$ is a row vector of length N_{p+1}, consisting of $m^{(j)}(\bar{x}_i)$ with $|j| = p+1$ and $\bar{x}_i$ lies on a line connecting x_i and x_0. Using this result, a typical element of $HX'Wr/(nh^d)$ can be written as, using the same j and j' as above,

$$\frac{1}{nh^d}\sum_{i=1}^{n}\big((x_i - x_0)/h\big)^{(j)}(x_i - x_0)^{(j')}m^{(j')}(\bar{x}_i)K\big((x_i - x_0)/h\big)/(j!j'!),$$

where here, $|j'| = p+1$. Since $\|(x_i - x_0)^{(j')}\| = O(h^{p+1})$ when the kernel function used has a bounded support, if the $p+1$st order derivative of $m(x)$ at $x = x_0$ is bounded, then the bias term is of order h^{p+1}.

Note that when the $p+1$st derivative is Lipschitz continuous at $x = x_0$, the leading term of the bias can be expressed as

$$e_N'(HX'WXH)^{-1}HX'WX^{(p+1)}m^{(p+1)}(x_0).$$

Variance Conditional variance of $e_N'(X'WX)^{-1}X'W\epsilon$ is

$$e_N'(X'WX)^{-1}X'W\Sigma WX(X'WX)^{-1}e_N,$$

where Σ is an $n \times n$ diagonal matrix with the ith diagonal element $\sigma^2(x_i) = E(\epsilon_i^2|x_i)$. This can be rewritten as

$$\begin{aligned}&e_N'H(HX'WXH)^{-1}HX'W\Sigma WXH(HX'WXH)^{-1}He_N\\&\quad= e_N'(HX'WXH)^{-1}HX'W\Sigma WXH(HX'WXH)^{-1}e_N.\end{aligned}$$

Combining the earlier calculation about $HX'WXH/(nh^d)$ with the observation that the typical element of $HX'W\Sigma WXH/(nh^d)$ can be written as

$$\frac{1}{nh^d}\sum_{i=1}^{n}\big((x_i - x_0)/h\big)^{(j)}\big((x_i - x_0)/h\big)^{(j')}\sigma^2(x_i)K^2\big((x_i - x_0)/h\big)/(j!j'!),$$

we see that the variance is of order $1/(nh^d)$. Note that when the conditional variance function is Lipschitz continuous at x_0, the highest order term of the conditional variance can be expressed as

$$e_N'(HX'WXH)^{-1}HX'W^2XH(HX'WXH)^{-1}e_N\sigma^2(x_0).$$

These finite sample expressions of the bias term and the conditional variance term will later be used to approximate the mean squared error, which can be used to optimally choose the bandwidth h.

The asymptotic properties of the local polynomial estimator has been developed by many authors, but the following results due to Masry (1996a, 1996b) seem to be the most comprehensive. We assume stationarity of $\{(X_t, Y_t)\}$, and define the local polynomial regression estimator of $E(Y_{t+s}|X_t = x) = m(x)$ and its derivatives at $x = x_0$ where $x_0 \in \mathbb{R}^d$.

Let $f(x)$ denote the Lebesgue density of X_t, $f(x, x', \ell)$ denote the joint Lebesgue density of X_t and $X_{t+\ell}$, $j = (j_1, \ldots, j_d)$,

$$D^j m(x) = \frac{\partial^{|j|}m(x)}{\partial^{j_1}x_1 \cdots \partial^{j_d}x_d},$$

its local polynomial estimator of order p by $\hat\beta_{|j|,j}(x)$, and define for $(0, \ldots, 0) \in \mathbb{R}^d$, $\hat\beta_{0,(0,\ldots,0)}(x) = \hat\beta^{(0)}$. Masry (1996b) establishes the conditions under which local polynomial estimator converges uniformly over a compact set.

THEOREM 4.1. *Let D be a compact subset of $\mathbb{R}^d$. If*

(1) *the kernel function $K(\cdot)$ is bounded with compact support (there exists $A > 0$ such that $K(u) = 0$ for $\|u\| > A$) and there exists $C > 0$ such that for any $(j_1, \ldots, j_d)$ such that $0 \leqslant j_1 + \cdots + j_d \leqslant 2p + 1$*

$$\big|u_1^{j_1} \cdots u_d^{j_d} K(u) - v_1^{j_1} \cdots v_d^{j_d} K(v)\big| \leqslant C\|u - v\|,$$

(2) *the stationary process* $\{(X_t, Y_t)\}$ *is strongly mixing with the mixing coefficient* $\alpha(k)$ *satisfying*

$$\sum_{j=1}^{\infty} j^a \alpha(j)^{1-2/\nu} < \infty$$

for some $\nu > 2$ *and* $a > 1 - 2/\nu$,

(3) *there exists* $C > 0$ *such that* $f(x) < C$, $f(x)$ *is uniformly continuous on* $\mathbb{R}^d$, *and* $\inf_{x \in D} f(x) > 0$,

(4) *there exists* $C > 0$ *such that* $f(u, v, \ell) < C$,

(5) *the conditional density* $f_{X_0|Y_s}(x|y)$ *of* X_0 *given* Y_s *exists and is uniformly bounded,*

(6) *the conditional density* $f_{(X_0, X_\ell)|(Y_s, Y_{s+\ell})}(x, x'|y, y')$ *of* (X_0, X_ℓ) *given* $(Y_s, Y_{s+\ell})$ *exists and is uniformly bounded for all* $\ell \geqslant 1$,

(7) *the* $p + 1$*st order of derivative of* $m(x)$ *is uniformly bounded and the* $p + 1$*st order derivative is Lipschitz continuous, and*

(8) $E(|Y|^\sigma) < \infty$ *for some* $\sigma > \nu$,

then

$$\sup_{x \in D} \left| \hat{\beta}_{|j|,j}(x) - D^j m(x) \right| = O\left(\left(\ln n / \left(n h^{d+2|j|} \right) \right)^{1/2} \right) + O\left(h^{p-|j|+1} \right).$$

Point-wise variance goes down with rate $1/(nh^d)$ as discussed above when $|j| = 0$. The $\ln n$ factor is the penalty we need to pay for uniform convergence.

Masry (1996a) establishes the asymptotic normality of the local polynomial estimator in an interior point of the support of X_t.[36] Let M and Γ be $N \times N$ matrices with $N_u \times N_v$, sub-matrices $M_{u,v}$ and $\Gamma_{u,v}$ for $u, v = 0, \ldots, p$, respectively, where the typical elements of $M_{u,v}$ is $\int x_1^{j_1+j_1'} \cdots x_d^{j_d+j_d'} K(x)\,\mathrm{d}x/(j!j'!)$ with $|j| = u$ and $|j'| = v$ and the typical element of $\Gamma_{u,v}$ is $\int x_1^{j_1+j_1'} \cdots x_d^{j_d+j_d'} K^2(x)\,\mathrm{d}x/(j!j'!)$ with $|j| = u$ and $|j'| = v$. Analogously define $M_{u,p+1}$ for $u = 0, \ldots, p$ and define the $N \times N_{p+1}$ matrix B as

$$\begin{pmatrix} M_{0,p+1} \\ M_{1,p+1} \\ \vdots \\ M_{p,p+1} \end{pmatrix}$$

and recall that we write $m^{(p+1)}(x)$ to denote a vector of $D^j m(x)$ with $|j| = p + 1$ in the lexicographic order discussed above.[37]

[36] The following results imposes comparable conditions as those above, although Masry (1996a) establishes results under somewhat weaker conditions on the kernel functions and results include cases under ρ-mixing as well.

[37] Our definition of M is different from that in the Masry's paper by $j!j'!$ for each element of M and thus the asymptotic bias and variance expressions differ as well reflecting only the difference in the notations.

Note that matrices M, Γ, and B are the probability limits of $HX'WXH/(nh^d)$, $HX'W^2XH/(nh_n^d)$, and $HX'WX^{(p+1)}/(nh^d)$, respectively, when x_0 is an interior point of the support of X_t.

THEOREM 4.2. *Suppose x_0 is an interior point of the support of X_t. Let $h = O(n^{-1/(d+2p+2)})$ as $n \to \infty$. If the conditional distribution and the conditional variance of Y_s given $X_0 = x$ are continuous at $x = x_0$, $f(x)$ is continuous at x_0, $f(x_0) > 0$ and if*

(1) *the kernel function $K(\cdot)$ is bounded with compact support,*
(2) *the stationary process $\{(X_t, Y_t)\}$ is strongly mixing with the mixing coefficient $\alpha(k)$ satisfying*

$$\sum_{j=1}^{\infty} j^a \alpha(j)^{1-2/\nu} < \infty$$

for some $\nu > 2$ and $a > 1 - 2/\nu$, and there exists $\nu_n = o((nh^d)^{1/2})$ such that $(n/h^d)^{1/2}\alpha(\nu_n) \to 0$ as $n \to \infty$,
(3) *there exists $C > 0$ such that $f(x) < C$,*
(4) *there exists $C > 0$ such that $f(u, v, \ell) < C$,*
(5) *the conditional density $f_{(X_0,X_\ell)|(Y_s,Y_{s+\ell})}(x, x'|y, y')$ of (X_0, X_ℓ) given $(Y_s, Y_{s+\ell})$ exists and is uniformly bounded for all $\ell \geqslant 1$,*
(6) *the $p + 1$st order of derivative of $m(x)$ is uniformly bounded and the $p + 1$st order derivative is Lipschitz continuous, and*
(7) *$E(|Y|^\nu) < \infty$ for ν defined above,*

then

$$\left(nh^{d+2|j|}\right)^{1/2}\left(\left[\hat{\beta}_{|j|,j}(x_0) - D^j m(x_0)\right] - \left(M^{-1}Bm^{(p+1)}(x_0)\right)_i h^{p+1-|j|}\right)$$

converges in distribution to the zero mean random variable with variance

$$\frac{\sigma^2(x_0)}{f(x_0)}\left(M^{-1}\Gamma M^{-1}\right)_{i,i}$$

where i denotes the order in which j appear in matrix M.

The convergence rate coincides with the optimal rate computed by Stone (1982). The theorem specifies the rate at which h should converge to 0, but does not specify how to choose h. Section 6 discusses how to choose the smoothing parameter.

Note that the first order bias term

$$\left(M^{-1}Bm^{(p+1)}(x_0)\right)_i h^{p+1-|j|}$$

depends on the $p + 1$st order derivatives but does *not*, in general, depend on the distribution of the conditioning variable, other than the fact that $f(x_0) > 0$ has been used in arriving at the formula. When the kernel function used is symmetric and $p - |j|$ is even, then the bias term can be shown to be of order $h^{p+2-|j|}$ and involves the derivative of regressor density.[38] This corresponds to the case of the kernel regression estimator.[39]

The order of the variance depends on the dimension of the function being estimated and the order of the derivative of the target function, but does not depend on the degree of the polynomial used in estimation. However, the constant term in the variance expression does depend on the degree of the polynomial used. It has been observed that the constant term does not change when p moves from a lower even number to the next odd number, for example from 0 to 1. It does go up when moving up from an odd number to the next even number, for example from 1 to 2.[40] Thus, moving up by one from an even number to an odd number reduces the bias, but does not add to the variance. So when there is a choice, we should choose p to be an odd number. In particular, it is better to use a local linear estimator to estimate the conditional mean function rather than a kernel regression estimator. Note that this is a result at interior points and also when the underlying function is at least $(p + 1)$-times continuously differentiable.

Another point to note about the form of the first order variance is that it is the same regardless of whether the errors are allowed to be correlated or not. This is a standard but an unpleasant result in nonparametric asymptotic analysis as pointed out by Robinson (1983) for the case of kernel density estimation. It is unpleasant, because, for any finite number of observations, the observations that fall in the fixed neighborhood of x_0 would be correlated especially in high frequency data analysis. See Conley, Hansen and Liu (1997) for a bootstrap approach to assess the variability.[41]

Here, we have discussed local polynomial estimation of the conditional mean function. For a discussion of locally linear estimation of the conditional quantile function, see Chaudhuri (1991a, 1991b) and Yu and Jones (1998).

5. Semiparametric estimation

We review some semiparametric estimation methods used in econometrics. As discussed in Section 2, the curse-of-dimensionality problem associated with nonparametric density and conditional mean function estimators makes the methods impractical in applications with many regressors and modest size samples. Semiparametric modeling approaches offer a middle ground between fully nonparametric and fully parametric approaches. They achieve faster rates of convergence for conditional mean functions or other parameters of interest by employing one of the three approaches discussed earlier: by imposing some parametric restrictions, by changing the target parameters, or

[38] See Fan and Gijbels (1996, Theorem 3.1) for a discussion of a univariate case.

[39] See Härdle and Linton (1994).

[40] See Ruppert and Wand (1994) and Fan and Gijbels (1996, Section 3.3).

[41] Another approach may be to compute the finite sample variance formula and estimate it analogously to the Newey–West approach.

by imposing quantile restrictions in the case of limited dependent variable models. The nonparametric density and conditional mean function estimators described in the last section form the building blocks of a variety of semiparametric estimators.

In Section 2, we considered one semiparametric model – the partially linear model – and described its application to the problems of estimating consumer demand functions and to controlling for sample selection. Here we consider that model in greater detail as well as other classes of semiparametric models for conditional mean function estimation, including additive separable models, index models, and average derivative models with and without index restrictions. We also review the censored LAD estimator of Powell (1984) and the Maximum Score estimator of Manski (1975, 1985) for the limited dependent variable models as examples of exploiting quantile restrictions. These methods embody distinct ideas that are applicable in other contexts. A detailed discussion of techniques for deriving the distribution theory is left for Section 7.

5.1. *Conditional mean function estimation with an additive structure*

Suppose the relationship of interest is $E(Y|X = x) = g(x)$, where X is a random vector of length d and g is an unknown function from $\mathbb{R}^d$ into $\mathbb{R}$. As described earlier, we face the curse of dimensionality if the fully nonparametric estimator of $g(x)$ were to be used. Another problem is that nonparametrically estimated g functions become difficult to interpret when the estimated surface can no longer be visualized and the effect of any regressor on the dependent variable depends on the values of all the other regressors.

We consider three classes of semiparametric estimators for $g(x)$ that impose different kinds of modeling restrictions designed to overcome the curse-of-dimensionality problem and to make estimates easier to interpret. The first class, *additively separable models*, restricts $g(x)$ to lie in the space of functions that can be written as an additively separable function of the regressors. The second class, *single index models*, assumes that X affects Y only through an index $X'\beta$. That is, $g(x) = g(x'\beta)$. *Multiple index models* allow the conditional mean of Y to depend on multiple indices. The third class, *partially linear models*, assumes that the function $g(x)$ can be decomposed into a linear component and a nonparametric component, thereby extending the traditional linear modeling framework to include a nonparametric term. Partially linear restrictions are often imposed in connection with index model restrictions, giving rise to partially linear, single or multiple index models.

5.1.1. *Additively separable models*

An additively separable model restricts $g(x)$ to be additively separable in the components of the vector X:

$$E(Y|X = x) = \alpha + g_1(x_1) + g_2(x_2) + g_3(x_3) + \cdots + g_d(x_d),$$

where the $g_j(x_j)$, $j = 1, \dots, d$, are assumed to be unknown and are nonparametrically estimated. A key advantage of imposing additive separability is that the nonparametric estimators of the $g_j(x_j)$ functions as well as of the conditional mean function $E(Y|X = x)$ can be made to converge at the univariate nonparametric rate. Another advantage is interpretive: the model allows for graphical depiction of the effect of x_j on y holding other regressors constant. The separability assumption is also not as restrictive as it may seem, because some regressors could be interactions of other regressors (e.g. $x_3 = x_1 x_2$). However, for $g_i(x_i)$ to be nonparametrically identified, it is necessary to rule out general forms of collinearity between the regressors. That is, we could not allow $x_1 = \psi(x_k)$ for some ψ function, for example, and still separately identify $g_1(x), \dots, g_d(x)$.[42]

Estimation methods

Back-fitting algorithms As described in Hastie and Tibshirani (1990), additively separable models can be solved through an algorithm called *back-fitting*.

The algorithm involves three steps:

(i) Choose initial starting values for α and for g_j. A good starting value might set $\alpha^0 = \mathit{average}(Y)$ and g_j^0 equal to the values predicted by a linear in x least squares regression of Y on a constant and all the regressors.
(ii) For each $j = 1, \dots, d$, define $g_j = \hat{E}(y - \alpha - \sum_{k \neq j} g_k^0(x_k)\ |x_j)$, where g_k^0 is the most recent estimate of $g_k(x_k)$ (the starting value at the first iteration). The conditional expectation is estimated by a smoothing method, such as kernel or local linear regression, or series expansion or spline regression. At this stage, if it is desired that a functional form restriction be imposed on the shape of one or more of the g_j functions, then the restriction can be imposed by setting, for example, $\hat{E}(y - \alpha - \sum_{k \neq j} g_k^0(x_k)\ |x_j) = x_j \beta_j$.
(iii) Repeat step (ii) until convergence is reached (when the estimated $g_j(x_j)$ functions no longer change).[43]

Back-fitting can require many iterations to reach convergence, but it is relatively easy to implement and is available in the software package Splus. Disadvantages of the method are that consistency has not been shown when nonparametric smoothing methods are used in step (ii) and there is as of yet no general distribution theory available that can be used to evaluate the variation of the estimators.

An estimator based on integration An alternative approach to estimating the additively separable model, which is studied by Newey (1994b), Härdle and Linton (1996), Linton et al. (1997) and others. Although it is more difficult to implement than the back-fitting

[42] See the discussion of concurvity in Hastie and Tibshirani (1990).

[43] Also see Hastie and Tibshirani (1990) for discussion of a modified back-fitting algorithm that, in some circumstances, converges in fewer iterations.

procedure, because it requires a pilot estimator of the nonparametric model $g(x)$, the integration approach has the advantage of having a distribution theory available.

For notational simplicity, consider the additively separable model with two regressors $Y = \alpha + g_1(X_1) + g_2(X_2) + \varepsilon$. Define the integrated parameter

$$\tilde{g}_1(x_1) = \int g(x_1, x_2)\, \mathrm{d}F_{x_2}.$$

Note that this is generally *not* equal to $E(Y|X_1 = x_1)$ which would be

$$E(Y|X_1 = x_1) = \int g(x_1, x_2)\, \mathrm{d}F_{x_2|X_1=x_1}.$$

If X_1 and X_2 are independent, then the two parameters coincide. The integration estimator is given by

$$\hat{g}_1(x_1) = n^{-1} \sum_{i=1}^{n} \hat{g}(x_1, x_{2i}).$$

If the model is additive, then $\hat{g}_1(x_1)$ estimates $g_1(x_1)$ up to an additive constant. Reversing the roles of $x_1$and x_2 obtains an estimator for $g_2(x_2)$, again up to scale.

In general, we do not really believe that the underlying function $g(x_1, x_2)$ is additively separable but that we use the model as a convenient way to summarize data. From this perspective, the integration estimator proposes to examine the effect of one variable X_1 on the dependent variable after integrating out the rest of the variables $X_2, \ldots, X_d$ using the marginal distribution of $X_2, \ldots, X_d$, which would be exactly the correct procedure if the underlying function g is indeed additively separable between X_1 and $X_2, \ldots, X_d$.

The back fitting algorithm seems to be an attempt to obtain the solution to the least squares problem within the class of additively separable functions. These two sets of functions should coincide up to an additive constant term, if underlying function g is additively separable, if not, the two estimates in general would converge to different functions.

Newey (1994b) shows that the estimator $\hat{g}_1(x_1)$ converges at a one-dimensional nonparametric rate because of the averaging. As we have seen, the convergence rate decreases in a higher dimension space because the rate at which we obtain data decreases. Because there is no need to condition on $X_2, \ldots, X_d$ for examining $g_1(x_1)$, the convergence rate corresponds to that for one-dimensional cases.

As noted above, an advantage of estimating additive models through integration is that the distribution theory for the estimators has been developed.[44] A disadvantage of the integration estimator is that it requires that the higher dimensional estimate of the $g(x)$ be calculated prior to averaging, and existing distribution theory for the estimator requires that negative kernel functions be used for bias reduction.

[44] See, for example, Härdle and Linton (1996).

Generalized additive models The additive modeling framework has been generalized to allow for known or unknown transformations of the dependent variable, Y. That is, estimators are available for models of the form

$$\theta(Y) = \alpha + g_1(X_1) + g_2(X_2) + \cdots + g_d(X_d) + \varepsilon,$$

where the link function θ may be a known transformation (such as the Box–Cox transformation) or may be assumed to be unknown and nonparametrically estimated along with the g_j functions. Hastie and Tibshirani (1990) describe how to modify back-fitting procedures to accommodate binary response data and survival data, when the link function is known. For the case of an unknown θ function, Breiman and Friedman (1985) propose an estimation procedure called ACE (Alternating Conditional Expectation).[45] Linton et al. (1997) describe an instrumental variables procedure for estimating the θ function, which is based on the identifying assumption that the model is only additively separable for the correct transformation so that misspecification in θ shows up as a correlation between the error terms and the instruments. We are not aware of empirical applications of these methods in economics, although generalized additive models (GAMs) and ACE seem potentially very useful ways for empirical researchers to gain some flexibility in modeling the conditional mean function while at the same time avoiding the curse-of-dimensionality.

5.1.2. Single index model

The single index model restricts the function $g(x)$ under consideration to be

$$g(x) = \phi(x'\beta_0)$$

where ϕ is an unknown function. An estimator of the slope coefficients β_0 in the single index model that allows for discrete regressors and regressors which may be functionally related is studied by Ichimura (1993).

Consider the single index model in the conditional mean function:

$$E(Y|X = x) = \phi(x'\beta_0).$$

This model arises naturally in a variety of limited dependent variable models in which the observed dependent variable Y is modeled as a transformation of $X'\beta_0$ and an unobserved variable which is independent of X. See Heckman and Robb (1985) and Stoker (1986). Also, this model can be viewed simply as a generalization of the regression function.

[45] ACE is also discussed in Hastie and Tibshirani (1990). The ACE algorithm is available in the software package Splus.

Observe that writing $\varepsilon = Y - \phi(x'\beta_0)$,

$$m_W(b) \equiv E\{[Y - E(Y|X'b)]^2 W(X)\}$$
$$= E\{\varepsilon^2 W(X)\} + E\{[\phi(X'\beta_0) - E(Y|X'b)]^2 W(X)\}.$$

The computation makes clear that, for any function $W(x)$, the variation in Y has two sources: the variation in $X'\beta_0$ and that in ε. If we choose b to be proportional to β_0, then the contribution to the variation due to the variation in $X'\beta_0$ becomes zero in function $m_W(b)$ as $E(Y|X'b) = \phi(X'\beta_0)$ in that case. This observation lead to defining an estimator as

$$\min_b \frac{1}{n}\sum_{i=1}^{n}[y_i - E(y_i|x_i'b)]^2 W(x_i)$$

if we knew the conditional mean function $E(Y_i|X_i'b)$. As we do not know it, we need to replace it with its estimate. But because the conditional mean function cannot be estimated at points where the density of $X'b$ is low, we need to introduce trimming, for the other estimators we examine.

The trimming function in this case has a further complication. Even if the density of X is bounded away from zero, the density of $X'b$ is not, in general. This can be understood by considering two variables that each has the uniform distribution on the unit square and considering the density corresponding to the sum.

A simple way around this problem is to define the trimming function as follows:

$$I_i = 1\{x_i \in \mathcal{X}\},$$

where $\mathcal{X}$ denotes a fixed interior point of the support of X_i by at least certain distance. Note that over this set $\mathcal{X}$, by construction the density of x is bounded away from zero and that the density of $X'b$ is also bounded away from zero.

Another point to note is that for any constant value $c \neq 0$, $E(Y|X'b = x'b) = E(Y|X'(cb) = x'(cb))$ so that we cannot identify the length of β_0. Thus we define the estimator to be the minimizer of the following objective function after replacing $E(Y_i|X_i'b)$ with a nonparametric estimator of it:

$$\min_{b\in\{b:\, b_1>0,\, b'b=1\}} \frac{1}{n}\sum_{i=1}^{n}[y_i - \hat{E}(y_i|x_i'b)]^2 W(x_i) I_i.$$

In implementation, two forms of normalization are used; in some cases $\beta'\beta = 1$ is imposed and in other cases one of the coefficient is set to 1.[46] In either case, the Var–Cov matrix of the estimator is $V^{-}\Omega V^{-}$, where

$$V = E\{[\varphi'(x'\beta_0)]^2[\tilde{x} - E(\tilde{x}|x'\beta_0)][\tilde{x} - E(\tilde{x}|x'\beta_0)]'\},$$

[46] We consider $W(x) = 1$ for simplicity below. See Ichimura (1993) for the weighted case. In general we need to modify the standard estimation of $E(Y|X'b)$ to achieve efficiency by weighting.

$$\Omega = E\{\sigma^2(X)[\varphi'(X'\beta_0)]^2[\tilde{X} - E(\tilde{X}|X'\beta_0)][\tilde{X} - E(\tilde{X}|X'\beta_0)]'\},$$
$$\sigma^2(X) = V(Y|X)$$

and all of the expectations are taken over a given set $\mathcal{X}$ over which the density of $X'\beta_0$ is assumed to be bounded away from 0. When $\beta'\beta = 1$, $\tilde{x} = x$ and when one of the coefficients is set to 1, $\tilde{x}$ is the original regressors except the regressor whose coefficient is set to 1. For the first normalization, note that $\Omega\beta_0 = 0$ and $V\beta_0 = 0$ hold so that V and Ω are not invertible.

There are two sources of efficiency loss. One is that the variation in $\tilde{X} - E(\tilde{X}|X'\beta_0)$ is used rather than the variation in $\tilde{X}$. The other is that heteroskedasticity is not accounted for in the estimation. The first problem arises as ϕ is unknown, and hence is genuine to the formulation of the problem. The second problem can be resolved by weighting if the model is truly single index. Oftentimes, however, we use the single index model as a convenient approximation to a more general function. Ichimura and Lee (2006) shows that if the single index model is used when the underlying model is not single index, the SLS estimator still is consistent to a vector which best approximates the conditional mean function within the single index model, and it is asymptotically normal, but its asymptotic variance contains an additional term. They discuss how to estimate the asymptotic variance term including this additional term and hence how to make the estimator robust to misspecification. Here the discussion used the linear single index, but the same idea applies to the nonlinear index model and also to the case of multiple indices. See Ichimura and Lee (1991).

When the dependent variable is discrete, the more natural objective function is likelihood based. Klein and Spady (1993) examine the case of binary choice models and propose an estimator that is efficient among semiparametric estimators.

Blundell and Powell (2003) considers the single index model with an endogenous regressor and Ichimura and Lee (2006) considers the estimation of the conditional quantile function when the conditional quantile function is modeled as a single index function.

5.1.3. Partially linear regression model

The partially linear regression model extends the linear regression model to include a nonparametric component and specifies:

$$Y = X'\beta_0 + \varphi(Z) + \varepsilon$$

where $X \in R^p$ and $Z \in R^q$ do not have common variables. If they do, then the common variables would be regarded as a part of Z but not X because the coefficients that correspond to the common variables would be not identifiable. If there are no cross terms of z among X's, then the model presumes additive separability of $\varphi(Z)$ and X, which may be too restrictive in some applications.

This framework is convenient for a model with many regressors, where fully nonparametric estimation is often impractical. It is also a good choice for a model that contains discrete regressors along with a few continuous ones. As discussed in Section 2, this model has been broadly applied in economics, mainly to the problem of estimating Engel curves and to the problem of controlling for sample selection bias. Estimators for the partially linear model are studied in Heckman (1980, 1990), Shiller (1984), Stock (1991), Wahba (1984), Engle et al. (1986), Chamberlain (1986b), Powell (1987), Newey (1988), Robinson (1988), Ichimura and Lee (1991), Andrews (1991), Cosslett (1991), Choi (1992), Ahn and Powell (1993), Honoré and Powell (1994), Yatchew (1997), Heckman et al. (1998), Heckman, Ichimura and Todd (1998b) and others.

As we saw, the nonparametric convergence rate would depend on the number of continuous regressors in (X, Z). In the partially linear regression framework, the convergence rate of the estimator of φ also depends on the number of continuous regressors among z. Remarkably, the $n^{1/2}$-consistent estimation of β can be carried out regardless of the number of continuous regressors in (X, Z) provided there is enough smoothness in underlying function, as shown by Robinson (1988).

To consider the estimator Robinson studied, observe that

$$E(Y|Z = z) = E(X'|Z = z)\beta_0 + \varphi(z)$$

so that

$$Y - E(Y|Z = z) = \big(X - E(X|Z = z)\big)'\beta_0 + \varepsilon.$$

If we knew $E(Y|Z = z)$ and $E(X|Z = z)$ then one could estimate β_0 by the ordinary least squares method of $Y - E(Y|Z = z)$ on $X - E(X|Z = z)$. Because we do not know them, we can estimate them by some nonparametric method. Call them $\hat{E}(Y|Z = z)$ and $\hat{E}(X|Z = z)$, and estimate β_0 by

$$\left(\sum_{i=1}^{N}\big[x_i - \hat{E}(x_i|z_i)\big]\big[x_i - \hat{E}(x_i|z_i)\big]'\right)^{-1}\sum_{i=1}^{N}\big[x_i - \hat{E}(x_i|z_i)\big]\big[y_i - \hat{E}(y_i|z_i)\big].$$

Since the conditional mean functions will not be estimated well where the density of Z is low, Robinson makes use of a trimming function $\hat{I}_i = 1\{\hat{f}(z_i) > b_n\}$, where $\hat{f}(z)$ is a kernel density estimator, for a given sequence of numbers $\{b_n\}$.[47] The estimator is defined as

$$\hat{\beta} = \left(\sum_{i=1}^{N}\big[x_i - \hat{E}(x_i|z_i)\big]\big[x_i - \hat{E}(x_i|z_i)\big]'\hat{I}_i\right)^{-1} \times \sum_{i=1}^{N}\big[x_i - \hat{E}(x_i|z_i)\big]\big[y_i - \hat{E}(y_i|z_i)\big]\hat{I}_i.$$

The estimation method is reminiscent of a double residual regression interpretation of the OLS estimator: consider the OLS estimation of

$$Y = X'\beta_0 + Z'\gamma + \varepsilon.$$

47 This trimming method is also used by Bickel (1982).

As it is well known the OLS estimator of β_0 is the OLS estimator of u_y on u_x where u_y is the OLS residual of running Y on Z and u_x is the OLS residual of running X on Z.[48] Here, the first stage is replaced by nonparametric regressions.

Let α and μ be nonnegative real numbers and m be the integer such that $m-1 \leqslant \mu \leqslant m$. For such $\mu > 0$, $\Im_\mu^\alpha$ is the class of functions g: $R^q \to R$ satisfying: g is $(m-1)$-times partially differentiable for all z; for some $\rho > 0$, $\sup_{y\in\{y;\ |y-z|<\rho\}} |g(y) - g(z) - Q_{m-1}(y,z)|/|y-z|^\mu \leqslant h(z)$, where $Q_0 = 0$ and for $m \geqslant 2$, $Q_{m-1}(y,z)$ is the $(m-1)$th-degree homogeneous polynomial in $y-z$ with coefficients the partial derivatives of g at z of order 1 through $m-1$; and $g(z)$, its partial derivatives of order $(m-1)$ and less, and $h(z)$, all have αth moments.

Robinson uses kernel regression estimator with independent kernel functions. He introduces the following notation: K_l, $l \geqslant 1$, is the class of even functions $k: R \to R$ satisfying

$$\int_{-\infty}^{\infty} u^i k(u)\, du = \begin{cases} 1 & \text{if } i = 0, \\ 0 & \text{if } i = 1, \dots, l-1, \end{cases}$$

$$k(u) = O\big(\big(1 + |u|^{l+1+\delta}\big)^{-1}\big), \quad \text{for some } \delta > 0.$$

In the statement below, k is the kernel function, a is the bandwidth for estimating regression function and density, and b is the trimming value, q is the dimension of z. Both a and b depend on N although the notation does not explicitly express it.

THEOREM 5.1 *(Robinson). Let the following conditions hold*:

(i) (X_i, Y_i, Z_i), $i = 1, 2 \dots$, *are independent and distributed as* (X, Y, Z);
(ii) *the model specification is correct*;
(iii) ε *is independent of* (X, Z);
(iv) $E(\varepsilon^2) = \sigma^2 < \infty$;
(v) $E(|X|^4) < \infty$;
(vi) Z *admits a pdf* f *such that* $f \in \Im_\lambda^\infty$, *for some* $\lambda > 0$;
(vii) $E(X|Z = z) \in \Im_\mu^2$, *for some* $\mu > 0$;
(viii) $\varphi(z) \in \Im_\nu^4$, *for some* $\nu > 0$;
(ix) *as* $N \to \infty$, $Na^{2q}b^4 \to \infty$, $na^{2\min(\lambda+1,\mu)+2\min(\lambda+1,\nu)}b^{-4} \to 0$, $a^{\min(\lambda+1,2\lambda,\mu,\nu)}b^{-2} \to 0$, $b \to 0$;
(x) $k \in K_{\max(l+m-1,l+n-1)}$, *for the integers* l, m, n *such that* $l-1 < \lambda \leqslant l$, $m-1 < \mu \leqslant m$, *and* $n-1 < \nu \leqslant n$.

Then the condition that

$$\Phi \equiv E\big\{\big[x - E(x|z)\big]\big[x - E(x|z)\big]'\big\} \quad \textit{is positive definite}$$

is necessary and sufficient for $\sqrt{N}(\hat\beta - \beta) \xrightarrow{d} N(0, \sigma^2\Phi^{-1})$ *and*

$$\hat\sigma^2\left(N^{-1}\sum_{i=1}^{N}\big[x_i - \hat E(x_i|z_i)\big]\big[x_i - \hat E(x_i|z_i)\big]'\hat I_i\right)^{-1} \xrightarrow{p} \sigma^2\Phi^{-1},$$

[48] Frisch–Waugh double residual regression. See Goldberger (1968) and Malinvaud (1970).

where

$$\hat{\sigma}^2 = N^{-1}\sum_{i=1}^{N}\big[y_i - \hat{E}(y_i|z_i) - \big(x_i - \hat{E}(x_i|z_i)\big)'\hat{\beta}\big]^2.$$

As stated earlier, the convergence rate of $\hat{\beta}$ is $\sqrt{N}$, which does not depend on the dimension of Z, despite the presence of φ. The theorem is stated for the kernel regression estimator, but the result also holds for other nonparametric estimators as discussed in Section 7.

If $\hat{E}$ is a linear in dependent variable estimator, then $\hat{\sigma}^2$ can be rewritten as

$$N^{-1}\sum_{i=1}^{N}\big[y_i - x_i'\hat{\beta} - \hat{E}\big(y_i - x_i'\hat{\beta}|z_i\big)\big]^2,$$

which is a natural estimator of σ^2.

Compared to the OLS estimation without φ under homoskedasticity, the variance is higher because

$$\operatorname{Var}(x) = \Phi + \operatorname{Var}\big(E(x|z)\big).$$

When there is heteroskedasticity, so that (iii) does not hold, under analogous conditions

$$\sqrt{N}(\hat{\beta} - \beta) \xrightarrow{d} N\big(0, \Phi^{-1}\Omega\Phi^{-1}\big),$$

where

$$\Omega = E\big\{\varepsilon^2\big[x - E(x|z)\big]\big[x - E(x|z)\big]'\big\}.$$

The partially linear regression model also resembles the conditional mean function in the sample selection model. If the outcome equation is specified as $Y = X'\beta + u$ and the selection equation is specified by the latent model of the form $1(z'\theta + v > 0)$, where (u, v) and (X, Z) are independent, then without specifying the joint distribution of (u, v), the following relationship holds:

$$Y = X'\beta_0 + \varphi(Z'\theta) + \varepsilon,$$
$$E(\varepsilon|X, Z) = 0.$$

Note that in this case, there is more structure on the φ function and that θ (up to a scalar) can be estimated from the data on whether Y is observed. Without this structure, as discussed above, the partially linear regression model only identifies coefficients of X variables that are not in the Z variables.

Powell (1987) made use of this observation, modified Robinson's estimator so that there is no need for trimming, and discussed estimation of β_0. Ahn and Powell (1993) extended this approach further based on the observation that in the sample selection model one can write the conditional mean function as

$$Y = X'\beta_0 + \varphi\big(P(Z)\big) + \varepsilon,$$
$$E(\varepsilon|X, Z) = 0,$$

where $P(z)$ is the probability of being selected into samples, which can be estimated from the data about selection.[49] Ichimura and Lee (1991) propose a way of simultaneously estimating β and θ with truncated data. Yatchew (1997) proposes using the differencing idea of Powell (1987) without averaging. Heckman et al. (1998), Heckman, Ichimura and Todd (1998b) study estimation of β and $\varphi(P(z))$, allowing for parametrically estimated $P(z)$ and data-dependent bandwidths. The estimator they study is basically the same as the estimator studied by Robinson, but they use the local polynomial estimator instead of the kernel regression estimator. Instead of Z, they have a parametric form $P(z'\theta)$ where θ is estimated by $\hat{\theta}$ from the data on selection, use trimming based on an estimated low percentile (usually 1 or 2%) of $P(z_i'\hat{\theta})$, denoted as $\hat{q}_n$ so that the trimming function is written as $\hat{I}_i = 1(\hat{f}(\hat{P}_i) > \hat{q}_n)$ where $\hat{f}(\cdot)$ is the kernel density estimator of the density of $P(z'\theta)$, and the smoothing parameter can be data dependent. Estimation of φ is done using the estimated β to purge Y of its dependence on X. That is, we can estimate $\varphi(p_0)$ by a local linear regression of $Y_i - X_i'\hat{\beta}$ on $\hat{P}_i$ evaluated at p_0, which we denote by $\hat{\varphi}(p_0)$.

The following theorem summarizes the results by Heckman, Ichimura and Todd (1998b). D_i denotes the indicator of whether the ith observation is in the sample or not.

THEOREM 5.2. *Assume that*:

(i) *data* $\{(X_i, Y_i, Z_i, D_i)\}$ *are i.i.d.*, $E\{\|x_i\|^{2+\varepsilon} + \|z_i\|^{2+\varepsilon}\} < \infty$ *for some* $\varepsilon > 0$, *and* $E\{|y_i|^3\} < \infty$,

(ii) $\sqrt{n}(\hat{\theta} - \theta_0) = n^{-1/2}\sum_{i=1}^n \psi(z_i, d_i) + o_p(1)$, *where* $n^{-1/2}\sum_{i=1}^n \psi(z_i)$ *converges in distribution to a normal random vector,*

(iii) *the kernel function* $K(\cdot)$ *is supported on* $[-1, 1]$ *and it is twice continuously differentiable,*

(iv) $P(z_i'\theta)$ *is twice continuously differentiable with respect to* θ *and both derivatives have second moments,*

(v) $E(X|P)$, $E\{\varphi(P)\}$ *are twice continuously differentiable with respect to* θ,

(vi) $H_1 = E\{[X - E(X|P)][X - E(X|P)]'I\}$ *evaluated at the true* $\theta = \theta_0$ *is nonsingular,*

(vii) *the density of* $P(Z'\theta)$, f_θ, *is uniformly bounded and uniformly continuous in the neighborhood of* θ_0 *and for any* $\varepsilon > 0$ *there exists* $\delta > 0$ *such that if* $\|\theta - \theta_0\| < \delta$ *then* $\sup_{0\leqslant s\leqslant 1} |f_\theta(s) - f_{\theta_0}(s)| < \varepsilon$,

[49] Establishing the asymptotic distribution theory for an estimator that involves trimming which uses estimated θ or estimated $P(z)$ would be a nontrivial task. Powell (1987) and Ahn and Powell (1993) avoided the need for trimming by a clever re-weighting scheme. This approach have been developed to be applicable to broader models by Honoré and Powell (1994, 2005), and Aradillas-Lopez, Honoré and Powell (2005).

(viii) $na_n^3/\log n \to \infty$ *and* $na_n^8 \to 0$.

Then

$$n^{1/2}(\hat{\beta} - \beta_0) = n^{-1/2}\sum_{i=1}^{n} H_1^{-1}\{[X_i - E(X|P_i)]\varepsilon_i I_i + H_2\psi(Z_i, D_i)\} + o_p(1)$$

where $H_2 = E\{[X - E(X|P)]P(Z'\theta_0)[Z - E(Z|P)]'I\}$.

If in addition to the assumptions above, the following assumptions hold:

(ix) φ *is twice continuously differentiable,*

(x) $f_{\theta_0}(p_0) > 0$,

(xi) *the bandwidth sequence satisfies* $\hat{a}_n = \hat{\alpha}_n n^{-1/5}$, $\operatorname{plim} \hat{\alpha}_n = \alpha_0 > 0$,

(xii) $\sigma^2(p_0) = E[|Y - X'\beta|^2 | P = p_0]$ *is finite and continuous at* p_0,

then

$$n^{2/5}\big(\hat{\varphi}(p_0) - \varphi(p_0)\big) \sim N(B, V)$$

where

$$B = \frac{1}{2}\varphi''(p_0)\left[\int s^2 K(s)\,\mathrm{d}s\right]\alpha_0^2,$$

$$V = \frac{\operatorname{Var}(Y - X'\beta | P = p_0)}{f_{\theta_0}(p_0)\alpha_0}\int K^2(s)\,\mathrm{d}s,$$

where $\varphi''(p_0)$ *is the second derivative of the regression function.*

5.2. *Improving the convergence rate by changing the parameter of interest*

The prototypical way to improving the convergence rate is by averaging. If we give up estimating a function at a point and instead average the point estimates over a region, we can, under some conditions, improve the convergence rate. This point is clear enough for the case of the conditional mean function $m(x) = E(Y|X = x)$. We saw that the convergence rate of the estimator of the conditional mean function depends on the number of continuous conditioning variables and the underlying smoothness of the conditional mean function with respect to these variables. Let $X = (X_1, X_2)$. Instead of estimating $m(x_1, x_2)$, one can estimate $m(x_1, A) = E(Y|X_1 = x_1, X_2 \in A)$ for some region A. In this case, since it is equivalent to having less continuous regressors, the convergence would only depend on the number of continuous regressors among X_1.

An analogous result holds for the estimation of the average of a nonparametric estimator of the derivative of a function. The average derivative estimator is examined by Stoker (1986) and its asymptotic distribution theory, in modified forms, is established by Powell, Stock and Stoker (1989), Robinson (1989), and Härdle and Stoker (1989). Newey and Stoker (1993) discusses efficiency issues. A nice application is Deaton and Ng (1998).

Note that when $E(Y|X) = g(X)$, the solution to

$$\min_b E\{[Y - X'b]^2\} = \min_b E\{[g(X) - X'b]^2\} + E[\operatorname{Var}(Y|X)]$$

corresponds to the OLS estimator. Here, $b^* = E(XX')^{-1}E[XY]$ can be interpreted as the best predictor of the form $X'b^*$ as observed by White (1980).

Because we are also interested in measuring the marginal effect of a change in regressors to dependent variables, $\partial g/\partial x$, we may want to estimate δ_k that solves

$$\min_{\delta_k} E\{(\partial g/\partial x - \delta_k)^2\}$$

for each $k = 1, \ldots, d$. The solution is $\delta_k^* = E\{\partial g/\partial x\}$. Stoker (1986) proposed estimation of δ_k^*.

Another case δ_k^* is of interest is when $g(x) = \phi(x'\beta_0)$. Stoker observed that many limited dependent variable models have this property. In this case

$$\partial g/\partial x = \phi'(x'\beta_0) \cdot \beta_0.$$

Thus $E(\partial g/\partial x) = c \cdot \beta_0$ for some constant c: estimation of the average derivative corresponds to β_0 parameter up to a constant term.

However, the interpretation of the average derivative as β_0 parameter up to a constant term depends on the assumption that (i) there is no discrete regressors among regressors and (ii) there is no functional relationship among regressors. These two assumptions may make the direct application of the average derivative method unsuitable for many limited dependent variable models. This issue is not relevant if we interpret the average derivative in a nonparametric context.

As we discussed earlier, $g(x)$ and its derivatives can be estimated consistently by nonparametric estimators. But as noted there, the convergence rate is very slow especially when K is large and/or when we estimate higher order derivatives. It turns out that δ_k^* can be estimated $1/\sqrt{n}$-consistently, the typical rate at which parametric estimators converge.

Let $\hat{\Delta}(x)$ be a nonparametric estimator of $\partial g/\partial x$ at a point x. Then a natural estimator of $\delta^* = (\delta_1^*, \delta_2^*, \ldots, \delta_d^*)'$ is

$$\frac{1}{n}\sum_{i=1}^{n} \hat{\Delta}(x_i).$$

Stoker (1986) does not examine this estimator but instead bases his estimator on an integration by parts argument. We present his argument for the one dimension case but the same argument goes through for a higher dimension, with an appropriate boundary conditions as made explicit in the computation below:

$$\begin{aligned}
E(g') &= \int_{-\infty}^{\infty} g'(x) f(x)\,\mathrm{d}x \\
&= g(x)f(x)|_{-\infty}^{\infty} - \int_{-\infty}^{\infty} g(x) f'(x)\,\mathrm{d}x \\
&= -\int_{-\infty}^{\infty} g(x)\frac{f'(x)}{f(x)} f(x)\,\mathrm{d}x = -E\left(Y\frac{f'}{f}\right).
\end{aligned}$$

Thus by making use of a nonparametric estimator of $f(x)$ and its derivative, one can estimate the average derivative. As the ratio f'/f will not be estimable where f is low, the estimator is defined making use of a trimming function $\hat{I}_i = 1\{\hat{f}(x_i) > b_n\}$ for a given sequence of numbers $\{b_n\}$.

$$\hat{\delta} = \frac{1}{n}\sum_{i=1}^{n} \frac{-\partial \hat{f}(x_i)/\partial x}{\hat{f}(x_i)} y_i \hat{I}_i, \qquad \text{where}$$

$$\hat{f}(x) = \frac{1}{n}\sum_{j=1}^{n} \frac{1}{a_n^K} K\left(\frac{x - x_j}{a_n}\right).$$

The estimator can be obtained directly without any optimization. Härdle and Stoker (1989) show:

THEOREM 5.3. *Consider* $y_i = g(x_i) + \varepsilon_i$ *with* $E(\varepsilon_i|x_i) = 0$ *under iid sampling. Assume that*:

(1) *The regressors have density* $f(x)$ *where the support of* f *is a convex subset of* R^K.
(2) $f(x) = 0$ *at the boundary of the support.*
(3) $g(x)$ *is continuously differentiable almost everywhere.*
(4) $E\{y^2(\partial \log f(x)/\partial x)(\partial \log f(x)/\partial x)'\}$ *and* $E\{(\partial g/\partial x)(\partial g/\partial x)'\}$ *are finite and* $E(y^2|x)$ *is continuous.*
(5) $f(x)$ *is differentiable up to* $p \geqslant K + 2$.
(6) $f(x)$ *and* $g(x)$ *obey local Lipschitz conditions, i.e. for* v *in neighborhood of* 0, *there exist functions* ω_f, $\omega_{f'}$, $\omega_{g'}$, *and* $\omega_{\ell g}$ *such that*

$$\left|f(x+v) - f(x)\right| \leqslant \omega_f(x)|v|,$$
$$\left|f'(x+v) - f'(x)\right| \leqslant \omega_{f'}(x)|v|,$$
$$\left|g'(x+v) - g'(x)\right| \leqslant \omega_{g'}(x)|v|,$$
$$\left|\frac{\partial \log f(x+v)}{\partial x} g(x+v) - \frac{\partial \log f(x)}{\partial x} g(x)\right| \leqslant \omega_{\ell g}(x)|v|$$

where second moments of ω_f, $\omega_{f'}$, $\omega_{g'}$, *and* $\omega_{\ell g}$ *are finite.*
(7) *Let* $A_n = \{x|f(x) > b_n\}$. *As* $n \to \infty$,

$$\int_{A_n^c} g(x)\frac{\partial f(x)}{\partial x}\,\mathrm{d}x = o\left(n^{-1/2}\right).$$

(8) *Let* $f^{(p)}$ *denote the pth order derivative of* f. $f^{(p)}$ *is locally Hölder continuous: there exist* $\gamma > 0$ *and* $c(x)$ *such that*

$$\left|f^{(p)}(x+v) - f^{(p)}(x)\right| \leqslant c(x)|v|^{\gamma},$$

where second moments of $f^{(p)}$ *and* $c(x)$ *are finite.*

(9) *The kernel function* $K(u)$, $u \in R^K$, *has finite support, is symmetric, has* $(p+\gamma)$*-absolute moments, and* $K(u)=0$ *at the boundary points, and* $K(u)$ *is of order p, i.e.* $\int_{R^K} K(u)\,\mathrm{d}u = 1$,

$$\int_{R^K} u_1^{\ell_1} u_2^{\ell_2} \cdots u_\rho^{\ell_\rho} K(u_1, u_2, \ldots, u_K)\,\mathrm{d}u = 0 \quad \textit{where}$$
$$\ell_1 + \cdots + \ell_\rho < p, \textit{ for all } \rho \leqslant K, \textit{ and}$$
$$\int_{R^K} u_1^{\ell_1} u_2^{\ell_2} \cdots u_\rho^{\ell_\rho} K(u_1, u_2, \ldots, u_K)\,\mathrm{d}u \neq 0 \quad \textit{where}$$
$$\ell_1 + \cdots + \ell_\rho = p, \textit{ for all } \rho \leqslant K.$$

(10) *As* $n \to \infty$, $a_n \to 0$, $b_n \to 0$, $a_n/b_n \to 0$ *and for some* $\varepsilon > 0$, $n^{1-\varepsilon} a_n^{2K-2} b_n^4 \to \infty$, *and* $n a_n^{2p-2} \to 0$.

Then

$$\sqrt{n}(\hat{\delta} - \delta) \xrightarrow{d} N(0, \Sigma),$$

where

$$\Sigma = E\left\{\left[\frac{\partial g}{\partial x} - E\left(\frac{\partial g}{\partial x}\right)\right]\left[\frac{\partial g}{\partial x} - E\left(\frac{\partial g}{\partial x}\right)\right]'\right\} + E\left\{\sigma_\varepsilon^2 \frac{\partial \log f(x)}{\partial x}\frac{\partial \log f(x)}{\partial x'}\right\}.$$

Although b_n has to converge to zero, there is no restriction on the speed at which that convergence has to happen in this condition. The speed requirement comes from assumption (7). As $n a_n^{2p-2} \to 0$, the parameter a_n does need to converge to zero sufficiently fast. In order for these bandwidth requirements to be mutually consistent, the density f needs to approach 0 sufficiently smoothly.

As observed above, the estimator is based on some boundary conditions. When the boundary conditions do not hold, then direct estimation of the average of a nonparametric estimator of the derivative would be preferable. Also, in deriving the theoretical properties of the estimator, negative kernel functions are used to "kill" the bias term asymptotically. Additionally, $E(\varepsilon|x) = 0$ is needed, so that models with endogenous regressors cannot be treated with this estimator. Lastly, if some of the regressors are discrete, the derivative is clearly not defined. Even in this case, however, if one restricts taking derivative with respect to the continuous regressors, then the arguments would go through without a modification. See Härdle and Stoker (1989) for estimation of the asymptotic variance–covariance matrix. Newey and Stoker (1993) showed that the estimator has the variance and covariance matrix that coincides with the smallest variance–covariance matrix within nonparametric estimators that are $1/\sqrt{n}$-consistent to δ^*.

5.3. *Usage of different stochastic assumptions*

As we discussed in the context of the censored regression model, a quantile restriction leads to $n^{1/2}$-consistent estimator even in the presence of an infinite dimensional nuisance parameter. This important result was shown by Powell (1984). A conditional mean restriction is not sufficient. The same idea applied to the binary response model does not lead to $n^{1/2}$-consistent estimator. We will see why below via a discussion of Manski's (1975, 1985) maximum score estimator.

5.3.1. Censored regression model

The model we study is

$$y_t^* = x_t'\beta_0 - \varepsilon_t,$$
$$y_t = \begin{cases} y_t^* & \text{if } y_t^* > 0, \\ 0 & \text{if } y_t^* \leqslant 0, \end{cases}$$

where the conditional median of ε is assumed to be 0. In econometric literature, Powell (1984) is the first to explicitly recognize essentially the parametric nature of the conditional quantile function under the censored regression model even though the conditional distribution of ε is restricted to have the conditional median to be 0.

There are two observations that lead to Powell's estimator. First, when $x_t'\beta_0 > 0$ the median of observed dependent variable is still $x_t'\beta_0$ and when $x_t'\beta_0 < 0$ the median of observed dependent variable is 0 so that the median of the observed dependent variable is known to have the following parametric form:

$$\max\{0, x_t'\beta_0\}.$$

Second, the minimizer of $\sum_{t=1}^T |y_t - a|$ over a estimates the median consistently. Thus the estimator is defined as the minimizer of

$$\inf_b \sum_{t=1}^T \left| y_t - \max\{0, x_t'b\}\right|.$$

Powell (1984) showed that the estimator is $n^{1/2}$-consistent and asymptotically normal:

$$\sqrt{T}(\hat\beta - \beta_0) \xrightarrow{d} N\left(0, \lim_{T\to\infty} C_T^{-1} M_T C_T^{-1}\right)$$

where

$$C_T = E\left\{T^{-1}\sum_{t=1}^T 2f_t(0|x_t)\cdot 1(x_t'\beta_0 > 0)x_t x_t'\right\} \quad \text{and}$$

$$M_T = E\left\{T^{-1}\sum_{t=1}^T 1(x_t'\beta_0 > 0)x_t x_t'\right\}.$$

When $f_t(0|x_t) = f(0)$, $C_T = 2f(0)$ and thus

$$\sqrt{T}(\hat\beta - \beta_0) \xrightarrow{d} N\left(0, \lim_{T\to\infty} \frac{1}{4f(0)} M_T^{-1}\right).$$

Under this assumption Powell provides consistent estimator of $f(0)$ and $\lim_{T\to\infty} M_T$. When we have i.i.d. sampling $f(0|x)$ can be estimated consistently and thus C_T also, under some regularity conditions.

5.3.2. *Binary response model*

For the case of binary response, the model is:

$$y_i = 1\left(x_i'\beta_0 - \varepsilon_i > 0\right).$$

Observe that

$$E(y_i|x_i) = F_\varepsilon\left(x_i'\beta_0|x_i\right),$$

where F_ε is the cumulative distribution function of ε. If the median of ε_i given x_i is 0, that is, if

$$F_\varepsilon(s|x_i) = 1/2 \quad \text{if and only if} \quad s = 0,$$

then the median of y_i given x_i is 1 if $x_i'\beta_0 > 0$ and 0 if $x_i'\beta_0 < 0$. That is the conditional median function of y_i is known to be parametric and the form is $1(x_i'\beta_0 > 0)$. Thus, based on the quantile regression idea, a natural estimator is to find the minimizer of the following objective function

$$\sum_{i=1}^{n}\left|y_i - 1\left(x_i'\beta > 0\right)\right|,$$

as in the censored LAD estimator. As Manski (1985) discusses, minimizing this objective function is equivalent to maximizing the maximum score objective function of Manski (1985):

$$\sum_{i=1}^{n}(2y_i - 1)\,\text{sign}\left(x_i'\beta\right),$$

where $\text{sign}(s)$ equals 1 if $s > 0$ and -1 if $s < 0$ and equals 0 if $s = 0$. Unlike the objective function of the censored LAD estimator, this objective function changes the value around the points $x_i'\beta = 0$. As the observations corresponding to this line is measure zero when there is a continuous regressor, the convergence rate is not $n^{-1/2}$. Kim and Pollard (1990) showed that in fact the estimator converges with rate $n^{-1/3}$. Note that this convergence rate corresponds to that of nonparametric estimators which do not exploit smoothness. Horowitz (1992) showed how to exploit the smoothness of the underlying conditional CDF and improved the convergence rate when the underlying CDF is smooth. His estimator replaces the unsmooth sign function by a smooth function.[50]

[50] Horowitz (1992) implementation does not exactly correspond to a smoothed version of the Manski's objective function as Horowitz replaces the sign function with a smooth CDF function.

6. Smoothing parameter choice and trimming

The flexible estimators described in Sections 4 and 5 are specified up to some choice of smoothing parameter. For local estimators, the smoothing parameter choice corresponds to choosing the bandwidth parameter. For global estimators, the smoothing parameter choice corresponds to choosing the bases functions to include in the expansion. For semiparametric estimators, in addition to choosing the smoothing parameter, implementation of the estimators also requires choosing a method of trimming the data, as discussed in Section 5. In this section, we discuss the problem of smoothing parameter choice in the context of density and conditional mean function estimation and also in the context of semiparametric estimation. We also discuss trimming methods.

One way of choosing smoothing parameters is to use graphical diagnostics, which reveal how an estimated surface changes in response to varying the smoothing parameters. For a simple problem, some argue that this can be a reasonable way of selecting smoothing parameters. But this procedure is subjective and hence the choice would be hard to justify formally or communicate to others. In addition, even at the subjective level, it is questionable if we can visualize something corresponding to bias and variance of the estimator. Moreover, for higher dimensional problems or for cases where nonparametric estimators are being used as input into a semiparametric estimation problem, an implicit criteria the graphical approach uses is not necessarily appropriate and is too user-intensive to be practical. A more automatic bandwidth selection method is needed. For nonparametric density and regression estimation, the importance of developing data-based methods to guide researchers in selecting bandwidths is well recognized and a variety of bandwidth selectors have been proposed in the statistics and econometrics literatures. All the methods select the bandwidth to minimize error in estimation with respect to a certain criteria. They differ in the criteria used for measuring estimation error.

We summarize results in the literature as well as our own Monte Carlo studies evaluating the performance of different smoothing parameter selection methods. Our discussion is limited to the bandwidth selection methods for the kernel density estimator and local polynomial estimators.

There are two types of smoothing parameters: constant, or sometimes referred to as global, and variable. A global smoothing parameter is held fixed for the entire domain of the function being estimated and a variable smoothing parameter is allowed to vary at each point of the domain.[51]

For the density estimation, we discuss global bandwidth choice for the kernel density estimator. The advantage of a variable bandwidth is that it adapts better to the design of the data. A disadvantage, in the case of the kernel density estimation, is that once the bandwidth is allowed to depend on the data, the resulting estimator is no longer guaranteed to be a density. For regression estimation, this problem does not exist so we will consider both global and local bandwidth selectors.

[51] Fan and Gijbels (1992) studies a bandwidth selection method which differ for each data point and refers to the method as a "global variable" method.

6.1. Methods for selecting smoothing parameters in the kernel density estimation

As was discussed earlier, the efficiency of the kernel density estimator

$$f_n(x;h) = \frac{1}{nh}\sum_{i=1}^{n} K\left(\frac{x - X_i}{h}\right)$$

depends more on the choice of bandwidth h than on the choice of kernel function $K(\cdot)$ within a class of commonly used kernels. Therefore, in the following discussion we take the choice of kernel function as given and focus on the question of how to choose the smoothing parameter.

The three bandwidth selection methods we discuss are the rule of thumb (ROT) method, the least square cross validation method (LSCV), and the smoothed bootstrap (SB) method by Taylor (1989).

The ROT method is chosen for its simplicity in implementation. The other two methods are chosen for their theoretical coherence as well as reliable performance in Monte Carlo studies.

The loss function underlying all three methods of selecting the bandwidth of the kernel density estimator is the highest order of the integrated mean squared error:

$$\int E\left\{\left(f_n(x;h) - f(x)\right)^2\right\} \mathrm{d}x = \int \left[\mathrm{Var}\left(\left(f_n(x;h)\right)\right) + \mathrm{Bias}^2(x)\right] \mathrm{d}x,$$

where $\mathrm{Bias}(x) = E[f_n(x;h)] - f(x)$ and here and below, the integration is taken over the whole real line.

Three methods differ in ways to approximate this objective function. If we wish to choose the bandwidth local to a particular point x, then clearly we should examine $E\{(f_n(x;h) - f(x))^2\}$ at the point x rather than examining the overall measure such as above.

Rule of thumb Under suitable regularity conditions the IMSE can be approximated by the sum of two terms:

$$AIMSE(h) = \frac{c_{2K}}{nh} + \frac{\sigma_K^2}{4} h^4 \int \left[f''(x)\right]^2 \mathrm{d}x,$$

where $c_{2K} = \int K^2(s)\,\mathrm{d}s$ and $\sigma_K^2 = \int s^2 K(s)\,\mathrm{d}s$. The first term represents the variance and the second term represents the bias term.[52]

[52] The highest order approximation to the MSE at point x is

$$\frac{c_{2K}}{nh} f(x) + \frac{1}{4} h^4 \sigma_K^2 \left[f''(x)\right]^2.$$

There is a different trade-off between variance bias at each point reflecting different values of $f(x)$ and $f''(x)$. Thus it seems more desirable to choose a point-wise bandwidth.

The h that minimizes the AIMSE is

$$h_{AIMSE} = \left[\frac{c_{2K}}{\sigma_K^2} \frac{1}{[\int [f''(x)]^2 \, dx]} \right]^{1/5} n^{-1/5}. \tag{6.1}$$

The optimal bandwidth decreases with the size of the sample and increases when the effect of bias on the AMISE is greater; i.e. when $\int [f''(x)]^2 \, dx$ is larger.

From Equation (6.1) we see that estimating the global optimal plug-in bandwidth that minimizes the *AIMSE* requires obtaining an estimate of $\int [f''(x)]^2 \, dx$.

ROT estimates the unknown quantity by assuming a value based on a parametric family, usually the $N(\mu, \sigma^2)$ distribution. Under normality,

$$\int f''(x)^2 \, dx = \sigma^{-5} \frac{3}{8\sqrt{\pi}} \approx 0.212\sigma^{-5}.$$

If in addition a normal kernel is used, the ROT bandwidth is approximately equal to $1.06\sigma n^{-1/5}$.

Because the scale parameter σ is potentially sensitive to outliers, Silverman (1986) suggests using a more robust *rule-of-thumb* estimator, where the interquartile range of the data replaces the sample standard deviation as a scale parameter. It is given by $h_{ROT} = 1.06 \min(\hat{\sigma}, \hat{R}/1.34) n^{-1/5}$, where $\hat{\sigma}$ is the sample standard deviation and $\hat{R}$ the estimated interquartile range (for Gaussian data, $\hat{R} \approx 1.34\hat{\sigma}$).[53]

Clearly, when the underlying density is not normal, the ROT method does not consistently estimate the h_{AIMSE} and hence is suboptimal. However, because it converges to 0 with an appropriate rate, it does yield a consistent and asymptotically normal kernel density estimator when the underlying density is twice continuously differentiable.

Least square cross validation The least square cross validation (LSCV) discussed by Stone (1974) chooses the bandwidth that minimizes the estimated integrated squared error (ISE):

$$ISE = \int \left[f_n(x; h) - f(x) \right]^2 dx.$$

Hall (1982) showed that under regularity conditions

$$ISE = IMSE + o_p\left(h^4 + (nh)^{-1}\right)$$

so that minimizing the ISE and minimizing the IMSE is equivalent to the first order under some regularity conditions.

Note that

$$ISE = \int \left[f_n(x; h) \right]^2 dx - 2 \int f_n(x; h) f(x) \, dx + \int \left[f(x) \right]^2 dx$$

[53] The *rule-of-thumb* method can of course be tailored to a particular application. For example, if a researcher strongly suspected bimodality in the density, he/she may want to use a bimodal parametric density for the plug-in estimator.

and that the last term does not depend on h so minimizing the sum of the first two terms is equivalent to minimizing the ISE. Although the second term is not computable because $f(x)$ is not known, its unbiased estimator can be constructed by

$$-2\frac{1}{n}\sum_{i=1}^{n} f_{ni}(X_i; h),$$

where $f_{ni}(x; h) = (n-1)^{-1}\sum_{j\neq i} K((x - X_i)/h)/h$.

Thus the LSCV chooses the bandwidth that minimizes

$$AISE(h) = \int \left[f_n(x; h)\right]^2 \mathrm{d}x - 2\frac{1}{n}\sum_{i=1}^{n} f_{ni}(X_i; h).$$

Note that if we use $f_n(x; h)$ in place of $f_{ni}(x; h)$, then the LSCV yields an inconsistent method. To see this observe that

$$\int \left[f_n(x; h)\right]^2 \mathrm{d}x = \frac{\int K^2(s)\,\mathrm{d}s}{nh} + \frac{1}{n^2 h}\sum_{i=1}^{n}\sum_{j\neq i} K * K\big((X_i - X_j)/h\big),$$

where $K * K(u) = \int K(u-s)K(s)\,\mathrm{d}s$. So if there is no duplication in the observations $\{X_i\}_{i=1}^n$ and

$$\int K^2(s)\,\mathrm{d}s < 2K(0)$$

and $\lim_{|s|\to\infty} |s|K(s) = 0$ as well as $\lim_{|s|\to\infty} |s|K * K(s) = 0$, then choosing h small will make the objective function small. Since this holds regardless of $f(x)$, the LSCV yields an inconsistent method. Note that $\int K^2(s)\,\mathrm{d}s < 2K(0)$ holds for most kernel functions such as those densities that has a single peak at 0.[54]

When there is no duplication of observations, on the other hand, the "delete one" modification fixes the problem as defined above. However, the same issue which was avoided by the "delete one" modification arises when there are duplication of observations. Because the duplication of observations arises naturally if there is discretization, one needs to be aware of this potential problem when applying the LSCV.

Hall (1983) and Stone (1984) justified LSCV as a data dependent method to choose the optimal bandwidth. In particular, Stone (1984) showed that, only assuming boundedness of $f(x)$ (and its marginals, for the multivariate case),

$$\frac{ISE(h_{LSCV})}{ISE(h_{\mathrm{opt}})} \to 1$$

as $n \to \infty$ with probability 1, where h_{opt} minimizes $ISE(h)$.

[54] For these functions $\int K^2(x)\,\mathrm{d}x$ can be regarded as the mean of $K(x)$ and it has to be lower than its maximum $K(0)$.

Smoothed bootstrap The smoothed bootstrap method of Taylor (1989) is motivated by the formula obtained when estimating $\int E\{[f_n(x;h) - f(x)]^2\}\,dx$ by a bootstrap sample generated from $f_n(x;h)$. That is, writing X_i^* to be sampled from distribution $f_n(x;h)$, one can estimate $\int E\{[f_n(x;h) - f(x)]^2\}\,dx$ by

$$E^*\left\{\frac{1}{nh}\sum_{i=1}^{n} K\big((x - X_i^*)/h\big) - \frac{1}{nh}\sum_{i=1}^{n} K\big((x - X_i)/h\big)\right\}^2.$$

Taylor (1989) observes that this can be explicitly computed when Gaussian kernel is used and its integration over x is:

$$\frac{1}{2n^2h(2\pi)^{1/2}}\left[\sum_{i=1}^{n}\sum_{j=1}^{n}\exp\left\{-\frac{X_j - X_i}{8h^2}\right\} - \frac{4}{3^{1/2}}\sum_{i=1}^{n}\sum_{j=1}^{n}\exp\left\{-\frac{X_j - X_i}{6h^2}\right\}\right.$$
$$\left. + 2^{1/2}\sum_{i=1}^{n}\sum_{j=1}^{n}\exp\left\{-\frac{X_j - X_i}{4h^2}\right\} + n2^{1/2}\right].$$

He modifies the above formula to sum over $i \neq j$. The modified objective function, $B^*(h)$, say, is then minimized to define the data dependent bandwidth.

Taylor (1989) shows that

$$\mathrm{Var}\{B^*(h)\} = \frac{0.026}{8n^2h\pi^{1/2}}\int [f(x)]^2\,dx + O(h/n^2).$$

It is an order of magnitude less than the corresponding object for the LSCV, $\mathrm{Var}(AISE(h))$ computed by Scott and Terrell (1987):

$$\mathrm{Var}\big(AISE(h)\big) = \frac{4}{n}\left[\int [f(x)]^3\,dx - \left\{\int [f(x)]^2\,dx\right\}\right] + O\big(1/(n^2h) + h^4/n\big).$$

A brief discussion of other methods Other methods which perform well in Monte Carlo studies is the method of Jones and Sheather (1991) and its modification by Jones, Marron and Sheather (1996). We did not discuss this method here as the method seems theoretically incoherent. Like the ROT method, their approach targets the optimal bandwidth when the underlying density is twice continuously differentiable. But the method presumes that the density has higher order derivatives so that the target is not necessarily an interesting object from a theoretical point of view.

From a statistical perspective, the least square based objective functions we have discussed above may seem ad hoc. Indeed the literature has considered likelihood based methods to selecting the bandwidth as well. However, Schuster and Gregory (1981) showed that when the tail of the target density is thicker than exponential decay, then choosing the bandwidth by the likelihood based cross validation leads to an inconsistent density estimator.

Empirical performance Several published studies examine bandwidth performance in real data examples and in Monte Carlo settings. They include Jones, Marron and Sheather (1992) (hereafter JMS), Cao, Cuevas and Gonzalez-Mantiega (1994), Park and Turlach (1992), Park and Marron (1990), Härdle (1991), Cleveland and Loader (1996) and Loader (1995). Below we summarize commonalities and disparities in findings across studies and then present some findings from our own Monte Carlo study. More empirical evidence needs to be accumulated to better understand how different methods compare under data designs that commonly arise in economics.

In their evaluation of rule-of-thumb (ROT) methods, Silverman (1986), JMS (1996) and Härdle (1991) conclude that a ROT estimator with a normal reference density has a tendency to over-smooth, or choose too large a bandwidth, particularly when the data are highly skewed or is multi-modal. In two separate examples, JMS (1996) and Härdle (1991) find that the ROT estimator is unable to detect a simple case of bimodality.[55]

The LSCV estimator tends to suffer from the opposite problem: under-smoothing. JMS conclude that because of under-smoothing, the LSCV procedure leads to high variability and overall unreliability in choosing the optimal bandwidth. Hall and Marron (1991) partly explain the under-smoothing tendency by showing that LSCV frequently gives local minima and the tendency to under-smooth likely comes from not finding the global minimum. Park and Marron (1990) and Loader (1995) point out that LSCV is nonetheless the method of choice for cases where the researcher is only willing to maintain a limited degree of smoothness on the true density. Most other bandwidth selection methods require smoothness assumptions on higher order derivatives. In Loader's simulations, the LSCV approach performs well. This was also the finding in our own simulations.

The smoothed bootstrap (SB) selector has only been studied in a few papers. JMS find its performance to be close to that of the Sheather and Jones' method. Faraway and Jhun (1990) compare the SB and LSCV procedures and find that SB performs better, which they attribute mostly to its lower variability. For further evidence on relative performance of bandwidth selectors, see Hall et al. (1991), and Park, Kim and Marron (1994), and Loader (1995).

6.2. *Methods for selecting smoothing parameters in the local polynomial estimator of a regression function*

Here, we consider the problem of choosing the smoothing parameter for a local polynomial estimator of a fixed degree; typically equal to one (i.e. local linear regression). In particular we discuss a rule of thumb method by Fan and Gijbels (1996), least square cross validation, and Fan and Gijbels's method (1995) of residual square criteria (RSC). These methods do not require an initial bandwidth selection. We also discuss Fan and

[55] This drawback could possibly be overcome by using a more flexible parametric family as a reference in constructing the plug-in estimate of $\int [f''(x)]^2 \, dx$. For example, a mixture of normals could be used.

Gijbels's (1995) finite sample approximation method as a prototype of an attempt to improve on these methods.

These methods are the standard bandwidth selection methods, but limitations of these methods are also discussed in view of the alternatives proposed by Fan et al. (1996), Doksum, Peterson and Samarov (2000), and Prewitt and Lohr (2006).

6.2.1. *A general discussion*

All the methods we discuss estimate in some ways the asymptotic mean square error (AMSE) of estimating $D^j m(x_0)$ ($j = (j_1, \ldots, j_d)$), at a point for the case of the local bandwidth or its integral and with some weights for the case of the global bandwidth. For the local polynomial estimator of order p when the underlying one-dimensional regression function is at least $p + 1$ times continuously differentiable, the AMSE at a point can be obtained by inspecting Theorem 2:

$$AMSE(x_0) = \left[\left(M^{-1} B m^{(p+1)}(x_0)\right)_\ell\right]^2 h^{2(p+1-|j|)} + \frac{\sigma^2(x_0)/f(x_0)}{nh^{d+2|j|}}\left(M^{-1}\Gamma M^{-1}\right)_{\ell,\ell}$$

where ℓ is the order in which j appear. Note that in using this formula, we assume that $p - |j|$ is odd so that the bias term does not vanish.

Thus the asymptotically optimum point-wise bandwidth is

$$h_{\text{opt},p,j}(x_0) = \left[\frac{[(d+2|j|)(M^{-1}\Gamma M^{-1})_{\ell,\ell}\sigma^2(x_0)/f(x_0)]}{2(p+1-|j|)[(M^{-1}Bm^{(p+1)}(x_0))_\ell]^2 n}\right]^{1/(2p+d+2)}.$$

The optimum bandwidth depends on three factors: the conditional variance, the density of regressors, and the $(p + 1)$st derivative of the underlying function. The $(p + 1)$st derivative enters because we consider the local polynomial estimator of order p and the size of the $(p+1)$st derivative captures a local deviation from the pth order model used. When there is a larger variance (high $\sigma^2(x_0)$), less data (low $f(x_0)$), or less deviation from the model (high $\|m^{(p+1)}(x_0)\|$), then we want to use a wider bandwidth.

Sometimes, statistical packages choose a fixed proportion of the data nearest to the point of evaluation (x_0) by default. This approach will effectively choose a wider bandwidth at a lower density region. In view of the result above, this may be appropriate when the variance and the model approximation is roughly constant. However, generally the approach cannot be an optimal way to choose the bandwidth as it does not have a way to accommodate the two other factors affecting the optimal bandwidth. In addition, the method is silent about the appropriate level of proportionality.

6.2.2. *One step methods*

Rule of thumb Fan and Gijbels (1996) proposes a ROT method for choosing a global bandwidth. Optimum global bandwidth is obtained by minimizing the integrated version of the $AMSE(x)$ using some weight function, say $w(x)$ over x:

$$AMSE = \int \left[\left(M^{-1} B m^{(p+1)}(x) \right)_{\ell} \right]^2 w(x)\,\mathrm{d}x h^{2(p+1-|j|)} + \frac{\int [\sigma^2(x)/f(x)] w(x)\,\mathrm{d}x}{n h^{d+2|j|}} \left(M^{-1} \Gamma M^{-1} \right)_{\ell,\ell}.$$

Thus the optimum global bandwidth is expressed exactly as the local one except that each of the functions in the expression above are replaced by the integrated versions:

$$h_{\text{opt,global},p,j} = \left[\frac{(d+2|j|)(M^{-1}\Gamma M^{-1})_{\ell,\ell} \int [\sigma^2(x)/f(x)] w(x)\,\mathrm{d}x}{2(p+1-|j|) \int [(M^{-1} B m^{(p+1)}(x))_{\ell}]^2 w(x)\,\mathrm{d}x n} \right]^{1/(2p+d+2)}.$$

They propose to use $w(x) = f(x) w_0(x)$ for a given $w_0(x)$, estimate $m(x)$ by a global polynomial of order $p+3$, $\hat{m}_{p+3}(x)$ so that the $(p+1)$st derivative $\hat{m}_{p+3}^{(p+1)}(x)$ has enough flexibility, and use the residuals $y_i - \hat{m}_{p+3}(x_i)$ from the global polynomial regression to estimate the global residual variance, say $\hat{\sigma}^2$ and defined the ROT bandwidth:

$$h_{ROT,p,j} = \left[\frac{(d+2|j|)(M^{-1}\Gamma M^{-1})_{i,i} \hat{\sigma}^2 \int w_0(x)\,\mathrm{d}x}{2(p+1-|j|) \sum_{i=1}^{n} [(M^{-1} B \hat{m}_{p+3}^{(p+1)}(x_i))_{\ell}]^2 w_0(x_i)} \right]^{1/(2p+d+2)}.$$

Effectively, the method presumes homoskedasticity. Note that $\int [(M^{-1} B m^{(p+1)}(x))_{\ell}]^2 \times w(x)\,\mathrm{d}x n$ is replaced by its consistent estimator

$$\sum_{i=1}^{n} \left[\left(M^{-1} B \hat{m}_{p+3}^{(p+1)}(x_i) \right)_{\ell} \right]^2 w_0(x_i).$$

In implementation, they used a constant function on the support of the regressors as w_0.

Least square cross validation The LSCV bandwidth is a method for obtaining the optimum bandwidth for estimating the conditional mean function. A global bandwidth is chosen to minimize a weighted sum of the squared prediction errors:

$$h_{LSCV} = \arg\min_h \frac{1}{n} \sum_{i=1}^{n} \left(y_i - \hat{m}_{i,h}(x_i) \right)^2 w_0(x_i),$$

where $\hat{m}_{i,h}(x_i)$ is the local polynomial regression function estimator computed without using the ith observation but evaluated at x_i. The ith observation has to be omitted, because if we use all observations to estimate the conditional mean function, by choosing the bandwidth very small, one can always make the objective function 0.[56]

[56] When there are duplicate observations in the sense that the (y_i, x_i) pair is the same for multiple observations, then the "leave-one-out" $\hat{m}_{i,h}(x_i)$ estimator needs to be modified to also exclude duplicate observations. Otherwise the problem the leave-one-out approach aims to avoid would not be avoided.

Another consideration in carrying out LSCV is that the local linear estimator in one dimension is defined only when there are at least two data points within the support of the kernel weight function. This effectively places a lower bound on the values of bandwidths that can be considered.[57]

Note the importance of using $w_0(x)$ in the objective function. Without the weight function LSCV chooses a global bandwidth with $w(x) = f(x)$. Thus unless the regressor distribution is bounded, the objective function may not converge to a meaningful object when the conditional variance is bounded away from zero, for example.

Residual squares criterion Fan and Gijbels (1995) proposes an objective function for choosing the bandwidth appropriate for estimating the conditional mean function and its derivatives by the local polynomial estimator of order p in one-dimensional problems. Note that in one-dimensional problems the $AMSE(x_0)$ simplifies to

$$\begin{aligned} AMSE(x_0) &= \left[\left(M^{-1}B\right)_\ell m^{(p+1)}(x_0)\right]^2 h^{2(p+1-|j|)} \\ &\quad + \frac{\sigma^2(x_0)/f(x_0)}{nh^{d+2|j|}}\left(M^{-1}\Gamma M^{-1}\right)_{\ell,\ell} \end{aligned}$$

because $m^{(p+1)}(x_0)$ is a scalar. Thus, the bandwidth optimal for estimating the regression function can be adjusted by a known factor to produce the optimum bandwidth suitable for estimating the derivatives of the regression function. They study

$$RSC(x_0) = \frac{\sum_{i=1}^n (y_i - \hat{y}_i)^2 K_h(x_i - x_0)}{\operatorname{trace}\{W - WX(X'WX)^{-1}X'W\}}\left(1 + (p+1)\hat{V}\right),$$

where $\hat{y} = (\hat{y}_1, \ldots, \hat{y}_n)' = X\hat{\beta}$ is the local polynomial fit using all the estimated coefficients, $\hat{V}$ is the 1–1 element of $(X'WX)^{-1}(X'W^2X)(X'WX)^{-1}$. The minimizer of this objective function multiplied by a known factor is the local RSC bandwidth. The multiplying factor depends on p and the order of the derivative being estimated. They show that this method selects the locally optimum bandwidth asymptotically.[58]

To understand the objective function we examine each term of the expression separately. Note that since $\hat{\beta} = (X'WX)^{-1}X'Wy$, the denominator, ignoring the $1 + (p+1)V$ term can be written as

$$\begin{aligned} & y'\left(I - WX(X'WX)^{-1}X'\right)W\left(I - X(X'WX)^{-1}X'W\right)y \\ &\quad = y'\left(W - WX(X'WX)^{-1}X'W\right)y. \end{aligned}$$

Recall that $y = X\beta_0 + r + \epsilon$. Since the term related to $X\beta_0$ vanishes and ignoring the cross terms of r and ϵ as they are smaller order, the leading two terms are

$$r'\left(W - WX(X'WX)^{-1}X'W\right)r \quad \text{and} \quad \epsilon'\left(W - WX(X'WX)^{-1}X'W\right)\epsilon.$$

[57] By restricting the range of the bandwidth to be above a certain smallest value, we may not need to use the delete-one-method, which is computationally costly.

[58] See Fan and Gijbels (1995, Table 1) for the adjustment factors.

For the local linear case the first term divided by the trace in the denominator of the definition of RSC converges to $[m^{(p+1)}(x_0)]^2 h^{2(p+1)}$ times a constant (say C) and the second term divided by the same trace converges to $\sigma^2(x_0)$.

As we saw, the $\hat{V}$ is approximately constant (say C') divided by $(nh)f(x_0)$. Thus

$$\left(C\left[m^{(p+1)}(x_0)\right]^2 h^{2(p+1)} + \sigma^2(x_0)\right)\left(1 + \frac{(1+p)C'}{nhf(x_0)}\right)$$
$$= \sigma^2(x_0) + C\left[m^{(p+1)}(x_0)\right]^2 h^{2(p+1)} + \frac{(1+p)C'\sigma^2(x_0)}{nhf(x_0)} + o\left(h^4 + 1/(nh)\right).$$

The minimizer is proportional to the optimum bandwidth by a known factor as desired.

They advocate using the integrated version of the $RSC(x_0)$ over an interval to select a global bandwidth. In fact even for the local bandwidth, they advocate using locally integrated version of $RSC(x_0)$ objective function. Clearly the adjustment term does not change.

6.2.3. *Two step methods*

The methods discussed above do not require that an initial bandwidth be specified. As discussed, other methods proposed in the literature attempt to improve on these procedures by using the first stage estimates as inputs into a second stage.

The methods estimate the bias and variance terms. Note that to estimate the bias term, which involves the $(p+1)$st order derivative, we need to assume that the function is smoother than required for estimating the regression function itself. For example, when a twice continuously differentiable function is being estimated by the local linear regression estimator, the bias term depends on the second order derivative. To compute the optimum bandwidth for estimating the second order derivative, the underlying function is assumed to be at least $(p+1)$-times continuously differentiable, or in this case at least three times continuously differentiable. But for a function with that degree of smoothness, the local linear estimator does not achieve the optimum rate of convergence. Thus the bandwidth computed does not have an overall optimality property. In this case, we will be estimating the optimal bandwidth optimum given that the local linear estimator is used in estimation.

Fan and Gijbels's finite sample method Fan and Gijbels (1995) propose to use their RSC bandwidths to construct a "refined" bandwidth. Instead of using the asymptotic formula, they propose to use the finite sample counter-part discussed in Section 4. The bias is

$$(X'WX)^{-1}X'Wr$$

and the variance is

$$(X'WX)^{-1}X'W^2X(X'WX)^{-1}\sigma^2(x_0).$$

Because $r = m - X\beta_0$, the bias is not known. But it can be approximated by

$$(X'WX)^{-1}X'W\tau,$$

where the τ is a vector of length n with the ith element to be

$$(x_i - x_0)^{(p+1)}/(p+1)!\beta^{(p+1)} + \cdots + (x_i - x_0)^{(p+a)}/(p+a)!\beta^{(p+a)}.$$

They advocate using $a = 2$ or 3 as a target bias expression. Writing $S_n = X'WX$ and $S_{n,s,t} = [X^{(s)\prime}/s!]W[X^{(t)}/t!]$, we can write $(X'WX)^{-1}X'W\tau$ as

$$S_n^{-1}\begin{pmatrix} S_{n,0,p+1}\beta^{(p+1)} + \cdots + S_{n,0,p+a}\beta^{(p+a)} \\ \vdots \\ S_{n,p,p+1}\beta^{(p+1)} + \cdots + S_{n,p,p+a}\beta^{(p+a)} \end{pmatrix}.$$

The unknown terms $\beta^{(p+1)}, \ldots, \beta^{(p+a)}$ can be estimated using the local polynomial estimator of degree $p + a$. For this step, RSC method is being advocated. They also note that the finite sample performance was better when the terms corresponding to $S_{n,s,p+t}$ where $s + t > p + a$ are set to 0. These terms are smaller order terms than the target bias expression.

The conditional variance is estimated by the same expression corresponding to the first expression of the RSC objective function:

$$\frac{\sum_{i=1}^{n}(y_i - \hat{y}_{p+a_i})^2 K_h(x_i - x_0)}{\operatorname{trace}\{W - WX_{p+a}(X'_{p+a}WX_{p+a})^{-1}X'_{p+a}W\}},$$

where X_{p+a} corresponds to regressors of the $(p+a)$th degree local polynomial estimator and $\hat{y}_{p+a} = X_{p+a}\hat{\beta}_{p+a}$. Because the higher degree local polynomial estimator is used, the bias contribution is of order h^{p+a+1} and thus can be ignored. The estimated bias and variance terms are then used to form the estimated mean square error used to choose the bandwidth.

Other methods Ruppert (1997) proposes instead to estimate the bias term by estimating the OLS regression:

$$\hat{m}_h^{(j)}(x_0) = c_0(x_0) + c_{p+1-|j|}(x_0)h^{p+1-|j|} + \cdots + c_{p+a-|j|}h^{p+a-|j|}$$

using different h values as regressors and the corresponding $\hat{m}_h^{(j)}(x_0)$ values as the dependent variable. This formulation is motivated by the asymptotic bias calculation. The estimated terms after the first one are used to estimate the bias. Ruppert (1997) replaces Fan and Gijbels's bias estimator in the finite sample method with this estimator in approximating the asymptotic mean square error.

Note that the point-wise optimum bandwidth becomes infinite when $m^{(p+1)}(x_0) = 0$, even though this may hold only at x_0, so that the pth order approximation does not hold globally. This is a limitation of considering the optimum bandwidth point-wise. Fan et al. (1996) considers modeling the local bandwidth globally using the LSCV objective function. While they describe the method for the kernel regression estimator, the method is clearly applicable to local polynomial estimator. Their objective function is

$$\sum_{i=1}^{n}\left[y_i - m_i\left(x_i, h(x_i)\right)\right]^2$$

where in their case

$$m_i\left(x, h(x)\right) = \frac{\sum_{j \neq i} y_j K((x - x_j)/h(x))}{\sum_{j \neq i} K((x - x_j)/h(x))}$$

and $h(x) = h_0 g(x)$ for some $g(x)$ to be in a prespecified class of functions. This approach avoids approaching the problem point-wise and also makes the global LSCV method a local method.

Doksum, Peterson and Samarov (2000) argues that the asymptotic formula used to construct approximation to the asymptotic mean square error is valid only for small bandwidths. They show that for larger bandwidths, a finite differencing gives a better approximation.

Prewitt and Lohr (2006) develops a way to eliminate a too small bandwidth from being considered, using the ratio of the largest to the smallest eigenvalues of the matrix $X'WX/(nh^d)$, drawing an analogy between local polynomial methods and regular linear regression analysis. This approach could be applied to prevent to guard against too small a bandwidth being chosen by any of the above methods.

6.3. How to choose smoothing parameters in semiparametric models

Relatively few papers have examined the problem of how to choose smoothing parameters in implementing semiparametric models.[59] Here we provide a brief account of some of the developments in this area of research.

6.3.1. Optimal bandwidth choice in average derivative estimation

The problem of choosing the optimal bandwidth in average derivative estimation is considered in Powell and Stoker (1996), Härdle et al. (1992), Härdle and Tsybakov (1993), and Nishiyama and Robinson (2000, 2001). Härdle et al. (1992) study bandwidth choice for the estimation of univariate unweighted average derivatives. Härdle and Tsybakov (1993) and Powell and Stoker (1996) study a variety of weighted average derivative estimators for higher dimensions under a variety of weighting schemes using asymptotic mean square error as a criterion. Nishiyama and Robinson (2000, 2001) propose to use an approximation to the asymptotic normality as a criterion.

[59] See Härdle, Hall and Ichimura (1993), Härdle et al. (1992), Härdle and Tsybakov (1993), Hall and Horowitz (1990), Hall and Marron (1987), Horowitz (1992), Ichimura and Linton (2005), Linton (1995a, 1996), Nishiyama and Robinson (2000, 2001), Powell and Stoker (1996), Stoker (1996), and Robinson (1991).

Here, we describe the approach taken in Powell and Stoker (1996) as a prototype analysis of an optimal plug-in bandwidth selection that minimizes the leading terms of the asymptotic mean-squared error of a semiparametric estimator. Recall from Section 5 of the chapter that an indirect density weighted average derivative estimator takes the form

$$\hat{\delta}_{WIAD} = -\frac{2}{n}\sum_{i=1}^{n}\frac{\partial \hat{f}(x)}{\partial x} y_i.$$

As shown in Powell and Stoker (1996), this estimator can alternatively be written as

$$\binom{N}{2}^{-1}\sum_{i<j} p(z_i, z_j, h),$$

where $z_i = (x_i, y_i)$, for a d-dimensional vector x_i and a scalar y_i, $p(z_i, z_j, h) = -h^{-d-1}K'(\frac{x_i - x_k}{h})(y_i - y_j)$ and $K(\cdot)$ is a kernel function satisfying $K(u) = K(-u)$, $K'(\cdot)$ denotes the d-dimensional vector of partial derivatives of $K(\cdot)$, $\int K(u)\,du = 1$, $\int K(u)u^l\,du = 0$ for $l < \alpha$, $\int K(u)u^\alpha\,du \neq 0$ (for commonly used kernel functions, $\alpha = 2$). A requirement for asymptotic normality of the estimator is $2\alpha > d + 2$. Define

$$\hat{r}(z_i, h) = \frac{1}{N-1}\sum_{j\neq i} p(z_i, z_j, h),$$

$r_0(z) = \lim_{h\to 0} E[\hat{r}(z, h)]$. Note that

$$E\big[\hat{r}(z, h)\big] - r_0(z) = s(z)h^\alpha + o\big(h^\alpha\big)$$

for some $s(z)$ under the assumption on the kernel function, among others and

$$E\big(\big\|p(z, z_j, h)\big\|^2\big) = q(z)h^{-\gamma} + o\big(h^{-\gamma}\big).$$

For the average derivative case, $\gamma = d + 2$ and

$$q(z) = \big[\big(y - E(y|x)\big)^2 + \operatorname{Var}(y|x)\big]f(x)\sum_{j=1}^{k}\int K_j^2(s)\,\mathrm{d}s$$

where K_j denote the jth element of K'. As shown in Powell and Stoker (1996), the leading terms of the mean-squared error of $\hat{\delta}_{WIAD}$ are

$$\big[E\big(s(z_i)\big)\big]^2 h^{2\alpha} + 4n^{-1}\operatorname{Var}\big[r_0(z_i)\big] + 2n^{-1}C_0h^\alpha + 2n^{-2}E\big[q(z_i)\big]h^{-(d+2)}$$
$$+ o\big(h^{2\alpha}\big) + o\big(h^\alpha/n\big) + o\big(1/\big(n^2h^{d+2}\big)\big).$$

Minimizing over h (noting that the variance term does not depend on the bandwidth) and keeping only the leading terms gives the optimal plug-in bandwidth selector[60]:

$$h_{\text{opt}} = \left[\frac{(d+2)E[q(z_i)]}{\alpha[E(s(x))]^2}\right]^{1/(2\alpha+d+2)}\left[\frac{1}{n}\right]^{2/(2\alpha+d+2)}.$$

[60] See Proposition 4.1 in Powell and Stoker (1996).

The method calls for using a high order kernel so that $2\alpha > d + 2$. However, a simulation study conducted by Horowitz and Härdle (1996) found that using a second order kernel produced more stable results.

Robinson (1995) showed that the normal approximation to the asymptotic distribution of the density weighted averaged derivative estimator could be worse than for the standard parametric case, depending on the bandwidth. In particular, he showed that, under some regularity conditions, the approximation error is of order

$$n^{-1/2} + n^{-1}h^{-d-2} + n^{1/2}h^{\alpha} + h^{M-1},$$

where M denotes the order of differentiability of the conditional mean function of y given x. Thus, the bandwidth required to make the order of approximation comparable to the parametric case of $n^{-1/2}$ is, for some $C \in (1, \infty)$ when $M - 1 \geqslant \alpha/2$,

$$\left(Cn^{1/(2d+4)}\right)^{-1} \leqslant h \leqslant Cn^{-\alpha}.$$

The optimum bandwidth proposed by Powell and Stoker (1996) does not satisfy the second inequality (the bias contribution to the normal approximation dominates), so using the bandwidth will make the normal approximation to be suboptimal. Nishiyama and Robinson (2000, 2001) derived the optimum bandwidth when approximation to the normality is the criterion.

Given that the normal approximation is worse than the parametric cases, Nishiyama and Robinson (2005) examine the bootstrap approximation and provide sufficient conditions under which the bootstrap approximates the asymptotic distribution to a higher order. While the work is carried out in detail for the particular case of the average derivative estimator, no doubt the technologies developed would be useful for investigating properties of other estimators.

6.3.2. *Other works*

Härdle, Hall and Ichimura (1993) study the semiparametric least squares estimation of the single index model and propose to optimize over the bandwidth as well as the unknown coefficient. They propose a way of choosing the bandwidth that is asymptotically optimal for estimating the conditional mean function. It is not in general optimal for estimating the unknown coefficient, although the asymptotic distribution theory will still be valid with that choice of bandwidth.

Hall and Horowitz (1990), Horowitz (1992), Ichimura and Linton (2005) and Linton (1995a) study optimum bandwidth selection for estimation of censored regression models, binary choice models, program evaluation models and the partially linear regression models, respectively. All these papers use the leading terms of the asymptotic mean square error terms as the criterion in choosing the optimum bandwidth.

Compared to the literature in the nonparametric estimation, the literature in selecting the smoothing parameter for estimators of semiparametric model parameters is sparse. Much more research needs to be done in this direction. Without specifying ways of choosing the bandwidth parameter, the estimators are not well defined.

6.4. Trimming

6.4.1. What is trimming?

In the context of computing a statistic, trimming refers to a practice to systematically discarding the contribution of estimated function values to the statistic when some properties hold at the points the function is being evaluated. Usually the term "trimming function" refers to an indicator function indicating which points to include, rather than which points to discard.

6.4.2. Three reasons for trimming

There are three reasons for trimming. First, a parameter studied may not make sense without trimming. Second, a statistic may not make sense without trimming, or third, the statistics may not have desirable properties asymptotically without trimming.

As an example for the first case, consider estimating the conditional mean function $m(x)$. Recall that this function is defined at any point in the support, S, of the conditioning random vector so more precisely we should write it as $m(x) \cdot 1\ (x \in S)$. If we are to estimate the conditional mean function at observed data points, the indicator function is always 1, so that we can ignore the trimming function, but otherwise, the definition of the parameter calls for it. Parameters examined in Section 2 provide some other examples where trimming is needed. We saw there that the identifiable parameter under the matching assumption needed to satisfy the common support condition. Therefore, the definition of the average treatment on treated parameter, for example, incorporated the trimming function as in

$$\frac{E\{(Y_1 - Y_0)1(X \in S)|D = 1\}}{E\{1(X \in S)|D = 1\}},$$

where S denotes the common support of regressors X.

As an example for the second reason for trimming, recall the definition of the kernel regression estimator using the Epanechnikov kernel with optimal bandwidth. With this estimator, there is a positive probability that the denominator is zero, so that the estimator is not necessarily well defined. The estimator is well defined only if there is a data point in the appropriate neighborhood.

There are at least two distinct technical reasons for trimming in order to establish desirable properties of the statistics under consideration. First, to secure local data and second, to avoid the boundary value problem. Consider the same estimator and assume we want to show that the estimator converges with a rate uniformly over a given domain. Then at any point over the domain, the density of the conditioning vector needs to be bounded away from 0 by the amount dictated by the convergence rate of the estimator we wish to obtain. For one thing, if the density is too low, then we cannot hope to obtain the local observation comparable to other regions. From a theoretical point of view, we can assume that the density is bounded away from 0, but of course in application, the condition does not necessarily hold and hence we have to introduce trimming. We may also need to ensure that the function is not evaluated at points too close to the boundary value.

The third case for trimming often arises in examining semiparametric estimators which use nonparametric estimators in their construction. In establishing asymptotic properties of the semiparametric estimator, a uniform convergence rate of the nonparametric estimator is used.

The need for trimming for all cases is uncontroversial. But we have heard some claims for ignoring trimming "in practice" as "it does not matter very much". While it would be nice if it were true, we emphasize that at this point we know of no systematic empirical or theoretical study which substantiates the claim.

6.4.3. How trimming is done

Sometimes trimming is specified using an a priori chosen set over which some desirable properties hold, such as the density being bounded away from zero. There is no provision for how we should choose such a set given a finite amount of observations.

Bickel (1982) introduced the trimming function that does not depend on a priori knowledge of the shape of the support in the context of adaptive estimation. In carrying out trimming of certain data points with low density, he used an estimated density. A deterministic sequence which converges to zero is used to decide which points correspond to "low" density points.

While theoretically this procedure can be carried out without knowing anything about the density, in finite sample, the procedure might inadvertently trim out a high fraction of observations. To avoid this problem, Heckman et al. (1998) proposed defining a trimming function using a quantile of the estimated density.

An additional complication arises for the case of the index model. Consider for concreteness the linear index model. In this case, we need to find points of low density corresponding to any index defined by a linear combination of the regressors. It may seem enough to trim observations based on the joint density of the regressors but that is not the case. To see this consider two independent regressors both distributed uniformly over unit intervals. On the support, the density of the regressors are bounded away from zero. But any linear combination of the two regressors will not be bounded away from zero at the minimum and the maximum points, when two regressors are involved in the linear combination. This is because the density is low when the length of the line segment that leads to the same value for the linear combination is short. At the points that have the minimum and the maximum values of the linear combination, the corresponding length of the line segments are zero.

In addition to the density being bounded away from zero, trimming needs to guarantee that the points of estimation are interior points of the support, so that the length of the line segments will be away from zero. Clearly, one can presume a priori knowledge about the support and define trimming function using the knowledge.

One way to define the trimming function empirically is to use the estimated density as previously described. In this case, we need to keep points only if the density values are above certain value and that in a neighborhood there are no points with density values below the prespecified value. The prespecified value can be defined using the quantiles of the estimated density as in the previous case.

Given that the index models are used when we do not have enough observations to use fully nonparametric models, the above trimming approach may be unattractive, because it uses fully nonparametric density estimator. An alternative approach which only involves one-dimensional density estimation is to search over the lowest one-dimensional density estimate at each point. We only keep a point if the point does not correspond to a low density point for any linear combination of regressors. Clearly this approach is computationally intensive. A practical alternative to this approach may be to try out the density estimation of the index defined by the bases of the space of the coefficients and keep all points which are above the prespecified low density values.

Asymptotic analysis becomes complicated with data dependent trimming. A simple method is provided by Ichimura (1995).

7. Asymptotic distribution of semiparametric estimators

In this section, we gather some basic asymptotic results that are useful in deriving the asymptotic distribution for semiparametric estimators. The structure underlying the asymptotic distribution of semiparametric estimators has been clarified greatly through the works of Aït-Sahalia (1992), Andrews (1994), Newey (1994a), Sherman (1994a, 1994b), Ai and Chen (2003), Chen, Linton and Van Keilegom (2003), and Ichimura and Lee (2006). Using these results, the asymptotic variance–covariance matrix of most of the semiparametric estimators can be easily computed. Chen (in this handbook) describes this development for the semiparametric GMM estimators, so we will describe the developments with regard to semiparametric M-estimators, summarizing the results obtained by Ichimura and Lee (2006).

Let Z denote the random variable of dimension $\mathbf{R}^{d_z}$ with the support $\mathcal{S}$. Also, let θ_0 be an element of a finite dimensional parameter space $\Theta \subset \mathbf{R}^{d_\theta}$ that minimizes $E[m(Z, \theta, f_0(\cdot, \theta))]$, for an unknown, d_f-vector-valued function $f_0 \in \mathcal{F}$, where $\mathcal{F}$ is a Banach space of d_f-vector-valued function of Z on the domain $\mathcal{U}$ with the supremum norm. We assume that for each $\theta \in \Theta$, $f(\cdot, \theta) \in \mathcal{F}$. Note that function $f(\cdot, \theta)$ is a function of Z, but the $\cdot$ argument may be different from Z. This is the reason for introducing the notation of $\mathcal{U}$. We will discuss this again with an example.

We denote the Euclidean norm by $\|\cdot\|$, $\|f\|_{\mathcal{F}} = \sup_{\theta \in \Theta} \sup_{z \in \mathcal{S}} \|f(z, \theta)\|$ for any $f(\cdot, \theta) \in \mathcal{F}$, and $\|(\theta, f)\|_{\Theta \times \mathcal{F}} = \|\theta\| + \|f\|_{\mathcal{F}}$. When f depends on θ, $\|f(\cdot, \theta)\|_\infty$ is understood to be the supremum norm with θ fixed.

Let the function $m(Z, \theta, f)$ denote a known, real-valued function that may depend on the data Z and parameter θ directly and also possibly indirectly through f, for example, if f depends on θ. The function m can depend on f only via a particular value Z, in which case m is a regular function with respect to $f(Z,\theta)$, or it can depend on an entire function $f(\cdot,\theta)$, in which case m is a functional with respect to f for each Z and θ. In any case, we assume that $m(z,\theta,f)$ is defined over $\mathbf{S}\times\Theta\times\mathcal{F}$.

Assume that for each θ, a nonparametric estimator $\hat{f}_n(\cdot,\theta)$ of $f_0(\cdot,\theta)$ is available. We define an M-estimator of θ_0 as the minimizer of

$$\hat{S}_n(\theta)\equiv n^{-1}\sum_{i=1}^{n} m\big(Z_i,\theta,\hat{f}_n(\cdot,\theta)\big),$$

under the assumption that the observed data $\{Z_i\colon i=1,\dots,n\}$ are a random sample of Z. Let $\hat{\theta}_n$ denote the resulting estimator of θ_0.

Examples that fit within this framework include the estimators studied by Robinson (1988), Powell, Stock and Stoker (1989), Ichimura (1993), and Klein and Spady (1993) among many others, but the framework is also general enough to include the single-index quantile regression estimator, as discussed in Ichimura and Lee (2006).

Here, we will use the semiparametric least squares (SLS) estimator of Ichimura (1993) as a working example to illustrate how the assumptions and theorems can be applied to derive the distribution theory. In the SLS case, $Z=(Y,X)$ and

$$m\big(Z,\theta,f(\cdot,\theta)\big)=\big(Y-f(X'\theta,\theta)\big)^2 1(X\in\mathcal{X})/2.$$

We assume $E(Y|X)=\phi(X'\theta_0)$. In this example, θ enters m only via f and m depends on f only via its value at X. Note that the $\cdot$ argument in this case is one-dimensional, although X is in general a vector. In this example, $\mathcal{U}$ is the support of $X'\theta$.

To state the assumptions and results of Ichimura and Lee (2006), we need to introduce some more notation. For any $\delta_1>0$ and $\delta_2>0$, define $\Theta_{\delta_1}=\{\theta\in\Theta\colon \|\theta-\theta_0\|<\delta_0\}$ and $\mathcal{F}_{\delta_1,\delta_2}=\{f\in\mathcal{F}\colon \sup_{\theta\in\Theta_{\delta_1}}\|f(\cdot,\theta)-f_0(\cdot,\theta_0)\|_{\infty<\delta_2}\}$.

7.1. Assumptions

The function m is not required to be differentiable, but is assumed to satisfy the following conditions.

ASSUMPTION 7.1. For any (θ_1,f_1) and (θ_2,f_2) in $\Theta_{\delta_1}\times\mathcal{F}_{\delta_1,\delta_2}$, there exist linear operators $\Delta_1(z)\cdot(\theta_1-\theta_2)$ and $\Delta_2(z,f_1(\cdot)-f_2(\cdot))$ and a function $\dot{m}(z,\delta_1,\delta_2)$ satisfying

$$\text{(a)}\quad \big|m\big(z,\theta_1,f_1(\cdot)\big)-m\big(z,\theta_2,f_2(\cdot)\big)-\Delta_1(z)(\theta_1-\theta_2)-\Delta_2\big(z,f_1(\cdot)-f_2(\cdot)\big)\big| \leqslant \big[\|\theta_1-\theta_2\|+\big\|f_1(\cdot)-f_2(\cdot)\big\|_\infty\big]\dot{m}(z,\delta_1,\delta_2),$$

and

$$\text{(b)}\quad E\big[\dot{m}^2(Z,\delta_1,\delta_2)\big]^{1/2}\leqslant C\big(\delta_1^{\alpha_1}+\delta_2^{\alpha_2}\big)$$

for some constants $C<\infty$, $\alpha_1>0$, and $\alpha_2>0$.[61]

[61] Here, Δ_1, Δ_2, and $\dot{m}$ may depend on $(\theta_2,f_2(\cdot))$. However, we suppress the dependence on $(\theta_2,f_2(\cdot))$ for the sake of simplicity in notation.

Ichimura and Lee (2006) verify the condition for the single-index semiparametric quantile regression estimator. The condition is easier to verify for differentiable cases. Note that $\Delta_1(z)$ and $\Delta_2(z)$ correspond to the "derivatives" of m with respect to θ and f, respectively. Because m is generally a functional in f, the first "derivative" with respect to f is a linear operator, whereas the "derivative" with respect to θ can be expressed as a finite dimensional vector.

For SLS, the function m depends on f only via $f(X'\theta, \theta)$, so that both "derivatives" correspond to a finite dimensional vector. One can guess the forms of $\Delta_1(z)$ and $\Delta_2(z)$ by taking derivatives and evaluating them at the true values. Because the function m does not depend on θ directly, $\Delta_1(z) = 0$ and $\Delta_2(z) = -(Y - f_0(X'\theta_0, \theta_0))$. One can verify that with these functions, the assumption holds with $\dot{m}(z, \delta_1, \delta_2) = \delta_2$, so that $\alpha_2 = 1$.

While the function m is allowed to be nondifferentiable, its expected value is assumed to be differentiable with respect to θ and f (as assumed in Pollard (1985)). Denote the expected value by $m^*(\theta, f) = E[m(Z, \theta, f)]$.

ASSUMPTION 7.2. $m^*(\theta, f)$ is twice continuously Fréchet differentiable in an open, convex neighborhood of $(\theta_0, f_0(\cdot, \theta_0))$ with respect to a norm $\|(\theta, f)\|_{\Theta\times\mathcal{F}}$.

For the SLS example, the Fréchet derivative with respect to θ is zero and hence the cross derivative is also. The Fréchet derivative with respect to f is $D_f m^*(\theta, f)(h) = -E[(Y - f(X))h(X)1\{X \in \mathcal{X}\}]$ and the second Fréchet derivative with respect to f is $D_{f,f} m^*(\theta, f)(h_1, h_2) = E[h_1(X)h_2(X)1\{X \in \mathcal{X}\}]$.

The class of functions $\mathcal{F}$ needs to be restricted as well. To characterize the nature of the restriction, we first introduce a few additional notations. Let $\underline{\alpha}$ denote the greatest integer strictly smaller than α, $j = (j_1, \ldots, j_d)$, and let

$$\|g\|_\alpha = \max_{|j|\leqslant\underline{\alpha}} \sup_x \left|D^j g(x)\right| + \max_{|j|=\underline{\alpha}} \sup_{x,y} \frac{|D^j g(x) - D^j g(y)|}{\|x - y\|^{\alpha-\underline{\alpha}}},$$

where the suprema are taken over all x, y in the interior of $\mathcal{U}$ with $x \neq y$. Then $C_M^\alpha(\mathcal{U})$ is defined as the set of all continuous functions $g : \mathcal{U} \subset \mathbf{R}^d \mapsto \mathbf{R}$ with $\|g\|_\alpha \leqslant M$.

ASSUMPTION 7.3. $f_0(\cdot, \theta)$ is twice continuously differentiable on Θ_{δ_1} with bounded derivatives on $\mathcal{U}$ and $\mathcal{F}$ is a subset of $C_M^\alpha(\mathcal{U})$, where $\mathcal{U}$ is a finite union of bounded convex subsets of $\mathbf{R}^{d_u}$ with nonempty interior where $\alpha > d_u/2$.

For SLS, $f_0(u, \theta) = E(Y|X'\theta = u)$. The assumption requires that f_0 is twice continuously differentiable with respect to θ. In the SLS case, $d_u = 1$, so we do not require differentiability with respect to u.

The next set of assumptions are restrictions on the estimator of f_0.

ASSUMPTION 7.4.

(a) For any $\theta \in \Theta_{\delta_1}$, $\hat{f}_n(\cdot, \theta) \in C_M^\alpha(\mathcal{X})$ with probability approaching one.

(b) $\sup_{\theta\in\Theta_{\delta_1}} \|\hat{f}_n(\cdot,\theta) - f_0(\cdot,\theta)\|_\infty = O_p(\tilde{\delta}_2)$ for $\tilde{\delta}_2$ satisfying $n^{1/2}\tilde{\delta}_2^{1+\alpha_2} \to 0$.

(c) For any $\varepsilon > 0$ and $\delta > 0$, independent of θ, there exists n_0 such that for all $n \geqslant n_0$, the following holds:

$$\Pr\bigl\{\bigl\|\bigl[\hat{f}_n(\cdot,\theta) - \hat{f}_n(\cdot,\theta_0)\bigr] - \bigl[f_0(\cdot,\theta) - f_0(\cdot,\theta_0)\bigr]\bigr\|_\infty \leqslant \delta\|\theta-\theta_0\|\bigr\} \geqslant 1-\varepsilon.$$

Condition (b) requires that $\hat{f}_n(\cdot,\theta)$ converge uniformly in probability. If $\alpha_2 = 1$ (smooth m), then $\tilde{\delta}_2 = o(n^{-1/4})$; when $\alpha_2 = 0.5$ (nonsmooth m), then $\tilde{\delta}_2 = o(n^{-1/3})$. In general, $\hat{f}_n(\cdot,\theta)$ needs to converge at a faster rate when m is less smooth.

Condition (c) is satisfied if $\hat{f}_n(\cdot,\theta)$ is differentiable with respect to θ and the derivative converges uniformly to $\partial f_0(\cdot,\theta)/\partial\theta$ over both arguments. This is shown by Ichimura (1993) for the SLS example. Ichimura and Lee's (1991) results in the appendix are useful in proving analogous results in other kernel based estimators.

The next set of assumptions are joint conditions on the second Fréchet derivative of $m^*(\theta, f)$ with respect to f and the estimator of f_0. Write $D_{f,f}m^*(\theta, f) = \int w(\theta, f(\cdot,\theta))h_1(\cdot)h_2(\cdot)\,\mathrm{d}P$, where P is the measure of Z.

Assumption 7.5. One of the following three conditions holds:

(i) $w(\theta, f(\cdot,\theta))$ does not depend on θ or $f(\cdot,\theta)$ and is bounded.

(ii) $\|w(\theta, f(\cdot,\theta)) - w(\theta_0, f_0(\cdot,\theta_0))\| \leqslant C_w\|\theta-\theta_0\|$ for some finite constant C_w and $\sup_{\theta\in\Theta_{\delta_1}} \|\hat{f}_n(\cdot,\theta) - f_0(\cdot,\theta)\|_\infty = o_p(n^{-1/4})$.

(iii) $\|w(\theta, f(\cdot,\theta)) - w(\theta_0, f_0(\cdot,\theta_0))\| \leqslant C_w[\|\theta-\theta_0\| + \|f(\cdot,\theta) - f_0(\cdot,\theta_0)\|_\infty]$ for some finite constant C_w

We saw that for SLS, case (i) applies.

The following assumption is made first to accommodate cases where estimation of f_0 has an effect on the asymptotic distribution of the estimator of θ_0. Later, sufficient conditions for this higher level assumption are discussed.

Assumption 7.6.

(a) As a function of θ, $D_f m^*(\theta, f_0(\cdot,\theta))[\hat{f}_n(\cdot,\theta) - f_0(\cdot,\theta)]$ is twice continuously differentiable on Θ_{δ_1} with probability approaching one.

(b) There exists a nonsingular d_θ-row-vector-valued $\Gamma_1(z)$ such that $E[\Gamma_1(Z)] = 0$, $E[\Gamma_1(Z)\Gamma_1^T(Z)] < \infty$

$$\frac{\mathrm{d}}{\mathrm{d}\theta^T}\bigl(D_f m^*\bigl(\theta, f_0(\cdot,\theta)\bigr)\bigl[\hat{f}_n(\cdot,\theta) - f_0(\cdot,\theta)\bigr]\bigr)\big|_{\theta=\theta_0} = n^{-1}\sum_{i=1}^{n}\Gamma_1(Z_i) + o_p\bigl(n^{-1/2}\bigr). \tag{7.1}$$

In (b), $\Gamma_1(z)$ captures the effects of the first stage estimation of f_0. Two cases where the derivative is easy to compute are: when f_0 does not depend on θ and when $D_f m^*(\theta, f_0(\cdot,\theta))[\hat{f}_n(\cdot,\theta) - f_0(\cdot,\theta)]$ is identically zero. For SLS estimator, $D_f m^*(\theta, f_0(\cdot,\theta))[\hat{f}_n(\cdot,\theta) - f_0(\cdot,\theta)]$ is identically zero so that there is no first order effect of estimating f_0.

The following proposition proved in Ichimura and Lee (2006) provides a set of sufficient conditions for computing the adjustment term that appears in Assumption 7.6.

PROPOSITION 7.1. *Assume that*

(a) $$D_f m^*(\theta, f_0(\cdot,\theta))[h(\cdot)] = \int h(\cdot) g(\cdot,\theta)\, \mathrm{d}P; \tag{7.2}$$

(b) *$g(\cdot,\theta)$ is twice continuously differentiable with respect to θ with probability one*;
(c) *$\hat{f}_n(\cdot,\theta)$ has an asymptotic linear form: for any $\theta \in \Theta_{\delta_1}$,*

$$\hat{f}_n(\cdot,\theta) - f_0(\cdot,\theta) = n^{-1} \sum_{j=1}^{n} \varphi_{nj}(\cdot,\theta) + b_n(\cdot,\theta) + R_n(\cdot,\theta), \tag{7.3}$$

where $\varphi_{nj}(\cdot,\theta)$ is a stochastic term that has expectation zero (with respect to the jth observation), $b_n(\cdot,\theta)$ is a bias term satisfying $\sup_{z,\theta} \|b_n(z,\theta)\| = o(n^{-1/2})$, and $R_n(\cdot,\theta)$ is a remainder term satisfying $\sup_{z,\theta} \|R_n(z,\theta)\| = o_p(n^{-1/2})$;
(d) *$\hat{f}_n(\cdot,\theta)$ is twice continuously differentiable with respect to θ with probability approaching one and $\partial \hat{f}_n(\cdot,\theta)/\partial\theta$ also has an asymptotic linear form*:

$$\frac{\partial \hat{f}_n(\cdot,\theta)}{\partial\theta} - \frac{\partial f_0(\cdot,\theta)}{\partial\theta} = n^{-1} \sum_{j=1}^{n} \tilde{\varphi}_{nj}(\cdot,\theta) + o_p(n^{-1/2}), \tag{7.4}$$

uniformly over (z,θ), where $\tilde{\varphi}_{nj}(\cdot,\theta)$ is a stochastic term that has expectation zero (with respect to the jth observation); and
(e) *there exists a d_θ-row-vector-valued $\Gamma_1(z)$ such that $E[\Gamma_1(Z)] = 0$ and*

$$\max_{1\leqslant i\leqslant n} \|\Gamma_{n1}(Z_i) - \Gamma_1(Z_i)\| = o_p(n^{-1/2}),$$

where

$$\Gamma_{n1}(Z_i) = \int \tilde{\varphi}_{ni}(\cdot,\theta_0) g(\cdot,\theta_0)\, \mathrm{d}P + \int \varphi_{ni}(\cdot,\theta_0) \frac{\partial g(\cdot,\theta_0)}{\partial\theta}\, \mathrm{d}P. \tag{7.5}$$

Then Assumption 7.6 is satisfied.

7.2. Main results on asymptotic distribution

First some notation. Let $\Delta_{10}(z)$ and $\Delta_{20}(z,h)$ denote $\Delta_1(z)$ and $\Delta_2(z,h)$ in Assumption 7.1 with $(\theta_1, f_1) = (\theta, f)$ and $(\theta_2, f_2) = (\theta_0, f_0(\cdot,\theta_0))$. Thus, $\Delta_{10}(z)(\theta - \theta_0) + \Delta_{20}(z, f(\cdot,\theta) - f_0(\cdot,\theta_0))$ is a linear approximation of $m(z,\theta,f(\cdot,\theta)) - m(z,\theta_0,$

$f_0(\cdot, \theta_0))$. Define $\Delta_{20}^*[h] = E[\Delta_{20}(Z, h)]$ for fixed h. Also define a d_θ-row-vector-valued function $\Gamma_0(z)$ such that

$$\Gamma_0(z) = \Delta_{10}(z) - E\big[\Delta_{10}(Z)\big] + \Delta_{20}\left[z, \frac{\partial f_0(\cdot, \theta_0)}{\partial \theta^T}\right] - \Delta_{20}^*\left[\frac{\partial f_0(\cdot, \theta_0)}{\partial \theta^T}\right] + \Gamma_1(z),$$

$\Omega_0 = E[\Gamma_0(Z)^T \Gamma_0(Z)]$, and

$$V_0 = \left.\frac{\mathrm{d}^2 m^*(\theta, f_0(\cdot, \theta))}{\mathrm{d}\theta\, \mathrm{d}\theta^T}\right|_{\theta=\theta_0}.$$

Notice that V_0 is the Hessian matrix of $m^*(\theta, f_0(\cdot, \theta))$ with respect to θ, evaluated at $\theta = \theta_0$.

The following theorem gives the asymptotic distribution of $\hat{\theta}_n$.

THEOREM 7.2. *Assume that θ_0 is an interior point of Θ, θ_0 is a unique minimizer of $m^*(\theta, f_0(\cdot, \theta))$, and $\hat{\theta}_n$ is a consistent estimator of θ_0. Moreover, assume that $\{Z_i\colon i = 1, \ldots, n\}$ are a random sample of Z. Let Assumptions 7.1–7.6 hold. Assume that there exists $C(z)$ satisfying $\|\Delta_{20}[z, h(\cdot, \theta)]\| \leqslant C(z)\|h(\cdot, \theta)\|_\infty$ for any θ and $\|C(Z)\|_{L^2(P)} < \infty$. Also, assume that Ω_0 exists and V_0 is a positive definite matrix. Then*

$$n^{1/2}(\hat{\theta}_n - \theta_0) \to_d \mathbf{N}\big(0, V_0^{-1} \Omega_0 V_0^{-1}\big).$$

Let $\partial_1 m^*(\theta, f)$ denote a vector of the usual partial derivatives of $m^*(\theta, f)$ with respect to the first argument θ. In this notation, $\partial_1 m^*(\theta, f(\cdot, \theta))$ denotes the partial derivative of $m^*(\theta, f)$ with respect to the first argument θ, evaluated at $(\theta, f) = (\theta, f(\cdot, \theta))$. Similarly, let $\partial_1^2 m^*(\theta, f)$ denote the usual Hessian matrix of $m^*(\theta, f)$ with respect to θ, holding f constant. Using this notation, note that by the chain rule, the expression of V_0 can be written as[62]

$$\begin{aligned}
V_0 &= \left.\frac{\mathrm{d}^2 m^*(\theta, f_0(\cdot, \theta))}{\mathrm{d}\theta\, \mathrm{d}\theta^T}\right|_{\theta=\theta_0} \\
&= \partial_1^2 m^*\big(\theta_0, f_0(\cdot, \theta_0)\big) + D_{ff} m^*\big(\theta_0, f_0(\cdot, \theta_0)\big)\left[\frac{\partial f_0(\cdot, \theta_0)}{\partial \theta}, \frac{\partial f_0(\cdot, \theta_0)}{\partial \theta^T}\right] \\
&\quad + 2\left\{D_f\big[\partial_1 m^*\big(\theta_0, f_0(\cdot, \theta_0)\big)^T\big]\left[\frac{\partial f_0(\cdot, \theta_0)}{\partial \theta}\right]\right\} \\
&\quad + D_f m^*\big(\theta_0, f_0(\cdot, \theta_0)\big)\left[\frac{\partial^2 f_0(\cdot, \theta_0)}{\partial \theta \partial \theta^T}\right].
\end{aligned}$$

62 See Ichimura and Lee (2006, Appendix) for the expression of V_0 when $d_f > 1$.

For the SLS case, note that $\partial_1 m^*(\theta, f_0(\cdot, \theta)) = 0$ and that $D_f m^*(\theta_0, f_0(\cdot, \theta_0))(h) = 0$ so that

$$V_0 = D_{ff} m^*\big(\theta_0, f_0(\cdot, \theta_0)\big)\left[\frac{\partial f_0(\cdot, \theta_0)}{\partial \theta}, \frac{\partial f_0(\cdot, \theta_0)}{\partial \theta^T}\right].$$

Because $\partial f_0(X'\theta, \theta)/\partial\theta$ evaluated at θ_0 is $\phi'(X'\theta_0)[\tilde{X} - E(\tilde{X}|X'\theta_0)]$, where $\tilde{X}$ is all X except for the variable whose associated coefficient is set to 1 (required for normalization). Thus,

$$V_0 = E\big\{\big[\phi'(X'\theta_0)\big]^2 1\{X \in \mathcal{X}\}\big[\tilde{X} - E(\tilde{X}|X'\theta_0)\big]\big[\tilde{X} - E(\tilde{X}|X'\theta_0)\big]'\big\}$$

and

$$\Omega_0 = E\big\{\big[\phi'(X'\theta_0)\big]^2 \epsilon^2 1\{X \in \mathcal{X}\}\big[\tilde{X} - E(\tilde{X}|X'\theta_0)\big]\big[\tilde{X} - E(\tilde{X}|X'\theta_0)\big]'\big\}$$

where $\epsilon = Y - \phi(X'\theta_0)$.

As indicated above, when f_0 does not depend on θ, one can easily compute the adjustment term $\Gamma_1(z)$. It turns out that one can relax the smoothness condition on function m with respect to f as well. The following assumptions are invoked in the theorem below, which gives the asymptotic distribution of $\hat{\theta}_n$ when the first-stage nonparametric estimator $\hat{f}_n(\cdot, \theta)$ does not depend on θ.

ASSUMPTION 7.7. For any (θ_1, f) and (θ_2, f) in $\Theta_{\delta_1} \times \mathcal{F}_{\delta_2}$, there exist a d_θ-row-vector-valued function $\Delta_1(z, \theta_2, f)$ and a function $\dot{m}(z, \delta_1)$ satisfying

$$\text{(a)}\quad \big|m\big(z, \theta_1, f(\cdot)\big) - m\big(z, \theta_2, f(\cdot)\big) - \Delta_1(z, \theta_2, f)(\theta_1 - \theta_2)\big| \leqslant \|\theta_1 - \theta_2\| \dot{m}(z, \delta_1),$$

$$\text{(b)}\quad \big\|\dot{m}(Z, \delta_1)\big\|_{L^2(P)} \leqslant C\delta_1^{\alpha_1} \quad \text{for some constants } C < \infty \text{ and } \alpha_1 > 0,$$

and

$$\text{(c)}\quad \sup_{f \in \mathcal{F}_{\delta_2}} \left\| n^{-1} \sum_{i=1}^n \big\{\Delta_1(Z_i, \theta_0, f) - E\big[\Delta_1(Z, \theta_0, f)\big]\big\} - \big\{\Delta_1(Z_i, \theta_0, f_0) - E\big[\Delta_1(Z, \theta_0, f_0)\big]\big\} \right\| = o_p\big(n^{-1/2}\big) \quad \text{for any } \delta_2 \to 0.$$

ASSUMPTION 7.8.

(a) $f_0(\cdot)$ is an element of $\mathcal{C}_M^\alpha(\mathcal{X})$ for some $\alpha > d_1/2$, where d_1 is the dimension of the argument of $f_0(\cdot)$ and $\mathcal{X}$ is a finite union of bounded, convex subsets of $\mathbf{R}^{d_1}$ with nonempty interior.

(b) $\hat{f}_n(\cdot) \in \mathcal{C}_M^\alpha(\mathcal{X})$ with probability approaching one.

(c) $\|\hat{f}_n(\cdot) - f_0(\cdot)\|_\infty = o_p(1)$.

We next state the theorem providing the asymptotic distribution of $\hat{\theta}_n$ when the first-stage nonparametric estimator $\hat{f}_n(\cdot, \theta)$ does not depend on θ.

THEOREM 7.3. *Assume that θ_0 is an interior point of Θ, θ_0 is a unique minimizer of $m^*(\theta, f_0(\cdot))$, and $\hat{\theta}_n$ is a consistent estimator of θ_0. Moreover, assume that $\{Z_i\colon i = 1, \dots, n\}$ are a random sample of Z. Let Assumptions 7.2, 7.5, 7.6, and 7.8 hold. Assume that either Assumption 7.1 or Assumption 7.7 holds. Also, assume that $\Omega_0 = E[\Gamma_0(Z)^T \Gamma_0(Z)^T]$ exists and V_0 is a positive definite matrix, where*

$$\Gamma_0(z) = \Delta_1(z, \theta_0, f_0) - E\big[\Delta_1(Z, \theta_0, f_0)\big] + \Gamma_1(z)$$

and

$$V_0 = \frac{\partial^2 m^*(\theta_0, f_0(\cdot))}{\partial\theta\,\partial\theta^T}.$$

Then

$$n^{1/2}(\hat{\theta}_n - \theta_0) \to_d \mathbf{N}\big(0, V_0^{-1}\Omega_0 V_0^{-1}\big).$$

8. Computation

Flexible modeling methods are computationally more demanding than traditional approaches. Among the various classes of flexible estimators, local methods tend to be the most computationally intensive, because they require solving separate problems at each point at which the density or function is evaluated. The computational burden is particularly great when cross-validation or bootstrap methods are used to select smoothing parameters and/or bootstrap methods are used to evaluate the variation of the estimators. Because local density and regression estimators form the ingredients for many semiparametric procedures, the semiparametric methods can also be highly computationally intensive.

Fortunately, the processing speeds of today's computers make nonparametric and semiparametric modeling methods feasible in many applications with sample sizes of a few thousand, despite their additional computational burden. But when sample sizes get large, say on the order of 10,000 or more, then computing estimates and standard errors can become a major task, and time considerations may drive the choice of bandwidth selector and variance estimator. In such cases, one can take advantage of approximation methods that were suggested by Silverman (1982a) and further studied in Fan and Marron (1994), Hall and Wand (1996), Jones and Lotwick (1984), Wand (1994) and others for speeding up computations in local regression and density estimation. These methods allow for great gains in speed and provide a way of controlling the accuracy of the approximation.

8.1. Description of an approximation method

The approximation method first grids the x-axis and computes the estimates only at grid points. Computation over grids is done efficiently using fast Fourier transformation. The method then interpolates to find function values between the grid-point estimates. The number of grid points, M, is chosen by the researcher. We first describe the most simple version of the binning method, in the context of obtaining a local linear regression estimate. Then we describe a fast Fourier implementation of the binning method, first for density estimation and then for local regression. The FF transformation effectively factors the data component and the bandwidth component in the frequency domain. This allows computation across different bandwidths to be done in a more efficient way, because the data component of the computation can be done only once and reused when computing the values at different bandwidths.

8.1.1. A simple binning estimator

Let $x_1 \ldots x_n$ denote n actual data points at which we wish to evaluate the conditional mean function for the model

$$y = m(x) + \varepsilon.$$

The local linear regression estimator at a point x is given by

$$\hat{E}_n(y_i|x) = \frac{\sum_{j=1}^n y_j K_j \sum_{k=1}^n K_k(x-x_k)^2 - \sum_{j=1}^n y_j K_j(x-x_j)\sum_{k=1}^n K_k(x-x_k)}{\sum_{j=1}^n K_j \sum_{k=1}^n K_k(x-x_k)^2 - [\sum_{j=1}^n K_j(x-x_j)]^2},$$

where $K_j = K((x-x_j)/h_n)$. Calculating the local regression estimator requires estimating terms of the form

$$\sum_{i=1}^n y_i(x-x_i)^l K\big((x-x_i)/h_n\big) \tag{8.1}$$

for $l = 0, 1, 2$ for the n data points at which the function is evaluated.

The binning method reduces the computational burden of evaluating these kernel values by making an equally spaced grid over the support of the conditioning variable, evaluating the function only at the grid points and interpolating to estimate the value of the function at other points. Denote the N grid points by $z_1, \ldots, z_N$. Binning can be implemented by first assigning each data point (x_i) and point of evaluation (x) to their nearest grid points (z_j and $z_{j'}$, respectively) and approximating (8.1) by

$$\sum_{j=1}^N \sum_{i\in I_j} y_i(z_{j'}-z_j)^l K\big((z_{j'}-z_j)/h_n\big),$$

where $z_{j'}$ are now the N grid points of evaluation, z_j are the grid points to which the data points have been assigned and I_j are the set of indices that are binned into the jth bin.

A consequence of choosing equally-spaced grid points is that the distance between z_1 and z_3 is the same as between z_{N-2} and z_N, etc. Letting Δ denote the smallest distance between two grid points, we only need to evaluate the kernel at N values:

$$K(\Delta/h), K(2\Delta/h), K(3\Delta/h), \ldots, K(N\Delta/h)$$

which reduces the required number of evaluations of the kernel function to N from n^2 (the number required under a naive strategy of evaluating the kernel for each possible combination of data-points).

Fan and Marron (1994) introduce a modification of this simple binning idea, called linear binning. Linear binning assigns each data point or point of evaluation to multiple grid points, weighting each in proportion to their distance from the grid points. Fan and Marron (1994) show that for the linear binning estimator, the approximation error can be bounded by δ^4, where δ is the bin or grid width. The FFT implementation described below uses the linear binning idea.

8.1.2. Fast Fourier transform (FFT) binning for density estimation

The binning method described above is adequate for many univariate estimation problems. But for multivariate as well as univariate estimation problems, a more efficient FFT implementation of binning is available. We describe how the FFT can be used to increase the efficiency of the binning estimator in the context of estimating a density, and then discuss how to apply it for local linear regression estimation. The FFT reduces the number of computations by taking advantage of periodicity in complex functions.

The Fourier transform of a density $g(t)$ is

$$\tilde{g}(s) = (2\pi)^{-1/2} \int_{-\infty}^{\infty} e^{ist} g(t)\,\mathrm{d}t. \tag{8.2}$$

Let $\hat{f}_n(x)$ be a standard kernel density estimator, $\hat{f}_n(x) = (nh_n)^{-1} \sum_{j=1}^{n} K((t - x_j)/h_n)$. The F-transform of $\hat{f}_n(x)$ is

$$\begin{aligned}
\tilde{\hat{f}}_n(s) &= (2\pi)^{-1/2}(nh_n)^{-1} \sum_{j=1}^{n} \int e^{ist} K\big((t - x_j)/h_n\big)\,\mathrm{d}t \\
&= (2\pi)^{-1/2} n^{-1} \sum_{j=1}^{n} \int e^{is(x_j + h_n u)} K(u)\,\mathrm{d}u \\
&= \left\{ n^{-1} \sum_{j=1}^{n} e^{isx_j} \right\} \cdot \left\{ (2\pi)^{-1/2} \int e^{ish_n u} K(u)\,\mathrm{d}u \right\}
\end{aligned}$$

where the last two equalities follow after doing a change of variables $u = (t - x_j)/h_n$. The first term in brackets depends only on the data. The second is the F-transform of the $K(sh_n)$, which depends on the kernel and bandwidth choice. Under certain choices for K, there is an explicit solution for the second term. For example, if K is normal it equals $(2\pi)^{-1/2} \exp\{(-s^2h_n^2)/2\}$.

The separation of (8.2) into two terms – one that depends solely on the data and one on the smoothing parameters – has a major computational advantage for algorithms, such as cross-validation, which require evaluating the function for several different bandwidth parameters, since the data component needs to be evaluated only once.

To be able to quickly evaluate the data component, we wish to find an approximation to the first term, $(2\pi)^{-1/2}n^{-1}\sum_{j=1}^{n} e^{isx_j}$. Then $f_n(s)$ will be estimated by applying FF inversion to $\tilde{\hat{f}}_n(s)$.

For large n, $(2\pi)^{-1/2}n^{-1}\sum_{j=1}^{n} e^{isx_j}$ converges to $(2\pi)^{-1/2}\int_{-\infty}^{\infty} e^{isx} g(x)\,\mathrm{d}x$. Usually it is not possible to explicitly obtain the integral, but it can be approximated over a discrete set of points. Let $t_k = k\Delta$ denotes grid points over the interval $[-\infty, \infty]$, Δ a bin width, $k = -(N-1), \ldots, 0, \ldots, (N-1)$, and let $g_k = g(t_k)$. The discrete FFT approximation to the integral evaluated at a point $s_n = n/(N\Delta)$, $n = -N/2, \ldots, N/2$ is

$$\tilde{g}(s_n) = (2\pi)^{-1/2} \sum_{k=-(N-1)}^{(N-1)} e^{is_n t_k} g_k \Delta.$$

The last expression can be written as

$$\tilde{g}(s_n) = (2\pi)^{-1/2}\Delta \sum_{k=-(N-1)}^{(N-1)} e^{\frac{ink\Delta}{N\Delta}} g_k.$$

We can use the fact that $e^{i\alpha}$ is a cyclical function to reduce the number of calculations to $N \log_2 N$. Writing the last expression as

$$(2\pi)^{-1/2}\Delta\left\{\sum_{k=-(N-1)}^{-1} e^{\frac{ink}{N}} g_k + g_0 + \sum_{k=1}^{(N-1)} e^{\frac{ink}{N}} g_k\right\}. \tag{8.3}$$

We now consider just the third term in brackets, since all the same considerations apply to the first. We can write it as

$$\begin{aligned}
\sum_{k=1}^{(N-1)} e^{\frac{ink}{N}} g_k &= \sum_{k=1}^{(\frac{N}{2}-1)} e^{\frac{in(2k+1)}{N}} g_{(2k+1)} + \sum_{k=1}^{(\frac{N}{2}-1)} e^{\frac{in(2k)}{N}} g_{(2k)} \\
&= e^{\frac{in}{N}} \sum_{k=1}^{(\frac{N}{2}-1)} e^{\frac{ink}{N/2}} g_{(2k+1)} + \sum_{k=1}^{(\frac{N}{2}-1)} e^{\frac{ink}{N/2}} g_{(2k)}.
\end{aligned}$$

Repeat this process until the summation only includes one term:

$$= e^{\frac{in}{N}} \sum_{k=1}^{(\frac{N}{4}-1)} e^{\frac{in(2k+1)}{N/2}} g_{(2(2k+1)+1)} + e^{\frac{in}{N}} \sum_{k=1}^{(\frac{N}{4}-1)} e^{\frac{in(2k)}{N/2}} g_{(2(2k)+1)}$$

$$+\sum_{k=1}^{(\frac{N}{4}-1)} e^{\frac{in(2k+1)}{N/2}} g_{(2(2k+1))} + \sum_{k=1}^{(\frac{N}{4}-1)} e^{\frac{in2k}{N/2}} g_{(2(2k))}$$

$$= e^{\frac{in}{N}} e^{\frac{in}{N/2}} \sum_{k=1}^{(\frac{N}{4}-1)} e^{\frac{ink}{N/4}} g_{(4k+3)} + e^{\frac{in}{N}} \sum_{k=1}^{(\frac{N}{4}-1)} e^{\frac{ink}{N/4}} g_{(4k+1)}$$

$$+ e^{\frac{in}{N/2}} \sum_{k=1}^{(\frac{N}{4}-1)} e^{\frac{ink}{N/4}} g_{(4k+2)} + \sum_{k=1}^{(\frac{N}{4}-1)} e^{\frac{ink}{N/4}} g_{(4k)} \quad \text{etc.}$$

After making these substitutions, we get

$$= g_{(0)}\big(e^{in/N}\big)^0 + g_{(1)}\big(e^{in/N}\big)^1 + g_{(2)}\big(e^{in/N}\big)^2 + \cdots + g_{(2^r)}\big(e^{in/N}\big)^{2r},$$

where 2^r is the total number of grid points ($2^r = M$).

Consider the number of calculations required for each of these terms for $n = 0, \ldots, N/2$. (Negative terms are complex conjugates.) Here

$g_{(1)}\big(e^{in/N}\big)$, $n = 0, \ldots, N/2$, requires N complex multiplications,

$g_{(2)}\big(e^{in/N}\big)^2$, $n = 0, \ldots, N/2$, requires $N/2$ complex multiplications,

$g_{(3)}\big(e^{in/N}\big)^3$, $n = 0, \ldots, N/2$, requires $N/3$ complex multiplications,

$\vdots$

$g_{(2^r)}\big(e^{in/N}\big)^{2^r}$, $n = 0, \ldots, N/2$, requires N/N complex multiplications.

Thus, we need no more than $N + N/2 + N/3 + \cdots + N/N = N \log_2 N$ complex multiplications.

Making the grid To implement the method described above, consider an interval $[a, b]$ in which the data lie. The FFT method imposes periodic boundary conditions, so the interval needs to be chosen large enough. For a normal kernel, it suffices to choose a and b that satisfy

$$a < \min(x_j) - 3h_n,$$
$$b > \max(x_j) + 3h_n,$$

where h_n is the bandwidth [Silverman (1986)]. Also, let $M = 2^r$ for some integer r denote the total number of grid points and let δ be the bin width, $\delta = (b - a)/M$. The grid points are given by $t_k = a + k\delta$, for $k = 0, 1, \ldots, M - 1$. If the data point falls onto the grid interval $[t_k, t_{k+1}]$, we assign a weight $\underline{\xi}_k = \delta^{-2}n^{-1}(t_{k+1} - x_j)$ to t_k and a weight $\bar{\xi}_{k+1} = \delta^{-2}n^{-1}(x_j - t_k)$ to t_{k+1}. The weights over all the data points (x_j, $j = 1, \ldots, n$) are accumulated at each grid point. Let

$$\underline{\xi}_k = \delta^{-2}n^{-1}\sum_{j=1}^{n}(t_{k+1} - x_j)1\big(x_j \in [t_k, t_{k+1}]\big),$$

$$\bar{\xi}_k = \delta^{-2} n^{-1} \sum_{j=1}^{n} (x_j - t_{k-1}) 1\bigl(x_j \in [t_{k-1}, t_k]\bigr),$$

$$\xi_k = \underline{\xi}_k + \bar{\xi}_k.$$

The ξ_k weights satisfy $\sum_{k=0}^{M} \xi_k = \delta^{-1}$.

In this notation, we can write the binning approximation for $(2\pi)^{-1/2} n^{-1} \sum_{j=1}^{n} e^{i s_n x_j}$ as

$$\begin{aligned} &\approx (2\pi)^{-1/2} \sum_{k=0}^{M-1} \delta \xi_k e^{i s_n t_k} \\ &= (2\pi)^{-1/2} \sum_{k=0}^{M-1} \delta \xi_k e^{i s_n (a + k\delta)}. \end{aligned}$$

s_n are taken to be $s_n = n/M\delta$ for $n = -M/2, \ldots, M/2$:

$$\begin{aligned} &= (2\pi)^{-1/2} \sum_{k=0}^{M-1} \delta \xi_k e^{i \frac{n}{M\delta}(a + k\delta)} \\ &= (2\pi)^{-1/2} e^{\frac{ia}{M\delta}} \left\{ \sum_{k=0}^{M-1} \delta \xi_k e^{\frac{ink}{M}} \right\}. \end{aligned}$$

This last expression is in the form needed to apply FFT. Jones and Lotwick (1983) show that the MISE of this approximation is $O(\delta^4)$.

8.2. *Performance evaluation*

In this section, we evaluate the gains in speed in a set-up where we are performing local linear regression and choosing smoothing parameters through least squares cross-validation (the LSCV method described in Section 6). The computational method effectively factors the data component and the bandwidth component in the frequency domain, so that computation across different bandwidths can be done efficiently by reusing the data component of the computation. We show how these techniques work very well and make it feasible to do nonparametric and semiparametric estimation with sample sizes well over 100,000.

The following result is obtained for data generated by $y = \exp x$ without error, where x has the standard normal distribution. Grids are constructed between -3 and 3. We estimate $E\{y|x\}$ at all data points using the local linear regression method and use LSCV to select the globally optimum bandwidth. The machine we used is a DEC 5000/240.

Table 1 compares the speed and the average root percentage mean squared errors compared to the method without approximating (reported in the second row of each cell) for different size samples and for different grid sizes, M.

Table 1
Speed/accuracy comparisons

	$n = 1000$	$n = 10{,}000$	$n = 100{,}000$
$M = 100$	1.02 sec 0.25%	14.7 sec 0.27%	185.8 sec 0.40%
$M = 500$	1.81 sec 0.047%	11.5 sec 0.048%	145.1 sec 0.049%
$M = 1000$	2.45 sec 0.021%	11.5 sec 0.036%	137.4 sec 0.041%
No approx.	175.2 sec	22,257 sec	N/A

Speed does not necessarily increase with the gain in accuracy, because the computation involves optimization over the bandwidth. The time it takes for convergence, in our experience, goes down as M increases. As one can see for the case of 10,000 observations we can reduce the computation time to 0.036% of the time it would otherwise take. For the case of 100,000 observations and for this workstation, the computation would have been a major task running over days as opposed to about 3 minutes with the approximation method.

9. Conclusions

In this chapter, we have reviewed recent advances in nonparametric and semiparametric estimation, with emphasis on applicability of methods in empirical research. Our discussion focused on the modeling and estimation of densities, conditional mean functions and derivatives of functions. The examples of Section 2 illustrated how flexible modeling methods have been adopted in previous empirical studies, either as an estimation method in their own right or as a way of checking parametric modeling assumptions. Section 3 highlighted key concepts in semiparametric and nonparametric modeling that do not have counterparts in parametric modeling, such as the dependence of rates of convergence on the dimension of the estimation problem, the notion of models with an infinite number of parameters, the criteria used to define optimal convergence rates, and the existence of so-called "dimension-free" semiparametric estimators.

Section 4 of the chapter described a number of nonparametric approaches for estimating densities and conditional mean functions. Although nonparametric estimators are sometimes deemed infeasible because of slow convergence rates, they are nonetheless of keen interest because they form the building blocks of many semiparametric methods. We introduced some likelihood based and method of moments based approaches and presented a unifying framework for thinking about how apparently different estimators relate to one another. The asymptotic distribution theory for the commonly used local polynomial regression estimator was also presented.

Section 5 studied application of a variety of semiparametric models that offer a middle ground between fully parametric and nonparametric approaches. By imposing some parametric restrictions, they typically achieve faster convergence rates than nonparametric estimators. By remaining flexible with regard to certain aspects of the model, semiparametric estimators are consistent under a broader class of models than are fully parametric estimators. In some cases, flexibility can be achieved without sacrificing rates of convergence. However we note that semiparametric models are generally not embedded in a sequence of models in which an arbitrary function can be approximated. It is desirable to consider such embedding and construct tests against such sequences when semiparametric models are used. Stone's extended linear model provides such a framework for the additive separable models.

In Section 6 we addressed questions that arise in implementing nonparametric methods, with regard to optimal choices of smoothing parameters and how best to implement trimming procedures. We reviewed a large and growing literature on bandwidth selectors for nonparametric density and regression estimators. Section 6 also considers the bandwidth selection problem in the context of semiparametric models, although that literature is still in its infancy. We described a few bandwidth selectors that have been proposed for index models and for the partially linear model.

Section 7 presented a way to compute asymptotic variance of the semiparametric M-estimators. Section 8 provided a brief introduction to some computational methods that have been introduced to ease the computational burden of nonparametric estimators when applied to large datasets. These methods show much promise, but their performance has yet to be widely studied in economic applications.

It is our hope that the topics of this chapter have provided an overview of how empirical researchers can best take advantage of recent developments in nonparametric and semiparametric modeling.

References

Abbring, J.H., Heckman, J.J. (2007). "Econometric evaluation of social programs, Part III: Distributional treatment effects, dynamic treatment effects, dynamic discrete choice, and general equilibrium policy evaluation". In: Heckman, J.J., Leamer, E. (Eds.), Handbook of Econometrics, vol. 6B. Elsevier (Chapter 72).

Ahmad, I.A. (1976). "On asymptotic properties of an estimate of a functional of a probability density". Scandinavian Actuarial Journal, 176–181.

Ahn, H., Powell, J.L. (1993). "Semiparametric estimation of censored sample selection models with a nonparametric selection mechanism". Journal of Econometrics 58 (1–2), 3–29.

Ai, C., Blundell, R., Chen, X. (2000). "Semiparametric Engel curves with endogenous expenditure". Mimeo. UCL.

Ai, C., Chen, X. (2003). "Efficient estimation of models with conditional moment restrictions containing unknown functions". Econometrica 71, 1795–1843.

Aït-Sahalia, Y. (1992). "The delta method for nonparametric kernel functionals". Mimeo.

Altonji, J., Ichimura, H. (1998). "Estimating derivatives in nonseparable models with limited dependent variables". Mimeo.

Andrews, D. (1991). "Asymptotic normality of series estimators for various nonparametric and semiparametric models". Econometrica 59, 307–345.

Andrews, D. (1994). "Empirical process methods in econometrics". In: Engle, R.F., McFadden, D.L. (Eds.), Handbook of Econometrics, vol. 4, pp. 2247–2294.

Aradillas-Lopez, A., Honoré, B., Powell, J.L. (2005). "Pairwise difference estimation of nonlinear models with nonparametric functions". Mimeo.

Arellano, M., Honoré, B. (2001). "Panel data models: Some recent developments". In: Heckman, J., Leamer, E. (Eds.), Handbook of Econometrics, vol. 5. North-Holland.

Ashenfelter, O. (1978). "Estimating the effect of training programs on earnings". Review of Economics and Statistics 60, 47–57.

Ashenfelter, O., Card, D. (1985). "Using the longitudinal structure of earnings to estimate the effect of training programs". Review of Economics and Statistics 67, 648–660.

Banks, J., Blundell, R., Lewbel, A. (1997). "Quadratic Engel curves and consumer demand". Review of Economics and Statistics 79, 527–539.

Barron, A.R. (1993). "Universal approximation bounds for superpositions of a sigmoidal function". IEEE Transactions in Information Theory 39, 930–945.

Bassi, L. (1984). "Estimating the effects of training programs with nonrandom selection". Review of Economics and Statistics 66, 36–43.

Berlinet, A., Thomas-Agnan, C. (2003). Reproducing Kernel Hilbert Spaces in Probability and Statistics. Kluwer Academic Publishers, Boston.

Bickel, P. (1982). "On adaptive estimation". Annals of Statistics 10, 647–671.

Bickel, P.J., Klaassen, C.A.J., Ritov, Y., Wellner, J.A. (1993). Efficient and Adaptive Estimation for Semiparametric Models. Johns Hopkins University Press, Baltimore and London.

Bierens, H.J. (1985). "Kernel estimators of regression functions". In: Bewley, T. (Ed.), Advances in Econometrics. Cambridge University Press, New York.

Blundell, R., Duncan, A. (1998). "Kernel regression in empirical microeconomics". The Journal of Human Resources 33, 62–87.

Blundell, R., Powell, J. (2003). "Endogeneity in semiparametric binary response models". Mimeo.

Blundell, R., Browning, M., Crawford, I.A. (2003). "Nonparametric Engel curves and revealed preference". Econometrica 71, 205–240.

Blundell, R., Chen, X., Kristensen, D. (2003). "Semi-nonparametric IV estimation of shape invariant Engel curves". Mimeo.

Breiman, L., Friedman, J.H. (1985). "Estimating optimal transformations for multiple regression and correlation". Journal of the American Statistical Association 80, 580–619.

Buchinsky, M. (1994). "Changes in the US wage structure 1963–1987: Application of quantile regression". Econometrica 62, 405–454.

Buchinsky, M. (1995). "Quantile regression, Box–Cox transformation model, and the US wage structure, 1963–1987". Journal of Econometrics 65, 109–154.

Buchinsky, M. (1998). "The dynamics of changes in the female wage distribution in the USA: A quantile regression approach". Journal of Applied Econometrics 13, 1–30.

Buchinsky, M., Hahn, J. (1998). "An alternative estimator for the censored quantile regression model". Econometrica 66, 653–671.

Cao, R., Cuevas, A., Gonzalez-Mantiega, W. (1994). "A comparative study of several smoothing methods in density estimation". Computational Statistics and Data Analysis 17, 153–176.

Chamberlain, G. (1986a). "Asymptotic efficiency in semi-parametric models with censoring". Journal of Econometrics 32, 189–218.

Chamberlain, G. (1986b). "Notes on semiparametric regression". Unpublished manuscript. Harvard University.

Chamberlain, G. (1995). "Quantile regression, censoring, and the structure of wages". In: Sims, C. (Ed.), Advances in Econometrics: Sixth World Congress, vol. 1. Cambridge University Press.

Chaudhuri, P. (1991a). "Global nonparametric estimation of conditional quantile functions and their derivatives". Journal of Multivariate Analysis 39, 246–269.

Chaudhuri, P. (1991b). "Nonparametric estimates of regression quantiles and their local Bahadur representation". Annals of Statistics 19, 760–777.
Chen, X. (2007). "Large sample sieve estimation of semi-nonparametric models". In: Heckman, J.J., Leamer, E. (Eds.), Handbook of Econometrics, vol. 6B. Elsevier (Chapter 76).
Chen, X., White, H. (1999). "Improved rates and asymptotic normality for nonparametric neural network estimators". IEEE Transactions in Information Theory 45, 682–691.
Chen, X., Linton, O., Van Keilegom, I. (2003). "Estimation of semiparametric models when the criterion function is not smooth". Econometrica 71, 1591–1608.
Choi, K. (1992). "The semiparametric estimation of the sample selection model using series expansion and the propensity score". PhD dissertation. University of Chicago.
Chui, C. (1992). An Introduction to Wavelets. Academic Press.
Cleveland, W.S., Loader, C. (1996). "Smoothing by local regression: Principles and methods". Unpublished manuscript. AT&T Bell Laboratories.
Conley, T.G., Hansen, L.P., Liu, W.-F. (1997). "Bootstrapping the long run". Macroeconomic Dynamics 1, 279–311.
Cosslett, S.R. (1987). "Efficiency bounds for distribution free estimators for the binary choice and the censored regression model". Econometrica 55, 559–585.
Cosslett, S.R. (1991). "Semiparametric estimation of a regression model with sample selectivity". In: Barnett, W.A., Powell, J., Tauchen, G. (Eds.), Nonparametric and Semiparametric Methods in Economics and Statistics. Cambridge University Press, Cambridge, pp. 175–197.
Daubechies, I. (1992). Ten Lectures on Wavelets. CBMS–NSF Regional Conference Series in Applied Mathematics. Society for Industrial and Applied Mathematics, Philadelphia.
Davidson, R., MacKinnon, J.G. (1982). "Some non-nested hypotheses tests and the relations among them". The Review of Economic Studies 49, 551–565.
Deaton, A. (1996). Microeconometric Analysis for Development Policy: Approach to Analyzing Household Surveys. World Bank/The Johns Hopkins University Press.
Deaton, A., Ng, S. (1998). "Parametric and nonparametric approaches in price and tax reform". Journal of the American Statistical Association 93, 900–910.
Deaton, A., Paxson, C. (1998). "Economies of scale, household size and the demand for food". Journal of Political Economy 106, 897–930.
Delgado, M.A., Robinson, P. (1992). "Nonparametric and semiparametric methods for economic research". Journal of Economic Surveys 3, 201–249.
DiNardo, J., Fortin, N., Lemiex, T. (1996). "Labor market institutions and the distribution of wages, 1973–1992: A semiparametric approach". Econometrica 64, 1001–1044.
Doksum, K., Peterson, D., Samarov, A. (2000). "On variable bandwidth selection in local polynomial regression". Journal of Royal Statistical Society, Series B 62, 431–448.
Engle, R., Granger, C.W., Rice, J., Weiss, A. (1986). "Semiparametric estimates of the relation between weather and electricity demand". Journal of the American Statistical Association 81, 310–320.
Epanechnikov, V.A. (1969). "Non-parametric estimation of a multivariate probability density". Theory of Probability and Its Applications 14, 153–158.
Eubank, R.L. (1999). Nonparametric Regression and Spline Smoothing, second ed. Dekker, New York.
Fan, J. (1992). "Design adaptive nonparametric regression". Journal of the American Statistical Association 87, 998–1004.
Fan, J., Gijbels, I. (1992). "Variable bandwidth and local linear regression smoothers". Annals of Statistics 20, 2008–2036.
Fan, J., Gijbels, I. (1995). "Data-driven bandwidth selection in local polynomial fitting: Variable bandwidth and spatial adaptation". Journal of Royal Statistical Society, Series B 57, 371–394.
Fan, J., Gijbels, I. (1996). Local Polynomial Modeling and Its Applications. Chapman and Hall, New York.
Fan, J., Marron, J.S. (1994). "Fast implementations of nonparametric curve estimation". Journal of Computational and Graphical Statistics 3, 35–56.
Fan, J., Hall, P., Martin, M., Patil, P. (1996). "On local smoothing of nonparametric curve estimators". Journal of American Statistical Association 91, 258–266.

Faraway, J.J., Jhun, M. (1990). "Bootstrap choice of bandwidth for density estimation". Journal of the American Statistical Association 85, 1119–1122.

Fraker, T., Maynard, R. (1987). "The adequacy of comparison group designs for evaluations of employment related programs". The Journal of Human Resources 22, 194–227.

Goldberger, A. (1968). Topics in Regression Analysis. Wiley, New York.

Green, P.J., Silverman, B.W. (1994). Nonparametric Regression and Generalized Linear Models. Chapman and Hall.

Gronau, R. (1973a). "New econometric approaches to fertility". Journal of Political Economy 81, 168–199.

Gronau, R. (1973b). "The intrafamily allocation of time: The value of the housewive's time". The American Economic Review 63, 634–651.

Hall, P. (1982). "Limit theorems for stochastic measures of the accuracy of density estimation". Stochastic Process Applications 13, 11–25.

Hall, P. (1983). "Large sample optimality of least-squares cross-validation in density estimation". Annals of Statistics 11, 1156–1174.

Hall, P., Horowitz, J.L. (1990). "Bandwidth selection in semiparametric estimation of censored linear regression models". Econometric Theory 6, 123–150.

Hall, P., Marron, J.S. (1987). "Extent to which least-squares cross-validation minimizes integrated squared error in nonparametric density estimation". Probability Theory and Related Fields 74, 567–581.

Hall, P., Marron, J.S. (1991). "Local minima in cross-validation functions". Journal of the Royal Statistical Society, Series B 53, 245–252.

Hall, P., Patil, P. (1995). "Formulae for mean integrated squared error of nonlinear wavelet-based density estimators". Annals of Statistics 23, 905–928.

Hall, P., Wand, M.P. (1996). "On the accuracy of binned kernel density estimates". Journal of Multivariate Analysis 56, 165–184.

Hall, P., Sheather, S., Jones, M., Marron, J. (1991). "On optimal data-based bandwidth selection in kernel density estimation". Biometrika 78, 263–269.

Hansen, L.P. (1982). "Large sample properties of generalized method of moments estimators". Econometrica 50, 1029–1059.

Härdle, W. (1990). Applied Nonparametric Regression. Cambridge University Press.

Härdle, W. (1991). Smoothing Techniques with Implementation in *S*. Springer-Verlag, New York.

Härdle, W., Gasser, T. (1984). "Robust nonparametric function fitting". Journal of the Royal Statistical Society, Series B 46, 42–51.

Härdle, W., Linton, O. (1994). "Applied nonparametric methods". In: Handbook of Econometrics, vol. 4. Elsevier, Amsterdam, pp. 2295–2339.

Härdle, W., Linton, O.B. (1996). "Estimating additive regression with known links". Biometrika 83, 529–540.

Härdle, W., Stoker, T. (1989). "Investigating smooth multiple regression by the method of average derivatives". Journal of American Statistical Association 84, 986–995.

Härdle, W., Tsybakov, A.B. (1993). "How sensitive are average derivatives?". Journal of Econometrics 58, 31–48.

Härdle, W., Hildenbrand, W., Jerison, M. (1991). "Empirical evidence on the law of demand". Econometrica 59, 1525–1549.

Härdle, W., Hart, J., Marron, J.S., Tsybakov, A.B. (1992). "Bandwidth choice for average derivative estimation". Journal of the American Statistical Association 87, 218–226.

Härdle, W., Hall, P., Ichimura, H. (1993). "Optimal semiparametric estimation in single index models". Annals of Statistics 21, 157–178.

Hasminskii, R.Z., Ibragimov, I.A. (1979). "On the nonparametric estimation of functionals". In: Mandl, M., Husková, M. (Eds.), Proceedings of the Second Prague Symposium on Asymptotic Statistics. North-Holland, Amsterdam, pp. 41–51.

Hastie, T.J., Tibshirani, R.J. (1990). Generalized Additive Models. Chapman and Hall.

Hausman, J. (1978). "Specification tests in econometrics". Econometrica 46, 1251–1272.

Heckman, J.J. (1976). "The common structure of statistical models of truncation, sample selection, and limited dependent variables and a simple estimator for such models". Annals of Economic and Social Measurement 5, 475–492.

Heckman, J.J. (1980). "Addendum to sample selection bias as specification error". In: Stromsdorfer, E., Frakas, G. (Eds.), Evaluation Studies Review Annual. Sage, San Francisco.

Heckman, J.J. (1990). "Varieties of selection bias". American Economic Review 80, 313–328.

Heckman, J.J., Hotz, J. (1989). "Choosing among alternative nonexperimental methods for estimating the impact of social programs: The case of manpower training". Journal of the American Statistical Association 84, 862–880.

Heckman, J.J., Robb, R. (1985). "Alternative methods for evaluating the impact of interventions". In: Heckman, J., Singer, B. (Eds.), Longitudinal Analysis of Labor Market Data. Cambridge University Press.

Heckman, J.J., Smith, J. (1995). "Assessing the case for randomized social experiments". Journal of Economic Perspectives 9, 85–100.

Heckman, J.J., Ichimura, H., Todd, P. (1997). "Matching as an econometric evaluation estimator: Evidence from evaluating a job training program". Review of Economic Studies 64, 605–654.

Heckman, J.J., Ichimura, H., Smith, J., Todd, P. (1998). "Nonparametric characterization of selection bias using experimental data". Econometrica 66, 1017–1098.

Heckman, J.J., Ichimura, H., Todd, P. (1998a). "Matching as an econometric evaluation estimator". Review of Economic Studies 65, 261–294.

Heckman, J.J., Ichimura, H., Todd, P. (1998b). "Implementing the partially linear regression model". Unpublished manuscript.

Heckman, J.J., Lochner, L., Todd, P. (2005). "Earnings functions, rates of return and treatment effects: The Mincer equation and beyond". In: Handbook of Education Economics. In press.

Heckman, J.J., Vytlacil, E.J. (2007a). "Econometric evaluation of social programs, Part I: Causal models, structural models and econometric policy evaluation". In: Heckman, J.J., Leamer, E. (Eds.), Handbook of Econometrics, vol. 6B. Elsevier (Chapter 70).

Heckman, J.J., Vytlacil, E.J. (2007b). "Econometric evaluation of social programs, Part II: Using the marginal treatment effect to organize alternative economic estimators to evaluate social programs and to forecast their effects in new environments". In: Heckman, J.J., Leamer, E. (Eds.), Handbook of Econometrics, vol. 6B. Elsevier (Chapter 71).

Hjort, N.L., Jones, M.C. (1996). "Local parametric nonparametric density estimation". Annals of Statistics 24, 1619–1647.

Honoré, B., Powell, J. (1994). "Pairwise difference estimators of censored and truncated regression models". Journal of Econometrics 64, 241–278.

Honoré, B., Powell, J. (2005). "Pairwise difference estimation of nonlinear models". In: Andrews, D., Stock, J. (Eds.), Identification and Inference for Econometric Models. Cambridge University Press, New York.

Horowitz, J.L. (1992). "A smoothed maximum score estimator for the binary response model". Econometrica 60, 505–531.

Horowitz, J.L. (1998). Semiparametric Methods in Econometrics. Lecture Notes in Statistics, vol. 131. Springer-Verlag, New York and Heidelberg.

Horowitz, J.L., Härdle, W. (1996). "Direct semiparametric estimation of single-index models with discrete covariates". Journal of American Statistical Association 91, 1632–1640.

Horowitz, J.L., Lee, S. (2005). "Nonparametric estimation of an additive quantile regression model". Journal of the American Statistical Association 100, 1238–1249.

Huang, J.Z. (1998). "Projection estimation in multiple regression with application to functional ANOVA models". Annals of Statistics 26, 242–272.

Huang, J.Z. (2003). "Local asymptotics for polynomial spline regression". Annals of Statistics 31, 1600–1635.

Huang, S.-Y. (1999). "Density estimation by wavelet-based reproducing kernels". Statistica Sinica 9, 137–151.

Ichimura, H. (1993). "Semiparametric least squares estimation of single index models (SLS) and weighted SLS estimation of single index models". Journal of Econometrics 58, 71–120.

Ichimura, H. (1995). "Asymptotic distribution theory for semiparametric and nonparametric estimators with data dependent smoothing parameters". Unpublished manuscript. University of Pittsburgh.
Ichimura, H., Lee, L.-F. (1991). "Semiparametric least squares estimation of multiple index models: Single equation estimation". In: Barnett, W.A., Powell, J., Tauchen, G. (Eds.), Nonparametric and Semiparametric Methods in Economics and Statistics. Cambridge University Press, Cambridge, England, pp. 3–49.
Ichimura, H., Linton, O. (2005). "Asymptotic expansions for some semiparametric program evaluation estimators". In: Andrews, D., Stock, J. (Eds.), Identification and Inference for Econometric Models. Cambridge University Press, New York.
Ichimura, H., Lee, S. (2006). "Characterization of the asymptotic distribution of semiparametric M-estimators". Mimeo. University of Tokyo.
Ichimura, H., Taber, C. (2000). "Direct estimation of policy impacts". NBER Technical Working Paper 254.
Jones, M.C., Lotwick, H.W. (1983). "On the errors involved in computing the empirical characteristic function". Journal of Statistical Computation and Simulation 17, 133–149.
Jones, M.C., Lotwick, H.W. (1984). "A remark on algorithm AS 176 kernel density estimation using the fast Fourier transform". Applied Statistics 33, 120–122.
Jones, M.C., Sheather, S.J. (1991). "A reliable data-based bandwidth selection method for kernel density estimation". Journal of the Royal Statistical Society, Series B 53, 683–690.
Jones, M.C., Marron, J.S., Sheather, S.J. (1992). "Progress in data-based bandwidth selection for kernel density estimation". Manuscript.
Jones, M.C., Marron, J.S., Sheather, S.J. (1996). "A brief survey of bandwidth selection for density estimation". Journal of the American Statistical Association 91, 401–407.
Klein, R.W., Spady, R.H. (1993). "An efficient semiparametric estimator for binary response models". Econometrica 61, 387–421.
Kim, J., Pollard, D. (1990). "Cube root asymptotics". Annals of Statistics 18, 191–219.
Koenker, R. (2005). Quantile Regression. Cambridge University Press.
Koenker, R., Bassett, G. (1978). "Regression quantiles". Econometrica 46, 33–50.
Lee, M.-J. (1996). Methods of Moments and Semiparametric Econometrics for Limited Dependent Variable Models. Springer-Verlag.
Lewis, H.G. (1974). "Comments on selectivity biases in wage comparisons". Journal of Political Economy 82, 1145–1155.
Linton, O.B. (1995a). "Second order approximation in a partially linear regression model". Econometrica 63, 1079–1113.
Linton, O.B. (1995b). "Estimation in semiparametric models: A review". In: Phillips, P.C.B., Maddala, G.S. (Eds.), A Volume in Honor of C.R. Rao. Blackwell.
Linton, O.B. (1996). "Edgeworth approximation for MINPIN estimators in semiparametric regressions models". Econometric Theory 12, 30–60.
Linton, O.B. (1997). "Efficient estimation of additive nonparametric regression models". Biometrika 84, 469–474.
Linton, O.B., Nielsen, J.P. (1995). "A kernel method of estimating structured nonparametric regression based on marginal integration". Biometrika 82, 93–100.
Linton, O.B., Chen, R., Wang, N., Härdle, W. (1997). "An analysis of transformations for additive nonparametric regression". Journal of the American Statistical Association 92, 1512–1521.
Loader, C. (1995). "Old faithful erupts: Bandwidth selection reviewed". Manuscript. AT&T Bell Laboratories.
Loader, C. (1996). "Local likelihood density estimation". Annals of Statistics 24, 1602–1618.
McFadden, D.L. (1985). Presidential address at the World Congress of the Econometric Society.
Malinvaud, E.B. (1970). Statistical Methods of Econometrics. North-Holland, Amsterdam.
Manski, C.F. (1975). "Maximum score estimation of the stochastic utility model of choice". Journal of Econometrics 3, 205–228.
Manski, C.F. (1985). "Semiparametric analysis of discrete response: Asymptotic properties of the maximum score estimator". Journal of Econometrics 27, 313–333.
Masry, E. (1996a). "Multivariate regression estimation: Local polynomial fitting for time series". Stochastic Processes and Their Applications 65, 81–101.

Masry, E. (1996b). "Multivariate local polynomial regression for time series: Uniform strong consistency and rates". Journal of Time Series Analysis 17, 571–599.

Matzkin, R. (1994). "Restrictions of economic theory in nonparametric methods". In: Engle, R.F., McFadden, D.L. (Eds.), Handbook of Econometrics, vol. 4, pp. 2524–2554.

Mincer, J. (1974). Schooling, Experience and Earnings. NBER Press, New York.

Moore, D.S., Yackel, J.W. (1977a). "Consistency properties of nearest neighbor density function estimators". Annals of Statistics 5, 143–154.

Moore, D.S., Yackel, J.W. (1977b). "Large sample properties of nearest neighbor density function estimators". In: Gupta, S.S., Moore, D.S. (Eds.), Statistical Decision Theory and Related Topics. Academic Press, New York.

Nadaraya, E.A. (1964). "On estimating regression". Theory of Probability and Its Applications 10, 186–190.

Newey, W.K. (1985). "Generalized method of moments specification tests". Journal of Econometrics 29, 229–256.

Newey, W.K. (1987). "Specification tests for distributional assumptions in the Tobit model". Journal of Econometrics 34, 125–145.

Newey, W.K. (1988). "Two-step series estimation of sample selection models". Working paper. MIT.

Newey, W.K. (1990). "Semiparametric efficiency bounds". Journal of Applied Econometrics 5, 99–135.

Newey, W.K. (1994a). "The asymptotic variance of semiparametric estimators". Econometrica 62, 1349–1382.

Newey, W.K. (1994b). "Kernel estimation of partial means". Econometric Theory 10, 233–253.

Newey, W.K. (1997). "Convergence rates and asymptotic normality for series estimators". Journal of Econometrics 79, 147–168.

Newey, W.K., Powell, J. (1990). "Efficient estimation of linear and type I censored regression models under conditional quantile restrictions". Econometric Theory 6, 295–317.

Newey, W., McFadden, D. (1994). "Large sample estimation and hypothesis testing". In: Engle, R.F., McFadden, D.L. (Eds.), Handbook of Econometrics, vol. 4, pp. 2113–2241.

Newey, W., Stoker, T. (1993). "Efficiency of weighted average derivative estimators". Econometrica 61, 1199–1223.

Newey, W.K., Powell, J., Walker, J. (1990). "Semiparametric estimation of selection models: Some empirical results". American Economic Review 80, 324–328.

Nishiyama, Y., Robinson, P. (2000). "Edgeworth expansions for semiparametric averaged derivatives". Econometrica 68, 931–980.

Nishiyama, Y., Robinson, P. (2001). "Studentization in edgeworth expansions for estimates of semiparametric single index models". In: Hsiao, C., Morimune, K., Powell, J. (Eds.), Nonlinear Statistical Modeling. Cambridge University Press, UK.

Nishiyama, Y., Robinson, P. (2005). "The bootstrap and the edgeworth correction for semiparametric average derivatives". Econometrica 73, 903–948.

Ochiai, T., Naito, K. (2003). "Asymptotic theory for the multiscale wavelet density derivative estimator". Communications in Statistics Theory and Methods 32, 1925–1950.

Olley, G.S., Pakes, A. (1996). "The dynamics of productivity in the telecommunications equipment industry". Econometrica 64, 1263–1297.

Pagan, A., Ullah, A. (1999). Nonparametric Econometrics. Cambridge University Press, Cambridge, MA.

Pakes, A., Pollard, D. (1989). "Simulation and asymptotics of optimization estimators". Econometrica 57, 1027–1057.

Park, B.U., Marron, J.S. (1990). "Comparison of data-driven bandwidth selectors". Journal of the American Statistical Association 85, 66–72.

Park, B.U., Turlach, B.A. (1992). "Reply to comments on practical performance of several data driven bandwidth selectors". Computational Statistics 7, 283–285.

Park, B.U., Kim, W.C., Marron, J.S. (1994). "Asymptotically best bandwidth selectors in kernel density estimation". Statistics and Probability Letters 19, 119–127.

Parzen, E. (1962). "On estimation of a probability density function and mode". Annals of Mathematical Statistics 33, 1065–1076.

Pollard, D. (1985). "New ways to prove central limit theorems". Econometric Theory 1, 295–314.
Powell, J. (1984). "Least absolute deviations estimator for the censored regression model". Journal of Econometrics 25, 303–325.
Powell, J. (1987). "Semiparametric estimation of bivariate latent variable models". Working Paper No. 8704. SSRI, University of Wisconsin–Madison.
Powell, J. (1994). "Estimation of semiparametric models". In: Engle, R.F., McFadden, D.L. (Eds.), Handbook of Econometrics, vol. 4, pp. 2443–2521.
Powell, J., Stoker, T. (1996). "Optimal bandwidth choice for density weighted averages". Journal of Econometrics 75, 291–316.
Powell, J., Stock, J., Stoker, T. (1989). "Semiparametric estimation of index coefficients". Econometrica 57 (6), 1403–1430.
Prakasa-Rao, B.L.S. (1983). Nonparametric Functional Estimation. Academic Press, Orlando.
Prewitt, K., Lohr, S. (2006). "Bandwidth selection in local polynomial regression using eigenvalues". Journal of Royal Statistical Society, Series B 68, 135–154.
Ritov, Y., Bickel, P. (1990). "Achieving information bounds in non and semiparametric models". Annals of Statistics 18, 925–938.
Robinson, P.M. (1983). "Nonparametric estimators for time series". Journal of Time Series Analysis 4, 185–207.
Robinson, P.M. (1988). "Root-N consistent nonparametric regression". Econometrica 56, 931–954.
Robinson, P.M. (1989). "Hypothesis testing in semiparametric and nonparametric models for econometric time series". Review of Economic Studies 56, 511–534.
Robinson, P.M. (1991). "Automatic frequency domain inference on semiparametric and nonparametric models". Econometrica 59, 1329–1363.
Robinson, P.M. (1995). "The normal approximation for semiparametric averaged derivatives". Econometrica 63, 667–680.
Rosenblatt, M. (1956). "Remarks on some nonparametric estimators of a density function". Annals of Mathematical Statistics 27, 832–837.
Rosenzweig, M., Wolpin, K.I. (2000). "Natural natural experiments". Journal of Economic Literature 38, 827–874.
Ruppert, D. (1997). "Empirical-bias bandwidths for local polynomial nonparametric regression and density estimation". Journal of American Statistical Association 92, 1049–1062.
Ruppert, D., Wand, M.P. (1994). "Multivariate locally weighted least squares regression". Annals of Statistics 22, 1346–1370.
Saitoh, S. (1989). Theory for Reproducing Kernels and Its Applications. Wiley, New York.
Schmalensee, R., Stoker, T. (1999). "Household gasoline demand in the United States". Econometrica 67, 645–662.
Schuster, E.F., Gregory, C.G. (1981). "On the nonconsistency of maximum likelihood nonparametric density estimators". In: Eddy, W.F. (Ed.), Computer Science and Statistics: Proceedings of the 13th Symposium on the Interface. Springer-Verlag, New York, pp. 295–298.
Schweder, T. (1975). "Window estimation of the asymptotic variance of rank estimators of location". Scandinavian Journal of Statistics 2, 113–126.
Scott, D.W. (1992). Multivariate Density Estimation. John Wiley & Sons, New York.
Scott, D.W., Terrell, G.R. (1987). "Biased and unbiased cross-validation in density estimation". Journal of American Statistical Association 82, 1131–1146.
Sherman, R. (1994a). "Maximal inequalities for degenerate U-processes with application to optimization estimators". Annals of Statistics 22, 439–459.
Sherman, R. (1994b). "U-processes in the analysis of a generalized semiparametric regression estimator". Econometric Theory 10, 372–395.
Shiller, R.J. (1984). "Smoothness priors and nonlinear regression". Journal of the American Statistical Association 72, 420–423.
Schoenberg, I.J. (1964). "Spline functions and the problem of graduation". Proceedings of the National Academy of Sciences 52, 947–950.

Silverman, B.W. (1982a). "Kernel density estimation using the fast Fourier transform method". Applied Statistics 31, 93–99.
Silverman, B.W. (1982b). "On the estimation of a probability density function by the maximum penalized likelihood method". Annals of Statistics 10, 795–810.
Silverman, B.W. (1986). Density Estimation for Statistics and Data Analysis. Chapman and Hall, London.
Smith, J., Todd, P. (2001). "Reconciling conflicting evidence on the performance of propensity score matching estimators". American Economic Review 91, 112–118.
Smith, J., Todd, P. (2005). "Does matching overcome Lalonde's critique of nonexperimental estimators?". Journal of Econometrics 125, 305–353. Rejoinder 125, 365–375.
Stein, C. (1956). "Efficient nonparametric testing and estimation". In: Proc. Third Berkeley Symp. Math. Statist. Prob., vol. 1. Univ. California Press, Berkeley, pp. 187–195.
Stern, S. (1996). "Semiparametric estimates of the supply and demand effects of disability on labor force participation". Journal of Econometrics 71, 49–70.
Stock, J. (1991). "Nonparametric policy analysis: An application to estimating hazardous waste cleanup benefits". In: Barnett, W.A., Powell, J., Tauchen, G. (Eds.), Nonparametric and Semiparametric Methods in Economics and Statistics. Cambridge University Press, Cambridge, England, pp. 77–98.
Stoker, T. (1986). "Consistent estimation of scaled coefficients". Econometrica 54, 1461–1481.
Stoker, T. (1991). "Equivalence of direct, indirect, and slope estimators of average derivatives". In: Barnett, W.A., Powell, J., Tauchen, G. (Eds.), Nonparametric and Semiparametric Methods in Economics and Statistics. Cambridge University Press, Cambridge, England, pp. 99–118.
Stoker, T. (1996). "Smoothing bias in the measurement of marginal effects". Journal of Econometrics 72, 49–84.
Stone, C. (1974). "Cross-validatory choice and assessment of statistical predictions (with discussion)". Journal of the Royal Statistical Society, Series B 36, 111–147.
Stone, C. (1977). "Consistent nonparametric regression (with discussion)". Annals of Statistics 5, 595–645.
Stone, C. (1980). "Optimal rates of convergence for nonparametric estimators". Annals of Statistics 8, 1348–1360.
Stone, C. (1982). "Optimal rates of convergence for nonparametric regression". Annals of Statistics 10, 1040–1053.
Stone, C. (1984). "An asymptotically optimal window selection rule for kernel density estimates". Annals of Statistics 12, 1285–1297.
Stone, C., Hansen, M., Kooperberg, C., Truong, Y. (1997). "Polynomial splines and their tensor products in extended linear modeling". Annals of Statistics 25, 1371–1425.
Tauchen, G. (1985). "Diagnostic testing and evaluation of maximum likelihood models". Journal of Econometrics 30, 415–443.
Taylor, C. (1989). "Bootstrap choice of the smoothing parameter in kernel density estimation". Biometrika 76, 705–712.
Tsybakov, A.B. (1982). "Robust estimates of a function". Problems of Information Transmission 18, 190–201.
Ullah, A., Vinod, H.D. (1993). Nonparametric Econometrics. Cambridge University Press.
Van der Vaart, A.W. (1998). Asymptotic Statistics. Cambridge University Press.
Van der Vaart, A.W., Wellner, J.A. (1996). Weak Convergence and Empirical Processes. Springer.
Wahba, G. (1984). "Partial spline models for the semi-parametric estimation of functions of several variables". In: Bradley, R.A., Hunter, J.S., Kendall, D.G., Watson, G.S. (Eds.), Statistical Analysis of Time Series. Institute of Statistical Mathematics, Tokyo.
Wahba, G. (1990). Spline Models for Observational Data. CBMS–NSF Regional Conference Series in Applied Mathematics. Society for Industrial and Applied Mathematics, Philadelphia.
Walter, G., Blum, J.R. (1979). "Probability density estimation using delta sequences". Annals of Statistics 7, 328–340.
Wand, M.P. (1994). "Fast computation of multivariate kernel estimators". Journal of Computational and Graphical Statistics 3, 433–445.

Watson, G.S. (1964). "Smooth regression analysis". Sankhya, Series A 26, 357–372.
Weinert, H. (Ed.) (1982). Reproducing Kernel Hilbert Spaces: Applications in Statistical Signal Processing. Hutchinson Ross, Stroudsburg, PA.
White, H. (1980). "Using least squares to approximate unknown regression functions". International Economic Review 21, 149–170.
Willis, R. (1986). "Wage determinants: A survey and reinterpretation of human capital earnings functions". In: Ashenfelter, O., Layard, R. (Eds.), Handbook of Labor Economics. Elsevier.
Wu, D.-M. (1974). "Alternative tests of independence between stochastic regressors and disturbances: Finite sample results". Econometrica 42, 529–546.
Yatchew, A. (1997). "An elementary estimator of the partial linear model". Economics Letters 57, 135–143.
Yatchew, A. (1998). "Nonparametric regression techniques in economics". Journal of Economic Literature 26, 669–721.
Yatchew, A. (2003). Semiparametric Regression for the Applied Econometrician. Cambridge University Press.
Yu, K., Jones, M.C. (1998). "Local linear quantile regression". Journal of the American Statistical Association 93, 228–237.
Zemanian, A.H. (1965). Distribution Theory and Transform Analysis. Dover Publications, Inc., New York.
Zhou, S., Shen, X., Wolfe, D.A. (1998). "Local asymptotics for regression splines and confidence regions". Annals of Statistics 26, 1760–1782.

Chapter 75

THE ECONOMETRICS OF DATA COMBINATION*

GEERT RIDDER

Department of Economics, University of Southern California, Los Angeles, USA
e-mail: ridder@usc.edu

ROBERT MOFFITT

Department of Economics, Johns Hopkins University, Baltimore, USA
e-mail: moffitt@jhu.edu

Contents

* We thank J. Angrist, J. Currie, J.J. Heckman, C.F. Manski, and a referee for helpful comments on an earlier draft.

Handbook of Econometrics, Volume 6B

DOI: 10.1016/S1573-4412(07)06075-8

Abstract

Economists who use survey or administrative data for inferences regarding a population may want to combine information obtained from two or more samples drawn from the population. This is the case if there is no single sample that contains all relevant variables. A special case occurs if longitudinal or panel data are needed but only repeated cross-sections are available.

In this chapter we survey sample combination. If two (or more) samples from the same population are combined, there are variables that are unique to one of the samples and variables that are observed in each sample. What can be learned by combining such samples, depends on the nature of the samples, the assumptions that one is prepared to make, and the goal of the analysis. The most ambitious objective is the identification and estimation of the joint distribution, but often we settle for the estimation of economic models that involve these variables or a subset thereof. Sometimes the goal is to reduce biases due to mismeasured variables.

We consider sample merger by matching on identifiers that may be imperfect in the case that the two samples have a substantial number of common units. For the case that the two samples are independent, we consider (conditional) bounds on the joint distribution. Exclusion restrictions will narrow these bounds. We also consider inference under the strong assumption of conditional independence.

Keywords

sample combination, matching, nonparametric identification, repeated cross-sections

JEL classification: C13, C14, C23, C21, C42, C81

1. Introduction

Economists who use survey or administrative data for inferences regarding a population may want to combine information obtained from two or more samples drawn from the population. This is the case if (i) there is no single sample that contains all relevant variables, (ii) one of the samples has all relevant variables, but the sample size is too small, (iii) the survey uses a stratified design. A special case of (i) occurs if longitudinal or panel data are needed, while only repeated cross sections are available.

There are good reasons why data sets often do not have all relevant variables. If the data are collected by interview, it is advisable to avoid long questionnaires. If the data come from an administrative file, usually only variables that are relevant for the eligibility for a program and for the determination of the benefits or payments associated with that program are included. Hence, unless a survey was designed to include all the relevant variables for a particular research project, there is no single data set that contains all variables of interest. However, often the variables are available in two or more separate surveys. In that case it is natural to try to combine the information in the two surveys to answer the research question.

In this chapter we survey sample combination. What can be learned by combining two or more samples depends on the nature of the samples and the assumptions that one is prepared to make. If two (or more) samples from the same population are combined, there are variables that are unique to one of the samples and variables that are observed in each sample. To be specific, consider a population and assume that for each member of the population we can define the variables Y, Z, X. Sample A contains the variables Y, Z and sample B the variables X, Z. The variables in Y are unique to sample A and those in X are unique to sample B. Hence, we have random samples from overlapping (in variables) marginal distributions.

How one uses this information depends on the goal of the study. We distinguish between

(i) Identification and estimation of the joint distribution of X, Y, Z. This was the original motivation for the type of sample merging that is discussed in Section 3.2. The hope was that with the merged sample the distributional impact of taxes and social programs could be studied. An example is a study of the effect of a change in the tax code on the distribution of tax payments. In principle, tax returns contain all the relevant variables. However, if the change depends on variables that did not enter the tax code before, or if it is desired to estimate the effect for specific subgroups that are not identifiable from the tax returns, the need arises to obtain the missing information from other sources. The joint distribution is also the object of interest in non-parametric (conditional) inference. This is obviously the most ambitious goal.

(ii) Estimation of economic models that involve X, Y, Z (or a subset of these variables). Such models are indexed by a vector of parameters θ that is of primary interest, and, as will become clear in Section 4.3, parametric restrictions are helpful (but not necessary) in securing identification by sample combination.

An example is the estimation of the effect of age at school entry on the years of schooling by combining data from the US censuses in 1960 and 1980 [Angrist and Krueger (1992)].

(iii) Estimation of an economic model with mismeasured variables. In this case sample A contains Y, X, Z and sample B X^*, Z with X^* the correct value and X the mismeasured value of the same variable, e.g. income. If X is self-reported income, this variable may be an imperfect indicator of true income X^*. A better indicator is available in administrative data, e.g. tax records. Hence, it is desirable to combine these samples to obtain a dataset that has both the correctly measured variable and Y. Again this was a motivation for the type of sample merger discussed in Section 3.2. In Section 4.5 we show that sample merger is not necessary to avoid measurement error bias.

For problems of type (i) there are a number of methods that merge the samples A and B into one sample that is treated as a random sample from the joint distribution of X, Y, Z. Because the common variables Z[1] are often not of independent interest, we assume for the moment that the researcher is satisfied with a random sample from the joint distribution of X, Y. Sample merging is discussed in Sections 2 and 3. Its success depends on two factors: (i) the number of members of the population that are in both samples, and (ii) the degree to which these common members can be identified from the common variables Z. In the simplest case Z identifies members of the population uniquely, for instance if Z is an individual's Social Security Number or some other unique identifier (measured without error). If the common members are a random sample from the population, then the merged sample is indeed a random sample from the population distribution of X, Y. Complications arise if the number of population members that are in both samples is substantial, but they cannot be identified without error. We discuss estimation in samples that have been merged. Because the matching process is not perfect the merging introduces a form of measurement or matching error. The analogy is almost complete because the bias is similar to the attenuation bias in models with mismeasured independent variables

The merger of samples has also been attempted in the case that the fraction of units that are in both samples is negligible. Indeed the techniques that have been used to merge such samples are the same as for samples with common units that cannot be identified with absolute certainty. Only under the strong assumption of conditional independence of Y and X given Z, we can treat the merged or matched sample as a random sample from the joint distribution of Y, Z, X (Section 4). As shown in Section 4 it is preferable not to merge the two samples, even if the assumption of conditional independence is correct. Under conditional independence we can estimate the joint distribution of Y, Z, X and any identified conditional model without merging the samples. If the assumption of conditional independence does not hold and our goal is to recover the joint

[1] Sometimes variables have to be transformed to make them equal in both samples. For instance, A may contain the age and B the year of birth.

distribution of Y, Z_0, X with Z_0 a subvector of Z, then the two samples give bounds on this joint distribution. Point identification is possible if we specify a parametric model for the conditional distribution of Y given X, Z_0, $f(y \mid x, z_0; \theta)$ or moments of that distribution, e.g. the conditional mean. In both cases, it is essential that some of the common variables in Z are not in Z_0, i.e. that there are exclusion restrictions. In Section 4.5 we also consider the case that one or more of the variables of a survey is subject to measurement error, while there is a second survey that has error free data on these variables, but does not contain data on the other relevant variables in the first survey. We show that the merger of the two samples is again not the solution, but that such data are helpful in reducing or even eliminating the errors-in-variables bias.

A special case of sample combination with some distinct variables are synthetic cohorts obtained from repeated cross sections. In that case Y and X are the same variables in two time periods and Z is the variable that identifies the cohort. This special case deserves separate consideration and is discussed in Section 5.

In Section 6 we consider the combination of samples with common variables that are drawn from possibly overlapping subpopulations of some target population. We distinguish between (i) all samples have the same set of variables, but they are drawn from distinct subpopulations, (ii) there is one sample that has all variables of interest and at least one other sample that is drawn from the same population, but contains a subset of the variables of interest. Case (i) occurs if the sample design is stratified. Often, a simple random sample from a population is not the most efficient sample design. If subpopulations are identifiable from the sampling frame, a design that oversamples heterogeneous subpopulations and undersamples homogeneous ones, requires fewer observations to achieve the same precision. Such a sample design is called a stratified design (with unequal probabilities of selection). It may even be that in a simple random sample certain subpopulations that are of particular interest will not be represented at all. For instance, if the dependent variable is the indicator of a rare event, there may be insufficient observations to study factors that affect the occurrence of the event. With a stratified sample design the samples from the strata must be combined. The procedure depends on the type of inference, in particular on whether the inference is on the conditional distribution of a (vector of) dependent variable(s) given a set of conditioning variables or not. If the strata are subsets of the support of the conditioning variables or of variables that are independent of the dependent variables given the conditioning variables, then the stratified sample can be treated as a random sample. If the inference is unconditional or if the strata are subsets of the support of the dependent variables, then we cannot treat the stratified sample as if it were a random sample. The correct procedure is to use some weighting scheme that uses the inverse probability of selection as the sampling weights [Horvitz and Thompson (1952)].

In case (ii) a small sample with all relevant variables is typically combined with a larger sample with fewer variables. The goal is to increase the precision of the estimates obtained from the small sample. The main difference between the sample combination considered in Sections 2–4 and in Section 6 is that in Sections 2–4 the issue is whether the distribution, moments or parameters of interest are identified from the combined samples. In Section 6 identification is usually ensured (see Section 6.2 for a discussion of the conditions) and the focus is on efficient inference.

A stratified sample is a special case of a sample in which the probability that a population unit is included in the sample depends on the variables of interest. In a stratified sample this probability is a known function of the variables that define the strata. The more general case in which this probability is not known and has to be estimated occurs for instance, if responses are missing for a fraction of the population. A special case is the estimation of treatment effects where the counterfactual outcome is missing. If the probability of observation depends on the independent variables, but not on the dependent variable, the data are Missing At Random (MAR). If we have a random sample from the marginal population distribution of the independent variables, either because we observe the independent variables even if the dependent variable is missing, or because we have an independent random sample from this distribution, then we can estimate parameters of the distribution of the dependent variable. Hirano, Imbens and Ridder (2003) have shown that the efficient estimator uses estimated sampling weights, even if these weights are known. This seems to be a generic result, because the efficient estimator in stratified samples also requires estimated weights.

This chapter provides a common framework for research in different fields of economics and statistics. It is mostly a survey, but we also point at some areas, for instance non-parametric identification of joint distributions by exclusion restrictions, that have not been explored yet. Although we survey empirical applications we have not attempted to include all studies that use some form of data combination. By bringing together research that until now was rather disjoint we hope to stimulate further research on data combination.

2. Merging samples with common units

An obvious way to combine information in two samples is to merge the samples. If the two samples have a substantial number of common units, the natural action is to link the records relating to the same unit. The linkage of records for the same unit is usually called *exact matching*. This term is misleading, because it suggests that the linkage is without errors. Record linkage is easy if both records contain a unique identifier, e.g. an individual's social security number, that is observed without error. Card, Hildreth and Shore-Sheppard (2001) match survey to administrative data, and find that even in the administrative data the social security numbers are often misreported. If the two surveys are independently drawn samples from two overlapping populations, the linked records are a sample from the intersection of the two populations.

2.1. Broken random samples

DeGroot, Feder and Goel (1971), DeGroot and Goel (1976) and DeGroot and Goel (1980) consider the reconstruction of a broken random sample, i.e. a random sample in which the identity of the members is observed with error. Besides its intrinsic interest, we discuss their method because of its similarity to methods used to merge samples that have no common units.

Consider a random sample of size N from a population and assume that the identity of the units in the random sample is observed with error, i.e. a record consist of $(Y_i, Z_{1i}, Z_{2j}, X_j)$ with

$$Z_{ki} = Z_i + \varepsilon_{ki}, \quad k = 1, 2. \tag{1}$$

The identifier Z is observed with error and unit i is erroneously linked to unit j. We ignore for the moment Y, X.[2] We also assume that $Z, \varepsilon_1, \varepsilon_2$ are jointly normally distributed,[3] and as a consequence the observed Z_1, Z_2 have a bivariate normal distribution with means μ_1, μ_2, standard deviations σ_1, σ_2, and correlation coefficient ρ. Let ϕ denote a permutation of $1, \ldots, N$ so that Z_{1i} is linked with $Z_{2\phi(i)}$. The loglikelihood of the sample $Z_{1i}, Z_{2\phi(i)}, i = 1, \ldots, N$, is

$$\begin{aligned} &\ln L\left(\mu_1, \mu_2, \sigma_1^2, \sigma_2^2, \rho, \phi\right) \\ &\quad = C - \frac{N}{2}\log\left(1-\rho^2\right) - \frac{N}{2}\log\sigma_1^2 - \frac{N}{2}\log\sigma_2^2 \\ &\qquad - \frac{1}{2(1-\rho)^2} \\ &\qquad \times \sum_{i=1}^{N}\left\{\frac{(z_{1i}-\mu_1)^2}{\sigma_1^2} + \frac{(z_{2\phi(i)}-\mu_2)^2}{\sigma_2^2} - 2\rho\frac{(z_{1i}-\mu_1)(z_{2\phi(i)}-\mu_2)}{\sigma_1\sigma_2}\right\}. \end{aligned} \tag{2}$$

Note that the vector ϕ is treated as a vector of parameters, i.e. the likelihood is the joint distribution if ϕ is the correct linkage. Maximizing the loglikelihood with respect to the means and variances yields the usual MLE for these parameters. If we substitute these MLE and maximize with respect to ρ we obtain the concentrated loglikelihood that only depends on ϕ

$$L(\phi) = C - \frac{N}{2}\log\left(1-\rho_\phi^2\right) \tag{3}$$

with ρ_ϕ the sample correlation coefficient between $Z_{1i}, Z_{2\phi(i)}, i = 1, \ldots, N$. This sample correlation coefficient depends on the permutation ϕ. It is easily verified for $N = 2$ and it can be shown for all N [Hájek and Šidak (1967)] that the average of the sample correlation coefficient over all permutations is equal to 0. Hence the smallest value for ρ_ϕ is $\rho_{\min} < 0$ and the largest $\rho_{\max} > 0$. If the order statistics of Z_1, Z_2 are denoted by $Z_{1(i)}, Z_{2(i)}$, then it is intuitively clear that the sample correlation coefficient is maximal if $Z_{1(i)}$ is linked with $Z_{2(i)}$, and minimal if $Z_{1(i)}$ is linked with $Z_{2(N-i+1)}$. The first permutation is denoted by $\phi_{\max}$, the second by $\phi_{\min}$. Because the concentrated

[2] If Y, X are correlated (given Z_1, Z_2) they could be helpful in reconstructing the correctly linked sample.

[3] This assumption can be relaxed, see DeGroot, Feder and Goel (1971).

loglikelihood increases with ρ_ϕ^2, the MLE of ρ is $\rho_{\max}$ if $\rho_{\max}^2 > \rho_{\min}^2$ and $\rho_{\min}$ if the reverse inequality holds. In the first case the likelihood is maximized if we link according to the order statistics, and in the second case if we link in the reverse order. As is obvious from the loglikelihood in (2) the nature of the linkage, i.e. the choice of ϕ, depends only on the sign of ρ. The MLE for ρ suggests the following rule to decide on this sign: if $\rho_{\max}^2 > \rho_{\min}^2$ then we estimate the sign of ρ as $+1$, while we use the opposite sign if the reverse inequality holds. DeGroot and Goel (1980) conduct some sampling experiments that show that for values of ρ of 0.9, i.e. a relatively small measurement error in the identifier, this procedure yields the correct sign in more than 75% of the replications (for sample sizes ranging from 5 to 500).

Obviously, if the Z_1, Z_2 are observations on a common identifier, we do not have to estimate the sign of ρ, because the correlation is positive, unless we make extreme assumptions on the correlation between the two measurement errors. The optimal linkage is then on the order statistic of Z_1 and Z_2. Maximization of the loglikelihood (2) with respect to the permutation ϕ is equivalent to maximization of

$$\sum_{i=1}^{N} z_{1i} z_{2\phi(i)} \tag{4}$$

and this is in turn equivalent to minimization of

$$\sum_{i=1}^{N} z_{1i}^2 + \sum_{i=1}^{N} z_{2i}^2 - 2\sum_{i=1}^{N} z_{1i} z_{2\phi(i)} = \sum_{i=1}^{N} (z_{1i} - z_{2\phi(i)})^2. \tag{5}$$

Hence the Euclidean or L^2 distance between the vectors of observed identifiers is minimized. As we shall see, this rule that is derived for the case of exact matching with mismeasured identifiers, is also used in the case that there are no common units in the samples.

If there are multiple identifiers, i.e. if Z is a K vector and Z_1, Z_2 have multivariate normal distributions with means μ_1, μ_2, variance matrices Σ_{11}, Σ_{22}, and covariance matrix Σ_{12}, the factor of the likelihood function that depends on the permutation ϕ is

$$\ln L(\mu, \Sigma_{12}) = \exp\left\{-\frac{1}{2}\sum_{i=1}^{N} z_{1i}' \Sigma^{12} z_{2\phi(i)}\right\}. \tag{6}$$

In this expression

$$\Sigma^{12} = -\Sigma_{11}^{-1}\Sigma_{12}\left(\Sigma_{22} - \Sigma_{21}\Sigma_{11}^{-1}\Sigma_{12}\right)^{-1}. \tag{7}$$

This likelihood factor is the probability that the permutation ϕ is the correct match and hence maximization of the likelihood function is equivalent to maximization of the probability of a correct match.

The maximization of the likelihood factor in (6) is equivalent to the maximization of

$$\sum_{i=1}^{N} z_{1i} C_{12} z_{2\phi(i)} \tag{8}$$

with $C_{12} = -\Sigma^{12}$. This is equivalent to the minimization of

$$\sum_{i=1}^{N}(z_{1i} - z_{2\phi(i)})' C_{12}(z_{1i} - z_{2\phi(i)}), \tag{9}$$

i.e. the quadratic distance with matrix C_{12} between the vectors of identifiers. The same distance measure is sometimes used if the samples have no common units and Z is a vector of common characteristics (see Section 3.2).

Because all units must be matched the maximization of (8) is equivalent to the minimization of

$$\sum_{i=1}^{N}\sum_{j=1}^{N} d_{ij} z_{1i} C_{12} z_{2j} \tag{10}$$

subject to for $i = 1, \ldots, N$, $j = 1, \ldots, N$,

$$\sum_{i=1}^{N} d_{ij} = \sum_{j=1}^{N} d_{ij} = 1 \tag{11}$$

and $d_{ij} = 0, 1$. This is a linear assignment problem, an integer programming problem for which efficient algorithms are available.

This procedure requires an estimate of Σ_{12}, the covariance matrix of Z_1 and Z_2. Note that in the case of a single identifier only the sign of this covariance was needed. If the errors in the identifiers are independent in the two samples, an estimate of the variance matrix of the true identifier vector Z suffices. The extension of DeGroot and Goel's MLE to the multivariate case has not been studied.

2.2. Probabilistic record linkage

2.2.1. Matching with imperfect identifiers

The ML solution to the reconstruction of complete records assumes that the mismeasured identifiers are ordered variables. The method of probabilistic record linkage can be used if the matching is based on (mismeasured) nominal identifiers, such as names, addresses or social security numbers. Probabilistic record linkage has many applications. It is used by statistical agencies to study the coverage of a census, by firms that have a client list that is updated regularly, and by epidemiologists who study the effect of a potentially harmful exposure [see Newcombe (1988), for a comprehensive survey of the applications]. In epidemiological studies a sample of individuals who have been exposed to an intervention is linked with a population register to determine the effects on fertility and/or mortality, the latter possibly distinguished by cause [Newcombe et al. (1959), Buehler et al. (2000), Fair et al. (2000)]. Probabilistic record linkage is also used in queries from a large file, e.g. finding matching fingerprints or DNA samples. The implementation of probabilistic record linkage depends on the specific features of the data. In this survey we only describe some general ideas. We use the setup of Fellegi and Sunter (1969), although we change it to stress the similarity with the reconstruction of broken random samples (Section 2.1) and statistical matching (Section 3.2).

Initially we assume that there is a single identifier Z that identifies each member of the population uniquely. We have two samples of sizes N_1 and N_2 from the population. These samples need not be of equal size and, although it is assumed that a substantial fraction of the units in both samples are common, the remaining units are unique to one of the samples. This is a second departure from the assumptions made in the case of a broken random sample. A key ingredient of probabilistic matching is the record generating model that describes how the observed identifiers in the records are related to the unique true identifier. It is obvious that errors in names and reported social security numbers cannot be described by a simple model with additive measurement error [Fellegi and Sunter (1969), Copas and Hilton (1990), and Newcombe, Fair and LaLonde (1992), develop alternative record generating models]. To keep the exposition simple, we will stick with the additive model of Equation (1). The main ideas can be explained with this model and are independent of a specific model of the record generating process.

The first step is to define a comparison vector W_{ij} for each pair i, j, with i with identifier Z_{1i} in the first and j with identifier Z_{2j} in the second random sample. An obvious choice is $W_{ij} = Z_{2j} - Z_{1i}$, but we can also include Z_1 and use the comparison vector $W_{ij} = (Z_{2j} - Z_{1i}, Z_{1i})'$. Define M_{ij} as the indicator of the event that i and j are matched, i.e. are the same unit. If we assume that the measurement errors in the two samples are independent of each other and of the true identifier Z, and that the identifiers of distinct units are independently distributed in the two samples, we have, for $W_{ij} = Z_{2j} - Z_{1i}$, with f the density of $\varepsilon_2 - \varepsilon_1$ and G_k the cdf of Z in sample k,

$$
\begin{aligned}
&h(w_{ij} \mid M_{ij} = 1) = f(w_{ij}),\\
&h(w_{ij} \mid M_{ij} = 0) = \iint f(w_{ij} - z' + z)\,\mathrm{d}G_1(z)\,\mathrm{d}G_2(z'). \qquad (12)
\end{aligned}
$$

For every pair i, j we consider the density ratio, provided that the denominator is greater than 0 (if the denominator is 0, the match can be made without error),

$$
\frac{h(w_{ij} \mid M_{ij} = 1)}{h(w_{ij} \mid M_{ij} = 0)}. \qquad (13)
$$

This ratio gives the relative likelihood that the comparison vector is from a matched pair. Just as in a statistical test of the null hypothesis that i, j refer to the same unit, we decide that the pair is matched if the density ratio exceeds a threshold. Note that with this matching rule unit i may be matched with more than one unit in sample 2 and unit j may be matched with more than one unit in sample 1.

To illustrate the procedure we consider a simple case. The distribution of the identifier is usually discrete. Here we assume that there is a superpopulation of identifiers from which the identifiers in the (finite) population are drawn. In particular, we assume that the Z's in both samples are independent draws from a normal distribution with mean μ and variance σ^2. A uniform distribution may be a more appropriate choice in many instances. The measurement errors are also assumed to be normally distributed with mean 0 and variances σ_1^2, σ_2^2.

Under these assumptions, the density ratio is

$$\frac{\phi(z_{2j} - z_{1i}; \sigma_1^2 + \sigma_2^2)}{\phi(z_{2j} - z_{1i}; 2\sigma^2 + \sigma_1^2 + \sigma_2^2)} = \sqrt{\frac{2\sigma^2 + \sigma_1^2 + \sigma_2^2}{\sigma_1^2 + \sigma_2^2}} \exp\left\{-\frac{\sigma^2}{(2\sigma^2 + \sigma_1^2 + \sigma_2^2)(\sigma_1^2 + \sigma_2^2)}(z_{2j} - z_{1i})^2\right\}. \tag{14}$$

The cutoff value for the density ratio can also be expressed as

$$(z_{2j} - z_{1i})^2 < C \tag{15}$$

and we match if this inequality holds. C is a constant that is chosen to control either the probability of a false or a missed match. If we take the first option we choose C such that

$$2\Phi\left(\frac{\sqrt{C}}{\sqrt{2\sigma^2 + \sigma_1^2 + \sigma_2^2}}\right) - 1 = \alpha. \tag{16}$$

The advantage of this choice is that the cutoff value can be computed with the (estimated) variances of the observed identifiers Z_{1i} and Z_{2j} which are $\sigma^2 + \sigma_1^2$ and $\sigma^2 + \sigma_2^2$, respectively. Estimation of the variances of the measurement errors is not necessary. If there are multiple identifiers, the criterion for matching i and j is

$$(z_{2j} - z_{1i})'\left((\Sigma_1 + \Sigma_2)^{-1} - (2\Sigma + \Sigma_1 + \Sigma_2)^{-1}\right)(z_{2j} - z_{1i}) < C, \tag{17}$$

i.e. the quadratic distance with the specified matrix between the observed identifiers is less than a threshold. To use this criterion we need estimates of Σ and $\Sigma_1 + \Sigma_2$. If $\Sigma \gg \Sigma_1 + \Sigma_2$ the criterion can be approximated by a quadratic form with matrix $(\Sigma_1 + \Sigma_2)^{-1}$, and the distance is chi-squared distributed for matches. In that case it is more convenient to choose C to control the probability of a missed match.

In general, the estimation of the parameters that enter the density ratio is the most problematic part of probabilistic linkage. Tepping (1968), Copas and Hilton (1990) and Belin and Rubin (1995) propose estimation methods that use a training sample in which it is known which pairs are matched to estimate the parameters of the distribution of the comparison vector among matched and unmatched pairs.

It is interesting to compare probabilistic record linkage to the method that was proposed for the reconstruction of a broken random sample. Instead of minimizing the (average) distance between the identifiers as in (5), we choose a cutoff value for the distance and match those pairs with a distance less than the cutoff value. In probabilistic record linkage a record may be linked with two or more other records. If the true identifiers are sufficiently distinct and/or if the measurement errors are relatively small the probability of this event is negligible. Alternatively, we can choose the record that has the largest match probability.

2.2.2. Matching errors and estimation

The term exact matching is a misnomer when dealing with samples that have been matched using identifiers that are subject to error. Matching error biases estimates of parameters. In this section we consider the case that a random sample from a population is matched (with error) to a register that contains each unit in the sample. There has been very little work on biases due to matching errors. Usually, matched samples are analyzed as if there are no mismatches. This section provides a framework that can be used to assess potential biases and to obtain unbiased estimates if some knowledge of the matching process is available.

We assume that a random sample of size N_1 is matched with a register of size N_2 that is a random sample from the target population or the complete target population ($N_2 > N_1$). For example, we have a sample of taxpayers that is matched with the register of tax returns. The sample contains a variable X and an identifier Z_1 that is measured with error and the register contains a variable Y and an identifier Z_2 that is also measured with error. The true identifier is denoted by Z. We want to study the relation between X and Y or in general statistics defined for the joint distribution of X, Y. In fact, we show that the joint distribution of X, Y is (non-parametrically) identified, if the matching probabilities are available.

The data are generated as follows. First, a sample of size N_2 is drawn from the joint distribution of X, Y, Z. This sample is the register. Next, we generate the mismeasured identifiers Z_1, Z_2, e.g. according to (1) or some other record generating model discussed in the previous section. We observe Y_j, Z_{2j}, $j = 1, \dots, N_2$. The next step is to draw $N_1 < N_2$ observations from the register without replacement. This is the sample, for which we observe X_i, Z_{1i}, $i = 1, \dots, N_1$. Note that in this case all members in the sample are represented in the register.

The bias induced by the matching errors depends on the relation between the mismeasured identifier and the variables of interest. For instance, if the identifier is a (misreported) social security number, then it is reasonable to assume that both the identifier Z and the observed values Z_1, Z_2 are independent of the variables of interest. If, in addition, there is a subsample with correctly reported identifiers $Z_1 = Z_2 = Z$, e.g. the subsample with $Z_1 = Z_2$ (this is an assumption), then this subsample is a random sample from the joint distribution of the variables of interest. However, often common variables beside the identifier are used to match units i and j with $z_{1i} \neq z_{2j}$, e.g. we match i and j if z_{1i} and z_{2j} are close and i and j have the same gender, age, and location etc. Note that the additional common variables need not be observed with error in the two samples. However, the probability that the match is correct depends on these additional common variables that in general are correlated with variables of interest. In this case, even if we can identify a subsample in which all matches are correct, this subsample is not a random sample from the joint distribution of the variables of interest.

Here we only consider the case that Z, Z_1, Z_2 are independent of X, Y. The general case can be analyzed in much the same way. Note that this is the simplest case for probabilistic record linkage. There is an interesting contrast with statistical matching, as discussed in the next section, because there the quality of the approximation relies heavily on the correlation between the identifiers and the variables of interest.

The quality of the matches depends on the matching method that in turn depends on the record generating model. We use the same example that was considered in Section 2.2.1. The record generating model is as in (1) and Z, ε_1 and ε_2 are all independently normally distributed. Under these assumptions i in the sample is matched with $\phi(i)$ in the register if and only if $|z_{2\phi(i)} - z_{1i}| < C$ with C determined e.g. as in (16) or by some other rule. We can derive an expression for the probability that the match is correct given that we use this matching rule, i.e. the probability of the event that $Z_i = Z_{\phi(i)}$ given that $|Z_{2\phi(i)} - Z_{1i}| \leqslant C$. Substitution of (1) and using the independence of the reporting errors and the true value gives by Bayes' theorem

$$\begin{aligned}
&\Pr(M_{i\phi(i)} = 1) \\
&\quad = \Pr\big(Z_i = Z_{\phi(i)} \mid |Z_{2\phi(i)} - Z_{1i}| \leqslant C\big) \\
&\quad = \frac{\Pr(Z_i = Z_{\phi(i)}) \Pr(|\varepsilon_{2\phi(i)} - \varepsilon_{1i}| < C)}{\Pr(Z_i = Z_{\phi(i)}) \Pr(|\varepsilon_{2\phi(i)} - \varepsilon_{1i}| < C) + \Pr(Z_i \neq Z_{\phi(i)}) \Pr(|Z_{\phi(i)} + \varepsilon_{2\phi(i)} - Z_i - \varepsilon_{1i}| < C)} \\
&\quad = \frac{\frac{1}{N_2}\Phi\big(\frac{C}{\sqrt{\sigma_1^2+\sigma_2^2}}\big)}{\frac{1}{N_2}\Phi\big(\frac{C}{\sqrt{\sigma_1^2+\sigma_2^2}}\big) + \frac{N_2-1}{N_2}\Phi\big(\frac{C}{\sqrt{\sigma_1^2+\sigma_2^2+2\sigma^2}}\big)}. \qquad (18)
\end{aligned}$$

This expression for the probability of a correct match under the given matching rule has a Bayesian flavor. The probability of a correct match, if a unit in the sample is matched at random with a unit in the register is $\frac{1}{N_2}$. This is also the limit of the probability of a correct match if $C \to \infty$. The probability decreases in C. If $C \downarrow 0$ we obtain the limit

$$\frac{\frac{1}{N_2}}{\frac{1}{N_2} + \frac{N_2-1}{N_2}\sqrt{\frac{\sigma_1^2+\sigma_2^2}{\sigma_1^2+\sigma_2^2+2\sigma^2}}} \qquad (19)$$

and this probability approaches 1 if the reporting error in the identifier is small. Hence, we improve on random matching by using the noisy identifiers. Of course, if we choose C too small, there will be few matches. As will be seen below, the variance of estimators is inversely proportional to the probability of a correct match, so that if our goal is to estimate parameters accurately we face a trade-off between the number of matched observations and the probability that the match is correct. Although this analysis is for a specific record generating model, the trade-off is present in all matched samples.

If we match i in the sample to $\phi(i)$ in the register, if $|Z_{2\phi(i)} - Z_{1i}| \leqslant C$, then the conditional probability of a correct match given the identifiers Z_1, Z_2 is

$$\begin{aligned}
&\Pr\big(M_{i\phi(i)} = 1 \mid Z_{1i}, Z_{2\phi(i)}\big) \\
&\quad = \Pr\big(Z_i = Z_{\phi(i)} \mid |Z_{2\phi(i)} - Z_{1i}| \leqslant C, Z_{1i}, Z_{2\phi(i)}\big)
\end{aligned}$$

$$= \frac{\Pr(M_{i\phi(i)} = 1)\phi_1(Z_{2\phi(i)} - Z_{1i})}{\Pr(M_{i\phi(i)} = 1)\phi_1(Z_{2\phi(i)} - Z_{1i}) + \Pr(M_{i\phi(i)} = 0)\phi_2(Z_{2\phi(i)} - Z_{1i})} \tag{20}$$

with

$$\phi_1(Z_{2\phi(i)} - Z_{1i}) = \phi\big(Z_{2\phi(i)} - Z_{1i} \,\big|\, |Z_{2\phi(i)} - Z_{1i}| \leqslant C; \sigma_1^2 + \sigma_2^2\big),$$
$$\phi_2(Z_{2\phi(i)} - Z_{1i}) = \phi\big(Z_{2\phi(i)} - Z_{1i} \,\big|\, |Z_{2\phi(i)} - Z_{1i}| \leqslant C; 2\sigma^2 + \sigma_1^2 + \sigma_2^2\big).$$

Now we are in a position to discuss estimation. Consider a pair $i, \phi(i)$ matched according to a matching rule, e.g. the rule above, from the $N_1 \times N_2$ possible pairs. The joint distribution of $X_i, Z_{1i}, Y_{\phi(i)}, Z_{2\phi(i)}$ has density $g(x_i, z_{1i}, y_{\phi(i)}, z_{2\phi(i)})$ with

$$g(x_i, z_{1i}, y_{\phi(i)}, z_{2\phi(i)}) = g(x_i, z_{1i}, y_{\phi(i)}, z_{2\phi(i)}, M_{i\phi(i)} = 1) + g(x_i, z_{1i}, y_{\phi(i)}, z_{2\phi(i)}, M_{i\phi(i)} = 0). \tag{21}$$

If the joint density of X, Y is $f(x, y)$, then because we assume that X, Y and Z, Z_1, Z_2 are independent,

$$g(x_i, z_{1i}, y_{\phi(i)}, z_{2\phi(i)}, M_{i\phi(i)} = 1) = f(x_i, y_{\phi(i)}) \Pr(M_{i\phi(i)} = 1 \mid z_{1i}, z_{2\phi(i)}) g(z_{1i}, z_{2\phi(i)}) \tag{22}$$

and

$$g(x_i, z_{1i}, y_{\phi(i)}, z_{2\phi(i)}, M_{i\phi(i)} = 0) = f_1(x_i) f_2(y_{\phi(i)}) \Pr(M_{i\phi(i)} = 0 \mid z_{1i}, z_{2\phi(i)}) g(z_{1i}, z_{2\phi(i)}). \tag{23}$$

Substituting (22) and (23) in (21), and using $g(x_i, z_{1i}, y_{\phi(i)}, z_{2\phi(i)}) = f(x_i, y_{\phi(i)}) \times g(z_{1i}, z_{2\phi(i)})$, we can solve for $f(x_i, y_{\phi(i)})$

$$\begin{aligned} f(x_i, y_{\phi(i)}) &= \frac{g(x_i, y_{\phi(i)}) - \Pr(M_{i\phi(i)} = 0 \mid z_{1i}, z_{2\phi(i)}) f_1(x_i) f_2(y_{\phi(i)})}{\Pr(M_{i\phi(i)} = 1 \mid z_{1i}, z_{2\phi(i)})} \\ &= f_1(x_i) f_2(y_{\phi(i)}) + \frac{g(x_i, y_{\phi(i)}) - f_1(x_i) f_2(y_{\phi(i)})}{\Pr(M_{i\phi(i)} = 1 \mid z_{1i}, z_{2\phi(i)})} \end{aligned} \tag{24}$$

if the denominator is greater than 0, which is the case for any sensible matching rule.

The distributions on the right-hand side of this expression are all observed. Hence this identification result is non-parametric, although it requires that the matching probabilities are known or that they can be estimated.

Often we are not interested in the joint distribution of Y, X, but in a population parameter θ_0 that is the unique solution to a vector of population moment conditions

$$\mathrm{E}\big[m(X_i, Y_i; \theta)\big] = 0. \tag{25}$$

These population moment conditions refer to the correctly matched observations. If two observations are incorrectly matched, they are stochastically independent. In general for $i \neq j$

$$\mathrm{E}\big[m(X_i, Y_j; \theta)\big] = 0 \tag{26}$$

is solved by $\theta_1 \neq \theta_0$. In other words, the parameter cannot be identified from the two marginal distributions.

The solution for the joint population distribution in (24) suggests the sample moment conditions that combine information from the sample and the register

$$\frac{1}{N_1}\sum_{i=1}^{N_1} \frac{m(x_i, y_{\phi(i)}; \theta)}{\Pr(M_{i\phi(i)} = 1 \mid z_{1i}, z_{2\phi(i)})} - \frac{1}{N_1^2}\sum_{j=1}^{N_1}\sum_{k=1}^{N_1} \frac{1 - \Pr(M_{j\phi(k)} = 1 \mid z_{1j}, z_{2\phi(k)})}{\Pr(M_{j\phi(k)} = 1 \mid z_{1j}, z_{2\phi(k)})} m(x_j, y_{\phi(k)}; \theta) \tag{27}$$

and the weighted GMM estimator of θ either makes (27) equal to 0 or is the minimizer of a quadratic form in these sample moment conditions. In this expression (but not in (24)) it is implicitly assumed that the probability that a unit in the sample is matched with two or more units in the register is negligible. This simplifies the notation.

We obtain a particularly simple result if we use the identifiers to match the sample to the register, but ignore them in the inference, i.e. in (21) we start with the joint distribution of $X_i, Y_{\phi(i)}$, so that

$$f(x_i, y_{\phi(i)}) = f_1(x_i) f_2(y_{\phi(i)}) + \frac{g(x_i, y_{\phi(i)}) - f_1(x_i) f_2(y_{\phi(i)})}{\Pr(M_{i\phi(i)} = 1)}.$$

This will give consistent, but less efficient, estimates. Let the probability of a correct match $\Pr(M_{i\phi(i)} = 1) = \lambda$. If X and Y have mean 0, then

$$\operatorname{cov}(X_i, Y_i) = \frac{\operatorname{cov}(X_i, Y_{\phi(i)})}{\lambda}. \tag{28}$$

With the same assumption we find for the moment conditions of a simple linear regression with an intercept

$$\mathrm{E}\big[(Y_i - \alpha - \beta X_i)X_i\big] = \frac{\mathrm{E}[(Y_{\phi(i)} - \alpha - \beta X_i)X_i] - (1-\lambda)[\mathrm{E}(Y_{\phi(i)})\mathrm{E}(X_i) - \alpha\mathrm{E}(X_i) - \beta\mathrm{E}(X_i^2)]}{\lambda}, \tag{29}$$

$$\mathrm{E}[Y_i - \alpha - \beta X_i] = \frac{\mathrm{E}[Y_{\phi(i)} - \alpha - \beta X_i] - (1-\lambda)[\mathrm{E}(Y_{\phi(i)}) - \alpha - \beta\mathrm{E}(X_i)]}{\lambda} = \mathrm{E}[Y_{\phi(i)} - \alpha - \beta X_i]. \tag{30}$$

Setting these conditions equal to 0 and solving for the parameters we find that

$$\beta = \frac{\operatorname{cov}(X_i, Y_{\phi(i)})}{\lambda \operatorname{var}(X_i)},$$

$$\alpha = \mathrm{E}(Y_{\phi(i)}) - \beta \mathrm{E}(X_i) \tag{31}$$

and, if we substitute the sample statistics for the population statistics, we obtain the estimator suggested by Neter, Maynes and Ramanathan (1965) and Scheuren and Winkler (1993). The results in this section generalize their results to arbitrary moment conditions and less restrictive assumptions on the sampling process. In particular, we show that the matching probabilities that are computed for probabilistic linkage can be used to compute the moment conditions for the matched population. This is important because the simulation results in Scheuren and Winkler (1993) show that the bias induced by false matches can be large.

The asymptotic variance of the estimator for β is

$$\mathrm{var}(\hat{\beta}) = \frac{\sigma^2}{N_1 \lambda^2 \, \mathrm{var}(X)}. \tag{32}$$

The variance decreases with the matching probability. The GMM estimator is consistent if the matching probability is positive.

3. Independent samples with common variables

3.1. Fréchet bounds and conditional Fréchet bounds on the joint distribution

Exact or probabilistic matching is not advisable if the fraction of units that are in both samples is small. If the fraction is negligible, we may treat the two random samples as independent samples that have no units in common. Although exact or probabilistic matching produces more informative data, the fear that linked files pose a threat to the privacy of individuals who, with some effort, may be identifiable from the linked records, has prevented the large scale matching of administrative and survey data.[4] As a consequence, often the only available samples that contain all relevant variables are relatively small random samples from a large population. It is safe to assume that these random samples have no common units.

The two independent random samples identify the marginal distributions of X, Z (sample A) and Y, Z (sample B). If there are no common variables Z, the marginal distributions put some restrictions on the joint distribution of X, Y. These Fréchet (1951) bounds on the joint distribution are not very informative. For example, if the marginal and joint distributions are all normal, there is no restriction on the correlation coefficient of X and Y, i.e. it can take any value between -1 and 1.

[4] Fellegi (1999) notes that public concern with file linkage varies over place and time and that, ironically, the concern is larger if the linkage is performed by government agencies than if private firms are involved. Modern data acquisition methods like barcode scanners and the internet result in large files that are suitable for linkage.

With common variables Z the Fréchet bounds can be improved. The bounds for the joint conditional cdf of X, Y given $Z = z$ are

$$\max\{F(x \mid z) + F(y \mid z) - 1, 0\} \leqslant F(x, y \mid z) \leqslant \min\{F(x \mid z), F(y \mid z)\}. \quad (33)$$

Taking the expectation over the distribution of the common variables Z we obtain

$$\mathrm{E}[\max\{F(x \mid Z) + F(y \mid Z) - 1, 0\}] \\ \leqslant F(x, y) \leqslant \mathrm{E}[\min\{F(x \mid Z), F(y \mid Z)\}]. \quad (34)$$

The bounds are sharp, because the lower and upper bounds, $\mathrm{E}[\max\{F(x \mid Z) + F(y \mid Z) - 1, 0\}]$ and $\mathrm{E}[\min\{F(x \mid Z), F(y \mid Z)\}]$ are joint cdf's of X, Y with marginal cdf's equal to $F(x)$ and $F(y)$. Note that because the expectation of the maximum is greater than the maximum of the expectations (the reverse relation holds for the expectation of the minimum), the Fréchet bounds with common variables are narrower than those without. If either X or Y are fully determined by Z, then the joint cdf is identified. To see this let the conditional distribution of X given $Z = z$ be degenerate in $x(z)$. Define $A(x) = \{z \mid x(z) \leqslant x\}$. Then $F(x \mid z) = 1$ if $z \in A(x)$ and $F(x \mid z) = 0$ if $z \in A(x)^c$. Substitution in (34) gives that the lower and upper bounds coincide and that

$$F(x, y) = \mathrm{E}[F(y \mid Z) \mid Z \in A(x)] \Pr(Z \in A(x)). \quad (35)$$

In the special case that the population distribution of X, Y, Z is trivariate normal, the only parameter that cannot be identified is the correlation between X and Y. We have

$$\rho_{XY} = \rho_{XY|Z}\sqrt{1 - \rho_{XZ}^2}\sqrt{1 - \rho_{YZ}^2} + \rho_{XZ}\rho_{YZ}. \quad (36)$$

This gives the bounds

$$\rho_{XZ}\rho_{YZ} - \sqrt{1 - \rho_{XZ}^2}\sqrt{1 - \rho_{YZ}^2} \\ \leqslant \rho_{XY} \leqslant \rho_{XZ}\rho_{YZ} + \sqrt{1 - \rho_{XZ}^2}\sqrt{1 - \rho_{YZ}^2}. \quad (37)$$

The lower bound reaches its minimum -1 if $\rho_{XZ} = -\rho_{YZ}$ (the upper bound is $1 - 2\rho_{XZ}^2$) and the upper bound reaches its maximum 1 if $\rho_{XZ} = \rho_{YZ}$ (the lower bound is $-1 + 2\rho_{XZ}^2$. Also if either ρ_{XZ} or ρ_{YZ} is equal to 1, then $\rho_{XY} = \rho_{XZ}\rho_{YZ}$. The length of the interval is $2\sqrt{1 - \rho_{XZ}^2}\sqrt{1 - \rho_{YZ}^2}$ and hence the bound is more informative if the correlation between either Z and X or Z and Y is high.

An example illustrates how much correlation between X, Y and Z is required to narrow bounds. Consider a linear regression model

$$Y = \alpha + \beta X + U \quad (38)$$

where X and U are independent and normally distributed. If σ_X, σ_Y denote the standard deviation of X and Y, respectively, we have

$$\frac{\sigma_Y}{\sigma_X} = \frac{|\beta|}{\sqrt{R^2}} \quad (39)$$

with R^2 the coefficient of determination of the regression. If we multiply the bounds in (37) by $\frac{\sigma_Y}{\sigma_X}$ we obtain an interval for the slope β. If p denotes the relative (with respect to β) length of the interval and we consider the case that the correlation between X and Z and Y and Z are equal, we obtain the following expression for the required correlation

$$\rho_{XZ} = \sqrt{1 - \frac{p\sqrt{R^2}}{2}}. \tag{40}$$

The correlation decreases with R^2 and the (relative) length of the interval for β. For instance, if we want a 0.20 relative length for a regression with an R^2 of 0.9, we need that $\rho_{XZ} = \rho_{YZ} = 0.95$. In general, the correlation that is needed to obtain informative bounds is rather high, and this illustrates the limited information about the relation between X and Y in the combined sample.

The Fréchet bounds on the joint cdf in (34) treat the variables X and Y symmetrically. As the notation suggests, often Y is the dependent and X the independent variable in a relation between these variables, and we focus on the conditional distribution of Y given X. An important reason to do this, is that we may assume that this conditional distribution is invariant under a change in the marginal distribution of X. For example, Cross and Manski (2002) consider the case that Y is the fraction of votes for a party and X is the indicator of an ethnic group. It is assumed that the ethnic groups vote in the same way in elections, but that the ethnic composition of the voters changes over time. If we have the marginal distributions of Y (election results by precinct) and X (ethnic composition by precinct), what can we say about future election results, if we have a prediction of the future composition of the population, i.e. the future marginal distribution of X?

Horowitz and Manski (1995) and Cross and Manski (2002) have derived bounds for the case that X is a discrete variable with distribution

$$\Pr(X = x_k) = p_k, \quad k = 1, \ldots, K. \tag{41}$$

We first derive their bounds for the case that there are no common variables Z. They consider bounds on the conditional expectation

$$\mathrm{E}\big[g\big(h(Y), X\big) \mid X = x\big]$$

with g bounded and monotone in h for almost all x. A special case is $g(h(Y), X) = I(Y \leqslant y)$ which gives the conditional cdf. Because the conditional expectation above is continuous and increasing in $F(y \mid x)$, in the sense that the expectation with respect to $F_1(y \mid x)$ is not smaller than that with respect to $F_2(Y \mid x)$, if $F_1(y \mid x)$ first-order stochastically dominates $F_2(y \mid x)$, we can derive bounds on this expectation from bounds on the conditional cdf.

In the sequel we derive bounds both on the conditional cdf $F(y \mid x)$ and on $F(y; x_k) = \Pr(Y \leqslant y, X = x_k)$. We first derive bounds on these cdf's for a given k.

Next we consider the K-vector of these cdf's. Note that by the law of total probability

$$\sum_{k=1}^{K} F(y; x_k) = F(y)$$

which imposes an additional restriction on the vector $F(y; x_k)$, $k = 1, \ldots, K$.

The Fréchet bounds on $F(y; x_k)$ are

$$\max\{F(y) - (1 - p_k), 0\} \leqslant F(y; x_k) \leqslant \min\{F(y), p_k\}. \tag{42}$$

For each k these bounds are sharp, because both the lower and upper bound are increasing in y, and they both increase from 0 to p_k, i.e. they are $\tilde{F}(y; x_k)$ for some random variables $\tilde{Y}$ and $\tilde{X}$.

The bounds in (42) imply that if $p_k \leqslant \frac{1}{2}$

$$\begin{aligned}
&0 \leqslant F(y; x_k) \leqslant F(y), \quad y < F^{-1}(p_k),\\
&0 \leqslant F(y; x_k) \leqslant p_k, \quad F^{-1}(p_k) \leqslant y < F^{-1}(1 - p_k),\\
&F(y) - (1 - p_k) \leqslant F(y; x_k) \leqslant p_k, \quad y \geqslant F^{-1}(1 - p_k),
\end{aligned} \tag{43}$$

with an obvious change if $p_k > \frac{1}{2}$. Upon division by p_k we obtain bounds on the conditional cdf of Y given $X = x_k$

$$\begin{aligned}
&0 \leqslant F(y \mid x_k) \leqslant \frac{F(y)}{p_k}, \quad y < F^{-1}(p_k),\\
&0 \leqslant F(y \mid x_k) \leqslant 1, \quad F^{-1}(p_k) \leqslant y < F^{-1}(1 - p_k),\\
&\frac{F(y) - (1 - p_k)}{p_k} \leqslant F(y \mid x_k) \leqslant 1, \quad y \geqslant F^{-1}(1 - p_k).
\end{aligned} \tag{44}$$

The bounds have an appealing form. The lower bound is the left truncated cdf of Y where the truncation point is the $(1-p_k)$th quantile of the distribution of Y and the upper bound is the right truncated cdf with truncation point equal to the p_kth quantile. These bounds on the conditional cdf of Y were derived by Horowitz and Manski (1995) and Cross and Manski (2002). They are essentially Fréchet bounds on the joint distribution.

Next, we consider bounds on the vector $F(y; .) = (F(y; x_1) \ldots F(y; x_K))'$. For $K = 2$ the bounds in (42) are (without loss of generality we assume $p_1 < \frac{1}{2}$, i.e. $p_2 = 1 - p_1 > p_1$)

$$\begin{aligned}
&0 \leqslant F(y; x_1) \leqslant F(y), \quad y < F^{-1}(p_1),\\
&0 \leqslant F(y; x_1) \leqslant p_1, \quad F^{-1}(p_1) \leqslant y < F^{-1}(p_2),\\
&F(y) - p_2 \leqslant F(y; x_1) \leqslant p_1, \quad y \geqslant F^{-1}(p_2),\\
&0 \leqslant F(y; x_2) \leqslant F(y), \quad y < F^{-1}(p_1),\\
&F(y) - p_1 \leqslant F(y; x_2) \leqslant F(y), \quad F^{-1}(p_1) \leqslant y < F^{-1}(p_2),\\
&F(y) - p_1 \leqslant F(y; x_2) \leqslant p_2, \quad y \geqslant F^{-1}(p_2).
\end{aligned} \tag{45}$$

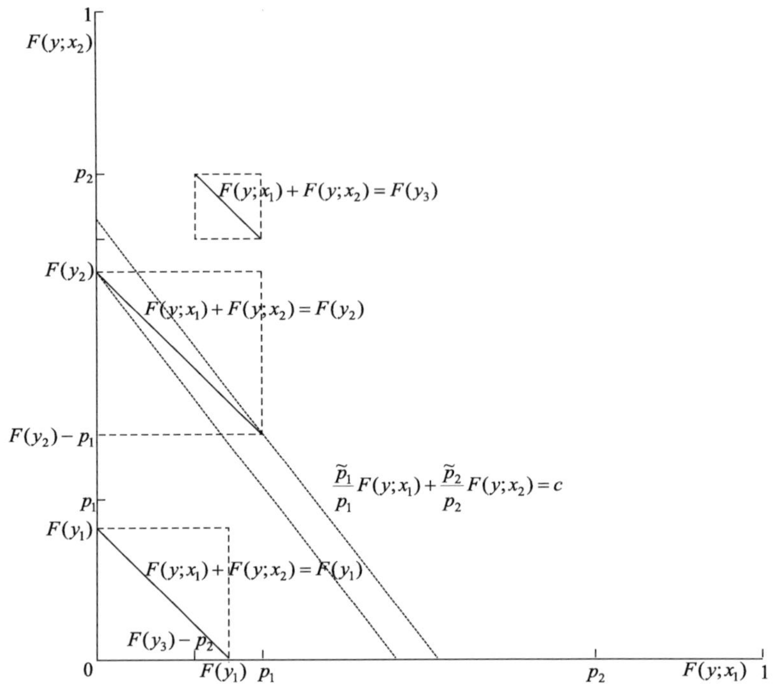

Figure 1. Bounds on $(F(y;x_1), F(y;x_2))$ for three values of y.

By the law of total probability $F(y;.)$ satisfies for all y

$$\sum_{k=1}^{K} F(y;x_k) = F(y). \tag{46}$$

Hence, the vector of conditional cdf's is in a set that is the intersection of the Fréchet bounds in (45) and the hyperplane in (46). The resulting bounds on $(F(y;x_1), F(y;x_2))$ are given in Figure 1 for three values of y with $y_1 < F^{-1}(p_1)$, $F^{-1}(p_1) \leqslant y_2 < F^{-1}(p_2)$, and $y_3 \geqslant F^{-1}(p_2)$. The Fréchet bounds on $(F(y;x_1), F(y;x_2))$ are the squares. The law of total probability selects two vertices of these squares as the extreme points of the set of $(F(y;x_1), F(y;x_2))$ that satisfy both the Fréchet bounds and the law of total probability. Bounds on the conditional cdf's $F(y \mid x_1)$ and $F(y \mid x_2)$ are obtained upon division by p_1 and p_2, respectively. This amounts to a change in the units in Figure 1 and except for that the figure is unchanged.

From (45) the lower bound on $F(y;x_1)$ is

$$F_L(y;x_1) = \begin{cases} 0, & y < F^{-1}(p_2), \\ F(y) - p_2, & y \geqslant F^{-1}(p_2), \end{cases}$$

and the upper bound is

$$F_U(y;x_1) = \begin{cases} F(y), & y < F^{-1}(p_1), \\ p_1, & y \geqslant F^{-1}(p_1). \end{cases}$$

Note that both the lower and upper bound increase from 0 to p_1 with y, and hence are equal to $\tilde{F}(y;x_1)$ for some random variables $\tilde{Y}$ and $\tilde{X}$. The corresponding upper and lower bounds on $F(y;x_2)$ are $F_U(y;x_2) = F(y) - F_L(y;x_1)$ and $F_L(y;x_2) = F(y) - F_U(y;x_1)$, and these bounds are equal to $\tilde{F}(y;x_2)$ for some random variables $\tilde{Y}$ and $\tilde{X}$. This establishes that the bounds are sharp. A general proof of this statement can be found in Cross and Manski.

The bounds on the conditional cdf's $F(y \mid x_1)$ and $F(y \mid x_2)$ are also given in Figure 2. By the law of total probability, the lower bound of $F(y \mid x_1)$ corresponds with upper bound of $F(y \mid x_2)$ and the other way around. Note that the bounds are narrower for $F(y \mid x_2)$ because x_2 has a higher probability than x_1. From this figure we can obtain bounds on the conditional median of Y given X. We find that the change in this conditional median has bounds

$$\begin{aligned} F^{-1}\left(\frac{1}{2} - \frac{1}{2}p_1\right) - F^{-1}\left(1 - \frac{1}{2}p_1\right) &\leqslant \operatorname{med}(Y \mid x_2) - \operatorname{med}(Y \mid x_1) \\ &\leqslant F^{-1}\left(\frac{1}{2} + \frac{1}{2}p_1\right) - F^{-1}\left(\frac{1}{2}p_1\right). \end{aligned} \tag{47}$$

Note that the lower bound is negative and the upper bound positive for all p_1, so that it is impossible to sign the change of the conditional median with this information. This suggests that the relation between Y and X cannot be inferred from two marginal distributions without common variables.

If $K \geqslant 3$ the bounds can be derived in the same way. First, we order the p_k by increasing size. Next, we find the hypercubes that correspond to the Fréchet bounds on $F(y; .)$. As in Figure 1 the vertices depend on the value of y, i.e. for which k we have $F^{-1}(p_k) \leqslant y < F^{-1}(p_{k+1})$. Finally, we select the vertices that satisfy the law of total probability. These are the extreme points of the set of admissible $F(y;x_k)$, $k = 1, \ldots, K$. To be precise, the set is the convex hull of these extreme points. As we shall see below, for prediction purposes it is sufficient to find the vertices.

The main reason for bounds on the conditional cdf of Y given X, instead of on the joint cdf of Y, X, is that it is usually assumed that the conditional cdf is invariant with respect to changes in the distribution of X. Of course, this is a common assumption in conditional econometric models with fixed parameters. An obvious application is to conditional prediction. Cross and Manski consider the prediction of the outcome of a future election assuming that the voting behavior of demographic groups remains the same, but that the composition of the population changes and the future composition of the population can be predicted accurately.

The predicted distribution of the future outcome $\tilde{F}(y)$ satisfies

$$\tilde{F}(y) = F(y;x_1)\frac{\tilde{p}_1}{p_1} + F(y;x_2)\frac{\tilde{p}_2}{p_2} \tag{48}$$

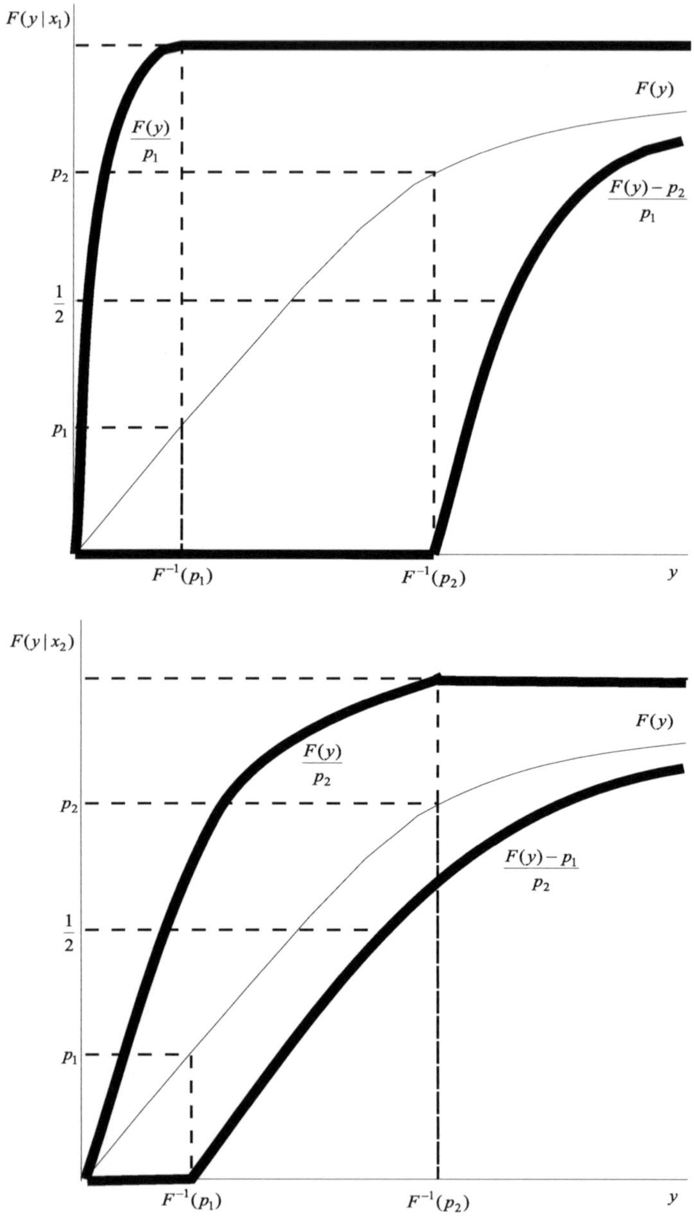

Figure 2. Bounds on $F(y \mid x_1)$ and $F(y \mid x_2)$.

with $\tilde{p}_1$ the future fraction with $X = x_1$. Again, without loss of generality we assume $p_1 < \frac{1}{2}$. We can further distinguish between $\tilde{p}_1 \leqslant p_1$ and $\tilde{p}_1 > p_1$. In the former case the bounds on the predicted cdf can be found as in Figure 1. In that figure we indicate the bounds for $F^{-1}(p_1) \leqslant y < F^{-1}(p_2)$. The bounds are obtained by intersecting the set of feasible $(F(y; x_1), F(y; x_2))$ with (48). We find

$$\frac{\tilde{p}_1}{p_1}F(y) \leqslant \tilde{F}(y) \leqslant \min\left\{\frac{\tilde{p}_2}{p_2}F(y), 1\right\}, \quad y < F^{-1}(p_1),$$
$$1 - \frac{\tilde{p}_2}{p_2}\big(1 - F(y)\big) \leqslant \tilde{F}(y) \leqslant \min\left\{\frac{\tilde{p}_2}{p_2}F(y), 1\right\}, \quad F^{-1}(p_1) \leqslant y < F^{-1}(p_2),$$
$$1 - \frac{\tilde{p}_2}{p_2}\big(1 - F(y)\big) \leqslant \tilde{F}(y) \leqslant 1 - \frac{\tilde{p}_1}{p_1}\big(1 - F(y)\big), \quad y \geqslant F^{-1}(p_2). \tag{49}$$

As is obvious from Figure 1, the bounds increase with the difference between p_1 and $\tilde{p}_1$. For $K \geqslant 3$ the bounds on the predicted cdf are found by evaluating

$$\sum_{k=1}^{K} \frac{\tilde{p}_k}{p_k} F(y; x_k) \tag{50}$$

at the extreme points of the set of feasible $F(y; .)$.

As noted, a key assumption in the derivation of the bounds is that X is a discrete variable. From (44) it is obvious that the bounds on the conditional cdf become uninformative if p_k goes to 0, i.e. the bounds become $0 \leqslant F(y \mid x_k) \leqslant 1$ for all y. Hence, if X is close to continuous the bounds on the conditional cdf's are not useful. If the support of Y is bounded, e.g. if it is a dichotomous variable, then the bounds on the support can be used to obtain bounds on conditional expectations. Such bounds are of a different nature and beyond the scope of this chapter.

3.2. Statistical matching of independent samples

The Fréchet bounds exhaust the information on the joint distribution of X, Y. If we merge the samples A and B no information is added, and our knowledge of the joint distribution of X and Y does not increase. How much we can learn about the joint distribution of X, Y is completely determined by the relation between X and Z in sample A and that between Y and Z in sample B.

In spite of this, the temptation to match two samples that do not have common units as if they were two samples with a substantial degree of overlap has been irresistible. A number of authors have proposed methods for this type of file matching [Okner (1972), Ruggles and Ruggles (1974), Radner (1974), Ruggles, Ruggles and Wolff (1977), Barr and Turner (1978), Kadane (1978); see also the survey in Radner et al. (1980)]. These methods are direct applications of those that are used in the reconstruction of broken random samples and probabilistic matching. Let the sample A be $x_i, z_{1i}, i = 1, \ldots, N_1$, and the sample B be $y_i, z_{2i}, i = 1, \ldots, N_2$. The vectors z_1 and z_2 contain the same variables and the subscript only indicates whether the observation is in sample A or B. Because the samples A and B do not contain common units, the fact that z_{1i} and z_{2j} are close does not imply that they refer to the same unit or even similar (except for these variables) units. If we match unit i in A to unit j in B we must decide which of the vectors z_{1i} or z_{2j} we include in the matched file. If we use the observation for file A, then this file is referred as the base file, and file B is called the supplemental file.

The two methods that have been used in the literature are constrained and unconstrained matching. Both methods require the specification of a distance function $D(z_{1i}, z_{2j})$. In (9) (for broken random sample) and (17) (for probabilistic record linkage) we specify the distance function as a quadratic function of the difference, but other choices are possible.[5] In practice, one must also decide on which variables to include in the comparison, i.e. in the z vector. The Fréchet bounds suggest that the joint distribution of X, Y is best approximated, if the correlation between either X or Y and Z or the R^2 in a regression of either X or Y on Z is maximal. Often, the units that can be matched are restricted to, e.g. units that have the same gender. In that case gender is called a cohort variable.

With constrained matching every unit in sample A is matched to exactly one unit in sample B. Often A and B do not have an equal number of units. However, both are random samples from a population and hence the sampling fraction for both samples is known (assume for the moment that the sample is obtained by simple random sampling). The inverse of the sampling fraction is the sample weight, w_A for sample A and w_B for sample B. Assume that the weights are integers. Then we can replicate the units in sample A w_A times and those in sample B w_B times to obtain two new samples that have the same number of units M (equal to the population size). Now we match the units in these samples as if they were a broken random sample, i.e. we minimize over d_{ij}, $i = 1, \ldots, M$, $j = 1, \ldots, M$, with $d_{ij} = 1$ if i and j are matched

$$\sum_{i=1}^{M} \sum_{j=1}^{M} d_{ij} D(z_{1i}, z_{2j}) \tag{51}$$

subject to

$$\sum_{k=1}^{M} d_{ik} = 1,$$

$$\sum_{k=1}^{M} d_{kj} = 1, \tag{52}$$

for all $i = 1, \ldots, M$, $j = 1, \ldots, M$. If we choose distance function (9) we obtain the same solution as in a broken random sample. Of course, there is little justification for this matching method if the samples A and B have no common units.

[5] Rodgers (1984) finds no systematic differences in the performance of distance functions, although he comments that the Mahalanobis distance using an estimated variance matrix does not perform well.

The method of constrained matching was first proposed by Barr and Turner (1978). An advantage of this method is that the marginal distributions of X and Y in the merged file are the same as those in the samples A and B. A disadvantage is that the optimization problem in (51) is computationally burdensome.

In unconstrained matching the base file A and the supplemental file B are treated asymmetrically. To every unit i in file A we match the unit j in file B, possibly restricted to some subset defined by cohort variables, that minimizes $D(z_{1i}, z_{2j})$. It is possible that some unit in B is matched to more than one unit in A, and that some units in B are not matched to any unit in A. As a consequence, the distribution of Z_2, Y in the matched file may differ from that in the original sample B. Note that if we use the distance function (17), unconstrained matching is formally identical to probabilistic record linkage. Of course, there is no justification for this method, if the samples A and B have no common units. The first application of unconstrained matching was by Okner (1972) who used the 1967 Survey of Economic Opportunity as the base file and the 1966 Tax File as the supplemental file to create a merged file that contained detailed data on the components of household income.

The merger of two files using either unconstrained or constrained matching has been criticized since its first use. In his comment on Okner's (1972) method, Sims (1972) noted that an implicit assumption on the conditional dependence of X, Y given Z is made, usually the assumption that X, Y are independent conditional on Z. A second problem is best explained if we consider matching as an imputation method for missing data. File A contains X, Z_1 and Y is missing. If we assume conditional independence, an imputed value of Y is a draw from the conditional distribution of Y given $Z_1 = z_1$. Such a draw can be obtained from file B, if for one of the units in file B $Z_2 = z_1$. If such a unit is not present in file B, we choose a unit with a value of Z_2 close to z_1. This is an imperfect imputation, and we can expect that the relation between Z_1 and Y in the merged file is biased. Indeed, Rodgers (1984) reports that the covariance between Z_1 and Y is underestimated, as one would expect. An alternative would be to estimate the relation between Y and Z_2 in sample B, e.g. by a linear regression, and use the predicted value for $Z_1 = z_1$, or preferably a draw from the estimated conditional distribution of Y given $Z_1 = z_1$, i.e. include the regression disturbance variability in the imputation.[6] The imputation becomes completely dependent on model assumptions, if the support of Z_1 is larger than that of Z_2. In general the distribution of X, Y, Z can only be recovered on the intersection of the supports of Z_1 and Z_2. If both samples are random samples from the same population, as we assume here, then the supports coincide.

It is possible to evaluate the quality of the data produced by a statistical match, by matching two independent subsamples from a larger dataset. The joint distribution in the matched sample can be compared to the joint distribution in the original dataset. Evaluation studies have been performed by, among others, Ruggles, Ruggles and Wolff (1977), and Rodgers and DeVol (1982). It comes as no surprise that the conclusion from

[6] Even better: also include the variability due to parameter uncertainty.

these evaluations is that the joint distribution of X, Y cannot be estimated from the joint marginal distributions of X, Z and Y, Z.

As noted, matching can be considered as an imputation method for missing data. Rubin (1986) has suggested that instead of merging the files A and B, it is preferable to concatenate them, and to impute the missing Y in file A and missing X in file B using the estimated relations between X and Z_1 (file A) and Y and Z_2 (file B). In particular, he suggests not to use a single draw from the (estimated) conditional distribution of X given $Z_1 = z_2$ and of Y given $Z_2 = z_1$, effectively assuming conditional independence, but to add draws from the distributions of X given $Z_1 = z_2, Y = y$ and Y given $Z_2 = z_1$, $X = x$ assuming a range of values for the conditional correlation. The resulting datasets reflects the uncertainty on the conditional correlation and the variability of parameter estimates over the imputations indicates the sensitivity of these estimates to assumptions on the conditional correlation. Further developments along these lines can be found in Raessler (2002).

4. Estimation from independent samples with common variables

4.1. Types of inference

Without further assumptions the (conditional) Fréchet bounds on the joint cdf is all that can be learned from the two samples. These bounds are usually not sufficiently narrow, unless the common variables are highly correlated with Y and X. In this section we explore what additional assumptions are needed to improve the inference.

We consider (i) conditional independence, and (ii) exclusion restrictions. Exclusion restrictions refer to the situation that the distribution of Y given X, Z is independent of a subvector Z_0^c of Z, and hence depends only on the other variables Z_0 in Z. We also consider both non-parametric inference, i.e. the goal is to estimate the joint distribution of Y, X, Z_0 or the conditional distribution of Y given X, Z_0 or moments of these distributions, and parametric inference, i.e. the joint distribution of Y, X, Z_0 or the conditional distribution of Y given X, Z_0 is in a parametric class. Parametric assumptions play an important role in inference from independent samples, a theme that is repeated in Section 5 on inference in repeated cross sections.

None of the methods discussed below requires that the two samples are merged. All computations can be done on the two samples separately.

4.2. Semi- and non-parametric inference

4.2.1. Conditional independence

If Y, X are stochastically independent given the common variables Z, then the joint density of X, Y is

$$f(x, y) = \mathrm{E}\big(f(x \mid Z) f(y \mid Z)\big). \tag{53}$$

Although the joint distribution is identified, often we just want to compute an expectation $\mathrm{E}(g(X, Y))$. We have

$$\mathrm{E}\big(g(X, Y)\big) = \mathrm{E}_{YZ}\big(\mathrm{E}\big(g(X, Y) \mid Y, Z\big)\big) = \mathrm{E}_{YZ}\big(\mathrm{E}\big(g(X, Y) \mid Z\big)\big), \tag{54}$$

where the last equality holds by conditional independence. Note that the inner conditional expectation is with respect to the distribution of X given Z that is identified from sample A, and that the outer expectation is with respect to the joint distribution of Y, Z that is identified from sample B. We implicitly assume that the distributions of Z_1 and Z_2 in the samples A and B are identical. This is true if both samples are from the same population.

For a fixed value of Y, we can estimate the inner conditional expectation by a non-parametric regression (e.g. kernel or series) estimator of $g(X, y)$ on Z using sample A. The estimator of $\mathrm{E}(g(X, Y))$ is then obtained by averaging this regression estimator over Y, Z in sample B. The analysis of this estimator is beyond the scope of this chapter. It is similar to the semi-parametric imputation estimator proposed by Imbens, Newey and Ridder (2004) and Chen, Hong and Tarozzi (2004) who establish semi-parametric efficiency for their estimator. Their results can be directly applied to this estimator. In the literature it has been suggested that for the estimation of $\mathrm{E}(g(X, Y))$ we must first estimate the joint distribution of X, Y [see Sims (1972) and Rubin (1986)], but this is not necessary. Note that a similar method can be used to estimate $\mathrm{E}(g(X, Y, Z_0))$ with Z_0 a subvector of Z.

4.2.2. Exclusion restrictions

If we are not prepared to assume that X, Y are conditionally independent given Z, we can only hope for bounds on the expected value $\mathrm{E}(g(X, Y, Z_0))$. Such bounds are given by Horowitz and Manski (1995) and Cross and Manski (2002) and can be derived in the same way as the bounds in Section 3.1. In particular, they derive bounds on $\mathrm{E}[g(h(Y, Z_0), X, Z_0) \mid X = x, Z_0 = z_0]$ with g bounded and monotone in h for (almost all) x, z_0.

We consider two possibilities: (i) the conditional distribution of Y given X, Z depends on all variables in Z, (ii) this conditional distribution only depends on a subvector Z_0 of Z and is independent of the other variables Z_0^c in Z. Note that the possibilities are expressed in terms of the conditional distribution of Y given X (and Z or Z_0). This suggests that Y is considered as the dependent variable and that X, Z are explanatory variables.

If assumption (i) applies, the bounds derived above are bounds on $F(y; . \mid Z = z)$ or $F(y \mid ., Z = z)$. If we are interested in $F(y; .)$ or $F(y \mid .)$, we have to average over the marginal distribution of Z or the conditional distribution of Z given $X = x_k$ ($F(y \mid X = x_k, Z)$ has to be averaged over this distribution). As noted in Section 3.1 this averaging results in narrower bounds, but as noted in that section the correlation between Y and Z and X and Z must be high to obtain informative bounds.

Assumption (ii) that states that the vector of common variables Z_0^c can be omitted from the relation between Y and X, Z is more promising. As stated, assumption (ii) focuses on conditional (in)dependence of Y and Z_0^c given X, Z_0. Alternatively, the assumption can be expressed as conditional mean (in)dependence or conditional quantile (in)dependence. In that case, we identify or obtain bounds on the conditional mean or quantile. We only discuss conditional (in)dependence. The derivation of bounds on the conditional mean from bounds on the conditional cdf is complicated by the fact that the conditional mean is not a continuous function of the conditional cdf. However, if the assumptions are expressed as restrictions on the conditional mean, this does not matter.

Assumption (ii) is an exclusion restriction. If we decompose $Z = (Z_0' Z_0^{c'})'$, then Z_0^c is excluded from the conditional distribution of Y given X, Z. Exclusion restrictions are powerful and often are sufficient to identify $F(y \mid x, z_0)$. We maintain the assumption that X is discrete. This simplifies the analysis substantially. This is not surprising, because non-parametric identification under exclusion restrictions is an inverse problem, and it is well known that inverse problems are much harder for continuous distributions [see, e.g. Newey and Powell (2003)]. First, we consider conditions under which $F(y \mid x, z_0)$ is non-parametrically identified. Next, we consider the underidentified case, and we show that we can find bounds that improve on the bounds that hold without an exclusion restriction.

Without loss of generality we omit Z_0. The common variable Z is excluded from the conditional cdf of Y given X, Z. We denote

$$\Pr(X = x_k \mid Z = z) = p_k(z). \tag{55}$$

With the exclusion restriction we have that for all z,

$$F(y \mid z) = \sum_{k=1}^{K} F(y \mid x_k) p_k(z). \tag{56}$$

If Z is also discrete, (56) is a linear system of equations with unknowns $F(y \mid x_k)$, i.e. K unknowns. Hence, this system has a unique solution if Z takes at least $L \geqslant K$ values and the $L \times K$ matrix, with (l, k)th component $p_k(z_l)$ has rank equal to K. In that case $F(y \mid .)$ is exactly identified. If the rank of this matrix is strictly greater than K (this requires that $L > K$), then the equation has no solution. Hence, if $L > K$ a test of the rank of the matrix, and in particular a test whether the rank is equal to K is a test of the overidentifying restrictions, or in other words, a test of the exclusion restriction. If the exclusion restriction is rejected, we can allow the conditional cdf of Y given X, Z to depend on Z. For instance, if X takes two values and Z contains two variables, of which the first takes two values and the second four, then we obtain an exactly identified model by allowing the conditional cdf to depend on the first variable in Z.

If X and Z take two values, i.e. $K = L = 2$, the solution to (56) is

$$F(y \mid x_1) = \frac{p_2(z_1) F(y \mid z_2) - p_2(z_2) F(y \mid z_1)}{p_1(z_2) - p_1(z_1)},$$

$$F(y \mid x_2) = \frac{p_1(z_2)F(y \mid z_1) - p_1(z_1)F(y \mid z_2)}{p_1(z_2) - p_1(z_1)}. \tag{57}$$

Note that this implies that

$$F(y \mid x_2) - F(y \mid x_1) = \frac{F(y \mid z_2) - F(y \mid z_1)}{p_1(z_2) - p_1(z_1)}. \tag{58}$$

If conditional cdf's are replaced by conditional expectations, this is the Wald estimator [Wald (1940)], which is the Instrumental Variable (IV) estimator for a dichotomous endogenous variable with a dichotomous instrument.

Solving (56) for the case that X is continuous is much harder. In effect, we have to find the components of a mixture in the case that the mixing distribution is known. The problem is that the solution is not continuous in $F(y \mid .)$ unless restrictions are imposed on these conditional distributions. For instance, if Z is independent of Y, X (exclusion restriction) and the joint distribution of Y, X is normal, then the covariance of Y, X can be recovered from

$$\mathrm{E}(Y \mid Z = z) = \mu_Y + \Sigma_{YX}\Sigma_{XX}^{-1}\bigl(\mathrm{E}(X \mid Z = z) - \mu_X\bigr). \tag{59}$$

with μ the mean and Σ the covariance matrix of the joint normal distribution. Further details on weaker restrictions can be found in Newey and Powell (2003).

The similarity of the non-parametric two-sample estimator and the corresponding IV estimator with endogenous X and Z as instrumental variable, can lead (and as will be noted in Section 4.4 has led) to much confusion. In particular, it does not mean that we should consider X as an endogenous variable.

If $L < K$ the conditional cdf $F(y \mid .)$ is not identified. In that case we can use the results in Horowitz and Manski (1995) and Cross and Manski (2002) to obtain bounds (see the discussion in Section 3.1). The exclusion restriction imposes additional restrictions on the conditional cdf. Figure 3 illustrates these bounds for the case $K = 3$, $L = 2$. In this figure the two triangles give the sets of $F(y \mid x_1), F(y \mid x_2), F(y \mid x_3)$ that are consistent with sample information if $Z = z_1$ or $Z = z_2$. Because Z takes both values and is excluded from the conditional distribution of Y given $X = x$, $F(y \mid x_1), F(y \mid x_2), F(y \mid x_3)$ has to be in the intersection of these triangles. Note that the extreme points are the Wald estimators of $F(y \mid x_1), F(y \mid x_3)$ and $F(y \mid x_2), F(y \mid x_3)$ for the case that $F(y \mid x_2)$ and $F(y \mid x_1)$ are set to 0, respectively. In general the extreme points are Wald estimators for conditional cdf's that are obtained by imposing identifying restrictions. Figure 3 is drawn for $p_k(z_l) \leqslant \frac{1}{2}$, $k = 1, 2, 3$, $l = 1, 2$, and $y < \min\{F^{-1}(p_k(z_l)),\ k = 1, 2, 3,\ l = 1, 2\}$. The other bounds can be obtained in the same way. Note that the exclusion restriction gives a narrower bound. To see this, compare the bound on $F(y \mid x_1)$ in the figure to those for $Z = z_1$ or $Z = z_2$, which are 0 (lower bound) and $\frac{F(y|z_1)}{p_1(z_1)}$ and $\frac{F(y|z_2)}{p_1(z_2)}$ (upper bound), respectively.

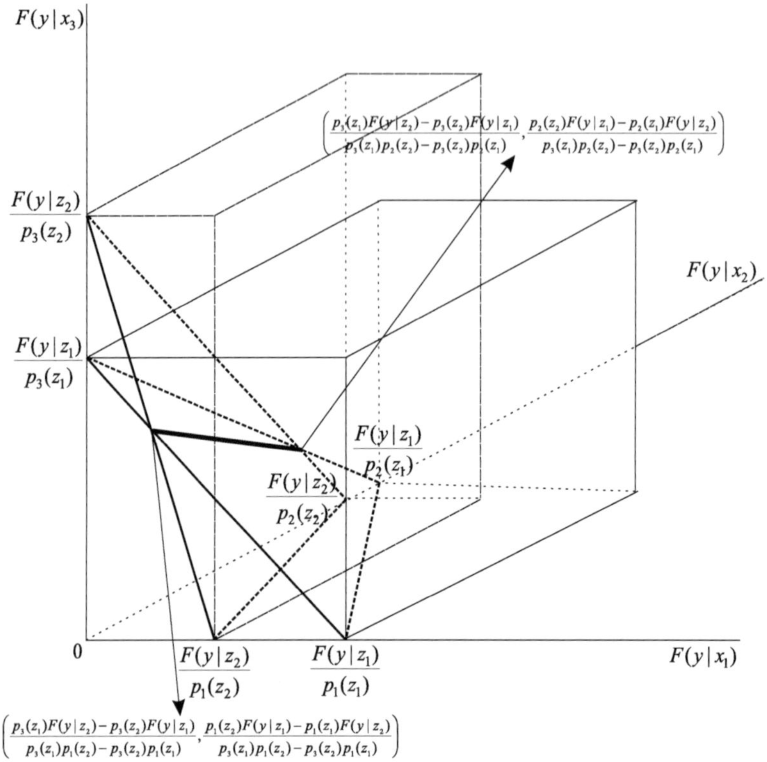

Figure 3. Bounds on $F(y \mid x_1)$, $F(y \mid x_2)$, $F(y \mid x_3)$ in underidentified case; $p_k(z_l) \leqslant \frac{1}{2}$, $k = 1, 2, 3$, $l = 1, 2$, and $y < \min\{F^{-1}(p_k(z_l)),\ k = 1, 2, 3,\ l = 1, 2\}$.

4.3. Parametric inference

4.3.1. Conditional independence

Often two samples are merged to estimate a parametric relation between a dependent variable Y, present in one sample, and a vector of independent variables X some of which may be only present in an independent sample. We assume that sample A contains X, Z, sample B contains Y, Z and that we estimate a relation between Y and X, Z_0 with Z_0 a subvector of Z. This relation has a vector of parameters θ and we assume that the population parameter vector θ_0 is the unique solution to the population moment conditions

$$\mathrm{E}\big(m(Y, X, Z_0; \theta)\big) = 0. \tag{60}$$

This framework covers Maximum Likelihood (ML) and Generalized Method of Moments (GMM). Initially, we assume that X and Y are conditionally independent given Z.

Under conditional independence we have

$$\begin{aligned} \mathrm{E}\big(m(Y, X, Z_0; \theta)\big) &= \mathrm{E}_{YZ}\big(\mathrm{E}_X\big(m(Y, X, Z_0; \theta) \mid Y, Z\big)\big) \\ &= \mathrm{E}_{YZ}\big(\mathrm{E}_X\big(m(Y, X, Z_0; \theta) \mid Z\big)\big). \end{aligned} \tag{61}$$

If we have an estimate of the conditional distribution of X given Z, identified in sample A, we can estimate $\mathrm{E}(m(y, X, z_0; \theta) \mid Z = z)$ for fixed values $Y = y$ and $Z = z$ using the data from sample A. The sample moment conditions corresponding to (61) are

$$\frac{1}{N_2} \sum_{j=1}^{N_2} \widehat{\mathrm{E}_{X|Z}}\big(m(Y_j, X, Z_{02j}; \theta) \mid Z_{2j}\big) = 0, \tag{62}$$

where the hat indicates that the conditional expectation is estimated using the data from sample A.

As an example consider the regression model

$$Y = \beta_1 X + \beta_2 Z_0 + \varepsilon. \tag{63}$$

The scalar dependent variable Y and a vector of common variables Z_1 are observed in sample A. The (scalar) independent variable X and a vector of the common variables Z_2 are observed in sample B (the subscript on Z indicates the sample). We assume that Z_1 and Z_2 are independently and identically distributed. The scalar variable Z_0 is a component of Z. The parameters β_1, β_2 are identified by

$$\mathrm{E}(\varepsilon \mid X, Z) = 0. \tag{64}$$

In general this assumption is too strong, because it generates more moment conditions than are needed to identify the regression parameters. These parameters are identified, even if (scalar) X is correlated with ε, provided that Z has two variables that are not correlated with ε. In general, Z is chosen to ensure that the variables in the relation that are in sample A and those that are in sample B are conditionally independent given Z, and Z may contain many variables. It is not even necessary to assume that all the variables in Z are exogenous, as suggested by (64). If X is exogenous, only Z_0 (or one other variable in Z) has to be exogenous.

We first consider the case that both X and Z_0 are exogenous. The population moment conditions are

$$\begin{aligned} &\mathrm{E}\big[(Y - \beta_1 X - \beta_2 Z_0) X\big] = 0, \\ &\mathrm{E}\big[(Y - \beta_1 X - \beta_2 Z_0) Z_0\big] = 0. \end{aligned} \tag{65}$$

Under conditional independence these can be written as

$$\mathrm{E}_{YZ_2}\big[Y\mathrm{E}_{X|Z_1}(X \mid Z_2) - \beta_1 \mathrm{E}_{X|Z_1}\big(X^2 \mid Z_2\big) - \beta_2 Z_{02} \mathrm{E}_{X|Z_1}(X \mid Z_2)\big] = 0, \tag{66}$$

$$\mathrm{E}_{YZ_2}\big[\big(Y - \beta_1 \mathrm{E}_{X|Z_1}(X \mid Z_2) - \beta_2 Z_{02}\big) Z_{02}\big] = 0. \tag{67}$$

In these expressions $\mathrm{E}_{X|Z_1}(X \mid Z_2)$ is the conditional expectation of X given Z_1 that can be estimated from sample A and that is a function of Z_1, with Z_2 substituted for Z_1.

In other words, it is the imputed X in sample B based on Z_2 observed in sample B and using the conditional expectation of X given Z_1 in sample A.

If we substitute the sample moments for $\mathrm{E}_{YZ_2}[Y\mathrm{E}_{X|Z_1}(X \mid Z_2)]$, $\mathrm{E}_{YZ_2}[\mathrm{E}_{X|Z_1}(X \mid Z_2)]$, $\mathrm{E}_{YZ_2}[\mathrm{E}_{X|Z_1}(X^2 \mid Z_2)]$, and $\mathrm{E}_{YZ_2}[Z_{02}\mathrm{E}_{X|Z_1}(X \mid Z_2)]$, we obtain the sample moment conditions that can be solved to obtain the estimator of the regression coefficients. From GMM theory [Hansen (1982)] it follows that this estimator is consistent and asymptotically normal. If the number of moment conditions exceeds the number of parameters, we obtain an efficient estimator by minimizing a quadratic form in the sample moment conditions with the inverse of the variance matrix of these conditions as weighting matrix.

It is interesting to note that the GMM estimator obtained from (66)–(67) is not the imputation estimator obtained by replacing the unobserved X in sample B by its imputed value. The imputation estimator is not even available, if X and Z_0 are both exogenous and $Z = Z_0$.

If Z contains at least one additional exogenous variable, Z_0^c, we can choose to use the moment condition corresponding to Z_0^c, instead of the moment condition corresponding to X, even if X is exogenous. In that case we can replace the moment conditions (65) by

$$\begin{aligned} &\mathrm{E}\big[(Y - \beta_1 X - \beta_2 Z_0)Z_0^c\big] = 0, \\ &\mathrm{E}\big[(Y - \beta_1 X - \beta_2 Z_0)Z_0\big] = 0. \end{aligned} \tag{68}$$

Because the Z's are in both samples, all expected values in these population moment conditions can be obtained from sample A $(\mathrm{E}(XZ_0), \mathrm{E}(XZ_0^c))$, sample B $(\mathrm{E}(YZ_0), \mathrm{E}(YZ_0^c))$ or both $(\mathrm{E}(Z_0^2), \mathrm{E}(Z_0 Z_0^c))$. Hence, in this case we need not make the assumption of conditional independence of X and Y given Z. Note that this is true, irrespective of whether X is endogenous or not. Key are the availability of additional common variables that can replace X in the moment conditions and the additive separability of variables that are in different samples in the residual $Y - \beta_1 X - \beta_2 Z_0$. We shall explore this below.

In the example the distribution of X given Z was not needed to obtain the GMM estimator, because the moment conditions were quadratic in X and only $\mathrm{E}(X \mid Z)$ and $\mathrm{E}(X^2 \mid Z)$ had to be estimated. In general, this will not be the case, and an assumption on this conditional distribution is needed. Econometricians are usually reluctant to specify the distribution of exogenous variables, and for that reason we may consider a semi-parametric alternative in which $\mathrm{E}_{X|Z_1}(m(y, X, z_0; \theta) \mid Z = z)$ is estimated by a non-parametric regression (series or kernel estimator) of $m(y, X_i, z_0; \theta)$ on Z_{1i} in sample A. This gives $\hat{\mathrm{E}}_{X|Z}(m(y, X, z_0; \theta))$ which is substituted to obtain the sample moment conditions as an average in sample B. This estimator is similar to the estimator considered in Chen, Hong and Tarozzi (2004) and Imbens, Newey and Ridder (2004), and their results can be used to analyze this estimator.

4.3.2. Exclusion restrictions

In Section 4.2.2 we discussed conditions under which exclusion restrictions are sufficient for the non-parametric identification of the conditional distribution of Y given X, Z_0. In this section we consider parametric inference. The assumptions we impose are convenient, but stronger than needed. In particular, we restrict the discussion to additively separable moment conditions. The existing literature only considers this case. If the exclusion restrictions identify the joint distribution as explained in Section 4.2.2, the separability assumption can be relaxed. This has not been studied, and developing procedures for this case is beyond the scope of this chapter.

The setup and notation is as in Section 4.2.2 with Z_0^c the components of Z that are not in the relation and satisfy (69), i.e. that are exogenous for the relation between Y and X, Z_0. We consider moment conditions that can be written as

$$\mathrm{E}\big(\big(f(Y;\theta) - g(X, Z_0;\theta)\big)h\big(Z_0, Z_0^c\big)\big) = 0 \tag{69}$$

with f, g, h known functions and θ a vector of parameters. If Y is scalar, then so is g. The dimension of h is not smaller than that of θ. In general, this implies that the dimension of Z_0^c has to exceed that of X,[7] i.e. the number of common exogenous variables that are excluded from the relation cannot be smaller than the number of variables in X. If we assume that some variables in either X or Z_0 are endogenous we need as many additional variables in Z_0^c as there are endogenous variables among X, Z_0.

The estimator based on the population moment conditions (69) is called the Two-Sample Instrumental Variable (2SIV) estimator. In the case that all variables are observed in a single sample, the estimator based on the moment conditions in (69) is related to Amemiya's nonlinear simultaneous equations estimator [see, e.g. Amemiya (1985, Chapter 8)].

We discuss three examples of models that give moment conditions as in (69): the linear regression model, the probability model for discrete dependent variables, and the mixed proportional hazard model for duration data. In all models we take $h(Z_0, Z_0^c) = (Z_0' Z_0^{c'})'$. For the linear regression model the moment conditions are

$$\mathrm{E}\big(Y - \beta_0 - \beta_1' X - \beta_2' Z_0\big) = 0, \tag{70}$$

$$\mathrm{E}\big(\big(Y - \beta_0 - \beta_1' X - \beta_2' Z_0\big)Z_0\big) = 0, \tag{71}$$

$$\mathrm{E}\big(\big(Y - \beta_0 - \beta_1' X - \beta_2' Z_0\big)Z_0^c\big) = 0. \tag{72}$$

Note that we can replace X by $\mathrm{E}(X \mid Z_0, Z_0^c)$.[8] We can even replace X by the linear approximation to this conditional expectation, i.e. by $\pi_0 + \pi_1' Z_0 + \pi_2' Z_0^c$ where the vector π minimizes $\mathrm{E}[(X - \pi_0 - \pi_1' Z_0 - \pi_2' Z_0^c)^2]$. This gives the estimating equations of

[7] If Z_0 is exogenous, then functions, e.g. powers, of Z_0 are also exogenous. To avoid identification by functional form, we need the additional exogenous variables in Z_0^c.

[8] This is a consequence of the equivalence of 2SLS and IV in this type of models.

the two-stage linear imputation estimator first suggested by Klevmarken (1982). In the first stage, the vector of independent variables X is regressed on the common exogenous variables Z_0, Z_0^c using data from sample A. This estimated relation is used to compute the predicted value of X in sample B, using the common variables as observed in sample B. These predicted values are substituted in the estimating equations that now only contain variables observed in sample B.

The second example is the probability model for discrete dependent variables. If we consider a dummy dependent variable then we specify

$$\Pr(Y = 1 \mid X, Z_0) = G(\beta_0 + \beta_1' X + \beta_2' Z_0) \tag{73}$$

with G a cdf of some continuous distribution, e.g. the standard normal (Probit) or logistic cdf (Logit). The moment conditions are

$$\mathrm{E}(Y - G(\beta_0 + \beta_1' X + \beta_2' Z_0)) = 0, \tag{74}$$

$$\mathrm{E}(Y - G(\beta_0 + \beta_1' X + \beta_2' Z_0) Z_0) = 0, \tag{75}$$

$$\mathrm{E}(Y - G(\beta_0 + \beta_1' X + \beta_2' Z_0) Z_0^c) = 0. \tag{76}$$

Except for the logit model, these moment conditions do not give the efficient estimator of β. To obtain the efficient estimator we must multiply the residual by

$$\frac{g(\beta_0 + \beta_1' X + \beta_2' Z_0)}{G(\beta_0 + \beta_1' X + \beta_2' Z_0)(1 - G(\beta_0 + \beta_1' X + \beta_2' Z_0))}. \tag{77}$$

The resulting moment equation cannot be computed from the separate samples. Ichimura and Martinez-Sanchis (2005) discuss this case and also derive bounds on the parameters if there is no point identification.

The last example is the Mixed Proportional Hazard (MPH) model for duration data. In that model the hazard rate h of the duration Y is specified as

$$h(y \mid x, V; \theta) = \lambda(y; \theta_1) \exp\{\theta_2' X + \theta_3' Z_0\} V \tag{78}$$

with λ the baseline hazard and V a random variable that is independent of Z_0, Z_1 and that captures the effect of omitted variables. By (78) we have that

$$\ln \Lambda(Y; \theta_1) + \theta_2' X + \theta_3' Z_0 = U \tag{79}$$

with U independent of Z_0, Z_1 and Λ the integral of λ. This gives the moment conditions

$$\mathrm{E}((\ln \Lambda(Y; \theta_1) + \theta_2' X + \theta_3' Z_0) Z_0) = 0, \tag{80}$$

$$\mathrm{E}((\ln \Lambda(Y; \theta_1) + \theta_2' X + \theta_3' Z_0) Z_0^c) = 0. \tag{81}$$

The number of variables in Z_0^c must at least be equal to the number of parameters in $(\theta_1' \theta_2')'$.[9] Alternatively, we can identify θ_1 by making assumptions on the functional

[9] If we assume the baseline hazard is Weibull we can identify the regression parameters up to scale. These parameters can be identified, if we choose a functional form for the baseline hazard that is not closed under a power transformation.

form of the regression function. For instance, if we maintain the hypothesis that the regression function is linear, we can use powers of the variables in Z_0^c in the moment conditions. In that case no additional common variables are needed.[10] Besides the MPH model, we can estimate other transformation models from two independent samples. Examples are the Box–Cox transform [Box and Cox (1964)] and the transform suggested by Burbidge, Magee and Robb (1988).[11]

These three examples correspond to linear regression, nonlinear regression and transformation models. Other models, as the Tobit model, can also be estimated with this type of data. For the Tobit model we can employ the two-part estimation method that yields moment conditions as in (69). Only in the linear regression model is the GMM estimator equivalent to a (linear) imputation estimator. In the other examples, imputation yields biased estimates.

The additional common variables Z_0^c must be exogenous. They also have to be correlated with the variables in X. In other words, they must satisfy the requirements for valid instruments for X, irrespective of whether the variables in X are exogenous or endogenous. As noted before, the separability of the moment conditions is a sufficient, but not necessary condition for identification.

The asymptotic distribution theory of the 2SIV estimator based on (69) raises some new issues. First, we introduce some notation. Let

$$m(\theta) = \big(f(Y;\theta) - g(X, Z_0;\theta)\big)h\big(Z_0, Z_0^c\big) \tag{82}$$

and for $i = 1, \ldots, N_1$, $j = 1, \ldots, N_2$,

$$\begin{aligned} m_{2j}(\theta) &= f(Y_j;\theta)h\big(Z_{02j}, Z_{02j}^c\big), \\ m_{1i}(\theta) &= g(X_i, Z_{01i};\theta)h\big(Z_{01i}, Z_{01i}^c\big) \end{aligned} \tag{83}$$

with the second subscript in, e.g. Z_{01i} indicating that the common included exogenous variable Z_0 is observed in sample A etc. Using this notation, the sample moment conditions are

$$m_N(\theta) = \frac{1}{N_2}\sum_{j=1}^{N_2} m_{2j}(\theta) - \frac{1}{N_1}\sum_{i=1}^{N_1} m_{1i}(\theta). \tag{84}$$

We make the following assumptions (the derivatives in the assumptions are assumed to exist and to be continuous in θ):

(A1) The common variables in samples A and B, the random vectors Z_{01}, Z_{01}^c and Z_{02}, Z_{02}^c are independently but identically distributed.

[10] Provided that the identification condition (A3) below is satisfied.

[11] The latter transform is used by Carroll, Dynan and Krane (1999) who use two independent samples to estimate their regression model. Because their model has a 'missing parameter' and not a missing regressor, they do not use 2SIV.

(A2) If $N_1, N_2 \to \infty$

$$\frac{\partial m_N}{\partial \theta'}(\theta) \xrightarrow{p} \mathrm{E}\left(\frac{\partial m}{\partial \theta'}(\theta)\right)$$

uniformly for $\theta \in \Theta$ with Θ the parameter space.

(A3) The rank of the matrix $\mathrm{E}(\frac{\partial m}{\partial \theta'}(\theta_0))$ is equal to the dimension of θ.

Assumption (A1) ensures that the limit in (A2) holds pointwise for every $\theta \in \Theta$. Assumption (A3) is the identification condition. The probability limit of the derivative of the moment conditions is

$$\mathrm{E}\left(\frac{\partial m}{\partial \theta'}(\theta)\right) = \mathrm{E}\left(\frac{\partial f(Y;\theta)}{\partial \theta'} h\left(Z_{02}, Z_{02}^c\right)\right) - \mathrm{E}\left(\frac{\partial g(X, Z_{01};\theta)}{\partial \theta'} h\left(Z_{01}, Z_{01}^c\right)\right). \tag{85}$$

This matrix can be estimated consistently from the samples A and B, because the expectations only involve variables that are observed in the same sample.

The 2SIV is formally defined by

$$\hat{\theta}_N = \arg\min_{\theta \in \Theta} m_N(\theta)' W_N m_N(\theta) \tag{86}$$

with W_N a weighting matrix that satisfies

$$W_N \xrightarrow{p} W \tag{87}$$

with W a positive definite matrix and $N \to \infty$ if $N_1, N_2 \to \infty$. In Appendix A we show that assumptions (A1)–(A3) are sufficient for weak consistency of the 2SIV.

If (A1) does not hold, the 2SIV is biased. The probability limit is the minimizer of

$$\begin{aligned}&(\theta - \theta_0)' \mathrm{E}\left[\frac{\partial m'}{\partial \theta}(\theta_*)\right] W \mathrm{E}\left[\frac{\partial m}{\partial \theta'}(\theta_*)\right](\theta - \theta_0) \\ &\quad + 2\mathrm{E}\left[m(\theta_0)\right]' W \mathrm{E}\left[\frac{\partial m}{\partial \theta'}(\theta_*)\right](\theta - \theta_0) + \mathrm{E}\left[m(\theta_0)\right]' W \mathrm{E}\left[m(\theta_0)\right]\end{aligned} \tag{88}$$

but the last two terms do not vanish. We can use this expression to find the asymptotic bias of the 2SIV estimator.

The optimal weight matrix W is the inverse of the variance matrix of $m_N(\theta_0)$. To derive the asymptotic variance matrix we have to make an assumption on the rate at which the sample sizes increase. Such an assumption was not needed to establish weak consistency of the 2SIV estimator. We assume

(A4) $\lim_{N_1 \to \infty, N_2 \to \infty} \frac{N_2}{N_1} = \lambda$ with $0 < \lambda < \infty$.

Consider, using the fact that $\mathrm{E}(m(\theta_0)) = 0$ if (A1) is true,

$$\begin{aligned}\sqrt{N_2} m_N(\theta_0) &= \frac{1}{\sqrt{N_2}} \sum_{j=1}^{N_2} \left(m_{2j}(\theta_0) - \mathrm{E}\left(m_{2j}(\theta_0)\right)\right) \\ &\quad - \sqrt{\frac{N_2}{N_1}} \frac{1}{\sqrt{N_1}} \sum_{i=1}^{N_1} \left(m_{1i}(\theta_0) - \mathrm{E}\left(m_{1i}(\theta_0)\right)\right).\end{aligned} \tag{89}$$

Hence, the asymptotic variance matrix of the moment conditions is

$$M(\theta_0) = \lim_{N_2 \to \infty} \mathrm{E}\big[N_2 m_N(\theta_0) m_N(\theta_0)'\big] = \lambda \operatorname{Var}\big(m_{2j}(\theta_0)\big) + \operatorname{Var}\big(m_{1i}(\theta_0)\big) \tag{90}$$

and the inverse of this matrix is the optimal choice for $W(\theta_0)$. This matrix can be easily estimated if we have an initial consistent estimator. Note that by the central limit theorem for i.i.d. random variables (if the asymptotic variance is finite) $\sqrt{N_2} m_N(\theta_0)$ converges to a normal distribution with mean 0. However, if (A1) does not hold and as a consequence $\mathrm{E}(m(\theta_0)) \neq 0$, the mean diverges. This will affect the interpretation of the test of overidentifying restrictions that will be discussed below.

Under (A1)–(A4)

$$\sqrt{N_2}(\hat{\theta}_N - \theta_0) \xrightarrow{d} N\big(0, V(\theta_0)\big) \tag{91}$$

with

$$\begin{aligned} V(\theta_0) = {} & \left[\mathrm{E}\left(\frac{\partial m'}{\partial \theta}(\theta_0)\right) W(\theta_0) \mathrm{E}\left(\frac{\partial m}{\partial \theta'}(\theta_0)\right)\right]^{-1} \\ & \cdot \mathrm{E}\left(\frac{\partial m'}{\partial \theta}(\theta_0)\right) W(\theta_0)\big(\lambda \operatorname{Var}\big(m_{2j}(\theta_0)\big) \\ & + \operatorname{Var}\big(m_{1i}(\theta_0)\big)\big) W(\theta_0) \mathrm{E}\left(\frac{\partial m}{\partial \theta'}(\theta_0)\right) \\ & \cdot \left[\mathrm{E}\left(\frac{\partial m'}{\partial \theta}(\theta_0)\right) W(\theta_0) \mathrm{E}\left(\frac{\partial m}{\partial \theta'}(\theta_0)\right)\right]^{-1}. \end{aligned} \tag{92}$$

See Appendix A for a proof.

The preceding discussion suggest a two-step procedure. In the first step we use a known weight matrix, e.g. $W_N = I$. The resulting 2SIV estimator is consistent, but not efficient. In the second step, we first estimate the optimal weight matrix, the inverse of (90). This matrix only depends on the first-step consistent estimator and moments that can be computed from the two independent samples A and B (for λ we substitute $\frac{N_2}{N_1}$). Next, we compute the efficient 2SIV estimator (86) with this weight matrix. This estimator has asymptotic variance

$$\left[\mathrm{E}\left(\frac{\partial m'}{\partial \theta}(\theta_0)\right)\big(\lambda \operatorname{Var}\big(m_{2j}(\theta_0)\big) + \operatorname{Var}\big(m_{1i}(\theta_0)\big)\big) \mathrm{E}\left(\frac{\partial m}{\partial \theta'}(\theta_0)\right)\right]^{-1} \tag{93}$$

which can be estimated from the independent samples.

In general, the efficient 2SIV estimator is less efficient than efficient estimators based on a sample that contains all the variables. In the case that the information matrix only depends on variables in sample A, we can estimate the variance of the efficient estimator, even if the estimator itself cannot be computed from the independent samples. The inverse of the information matrix gives an indication of the efficiency loss, due to the fact that we do not have a sample that has all variables.

If the number of moment conditions is larger than the number of parameters, we can test the overidentifying restrictions. The test statistic is

$$T_N = N_2 m_N(\hat{\theta}_N)' \left[\frac{N_2}{N_1} \widehat{\mathrm{Var}}\big(m_{2j}(\hat{\theta}_N)\big) + \widehat{\mathrm{Var}}\big(m_{1i}(\hat{\theta}_N)\big) \right]^{-1} m_N(\hat{\theta}_N), \tag{94}$$

where $\widehat{\mathrm{Var}}$ denotes the sample variance. If (A1)–(A4) hold, then $T_N \xrightarrow{d} \chi^2(\dim(m) - \dim(\theta))$. Appendix A contains a proof.

As noted before, rejection of the overidentifying restrictions indicates that either some of the common variables that are used as instruments are not exogenous or that they are not identically distributed in the samples A and B.

Although the technique of choice for estimating relations from combined samples has been GMM, Maximum Likelihood can be used as well. A reason for the preference for GMM (or IV) may be that in that framework it is easier to obtain consistent estimates of structural parameters if some of the regressors are endogenous. Orthogonality conditions for equation errors and instrumental variables are more natural in GMM. To define the Two-Sample Maximum Likelihood (2SML) estimator we start with a parametric model for the conditional distribution of Y given X, Z_0, $f(y \mid x, z_0; \theta)$. Because X is not observed in sample A, we use sample B to estimate the conditional density of X given Z_0, Z_1. We can use a parametric or a non-parametric estimator for the latter conditional density. The likelihood contributions are obtained from the conditional density of Y given Z_0, Z_1

$$f(y \mid z_0, z_1; \theta) = \int f(y \mid x, z_0; \theta) g(x \mid z_0, z_1)\, \mathrm{d}x. \tag{95}$$

With a parametric estimator for $g(x \mid z_0, z_1)$ the 2SML estimator is a conventional MLE with all the usual properties. The properties of the 2SML with a non-parametric estimator of this conditional density have not been studied. In Section 4.2.2 we considered non-parametric identification of $f(y \mid x_1, z_0)$, and non-parametric identification is sufficient for parametric identification. Again Chen, Hong and Tarozzi (2004) and Imbens, Newey and Ridder (2004) provide the framework in which the 2SML can be analyzed.

2SIV or 2SML are used if some of the explanatory variables in a relation are not measured in the same sample as the dependent variable. Another situation occurs in models with generated regressors, in which the parameters of the generated regressor cannot be estimated from the same sample. An important example of a generated regressor is the sample selection correction function. An example is the estimation of a wage equation on a sample of working individuals. This yields biased estimates of the regression coefficients if a positive fraction of the population under consideration does not work. A method to reduce this bias is to include a sample selection correction function [Heckman (1979)]. The parameters of this function cannot be estimated from the sample of working individuals. However, if an independent sample is available that contains both working and nonworking individuals but no information on wages, then the parameters can be estimated from this sample. This allows us to compute the sample selection correction for the working individuals.

Another example of a generated regressor is Carroll, Dynan and Krane (1999) who estimate the effect of the probability of becoming unemployed on the wealth to income ratio. They estimate the wealth equation with data from the Survey of Consumer Finances (SCF). However, the SCF has no information on unemployment. The probability of becoming unemployed is estimated from the Current Population Survey (CPS) and because the variables that enter this probability are also observed in the SCF, this probability can be imputed in the SCF. Note that in these examples there are no missing variables. Only the parameters that enter the generated regressor are estimated from an independent sample. This type of data combination can be treated as any estimation problem with a generated regressor [Pagan (1984)]. The fact that the parameter is estimated from an independent sample even simplifies the distribution theory.

4.4. *The origin of two-sample estimation and applications*

Of the methods discussed in this section only the 2SIV estimator is prominent in econometrics. The first author who suggested this estimator was Klevmarken (1982). Since then it was rediscovered independently by Angrist and Krueger (1992) and Arellano and Meghir (1992).[12] Klevmarken derives the 2SIV estimator for a single equation that is part of a system of linear simultaneous equations. In our notation he considers

$$Y = \beta_0 + \beta_1' X + \beta_2' Z_0 + \varepsilon \tag{96}$$

with X observed in sample A and Y in sample B, while Z_0 is a subvector of the common variables Z. He also assumes that all the variables in X are endogenous,[13] that all the common variables Z are exogenous and that Z contains all exogenous variables.[14] If we compare these assumptions with ours, we see that Klevmarken's assumptions are far too strong and limit the application of 2SIV to rather special cases. In particular, the assumption that Z contains all exogenous variables seems to be inspired by a desire to give a structural interpretation to the first-stage imputation regression, in which X is regressed on the exogenous variables in Z. Such an interpretation is not needed, and hence the only requirement is the order condition discussed in the previous subsection. Moreover, not all common variables need to be exogenous, as long as this order condition is satisfied. Finally, some of the variables in X may be exogenous. Klevmarken states that we can only allow for exogenous variables if the joint distribution of X and Z is multivariate normal, which ensures that the conditional mean of X given Z is linear in Z. As the derivation in the previous subsection shows, a linear conditional mean is not essential for the 2SIV estimator. In the linear regression model replacing

[12] These authors do not cite Klevmarken's contribution.

[13] Klevmarken (1982, p. 160).

[14] Klevmarken (1982, p. 159).

the conditional expectation by the linear population projection on Z will not affect the moment conditions[15] and hence the assumption of multivariate normality is not needed. Carroll and Weil (1994) start from the same model as Klevmarken. They claim[16] that to compute the variance matrix of the 2SIV estimator it is required that in one of the datasets we observe Y, X, Z. The discussion in the previous subsection shows that this is not necessary. The problem with their approach is that their estimator of the variance matrix requires the residuals of the regression and these cannot be recovered from the independent samples.

At this point, we should clarify the role of endogenous and exogenous regressors in 2SIV estimation. The natural solution to missing variables in a statistical relation is imputation of these variables. Indeed, the 2SIV estimator in the linear regression model can be seen as an imputation estimator. Econometricians are used to imputation if the regression contains some endogenous variables. In the Two-Stage Least Squares (2SLS) estimator the endogenous variables are replaced by a predicted or imputed value. Hence, it is not surprising that 2SIV was originally developed for linear regression models with endogenous regressors. Our derivation shows that such a restriction is not necessary, and in particular, that the 2SIV only imputes missing variables, if the model is a linear regression. In the general case specified in (69), there is no imputation of missing variables.

After Klevmarken (1982) the 2SIV estimator was reinvented independently by Arellano and Meghir (1992) and Angrist and Krueger (1992). Arellano and Meghir consider moment restrictions of the form (we use our earlier notation with Z_1, Z_2 the common variables Z as observed in sample A and B, respectively)

$$\begin{aligned} &\mathrm{E}\big(m(X, Z_1; \theta)\big) = 0, \\ &\mathrm{E}\big(m(Y, Z_2; \theta)\big) = 0, \end{aligned} \tag{97}$$

i.e. the moment restrictions are defined for the samples A and B separately. These separate moment restrictions are obtained if we consider the linear regression model (96). If we relate the X to the exogenous common variables Z

$$X = \Pi Z + \eta, \tag{98}$$

we can substitute this in (96) to obtain

$$Y = \beta_0 + \beta_1' \Pi Z + \beta_2' Z_0 + \varepsilon + \beta_1' \eta. \tag{99}$$

If the order condition is satisfied, we can estimate β from the linear regression in (99). In particular, (98) can be estimated from sample A and (99) from sample B. The corresponding moment conditions are

[15] Provided that the distribution of the common variables in the two samples is the same.

[16] See the Technical Appendix to in their paper.

$$\mathrm{E}\big((X_1 - \Pi Z_1)' Z_1\big) = 0,$$
$$\mathrm{E}\big(\big(Y - \beta_0 - \beta_1' \Pi Z_2 - \beta_2' Z_{02}\big) Z_2\big) = 0 \tag{100}$$

and this has the form (97). Note again that the linear first step can be seen as a linear population projection and is valid even if the conditional expectation of X_1 given Z is not linear (provided that Z_1 and Z_2 have the same distribution). Also the moment restrictions are nonlinear in the structural parameters β. Arellano and Meghir (1992) propose to estimate β_0, $\pi = \Pi'\beta_1$ and β_2, and to use Chamberlain's (1982) minimum distance estimator in a second stage to obtain an estimate of the structural parameters. Their estimator is equivalent to the imputation estimator. In particular, it can only be used if the X enters linearly in the moment conditions, and it cannot be used if we estimate a model with a nonlinear (in X) moment condition.

Arellano and Meghir apply their estimator to a female labor supply equation. In this equation the dependent variable, hours, is observed in the UK Labor Force Survey (LFS), the European counterpart of the US Current Population Survey. Two of the independent variables, the wage rate and other income, are obtained from a budget survey, the Family Expenditure Survey (FES). This situation is common: budget surveys contain detailed information on the sources of income, while labor market surveys contain information on labor supply and job search. An indicator whether the woman is searching for (another) job is one of the explanatory variables. Arellano and Meghir estimate the labor supply equation using the LFS data after imputing the wage rate and other income, using a relation that is estimated with the FES data. The common variables (or instruments) that are used in the imputation, but are excluded in the labor supply equation are education and age of husband and regional labor market conditions.

Angrist and Krueger (1992) consider the linear regression model

$$Y = \beta_0 + \beta_1' X + \varepsilon \tag{101}$$

with X, Z_1 observed in sample A and Y, Z_2 in sample B with A and B independent samples from a common population. They assume that all common variables are exogenous, and they implicitly assume that the number of (exogenous) common variables exceeds the number of variables in X, i.e. that the order condition is satisfied. Under these conditions the 2SIV estimator is based on a special case of the moment conditions in (70)–(72).

Angrist and Krueger apply the 2SIV estimator to study the effect of the age at school entry on completed years of schooling. Children usually go to school in the year in which they turn 6. If this rule were followed without exceptions, then the age at school entry would be determined by the birthdate. However, exceptions occur and there is some parental control over the age at school entry which makes this variable potentially endogenous. Angrist and Krueger assume that the date of birth is not correlated with any characteristic of the child and hence has no direct effect on completed years of schooling. Because there is no dataset that contains both age at school entry and completed years of schooling, Angrist and Krueger combine information in two US censuses, the 1960 and the 1980 census. Because they use 1% (1960) and 5% (1980) samples they assume that the number of children who are in both samples is negligible. They compute the age at school entry from the 1960 census and the completed years of schooling from the 1980 census. The common variable (and instrument) is the quarter in which the child is born.

Other applications of 2SIV are Carroll and Weil (1994), Lusardi (1996), Dee and Evans (2003), and Currie and Yelowitz (2000). Carroll and Weil (1994) combine data from the 1983 Survey of Consumer Finances (SCF) that contains data on savings and wealth and the Panel Study of Income Dynamics (PSID) that contains data on income growth to study the relation between the wealth income ratio and income growth. The common variables are education, occupation, and age of the head of the household. Lusardi (1996) estimates an Euler equation that relates the relative change in consumption to the predictable component of income growth. Because the consumption data in the PSID are unreliable, she uses the Consumer Expenditure Survey (CEX) to obtain the dependent variable. She also shows that the income data in the CEX are measured with error (and that number of observations with missing income is substantial) and for that reason she uses the PSID to measure income growth. She experiments with different sets of common exogenous variables that contain household characteristics (marital status, gender, ethnicity, presence of children, number of earners), education and occupation (interacted with age), education (interacted with age). Dee and Evans (2003) study the effect of teen drinking on educational attainment. The problem they face is that there is no dataset that has both information on teen drinking and on later educational outcomes. Moreover, drinking may be an endogenous variable, because teenagers who do poorly in school may be more likely to drink. Data on teen drinking are obtained from the 1977–1992 Monitoring the Future (MTF) surveys, while data on educational outcomes are obtained from the 5% public use sample from the 1990 US census. The common exogenous variables are the minimum legal drinking age that differs between states, but more importantly increased over the observation period, state beer taxes, ethnicity, age and gender. The indicator of teen age drinking is considered to be endogenous. Currie and Yelowitz (2000) consider the effect of living in public housing on outcomes for children. The outcome variables, living in high density housing, overcrowding in the house, being held back at school, are from the 1990 census. The indicator of living in public housing is from the pooled 1990–1995 March supplements to the Current Population Survey (CPS). This indicator is assumed to be endogenous in the relation with the outcome variables. The common exogenous variable is the sex composition of the household where households with two children of different gender are more likely to live in public housing because they qualify for larger units.

4.5. *Combining samples to correct for measurement error*

One of the reasons to merge datasets is that the variables in one of the sets is measured more accurately. An example is the study by Okner (1972) who merged the 1967 Survey of Economic Opportunity with the 1966 Tax File using file matching, because the income measures reported in the SEO were thought to be inaccurate. In this section we show that even for this purpose the datafiles need not be merged, and that we can correct for measurement error in one (or more) of the explanatory variables with only marginal error free information.

The procedure that we describe works even if there are no common variables in the two datasets. If there are common variables and if these are exogenous and not correlated with the measurement error, we can use the 2SIV estimator to obtain consistent estimates of the coefficients in a linear relation where some independent variables are measured with error.

There is a larger literature on the use of validation samples to correct for measurement error. In a validation sample both X_1 and the true value X_1^* (and X_2) are observed. This allows for weaker assumptions on the measurement error process. In particular, the measurement error can be correlated with X_1^* and with X_2. This type of sample combination is beyond the scope of the present chapter. Validation samples are rare, because they require the matching of survey and administrative data. Chen, Hong and Tamer (2005) propose a method for the use of validation samples if variables are measured with error.

We consider a simple example of a conditional distribution with pdf $f(y \mid x_1^*, x_2; \theta)$. There are two explanatory variables X_1^*, X_2 where X_2 is observed without error and the error-free X_1^* is not observed. Instead, we observe X_1 that is related to X_1^* as specified below. The observed conditional distribution of Y given X_1, X_2 is

$$f(y \mid x_1, x_2; \theta) = \int f(y \mid x_1^*, x_2; \theta) g\bigl(x_1^* \mid x_1, x_2\bigr) \, \mathrm{d}x_1^* \tag{102}$$

if X_1^* is continuous and the integral is replaced by a sum if X_1^* is discrete. To determine the observed conditional distribution we need to specify or identify $g(x_1^* \mid x_1, x_2)$. We show that this conditional density can be identified from a separate dataset that only contains observations from the distribution of X_1^*, i.e. observations from the marginal distribution of the error-free explanatory variable. Hence we have a sample A that contains Y, X_1, X_2 and an independent sample B that contains only X_1^*.

We consider a special case that allows for a closed-form solution. In particular, we assume that both X_1^* and X_1 are 0–1 dichotomous variables. The relation between these variables, the measurement error model, can be specified in a number of ways. We only allow for measurement error models that are identified from observations from the marginal distribution of X_1 observed in sample A and the marginal distribution of X_1^*, observed in the independent sample B. An example of such a measurement error model is classical measurement error which assumes

$$\Pr\bigl(X_1 = 1 \bigm| X_1^* = 1, X_2\bigr) = \Pr\bigl(X_1 = 0 \bigm| X_1^* = 0, X_2\bigr) = \lambda, \tag{103}$$

i.e. the probability of misclassification is independent of X_1^*. Moreover, (103) implies that X_1 is independent of X_2 given X_1^*. Solving for λ we find

$$\lambda = \frac{\Pr(X_1 = 1) + \Pr(X_1^* = 1) - 1}{2\Pr(X_1^* = 1) - 1}. \tag{104}$$

Hence, λ is indeed identified from the marginal distributions of X_1 and X_1^*.

Note that (104) only gives solutions between 0 and 1 if

$$\Pr(X_1 = 1) < \Pr(X_1^* = 1) \tag{105}$$

if $\Pr(X_1^* = 1) > 1/2$, or if

$$\Pr(X_1 = 1) > \Pr(X_1^* = 1) \tag{106}$$

if $\Pr(X_1^* = 1) > 1/2$. This is equivalent to

$$\begin{aligned}\Pr(X_1 = 1)\bigl(1 - \Pr(X_1 = 1)\bigr) &= \operatorname{Var}(X_1) > \operatorname{Var}(X_1^*)\\ &= \Pr(X_1^* = 1)\bigl(1 - \Pr(X_1^* = 1)\bigr).\end{aligned} \tag{107}$$

In other words, the observed X has a larger variance than the true X_1^*, as is generally true for classical measurement error models. This restriction on the observable marginal distributions must be satisfied, if we want to consider the classical measurement error model.

The second measurement error model assumes that misclassification only occurs if X_1^* is equal to 1,[17] maintaining the assumption that X_1 is independent of X_2 given X_1^*. Hence

$$\begin{aligned}&\Pr(X_1 = 0 \mid X_1^* = 0, X_2) = 1,\\ &\Pr(X_1 = 1 \mid X_1^* = 1, X_2) = \lambda.\end{aligned} \tag{108}$$

With this assumption we find

$$\lambda = \frac{\Pr(X_1 = 1)}{\Pr(X_1^* = 1)}. \tag{109}$$

As in the case of classical measurement error, this measurement error model implies an observable restriction on the two observed marginal distributions, in the case $\Pr(X_1 = 1) \leqslant \Pr(X_1^* = 1)$.

Both measurement error models are special cases of the general misclassification error model

$$\begin{aligned}&\Pr(X_1 = 0 \mid X_1^* = 0, X_2) = \lambda_0,\\ &\Pr(X_1 = 1 \mid X_1^* = 1, X_2) = \lambda_1.\end{aligned} \tag{110}$$

Again we assume that X_1 is independent of X_2 given X_1^*. In this general model the parameters λ_0, λ_1 are not identified from the marginal distributions of X_1 and X_1^*. Hence we must fix one of these parameters or their ratio, as is done in the measurement error models that we introduced in this section. We also assume that the misclassification is independent of X_2.

Of course, it is not sufficient to identify the measurement error distribution. The conditional density of Y given X_1, X_2, which is the basis for likelihood inference, is

[17] The misclassification can also only occur if X_1^* is 0.

obtained from the density of Y given X_1^*, X_2, which contains the parameters of interest, if we integrate the unobserved X_1^* with respect to the density of X_1^* given the observed X_1, X_2 (see (102)). Hence, the key is the identification of the distribution of X_1^* given X_1, X_2.

This conditional distribution is identified from the measurement error model that in turn is identified from the marginal distributions of X_1 and X_1^* and the joint distribution of X_1, X_2. The solution depends on the measurement error model. Here we give the solution, if we assume that the measurement error is classical, but the solution for other (identified) measurement error models is analogous. In the sequel we use subscripts to indicate the variables in the distribution.

Consider

$$\begin{aligned} g_{x_1,x_1^*,x_2}(x_1, x_1^*, x_2) &= g_{x_1}(x_1 \mid x_1^*, x_2) g_{x_1^*,x_2}(x_1^*, x_2) \\ &= g_{x_1}(x_1 \mid x_1^*) g_{x_1^*,x_2}(x_1^*, x_2) \end{aligned} \tag{111}$$

because X_1 is independent of X_2 given X_1^*. After substitution of (103) we obtain

$$g_{x_1,x_1^*,x_2}(x_1, x_1^*, x_2) = \begin{cases} \lambda g_{x_1^*,x_2}(x_1^*, x_2), & x_1 = x_1^*, \\ (1-\lambda) g_{x_1^*,x_2}(x_1^*, x_2), & x_1 \neq x_1^*. \end{cases} \tag{112}$$

The marginal distribution of X_1, X_2, which can be observed, is

$$g_{x_1,x_2}(x_1, x_2) = \lambda g_{x_1^*,x_2}(x_1, x_2) + (1-\lambda) g_{x_1^*,x_2}(1 - x_1, x_2). \tag{113}$$

Solving for $g_{x_1^*,x_2}(x_1^*, x_2)$ we find

$$g_{x_1^*,x_2}(x_1^*, x_2) = \frac{(1-\lambda) g_{x_1,x_2}(1 - x_1^*, x_2) - \lambda g_{x_1,x_2}(x_1^*, x_2)}{1 - 2\lambda}. \tag{114}$$

Substitution in (112) gives the joint density of X_1, X_1^*, X_2. The conditional density of X_1^* given X_1, X_2 is obtained if we divide the result by $g_{x_1,x_2}(x_1, x_2)$.

With a dichotomous X_1 we obtain a simple closed form solution. If X_1 is continuous, we can still identify the distribution of X_1^* given X_1, X_2 if the measurement error model is identified from the marginal distributions of X_1 and X_1^*, as is the case if we assume classical measurement error. Hu and Ridder (2003) show that the identification involves two sequential deconvolution problems. They also develop the distribution theory of the resulting estimator.

5. Repeated cross sections

5.1. General principles

Repeated cross sections consist of independent samples drawn from a population at multiple points in time $t = 1, \ldots, T$. There are many such data sets in the US and other countries, and more than true panel data sets in some. In the US, the Current

Population Survey (CPS) is a leading example, as is the General Social Survey, and even the Survey of Income and Program Participation, if data from different cohorts are employed. There are also examples of firm-level data sets of this kind. In the UK, the Family Expenditure Survey (FES) is a prominent example. In continental Europe, CPS-like cross sections are often used, as are repeated cross-sectional labor force surveys. In developing countries, such labor force surveys are often available as well as several of the World Bank LSMS surveys which have multiple waves.

Although repeated cross section (RCS) data have the obvious disadvantage relative to panel data of not following the same individuals over time, they have certain advantages over panel data. Attrition and nonresponse problems are generally much less severe, for example, and often RCS data have much larger sample sizes than available panels. In many cases RCS data are available farther back in calendar time than longitudinal data because governments began collecting repeated cross sections prior to collecting panel data. In some cases, RCS data are available for a broader and more representative sample of the population than true panel data, at least in cases where the latter only sample certain groups (e.g. certain cohorts as in the US NLS panels).

Although the cross sections can be pooled and cross-sectional models can be estimated on them, the more interesting question is whether they can be used to estimate models of the type estimable with true panel data. To consider this question, assume that in each cross section t we observe a sample from the distribution W_t, Z_t where W_t is a vector of variables that are only measured in each cross section and Z_t is a vector of variables which are measured in all cross sections, and hence can be used to match the individuals across the different waves (individual subscripts $i = 1, \dots, N$ are omitted for now). Both W_t and Z_t may contain variables which are identical at all t (i.e. time invariant variables) although in most applications all time invariant variables will be measured at all t and hence will be in Z_t. We assume that the population is sufficiently large and the sample sufficiently small that there are no common individuals in the cross sections. Further, we assume that the population from which the samples are drawn is closed,[18] and thus we ignore out in- and out-migration, births, and mortality.

At issue is what distributions and what types of models can be identified from the set of cross sections. The unconditional joint distribution of $W_1, \dots, W_T$ is not identified except in the trivial case in which the elements are independent. Models which require for identification only moments from each cross section, and which therefore do not require knowledge of the joint distribution, are identified but do not make particular use of the repeated cross section (RCS) nature of the data except perhaps for investigations of time-varying parameters. The models of interest and under discussion here are those which require identification of the joint distribution or of some aspect of it.

Identification necessarily requires restrictions. Non-parametric identification of conditional distributions $f(W_t \mid W_\tau)$, $t \neq \tau$, follows from the general principles and

[18] This ensures that the relation between a dependent and independent variables does not change over time due to in- and outflow from the population, and we can make this assumption, instead of that of a closed population.

restrictions elucidated in Section 4.2.2 above, with the change of notation from Y to W_t and from X to W_τ. With the common variable Z_t available in each cross section and used for matching, bounds on those conditional distributions can be established. If Z_t or some elements of it are excluded from the relation between W_t and W_τ, and Z_t is discrete, the conditional distributions are exactly identified provided a rank condition is met which relates the number of points in the support of Z_t to the number of conditional distributions to be estimated.

We shall focus in this section primarily on parametric models for which independence of $W_1, \ldots, W_T$ is not assumed but which contain exclusion restrictions. While there are in general many models which can be identified under different restrictions, we will work with a model similar to that in Section 4.3.2 above:

$$f(Y_t;\theta) = g_1(X_t, Z_0;\theta) + g_2(Y_{t-1}, Z_0;\theta) + \varepsilon_t \tag{115}$$

and with associated GMM moment condition, following on (69), of:

$$\mathrm{E}\big[\big(f(Y_t;\theta) - g_1(X_t, Z_0;\theta) - g_2(Y_{t-1}, Z_0;\theta)\big)h(Z_0, Z_{1t})\big] = 0, \tag{116}$$

where f, g_1, g_2, and h are known (possibly up to parameters) functions and θ a vector of parameters. The vector Z_0 is a vector of common time-invariant variables in the cross sections which are included in the g_1 and g_2 relations.[19] In most applications, $f(Y_t;\theta) = Y_t$. The function g_1 contains only X_t and Z_0 and hence appears to be estimable from a single cross section, but, as will be shown below, this is problematic in fixed effects models because X_t is correlated with the error in that case. The functions g_1 and g_2 must be separable because X_t and Y_{t-1} do not appear in the same cross section.

Individuals across cross sections are identified by variables Z_0 and Z_{1t}, with the latter excluded from the relation between Y_t and X_t, Y_{t-1}, Z_0. In most applications to date, $Z_{1t} = t$ or a set of time dummies.[20] The critical exclusion restriction in all RCS models is that Z_{1t} and its interactions with Z_0 do not enter in g_1 and g_2, and yet these variables are correlated with those functions. For the $Z_{1t} = t$ case, this implies that variables that change predictably with time, as individual age, year, unemployment duration, or firm lifetimes (depending on the application) cannot enter g_1 and g_2. Thus the essential restriction in RCS estimation is that intertemporal stability exist in the true relationship. Such a restriction is not needed when true panel data are available. Note as well that the number of independent components in h must not be smaller than the dimension of θ and, in most models, must be larger than the dimension of X_t, Y_{t-1}, and Z_0. This also can be a fairly limiting condition in practice if the number of cross sections available is

[19] These variables can be time-varying but this is rare in applications so we consider only the case where they are time-constant. None of the results we discuss below are substantially changed by this restriction.

[20] However, it is possible that some history information is available in each cross section which means that these time-varying variables (e.g. employment or marital status histories in the case of household survey data; ages of children are another) are potential additional instruments.

small relative to the number of parameters whose identification requires instrumenting with functions of t.

In linear models the GMM estimator can be implemented as a two-step estimator. First, project X_t and Y_{t-1} on $h(Z_0, Z_{1t})$, i.e. obtain $\mathrm{E}(X_t \mid h(Z_0, Z_{1t}))$ and $\mathrm{E}(Y_{t-1} \mid h(Z_0, Z_{1t}))$.[21] Second, regress Y_t on these projections and on Z_0. If there are no Z_0 in the data and $h(Z_{1t})$ is a set of time dummies, this is equivalent to an aggregate time-series regression where the time means of Y_t are regressed upon the time means of X_t and Y_{t-1}. In this case the number of cross sections has to be at least 3. Most interesting cases arise however when Z_0 variables are available; in household survey data, these may be birth year (= cohort), education, race, sex, and so on. If these variables are all discrete and $h(Z_{1t}, Z_0)$ is assumed to be a vector of indicators for a complete cross-classification Z_0 and time, estimation using (116) is equivalent to a regression of the cell means of Y_t on the cell means of X_t, Y_{t-1}, and the dummy variables Z_0. Note that in that case we need fewer cross sections. However, if a parametric form of h is assumed, this aggregation approach is not necessary, and if the model is nonlinear (including the binary choice and related models), the two-step aggregation approach is not possible in the first place. In that case the estimator is the possibly overidentified GMM estimator defined by the moment conditions in (116).

Two leading examples fit into this framework. One is the linear first-order autoregression (with individual i subscripts now added)

$$Y_{it} = \alpha + \beta Y_{i,t-1} + \gamma X_{it} + \delta Z_{0i} + \varepsilon_{it}. \tag{117}$$

With time dummies as excluded variables the number of observations is equal to the number of cross sections and this imposes restrictions on the time-variation of the parameters of (117). The restriction that the instrument must be relevant implies that the mean of $\mathrm{E}(Y_{t-1} \mid Z_0, t)$ must vary with t. If Y_{t-1} is correlated with ε_t, an instrument Z_{1t} must be found which is orthogonal to ε_t.

A second example is the linear individual effects model

$$Y_{it} = \gamma X_{it} + \delta Z_{0i} + f_i + \varepsilon_{it}, \tag{118}$$

where f is an individual effect which is potentially correlated with X_t and Z_0. The within-estimator commonly used with true panel data cannot be implemented with RCS data because it requires knowledge of Y_t at multiple t. RCS IV estimation using (116) proceeds by using the elements of h as instruments for X_t, which again requires some minimal time-invariance of the parameters of (118). Consistency (see below) is based on the presumption that time-varying variables like those in Z_{1t} must be orthogonal to time-invariant variables like f. For instrument relevance, $\mathrm{E}(X_t \mid Z_0, t)$ must vary with t.

Estimation of the model in (118) by the aggregation method mentioned previously was proposed by Deaton (1985). He considers cohort data, so that time in his case is

[21] Projections onto Z_0 and Z_{1t} directly are an alternative.

age. Deaton considered Z_0 to contain only birth year (= cohort) indicators and h to be a set of all cohort-age indicators. He then proposed constructing a data set of cohort profiles of mean Y and X (a 'pseudo' panel data set) and estimating (118) by regressing the age-cohort means of Y on those of X and on cohort dummies (or by the within-estimator for fixed effects models applied to these aggregate observations).

5.2. Consistency and related issues

The conditions for consistency of moment estimators in the form (116) are well known in general [Hansen (1982)]. The special form they take in the two sample case were considered in Section 4.3.2 above, where weak consistency was proven. For the RCS case, aside from the usual rank conditions and conditions on convergence of matrices to positive definite forms, we have the condition that the instruments are not correlated with the random error

$$\mathrm{E}\big[\eta_{it} h(Z_{0i}, Z_{it})\big] = 0,$$

where $\eta_{it} = f(Y_{it};\theta) - g_1(X_{it}, Z_{0i};\theta) - g_2(Y_{i,t-1}, Z_{0i};\theta)$. If there is an individual effect, we have that $\eta_{it} = f_i + \varepsilon_{it}$ and hence we require that $\mathrm{E}[\varepsilon_{it} h(Z_{0i}, Z_{it})] = 0$, and $\mathrm{E}[f_i h(Z_{0i}, Z_{it})] = 0$. The first assumption must hold even with the presence of Y_{t-1} in the equation and represents an IV solution familiar to panel data models with dynamics and lagged endogenous variables. However, with a lagged dependent variable in the equation the errors in successive periods have a MA(1) structure because the errors in not observing the same individuals in each cross section are correlated [McKenzie (2004)].

The assumption on the individual effect f_i that may be correlated with X_{it} is the more problematic assumption. If h is a set of time dummies, then a sufficient condition is that the (population) mean of f_i does not change over time. If we have repeated cross sections of size N_t in period $t = 1, \dots, T$, then this implies that[22]

$$\bar{f}_t = \frac{1}{N_t} \sum_{i=1}^{N_t} f_i \xrightarrow{p} 0.$$

Hence, if $\min\{N_1, \dots, N_T\} \to \infty$, then the limit of the time averaged regression without a lagged dependent variable is

$$Y_t^* = \alpha + \gamma X_t^* + \varepsilon_t^*$$

with ε_t^* a common time shock in the ε_{it} and $*$ indicating population averages of the variables. OLS applied to this equation gives consistent estimators of the regression parameters, and this establishes that the GMM estimator that uses moment condition (116) is consistent if $\min\{N_1, \dots, N_T\} \to \infty$, i.e. for large N asymptotics.

22 Without loss of generality we can take the common time constant limit equal to 0.

For the same model and assumptions on the random error, time dummies are not valid instruments if N_t is fixed and T becomes large. Note that in this case the number of instruments is equal to T and hence goes to infinity. The problem is obvious if we consider the second stage regression that involves the projections on the instruments, i.e. the averages in the repeated cross sections

$$\overline{Y}_t = \alpha + \gamma \overline{X}_t + \overline{f}_t + \bar{\varepsilon}_t.$$

Hence

$$\mathrm{E}[\overline{X}_t \overline{f}_t] = \frac{1}{N_t} \mathrm{E}[X_{it} f_i] \neq 0$$

for finite N_t.

There is another asymptotic that can be considered as well, which is an asymptotic in the number of cohorts [Deaton (1985), Verbeek (1996)]. Up to this point we have assumed that a single population of N individuals is followed over time for T periods, which is equivalent to a single cohort (or a fixed set of birth years). Now let us consider increasing the number of such cohort groups (c) by moving over calendar time, or possibly space, and increasing the number of pseudo-panels in the data. Each new panel has N individuals and is observed for T periods. Once again, with fixed N, the average individual effect will be correlated with the average covariate, so that the GMM estimator is biased.

Deaton (1985) has proposed a modification of the estimator for the linear fixed effects model which contains a bias adjustment for the finite, fixed N case and which is consistent for the large T case, an estimator that has been much discussed in the literature. Deaton notes that estimation of the aggregated estimation equation

$$\overline{Y}_{ct} = \gamma \overline{X}_{ct} + \delta_c + \bar{\varepsilon}_{ct}, \tag{119}$$

where means are taking over observations within each cohort (c) and year (t) cell yields biased estimates for finite N because $\overline{f}_{ct}$ is correlated with $\overline{X}_{ct}$. Deaton instead considers the "population" equation

$$Y^*_{ct} = \gamma X^*_{ct} + \delta_c + \varepsilon^*_{ct}, \tag{120}$$

where variables with asterisks represent population values, i.e. values that would obtain if the cohort would be infinitely large. Note that δ_c absorbs a nonzero mean of the f_i in cohort c.

For the estimation of (120) $\overline{X}_{ct}$ and $\overline{Y}_{ct}$ must be inserted to proxy their population counterparts but they do so with error. Deaton suggests that the measurement error for each be estimated by the within-cell variances of X and Y using the individual data and that a finite-sample adjustment be made when estimating the coefficient vector.

Deaton does not set up his model in the GMM framework but it can be done so. Although he discusses his estimator as an errors-in-variables estimator, it is more in line with our discussion to consider it as a finite N bias-corrected version of the GMM estimator. To focus on the key issues, assume that only one cohort of N individuals is observed for T periods. The individual model is

$$y_{it} = \delta + \beta x_{it} + f_{it} + \varepsilon_{it}. \tag{121}$$

The second stage equation when using time dummies as instruments is

$$\bar{y}_t = \beta \bar{x}_t + \overline{f}_t + \bar{\varepsilon}_t. \tag{122}$$

Consequently,

$$\mathrm{Cov}(\bar{y}_t, \bar{x}_t) = \beta\,\mathrm{Var}(\bar{x}_t) + \mathrm{Cov}(\overline{f}_t, \bar{x}_t). \tag{123}$$

The bias term in (123) is

$$\mathrm{Cov}(\overline{f}_t, \bar{x}_t) = \frac{\mathrm{Cov}(f_i, x_{it})}{N}. \tag{124}$$

This bias term is small if N is large or if the correlation between the regressor and the individual effect is small. The Deaton finite sample adjustment can be derived by noting that $f_{it} = y_{it} - \beta x_{it} - \varepsilon_{it}$ and that, therefore, $\mathrm{Cov}(f_{it}, x_{it}) = \mathrm{Cov}(y_{it}, x_{it}) - \beta\,\mathrm{Var}(x_{it})$. Hence $\mathrm{Cov}(\overline{f}_t, \bar{x}_t) = \frac{\sigma_{yx} - \beta\sigma_x^2}{N}$ where σ_{yx} and σ_x^2 are the covariance of x and y and the variance of x for the individual observations in a time period. Inserting this into (123) and solving for β, we obtain the Deaton estimator if we replace the population variances and covariances with sample variances and covariances:

$$\hat{\beta} = \frac{\mathrm{Cov}(\bar{y}_t, \bar{x}_t) - \frac{\sigma_{yx}}{N}}{\mathrm{Var}(\bar{x}_t) - \frac{\sigma_x^2}{N}}. \tag{125}$$

As $N \to \infty$ the bias and the bias correction terms go to 0 and the least squares estimate of the aggregate model is consistent. Deaton noted that the estimator is also consistent as $T \to \infty$ and Verbeek and Nijman (1992, 1993) show that this estimator is consistent as $C \to \infty$ provided a minor change is made in the bias correction. Verbeek and Nijman also note that the Deaton estimator increases variance at the same time that it reduces bias, giving rise to a mean-squared error tradeoff that can be addressed by not subtracting off the "full" bias correction in (125). Devereux (2003) shows that the Deaton estimator is closely related to estimators which adjust for finite sample bias in IV estimation and that, in fact, the estimator is equivalent to the Jacknife Instrumental Variables estimator and is closely related to k-class estimators. Devereux also proposes a modification of the Deaton estimator which is approximately unbiased but has a smaller finite sample variance.

There have been some explorations in the literature seeking to determine how large N must be for the finite sample adjustments to be avoided by Monte Carlo simulations. Verbeek and Nijman (1992) suggest that cell sizes of 100 to 200 are sufficient, while Devereux (2003) suggests that they should be higher, possibly 2000 or more. The necessary N is sensitive to the specification of the model. Devereux also conducts an exercise which subsamples the available N in a model to gauge the degree of bias.

There has also been a discussion in the literature of how to divide the available data into cohort groups, given that most data sets do not have sufficient samples to divide the data completely by discrete values of birth year [Verbeek and Nijman (1992, 1993)]. Dividing the sample into more birth cohorts increases C while decreasing the sample size per cohort. In the applied literature, groupings of birth cohorts and formation of cells for the aggregated estimation has been, by and large, ad hoc. Moffitt (1993) suggests that aggregation not be conducted at all but rather that the individual data be employed and a parametric function of birth year and t be estimated to smooth the instrument to achieve efficiency, but he does not present any formal criteria for how to do so. A better framework for analyzing these issues is that which considers alternative specifications of the instrument which trade off bias and variance. Donald and Newey (2001) present one such analysis.

The literature has also addressed dynamic fixed effects models. In this case we are interested in the individual model

$$Y_{it} = \alpha + \beta Y_{i,t-1} + \delta Z_{0i} + f_i + \varepsilon_{it} \tag{126}$$

which is a combination of (117) and (118). The desirability of different instrument sets Z_{1i} depends once again on the asymptotics involved. But when asymptotics are taken in N (the number of observations per cohort), the consistency properties of different instrument sets are almost identical to those for true panel data [Sevestre and Trognon (1996), Arellano and Honoré (2001)]. Using simple functions of t as instruments, for example, will yield inconsistent estimates for the same reasons that conventional fixed effects methods in true panel data yield inconsistent estimates in the presence of both fixed effects and lagged regressors. As in the case of true panel data, additional instruments which generate first-differenced estimators and which use lagged values of the dependent variable can yield consistent estimates.

Collado (1997) and McKenzie (2004) consider this model and discuss various applications of IV to the model, using the same principles in the literature on true panel data, using lagged values of the dependent variable as instruments and possibly using the larger instrument set implied by the Arellano–Bond estimator. Collado and McKenzie also propose Deaton-style bias-correction terms to correct for the finite N problem discussed above. Collado shows that her estimator is consistent in C and, for a different bias-correction, consistent in T. McKenzie considers a sequential asymptotic in which N is first allowed to go to infinity conditional on fixed T and then limits are taken w.r.t. T.

5.3. *Binary choice models*

In the binary choice model we return to (115) and let $f(Y_t;\theta) = Y_t^*$, $Y_t = I(Y_t^* \geqslant 0)$, and F be the c.d.f. of $-\varepsilon_t$. Then $\Pr(Y_t = 1 \mid X_t, Z_0, Y_{t-1};\theta) = F(g_1(X_t, Z_0;\theta) + g_2(Y_{t-1}, Z_0;\theta))$ so that

$$Y_{it} = F\big(g_1(X_{it}, Z_{0i};\theta) + g_2(Y_{i,t-1}, Z_{0i};\theta)\big) + \nu_{it}, \tag{127}$$

which does not fit into the framework of the moment condition in (117) because X_t and Y_{t-1} are not separable. Let us therefore initially assume $g_2 = 0$ and consider lagged indicators below. Now (117) applies directly assuming the availability of a suitable exclusion restriction, as before. The moment conditions are a simple extension of those shown in Equations (74)–(76). The method is applicable to the individual effects binary choice model or to a binary choice model with endogenous X_t with the restrictions that hold in the cross section case. For instance, in parametric estimation where the F distribution is assumed to be known, a distributional assumption is needed for the individual effect in order to derive F, e.g., if f is the individual effect component of ε_t,

$$f_i = v(Z_{0i}; \phi) + \eta_i, \tag{128}$$

where v is assumed to be of known form and where η_i has a known parametric distribution from which the c.d.f. of the composite error $\eta_i - \varepsilon_{it}$ can be derived.

If X_t is endogenous and if the instrument is a set of time dummies, possibly interacted with Z_0, the nonlinearity of the conditional expectation function means that GMM is not equivalent to any type of aggregate regression of cell means of Y on cell means of X and Z. However, with a stronger assumption, a version of such an approach is possible [Moffitt (1993)]. The necessary assumption, in addition to (128), is

$$X_{it} = w(Z_{0i}, Z_{1it}; \psi) + \omega_{it}, \tag{129}$$

where w is a function of known parametric form and ω_{it} is an error term with a parametric distributional form that may be correlated with ε_{it}. The assumption that the exact form of dependence of the endogenous variable on the instruments is known and that the conditional distribution of the regressor follows a specific parametric form are very strong. In the simplest case, g_1 is linear in X_t and Z_0 and w is linear in Z_0 and Z_{1t}, and ε_t and ω_t are assumed to be bivariate normal. Then a variety of estimating techniques are possible, drawing on the literature on endogenous regressors in limited dependent variable models [Amemiya (1978), Heckman (1978), Nelson and Olsen (1978), Rivers and Vuong (1988), Smith and Blundell (1986); see Blundell and Smith (1993) for a review]. Options include replacing X_t in g_1 with its predicted value from (129); inserting an estimated residual from (129) into (127); and estimating (153) and (155) in reduced form by inserting (129) into (127). In this approach, the parameters of (127) are estimated by maximum likelihood, which implies that the instrument vector h in (116) is the binary choice instrument vector that is equal to $\frac{F'}{(1-F)F}$ times the derivative of the argument of F w.r.t. θ.

To consider the model with Y_{t-1} let us first consider the case in which $X_t = X$ is time invariant, in which case it can be folded into Z_0 and we can let $g_1 = 0$ without loss of generality. Then we have

$$\mathrm{E}(Y_{it} \mid Z_{0i}, Y_{i,t-1}) = F\big(g_2(Y_{i,t-1}, Z_{0i}; \theta)\big), \tag{130}$$

where we have assumed that ε_{it} is distributed independently of $Y_{i,t-1}$, i.e. there is no serial correlation. Instrumental variable estimation of (130) conducted by replacing Y_{t-1}

by a predicted value and applying maximum likelihood to the resulting model is known to be inconsistent because Y_{t-1} is binary and hence its prediction error follows a non-normal, two-point discrete distribution. An alternative procedure is to integrate Y_{t-1} out of the equation. Letting $p_t(Z_0)$ be the marginal probability $\Pr(Y_t = 1 \mid Z_0)$, we have

$$\begin{aligned} E(Y_t \mid Z_0) &= p_t(Z_0) \\ &= p_{t-1}(Z_0)\Pr(Y_t = 1 \mid Z_0, Y_{t-1} = 1) \\ &\quad + \bigl(1 - p_{t-1}(Z_0)\bigr)\Pr(Y_t = 1 \mid Z_0, Y_{t-1} = 0) \\ &= p_{t-1}(Z_0)F\bigl(g_2(1, Z_0; \theta)\bigr) + \bigl(1 - p_{t-1}(Z_0)\bigr)F\bigl(g_2(0, Z_0; \theta)\bigr) \\ &= p_{t-1}(Z_0)\bigl(1 - \lambda(Z_0; \theta)\bigr) + \bigl(1 - p_{t-1}(Z_0)\bigr)\mu(Z_0; \theta) \\ &= \mu(Z_0; \theta) + \eta(Z_0; \theta)p_{t-1}(Z_0), \end{aligned} \tag{131}$$

where $\lambda(Z_0; \theta) = \Pr(Y_t = 0 \mid Z_0, Y_{t-1} = 1) = F(g_2(1, Z_0; \theta))$ is the exit rate from $Y_{t-1} = 1$ to $Y_t = 0$, $\mu(Z_0; \theta) = \Pr(Y_t = 1 \mid Z_0, Y_{t-1} = 0) = F(g_2(0, Z_0; \theta))$ is the exit rate from $Y_{t-1} = 0$ to $Y_t = 1$, and $\eta(Z_0; \theta) = 1 - \lambda(Z_0; \theta)\mu(Z_0; \theta)$. Equation (131) is a familiar flow identity from renewal theory showing how the marginal probability at $t - 1$ is transformed by the two transition probabilities into the marginal probability at t. It suggests a procedure by which the reduced form model $Y_t = \mu(Z_0; \theta) + \eta(Z_0; \theta)p_{t-1}(Z_0) + \nu_t$ is estimated by nonlinear least squares (given the nonlinearity of the two transition probabilities in θ) or GMM using a first-stage estimate of $p_{t-1}(Z_0)$ similar to the case of a generated regressor. Because the marginals at every t are estimable from the RCS data, such a first-stage estimate is obtainable. Identification of the transition probabilities is achieved by restricting their temporal dependence (indeed, in (131) they are assumed to be time invariant); identification is lost if the two transition probabilities vary arbitrarily with t [Moffitt (1993)]. The model is equivalent to a two-way contingency table where the marginals are known; the data furnish a sample of tables and the restrictions on how the joint distribution varies across the sample yields identification.

The first-stage estimation of $p_{t-1}(Z_0)$ can be obtained from an approximation of the function or the structure of the model can be used to recursively solve for $p_{t-1}(Z_0)$ back to the start of the process. Assuming that $p_0 = 0$ and that the process begins with $t = 1$, and continuing to assume time-invariant hazards,

$$\begin{aligned} p_{t-1}(Z_0) &= \mu(Z_0; \theta)\left[1 + \sum_{\tau=1}^{t-2} \eta(Z_0; \theta)^{t-1-\tau}\right] \\ &= \mu(Z_0; \theta)\frac{1 - \eta(Z_0; \theta)^{t-1}}{1 - \eta(Z_0; \theta)} \end{aligned} \tag{132}$$

which can be jointly estimated with (131) imposing the commonality of the functions[23] Alternatively, (131) can be expressed in fully solved back form and estimated as well.

[23] Alternatively an initial conditions can be specified as a marginal p in the first period.

Equation (131) has been used as the basis of RCS estimation at the aggregate level. Miller (1952) considered estimation of (131) with time-series data on the proportions of a variable, p_t which is special case of RCS data. Without data on individual regressors Z_0, he suggested simple least squares estimation of

$$p_t = \mu + \eta p_{t-1} + \nu_t. \tag{133}$$

Madansky (1959) proved that the least squares estimators of the two hazards are consistent for fixed N as $T \to \infty$ and for fixed T as $N \to \infty$. Lee, Judge and Zellner (1970) and MacRae (1977) proposed various types of restricted least squares estimators to ensure that the estimated hazards do not fall outside the unit interval. This problem would not arise in the approach here, which specifies the hazards in proper probability form.

Estimation of the Markov model with RCS data is considerably complicated if there is serial correlation in the errors or if time-varying X_t are allowed. With serial correlation of the errors, the two transition probabilities require knowledge of the functional dependence of ε_t on Y_{t-1}. The most straightforward approach would require replacing the simple transition probabilities we have shown here with joint probabilities of the entire sequences of states $Y_{t-1}, Y_{t-2}, \ldots, Y_1$ which in turn would be a nonlinear function of Z_0 and the parameters of the assumed joint distribution of $\varepsilon_{t-1}, \varepsilon_{t-2}, \ldots, \varepsilon_1$. This treatment would be parallel to maximum likelihood estimation with true panel data in random effects and similar models where the joint distribution is likewise integrated out. With time-varying X_t, the approach in (131) is problematic because

$$\mathrm{E}(Y_t \mid X_t, Z_0) = \mu(X_t, Z_0; \theta) + \eta(X_t, Z_0; \theta) p_{t-1}(X_t, Z_0), \tag{134}$$

where $\mu(X_t, Z_0; \theta) = F(g_1(X_t, Z_0; \theta) + g_2(0, Z_0; \theta))$ and $\lambda(X_t, Z_0; \theta) = 1 - F(g_1(X_t, Z_0; \theta) + g_2(1, Z_0; \theta))$. The difficulty is that $p_{t-1}(X_t, Z_0)$ is not identified from the data. Estimation would require the assumption of a Markov or other process for X_t which could be used to formulate a function $p_{t-1}(X_t, Z_0)$ which could be identified from the data.

5.4. Applications

Despite the large number of RCS data sets in the US and abroad, the methods described in this section have been applied relatively infrequently. The vast majority of uses of RCS data simply estimate pooled cross-sectional parameters without matching individuals across waves by birth cohort, education, or other individual time-invariant covariates. A rather large literature on program evaluation in the US uses RCS data with area fixed effects in a period where policies differ across areas and over time and policy effects are estimated from the cross-area covariation in the change in policies and in the outcome (migration is ignored). This literature likewise does not make use of the techniques discussed here.

Of the applications that have been conducted, virtually all have used the Deaton linear fixed effects aggregation approach rather than the more general GMM-IV approach described here. Most of the applications have been to life cycle models, which is a natural area of application because age profiles are central to the theory and the Deaton approach is explicit in formulating aggregate cohort profiles of that type. Browning, Deaton and Irish (1985) estimated a life cycle model of labor supply and consumption using seven waves of the FES and were the first to demonstrate the estimation of the fixed effects model, which arises naturally from the first order conditions of separable lifetime utility functions, by aggregation into cohort profiles. Subsequent FES analyses include Blundell, Browning and Meghir (1994), who estimated Euler equations under uncertainty for aggregate cohort profiles of consumption, using instrumental variables with lags to control for the endogeneity of lagged consumption; Attanasio and Weber (1994), who estimated life cycle consumption profiles with aggregate cohort means but allowed calendar-time varying effects in an attempt to explain macro trends in UK consumption; and Alessie, Devereux and Weber (1997), who added borrowing constraints to the model. Analyses using RCS methods to other data sets are small in number. Attanasio (1998) used the US Consumer Expenditure Survey to construct aggregate cohort profiles of saving rates in an attempt to explain the decline in saving rates in the US. Blow and Preston (2002) used a UK tax data set that did not contain information on age to estimate the effect of taxes on earnings of the self-employed, and followed the aggregation approach grouping on region of residence and occupation. Paxson and Waldfogel (2002) used the Deaton method but applied to state-specific means over time in the US, regressing state-specific measures of measures of child mistreatment on a number of state-level variables and mean socioeconomic characteristics obtained from the CPS as well as state and year fixed effects. The authors applied the Deaton finite-sample correction to the regressor matrix containing the moments for the aggregate CPS regressors and reported large increases in estimated coefficients as a result. Finally, Heckman and Robb (1985) showed that treatment effects models can be estimated with RCS data even if information on who has been trained and who has not is not available in post-training cross sections if the fraction who are trained is known.

There have been a few applications of the Markov model described above. Pelzer, Eisinga and Franses (2002, 2004) have implemented the maximum likelihood estimator suggested in Moffitt (1993) and discussed above, adding unobserved heterogeneity, for two applications. The papers also discuss alternative computational methods and algorithms. In the first application, the authors used a true panel data set with five waves to estimate a Markov model for changes in voter intentions (Democrat vs Republican), treating the panel as a set of repeated cross sections. They then validated the model by estimating model on the true panel, and found that the coefficients on the regressor variables were quite similar in both methods but that the intercept was quite different. In the second application, the authors examined transition rates in personal computer ownership in the Netherlands over a 16-year period, but again using a true panel data set which was initially treated as a set of repeated cross sections. The authors again found the regressor coefficients to be quite close in both cases. The authors also note that the RCS Markov model is formally identical to problem of ecological inference, or the problem of how to infer individual relationships from grouped data [Goodman (1953), King (1997)]. In the ecological inference problem, a set of grouped observations furnishes data on the marginals of binary dependent and independent variables (the "aggregate" data) and restrictions on how the joint distribution (the "individual data") varies across groups is used for identification.

Güell and Hu (2003) studied the estimation of hazard functions for leaving unemployment using RCS data containing information on the duration of the spell, allowing matching across cross sections on that variable. The authors used a GMM procedure very similar to that proposed here. The similarity to the RCS Markov model discussed here is superficial, however, for the matching on duration permits direct identification of transition rates. The authors apply the method to quarterly Spanish labor force survey data, which recorded spell durations, over a 16 year period, and estimate how exit rates from unemployment have changed with calendar time and what that implies for the distribution of unemployment. A simpler but similar exercise by Peracchi and Welch (1994) used matched CPS files in adjacent years over the period 1968–1990 to measure labor force transitions between full-time, part-time, and no work, and then assemble the transition rates into an RCS data set which they use to estimate transition rates by cohort as a function of age, year, and other variables.

6. Combining biased samples and marginal information

6.1. Biased samples and marginal information

In the previous sections we combined random samples from the same population that had (some) population members and/or variables in common. In this section we study the combination of samples that are drawn from distinct, but possibly overlapping subpopulations. The most common case is that of a stratified sample. In a stratified sample the population is divided into nonoverlapping subpopulations, the strata, and separate random samples, usually with different sampling fractions, are drawn from these strata. A stratified random sample usually achieves the same precision, as measured by the variance of estimates, with a smaller sample size.

If the sampling fraction differs between strata, the members of the population have an unequal probability of being observed. If the probability of observation depends on the variable of interest, or on variables that are correlated with the variable of interest, then the stratified sample gives a biased estimate of the distribution of the variable of interest and any parameter defined for this distribution.

A stratified sample is a special case of a biased sample. A biased sample is a sample in which the probability of observation depends on the variable(s) of interest. Let Y be the vector of variables of interest. In a biased sample the probability of observation is proportional with $W(Y)$. The function W is called the biasing function. The density of

Y in the sample is[24]

$$g(y) = \frac{W(y)f(y)}{\int_{-\infty}^{\infty} W(v)f(v)\,\mathrm{d}v}. \tag{135}$$

Special cases of biasing functions are $W(y) = I_S(y)$ with I_S the indicator of the subset S of the support of Y, i.e. a stratum of the population, and $W(y) = y$, i.e. the probability of selection is proportional to Y. If Y is a duration, the second biased sample is called a length-biased sample. A length-biased sample is a biased sample from the full distribution and not a sample from a subpopulation. Estimation from a pure length-biased sample does not involve sample combination.

For biased samples the distinction between the dependent variable(s) Y and the independent variable(s) X is important. In particular, it makes a difference if the distribution of interest is that of Y or the conditional distribution of Y given X. If the biasing function $W(y, x)$ is a function of x only, the joint density of Y given X in the sample is

$$g(y, x) = \frac{W(x)f(y \mid x)f(x)}{\int_{-\infty}^{\infty} W(w)f(w)\,\mathrm{d}w}. \tag{136}$$

The marginal distribution of X in the sample has density

$$g(x) = \frac{W(x)f(x)}{\int_{-\infty}^{\infty} W(w)f(w)\,\mathrm{d}w} \tag{137}$$

so that the conditional density of Y given X in the sample is the population conditional density $f(y \mid x)$. Hence, if we are interested in the conditional distribution of Y given X (or parameters defined for this distribution) and the biasing function is a function of X only, the biased sample directly identifies the conditional distribution of Y given X. In all other cases, we cannot ignore the fact that we have a biased sample.

In Section 6.2 we consider parametric and non-parametric identification in biased samples. In leading cases parametric restrictions secure identification while there is non-parametric underidentification. This precludes tests of these parametric restrictions. Non-parametric identification requires that the biased samples are 'overlapping' (in a sense that will be made precise). Necessary and sufficient conditions for the non-parametric identification of the distribution of Y or the joint distribution of Y, X are given by Gill, Vardi and Wellner (1988). These conditions apply if the biased samples have the same variables. However they cannot be used if some of the subsamples only have a subset of the variables in Y, X. It is even possible that we do not observe the subsample itself, but only moments of the variables in the subsample. In these cases non-parametric identification has to be established on a case by case basis.

Efficient estimation from a combination of biased samples is considered in Section 6.3. First, we consider efficient non-parametric estimation of the cdf of Y or that

[24] Here and in the sequel g and f are either pdf's or mass functions, i.e. densities with respect to the counting measure.

of Y, X from a combination of biased samples that non-parametrically identifies these distributions. Next, we consider the special case of an endogenously stratified sample and parametric inference on the conditional distribution of Y given X, if the parameters in this distribution are identified.[25] Finally, we consider the case that a (possibly biased) sample is combined with information from other samples that only specify selected moments of a subset of the variables in Y, X. If the main sample is a random sample then the parameters are identified from this sample and the additional information overidentifies the parameters. The additional degrees of freedom can be used to increase the precision of the estimates or they can be used to test the (parametric) model for the conditional distribution of Y given X. If the additional information just identifies the parameters there is no gain in precision. Finally, the first sample and additional information may not identify the parameters. In that case the combination may provide narrower bounds on these parameters. An alternative is to define a population that is consistent with all available information and to estimate parameters defined for this population. These parameters are equal to the population parameters in the identified case [Imbens and Hellerstein (1999)].

This final approach has all the earlier efficient parametric estimators as special cases. It also covers the combination of biased samples with samples that have marginal information on a subset of the variables in Y, X. An example is the contaminated sampling problem considered by Lancaster and Imbens (1996) who consider the combination of a sample from the distribution of X given $Y = 1$, Y is a 0–1 variable, with a random sample from the marginal distribution of X.

The theory of biased samples is now fairly complete. The general theory of identification is summarized in Gill, Vardi and Wellner (1988) who also discuss efficient non-parametric estimation of the marginal cdf of Y or the joint cdf of Y, X. In econometrics the emphasis has been on parametric inference in the conditional distribution of Y given X. The efficient MLE was developed by Imbens (1992). Imbens and Lancaster (1996) consider the general case. The history of this problem is interesting, because the contributions were made by researchers with different backgrounds, which reflects the prevalence of biased samples in different areas. Cox (1969) considered non-parametric inference in length-biased samples. This was followed by a number of contributions by Vardi (1982, 1985), culminating in Gill, Vardi and Wellner (1988). In econometrics the problem was first studied in discrete-choice models [Manski and Lerman (1977)]. Further contributions are Manski and McFadden (1981), Cosslett (1981b, 1981a), Morgenthaler and Vardi (1986), and Imbens (1992). The case that the dependent variable Y is continuous was studied by Hausman and Wise (1981) and Imbens and Lancaster (1996). Related problems that will be considered in this section are case-control studies [Prentice and Pyke (1979), Breslow and Day (1980)], contaminated samples [Hsieh, Manski and McFadden (1985), Lancaster and Imbens

[25] Parametric identification suffices, but preferably the conditional distribution of Y given X should be non-parametrically identified, and for this the strata need to be overlapping.

(1996)] and the combination of micro and macro data [Imbens and Lancaster (1994), Imbens and Hellerstein (1999)].

6.2. Identification in biased samples

General results on non-parametric identification of the population cdf from combined biased samples are given by Vardi (1985) and Gill, Vardi and Wellner (1988). Initially, we make no distinction between dependent and independent variables. Let the population distribution of the random vector Y have cdf F. Instead of a random sample from the population with cdf F, we have K random but biased samples from distributions with cdf's G_k, $k = 1, \dots, K$. The relation between G_k and F is given by

$$G_k(y) = \frac{\int_{-\infty}^{y} W_k(y)\,\mathrm{d}F(y)}{\int_{-\infty}^{\infty} W_k(v)\,\mathrm{d}F(v)}. \tag{138}$$

In this expression W_k is a biasing function. This function is assumed to be known and nonnegative (it may be 0 for some values of y). An obvious interpretation of this function is that it is proportional to the probability of selection. If f is the density of F, then the probability of observing y in the kth biased sample is proportional to $W_k(y) f(y)$. Because we specify the probability of selection up to a multiplicative constant we must divide by the integral of $W_k(y) f(y)$ to obtain a proper cdf.

It is obvious that we can only recover the population cdf for values of y where at least one of the weight functions is positive. The region where F is identified, $\mathcal{S}$, is defined by

$$\mathcal{S} = \left\{ y \;\middle|\; \sum_{k=1}^{K} W_k(y) > 0 \right\}. \tag{139}$$

If $\mathcal{S}$ is a strict subset of the support of Y we can only recover the conditional cdf of Y given $Y \in \mathcal{S}$. For values of y with $W_k(y) > 0$, the population pdf can be found from

$$g_k(y) = \frac{W_k(y)}{\overline{W}_k} f(y) \tag{140}$$

with

$$\overline{W}_k = \int_{-\infty}^{\infty} W_k(w)\,\mathrm{d}F(w). \tag{141}$$

If f satisfies (140), then so does $c.f$ for any positive constant c. Because f is a density, the sum or integral over its support is 1, and this restriction determines the constant.

Let $\bar{g}(y)$ be the density of a randomly selected observation from the pooled sample. If the subsample sizes are determined by a multinomial distribution with parameters λ_k, $k = 1, \dots, K$, and N (the size of the pooled sample), then we have a multinomial sampling plan. The density of a randomly selected observation from the pooled sample is $\bar{g}(y) = \sum_{i=1}^{K} \lambda_k g_k(y)$. In the case that the subsample sizes are fixed, we substitute

$\frac{N_k}{N}$ for λ_k to obtain the density of a randomly selected observation in the pooled sample. This implies that the identification results for multinomial sampling and for fixed subsample sizes are identical.

From (140) we solve for f as a function of $\bar{g}$

$$f(y) = \frac{1}{\sum_{k=1}^{K} \lambda_k \frac{W_k(y)}{W_k}} \bar{g}(y). \tag{142}$$

This solution does not express f in terms of observable quantities, because it depends on the unknown W_k's. The W_k, $k = 1, \ldots, K$, are determined by the following system of equations that is obtained by multiplying (142) by $W_k(y)$ and by integrating the resulting expression over y

$$1 = \frac{1}{W_k} \int_{-\infty}^{\infty} \frac{W_k(y)}{\sum_{l=1}^{K} \lambda_l \frac{W_l(y)}{W_l}} \bar{g}(y)\,\mathrm{d}y \tag{143}$$

for $k = 1, \ldots, K$. Note that this set of equations only determines the W_k's up to a multiplicative factor. To obtain a solution we choose an arbitrary subsample, e.g. subsample 1, and we set $W_1 = 1$.

By rewriting (142) (we divide by 1), we find

$$f(y) = \frac{\frac{1}{\sum_{k=1}^{K} \lambda_k \frac{W_k(y)}{W_k}} \bar{g}(y)}{\int_{-\infty}^{\infty} \frac{1}{\sum_{k=1}^{K} \lambda_k \frac{W_k(v)}{W_k}} \bar{g}(v)\,\mathrm{d}v}. \tag{144}$$

We see that f only depends on the ratios $\frac{W_k}{W_1}$, $k = 2, \ldots, K$. We can now restate the identification problem: The population pdf f (with cdf F) is non-parametrically identified from the K biased samples if and only if the equation system (143) and (144) has a unique solution for f and W_k, $k = 2, \ldots, K$ (in the equations we set $W_1 = 1$). If desired we can recover W_1 from (141) with $k = 1$.

We consider the solution in more detail for the case of two biased samples, i.e. $K = 2$. Define the set V_{12} by

$$V_{12} = \{ y \mid W_1(y) W_2(y) > 0 \}. \tag{145}$$

Note that if the weight functions are stratum indicators, the V_{12} contains all y that are common to both strata. For all $y \in V_{12}$

$$\frac{W_2}{W_1} = \frac{g_1(y)}{g_2(y)} \frac{W_2(y)}{W_1(y)}. \tag{146}$$

Note that the functions on the right-hand side are all known or estimable from the biased samples. Hence, the ratio $\frac{W_2}{W_1}$ is (over)identified on V_{12}. This ratio can be substituted in (144) to obtain f. If the set V_{12} is empty, then it is not possible to identify the ratio $\frac{W_2}{W_1}$ and f.

If $K \geqslant 3$ we look for biased samples k, l for which the set $V_{kl} = \{y \mid W_k(y)W_l(y) > 0\}$ is not empty, i.e. for which

$$\int_{-\infty}^{\infty} W_k(y)W_l(y)\,\mathrm{d}F(y) > 0. \tag{147}$$

The same argument as for $K = 2$ shows that for such a pair of subsamples k, l we can identify the conditional distribution of Y given that Y is in the set where $W_k(y) + W_l(y) > 0$. Samples for which (147) holds are called connected. Because the result holds for all pairs k, l we can characterize the region of identification of the population distribution. Let $\mathcal{K}_m$, $m = 1, \ldots, M$, be disjoint index sets of connected subsamples. The union of these index sets is the set of all subsamples $\{1, \ldots, K\}$. The population distribution is identified on the regions $\mathcal{S}_m$, $m = 1, \ldots, M$, with $\mathcal{S}_m = \{y \mid \sum_{k \in \mathcal{K}_m} W_k(y) > 0\}$, i.e. we can identify the conditional distributions of Y given that $Y \in \mathcal{S}_m$. If there is only one region of identification that coincides with the support of Y, the population distribution is identified on its support.

Until now we did not distinguish between the dependent variable(s) Y and independent variables X. The theory developed above applies directly if biased samples from the joint distribution of Y, X are combined. The special case that the biasing function only depends on X has already been discussed. There are however other possibilities, e.g. that in some subsample only Y or only X is observed. A sample from the marginal distribution of X or Y cannot be considered as a biased sample from the joint distribution of X, Y, so that the general theory cannot be used. A simple example illustrates this point.[26]

Assume that X and Y are both discrete with 2 and K values and assume that we have random samples from strata defined by Y. The biasing functions are $W_k(y, x) = I_{y=k}(y, x)$, $k = 1, \ldots, K$. The subsamples are not connected and we cannot identify the joint distribution of X, Y. Now assume that we have an additional random sample from the distribution of X. It seems that the 'biasing' function for this sample is $I_{x=1,2}(y, x)$ and this additional subsample is connected with each of the other subsamples. We conclude that the joint distribution is identified. This conclusion is not correct, because the marginal density of X satisfies by the law of total probability

$$f_X(1) = \sum_{k=1}^{K} f(1 \mid k) f_Y(k). \tag{148}$$

If $K = 2$ we can identify the marginal distribution of Y and therefore the joint distribution of Y, X from the biased samples and the marginal distribution of X. If $K > 2$, there will be observationally equivalent solutions and we cannot identify the joint distribution. If the additional sample is from the marginal distribution of Y we can identify the joint distribution. Note that $W_k = f_Y(k)$ so that this case corresponds to prior information

[26] Although Gill, Vardi and Wellner (1988) do not claim that their identification theorem applies with marginal information, they give suggestive examples, e.g. their Example 4.4.

on the W_k's. In general, samples from marginal distributions provide prior information on the W_k's, e.g. (148) imposes as many restrictions as the number of distinct values taken by X. Currently there is no general theory of non-parametric identification with marginal information that is comparable to the Gill, Vardi and Wellner (1988) theory.

We now consider some examples:

Endogenous stratification First, we consider the marginal distribution of Y. Let $\mathcal{S}_k$, $k = 1, \dots, K$, be a partition of the support of Y, and let $W_k(y) = I_{\mathcal{S}_k}$. The population cdf of Y is not identified, because the biased samples are not connected. If we have a supplementary random sample from the distribution of Y, the biased samples are connected and the cdf is identified. Next, consider the conditional distribution of Y given X. If the subpopulations partition the support of the joint distribution of Y, X, then the joint and conditional cdf are identified with a supplementary sample from the joint distribution. This conditional cdf is in general not identified if the supplementary sample is from the marginal distribution of Y. If the subpopulations are defined as a partition of the support of Y, then an additional random sample from the marginal distribution of Y suffices for identification of the joint and conditional cdf of Y, X, because the W_k can be obtained from the marginal distribution of Y. A special case is a case-control study in which Y is 0–1 and the strata are defined by Y.

Case-control with contaminated controls Consider the case that Y is a 0–1 variable. We combine a random sample from the subpopulation defined by $Y = 1$, i.e. a random sample from the conditional distribution of X given $Y = 1$, with random samples from the marginal distributions of X and Y. By the law of total probability $f(x) = f(x \mid y = 1)\Pr(Y = 1) + f(x \mid y = 0)(1 - \Pr(Y = 1))$. The marginal distribution of Y identifies $\Pr(Y = 1)$ and combining this with the marginal distribution of X identifies $f(x \mid y = 0)$. Hence, the joint distribution of X, Y is identified. A sample from the marginal distribution of X does not identify the joint distribution of Y, X nor the marginal distribution of Y given X.

Non-parametric identification of the conditional distribution of Y given X is desirable, even if we assume that the conditional cdf is a member of a parametric family $F(y \mid x; \theta)$. Often, parametric assumptions identify θ from a single biased sample. Consider

$$f(y, x; \theta) = f(y \mid x; \theta)h(x) = W_k \frac{g_k(y, x)}{W_k(y, x)} \tag{149}$$

for all $(y, x), (y', x') \in S_k$ with $S_k = \{(y, x) \mid W_k(y, x) > 0\}$ we have

$$\frac{f(y \mid x; \theta)}{f(y' \mid x'; \theta)} = \frac{g_k(y, x)}{g_k(y', x')} \frac{W_k(y', x')}{W_k(y, x)}. \tag{150}$$

For instance, if the model is a probit model with $\Pr(Y = 1 \mid x; \theta) = \Phi(\theta_0 + \theta_1 x)$ for a dummy dependent Y, and W_k is the indicator of the stratum $Y = 1$, then θ_0, θ_1 are identified from this biased sample. To see this we consider the case that x is continuous and that 0 and 1 are in the support of x. Fix x' in (150) and consider the derivative with respect to x of the logarithm of the resulting expression. Evaluating the result fot $x = 0$ and $x = 1$ gives a (nonlinear) system of two equations in θ_0, θ_1 that can be solved for these two parameters. A more comprehensive discussion of parametric identification in choice-based samples can be found in Lancaster (1992). We do not discuss this type of identification any further, because it should be avoided.

Nonresponse in sample surveys or attrition in panel data also results in biased samples from the underlying population. For conditional inference, the key question is whether the response/attrition depends on Y. Note that in this case the biasing function is in general unknown. The large literature on sample selectivity goes back to Heckman (1979). Sample combination can be used to put restrictions on the biasing function, in this case the probability of response. Hirano et al. (2001) consider the combination of a panel survey with selective attrition and a refreshment sample. Manski (2003, Section 1.4), derives bounds on the population distribution under weak assumptions on the missing data process. This type of biased samples is beyond the scope of this survey.

6.3. *Non-parametric and efficient estimation in biased samples*

6.3.1. *Efficient non-parametric estimation in biased samples*

The efficient non-parametric estimator of the population cdf from a set of biased samples was first derived by Vardi (1985). Gill, Vardi and Wellner (1988) give a rigorous analysis of this estimator and prove that it is asymptotically efficient.[27]

Vardi's estimator is the solution to the empirical counterparts of Equations (144) and (143). The estimator of the cdf is

$$\hat{F}(y) = \frac{\int_0^y \frac{1}{\sum_{k=1}^K \lambda_k \frac{W_k(v)}{\hat{W}_k}} \, \mathrm{d}\hat{\bar{G}}(v)}{\int_{-\infty}^{\infty} \frac{1}{\sum_{k=1}^K \lambda_k \frac{W_k(v)}{\hat{W}_k}} \, \mathrm{d}\hat{\bar{G}}(v)}, \tag{151}$$

$$1 = \frac{1}{\hat{W}_k} \int_{-\infty}^{\infty} \frac{W_k(y)}{\sum_{l=1}^K \lambda_l \frac{W_l(y)}{\hat{W}_l}} \, \mathrm{d}\hat{\bar{G}}(y), \quad k = 2, \ldots, K. \tag{152}$$

In these equations $\lambda_k = \frac{N_k}{N}$. Integration with respect to the empirical cdf is just averaging over the combined sample.

If the cdf is non-parametrically identified, then the system of $K-1$ equations in $K-1$ unknowns (152) has a unique solution. This solution is substituted in (151) to obtain the non-parametric estimator of the cdf.

[27] In the sense that its limit process has a covariance function that reaches the lower bound for all regular estimators.

Gill, Vardi and Wellner (1988) show that the empirical cdf is consistent (at rate $n^{\frac{1}{2}}$) and asymptotically normal with a covariance function that can be easily estimated.[28]

In the case of endogenous stratification we have $W_k(y) = I_{\mathcal{S}_k}(y)$ with $\mathcal{S}_k$, $k = 1, \dots, K$, a partition of the set of values taken by Y. To ensure identification we have an additional random sample and we call this stratum $K+1$ with $W_{K+1}(y) = 1$ for all y. We normalize with respect to this stratum so that in (152) we have K equations in the unknowns $\hat{W}_1, \dots, \hat{W}_K$. They are

$$1 = \frac{1}{\hat{W}_k} \int_{-\infty}^{\infty} \frac{W_k(y)}{\sum_{l=1}^{K+1} \lambda_l \frac{W_l(y)}{\hat{W}_l} + \lambda_{K+1}} \, \mathrm{d}\hat{\bar{G}}(y), \quad k = 1, \dots, K. \tag{153}$$

Because integration with respect to the empirical cdf $\hat{\bar{G}}$ is just averaging over the complete data we obtain

$$\begin{aligned} 1 &= \frac{1}{\hat{W}_k} \frac{1}{N} \sum_{i=1}^{N} \frac{W_k(y_i)}{\sum_{l=1}^{K+1} \lambda_l \frac{W_l(y_i)}{\hat{W}_l} + \lambda_{K+1}} \\ &= \frac{1}{\hat{W}_k} \frac{1}{N} \sum_{i=1}^{N} \frac{1}{\lambda_k \frac{1}{\hat{W}_k} + \lambda_{K+1}} I_{\mathcal{S}_k}(y_i). \end{aligned} \tag{154}$$

If N_k, $k = 1, \dots, K+1$, is the sample size in the strata, $N = N_1 + \cdots + N_{K+1}$, and $\hat{N}_{K+1,k}$ is the number of observations in the random sample that is in $\mathcal{S}_k$, we have $\sum_{i=1}^{N} I_{\mathcal{S}_k}(y_i) = N_k + \hat{N}_{K+1,k}$

$$1 = \frac{N_k + \hat{N}_{K+1,k}}{N_k + N_{K+1}\hat{W}_k}, \quad k = 1, \dots, K, \tag{155}$$

with solution

$$\hat{W}_k = \frac{\hat{N}_{K+1,k}}{N_{K+1}}. \tag{156}$$

Hence the non-parametric estimator of the empirical cdf is just the sum of the empirical cdf of the random sample and the weighted empirical cdf in the strata with weights $\frac{\lambda_k}{\hat{W}_k}$, i.e. the ratio of the fraction of stratum k in the sample and population.

6.3.2. *Efficient parametric estimation in endogenously stratified samples*

We restrict the discussion to parametric models that specify the conditional density $f(y \mid x; \theta)$. A special case is the discrete choice model where y is a categorical

[28] If the dimension of $y \geqslant 2$ the result applies to the empirical measure that counts the number of outcomes in a set $E \subset \Re^M$ with M the dimension of y. There are restrictions on the choice of E, e.g. the orthants $y \leqslant c$ will do, in order to obtain uniform convergence.

variable. The sample space $\mathcal{Y} \times \mathcal{X}$ is divided into strata $\mathcal{S}_k$. These strata need not be disjoint. Indeed the analysis in Section 6.2 shows that to ensure non-parametric identification of $f(y \mid x)$ the strata should be overlapping. A special case occurs if Y is discrete and $\mathcal{S}_y = \{y\} \times \mathcal{X}$ for $y = 1, \ldots, M$. Such a sample is called a choice-based or response-based sample. In econometrics, estimation in endogenously stratified samples was first discussed in choice-based samples [Manski and Lerman (1977), Manski and McFadden (1981), Cosslett (1981b)]. The surprisingly simple efficient estimator in such samples was also first discovered for choice-based samples [Imbens (1992)] and later generalized to arbitrary endogenously stratified samples [Imbens and Lancaster (1996)]. We use a suggestion by Lancaster (1992) who showed that in choice-based samples the efficient estimator is the Conditional Maximum Likelihood (CML) estimator, if we substitute the observed stratum fractions, even if these fractions are specified by the sample design. This is true in any endogenously stratified sample. This simple result is similar to the observation of Wooldridge (1999) and Hirano, Imbens and Ridder (2003) who show that in stratified sampling the estimated or observed sample weights are preferred over the weights computed from the sampling probabilities that are used in the sample design. In the sequel we assume that the parameters in the conditional distribution of Y given X are identified, preferably because this conditional distribution is non-parametrically identified.

We assume that sampling is in two stages (i) a stratum $\mathcal{S}_k$ is selected with probability H_k, (ii) a random draw is obtained from $f(y, x \mid (Y, X) \in \mathcal{S}_k)$ which we denote as $f(y, x \mid \mathcal{S}_k)$. This is called multinomial sampling. In stratified sampling the number of observations in each stratum $\mathcal{S}_k$ is fixed in advance. Imbens and Lancaster (1996) show that inferences for both sampling schemes are the same, because the associated likelihood functions are proportional. Let S be the stratum indicator that is equal to k if the observation is in $\mathcal{S}_k$.

The joint density of Y, X, S in the sample is

$$g(s, y, x) = H_s f(y, x \mid \mathcal{S}_k) = H_s \frac{f(y \mid x; \theta) f(x)}{Q_s} \tag{157}$$

with

$$Q_s = \int_{\mathcal{S}_k} f(y \mid x; \theta) f(x) \, \mathrm{d}y \, \mathrm{d}x,$$

where we implicitly assume that Y is continuous. If not, just replace integration by summation. Now define

$$\mathcal{S}_k(x) = \bigl\{ y \bigm| (y, x) \in \mathcal{S}_k \bigr\}$$

and

$$\begin{aligned} R(k, x, \theta) &= \Pr\bigl((Y, X) \in \mathcal{S}_k \bigm| X = x\bigr) = \Pr\bigl(Y \in \mathcal{S}_k(x) \bigm| X = x\bigr) \\ &= \int_{\mathcal{S}_k(x)} f(y \mid x; \theta) \, \mathrm{d}y. \end{aligned}$$

Obviously $Q_k = \mathrm{E}(R(k, X, \theta))$.

The marginal density of X in the sample is obtained from (157) by integration with respect to y over $\mathcal{S}_k(x)$ (which may be an empty set for some x and k) and summation over k

$$g(x) = f(x) \sum_{k=1}^{K} \frac{H_k}{Q_k} R(k, x, \theta).$$

The sample density of X depends on the parameters θ. In endogenously stratified samples this distribution contains information on X. The conditional density of S, Y given X in the sample is

$$g(s, y \mid x) = \frac{f(y \mid x; \theta) \frac{H_s}{Q_s}}{\sum_{k=1}^{K} \frac{H_k}{Q_k} R(k, x, \theta)}. \tag{158}$$

An obvious method to obtain an efficient estimator of θ is by maximizing the likelihood function based on (157)

$$\ln L(\theta) = \sum_{i=1}^{N} \ln g(s_i, y_i, x_i) = \sum_{i=1}^{N} \ln f(y_i \mid x_i; \theta) f(x_i) + \ln\left(\frac{H_{s_i}}{Q_{s_i}}\right).$$

This likelihood requires the evaluation of Q_k that depends on θ and also on the marginal population density of X, $f(x)$. This is computationally unattractive, and worse it requires the specification of the density of the independent variables.

For that reason we consider an alternative method to obtain the MLE. This method consists of three steps. First, we assume that the distribution of X is discrete with L points of support, i.e.

$$\Pr(X = x_l) = f(x_l) = \pi_l, \quad l = 1, \ldots, L.$$

Next, we reparameterize from the discrete distribution of X in the population π_l to its discrete distribution in the sample λ_l. The stratum probabilities Q_k can also be expressed in λ_l. After this reparametrization the log likelihood is the sum of the conditional loglikelihood and the marginal loglikelihood of the observations on X. The first factor depends on λ_l only through the stratum probabilities Q_k.

The third step is that, if we maximize the conditional loglikelihood with respect to $H_1, \ldots, H_K$ and evaluate the first-order conditions at the MLE of these 'parameters', the restrictions on the stratum probabilities Q_k are satisfied. Hence maximizing the conditional loglikelihood with respect to θ and $H_1, \ldots, H_K$ is equivalent to maximization of the sample loglikelihood with respect to θ. This conclusion does not depend on the assumption that X has a discrete distribution. Following Chamberlain (1987) we conclude that the CMLE is efficient. Note that this is true if we replace the multinomial sampling probabilities H_k in the conditional loglikelihood by their sample values $\frac{N_k}{N}$ with N_k the number of observations in stratum k. The CMLE is not efficient if we use the probabilities H_k that were actually used in the multinomial sampling.

The discrete distribution of X in the sample is

$$g(x_l) = \lambda_l = \pi_l \left[\sum_{k=1}^{K} \frac{H_k}{Q_k} R(k, x_l, \theta) \right].$$

Hence

$$Q_k = \sum_{l=1}^{L} R(k, x_l, \theta)\pi_l = \sum_{l=1}^{L} \frac{R(k, x_l, \theta)}{\sum_{m=1}^{K} \frac{H_m}{Q_m} R(m, x_l, \theta)} \lambda_l$$

which can be written as a sample average

$$1 = \frac{1}{N} \sum_{i=1}^{N} \frac{R(k, x_i, \theta) \frac{1}{Q_k}}{\sum_{m=1}^{K} \frac{H_m}{Q_m} R(m, x_i, \theta)}. \tag{159}$$

The conditional loglikelihood is

$$\ln L_c(\theta) = \sum_{i=1}^{N} \ln f(y_i \mid x_i; \theta) - \sum_{i=1}^{N} \ln \left\{ \sum_{k=1}^{K} \frac{H_k}{Q_k} R(k, x_i, \theta) \right\} + \sum_{k=1}^{K} N_k \ln \frac{H_k}{Q_k}.$$

The first-order condition for H_k is

$$\frac{N_k}{H_k} = \sum_{i=1}^{N} \frac{R(k, x_i, \theta) \frac{1}{Q_k}}{\sum_{m=1}^{K} \frac{H_m}{Q_m} R(m, x_i, \theta)}.$$

If we substitute the MLE $\hat{H}_k = \frac{N_k}{N}$ in this equation and in (159) we see that they are identical and we conclude that the restrictions for Q_k are satisfied at the MLE (but not if we substitute H_k).

Note that if (159) holds for all $k = 1, \ldots, K$, multiplication by H_k and summation over k gives that $\sum_{l=1}^{L} \lambda_l = 1$. Again this condition is satisfied if the first-order conditions for maximization of the conditional loglikelihood with respect to $H_1, \ldots, H_K$ are evaluated at the MLE of these 'parameters'.

Hence the efficient estimator of θ is found by maximizing the conditional loglikelihood with respect to θ and $H_1, \ldots, H_K$. The first order conditions are evaluated at the MLE of $H_1, \ldots, H_K$ and solved for θ and $Q_1, \ldots, Q_K$. These first-order conditions set the sample average of the following functions equal to 0

$$m_1(s, y, x; \theta, Q) = \frac{\frac{\partial}{\partial \theta} f(y \mid x; \theta)}{f(y \mid x; \theta)} - \frac{\sum_{k=1}^{K} \frac{\hat{H}_k}{Q_k} \frac{\partial}{\partial \theta} R(k, x, \theta)}{\sum_{k=1}^{K} \frac{\hat{H}_k}{Q_k} R(k, x, \theta)}, \tag{160}$$

$$m_{2k}(s, y, x; \theta, Q) = Q_k - \frac{R(k, x, \theta)}{\sum_{m=1}^{K} \frac{\hat{H}_m}{Q_m} R(m, x, \theta)}, \tag{161}$$

for $k = 1, \ldots, K$ and $\hat{H}_k = \frac{N_k}{N}$. Hence the efficient estimator is a GMM estimator that satisfies moment conditions based on these moment functions. An additional moment function that gives $\hat{H}_k$ can be added, but the corresponding moment condition is independent of the other moment conditions. Hence we can treat the $\hat{H}_k$ as given.

The variance of the efficient estimator can be found by the usual GMM formula. The GMM formulation is convenient if we add additional sample information. This is just another moment condition.

6.3.3. Efficient parametric estimation with marginal information

Random sample with marginal information First we consider the case that a random sample $Y_i, X_i, i = 1, \ldots, N$, is combined with marginal information. The marginal information consists of moments $\mathrm{E}(h(Y, X)) = \bar{h}$ with h a known function of dimension K and $\bar{h}$ an K vector of constants. The expectation is over the population distribution of X, Y. Hence we combine information in two random samples, one of which comprises the whole population. Although these random samples cannot be independent, we can think of this as the combination of a relatively small random sample with a very large one. The sampling variance in the second sample is negligible. This is the setup considered by Imbens and Lancaster (1994).

Without loss of generality we set $\bar{h}$ equal to 0. The goal is to estimate the parameter vector θ in the conditional distribution of Y given X with conditional density $f(y \mid x; \theta)$. Because we have a random sample, identification is not an issue. However, the additional moments overindentify the parameters, and these additional moment restrictions increase the precision of the estimation or can be used to create more powerful specification tests.

The score vector is

$$m_1(y, x; \theta) = \frac{\partial \ln f(y \mid x; \theta)}{\partial \theta}. \tag{162}$$

Of course setting the sample average of the score equal to 0 gives the MLE that is an efficient estimator without additional information. The additional information can be expressed as

$$\mathrm{E}\big(h(Y, X)\big) = \iint h(y, x) f(y \mid x; \theta)\, \mathrm{d}y\, g(x)\, \mathrm{d}x = 0. \tag{163}$$

This gives a restriction on θ. The efficient estimator that uses this restriction is the restricted MLE that is obtained by maximizing the loglikelihood subject the constraint in (163).

The implementation of the restricted MLE requires the specification of the marginal density of X. Applied researchers are usually unwilling to make parametric assumptions on this marginal distribution, and for that reason it is convenient that such a specification is not needed. Rewrite (163) as an average over the sample

$$\frac{1}{N}\sum_{i=1}^{N}\int h(y, X_i) f(y \mid X_i; \theta)\,\mathrm{d}y = \frac{1}{N}\sum_{i=1}^{N} m_2(Y_i, X_i; \theta). \tag{164}$$

Imbens and Lancaster (1994) show that the optimal GMM estimator with weight matrix equal to the inverse of the variance matrix of the moment restrictions has an asymptotic variance that is equal to that of the restricted MLE.[29]

Their simulation study and empirical example show that the efficiency gains can be substantial. The precision of the estimator of the regression coefficient of X_j increases if the marginal information is the joint population distribution of grouped Y and grouped X_k. For instance, if Y is the employment indicator and X_j is age, the joint population distribution of employment status and age category (but no other variable) is highly informative on the age coefficient in an employment probit or logit. If the model has no interactions the pairwise population joint distributions of the dependent and the independent variables reduce the variances of the regression coefficients. Also in the case of a dummy dependent variable the marginal information is very useful if one of the outcomes is rare.

The additional moments (164) involve an integral over y (if Y is continuous). If one wants to avoid this integral one would be tempted to use the additional moment

$$\frac{1}{N}\sum_{i=1}^{N} h(Y_i, X_i) = \frac{1}{N}\sum_{i=1}^{N} m_3(Y_i, X_i; \theta) \tag{165}$$

instead of (164). The resulting GMM estimator is less efficient than the restricted MLE. This can be seen if one considers the case without covariates X and a scalar h and θ. In that case the moment condition in (164) restricts the parameter to its population value, while the moment condition in (165) does not remove the sampling variation in the restricted MLE. To achieve efficiency one should use (164) as the second set of moment conditions.

In the case that the conditional density is not specified, the moment conditions in (164) are not available and one if forced to use (165) together with the moment conditions based on $m(y, x; \theta)$ that is a vector of moment conditions that identifies θ and could be used to estimate the parameters if one only had the random sample from the population. The moment conditions (164) do not depend on θ, but because they are correlated with the moment conditions in (164). Hence imposing them along with (164) improves the precision of the estimators.

As noted the additional moments can be used for an often powerful test of the parametric model $f(y \mid x; \theta)$. The obvious test is the GMM overidentification test based on the moment conditions (162) and (164). The test statistic is the minimal value of the optimal GMM minimand and it has under the null hypothesis of correct specification,

[29] An alternative definition is the restricted MLE with (164) as the restriction.

a chi-squared distribution with K (dimension of h) degrees of freedom. It should be noted that the test also rejects if the random sample is not from the same population that is used to compute $\mathrm{E}(h(Y, X))$. To deal with this one could consider a joint test based on the moment conditions (162), (164) and (165) that tests both for the compatibility of the information and the specification. This test statistic has $2K$ degrees of freedom.

Van den Berg and van der Klaauw (2001) consider the estimation of a model for unemployment durations where the aggregate information consists of unemployment rates. Their approach is a direct application of the restricted MLE with the additional complication that they allow for measurement error in the aggregate data.

Biased samples with marginal information Imbens and Hellerstein (1999) show[30] that the optimal GMM estimator, based on (162) and (165), i.e. we consider the case that the conditional density of Y given X is not specified, but θ is estimated from a set of moment conditions, is equivalent to a weighted GMM estimator that solves

$$\sum_{i=1}^{N} w_i m_1(Y_i, X_i; \theta) = 0 \tag{166}$$

with weights $w_i, i = 1, \ldots, N$, defined as the solution to

$$\max \sum_{i=1}^{N} \ln w_i \quad \text{s.t.} \quad \sum_{i=1}^{N} w_i = 1, \quad \sum_{i=1}^{N} w_i h(Y_i, X_i) = \bar{h}. \tag{167}$$

The weights are equal to

$$w_i = w(Y_i, X_i) = \frac{1}{N(1 + \hat{\lambda}' h(Y_i, X_i))} \tag{168}$$

with $\hat{\lambda}$ the Lagrange multiplier on the second restriction. It is the solution to

$$\frac{1}{N} \sum_{i=1}^{N} \frac{h(Y_i, X_i)}{1 + \hat{\lambda}' h(Y_i, X_i)} = 0. \tag{169}$$

Now consider the case that a biased sample is combined with marginal information from the population. As an illustration we consider the example of a 0–1 dependent variable with conditional density $f(y \mid x; \theta) = G(x'\theta)^y (1 - G(x'\theta))^{1-y}$. The endogenously stratified sample has strata $\mathcal{S}_1 = 1 \times \mathcal{X}$ and $\mathcal{S}_2 = 0 \times \mathcal{X}$ with $\mathcal{X}$ the support of X. The multinomial sampling probabilities are H_1, H_2 and the population fractions of the two strata are Q_1, Q_2. Also $h(y, x) = y - Q_1$. In large samples $\hat{\lambda}$ in (169) converges to the solution to the equation that is obtained by replacing the sample average in (169)

[30] To be precise, they only consider linear regression with additional moment restrictions, but their argument applies generally.

by the corresponding expectation over the sample distribution

$$\int \sum_{y=0}^{1} \frac{y - Q_1}{1 + \lambda(y - Q_1)} \left(\frac{H_1}{Q_1} G(x'\theta) \right)^y \left(\frac{H_2}{Q_2} (1 - G(x'\theta)) \right)^{1-y} g(x)\,\mathrm{d}x = 0. \tag{170}$$

The solution is

$$\lambda = \frac{H_1 - Q_1}{Q_1 Q_2} \tag{171}$$

so that the weights that depend on the value of y only are

$$w(y, x) = \frac{1}{N} \frac{1}{1 + \frac{H_1 - Q_1}{Q_1 Q_2}(y - Q_1)} = \frac{1}{N} \left(\frac{Q_1}{H_1} \right)^y \left(\frac{Q_2}{H_2} \right)^{1-y}. \tag{172}$$

These weights are used in the score based on the full sample to obtain the weighted likelihood equation

$$\sum_{i=1}^{N} w(Y_i, X_i) \left(Y_i \frac{\partial \ln G(X_i'\theta)}{\partial \theta} + (1 - Y_i) \frac{\partial \ln(1 - G(X_i'\theta))}{\partial \theta} \right) = 0. \tag{173}$$

This corresponds to the Weighted Exogenous Sampling MLE of Manski and Lerman (1977). This estimator is not fully efficient because it does not use the parametric model in the additional moment condition.

We conclude that if the additional population moments combined with the biased sample identify the population parameters, then the weighted estimator proposed by Imbens and Hellerstein (1999) is the efficient GMM that imposes the population moments. If the conditional density is specified, the estimator is not fully efficient. Hence their weighted estimator provides a constructive method to combine biased samples with population moments. Devereux and Tripathi (2004) consider the combination of sample in which some of the variables in Y, X are censored or truncated with a sample in which all these variables or fully observed. They show that the efficient GMM estimator is a weighted GMM estimator. For instance, in the case of Y censored at C the weights are $w = \frac{I(Y \neq C)}{p + (1-p) I(Y < C)}$ with p the fraction of the combined sample with fully observed Y. The assumption that in one of the samples all variables are fully observed is restrictive.

If the combination of the biased sample(s) and the population moment does not identify the population parameters, the weighted GMM estimator converges to the solution of

$$\iint m_1(y, x; \theta) \frac{f_s(y, x)}{1 + \lambda' h(y, x)} \,\mathrm{d}y\,\mathrm{d}x \tag{174}$$

with λ the solution of (169) if we replace the (biased) sample average by the (biased) sample expected value. Hence the GMM estimator is consistent for the parameters in a distribution that satisfies the population moments and is also consistent with the biased sample. It is obtained from the distribution in the biased sample by weighting, which is the general approach (see Section 6.3.2). The weights reproduce the population distribution if the parameters are identified. If not, they produce a GMM estimate that is consistent with the available information. However, in that case the weight (and hence the GMM estimator) are not unique. In the optimization problem (167) we can replace $\ln w_i$ by $K(w_i)$ with K any concave function. This reflects the fact that the parameters are not point identified.

Appendix A

THEOREM 1. *If assumptions* (A1)–(A3) *hold, then the* 2SIV *estimator is weakly consistent.*

PROOF. We have by adding and subtracting $m_N(\theta_0)$

$$m_N(\theta)' W_N m_N(\theta) = \big(m_N(\theta) - m_N(\theta_0)\big)' W_N \big(m_N(\theta) - m_N(\theta_0)\big) + 2 m_N(\theta_0)' W_N \big(m_N(\theta) - m_N(\theta_0)\big) + m_N(\theta_0)' W_N m_N(\theta_0). \tag{175}$$

By the mean value theorem

$$m_N(\theta) = m_N(\theta_0) + \frac{\partial m_N}{\partial \theta'}(\theta_*)(\theta - \theta_0) \tag{176}$$

with θ_* between θ and θ_0. Substitution in (175) and taking the limit $N_1, N_2 \to \infty$ gives

$$(\theta - \theta_0)' \mathrm{E}\left[\frac{\partial m'}{\partial \theta}(\theta_*)\right] W \mathrm{E}\left[\frac{\partial m}{\partial \theta'}(\theta_*)\right](\theta - \theta_0) + 2\mathrm{E}\big[m(\theta_0)\big]' W \mathrm{E}\left[\frac{\partial m}{\partial \theta'}(\theta_*)\right](\theta - \theta_0) + \mathrm{E}\big[m(\theta_0)\big]' W \mathrm{E}\big[m(\theta_0)\big] \tag{177}$$

and this limit is attained uniformly in θ. If (A1) holds, then $\mathrm{E}(m(\theta_0)) = 0$, so that the last two terms on the right-hand side are equal to 0. Because $\mathrm{E}[\frac{\partial m'}{\partial \theta}(\theta)]$ is continuous in θ this matrix has full rank in a neighborhood of θ_0. In that neighborhood θ_0 is the unique minimizer. By Van der Vaart (1998, Theorem 5.7), this implies that the 2SIV estimator converges in probability to θ_0. □

THEOREM 2. *If assumptions* (A1)–(A4) *hold, then*

$$\sqrt{N_2}(\hat{\theta}_N - \theta_0) \xrightarrow{d} N\big(0, V(\theta_0)\big) \tag{178}$$

with

$$V(\theta_0) = \left[\mathrm{E}\left(\frac{\partial m'}{\partial \theta}(\theta_0)\right) W(\theta_0) \mathrm{E}\left(\frac{\partial m}{\partial \theta'}(\theta_0)\right)\right]^{-1}$$

$$\cdot \mathrm{E}\left(\frac{\partial m'}{\partial \theta}(\theta_0)\right) W(\theta_0)\big(\lambda \operatorname{Var}\big(m_{1j}(\theta_0)\big)$$

$$+ \operatorname{Var}\big(m_{2i}(\theta_0)\big)\big) W(\theta_0) \mathrm{E}\left(\frac{\partial m}{\partial \theta'}(\theta_0)\right)$$

$$\cdot \left[\mathrm{E}\left(\frac{\partial m'}{\partial \theta}(\theta_0)\right) W(\theta_0) \mathrm{E}\left(\frac{\partial m}{\partial \theta'}(\theta_0)\right)\right]^{-1}. \tag{179}$$

PROOF. The first-order conditions give

$$0 = \frac{\partial m_N'}{\partial \theta}(\hat{\theta}_N) W_N \sqrt{N_2} m_N(\hat{\theta}_N). \tag{180}$$

By the mean value theorem we have for some $\bar{\theta}_N$ between θ_0 and $\hat{\theta}_N$

$$\sqrt{N_2} m_N(\hat{\theta}_N) = \sqrt{N_2} m_N(\theta_0) + \frac{\partial m_N}{\partial \theta'}(\bar{\theta}_N) \sqrt{N_2}(\hat{\theta}_N - \theta_0). \tag{181}$$

Substitution in (180) and solving for $\sqrt{N_2}(\hat{\theta}_N - \theta_0)$ gives

$$\begin{aligned} &\sqrt{N_2}(\hat{\theta}_N - \theta_0) \\ &\quad = -\left[\frac{\partial m_N'}{\partial \theta}(\hat{\theta}_N) W_N \frac{\partial m_N}{\partial \theta'}(\bar{\theta}_N)\right]^{-1} \frac{\partial m_N'}{\partial \theta}(\hat{\theta}_N) W_N \sqrt{N_2} m_N(\theta_0). \end{aligned} \tag{182}$$

The proof is completed by noting that $\frac{\partial m_N}{\partial \theta}(\theta)$ is continuous in θ, and by using the central limit theorem for i.i.d. random variables to obtain the asymptotic distribution of $\sqrt{N_2} m_N(\theta_0)$. □

THEOREM 3. *If* (A1)–(A4) *hold, then* $T_N \xrightarrow{d} \chi^2(\dim(m) - \dim(\theta))$.

PROOF. Substitution of (182) in (181) gives

$$\begin{aligned} &\sqrt{N_2} m_N(\hat{\theta}_N) \\ &\quad = \left[I - \frac{\partial m_N}{\partial \theta'}(\bar{\theta}_N)\left[\frac{\partial m_N'}{\partial \theta}(\hat{\theta}_N) W_N \frac{\partial m_N}{\partial \theta'}(\bar{\theta}_N)\right]^{-1} \frac{\partial m_N'}{\partial \theta}(\hat{\theta}_N) W_N\right] \sqrt{N_2} m_N(\theta_0). \end{aligned} \tag{183}$$

Using the notation $A(\theta) = \frac{\partial m_N'}{\partial \theta}(\theta)$ and the assumption that this matrix is continuous in θ, we have

$$\sqrt{N_2} m_N(\hat{\theta}_N) = \big[I - A(\theta_0)'\big(A(\theta_0) W A(\theta_0)'\big)^{-1} A(\theta_0) W\big] \sqrt{N_2} m_N(\theta_0) + o_p(1). \tag{184}$$

Upon substitution of (184) in (94)

$$T_N = \sqrt{N_2} m_N(\theta_0)'\big[I - W' A(\theta_0)'\big(A(\theta_0) W A(\theta_0)'\big)^{-1} A(\theta_0)\big] W$$

$$\cdot \left[I - A(\theta_0)' \left(A(\theta_0) W A(\theta_0)' \right)^{-1} A(\theta_0) W \right] \sqrt{N_2} m_N(\theta_0) + o_p(1)$$
$$= \sqrt{N_2} m_N(\theta_0)' \left[W - W' A(\theta_0)' \left(A(\theta_0) W A(\theta_0)' \right)^{-1} A(\theta_0) W \right] \sqrt{N_2} m_N(\theta_0)$$
$$+ o_p(1). \tag{185}$$

If $W = M(\theta_0)^{-1}$, we can find a matrix $M(\theta_0)^{-\frac{1}{2}}$ with $M(\theta_0)^{-1} = M(\theta_0)^{-\frac{1}{2}} M(\theta_0)^{-\frac{1}{2}}$. Then

$$T_N = \sqrt{N_2} m_N(\theta_0)' M(\theta_0)^{-\frac{1}{2}}$$
$$\cdot \left[I - M(\theta_0)^{-\frac{1}{2}} A(\theta_0)' \left(A(\theta_0) M(\theta_0)^{-1} A(\theta_0)' \right)^{-1} A(\theta_0) M(\theta_0)^{-\frac{1}{2}} \right]$$
$$\cdot M(\theta_0)^{-\frac{1}{2}} \sqrt{N_2} m_N(\theta_0) + o_p(1). \tag{186}$$

Because $\sqrt{N_2} m_N(\theta_0)' M(\theta_0)^{-\frac{1}{2}} \xrightarrow{d} N(0, I)$ and the matrix between [.] is idempotent with rank equal to $\dim(m_N) - \dim(\theta)$, the result follows. □

References

Alessie, R., Devereux, M., Weber, G. (1997). "Intertemporal consumption, durables and liquidity constraints: A cohort analysis". European Economic Review 41, 37–59.

Amemiya, T. (1978). "The estimation of a simultaneous-equation generalized probit model". Econometrica 46 (5), 1193–1205.

Amemiya, T. (1985). Advanced Econometrics. Harvard University Press, Cambridge, MA.

Angrist, J.D., Krueger, A.B. (1992). "The effect of age at school entry on educational attainment: An application of instrumental variables with moments from two samples". Journal of the American Statistical Association 87, 328–336.

Arellano, M., Honoré, B. (2001). "Panel data models: Some recent developments". In: Heckman, J., Leamer, E. (Eds.), Handbook of Econometrics, vol. 5. Elsevier, Amsterdam.

Arellano, M., Meghir, C. (1992). "Female labour supply and on-the-job-search: An empirical model estimated using complementary data sets". Review of Economic Studies 59, 537–557.

Attanasio, O. (1998). "A cohort analysis of saving behavior by US households". Journal of Human Resources 33, 575–609.

Attanasio, O., Weber, G. (1994). "The UK consumption boom of the late 1980's: Aggregate implications of microeconometric evidence". Economic Journal 104, 1269–1302.

Barr, R.S., Turner, J.S. (1978). "A new, linear programming approach to microdata file merging". In: Compendium of Tax Research, 1978 ed. Office of Tax Analysis, Department of the Treasury, Washington, DC, pp. 131–155.

Belin, T.R., Rubin, D.B. (1995). "A method for calibrating false-match rates in record linkage". Journal of the American Statistical Association 90, 694–707.

Blow, L., Preston, I. (2002). "Deadweight loss and taxation of earned income: Evidence from tax records of the UK self-employed". IFS Working Paper 15. London.

Blundell, R., Browning, M., Meghir, C. (1994). "Consumer demand and the lifecycle allocation of household expenditures". Review of Economic Studies 61, 57–80.

Blundell, R., Smith, R. (1993). "Simultaneous microeconometric models with censored and qualitative dependent variables". In: Maddala, G.S., Rao, C.R., Vinod, H.D. (Eds.), Handbook of Statistics: Econometrics, vol. 11. Elsevier, Amsterdam.

Box, G.E.P., Cox, D.R. (1964). "An analysis of transformations". Journal of the Royal Statistical Society B 26, 211–252.

Breslow, N.E., Day, N.E. (1980). Statistical Methods on Cancer Research, Volume 1: Case-control Studies. International Agency for Cancer Research, Lyon.
Browning, M., Deaton, A., Irish, M. (1985). "A profitable approach to labor supply and commodity demands over the life cycle". Econometrica 53, 503–544.
Buehler, J.W., Prager, K., Hogue, C.J., Shamsuddin, K., Lieberman, E., Young, T.K., Kliewer, E., Blanchard, O.J., Mayer, T. (2000). "The role of linked birth and infant death certificates in maternal and child health epidemiology in the United States". American Journal of Preventive Medicine 19, 3–11.
Burbidge, J.B., Magee, L., Robb, A.L. (1988). "Alternative transformations to handle extreme values of the dependent variable". Journal of the American Statistical Association 83, 123–127.
Card, D., Hildreth, A.K.G., Shore-Sheppard L.D. (2001). "The measurement of Medicaid coverage in the SIPP: Evidence from California, 1990–1996". Working Paper. NBER 8514.
Carroll, C.D., Weil, D.N. (1994). "Saving and growth: A reinterpretation". Carnegie–Rochester Conference Series on Public Policy 40, 133–191.
Carroll, C.D., Dynan, K.E., Krane, S.D. (1999). "Unemployment risk and precautionary wealth: Evidence from household's balance sheetd". Finance and Economics Discussion Series, 1999-15. Federal Reserve Board, Washington, DC.
Chamberlain, G. (1982). "Multivariate regression models for panel data". Journal of Econometrics 18, 5–46.
Chamberlain, G. (1987). "Asymptotic efficiency in estimation with conditional moment restrictions". Econometrica 34, 305–334.
Chen, X., Hong, H., Tamer, E. (2005). "Measurement error models with auxiliary data". Review of Economic Studies 72, 343–366.
Chen, X., Hong, H., Tarozzi, A. (2004). "Semiparametric efficiency in GMM models of nonclassical measurement error, missing data and treatment effects".
Collado, L. (1997). "Estimating dynamic models from time series of independent cross-sections". Journal of the Econometrics 82, 37–62.
Copas, J.B., Hilton , F.J. (1990). "Record linkage: Statistical methods for matching computer records". Journal of the Royal Statistical Society A 153, 287–320.
Cosslett, S.R. (1981a). "Efficient estimation of discrete choice models". In: Manski, C.F., McFadden, D. (Eds.), Structural Analysis of Discrete Data. MIT Press, Cambridge, MA.
Cosslett, S.R. (1981b). "Maximum likelihood estimator for choice-based samples". Econometrica 49 (5), 1289–1316.
Cox, D.R. (1969). "Some sampling problems in technology". In: Johnson, N.L., Smith Jr., H. (Eds.), New Developments in Survey Sampling. Wiley–Interscience, New York, pp. 506–527.
Cross, P.J., Manski, C.F. (2002). "Regressions, short and long". Econometrica 70, 357–368.
Currie, J., Yelowitz, A. (2000). "Are public housing projects good for kids?". Journal of Public Economics 75, 99–124.
Deaton, A. (1985). "Panel data from time series of cross sections". Journal of Econometrics 30, 109–126.
Dee, T.S., Evans, W.N. (2003). "Teen drinking and educational attainment: Evidence from Two-Sample Instrumental Variables (TSIV) estimates". Journal of Labor Economics 21, 178–209.
DeGroot, M.H., Goel, P.K. (1976). "The matching problem for multivariate normal data". Sankhya 38, 14–29.
DeGroot, M.H., Goel, P.K. (1980). "Estimation of the correlation coefficient from a broken random sample". Annals of Statistics 8, 264–278.
DeGroot, M.H., Feder, P.I., Goel, P.K. (1971). "Matchmaking". Annals of Mathematical Statistics 42, 578–593.
Devereux, P.J. (2003). "Small sample bias in synthetic cohort models of labor supply". Mimeo.
Devereux, P.J., Tripathi, G. (2004). "Combining datasets to overcome selection caused by censoring and truncation in moment based models". Mimeo. UCLA.
Donald, S., Newey, W. (2001). "Choosing the number of instruments". Econometrica 69, 1161–1191.
Fair, M., Cyr, M., Wen, S.W., Guyon, G., MacDonald, R.C., Buehler, J.W., Prager, K., Hogue, C.J., Shamsuddin, K., Lieberman, E., Young, T.K., Kliewer, E., Blanchard, O.J., Mayer, T. (2000). "An assessment of the validity of a computer system for probabilistic record linkage of birth and death records in Canada. The fetal and infant health study group". Chronic Diseases in Canada 21, 8–13.

Fellegi, I.P. (1999). "Record linkage and public policy". In: Record Linkage Techniques-1997. National Academy Press, Washington, DC, pp. 3–12.

Fellegi, I.P., Sunter, A.B. (1969). "A theory of record linkage". Journal of the American Statistical Association 64, 1183–1210.

Fréchet, M. (1951). "Sur les tableaux de correlation dont les marges sont données". Annales de Université, Lyons Sect. A 14, 53–77.

Gill, R.D., Vardi, Y., Wellner, J.A. (1988). "Large sample theory of empirical distributions in biased sampling models". Annals of Statistics 18, 1069–1112.

Goodman, L. (1953). "Ecological regressions and behavior of individuals". American Sociological Review 18, 663–664.

Güell, M., Hu, L. (2003) "Estimating the probability of leaving unemployment using uncompleted spells from repeated cross-section data". Working Paper 473. Industrial Relations Section, Princeton.

Hajek, J., Sidak, Z. (1967). Theory of Rank Tests. Academic Press, New York.

Hansen, L.P. (1982). "Large sample properties of generalized method of moments estimators". Econometrica 50, 1029–1054.

Hausman, J., Wise, D. (1981). "Stratification on endogenous variables and estimation: The Gary income maintenance experiment". In: Manski, C.F., McFadden, D. (Eds.), Structural Analysis of Discrete Data. MIT Press, Cambridge, MA, pp. 364–391.

Heckman, J.J. (1978). "Dummy endogenous variables in a simultaneous equation system". Econometrica 46 (6), 931–959.

Heckman, J.J. (1979). "Sample selection bias as a specification error". Econometrica 47, 153–161.

Heckman, J.J., Robb, R. (1985). "Alternative methods for evaluating the impact of interventions". In: Heckman, J., Singer, B. (Eds.), Longitudinal Analysis of the Labor Market. Cambridge University Press, Cambridge.

Hirano, K., Imbens, G., Ridder, G. (2003). "Efficient estimation of average treatment effects using the estimated propensity score". Econometrica 71, 1161–1189.

Hirano, K., Imbens, G.W., Ridder, G., Rubin, D.B. (2001). "Combining panel data with attrition and refreshment samples". Econometrica 69, 1645–1659.

Horowitz, J., Manski, C.F. (1995). "Identification and robustness with contaminated and corrupted data". Econometrica 63, 281–302.

Horvitz, D.G., Thompson, D.J. (1952). "A generalization of sampling without replacement from a finite universe". Journal of the American Statistical Association 47, 663–685.

Hsieh, D.A., Manski, C.F., McFadden, D. (1985). "Estimation of response probabilities from augmented retrospective observations". Journal of the American Statistical Association 80, 651–662.

Hu, Y., Ridder, G. (2003). "Estimation of nonlinear models with measurement errors using marginal information". Working Paper. CLEO, University of Southern California.

Ichimura, H., Martinez-Sanchis, E. (2005). "Identification and estimation of GMM models by a combination of two data sets". Mimeo. University College London.

Imbens, G.W. (1992). "An efficient method of moments estimator for discrete choice models with choice-based sampling". Econometrica 60, 1187–1214.

Imbens, G.W., Hellerstein, J. (1999). "Imposing moment restrictions from auxiliary data by weighting". Review of Economics and Statistics 81, 1–14.

Imbens, G.W., Lancaster, T. (1994). "Combining micro and macro data in microeconometric models". Review of Economic Studies 61, 655–680.

Imbens, G.W., Lancaster, T. (1996). "Efficient estimation and stratified sampling". Journal of Econometrics 74, 289–318.

Imbens G.W., Newey, W.K., Ridder, G. (2004). "Mean-squared-error calculations for Average Treatment Effects". Mimeo.

Kadane, J.B. (1978). "Some problems in merging data files". In: Compendium of Tax Research, 1978 ed. Office of Tax Analysis, Department of the Treasury, Washington, DC, pp. 159–179.

King, G. (1997). A Solution to the Ecological Inference Problem: Reconstructing Individual Behavior from Aggregate Data. Princeton University Press, Princeton.

Klevmarken, W.A. (1982). "Missing variables and two-stage least-squares estimation from more than one data set". In: 1981 Proceedings of the American Statistical Association, Business and Economic Statistics Section. Pp. 156–161.
Lancaster, A.D. (1992). "A survey of inference in choice-based samples". Working Paper. Department of Economics, Brown University.
Lancaster, A.D., Imbens, G.W. (1996). "Case-control studies with contaminated controls". Journal of Econometrics 71, 145–160.
Lee, T., Judge, G., Zellner, A. (1970). Estimating the Parameters of the Markov Probability Model from Aggregate Time Series Data. North-Holland, Amsterdam.
Lusardi, A. (1996). "Permanent income, current income, and consumption: Evidence from two panel data sets". Journal of Business and Economic Statistics 14, 81–90.
MacRae, E.C. (1977). "Estimation of time-varying Markov processes with aggregate data". Econometrica 45, 183–198.
Madansky, A. (1959). "Least squares estimation in finite Markov processes". Psychometrika 17, 149–167.
Manski, C. (2003). Partial Identification of Probability Distributions. Springer-Verlag, New York.
Manski, C.F., Lerman, S. (1977). "The estimation of choice probabilities from choice based samples". Econometrica 45, 1977–1988.
Manski, C.F., McFadden, D. (1981). "Alternative estimators and sample designs for discrete choice data". In: Manski, C.F., McFadden, D. (Eds.), Structural Analysis of Discrete Data. MIT Press, Cambridge, MA.
McKenzie, D. (2004). "Asymptotic theory for heterogeneous dynamic pseudo-panels". Journal of Econometrics 120, 235–262.
Miller, G. (1952). "Finite Markov processes in psychology". Psychometrika 24, 137–144.
Moffitt, R. (1993). "Identification and estimation of dynamic models with a time series of repeated cross sections". Journal of Econometrics 59, 99–123.
Morgenthaler, S., Vardi, Y. (1986). "Choice-based samples: A non-parametric approach". Journal of Econometrics 32, 109–125.
Nelson, F., Olsen, L. (1978). "Specification and estimation of a simultaneous equation model with limited dependent variables". International Economic Review 19, 695–705.
Neter, J., Maynes, E.S., Ramanathan, R. (1965). "The effect of mismatching on the measurement of response errors". Journal of the American Statistical Association 60, 1005–1027.
Newcombe, H.B. (1988). Handbook of Record Linkage: Methods for Health and Statistical Studies, Administration and Business. Oxford University Press, Oxford.
Newcombe, H.B., Fair, M.E., LaLonde, P. (1992). "The use of names for linking personal records". Journal of the American Statistical Association 87, 1193–1208.
Newcombe, H.B., Kennedy, J.M., Axford, S.J., James, A.P. (1959). "Automatic linkage of vital records". Science 130, 954–959.
Newey, W.K., Powell, J.L. (2003). "Instrumental variables estimation for non-parametric models". Econometrica 71, 1565–1578.
Okner, B.A. (1972). "Constructing a new data base from existing microdata sets: The 1966 merge file". Annals of Economic and Social Measurement 1, 325–362.
Pagan, A. (1984). "Econometric issues in the analysis of regressions with generated regressors". International Economic Review 25, 221–247.
Paxson, C., Waldfogel, J. (2002). "Work, welfare and child maltreatment". Journal of Labor Economics 20, 435–474.
Pelzer, B., Eisinga, R., Franses, P.H. (2002). "Inferring transition probabilities from repeated cross sections". Political Analysis 18, 113–133.
Pelzer, B., Eisinga, R., Franses, P.H. (2004). "Ecological panel inference from repeated cross sections". In: King, G., Rosen, O., Tanner, M. (Eds.), Ecological Inference. New Methodological Strategies. Cambridge University Press, Cambridge.
Perrachi, F., Welch, F. (1994). "Trends in labor force transitions of older men and women". Journal of Labor Economics 12, 210–242.

Prentice, R., Pyke, R. (1979). "Logistic disease incidence models and case-control studies". Biometrika 66, 403–411.
Radner, D.B. (1974). "The statistical matching of microdata sets: The Bureau of Economic Analysis 1964 Current Population Survey-Tax model match". PhD Thesis. Department of Economics, Yale University.
Radner, D.B., Allen, R., Gonzalez, M.E., Jabine, T.B., Muller, H.J. (1980). "Report on exact and statistical matching techniques". Statistical Policy Working Paper no. 5. US Department of Commerce, Washington DC.
Raessler, S. (2002). Statistical Matching: A Frequentist Theory, Practical Applications, and Alternative Bayesian Approaches. Springer, New York.
Rivers, D., Vuong, Q. (1988). "Limited information estimators and exogeneity tests for simultaneous probit models". Journal of Econometrics 39, 347–366.
Rodgers, W.L. (1984). "An evaluation of statistical matching". Journal of Business and Economic Statistics 2, 91–102.
Rodgers, W., DeVol, E. (1982). "An evaluation of statistical matching". In: 1981 Proceedings of the American Statistical Association, Section on Survey Research Methods. Pp. 128–132.
Rubin, D.B. (1986). "Statistical matching using file concatenation with adjusted weights and multiple imputations". Journal of Business and Economic Statistics 4, 87–94.
Ruggles, N., Ruggles, R. (1974). "A strategy for merging and matching microdata sets". Annals of Economic and Social Measurement 3, 353–371.
Ruggles, N., Ruggles, R., Wolff, E. (1977). "Merging microdata: Rationale, practice, and testing". Annals of Economic and Social Measurement 6, 407–429.
Scheuren, F., Winkler, W.E. (1993). "Regression analysis of data files that are computer matched". Survey Methodology 19, 39–58.
Sevestre, P., Trognon, A. (1996). "Dynamic linear models". In: Mátyás, L., Sevestre, P. (Eds.), The Econometrics of Panel Data: A Handbook of the Theory with Applications, second ed. Kluwer, Dordrecht.
Sims, C.A. (1972). "Comments". Annals of Economic and Social Measurement 1, 343–345.
Smith, R., Blundell, R. (1986). "An exogeneity test for a simultaneous equation Tobit model with an application to labor supply". Econometrica 54, 679–685.
Tepping, B.J. (1968). "A model for optimal linkage of records". Journal of the American Statistical Association 63, 1321–1332.
Van den Berg, G.J., van der Klaauw, B. (2001). "Combining micro and macro unemployment duration data". Journal of Econometrics 102, 271–309.
Van der Vaart, A. (1998). Asymptotic Statistics. Cambridge University Press, Cambridge, UK.
Vardi, Y. (1982). "Non-parametric estimation in the presence of length bias". Annals of Statistics 10, 616–620.
Vardi, Y. (1985). "Empirical distributions in selection bias models". Annals of Statistics 13, 178–203.
Verbeek, M. (1996). "Pseudo panel data". In: Matyas, L., Sevestre, P. (Eds.), The Econometrics of Panel Data. Kluwer.
Verbeek, M., Nijman, T. (1992). "Can cohort data be treated as genuine panel data?". Empirical Economics 17, 9–23.
Verbeek, M., Nijman, T. (1993). "Minimum MSE estimation of a regression model with fixed effects from a series of cross sections". Journal of Econometrics 59, 125–136.
Wald, A. (1940). "The fitting of straight lines if both variables are subject to error". Annals of Mathematical Statistics 11, 284–300.
Wooldridge, J. (1999). "Asymptotic properties of weighted M-estimators for variable probability samples". Econometrica 67, 1385–1406.

Chapter 76

LARGE SAMPLE SIEVE ESTIMATION OF SEMI-NONPARAMETRIC MODELS*

XIAOHONG CHEN

Department of Economics, Yale University, Box 208281, New Haven, CT 06520, USA
e-mail: xiaohong.chen@yale.edu

Contents

* The author thanks C. Ai, J. Heckman, B. Honore, J. Huang, G. Imbens, R. Matzkin, W. Newey, J. Powell and H. White for valuable suggestions, J. Huang for showing his work on concave extended linear models, and two anonymous referees for critical comments that lead to thorough revisions. She also thanks K. Hyndman, A. Ingster, M. Kredler, D. Pouzo and R. Sela for proof-reading, M. Garibotti, D. Pouzo and V. Tsyrennikov for simulations and other PhD students who went through earlier versions used as the lecture notes for *Topics in Econometrics* during the Fall 2002, Fall 2003, Spring 2005 and Fall 2005 sessions at New York University. The author acknowledges financial support from the National Science Foundation and the C.V. Starr Center at NYU. Any errors or omissions are the responsibility of the author.

Handbook of Econometrics, Volume 6B

DOI: 10.1016/S1573-4412(07)06076-X

Abstract

Often researchers find parametric models restrictive and sensitive to deviations from the parametric specifications; semi-nonparametric models are more flexible and robust, but lead to other complications such as introducing infinite-dimensional parameter spaces that may not be compact and the optimization problem may no longer be well-posed. The method of sieves provides one way to tackle such difficulties by optimizing an empirical criterion over a sequence of approximating parameter spaces (i.e., sieves); the sieves are less complex but are dense in the original space and the resulting optimization problem becomes well-posed. With different choices of criteria and sieves, the method of sieves is very flexible in estimating complicated semi-nonparametric models with (or without) endogeneity and latent heterogeneity. It can easily incorporate prior information and constraints, often derived from economic theory, such as monotonicity, convexity, additivity, multiplicity, exclusion and nonnegativity. It can simultaneously estimate the parametric and nonparametric parts in semi-nonparametric models, typically with optimal convergence rates for both parts.

This chapter describes estimation of semi-nonparametric econometric models via the method of sieves. We present some general results on the large sample properties of the sieve estimates, including consistency of the sieve extremum estimates, convergence rates of the sieve M-estimates, pointwise normality of series estimates of regression functions, root-n asymptotic normality and efficiency of sieve estimates of smooth functionals of infinite-dimensional parameters. Examples are used to illustrate the general results.

Keywords

sieve extremum estimation, series, sieve minimum distance, semiparametric two-step estimation, endogeneity in semi-nonparametric models

JEL classification: C13, C14, C20

1. Introduction

Semiparametric and nonparametric modelling techniques have grown increasingly popular in both theoretical and applied econometrics.[1] This is partly because economic theory seldom suggests any parametric functional relationships among economic variables, nor does it suggest particular parametric forms for error distributions. An additional reason for the growing popularity of semi-nonparametric models is the declining computational cost of collecting and analyzing large economic data sets. All of the chapters in the book edited by Barnett, Powell and Tauchen (1991) and several chapters[2] in the Handbook of Econometrics Volume 4 edited by Engle and McFadden (1994) have already reviewed the work in semiparametric and nonparametric econometrics that has been conducted up to the mid-1990s. More recently, Horowitz (1998) has provided a comprehensive treatment of four leading classes of semiparametric econometric models estimated via the kernel method. Pagan and Ullah (1999), Härdle et al. (2004) and Li and Racine (2007) have surveyed the most well-known existing theoretical and empirical work on the estimation and testing of semiparametric and nonparametric econometric models via the methods of kernel, local linear regression and series. This chapter will review some recent developments in large sample theory on estimation of semi-nonparametric models via the *method of sieves* [Grenander (1981)].

Semi-nonparametric models involve unknown parameters that lie in infinite-dimensional parameter spaces; hence it can be computationally difficult to estimate such models using finite samples. Moreover, even if one could solve the problem of optimizing a sample criterion over an infinite-dimensional parameter space, the resulting estimator may have undesirable large sample properties such as inconsistency and/or a very slow rate of convergence; this is because the problem of optimization over an infinite-dimensional noncompact space may no longer be well-posed. To resolve this problem, the method of sieves optimizes a criterion function over a sequence of significantly less complex, and often finite-dimensional, parameter spaces, which we call *sieves*. To ensure consistency of the method, we require that the complexity of sieves increases with the sample size so that in the limit the sieves are dense in the original parameter space.[3]

The infinite-dimensional unknown parameter in a nonparametric or semiparametric model can often be viewed as a member of some function space with certain regularities (e.g., having bounded second derivatives, monotone, concave). Thus, many deterministic approximation results developed in mathematics and computer science can be used to

[1] In this chapter, an econometric model is termed "*parametric*" if all of its parameters are in finite-dimensional parameter spaces; a model is "*nonparametric*" if all of its parameters are in infinite-dimensional parameter spaces; a model is "*semiparametric*" if its parameters of interests are in finite-dimensional spaces but its nuisance parameters are in infinite-dimensional spaces; a model is "*semi-nonparametric*" if it contains both finite-dimensional and infinite-dimensional unknown parameters of interests.

[2] See the ones written by Newey and McFadden (1994), Andrews (1994a), Powell (1994), Härdle and Linton (1994), Matzkin (1994), Manski (1994) and others.

[3] These terms will become much clearer in the next two sections.

suggest sieves that provide good and computable approximations to an unknown function. For example, the sieves or approximating spaces can be constructed using linear spans of power series, Fourier series, splines or many other basis functions; see e.g. Judd (1998, Chapters 6 and 12) for numerical implementation of such sieves for problems in economics and finance. Since these approximating spaces can often be characterized by a finite number of "parameters", a nonparametric or semiparametric estimation problem is often reduced to a parametric one when the method of sieves is implemented. However, to obtain the desired theoretical properties of the estimator, it is necessary that the number of parameters increase slowly with the sample size. It is this feature that gives the sieve method its added flexibility and robustness over classical parametric methods which assume fixed, finite-dimensional parameter spaces.

One attractive feature of the method of sieves is that it is easy to implement. The sieve method is particularly convenient when the unknown functions enter the criterion function (or moment condition) nonlinearly, satisfy some known restrictions such as monotonicity, concavity, additivity, multiplicity and exclusion, or when the error distribution has known tail behavior such as fat tails. With different choices of criteria and sieves, the method of sieves provides a flexible and computationally feasible approach to estimate complicated semi-nonparametric models with (or without) constraints, endogeneity and latent heterogeneity. Moreover, it can simultaneously estimate the parametric and nonparametric components in semi-nonparametric models, and can often achieve optimal convergence rates for both parts. We shall demonstrate these with some examples in the subsequent sections.

Although the method of sieves is easy to implement and the sieve estimators typically have desirable large sample properties, its theoretical properties cannot be justified by applying the classical theory for parametric models. Any appropriate large sample theory for the sieve method should not only account for the approximation errors, which arise because we replace the original parameter space with the simpler sieve space, but also control for the complexity of the sieve parameter spaces, which increases with the sample size. Consequently, the large sample properties of the sieve method are in general difficult to derive, which may partly explain why currently there are fewer econometric applications using such techniques than those using the kernel method. However, we should mention that the sieve estimation method admits, as special cases, many standard estimation methods (such as series-based method) in econometrics. As a result, some large sample results appear in the literature in papers that do not mention the word "sieve" at all.

In this chapter we shall present some general results on large sample estimation theory using the method of sieves and illustrate how to apply these results with examples. Instead of presenting the current sieve estimation theory at its greatest generality, we have chosen to review results that are relatively accessible but general enough to cover most semi-nonparametric econometric applications. References are given for the results that are not presented in detail.

The rest of this chapter is organized as follows. In Section 2, we first present several examples of semi-nonparametric econometric models. We then define the sieve extremum estimation and its special cases including sieve M-estimation, sieve maximum likelihood estimation (MLE), sieve generalized least squares (GLS), sieve minimum distance (MD) and others. The various criterion functions are illustrated using examples. In addition, we introduce the popular *series* estimators as the sieve M-estimators obtained when the criterion functions are concave and the sieve spaces are finite-dimensional linear.[4] We then review typical function spaces and sieve spaces used in econometrics, and conclude this section with a small Monte Carlo study to demonstrate the implementation of the sieve extremum estimation.[5] Section 3 focuses on the large sample properties of sieve estimation of infinite-dimensional unknown parameters. We first provide a new consistency theorem for general sieve extremum estimation where the original parameter space may not be compact and the problem may not be well-posed. This theorem implies consistency of sieve M-estimators and of sieve MD-estimators in two remarks. We then present a convergence rate result for sieve M-estimators and illustrate how to apply the result with some examples. We also review the convergence rate and the pointwise asymptotic normality results for the series estimators. In Section 4, we present general results on $\sqrt{n}$-asymptotic normality of sieve estimators of smooth functionals of unknown infinite-dimensional parameters, where n denotes the sample size. Here we first discuss the popular two-step semiparametric procedures in which the first step unknown functions could be estimated by any nonparametric procedures such as kernel, local linear regression and sieve methods, and the second step unknown parametric components are estimated by the generalized method of moments (GMM). The theorem on $\sqrt{n}$-asymptotic normality of the second step GMM estimator is a slight refinement of the existing ones in the semiparametric literature. We then review the $\sqrt{n}$-asymptotic normality of the sieve M-estimation of smooth functionals of unknown functions, as well as the semiparametric efficiency of the sieve MLE. Finally we present the recent theory on the sieve MD estimation for the parametric components in semi-nonparametric conditional moment models where the unknown functions could depend on endogenous variables. Section 5 points out additional topics on statistical inference via the method of sieves that are not reviewed here due to the lack of space.

Throughout this chapter, we assume that there is an underlying complete probability space, the data $\{Z_t = (Y_t', X_t')': t \geqslant 1\}$ are strictly stationary ergodic,[6] and all probability calculations are done under the true probability measure P_o. For random variables V_n and positive numbers b_n, $n \geqslant 1$, we define $V_n = O_P(b_n)$ as $\lim_{c\to\infty} \limsup_n P(|V_n| \geqslant$

[4] We note that this definition of series estimators differs slightly from those in the current econometrics literature.

[5] See the chapter by Ichimura and Todd (2007) for more details on the implementation of semi-nonparametric estimators.

[6] In this chapter, the notation $'$ denotes the transpose of a vector. See Hansen (1982), White (1984) or Wooldridge (1994) for the definition of a strictly stationary ergodic process. We make this assumption to simplify the presentation. See White and Wooldridge (1991) on sieve extremum estimation for general dependent heterogeneous processes.

$cb_n) = 0$, and define $V_n = o_P(b_n)$ as $\lim_n P(|V_n| \geqslant cb_n) = 0$ for all $c > 0$. The notation $\text{plim}_{n\to\infty} V_n = 0$ also means that $V_n = o_P(1)$ (i.e., V_n converges to 0 in probability). Similarly $V_n = o_{a.s.}(1)$ means that V_n converges to 0 almost surely. For two sequences of positive numbers b_{1n} and b_{2n}, the notation $b_{1n} \asymp b_{2n}$ means that the ratio b_{1n}/b_{2n} is bounded below and above by positive constants that are independent of n.

2. Sieve estimation: Examples, definitions, sieves

As alluded to in the introduction, the method of sieves consists of two key ingredients: a criterion function and sieve parameter spaces (a sequence of approximating spaces). Both the criterion functions and the sieve spaces can be very flexible. In particular, almost all of the classical criterion functions stated in Newey and McFadden (1994), so long as they still allow for identification, can be used as criterion functions in the method of sieve estimation. Therefore, the main new ingredient is the choice of sieve parameter spaces, which will be discussed in this section.

2.1. Empirical examples of semi-nonparametric econometric models

It is impossible to list all of the existing and potential semi-nonparametric models and their empirical applications in econometrics. In this subsection we present three empirical examples as illustration; additional ones can be found in Manski (1994), Powell (1994), Matzkin (1994), Horowitz (1998), Pagan and Ullah (1999), Blundell and Powell (2003) and other surveys on this topic.

EXAMPLE 2.1 *(Single spell duration models with unobserved heterogeneity).* Classical single spell duration models in search unemployment [Flinn and Heckman (1982)], job turnover [Jovanovic (1979)], labor supply [Heckman and Willis (1977)] and others often suggest a functional form for the structural duration distribution conditional on individual heterogeneity. More specifically, let $G(\tau|u,x)$ be the structural distribution function of duration T conditional on a scalar of unobserved heterogeneity $U = u$ and a vector of observed heterogeneity $X = x$. The distribution of observed duration given $X = x$ is

$$F(\tau|x) = \int G(\tau|u,x)\,\mathrm{d}h(u),$$

where the unobserved heterogeneity U is modelled as a random factor with distribution function $h(\cdot)$. An i.i.d. sample of observations $\{T_i, X_i\}_{i=1}^n$ allows us to recover the true $F(\tau|x)$ uniquely. Theoretical models often imply parametric functional forms of G up to unknown finite-dimensional parameters β. Denote $g(\cdot|\beta,u,x)$ as the probability density function of $G(\cdot|\beta,u,x)$. Conventional parametric MLE method assumes that the unobserved heterogeneity follows some known distribution h_γ up to some unknown finite-dimensional parameters γ. Under this assumption it then estimates the unknown parameters β,γ by $\arg\max_{\beta,\gamma} \frac{1}{n}\sum_{i=1}^n \log\{\int g(T_i|\beta,u,X_i)\,\mathrm{d}h_\gamma(u)\}$.

Heckman and Singer (1984) point out that both theoretical and empirical examples indicate that the parametric MLE estimates of structural parameters β in these duration models are inconsistent if the distribution of the unobserved heterogeneity is misspecified. Instead, they propose the following semi-nonparametric single spell duration model

$$F(\tau|\beta, h, x) = \int G(\tau|\beta, u, x)\,\mathrm{d}h(u), \tag{2.1}$$

where the distribution h of unobserved heterogeneity is left unspecified. Heckman and Singer (1984) establish the identification of (β', h), and propose a sieve MLE method to estimate (β', h) jointly. They also show that their estimator is consistent.

The Heckman–Singer model is a typical example of a broad class of semi-nonparametric models that specify the (conditional) distribution associated with the observed economic variables semi-nonparametrically, where the specific semi-nonparametric form can be derived from independence of errors and regressors such as in discrete choice models, transformation models, sample selection models, mixture models, random censoring, nonlinear measurement errors and others. More generally, one could consider semi-nonparametric models based on quantile independence, symmetry or other qualitative restrictions on distributions. See Horowitz (1998), Manski (1994), Powell (1994) and Bickel et al. (1993) for examples.

EXAMPLE 2.2 *(Shape-invariant system of Engel curves).* Blundell, Browning and Crawford (2003) have shown that a system of Engel curves that satisfies Slutsky's symmetry condition and allows for demographic effects on budget shares in a given year must take the following form:

$$Y_{1\ell i} = h_{1\ell}\big(Y_{2i} - h_0(X_{1i})\big) + h_{2\ell}(X_{1i}) + \varepsilon_{\ell i}, \quad \ell = 1, \ldots, N,$$

where $Y_{1\ell i}$ is the ith household budget share on ℓth goods, Y_{2i} is the ith household log-total nondurable expenditure, X_{1i} is a vector of the ith household demographic variables that affect the household's nondurable consumption. Note that $h_0(X_{1i})$ is common among all the goods and is called an "equivalence scale" in the consumer demand literature. Citing strong empirical evidence and many existing works, Blundell, Browning and Crawford (2003) have argued that popular parametric linear and quadratic forms for $h_{1\ell}(\cdot)$ are inadequate, and that consumer demand theory only suggests the purely nonparametric specification:

$$\begin{aligned} &E\big[Y_{1\ell i} - \big\{h_{1\ell}\big(Y_{2i} - h_0(X_{1i})\big) + h_{2\ell}(X_{1i})\big\}\big|X_{1i}, Y_{2i}\big] \\ &\quad = E[\varepsilon_{\ell i}|X_{1i}, Y_{2i}] = 0, \end{aligned} \tag{2.2}$$

where $h_{1\ell}$, $h_{2\ell}$ and h_0 are all unknown functions. For the identification of all these unknown functions $\theta = (h_0, h_{11}, \ldots, h_{1N}, h_{21}, \ldots, h_{2N})'$ satisfying (2.2), it suffices to assume that at least one of $h_{1\ell}, \ell = 1, \ldots, N$, is nonlinear and that $h_{2\ell}(x_1^*) = 0$, $\ell = 1, \ldots, N$, for some x_1^* in the support of X_1.

Unfortunately, when X_{1i} contains too many household demographic variables (say when $\dim(X_{1i}) \geqslant 3$), the fully nonparametric specification (2.2) cannot lead to precise estimates of the unknown functions $h_0, h_{21}, \ldots, h_{2N}$ due to the so-called "curse of dimensionality". Therefore, applied researchers must impose more structure on the model. Using the British family expenditure survey (FES) data, Blundell, Duncan and Pendakur (1998) found the following semi-nonparametric specification to be reasonable:

$$E\left[Y_{1\ell i} - \left\{h_{1\ell}\left(Y_{2i} - g\left(X_{1i}'\beta_1\right)\right) + X_{1i}'\beta_{2\ell}\right\}\middle|X_{1i}, Y_{2i}\right] = 0, \tag{2.3}$$

where $h_{1\ell}$, $\ell = 1, \ldots, N$, are still unknown functions, but now $h_0(X_{1i}) = g(X_{1i}'\beta_1)$ and $h_{2\ell}(X_{1i}) = X_{1i}'\beta_{2\ell}$ are known up to unknown finite-dimensional parameters β_1 and $\beta_{2\ell}$. Here the parameters of interest are $\theta = (\beta_1', \beta_{21}', \ldots, \beta_{2N}', h_{11}, \ldots, h_{1N})'$. This semi-nonparametric specification has been estimated by Blundell, Duncan and Pendakur (1998) using the kernel method and Blundell, Chen and Kristensen (2007) using the sieve method.

Both the specifications (2.2) and (2.3) assume that the total nondurable expenditure Y_{2i} is exogenous. However, this assumption has been rejected empirically. Noting the endogeneity of total nondurable expenditure, Blundell, Chen and Kristensen (2007) considered the following semi-nonparametric instrumental variables (IV) regression:

$$E\left[Y_{1\ell i} - \left\{h_{1\ell}\left(Y_{2i} - g\left(X_{1i}'\beta_1\right)\right) + X_{1i}'\beta_{2\ell}\right\}\middle|X_{1i}, X_{2i}\right] = 0, \tag{2.4}$$

where the parameters of interest are still $\theta = (\beta_1', \beta_{21}', \ldots, \beta_{2N}', h_{11}, \ldots, h_{1N})'$, and X_{2i} is the gross earnings of the head of the ith household which is used as an instrument for the total nondurable expenditure Y_{2i}. They estimated this model via the sieve method and their empirical findings demonstrate the importance of accounting for the endogenous total expenditure semi-nonparametrically.

EXAMPLE 2.3 *(Consumption-based asset pricing models).* A standard consumption-based asset pricing model assumes that at time zero a representative agent maximizes the expected present value of the total utility function $E_0\{\sum_{t=0}^{\infty}\delta^t u(C_t)\}$, where δ is the time discount factor and $u(C_t)$ is period t's utility. The consumption-based asset pricing model comes from the first-order conditions of a representative agent's optimal consumption choice problem. These first-order conditions place restrictions on the joint distribution of the intertemporal marginal rate of substitution in consumption and asset returns. They imply that for any traded asset indexed by ℓ, with a gross return at time $t+1$ of $R_{\ell,t+1}$, the following Euler equation holds:

$$E(M_{t+1}R_{\ell,t+1}|\mathbf{w}_t) = 1, \quad \ell = 1, \ldots, N, \tag{2.5}$$

where M_{t+1} is the intertemporal marginal rate of substitution in consumption, and $E(\cdot|\mathbf{w}_t)$ denotes the conditional expectation given the information set at time t (which is the sigma-field generated by $\mathbf{w}_t$). More generally, any nonnegative random variable M_{t+1} satisfying Equation (2.5) is called a stochastic discount factor (SDF); see Hansen and Richard (1987) and Cochrane (2001).

Hansen and Singleton (1982) have assumed that the period t utility takes the power specification $u(C_t) = [(C_t)^{1-\gamma} - 1]/[1-\gamma]$, where γ is the curvature parameter of the utility function at each period, which implies that the SDF takes the form $M_{t+1} = \delta(\frac{C_{t+1}}{C_t})^{-\gamma}$ and the Euler equation becomes:

$$E\left(\delta_o\left(\frac{C_{t+1}}{C_t}\right)^{-\gamma_o} R_{\ell,t+1} - 1 \middle| \mathbf{w}_t\right) = 0, \quad \ell = 1, \ldots, N, \tag{2.6}$$

where the unknown scalar parameters δ_o, γ_o can be estimated by Hansen's (1982) generalized method of moment (GMM). However, this classical power utility-based asset pricing model (2.6) has been rejected empirically.

Many subsequent papers have tried to relax the model (2.6) to fit the data better by introducing durable goods, habit formation or a nonseparable preference specification. The first class of papers proposes various parametric forms of the SDF, M_{t+1}, that are more flexible than $M_{t+1} = \delta(\frac{C_{t+1}}{C_t})^{-\gamma}$; see e.g. Eichenbaum and Hansen (1990), Constantinides (1990), Campbell and Cochrane (1999). The second class of papers has made the SDF, M_{t+1}, a purely nonparametric function of a few state variables; see e.g. Gallant and Tauchen (1989), Newey and Powell (1989) and Bansal and Viswanathan (1993). Recently, Chen and Ludvigson (2003) have specified the SDF, M_{t+1}, to be semi-nonparametric in order to incorporate some preference parameters. In particular, they combine the power utility specification with a nonparametric internal habit formation: $E_0\{\sum_{t=0}^{\infty}\delta^t[(C_t - H_t)^{1-\gamma} - 1]/[1-\gamma]\}$, where $H_t = H(C_t, C_{t-1}, \ldots, C_{t-L})$ is the period t habit level. Here $H(\cdot)$ is a homogeneous of degree one unknown function of current and past consumption, and can be rewritten as $H(C_t, C_{t-1}, \ldots, C_{t-L}) = C_t h_o(\frac{C_{t-1}}{C_t}, \ldots, \frac{C_{t-L}}{C_t})$ with $h_o(\cdot)$ unknown. It is obvious that one needs to impose $0 \leqslant h_o(\cdot) < 1$ so that $0 \leqslant H_t < C_t$. The following external habit specification is a special case of their model:

$$E\left(\delta_o\left(\frac{C_{t+1}}{C_t}\right)^{-\gamma_o} \frac{\left(1 - h_o\left(\frac{C_t}{C_{t+1}}, \ldots, \frac{C_{t+1-L}}{C_{t+1}}\right)\right)^{-\gamma_o}}{\left(1 - h_o\left(\frac{C_{t-1}}{C_t}, \ldots, \frac{C_{t-L}}{C_t}\right)\right)^{-\gamma_o}} R_{\ell,t+1} - 1 \middle| \mathbf{w}_t\right) = 0, \tag{2.7}$$

for $\ell = 1, \ldots, N$, where $\gamma_o > 0$, $\delta_o > 0$ are unknown scalar preference parameters, $h_o(\cdot) \in [0, 1)$ is an unknown function and $H_{t+1} = C_{t+1}h_o(\frac{C_t}{C_{t+1}}, \ldots, \frac{C_{t+1-L}}{C_{t+1}})$ is the habit level at time $t+1$. Chen and Ludvigson (2003) have applied the sieve method to estimate this model and its generalization which allows for internal habit formation of unknown form. Their empirical findings, using quarterly data, are in favor of flexible nonlinear internal habit formation.

Semi-nonparametric conditional moment models. We note that Examples 2.2 and 2.3 and many other economic models imply semi-nonparametric conditional moment restrictions of the form

$$E\left[\rho(Z_t; \theta_o) \middle| X_t\right] = 0, \quad \theta_o \equiv \left(\beta_o', h_o'\right)', \tag{2.8}$$

where $\rho(\cdot;\cdot)$ is a column vector of residual functions whose functional forms are known up to unknown parameters, $\theta \equiv (\beta', h')'$, and $\{Z_t' = (Y_t', X_t')\}_{t=1}^n$ is the data where Y_t is a vector of endogenous variables and X_t is a vector of conditioning variables. Here $E[\rho(Z_t, \theta)|X_t]$ denotes the conditional expectation of $\rho(Z_t, \theta)$ given X_t, and the true conditional distribution of Y_t given X_t is unspecified (and is treated as a nuisance function). The parameters of interest $\theta_o \equiv (\beta_o', h_o')'$ contain a vector of finite-dimensional unknown parameters β_o and a vector of infinite-dimensional unknown functions $h_o(\cdot) = (h_{o1}(\cdot), \ldots, h_{oq}(\cdot))'$, where the arguments of $h_{oj}(\cdot)$ could depend on Y, X, known index function $\delta_j(Z, \beta_o)$ up to unknown β_o, other unknown function $h_{ok}(\cdot)$ for $k \neq j$, or could also depend on unobserved random variables. Motivated by the asset pricing and rational expectations models, Hansen (1982, 1985) studied the conditional moment restriction $E[\rho(Z_t; \beta_o)|X_t] = 0$ (i.e., without unknown h_o) for stationary ergodic time series data (where typically $Z_t' = (Y_t', X_t')$ and X_t includes lagged Y_t and other pre-determined variables known at time t). Chamberlain (1992), Newey and Powell (2003), Ai and Chen (2003) and Chen and Pouzo (2006) studied the general case $E[\rho(Z_t; \beta_o, h_o)|X_t] = 0$ for i.i.d. data.

The semi-nonparametric conditional moment models given by (2.8) can be classified into two broad subclasses. The first subclass consists of *models without endogeneity* in the sense that $\rho(Z_t, \theta) - \rho(Z_t, \theta_o)$ does not depend on any endogenous variables (Y_t); hence the true parameter θ_o can be identified as the unique maximizer of $Q(\theta) = -E[\rho(Z_t, \theta)'\{\Sigma(X_t)\}^{-1}\rho(Z_t, \theta)]$, where $\Sigma(X_t)$ is a positive definite weighting matrix. The second subclass consists of *models with endogeneity* in the sense that $\rho(Z_t, \theta) - \rho(Z_t, \theta_o)$ does depend on endogenous variables (Y_t). Here the true parameter θ_o can be identified as the unique maximizer of

$$Q(\theta) = -E\big[m(X_t, \theta)'\{\Sigma(X_t)\}^{-1}m(X_t, \theta)\big] \quad \text{with } m(X_t, \theta) \equiv E\big[\rho(Z_t, \theta)\big|X_t\big].$$

Although the second subclass includes the first subclass as a special case, when θ contains unknown functions, it is much easier to derive asymptotic properties for various nonparametric estimators of θ identified by the conditional moment models belonging to the first subclass. The first subclass includes, as special cases, many semi-nonparametric regression models that have been well studied in econometrics. For example, it includes the specifications (2.2) and (2.3) of Example 2.2, the partially linear regression $E[Y_i - X_{1i}'\beta_o - h_o(X_{2i})|X_{1i}, X_{2i}] = 0$ of Engle et al. (1986) and Robinson (1988), the index regression $E[Y_i - h_o(X_i'\beta_o)|X_i] = 0$ of Powell, Stock and Stoker (1989), Ichimura (1993) and Klein and Spady (1993), the varying coefficient model $E[Y_i - \sum_{j=1}^q h_{oj}(D_{ji})X_{ji}|(D_{ki}, X_{ki}), k = 1, \ldots, q] = 0$ of Chen and Tsay (1993), Cai, Fan and Yao (2000) and Chen and Conley (2001), and the additive model with a known link (F) function $E[Y_i - F(\sum_{j=1}^q h_{oj}(X_{ji}))|X_{1i}, \ldots, X_{qi}] = 0$ of Horowitz and Mammen (2004).

The second subclass includes, as special cases, the specification (2.4) of Example 2.2, Example 2.3, semi-nonparametric asset pricing and rational expectation models, and simultaneous equations with flexible parameterization. A leading, yet difficult example of this subclass, is the purely nonparametric instrumental variables (IV) regression

$E[Y_{1i} - h_o(Y_{2i})|X_i] = 0$ studied by Newey and Powell (2003), Darolles, Florens and Renault (2002), Blundell, Chen and Kristensen (2007), Hall and Horowitz (2005) and Carrasco, Florens and Renault (2006). A more difficult example is the nonparametric IV quantile regression $E[1\{Y_{1i} \leqslant h_o(Y_{2i})\} - \gamma|X_i] = 0$ for some known $\gamma \in (0, 1)$ considered by Chernozhukov, Imbens and Newey (2007), Horowitz and Lee (2007) and Chen and Pouzo (2006). See Blundell and Powell (2003), Florens (2003), Newey and Powell (1989), Carrasco, Florens and Renault (2006) and Chen and Pouzo (2006) for additional examples.

2.2. *Definition of sieve extremum estimation*

2.2.1. *Ill-posed versus well-posed problem, sieve extremum estimation*

Let Θ be an infinite-dimensional parameter space endowed with a (pseudo-) metric d. A typical semi-nonparametric econometric model specifies that there is a population criterion function $Q : \Theta \to \mathcal{R}$, which is uniquely maximized at a (pseudo-) true parameter $\theta_o \in \Theta$.[7] The choice of $Q(\cdot)$ and the existence of θ_o are suggested by the identification of an econometric model. The (pseudo-) true parameter $\theta_o \in \Theta$ is unknown but is related to a joint probability measure $P_o(z_1, \ldots, z_n)$, from which a sample of size n observations $\{Z_t\}_{t=1}^n$, $Z_t \in \mathcal{R}^{d_z}$, $1 \leqslant d_z < \infty$, is available. Let $\widehat{Q}_n : \Theta \to \mathcal{R}$ be an empirical criterion, which is a measurable function of the data $\{Z_t\}_{t=1}^n$ for all $\theta \in \Theta$, and converges to Q in some sense (to be more precise in Subsection 3.1) as the sample size $n \to \infty$. One general way to estimate θ_o is by maximizing $\widehat{Q}_n$ over Θ; the maximizer, $\arg\sup_{\theta \in \Theta} \widehat{Q}_n(\theta)$, assuming it exists, is then called the *extremum* estimate. See e.g. Amemiya (1985, Chapter 4), Gallant and White (1988b), Newey and McFadden (1994) and White (1994).

When Θ is infinite-dimensional and possibly not compact with respect to the (pseudo-) metric d,[8] maximizing $\widehat{Q}_n$ over Θ may not be well-defined; or even if a maximizer $\arg\sup_{\theta \in \Theta} \widehat{Q}_n(\theta)$ exists, it is generally difficult to compute, and may have undesirable large sample properties such as inconsistency and/or a very slow rate of convergence. These difficulties arise because the problem of optimization over an infinite-dimensional noncompact space may no longer be well-posed. Throughout this chapter, we say the optimization problem is *well-posed*, if for all sequences $\{\theta_k\}$ in Θ such that $Q(\theta_o) - Q(\theta_k) \to 0$, then $d(\theta_o, \theta_k) \to 0$; is *ill-posed* (or *not well-posed*) if there exists a sequence $\{\theta_k\}$ in Θ such that $Q(\theta_o) - Q(\theta_k) \to 0$ but $d(\theta_o, \theta_k) \nrightarrow 0$.[9] For a given

[7] Although we often call θ_o the "true" parameter in this survey chapter, it in fact could be a pseudo-true parameter value, depending on the specification of the econometrics model and the choice of Q. See Ai and Chen (2007) for estimation of misspecified semi-nonparametric models.

[8] In an infinite-dimensional metric space $(\mathcal{H}, d)$, a compact set is a d-closed and totally bounded set. (A set is totally bounded if for any $\varepsilon > 0$, there exist finitely many open balls with radius ε that cover the set.) A d-closed and bounded set is compact only in a finite-dimensional Euclidean space.

[9] See Carrasco, Florens and Renault (2006) and Vapnik (1998) for surveys on ill-posed inverse problems in linear nonparametric models.

semi-nonparametric model, suppose the criterion $Q(\theta)$ and the space Θ are chosen such that $Q(\theta)$ is uniquely maximized at θ_o in Θ. Then whether the problem is ill-posed or well-posed depends on the choice of the pseudo-metric d. This is because different metrics on an infinite-dimensional space Θ may not be equivalent to each other.[10] In particular, it is likely that some standard norm (say $\|\theta_o - \theta\|_s$) on Θ is not continuous in $Q(\theta_o) - Q(\theta)$ and the problem is ill-posed under $\|\cdot\|_s$, but there is another pseudo-metric (say $\|\theta_o - \theta\|_w$) on Θ that is continuous in $Q(\theta_o) - Q(\theta)$, hence the problem becomes well-posed under this $\|\cdot\|_w$; such a pseudo-metric is typically weaker than $\|\cdot\|_s$ (i.e., $\|\theta_o - \theta\|_s \to 0$ implies $\|\theta_o - \theta\|_w \to 0$). See Ai and Chen (2003, 2007) for more discussions.[11]

No matter whether the semi-nonparametric problems are well-posed or ill-posed, the method of sieves provides one general approach to resolve the difficulties associated with maximizing $\widehat{Q}_n$ over an infinite-dimensional space Θ by maximizing $\widehat{Q}_n$ over a sequence of approximating spaces Θ_n, called *sieves* by Grenander (1981), which are less complex but are dense in Θ. Popular sieves are typically compact, nondecreasing ($\Theta_n \subseteq \Theta_{n+1} \subseteq \cdots \subseteq \Theta$) and are such that for any $\theta \in \Theta$ there exists an element $\pi_n\theta$ in Θ_n satisfying $d(\theta, \pi_n\theta) \to 0$ as $n \to \infty$, where the notation π_n can be regarded as a projection mapping from Θ to Θ_n.

An *approximate sieve extremum estimate*, denoted by $\hat{\theta}_n$, is defined as an approximate maximizer of $\widehat{Q}_n(\theta)$ over the sieve space Θ_n, i.e.,

$$\widehat{Q}_n(\hat{\theta}_n) \geqslant \sup_{\theta \in \Theta_n} \widehat{Q}_n(\theta) - O_P(\eta_n), \quad \text{with } \eta_n \to 0 \text{ as } n \to \infty. \tag{2.9}$$

When $\eta_n = 0$, we call $\hat{\theta}_n$ in (2.9) the *exact* sieve extremum estimate.[12] The sieve extremum estimation method clearly includes the standard extremum estimation method by setting $\Theta_n = \Theta$ for all n.

REMARK 2.1. Following White and Wooldridge (1991, Theorem 2.2), one can show that $\hat{\theta}_n$ in (2.9) is well defined and measurable under the following mild sufficient conditions: (i) $\widehat{Q}_n(\theta)$ is a measurable function of the data $\{Z_t\}_{t=1}^n$ for all $\theta \in \Theta_n$; (ii) for any data $\{Z_t\}_{t=1}^n$, $\widehat{Q}_n(\theta)$ is upper semicontinuous on Θ_n under the metric $d(\cdot,\cdot)$; and (iii) the sieve space Θ_n is compact under the metric $d(\cdot,\cdot)$. Therefore, in the rest of this chapter we assume that $\hat{\theta}_n$ in (2.9) exists and is measurable.

For a semi-nonparametric econometric model, $\theta_o \in \Theta$ can be decomposed into two parts $\theta_o = (\beta_o', h_o')' \in B \times \mathcal{H}$, where B denotes a finite-dimensional compact parameter space, and $\mathcal{H}$ an infinite-dimensional parameter space. In this case, a natural sieve

[10] This is in contrast to the fact that all the norms are equivalent on a finite-dimensional Euclidean space.

[11] The use of a weaker pseudo-metric enables Ai and Chen (2003) to obtain root-n normality of $\hat{\beta}$ for β_o identified via the model $E[\rho(Z_t; \beta_o, h_o)|X_t] = 0$, even when $h_o()$ is a function of the endogenous variable Y and the estimation problem may be ill-posed under the standard mean squared error metric $\sqrt{E[h(Y) - h_o(Y)]^2}$.

[12] Since the complexity of the sieve space Θ_n increases with the sample size, it is obvious that the maximization of $\widehat{Q}_n(\theta)$ over Θ_n need not be exact and the approximate maximizer $\hat{\theta}_n$ in (2.9) will be enough for consistency; see the consistency theorem in Subsection 3.1.

space will be $\Theta_n = B \times \mathcal{H}_n$ with $\mathcal{H}_n$ being a sieve for $\mathcal{H}$, and the resulting estimate $\hat{\theta}_n = (\hat{\beta}_n, \hat{h}_n)$ in (2.9) will sometimes be called a simultaneous (or joint) sieve extremum estimate. For a semi-nonparametric model, we can also estimate the parameters of interest (β_o, h_o) by the *approximate profile sieve extremum estimation* that consists of two steps:

Step 1. For an arbitrarily fixed value $\beta \in B$, compute

$$\widehat{Q}_n\big(\beta, \tilde{h}(\beta)\big) \geqslant \sup_{h \in \mathcal{H}_n} \widehat{Q}_n(\beta, h) - O_P(\eta_n)$$

with $\eta_n = o(1)$;

Step 2. Estimate β_o by $\hat{\beta}_n$ solving $\widehat{Q}_n(\hat{\beta}, \tilde{h}(\hat{\beta})) \geqslant \max_{\beta \in B} \widehat{Q}_n(\beta, \tilde{h}(\beta)) - O_P(\eta_n)$, and then estimate h_o by $\hat{h}_n = \tilde{h}(\hat{\beta}_n)$.

Depending on the specific structure of a semi-nonparametric model, the profile sieve extremum estimation procedure may be easier to compute.

2.2.2. *Sieve M-estimation*

When $\widehat{Q}_n(\theta)$ can be expressed as a sample average of the form

$$\sup_{\theta \in \Theta_n} \widehat{Q}_n(\theta) = \sup_{\theta \in \Theta_n} \frac{1}{n} \sum_{t=1}^{n} l(\theta, Z_t),$$

with $l : \Theta \times \mathcal{R}^{d_z} \to \mathcal{R}$ being the criterion based on a single observation, we also call the $\hat{\theta}_n$ solving (2.9) as an approximate *sieve maximum-likelihood-like* (M-) estimate.[13] This includes sieve maximum likelihood estimation (MLE), sieve least squares (LS), sieve generalized least squares (GLS) and sieve quantile regression as special cases.

EXAMPLE 2.1 *(Continued)*. Heckman and Singer (1984) estimated the unknown true parameters $\theta_o = (\beta_o', h_o)' \in \Theta$ in their semiparametric specification, (2.1), of Example 2.1 by the sieve MLE:

$$\sup_{\theta \in \Theta_n} \widehat{Q}_n(\theta) = \sup_{\beta \in B, h \in \mathcal{H}_n} \frac{1}{n} \sum_{i=1}^{n} \log\left(\int g(T_i | \beta, u, X_i) \, \mathrm{d}h(u)\right),$$

where as $n \to \infty$, the sieve space, $\mathcal{H}_n$, becomes dense in the space of probability distribution functions over $\mathcal{R}$.

[13] Our definition follows that in Newey and McFadden (1994). Some statisticians such as Birgé and Massart (1998) call this a sieve minimum contrast estimate.

EXAMPLE 2.2 *(Continued)*. The nonparametric exogenous expenditure specification (2.2) of Example 2.2 can be estimated by the sieve nonlinear LS:

$$\sup_{\theta\in\Theta_n} \widehat{Q}_n(\theta) = \sup_{h\in\mathcal{H}_n} \frac{-1}{n}\sum_{i=1}^{n}\sum_{\ell=1}^{N}\left[Y_{1\ell i} - \left\{h_{1\ell}\left(Y_{2i} - h_0(X_{1i})\right) + h_{2\ell}(X_{1i})\right\}\right]^2,$$

with $\theta = h = (h_0, h_{11}, \ldots, h_{1N}, h_{21}, \ldots, h_{2N})'$ the unknown parameters and $\Theta_n = \mathcal{H}_n = \mathcal{H}_{0,n} \times \prod_{\ell=1}^{N} \mathcal{H}_{1\ell,n} \times \prod_{\ell=1}^{N} \mathcal{H}_{2\ell,n}$ the sieve space,[14] where we impose the identification condition $h_{2\ell}(x_1^*) = 0$ on the sieve space $\mathcal{H}_{2\ell,n}$ for $\ell = 1, \ldots, N$. The semi-nonparametric exogenous expenditure specification (2.3) of Example 2.2 can be also estimated by the sieve nonlinear LS:

$$\sup_{\theta\in\Theta_n} \widehat{Q}_n(\theta) = \sup_{\beta\in B,\, h\in\mathcal{H}_n} \frac{-1}{n}\sum_{i=1}^{n}\sum_{\ell=1}^{N}\left[Y_{1\ell i} - \left\{h_{1\ell}\left(Y_{2i} - g\left(X_{1i}'\beta_1\right)\right) + X_{1i}'\beta_{2\ell}\right\}\right]^2,$$

with $\theta = (\beta', h')' = (\beta_1', \beta_{21}', \ldots, \beta_{2N}', h_{11}, \ldots, h_{1N})'$ the unknown parameters and $\Theta_n = B \times \mathcal{H}_n = B_1 \times \prod_{\ell=1}^{N} B_{2\ell} \times \prod_{\ell=1}^{N} \mathcal{H}_{1\ell,n}$ the sieve space.

More generally, we can apply the sieve GLS criterion

$$\sup_{\theta\in\Theta_n} \widehat{Q}_n(\theta) = \sup_{\theta\in\Theta_n} \frac{-1}{n}\sum_{i=1}^{n} \rho(Z_i,\theta)'\left\{\Sigma(X_i)\right\}^{-1}\rho(Z_i,\theta)$$

to estimate all the models belonging to the first subclass of the conditional moment restrictions (2.8) where $\rho(Z_i,\theta) - \rho(Z_i,\theta_o)$ does not depend on endogenous variables Y_i, here $\Sigma(X_i)$ is a positive definite weighting matrix function such as the identity matrix. See Remark 4.3 in Subsection 4.3 for optimally weighted version of this procedure.

2.2.3. *Series estimation, concave extended linear models*

In this chapter, we call a special case of sieve M-estimation *series* estimation, which is sieve M-estimation with *concave* criterion functions $\widehat{Q}_n(\theta) = \frac{1}{n}\sum_{t=1}^{n} l(\theta, Z_t)$ and *finite-dimensional linear* sieve spaces Θ_n. We say the criterion is concave if $\widehat{Q}_n(\tau\theta_1 + (1-\tau)\theta_2) \geqslant \tau\widehat{Q}_n(\theta_1) + (1-\tau)\widehat{Q}_n(\theta_2)$ for any $\theta_1, \theta_2 \in \Theta$ and any scalar $\tau \in (0, 1)$. Of course this definition only makes sense when the parameter space Θ is convex (i.e., for any $\theta_1, \theta_2 \in \Theta$, we have $\tau\theta_1 + (1-\tau)\theta_2 \in \Theta$ for any scalar $\tau \in (0, 1)$). We say a sieve Θ_n is finite-dimensional linear if it is a linear span of finitely many known basis functions; see Subsection 2.3.1 for examples.

Although our definition of series estimation may differ from those in the current econometrics literature, it is closely related to the definition of the sieve M-estimation of "*concave extended linear models*" in the statistics literature; see e.g. Hansen (1994), Stone et al. (1997), and Huang (2001). Consider a $\mathcal{Z}$-valued random variable Z, where

[14] Throughout this chapter $\prod_{\ell=1}^{N} \mathcal{H}_{\ell,n}$ denotes a Cartesian product $\mathcal{H}_{1,n} \times \cdots \times \mathcal{H}_{N,n}$.

$\mathcal{Z}$ is an arbitrary set. The probability density $p_o(z)$ of Z depends on a true but unknown parameter θ_o. All the concave extended linear models have three common ingredients: (1) a (possibly infinite-dimensional) linear parameter space Θ; (2) the criterion evaluated at a single observation is concave; that is, given any $\theta_1, \theta_2 \in \Theta$, $l(\tau\theta_1 + (1-\tau)\theta_2, z) \geqslant \tau l(\theta_1, z) + (1-\tau)l(\theta_2, z)$ for any scalar $\tau \in (0, 1)$ and any value $z \in \mathcal{Z}$; (3) the population criterion $Q(\theta) = E[l(\theta, Z)]$ is strictly concave; that is, given any two essentially different functions $\theta_1, \theta_2 \in \Theta$, $E[l(\tau\theta_1 + (1-\tau)\theta_2, Z)] > \tau E[l(\theta_1, Z)] + (1-\tau)E[l(\theta_2, Z)]$ for any scalar $\tau \in (0, 1)$.

The sieve M-estimation of a concave extended linear model can be implemented by maximizing $\widehat{Q}_n(\theta) = \frac{1}{n}\sum_{t=1}^{n} l(\theta, Z_t)$ over a finite-dimensional linear sieve space Θ_n without any constraints. The resulting estimator is called a series estimator in this paper. Therefore, for the same concave criterion function, a sieve M-estimator is a series estimator if the sieve spaces Θ_n are finite-dimensional linear (such as the ones listed in Subsections 2.3.1 and 2.3.2), but is not a series estimator if the sieve spaces Θ_n are not finite-dimensional linear (such as the ones listed in Subsections 2.3.3 and 2.3.4). Although this definition of a series estimator might look restrictive, it will make the descriptions of large sample properties much easier in Section 3.

For series estimation, concavity of the criterion function plays a central role. In particular, the sieve spaces used in estimation are not required to be compact and can be any unrestricted finite-dimensional linear spaces. Such sieves not only make it easy to compute the estimators, but also make it convenient to discuss orthogonal projections and functional analysis of variance (ANOVA) decompositions (such as additivity) in the nonparametric multivariate regression framework; see e.g. Stone (1985, 1986), Andrews and Whang (1990), Huang (1998a).

In order to apply the series estimation to a semi-nonparametric model, one needs to first find a concave criterion function that identifies the unknown parameters of interest. We now present several such examples.

EXAMPLE 2.4 *(Multivariate LS regression).* We consider the estimation of an unknown multivariate conditional mean function $\theta_o(\cdot) = h_o(\cdot) = E(Y|X = \cdot)$. Here $Z = (Y, X)$, Y is a scalar, X has support $\mathcal{X}$ that is a bounded subset of $\mathcal{R}^d$, $d \geqslant 1$. Suppose $h_o \in \Theta$, where Θ is a linear subspace of the space of functions h with $E[h(X)^2] < \infty$. Let $l(h, Z) = -[Y - h(X)]^2$ and $Q(\theta) = -E\{[Y - h(X)]^2\}$; then both are concave in h and Q is strictly concave in $h \in \Theta$.

Let $\{p_j(X), j = 1, 2, \ldots\}$ denote a sequence of known basis functions that can approximate any real-valued square integrable functions of X well; see Subsection 2.3.1 or Newey (1997) for specific examples of such basis functions. Then

$$\Theta_n = \mathcal{H}_n = \left\{h : \mathcal{X} \to \mathcal{R},\ h(x) = \sum_{j=1}^{k_n} a_j p_j(x) \colon a_1, \ldots, a_{k_n} \in \mathcal{R}\right\}, \tag{2.10}$$

with $\dim(\Theta_n) = k_n \to \infty$ slowly as $n \to \infty$, is a finite-dimensional linear sieve for Θ, and $\hat{h} = \arg\max_{h \in \mathcal{H}_n} \frac{-1}{n}\sum_{t=1}^{n}[Y_t - h(X_t)]^2$ is a series estimator of the conditional mean $h_o(\cdot) = E(Y|X = \cdot)$. Moreover, this series estimator $\hat{h}$ has a simple closed-form expression:

$$\hat{h}(x) = p^{k_n}(x)'(P'P)^{-}\sum_{i=1}^{n} p^{k_n}(X_i)Y_i, \quad x \in \mathcal{X}, \tag{2.11}$$

with $p^{k_n}(X) = (p_1(X), \ldots, p_{k_n}(X))'$, $P = (p^{k_n}(X_1), \ldots, p^{k_n}(X_n))'$ and $(P'P)^{-}$ the Moore–Penrose generalized inverse. The estimator $\hat{h}$ given in (2.11) will be called a series LS estimator or a linear sieve LS estimator.

EXAMPLE 2.5 *(Multivariate quantile regression).* Let $\alpha \in (0, 1)$. We consider the estimation of an unknown multivariate αth quantile function $\theta_o(\cdot) = h_o(\cdot)$ such that $E[1\{Y \leqslant h_o(X)\}|X] = \alpha$. Here $Z = (Y, X)$, X has support $\mathcal{X}$ that is a bounded subset of $\mathcal{R}^d$, $d \geqslant 1$. Suppose $h_o \in \Theta$, where Θ is a linear subspace of the space of functions h with $E[h(X)^2] < \infty$. Let $l(h, Z) = [1\{Y \leqslant h(X)\} - \alpha][Y - h(X)]$,[15] and $Q(\theta) = E\{[1\{Y \leqslant h(X)\} - \alpha][Y - h(X)]\}$, then both are concave in h and Q is strictly concave in $h \in \Theta$.

Let $\Theta_n = \mathcal{H}_n$ be a finite-dimensional linear sieve such as the one given in (2.10). Then $\hat{h} = \arg\max_{h\in\mathcal{H}_n} \frac{1}{n}\sum_{t=1}^{n}[1\{Y_t \leqslant h(X_t)\} - \alpha][Y_t - h(X_t)]$ is a series estimator of the conditional quantile function h_o.

EXAMPLE 2.6 *(Log-density estimation).* Let f_o be the true unknown positive probability density of Z on $\mathcal{Z}$ and suppose that we want to estimate the log-density, $\log f_o$. Since $\log f_o$ is subject to the nonlinear constraint $\int_{\mathcal{Z}} \exp\{\log f_o(z)\}\,dz = 1$, it is more convenient to write $\log f_o = h_o - \log\int_{\mathcal{Z}} \exp h_o(z)\,dz$, and treat h_o as an unknown function in some linear space. Since $\log f_o = [h_o + c] - \log\int_{\mathcal{Z}} \exp[h_o(z) + c]\,dz$ for any constant c, we need some location normalization to ensure the identification of h_o. By imposing a linear constraint such as $\int_{\mathcal{Z}} h(z)\,dz = 0$ (or $h(z^*) = 0$ for a fixed $z^* \in \mathcal{Z}$), we can determine h uniquely and make the mapping $h \mapsto \log f$ one-to-one. Therefore, we assume $h_o \in \Theta$, where Θ is a linear subspace of the space of real-valued functions h with $E[h(Z)^2] < \infty$ and $\int_{\mathcal{Z}} h(z)\,dz = 0$. The log-likelihood evaluated at a single observation Z is given by $l(h, Z) = h(Z) - \log\int_{\mathcal{Z}} \exp h(z)\,dz$. Stone (1990) has shown that $l(h, Z)$ is concave and $Q(\theta) = E\{h(Z) - \log\int_{\mathcal{Z}} \exp h(z)\,dz\}$ is strictly concave in $h \in \Theta$.

Let $\{p_j(Z), j = 1, 2, \ldots\}$ denote a sequence of known basis functions that can approximate any real-valued square integrable functions of Z well. Then

$$\Theta_n = \mathcal{H}_n = \left\{h : \mathcal{Z} \to \mathcal{R},\ h(z) = \sum_{j=1}^{k_n} a_j p_j(z)\colon \int_{\mathcal{Z}} h(z)\,dz = 0,\ a_1, \ldots, a_{k_n} \in \mathcal{R}\right\},$$

15 This is a "check" function in Koenker and Bassett (1978).

with $\dim(\Theta_n) = k_n \to \infty$ slowly as $n \to \infty$, is a finite-dimensional linear sieve for Θ, and

$$\hat{h} = \arg\max_{h \in \mathcal{H}_n} \frac{1}{n} \sum_{i=1}^{n} \left[h(Z_i) - \log \int_{\mathcal{Z}} \exp h(z)\, \mathrm{d}z \right]$$

is a series estimator of the log-density function h_o.

It is easy to see that log-conditional density and log-spectral density estimation can be carried out in the same way; see e.g. Stone (1994) and Kooperberg, Stone and Truong (1995b).

EXAMPLE 2.7 *(Estimation of conditional hazard function).* Consider a positive survival time T, a positive censoring time C, the observed time $Y = \min(T, C)$ and an $\mathcal{X}$-valued random vector X of covariates. Let $Z = (X', Y, 1(T \leqslant C))'$ denote a single observation. Suppose T and C are conditionally independent given X, and that $\Pr(C \leqslant \tau_0) = 1$ for a known positive constant τ_0. Let $f_o(\tau|x)$ and $F_o(\tau|x)$, $\tau > 0$, be the true unknown conditional density function and conditional distribution function, respectively, of T given $X = x$. Then the ratio $f_o(\tau|x)/[1 - F_o(\tau|x)]$, $\tau > 0$, is called the conditional hazard function of T given $X = x$. We want to estimate the log-conditional hazard function $h_o(\tau, x) = \log\{f_o(\tau|x)/[1 - F_o(\tau|x)]\}$. Since the likelihood at a single observation Z equals

$$\begin{aligned} &\left[f(Y|X)\right]^{1(T \leqslant C)} \left[1 - F(Y|X)\right]^{1(T > C)} \\ &\quad = \left[\exp\{h(Y, X)\}\right]^{1(T \leqslant C)} \exp\left(-\int_0^Y \exp\{h(\tau, X)\}\, \mathrm{d}\tau\right), \end{aligned}$$

the log-likelihood evaluated at a single observation is given by

$$l(h, Z) = 1(T \leqslant C) h(Y, X) - \int_0^Y \exp\{h(\tau, X)\}\, \mathrm{d}\tau.$$

Kooperberg, Stone and Truong (1995a) showed that the $l(h, Z)$ is concave in h and $Q(\theta) = E\{l(h, Z)\}$ is strictly concave in h.

Suppose $h_o \in \Theta$, where Θ is a linear subspace of the space of real-valued functions h with $E[h(Y, X)^2] < \infty$. Let $\{p_j(Y, X),\ j = 1, 2, \ldots\}$ denote a sequence of known basis functions that can approximate any real-valued square integrable functions of (Y, X) well. Then

$$\begin{aligned} \Theta_n &= \mathcal{H}_n \\ &= \left\{ h : (0, \tau_0] \times \mathcal{X} \to \mathcal{R},\ h(\tau, x) = \sum_{j=1}^{k_n} a_j p_j(\tau, x) \colon a_1, \ldots, a_{k_n} \in \mathcal{R} \right\}, \end{aligned}$$

with $\dim(\Theta_n) = k_n \to \infty$ slowly as $n \to \infty$, is a finite-dimensional linear sieve for Θ, and

$$\hat{h} = \arg\max_{h \in \mathcal{H}_n} \frac{1}{n} \sum_{i=1}^{n} \left[1(T_i \leqslant C_i) h(Y_i, X_i) - \int_0^{Y_i} \exp\{h(\tau, X_i)\} \, d\tau \right]$$

is a series estimator of the log-conditional hazard function h_o.

Finally, we should point out that not all semi-nonparametric M-estimation problems can be reparameterized into series estimation problems. For example, the nonparametric exogenous expenditure specification (2.2) of Example 2.2 does not belong to the concave extended linear models, since, in this specification, the unknown function $h_0(X_1)$ enters the other unknown functions $h_{1\ell}(Y_2 - h_0(X_1))$, $\ell = 1, \ldots, L$, nonlinearly as an argument. Nevertheless, as described in the previous subsection, this model can still be estimated by the general sieve M-estimation method.

2.2.4. *Sieve MD estimation*

When $-\widehat{Q}_n(\theta)$ can be expressed as a quadratic distance from zero, we call the $\hat{\theta}_n$ solving (2.9) an approximate *sieve minimum distance* (MD) estimate.

One typical quadratic form is

$$\sup_{\theta \in \Theta_n} \widehat{Q}_n(\theta) = \sup_{\theta \in \Theta_n} -\frac{1}{n} \sum_{t=1}^{n} \hat{m}(X_t, \theta)' \{\widehat{\Sigma}(X_t)\}^{-1} \hat{m}(X_t, \theta) \tag{2.12}$$

with $\hat{m}(X_t, \theta_o) \to 0$ in probability. Here $\hat{m}(X_t, \theta)$ is a nonparametrically estimated moment restriction function of fixed, finite dimension, and $\widehat{\Sigma}(X_t)$ is a possibly nonparametrically estimated weighting matrix of the same dimension as that of $\hat{m}(X_t, \theta)$. The weighting matrix, $\widehat{\Sigma}$, is introduced for the purpose of efficiency,[16] and $\widehat{\Sigma}(X_t) \to \Sigma(X_t)$ in probability, where $\Sigma(X_t)$ is a positive definite matrix (of the same fixed, finite dimension as that of $\widehat{\Sigma}(X_t)$). We can apply the sieve MD criterion, (2.12), to estimate all the models belonging to the conditional moment restrictions $E[\rho(Z, \theta_o)|X] = 0$, regardless of whether or not $\rho(Z_t, \theta) - \rho(Z_t, \theta_o)$ depends on endogenous variables Y_t. In particular, $\hat{m}(X_t, \theta)$ could be any nonparametric estimate of the conditional mean function $m(X_t, \theta) = E[\rho(Z, \theta)|X = X_t]$; see e.g. Newey and Powell (1989, 2003) and Ai and Chen (1999, 2003).

Another typical quadratic form is the sieve GMM criterion

$$\sup_{\theta \in \Theta_n} \widehat{Q}_n(\theta) = \sup_{\theta \in \Theta_n} -\hat{g}_n(\theta)' \widehat{W} \hat{g}_n(\theta) \tag{2.13}$$

[16] See Ai and Chen (2003) or Subsection 4.3 for details on semiparametric efficiency.

with $\hat{g}_n(\theta_o) \to 0$ in probability. Here $\hat{g}_n(\theta)$ is a sample average of some unconditional moment conditions of increasing dimension, and $\widehat{W}$ is a possibly random weighting matrix of the same increasing dimension as that of $\hat{g}_n(\theta)$. As above, the weighting matrix $\widehat{W}$ is introduced for the purpose of efficiency, and $\widehat{W} - W_n \to 0$ in probability, with W_n being a positive definite matrix (of the same increasing dimension as that of $\widehat{W}$). Note that $E[\rho(Z,\theta_o)|X] = 0$ if and only if the following increasing number of unconditional moment restrictions hold:

$$E\big[\rho(Z_t,\theta_o)p_{0j}(X_t)\big] = 0, \quad j = 1, 2, \ldots, k_{m,n}, \tag{2.14}$$

where $\{p_{0j}(X),\ j = 1, 2, \ldots, k_{m,n}\}$ is a sequence of known basis functions that can approximate any real-valued square integrable functions of X well as $k_{m,n} \to \infty$. Let $p^{k_{m,n}}(X) = (p_{01}(X), \ldots, p_{0k_{m,n}}(X))'$. It is now obvious that the conditional moment restrictions (2.8) $E[\rho(Z,\theta_o)|X] = 0$ can be estimated via the sieve GMM criterion (2.13) using $\hat{g}_n(\theta) = \frac{1}{n}\sum_{t=1}^{n} \rho(Z_t,\theta) \otimes p^{k_{m,n}}(X_t)$.

Not only it is possible for both the sieve MD, (2.12), and the sieve GMM, (2.13), to estimate all the models belonging to the conditional moment restrictions (2.8), but they are also very closely related. For example, when applying the sieve MD (2.12) procedure, we could use the series LS estimator (2.15) as an estimator of the conditional mean function $m(X,\theta) = E[\rho(Z,\theta)|X]$:

$$\hat{m}(X,\theta) = \sum_{j=1}^{n} \rho(Z_j,\theta)p^{k_{m,n}}(X_j)'(P'P)^- p^{k_{m,n}}(X), \tag{2.15}$$

with $P = (p^{k_{m,n}}(X_1), \ldots, p^{k_{m,n}}(X_n))'$ where $k_{m,n} \to \infty$ slowly as $n \to \infty$, and $(P'P)^-$ the Moore–Penrose inverse. The resulting sieve MD (2.12) with identity weighting $\widehat{\Sigma}(X_t) = I$ will become the following sieve GMM (2.13):

$$\min_{\theta\in\Theta_n} \left(\sum_{i=1}^{n} \rho(Z_i,\theta) \otimes p^{k_{m,n}}(X_i)\right)' \big(I \otimes (P'P)^-\big)\left(\sum_{i=1}^{n} \rho(Z_i,\theta) \otimes p^{k_{m,n}}(X_i)\right), \tag{2.16}$$

where $\otimes$ denotes the Kronecker product; see Ai and Chen (2003) for details.

EXAMPLE 2.2 *(Continued).* The semi-nonparametric endogenous expenditure specification (2.4) of Example 2.2 can be estimated by the sieve MD (2.12), with $\hat{m}(X_i,\theta) = (\hat{m}_1(X_i,\theta), \ldots, \hat{m}_N(X_i,\theta))'$,

$$\begin{aligned}&\hat{m}_\ell(X_i,\theta)\\ &\quad= \sum_{j=1}^{n}\big[Y_{1\ell j} - \big\{h_{1\ell}\big(Y_{2j} - g\big(X_{1j}'\beta_1\big)\big) + X_{1j}'\beta_{2\ell}\big\}\big]p^{k_{m,n}}(X_j)'(P'P)^- p^{k_{m,n}}(X_i),\end{aligned}$$

where $\theta = (\beta', h')' = (\beta_1', \beta_{21}', \ldots, \beta_{2N}', h_{11}, \ldots, h_{1N})'$ is the vector of unknown parameters, and $\Theta_n = B \times \mathcal{H}_n = B_1 \times \prod_{\ell=1}^{N} B_{2\ell} \times \prod_{\ell=1}^{N} \mathcal{H}_{1\ell,n}$ is the sieve space; see Blundell, Chen and Kristensen (2007) for details.

EXAMPLE 2.3 *(Continued)*. The semi-nonparametric external habit specification (2.7) of Example 2.3 can be estimated by the sieve GMM criterion (2.16), with $\rho(Z_t, \theta) = (\rho_1(Z_t, \theta), \ldots, \rho_N(Z_t, \theta))'$,

$$\rho_\ell(Z_t, \theta) = \delta\left(\frac{C_t}{C_{t+1}}\right)^\gamma \frac{\left(1 - h\left(\frac{C_t}{C_{t+1}}, \ldots, \frac{C_{t+1-L}}{C_{t+1}}\right)\right)^{-\gamma}}{\left(1 - h\left(\frac{C_{t-1}}{C_t}, \ldots, \frac{C_{t-L}}{C_t}\right)\right)^{-\gamma}} R_{\ell,t+1} - 1,$$

$$\ell = 1, \ldots, N,$$

$$Z_t = \left(\frac{C_t}{C_{t+1}}, \ldots, \frac{C_{t+1-L}}{C_{t+1}}, \frac{C_{t-1}}{C_t}, \ldots, \frac{C_{t-L}}{C_t}, R_{1,t+1}, \ldots, R_{N,t+1}, X_t\right),$$

$$X_t = \mathbf{w}_t,$$

where $\theta = (\beta', h)' = (\delta, \gamma, h)'$ is the vector of unknown parameters, and $\Theta_n = B \times \mathcal{H}_n = B_\delta \times B_\gamma \times \mathcal{H}_n$ is the sieve space, here $0 \leqslant h < 1$ is imposed on the sieve space $\mathcal{H}_n$. Obviously, this model (2.7) can also be estimated by the sieve MD (2.12), with $\hat{m}(X_t, \theta) = \hat{m}(\mathbf{w}_t, \theta)$ being a nonparametric estimator such as the series LS estimator (2.15) of $E[\rho(Z_t, \theta)|X_t = \mathbf{w}_t]$; see Chen and Ludvigson (2003) for details.[17]

2.3. Typical function spaces and sieve spaces

Here we will present some commonly used sieves whose approximation properties are already known in the mathematical literature on approximation theory.

2.3.1. Typical smoothness classes and (finite-dimensional) linear sieves

We first review the most popular smoothness classes of functions used in the nonparametric estimation literature; see e.g. Stone (1982, 1994), Robinson (1988), Newey (1997) and Horowitz (1998). Suppose for the moment that $\mathcal{X} = \mathcal{X}_1 \times \cdots \times \mathcal{X}_d$ is the Cartesian product of compact intervals $\mathcal{X}_1, \ldots, \mathcal{X}_d$. Let $0 < \gamma \leqslant 1$. A real-valued function h on $\mathcal{X}$ is said to satisfy a Hölder condition with exponent γ if there is a positive number c such that $|h(x) - h(y)| \leqslant c|x - y|_e^\gamma$ for all $x, y \in \mathcal{X}$; here $|x|_e = (\sum_{l=1}^d x_l^2)^{1/2}$ is the Euclidean norm of $x = (x_1, \ldots, x_d) \in \mathcal{X}$. Given a d-tuple $\alpha = (\alpha_1, \ldots, \alpha_d)$ of nonnegative integers, set $[\alpha] = \alpha_1 + \cdots + \alpha_d$ and let D^α denote the differential operator defined by

$$D^\alpha = \frac{\partial^{[\alpha]}}{\partial x_1^{\alpha_1} \ldots \partial x_d^{\alpha_d}}.$$

[17] There are also semi-nonparametric recursive method of moment procedures that enable us to estimate nonlinear time series models with latent variables. See e.g. Chen and White (1998, 2002), Pastorello, Patilea and Renault (2003) and Linton and Mammen (2005).

Let m be a nonnegative integer and set $p = m + \gamma$. A real-valued function h on $\mathcal{X}$ is said to be *p-smooth* if it is m times continuously differentiable on $\mathcal{X}$ and $D^\alpha h$ satisfies a Hölder condition with exponent γ for all α with $[\alpha] = m$.

Denote the class of all p-smooth real-valued functions on $\mathcal{X}$ by $\Lambda^p(\mathcal{X})$ (called a Hölder class), and the space of all m-times continuously differentiable real-valued functions on $\mathcal{X}$ by $C^m(\mathcal{X})$. Define a Hölder ball with smoothness $p = m + \gamma$ as

$$\Lambda_c^p(\mathcal{X}) = \Big\{ h \in C^m(\mathcal{X}) \colon \sup_{[\alpha]\leqslant m} \sup_{x\in\mathcal{X}} \big|D^\alpha h(x)\big| \leqslant c,$$
$$\sup_{[\alpha]=m} \sup_{x,y\in\mathcal{X},\, x\neq y} \frac{|D^\alpha h(x) - D^\alpha h(y)|}{|x-y|_e^\gamma} \leqslant c \Big\}.$$

The Hölder (or p-smooth) class of functions are popular in econometrics because a *p-smooth* function can be approximated well by various linear sieves.

A sieve is called a "(finite-dimensional) linear sieve" if it is a linear span of finitely many known basis functions. Linear sieves, including power series, Fourier series, splines and wavelets, form a large class of sieves useful for sieve extremum estimation. We now provide some examples of commonly used linear sieves for univariate functions with support $\mathcal{X} = [0, 1]$.

Polynomials. Let $\mathrm{Pol}(J_n)$ denote the space of polynomials on $[0, 1]$ of degree J_n or less; that is,

$$\mathrm{Pol}(J_n) = \Big\{ \sum_{k=0}^{J_n} a_k x^k,\ x \in [0,1] \colon a_k \in \mathcal{R} \Big\}.$$

Trigonometric polynomials. Let $\mathrm{TriPol}(J_n)$ denote the space of trigonometric polynomials on $[0, 1]$ of degree J_n or less; that is,

$$\mathrm{TriPol}(J_n) = \Big\{ a_0 + \sum_{k=1}^{J_n} \big[a_k \cos(2k\pi x) + b_k \sin(2k\pi x)\big],\ x \in [0,1] \colon a_k, b_k \in \mathcal{R} \Big\}.$$

Let $\mathrm{CosPol}(J_n)$ denote the space of cosine polynomials on $[0, 1]$ of degree J_n or less; that is,

$$\mathrm{CosPol}(J_n) = \Big\{ a_0 + \sum_{k=1}^{J_n} a_k \cos(k\pi x),\ x \in [0,1] \colon a_k \in \mathcal{R} \Big\}.$$

Let $\mathrm{SinPol}(J_n)$ denote the space of sine polynomials on $[0, 1]$ of degree J_n or less; that is,

$$\mathrm{SinPol}(J_n) = \Big\{ \sum_{k=1}^{J_n} a_k \sin(k\pi x),\ x \in [0,1] \colon a_k \in \mathcal{R} \Big\}.$$

We note that the classical trigonometric sieve, TriPol(J_n), is well suited for approximating periodic functions on $[0, 1]$, while the cosine sieve, CosPol(J_n), is well suited for approximating aperiodic functions on $[0, 1]$ and the sine sieve, SinPol(J_n), can approximate functions vanishing at the boundary points (i.e., when $h(0) = h(1) = 0$).

Univariate splines. Let J_n be a positive integer, and let $t_0, t_1, \ldots, t_{J_n}, t_{J_n+1}$ be real numbers with $0 = t_0 < t_1 < \cdots < t_{J_n} < t_{J_n+1} = 1$. Partition $[0, 1]$ into $J_n + 1$ subintervals $I_j = [t_j, t_{j+1})$, $j = 0, \ldots, J_n - 1$, and $I_{J_n} = [t_{J_n}, t_{J_n+1}]$. We assume that the knots $t_1, \ldots, t_{J_n}$ have bounded mesh ratio:

$$\frac{\max_{0 \leqslant j \leqslant J_n}(t_{j+1} - t_j)}{\min_{0 \leqslant j \leqslant J_n}(t_{j+1} - t_j)} \leqslant c \quad \text{for some constant } c > 0. \tag{2.17}$$

Let $r \geqslant 1$ be an integer. A function on $[0, 1]$ is a *spline of order* r, equivalently, *of degree* $m \equiv r - 1$, *with knots* $t_1, \ldots, t_{J_n}$ if the following hold: (i) it is a polynomial of degree m or less on each interval I_j, $j = 0, \ldots, J_n$; and (ii) (for $m \geqslant 1$) it is $(m - 1)$-times continuously differentiable on $[0, 1]$. Such spline functions constitute a linear space of dimension $J_n + r$. For detailed discussions of univariate splines; see de Boor (1978) and Schumaker (1981). For a fixed integer $r \geqslant 1$, we let Spl(r, J_n) denote the space of splines of order r (or of degree $m \equiv r - 1$) with J_n knots satisfying (2.17). Since

$$\mathrm{Spl}(r, J_n) = \left\{ \sum_{k=0}^{r-1} a_k x^k + \sum_{j=1}^{J_n} b_j \left[\max\{x - t_j, 0\}\right]^{r-1},\ x \in [0, 1]\colon a_k, b_j \in \mathcal{R} \right\},$$

we also call Spl(r, J_n) the polynomial spline sieve of degree $m \equiv r - 1$.

In this chapter, $L_2(\mathcal{X}, leb)$ denotes the space of real-valued functions h such that $\int_{\mathcal{X}} |h(x)|^2 \, \mathrm{d}x < \infty$.

Wavelets. Let $m \geqslant 0$ be an integer. A real-valued function ψ is called a "mother wavelet" of degree m if it satisfies the following: (i) $\int_{\mathcal{R}} x^k \psi(x) \, \mathrm{d}x = 0$ for $0 \leqslant k \leqslant m$; (ii) ψ and all its derivatives up to order m decrease rapidly as $|x| \to \infty$; (iii) $\{2^{j/2}\psi(2^j x - k)\colon j, k \in \mathbb{Z}\}$ forms a Riesz basis of $L_2(\mathcal{R}, leb)$, in the sense that the linear span of $\{2^{j/2}\psi(2^j x - k)\colon j, k \in \mathbb{Z}\}$ is dense in $L_2(\mathcal{R}, leb)$ and there exist positive constants $c_1 \leqslant c_2 < \infty$ such that

$$c_1 \sum_{j=-\infty}^{\infty} \sum_{k=-\infty}^{\infty} |a_{jk}|^2 \leqslant \left\| \sum_{j=-\infty}^{\infty} \sum_{k=-\infty}^{\infty} a_{jk} 2^{j/2} \psi(2^j x - k) \right\|^2_{L_2(\mathcal{R}, leb)} \leqslant c_2 \sum_{j=-\infty}^{\infty} \sum_{k=-\infty}^{\infty} |a_{jk}|^2$$

for all doubly bi-infinite square-summable sequences $\{a_{jk}\colon j, k \in \mathbb{Z}\}$.

A scaling function ϕ is called a "father wavelet" of degree m if it satisfies the following: (i) $\int_{\mathcal{R}} \phi(x) \, \mathrm{d}x = 1$; (ii) ϕ and all its derivatives up to order m decrease rapidly as $|x| \to \infty$; (iii) $\{\phi(x-k)\colon k \in \mathbb{Z}\}$ forms a Riesz basis for a closed subspace of $L_2(\mathcal{R}, leb)$.

Orthogonal wavelets. Given an integer $m \geqslant 0$, there exist a father wavelet ϕ of degree m and a mother wavelet ψ of degree m, both compactly supported, such that for any integer $j_0 \geqslant 0$, any function g in $L_2(\mathcal{R}, leb)$ has the following wavelet m-regular multiresolution expansion:

$$g(x) = \sum_{k=-\infty}^{\infty} a_{j_0 k}\phi_{j_0 k}(x) + \sum_{j=j_0}^{\infty}\sum_{k=-\infty}^{\infty} b_{jk}\psi_{jk}(x), \quad x \in \mathcal{R},$$

where

$$a_{jk} = \int_{\mathcal{R}} g(x)\phi_{jk}(x)\,\mathrm{d}x, \quad \phi_{jk}(x) = 2^{j/2}\phi\big(2^j x - k\big),\ x \in \mathcal{R},$$
$$b_{jk} = \int_{\mathcal{R}} g(x)\psi_{jk}(x)\,\mathrm{d}x, \quad \psi_{jk}(x) = 2^{j/2}\psi\big(2^j x - k\big),\ x \in \mathcal{R},$$

and $\{\phi_{j_0 k},\ k \in \mathbb{Z};\ \psi_{jk},\ j \geqslant j_0,\ k \in \mathbb{Z}\}$ is an orthonormal[18] basis of $L_2(\mathcal{R}, leb)$; see Meyer (1992, Theorem 3.3).

For $j \geqslant 0$ and $0 \leqslant k \leqslant 2^j - 1$, denote the periodized wavelets on [0, 1] by

$$\phi^*_{jk}(x) = 2^{j/2}\sum_{l\in\mathbb{Z}}\phi\big(2^j x + 2^j l - k\big),$$
$$\psi^*_{jk}(x) = 2^{j/2}\sum_{l\in\mathbb{Z}}\psi\big(2^j x + 2^j l - k\big), \quad x \in [0, 1].$$

For $j_0 \geqslant 0$, the collection $\{\phi^*_{j_0 k},\ k = 0, \ldots, 2^{j_0} - 1;\ \psi^*_{jk},\ j \geqslant j_0,\ k = 0, \ldots, 2^j - 1\}$ is an orthonormal basis of $L_2([0, 1], leb)$ [see Daubechies (1992)]. We consider the finite-dimensional linear space spanned by this wavelet basis. For an integer $J_n > j_0$, set

$$\mathrm{Wav}\big(m, 2^{J_n}\big) = \left\{\sum_{k=0}^{2^{j_0}-1}\alpha_{j_0 k}\phi^*_{j_0 k}(x) + \sum_{j=j_0}^{J_n-1}\sum_{k=0}^{2^j-1}\beta_{jk}\psi^*_{jk}(x),\right.$$
$$\left. x \in [0, 1]\colon \alpha_{j_0 k}, \beta_{jk} \in \mathcal{R}\right\}$$

or, equivalently [see Meyer (1992)],

$$\mathrm{Wav}\big(m, 2^{J_n}\big) = \left\{\sum_{k=0}^{2^{J_n}-1}\alpha_k\phi^*_{J_n k}(x),\ x \in [0, 1]\colon \alpha_k \in \mathcal{R}\right\}.$$

[18] I.e., $\int_{\mathcal{R}}\psi_{jk}(x)\psi_{jk}(x)\,\mathrm{d}x = 1$ and $\int_{\mathcal{R}}\psi_{jk}(x)\psi_{j'k'}(x)\,\mathrm{d}x = 0$ for $j \neq j'$ or $k \neq k'$; also $\int_{\mathcal{R}}\phi_{j_0 k}(x)\phi_{j_0 k}(x)\,\mathrm{d}x = 1$ and $\int_{\mathcal{R}}\phi_{j_0 k}(x)\phi_{j_0 k'}(x)\,\mathrm{d}x = 0$ for $k \neq k'$; in addition $\int_{\mathcal{R}}\phi_{j_0 k}(x)\psi_{jk'}(x)\,\mathrm{d}x = 0$ for $j \geqslant j_0$.

Tensor product spaces. Let $\mathcal{U}_\ell$, $1 \leqslant \ell \leqslant d$, be compact sets in Euclidean spaces and $\mathcal{U} = \mathcal{U}_1 \times \cdots \times \mathcal{U}_d$ be their Cartesian product. Let $\mathbb{G}_\ell$ be a linear space of functions on $\mathcal{U}_\ell$ for $1 \leqslant \ell \leqslant d$, each of which can be any of the sieve spaces described above, among others. The tensor product, $\mathbb{G}$, of $\mathbb{G}_1, \ldots, \mathbb{G}_d$ is defined as the space of functions on $\mathcal{U}$ spanned by the functions $\prod_{\ell=1}^{d} g_\ell(x_\ell)$, where $g_\ell \in \mathbb{G}_\ell$ for $1 \leqslant \ell \leqslant d$. We note that $\dim(\mathbb{G}) = \prod_{\ell=1}^{d} \dim(\mathbb{G}_\ell)$. Tensor-product construction is a standard way to generate linear sieves of multivariate functions from linear sieves of univariate functions.

Linear sieves are attractive because of their simplicity and ease of implementation. Moreover, linear sieves can approximate functions in a Hölder space, $\Lambda^p(\mathcal{X})$, well. In the following we let θ denote a real-valued function with a bounded domain $\mathcal{X} \subset \mathcal{R}^d$, $\|\theta\|_\infty \equiv \sup_{x\in\mathcal{X}} |\theta(x)|$ denote its L_∞ norm, and $\|\theta\|_{2,leb} \equiv \{\int_{\mathcal{X}}[\theta(x)]^2\,\mathrm{d}x / \operatorname{vol}(\mathcal{X})\}^{1/2}$ be the scaled L_2 norm relative to the Lebesgue measure of $\mathcal{X}$. Define the sieve approximation errors to $\theta_o \in \Lambda^p(\mathcal{X})$ in $L_\infty(\mathcal{X}, leb)$-norm and $L_2(\mathcal{X}, leb)$-norm as

$$\rho_{\infty n} \equiv \inf_{g\in\Theta_n} \|g - \theta_o\|_\infty \quad \text{and} \quad \rho_{2n} \equiv \inf_{g\in\Theta_n} \|g - \theta_o\|_{2,leb}.$$

It is obvious that $\rho_{2n} \leqslant \rho_{\infty n}$. For a multivariate function $\theta_o \in \Theta = \Lambda^p([0,1]^d)$, we consider the tensor product linear sieve space Θ_n, which is constructed as a tensor product space of some commonly used univariate linear approximating spaces $\Theta_{n1}, \ldots, \Theta_{nd}$. Let $\dim(\Theta_n) = k_n$ and $[p]$ be the biggest integer satisfying $[p] < p$. Then we have the following tensor product sieve approximation error rates for $\theta_o \in \Lambda^p([0,1]^d)$:

Polynomials. If each $\Theta_{n\ell} = \operatorname{Pol}(J_n)$, then $\rho_{\infty n} = O(J_n^{-p}) = O(k_n^{-p/d})$ [see e.g. Section 5.3.2 of Timan (1963)].

Trigonometric polynomials. If θ_o can be extended to a periodic function, and if each $\Theta_{n\ell} = \operatorname{TriPol}(J_n)$, then $\rho_{\infty n} = O(J_n^{-p}) = O(k_n^{-p/d})$ [see e.g. Section 5.3.1 of Timan (1963)].

Splines. If each $\Theta_{n\ell} = \operatorname{Spl}(r, J_n)$ with $r \geqslant [p]+1$, then $\rho_{\infty n} = O(J_n^{-p}) = O(k_n^{-p/d})$ [see (13.69) and Theorem 12.8 of Schumaker (1981)].

Orthogonal wavelets. If each $\Theta_{n\ell} = \operatorname{Wav}(m, 2^{J_n})$ with $m > p$, then $\rho_{\infty n} = O(2^{-pJ_n}) = O(k_n^{-p/d})$ [see Proposition 2.5 of Meyer (1992)].

2.3.2. *Weighted smoothness classes and (finite-dimensional) linear sieves*

In semi-nonparametric econometric applications, sometimes the parameters of interest are functions with unbounded supports. Here we present two finite-dimensional linear sieves that can approximate functions with unbounded supports well. In the following we let $L_p(\mathcal{X}, \omega)$, $1 \leqslant p < \infty$, denote the space of real-valued functions h such that $\int_{\mathcal{X}} |h(x)|^p \omega(x)\,\mathrm{d}x < \infty$ for a smooth weight function $\omega : \mathcal{X} \mapsto (0, \infty)$.

Hermite polynomials. Hermite polynomial series $\{H_k\colon k = 1, 2, \ldots\}$ is an orthonormal basis of $L_2(\mathcal{R}, \omega)$ with $\omega(x) = \exp\{-x^2\}$. It can be obtained by applying the Gram–Schmidt procedure to the polynomial series $\{x^{k-1}\colon k = 1, 2, \ldots\}$ under the inner product $\langle f, g\rangle_\omega = \int_{\mathcal{R}} f(x)g(x)\exp\{-x^2\}\,\mathrm{d}x$. That is, $H_1(x) = 1/\sqrt{\int_{\mathcal{R}} \exp\{-x^2\}\,\mathrm{d}x} = \pi^{-1/4}$, and for all $k \geqslant 2$,

$$H_k(x) = \frac{x^{k-1} - \sum_{j=1}^{k-1}\langle x^{k-1}, H_j\rangle_\omega H_j(x)}{\sqrt{\int_{\mathcal{R}}[x^{k-1} - \sum_{j=1}^{k-1}\langle x^{k-1}, H_j\rangle_\omega H_j(x)]^2\exp\{-x^2\}\,\mathrm{d}x}}.$$

Let $\mathrm{HPol}(J_n)$ denote the space of Hermite polynomials on $\mathcal{R}$ of degree J_n or less:

$$\mathrm{HPol}(J_n) = \left\{\sum_{k=1}^{J_n+1} a_k H_k(x)\exp\left\{-\frac{x^2}{2}\right\},\ x \in \mathcal{R}\colon a_k \in \mathcal{R}\right\}.$$

Then any function in $L_2(\mathcal{R}, leb)$ can be approximated by the $\mathrm{HPol}(J_n)$ sieve as $J_n \to \infty$.

When the $\mathrm{HPol}(J_n)$ sieve is used to approximate an unknown $\sqrt{\theta_o}$, where θ_o is a probability density function over $\mathcal{R}$, the corresponding sieve maximum likelihood estimation is also called SNP in econometrics; see e.g. Gallant and Nychka (1987), Gallant and Tauchen (1989) and Coppejans and Gallant (2002).

Laguerre polynomials. Laguerre polynomial series $\{L_k\colon k = 1, 2, \ldots\}$ is an orthonormal basis of $L_2([0, \infty), \omega)$ with $\omega(x) = \exp\{-x\}$. It can be obtained by applying the Gram–Schmidt procedure to the polynomial series $\{x^{k-1}\colon k = 1, 2, \ldots\}$ under the inner product $\langle f, g\rangle_\omega = \int_0^\infty f(x)g(x)\exp\{-x\}\,\mathrm{d}x$. Let $\mathrm{LPol}(J_n)$ denote the space of Laguerre polynomials on $[0, \infty)$ of degree J_n or less:

$$\mathrm{LPol}(J_n) = \left\{\sum_{k=1}^{J_n+1} a_k L_k(x)\exp\left\{-\frac{x}{2}\right\},\ x \in [0, \infty)\colon a_k \in \mathcal{R}\right\}.$$

Then any function in $L_2([0, \infty), leb)$ can be approximated by the $\mathrm{LPol}(J_n)$ sieve as $J_n \to \infty$.

2.3.3. *Other smoothness classes and (finite-dimensional) nonlinear sieves*

Nonlinear sieves can also be used for sieve extremum estimation. A popular class of nonlinear sieves in econometrics is single hidden layer feedforward Artificial Neural Networks (ANN). Here we present three typical forms of ANNs; see Hornik et al. (1994) for additional ones.

Sigmoid ANN. Define

$$\mathrm{sANN}(k_n) = \left\{\sum_{j=1}^{k_n} \alpha_j S(\gamma_j' x + \gamma_{0,j})\colon \gamma_j \in \mathcal{R}^d,\ \alpha_j, \gamma_{0,j} \in \mathcal{R}\right\},$$

where $S:\mathcal{R} \to \mathcal{R}$ is a sigmoid activation function, i.e., a bounded nondecreasing function such that $\lim_{u\to-\infty} S(u) = 0$ and $\lim_{u\to\infty} S(u) = 1$. Some popular sigmoid activation functions include

- Heaviside $S(u) = 1\{u \geqslant 0\}$;
- logistic $S(u) = 1/(1+\exp\{-u\})$;
- hyperbolic tangent $S(u) = (\exp\{u\} - \exp\{-u\})/(\exp\{u\} + \exp\{-u\})$;
- Gaussian sigmoid $S(u) = (2\pi)^{-1/2}\int_{-\infty}^{u} \exp(-y^2/2)\,dy$;
- cosine squasher $S(u) = \frac{1+\cos(u+3\pi/2)}{2} 1\{|u| \leqslant \pi/2\} + 1\{u > \pi/2\}$.

Let $\mathcal{X}$ be a compact set in $\mathcal{R}^d$, and $C(\mathcal{X})$ be the space of continuous functions mapping from $\mathcal{X}$ to $\mathcal{R}$. Gallant and White (1988a) first established that the sANN sieve with the cosine squasher activation function is dense in $C(\mathcal{X})$ under the sup-norm. Cybenko (1990) and Hornik, Stinchcombe and White (1989) show that the sANN(k_n), with any sigmoid activation function, is dense in $C(\mathcal{X})$ under the sup-norm.

Let $\mathcal{H} = \{h \in L_2(\mathcal{X}, leb)\colon \int_{\mathcal{R}^d} |w||\tilde{h}(w)|\,dw < \infty\}$. This means $h \in \mathcal{H}$ if and only if it is square integrable and its Fourier transform $\tilde{h}$ has finite first moment, where $\tilde{h}(w) \equiv \int \exp(-iwx)h(x)\,dx$ is the Fourier transform of h. Barron (1993) established that for any $h_o \in \mathcal{H}$, the sANN(k_n) sieve approximation error rate in $L_2(\mathcal{X}, leb)$-norm ρ_{2n} is no slower than $O([k_n]^{-1/2})$, which was later improved to $O([k_n]^{-1/2-1/(2d)})$ in Makovoz (1996) for the sANN(k_n) with the Heaviside sigmoid function, and to $O([k_n]^{-1/2-1/(d+1)})$ in Chen and White (1999) for the sANN(k_n) with general sigmoid function.

General ANN. Define

$$\text{gANN}(k_n) = \left\{\sum_{j=1}^{2^r k_n} \alpha_j \big[\max\{|\gamma_j|_e, 1\}\big]^{-m} \psi(\gamma_j' x + \gamma_{0,j})\colon \gamma_j \in \mathcal{R}^d,\ \alpha_j, \gamma_{0,j} \in \mathcal{R}\right\},$$

where $\psi:\mathcal{R} \to \mathcal{R}$ is any activation function but not a polynomial with fixed degree. In particular, we often let ψ be a smooth function in a Hölder space $\Lambda^m(\mathcal{R})$ and satisfy $0 < \int_{\mathcal{R}} |D^r\psi(x)|\,dx < \infty$ for some $r \geqslant m$. This includes all the above sigmoid activation functions as special cases (with $m = 0$ and $r = 1$); see Hornik et al. (1994) for additional examples.

Let

$$\mathcal{H} = \left\{h \in L_2(\mathcal{X}, \mu)\colon h(x) = \int \exp(ia'x)\,d\sigma_h(a), \int_{\mathcal{R}^d} \big[\max\{|a|_e, 1\}\big]^{m+1} d|\sigma_h|_{tv}(a) < \infty\right\},$$

where σ_h is a complex-valued measure, and $|\sigma_h|_{tv}$ denotes the total variation of σ_h. Let $W_2^m(\mathcal{X}, \mu)$ be the weighted Sobolev space of functions, where functions as well as all their partial derivatives (up to mth order) are $L_2(\mathcal{X}, \mu)$-integrable for a finite measure μ. It is known that a function in $\mathcal{H}$ also belongs to $W_2^m(\mathcal{X}, \mu)$. Denote $\|h\|_{m,\mu} = \{\int h(x)^2 \, d\mu(x) + \int |D^m h(x)|_e^2 \, d\mu(x)\}^{1/2}$ as the weighted Sobolev norm. Hornik et al. (1994) established that for any $h_o \in \mathcal{H}$, the gANN(k_n) sieve approximation error rate in the weighted Sobolev norm ($\|\cdot\|_{m,\mu}$) is no slower than $O([k_n]^{-1/2})$, which was later improved to $O([k_n]^{-1/2-1/(d+1)})$ in Chen and White (1999).

Gaussian radial basis ANN. Let $\mathcal{X} = \mathcal{R}^d$. Define

$$\text{rbANN}(k_n) = \left\{\alpha_0 + \sum_{j=1}^{k_n} \alpha_j G\left(\frac{\{(x-\gamma_j)'(x-\gamma_j)\}^{1/2}}{\sigma_j}\right): \gamma_j \in \mathcal{R}^d, \right.$$
$$\left. \alpha_j, \sigma_j \in \mathcal{R},\ \sigma_j > 0\right\},$$

where G is the standard Gaussian density function. Let $W_1^m(\mathcal{X})$ be the Sobolev space of functions, where functions as well as all their partial derivatives (up to mth order) are $L_1(\mathcal{X}, leb)$-integrable. Meyer (1992) shows that rbANN(k_n) is dense in the smoothness class $W_1^m(\mathcal{X})$. Girosi (1994) established that for any $h_o \in \mathcal{H}$, the rbANN(k_n) sieve approximation error rate in $L_2(\mathcal{X}, leb)$-norm ρ_{2n} is no slower than $O([k_n]^{-1/2})$, which was later improved to $O([k_n]^{-1/2-1/(d+1)})$ in Chen, Racine and Swanson (2001).

Additional examples of nonlinear sieves include spline sieves with data-driven choices of knot locations (or free-knot splines), and wavelet sieves with thresholding. Nonlinear sieves are more flexible and may enjoy better approximation properties than linear sieves; see e.g. Chen and Shen (1998) for the comparison of linear vs. nonlinear sieves.

2.3.4. *Infinite-dimensional (nonlinear) sieves and method of penalization*

Most commonly used sieve spaces are finite-dimensional truncated series such as those listed above. However, the general theory on sieve extremum estimation can also allow for infinite-dimensional sieve spaces. For example, consider the smoothness class $\Theta = \Lambda^p(\mathcal{X})$ with $\mathcal{X} = [0, 1]$, $p > 1/2$. It is well known that any function $\theta \in \Theta$ can be expressed as an infinite Fourier series $\theta(x) = \sum_{k=1}^{\infty}[a_k \cos(kx) + b_k \sin(kx)]$, and its derivative with fractional power $\gamma \in (0, p]$ can also be defined in terms of Fourier series:

$$\theta^{(\gamma)}(x) = \sum_{k=1}^{\infty} k^\gamma \left[\left(a_k \cos\frac{\pi\gamma}{2} + b_k \sin\frac{\pi\gamma}{2}\right)\cos(kx) \right.$$
$$\left. + \left(b_k \cos\frac{\pi\gamma}{2} - a_k \sin\frac{\pi\gamma}{2}\right)\sin(kx)\right].$$

Similarly, any function $\theta \in \Theta = \Lambda^p(\mathcal{X})$ and its fractional derivatives can be expressed as infinite series of splines and wavelets; see e.g. Meyer (1992). Let pen$(\theta) =$

$(\int_{\mathcal{X}} |\theta^{(p)}(x)|^q \, dx)^{1/q}$ for $p > 1/2$ and some integer $q \geqslant 1$. Then we can take the sieves to be $\Theta_n = \{\theta \in \Theta\colon \operatorname{pen}(\theta) \leqslant b_n\}$ with $b_n \to \infty$ as $n \to \infty$ arbitrarily slowly; see e.g. Shen (1997). The choice of q is typically related to the criterion function $\widehat{Q}_n(\theta)$, such as $q = 2$ for conditional mean regression [Wahba (1990)], $q = 1$ [Koenker, Ng and Portnoy (1994)] and total variation norm [Koenker and Mizera (2003)] for quantile regressions.

More generally, if the parameter space Θ is a typical function space such as a Hölder, Sobolev or Besov space, then any function $\theta \in \Theta$ can be expressed as infinite series of some known Riesz basis $\{B_k(\cdot)\}_{k=1}^{\infty}$. An infinite-dimensional sieve space could take the form:

$$\Theta_n = \left\{\theta \in \Theta\colon \theta(\cdot) = \sum_{k=1}^{\infty} a_k B_k(\cdot),\ \operatorname{pen}(\theta) \leqslant b_n\right\} \quad \text{with } b_n \to \infty \text{ slowly,} \tag{2.18}$$

where $\operatorname{pen}(\theta)$ is a smoothness (or roughness) penalty term.

REMARK 2.2. When $\widehat{Q}_n(\theta)$ is concave and $\operatorname{pen}(\theta)$ is convex, the sieve extremum estimation, $\sup_{\theta \in \Theta_n} \widehat{Q}_n(\theta)$ with Θ_n given in (2.18), becomes equivalent to the *penalized extremum estimation*

$$\max_{\theta \in \Theta} \left\{\widehat{Q}_n(\theta) - \lambda_n \operatorname{pen}(\theta)\right\} \tag{2.19}$$

where the Lagrange multiplier λ_n is chosen such that the solution satisfies $\operatorname{pen}(\hat{\theta}) = b_n$. See e.g. Eggermont and LaRiccia (2001, Subsection 1.6).

2.3.5. Shape-preserving sieves

There are many sieves that can preserve the shape, such as nonnegativity, monotonicity and convexity, of the unknown function to be approximated. See e.g. DeVore (1977a, 1977b) on shape-preserving spline and polynomial sieves, Anastassiou and Yu (1992a, 1992b) and Dechevsky and Penev (1997) on shape-preserving wavelet sieves. Here we mention one of such shape-preserving sieves.

Cardinal B-spline wavelets. The cardinal B-spline of order $r \geqslant 1$ is given by

$$B_r(x) = \frac{1}{(r-1)!} \sum_{j=0}^{r} (-1)^j \binom{r}{j} \left[\max(0, x - j)\right]^{r-1}, \tag{2.20}$$

which has support $[0, r]$, is symmetric at $r/2$ and is a piecewise polynomial of highest degree $r - 1$. It satisfies $B_r(x) \geqslant 0$, $\sum_{k=-\infty}^{+\infty} B_r(x - k) = 1$ for all $x \in \mathcal{R}$, which is crucial to preserve the shape of the unknown function to be approximated. Its derivative satisfies $\frac{\partial}{\partial x} B_r(x) = B_{r-1}(x) - B_{r-1}(x - 1)$. See Chui (1992, Chapter 4) for a recursive construction of cardinal B-splines and their properties.

We can construct a cardinal B-spline wavelet basis for the space $L_2(\mathcal{R}, leb)$ as follows. Let $\phi_r(x) = B_r(x)$ be the father wavelet (or the scaling function). Then there is a "unique" mother wavelet function ψ_r with minimum support $[0, 2r-1]$ and is given by

$$\psi_r(x) = \sum_{\ell=0}^{3r-2} q_\ell B_r(2x-\ell), \quad q_\ell = (-1)^\ell 2^{1-r} \sum_{j=0}^{r} \binom{r}{j} B_{2r}(\ell+1-j).$$

Let

$$\phi_{r,jk}(x) = 2^{j/2} B_r\big(2^j x - k\big), \quad \psi_{r,jk}(x) = 2^{j/2}\psi_r\big(2^j x - k\big), \quad x \in \mathcal{R}.$$

Then for an integer $j_0 \geqslant 0$, $\{\phi_{r,j_0 k},\ k \in \mathbb{Z};\ \psi_{r,jk},\ j \geqslant j_0,\ k \in \mathbb{Z}\}$ is a Riesz basis of $L_2(\mathcal{R}, leb)$. Moreover, any function g in $L_2(\mathcal{R}, leb)$ has the following spline-wavelet $m = r-1$ regular multiresolution expansion:

$$g(x) = \sum_{k=-\infty}^{\infty} a_{j_0 k} 2^{j_0/2} B_r\big(2^{j_0} x - k\big) + \sum_{j=j_0}^{\infty} \sum_{k=-\infty}^{\infty} b_{jk}\psi_{r,jk}(x), \quad x \in \mathcal{R},$$

see Chui (1992, Chapter 6). For an integer $J_n > j_0 = 0$, set

$$\begin{aligned}\mathrm{SplWav}\big(r-1, 2^{J_n}\big) = \Bigg\{ &\sum_{k=-\infty}^{\infty} a_{0k} B_r(x-k) \\ &+ \sum_{j=0}^{J_n-1} \sum_{k=-\infty}^{\infty} \beta_{jk}\psi_{r,jk}(x),\ x \in \mathcal{R}\colon a_{0k}, \beta_{jk} \in \mathcal{R}\Bigg\}\end{aligned}$$

or, equivalently,[19]

$$\mathrm{SplWav}\big(r-1, 2^{J_n}\big) = \Bigg\{ \sum_{k=-\infty}^{\infty} \alpha_k 2^{J_n/2} B_r\big(2^{J_n} x - k\big),\ x \in \mathcal{R}\colon \alpha_k \in \mathcal{R}\Bigg\}.$$

Any nondecreasing continuous function on $\mathcal{R}$ can be approximated well by the $\mathrm{SplWav}(r-1, 2^{J_n})$ sieve with nondecreasing sequence $\{\alpha_k\}$ (i.e., $\alpha_k \leqslant \alpha_{k+1}$). In particular, let

$$\begin{aligned}\mathrm{MSplWav}\big(r-1, 2^{J_n}\big) = \Bigg\{ &g(x) = \sum_{k=-\infty}^{\infty} \alpha_k 2^{J_n/2} B_r\left(2^{J_n} x - k + \frac{r}{2}\right)\colon \\ &\alpha_k \leqslant \alpha_{k+1}\Bigg\}\end{aligned}$$

19 See Chen, Hansen and Scheinkman (1998) for the approximation property of this sieve for twice differentiable functions on $\mathcal{R}$.

denote the monotone spline wavelet sieve. Then for any bounded nondecreasing continuous function θ_o on $\mathcal{R}$, the MSplWav$(r-1, 2^{J_n})$, $r \geqslant 1$, sieve approximation error rate in sup-norm is $O(2^{-J_n})$; for any bounded nondecreasing continuously differentiable function θ_o on $\mathcal{R}$, the MSplWav$(r-1, 2^{J_n})$, $r \geqslant 2$, sieve approximation error rate in sup-norm is $O(2^{-2J_n})$; see e.g. Anastassiou and Yu (1992a).

2.3.6. Choice of a sieve space

The choice of a sieve space $\Theta_n = B \times \mathcal{H}_n$ depends on how well it approximates $\Theta = B \times \mathcal{H}$ and how easily one can compute $\max_{\theta \in \Theta_n} \widehat{Q}_n(\theta)$.

In general, it will be easier to compute $\max_{\theta \in \Theta_n} \widehat{Q}_n(\theta)$ when the sieve space, $\Theta_n = B \times \mathcal{H}_n$, is an unconstrained finite-dimensional linear space. Moreover, if the criterion function, $\widehat{Q}_n(\theta)$, is concave, one can choose such a linear sieve, just as in the series estimation of a concave extended linear model described in Subsection 2.2.2.

However, the ease of computation should not be the only concern when one decides which sieve to use in practice. This is because the large sample performance of a sieve estimate also depends on the approximation properties of the chosen sieve. Unfortunately, a finite-dimensional linear sieve does not always possess better approximation properties than some nonlinear sieves. For example, let us consider the estimation of a multivariate conditional mean function $h_o(\cdot) = E[Y_t | X_t = \cdot] \in \Theta$. Let Θ_n be a sieve space. Then $\hat{\theta} = \hat{h} = \arg\max_{h \in \Theta_n} \frac{-1}{n} \sum_{t=1}^{n} [Y_t - h(X_t)]^2$ is a sieve M-estimator of h_o. If $\Theta = \Lambda^p([0,1]^d)$ is the space of p-smooth functions with $p > d/2$, then one can take Θ_n to be any of the finite-dimensional linear sieve space in Subsection 2.3.1, and the resulting estimator $\hat{h}$ is a series estimator. However, if $\Theta = W_1^1([0,1]^d)$ as defined in Subsection 2.3.3, then it is better to choose the sieve space, Θ_n, to be the nonlinear Gaussian radial basis ANN in Subsection 2.3.3; the resulting estimator is still a sieve M-estimator but not a series estimator. See Section 3 for additional examples.

How well a sieve, Θ_n, approximates Θ often depends on the support, the smoothness, the shape restrictions of functions in Θ and the structure, such as additivity, nonnegativity, exclusion restrictions, imposed by the econometric model. For example, a Hermite polynomial sieve can approximate a multivariate unknown smooth density with unbounded supports and relatively thin tails well, but a power series sieve and a Fourier series sieve cannot. This is why Gallant and Nychka (1987) considered Hermite polynomial sieve MLE since they wanted to approximate multivariate densities that are smooth, have unbounded supports and include the multivariate normal density as a special case. As another example, a first-order monotone spline sieve can approximate any bounded monotone but nondifferentiable function well, and a third-order cardinal B-spline wavelet sieve can approximate any bounded monotone differentiable function well. In Example 2.1, Heckman and Singer (1984, pp. 300 and 301) did not want to impose any assumptions on the distribution function $h(\cdot)$ of the latent random factor, hence they applied a first-order monotone spline sieve to approximate it. In their estimation of the first eigenfunction of the conditional expectation operator associated with a fully nonparametric scalar diffusion model, Chen, Hansen and Scheinkman (1998) applied a shape-preserving third order cardinal B-spline wavelet sieve to approximate the unknown first eigenfunction, since the first eigenfunction is known to be monotone and twice continuously differentiable. As a final example, in their sieve MD estimation of the semi-nonparametric external habit model (2.7) of Example 2.3, Chen and Ludvigson (2003) used the sANN sieve with logistic activation function to approximate the unknown habit function $H(C_t, C_{t-1}, \ldots, C_{t-L}) = C_t h(\frac{C_{t-1}}{C_t}, \ldots, \frac{C_{t-L}}{C_t})$. This is partly because when $L \geqslant 3$, the unknown smooth function $h : \mathcal{R}^L \to [0, 1)$ can be approximated by a sANN sieve well, and partly because it is very easy to impose the habit constraint $0 \leqslant H(C_t, C_{t-1}, \ldots, C_{t-L}) < C_t$ when $h(\frac{C_{t-1}}{C_t}, \ldots, \frac{C_{t-L}}{C_t})$ is approximated by the sANN sieve with logistic activation function.

For a sieve estimate to be consistent with a fast rate of convergence, it is important to choose sieves with good approximation error rates as well as controlled complexity.[20] Nevertheless, for econometric applications where the only prior information on the unknown functions is their smoothness and supports, the choice of a sieve space is not important, as long as the chosen sieve space has the desired approximation error rate.

2.4. A small Monte Carlo study

To illustrate how to implement the sieve extremum estimation, we present a small Monte Carlo simulation carried out using Matlab and Fortran. The true model is: $Y_1 = X_1\beta_o + h_{o1}(Y_2) + h_{o2}(X_2) + U$ with $\beta_o = 1$, $h_{o1}(Y_2) = 1/[1 + \exp\{-Y_2\}]$ and $h_{o2}(X_2) = \log(1 + X_2)$. We assume that Y_2 is endogenous and $Y_2 = X_1 + X_2 + X_3 + R \times U + e$ with either $R = 0.9$ (strong correlation) or 0.1 (weak correlation). Suppose that the regressors X_1, X_2, X_3 are independent and uniformly distributed over $[0, 1]$, and that e is independent of (X, U) and normally distributed with mean zero and variance 0.1. (We have also tried $E[e^2] = 0.05, 0.25$, the simulation results share very similar patterns to the ones when $E[e^2] = 0.1$, hence are not reported here.) Conditional on $X = (X_1, X_2, X_3)'$, U is normally distributed with mean zero and variance $(X_1^2 + X_2^2 + X_3^2)/3$. Let $Z = (Y_1, Y_2, X')'$. A random sample of $n = 1000$ data $\{Z_i\}_{i=1}^n$ is generated from this design. An econometrician observes the simulated data $\{Z_i\}_{i=1}^n$, and wants to estimate $\theta_o = (\beta_o, h_{o1}, h_{o2})'$, obeying the conditional moment restriction:

$$E\big[Y_{1i} - \big\{X_{1i}\beta_o + h_{o1}(Y_{2i}) + h_{o2}(X_{2i})\big\}\big|X_i\big] = 0. \tag{2.21}$$

This model is a generalization of the partially linear IV regression $E[Y_1 - \{X_1\beta_o + h_{o1}(Y_2)\}|X] = 0$ example of Ai and Chen (2003) to a partially additive IV regression. Since $h_{o1}(Y_2)$ is an unknown function of the endogenous variable Y_2, both examples belong to the so-called ill-posed inverse problems.

Let $\rho(Z, \theta) = Y_1 - \{X_1\beta + h_1(Y_2) + h_2(X_2)\}$ with $\theta = (\beta, h_1, h_2)'$. We say that the parameters $\theta_o = (\beta_o, h_{o1}, h_{o2})'$ are identified if $E[\rho(Z, \theta)|X] = 0$ only when $\theta = \theta_o$.

[20] This will become clear from the large sample theory discussed later in Section 3.

As a sufficient condition for the identification of θ_o, we assume that $\mathrm{Var}(X_1) > 0$, $h_1(y_2)$ is a bounded function with $\sup_{y_2}|h_1(y_2)| \leqslant 1$ and that $h_2(x_2)$ satisfies $h_2(0.5) = \log(3/2)$. In particular, we assume that $\theta_o = (\beta_o, h_{o1}, h_{o2})' \in \Theta = B \times \mathcal{H}_1 \times \mathcal{H}_2$ with B a compact interval in $\mathcal{R}$, $\mathcal{H}_1 = \{h_1 \in C^2(\mathcal{R})\colon \sup_{y_2}|h_1(y_2)| \leqslant 1, \int [D^2 h_1(y_2)]^2\,\mathrm{d}y_2 < \infty\}$ and $\mathcal{H}_2 = \{h_2 \in C^2([0,1])\colon h_2(0.5) = \log(3/2), \int [D^2 h_2(x_2)]^2\,\mathrm{d}x_2 < \infty\}$.

Since this model (2.21) fits into the second subclass of the conditional moment restrictions (2.8) with $E[\rho(Z,\theta_o)|X] = 0$, we can apply the sieve MD criterion (2.12) to estimate $\theta_o = (\beta_o, h_{o1}, h_{o2})$. We take $\Theta_n = B \times \mathcal{H}_{1n} \times \mathcal{H}_{2n}$ as the sieve space, where

$$\mathcal{H}_{1n} = \left\{h_1(y_2) = \Pi_1' B^{k_{1,n}}(y_2)\colon \int \left[D^2 h_1(y_2)\right]^2 \mathrm{d}y_2 \leqslant c_1 \log n\right\},$$

$B^{k_{1,n}}(y_2)$ is either a polynomial spline basis with equally spaced (according to empirical quantile of Y_2) knots, or a 3rd order cardinal B-spline basis, or a Hermite polynomial basis,[21] and $\dim(\Pi_1) = k_{1,n}$ is the number of unknown sieve coefficient of h_1. Similarly,

$$\mathcal{H}_{2n} = \left\{h_2(x_2) = \Pi_2' B^{k_{2,n}}(x_2)\colon \int \left[D^2 h_2(x_2)\right]^2 \mathrm{d}x_2 \leqslant c_2 \log n,\right.$$
$$\left. h_2(0.5) = \log(3/2)\right\},$$

$B^{k_{2,n}}(x_2)$ is either a polynomial spline basis with equally spaced (according to empirical quantile of X_2) knots, or a 3rd order cardinal B-spline basis, and $\dim(\Pi_2) = k_{2,n}$ is the number of unknown sieve coefficients of h_2. In the Monte Carlo study, we have tried $k_{1,n} = 4, 5, 6, 8$ and $k_{2,n} = 4, 5, 6$.

As an illustration, we only consider the sieve MD estimation (2.12) using the identity weighting $\widehat{\Sigma}(X) = I$,[22] and the series LS estimator as the $\hat{m}(X,\theta)$ for the conditional mean function $E[\rho(Z,\theta)|X]$, thus the criterion becomes

$$\min_{\beta\in B,\, h_1\in\mathcal{H}_{1n},\, h_2\in\mathcal{H}_{2n}} \frac{1}{n}\sum_{i=1}^{n}\left\{\hat{m}(X_i,\theta)\right\}^2, \quad \text{with}$$

$$\hat{m}(X,\theta) = \sum_{j=1}^{n}\left[Y_{1j} - \left\{X_{1j}\beta + h_1(Y_{2j})\right.\right.$$
$$\left.\left. + h_2(X_{2j})\right\}\right] p^{k_{m,n}}(X_j)'(P'P)^{-} p^{k_{m,n}}(X),$$

where in the simulation $p^{k_{m,n}}(X)$ is taken to be the 4th degree polynomial spline sieve, with basis $\{1, X_1, X_1^2, X_1^3, X_1^4, [\max(X_1 - 0.5, 0)]^4, X_2, X_2^2, X_2^3, X_2^4, [\max(X_2 - 0.5, 0)]^4, X_3, X_3^2, X_3^3, X_3^4, [\max(X_3 - 0.1, 0)]^4, [\max(X_3 - 0.25, 0)]^4, [\max(X_3 -$

[21] See Blundell, Chen and Kristensen (2007) for a more detailed description on the choice of $\mathcal{H}_{1n}$.

[22] See Subsection 4.3 or Ai and Chen (2003) for the sieve MD procedure with the optimal weighting matrix.

$0.5, 0)]^4$, $[\max(X_3 - 0.75, 0)]^4$, $[\max(X_3 - 0.90, 0)]^4$, X_1X_3, X_2X_3, $X_1[\max(X_3 - 0.25, 0)]^4$, $X_2[\max(X_3-0.25, 0)]^4$, $X_1[\max(X_3-0.75, 0)]^4$, $X_2[\max(X_3-0.75, 0)]^4\}$. We note that the above criterion is equivalent to a constrained 2 Stage Least Squares (2SLS) with $k_{m,n} = 26$ instruments and $\dim(\Theta_n) = 1 + k_{1,n} + k_{2,n}$ ($< k_{m,n}$) unknown parameters:

$$\min_{\beta\in B,\, h_1\in\mathcal{H}_{1n},\, h_2\in\mathcal{H}_{2n}} [\mathbf{Y}_1 - \mathbf{X}_1\beta - \mathbf{B}\Pi]' P(P'P)^- P'[\mathbf{Y}_1 - \mathbf{X}_1\beta - \mathbf{B}\Pi],$$

where $\mathbf{Y}_1 = (Y_{11}, \ldots, Y_{1n})'$, $\mathbf{X}_1 = (X_{11}, \ldots, X_{1n})'$, $\Pi = (\Pi_1', \Pi_2')'$, $\mathbf{B}_1 = (B^{k_{1,n}}(Y_{21}), \ldots, B^{k_{1,n}}(Y_{2n}))'$, $\mathbf{B}_2 = (B^{k_{2,n}}(X_{21}), \ldots, B^{k_{2,n}}(X_{2n}))'$ and $\mathbf{B} = (\mathbf{B}_1', \mathbf{B}_2')'$.

Since $\rho(Z, \theta)$ is linear in $\theta = (\beta, h_1, h_2)'$, the joint sieve MD estimation is equivalent to the profile sieve MD estimation for this model. We can first compute a profile sieve estimator for $h_1(y_2)+h_2(x_2)$. That is, for any fixed β, we compute the sieve coefficients Π by minimizing $\sum_{i=1}^n \{\hat{m}(X_i, \theta)\}^2$ subject to the smoothness constraints imposed on the functions h_1 and h_2:

$$\min_{\Pi:\ \int [D^2 h_\ell(y)]^2\, dy \leqslant c_\ell \log n,\ \ell=1,2} [\mathbf{Y}_1 - \mathbf{X}_1\beta - \mathbf{B}\Pi]' P(P'P)^- P'[\mathbf{Y}_1 - \mathbf{X}_1\beta - \mathbf{B}\Pi] \tag{2.22}$$

for some upper bounds $c_\ell > 0$, $\ell = 1, 2$. Let $\widetilde{\Pi}(\beta)$ be the solution to (2.22) and $\tilde{h}_1(y_2; \beta) + \tilde{h}_2(x_2; \beta) = (B^{k_{1,n}}(y_2)', B^{k_{2,n}}(x_2)')\widetilde{\Pi}(\beta)$ be the profile sieve estimator of $h_1(y_2) + h_2(x_2)$. Next, we estimate β by $\hat{\beta}_{\mathrm{iv}}$ which solves the following 2SLS problem:

$$\min_\beta \bigl[\mathbf{Y}_1 - \mathbf{X}_1\beta - \mathbf{B}\widetilde{\Pi}(\beta)\bigr]' P(P'P)^- P'\bigl[\mathbf{Y}_1 - \mathbf{X}_1\beta - \mathbf{B}\widetilde{\Pi}(\beta)\bigr]. \tag{2.23}$$

Finally we estimate $h_{o1}(y_2) + h_{o2}(x_2)$ by

$$\hat{h}_1(y_2) + \hat{h}_2(x_2) = \bigl(B^{k_{1,n}}(y_2)', B^{k_{2,n}}(x_2)'\bigr)\widetilde{\Pi}(\hat{\beta}_{\mathrm{iv}}),$$

and then estimate h_{o1} and h_{o2} by imposing the location constraint $h_2(0.5) = \log(3/2)$:

$$\hat{h}_{2,\mathrm{iv}}(x_2) = B^{k_{2,n}}(x_2)'\widetilde{\Pi}_2(\hat{\beta}_{\mathrm{iv}}) - B^{k_{2,n}}(0.5)'\widetilde{\Pi}_2(\hat{\beta}_{\mathrm{iv}}) + \log(3/2),$$
$$\hat{h}_{1,\mathrm{iv}}(y_2) = B^{k_{1,n}}(y_2)'\widetilde{\Pi}_1(\hat{\beta}_{\mathrm{iv}}) + B^{k_{2,n}}(0.5)'\widetilde{\Pi}_2(\hat{\beta}_{\mathrm{iv}}) - \log(3/2).$$

We note that although this model (2.21) belongs to the nasty ill-posed inverse problem, the above profile sieve MD procedure is very easy to compute, and in fact, $\hat{\beta}_{\mathrm{iv}}$ and $\widetilde{\Pi}(\hat{\beta}_{\mathrm{iv}})$ have closed form solutions. To see this, we note that (2.22) is equivalent to

$$\min_{\Pi,\lambda_\ell} (\mathbf{Y}_1 - \mathbf{X}_1\beta - \mathbf{B}\Pi)' P(P'P)^- P'(\mathbf{Y}_1 - \mathbf{X}_1\beta - \mathbf{B}\Pi)$$
$$+ \sum_{\ell=1}^{2} \lambda_\ell \bigl\{\Pi_\ell' C_\ell \Pi_\ell - c_\ell \log n\bigr\},$$

where for $\ell = 1, 2$, $C_\ell = \int [D^2 B^{k_{\ell,n}}(y)][D^2 B^{k_{\ell,n}}(y)]'\, dy$, $\Pi_\ell' C_\ell \Pi_\ell = \int [D^2 h_\ell(y)]^2\, dy$ and $\lambda_\ell \geqslant 0$ is the Lagrange multiplier. However, we do not want to specify the upper bounds $c_\ell > 0, \ell = 1, 2$, instead we choose some small values as the penalization weights λ_1, λ_2, and solve the following problems:

$$\min_{\Pi}(\mathbf{Y}_1 - \mathbf{X}_1\beta - \mathbf{B}\Pi)'P(P'P)^- P'(\mathbf{Y}_1 - \mathbf{X}_1\beta - \mathbf{B}\Pi) + \sum_{\ell=1}^{2} \lambda_\ell \Pi_\ell' C_\ell \Pi_\ell. \tag{2.24}$$

Denote $C(\lambda_1, \lambda_2) = \left[\begin{smallmatrix} \lambda_1 C_1 & 0 \\ 0 & \lambda_2 C_2 \end{smallmatrix}\right]$ as the smoothness penalization matrix. The minimization problem (2.24) has a simple closed form solution:

$$\begin{aligned}\widetilde{\Pi}(\beta) &= \big(\mathbf{B}'P(P'P)^- P'\mathbf{B} + C(\lambda_1, \lambda_2)\big)^- \mathbf{B}'P(P'P)^- P'[\mathbf{Y}_1 - \mathbf{X}_1\beta] \\ &= W[\mathbf{Y}_1 - \mathbf{X}_1\beta],\end{aligned}$$

with $W = (\mathbf{B}'P(P'P)^- P'\mathbf{B} + C(\lambda_1, \lambda_2))^- \mathbf{B}'P(P'P)^- P'$. Substituting the solution $\widetilde{\Pi}(\beta)$ into the 2SLS problem (2.23), we obtain

$$\begin{aligned}\hat{\beta}_{\mathrm{iv}} &= \big[\mathbf{X}_1'(I - \mathbf{B}W)'P(P'P)^- P'(I - \mathbf{B}W)\mathbf{X}_1\big]^{-1}\mathbf{X}_1' \\ &\quad \times (I - \mathbf{B}W)'P(P'P)^- P'(I - \mathbf{B}W)\mathbf{Y}_1,\end{aligned}$$

and $\widetilde{\Pi}(\hat{\beta}_{\mathrm{iv}}) = W[\mathbf{Y}_1 - \mathbf{X}_1\hat{\beta}_{\mathrm{iv}}]$.

Table 1
Different endogeneity, Spl(3, 2) for h_2, $k_{2n} = 5$, $\lambda_2 = 0.0001$

R	β	SE(β)	IBias$^2(h_1)$	IMSE(h_1)	IBias$^2(h_2)$	IMSE(h_2)
		Spl(3, 2)	$k_{1n} = 5$	$\lambda_1 = 0.005$		
0.0	1.0081	0.0909	0.0003	0.0427	0.0000	0.0026
0.1	1.0021	0.0907	0.0003	0.0446	0.0000	0.0026
0.9	0.9404	0.0947	0.0148	0.0926	0.0003	0.0030
		Spl(3, 1)	$k_{1n} = 4$	$\lambda_1 = 0.001$		
0.0	1.0076	0.0891	0.0002	0.0225	0.0000	0.0025
0.1	1.0010	0.0886	0.0002	0.0229	0.0000	0.0025
0.9	0.9398	0.0941	0.0160	0.0623	0.0003	0.0029
		HPol(4)	$k_{1n} = 5$	$\lambda_1 = 0.005$		
0.0	1.0089	0.0906	0.0003	0.0395	0.0000	0.0026
0.1	1.0029	0.0901	0.0003	0.0397	0.0000	0.0026
0.9	0.9418	0.0948	0.0121	0.0830	0.0003	0.0030
		HPol(3)	$k_{1n} = 4$	$\lambda_1 = 0.001$		
0.0	1.0078	0.0890	0.0002	0.0202	0.0000	0.0025
0.1	1.0012	0.0885	0.0002	0.0205	0.0000	0.0025
0.9	0.9401	0.0941	0.0112	0.0546	0.0003	0.0029

Table 2
Different penalization levels and sieve terms, $R = 0.9$

(λ_1, λ_2)	β	SE(β)	IBias$^2(h_1)$	IMSE(h_1)	IBias$^2(h_2)$	IMSE(h_2)
Spl(3, 1) for h_1 and h_2, $k_{1n} = k_{2n} = 4$						
(0.001, 0.0)	0.9366	0.0941	0.0176	0.0612	0.0003	0.0018
(0.05, 0.001)	0.9324	0.0867	0.0185	0.0568	0.0003	0.0016
Spl(3, 3) for h_1 and h_2, $k_{1n} = k_{2n} = 6$						
(0.001, 0.0)	0.9451	0.0984	0.0124	0.1594	0.0003	0.0032
(0.05, 0.001)	0.9441	0.0954	0.0125	0.0720	0.0003	0.0028

For $R = 0.9$, 0.1 and 0.0, a sample of 1000 data points were generated according to the above design. The sieve MD procedure was applied to the data with identity weighting matrix $\widehat{\Sigma}(X) = I$ and the penalization weights $\lambda_1 = 0.005$ (or 0.001) and $\lambda_2 = 0.0001$ (or 0) for simplicity. The estimated coefficients were recorded. Then, a new sample of 1000 data points were drawn and the estimated coefficients were computed again. This procedure was repeated 400 times. The mean (M) and standard error (SE) of the β_o estimator across the 400 simulations are reported in Tables 1–2. To evaluate the performance of the sieve MD estimators of the nonparametric components $h_{o1}(Y_2)$ and $h_{o2}(X_2)$, we report their integrated squared biases (IBias^2) and the integrated mean squared errors (IMSE) across the 400 simulations in Tables 1–2.[23] Table 1 summarizes the performance of the estimators across different degrees of endogeneity and different sieves for $h_1(Y_2)$. Table 2 summarizes the sensitivity of the estimators (under $R = 0.9$) to different sieve number of terms and penalization parameters for both $h_1(Y_2)$ and $h_2(X_2)$. We also plot the estimated functions $h_{o1}(Y_2)$ and $h_{o2}(X_2)$ corresponding to the strong correlation case ($R = 0.9$) in Figure 1, where the solid lines represent the true functions and the dashed (or dotted) lines denote the sieve MD (or sieve IV) estimates.

Tables 1–2 and Figure 1 indicate that even under strong correlation, the sieve MD estimates of β_o and $h_{o2}(X_2)$ perform well. We find that the sieve IV estimates of β_o and $h_{o2}(X_2)$ are not sensitive to the choices of the penalization parameters λ_1, λ_2, nor to the choices of sieve bases for $h_{o1}(Y_2)$. The sieve IV estimate of $h_{o1}(Y_2)$ is also not very sensitive to the choices of sieve bases, although it is slightly more sensitive to the penalization parameter λ_1 under strong correlation. Since under strong correlation, the

[23] The IBias$^2(h_1)$ and IMSE(h_1) in Table 1 are calculated as follows. Let $\hat{h}_i$ be the estimate of h_{o1} from the ith simulated data set, and $\bar{h}(y) = \sum_{i=1}^{400} \hat{h}_i(y)/400$ be the pointwise average across 200 simulations. We calculate the pointwise squared bias as $[\bar{h}(y) - h_{o1}(y)]^2$, and the pointwise variance as $400^{-1} \sum_{i=1}^{400} [\hat{h}_i(y) - \bar{h}(y)]^2$. The integrated squared bias is calculated by numerically integrating the pointwise squared bias from $\underline{y}$ to $\bar{y}$ which are respectively the 2.5th and 97.5th empirical percentiles of Y_2; The integrated MSE are computed in a similar way.

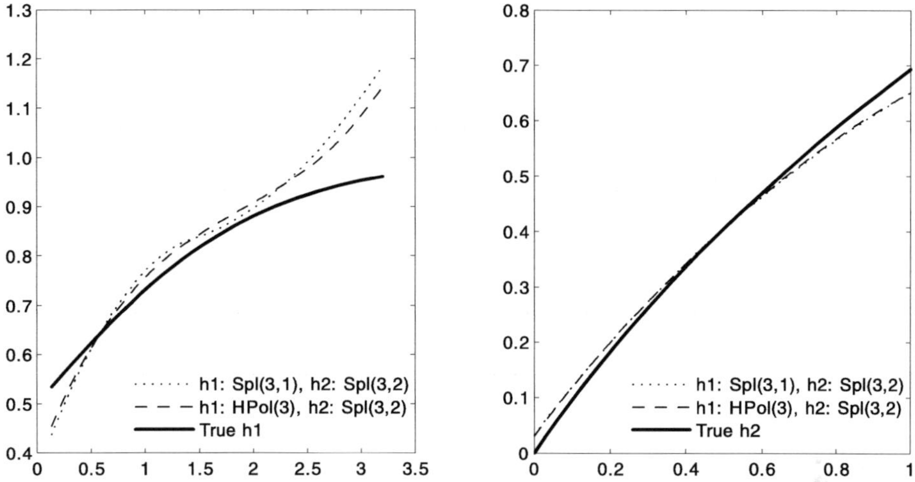

Figure 1. True and estimated functions with $R = 0.9$, $\lambda_1 = 0.001$, $\lambda_2 = 0.0001$.

estimation of $h_{o1}(Y_2)$ is a nasty ill-posed inverse problem, as the penalization parameter λ_1 gets smaller, the integrated squared bias of $h_{o1}()$ does not change much but the integrated variance of $h_{o1}()$ increases more. The additional Monte Carlo results for other sieve bases such as 3rd order cardinal B-splines and for different combinations of sieve number of terms and penalization levels share similar patterns to the ones reported here. These findings are also consistent with the more detailed Monte Carlo studies in Blundell, Chen and Kristensen (2007).

2.5. *An incomplete list of sieve applications in econometrics*

We conclude this section by listing a few applications of the sieve extremum estimation in econometrics.[24] Most of the existing applications are done in microeconometrics. Elbadawi, Gallant and Souza (1983) studied Fourier series LS estimation of demand elasticity. Cosslett (1983) proposed nonparametric ML estimation of a binary choice model. Heckman and Singer (1984) considered sieve ML estimation of a duration model where the unknown error distribution is approximated by a first-order spline. Their estimation procedure was also applied in Cameron and Heckman (1998) to a life-cycle schooling problem. Duncan (1986) used spline sieve MLE in estimating a censored regression. Hausman and Newey (1995) considered power series and spline series LS estimation of consumer surplus. Hahn (1998) and Imbens, Newey and Ridder (2005)

[24] Although restricting our attention to economic applications only, it is still impossible to mention all the existing applications of sieve methods in econometrics. Any omissions reflect my lack of awareness and are purely unintentional.

used power series and splines in the two-step efficient estimation of the average treatment effect models. Newey, Powell and Vella (1999), and Pinkse (2000) considered series estimation of a triangular system of simultaneous equations. To estimate semi-parametric generalizations of Heckman's (1979) sample selection model, Gallant and Nychka (1987) proposed the Hermite polynomial sieve MLE, while Newey (1988) and Das, Newey and Vella (2003) applied the series LS estimation method. Recently, Newey (2001) used the sieve MD procedure to estimate a nonlinear measurement error model. Blundell, Chen and Kristensen (2007) considered a profile sieve MD procedure to estimate shape-invariant Engel curves with nonparametric endogenous expenditure. Coppejans (2001) proposed sieve ML estimation of a binary choice model. Khan (2005) considered a sieve LS estimation of a probit binary choice model with unknown heteroskedasticity. Hirano, Imbens and Ridder (2003) proposed a sieve logistic regression to estimate propensity score for treatment effect models. Mahajan (2004) estimated a semiparametric single index model with binary misclassified regressors via sieve MLE. Chen, Fan and Tsyrennikov (2006) studied sieve MLE of semi-nonparametric multivariate copula models. Chen, Hong and Tamer (2005) made use of spline sieves to estimate nonlinear nonclassical measurement error models with an auxiliary sample. Their estimation procedure was shown in Chen, Hong and Tarozzi (2007) to be semiparametrically efficient for general nonlinear GMM models of nonclassical measurement errors, missing data and treatment effects. Hu and Schennach (2006) apply sieve MLE to estimate a nonlinear nonclassical measurement error model with instruments. Brendstrup and Paarsch (2004) applied Hermite and Laguerre polynomial sieve MLE to estimate sequential asymmetric English auctions. Bierens (in press) and Bierens and Carvalho (in press) applied Legendre polynomial sieve MLE respectively to estimate an interval-censored mixed proportional hazard model and a competing risks model of recidivism.

There have also been many applications of the method of sieves in time series econometrics. Engle et al. (1986) forecasted electricity demand using a partially linear spline regression. Engle and Gonzalez-Rivera (1991) applied sieve MLE to estimate ARCH models where the unknown density of the standardized innovation is approximated by a first order spline sieve. Gallant and Tauchen (1989) and Gallant, Hsieh and Tauchen (1991) employed Hermite polynomial sieve MLE to study asset pricing and foreign exchange rates. Gallant and Tauchen (1996, 2004) have proposed the combinations of Hermite polynomial sieve and simulated method of moments to effectively solve many complicated asset pricing models with latent factors, and their methods have been widely applied in empirical finance. Bansal and Viswanathan (1993), Bansal, Hsieh and Viswanathan (1993) and Chapman (1997) considered sieve approximation of the whole stochastic discount factor (or pricing kernel) as a function of a few macroeconomic factors. White (1990) and Granger and Teräsvirta (1993) suggested nonparametric LS forecasting via sigmoid ANN sieve. Hutchinson, Lo and Poggio (1994) applied radial basis ANN to option pricing. Chen, Racine and Swanson (2001) used partially linear ANN and ridgelet sieves to forecast US inflation. McCaffrey et al. (1992) estimated the Lyapunov exponent of a chaotic system via ANN sieves.[25] Chen and Ludvigson (2003) employed a sigmoid ANN sieve to estimate the unknown habit function in a consumption asset pricing model. Polk, Thompson and Vuolteenaho (2003) applied sigmoid ANN to compute conditional quantile in testing stock return predictability. Chen, Hansen and Scheinkman (1998) employed a shape-preserving spline-wavelet sieve to estimate the eigenfunctions of a fully nonparametric scalar diffusion model from discrete-time low-frequency observations. Chen and Conley (2001) made use of the same sieve to estimate a spatial temporal model with flexible conditional mean and conditional covariance. Phillips (1998) applied orthonormal basis to analyze spurious regressions. Engle and Rangel (2004) proposed a new Spline GARCH model to measure unconditional volatility and have applied it to equity markets for 50 countries for up to 50 years of daily data. See Fan and Yao (2003) for additional applications to financial time series models.

3. Large sample properties of sieve estimation of unknown functions

We already know that the sieve method is very general and easily implementable. In this section, we shall first establish that, under mild regularity conditions, the sieve extremum estimation will consistently estimate both finite-dimensional and infinite-dimensional unknown parameters. However, for econometric and statistical inference, one would like to know how accurate a consistent sieve estimator might be given a finite data set and what its limiting distribution is. Unfortunately there does not yet exist a general theory of pointwise limiting distribution for a sieve extremum estimator of an unknown function. There are a few results on pointwise limiting distribution for series estimators of densities and LS regression functions, which we shall review at the end of this section. However, all is not lost. We do have a well developed theory on $\sqrt{n}$-asymptotic normality of sieve estimators of smooth functionals[26] of unknown functions.

As we shall see in Section 4, in order to derive $\sqrt{n}$-asymptotic normality and semiparametric efficiency of sieve estimators of parametric components in a semi-nonparametric model, the sieve estimators of the nonparametric components should converge to the true unknown functions at rates faster than $n^{-1/4}$ under certain metric. This motivates the importance of establishing rates of convergence for sieve estimators of unknown functions even when the unknown functions are nuisance parameters (i.e., not the parameters of interest). Moreover, when an unknown function is also a parameter of interest in a nonparametric or a semi-nonparametric model, the convergence rate

[25] Their work is closely related to the estimation of derivative of a multivariate unknown regression function via ANN sieves in Gallant and White (1992). Shintani and Linton (2004) proposed a nonparametric test of chaos via ANN sieves.

[26] See Section 4 for the definition of a "smooth functional". Here it suffices to know that regular finite-dimensional parameters and average derivatives of unknown functions are examples of smooth functionals.

will provide useful information on the accuracy of a sieve estimator for a given finite sample size. Unfortunately, to date there is no unified theory on rates of convergence for the general sieve extremum estimators of unknown functions either.[27] Nevertheless, the theory on convergence rates of sieve M-estimators is by now well developed.

In this section we first provide a new consistency theorem on general sieve extremum estimation in Subsection 3.1. We then review the existing results on convergence rates and pointwise limiting distributions for sieve M-estimators of unknown functions. We begin this discussion with a survey of the convergence rate results for general sieve M-estimators of unknown functions in Subsection 3.2 and illustrate how to verify the technical conditions assumed for the general result with two examples. Although series estimation is a special case of sieve M-estimation, due to its special properties (i.e., concave criterion and finite-dimensional linear sieve space), the convergence rate of a series estimator can be derived under alternative sufficient conditions, which will be reviewed in Subsection 3.3. Subsection 3.4 presents the existing results on the pointwise normality of the series estimator in the special case of a LS regression function.

3.1. *Consistency of sieve extremum estimators*

For an infinite-dimensional, possibly noncompact parameter space Θ, Geman and Hwang (1982) obtained the consistency of sieve MLE with i.i.d. data; White and Wooldridge (1991) obtained the consistency of sieve extremum estimates with dependent and heterogeneous data. For an infinite-dimensional, compact parameter space Θ, Gallant (1987) and Gallant and Nychka (1987) derived the consistency of sieve M-estimates; Newey and Powell (2003) and Chernozhukov, Imbens and Newey (2007) established the consistency of sieve MD estimates. In the following, we present a new consistency theorem for approximate sieve extremum estimates that allows for noncompact infinite-dimensional Θ and is applicable to ill-posed semi-nonparametric problems.[28]

Let $d(\cdot,\cdot)$ be a (pseudo) metric on Θ. In particular, when $\Theta = B \times \mathcal{H}$ where B is a subset of some Euclidean space and $\mathcal{H}$ is a subset of some normed function space, we

[27] To the best of our knowledge, currently there is one unpublished paper [Chen and Pouzo (2006)] that derives the convergence rates for the sieve MD estimates $\hat{\theta}_n$ of $\theta_o = (\beta_o, h_o)$ satisfying the semi-nonparametric conditional moment models $E[\rho(Z, \beta_o, h_o(\cdot))|X] = 0$, where the unknown $h_o(\cdot)$ could depend on the endogenous variables Y or latent variables. Earlier, Ai and Chen (2003) obtained a faster than $n^{-1/4}$ convergence rate under a weaker metric. There are also a few papers on convergence rates of sieve MD estimate of h_o in specific models; see e.g. Blundell, Chen and Kristensen (2007) and Hall and Horowitz (2005) for the model $E[Y_1 - h_o(Y_2)|X] = 0$. Van der Vaart and Wellner (1996, Theorem 3.4.1) stated an abstract rate result for sieve extremum estimation. However, their conditions rule out ill-posed semi-nonparametric problems, and require a maximal inequality with rate for the process $\sqrt{n}(\widehat{Q}_n - Q)$, which is currently not available for a general criterion $\widehat{Q}_n$. Hence, it is fair to say that a general theory on rates of convergence for sieve extremum estimators is currently lacking.

[28] Based on a recent theorem of Stinchcombe (2002), the consistency of sieve extremum estimates is a generic property.

can use $d(\theta,\tilde{\theta}) = |\beta - \tilde{\beta}|_e + \|h - \tilde{h}\|_{\mathcal{H}}$, where $|\cdot|_e$ denotes the Euclidean norm, and $\|\cdot\|_{\mathcal{H}}$ is a norm imposed on the function space $\mathcal{H}$. For example, if $\mathcal{H} = C^m(\mathcal{X})$ with a bounded $\mathcal{X}$, we could take $\|h\|_{\mathcal{H}}$ to be $\|h\|_\infty$ or $\|h\|_{2,leb}$.

CONDITION 3.1 *(Identification).*
(i) $Q(\theta_o) > -\infty$, and if $Q(\theta_o) = +\infty$ then $Q(\theta) < +\infty$ for all $\theta \in \Theta_k \setminus \{\theta_o\}$ for all $k \geqslant 1$;
(ii) there are a nonincreasing positive function $\delta()$ and a positive function $g()$ such that for all $\varepsilon > 0$ and for all $k \geqslant 1$,

$$Q(\theta_o) - \sup_{\{\theta\in\Theta_k:\ d(\theta,\theta_o)\geqslant\varepsilon\}} Q(\theta) \geqslant \delta(k)g(\varepsilon) > 0.$$

CONDITION 3.2 *(Sieve spaces).* $\Theta_k \subseteq \Theta_{k+1} \subseteq \Theta$ for all $k \geqslant 1$; and there exists a sequence $\pi_k\theta_o \in \Theta_k$ such that $d(\theta_o, \pi_k\theta_o) \to 0$ as $k \to \infty$.

CONDITION 3.3 *(Continuity).*
(i) For each $k \geqslant 1$, $Q(\theta)$ is upper semicontinuous on Θ_k under the metric $d(\cdot,\cdot)$;
(ii) $|Q(\theta_o) - Q(\pi_{k(n)}\theta_o)| = o(\delta(k(n)))$.

CONDITION 3.4 *(Compact sieve space).* The sieve spaces, Θ_k, are compact under $d(\cdot,\cdot)$.

CONDITION 3.5 *(Uniform convergence over sieves).*
(i) For all $k \geqslant 1$, $\operatorname{plim}_{n\to\infty} \sup_{\theta\in\Theta_k} |\widehat{Q}_n(\theta) - Q(\theta)| = 0$;
(ii) $\hat{c}(k(n)) = o_P(\delta(k(n)))$ where $\hat{c}(k(n)) \equiv \sup_{\theta\in\Theta_{k(n)}} |\widehat{Q}_n(\theta) - Q(\theta)|$;
(iii) $\eta_{k(n)} = o(\delta(k(n)))$.

THEOREM 3.1. *Let $\hat{\theta}_n$ be the approximate sieve extremum estimator defined by* (2.9). *If Conditions* 3.1–3.5 *hold, then $d(\hat{\theta}_n, \theta_o) = o_P(1)$.*

PROOF. By Remark 2.1, $\hat{\theta}_n$ is well defined and measurable. For all $\varepsilon > 0$, under Conditions 3.3(i) and 3.4, $\sup_{\{\theta\in\Theta_{k(n)}:\ d(\theta,\theta_o)\geqslant\varepsilon\}} Q(\theta)$ exists. By definition, we have for all $\varepsilon > 0$,

$$\begin{aligned}\Pr\big(d(\hat{\theta}_n,\theta_o) > \varepsilon\big) &\leqslant \Pr\Big(\sup_{\{\theta\in\Theta_{k(n)}:\ d(\theta,\theta_o)\geqslant\varepsilon\}} \widehat{Q}_n(\theta) \geqslant \widehat{Q}_n(\pi_{k(n)}\theta_o) - O(\eta_{k(n)})\Big)\\ &\leqslant P_1 + P_2,\end{aligned}$$

where

$$\begin{aligned}P_1 &\equiv \Pr\Big(\sup_{\{\theta\in\Theta_{k(n)}:\ d(\theta,\theta_o)\geqslant\varepsilon\}} \big|\widehat{Q}_n(\theta) - Q(\theta)\big| > \hat{v}\big(k(n)\big)\Big)\\ &\leqslant \Pr\Big(\sup_{\theta\in\Theta_{k(n)}} \big|\widehat{Q}_n(\theta) - Q(\theta)\big| > \hat{v}\big(k(n)\big)\Big),\end{aligned}$$

and

$$P_2 \equiv \Pr\Big(\sup_{\{\theta\in\Theta_{k(n)}:\, d(\theta,\theta_o)\geqslant\varepsilon\}} Q(\theta) \geqslant Q(\pi_{k(n)}\theta_o) - 2\hat{\nu}\big(k(n)\big) - O(\eta_{k(n)})\Big)$$

$$= \Pr\Big(2\hat{\nu}\big(k(n)\big) + \big\{Q(\theta_o) - Q(\pi_{k(n)}\theta_o)\big\} + O(\eta_{k(n)}) \geqslant Q(\theta_o) - \sup_{\{\theta\in\Theta_{k(n)}:\, d(\theta,\theta_o)\geqslant\varepsilon\}} Q(\theta)\Big).$$

Choosing $\hat{\nu}(k(n)) = \hat{c}(k(n))$ it follows that the $P_1 = 0$ by definition of $\hat{c}(k(n))$ and Condition 3.5(i), and $P_2 \leqslant \Pr[2\hat{c}(k(n)) + \{Q(\theta_o) - Q(\pi_{k(n)}\theta_o)\} + O(\eta_{k(n)}) \geqslant \delta(k(n))g(\varepsilon)] \to 0$ by Conditions 3.1 and 3.5(ii). □

REMARK 3.1. (1) Theorem 3.1 is applicable to both well-posed and ill-posed semi-nonparametric models. When the problem (such as the nonparametric IV regression $E[Y_1 - h_o(Y_2)|X] = 0$) is ill-posed, one may have $\liminf_k \delta(k) = 0$, which is still allowed by Conditions 3.1(ii), 3.3(ii) and 3.5(ii)(iii). See Chen and Pouzo (2006) for alternative general consistency theorems for sieve extremum estimates that allow for ill-posed problems.

(2) If $\liminf_k \delta(k) > 0$, then Condition 3.5(iii) is automatically satisfied with $\eta_{k(n)} = o(1)$, Condition 3.5(ii) is implied by Condition 3.5(i), and Condition 3.3(ii) is implied by Condition 3.2 and Condition 3.3(ii)$'$:

CONDITION 3.3(ii)$'$. $Q(\theta)$ is continuous at θ_o in Θ.

(3) Theorem 3.1 is an extension of Corollary 2.6 of White and Wooldridge (1991). Their corollary implies $d(\hat{\theta}_n, \theta_o) = o_P(1)$ under Conditions 3.4, 3.5(i) and Conditions 3.1$'$, 3.2$'$ and 3.3$'$:

CONDITION 3.1$'$.
(i) $Q(\theta)$ is continuous at θ_o in Θ, $Q(\theta_o) > -\infty$;
(ii) for all $\varepsilon > 0$, $Q(\theta_o) > \sup_{\{\theta\in\Theta:\, d(\theta,\theta_o)\geqslant\varepsilon\}} Q(\theta)$.

CONDITION 3.2$'$. $\Theta_k \subseteq \Theta_{k+1} \subseteq \Theta$ for all $k \geqslant 1$; and for any $\theta \in \Theta$ there exists $\pi_k\theta \in \Theta_k$ such that $d(\theta, \pi_k\theta) \to 0$ as $k \to \infty$.

CONDITION 3.3$'$. For each $k \geqslant 1$,
(i) $\widehat{Q}_n(\theta)$ is a measurable function of the data $\{Z_t\}_{t=1}^n$ for all $\theta \in \Theta_k$; and
(ii) for any data $\{Z_t\}_{t=1}^n$, $\widehat{Q}_n(\theta)$ is upper semicontinuous on Θ_k under the metric $d(\cdot,\cdot)$.

We note that under Condition 3.2, Condition 3.1$'$(ii) implies that Condition 3.1(ii) is satisfied with $\delta(k) = const. > 0$, hence Remark 3.1(2) is applicable and $d(\hat{\theta}_n, \theta_o) =$

$o_P(1)$. Unfortunately, Condition 3.1′(ii) may fail to be satisfied in some ill-posed semi-nonparametric models when Θ is a noncompact infinite-dimensional parameter space.

(4) Condition 3.1′ is satisfied by Condition 3.1″:

CONDITION 3.1″.
(i) Θ is compact under $d(\cdot,\cdot)$, and $Q(\theta)$ is upper semicontinuous on Θ under $d(\cdot,\cdot)$;
(ii) $Q(\theta)$ is uniquely maximized at θ_o in Θ, $Q(\theta_o) > -\infty$.

As a consequence of Theorem 3.1, we obtain: $d(\hat{\theta}_n, \theta_o) = o_P(1)$ under Conditions 3.1″, 3.2, 3.4 and 3.5(i). This result is very similar to Lemmas A.1 in Newey and Powell (2003) and Chernozhukov, Imbens and Newey (2007).

REMARK 3.2. If $\hat{\theta}_n$ satisfies $\widehat{Q}_n(\hat{\theta}_n) \geqslant \sup_{\theta\in\Theta_n} \widehat{Q}_n(\theta) - O_{a.s.}(\eta_n)$, then $d(\hat{\theta}_n, \theta_o) = o_{a.s.}(1)$ under Conditions 3.1–3.4 and Condition 3.5″:

CONDITION 3.5″.
(i) For all $k \geqslant 1$, $\sup_{\theta\in\Theta_k} |\widehat{Q}_n(\theta) - Q(\theta)| = o_{a.s.}(1)$;
(ii) $\hat{c}(k(n)) = o_{a.s.}(\delta(k(n)))$;
(iii) $\eta_{k(n)} = o(\delta(k(n)))$.

This extends Gallant's (1987) theorem to almost sure convergence of approximate sieve extremum estimates, allowing for noncompact infinite-dimensional Θ and for ill-posed semi-nonparametric models.

Note that when $\Theta_k = \Theta$ is compact, the conditions for Theorem 3.1 become the standard assumptions imposed for consistency of parametric extremum estimation in Newey and McFadden (1994) and White (1994). For semi-nonparametric models, the entire parameter space Θ contains infinite-dimensional unknown functions and is generally noncompact. Nevertheless, one can easily construct compact approximating parameter spaces (sieves) Θ_k. Moreover, it is relatively easy to verify the uniform convergence over compact sieve spaces,[29] while "$\text{plim}_{n\to\infty} \sup_{\theta\in\Theta} |\widehat{Q}_n(\theta) - Q(\theta)| = 0$" may fail when the space Θ is too "large" or too "complex".

We now review some notions of complexity of a function class. Let $L_r(P_o)$, $r \in [1,\infty)$, denote the space of real-valued random variables with finite rth moments and $\|\cdot\|_r$ denote the $L_r(P_o)$-norm. Let $\mathcal{F}_n = \{g(\theta,\cdot)\colon \theta \in \Theta_n\}$ be a class of real-valued, $L_r(P_o)$-measurable functions indexed by $\theta \in \Theta_n$. One notion of complexity of the class $\mathcal{F}_n$ is the $L_r(P_o)$-*covering numbers without bracketing*, which is the minimal number of w-balls $\{\{f\colon \|f - g_j\|_r \leqslant w\},\ \|g_j\|_r < \infty,\ j = 1,\dots,N\}$ that cover $\mathcal{F}_n$, denoted

[29] One could modify the proof of Corollary 2.2 in Newey (1991) or the proof of Lemma 1 in Andrews (1992) to provide sufficient conditions for Condition 3.5(i) in terms of Conditions 3.3(i) and 3.4 and the pointwise convergence over Θ_k.

as $N(w, \mathcal{F}_n, \|\cdot\|_r)$. Likewise, we can define $N(w, \mathcal{F}_n, \|\cdot\|_{n,r})$ as the $L_r(P_n)$-(random) covering numbers without bracketing, where $\|\cdot\|_{n,r}$ denotes the $L_r(P_n)$-norm and P_n denotes the empirical measure of a random sample $\{Z_i\}_{i=1}^n$. Sometimes the covering numbers of $\mathcal{F}_n$ can grow to infinity very fast as n grows; it is then more convenient to measure the complexity of $\mathcal{F}_n$ using the notion of *$L_r(P_o)$-metric entropy without bracketing*, $H(w, \mathcal{F}_n, \|\cdot\|_r) \equiv \log(N(w, \mathcal{F}_n, \|\cdot\|_r))$, and the $L_r(P_n)$-(random) metric entropy without bracketing, $H(w, \mathcal{F}_n, \|\cdot\|_{n,r}) \equiv \log(N(w, \mathcal{F}_n, \|\cdot\|_{n,r}))$. Detailed discussions of metric entropy can be found in Pollard (1984), Andrews (1994a), van der Vaart and Wellner (1996) and van de Geer (2000).

When the function class Θ is too complex in terms of its metric entropy being too large, then the uniform convergence over the entire parameter space Θ may fail, but the uniform convergence over a sieve space Θ_n (i.e., Condition 3.5(i)) can still be satisfied. For example, when $\widehat{Q}_n(\theta) = n^{-1}\sum_{t=1}^n l(\theta, Z_t)$ and $\{Z_t\}_{t=1}^n$ is i.i.d., $E\{\sup_{\theta\in\Theta_n} |l(\theta, Z_t)|\} < \infty$, then Condition 3.5(i) is satisfied if and only if $H(w, \{l(\theta, \cdot)\colon \theta \in \Theta_n\}, \|\cdot\|_{n,1}) = o_P(n)$ for all $w > 0$; see Pollard (1984). When the space Θ is infinite-dimensional and not totally bounded, $H(w, \{l(\theta, \cdot)\colon \theta \in \Theta\}, \|\cdot\|_{n,1}) = O_P(n)$ may occur; hence $\sup_{\theta\in\Theta} |\widehat{Q}_n(\theta) - Q(\theta)| \neq o_P(1)$. For such a case, the extremum estimator obtained by maximizing over the entire parameter space Θ, $\arg\sup_{\theta\in\Theta} \widehat{Q}_n(\theta)$, may fail to exist or be inconsistent.

Conditions 3.1–3.4 of Theorem 3.1 are basic regularity conditions; one can provide more primitive sufficient assumptions for Condition 3.5 in specific applications. In the next remarks we present simple consistency results for sieve M-estimators and sieve MD-estimators. Let $N(w, \Theta_n, d)$ denote the minimal number of w-radius balls (under the metric d) that cover the sieve space Θ_n.

REMARK 3.3 *(Consistency of sieve M-estimator $\hat{\theta}_n = \arg\sup_{\theta\in\Theta_n} n^{-1}\sum_{t=1}^n l(\theta, Z_t) - o_P(1)$).* Suppose that Conditions 3.2 and 3.4 hold, that Condition 3.1 is satisfied with $Q(\theta) = E\{l(\theta, Z_t)\}$ and $\liminf_{k(n)} \delta(k(n)) > 0$, and that $E\{l(\theta, Z_t)\}$ is continuous at $\theta = \theta_o \in \Theta$. Then $d(\hat{\theta}_n, \theta_o) = o_P(1)$ under the following Condition 3.5M:

CONDITION 3.5M.

(i) $\{Z_t\}_{t=1}^n$ is i.i.d., $E\{\sup_{\theta\in\Theta_n} |l(\theta, Z_t)|\}$ is bounded;

(ii) there are a finite $s > 0$ and a random variable $U(Z_t)$ with $E\{U(Z_t)\} < \infty$ such that $\sup_{\theta,\theta'\in\Theta_n\colon d(\theta,\theta')\leqslant\delta} |l(\theta, Z_t) - l(\theta', Z_t)| \leqslant \delta^s U(Z_t)$;

(iii) $\log N(\delta^{1/s}, \Theta_n, d) = o(n)$ for all $\delta > 0$.

Remark 3.3 is a direct consequence of Theorem 3.1 and Pollard's (1984) Theorem II.24. This is because Condition 3.5M(i) and (ii) imply $H(w, \{l(\theta, \cdot)\colon \theta \in \Theta_n\}, \|\cdot\|_{n,1}) \leqslant \log N(\delta^{1/s}, \Theta_n, d)$, hence Condition 3.5M implies Condition 3.5(i). See White and Wooldridge (1991, Theorem 2.5) and Ai and Chen (2007, Lemma A.1) for more general sufficient assumptions for Condition 3.5.

REMARK 3.4 *(Consistency of sieve MD-estimator $\hat{\theta}_n = \arg\inf_{\theta\in\Theta_n} \frac{1}{n}\sum_{t=1}^{n} \hat{m}(X_t,\theta)' \times \{\widehat{\Sigma}(X_t)\}^{-1}\hat{m}(X_t,\theta) + o_P(1)$).* Suppose that Conditions 3.2 and 3.4 hold, that $m(X_t,\theta) \equiv E\{\rho(Z_t,\theta)|X_t\} = 0$ only when $\theta = \theta_o \in \Theta$, that for all X_t, $m(X_t,\theta)$ is continuous in θ_o under the metric $d(\cdot,\cdot)$, and that $\liminf_{k(n)} \delta(k(n)) > 0$. Then $d(\hat{\theta}_n,\theta_o) = o_P(1)$ under the following Condition 3.5MD:

CONDITION 3.5MD.

(i) $\{Z_t\}_{t=1}^{n}$ is i.i.d., $E\{\sup_{\theta\in\Theta_n} |m(X_t,\theta)'m(X_t,\theta)|\}$ is bounded;

(ii) there are a finite $s > 0$ and a $U(X_t)$ with $E\{[U(X_t)]^2\} < \infty$ such that $\sup_{\theta,\theta'\in\Theta_n:\, d(\theta,\theta')\leqslant\delta} |m(X_t,\theta) - m(X_t,\theta')| \leqslant \delta^s U(X_t)$;

(iii) $\log N(\delta^{1/s}, \Theta_n, d) = o(n)$ for all $\delta > 0$;

(iv) uniformly over X_t, $\widehat{\Sigma}(X_t) = \Sigma(X_t) + o_P(1)$ for a positive definite and finite $\Sigma(X_t)$;

(v) $\frac{1}{n}\sum_{i=1}^{n} |\hat{m}(X_i,\theta) - m(X_i,\theta)|^2 = o_P(1)$ uniformly over $\theta \in \Theta_n$.

See Chen and Pouzo (2006) for a proof of Remark 3.4; they also provide sufficient conditions for the consistency of sieve MD-estimator $\hat{\theta}_n$ without imposing $\liminf_{k(n)} \delta(k(n)) > 0$. Also see Newey and Powell (2003) and Ai and Chen (1999, 2003, 2007) for primitive sufficient conditions for Condition 3.5MD(iv) and (v) where $\widehat{\Sigma}(X_t)$ and $\hat{m}(X_t,\theta)$ are kernel or series estimates of $\Sigma(X_t)$ and $m(X_t,\theta)$, respectively.

Finally, Theorem 3.1 is also applicable to derive convergence of sieve extremum estimates to some pseudo-true values in misspecified semi-nonparametric models; see Lemma 3.1 of Ai and Chen (2007) for such an application.

3.2. Convergence rates of sieve M-estimators

There are many results on convergence rates of sieve M-estimators of unknown functions. For i.i.d. data, Van de Geer (1995) obtained the rate for sieve LS regression. Shen and Wong (1994), and Birgé and Massart (1998) derived the rates for general sieve M-estimation. Van de Geer (1993) and Wong and Shen (1995) obtained the rates for sieve MLE. For time series data, Chen and Shen (1998) derived the rate for sieve M-estimation of stationary beta-mixing models.[30] The general theory on convergence rates is technically involved and relies on the theory of empirical processes. In this section we present a simple version of the rate results for sieve M-estimation whose conditions are easy to verify. However, readers who are interested in the most general theory on convergence rates of sieve M-estimates are encouraged to read the papers by Shen and Wong (1994), Wong and Shen (1995) and Birgé and Massart (1998).

[30] It is impossible to mention here all the existing results on convergence rates of sieve M-estimates. There are many papers on convergence rates of particular sieves, such as the work on polynomial spline regression and density estimation by Stone and his collaborators, see Subsection 3.3 for details; the work on wavelets by Donoho, Johnstone and others [see e.g., Donoho et al. (1995)]; the work on neural networks by Barron (1993), White (1990) and others.

Recall $\theta_o \in \Theta$ and that the approximate sieve M-estimate $\hat{\theta}_n$ solves:

$$n^{-1}\sum_{t=1}^{n} l(\hat{\theta}_n, Z_t) \geqslant \sup_{\theta\in\Theta_n} n^{-1}\sum_{t=1}^{n} l(\theta, Z_t) - O_P\left(\varepsilon_n^2\right) \quad \text{with } \varepsilon_n \to 0. \tag{3.1}$$

Let $d(\theta_o, \theta)$ be a (pseudo-) metric on Θ such that $d(\theta_o, \hat{\theta}_n) = o_P(1)$. Let $K(\theta_o, \theta) \equiv E(l(\theta_o, Z_t) - l(\theta, Z_t))$.[31] Let $\|\theta_o - \theta\|$ be a metric on Θ such that $\|\theta_o - \theta\| \leqslant const.d(\theta_o, \theta)$ for all $\theta \in \Theta$, and $\|\theta_o - \theta\| \asymp K^{1/2}(\theta_o, \theta)$ for $\theta \in \Theta$ with $d(\theta_o, \theta) = o(1)$. We shall give a convergence rate for sieve estimate $\hat{\theta}_n$ under $\|\theta_o - \theta\|$, and thus automatically give an upper bound on $\bar{d}(\theta_o, \hat{\theta}_n)$, where $\bar{d}$ is any other metric on Θ satisfying $\bar{d}(\theta_o, \theta) \leqslant const.K^{1/2}(\theta_o, \theta)$.

In order for $\hat{\theta}_n$ to converge to θ_o at a fast rate under the metric $\|\theta_o - \hat{\theta}_n\|$, not only does the sieve approximation error rate, $\|\theta_o - \pi_n\theta_o\|$, have to approach zero suitably fast, but additionally, the sieve space, Θ_n, must not be too complex. We have already introduced $L_r(P_o)$-covering numbers (metric entropy) without bracketing as a complexity measure of a class $\mathcal{F}_n = \{g(\theta, \cdot): \theta \in \Theta_n\}$, we now consider another measure of complexity. Let $\mathcal{L}_r$ be the completion of $\mathcal{F}_n$ under the norm $\|\cdot\|_r$. For any given $w > 0$, if there exists a collection of functions (brackets) $\{g_1^l, g_1^u, \ldots, g_N^l, g_N^u\} \subset \mathcal{L}_r$ such that $\max_{1\leqslant j\leqslant N} \|g_j^u - g_j^l\|_r \leqslant w$ and for any $g \in \mathcal{F}_n$, there exists $j \in \{1, \ldots, N\}$ with $g_j^l \leqslant g \leqslant g_j^u$ a.e.-P_o, then the minimal number of such brackets, $N_{[\,]}(w, \mathcal{F}_n, \|\cdot\|_r) \equiv \min(N: \{g_1^l, g_1^u, \ldots, g_N^l, g_N^u\})$, is called the *$L_r(P_o)$-covering numbers with bracketing*. Likewise, $H_{[\,]}(w, \mathcal{F}_n, \|\cdot\|_r) \equiv \log(N_{[\,]}(w, \mathcal{F}_n, \|\cdot\|_r))$ is called the *$L_r(P_o)$-metric entropy with bracketing* of the class $\mathcal{F}_n$. See Pollard (1984), Andrews (1994a), Van der Vaart and Wellner (1996) and Van de Geer (2000) for more details.

We now present a result of Chen and Shen (1996) for i.i.d. data; see Chen and Shen (1998) for the stationary beta-mixing case and Chen and White (1999) for the stationary uniform-mixing case.[32]

CONDITION 3.6. $\{Z_t\}_{t=1}^n$ is an i.i.d. or m-dependent sequence.

CONDITION 3.7. There is $C_1 > 0$ such that for all small $\varepsilon > 0$,

$$\sup_{\{\theta\in\Theta_n:\ \|\theta_o-\theta\|\leqslant\varepsilon\}} \operatorname{Var}\bigl(l(\theta, Z_t) - l(\theta_o, Z_t)\bigr) \leqslant C_1\varepsilon^2.$$

CONDITION 3.8. For any $\delta > 0$, there exists a constant $s \in (0, 2)$ such that

$$\sup_{\{\theta\in\Theta_n:\ \|\theta_o-\theta\|\leqslant\delta\}} \bigl|l(\theta, Z_t) - l(\theta_o, Z_t)\bigr| \leqslant \delta^s U(Z_t),$$

with $E([U(Z_t)]^\gamma) \leqslant C_2$ for some $\gamma \geqslant 2$.

[31] If the criterion is a log-likelihood, then $K(\theta_o, \theta)$ is simply the Kullback–Leibler information.

[32] See Fan and Yao (2003) for description of various nonparametric methods applied to nonlinear time series models.

Conditions 3.6 and 3.7 imply that, within a neighborhood of θ_o,

$$\mathrm{Var}\left(n^{-1/2}\sum_{t=1}^{n}\big(l(\theta, Z_t) - l(\theta_o, Z_t)\big)\right)$$

behaves like $\|\theta_o - \theta\|^2$. Condition 3.8 implies that, when restricting to a local neighborhood of θ_o, $l(\theta, Z_t)$ is "continuous" at θ_o with respect to a metric $\|\theta_o - \theta\|$, which is locally equivalent to $K^{1/2}$. Conditions 3.7 and 3.8 are usually easily verifiable by exploiting the specific form of the criterion function.

Denote $\mathcal{F}_n = \{l(\theta, Z_t) - l(\theta_o, Z_t)\colon \|\theta_o - \theta\| \leqslant \delta,\ \theta \in \Theta_n\}$, and for some constant $b > 0$, let[33]

$$\delta_n = \inf\left\{\delta \in (0,1)\colon \frac{1}{\sqrt{n}\delta^2}\int_{b\delta^2}^{\delta}\sqrt{H_{[\,]}\big(w, \mathcal{F}_n, \|\cdot\|_2\big)}\,\mathrm{d}w \leqslant const.\right\}.$$

To calculate δ_n, an upper bound on $H_{[\,]}(w, \mathcal{F}_n, \|\cdot\|_2)$ is often enough, and, fortunately for us, much of the work has already been done. For instance, according to Lemma 2.1 of Ossiander (1987) we have that, $H_{[\,]}(w, \mathcal{F}_n, \|\cdot\|_2) \leqslant H(w, \mathcal{F}_n, \|\cdot\|_\infty)$. Moreover, Condition 3.8 implies that

$$H_{[\,]}\big(w, \mathcal{F}_n, \|\cdot\|_2\big) \leqslant \log N\big(w^{1/s}, \Theta_n, \|\cdot\|\big).$$

For finite-dimensional linear sieves such as those listed in Subsection 2.3.1 we have $\log N(\epsilon, \Theta_n, \|\cdot\|) \leqslant const.\dim(\Theta_n)\log(\frac{1}{\epsilon})$ [see e.g. Chen and Shen (1998)]; and for neural network and ridgelet nonlinear sieves we have $\log N(\epsilon, \Theta_n, \|\cdot\|) \leqslant const.\dim(\Theta_n)\log(\frac{\dim(\Theta_n)}{\epsilon})$ [see e.g. Chen and White (1999)].

THEOREM 3.2. *Let $\hat\theta_n$ be the approximate sieve M-estimator defined by* (3.1). *If Conditions* 3.6–3.8 *hold, then*

$$\|\theta_o - \hat\theta_n\| = O_P(\varepsilon_n), \quad \text{with } \varepsilon_n = \max\big\{\delta_n, \|\theta_o - \pi_n\theta_o\|\big\}.$$

We note that δ_n increases with the complexity of the sieve Θ_n and can be interpreted as a measure of the standard deviation term, while the deterministic approximation error $\|\theta_o - \pi_n\theta_o\|$ decreases with the complexity of the sieve Θ_n and is a measure of the bias. The best convergence rate can be obtained by choosing the complexity of the sieve Θ_n such that $\delta_n \asymp \|\theta_o - \pi_n\theta_o\|$.

Chen and Shen (1998) have demonstrated how to apply the time series version of this theorem with three examples: first, they considered a multivariate nonparametric regression with either a neural network sieve, a wavelet sieve or a spline sieve; second, a partially additive time series model via spline and Fourier series sieves; and third,

[33] There is a typo in Chen and Shen (1998, p. 297), where the "sup" in the definition of δ_n should be replaced by the "inf". Nevertheless, all the other calculations of δ_n in Chen and Shen (1998) are correct.

a transformation model with an unknown link via a monotone spline sieve. Chen and White (1999) considered a time series nonparametric conditional quantile regression via neural network sieve and multivariate conditional density estimation via neural network sieve. Chen and Conley (2001) applied this theorem to a varying coefficient VAR model with a flexible spatial conditional covariance. In the following we illustrate the verification of the conditions of Theorem 3.2 with two examples.

3.2.1. *Example: Additive mean regression with a monotone constraint*

Suppose that the i.i.d. data $\{Y_t, X_t' = (X_{1t}, \ldots, X_{qt})\}_{t=1}^n$ are generated according to

$$Y_t = h_{o1}(X_{1t}) + \cdots + h_{oq}(X_{qt}) + e_t, \qquad E[e_t | X_t] = 0.$$

Let $\theta_o = (h_{o1}, \ldots, h_{oq})' \in \Theta = \mathcal{H}$ be the parameters of interest with $\mathcal{H} = \mathcal{H}^1 \times \cdots \times \mathcal{H}^q$ to be specified in Assumption 3.1. For simplicity, we assume that $\dim(X_j) = 1$ for $j = 1, \ldots, q$, $\dim(X) = q$ and $\dim(Y) = 1$. We estimate the regression function $\theta_o(X) = \sum_{j=1}^q h_{oj}(X_{jt})$ by maximizing over a sieve $\Theta_n = \mathcal{H}_n$ the criterion $\widehat{Q}_n(\theta) = n^{-1} \sum_{t=1}^n l(\theta, Z_t)$, where $l(\theta, Z_t) = -(1/2)[Y_t - \sum_{j=1}^q h_j(X_{jt})]^2$ and $Z_t = (Y_t, X_t')'$. Let $\|\theta - \theta_o\|^2 = E(\theta(X_t) - \theta_o(X_t))^2 = E\{\sum_{j=1}^q [h_j(X_{jt}) - h_{oj}(X_{jt})]\}^2$.

ASSUMPTION 3.1.

(i) $h_{o1} \in \mathcal{H}^1 = C([b_{11}, b_{21}]) \cap \{h\colon \text{nondecreasing}\}$;
(ii) for $j = 2, \ldots, q$, $h_{oj} \in \mathcal{H}^j = \Lambda_{c_j}^{p_j}([b_{1j}, b_{2j}])$ with $p_j > 1/2$; and $h_{oj}(x_j^*) = 0$ for some known $x_j^* \in (b_{1j}, b_{2j})$.

ASSUMPTION 3.2. $\sigma^2(X) \equiv E[e^2 | X]$ is bounded.

Assumption 3.1(ii) is sufficient for identification, and Assumption 3.2 is a simple regularity condition that has been imposed in many papers; see e.g. Newey (1997).

The sieve will be chosen to have the form $\mathcal{H}_n = \mathcal{H}_n^1 \times \cdots \times \mathcal{H}_n^q$. First we let $\mathcal{H}_n^1$ be a shape-preserving sieve such as the monotone spline wavelet sieve MSplWav$(r_1 - 1, 2^{J_{1n}})$ with $r_1 \geqslant 1$ and $k_{1n} = 2^{J_{1n}}$ in Subsection 2.3.5. For $j = 2, \ldots, q$, we let $\mathcal{H}_n^j = \{h_j \in \Theta_{jn}\colon h_j(x_j^*) = 0,\ \|h_j\|_\infty \leqslant c_j\}$ where Θ_{jn} can be any of the finite-dimensional linear sieve examples in Subsection 2.3.1 such as $\Theta_{jn} = \text{Pol}(k_{jn})$ or TriPol(k_{jn}) or Spl(r_j, k_{jn}) with $r_j \geqslant [p_j] + 1$, or Wav$(m_j, 2^{J_{jn}})$ with $m_j > p_j$ and $k_{jn} = 2^{J_{jn}}$.

In the following result we denote $p_1 = 1$ and $p = \min\{p_1, p_2, \ldots, p_q\}$.

PROPOSITION 3.3. *Let $\hat{\theta}_n$ be the sieve M-estimate. Suppose that Assumptions* 3.1 and 3.2 *hold. Let $k_{jn} = O(n^{1/(2p_j+1)})$ for $j = 1, \ldots, q$. Then $\|\hat{\theta}_n - \theta_o\| = O_P(n^{-p/(2p+1)})$ with $p = \min\{p_1, \ldots, p_q\}$.*

PROOF. Theorem 3.2 is readily applicable to prove this result. It is easy to see that $K(\theta_o, \theta) \asymp \|\theta - \theta_o\|^2$. Condition 3.6 is assumed. Now we check Conditions 3.7 and 3.8.

Since $l(\theta, Z_t) - l(\theta_o, Z_t) = (\theta - \theta_o)[e_t + (\theta_o - \theta)/2]$, we have

$$E\big[l(\theta, Z_t) - l(\theta_o, Z_t)\big]^2 \leqslant 2E\big(\sigma^2(X_t)\big[\theta_o(X_t) - \theta(X_t)\big]^2\big) + (1/2)E\big(\big[\theta_o(X_t) - \theta(X_t)\big]^4\big)$$
$$\leqslant const.\|\theta - \theta_o\|^2 + (1/2)E\big(\big[\theta_o(X_t) - \theta(X_t)\big]^4\big).$$

By Theorem 1 of Gabushin (1967) when p is an integer and Lemma 2 in Chen and Shen (1998) for any $p > 0$, we have $\|\theta - \theta_o\|_\infty \leqslant c\|\theta - \theta_o\|^{2p/(2p+1)}$. Hence

$$E\big(\big[\theta_o(X_t) - \theta(X_t)\big]^4\big) \leqslant \sup_x\big[\theta(x) - \theta_o(x)\big]^2 E\big(\big[\theta_o(X_t) - \theta(X_t)\big]^2\big)$$
$$\leqslant C\|\theta - \theta_o\|^{2(1+[2p/(2p+1)])}.$$

So Condition 3.7 is satisfied for all $\varepsilon \leqslant 1$. On the other hand,

$$\big|l(\theta, Z_t) - l(\theta_o, Z_t)\big| \leqslant \|\theta - \theta_o\|_\infty\big[|e_t| + \big(\|\theta_o\|_\infty + \|\theta\|_\infty\big)/2\big] \quad \text{a.s.}$$

Using Lemma 2 in Chen and Shen (1998) we see that Condition 3.8 is then satisfied with $s = 2p/(2p + 1)$, $U(Z_t) = |e_t| + const.$ and $\gamma = 2$.

To apply Theorem 3.2, it remains to compute the deterministic approximation error rate $\|\theta_o - \pi_n\theta_o\|$ and the metric entropy with bracketing $H_{[\,]}(w, \mathcal{F}_n, \|\cdot\|_2)$ of the class $\mathcal{F}_n = \{l(\theta, Z_t) - l(\theta_o, Z_t)\colon \|\theta - \theta_o\| \leqslant \delta,\ \theta \in \Theta_n\}$. By definition, $\|\theta_o - \pi_n\theta_o\| \leqslant const. \max\{\|h_{oj} - \pi_n h_{oj}\|_\infty\colon j = 1, \ldots, q\}$. Let $C = \sqrt{E\{U(Z_t)^2\}}$, then for all $0 < \frac{w}{C} \leqslant \delta < 1$, $H_{[\,]}(w, \mathcal{F}_n, \|\cdot\|_2) \leqslant \sum_{j=1}^q \log N(\frac{w}{C}, \mathcal{H}_n^j, \|\cdot\|_\infty)$.

The final bit of calculation now depends on the choice of sieves. First, $\|h_{o1} - \pi_n h_{o1}\|_\infty = O((k_{1n})^{-1})$ by Anastassiou and Yu (1992a); and for $j = 2, \ldots, q$, $\mathcal{H}^j = \Lambda_{c_j}^{p_j}$, $\|h_{oj} - \pi_n h_{oj}\|_\infty = O((k_{jn})^{-p_j})$ by Lorentz (1966). Second, for all $j = 1, 2, \ldots, q$, $\log N(\frac{w}{C}, \mathcal{H}_n^j, \|\cdot\|_\infty) \leqslant const. \times k_{jn} \times \log(1 + \frac{4c_j}{w})$ by Lemma 2.5 in van de Geer (2000). Hence δ_n solves

$$\frac{1}{\sqrt{n}\delta_n^2}\int_{b\delta_n^2}^{\delta_n}\sqrt{H_{[\,]}(w, \mathcal{F}_n, \|\cdot\|_2)}\,dw$$
$$\leqslant \frac{1}{\sqrt{n}\delta_n^2}\max_{j=1,\ldots,q}\int_{b\delta_n^2}^{\delta_n}\sqrt{k_{jn} \times \log\left(1 + \frac{4c_j}{w}\right)}\,dw$$
$$\leqslant \frac{1}{\sqrt{n}\delta_n^2}\max_{j=1,\ldots,q}\sqrt{k_{jn}} \times \delta_n \leqslant const.$$

and the solution is $\delta_n \asymp \max_{j=1,\ldots,q}\sqrt{\frac{k_{jn}}{n}}$. By Theorem 3.2, $\|\hat{\theta}_n - \theta_o\| = O_P(\max_{j=1,\ldots,q}\{(k_{jn})^{-p_j}, \delta_n\})$. With the choice of $k_{jn} = O(n^{1/(2p_j+1)})$ for $j = 1, \ldots, q$, we obtain $\|\hat{\theta}_n - \theta_o\| = O_P(n^{-p/(2p+1)})$ with $p = \min\{p_1, \ldots, p_q\} > 0.5$. This immediately implies $\|\hat{h}_j - h_{oj}\|_2 = O_P(n^{-p/(2p+1)})$ for $j = 1, \ldots, q$. □

REMARK 3.5. (1) Since the parameter space $\mathcal{H} = \mathcal{H}^1 \times \cdots \times \mathcal{H}^q$ specified in Assumption 3.1 is compact with respect to the norm $\|\cdot\|$, we can take the original parameter space $\mathcal{H}$ as the sieve space $\mathcal{H}_n$. Applying Theorem 3.2 again, note that the approximation error $\|\pi_n\theta_o - \theta_o\| = 0$, we have $\|\hat{\theta}_n - \theta_o\| = O_P(\delta_n)$, where δ_n solves:

$$\frac{1}{\sqrt{n}\delta_n^2}\int_{b\delta_n^2}^{\delta_n}\sqrt{\sum_{j=1}^{q}\log N\big(w, \mathcal{H}^j, \|\cdot\|_\infty\big)}\,dw$$

$$\leqslant \frac{1}{\sqrt{n}\delta_n^2}\int_{b\delta_n^2}^{\delta_n}\sqrt{\sum_{j=1}^{q}\left(\frac{c_j}{w}\right)^{1/p_j}}\,dw \quad \text{by Birman and Solomjak (1967)}$$

$$\leqslant \frac{1}{\sqrt{n}\delta_n^2}\max_{j=1,\ldots,q} const.(\delta_n)^{1-\frac{1}{2p_j}} \leqslant const.$$

which is satisfied if $\delta_n = O(n^{-p/(2p+1)})$ with $p = \min\{p_1, \ldots, p_q\} > 0.5$. However, it is unclear how one can implement such an optimization over the entire parameter space $\mathcal{H}$ given a finite data set.

(2) Suppose that in Proposition 3.3 we replace Assumption 3.1(i) by $h_{o1} \in \Lambda_{c_1}^{p_1}([b_{11}, b_{21}])$ and let $\mathcal{H}_n^1 = \text{Pol}(k_{1n})$, or $\text{TriPol}(k_{1n})$, or $\text{Spl}(r_1, k_{1n})$ with $r_1 \geqslant [p_1]+1$, or $\text{Wav}(m_1, 2^{J_{1n}})$ with $m_1 > p_1$, $2^{J_{1n}} = k_{1n}$. Let $p = \min\{p_1, \ldots, p_q\} > 0.5$. Then we have $\|\hat{h}_j - h_{oj}\|_2 = O_P(n^{-p/(2p+1)})$ for $j = 1, \ldots, q$. Further, let $\|D^m\hat{h}_j - D^m h_{oj}\|_2 = \{E[D^m\hat{h}_j(X_{jt}) - D^m h_{oj}(X_{jt})]^2\}^{1/2}$ for an integer $m \geqslant 1$. If $p > m \geqslant 1$ then $\|D^m\hat{h}_j - D^m h_{oj}\|_2 = O_P(k_{jn}^{-(p-m)}) = O_P(n^{-(p-m)/(2p+1)})$ for $j = 1, \ldots, q$. This convergence rate achieves the optimal one derived in Stone (1982).

3.2.2. *Example: Multivariate quantile regression*

Suppose that the i.i.d. data $\{Y_t, X_t\}_{t=1}^n$ are generated according to

$$Y_t = \theta_o(X_t) + e_t, \qquad P[e_t \leqslant 0|X_t] = \alpha \in (0, 1),$$

where $X_t \in \mathcal{X} = \mathcal{R}^d$, $d \geqslant 1$. We estimate the conditional quantile function $\theta_o(\cdot)$ by maximizing over Θ_n the criterion $\widehat{Q}_n(\theta) = n^{-1}\sum_{t=1}^n l(\theta, Y_t, X_t)$, where $l(\theta, Y_t, X_t) = \{1(Y_t < \theta(X_t)) - \alpha\}[Y_t - \theta(X_t)]$. Let $\|\theta - \theta_o\|^2 = E(\theta(X_t) - \theta_o(X_t))^2$ and $W_1^1(\mathcal{X})$ be the Sobolev space defined in Subsection 2.3.3.

ASSUMPTION 3.3. $\theta_o \in \Theta = W_1^1(\mathcal{X})$.

ASSUMPTION 3.4. Let $f_{e|X}$ be the conditional density of e_t given X_t satisfying $0 < \inf_{x\in\mathcal{X}} f_{e|X=x}(0) \leqslant \sup_{x\in\mathcal{X}} f_{e|X=x}(0) < \infty$ and $\sup_{x\in\mathcal{X}} |f_{e|X=x}(z) - f_{e|X=x}(0)| \to 0$ as $|z| \to 0$.

It is known that the tensor product of finite-dimensional linear sieves such as those in Subsection 2.3.1 will not be able to approximate functions in $W_1^m(\mathcal{X})$, $m \geqslant 1$, well, hence the sieve convergence rates based on those linear sieves will be slower than those based on nonlinear sieves; see e.g. Chen and Shen (1998, Proposition 1, Case 1.3(ii)) for such an example. For time series regression models, Chen and White (1999), Chen, Racine and Swanson (2001) have shown that neural network sieves lead to faster convergence rates for functions in $W_1^m(\mathcal{X})$. Thus we consider the following Gaussian radial basis ANN sieve Θ_n for the unknown $\theta_o \in W_1^1(\mathcal{X})$:

$$\Theta_n = \left\{\alpha_0 + \sum_{j=1}^{k_n} \alpha_j G\left(\frac{\{(x-\gamma_j)'(x-\gamma_j)\}^{1/2}}{\sigma_j}\right),\right.$$
$$\left.\sum_{j=0}^{k_n} |\alpha_j| \leqslant c_0,\ |\gamma_j| \leqslant c_1,\ 0 < \sigma_j \leqslant c_2\right\},$$

where G is the standard Gaussian density function.

PROPOSITION 3.4. *Let $\hat{\theta}_n$ be the sieve M-estimate. Suppose that Assumptions* 3.3 and 3.4 *hold. Let $k_n^{2(1+1/(d+1))}\log(k_n) = O(n)$. Then*

$$\|\hat{\theta}_n - \theta_o\| = O_P\big([n/\log n]^{-(1+2/(d+1))/[4(1+1/(d+1))]}\big).$$

PROOF. Theorem 3.2 is readily applicable to prove this result. Condition 3.6 is directly assumed. By the above assumptions on conditional density $f_{e|X}$, it is easy to check that $K(\theta_o, \theta) \asymp E(\theta(X_t) - \theta_o(X_t))^2$; see Chen and White (1999, pp. 686–687) for details. Now let us check Conditions 3.7 and 3.8. Note that $|l(\theta, Y_t, X_t) - l(\theta_o, Y_t, X_t)| \leqslant \max(\alpha, 1-\alpha)|\theta(X_t) - \theta_o(X_t)|$, we have

$$\begin{aligned}\operatorname{Var}\big(l(\theta, Y_t, X_t) - l(\theta_o, Y_t, X_t)\big) &\leqslant E\big[l(\theta, Y_t, X_t) - l(\theta_o, Y_t, X_t)\big]^2 \\ &\leqslant E\big[\theta(X_t) - \theta_o(X_t)\big]^2,\end{aligned}$$

and thus Condition 3.7 is satisfied. Moreover, we have

$$\sup_{\{\theta\in\Theta_n:\ \|\theta-\theta_o\|\leqslant\delta\}} \big|l(\theta, Y_t, X_t) - l(\theta_o, Y_t, X_t)\big| \leqslant \sup_{\{\theta\in\Theta_n:\ \|\theta-\theta_o\|\leqslant\delta\}} \big|\theta(X_t) - \theta_o(X_t)\big|,$$

and $\|\theta - \theta_o\|_\infty \leqslant c\|\theta - \theta_o\|^{2/3}$ by Theorem 1 of Gabushin (1967). Hence, Condition 3.8 is satisfied with $s = 2/3$, $U(X_t) \equiv c$.

Now by results in Chen, Racine and Swanson (2001),

$$\|\theta_o - \pi_n\theta_o\| \leqslant const.(k_n)^{-1/2-1/(d+1)}$$

and $\log N(w, \Theta_n, \|\cdot\|_\infty) \leqslant const.k_n \log(\frac{k_n}{w})$. With $k_n^{2(1+1/(d+1))}\log(k_n) = O(n)$, it is easy to see that $\|\hat{\theta}_n - \theta_o\| = O_P([n/\log n]^{-(1+2/(d+1))/[4(1+1/(d+1))]})$ by applying Theorem 3.2. □

3.3. Convergence rates of series estimators

In this subsection we present the convergence rate of the series estimators for the concave extended linear models. Recall that in this framework, the parameter space, Θ, is a linear space which is often a subspace of the space of square integrable functions, the sample criterion function $\widehat{Q}_n(\theta) = n^{-1}\sum_{i=1}^{n} l(\theta, Z_i)$ is concave in $\theta \in \Theta$ almost surely and the population criterion function $Q(\theta) = E[l(\theta, Z_i)]$ is strictly concave in $\theta \in \Theta$. The results reported here are largely based on those of Huang (1998a, 2001) and Newey (1997).

Throughout this subsection, $\{Z_i\}_{i=1}^{n}$ is i.i.d. and θ denotes a real-valued function with a bounded domain, $\mathcal{X} \subset \mathcal{R}^d$. We use $\|\hat{\theta} - \theta_o\|$ to measure the discrepancy between $\hat{\theta}$ and θ_o.

CONDITION 3.9. $\|\theta\| \asymp \|\theta\|_{2,leb}$ for any Lebesgue square-integrable function θ.

In the multivariate LS regression of Example 2.4, $\theta_o(X) = E[Y|X]$, a natural choice for the norm is $\|\theta\| = \|\theta\|_2 = \{E[\theta(X)^2]\}^{1/2}$. If the density of X is bounded away from zero and infinity, then Condition 3.9 is satisfied. In general a natural choice of the norm, $\|\cdot\|$, will depend on the specific application and on the data generating process.

We impose the following condition on the linear sieve space.

CONDITION 3.10. The finite-dimensional linear sieve space, Θ_n, is theoretically identifiable in the sense that any $\theta \in \Theta_n$ with $\|\theta\| = 0$ implies that $\theta(u) = 0$ everywhere.

Under Condition 3.9, Condition 3.10 is trivially satisfied by commonly used linear approximation spaces such as those given in Subsection 2.3.1.

CONDITION 3.11. $\theta_o = \arg\max_{\Theta} E[l(\theta, Z)]$ satisfies $\|\theta_o\|_\infty \leqslant K_o < \infty$.

CONDITION 3.12. For any bounded functions $\theta_1, \theta_2 \in \Theta$, $E[l(\theta_1 + \tau(\theta_2 - \theta_1), Z)]$ is twice continuously differentiable with respect to $\tau \in [0, 1]$. For any constant $0 < K < \infty$, $\frac{\partial^2}{\partial\tau^2} E[l(\theta_1 + \tau(\theta_2 - \theta_1), Z)] \asymp -\|\theta_2 - \theta_1\|^2$ for $\theta_1, \theta_2 \in \Theta$ with $\|\theta_1\|_\infty \leqslant K$ and $\|\theta_2\|_\infty \leqslant K$ and $0 \leqslant \tau \leqslant 1$.

Given the above conditions, we can define $\bar{\theta}_n \equiv \arg\max_{\theta\in\Theta_n} E[l(\theta, Z)]$, and it is easy to see that $\|\bar{\theta}_n - \theta_o\| \asymp \inf_{\theta\in\Theta_n} \|\theta - \theta_o\|$.

CONDITION 3.13. For any pair of functions $\theta_1, \theta_2 \in \Theta_n$, $l(\theta_1 + \tau(\theta_2 - \theta_1), Z)$ is twice continuously differentiable with respect to τ. Moreover,

(i)

$$\sup_{g\in\Theta_n} \frac{|\frac{\partial}{\partial\tau} l(\bar{\theta}_n + \tau g, Z)|_{\tau=0}|}{\|g\|} = O_P\left(\sqrt{\frac{\dim(\Theta_n)}{n}}\right);$$

(ii) for any constant $0 < K < \infty$, there is a $c > 0$ such that $\frac{\partial^2}{\partial\tau^2} l(\theta_1 + \tau(\theta_2 - \theta_1), Z) \leqslant -c\|\theta_2 - \theta_1\|^2$ for any $\theta_1, \theta_2 \in \Theta_n$ with $\|\theta_1\|_\infty \leqslant K$ and $\|\theta_2\|_\infty \leqslant K$ and $0 \leqslant \tau \leqslant 1$, except on an event whose probability tends to zero as $n \to \infty$.

Denote $k_n = \dim(\Theta_n)$, $A_n \equiv \sup_{\theta\in\Theta_n, \|\theta\|_{2,leb}\neq 0}(\|\theta\|_\infty/\|\theta\|_{2,leb})$ and $\rho_{2n} \equiv \inf_{\theta\in\Theta_n}\|\theta - \theta_o\|_{2,leb}$. Under Conditions 3.9–3.11, we have $\rho_{2n} \asymp \inf_{\theta\in\Theta_n}\|\theta - \theta_o\|$. The following result is a special case of Huang (2001) for the sieve estimator of a concave extended linear model.

THEOREM 3.5. *Suppose Conditions* 3.9–3.13 *hold. Let* $\lim_{n\to\infty} A_n\rho_{2n} = 0$ *and* $\lim_{n\to\infty} A_n^2 k_n/n = 0$. *Then the series estimator,* $\hat{\theta}$, *exists uniquely with probability approaching one as* $n \to \infty$, *and*

$$\|\hat{\theta} - \theta_o\| = O_P\left(\sqrt{\frac{k_n}{n}} + \rho_{2n}\right).$$

This theorem could be regarded as a special case of Theorem 3.2 by taking $\delta_n \asymp \sqrt{\frac{k_n}{n}}$ and $\|\pi_n\theta_o - \theta_o\| \asymp \rho_{2n}$. To see this, first note that under Conditions 3.9–3.11 there is an essentially unique element $\pi_n\theta_o \in \Theta_n$ such that $\|\pi_n\theta_o - \theta_o\| = \inf_{\theta\in\Theta_n}\|\theta - \theta_o\|$, and $\|\pi_n\theta_o - \theta_o\| \asymp \|\pi_n\theta_o - \theta_o\|_{2,leb} \asymp \rho_{2n}$, which is the approximation error rate. Second, within the framework of concave extended linear models, for a finite-dimensional linear sieve Θ_n we have $\log N(w, \Theta_n, \|\cdot\|_\infty) \leqslant const.k_n \log(\frac{1}{w})$, hence $\delta_n \asymp \sqrt{\frac{k_n}{n}}$.

The constant $A_n \geqslant 1$ is a measure of irregularity of the finite-dimensional linear sieve space, Θ_n. Since we require that Θ_n be theoretically identifiable and functions in Θ_n be bounded, A_n is finite. In fact, let $\{\phi_j, j = 1, \ldots, k_n\}$ be an orthonormal basis of Θ_n relative to the theoretical inner product. Then, by the Cauchy–Schwarz inequality, $A_n \leqslant \{\sum_{j=1}^{k_n}\|\phi_j\|_\infty^2\}^{1/2} < \infty$. It is obvious that $\|\theta\|_\infty \leqslant A_n\|\theta\|_{2,leb}$ for all $\theta \in \Theta_n$. The linear sieve spaces are usually chosen to be among commonly used approximating spaces such as those described in Subsection 2.3.1 and the associated constant A_n is readily obtained by using results in the approximation theory literature. Here are some examples.

Polynomials. If $\Theta_n = \mathrm{Pol}(J_n)$ and $\mathcal{X} = [0, 1]$, then $A_n \asymp J_n$ [see Theorem 4.2.6 of DeVore and Lorentz (1993)].

Trigonometric polynomials. If $\Theta_n = \mathrm{TriPol}(J_n)$ and $\mathcal{X} = [0, 1]$, then $A_n \asymp J_n^{1/2}$ [see Theorem 4.2.6 of DeVore and Lorentz (1993)].

Univariate splines. If $\Theta_n = \mathrm{Spl}(r, J_n)$ and $\mathcal{X} = [0, 1]$, then $A_n \asymp J_n^{1/2}$ [see Theorem 5.1.2 of DeVore and Lorentz (1993)].

Orthogonal wavelets. If $\Theta_n = \mathrm{Wav}(m, 2^{J_n})$ and $\mathcal{X} = [0, 1]$, then $A_n \asymp 2^{J_n/2}$ [see Lemma 2.8 of Meyer (1992)].

Tensor product spaces. Let Θ_n be the tensor product of $\Theta_{n1}, \ldots, \Theta_{nd}$. The constant A_n associated with the tensor product linear sieve space, Θ_n, can be determined from the corresponding constants for its components. Set

$$a_{n\ell} = \sup_{\theta \in \Theta_{n\ell},\, \|\theta\|_{2,leb} \neq 0} \left(\|\theta\|_\infty / \|\theta\|_{2,leb}\right)$$

for $1 \leqslant \ell \leqslant d$. It is shown in Huang (1998a) that $A_n \leqslant const. \prod_{\ell=1}^d a_{n\ell}$.

We conclude this subsection with an application to the multivariate LS regression of Example 2.4.

ASSUMPTION 3.5.

(i) X has a compact support $\mathcal{X}$ and has a density that is bounded away from zero and infinity on $\mathcal{X}$, where $\mathcal{X} \subset \mathcal{R}^d$ is a Cartesian product of compact intervals $\mathcal{X}_1, \ldots, \mathcal{X}_d$;
(ii) $\mathrm{Var}(Y|X = \cdot)$ is bounded on $\mathcal{X}$;
(iii) $h_o(\cdot) = E[Y|X = \cdot] \in \Lambda^p(\mathcal{X})$ with $p > d/2$.

Theorem 3.5 can treat a general finite-dimensional linear sieve space Θ_n. For simplicity, however, we consider here only the case when the sieve space, Θ_n, in Example 2.4 is constructed as a tensor product space of some commonly used univariate linear approximating spaces $\Theta_{n1}, \ldots, \Theta_{nd}$. Then $k_n = \dim(\Theta_n) = \prod_{\ell=1}^d \dim(\Theta_{n\ell})$.

PROPOSITION 3.6. *Suppose Assumption* 3.5 *holds. Let $\hat{h}_n$ be the series estimate of h_o in Example* 2.4, *with the sieve, Θ_n, being the tensor-product of the univariate sieve spaces $\Theta_{n1}, \ldots, \Theta_{nd}$. For $\ell = 1, \ldots, d$,*

- *if $\Theta_{n\ell} = \mathrm{Pol}(J_n)$, $p > d$ and $J_n^{3d}/n \to 0$, then $\|\hat{h}_n - h_o\| = O_P(\sqrt{J_n^d/n} + J_n^{-p})$;*
- *if $\Theta_{n\ell} = \mathrm{TriPol}(J_n)$, $p > d/2$ and $J_n^{2d}/n \to 0$, then $\|\hat{h}_n - h_o\| = O_P(\sqrt{J_n^d/n} + J_n^{-p})$;*
- *if $\Theta_{n\ell} = \mathrm{Spl}(r, J_n)$ with $r \geqslant [p] + 1$, $p > d/2$ and $J_n^{2d}/n \to 0$, then $\|\hat{h}_n - h_o\| = O_P(\sqrt{J_n^d/n} + J_n^{-p})$.*

Let $J_n = O(n^{1/(2p+d)})$, then $\|\hat{h}_n - h_o\| = O_P(n^{-p/(2p+d)})$.

We note that this proposition can also be obtained as a direct consequence of Theorem 1 in Newey (1997).[34] The choice of $J_n \asymp n^{1/(2p+d)}$ balances the variance (J_n^d/n) and the squared bias (J_n^{-2p}) trade-off: $J_n^d/n \asymp J_n^{-2p}$. The resulting rate of convergence

[34] Proposition 3.6 is about the convergence rates under $\|\cdot\|_2$-norm for LS regressions. There are also a few results on the convergence rates under $\|\cdot\|_\infty$-norm for LS regressions; see e.g. Stone (1982), Newey (1997) and de Jong (2002).

$n^{-2p/(2p+d)}$ is actually optimal in the context of regression and density estimations: no estimate has a faster rate of convergence uniformly over the class of p-smooth functions [Stone (1982)]. The rate of convergence depends on two quantities: the specified smoothness p of the target function θ_o and the dimension d of the domain on which the target function is defined. Note the dependence of the rate of convergence on the dimension d: given the smoothness p, the larger the dimension, the slower the rate of convergence; moreover, the rate of convergence tends to zero as the dimension tends to infinity. This provides a mathematical description of a phenomenon commonly known as the "curse of dimensionality". Imposing additivity on an unknown multivariate function can imply faster rates of convergence of the corresponding estimate; see Subsection 3.2.1, Stone (1985, 1986), Andrews and Whang (1990), Huang (1998b) and Huang et al. (2000).

3.4. Pointwise asymptotic normality of series LS estimators

To date, we have a relatively complete theory on the rates of convergence for sieve M-estimators. The corresponding asymptotic distribution theory, however, is incomplete and requires much future work. All of the currently available results are for series estimators of densities and the LS regression functions. Asymptotic normality of the series LS estimators has been studied in Andrews (1991b), Gallant and Souza (1991), Newey (1994b, 1997), Zhou, Shen and Wolfe (1998), and Huang (2003). Stone (1990) and Strawderman and Tsiatis (1996) have given asymptotic normality results for polynomial spline estimators in the context of density estimation and hazard estimation, respectively.[35]

We focus on Example 2.4 throughout this subsection. That is, we assume that the data $\{Z_i = (Y_i, X_i')'\}_{i=1}^n$ are i.i.d., and the parameter of interest, $\theta_o(\cdot) = h_o(\cdot) = E[Y|X = \cdot]$, is a real-valued regression function with a bounded domain $\mathcal{X} \subset \mathcal{R}^d$.

3.4.1. Asymptotic normality of the spline series LS estimator

Here we present a result by Huang (2003) on the pointwise asymptotic normality of the spline series LS estimator.

ASSUMPTION 3.6.

(i) $\operatorname{Var}(Y|X = \cdot)$ is bounded away from zero on $\mathcal{X}$;

(ii)

$$\sup_{x\in\mathcal{X}} E\big[\{Y - h_o(X)\}^2 \times 1\big(|Y - h_o(X)| > \lambda\big)\big|X = x\big] \to 0 \quad \text{as } \lambda \to \infty.$$

[35] See Portnoy (1997) for a closely related result on the asymptotic normality for smoothing spline quantile estimators.

In the following, $\Phi(\cdot)$ denotes the standard normal distribution function, and $\mathrm{SD}(\hat{h}(x)|X_1,\ldots,X_n) = \{\mathrm{Var}(\hat{h}(x)|X_1,\ldots,X_n)\}^{1/2}$.

THEOREM 3.7. *[See Huang (2003).] Suppose Assumptions* 3.5 and 3.6 *hold. Let $\hat{h}_n$ be the series estimate of h_o in Example* 2.4, *with the sieve, Θ_n, being the tensor-product of the univariate spline sieve spaces $\Theta_{n\ell} = \mathrm{Spl}(r, J_n)$, $r \geqslant [p]+1$, $1 \leqslant \ell \leqslant d$. If $\lim_{n\to\infty} J_n^d \log n/n = 0$ and $\lim_{n\to\infty} J_n/n^{1/(2p+d)} = \infty$, then*

$$\Pr\bigl(\hat{h}(x) - h_o(x) \leqslant t \times \mathrm{SD}\bigl(\hat{h}(x)\big|X_1,\ldots,X_n\bigr)\bigr) \to \Phi(t), \quad t \in \mathcal{R}.$$

Asymptotic distribution results such as Theorem 3.7 can be used to construct asymptotic confidence intervals. Let $\widehat{\mathrm{SD}}(\hat{h}(x)|X_1,\ldots,X_n)$ be a consistent estimate of $\mathrm{SD}(\hat{h}(x)|X_1,\ldots,X_n)$; see Andrews (1991b) and Newey (1997) for such an estimate. Let $\hat{h}^l_\alpha(x) = \hat{h}(x) - z_{1-\alpha/2}\widehat{\mathrm{SD}}(\hat{h}(x)|X_1,\ldots,X_n)$ and $\hat{h}^u_\alpha(x) = \hat{h}(x) + z_{1-\alpha/2}\widehat{\mathrm{SD}}(\hat{h}(x)|X_1,\ldots,X_n)$, where $z_{1-\alpha/2}$ is the $(1-\alpha/2)$th quantile of the standard normal distribution. If the conditions of Theorem 3.7 hold, then $[\hat{h}^l_\alpha(x), \hat{h}^u_\alpha(x)]$ is an asymptotic $1-\alpha$ confidence interval of $h_o(x)$; that is, $\lim_{n\to\infty} P(\hat{h}^l_\alpha(x) \leqslant h_o(x) \leqslant \hat{h}^u_\alpha(x)) = 1-\alpha$.

Recall that for the tensor product spline sieve Θ_n, $k_n = \dim(\Theta_n) \asymp J_n^d$. If $h_o(\cdot)$ is p-smooth, then the tensor product spline sieve has the bias order $J_n^{-p} \asymp k_n^{-p/d}$. The condition $\lim_{n\to\infty} J_n/n^{1/(2p+d)} = \infty$ in Theorem 3.7 implies that the bias term is asymptotically negligible relative to the standard deviation of the estimate. Such a condition, $\lim_{n\to\infty} k_n/n^{d/(2p+d)} = \infty$, is usually called undersmoothing (or overfitting); that is, the total number of sieve parameters (k_n) required for undersmoothing is more than what is required to achieve Stone's (1982) optimal rate of convergence.

3.4.2. *Asymptotic normality of functionals of series LS estimator*

We now review the asymptotic normality results in Newey (1997) for any series estimation of functionals of the LS regression function. Let $a: \Theta \to \mathcal{R}$ be a functional, and we want to estimate $a(h_o)$, where $h_o(\cdot) = E[Y|X = \cdot] \in \Theta$. Recall that $\hat{h}(\cdot) = p^{k_n}(\cdot)'(P'P)^- \sum_{i=1}^n p^{k_n}(X_i)Y_i$ is the series LS estimator of $h_o(\cdot)$, with $p^{k_n}(X)$ being the finite-dimensional linear sieve (2.10), see Example 2.4. Then $a(\hat{h})$ will be a natural estimator for $a(h_o)$.

Let $s \geqslant 0$ be an integer, and define a strong norm on Θ as $\|h\|_{s,\infty} = \max_{[\gamma]\leqslant s} \sup_{x\in\mathcal{X}} |D^\gamma h(x)|$. Also, let $\zeta_0(k_n) \equiv \sup_{x\in\mathcal{X}} |p^{k_n}(x)|_e$, $\zeta_s(k_n) \equiv \max_{[\gamma]\leqslant s} \sup_{x\in\mathcal{X}} |D^\gamma p^{k_n}(x)|_e$, where $|\cdot|_e$ is the Euclidean norm.

ASSUMPTION 3.7.

(i) $\mathrm{Var}(Y|X=\cdot)$ is bounded away from zero on $\mathcal{X}$; $\sup_{x\in\mathcal{X}} E[\{Y - h_o(X)\}^4|X = x] < \infty$;

(ii) the smallest eigenvalue of $E[p^{k_n}(X)p^{k_n}(X)']$ is bounded away from zero uniformly in k_n;

(iii) for an integer $s \geqslant 0$ there are $\alpha > 0$, $\beta^*_{k_n}$ such that $\inf_{g\in\Theta_n} \|g - h_o\|_{s,\infty} = \|p^{k_n}(\cdot)'\beta^*_{k_n} - h_o(\cdot)\|_{s,\infty} = O(k_n^{-\alpha})$.

ASSUMPTION 3.8. Either

(i) $\lim_{n\to\infty} k_n\{\zeta_0(k_n)\}^2/n = 0$, and $a(h)$ is linear in $h \in \Theta$; or

(ii) for s as in Assumption 3.7, $\lim_{n\to\infty} k_n^2\{\zeta_s(k_n)\}^4/n = 0$, and there exists a function $D(h;\tilde{h})$ that is linear in $h \in \Theta$ such that for some $c_1, c_2, \varepsilon > 0$ and for all $\tilde{h}, \bar{h}$ with $\|\tilde{h} - h_o\|_{s,\infty} < \varepsilon$, $\|\bar{h} - h_o\|_{s,\infty} < \varepsilon$, it is true that

$$\left|a(h) - a(\tilde{h}) - D(h - \tilde{h};\tilde{h})\right| \leqslant c_1\left\{\|h - \tilde{h}\|_{s,\infty}\right\}^2; \quad \text{and}$$
$$\left|D(h;\tilde{h}) - D(h;\bar{h})\right| \leqslant c_2\|h\|_{s,\infty}\|\tilde{h} - \bar{h}\|_{s,\infty}.$$

ASSUMPTION 3.9.

(i) There is a positive constant c such that $|D(h;h_o)| \leqslant c\|h\|_{s,\infty}$ for s from Assumption 3.7;

(ii) there is an $h_n \in \Theta_n$ such that $E[h_n(X)^2] \to 0$ but $D(h_n;h_o)$ is bounded away from zero.

Assumption 3.7(iii) is a condition on the sieve approximation error under the strong norm $\|h\|_{s,\infty}$. Assumption 3.8 implies that $a(h)$ is Frechet differentiable in h with respect to the norm $\|h\|_{s,\infty}$. Assumption 3.9 says that the derivative $D(h;h_o)$ is continuous in the norm $\|h\|_{s,\infty}$ but not in the mean-square norm $\|h\|_2 = \{E[h(X)^2]\}^{1/2}$. The lack of mean-square continuity will imply that the estimator $a(\hat{h})$ is not $\sqrt{n}$-consistent for $a(h_o)$; see Newey (1997) for detailed discussions. In the following we denote $\Sigma = E[p^{k_n}(X)p^{k_n}(X)'\operatorname{Var}(Y|X)]$,

$$A = \left.\frac{\partial a(p^{k_n}(X)'\beta)}{\partial\beta}\right|_{\beta^*_{k_n}} \quad \text{and}$$
$$V_{k_n} = A'\left\{E\left[p^{k_n}(X)p^{k_n}(X)'\right]\right\}^{-1}\Sigma\left\{E\left[p^{k_n}(X)p^{k_n}(X)'\right]\right\}^{-1}A.$$

We let $\xrightarrow{d}$ denote convergence in distribution and $\mathcal{N}(0,1)$ denote a scalar random variable drawn from a standard normal distribution.

THEOREM 3.8. *[See Newey (1997).] Suppose Assumptions* 3.5(i)(ii), 3.7–3.9 *hold. Let $\hat{h}_n$ be the series estimate of h_o in Example* 2.4, *with the sieve Θ_n being the linear sieve* (2.10). *If $\lim_{n\to\infty}\sqrt{n}k_n^{-\alpha} = 0$, then*

$$\sqrt{\frac{n}{V_{k_n}}}\left(a(\hat{h}) - a(h_o)\right) \xrightarrow{d} \mathcal{N}(0,1).$$

We note that for the linear functional $a(h_o) = h_o(x)$, this theorem implies pointwise asymptotic normality of any series LS estimators $\hat{h}(x)$ satisfying Assumptions 3.5(i)(ii), 3.7, 3.8(i) and 3.9(ii). When we specialize this theorem further to the tensor product spline series estimator of $h_o(x)$, then Assumption 3.8(i) requires $\lim_{n\to\infty} k_n^2/n = 0$, which is stronger than the condition $\lim_{n\to\infty} k_n \log n/n = 0$ in Theorem 3.7. However, Theorem 3.7 is applicable only to the spline series LS estimator, while the results by Newey (1994b, 1997) are much more general.

The normality results reported in this section are only valid for i.i.d. data; see Andrews (1991b) for asymptotic normality of linear functionals of the series LS estimators based on time series dependent observations.

4. Large sample properties of sieve estimation of parametric parts in semiparametric models

In the general sieve extremum estimation framework of Section 2, a model typically contains a parameter vector $\theta = (\beta, h)$, where β is a vector of finite-dimensional parameters and h is a vector of infinite-dimensional parameters. When both β and h are parameters of interest we call the model "semi-nonparametric". When h is a vector of nuisance parameters, then, following Powell (1994) and others, we will call the model "semiparametric".

For weakly dependent observations, semiparametric models can be classified into two categories: (i) β cannot be estimated at a $\sqrt{n}$-rate, i.e., β has zero information bound; see van der Vaart (1991); and (ii) β can be estimated at a $\sqrt{n}$-rate. Models belonging to category (i) should be correctly viewed as nonparametric. However, since these models can still be estimated by the method of sieves, the general sieve convergence rate results can be applied to derive slower than $\sqrt{n}$-rates for the sieve estimates of β. To date there is little research about whether or not the sieve estimate of β can reach the optimal convergence rate and what its limiting distribution is. It is worth mentioning that for Heckman and Singer's (1984) model, Ishwaran (1996a) established that the β-parameters cannot be estimated at $\sqrt{n}$-rate, while Ishwaran (1996b) constructed another estimator of β that converges at the optimal rate but is not a sieve MLE. Prior to the work of Ishwaran (1996a, 1996b), Honoré (1990, 1994) proposed a clever estimator of β that is not a sieve MLE either and computed its convergence rate. It is still an open question whether or not Heckman and Singer's (1984) sieve MLE estimator could reach Ishwaran's optimal rate.[36]

There is a large literature on semiparametric estimation of β for models belonging to category (ii); see Bickel et al. (1993), Newey and McFadden (1994), Powell (1994),

[36] There are other important results in econometrics about specific models belonging to category (i). For example, Manski (1985) proposed a maximum score estimator of a binary choice model with zero median restriction; Kim and Pollard (1990) derived the $n^{1/3}$ consistency of Manski's estimator; Horowitz (1992) proposed a smoothed maximum score estimator for Manski's model, and proved that his smoothed estimator converges faster than $n^{1/3}$ and is asymptotically normal; Andrews and Schafgans (1998) proposed a slower than $\sqrt{n}$ rate kernel estimator of the intercept in Heckman's sample selection model; Honoré and Kyriazidou (2000) developed a slower than $\sqrt{n}$ rate kernel estimator of a discrete choice dynamic panel data model. See Powell (1994), Horowitz (1998), Pagan and Ullah (1999) for more examples.

Horowitz (1998) and Pagan and Ullah (1999) for reviews. Most of these results are derived using the so-called two-step procedure: Step one estimates h nonparametrically by $\hat{h}$, while step two estimates β via either M-estimation, GMM or more generally, MD-estimation with the unknown h replaced by $\hat{h}$. A few general results deal with the simultaneous estimation of β and h. For example, the sieve simultaneous procedure jointly estimates β and h by maximizing a sample criterion function $\widehat{Q}_n(\beta, h)$ over the sieve parameter space $\Theta_n = B \times \mathcal{H}_n$. The earlier applications of sieve MLE in econometrics, such as the papers by Duncan (1986) and Gallant and Nychka (1987) took this approach.

In Subsection 4.1 we review existing theory on the $\sqrt{n}$-asymptotic normality of the two-step estimates of β. In Subsection 4.2, we present recent advances on the $\sqrt{n}$-asymptotic normality and efficiency of the sieve simultaneous M-estimates of β. In Subsection 4.3, we mention the $\sqrt{n}$-asymptotic normality and efficiency of the simultaneous sieve MD estimates of β.

4.1. Semiparametric two-step estimators

There are several general theory papers in econometrics about the semiparametric two-step procedure. Andrews (1994b) proposed the MINPIN estimator of β, which is the extremum estimator of β where the empirical criterion function depends on the first step nonparametric estimator of h. Andrews (1994b) also provided a set of relatively high level conditions to ensure the $\sqrt{n}$-normality of his MINPIN estimator of β. Ichimura and Lee (2006) presented a set of relatively low level conditions to ensure the $\sqrt{n}$-normality of the semiparametric two-step M-estimator of β. Newey (1994a), Pakes and Olley (1995), and Chen, Linton and van Keilegom (2003) have studied the properties of the semiparametric two-step GMM estimator of β. In addition to providing a general way to compute the asymptotic variance of the second step β estimate, Newey (1994a) showed that the second stage estimation of β and its asymptotic variance do not depend on the particular choice of the nonparametric estimation technique in the first step, but only depend on the convergence rate of the first step estimation.

4.1.1. Asymptotic normality

In the following we state two results which are slight modifications of those in Chen, Linton and van Keilegom (2003), in which the empirical criterion function can be nonsmooth with respect to both β and h. Let $M : B \times \mathcal{H} \mapsto \mathcal{R}^{d_m}$ be a nonrandom, vector-valued measurable function, where B is a compact subset in $\mathcal{R}^{d_\beta}$ with $d_m \geqslant d_\beta$. The identifying assumption is that $M(\beta, h_o(\cdot, \beta)) = 0$ at $\beta = \beta_o \in B$ and $M(\beta, h_o(\cdot, \beta)) \neq 0$ for all $\beta \neq \beta_o$. We denote $\beta_o \in B$ and $h_o \in \mathcal{H}$ as the true unknown finite- and infinite-dimensional parameters, where the function $h_o \in \mathcal{H}$ can depend on the parameters β and the data Z. We usually suppress the arguments of the function h_o for notational convenience; thus: $(\beta, h) \equiv (\beta, h(\cdot, \beta))$, $(\beta, h_o) \equiv (\beta, h_o(\cdot, \beta))$ and $(\beta_o, h_o) \equiv (\beta_o, h_o(\cdot, \beta_o))$. We assume that $\mathcal{H}$ is a vector space of functions endowed with a pseudo-metric $\|\cdot\|_{\mathcal{H}}$, which is a sup-norm metric with respect to the β-argument and a pseudo-metric with respect to all the other arguments. Suppose that there also exists a random vector-valued function $M_n : B \times \mathcal{H} \to \mathcal{R}^{d_m}$ depending on the data $\{Z_i\colon i = 1, \ldots, n\}$, such that $M_n(\beta, h_o)' W M_n(\beta, h_o)$ is close to $M(\beta, h_o)' W M(\beta, h_o)$ for some symmetric positive-definite matrix W. Suppose that for each β there is an initial nonparametric estimator $\hat{h}(.)$ for $h_o(.)$. Denote W_n as a possibly random weighting matrix such that $W_n - W = o_P(1)$. Then β_o can be estimated by $\hat{\beta}$, which solves the sample minimum distance problem[37]:

$$\min_{\beta\in B} M_n(\beta, \hat{h})' W_n M_n(\beta, \hat{h}). \tag{4.1}$$

For any $\beta \in B$, we say that $M(\beta, h)$ is pathwise differentiable at h in the direction $[\bar{h} - h]$ if $\{h + \tau(\bar{h} - h)\colon \tau \in [0, 1]\} \subset \mathcal{H}$ and $\lim_{\tau\to 0}[M(\beta, h + \tau(\bar{h} - h)) - M(\beta, h)]/\tau$ exists; we denote the limit by $\Gamma_2(\beta, h)[\bar{h} - h]$.

THEOREM 4.1. *Suppose that $\beta_o \in \operatorname{int}(B)$ satisfies $M(\beta_o, h_o) = 0$, that $\hat{\beta} - \beta_o = o_P(1)$, $W_n - W = o_P(1)$, and that:*

(4.1.1) $\|M_n(\hat{\beta}, \hat{h})\| = \inf_{\|\beta-\beta_o\|\leqslant\delta_n} \|M_n(\beta, \hat{h})\| + o_P(1/\sqrt{n})$ *for some positive sequence* $\delta_n = o(1)$.

(4.1.2) (i) *The ordinary partial derivative $\Gamma_1(\beta, h_o)$ in β of $M(\beta, h_o)$ exists in a neighborhood of β_o, and is continuous at $\beta = \beta_o$*; (ii) *the matrix $\Gamma_1 \equiv \Gamma_1(\beta_o, h_o)$ is such that $\Gamma_1' W \Gamma_1$ is nonsingular.*

(4.1.3) *The pathwise derivative $\Gamma_2(\beta, h_o)[h - h_o]$ of $M(\beta, h_o)$ exists in all directions $[h - h_o]$ and satisfies*:

$$\big\|\Gamma_2(\beta, h_o)[h - h_o] - \Gamma_2(\beta_o, h_o)[h - h_o]\big\| \leqslant \|\beta - \beta_o\| \times o(1)$$

for all β with $\|\beta - \beta_o\| = o(1)$, all h with $\|h - h_o\|_{\mathcal{H}} = o(1)$. Either

(4.1.4) $\|M(\beta, \hat{h}) - M(\beta, h_o) - \Gamma_2(\beta, h_o)[\hat{h} - h_o]\| = o_P(n^{-1/2})$ *for all β with $\|\beta - \beta_o\| = o(1)$; or*

(4.1.4)′ (i) *there are some constants $c \geqslant 0$, $\epsilon \in (0, 1]$ such that*

$$\big\|M(\beta, h) - M(\beta, h_o) - \Gamma_2(\beta, h_o)[h - h_o]\big\| \leqslant c\|h - h_o\|_{\mathcal{H}}^{1+\epsilon}$$

for all β with $\|\beta - \beta_o\| = o(1)$ and all h with $\|h - h_o\|_{\mathcal{H}} = o(1)$; and (ii) $c\|\hat{h} - h_o\|_{\mathcal{H}}^{1+\epsilon} = o_P(n^{-1/2})$.

(4.1.5) *For all sequences of positive numbers $\{\delta_n\}$ with $\delta_n = o(1)$,*

$$\sup_{\|\beta-\beta_o\|<\delta_n,\ \|h-h_o\|_{\mathcal{H}}<\delta_n} \frac{\|M_n(\beta, h) - M(\beta, h) - M_n(\beta_o, h_o)\|}{n^{-1/2} + \|M_n(\beta, h)\| + \|M(\beta, h)\|} = o_P(1).$$

(4.1.6) *For some finite matrix V_1, $\sqrt{n}\{M_n(\beta_o, h_o) + \Gamma_2(\beta_o, h_o)[\hat{h} - h_o]\} \xrightarrow{d} \mathcal{N}[0, V_1]$. Then $\sqrt{n}(\hat{\beta} - \beta_o) \xrightarrow{d} \mathcal{N}[0, (\Gamma_1' W \Gamma_1)^{-1} \Gamma_1' W V_1 W \Gamma_1 (\Gamma_1' W \Gamma_1)^{-1}]$.*

[37] See Theorem 1 in Chen, Linton and van Keilegom (2003) for the consistency property of $\hat{\beta} - \beta_o = o_P(1)$.

REMARK 4.1. This theorem can be established by following the proof of Theorem 2 in Chen, Linton and van Keilegom (2003). Note that condition (4.1.4) is implied by condition (4.1.4)$'$, while condition (4.1.4)$'$ with $\epsilon = 1$ becomes the one imposed in Newey (1994a) and Chen, Linton and van Keilegom (2003). When $M(\beta, h)$ is highly nonlinear in h and/or when the argument "$\cdot$" of $h(\cdot, \beta)$ has unbounded support, then condition (4.1.4)$'$(i) with $\epsilon = 1$ may fail to hold, but condition (4.1.4)$'$ with $0 < \epsilon < 1$ is typically satisfied. See Chen, Hong and Tarozzi (2007) for such an example in the two-step GMM estimation for nonclassical measurement error models and missing data problems. Of course a smaller ϵ has to be compensated by a faster rate of convergence of $\hat{h}$ to h_o in condition (4.1.4)$'$(ii) $\|\hat{h} - h_o\|_{\mathcal{H}} = o_P(n^{-1/2(1+\epsilon)})$. In the extreme case when $\|\hat{h} - h_o\|_{\mathcal{H}} = O_P(n^{-1/2})$, which is the case if h_o is a probability distribution function, then condition (4.1.4) is implied by condition

(4.1.4)$''$ (i) $\|M(\beta, h) - M(\beta, h_o) - \Gamma_2(\beta, h_o)[h - h_o]\| = \|h - h_o\|_{\mathcal{H}} \times o(1)$ *for all* β *with* $\|\beta - \beta_o\| = o(1)$ *and all* h *with* $\|h - h_o\|_{\mathcal{H}} = o(1)$; *and* (ii) $\|\hat{h} - h_o\|_{\mathcal{H}} = O_P(n^{-1/2})$.

Many econometric models correspond to $M(\beta, h) = E[m(Z_i, \beta, h)]$, $M_n(\beta, h) = n^{-1}\sum_{i=1}^n m(Z_i, \beta, h)$, where $m : \mathcal{R}^{d_z} \times B \times \mathcal{H} \to \mathcal{R}^{d_m}$ is a measurable, vector-valued function such that $E[m(Z_i, \beta, h_o(\cdot, \beta))] = 0$ if and only if $\beta = \beta_o \in B$, a subset of $\mathcal{R}^{d_\beta}$. In this situation, Theorem 3 in Chen, Linton and van Keilegom (2003) provides a set of easily-verifiable sufficient conditions for the stochastic equicontinuity condition (4.1.5) with i.i.d. data $\{Z_i\}$. The following lemma extends their result to strictly stationary processes. Let $\mathcal{F} = \{m(z, \beta, h): \beta \in B, h \in \mathcal{H}\}$ denote the class of measurable functions indexed by (β, h), and $H_{[\,]}(w, \mathcal{F}, \|\cdot\|_r)$ be the $L_r(P_o)$-metric entropy with bracketing of the class $\mathcal{F}$.

LEMMA 4.2. *Suppose that* $\{Z_t: t \geqslant 1\}$ *is strictly stationary, that* $M(\beta, h) = E[m(Z_t, \beta, h)]$ *and* $M_n(\beta, h) = n^{-1}\sum_{i=1}^n m(Z_t, \beta, h)$, *and that the arguments of the* $h(\cdot)$ *in* $m(Z_t, \beta, h(\cdot))$ *only depend on* β *and finitely many* Z_t. *Suppose that each component* m_j *of* $m = (m_1, \ldots, m_{d_m})'$ *satisfies*:

(4.2.1) $m_j(\cdot, \beta, h)$ *is locally uniformly* $L_r(P_o)$-*continuous with respect to* β, h *in the sense*:

$$\left(E\left[\sup_{(\beta', h'):\ \|\beta' - \beta\| < \delta,\ \|h' - h\|_{\mathcal{H}} < \delta} \left|m_{lcj}(Z, \beta', h') - m_{lcj}(Z, \beta, h)\right|^r\right]\right)^{1/r} \leqslant K_j \delta^{s_j}$$

for all $(\beta, h) \in B \times \mathcal{H}$, *all small positive value* $\delta = o(1)$, *and for some constants* $s_j \in (0, 1]$, $K_j > 0$ *and* $r \geqslant 1$.

Then: (i) $H_{[\,]}(w, \mathcal{F}_j, \|\cdot\|_r) \leqslant \log N([\frac{\varepsilon}{2K_j}]^{1/s_j}, B, \|\cdot\|) + \log N([\frac{\varepsilon}{2K_j}]^{1/s_j}, \mathcal{H}, \|\cdot\|_{\mathcal{H}})$ *for* $j = 1, \ldots, d_m$.

Furthermore, suppose that

(4.2.2) B *is a compact subset of* $\mathcal{R}^{d_\beta}$, *and* $\int_0^\infty \sqrt{\log N(\varepsilon^{1/s_j}, \mathcal{H}, \|\cdot\|_{\mathcal{H}})}\, \mathrm{d}\varepsilon < \infty$ *for* $j = 1, \ldots, d_m$.

(4.2.3) *Either* $\{Z_t\}_{t=1}^n$ *is i.i.d. and* (4.2.1) *holds with* $r \geqslant 2$, *or* $\{Z_t\}_{t=1}^n$ *is beta-mixing with a mixing decay rate satisfying* $\sum_{t=1}^{\infty} t^{2/(r-2)}\beta_t < \infty$ *for some* $r > 2$, *and* (4.2.1) *holds with* $r > 2$.

Then: (ii) *for all positive* δ_n *with* $\delta_n = o(1)$,

$$\sup_{\|\beta-\beta_o\|<\delta_n,\ \|h-h_o\|_{\mathcal{H}}<\delta_n} \left\| M_n(\beta, h) - M(\beta, h) - \left\{M_n(\beta_o, h_o) - M(\beta_o, h_o)\right\}\right\| = o_P\left(n^{-1/2}\right). \tag{4.2}$$

PROOF. Result (i) is already derived in the proof of Theorem 3 in Chen, Linton and van Keilegom (2003). Result (ii) for i.i.d. case is Theorem 3 of Chen, Linton and van Keilegom (2003). Now for stationary beta-mixing case, conditions (4.2.1)–(4.2.3) imply that $\int_0^\infty \sqrt{H_{[\,]}(w, \mathcal{F}, \|\cdot\|_r)}\,\mathrm{d}w < \infty$ with $r > 2$. This and $\sum_{t=1}^{\infty} t^{2/(r-2)}\beta_t < \infty$ imply that all the assumptions in Doukhan, Massart and Rio (1995) for the Donsker theorem on stationary beta-mixing are satisfied, which in turn implies the stochastic equicontinuity (4.2) result (ii). □

Both Theorem 3 in Chen, Linton and van Keilegom (2003) and Lemma 4.2 are extensions of the "type II class" and "type IV class" defined in Andrews (1994a) from $\beta \in B$ to $(\beta, h) \in B \times \mathcal{H}$. Condition (4.2.1) allows for discontinuous moment functions in (β, h) such as sign and indicator functions of (β, h).

Given the results of Newey (1994a), Chen, Linton and van Keilegom (2003) and Theorem 4.1, the choice of estimation of h in the first step should mainly depend on the ease of implementation. Recently, for the partially linear quantile regression $Y_t = X_{0t}'\beta_o + h_o(X_{1t}) + e_t$, $P[e_t \leqslant 0|X_t] = \alpha \in (0, 1)$, Lee (2003) proposed a two-step, $\sqrt{n}$ asymptotically normal and efficient estimator of β, where the first step involved a high-dimensional kernel quantile regression of Y_t on $X = (X_0', X_1')'$. Chen, Linton and van Keilegom (2003) considered a modification of Lee's model to a partially linear quantile regression with some endogenous regressors, and proposed another $\sqrt{n}$ asymptotically normal estimator of β by two-step GMM where the first step nonparametric estimation only involves $h(X_{1t})$. We can extend their models further to a partially additive quantile regression:

$$Y_t = X_{0t}'\beta_o + \sum_{j=1}^{q} h_{oj}(X_{jt}) + e_t, \qquad P[e_t \leqslant 0|X_t] = \alpha \in (0, 1).$$

If $h_{o1}, \ldots, h_{oq}$ were known, then β_o could be estimated based on the moment restriction $E[m(Z_i, \beta, h_o)] = 0$ iff $\beta = \beta_o$ with $m(Z_i, \beta, h_o) = X_0\{\alpha - 1(Y \leqslant X_{0t}'\beta + \sum_{j=1}^{q} h_{oj}(X_{jt})\}$. Clearly, to estimate β by semiparametric two-step GMM using the sample moment $n^{-1}\sum_{i=1}^{n} m(Z_i, \beta, \hat{h})$, it would be much easier if $\hat{h} = (\hat{h}_1, \ldots, \hat{h}_q)$ were a sieve estimate, say obtained by $\max_{h\in\mathcal{H}_n} \widehat{Q}_n(\beta, h) = n^{-1}\sum_{t=1}^{n} l(\beta, h, Y_t, X_t)$ for any arbitrarily fixed β, where

$$l(\beta, h, Y_t, X_t) = \left\{1\left(Y_t < X_{0t}'\beta + \sum_{j=1}^{q} h_j(X_{jt})\right) - \alpha\right\}\left[Y_t - X_{0t}'\beta - \sum_{j=1}^{q} h_j(X_{jt})\right],$$

and $\mathcal{H}_n = \mathcal{H}_n^1 \times \cdots \times \mathcal{H}_n^q$ as in Subsection 3.2.1, rather than a high-dimensional kernel quantile regression. Andrews (1994b), Newey (1994a, 1994b), Newey, Powell and Vella (1999) and Das, Newey and Vella (2003) have made the same recommendation in the context of two-step estimation with an additive LS regression in the first step.

There is also a large literature on the general theory of efficient estimation of β via various two-step procedures. For instance, the profile MLE estimation of β [which can be viewed as an important subclass of Andrews' (1994b) MINPIN procedure] can lead to efficient estimation of β; see e.g. Severini and Wong (1992), Ai (1997) and Murphy and van der Vaart (2000). Other two-step procedures which lead to the efficient estimation of β include those based on the efficient score equation approach; see Bickel et al. (1993) and Newey (1990a), and the optimally weighted GMM approach; see Newey (1990a, 1990b, 1993). See Powell (1994) and Pagan and Ullah (1999) for other examples. Clearly, these efficient procedures can be combined with a first step nonparametric estimation of h via the method of sieves.

4.2. Sieve simultaneous M-estimation

There are few general theory papers about the sieve simultaneous M-estimation of β and h; see Wong and Severini (1991), Shen (1997), Chen and Shen (1998). This procedure jointly estimates β and h by maximizing a sample criterion function $\widehat{Q}_n(\beta, h)$ over the sieve parameter space $\Theta_n = B \times \mathcal{H}_n$, where $\widehat{Q}_n(\beta, h)$ takes a sample average form $\frac{1}{n}\sum_{i=1}^{n} l(\beta, h, Z_i)$. Wong and Severini (1991) established $\sqrt{n}$-asymptotic normality and efficiency of smooth functionals of nonparametric MLE with parameter space $\Theta_n \equiv \Theta = B \times \mathcal{H}$. Shen (1997) extended their results to sieve MLE and to allow for highly curved (nonlinear) least favorable directions. Chen and Shen (1998) extend the result of Shen (1997) to general sieve M-estimation with stationary weakly dependent data.

4.2.1. Asymptotic normality of smooth functionals of sieve M-estimators

Let $\hat{\theta}_n = (\hat{\beta}_n, \hat{h}_n) = \arg\max_{(\beta,h)\in B\times\mathcal{H}_n} \frac{1}{n}\sum_{i=1}^{n} l(\beta, h, Z_i)$ denote the sieve M-estimate of $\theta_o = (\beta_o, h_o)$. In this subsection we present a simple $\sqrt{n}$-asymptotic normality theorem for the plug-in estimate of a smooth functional of θ_o. See Shen (1997) and Chen and Shen (1998) for the general version.

Suppose that $\Theta = B \times \mathcal{H}$ is convex in θ_o so that $\theta_o + \tau[\theta - \theta_o] \in \Theta$ for all small $\tau \in [0, 1]$ and for all fixed $\theta \in \Theta$. Suppose that the directional derivative

$$\frac{\partial l(\theta_o, z)}{\partial \theta}[\theta - \theta_o] \equiv \lim_{\tau \to 0} \frac{l(\theta_o + \tau[\theta - \theta_o], z) - l(\theta_o, z)}{\tau}$$

is well defined for almost all z in the support of Z.

Let $\Theta = B \times \mathcal{H}$ be equipped with a norm $\|\cdot\|$. Suppose the functional of interest, $f : \Theta \to \mathcal{R}$, is smooth in the sense that

$$\frac{\partial f(\theta_o)}{\partial \theta}[\theta - \theta_o] \equiv \lim_{\tau \to 0} \frac{f(\theta_o + \tau[\theta - \theta_o]) - f(\theta_o)}{\tau}$$

is well defined and

$$\left\| \frac{\partial f(\theta_o)}{\partial \theta} \right\| \equiv \sup_{\{\theta \in \Theta: \|\theta - \theta_o\| > 0\}} \frac{|\frac{\partial f(\theta_o)}{\partial \theta}[\theta - \theta_o]|}{\|\theta - \theta_o\|} < \infty.$$

Next, suppose that $\|\cdot\|$ induces an inner product $\langle \cdot, \cdot \rangle$ on the completion of the space spanned by $\Theta - \theta_o$, denoted as $\bar{V}$. By the Riesz representation theorem, there exists $v^* \in \bar{V}$ such that, for any $\theta \in \Theta$,

$$\frac{\partial f(\theta_o)}{\partial \theta}[\theta - \theta_o] = \langle \theta - \theta_o, v^* \rangle \quad \text{iff} \quad \left\| \frac{\partial f(\theta_o)}{\partial \theta} \right\| < \infty.$$

Suppose that the sieve M-estimate $\hat{\theta}_n$ converges to θ_o at a rate faster than δ_n (i.e., $\|\hat{\theta}_n - \theta_o\| = o_P(\delta_n)$). Let ε_n denote any sequence satisfying $\varepsilon_n = o(n^{-1/2})$, and $\mu_n(g(Z)) = \frac{1}{n}\sum_{t=1}^{n}\{g(Z_t) - E(g(Z_t))\}$ denote the empirical process indexed by the function g. Recall that $K(\theta_o, \theta) \equiv E[l(\theta_o, Z_i) - l(\theta, Z_i)]$.

CONDITION 4.1.

(i) There is $\omega > 0$ such that $|f(\theta) - f(\theta_o) - \frac{\partial f(\theta_o)}{\partial \theta}[\theta - \theta_o]| = O(\|\theta - \theta_o\|^{\omega})$ uniformly in $\theta \in \Theta_n$ with $\|\theta - \theta_o\| = o(1)$;

(ii) $\|\frac{\partial f(\theta_o)}{\partial \theta}\| < \infty$;

(iii) there is $\pi_n v^* \in \Theta_n$ such that $\|\pi_n v^* - v^*\| \times \|\hat{\theta}_n - \theta_o\| = o_P(n^{-1/2})$.

CONDITION 4.2.

$$\sup_{\{\theta \in \Theta_n: \|\theta - \theta_o\| \leqslant \delta_n\}} \mu_n\left(l(\theta, Z) - l(\theta \pm \varepsilon_n \pi_n v^*, Z) - \frac{\partial l(\theta_o, Z)}{\partial \theta}[\pm \varepsilon_n \pi_n v^*] \right) = O_P\left(\varepsilon_n^2\right).$$

CONDITION 4.3. $K(\theta_o, \hat{\theta}_n) - K(\theta_o, \hat{\theta}_n \pm \varepsilon_n \pi_n v^*) = \pm \varepsilon_n \langle \hat{\theta}_n - \theta_o, \pi_n v^* \rangle + o(n^{-1})$.

CONDITION 4.4.

(i) $\mu_n(\frac{\partial l(\theta_o, Z)}{\partial \theta}[\pi_n v^* - v^*]) = o_P(n^{-1/2})$;

(ii) $E\{\frac{\partial l(\theta_o, Z)}{\partial \theta}[\pi_n v^*]\} = o(n^{-1/2})$.

CONDITION 4.5. $n^{1/2}\mu_n(\frac{\partial l(\theta_o, Z)}{\partial \theta}[v^*]) \xrightarrow{d} \mathcal{N}(0, \sigma_{v^*}^2)$, with $\sigma_{v^*}^2 > 0$.

We note that for classical nonlinear M-estimation such as those reviewed in Newey and McFadden (1994), Conditions 4.1(i)(ii), 4.2, 4.3 and 4.5 are still required (albeit in slightly different expressions), while Conditions 4.1(iii) and 4.4 are automatically satisfied since $\pi_n v^* = v^*$ for the standard nonlinear M-estimation. Note that for i.i.d. data Condition 4.5 is satisfied whenever $\sigma_{v^*}^2 = \mathrm{Var}(\frac{\partial l(\theta_o, Z)}{\partial\theta}[v^*]) > 0$. If $l(\theta, Z)$ is also pathwise differentiable in $\theta \in \Theta_n$ with $\|\theta - \theta_o\| = o(1)$, then Conditions 4.2 and 4.3 are implied by Conditions 4.2′ and 4.3′ respectively, where

CONDITION 4.2′.

$$\sup_{\{\bar\theta\in\Theta_n:\ \|\bar\theta-\theta_o\|\leqslant\delta_n\}} \mu_n\left(\frac{\partial l(\bar\theta, Z)}{\partial\theta}[\pi_n v^*] - \frac{\partial l(\theta_o, Z)}{\partial\theta}[\pi_n v^*]\right) = o_P\left(n^{-1/2}\right).$$

CONDITION 4.3′. $E\{\frac{\partial l(\hat\theta_n, Z)}{\partial\theta}[\pi_n v^*]\} = \langle\hat\theta_n - \theta_o, \pi_n v^*\rangle + o(n^{-1/2})$.

Condition 4.2 (or 4.2′) can be verified by applying Lemma 4.2. Condition 4.3 (or 4.3′) can be verified when a Hilbert norm $\|\theta - \theta_o\|$ is chosen.

Conditions 4.2–4.4 may need to be modified when the parameter space Θ is not convex; see Shen (1997) and Chen and Shen (1998) for the needed modification.

THEOREM 4.3. *Suppose Conditions* 4.1–4.5 *hold, and* $\|\hat\theta_n - \theta_o\|^{\omega} = o_P(n^{-1/2})$. *Then, for the sieve M-estimate* $\hat\theta_n$, $n^{1/2}(f(\hat\theta_n) - f(\theta_o)) \xrightarrow{d} \mathcal{N}(0, \sigma_{v^*}^2)$.

The proof of Theorem 4.3 follows trivially from those in Shen (1997) and Ai and Chen (1999). In applications, one needs to specify a Hilbert norm $\|\theta - \theta_o\|$ in order to compute the representer v^*. Wong and Severini (1991) and Shen (1997) have used the Fisher norm, $\|\theta - \theta_o\|^2 = E\{\frac{\partial l(\theta_o, Z_i)}{\partial\theta}[\theta - \theta_o]\}^2$, for the sieve MLE procedure. Ai and Chen (1999, 2003) have introduced a Fisher-like norm for their sieve MD and sieve GLS procedures. In the next subsection we specialize Theorem 4.3 to derive root-n asymptotic normality of parametric parts in sieve GLS problems.

4.2.2. Asymptotic normality of sieve GLS

Recall that for all the models belonging to the first subclass of the conditional moment restrictions (2.8), $E\{\rho(Z, \theta_o)|X\} = 0$, where $\rho(Z, \theta) - \rho(Z, \theta_o)$ does not depend on endogenous variables Y, we can estimate $\theta_o = (\beta_o, h_o) \in B \times \mathcal{H}$ by the sieve GLS procedure:

$$\hat\theta_n = (\hat\beta_n, \hat h_n) = \arg\min_{(\beta,h)\in B\times\mathcal{H}_n} \frac{1}{n}\sum_{i=1}^{n} \rho(Z_i, \beta, h)'\Sigma(X_i)^{-1}\rho(Z_i, \beta, h),$$

where $\Sigma(X_i)$ is a positive definite weighting matrix. When $\Sigma(X_i)$ is known such as the identity matrix, this belongs to the sieve M-estimation with $l(\theta, Z_i) = -\rho(Z_i, \theta)'\Sigma(X_i)^{-1}\rho(Z_i, \theta)/2$. See Subsection 4.3 and Remark 4.3 for estimation of the optimal weighting matrix $\Sigma_o(X_i) \equiv \mathrm{Var}\{\rho(Z_i, \theta_o)|X_i\}$.

We now apply Theorem 4.3 to derive root-n asymptotic normality of the sieve GLS estimator $\hat{\beta}_n$. Define the norm $\|\theta-\theta_o\|^2 = E\{(\frac{\partial\rho(Z_i,\theta_o)}{\partial\theta}[\theta-\theta_o])\Sigma(X_i)^{-1}(\frac{\partial\rho(Z_i,\theta_o)}{\partial\theta}[\theta-\theta_o])\}$. For $j=1,\ldots,d_\beta$, let

$$D_{w_j}(X) = \left.\frac{\partial\rho(Z,\beta,h_o(\cdot))}{\partial\beta_j}\right|_{\beta=\beta_o} - \left.\frac{\partial\rho(X,\beta_o,h_o(\cdot)+\tau w_j(\cdot))}{\partial\tau}\right|_{\tau=0}$$
$$= \frac{\partial\rho(Z,\theta_o)}{\partial\beta_j} - \frac{\partial\rho(Z,\theta_o)}{\partial h}[w_j],$$

$w=(w_1,\ldots,w_{d_\beta})$, and $D_w(X) = (D_{w_1}(X),\ldots,D_{w_{d_\beta}}(X)) = \frac{\partial\rho(Z,\theta_o)}{\partial\beta'} - \frac{\partial\rho(Z,\theta_o)}{\partial h}[w]$ be a $(d_\rho\times d_\beta)$-matrix valued measurable function of X. Let $w^* = (w_1^*,\ldots,w_{d_\beta}^*)$, where for $j=1,\ldots,d_\beta$, w_j^* solves

$$E\{D_{w_j^*}(X)'\Sigma(X)^{-1}D_{w_j^*}(X)\} = \inf_{w_j} E\{D_{w_j}(X)'\Sigma(X)^{-1}D_{w_j}(X)\}.$$

Denote $D_{w^*}(X) = \frac{\partial\rho(Z,\theta_o)}{\partial\beta'} - \frac{\partial\rho(Z,\theta_o)}{\partial h}[w^*]$. Let

$$v_\beta^* = \left(E\{D_{w^*}(X)'\Sigma(X)^{-1}D_{w^*}(X)\}\right)^{-1}\lambda,$$

$v_h^* = -w^*v_\beta^*$ and $v^* = (v_\beta^*, v_h^*)$.

ASSUMPTION 4.1.
(i) $\beta_o \in \operatorname{int}(B)$;
(ii) $E[D_{w^*}(X)'\Sigma(X)^{-1}D_{w^*}(X)]$ is positive definite;
(iii) there is $\pi_n v^* \in \Theta_n$ such that $\|\pi_n v^* - v^*\| \times \|\hat{\theta}_n - \theta_o\| = o_P(n^{-1/2})$.

ASSUMPTION 4.2.
(i) $\Sigma(X)$ and $\Sigma_o(X) \equiv \operatorname{Var}\{\rho(Z_i,\theta_o)|X\}$ are positive definite and bounded uniform over X;
(ii) $\rho(Z,\theta)$ is twice continuously pathwise differentiable with respect to $\theta\in\Theta$ with $\|\theta-\theta_o\| = o(1)$;
(iii) Conditions 4.2′ and 4.3′ are satisfied with $\frac{\partial l(\bar{\theta},Z)}{\partial\theta}[\pi_n v^*] = -\rho(Z,\bar{\theta})'\times\Sigma(X)^{-1}\{\frac{\partial\rho(Z,\bar{\theta})}{\partial\theta}[\pi_n v^*]\}$ for all $\bar{\theta}\in\Theta_n$ with $\|\bar{\theta}-\theta_o\| = o(1)$;
(iv) $\{Z_i\}_{i=1}^n$ is i.i.d., $E\{\rho(Z,\theta_o)|X\} = 0$, $E\{\rho(Z,\theta)-\rho(Z,\theta_o)|X\} = \rho(Z,\theta)-\rho(Z,\theta_o)$ for all $\theta\in\Theta$.

PROPOSITION 4.4. *Let $\hat{\theta}_n$ be the sieve GLS estimate. Suppose Assumptions* 4.1–4.2 *hold. Then $n^{1/2}(\hat{\beta}_n-\beta_o) \xrightarrow{d} \mathcal{N}(0, V_1^{-1}V_2V_1^{-1})$ where*

$$V_1 = E[D_{w^*}(X)'\Sigma(X)^{-1}D_{w^*}(X)],$$
$$V_2 = E[D_{w^*}(X)'\Sigma(X)^{-1}\Sigma_o(X)\Sigma(X)^{-1}D_{w^*}(X)].$$

PROOF. Let $f(\theta) = \lambda'\beta$, where λ is an arbitrary unit vector in $\mathcal{R}^{d_\beta}$. Clearly, Condition 4.1(i) is satisfied with $\frac{\partial f(\theta_o)}{\partial\theta}[\theta - \theta_o] = (\beta - \beta_o)'\lambda$ and $\omega = \infty$. In addition, under Assumption 4.1(i)(ii), we have $v^* = (v^*_\beta, v^*_h)$ and

$$\|v^*\|^2 = \sup_{\{\theta\in\Theta:\ \|\theta-\theta_o\|>0\}} \frac{\{(\beta-\beta_o)'\lambda\}^2}{\|\theta-\theta_o\|^2}$$
$$= \lambda'\big(E\{D_{w^*}(X)'\Sigma(X)^{-1}D_{w^*}(X)\}\big)^{-1}\lambda < \infty.$$

Thus Condition 4.1 is implied by Assumption 4.1. Note that

$$\frac{\partial l(\theta_o, Z)}{\partial\theta}[\theta - \theta_o]$$
$$= -\rho(Z,\theta_o)'\Sigma(X)^{-1}\left(\frac{\partial\rho(Z,\theta_o)}{\partial\beta'}(\beta-\beta_o) + \frac{\partial\rho(Z,\theta_o)}{\partial h}[h - h_o]\right),$$

we have

$$E\left\{\frac{\partial l(\theta_o, Z)}{\partial\theta}[\pi_n v^*]\right\}$$
$$= -E\left\{\rho(Z,\theta_o)'\Sigma(X)^{-1}\left(\frac{\partial\rho(Z,\theta_o)}{\partial\beta'}(v^*_\beta) + \frac{\partial\rho(Z,\theta_o)}{\partial h}[\pi_n v^*_h]\right)\right\} = 0,$$

hence Condition 4.4(ii) is automatically satisfied. Since

$$\frac{1}{n}\sum_{t=1}^{n}\frac{\partial l(\theta_o, Z_t)}{\partial\theta}[\pi_n v^* - v^*]$$
$$= \frac{-1}{n}\sum_{t=1}^{n}\rho(Z_t,\theta_o)'\Sigma(X_t)^{-1}\left(\frac{\partial\rho(Z_t,\theta_o)}{\partial h}[\pi_n v^*_h - v^*_h]\right),$$

by Chebyshev inequality and Assumptions 4.1(iii) and 4.2(i), we have

$$\frac{1}{n}\sum_{i=1}^{n}\frac{\partial l(\theta_o, Z_i)}{\partial\theta}[\pi_n v^* - v^*] = o_P(n^{-1/2}),$$

hence Condition 4.4(i) is satisfied. Since data are i.i.d. and under Assumptions 4.1(ii) and 4.2(i),

$$\sigma^2_{v^*} = \mathrm{Var}\left\{\frac{\partial l(\theta_o, Z)}{\partial\theta}[v^*]\right\}$$
$$= \mathrm{Var}\left\{\rho(Z,\theta_o)'\Sigma(X)^{-1}\left(\frac{\partial\rho(Z,\theta_o)}{\partial\beta'} - \frac{\partial\rho(Z,\theta_o)}{\partial h}[w^*]\right)(v^*_\beta)\right\}$$
$$= (v^*_\beta)'E\{D_{w^*}(X)'\Sigma(X)^{-1}\Sigma_o(X)\Sigma(X)^{-1}D_{w^*}(X)\}(v^*_\beta)$$
$$= \lambda'V_1^{-1}V_2V_1^{-1}\lambda > 0,$$

Condition 4.5 is satisfied. By Theorem 4.3, we obtain, for any arbitrary unit vector $\lambda \in \mathcal{R}^{d_\beta}$, $n^{1/2}\lambda'(\hat{\beta}_n - \beta_o) \xrightarrow{d} \mathcal{N}(0, \sigma^2_{v*})$. Hence $\sqrt{n}(\hat{\beta}_n - \beta_o) \xrightarrow{d} \mathcal{N}(0, V_1^{-1} V_2 V_1^{-1})$. □

REMARK 4.2. The asymptotic variance, $V_1^{-1} V_2 V_1^{-1}$, of the sieve GLS estimator $\hat{\beta}_n$ can be consistently estimated by $\widehat{V}_1^{-1}\widehat{V}_2\widehat{V}_1^{-1}$, where

$$\widehat{V}_1 = \frac{1}{n}\sum_{i=1}^{n}\left(\frac{\partial\rho(Z_i,\hat{\theta}_n)}{\partial\beta'} - \frac{\partial\rho(Z_i,\hat{\theta}_n)}{\partial h}[\hat{w}]\right)' \times \Sigma(X_i)^{-1}\left(\frac{\partial\rho(Z_i,\hat{\theta}_n)}{\partial\beta'} - \frac{\partial\rho(Z_i,\hat{\theta}_n)}{\partial h}[\hat{w}]\right),$$

$$\widehat{V}_2 = \frac{1}{n}\sum_{i=1}^{n}\left(\frac{\partial\rho(Z_i,\hat{\theta}_n)}{\partial\beta'} - \frac{\partial\rho(Z_i,\hat{\theta}_n)}{\partial h}[\hat{w}]\right)' \times \Sigma(X_i)^{-1}\widehat{\Sigma}_o(X_i)\Sigma(X_i)^{-1}\left(\frac{\partial\rho(Z_i,\hat{\theta}_n)}{\partial\beta'} - \frac{\partial\rho(Z_i,\hat{\theta}_n)}{\partial h}[\hat{w}]\right),$$

$\hat{w} = (\hat{w}_1, \ldots, \hat{w}_{d_\beta})$ solves the following sieve minimization problem: for $j = 1, \ldots, d_\beta$,

$$\min_{w_j \in \mathcal{H}_n} \sum_{i=1}^{n}\left(\frac{\partial\rho(Z_i,\hat{\theta}_n)}{\partial\beta_j} - \frac{\partial\rho(Z_i,\hat{\theta}_n)}{\partial h}[w_j]\right)' \times \left[\Sigma(X_i)\right]^{-1}\left(\frac{\partial\rho(Z_i,\hat{\theta}_n)}{\partial\beta_j} - \frac{\partial\rho(Z_i,\hat{\theta}_n)}{\partial h}[w_j]\right),$$

and $\widehat{\Sigma}_o(X_i)$ can be any consistent nonparametric estimator of $\Sigma_o(X_i)$; see Ai and Chen (1999) for kernel estimator and Ai and Chen (2003, 2007) for series LS estimator of $\Sigma_o(X_i)$.

4.2.3. Example: Partially additive mean regression with a monotone constraint

Suppose that the i.i.d. data $\{Y_t, X'_t = (X'_{0t}, X_{1t}, \ldots, X_{qt})\}_{t=1}^n$ are generated according to

$$Y_i = X'_{0i}\beta_o + h_{o1}(X_{1i}) + \cdots + h_{oq}(X_{qi}) + e_i, \qquad E[e_i|X_i] = 0.$$

Let $\theta_o = (\beta'_o, h_{o1}, \ldots, h_{oq})' \in \Theta = B \times \mathcal{H}$ be the parameters of interests, where B is a compact subset of $\mathcal{R}^{d_\beta}$ and $\mathcal{H}$ is the same as that in Subsection 3.2.1. Since $h_{o1}(\cdot)$ can have a constant we assume that X_0 does not contain the constant regressor, $\dim(X_0) = d_\beta$, $\dim(X_j) = 1$ for $j = 1, \ldots, q$, $\dim(X) = d_\beta + q$, and $\dim(Y) = 1$. We estimate the regression function $\theta_o(X) = X'_{0t}\beta_o + \sum_{j=1}^q h_{oj}(X_{jt})$ by maximizing over $\Theta_n = B \times \mathcal{H}_n$ the criterion $\widehat{Q}_n(\theta) = n^{-1}\sum_{t=1}^n l(\theta, Y_t, X_t)$, where $l(\theta, Y_t, X_t) =$

$-\frac{1}{2}[Y_t - X'_{0t}\beta - \sum_{j=1}^{q} h_j(X_{jt})]^2$. Let $\|\theta - \theta_o\|^2 = E\{X'_{0t}(\beta - \beta_o) + \sum_{j=1}^{q}[h_j(X_{jt}) - h_{oj}(X_{jt})]\}^2$.

Note that $D_{w^*}(X)' = X_0 - \sum_{k=1}^{q} w^{*k}(X_k)$, where $w^{*k}(X_k)$, $k = 1, \ldots, q$, solves

$$\inf_{w^k, k=1,\ldots,q:\ E[|X_0 - \sum_{k=1}^{q} w^k(X_k)|_e^2]>0} E\left[\left(X_0 - \sum_{k=1}^{q} w^k(X_k)\right)\left(X_0 - \sum_{k=1}^{q} w^k(X_k)\right)'\right].$$

PROPOSITION 4.5. *Suppose that Assumption* 3.1 *and the following hold*:

(i) $\beta_o \in \operatorname{int}(B)$;
(ii) $\Sigma_o(X)$ *is positive and bounded*;
(iii) $E[X_0 X_0']$ *is positive definite*; $E[D_{w^*}(X)' D_{w^*}(X)]$ *is positive definite*;
(iv) *each element of* w^{*j} *belongs to the Hölder space* Λ^{m_j} *with* $m_j > 1/2$ *for* $j = 1, \ldots, q$.

Let $k_{jn} = O(n^{1/(2p_j+1)})$ *for* $j = 1, \ldots, q$. *Then* $n^{1/2}(\hat{\beta}_n - \beta_o) \xrightarrow{d} \mathcal{N}(0, V_1^{-1} V_2 V_1^{-1})$ *where* $V_1 = E[D_{w^*}(X)' D_{w^*}(X)]$, $V_2 = E[D_{w^*}(X)' \Sigma_o(X) D_{w^*}(X)]$.

PROOF. We obtain the result by applying Proposition 4.4. Let $\Theta_n = B \times \mathcal{H}_n$ and $\mathcal{H}_n = \mathcal{H}_n^1 \times \cdots \times \mathcal{H}_n^q$, where $\mathcal{H}_n^j$, $j = 1, 2, \ldots, q$, are the same as those in Subsection 3.2.1. By the same proof as that for Proposition 3.3, we have $\|\hat{\theta}_n - \theta_o\| = O_P(n^{-p/(2p+1)})$ provided that $p = \min\{p_1, \ldots, p_q\} > 0.5$. This and assumption (iv) imply Assumption 4.1(iii). Condition 4.3′ is trivially satisfied given the definition of the metric $\|\cdot\|$. It remains to verify Condition 4.2′:

$$\mu_n\left(\left\{X_0'[v_\beta^*] + \sum_{j=1}^{q}[\pi_n v_{h_j}^*(X_j)]\right\}\left\{X_0'[\beta - \beta_o] + \sum_{j=1}^{q}[h_j(X_j) - h_{oj}(X_j)]\right\}\right) = o_P(n^{-1/2}),$$

uniformly over $\theta \in \Theta_n$ with $\|\theta - \theta_o\| \leqslant \delta_n = O(n^{-p/(2p+1)})$. Applying Theorem 3 in Chen, Linton and van Keilegom (2003) (or Lemma 4.2 for i.i.d. case), assumptions (i)–(iv) and Assumption 3.1 ($h_j \in \mathcal{H}^j = \Lambda_c^{m_j}$ with $m_j > 1/2$ for all $j = 1, \ldots, q$) imply Condition 4.2′; also see van der Vaart and Wellner (1996). □

Notice that for the well-known partially linear regression model $Y_i = X'_{0i}\beta_o + h_{o1}(X_{1i}) + e_i$, $E[e_i | X_i] = 0$, we can explicitly solve for $D_{w^*}(X)' \equiv X_0 - w^{*1}(X_1)$ with $w^{*1}(X_1) = E\{X_0 | X_1\}$. Hence assumption (iv) will be satisfied if $E\{X_0 | X_1\}$ is smooth enough. See Remark 4.3 for semiparametric efficient estimation of β_o.

4.2.4. Efficiency of sieve MLE

Wong (1992), and Wong and Severini (1991) established asymptotic efficiency of plug-in nonparametric MLE estimates of smooth functionals. Shen (1997) extended their results to sieve MLE. We review the results of Wong (1992) and Shen (1997) in this subsection. Related work can be found in Begun et al. (1983), Ibragimov and Hasminskii (1991), Bickel et al. (1993).

Here the criterion is $\widehat{Q}_n(\theta) = \frac{1}{n}\sum_{i=1}^n l(Z_i, \theta)$, where $l(Z_i, \theta) = \log p(Z_i, \theta)$ is a log-likelihood evaluated at the single observation Z_i. We use the Fisher norm: $\|\theta - \theta_o\|^2 = E\{\frac{\partial \log p(Z_i, \theta_o)}{\partial \theta}[\theta - \theta_o]\}^2$. Recall that a probability family $\{P_\theta\colon \theta \in \Theta\}$ is *locally asymptotically normal* (LAN) at θ_o, if (1) for any g in the linear span of $\Theta - \theta_o$, $\theta_o + tn^{-1/2}g \in \Theta$ for all small $t \geqslant 0$, and (2)

$$\frac{\mathrm{d}P_{\theta_o+n^{-1/2}g}}{\mathrm{d}P_{\theta_o}}(Z_1, \ldots, Z_n) = \exp\left\{\Sigma_n(g) - \frac{1}{2}\|g\|^2 + R_n(\theta_o, g)\right\},$$

where $\Sigma_n(g)$ is linear in g, $\Sigma_n(g) \xrightarrow{d} \mathcal{N}(0, \|g\|^2)$ and $\operatorname{plim}_{n\to\infty} R_n(\theta_o, g) = 0$ (both limits are under the true probability measure $P_o = P_{\theta_o}$); see e.g. LeCam (1960).

To avoid the "super-efficiency" phenomenon, certain conditions on the estimates are required. In estimating a smooth functional in the infinite-dimensional case, Wong (1992, p. 58) defines the class of *pathwise regular* estimates in the sense of Bahadur (1964). An estimate $T_n(Z_1, \ldots, Z_n)$ of $f(\theta_o)$ is *pathwise regular* if for any real number $\tau > 0$ and any g in the linear span of $\Theta - \theta_o$, we have

$$\limsup_{n\to\infty} P_{\theta_{n,\tau}}\big(T_n < f(\theta_{n,\tau})\big) \leqslant \liminf_{n\to\infty} P_{\theta_{n,-\tau}}\big(T_n < f(\theta_{n,-\tau})\big),$$

where $\theta_{n,\tau} = \theta_o + n^{-1/2}\tau g$.

THEOREM 4.6. *[See Wong (1992), Shen (1997).] In addition to LAN, suppose the functional $f: \Theta \to \mathcal{R}$ is Frechet-differentiable at θ_o with $0 < \|\frac{\partial f(\theta_o)}{\partial \theta}\| < \infty$. Then for any pathwise regular estimate T_n of $f(\theta_o)$, and any real number $\tau > 0$,*

$$\limsup_{n\to\infty} P_o\big(\sqrt{n}|T_n - f(\theta_o)| \leqslant \tau\big) \leqslant P_o\left(\left|\mathcal{N}\left(0, \left\|\frac{\partial f(\theta_o)}{\partial \theta}\right\|^2\right)\right| \leqslant \tau\right)$$

where $\mathcal{N}(0, \|\frac{\partial f(\theta_o)}{\partial \theta}\|^2)$ is a scalar random variable drawn from a normal distribution with mean 0 and variance $\|\frac{\partial f(\theta_o)}{\partial \theta}\|^2$.

THEOREM 4.7. *[See Shen (1997).] In addition to the conditions to ensure $n^{1/2}(f(\hat{\theta}_n) - f(\theta_o)) \xrightarrow{\mathrm{P}_{\theta_o}} \mathcal{N}(0, \sigma_{v*}^2)$ with $\sigma_{v*}^2 = \|\frac{\partial f(\theta_o)}{\partial \theta}\|^2$, if LAN holds, then for the plug-in sieve MLE estimates of $f(\theta)$, any real number $\tau > 0$, and any g in the linear span of $\Theta - \theta_o$,*

$$n^{1/2}\big(f(\hat{\theta}_n) - f(\theta_{n,\tau})\big) \xrightarrow{\mathrm{P}_{\theta_{n,\tau}}} \mathcal{N}(0, \sigma_{v*}^2),$$

where $\theta_{n,\tau} = \theta_o + n^{-1/2}\tau g$. Here $\xrightarrow{\mathrm{P}_\theta}$ means convergence in distribution under probability measure P_θ.

4.3. Sieve simultaneous MD estimation: Normality and efficiency

As we mentioned in Section 2.1, most structural econometric models belong to the semiparametric conditional moment framework: $E[\rho(Z, \beta_o, h_o(\cdot))|X] = 0$, where the difference $\rho(Z, \beta, h(\cdot)) - \rho(Z, \beta_o, h_o(\cdot))$ does depend on the endogenous variables Y. There are even fewer general theory papers on the sieve simultaneous MD estimation of β_o and h_o for this class of models; see Newey and Powell (1989, 2003) and Ai and Chen (1999, 2003). The sieve simultaneous MD procedure jointly estimates β_o and h_o by minimizing a sample quadratic form $\frac{1}{n}\sum_{i=1}^{n} \hat{m}(X_i, \beta, h)'[\widehat{\Sigma}(X_i)]^{-1}\hat{m}(X_i, \beta, h)$ over the sieve parameter space $\Theta_n = B \times \mathcal{H}_n$, where $\hat{m}(X_i, \beta, h)$ is any nonparametric estimator of the conditional mean function $m(X, \beta, h) \equiv E[\rho(Z, \beta, h(\cdot))|X]$, $\widehat{\Sigma}(X) \to \Sigma(X)$ in probability and $\Sigma(X)$ is a positive definite weighting matrix. Ai and Chen (1999, 2003) established the $\sqrt{n}$-asymptotic normality of this sieve MD estimator $\hat{\beta}$ of β_o.

For semiparametric efficient estimation of β_o, Ai and Chen (1999) proposed the three-step optimally weighted sieve MD procedure:

Step 1. Obtain an initial consistent sieve MD estimator $\hat{\theta}_n = (\hat{\beta}_n, \hat{h}_n)$ by

$$\min_{\theta=(\beta,h)\in B\times\mathcal{H}_n} \frac{1}{n}\sum_{i=1}^{n} \hat{m}(X_i, \theta)'\hat{m}(X_i, \theta),$$

where $\hat{m}(X_i, \theta)$ is any nonparametric estimator of the conditional mean function $m(X, \theta) \equiv E[\rho(Z, \beta, h(\cdot))|X]$.

Step 2. Obtain a consistent estimator $\widehat{\Sigma}_o(X)$ of the optimal weighting matrix $\Sigma_o(X) \equiv \mathrm{Var}[\rho(Z, \beta_o, h_o(\cdot))|X]$ using $\hat{\theta}_n = (\hat{\beta}_n, \hat{h}_n)$ and any nonparametric regression procedures (such as kernel, nearest-neighbor or series LS estimation).

Step 3. Obtain the optimally weighted estimator $\tilde{\theta}_n = (\tilde{\beta}_n, \tilde{h}_n)$ by solving

$$\min_{\theta=(\beta,h)\in B\times\mathcal{H}_n} \frac{1}{n}\sum_{i=1}^{n} \hat{m}(X_i, \theta)'\big[\widehat{\Sigma}_o(X_i)\big]^{-1}\hat{m}(X_i, \theta).$$

As an alternative way to efficiently estimate β_o, Ai and Chen (2003) proposed the locally continuously updated sieve MD procedure:

Step 1. Obtain an initial consistent sieve MD estimator $\hat{\theta}_n$ by

$$\min_{\theta\in B\times\mathcal{H}_n} \sum_{i=1}^{n} \hat{m}(X_i, \theta)'\hat{m}(X_i, \theta),$$

where $\hat{m}(X_i, \theta)$ is the series LS estimator (2.15) of $m(X, \theta) \equiv E[\rho(Z, \beta, h(\cdot))|X]$.

Step 2. Obtain the optimally weighted sieve MD estimator $\tilde{\theta}_n = (\tilde{\beta}_n, \tilde{h}_n)$ by

$$\min_{\theta=(\beta,h)\in N_{on}} \frac{1}{n}\sum_{i=1}^{n} \hat{m}(X_i, \theta)'\big[\widehat{\Sigma}_o(X_i, \theta)\big]^{-1}\hat{m}(X_i, \theta),$$

where N_{on} is a shrinking neighborhood of $\theta_o = (\beta_o, h_o)$ within the sieve space $B \times \mathcal{H}_n$, and $\widehat{\Sigma}_o(X_i, \theta)$ is any nonparametric estimator of the conditional variance function $\Sigma_o(X, \theta) \equiv \mathrm{Var}[\rho(Z, \beta, h(\cdot))|X]$. To compute this Step 2 one could use $\hat{\theta}_n = (\hat{\beta}_n, \hat{h}_n)$ from Step 1 as a starting point.

While Ai and Chen (1999) consider kernel estimation of the conditional mean $m(\cdot, \theta)$ and the conditional variance $\Sigma_o(\cdot, \theta)$, Ai and Chen (2003) propose series LS estimation of $m(\cdot, \theta)$ and $\Sigma_o(\cdot, \theta)$. Let $\{p_{0j}(X), j = 1, 2, \ldots, k_{m,n}\}$ be a sequence of known basis functions that can approximate any real-valued square integrable functions of X well as $k_{m,n} \to \infty$, $p^{k_{m,n}}(X) = (p_{01}(X), \ldots, p_{0k_{m,n}}(X))'$ and $P = (p^{k_{m,n}}(X_1), \ldots, p^{k_{m,n}}(X_n))'$. Then a series LS estimator of the conditional variance $\Sigma_o(X, \theta) \equiv \mathrm{Var}[\rho(Z, \theta)|X]$ is

$$\widehat{\Sigma}_o(X, \theta) \equiv \sum_{i=1}^{n} \rho(Z_i, \theta)\rho(Z_i, \theta)' p^{k_{m,n}}(X_i)'(P'P)^{-1} p^{k_{m,n}}(X).$$

Also, $\Sigma_o(X) = \mathrm{Var}[\rho(Z, \theta_o)|X]$ can be simply estimated by $\widehat{\Sigma}_o(X) \equiv \widehat{\Sigma}_o(X, \hat{\theta}_n)$.

We state the following result on semiparametric efficient estimation of β_o for the class of conditional moment restrictions $E[\rho(Z, \beta_o, h_o(\cdot))|X] = 0$; see Ai and Chen (2003) for details. For $j = 1, \ldots, d_\beta$, let

$$\begin{aligned} D_{w_j}(X) &\equiv \left.\frac{\partial E\{\rho(Z, \beta, h_o(\cdot))|X\}}{\partial \beta_j}\right|_{\beta=\beta_o} - \left.\frac{\partial E\{\rho(X, \beta_o, h_o(\cdot) + \tau w_j(\cdot))|X\}}{\partial \tau}\right|_{\tau=0} \\ &\equiv \frac{\partial m(X, \theta_o)}{\partial \beta_j} - \frac{\partial m(X, \theta_o)}{\partial h}[w_j], \end{aligned}$$

$$E\big\{D_{w_{oj}}(X)'\Sigma_o(X)^{-1}D_{w_{oj}}(X)\big\} = \inf_{w_j} E\big\{D_{w_j}(X)'\Sigma_o(X)^{-1}D_{w_j}(X)\big\},$$

$w_o = (w_{o1}, \ldots, w_{od_\beta})$, and $D_{w_o}(X) \equiv (D_{w_{o1}}(X), \ldots, D_{w_{od_\beta}}(X))$ be a $(d_\rho \times d_\beta)$-matrix valued measurable function of X.

THEOREM 4.8. *Let $\tilde{\beta}_n$ be either the three-step optimally weighted sieve MD estimator or the two-step locally continuously updated sieve MD estimator. Under the conditions stated in Ai and Chen* (2003, *Theorems* 6.1 *and* 6.2), *$\tilde{\beta}_n$ is semiparametric efficient and satisfies $\sqrt{n}(\tilde{\beta}_n - \beta_o) \xrightarrow{d} \mathcal{N}(0, V_o^{-1})$, with*

$$V_o = E\big[D_{w_o}(X)'\big[\Sigma_o(X)\big]^{-1}D_{w_o}(X)\big].$$

Ai and Chen (2003) also provide a simple consistent estimator, $\widehat{V}_o^{-1}$, for the asymptotic variance V_o^{-1} of $\tilde{\beta}_n$, where

$$\begin{aligned} \widehat{V}_o &= \frac{1}{n}\sum_{i=1}^{n}\left(\frac{\partial \hat{m}(X_i, \tilde{\theta}_n)}{\partial \beta'} - \frac{\partial \hat{m}(X_i, \tilde{\theta}_n)}{\partial h}[\hat{w}_o]\right)' \\ &\quad \times \big\{\widehat{\Sigma}_o(X_i)\big\}^{-1}\left(\frac{\partial \hat{m}(X_i, \tilde{\theta}_n)}{\partial \beta'} - \frac{\partial \hat{m}(X_i, \tilde{\theta}_n)}{\partial h}[\hat{w}_o]\right), \end{aligned}$$

$\hat{w}_o = (\hat{w}_{o1}, \ldots, \hat{w}_{od_\beta})$ solves the following sieve minimization problem:

$$\min_{w_j \in \mathcal{H}_n} \sum_{i=1}^{n} \left(\frac{\partial \hat{m}(X_i, \tilde{\theta}_n)}{\partial \beta_j} - \frac{\partial \hat{m}(X_i, \tilde{\theta}_n)}{\partial h}[w_j] \right)' \left[\widehat{\Sigma}_o(X_i) \right]^{-1} \times \left(\frac{\partial \hat{m}(X_i, \tilde{\theta}_n)}{\partial \beta_j} - \frac{\partial \hat{m}(X_i, \tilde{\theta}_n)}{\partial h}[w_j] \right)$$

for $j = 1, \ldots, d_\beta$, and

$$\frac{\partial \hat{m}(X, \theta)}{\partial \beta_j} - \frac{\partial \hat{m}(X, \theta)}{\partial h}[w_j] \equiv \sum_{i=1}^{n} \left(\frac{\partial \rho(Z_i, \theta)}{\partial \beta_j} - \frac{\partial \rho(Z_i, \theta)}{\partial h}[w_j] \right) p^{k_{m,n}}(X_i)'(P'P)^{-1} p^{k_{m,n}}(X).$$

REMARK 4.3. (1) Recently, Chen and Pouzo (2006) have extended the root-n normality and efficiency results of Ai and Chen (2003) to allow that the generalized residual functions $\rho(Z, \beta, h(\cdot))$ are not pointwise continuous in $\theta = (\beta, h)$.

(2) The three-step optimally weighted sieve MD leads to semiparametric efficient estimation of β_o for the model $E[\rho(Z, \beta_o, h_o(\cdot))|X] = 0$ regardless of whether $\rho(Z, \beta, h(\cdot)) - \rho(Z, \beta_o, h_o(\cdot))$ depends on the endogenous variables Y or not. However, when $\rho(Z, \beta, h(\cdot)) - \rho(Z, \beta_o, h_o(\cdot))$ does not depend on Y, to obtain an efficient estimator of β_o one can also apply the following simpler three-step sieve GLS procedure as suggested in Ai and Chen (1999):

Step 1. Obtain an initial consistent sieve GLS estimator $\hat{\theta}_n = (\hat{\beta}_n, \hat{h}_n)$ by

$$\min_{(\beta,h) \in B \times \mathcal{H}_n} \frac{1}{n} \sum_{i=1}^{n} \rho(Z_i, \beta, h(\cdot))' \rho(Z_i, \beta, h(\cdot)).$$

Step 2. Obtain a consistent estimator $\widehat{\Sigma}_o(X)$ of $\Sigma_o(X) = \mathrm{Var}[\rho(Z, \theta_o)|X]$ using $\hat{\theta}_n = (\hat{\beta}_n, \hat{h}_n)$ and any nonparametric regression procedures such as $\widehat{\Sigma}_o(X) = \widehat{\Sigma}_o(X, \hat{\theta}_n)$.

Step 3. Obtain the optimally weighted GLS estimator $\tilde{\theta}_n = (\tilde{\beta}_n, \tilde{h}_n)$ by solving

$$\min_{(\beta,h) \in B \times \mathcal{H}_n} \frac{1}{n} \sum_{i=1}^{n} \rho(Z_i, \beta, h(\cdot))' \left[\widehat{\Sigma}_o(X_i) \right]^{-1} \rho(Z_i, \beta, h(\cdot)).$$

That is, for all the models belonging to the first subclass of the conditional moment restrictions (2.8), $E\{\rho(Z, \beta_o, h_o)|X\} = 0$, where $\rho(Z, \theta) - \rho(Z, \theta_o)$ does not depend on endogenous variables Y, the simple three-step sieve GLS estimator $\tilde{\beta}_n$ also satisfies $\sqrt{n}(\tilde{\beta}_n - \beta_o) \xrightarrow{d} \mathcal{N}(0, V_o^{-1})$. Of course, the following continuously updated sieve GLS procedure will also lead to semiparametric efficient estimation of β_o:

$$(\tilde{\beta}_{\text{cgls}}, \tilde{h}_{\text{cgls}}) = \arg \min_{(\beta,h)\in B\times\mathcal{H}_n} \frac{1}{n}\sum_{i=1}^{n} \rho(Z_i, \beta, h(\cdot))'\big[\widehat{\Sigma}_o(X_i, \beta, h(\cdot))\big]^{-1}\rho(Z_i, \beta, h(\cdot)).$$

For the conditional moment restriction (without unknown function h_o), $E[\rho(Z, \beta_o)|X] = 0$, there are many alternative efficient estimation procedures for β_o, including the empirical likelihood of Donald, Imbens and Newey (2003), the generalized empirical likelihood (GEL) of Newey and Smith (2004), the kernel-based empirical likelihood of Kitamura, Tripathi and Ahn (2004), the continuously updated minimum distance procedure or the Euclidean conditional empirical likelihood of Antoine, Bonnal and Renault (2007), among others. It seems that one could extend their results to the more general conditional moment framework $E[\rho(Z, \beta_o, h_o())|X] = 0$, where the unknown function $h_o()$ is approximated by a sieve. In fact, Zhang and Gijbels (2003) have already considered the sieve empirical likelihood procedure for the special case $E[\rho(Z, \beta_o, h_o(X))|X] = 0$ where h_o is a function of conditioning variable X only; See Otsu (2005) for the general case.

Recently Ai and Chen (2007, 2004) have considered the semiparametric conditional moment framework $E[\rho_j(Z, \beta_o, h_o())|X_j] = 0$ for $j = 1, \ldots, J$ with finite J, where each conditional moment has its own conditioning set X_j that could differ across equations. This extension would be useful to estimating semiparametric structure models with incomplete information.

5. Concluding remarks

In this chapter, we have surveyed some recent large sample results on nonparametric and semiparametric estimation of econometric models via the method of sieves. We have restricted our attention to general consistency and convergence rates of sieve estimation of unknown functions and $\sqrt{n}$-asymptotic normality of sieve estimation of smooth functionals. Examples were used to illustrate the general sieve estimation theory. It is our hope that the examples adequately depicted the general sieve extremum estimation approach and its versatility. We conclude this chapter by pointing out additional topics on the method of sieves that have not been reviewed for lack of time and space.

First, although there is still lack of general theory on testing via the sieve method, there are some consistent specification tests using the method of sieves. For example, Hong and White (1995) tested a parametric regression model using series LS estimators; Hart (1997) presented many consistent tests using series estimators; Stinchcombe and White (1998) tested a parametric conditional moment restriction $E[\rho(Z, \beta_o)|X] = 0$ using neural network sieves and Li, Hsiao and Zinn (2003) tested semiparametric/nonparametric regression models using spline series estimators. Most recently Song (2005) proposed consistent tests of semi-nonparametric regression models via conditional martingale transforms where the unknown functions are estimated by the method of sieves. Additional references include Wooldridge (1992), Bierens (1990), Bierens and Ploberger (1997) and de Jong (1996). Also in principle, all of the existing test results based on kernel or local linear regression methods such as those in Robinson (1989), Fan and Li (1996), Lavergne and Vuong (1996), Chen and Fan (1999), Fan and Linton (1999), Aït-Sahalia, Bickel and Stoker (2001), Horowitz and Spokoiny (2001) and Fan, Zhang and Zhang (2001) can be done using the method of sieves.

Second, we have not touched on the issue of data-driven selection of sieve spaces. In practice, many existing model selection methods such as cross-validation (CV), generalized CV and AIC have been used in the current context due to the connection of the method of sieves with the parametric models; see the survey chapter by Ichimura and Todd (2007) on implementation details of semi-nonparametric estimators including series estimators, and the review by Stone et al. (1997) and Ruppert, Wand and Carroll (2003) on model selection with spline sieves for extended linear models. There are a few papers in statistics including Barron, Birgé and Massart (1999) and Shen and Ye (2002) that address data-driven selection among different sieve bases. There are many results on data-driven selection of the number of terms for a given sieve basis; see e.g. Li (1987), Andrews (1991a), Hurvich, Simonoff and Tsai (1998), Donald and Newey (2001), Coppejans and Gallant (2002), Phillips and Ploberger (2003), Fan and Peng (2004) and Imbens, Newey and Ridder (2005). In particular, Andrews (1991a) establishes the asymptotic optimality of CV as a method to select series terms for nonparametric least square regressions with heteroskedastic errors. Imbens, Newey and Ridder (2005) establishes a similar result for semiparametrically efficient estimation of average treatment effect parameters with a first step series estimation of conditional means. It would be very useful to extend their results to handle a more general class of semi-nonparametric models estimated via the method of sieves.

Third, so far there is little research on the higher order refinements of the large sample properties of the semiparametric efficient sieve estimators. Many authors, including Linton (1995) and Heckman et al. (1998), have pointed out that the first-order asymptotics of semiparametric procedures could be misleading and unhelpful. For the case of kernel estimators, some papers such as Robinson (1995), Linton (1995, 2001), Nishiyama and Robinson (2000, 2005), Xiao and Linton (2001) and Ichimura and Linton (2002) have obtained higher order refinements. It would be useful to extend these results to semiparametric efficient estimators using the method of sieves.

Finally, given the relative ease of implementation of the sieve method, but the general difficulty of deriving its large sample properties, it might be fruitful to combine the sieve method with the kernel or the local linear regression methods [see e.g. Fan and Gijbels (1996)]. Recent papers by Horowitz and Mammen (2004) and Horowitz and Lee (2005) have demonstrated the usefulness of this combination.

References

Ai, C. (1997). "A semiparametric maximum likelihood estimator". Econometrica 65, 933–964.

Ai, C., Chen, X. (2003). "Efficient estimation of models with conditional moment restrictions containing unknown functions". Econometrica 71, 1795–1843. Working paper version, 1999.

Ai, C., Chen, X. (1999). "Efficient sieve minimum distance estimation of semiparametric conditional moment models". Manuscript. London School of Economics.
Ai, C., Chen, X. (2004). "On efficient sequential estimation of semi-nonparametric moment models". Working paper. New York University.
Ai, C., Chen, X. (2007). "Estimation of possibly misspecified semiparametric conditional moment restriction models with different conditioning variables". Journal of Econometrics. In press.
Aït-Sahalia, Y., Bickel, P., Stoker, T. (2001). "Goodness-of-fit tests for kernel regression with an application to option implied volatilities". Journal of Econometrics 105, 363–412.
Amemiya, T. (1985). Advanced Econometrics. Harvard University Press, Cambridge.
Anastassiou, G., Yu, X. (1992a). "Monotone and probabilistic wavelet approximation". Stochastic Analysis and Applications 10, 251–264.
Anastassiou, G., Yu, X. (1992b). "Convex and convex-probabilistic wavelet approximation". Stochastic Analysis and Applications 10, 507–521.
Andrews, D. (1991a). "Asymptotic optimality of generalized C_L, cross-validation, and generalized cross-validation in regression with heteroskedastic errors". Journal of Econometrics 47, 359–377.
Andrews, D. (1991b). "Asymptotic normality of series estimators for nonparametric and semiparametric regression models". Econometrica 59, 307–345.
Andrews, D. (1992). "Generic uniform convergence". Econometric Theory, 241–257.
Andrews, D. (1994a). "Empirical process method in econometrics". In: Engle III, R.F., McFadden, D.F. (Eds.), Handbook of Econometrics, vol. 4. North-Holland, Amsterdam.
Andrews, D. (1994b). "Asymptotics for semi-parametric econometric models via stochastic equicontinuity". Econometrica 62, 43–72.
Andrews, D., Schafgans, M. (1998). "Semiparametric estimation of the intercept of a sample selection model". Review of Economic Studies 65, 497–517.
Andrews, D., Whang, Y. (1990). "Additive interactive regression models: Circumvention of the curse of dimensionality". Econometric Theory 6, 466–479.
Antoine, B., Bonnal, H., Renault, E. (2007). "On the efficient use of the informational content of estimating equations: Implied probabilities and Euclidean empirical likelihood". Journal of Econometrics 138, 488–512.
Bahadur, R.R. (1964). "On Fisher's bound for asymptotic variances". Ann. Math. Statist. 35, 1545–1552.
Bansal, R., Viswanathan, S. (1993). "No arbitrage and arbitrage pricing: A new approach". The Journal of Finance 48 (4), 1231–1262.
Bansal, R., Hsieh, D., Viswanathan, S. (1993). "A new approach to international arbitrage pricing". The Journal of Finance 48, 1719–1747.
Barnett, W.A., Powell, J., Tauchen, G. (1991). Non-parametric and Semi-parametric Methods in Econometrics and Statistics. Cambridge University Press, New York.
Barron, A.R. (1993). "Universal approximation bounds for superpositions of a sigmoidal function". IEEE Trans. Information Theory 39, 930–945.
Barron, A., Birgé, L., Massart, P. (1999). "Risk bounds for model selection via penalization". Probab. Theory Related Fields 113, 301–413.
Begun, J., Hall, W., Huang, W., Wellner, J.A. (1983). "Information and asymptotic efficiency in parametric-nonparametric models". The Annals of Statistics 11, 432–452.
Bickel, P.J., Klaassen, C.A.J., Ritov, Y., Wellner, J.A. (1993). Efficient and Adaptive Estimation for Semiparametric Models. The John Hopkins University Press, Baltimore.
Bierens, H. (1990). "A consistent conditional moment test of functional form". Econometrica 58, 1443–1458.
Bierens, H. (2006). "Semi-nonparametric interval-censored mixed proportional hazard models: Identification and consistency results". Econometric Theory. In press.
Bierens, H., Carvalho, J. (2006). "Semi-nonparametric competing risks analysis of recidivism". Journal of Applied Econometrics. In press.
Bierens, H., Ploberger, W. (1997). "Asymptotic theory of integrated conditional moment tests". Econometrica 65, 1129–1151.

Birgé, L., Massart, P. (1998). "Minimum contrast estimators on sieves: Exponential bounds and rates of convergence". Bernoulli 4, 329–375.

Birman, M., Solomjak, M. (1967). "Piece-wise polynomial approximations of functions in the class W_p^α". Mathematics of the USSR Sbornik 73, 295–317.

Blundell, R., Powell, J. (2003). "Endogeneity in nonparametric and semiparametric regression models". In: Dewatripont, M., Hansen, L.P., Turnovsky, S. (Eds.), Advances in Economics and Econometrics: Theory and Applications, vol. 2. Cambridge University Press, Cambridge, pp. 312–357.

Blundell, R., Browning, M., Crawford, I. (2003). "Non-parametric Engel curves and revealed preference". Econometrica 71, 205–240.

Blundell, R., Chen, X., Kristensen, D. (2007). "Semi-nonparametric IV estimation of shape-invariant Engel curves". Econometrica. In press.

Blundell, R., Duncan, A., Pendakur, K. (1998). "Semiparametric estimation and consumer demand". Journal of Applied Econometrics 13, 435–461.

Brendstrup, B., Paarsch, H. (2004). "Identification and estimation in sequential, asymmetric, English auctions". Manuscript, University of Iowa.

Cai, Z., Fan, J., Yao, Q. (2000). "Functional-coefficient regression models for nonlinear time series". Journal of American Statistical Association 95, 941–956.

Cameron, S., Heckman, J. (1998). "Life cycle schooling and dynamic selection bias". Journal of Political Economy 106, 262–333.

Campbell, J., Cochrane, J. (1999). "By force of habit: A consumption-based explanation of aggregate stock market behavior". Journal of Political Economy 107, 205–251.

Carrasco, M., Florens, J.-P., Renault, E. (2006). "Linear inverse problems in structural econometrics estimation based on spectral decomposition and regularization". In: Heckman, J.J., Leamer, E.E. (Eds.), Handbook of Econometrics, vol. 6. North-Holland, Amsterdam.

Chamberlain, G. (1992). "Efficiency bounds for semiparametric regression". Econometrica 60, 567–596.

Chapman, D. (1997). "Approximating the asset pricing kernel". The Journal of Finance 52 (4), 1383–1410.

Chen, X., Conley, T. (2001). "A new semiparametric spatial model for panel time series". Journal of Econometrics 105, 59–83.

Chen, X., Fan, Y. (1999). "Consistent hypothesis testing in semiparametric and nonparametric models for econometric time series". Journal of Econometrics 91, 373–401.

Chen, X., Ludvigson, S. (2003). "Land of addicts? An empirical investigation of habit-based asset pricing models". Manuscript. New York University.

Chen, X., Pouzo, D. (2006). "Efficient estimation of semi-nonparametric conditional moment models with possibly nonsmooth moments". Manuscript. New York University.

Chen, X., Shen, X. (1996). "Asymptotic properties of sieve extremum estimates for weakly dependent data with applications". Manuscript. University of Chicago.

Chen, X., Shen, X. (1998). "Sieve extremum estimates for weakly dependent data". Econometrica 66, 289–314.

Chen, R., Tsay, R. (1993). "Functional-coefficient autoregressive models". Journal of American Statistical Association 88, 298–308.

Chen, X., White, H. (1998). "Nonparametric adaptive learning with feedback". Journal of Economic Theory 82, 190–222.

Chen, X., White, H. (1999). "Improved rates and asymptotic normality for nonparametric neural network estimators". IEEE Tran. Information Theory 45, 682–691.

Chen, X., White, H. (2002). "Asymptotic properties of some projection-based Robbins–Monro procedures in a Hilbert space". Studies in Nonlinear Dynamics and Econometrics 6 (1). Article 1.

Chen, X., Fan, Y., Tsyrennikov, V. (2006). "Efficient estimation of semiparametric multivariate copula models". Journal of the American Statistical Association 101, 1228–1240.

Chen, X., Hansen, L.P., Scheinkman, J. (1998). "Shape-preserving estimation of diffusions". Manuscript. University of Chicago.

Chen, X., Hong, H., Tamer, E. (2005). "Measurement error models with auxiliary data". Review of Economic Studies 72, 343–366.

Chen, X., Hong, H., Tarozzi, A. (2007). "Semiparametric efficiency in GMM models of nonclassical measurement errors, missing data and treatment effects". The Annals of Statistics. In press.
Chen, X., Linton, O., van Keilegom, I. (2003). "Estimation of semiparametric models when the criterion function is not smooth". Econometrica 71, 1591–1608.
Chen, X., Racine, J., Swanson, N. (2001). "Semiparametric ARX neural network models with an application to forecasting inflation". IEEE Tran. Neural Networks 12, 674–683.
Chernozhukov, V., Imbens, G., Newey, W. (2007). "Instrumental variable identification and estimation of nonseparable models via quantile conditions". Journal of Econometrics 139, 4–14.
Chui, C. (1992). An Introduction to Wavelets. Academic Press, Inc., San Diego.
Cochrane, J. (2001). Asset Pricing. Princeton University Press, Princeton, NJ.
Constantinides, G. (1990). "Habit-formation: A resolution of the equity premium puzzle". Journal of Political Economy 98, 519–543.
Coppejans, M. (2001). "Estimation of the binary response model using a mixture of distributions estimator (MOD)". Journal of Econometrics 102, 231–261.
Coppejans, M., Gallant, A.R. (2002). "Cross-validated SNP density estimates". Journal of Econometrics 110, 27–65.
Cosslett, S. (1983). "Distribution-free maximum likelihood estimation of the binary choice model". Econometrica 51, 765–782.
Cybenko, G. (1990). "Approximation by superpositions of a sigmoid function". Mathematics of Control, Signals and Systems 2, 303–314.
Darolles, S., Florens, J.-P., Renault, E. (2002). "Nonparametric instrumental regression". Mimeo. GREMAQ, University of Toulouse.
Das, M., Newey, W.K., Vella, F. (2003). "Nonparametric estimation of sample selection models". Review of Economic Studies 70, 33–58.
Daubechies, I. (1992). Ten Lectures on Wavelets. SIAM, Philadelphia.
de Boor, C. (1978). A Practical Guide to Splines. Springer-Verlag, New York.
Dechevsky, L., Penev, S. (1997). "On shape-preserving probabilistic wavelet approximators". Stochastic Analysis and Applications 15, 187–215.
de Jong, R. (1996). "The Bierens test under data dependence". Journal of Econometrics 72, 1–32.
de Jong, R. (2002). "A note on 'Convergence rates and asymptotic normality for series estimators': Uniform convergence rates". Journal of Econometrics 111, 1–9.
DeVore, R.A. (1977a). "Monotone approximation by splines". SIAM Journal on Mathematical Analysis 8, 891–905.
DeVore, R.A. (1977b). "Monotone approximation by polynomials". SIAM Journal on Mathematical Analysis 8, 906–921.
DeVore, R.A., Lorentz, G.G. (1993). Constructive Approximation. Springer-Verlag, Berlin.
Donald, S., Newey, W. (2001). "Choosing the number of instruments". Econometrica 69, 1161–1191.
Donald, S., Imbens, G., Newey, W. (2003). "Empirical likelihood estimation and consistent tests with conditional moment restrictions". Journal of Econometrics 117, 55–93.
Donoho, D.L., Johnstone, I.M., Kerkyacharian, G., Picard, D. (1995). "Wavelet shrinkage: Asymptopia?". Journal of the Royal Statistical Society, Series B 57, 301–369.
Doukhan, P., Massart, P., Rio, E. (1995). "Invariance principles for absolutely regular empirical processes". Ann. Inst. Henri Poincaré – Probabilités et Statistiques 31, 393–427.
Duncan, G.M. (1986). "A semiparametric censored regression estimator". Journal of Econometrics 32, 5–34.
Eggermont, P., LaRiccia, V. (2001). Maximum Penalized Likelihood Estimation, Volume I: Density Estimation. Springer, New York.
Eichenbaum, M., Hansen, L.P. (1990). "Estimating models with intertemporal substitution using aggregate time series data". Journal of Business and Economic Statistics 8, 53–69.
Elbadawi, I., Gallant, A.R., Souza, G. (1983). "An elasticity can be estimated consistently without a prior knowledge of functional form". Econometrica 51, 1731–1751.
Engle, R., Gonzalez-Rivera, G. (1991). "Semiparametric ARCH models". Journal of Business and Economic Statistics 9, 345–359.

Engle, R.F., McFadden, D.L. (Eds.) (1994). Handbook of Econometrics, vol. 4. North-Holland, Amsterdam.

Engle, R., Rangel, G. (2004). "The spline GARCH model for unconditional volatility and its global macroeconomic causes". Working paper. New York University.

Engle, R., Granger, C., Rice, J., Weiss, A. (1986). "Semiparametric estimates of the relation between weather and electricity sales". Journal of the American Statistical Association 81, 310–320.

Fan, J., Gijbels, I. (1996). Local Polynomial Modelling and Its Applications. Chapman and Hall, London.

Fan, Y., Li, Q. (1996). "Consistent model specification tests: Omitted variables, parametric and semiparametric functional forms". Econometrica 64, 865–890.

Fan, Y., Linton, O. (1999). "Some higher order theory for a consistent nonparametric model specification test". Working paper LSE.

Fan, J., Peng, H. (2004). "On non-concave penalized likelihood with diverging number of parameters". The Annals of Statistics 32, 928–961.

Fan, J., Yao, Q. (2003). Nonlinear Time Series: Nonparametric and Parametric Methods. Springer-Verlag, New York.

Fan, J., Zhang, C., Zhang, J. (2001). "Generalized likelihood ratio statistics and Wilks phenomenon". The Annals of Statistics 29, 153–193.

Flinn, C., Heckman, J. (1982). "New methods for analyzing structural models of labor force dynamics". Journal of Econometrics 18, 115–168.

Florens, J.P. (2003). "Inverse problems and structural econometrics: The example of instrumental variables". In: Dewatripont, M., Hansen, L.P., Turnovsky, S. (Eds.), Advances in Economics and Econometrics: Theory and Applications, vol. 2. Cambridge University Press, Cambridge, pp. 284–311.

Gabushin, O. (1967). "Inequalities for norms of functions and their derivatives in the L_p metric". Matematicheskie Zametki 1, 291–298.

Gallant, A.R. (1987). "Identification and consistency in seminonparametric regression". In: Bewley, T.F. (Ed.), Advances in Econometrics, vol. I. Cambridge University Press, pp. 145–170.

Gallant, A.R., Nychka, D. (1987). "Semi-non-parametric maximum likelihood estimation". Econometrica 55, 363–390.

Gallant, A.R., Souza, G. (1991). "On the asymptotic normality of Fourier flexible form estimates". Journal of Econometrics 50, 329–353.

Gallant, A.R., Tauchen, G. (1989). "Semiparametric estimation of conditional constrained heterogenous processes: Asset pricing applications". Econometrica 57, 1091–1120.

Gallant, A.R., Tauchen, G. (1996). "Which moments to match?". Econometric Theory 12, 657–681.

Gallant, A.R., Tauchen, G. (2004). "EMM: A program for efficient method of moments estimation, Version 2.0 User's Guide". Working paper. Duke University.

Gallant, A.R., White, H. (1988a). "There exists a neural network that does not make avoidable mistakes". In: Proceedings of the IEEE 1988 International Conference on Neural Networks, vol. 1. IEEE, New York, pp. 657–664.

Gallant, A.R., White, H. (1988b). A Unified Theory of Estimation and Inference for Nonlinear Dynamic Models. Basil Blackwell, Oxford.

Gallant, A.R., White, H. (1992). "On learning the derivatives of an unknown mapping with multilayer feedforward networks". Neural Networks 5, 129–138.

Gallant, A.R., Hsieh, D., Tauchen, G. (1991). "On fitting a recalcitrant series: The pound/dollar exchange rate, 1974–83". In: Barnett, W.A., Powell, J., Tauchen, G. (Eds.), Non-parametric and Semi-parametric Methods in Econometrics and Statistics. Cambridge University Press, Cambridge, pp. 199–240.

Geman, S., Hwang, C. (1982). "Nonparametric maximum likelihood estimation by the method of sieves". The Annals of Statistics 10, 401–414.

Girosi, F. (1994). "Regularization theory, radial basis functions and networks". In: Cherkassky, V., Friedman, J.H., Wechsler, H. (Eds.), From Statistics to Neural Networks. Theory and Pattern Recognition Applications. Springer-Verlag, Berlin.

Granger, C.W.J., Teräsvirta, T. (1993). Modelling Nonlinear Economic Relationships. Oxford University Press, New York.

Grenander, U. (1981). Abstract Inference. Wiley Series, New York.
Härdle, W., Linton, O. (1994). "Applied nonparametric methods". In: Engle III, R.F., McFadden, D.F. (Eds.), Handbook of Econometrics, vol. 4. North-Holland, Amsterdam.
Härdle, W., Mueller, M., Sperlich, S., Werwatz, A. (2004). Nonparametric and Semiparametric Models. Springer, New York.
Hahn, J. (1998). "On the role of the propensity score in efficient semiparametric estimation of average treatment effects". Econometrica 66, 315–332.
Hall, P., Horowitz, J. (2005). "Nonparametric methods for inference in the presence of instrumental variables". The Annals of Statistics 33, 2904–2929.
Hansen, L.P. (1982). "Large sample properties of generalized method of moments estimators". Econometrica 50, 1029–1054.
Hansen, L.P. (1985). "A method for calculating bounds on the asymptotic covariance matrices of generalized method of moments estimators". Journal of Econometrics 30, 203–238.
Hansen, M.H. (1994). "Extended linear models, multivariate splines, and ANOVA". PhD Dissertation. Department of Statistics, University of California at Berkeley.
Hansen, L.P., Richard, S. (1987). "The role of conditioning information in deducing testable restrictions implied by dynamic asset pricing models". Econometrica 55, 587–613.
Hansen, L.P., Singleton, K. (1982). "Generalized instrumental variables estimation of nonlinear rational expectations models". Econometrica 50, 1269–1286.
Hart, J. (1997). Nonparametric Smoothing and Lack-of-Fit Tests. Springer-Verlag, New York.
Hausman, J., Newey, W. (1995). "Nonparametric estimation of exact consumer surplus and deadweight loss". Econometrica 63, 1445–1467.
Heckman, J. (1979). "Sample selection bias as a specification error". Econometrica 47, 153–161.
Heckman, J., Singer, B. (1984). "A method for minimizing the impact of distributional assumptions in econometric models for duration data". Econometrica 68, 839–874.
Heckman, J., Willis, R. (1977). "A beta logistic model for the analysis of sequential labor force participation of married women". Journal of Political Economy 85, 27–58.
Heckman, J., Ichimura, H., Smith, J., Todd, P. (1998). "Characterization of selection bias using experimental data". Econometrica 66, 1017–1098.
Hirano, K., Imbens, G., Ridder, G. (2003). "Efficient estimation of average treatment effects using the estimated propensity score". Econometrica 71, 1161–1189.
Hong, Y., White, H. (1995). "Consistent specification testing via nonparametric series regression". Econometrica 63, 1133–1159.
Honoré, B. (1990). "Simple estimation of a duration model with unobserved heterogeneity". Econometrica 58, 453–473.
Honoré, B. (1994). "A note on the rate of convergence of estimators of mixtures of Weibulls". Manuscript. Northwestern University.
Honoré, B., Kyriazidou, E. (2000). "Panel data discrete choice models with lagged dependent variables". Econometrica 68, 839–874.
Hornik, K., Stinchcombe, M., White, H. (1989). "Multilayer feedforward networks are universal approximators". Neural Networks 2, 359–366.
Hornik, K., Stinchcombe, M., White, H., Auer, P. (1994). "Degree of approximation results for feedforward networks approximating unknown mappings and their derivatives". Neural Computation 6, 1262–1275.
Horowitz, J. (1992). "A smoothed maximum score estimator for the binary response model". Econometrica 60, 505–531.
Horowitz, J. (1998). Semiparametric Methods in Econometrics. Springer-Verlag, New York.
Horowitz, J., Lee, S. (2005). "Nonparametric estimation of an additive quantile regression model". Journal of the American Statistical Association 100, 1238–1249.
Horowitz, J., Lee, S. (2007). "Nonparametric instrumental variables estimation of a quantile regression model". Econometrica 75, 1191–1208.
Horowitz, J., Mammen, E. (2004). "Nonparametric estimation of an additive model with a link function". The Annals of Statistics 32, 2412–2443.

Horowitz, J., Spokoiny, V. (2001). "An adaptive, rate-optimal test of a parametric mean-regression model against a nonparametric alternative". Econometrica 69, 599–631.
Hu, Y., Schennach, S. (2006). "Identification and estimation of nonclassical nonlinear errors-in-variables models with continuous distributions using instruments". Working paper. University of Texas, Austin.
Huang, J.Z. (1998a). "Projection estimation in multiple regression with application to functional ANOVA models". The Annals of Statistics 26, 242–272.
Huang, J.Z. (1998b). "Functional ANOVA models for generalized regression". Journal of Multivariate Analysis 67, 49–71.
Huang, J.Z. (2001). "Concave extended linear modeling: A theoretical synthesis". Statistica Sinica 11, 173–197.
Huang, J.Z. (2003). "Local asymptotics for polynomial spline regression". The Annals of Statistics 31, 1600–1635.
Huang, J.Z., Kooperberg, C., Stone, C.J., Truong, Y.K. (2000). "Functional ANOVA modeling for proportional hazards regression". The Annals of Statistics 28, 960–999.
Hurvich, C., Simonoff, J., Tsai, C. (1998). "Smoothing parameter selection in nonparametric regression using an improved Akaike information criterion". Journal of the Royal Statistical Society, Series B 60, 271–293.
Hutchinson, J., Lo, A., Poggio, T. (1994). "A non-parametric approach to pricing and hedging derivative securities via learning networks". The Journal of Finance 3, 851–889.
Ibragimov, I.A., Hasminskii, R.Z. (1991). "Asymptotically normal families of distributions and efficient estimation". The Annals of Statistics 19, 1681–1724.
Ichimura, H. (1993). "Semiparametric least squares (SLS), and weighted SLS estimation of single index models". Journal of Econometrics 58, 71–120.
Ichimura, H., Lee, S. (2006). "Characterization of the asymptotic distribution of semiparametric M-estimators". Manuscript. UCL.
Ichimura, H., Linton, O. (2002). "Asymptotic expansions for some semiparametric program evaluation estimators". Working paper IFS and LSE.
Ichimura, H., Todd, P. (2007). "Implementing nonparametric and semiparametric estimators". In: Heckman, J.J., Leamer, E. (Eds.), Handbook of Econometrics, vol. 6B. Elsevier. Chapter 74.
Imbens, G., Newey, W., Ridder, G. (2005). "Mean-squared-error calculations for average treatment effects". Manuscript. UC Berkeley.
Ishwaran, H. (1996a). "Identification and rates of estimation for scale parameters in location mixture models". The Annals of Statistics 24, 1560–1571.
Ishwaran, H. (1996b). "Uniform rates of estimation in the semiparametric Weibull mixture models". The Annals of Statistics 24, 1572–1585.
Jovanovic, B. (1979). "Job matching and the theory of turnover". Journal of Political Economy 87, 972–990.
Judd, K. (1998). Numerical Method in Economics. MIT University Press.
Khan, S. (2005). "An alternative approach to semiparametric estimation of heteroskedastic binary response models". Manuscript. University of Rochester.
Kim, J., Pollard, D. (1990). "Cube root asymptotics". The Annals of Statistics 18, 191–219.
Kitamura, Y., Tripathi, G., Ahn, H. (2004). "Empirical likelihood-based inference in conditional moment restriction models". Econometrica 72, 1667–1714.
Klein, R., Spady, R. (1993). "An efficient semiparametric estimator for binary response models". Econometrica 61, 387–421.
Koenker, R., Bassett, G. (1978). "Regression quantiles". Econometrica 46, 33–50.
Koenker, R., Mizera, I. (2003). "Penalized triograms: Total variation regularization for bivariate smoothing". Journal of the Royal Statistical Society, Series B 66, 145–163.
Koenker, R., Ng, P., Portnoy, S. (1994). "Quantile smoothing splines". Biometrika 81, 673–680.
Kooperberg, C., Stone, C.J., Truong, Y.K. (1995a). "Hazard regression". Journal of the American Statistical Association 90, 78–94.
Kooperberg, C., Stone, C.J., Truong, Y.K. (1995b). "Rate of convergence for logspline spectral density estimation". Journal of Time Series Analysis 16, 389–401.

Lavergne, P., Vuong, Q. (1996). "Nonparametric selection of regressors: The nonnested case". Econometrica 64, 207–219.
LeCam, L. (1960). "Local asymptotically normal families of distributions". Univ. California Publications in Statist. 3, 37–98.
Lee, S. (2003). "Efficient semiparametric estimation of a partially linear quantile regression model". Econometric Theory 19, 1–31.
Li, K. (1987). "Asymptotic optimality for C_p, C_L cross-validation, and generalized cross-validation: Discrete index set". The Annals of Statistics 15, 958–975.
Li, Q., Racine, J. (2007). Nonparametric Econometrics Theory and Practice. Princeton University Press. In press.
Li, Q., Hsiao, C., Zinn, J. (2003). "Consistent specification tests for semiparametric/nonparametric models based on series estimation methods". Journal of Econometrics 112, 295–325.
Linton, O. (1995). "Second order approximation in the partially linear regression model". Econometrica 63, 1079–1112.
Linton, O. (2001). "Edgeworth approximations for semiparametric instrumental variable estimators and test statistics". Journal of Econometrics 106, 325–368.
Linton, O., Mammen, E. (2005). "Estimating semiparametric ARCH(∞) models by kernel smoothing methods". Econometrica 73, 771–836.
Lorentz, G. (1966). Approximation of Functions. Holt, New York.
Mahajan, A. (2004). "Identification and estimation of single index models with misclassified regressors". Manuscript. Stanford University.
Makovoz, Y. (1996). "Random approximants and neural networks". Journal of Approximation Theory 85, 98–109.
Manski, C. (1985). "Semiparametric analysis of discrete response: Asymptotic properties of the maximum score estimator". Journal of Econometrics 27, 313–334.
Manski, C. (1994). "Analog estimation of econometric models". In: Engle III, R.F., McFadden, D.F. (Eds.), Handbook of Econometrics, vol. 4. North-Holland, Amsterdam.
Matzkin, R.L. (1994). "Restrictions of economic theory in nonparametric methods". In: Engle III, R.F., McFadden, D.F. (Eds.), Handbook of Econometrics, vol. 4. North-Holland, Amsterdam.
McCaffrey, D., Ellner, S., Gallant, A., Nychka, D. (1992). "Estimating the Lyapunov exponent of a chaotic system with nonparametric regression". Journal of the American Statistical Association 87, 682–695.
Meyer, Y. (1992). Ondelettes et operateurs I: Ondelettes. Hermann, Paris.
Murphy, S., van der Vaart, A. (2000). "On profile likelihood". Journal of the American Statistical Association 95, 449–465.
Newey, W.K. (1990a). "Semiparametric efficiency bounds". Journal of Applied Econometrics 5, 99–135.
Newey, W.K. (1990b). "Efficient instrumental variables estimation of nonlinear models". Econometrica 58, 809–837.
Newey, W.K. (1991). "Uniform convergence in probability and stochastic equicontinuity". Econometrica 59, 1161–1167.
Newey, W.K. (1993). "Efficient estimation of models with conditional moment restrictions". In: Maddala, G.S., Rao, C.R., Vinod, H.D. (Eds.), Handbook of Statistics, vol. 11. North-Holland, Amsterdam.
Newey, W.K. (1994a). "The asymptotic variance of semiparametric estimators". Econometrica 62, 1349–1382.
Newey, W.K. (1994b). "Series estimation of regression functionals". Econometric Theory 10, 1–28.
Newey, W.K. (1997). "Convergence rates and asymptotic normality for series estimators". Journal of Econometrics 79, 147–168.
Newey, W.K. (2001). "Flexible simulated moment estimation of nonlinear errors in variables models". Review of Economics and Statistics 83, 616–627.
Newey, W.K. (1988). "Two step series estimation of sample selection models". Manuscript. MIT Department of Economics.
Newey, W.K., McFadden, D.L. (1994). "Large sample estimation and hypothesis testing". In: Engle III, R.F., McFadden, D.L. (Eds.), Handbook of Econometrics, vol. 4. North-Holland, Amsterdam.

Newey, W.K., Powell, J.L. (1989). "Nonparametric instrumental variable estimation". Manuscript. Princeton University.
Newey, W.K., Powell, J.L. (2003). "Instrumental variable estimation of nonparametric models". Econometrica 71, 1565–1578. Working paper version, 1989.
Newey, W.K., Smith, R. (2004). "Higher order properties of GMM and generalized empirical likelihood estimators". Econometrica 72, 219–256.
Newey, W.K., Powell, J.L., Vella, F. (1999). "Nonparametric estimation of triangular simultaneous equations models". Econometrica 67, 565–603.
Nishiyama, Y., Robinson, P.M. (2000). "Edgeworth expansions for semiparametric averaged derivatives". Econometrica 68, 931–980.
Nishiyama, Y., Robinson, P.M. (2005). "The bootstrap and the Edgeworth correction for semiparametric averaged derivatives". Econometrica 73, 903–980.
Ossiander, M. (1987). "A central limit theorem under metric entropy with L_2 bracketing". The Annals of Probability 15, 897–919.
Otsu, T. (2005). "Sieve conditional empirical likelihood estimation of semiparametric models". Manuscript. Yale University.
Pagan, A., Ullah, A. (1999). Nonparametric Econometrics. Cambridge University Press.
Pakes, A., Olley, G.S. (1995). "A limit theorem for a smooth class of semiparametric estimators". Journal of Econometrics 65, 295–332.
Pastorello, S., Patilea, V., Renault, E. (2003). "Iterative and recursive estimation in structural non-adaptive models". Journal of Business & Economic Statistics 21, 449–509.
Phillips, P.C.B. (1998). "New tools for understanding spurious regressions". Econometrica 66, 1299–1325.
Phillips, P.C.B., Ploberger, W. (2003). "An introduction to best empirical models when the parameter space is infinite-dimensional". Oxford Bulletin of Economics and Statistics 65, 877–890.
Pinkse, J. (2000). "Nonparametric two-step regression estimation when regressors and errors are dependent". Canadian Journal of Statistics 28, 289–300.
Polk, C., Thompson, T.S., Vuolteenaho, T. (2003). "New forecasts of the equity premium". Manuscript. Harvard University.
Pollard, D. (1984). Convergence of Statistical Processes. Springer-Verlag, New York.
Portnoy, S. (1997). "Local asymptotics for quantile smoothing splines". The Annals of Statistics 25, 387–413.
Powell, J. (1994). "Estimation of semiparametric models". In: Engle III, R.F., McFadden, D.F. (Eds.), Handbook of Econometrics, vol. 4. North-Holland, Amsterdam.
Powell, J., Stock, J., Stoker, T. (1989). "Semiparametric estimation of index coefficients". Econometrica 57, 1403–1430.
Robinson, P. (1988). "Root-N-consistent semiparametric regression". Econometrica 56, 931–954.
Robinson, P. (1989). "Hypothesis testing in semiparametric and nonparametric models for econometric time series". Review of Economic Studies 56, 511–534.
Robinson, P. (1995). "The normal approximation for semiparametric averaged derivatives". Econometrica 63, 667–680.
Ruppert, D., Wand, M., Carroll, R. (2003). Semiparametric Regression. Cambridge University Press, Cambridge.
Schumaker, L. (1981). Spline Functions: Basic Theory. John Wiley & Sons, New York.
Severini, T., Wong, W.H. (1992). "Profile likelihood and conditionally parametric models". The Annals of Statistics 20, 1768–1802.
Shen, X. (1997). "On methods of sieves and penalization". The Annals of Statistics 25, 2555–2591.
Shen, X., Wong, W. (1994). "Convergence rate of sieve estimates". The Annals of Statistics 22, 580–615.
Shen, X., Ye, J. (2002). "Adaptive model selection". Journal of the American Statistical Association 97, 210–221.
Shintani, M., Linton, O. (2004). "Nonparametric neural network estimation of Lyapunov exponents and a direct test for chaos". Journal of Econometrics 120, 1–34.
Song, K. (2005). "Testing semiparametric conditional moment restrictions using conditional martingale transforms". Manuscript. Yale University, Department of Economics.

Stinchcombe, M. (2002). "Some genericity analyses in nonparametric econometrics". Manuscript, University of Texas, Austin, Department of Economics.
Stinchcombe, M., White, H. (1998). "Consistent specification testing with nuisance parameters present only under the alternative". Econometric Theory 14, 295–325.
Stone, C.J. (1982). "Optimal global rates of convergence for nonparametric regression". The Annals of Statistics 10, 1040–1053.
Stone, C.J. (1985). "Additive regression and other nonparametric models". The Annals of Statistics 13, 689–705.
Stone, C.J. (1986). "The dimensionality reduction principle for generalized additive models". The Annals of Statistics 14, 590–606.
Stone, C.J. (1990). "Large-sample inference for log-spline models". The Annals of Statistics 18, 717–741.
Stone, C.J. (1994). "The use of polynomial splines and their tensor products in multivariate function estimation (with discussion)". The Annals of Statistics 22, 118–184.
Stone, C.J., Hansen, M., Kooperberg, C., Truong, Y.K. (1997). "Polynomial splines and their tensor products in extended linear modeling (with discussion)". The Annals of Statistics 25, 1371–1470.
Strawderman, R.L., Tsiatis, A.A. (1996). "On the asymptotic properties of a flexible hazard estimator". The Annals of Statistics 24, 41–63.
Timan, A.F. (1963). Theory of Approximation of Functions of a Real Variable. MacMillan, New York.
Van de Geer, S. (1993). "Hellinger-consistency of certain nonparametric maximum likelihood estimators". The Annals of Statistics 21, 14–44.
Van de Geer, S. (1995). "The method of sieves and minimum contrast estimators". Mathematical Methods of Statistics 4, 20–38.
Van de Geer, S. (2000). Empirical Processes in M-estimation. Cambridge University Press.
Van der Vaart, A. (1991). "On differentiable functionals". The Annals of Statistics 19, 178–204.
Van der Vaart, A., Wellner, J. (1996). Weak Convergence and Empirical Processes: With Applications to Statistics. Springer-Verlag, New York.
Vapnik, V. (1998). Statistical Learning Theory. Wiley–Interscience, New York.
Wahba, G. (1990). Spline Models for Observational Data. CBMS–NSF Regional Conference Series. Philadelphia.
White, H. (1984). Asymptotic Theory for Econometricians. Academic Press.
White, H. (1990). "Connectionist nonparametric regression: Multilayer feedforward networks can learn arbitrary mappings". Neural Networks 3, 535–550.
White, H. (1994). Estimation, Inference and Specification Analysis. Cambridge University Press.
White, H., Wooldridge, J. (1991). "Some results on sieve estimation with dependent observations". In: Barnett, W.A., Powell, J., Tauchen, G. (Eds.), Non-parametric and Semi-parametric Methods in Econometrics and Statistics. Cambridge University Press, Cambridge, pp. 459–493.
Wong, W.H. (1992). "On asymptotic efficiency in estimation theory". Statistica Sinica 2, 47–68.
Wong, W.H., Severini, T. (1991). "On maximum likelihood estimation in infinite dimensional parameter spaces". The Annals of Statistics 19, 603–632.
Wong, W.H., Shen, X. (1995). "Probability inequalities for likelihood ratios and convergence rates for sieve MLE's". The Annals of Statistics 23, 339–362.
Wooldridge, J. (1992). "A test for functional form against nonparametric alternatives". Econometric Theory 8, 452–475.
Wooldridge, J. (1994). "Estimation and inference for dependent processes". In: Engle III, R.F., McFadden, D.F. (Eds.), Handbook of Econometrics, vol. 4. North-Holland, Amsterdam.
Xiao, Z., Linton, O. (2001). "Second order approximation for an adaptive estimator in a linear regression". Econometric Theory 17, 984–1024.
Zhang, J., Gijbels, I. (2003). "Sieve empirical likelihood and extensions of the generalized least squares". Scandinavian Journal of Statistics 30, 1–24.
Zhou, S., Shen, X., Wolfe, D.A. (1998). "Local asymptotics for regression splines and confidence regions". The Annals of Statistics 26, 1760–1782.

Chapter 77

LINEAR INVERSE PROBLEMS IN STRUCTURAL ECONOMETRICS ESTIMATION BASED ON SPECTRAL DECOMPOSITION AND REGULARIZATION*

MARINE CARRASCO

Université de Montréal, Canada

JEAN-PIERRE FLORENS

Toulouse School of Economics and Institut Universitaire de France

ERIC RENAULT

University of North Carolina, Chapel Hill, USA

Contents

* We thank Richard Blundell, Xiaohong Chen, Serge Darolles, James Heckman, Jan Johannes, François Laisney, Oliver Linton, Jean-Michel Loubes, Enno Mammen, Costas Meghir, Whitney Newey, Jean-François Richard, Anne Vanhems, and Ed Vytlacil for helpful discussions. Carrasco gratefully acknowledges financial support from the National Science Foundation, grant #SES-0211418.

Handbook of Econometrics, Volume 6B

DOI: 10.1016/S1573-4412(07)06077-1

Abstract

Inverse problems can be described as functional equations where the value of the function is known or easily estimable but the argument is unknown. Many problems in econometrics can be stated in the form of inverse problems where the argument itself is a function. For example, consider a nonlinear regression where the functional form is the object of interest. One can readily estimate the conditional expectation of the dependent variable given a vector of instruments. From this estimate, one would like to recover the unknown functional form.

This chapter provides an introduction to the estimation of the solution to inverse problems. It focuses mainly on integral equations of the first kind. Solving these equations is particularly challenging as the solution does not necessarily exist, may not be unique, and is not continuous. As a result, a regularized (or smoothed) solution needs to be implemented. We review different regularization methods and study the properties of the estimator. Integral equations of the first kind appear, for example, in the generalized method of moments when the number of moment conditions is infinite, and in the nonparametric estimation of instrumental variable regressions. In the last section of this chapter, we investigate integral equations of the second kind, whose solutions may not be unique but are continuous. Such equations arise when additive models and measurement error models are estimated nonparametrically.

Keywords

additive models, generalized method of moments, instrumental variables, integral equation, many regressors, nonparametric estimation, Tikhonov and Landweber–Fridman regularizations

JEL classification: C13, C14, C20

1. Introduction

1.1. Structural models and functional estimation

The objective of this chapter is to analyze functional estimation in structural econometric models. Different approaches exist to structural inference in econometrics and our presentation may be viewed as a nonparametric extension of the basic example of structural models, namely the static linear simultaneous equations model (SEM). Let us consider Y a vector of random endogenous variables and Z a vector of exogenous random variables. A SEM is characterized by a system

$$B_\theta Y + C_\theta Z = U \tag{1.1}$$

where B_θ and C_θ are matrices that are functions of an unknown "structural" parameter θ and $E[U \mid Z] = 0$. The reduced form is a multivariate regression model

$$Y = \Pi Z + V \tag{1.2}$$

where Π is the matrix of ordinary regression coefficients. The relation between reduced and structural form is, in the absence of higher moments restrictions, characterized by

$$B_\theta \Pi + C_\theta = 0. \tag{1.3}$$

The two essential issues of structural modeling, the identification and the overidentification problems, follow from the consideration of Equation (1.3). The uniqueness of the solution in θ for given Π defines the identification problem. The existence of a solution (or restrictions imposed on Π to guarantee the existence) defines the overidentification question. The reduced form parameter Π can be estimated by OLS and if a unique solution in θ exists for any Π, it provides the indirect least square estimate of θ. If the solution does not exist for any Π, θ can be estimated by a suitable minimization of $B_\theta \hat{\Pi} + C_\theta$ where $\hat{\Pi}$ is an estimator of Π.

In this chapter, we address the issue of functional extension of this construction. The data generating process (DGP) is described by a stationary ergodic stochastic process which generates a sequence of observed realizations of a random vector X.

The structural econometric models considered in this chapter are about the stationary distribution of X. This distribution is characterized by its cumulative distribution function (c.d.f.) F, while the functional parameter of interest is an element φ of some infinite dimensional Hilbert space. Following the notation of Florens (2003), the structural econometric model defines the connection between φ and F under the form of a functional equation:

$$A(\varphi, F) = 0. \tag{1.4}$$

This equation extends Equation (1.3) and the definitions of identification (uniqueness of this solution) and of overidentification (constraints on F such that a solution exists) are analogous to the SEM case. The estimation is also performed along the same line:

F can be estimated by the empirical distribution of the sample or by a more sophisticated estimator (like kernel smoothing) belonging to the domain of A. φ is estimated by solving (1.4) or, in the presence of overidentification, by a minimization of a suitable norm of $A(\varphi, F)$ after plugging in the estimator of F.

This framework may be clarified by some remarks.

1. All the variables are treated as random in our model and this construction seems to differ from the basic econometric models which are based on a distinction between exogenous or conditioning variables and endogenous variables. Actually this distinction may be used in our framework. Let X be decomposed into Y and Z and F into $F_Y(\cdot \mid Z = z)$ the conditional c.d.f. of Y given $Z = z$, and F_Z the marginal c.d.f. of Z. Then, the exogeneity of Z is tantamount to the conjunction of two conditions.

   Firstly, the solution φ of (1.4) only depends on $F_Y(\cdot \mid Z = z)$ and φ is identified by the conditional model only. Secondly if $F_Y(\cdot \mid Z = z)$ and F_Z are "variations free" in a given statistical model defined by a family of sampling distributions (intuitively no restrictions link $F_Y(\cdot \mid Z = z)$ and F_Z), no information on $F_Y(\cdot \mid Z = z)$ (and then on φ) is lost by neglecting the estimation of F_Z. This definition fully encompasses the usual definition of exogeneity in terms of cuts [see Engle, Hendry and Richard (1983), Florens and Mouchart (1985)]. Extension of that approach to sequential models and then to sequential or weak exogeneity is straightforward.
2. Our construction does not explicitly involve residuals or other unobservable variables. As will be illustrated in the examples below, most of the structural econometric models are formalized by a relationship between observable and unobservable random elements. A first step in the analysis of these models is to express the relationship between the functional parameters of interest and the DGP, or, in our terminology, to specify the relation $A(\varphi, F) = 0$. We start our presentation at the second step of this approach and our analysis is devoted to the study of this equation and to its use for estimation.
3. The overidentification is handled by extending the definition of the parameter in order to estimate overidentified models. Even if $A(\varphi, F) = 0$ does not have a solution for a given F, the parameter φ is still defined as the minimum of a norm of $A(\varphi, F)$. Then φ can be estimated from an estimation of F, which does not satisfy the overidentification constraints. This approach extends the original generalized method of moments (GMM) treatment of overidentification. Another way to take into account overidentification constraints consists in estimating F under these constraints (the estimator of F is the nearest distribution to the empirical distribution for which there exists a solution, φ, of $A(\varphi, F) = 0$). This method extends the new approach to GMM called the empirical likelihood analysis [see Owen (2001) and references therein]. In this chapter, we remain true to the first approach: if the equation $A(\varphi, F) = 0$ has no solution it will be replaced by the first-order condition of the minimization of a norm of $A(\varphi, F)$. In that

case, this first-order condition-defines a functional equation usually still denoted $A(\varphi, F) = 0$.

1.2. Notation

In this chapter, X is a random element of a finite or infinite dimensional space $\mathcal{X}$. In most of the examples, $\mathcal{X}$ is a finite dimensional euclidean space ($\mathcal{X} \subset \mathbb{R}^m$) and the distribution of X, denoted F is assumed to belong to a set $\mathcal{F}$. If F is absolutely continuous with respect to Lebesgue measure, its density is denoted by f. Usually, X is decomposed into several components, $X = (Y, Z, W) \in \mathbb{R}^p \times \mathbb{R}^q \times \mathbb{R}^r (p + q + r = m)$ and the marginal c.d.f.'s or probability density function (p.d.f.'s) are denoted by F_Y, F_Z, F_W and f_Y, f_X, f_W, respectively. Conditional c.d.f. are denoted by $F_Y(\cdot \mid Z = z)$ or $F_Y(\cdot \mid z)$ and conditional density by $f_Y(\cdot \mid Z = z)$ or $f_Y(\cdot \mid z)$. The sample may be an i.i.d. sample of X (denoted in that case $(x_i)_{i=1,\dots,n}$) or weakly dependent time series sample denoted $(x_t)_{t=1,\dots,T}$ in the dynamic case.

The paper focuses on the estimation of an infinite dimensional parameter denoted by φ, which is an element of a Hilbert space $\mathcal{H}$ (mathematical concepts are recalled in Section 2). In some particular cases, finite dimensional parameters are considered and this feature is underlined by the notation $\theta \in \Theta \subset \mathbb{R}^d$.

The structural model is expressed by an operator A from $\mathcal{H} \times \mathcal{F}$ into an Hilbert space $\mathcal{E}$ and defines the equation $A(\varphi, F) = 0$. The (possibly local) solution of this equation is denoted by

$$\varphi = \Psi(F). \tag{1.5}$$

For statistical discussions, a specific notation for the true value is helpful and F_0 will denote the true c.d.f. (associated with the density f_0 and with the true parameter φ_0 (or θ_0)). The estimators of the c.d.f. will be denoted by F_n in an i.i.d. setting or F_T in a dynamic environment.

The operator A may take various forms. Particular cases are linear operators with respect to F or to φ. The first case will be illustrated in the GMM example but most of the paper will be devoted to the study of linear operators relative to φ. In that case, equation $A(\varphi, F) = 0$ can be rewritten

$$A(\varphi, F) = K\varphi - r = 0 \tag{1.6}$$

where K is a linear operator from $\mathcal{H}$ to $\mathcal{E}$ depending on F and r is an element of $\mathcal{E}$ and is also a function of F. The properties of K are essential and we will present different examples of integral or differential operators. More generally, A may be nonlinear either with respect to F or to φ, but as usual in functional analysis, most of the analysis of nonlinear operators may be done locally (around the true value typically) and reduces to the linear case. Game theoretic models or surplus estimation give examples of nonlinear models.

The problem of solving Equation (1.4) enters in the class of inverse problems. An inverse problem consists of the resolution of an equation where the elements of the equations are imperfectly known. In the linear case, the equation is $K\varphi = r$ and F is not exactly known but only estimated. Thus, r is also imperfectly known. The econometric situation is more complex than most of the inverse problems studied in the statistical literature because K is also only imperfectly known. According to the classification proposed by Vapnik (1998), the stochastic inverse problems of interest in this chapter are more often than not characterized by equations where both the operator and the right-hand side term need to be estimated. Inverse problems are said to be well-posed if a unique solution exists and depends continuously on the imperfectly known elements of the equation. In our notation, this means that Ψ in (1.5) exists as a function of F and is continuous. Then if F is replaced by F_n, the solution φ_n of $A(\varphi_n, F_n) = 0$ exists and the convergence of F_n to F_0 implies the convergence of φ_n to φ_0 by continuity. Unfortunately a large class of inverse problems relevant to econometric applications are not well-posed [they are then said to be ill-posed in the Hadamard sense, see e.g. Kress (1999), Vapnik (1998)]. In this case, a regularization method needs to be implemented to stabilize the solution. Our treatment of ill-posed problems is close to that of Van Rooij and Ruymgaart (1999).

1.3. Examples

This section presents various examples of inverse problems motivated by structural econometric models. We will start with the GMM example, which is the most familiar to econometricians. Subsequently, we present several examples of linear (w.r.t. φ) inverse problems. The last three examples are devoted to nonlinear inverse problems.

1.3.1. Generalized method of moments (GMM)

Let us assume that X is m dimensional and the parameter of interest θ is also finite dimensional ($\theta \in \Theta \subset \mathbb{R}^d$). We consider a function

$$h : \mathbb{R}^m \times \Theta \to \mathcal{E} \tag{1.7}$$

and the equation connecting θ and F is defined by

$$A(\theta, F) = E\big(h(X, \theta)\big) = 0. \tag{1.8}$$

A particular case is given by $h(X, \theta) = \mu(X) - \theta$ where θ is exactly the expectation of a transformation μ of the data. More generally, θ may be replaced by an infinite dimensional parameter φ but we do not consider this extension here.

The GMM method was introduced by Hansen (1982) and has received numerous extensions [see Ai and Chen (2003) for the case of an infinite dimensional parameter]. GMM consists in estimating θ by solving an inverse problem linear in F but nonlinear in θ. It is usually assumed that θ is identified i.e. that θ is uniquely characterized by Equation (1.8). Econometric specifications are generally overidentified and a solution to (1.8) only exists for some particular F, including the true DGP F_0, under the hypothesis of correct specification of the model. The c.d.f. F is estimated by the empirical distribution and Equation (1.8) becomes:

$$\frac{1}{n}\sum_{i=1}^{n} h(x_i, \theta) = 0, \tag{1.9}$$

which has no solution in general. Overidentification is treated by an extension of the definition of θ as follows:

$$\theta = \arg\min_{\theta} \| B E(h) \|^2 \tag{1.10}$$

where B is a linear operator in $\mathcal{E}$ and $\| \ \|$ denotes the norm in $\mathcal{E}$. This definition coincides with (1.8) if F satisfies the overidentification constraints. Following Equation (1.10), the estimator is

$$\hat{\theta}_n = \arg\min_{\theta} \left\| B_n \left(\frac{1}{n}\sum_{i=1}^{n} h(x_i, \theta) \right) \right\|^2 \tag{1.11}$$

where B_n is a sequence of operators converging to B. If the number of moment conditions is finite, B_n and B are square matrices.

As θ is finite dimensional, the inverse problem generated by the first-order conditions of (1.10) or (1.11) is well-posed and consistency of the estimators follows from standard regularity conditions. As it will be illustrated in Section 6, an ill-posed inverse problem arises if the number of moment conditions is infinite and if optimal GMM is used. In finite dimensions, optimal GMM is obtained using a specific weighting matrix, $B = \Sigma^{-\frac{1}{2}}$, where Σ is the asymptotic variance of $\sqrt{n}(\frac{1}{n}\sum_{i=1}^{n} h(x_i, \theta))(\Sigma = \mathrm{Var}(h)$ in i.i.d. sampling). In the general case, optimal GMM requires the minimization of $\|g\|^2$ where

$$\Sigma^{\frac{1}{2}} g = E(h). \tag{1.12}$$

The function g is then the solution of a linear inverse problem. If the dimension of h is not finite, Equation (1.12) defines an ill-posed inverse problem, which requires a regularization scheme (see Section 3).

1.3.2. Instrumental variables

Instrumental regression is a possible strategy to perform nonparametric estimation when explanatory variables are endogenous. Let us decompose X into (Y, Z, W) where $Y \in \mathbb{R}$, $Z \in \mathbb{R}^q$, $W \in \mathbb{R}^r$. The subvectors Z and W may have common elements. The econometrician starts with a relation

$$Y = \varphi(Z) + U \tag{1.13}$$

where U is a random term which does not satisfy $E(U \mid Z) = 0$. This assumption is replaced by the more general hypothesis

$$E(U \mid W) = 0 \tag{1.14}$$

and W is called the set of instrumental variables. Condition (1.14) defines φ as the solution of an integral equation. In terms of density, (1.14) means that

$$A(\varphi, F) = \int \varphi(z) f_Z(z \mid W = w)\, \mathrm{d}z - \int y f_Y(y \mid W = w)\, \mathrm{d}y = 0. \tag{1.15}$$

Using previous notation, the first part of (1.15) is denoted $K\varphi$ and the second part is equal to r.

This expression is linear in φ and can be made linear in F by eliminating the denominator through a multiplication by $f_W(w)$. However, as will be seen later, this problem is essentially nonlinear in F because the treatment of overidentification and of regularization will necessarily reintroduce the denominator in (1.15).

Instrumental regression introduced in (1.15) can be generalized to local instrumental regression and to generalized local instrumental regression. These extensions are relevant in more complex models than (1.13), where in particular the error term may enter the equation in nonadditive ways [see for such a treatment, Florens et al. (2003)]. For example, consider the equation

$$Y = \varphi(Z) + Z\varepsilon + U \tag{1.16}$$

where Z is scalar and ε is a random unobservable heterogeneity component. It can be proved that, under a set of identification assumptions, φ satisfies the equations:

$$A_j(\varphi, F) = E\left(\frac{\partial\varphi(Z)}{\partial Z} \;\middle|\; W = w\right) - \frac{\frac{\partial}{\partial W_j} E(Y \mid W = w)}{\frac{\partial}{\partial W_j} E(Z \mid W = w)} = 0 \tag{1.17}$$

for any $j = 1, \ldots, r$. This equation, linear with respect to φ, combines integral and differential operators.

Instrumental variable estimation and its local extension define ill-posed inverse problems as will be seen in Section 5.

1.3.3. Deconvolution

Another classical example of an ill-posed inverse problem is given by the deconvolution problem. Let us assume that X, Y, Z are three scalar random elements such that

$$Y = X + Z. \tag{1.18}$$

Only Y is observable. The two components X and Z are independent. The density of the error term Z is known and denoted g. The parameter of interest is the density φ of X. Then φ is solution of

$$A(\varphi, F) = \int g(y - x)\varphi(x)\, \mathrm{d}x - h(y) = 0 \equiv K\varphi - r. \tag{1.19}$$

This example is comparable to the instrumental variables case but only the r.h.s. $r = h$ is unknown whereas the operator K is given.

1.3.4. Regression with many regressors

This example also constitutes a case of linear ill-posed inverse problems. Let us consider a regression model where the regressors are indexed by τ belonging to an infinite index set provided with a measure Π. The model is

$$Y = \int Z(\tau)\varphi(\tau)\Pi(\mathrm{d}\tau) + U \tag{1.20}$$

where $E(U \mid (Z(\tau))_\tau) = 0$ and φ is the parameter of interest and is infinite dimensional. Examples of regression with many regressors are now common in macroeconomics [see Stock and Watson (2002) or Forni and Reichlin (1998) for two presentations of this topic].

Let us assume that Y and $(Z(\tau))_\tau$ are observable. Various treatments of (1.20) can be done and we just consider the following analysis. The conditional moment equation $E(U \mid (Z(\tau))_\tau) = 0$ implies an infinite number of conditions indexed by τ:

$$E\bigl(Z(\tau)U\bigr) = 0, \quad \forall\tau,$$

or equivalently

$$\int E\bigl(Z(\tau)Z(\rho)\bigr)\varphi(\rho)\Pi(\mathrm{d}\rho) - E\bigl(YZ(\tau)\bigr) = 0, \quad \forall\tau. \tag{1.21}$$

This equation generalizes the usual normal equations of the linear regression to an infinite number of regressors. The inverse problem defined in (1.21) is linear in both F and φ but it is ill-posed. An intuitive argument to illustrate this issue is to consider the estimation using a finite number of observations of the second moment operator $E(Z(\tau)Z(\rho))$ which is infinite dimensional. The resulting multicollinearity problem is solved by a ridge regression. The "infinite matrix" $E(Z(\cdot)Z(\cdot))$ is replaced by $\alpha I + E(Z(\cdot)Z(\cdot))$ where I is the identity and α a positive number, or by a reduction of the set of regressors to the first principal components. These two solutions are particular examples of regularization methods (namely the Tikhonov and the spectral cut-off regularizations), which will be introduced in Section 3.

1.3.5. Additive models

The properties of the integral equations generated by this example and by the next one are very different from those of the three previous examples. We consider an additive regression model:

$$Y = \varphi(Z) + \psi(W) + U \tag{1.22}$$

where $E(U \mid Z, W) = 0$ and $X = (Y, Z, W)$ is the observable element. The parameters of interest are the two functions φ and ψ. The approach we propose here is related to the backfitting approach [see Hastie and Tibshirani (1990)]. Other treatments of additive models have been considered in the literature [see Pagan and Ullah (1999)].

Equation (1.22) implies

$$\begin{cases} E(Y \mid Z = z) = \varphi(z) + E(\psi(W) \mid Z = z), \\ E(Y \mid W = w) = E(\varphi(Z) \mid W = w) + \psi(w) \end{cases} \tag{1.23}$$

and by substitution

$$\begin{aligned} &\varphi(z) - E\big(E\big(\varphi(Z) \mid W\big) \mid Z = z\big) \\ &\quad = E(Y \mid Z = z) - E\big(E(Y \mid W) \mid Z = z\big) \end{aligned} \tag{1.24}$$

or, in our notations:

$$(I - K)\varphi = r$$

where $K = E(E(\cdot \mid W) \mid Z)$. Backfitting refers to the iterative method to solve Equation (1.23).

An analogous equation characterizes ψ. Actually even if (1.22) is not well specified, these equations provide the best approximation of the regression of Y given Z and W by an additive form. Equation (1.24) is a linear integral equation and even if this inverse problem is ill-posed because K is not one-to-one (φ is only determined up to a constant term), the solution is still continuous and therefore the difficulty is not as important as that of the previous examples.

1.3.6. *Measurement-error models or nonparametric analysis of panel data*

We denote η to be an unobservable random variable for which two measurements Y_1 and Y_2 are available. These measurements are affected by a bias dependent on observable variables Z_1 and Z_2. More formally:

$$\begin{cases} Y_1 = \eta + \varphi(Z_1) + U_1, & E(U_1 \mid \eta, Z_1, Z_2) = 0, \\ Y_2 = \eta + \varphi(Z_2) + U_2, & E(U_2 \mid \eta, Z_1, Z_2) = 0. \end{cases} \tag{1.25}$$

An i.i.d. sample $(y_{1i}, y_{2i}, \eta_i, z_{1i}, z_{2i})$ is drawn, but the η_i are unobservable. Equivalently this model may be seen as a two period panel data with individual effects η_i.

The parameter of interest is the "bias function" φ, identical for the two observations. In the experimental context, it is natural to assume that the joint distribution of the observables is independent of the order of the observations, or equivalently (Y_1, Z_1, Y_2, Z_2) are distributed as (Y_2, Z_2, Y_1, Z_1). This assumption is not relevant in a dynamic context.

The model is transformed in order to eliminate the unobservable variable by difference:

$$Y = \varphi(Z_2) - \varphi(Z_1) + U \tag{1.26}$$

where $Y = Y_2 - Y_1$, $U = U_2 - U_1$, and $E(U \mid Z_1, Z_2) = 0$.

This model is similar to an additive model except for the symmetry between the variables, and the fact that with the notation of (1.22), φ and ψ are identical. An application of this model can be found in Gaspar and Florens (1998) where y_{1i} and y_{2i} are two measurements of the ocean level in location i by a satellite radar altimeter, η_i is the true level and φ is the "sea state bias" depending on the waves' height and the wind speed (Z_{1i} and Z_{2i} are both two-dimensional).

The model is treated through the relation

$$E(Y \mid Z_2 = z_2) = \varphi(z_2) - E\big(\varphi(Z_1) \mid Z_2 = z_2\big), \tag{1.27}$$

which defines an integral equation $K\varphi = r$. The exchangeable property between the variables implies that conditioning on Z_1 gives the same equation (where Z_1 and Z_2 are exchanged).

1.3.7. Game theoretic model

This example and the next ones present economic models formalized by nonlinear inverse problems. As the focus of this chapter is on linear equations, these examples are given for illustration and will not be treated outside of this section. The analysis of nonlinear functional equations raises numerous questions: uniqueness and existence of the solution, asymptotic properties of the estimator, implementation of the estimation procedure and numerical computation of the solution. Most of these questions are usually solved locally by a linear approximation of the nonlinear problem deduced from a suitable concept of derivative. A strong concept of derivation (typically Frechet derivative) is needed to deal with the implicit form of the model, which requires the use of the implicit function theorem.

The first example of nonlinear inverse problems follows from the strategic behavior of the players in a game. Let us assume that for each game, each player receives a random signal or type denoted by ξ and plays an action X. The signal is generated by a probability described by its c.d.f. φ, and the players all adopt a strategy σ dependent on φ which associates X with ξ, i.e.

$$X = \sigma_\varphi(\xi).$$

The strategy σ_φ is determined as an equilibrium of the game (e.g. Nash equilibrium) or by an approximation of the equilibrium (bounded rationality behavior). The signal ξ is private knowledge for the player but is unobserved by the econometrician, and the c.d.f. φ is common knowledge for the players but is unknown for the statistician. The strategy σ_φ is determined from the rules of the game and by the assumptions on the behavior of the players. The essential feature of the game theoretic model from a statistical viewpoint is that the relation between the unobservable and the observable variables depends on the distribution of the unobservable component. The parameter of interest is the c.d.f. φ of the signals.

Let us restrict our attention to cases where ξ and X are scalar and where σ_φ is strictly increasing. Then the c.d.f. F of the observable X is connected with φ by

$$A(\varphi, F) = F \circ \sigma_\varphi - \varphi = 0. \tag{1.28}$$

If the signals are i.i.d. across the different players and different games, F can be estimated by a smooth transformation of the empirical distribution and Equation (1.28) is solved in φ. The complexity of this relation can be illustrated by the auction model. In the private value first price auction model, ξ is the value of the object and X the bid. If the number of bidders is $N+1$ the strategy function is equal to

$$X = \xi - \frac{\int_{\underline{\xi}}^{\xi} \varphi^N(u)\,\mathrm{d}u}{\varphi^N(\xi)} \tag{1.29}$$

where $[\underline{\xi}, \bar{\xi}]$ is the support of ξ and $\varphi^N(u) = [\varphi(u)]^N$ is the c.d.f. of the maximum private value among N players.

Model (1.28) may be extended to a non-i.i.d. setting (depending on exogenous variables) or to the case where σ_φ is partially unknown. The analysis of this model has been done by Guerre, Perrigne and Vuong (2000) in a nonparametric context. The framework of inverse problem is used by Florens, Protopopescu and Richard (1997).

1.3.8. Solution of a differential equation

In several models like the analysis of the consumer surplus, the function of interest is the solution of a differential equation depending on the data generating process.

Consider for example a class of problems where $X = (Y, Z, W) \in \mathbb{R}^3$ is i.i.d., F is the c.d.f. of X and the parameter φ verifies:

$$\frac{\mathrm{d}}{\mathrm{d}z}\varphi(z) = m_F\big(z, \varphi(z)\big) \tag{1.30}$$

when m_F is a regular function depending on F. A first example is

$$m_F(z, w) = E^F(Y \mid Z = z,\ W = w) \tag{1.31}$$

but more complex examples may be constructed in order to take into account the endogeneity of one or two variables. For example, Z may be endogenous and m_F may be defined by

$$E(Y \mid W_1 = w_1,\ W_2 = w_2) = E\big(m_F(Z, W_1) \mid W_1 = w_1,\ W_2 = w_2\big). \tag{1.32}$$

Microeconomic applications can be found in Hausman (1981, 1985) and Hausman and Newey (1995) where the function m_F represents the demand function for one good and φ measures the variation of the consumer surplus associated with a price change. A theoretical treatment is given by Vanhems (2006) and Loubes and Vanhems (2001).

1.3.9. Instrumental variables in a nonseparable model

Another example of a nonlinear inverse problem is provided by the following model:

$$Y = \varphi(Z, U) \tag{1.33}$$

where Z is an endogenous variable. The function φ is the parameter of interest. Denote $\varphi_z(u) = \varphi(z, u)$. Assume that $\varphi_z(u)$ is an increasing function of u for each z. Moreover, the distribution F_U of U is assumed to be known for identification purposes. Model (1.33) may arise in a duration model where Y is the duration [see Equation (2.2) of Horowitz (1999)]. One difference with Horowitz (1999) is the presence of an endogenous variable here. Assume there is a vector of instruments W, which are independent of U. Because U and W are independent, we have

$$P(U \leqslant u \mid W = w) = P(U \leqslant u) = F_U(u). \tag{1.34}$$

Denote f the density of (Y, Z) and

$$F(y, z \mid w) = \int_{-\infty}^{y} f(t, z \mid w)\,\mathrm{d}t.$$

F can be estimated using the observations (y_i, z_i, w_i), $i = 1, 2, \ldots, n$. By a slight abuse of notation, we use the notation $P(Y \leqslant y, Z = z \mid W = w)$ for $F(y, z \mid w)$. We have

$$\begin{aligned} P(U \leqslant u, Z = z \mid W = w) &= P\big(\varphi_z(Y)^{-1} \leqslant u,\ Z = z \mid W = w\big) \\ &= P\big(Y \leqslant \varphi_z(u),\ Z = z \mid W = w\big) \\ &= F\big(\varphi_z(u), z \mid w\big). \end{aligned} \tag{1.35}$$

Combining Equations (1.34) and (1.35), we obtain

$$\int F\big(\varphi_z(u), z \mid w\big)\,\mathrm{d}z = F_U(u). \tag{1.36}$$

Equation (1.36) belongs to the class of Urysohn equations of Type I [Polyanin and Manzhirov (1998)]. The estimation of the solution of Equation (1.36) is discussed in Florens (2005).

1.4. Organization of the chapter

Section 2 reviews the basic definitions and properties of operators in Hilbert spaces. The focus is on compact operators because they have the advantage of having a discrete spectrum. We recall some laws of large numbers and central limit theorems for Hilbert valued random elements. Finally, we discuss how to estimate the spectrum of a compact operator and how to estimate the operators themselves.

Section 3 is devoted to solving integral equations of the first kind. As these equations are ill-posed, the solution needs to be regularized (or smoothed). We investigate the properties of the regularized solutions for different types of regularizations.

In Section 4, we show under suitable assumptions the consistency and asymptotic normality of regularized solutions.

Section 5 details five examples: the ridge regression, the factor model, the infinite number of regressors, the deconvolution, and the instrumental variables estimation.

Section 6 has two parts. First, it recalls the main results relative to reproducing kernels. Reproducing kernel theory is closely related to that of the integral equations of the first kind. Second, we explain the extension of GMM to a continuum of moment conditions and show how the GMM objective function reduces to the norm of the moment functions in a specific reproducing kernel Hilbert space. Several examples are provided.

Section 7 tackles the problem of solving integral equations of the second kind. A typical example of such a problem is the additive model introduced earlier.

Finally, a web site containing an annotated bibliography and resources on inverse problems complements this chapter. It can be found on http://www.sceco.umontreal.ca/liste_personnel/carrasco/.

2. Spaces and operators

The purpose of this section is to introduce terminology and to state the main properties of operators in Hilbert spaces that are used in our econometric applications. Most of these results can be found in Debnath and Mikusinski (1999) and Kress (1999). Aït-Sahalia, Hansen and Scheinkman (2005) provide an excellent survey of operator methods for the purpose of financial econometrics.

2.1. Hilbert spaces

We start by recalling some of the basic concepts of analysis. In the sequel, $\mathbb{C}$ denotes the set of complex numbers. A vector space equipped by a norm is called a normed space. A sequence (φ_n) of elements in a normed space is called a Cauchy sequence if for every $\varepsilon > 0$ there exists an integer $N(\varepsilon)$ such that

$$\|\varphi_n - \varphi_m\| < \varepsilon$$

for all $n, m \geqslant N(\varepsilon)$, i.e., if $\lim_{n,m\to\infty} \|\varphi_n - \varphi_m\| = 0$. A space S is complete if every Cauchy sequence converges to an element in S. A complete normed vector space is called a Banach space.

Let $(E, \mathcal{E}, \Pi)$ be a probability space and

$$L^p_{\mathbb{C}}(E, \mathcal{E}, \Pi) = \left\{ f : E \to \mathbb{C} \text{ measurable s.t. } \|f\| \equiv \left(\int |f|^p \, \mathrm{d}\Pi \right)^{1/p} < \infty \right\}, \quad p \geqslant 1.$$

Then, $L^p_{\mathbb{C}}(E, \mathcal{E}, \Pi)$ is a Banach space. If we only consider functions valued in $\mathbb{R}$ this space is still a Banach space and is denoted in that case by L^p (we drop the subscript $\mathbb{C}$). In the sequel, we also use the following notation. If E is a subset of $\mathbb{R}^p$, then the σ-field $\mathcal{E}$ will always be the Borel σ-field and will be omitted in the notation $L^p(\mathbb{R}^q, \Pi)$. If Π has a density π with respect to Lebesgue measure, Π will be replaced by π. If π is uniform, it will be omitted in the notation.

DEFINITION 2.1 *(Inner product).* Let H be a complex vector space. A mapping $\langle,\rangle : H \times H \to \mathbb{C}$ is called an inner product in H if for any $\varphi, \psi, \xi \in H$ and $\alpha, \beta \in \mathbb{C}$ the following conditions are satisfied:

(a) $\langle \varphi, \psi \rangle = \overline{\langle \psi, \varphi \rangle}$ (the bar denotes the complex conjugate),
(b) $\langle \alpha\varphi + \beta\psi, \xi \rangle = \alpha\langle \varphi, \xi \rangle + \beta\langle \psi, \xi \rangle$,
(c) $\langle \varphi, \varphi \rangle \geqslant 0$ and $\langle \varphi, \varphi \rangle = 0 \Longleftrightarrow \varphi = 0$.

A vector space equipped by an inner product is called an inner product space.

EXAMPLE. The space $\mathbb{C}^N$ of ordered N-tuples $x = (x_1, \ldots, x_N)$ of complex numbers, with the inner product defined by

$$\langle x, y \rangle = \sum_{l=1}^{N} x_l \overline{y_l}$$

is an inner product space.

EXAMPLE. The space l^2 of all sequences $(x_1, x_2, \ldots)$ of complex numbers such that $\sum_{j=1}^{\infty} |x_j|^2 < \infty$ with the inner product defined by $\langle x, y \rangle = \sum_{j=1}^{\infty} x_j \overline{y_j}$ for $x = (x_1, x_2, \ldots)$ and $y = (y_1, y_2, \ldots)$ is an infinite dimensional inner product space.

EXAMPLE. The space $L^2_{\mathbb{C}}(E, \mathcal{E}, \Pi)$ associated with the inner product defined by

$$\langle \varphi, \psi \rangle = \int \varphi \overline{\psi} \, \mathrm{d}\Pi$$

is an inner product space. On the other hand, $L^p_{\mathbb{C}}(E, \mathcal{E}, \Pi)$ is not an inner product space if $p \neq 2$.

An inner product satisfies the Cauchy–Schwartz inequality, that is,

$$\left|\langle \varphi, \psi \rangle\right|^2 \leqslant \langle \varphi, \varphi \rangle \langle \psi, \psi \rangle$$

for all $\varphi, \psi \in H$. Remark that $\langle \varphi, \varphi \rangle$ is real because $\langle \varphi, \varphi \rangle = \overline{\langle \varphi, \varphi \rangle}$. It actually defines a norm $\|\varphi\| = \langle \varphi, \varphi \rangle^{1/2}$ (this is the norm induced by the inner product $\langle,\rangle$).

DEFINITION 2.2 *(Hilbert space).* If an inner product space is complete in the induced norm, it is called a Hilbert space.

A standard theorem in functional analysis guarantees that every inner product space H can be completed to form a Hilbert space $\mathcal{H}$. Such a Hilbert space is said to be the completion of H.

EXAMPLE. $\mathbb{C}^N$, l^2 and $L^2(\mathbb{R}, \Pi)$ are Hilbert spaces.

EXAMPLE (*Sobolev space*). Let $\Omega = [a, b]$ be an interval of $\mathbb{R}$. Denote by $\tilde{H}^m(\Omega)$, $m = 1, 2, \ldots$, the space of all complex-valued functions $\varphi \in \mathbb{C}^m$ such that for all $|l| \leqslant m$, $\varphi^{(l)} = \partial^l \varphi(\tau)/\partial \tau^l \in L^2(\Omega)$. The inner product on $\tilde{H}^m(\Omega)$ is

$$\langle \varphi, \psi \rangle = \int_a^b \sum_{l=0}^m \varphi^{(l)}(\tau)\overline{\psi^{(l)}(\tau)}\, \mathrm{d}\tau.$$

$\tilde{H}^m(\Omega)$ is an inner product space but it is not a Hilbert space because it is not complete. The completion of $\tilde{H}^m(\Omega)$, denoted $H^m(\Omega)$, is a Hilbert space.

DEFINITION 2.3 (*Convergence*). A sequence (φ_n) of vectors in an inner product space H is called strongly convergent to a vector $\varphi \in H$ if $\|\varphi_n - \varphi\| \to 0$ as $n \to \infty$.

Remark that if (φ_n) converges strongly to φ in H then $\langle \varphi_n, \psi \rangle \to \langle \varphi, \psi \rangle$ as $n \to \infty$, for every $\psi \in H$. The converse is false.

DEFINITION 2.4. Let H be an inner product space. A sequence (φ_n) of nonzero vectors in H is called an orthogonal sequence if $\langle \varphi_m, \varphi_n \rangle = 0$ for $n \neq m$. If in addition $\|\varphi_n\| = 1$ for all n, it is called an orthonormal sequence.

EXAMPLE. Let $\pi(x)$ be the p.d.f. of a normal with mean μ and variance σ^2. Denote by ϕ_j the Hermite polynomials of degree j:

$$\phi_j(x) = (-1)^j \frac{\frac{\mathrm{d}^j \pi}{\mathrm{d}x^j}}{\pi}. \tag{2.1}$$

The functions $\phi_j(x)$ form an orthogonal system in $L^2(\mathbb{R}, \pi)$.

Any sequence of vectors (ψ_j) in an inner product space that is linearly independent, i.e.,

$$\sum_{j=1}^{\infty} \alpha_j \psi_j = 0 \quad \Rightarrow \quad \alpha_j = 0 \quad \forall j = 1, 2, \ldots,$$

can be transformed into an orthonormal sequence by the method called Gram–Schmidt orthonormalization process. This process consists of the following steps. Given (ψ_j), define a sequence (φ_j) inductively as

$$\begin{aligned}
\varphi_1 &= \frac{\psi_1}{\|\psi_1\|}, \\
\varphi_2 &= \frac{\psi_2 - \langle \psi_2, \varphi_1 \rangle \varphi_1}{\|\psi_2 - \langle \psi_2, \varphi_1 \rangle \varphi_1\|} \\
&\vdots
\end{aligned}$$

$$\varphi_n = \frac{\psi_n - \sum_{l=1}^{n-1} \langle \psi_n, \varphi_l \rangle \varphi_l}{\| \psi_n - \sum_{l=1}^{n-1} \langle \psi_n, \varphi_l \rangle \varphi_l \|}.$$

As a result, (φ_j) is orthonormal and any linear combinations of vectors $\varphi_1, \dots, \varphi_n$ is also a linear combinations of $\psi_1, \dots, \psi_n$ and vice versa.

THEOREM 2.5 *(Pythagorean formula). If $\varphi_1, \dots, \varphi_n$ are orthogonal vectors in an inner product space, then*

$$\left\| \sum_{j=1}^{n} \varphi_j \right\|^2 = \sum_{j=1}^{n} \|\varphi_j\|^2.$$

From the Pythagorean formula, it can be seen that the α_j that minimize

$$\left\| \varphi - \sum_{j=1}^{n} \alpha_j \varphi_j \right\|$$

are such that $\alpha_j = \langle \varphi, \varphi_j \rangle$. Moreover

$$\sum_{j=1}^{n} \left| \langle \varphi, \varphi_j \rangle \right|^2 \leqslant \|\varphi\|^2. \tag{2.2}$$

Hence the series $\sum_{j=1}^{\infty} |\langle \varphi, \varphi_j \rangle|^2$ converges for every $\varphi \in H$. The expansion

$$\varphi = \sum_{j=1}^{\infty} \langle \varphi, \varphi_j \rangle \varphi_j \tag{2.3}$$

is called a generalized Fourier series of φ. In general, we do not know whether the series in (2.3) is convergent. Below we give a sufficient condition for convergence.

DEFINITION 2.6 *(Complete orthonormal sequence).* An orthonormal sequence (φ_j) in an inner product space H is said to be complete if for every $\varphi \in H$ we have

$$\varphi = \sum_{j=1}^{\infty} \langle \varphi, \varphi_j \rangle \varphi_j$$

where the equality means

$$\lim_{n \to \infty} \left\| \varphi - \sum_{j=1}^{n} \langle \varphi, \varphi_j \rangle \varphi_j \right\| = 0$$

where $\| \cdot \|$ is the norm in H.

A complete orthonormal sequence (φ_j) in an inner product space H is an orthonormal basis in H, that is every $\varphi \in H$ has a unique representation $\varphi = \sum_{j=1}^{\infty} \alpha_j \varphi_j$ where $\alpha_j \in \mathbb{C}$. If (φ_j) is a complete orthonormal sequence in an inner product space H then the set

$$\operatorname{span}\{\varphi_1, \varphi_2, \ldots\} = \left\{ \sum_{j=1}^{n} \alpha_j \varphi_j \colon \forall n \in \mathbb{N},\ \forall \alpha_1, \ldots, \alpha_n \in \mathbb{C} \right\}$$

is dense in H.

THEOREM 2.7. *An orthonormal sequence* (φ_j) *in a Hilbert space* $\mathcal{H}$ *is complete if and only if* $\langle \varphi, \varphi_j \rangle = 0$ *for all* $j = 1, 2, \ldots,$ *implies* $\varphi = 0$.

THEOREM 2.8 *(Parseval's formula). An orthonormal sequence* (φ_j) *in a Hilbert space* $\mathcal{H}$ *is complete if and only if*

$$\|\varphi\|^2 = \sum_{j=1}^{\infty} \left| \langle \varphi, \varphi_j \rangle \right|^2 \tag{2.4}$$

for every $\varphi \in \mathcal{H}$.

DEFINITION 2.9 *(Separable space).* A Hilbert space is called separable if it contains a complete orthonormal sequence.

EXAMPLE. A complete orthonormal sequence in $L^2([-\pi, \pi])$ is given by

$$\phi_j(x) = \frac{e^{ijx}}{\sqrt{2\pi}}, \qquad j = \ldots, -1, 0, 1, \ldots.$$

Hence, the space $L^2([-\pi, \pi])$ is separable.

THEOREM 2.10. *Every separable Hilbert space contains a countably dense subset.*

2.2. *Definitions and basic properties of operators*

In the sequel, we denote $K : \mathcal{H} \to \mathcal{E}$ the operator that maps a Hilbert space $\mathcal{H}$ (with norm $\|\cdot\|_{\mathcal{H}}$) into a Hilbert space $\mathcal{E}$ (with norm $\|\cdot\|_{\mathcal{E}}$).

DEFINITION 2.11. An operator $K : \mathcal{H} \to \mathcal{E}$ is called linear if

$$K(\alpha\varphi + \beta\psi) = \alpha K\varphi + \beta K\psi$$

for all $\varphi, \psi \in \mathcal{H}$ and all $\alpha, \beta \in \mathbb{C}$.

DEFINITION 2.12.

(i) The null space of $K : \mathcal{H} \to \mathcal{E}$ is the set $\mathcal{N}(K) = \{\varphi \in \mathcal{H}\colon\ K\varphi = 0\}$.

(ii) The range of $K : \mathcal{H} \to \mathcal{E}$ is the set $\mathcal{R}(K) = \{\psi \in \mathcal{E}\colon\ \psi = K\varphi \text{ for some } \varphi \in \mathcal{H}\}$.

(iii) The domain of $K : \mathcal{H} \to \mathcal{E}$ is the subset of $\mathcal{H}$ denoted $\mathcal{D}(K)$ on which K is defined.

(iv) An operator is called finite dimensional if its range is of finite dimension.

THEOREM 2.13. *A linear operator is continuous if it is continuous at one element.*

DEFINITION 2.14. A linear operator $K : \mathcal{H} \to \mathcal{E}$ is called bounded if there exists a positive number C such that

$$\|K\varphi\|_{\mathcal{E}} \leqslant C\|\varphi\|_{\mathcal{H}}$$

for all $\varphi \in \mathcal{H}$.

DEFINITION 2.15. The norm of a bounded operator K is defined as

$$\|K\| \equiv \sup_{\|\varphi\| \leqslant 1} \|K\varphi\|_{\mathcal{E}}.$$

THEOREM 2.16. *A linear operator is continuous if and only if it is bounded.*

EXAMPLE. The identity operator defined by $\mathcal{I}\varphi = \varphi$ for all $\varphi \in \mathcal{H}$ is bounded with $\|\mathcal{I}\| = 1$.

EXAMPLE. Consider the differential operator:

$$(D\varphi)(x) = \frac{\mathrm{d}\varphi(\tau)}{\mathrm{d}\tau} = \varphi'(\tau)$$

defined on the space $E_1 = \{\varphi \in L^2([-\pi, \pi])\colon\ \varphi' \in L^2([-\pi, \pi])\}$ with norm $\|\varphi\| = \sqrt{\int_{-\pi}^{\pi} |f(\tau)|^2\,\mathrm{d}\tau}$. For $\varphi_j(\tau) = \sin j\tau$, $j = 1, 2, \ldots,$ we have $\|\varphi_j\| = \sqrt{\int_{-\pi}^{\pi} |\sin(j\tau)|^2\,\mathrm{d}\tau} = \sqrt{\pi}$ and $\|D\varphi_j\| = \sqrt{\int_{-\pi}^{\pi} |j\cos(j\tau)|^2\,\mathrm{d}\tau} = j\sqrt{\pi}$. Therefore $\|D\varphi_j\| = j\|\varphi_j\|$ proving that the differential operator is not bounded.

THEOREM 2.17. *Every linear operator K from a finite dimensional normed space $\mathcal{H}$ into a normed space $\mathcal{E}$ is bounded.*

An important class of linear operators are valued in $\mathbb{C}$ and they are characterized by Riesz theorem. By Cauchy–Schwartz inequality, it follows that for any fixed vector g in an inner product space H, the formula $G(\varphi) = \langle \varphi, g \rangle$ defines a bounded linear functional on H. It turns out that if H is a Hilbert space, then every bounded linear functional is of this form.

THEOREM 2.18 *(Riesz). Let $\mathcal{H}$ be a Hilbert space. Then for each bounded linear function $G:\mathcal{H} \to \mathbb{C}$ there exists a unique element $g \in \mathcal{H}$ such that*

$$G(\varphi) = \langle \varphi, g \rangle$$

for all $\varphi \in \mathcal{H}$. The norms of the element g and the linear function G coincide

$$\|g\|_{\mathcal{H}} = \|G\|$$

where $\|\cdot\|_{\mathcal{H}}$ is the norm in $\mathcal{H}$ and $\|\cdot\|$ is the operator norm.

DEFINITION 2.19 *(Hilbert space isomorphism).* A Hilbert space $\mathcal{H}_1$ is said to be isometrically isomorphic (congruent) to a Hilbert space $\mathcal{H}_2$ if there exists a one-to-one linear mapping J from $\mathcal{H}_1$ to $\mathcal{H}_2$ such that

$$\langle J(\varphi), J(\psi) \rangle_{\mathcal{H}_2} = \langle \varphi, \psi \rangle_{\mathcal{H}_1}$$

for all $\varphi, \psi \in \mathcal{H}_1$. Such a mapping J is called a Hilbert space isomorphism (or congruence) from $\mathcal{H}_1$ to $\mathcal{H}_2$.

The terminology "congruence" is used by Parzen (1959, 1970).

THEOREM 2.20. *Let $\mathcal{H}$ be a separable Hilbert space.*

(a) *If $\mathcal{H}$ is infinite dimensional, then it is isometrically isomorphic to l^2.*
(b) *If $\mathcal{H}$ has a dimension N, then it is isometrically isomorphic to $\mathbb{C}^N$.*

A consequence of Theorem 2.20 is that two separable Hilbert spaces of the same dimension (finite or infinite) are isometrically isomorphic.

THEOREM 2.21. *Let $\mathcal{H}$ and $\mathcal{E}$ be Hilbert spaces and let $K:\mathcal{H} \to \mathcal{E}$ be a bounded operator. Then there exists a uniquely determined linear operator $K^*:\mathcal{E} \to \mathcal{H}$ with the property*

$$\langle K\varphi, \psi \rangle_{\mathcal{E}} = \langle \varphi, K^*\psi \rangle_{\mathcal{H}}$$

for all $\varphi \in \mathcal{H}$ and $\psi \in \mathcal{E}$. Moreover, the operator K^* is bounded and $\|K\| = \|K^*\|$. K^* is called the adjoint operator of K.

Riesz Theorem 2.18 implies that, in Hilbert spaces, the adjoint of a bounded operator always exists.

EXAMPLE 2.1 *(Discrete case).* Let π and ρ be two discrete probability density functions on $\mathbb{N}$. Let $\mathcal{H} = L^2(\mathbb{N}, \pi) = \{\varphi:\mathbb{N} \to \mathbb{R}, \varphi = (\varphi_l)_{l\in\mathbb{N}}$ such that $\sum_{l\in\mathbb{N}} \varphi_l^2 \pi(l) < \infty\}$ and $\mathcal{E} = L^2(\mathbb{N}, \rho)$. The operator K that associates to elements

$(\varphi_l)_{l\in\mathbb{N}}$ of $\mathcal{H}$ elements $(\psi_p)_{p\in\mathbb{N}}$ of $\mathcal{E}$ such that

$$(K\varphi)_p = \psi_p = \sum_{l\in\mathbb{N}} k(p,l)\varphi_l\pi(l)$$

is an infinite dimensional matrix. If $\mathcal{H}$ and $\mathcal{E}$ are finite dimensional, then K is simply a matrix and $K^* = K'$.

EXAMPLE 2.2 *(Integral operator).* An important kind of operator is the integral operator. Let $\mathcal{H} = L^2_{\mathbb{C}}(\mathbb{R}^q, \pi)$ and $\mathcal{E} = L^2_{\mathbb{C}}(\mathbb{R}^r, \rho)$ where π and ρ are p.d.f. The integral operator $K : \mathcal{H} \to \mathcal{E}$ is defined as

$$K\varphi(\tau) = \int k(\tau, s)\varphi(s)\pi(s)\,\mathrm{d}s. \tag{2.5}$$

The function k is called the kernel of the operator. If k satisfies

$$\iint \left|k(\tau, s)\right|^2 \pi(s)\rho(\tau)\,\mathrm{d}s\,\mathrm{d}\tau < \infty \tag{2.6}$$

(k is said to be a L^2-kernel) then K is a bounded operator and

$$\|K\| \leqslant \sqrt{\iint \left|k(\tau, s)\right|^2 \pi(s)\rho(\tau)\,\mathrm{d}s\,\mathrm{d}\tau}.$$

Indeed for any $\varphi \in \mathcal{H}$, we have

$$\begin{aligned}\|K\varphi\|^2_{\mathcal{E}} = \int \left|\int k(\tau, s)\varphi(s)\pi(s)\,\mathrm{d}s\right|^2 \rho(\tau)\,\mathrm{d}\tau &= \int \left|\langle k(\tau, \cdot), \varphi(\cdot)\rangle_{\mathcal{H}}\right|^2 \rho(\tau)\,\mathrm{d}\tau \\ &\leqslant \int \left\|k(\tau, \cdot)\right\|^2_{\mathcal{H}} \|\varphi\|^2_{\mathcal{H}} \rho(\tau)\,\mathrm{d}\tau\end{aligned}$$

by Cauchy–Schwarz inequality. Hence we have

$$\|K\varphi\|^2_{\mathcal{E}} \leqslant \|\varphi\|^2_{\mathcal{H}} \int \left\|k(\tau, \cdot)\right\|^2_{\mathcal{H}} \rho(\tau)\,\mathrm{d}\tau = \|\varphi\|^2_{\mathcal{H}} \iint \left|k(\tau, s)\right|^2 \pi(s)\rho(\tau)\,\mathrm{d}s\,\mathrm{d}\tau.$$

The upperbound for $\|K\|$ follows.

The adjoint K^* of the operator K is also an integral operator

$$K^*\psi(s) = \int k^*(s, \tau)\psi(\tau)\rho(\tau)\,\mathrm{d}\tau \tag{2.7}$$

with $k^*(s, \tau) = \overline{k(\tau, s)}$. Indeed, we have

$$\begin{aligned}\langle K\varphi, \psi\rangle_{\mathcal{E}} &= \int (K\varphi)(\tau)\overline{\psi(\tau)}\rho(\tau)\,\mathrm{d}\tau \\ &= \int \left(\int k(\tau, s)\varphi(s)\pi(s)\,\mathrm{d}s\right)\overline{\psi(\tau)}\rho(\tau)\,\mathrm{d}\tau\end{aligned}$$

$$
\begin{aligned}
&= \int \varphi(s)\Big(\int k(\tau, s)\overline{\psi(\tau)}\rho(\tau)\,\mathrm{d}\tau\Big)\pi(s)\,\mathrm{d}s \\
&= \int \varphi(s)\overline{\Big(\int k^*(s, \tau)\psi(\tau)\rho(\tau)\,\mathrm{d}\tau\Big)}\pi(s)\,\mathrm{d}s \\
&= \langle \varphi, K^*\psi\rangle_{\mathcal{H}}.
\end{aligned}
$$

There are two types of integral operators we are interested in, the covariance operator and the conditional expectation operator.

EXAMPLE 2.3 *(Conditional expectation operator).* When K is a conditional expectation operator, it is natural to define the spaces of reference as functions of unknown p.d.f.s. Let $(Z, W) \in \mathbb{R}^q \times \mathbb{R}^r$ be a r.v. with distribution $F_{Z,W}$, let F_Z, and F_W be the marginal distributions of Z and W, respectively. The corresponding p.d.f.s are denoted $f_{Z,W}$, f_Z, and f_W. Define

$$
\mathcal{H} = L^2(\mathbb{R}^q, f_Z) \equiv L_Z^2, \qquad \mathcal{E} = L^2(\mathbb{R}^r, f_W) \equiv L_W^2.
$$

Let K be the conditional expectation operator:

$$
\begin{aligned}
K : L_Z^2 &\to L_W^2 \\
\varphi &\to E\big[\varphi(Z) \mid W\big].
\end{aligned}
\tag{2.8}
$$

K is an integral operator with kernel

$$
k(w, z) = \frac{f_{Z,W}(z, w)}{f_Z(z) f_W(w)}.
$$

By Equation (2.7), its adjoint K^* has kernel $k^*(z, w) = k(w, z)$ and is also a conditional expectation operator:

$$
\begin{aligned}
K^* : L_W^2 &\to L_Z^2 \\
\psi &\to E\big[\psi(W) \mid Z\big].
\end{aligned}
$$

EXAMPLE 2.4 *(Restriction of an operator on a subset of $\mathcal{H}$).* Let $K : \mathcal{H} \to \mathcal{E}$ and consider the restriction denoted K_0 of K on a subspace $\mathcal{H}_0$ of $\mathcal{H}$. $K_0 : \mathcal{H}_0 \to \mathcal{E}$ is such that K_0 and K coincide on $\mathcal{H}_0$. It can be shown that the adjoint K_0^* of K_0 is the operator mapping $\mathcal{E}$ into $\mathcal{H}_0$ such that

$$
K_0^* = PK^* \tag{2.9}
$$

where P is the projection on $\mathcal{H}_0$. The expression of K_0^* will reflect the extra information contained in $\mathcal{H}_0$.

To prove (2.9), we use the definition of K^*:

$$
\begin{aligned}
\langle K\varphi, \psi\rangle_{\mathcal{E}} &= \langle \varphi, K^*\psi\rangle_{\mathcal{H}} \quad \text{for all } \varphi \in \mathcal{H}_0 \\
&= \langle \varphi, K_0^*\psi\rangle_{\mathcal{H}_0} \quad \text{for all } \varphi \in \mathcal{H}_0
\end{aligned}
$$

$$\Leftrightarrow \langle \varphi, K^*\psi - K_0^*\psi \rangle_{\mathcal{H}} = 0 \quad \text{for all } \varphi \in \mathcal{H}_0$$
$$\Leftrightarrow K^*\psi - K_0^*\psi \in \mathcal{H}_0^{\perp}$$
$$\Leftrightarrow K_0^*\psi = PK^*\psi.$$

A potential application of this result to the conditional expectation in Example 2.3 is the case where φ is known to be additive. Let $Z = (Z_1, Z_2)$. Then

$$\mathcal{H}_0 = \{\varphi(Z) = \varphi_1(Z_1) + \varphi_2(Z_2): \varphi_1 \in L^2_{Z_1}, \varphi_2 \in L^2_{Z_2}\}.$$

Assume that $E[\varphi_1(Z_1)] = E[\varphi_2(Z_2)] = 0$. We have $P\varphi = (\varphi_1, \varphi_2)$ with

$$\varphi_1 = (I - P_1P_2)^{-1}(P_1 - P_1P_2)\varphi,$$
$$\varphi_2 = (I - P_1P_2)^{-1}(P_2 - P_1P_2)\varphi,$$

where P_1 and P_2 are the projection operators on $L^2_{Z_1}$ and $L^2_{Z_2}$, respectively. If the two spaces $L^2_{Z_1}$ and $L^2_{Z_2}$ are orthogonal, then $\varphi_1 = P_1\varphi$ and $\varphi_2 = P_2\varphi$.

DEFINITION 2.22 *(Self-adjoint)*. If $K = K^*$ then K is called self-adjoint (or Hermitian).

Remark that if K is a self-adjoint integral operator, then $k(s, \tau) = \overline{k(\tau, s)}$.

THEOREM 2.23. *Let $K : \mathcal{H} \to \mathcal{H}$ be a self-adjoint operator then*

$$\|K\| = \sup_{\|\varphi\|=1} |\langle K\varphi, \varphi \rangle_{\mathcal{H}}|.$$

DEFINITION 2.24 *(Positive operator)*. An operator $K : \mathcal{H} \to \mathcal{H}$ is called positive if it is self-adjoint and $\langle K\varphi, \varphi \rangle_{\mathcal{H}} \geqslant 0$ for all φ in $\mathcal{H}$.

DEFINITION 2.25. A sequence (K_n) of operators $K_n : \mathcal{H} \to \mathcal{E}$ is called pointwise convergent if for every $\varphi \in \mathcal{H}$, the sequence $K_n\varphi$ converges in $\mathcal{E}$. A sequence (K_n) of bounded operators converges in norm to a bounded operator K if $\|K_n - K\| \to 0$ as $n \to \infty$.

DEFINITION 2.26 *(Compact operator)*. A linear operator $K : \mathcal{H} \to \mathcal{E}$ is called a compact operator if for every bounded sequence (φ_n) in $\mathcal{H}$, the sequence $(K\varphi_n)$ contains a convergent subsequence in $\mathcal{E}$.

THEOREM 2.27. *Compact linear operators are bounded.*

Not every bounded operator is compact. An example is given by the identity operator on an infinite dimensional space $\mathcal{H}$. Consider an orthonormal sequence (e_n) in $\mathcal{H}$. Then the sequence $\mathcal{I}e_n = e_n$ does not contain a convergent subsequence.

THEOREM 2.28. *Finite dimensional operators are compact.*

THEOREM 2.29. *If the sequence $K_n : \mathcal{H} \to \mathcal{E}$ of compact linear operators are norm convergent to a linear operator $K : \mathcal{H} \to \mathcal{E}$, i.e., $\|K_n - K\| \to 0$ as $n \to \infty$, then K is compact. Moreover, every compact operator is the limit of a sequence of operators with finite dimensional range.*

Hilbert–Schmidt operators are discussed in Dunford and Schwartz (1988, p. 1009), Dautray and Lions (1988, p. 41).

DEFINITION 2.30 *(Hilbert–Schmidt operator).* Let $\{\varphi_j,\ j = 1, 2, \ldots\}$ be a complete orthonormal set in a Hilbert space $\mathcal{H}$. An operator $K : \mathcal{H} \to \mathcal{E}$ is said to be a Hilbert–Schmidt operator if the quantity $\|\cdot\|_{\mathrm{HS}}$ defined by

$$\|K\|_{\mathrm{HS}} = \left\{ \sum_{j=1}^{\infty} \|K\varphi_j\|_{\mathcal{E}}^2 \right\}^{1/2}$$

is finite. The number $\|K\|_{\mathrm{HS}}$ is called the Hilbert–Schmidt norm of K. Moreover

$$\|K\| \leqslant \|K\|_{\mathrm{HS}} \tag{2.10}$$

and hence K is bounded.

From (2.10), it follows that HS norm convergence implies (operator) norm convergence.

THEOREM 2.31. *The Hilbert–Schmidt norm is independent of the orthonormal basis used in its definition.*

THEOREM 2.32. *Every Hilbert–Schmidt operator is compact.*

THEOREM 2.33. *The adjoint of a Hilbert–Schmidt operator is itself a Hilbert–Schmidt operator and $\|K\|_{\mathrm{HS}} = \|K^*\|_{\mathrm{HS}}$.*

Theorem 2.32 implies that Hilbert–Schmidt (HS) operators can be approached by a sequence of finite dimensional operators, which is an attractive feature when it comes to estimating K. Remark that the integral operator K defined by (2.5) and (2.6) is a Hilbert–Schmidt (HS) operator and its adjoint is also a HS operator. Actually, all Hilbert–Schmidt operators of $L^2(\mathbb{R}^q, \pi)$ in $L^2(\mathbb{R}^r, \rho)$ are integral operators. The following theorem is proved in Dautray and Lions (1988, p. 45).

THEOREM 2.34. *An operator of $L^2(\mathbb{R}^q, \pi)$ in $L^2(\mathbb{R}^r, \rho)$ is Hilbert–Schmidt if and only if it admits a kernel representation* (2.5) *conformable to* (2.6). *In this case, the kernel k is unique.*

EXAMPLE 2.1 *(Continued)*. Let K be an operator from $L^2(\mathbb{N},\pi)$ in $L^2(\mathbb{N},\rho)$ with kernel $k(l,p)$. K is a Hilbert–Schmidt operator if $\sum\sum k(l,p)^2\pi(l)\rho(p) < \infty$. In particular, the operator defined by $(K\varphi)_1 = \varphi_1$ and $(K\varphi)_p = \varphi_p - \varphi_{p-1}$, $p = 2, 3, \ldots,$ is not a Hilbert–Schmidt operator; it is not even compact.

EXAMPLE 2.3 *(Continued)*. By Theorem 2.34, a sufficient condition for K and K^* to be Hilbert–Schmidt and therefore compact is

$$\iint \left[\frac{f_{Z,W}(z,w)}{f_Z(z)f_W(w)}\right]^2 f_Z(z)f_W(w)\,\mathrm{d}z\,\mathrm{d}w < \infty.$$

EXAMPLE 2.5 *(Conditional expectation with common elements)*. Consider a conditional expectation operator from $L^2(X,Z)$ into $L^2(X,W)$ defined by

$$(K\varphi)(x,w) = E\big[\varphi(X,Z) \mid X = x,\ W = w\big].$$

Because there are common elements between the conditioning variable and the argument of the function φ, the operator K is not compact. Indeed, let $\varphi(X)$ be such that $E(\varphi^2) = 1$, we have $K\varphi = \varphi$. It follows that the image of the unit circle in $L^2(X,Z)$ contains the unit circle of $L^2(X)$ and hence is not compact. Therefore, K is not compact.

EXAMPLE 2.6 *(Restriction)*. For illustration, we consider the effect of restricting K on a subset of $L^2_{\mathbb{C}}(\mathbb{R}^q,\pi)$. Consider $\tilde{K}$ the operator defined by

$$\tilde{K} : L^2_{\mathbb{C}}(\mathbb{R}^q,\tilde{\pi}) \to L^2_{\mathbb{C}}(\mathbb{R}^r,\tilde{\rho}),$$
$$\tilde{K}\varphi = K\varphi$$

for every $\varphi \in L^2_{\mathbb{C}}(\mathbb{R}^q,\tilde{\pi})$, where $L^2_{\mathbb{C}}(\mathbb{R}^q,\tilde{\pi}) \subset L^2_{\mathbb{C}}(\mathbb{R}^q,\pi)$ and $L^2_{\mathbb{C}}(\mathbb{R}^r,\tilde{\rho}) \supset L^2_{\mathbb{C}}(\mathbb{R}^r,\rho)$. Assume that K is an HS operator defined by (2.5). Under which conditions is $\tilde{K}$ an HS operator? Let

$$\tilde{K}\varphi(s) = \int k(\tau,s)\varphi(s)\pi(s)\,\mathrm{d}s = \int k(\tau,s)\frac{\pi(s)}{\tilde{\pi}(s)}\varphi(s)\tilde{\pi}(s)\,\mathrm{d}s$$
$$\equiv \int \tilde{k}(\tau,s)\varphi(s)\tilde{\pi}(s)\,\mathrm{d}s.$$

Assume that $\tilde{\pi}(s) = 0$ implies $\pi(s) = 0$ and $\rho(\tau) = 0$ implies $\tilde{\rho}(\tau) = 0$. Note that

$$\int \left|\tilde{k}(\tau,s)\right|^2\tilde{\pi}(s)\tilde{\rho}(\tau)\,\mathrm{d}s\,\mathrm{d}\tau$$
$$= \int \left|k(\tau,s)\right|^2\frac{\pi(s)}{\tilde{\pi}(s)}\frac{\tilde{\rho}(\tau)}{\rho(\tau)}\pi(s)\rho(\tau)\,\mathrm{d}s\,\mathrm{d}\tau$$
$$< \sup_s\left|\frac{\pi(s)}{\tilde{\pi}(s)}\right| \sup_\tau\left|\frac{\tilde{\rho}(\tau)}{\rho(\tau)}\right| \int \left|k(\tau,s)\right|^2\pi(s)\rho(\tau)\,\mathrm{d}s\,\mathrm{d}\tau.$$

Hence the HS property is preserved if (a) there is a constant $c > 0$ such that $\pi(s) \leqslant c\tilde{\pi}(s)$ for all $s \in \mathbb{R}^q$ and (b) there is a constant d such that $\tilde{\rho}(\tau) \leqslant d\rho(\tau)$ for all $\tau \in \mathbb{R}^r$.

2.3. *Spectral decomposition of compact operators*

For compact operators, spectral analysis reduces to the analysis of eigenvalues and eigenfunctions. Let $K : \mathcal{H} \to \mathcal{H}$ be a compact linear operator.

DEFINITION 2.35. λ is an eigenvalue of K if there is a nonzero vector $\phi \in \mathcal{H}$ such that $K\phi = \lambda\phi$. ϕ is called the eigenfunction of K corresponding to λ.

THEOREM 2.36. *All eigenvalues of a self-adjoint operator are real. Eigenfunctions corresponding to different eigenvalues of a self-adjoint operator are orthogonal.*

THEOREM 2.37. *All eigenvalues of a positive operator are nonnegative.*

THEOREM 2.38. *For every eigenvalue λ of a bounded operator K, we have $|\lambda| \leqslant \|K\|$.*

THEOREM 2.39. *Let K be a self-adjoint compact operator, the set of its eigenvalues (λ_j) is countable and its eigenvectors (ϕ_j) can be orthonormalized. Its largest eigenvalue (in absolute value) satisfies $|\lambda_1| = \|K\|$. If K has infinitely many eigenvalues $|\lambda_1| \geqslant |\lambda_2| \geqslant \cdots$, then* $\lim_{j\to\infty} \lambda_j = 0$.

Let $K : \mathcal{H} \to \mathcal{E}$, K^*K and KK^* are self-adjoint positive operators on $\mathcal{H}$ and $\mathcal{E}$, respectively. Hence their eigenvalues are nonnegative by Theorem 2.37.

DEFINITION 2.40. Let $\mathcal{H}$ and $\mathcal{E}$ be Hilbert spaces, $K : \mathcal{H} \to \mathcal{E}$ be a compact linear operator and $K^* : \mathcal{E} \to \mathcal{H}$ be its adjoint. The square roots of the eigenvalues of the nonnegative self-adjoint compact operator $K^*K : \mathcal{H} \to \mathcal{H}$ are called the singular values of K.

The following results [Kress (1999), Theorem 15.16] apply to operators that are not necessarily self-adjoint.

THEOREM 2.41. *Let (λ_j) denote the sequence of the nonzero singular values of the compact linear operator K repeated according to their multiplicity. Then there exist orthonormal sequences ϕ_j of $\mathcal{H}$ and ψ_j of $\mathcal{E}$ such that*

$$K\phi_j = \lambda_j \psi_j, \qquad K^*\psi_j = \lambda_j \phi_j \tag{2.11}$$

for all $j \in N$. For each $\varphi \in \mathcal{H}$ we have the singular value decomposition

$$\varphi = \sum_{j=1}^{\infty} \langle \varphi, \phi_j \rangle \phi_j + Q\varphi \tag{2.12}$$

with the orthogonal projection operator $Q : \mathcal{H} \to \mathcal{N}(K)$ *and*

$$K\varphi = \sum_{j=1}^{\infty} \lambda_j \langle \varphi, \phi_j \rangle \psi_j. \tag{2.13}$$

$\{\lambda_j, \phi_j, \psi_j\}$ is called the singular system of K. Note that λ_j^2 are the nonzero eigenvalues of KK^* and K^*K associated with the eigenfunctions ψ_j and ϕ_j, respectively.

THEOREM 2.42. *Let* K *be the integral operator defined by* (2.5) *and assume condition* (2.6) *holds. Let* $\{\lambda_j, \phi_j, \psi_j\}$ *be as in* (2.11). *Then*:

(i) *The Hilbert–Schmidt norm of* K *can be written as*

$$\|K\|_{\mathrm{HS}} = \left\{ \sum_{j \in N} |\lambda_j|^2 \right\}^{1/2} = \left\{ \iint |k(\tau, s)|^2 \pi(s)\rho(\tau)\, \mathrm{d}s\, \mathrm{d}\tau \right\}^{1/2}$$

where each λ_j *is repeated according to its multiplicity.*

(ii) *(Mercer's formula)* $k(\tau, s) = \sum_{j=1}^{\infty} \lambda_j \psi_j(\tau)\overline{\phi_j(s)}$.

EXAMPLE *(Degenerate operator).* Consider an integral operator defined on $L^2([a, b])$ with a Pincherle–Goursat kernel i.e.

$$Kf(\tau) = \int_a^b k(\tau, s) f(s)\, \mathrm{d}s, \qquad k(\tau, s) = \sum_{l=1}^{n} a_l(\tau) b_l(s).$$

Assume that a_l and b_l belong to $L^2([a, b])$ for all l. By (2.6), it follows that K is bounded. Moreover, as K is finite dimensional, we have K compact by Theorem 2.28. Assume that the set of functions (a_l) is linearly independent. The equality $K\phi = \lambda\phi$ yields

$$\sum_{l=1}^{n} a_l(\tau) \int b_l(s)\phi(s)\, \mathrm{d}s = \lambda\phi(\tau),$$

hence $\phi(\tau)$ is necessarily of the form $\sum_{l=1}^{n} c_l a_l(\tau)$. The dimension of the range of K is therefore n and there are at most n nonzero eigenvalues.

EXAMPLE. Let $\mathcal{H} = L^2([0, 1])$ and the integral operator $Kf(\tau) = \int_0^1 (\tau \wedge s) f(s)\, \mathrm{d}s$ where $\tau \wedge s = \min(\tau, s)$. It is possible to explicitly compute the eigenvalues and eigenfunctions of K by solving $K\phi = \lambda\phi \iff \int_0^\tau s\phi(s)\, \mathrm{d}s + \tau \int_\tau^1 \phi(s)\, \mathrm{d}s = \lambda\phi(\tau)$. Using two successive differentiations with respect to τ, we obtain a differential equation $\phi(\tau) = -\lambda\phi''(\tau)$ with boundary conditions $\phi(0) = 0$ and $\phi'(1) = 0$. Hence the set of orthonormal eigenfunctions is $\phi_j(\tau) = \sqrt{2}\sin((\pi j \tau)/2)$ associated with the eigenvalues $\lambda_j = 4/(\pi^2 j^2)$, $j = 1, 3, 5, \ldots$. We can see that the eigenvalues converge to zero at an arithmetic rate.

EXAMPLE. Let π be the p.d.f. of the standard normal distribution and $\mathcal{H} = L^2(\mathbb{R}, \pi)$. Define K as the integral operator with kernel

$$k(\tau, s) = \frac{l(\tau, s)}{\pi(\tau)\pi(s)}$$

where $l(\tau, s)$ is the joint p.d.f. of the bivariate normal $\mathcal{N}\left(\binom{0}{0}, \begin{pmatrix} 1 & \rho \\ \rho & 1 \end{pmatrix}\right)$. Then K is a self-adjoint operator with eigenvalues $\lambda_j = \rho^j$ and has eigenfunctions that take the Hermite polynomial form ϕ_j, $j = 1, 2, \ldots$, defined in (2.1). This is an example where the eigenvalues decay exponentially fast.

2.4. *Random element in Hilbert spaces*

2.4.1. *Definitions*

Let $\mathcal{H}$ be a real separable Hilbert space with norm $\| \ \|$ induced by the inner product $\langle , \rangle$. Let $(\Omega, \mathcal{F}, P)$ be a complete probability space. Let $X : \Omega \to \mathcal{H}$ be a Hilbert space-valued random element (an $\mathcal{H}$-r.e.). X is integrable or has finite expectation $E(X)$ if $E(\|X\|) = \int_\Omega \|X\| \, \mathrm{d}P < \infty$, in that case $E(X)$ satisfies $E(X) \in \mathcal{H}$ and $E[\langle X, \varphi \rangle] = \langle E(X), \varphi \rangle$ for all $\varphi \in \mathcal{H}$. An $\mathcal{H}$-r.e. X is weakly second-order if $E[\langle X, \varphi \rangle^2] < \infty$ for all $\varphi \in \mathcal{H}$. For a weakly second-order $\mathcal{H}$-r.e. X with expectation $E(X)$, we define the covariance operator K as

$$\begin{aligned} &K : \mathcal{H} \to \mathcal{H}, \\ &K\varphi = E\big[\langle X - E(X), \varphi \rangle \big(X - E(X)\big)\big] \end{aligned}$$

for all $\varphi \in \mathcal{H}$. Note that $\operatorname{var}\langle X, \varphi \rangle = \langle K\varphi, \varphi \rangle$.

EXAMPLE. Let $\mathcal{H} = L^2([0, 1])$ with $\|g\| = [\int_0^1 g(\tau)^2 \, \mathrm{d}\tau]^{1/2}$ and $X = h(\tau, Y)$ where Y is a random variable and $h(\cdot, Y) \in L^2([0, 1])$ with probability one. Assume $E(h(\tau, Y)) = 0$, then the covariance operator takes the form:

$$\begin{aligned} K\varphi(\tau) &= E\big[\langle h(\cdot, Y), \varphi \rangle h(\tau, Y)\big] \\ &= E\left[\left(\int h(s, Y)\varphi(s) \, \mathrm{d}s\right) h(\tau, Y)\right] \\ &= \int E\big[h(\tau, Y)h(s, Y)\big]\varphi(s) \, \mathrm{d}s \\ &\equiv \int k(\tau, s)\varphi(s) \, \mathrm{d}s. \end{aligned}$$

Moreover, if $h(\tau, Y) = I\{Y \leqslant \tau\} - F(\tau)$ then $k(\tau, s) = F(\tau \wedge s) - F(\tau)F(s)$.

DEFINITION 2.43. An $\mathcal{H}$-r.e. Y has a Gaussian distribution on $\mathcal{H}$ if for all $\varphi \in \mathcal{H}$ the real-valued r.v. $\langle \varphi, Y \rangle$ has a Gaussian distribution on $\mathbb{R}$.

DEFINITION 2.44 *(Strong mixing)*. Let $\{X_{i,n},\ i = \dots, -1, 0, 1, \dots;\ n \geqslant 1\}$ be an array of $\mathcal{H}$-r.e., defined on the probability space $(\Omega, \mathcal{F}, P)$ and define $\mathcal{A}_{n,a}^{n,b} = \sigma(X_{i,n},\ a \leqslant i \leqslant b)$ for all $-\infty \leqslant a \leqslant b \leqslant +\infty$, and $n \geqslant 1$. The array $\{X_{i,n}\}$ is called a strong or α-mixing array of $\mathcal{H}$-r.e. if $\lim_{j\to\infty} \alpha(j) = 0$ where

$$\alpha(j) = \sup_{n\geqslant 1} \sup_{l} \sup_{A,B} \left[\left| P(A \cap B) - P(A)P(B) \right| :\ A \in \mathcal{A}_{n,-\infty}^{n,l},\ B \in \mathcal{A}_{n,l+j}^{n,+\infty} \right].$$

2.4.2. Central limit theorem for mixing processes

We want to study the asymptotic properties of $Z_n = n^{-1/2} \sum_{i=1}^n X_{i,n}$ where $\{X_{i,n}: 1 \leqslant 1 \leqslant n\}$ is an array of $\mathcal{H}$-r.e. Weak and strong laws of large numbers for near epoch dependent (NED) processes can be found in Chen and White (1996). Here we provide sufficient conditions for the weak convergence of processes to be denoted $\Rightarrow$ [see Davidson (1994) for a definition]. Weak convergence is stronger than the standard central limit theorem (CLT) as illustrated by a simple example. Let (X_i) be an i.i.d. sequence of zero mean weakly second-order elements of $\mathcal{H}$. Then for any Z in $\mathcal{H}$, $\langle X_i, Z\rangle$ is an i.i.d. zero mean sequence of $\mathbb{C}$ with finite variance $\langle KZ, Z\rangle$. Then standard CLT implies the asymptotic normality of $\frac{1}{\sqrt{n}} \sum_{i=1}^n \langle X_i, Z\rangle$. The weak convergence of $\frac{1}{\sqrt{n}} \sum_{i=1}^n X_i$ to a Gaussian process $\mathcal{N}(0, K)$ in $\mathcal{H}$ requires an extra assumption, namely $E\|X_1\|^2 < \infty$. Weak convergence theorems for NED processes that might have trending mean (hence are not covariance stationary) are provided by Chen and White (1998). Here, we report results for mixing processes proved by Politis and Romano (1994). See also van der Vaart and Wellner (1996) for i.i.d. sequences.

THEOREM 2.45. *Let $\{X_{i,n}: 1 \leqslant i \leqslant n\}$ be a double array of stationary mixing $\mathcal{H}$-r.e. with zero mean, such that for all n, $\|X_{i,n}\| < B$ with probability one, and $\sum_{j=1}^m j^2 \alpha(j) \leqslant K m^r$ for all $1 \leqslant m \leqslant n$ and n, and some $r < 3/2$. Assume, for any integer $l \geqslant 1$, that $(X_{1,n}, \dots, X_{l,n})$, regarded as a r.e. of $\mathcal{H}^l$, converges in distribution to say $(X_1, \dots, X_l)$. Moreover, assume $E[\langle X_{1,n}, X_{l,n}\rangle] \to E[\langle X_1, X_l\rangle]$ as $n \to \infty$ and*

$$\lim_{n\to\infty} \sum_{l=1}^{n} E\left[\langle X_{1,n}, X_{l,n}\rangle\right] = \sum_{l=1}^{\infty} E\left[\langle X_1, X_l\rangle\right] < \infty.$$

Let $Z_n = n^{-1/2} \sum_{i=1}^n X_{i,n}$. For any $\varphi \in \mathcal{H}$, let $\sigma_{\varphi,n}^2$ denote the variance of $\langle Z_n, \varphi\rangle$. Assume

$$\sigma_{\varphi,n}^2 \underset{n\to\infty}{\longrightarrow} \sigma_\varphi^2 \equiv \operatorname{Var}\left(\langle X_1, \varphi\rangle\right) + 2\sum_{i=1}^{\infty} \operatorname{cov}\left(\langle X_1, \varphi\rangle, \langle X_{1+i}, \varphi\rangle\right). \tag{2.14}$$

Then Z_n converges weakly to a Gaussian process $\mathcal{N}(0, K)$ in $\mathcal{H}$, with zero mean and covariance operator K satisfying $\langle K\varphi, \varphi\rangle = \sigma_\varphi^2$ for each $\varphi \in \mathcal{H}$.

In the special case when the $X_{i,n} = X_i$ form a stationary sequence, the conditions simplify considerably:

THEOREM 2.46. *Assume $X_1, X_2, \ldots,$ is a stationary sequence of $\mathcal{H}$-r.e. with mean μ and mixing coefficient α. Let $Z_n = n^{-1/2} \sum_{i=1}^{n} (X_i - \mu)$.*

(i) *If $E(\|X_1\|^{2+\delta}) < \infty$ for some $\delta > 0$, and $\sum_j [\alpha(j)]^{\delta/(2+\delta)} < \infty$*
(ii) *or if $X_1, X_2, \ldots,$ is i.i.d. and $E\|X_1\|^2 < \infty$.*

Then Z_n converges weakly to a Gaussian process $G \sim \mathcal{N}(0, K)$ in $\mathcal{H}$. The distribution of G is determined by the distribution of its marginals $\langle G, \varphi \rangle$ which are $\mathcal{N}(0, \sigma_\varphi^2)$ distributed for every $\varphi \in \mathcal{H}$ where σ_φ^2 is defined in (2.14).

Let $\{e_l\}$ be a complete orthonormal basis of $\mathcal{H}$. Then $\|X_1\|^2 = \sum_{l=1}^{\infty} \langle X_1, e_l \rangle^2$ and hence in the i.i.d. case, it suffices to check that $E\|X_1\|^2 = \sum_{l=1}^{\infty} E[\langle X_1, e_l \rangle^2] < \infty$.

The following theorem is stated in more general terms in Chen and White (1992).

THEOREM 2.47. *Let A_n be a random bounded linear operator from $\mathcal{H}$ to $\mathcal{H}$ and $A \neq 0$ be a nonrandom bounded linear operator from $\mathcal{H}$ to $\mathcal{H}$. If $\|A_n - A\| \to 0$ in probability as $n \to \infty$ and $Y_n \Rightarrow Y \sim \mathcal{N}(0, K)$ in $\mathcal{H}$. Then $A_n Y_n \Rightarrow AY \sim \mathcal{N}(0, AKA^*)$.*

In Theorem 2.47, the boundedness of A is crucial. In most of our applications, A will not be bounded and we will not be able to apply Theorem 2.47. Instead we will have to check the Liapunov condition [Davidson (1994)] "by hand".

THEOREM 2.48. *Let the array $\{X_{i,n}\}$ be independent with zero mean and variance sequence $\{\sigma_{i,n}^2\}$ satisfying $\sum_{i=1}^{n} \sigma_{i,n}^2 = 1$. Then $\sum_{i=1}^{n} X_{i,n} \xrightarrow{d} \mathcal{N}(0, 1)$ if*

$$\lim_{n \to \infty} \sum_{i=1}^{n} E\big[|X_{i,n}|^{2+\delta}\big] = 0 \quad \text{(Liapunov condition)}$$

for some $\delta > 0$.

2.5. *Estimation of an operator and its adjoint*

2.5.1. *Estimation of an operator*

In many cases of interest, an estimator of the compact operator, K, is given by a degenerate operator of the form

$$\hat{K}_n \varphi = \sum_{l=1}^{L_n} a_l(\varphi) \varepsilon_l \tag{2.15}$$

where $\varepsilon_l \in \mathcal{E}$, $a_l(\varphi)$ is linear in φ.

Examples:

1. *Covariance operator*

$$K\varphi(\tau_1) = \int E\big[h(\tau_1, X)h(\tau_2, X)\big]\varphi(\tau_2)\,\mathrm{d}\tau_2.$$

Replacing the expectation by the sample mean, one obtains an estimator of K:

$$\hat{K}_n\varphi(\tau_1) = \int\left(\frac{1}{n}\sum_{i=1}^{n} h(\tau_1, x_i)h(\tau_2, x_i)\right)\varphi(\tau_2)\,\mathrm{d}\tau_2 = \sum_{i=1}^{n} a_i(\varphi)\varepsilon_i$$

with

$$a_i(\varphi) = \frac{1}{n}\int h(\tau_2, x_i)\varphi(\tau_2)\,\mathrm{d}\tau_2 \quad \text{and} \quad \varepsilon_i = h(\tau_1, x_i).$$

Note that here K is self-adjoint and the rate of convergence of $\hat{K}_n$ to K is parametric.

2. *Conditional expectation operator*

$$K\varphi(w) = E\big[\varphi(Z) \mid W = w\big].$$

The kernel estimator of K with kernel ω and bandwidth c_n is given by

$$\hat{K}_n\varphi(w) = \frac{\sum_{i=1}^{n}\varphi(z_i)\omega\big(\frac{w-w_i}{c_n}\big)}{\sum_{i=1}^{n}\omega\big(\frac{w-w_i}{c_n}\big)} = \sum_{i=1}^{n} a_i(\varphi)\varepsilon_i$$

where

$$a_i(\varphi) = \varphi(z_i) \quad \text{and} \quad \varepsilon_i = \left[\frac{\omega\big(\frac{w-w_i}{c_n}\big)}{\sum_{i=1}^{n}\omega\big(\frac{w-w_i}{c_n}\big)}\right].$$

In this case, the rate of convergence of $\hat{K}_n$ is nonparametric, see Section 4.1.

2.5.2. *Estimation of the adjoint of a conditional expectation operator*

Consider a conditional expectation operator as described in Example 2.3. Let $K : L^2_Z \to L^2_W$ be such that $(K\varphi)(w) = E[\varphi(Z) \mid W = w]$ and its adjoint is $K^* : L^2_W \to L^2_Z$ with $(K\psi)(z) = E[\psi(W) \mid Z = z]$. Let $\hat{f}_{Z,W}$, $\hat{f}_Z(z)$, and $\hat{f}_W(w)$ be nonparametric estimators of $f_{Z,W}$, $f_Z(z)$, and $f_W(w)$ obtained either by kernel or sieves estimators. Assume that K and K^* are estimated by replacing the unknown p.d.f.s by their estimators, that is

$$\hat{K}_n\varphi(w) = \int \frac{\hat{f}_{Z,W}(z, w)}{\hat{f}_Z(z)}\varphi(z)\,\mathrm{d}z,$$

$$\widehat{(K^*)}_n\psi(z) = \int \frac{\hat{f}_{Z,W}(z, w)}{\hat{f}_W(w)}\psi(w)\,\mathrm{d}w.$$

Remark that $\widehat{(K^*)}_n \neq (\hat{K}_n)^*$ for $\mathcal{H} = L^2_Z$ and $\mathcal{E} = L^2_W$. Indeed, we do not have

$$\langle \hat{K}_n \varphi, \psi \rangle_{\mathcal{E}} = \langle \varphi, \widehat{(K^*)}_n \psi \rangle_{\mathcal{H}}. \tag{2.16}$$

There are two solutions to this problem. The first solution consists in choosing as space of references $\mathcal{H}_n = L^2(\mathbb{R}^q, \hat{f}_Z)$ and $\mathcal{E}_n = L^2(\mathbb{R}^r, \hat{f}_W)$. In which case, $\widehat{(K^*)}_n = (\hat{K}_n)^*$ for $\mathcal{H}_n$ and $\mathcal{E}_n$ because

$$\langle \hat{K}_n \varphi, \psi \rangle_{\mathcal{E}_n} = \langle \varphi, \widehat{(K^*)}_n \psi \rangle_{\mathcal{H}_n}. \tag{2.17}$$

The new spaces $\mathcal{H}_n$ and $\mathcal{E}_n$ depend on the sample size and on the estimation procedure. Another approach consists in defining $\mathcal{H} = L^2(\mathbb{R}^q, \pi)$ and $\mathcal{E} = L^2(\mathbb{R}^r, \rho)$ where π and ρ are known and satisfy: There exist $c, c' > 0$ such that $f_Z(z) \leqslant c\pi(z)$ and $f_W(w) \geqslant c'\rho(w)$. Then

$$K^*\psi(z) = \int \frac{f_{Z,W}(z,w)}{f_W(w)} \frac{\rho(w)}{\pi(z)} \psi(w)\,\mathrm{d}w \neq E\big[\psi(W) \mid Z = z\big].$$

In that case, $\widehat{(K^*)}_n = (\hat{K}_n)^*$ for $\mathcal{H}$ and $\mathcal{E}$ but the choice of π and ρ require some knowledge on the support and the tails of the distributions of W and Z.

An alternative solution to estimating K and K^* by kernel is to estimate the spectrum of K and to apply Mercer's formula. Let $\mathcal{H} = L^2_Z$ and $\mathcal{E} = L^2_W$. The singular system $\{\lambda_j, \phi_j, \psi_j\}$ of K satisfies

$$\lambda_j = \sup_{\phi_j, \psi_j} E\big[\phi_j(Z)\psi_j(W)\big], \quad j = 1, 2, \ldots, \tag{2.18}$$

subject to $\|\phi_j\|_{\mathcal{H}} = 1$, $\langle \phi_j, \phi_l \rangle_{\mathcal{H}} = 0$, $l = 1, 2, \ldots, j-1$, $\|\psi_j\|_{\mathcal{E}} = 1$, $\langle \psi_j, \psi_l \rangle_{\mathcal{E}} = 0$, $l = 1, 2, \ldots, j-1$. Assume the econometrician observes a sample $\{w_i, z_i\colon i = 1, \ldots, n\}$. To estimate $\{\lambda_j, \phi_j, \psi_j\}$, one can either estimate (2.18) by replacing the expectation by the sample mean or by replacing the joint p.d.f. by a nonparametric estimator.

The first approach was adopted by Darolles, Florens and Renault (1998). Let

$$\mathcal{H}_n = \left\{\varphi : \mathbb{R}^q \to \mathbb{R}, \int \varphi(z)^2\,\mathrm{d}\hat{F}_Z(z) < \infty\right\},$$

$$\mathcal{E}_n = \left\{\psi : \mathbb{R}^r \to \mathbb{R}, \int \psi(w)^2\,\mathrm{d}\hat{F}_W(w) < \infty\right\}$$

where $\hat{F}_Z$ and $\hat{F}_W$ are the empirical distributions of Z and W. That is $\|\varphi\|^2_{\mathcal{H}_n} = \frac{1}{n}\sum_{i=1}^n \varphi(z_i)^2$ and $\|\psi\|^2_{\mathcal{E}_n} = \frac{1}{n}\sum_{i=1}^n \psi(w_i)^2$. Darolles, Florens and Renault (1998) propose to estimate $\{\lambda_j, \phi_j, \psi_j\}$ by solving

$$\hat{\lambda}_j = \sup_{\hat{\phi}_j, \hat{\psi}_j} \frac{1}{n} \sum_{i=1}^n \big[\hat{\phi}_j(z_i)\hat{\psi}_j(w_i)\big], \quad j = 1, 2, \ldots, \tag{2.19}$$

subject to $\|\hat{\phi}_j\|_{\mathcal{H}_n} = 1$, $\langle \hat{\phi}_j, \hat{\phi}_l \rangle_{\mathcal{H}_n} = 0$, $l = 1, 2, \ldots, j-1$, $\|\hat{\psi}_j\|_{\mathcal{E}_n} = 1$, $\langle \hat{\psi}_j, \hat{\psi}_l \rangle_{\mathcal{E}_n} = 0$, $l = 1, 2, \ldots, j-1$, where $\hat{\phi}_j$ and $\hat{\psi}_j$ are elements of increasing dimensional spaces

$$\hat{\phi}_j(z) = \sum_{j=1}^{J} \alpha_j a_j(z), \qquad \hat{\psi}_j(w) = \sum_{j=1}^{J} \beta_j b_j(w)$$

for some bases $\{a_j\}$ and $\{b_j\}$. By Mercer's formula (2.13), K can be estimated by

$$\hat{K}_n \varphi(w) = \sum \hat{\lambda}_j \left(\int \hat{\phi}_j(z) \varphi(z) \, \mathrm{d}\hat{F}_Z \right) \hat{\psi}_j(w)$$

$$\widehat{(K^*)}_n \psi(z) = \sum \hat{\lambda}_j \left(\int \hat{\psi}_j(w) \psi(w) \, \mathrm{d}\hat{F}_W \right) \hat{\phi}_j(z).$$

Hence $\widehat{(K^*)}_n = (\hat{K}_n)^*$ for $\mathcal{H}_n$ and $\mathcal{E}_n$.

The second approach consists in replacing $f_{Z,W}$ by a nonparametric estimator $\hat{f}_{Z,W}$. Darolles, Florens and Gouriéroux (2004) use a kernel estimator, whereas Chen, Hansen and Scheinkman (1998) use B-spline wavelets. Let $\mathcal{H}_n = L^2(\mathbb{R}^q, \hat{f}_Z)$ and $\mathcal{E}_n = L^2(\mathbb{R}^r, \hat{f}_W)$ where $\hat{f}_Z$ and $\hat{f}_W$ are the marginals of $\hat{f}_{Z,W}$. Equation (2.18) can be replaced by

$$\hat{\lambda}_j = \sup_{\phi_j, \psi_j} \int \phi_j(z) \psi_j(w) \hat{f}_{Z,W}(z, w) \, \mathrm{d}z \, \mathrm{d}w, \quad j = 1, 2, \ldots, \tag{2.20}$$

subject to $\|\phi_j\|_{\mathcal{H}_n} = 1$, $\langle \phi_j, \phi_l \rangle_{\mathcal{H}_n} = 0$, $l = 1, 2, \ldots, j-1$, $\|\psi_j\|_{\mathcal{E}_n} = 1$, $\langle \psi_j, \psi_l \rangle_{\mathcal{E}_n} = 0$, $l = 1, 2, \ldots, j-1$. Denote $\{\hat{\lambda}_j, \hat{\phi}_j, \hat{\psi}_j\}$ the resulting estimators of $\{\lambda_j, \phi_j, \psi_j\}$. By Mercer's formula, K can be approached by

$$\hat{K}_n \varphi(w) = \sum \hat{\lambda}_j \left(\int \hat{\phi}_j(z) \varphi(z) \hat{f}_Z(z) \, \mathrm{d}z \right) \hat{\psi}_j(w),$$

$$\widehat{(K^*)}_n \psi(z) = \sum \hat{\lambda}_j \left(\int \hat{\psi}_j(w) \psi(w) \hat{f}_W(w) \, \mathrm{d}w \right) \hat{\phi}_j(z).$$

Hence $\widehat{(K^*)}_n = (\hat{K}_n)^*$ for $\mathcal{H}_n$ and $\mathcal{E}_n$. Note that in the three articles mentioned above, $Z = X_{t+1}$ and $W = X_t$ where $\{X_t\}$ is a Markov process. These papers are mainly concerned with estimation. When the data are the discrete observations of a diffusion process, the nonparametric estimations of a single eigenvalue–eigenfunction pair and of the marginal distribution are enough to recover a nonparametric estimate of the diffusion coefficient. The techniques described here can also be used for testing the reversibility of the process $\{X_t\}$, see Darolles, Florens and Gouriéroux (2004).

2.5.3. Computation of the spectrum of finite dimensional operators

Here, we assume that we have some estimators of K and K^*, denoted $\hat{K}_n$ and $\hat{K}_n^*$ such that $\hat{K}_n$ and $\hat{K}_n^*$ have finite range and satisfy

$$\hat{K}_n \varphi = \sum_{l=1}^{L_n} a_l(\varphi)\varepsilon_l, \tag{2.21}$$

$$\hat{K}_n^* \psi = \sum_{l=1}^{L_n} b_l(\psi)\eta_l \tag{2.22}$$

where $\varepsilon_l \in \mathcal{E}$, $\eta_l \in \mathcal{H}$, $a_l(\varphi)$ is linear in φ and $b_l(\psi)$ is linear in ψ. Examples of such operators are given in Section 2.5.1. Moreover the $\{\varepsilon_l\}$ and $\{\eta_l\}$ are assumed to be linearly independent. It follows that

$$\hat{K}_n^* \hat{K}_n \varphi = \sum_{l=1}^{L_n} b_l \left(\sum_{l'=1}^{L_n} a_{l'}(\varphi)\varepsilon_{l'} \right) \eta_l = \sum_{l,l'=1}^{L_n} a_{l'}(\varphi) b_l(\varepsilon_{l'}) \eta_l. \tag{2.23}$$

We calculate the eigenvalues and eigenfunctions of $\hat{K}_n^* \hat{K}_n$ by solving

$$\hat{K}_n^* \hat{K}_n \phi = \lambda^2 \phi.$$

Hence ϕ is necessarily of the form: $\phi = \sum_l \beta_l \eta_l$. Replacing in (2.23), we have

$$\lambda^2 \beta_l = \sum_{l',j=1}^{L_n} \beta_j a_{l'}(\eta_j) b_l(\varepsilon_{l'}). \tag{2.24}$$

Denote $\underline{\hat{\beta}} = [\beta_1, \ldots, \beta_{L_n}]$ the solution of (2.24). Solving (2.24) is equivalent to finding the L_n nonzero eigenvalues $\hat{\lambda}_1^2, \ldots, \hat{\lambda}_{L_n}^2$ and eigenvectors $\underline{\hat{\beta}}^1, \ldots, \underline{\hat{\beta}}^{L_n}$ of an $L_n \times L_n$-matrix C with principal element

$$c_{l,j} = \sum_{l'=1}^{L_n} a_{l'}(\eta_j) b_l(\varepsilon_{l'}).$$

The eigenfunctions of $\hat{K}_n^* \hat{K}_n$ are

$$\hat{\phi}_j = \sum_{l=1}^{L_n} \hat{\beta}_l^j \eta_l, \quad j = 1, \ldots, L_n,$$

associated with $\hat{\lambda}_1^2, \ldots, \hat{\lambda}_{L_n}^2$. $\{\hat{\phi}_j \colon j = 1, \ldots, L_n\}$ need to be orthonormalized. The estimators of the singular values are $\hat{\lambda}_j = \sqrt{\hat{\lambda}_j^2}$.

2.5.4. *Estimation of noncompact operators*

This chapter mainly focuses on compact operators, because compact operators can be approached by a sequence of finite dimensional operators and therefore can be easily estimated. However, it is possible to estimate a noncompact operator by an estimator, which is infinitely dimensional. A simple example is provided by the conditional expectation operator with common elements.

EXAMPLE 2.5 *(Continued).* This example is discussed in Hall and Horowitz (2005). Assume that the dimension of Z is p. The conditional expectation operator K can be estimated by a kernel estimator with kernel ω and bandwidth c_n

$$(\hat{K}\varphi)(x, w) = \frac{\sum_{i=1}^{n}[\int \frac{1}{c_n^p}\varphi(x, z)\omega(\frac{z-z_i}{c_n})\,\mathrm{d}z]\omega(\frac{x-x_i}{c_n})\omega(\frac{w-w_i}{c_n})}{\sum_{i=1}^{n}\omega(\frac{x-x_i}{c_n})\omega(\frac{w-w_i}{c_n})}.$$

We can see that $\hat{K}$ is an infinite dimensional operator because all functions $\varphi(x)$ that depend only on x are in the range of $\hat{K}$.

3. Regularized solutions of integral equations of the first kind

Let $\mathcal{H}$ and $\mathcal{E}$ be two Hilbert spaces considered only over the real scalars for the sake of notational simplicity. Let K be a linear operator on $\mathcal{D}(K) \subset \mathcal{H}$ into $\mathcal{E}$. This section discusses the properties of integral equations (also called Fredholm equations) of the first kind

$$K\varphi = r \tag{3.1}$$

where K is typically an integral compact operator. Such an equation in φ is in general an ill-posed problem by opposition to a well-posed problem. Equation (3.1) is said to be well-posed if (i) (*existence*) a solution exists, (ii) (*uniqueness*) the solution is unique, and (iii) (*stability*) the solution is continuous in r, that is φ is stable with respect to small changes in r. Whenever one of these conditions is not satisfied, the problem is said to be ill-posed. The lack of stability is particularly problematic and needs to be addressed by a regularization scheme. Following Wahba (1973) and Nashed and Wahba (1974), we introduce generalized inverses of operators in reproducing kernel Hilbert spaces (RKHS). Properties of RKHS will be studied more extensively in Section 6.

3.1. *Ill-posed and well-posed problems*

This introductory subsection gives an overview of the problems encountered when solving an equation $K\varphi = r$ where K is a linear operator, not necessarily compact. A more detailed encounter can be found in Groetsch (1993). We start with a formal definition of a well-posed problem.

DEFINITION 3.1. Let $K : \mathcal{H} \to \mathcal{E}$. The equation

$$K\varphi = r \tag{3.2}$$

is called well-posed if K is bijective and the inverse operator $K^{-1} : \mathcal{E} \to \mathcal{H}$ is continuous. Otherwise, the equation is called ill-posed.

Note that K is injective means $\mathcal{N}(K) = \{0\}$, and K is surjective means $\mathcal{R}(K) = \mathcal{E}$. In this section, we will restrict ourselves to the case where K is a bounded (and therefore continuous) linear operator. By Banach theorem [Kress (1999, p. 266)], if $K : \mathcal{H} \to \mathcal{E}$ is a bounded linear operator, K bijective implies that $K^{-1} : \mathcal{E} \to \mathcal{H}$ is bounded and therefore continuous. In this case, $K\varphi = r$ is well-posed.

An example of a well-posed problem is given by

$$(I - C)\varphi = r$$

where $C : \mathcal{H} \to \mathcal{H}$ is a compact operator and 1 is not an eigenvalue of C. This is an example of integral equations of the second kind that will be studied in Section 7.

We now turn our attention to ill-posed problems.

PROBLEM OF UNIQUENESS. If $\mathcal{N}(K) \neq \{0\}$, then to any solution of φ of (3.2), one can add an element φ_1 of $\mathcal{N}(K)$, so that $\varphi + \varphi_1$ is also a solution. A way to achieve uniqueness is to look for the solution with minimal norm.

PROBLEM OF EXISTENCE. A solution to (3.2) exists if and only if

$$r \in \mathcal{R}(K).$$

Since K is linear, $\mathcal{R}(K)$ is a subspace of $\mathcal{E}$, however it generally does not exhaust $\mathcal{E}$. Therefore, a traditional solution of (3.2) exists only for a restricted class of functions r. If we are willing to broaden our notion of solution, we may enlarge the class of functions r for which a type of generalized solution exists to a dense subspace of functions of $\mathcal{E}$.

DEFINITION 3.2. An element $\tilde{\varphi} \in \mathcal{H}$ is said to be a least squares solution of (3.2) if:

$$\|K\tilde{\varphi} - r\| \leqslant \|Kf - r\|, \quad \text{for any } f \in \mathcal{H}. \tag{3.3}$$

If the set S_r of all least squares solutions of (3.2) for a given $r \in \mathcal{E}$ is not empty and admits an element φ of minimal norm, then φ is called a pseudosolution of (3.2).

The pseudosolution, when it exists, is denoted $\varphi = K^{\dagger}r$ where $K^{\dagger}$ is by definition the Moore Penrose generalized inverse of K. However, the pseudosolution does not necessarily exist. The pseudosolution exists if and only if $Pr \in \mathcal{R}(K)$ where P is the orthogonal projection operator on $\overline{\mathcal{R}(K)}$, the closure of the range of K. Note that $Pr \in \mathcal{R}(K)$ if and only if

$$r = Pr + (1 - P)r \in \mathcal{R}(K) + \mathcal{R}(K)^{\perp}. \tag{3.4}$$

Therefore, a pseudosolution exists if and only if r lies in the dense subspace $\mathcal{R}(K) + \mathcal{R}(K)^{\perp}$ of $\mathcal{E}$.

We distinguish two cases:

1. *$\mathcal{R}(K)$ is closed.*
For any $r \in \mathcal{E}$, $\varphi = K^{\dagger}r$ exists and is continuous in r.

EXAMPLE. $(I - C)\varphi = r$ where C is compact and 1 is an eigenvalue of C. The problem is ill-posed because the solution is not unique but it is not severely ill-posed because the pseudosolution exists and is continuous.

2. *$\mathcal{R}(K)$ is not closed.*
The pseudosolution exists if and only if $r \in \mathcal{R}(K) + \mathcal{R}(K)^{\perp}$. But here, $\varphi = K^{\dagger}r$ is not continuous in r.

EXAMPLE. K is a compact infinite dimensional operator.

For the purpose of econometric applications, condition (3.4) will be easy to maintain since:

Either (K, r) denotes the true unknown population value, and then the assumption $r \in \mathcal{R}(K)$ means that the structural econometric model is well specified. Inverse problems with specification errors are beyond the scope of this chapter.

Or (K, r) denotes some estimators computed from a finite sample of size n. Then, insofar as the chosen estimation procedure is such that $\mathcal{R}(K)$ is closed (for instance because it is finite dimensional as in Section 2.5.1), we have $\mathcal{R}(K) + \mathcal{R}(K)^{\perp} = \mathcal{E}$.

The continuity assumption of K will come in general with the compactness assumption for population values and, for sample counterparts, with the finite dimensional property. Moreover, the true unknown value K_0 of K will be endowed with the *identification assumption*:

$$\mathcal{N}(K_0) = \{0\} \tag{3.5}$$

and the *well-specification assumption*:

$$r_0 \in \mathcal{R}(K_0). \tag{3.6}$$

Equations (3.5) and (3.6) ensure the existence of a unique true unknown value φ_0 of φ defined as the (pseudo)solution of the operator equation $K_0\varphi_0 = r_0$. Moreover, this solution is not going to depend on the choice of topologies on the two spaces $\mathcal{H}$ and $\mathcal{E}$.

It turns out that a compact operator K with infinite-dimensional range is a prototype of an operator for which $\mathcal{R}(K)$ is not closed. Therefore, as soon as one tries to generalize structural econometric estimation from a parametric setting (K finite dimensional) to a nonparametric one, which can be seen as a limit of finite dimensional problems (K compact), one is faced with an ill-posed inverse problem. This is a serious issue for the purpose of consistent estimation, since in general one does not know the true value

r_0 of r but only a consistent estimator $\hat{r}_n$. Therefore, there is no hope to get a consistent estimator $\hat{\varphi}_n$ of φ by solving $K\hat{\varphi}_n = \hat{r}_n$ that is $\hat{\varphi}_n = K^{\dagger}\hat{r}_n$, when $K^{\dagger}$ is not continuous. In general, the issue to address will be even more involved since $K^{\dagger}$ and K must also be estimated.

Let us finally recall a useful characterization of the Moore–Penrose generalized inverse of K.

PROPOSITION 3.3. *Under* (3.4), $K^{\dagger}r$ *is the unique solution of minimal norm of the equation* $K^{\star}K\varphi = K^{\star}r$.

In other words, the pseudosolution φ of (3.2) can be written in two ways:

$$\varphi = K^{\dagger}r = (K^{\star}K)^{\dagger}K^{\star}r.$$

For $r \in \mathcal{R}(K)$ (well-specification assumption in the case of true unknown values), $K^{\star}r \in \mathcal{R}(K^{\star}K)$ and then $(K^{\star}K)^{-1}K^{\star}r$ is well defined. The pseudosolution can then be represented from the singular value decomposition of K as

$$\varphi = K^{\dagger}r = (K^{\star}K)^{-1}K^{\star}r = \sum_{j=1}^{\infty} \frac{\langle r, \psi_j\rangle}{\lambda_j}\phi_j. \tag{3.7}$$

It is worth noticing that the spectral decomposition (3.7) is also valid for any $r \in \mathcal{R}(K) + \mathcal{R}(K)^{\perp}$ to represent the pseudosolution $\varphi = K^{\dagger}r = (K^{\star}K)^{\dagger}K^{\star}r$ since $r \in \mathcal{R}(K)^{\perp}$ is equivalent to $K^{\dagger}r = 0$.

Formula (3.7) clearly demonstrates the ill-posed nature of the equation $K\varphi = r$. If we perturb the right-hand side r by $r^{\delta} = r + \delta\psi_j$, we obtain the solution $\varphi^{\delta} = \varphi + \delta\phi_j/\lambda_j$. Hence, the ratio $\|\varphi^{\delta} - \varphi\|/\|r^{\delta} - r\| = 1/\lambda_j$ can be made arbitrarily large due to the fact that the singular values tend to zero. Since the influence of estimation errors in r is controlled by the rate of this convergence, Kress (1999, p. 280) says that the equation is "mildly ill-posed" if the singular values decay slowly to zero and that it is "severely ill-posed" if they decay rapidly. Actually, the critical property is the relative decay rate of the sequence $\langle r, \psi_j\rangle$ with respect to the decay of the sequence λ_j. To see this, note that the solution φ has to be determined from its Fourier coefficients by solving the equations

$$\lambda_j\langle\varphi, \phi_j\rangle = \langle r, \psi_j\rangle, \quad \text{for all } j.$$

Then, we may expect high instability of the solution φ if λ_j goes to zero faster than $\langle\varphi, \phi_j\rangle$. The properties of regularity spaces introduced below precisely document this intuition.

3.2. *Regularity spaces*

As stressed by Nashed and Wahba (1974), an ill-posed problem relative to $\mathcal{H}$ and $\mathcal{E}$ may be recast as a well-posed problem relative to new spaces $\mathcal{H}' \subset \mathcal{H}$ and $\mathcal{E}' \subset \mathcal{E}$, with topologies on $\mathcal{H}'$ and $\mathcal{E}'$, which are different from the topologies on $\mathcal{H}$ and $\mathcal{E}$, respectively. While Nashed and Wahba (1974) generally build these Hilbert spaces $\mathcal{H}'$ and $\mathcal{E}'$ as RKHS associated with an arbitrary self-adjoint Hilbert–Schmidt operator, we focus here on the RKHS associated with $(K^\star K)^\beta$, for some positive β. More precisely, assuming that K is Hilbert–Schmidt and denoting $(\lambda_j, \phi_j, \psi_j)$ its singular system (see Definition 2.40), we define the self-adjoint operator $(K^\star K)^\beta$ by

$$(K^\star K)^\beta \varphi = \sum_{j=1}^{\infty} \lambda_j^{2\beta} \langle \varphi, \phi_j \rangle \phi_j.$$

DEFINITION 3.4. The β-regularity space of the compact operator K is defined for all $\beta > 0$, as the RKHS associated with $(K^\star K)^\beta$. That is, the space:

$$\Phi_\beta = \left\{ \varphi \in \mathcal{N}(K)^\perp \text{ such that } \sum_{j=1}^{\infty} \frac{\langle \varphi, \phi_j \rangle^2}{\lambda_j^{2\beta}} < \infty \right\} \tag{3.8}$$

where a Hilbert structure is being defined through the inner product

$$\langle f, g \rangle_\beta = \sum_{j=1}^{\infty} \frac{\langle f, \phi_j \rangle \langle g, \phi_j \rangle}{\lambda_j^{2\beta}}$$

for f and $g \in \Phi_\beta$.

Note however that the construction of RKHS considered here is slightly more general than the one put forward in Nashed and Wahba (1974) since we start from elements of a general Hilbert space, not limited to be a L^2 space of functions defined on some interval of the real line. This latter example will be made explicit in Section 6. Moreover, the focus of our interest here will only be the regularity spaces associated with the true unknown value K_0 of the operator K. Then, the identification assumption will ensure that all the regularity spaces are dense in $\mathcal{H}$:

PROPOSITION 3.5. *Under the identification assumption $\mathcal{N}(K) = \{0\}$, the sequence of eigenfunctions $\{\phi_j\}$ associated with the nonzero singular values λ_j defines a Hilbert basis of $\mathcal{H}$. In particular, all the regularity spaces Φ_β, $\beta > 0$, contain the vectorial space spanned by the $\{\phi_j\}$ and, as such, are dense in $\mathcal{H}$.*

Proposition 3.5 is a direct consequence of the singular value decomposition (2.12). Generally speaking, when β increases, Φ_β, $\beta > 0$, is a decreasing family of subspaces of $\mathcal{H}$. Hence, β may actually be interpreted as the regularity level of the functions φ, as illustrated by the following result.

PROPOSITION 3.6. *Under the identification assumption ($\mathcal{N}(K) = \{0\}$), for any $\beta > 0$,*

$$\Phi_\beta = \mathcal{R}\left[(K^* K)^{\beta/2}\right].$$

In particular, $\Phi_1 = \mathcal{R}(K^*)$.

PROOF. By definition, the elements of the range of $(K^*K)^{\beta/2}$ can be written $f = \sum_{j=1}^{\infty} \lambda_j^{\beta} \langle \varphi, \phi_j \rangle \phi_j$ for some $\varphi \in \mathcal{H}$. Note that this decomposition also describes the range of K^* for $\beta = 1$. Then:

$$\|f\|_{\beta}^2 = \sum_{j=1}^{\infty} \frac{\langle \varphi, \phi_j \rangle^2}{\lambda_j^{2\beta}} \lambda_j^{2\beta} = \sum_{j=1}^{\infty} \langle \varphi, \phi_j \rangle^2 = \|\varphi\|^2 < \infty.$$

Hence $\mathcal{R}[(K^*K)^{\beta/2}] \subset \Phi_{\beta}$.

Conversely, for any $\varphi \in \Phi_{\beta}$, one can define:

$$f = \sum_{j=1}^{\infty} \frac{\langle \varphi, \phi_j \rangle}{\lambda_j^{\beta}} \phi_j$$

and then $(K^*K)^{\beta/2} f = \sum_{j=1}^{\infty} \langle \varphi, \phi_j \rangle \phi_j = \varphi$ since $\mathcal{N}(K) = \{0\}$. Hence, $\Phi_{\beta} \subset \mathcal{R}[(K^*K)^{\beta/2}]$. □

Since we mainly consider operators, K, which are integral operators with continuous kernels, applying the operator $(K^*K)^{\beta/2}$ has a smoothing effect, which is stronger for larger values of β. This is the reason why the condition $\varphi \in \Phi_{\beta}$ qualifies the level, β, of regularity or smoothness of φ. The associated smoothness properties are studied in further details in Loubes and Vanhems (2003). The space Φ_1 of functions is also put forward in Schaumburg (2004) when K denotes the conditional expectation operator for a continuous time Markov process X_t with Levy type generator sampled in discrete time. He shows that whenever a transformation $\varphi(X_t)$ of the diffusion process is considered with $\varphi \in \Phi_1$, the conditional expectation operator $E[\varphi(X_{t+h}) \mid X_t]$ admits a convergent power series expansion as the exponential of the infinitesimal generator.

The regularity spaces Φ_{β} are of interest here as Hilbert spaces (included in $\mathcal{H}$ but endowed with another scalar product) where our operator equation (3.2) is going to become well-posed. More precisely, let us also consider the family of regularity spaces Ψ_{β} associated with the compact operator K^*:

$$\Psi_{\beta} = \left\{ \psi \in \mathcal{N}(K^{\star})^{\perp} \text{ such that } \sum_{j=1}^{\infty} \frac{\langle \psi, \psi_j \rangle^2}{\lambda_j^{2\beta}} < \infty \right\}$$

Ψ_{β} is a Hilbert space endowed with the inner product:

DEFINITION 3.7. $\langle F, G \rangle_{\beta} = \sum_{j=1}^{\infty} \frac{\langle F, \psi_j \rangle \langle G, \psi_j \rangle}{\lambda_j^{2\beta}}$ for F and $G \in \Psi_{\beta}$.

Note that the spaces Ψ_{β} are not in general dense in $\mathcal{E}$ since $\mathcal{N}(K^{\star}) \neq \{0\}$. But they describe well the range of K when K is restricted to some regularity space:

PROPOSITION 3.8. *Under the identification assumption* $\mathcal{N}(K) = \{0\}$, $K(\Phi_{\beta}) = \Psi_{\beta+1}$ *for all positive* β. *In particular,* $\Psi_1 = \mathcal{R}(K)$.

PROOF. We know from Proposition 3.6 that when $\varphi \in \Phi_\beta$, it can be written: $\varphi = \sum_{j=1}^{\infty} \lambda_j^{\beta} \langle f, \phi_j \rangle \phi_j$ for some $f \in \mathcal{H}$. Then, $K\varphi = \sum_{j=1}^{\infty} \lambda_j^{\beta+1} \langle f, \phi_j \rangle \psi_j \in \Psi_{\beta+1}$. Hence $K(\Phi_\beta) \subset \Psi_{\beta+1}$.

Conversely, since according to a singular value decomposition like (2.12), the sequence $\{\psi_j\}$ defines a basis of $\mathcal{N}(K^\star)^\perp$, any element of $\Psi_{\beta+1}$ can be written as

$$\psi = \sum_{j=1}^{\infty} \langle \psi, \psi_j \rangle \psi_j \quad \text{with} \sum_{j=1}^{\infty} \frac{\langle \psi, \psi_j \rangle^2}{\lambda_j^{2\beta+2}} < \infty.$$

Let us then define $\varphi = \sum_{j=1}^{\infty} (1/\lambda_j) \langle \psi, \psi_j \rangle \phi_j$. We have

$$\sum_{j=1}^{\infty} \frac{\langle \varphi, \phi_j \rangle^2}{\lambda_j^{2\beta}} = \sum_{j=1}^{\infty} \frac{\langle \psi, \psi_j \rangle^2}{\lambda_j^{2\beta+2}} < \infty$$

and thus $\varphi \in \Phi_\beta$. Moreover, $K\varphi = \sum_{j=1}^{\infty} \langle \psi, \psi_j \rangle \psi_j = \psi$. This proves that $\Psi_{\beta+1} \subset K(\Phi_\beta)$. □

Therefore, when viewed as an operator from Φ_β into $\Psi_{\beta+1}$, K has a closed range defined by the space $\Psi_{\beta+1}$ itself. It follows that the ill-posed problem

$$K : \mathcal{H} \to \mathcal{E},$$
$$K\varphi = r$$

may be viewed as well-posed relative to the subspaces Φ_β into $\Psi_{\beta+1}$ and their associated norms. This means that

(i) First, we think about the pseudosolution $\varphi = K^\dagger r$ as a function of r evolving in $\Psi_{\beta+1}$, for some positive β.
(ii) Second, continuity of $\varphi = K^\dagger r$ with respect to r must be understood with respect to the norms $\|r\|_{\beta+1} = \langle r, r \rangle_{\beta+1}^{1/2}$ and $\|\varphi\|_\beta = \langle \varphi, \varphi \rangle_\beta^{1/2}$.

To get the intuition of this result, it is worth noticing that these new topologies define another adjoint operator $K_\beta^\star$ of K characterized by

$$\langle K\varphi, \psi \rangle_{\beta+1} = \langle \varphi, K_\beta^\star \psi \rangle_\beta,$$

and thus:

$$K_\beta^\star \psi = \sum_{j=1}^{\infty} (1/\lambda_j) \langle \psi, \psi_j \rangle \phi_j.$$

In particular, $K_\beta^\star \psi_j = \phi_j / \lambda_j$. In other words, all the eigenvalues of $K_\beta^\star K$ and $K K_\beta^\star$ are now equal to one and the pseudosolution is defined as

$$\varphi = K_\beta^\dagger r = K_\beta^\star r = \sum_{j=1}^{\infty} \frac{\langle r, \psi_j \rangle}{\lambda_j} \phi_j.$$

The pseudosolution depends continuously on r because $K_\beta^\dagger = K_\beta^\star$ is a bounded operator for the chosen topologies; it actually has a unit norm.

For the purpose of econometric estimation, we may be ready to assume that the true unknown value φ_0 belongs to some regularity space Φ_β. This just amounts to an additional smoothness condition about our structural functional parameter of interest. Then, we are going to take advantage of this regularity assumption through the rate of convergence of some regularization bias as characterized in the next subsection.

Note finally that assuming $\varphi_0 \in \Phi_\beta$, that is $r_0 \in \Psi_{\beta+1}$ for some positive β, is nothing but a small reinforcement of the common criterion of existence of a solution, known as Picard's theorem [see e.g. Kress (1999, p. 279)], which states that $r_0 \in \Psi_1 = \mathcal{R}(K)$. The spaces Φ_β and Ψ_β are strongly related to the concept of Hilbert scales, see Natterer (1984), Engel, Hanke and Neubauer (1996), and Tautenhahn (1996).

3.3. *Regularization schemes*

As pointed out in Section 3.1, the ill-posedness of an equation of the first kind with a compact operator stems from the behavior of the sequence of singular values, which converge to zero. This suggests trying to regularize the equation by damping the explosive asymptotic effect of the inversion of singular values. This may be done in at least two ways:

A first estimation strategy consists in taking advantage of the well-posedness of the problem when reconsidered within regularity spaces. Typically, a sieve kind of approach may be designed, under the maintained assumption that the true unknown value $r_0 \in \Psi_{\beta+1}$ for some positive β, in such a way that the estimator $\hat{r}_n$ evolves when n increases, in an increasing sequence of finite dimensional subspaces of $\Psi_{\beta+1}$. Note however that when the operator K is unknown, the constraint $\hat{r}_n \in \mathcal{N}(K^\star)^\perp$ may be difficult to implement. Hence, we will not pursue this route any further.

The approach adopted in this chapter follows the general regularization framework of Kress (1999, Theorem 15.21). It consists in replacing a sequence $\{1/\mu_j\}$ of explosive inverse singular values by a sequence $\{q(\alpha, \mu_j)/\mu_j\}$ where the *damping function* $q(\alpha, \mu)$ is chosen such that:

(i) $\{q(\alpha, \mu)/\mu\}$ remains bounded when μ goes to zero (damping effect),
(ii) for any given $\mu : \operatorname{Lim}_{\alpha \to 0} q(\alpha, \mu) = 1$ (asymptotic unbiasedness).

Since our inverse problem of interest can be addressed in two different ways:

$$\varphi = K^\dagger r = (K^\star K)^\dagger K^\star r,$$

the regularization scheme can be applied either to $K^\dagger$ $(\mu_j = \lambda_j)$ or to $(K^\star K)^\dagger$ $(\mu_j = \lambda_j^2)$. The latter approach is better suited for our purpose since estimation errors will be considered below at the level of $(K^\star K)$ and $K^\star r$, respectively. We maintain in this subsection the identification assumption $\mathcal{N}(K) = \{0\}$. We then define:

DEFINITION 3.9. A regularized version $\varphi_\alpha = A_\alpha K^\star r$ of the pseudosolution $\varphi = (K^\star K)^\dagger K^\star r$ is defined as

$$\varphi_\alpha = \sum_{j=1}^{\infty} \frac{1}{\lambda_j^2} q\big(\alpha, \lambda_j^2\big)\langle K^\star r, \phi_j\rangle \phi_j = \sum_{j=1}^{\infty} \frac{1}{\lambda_j} q\big(\alpha, \lambda_j^2\big)\langle r, \psi_j\rangle \phi_j$$
$$= \sum_{j=1}^{\infty} q\big(\alpha, \lambda_j^2\big)\langle \varphi, \phi_j\rangle \phi_j \tag{3.9}$$

where the real-valued function, q, is such that

$$\big|q(\alpha, \mu)\big| \leqslant d(\alpha)\mu, \qquad \lim_{\alpha\to 0} q(\alpha, \mu) = 1. \tag{3.10}$$

Note that (3.9) leaves unconstrained the values of the operator A_α on the space $\mathcal{R}(K^*)^\perp = \mathcal{N}(K)$. However, since $\mathcal{N}(K) = \{0\}$, A_α is uniquely defined as

$$A_\alpha \varphi = \sum_{j=1}^{\infty} \frac{1}{\lambda_j^2} q\big(\alpha, \lambda_j^2\big)\langle \varphi, \phi_j\rangle \phi_j \tag{3.11}$$

for all $\varphi \in \mathcal{H}$. Note that as q is real, A_α is self-adjoint. Then by (3.10), A_α is a bounded operator from $\mathcal{H}$ into $\mathcal{H}$ with

$$\|A_\alpha\| \leqslant d(\alpha). \tag{3.12}$$

In the following, we will always normalize the regularization parameter α such that $\alpha d(\alpha)$ has a positive finite limit c when α goes to zero. By construction, $A_\alpha K^* K\varphi \to \varphi$ as α goes to zero. When a genuine solution exists ($r = K\varphi$), the regularization induces a bias:

$$\varphi - \varphi_\alpha = \sum_{j=1}^{\infty} \big[1 - q\big(\alpha, \lambda_j^2\big)\big]\langle r, \psi_j\rangle (\phi_j/\lambda_j)$$
$$= \sum_{j=1}^{\infty} \big[1 - q\big(\alpha, \lambda_j^2\big)\big]\langle \varphi, \phi_j\rangle \phi_j. \tag{3.13}$$

The squared regularization bias is

$$\|\varphi - \varphi_\alpha\|^2 = \sum_{j=1}^{\infty} b^2\big(\alpha, \lambda_j^2\big)\langle \varphi, \phi_j\rangle^2, \tag{3.14}$$

where $b(\alpha, \lambda_j^2) = 1 - q(\alpha, \lambda_j^2)$ is the *bias function* characterizing the weight of the Fourier coefficient $\langle \varphi, \phi_j\rangle$. Below, we show that the most common regularization schemes fulfill the above conditions. We characterize these schemes through the definitions of the *damping weights* $q(\alpha, \mu)$ or equivalently, of the *bias function* $b(\alpha, \mu)$.

EXAMPLE *(Spectral cut-off)*. The spectral cut-off regularized solution is

$$\varphi_\alpha = \sum_{\lambda_j^2 \geqslant \alpha/c} \frac{1}{\lambda_j} \langle r, \psi_j \rangle \phi_j.$$

The explosive influence of the factor $(1/\mu)$ is filtered out by imposing $q(\alpha, \mu) = 0$ for small μ, that is $|\mu| < \alpha/c$. α is a positive regularization parameter such that no bias is introduced when $|\mu|$ exceeds the threshold α/c:

$$q(\alpha, \mu) = I\{|\mu| \geqslant \alpha/c\} = \begin{cases} 1 & \text{if } |\mu| \geqslant \alpha/c, \\ 0 & \text{otherwise.} \end{cases}$$

For any given scaling factor c, the two conditions of Definition 3.9 are then satisfied (with $d(\alpha) = c/\alpha$) and we get a bias function $b(\alpha, \lambda^2)$ which is maximized (equal to 1) when $\lambda^2 < \alpha/c$ and minimized (equal to 0) when $\lambda^2 \geqslant \alpha/c$.

EXAMPLE *(Landweber–Fridman)*. Landweber–Fridman regularization is characterized by

$$A_\alpha = c \sum_{l=0}^{1/\alpha - 1} (I - cK^*K)^l,$$

$$\varphi_\alpha = c \sum_{l=0}^{1/\alpha - 1} (I - cK^*K)^l K^* r.$$

The basic idea is similar to spectral cut-off but with a smooth bias function. Of course, one way to make the bias function continuous while meeting the conditions $b(\alpha, 0) = 1$ and $b(\alpha, \lambda^2) = 0$ for $\lambda^2 > \alpha/c$ would be to consider a piecewise linear bias function with $b(\alpha, \lambda^2) = 1 - (c/\alpha)\lambda^2$ for $\lambda^2 \leqslant \alpha/c$. Landweber–Fridman regularization makes it smooth, while keeping the same level and the same slope at $\lambda^2 = 0$ and zero bias for large λ^2, $b(\alpha, \lambda^2) = (1 - c\lambda^2)^{1/\alpha}$ for $\lambda^2 \leqslant 1/c$ and zero otherwise, that is

$$q(\alpha, \mu) = \begin{cases} 1 & \text{if } |\mu| > 1/c, \\ 1 - (1 - c\mu)^{1/\alpha} & \text{for } |\mu| \leqslant 1/c. \end{cases}$$

For any given scaling factor c, the two conditions of Definition 3.9 are then satisfied with again $d(\alpha) = c/\alpha$.

EXAMPLE *(Tikhonov regularization)*. Here, we have

$$A_\alpha = \left(\frac{\alpha}{c} I + K^*K\right)^{-1},$$

$$\varphi_\alpha = \left(\frac{\alpha}{c} I + K^*K\right)^{-1} K^* r = \sum_{j=1}^{\infty} \frac{\lambda_j}{\lambda_j^2 + \alpha/c} \langle r, \psi_j \rangle \phi_j$$

where c is some scaling factor. In contrast to the two previous examples, the bias function is never zero but decreases toward zero at a hyperbolic rate (when λ^2 becomes infinitely large), while still starting from 1 for $\lambda^2 = 0$:

$$b(\alpha, \lambda^2) = \frac{(\alpha/c)}{\lambda^2 + \alpha/c}$$

that is:

$$q(\alpha, \lambda^2) = \frac{\lambda^2}{\lambda^2 + \alpha/c}.$$

For any given scaling factor c, the two conditions of Definition 3.9 are again satisfied with $d(\alpha) = c/\alpha$.

We are going to show now that the regularity spaces Φ_β introduced in the previous subsection are well suited for controlling the regularization bias. The basic idea is a straightforward consequence of (3.15):

$$\|\varphi - \varphi_\alpha\|^2 \leqslant \Big[\sup_j b^2(\alpha, \lambda_j^2)\lambda_j^{2\beta}\Big]\|\varphi\|_\beta^2. \tag{3.15}$$

Therefore, the rate of convergence (when the regularization parameter α goes to zero) of the regularization bias will be controlled, for $\varphi \in \Phi_\beta$, by the rate of convergence of

$$M_\beta(\alpha) = \sup_j b^2(\alpha, \lambda_j^2)\lambda_j^{2\beta}.$$

The following definition is useful to characterize the regularization schemes.

DEFINITION 3.10 *(Geometrically unbiased regularization).* A regularization scheme characterized by a bias function $b(\alpha, \lambda^2)$ is said to be geometrically unbiased at order $\beta > 0$ if:

$$M_\beta(\alpha) = O(\alpha^\beta).$$

PROPOSITION 3.11. *The spectral cut-off and the Landweber–Fridman regularization schemes are geometrically unbiased at any positive order β. Tikhonov regularization scheme satisfies*

$$M_\beta(\alpha) = O(\alpha^{\min(\beta,2)}),$$

therefore it is geometrically unbiased only at order $\beta \in (0, 2]$.

PROOF. In the spectral cut-off case, there is no bias for $\lambda_j^2 > \alpha/c$ while the bias is maximum, equal to one, for smaller λ_j^2. Therefore:

$$M_\beta(\alpha) \leqslant (\alpha/c)^\beta.$$

In the Landweber–Fridman case, there is no bias for $\lambda_j^2 > 1/c$ but a decreasing bias $(1-c\lambda_j^2)^{1/\alpha}$ for λ_j^2 increasing from zero to $(1/c)$. Therefore, $M_\beta(\alpha) \leqslant [\mathrm{Sup}_{\lambda^2 \leqslant (1/c)}(1-c\lambda^2)^{2/\alpha}\lambda^{2\beta}]$. The supremum is reached for $\lambda^2 = (\beta/c)[\beta + (2/\alpha)]^{-1}$ and gives:

$$M_\beta(\alpha) \leqslant (\beta/c)^\beta\big[\beta + (2/\alpha)\big]^{-\beta} \leqslant (\beta/2)^\beta(\alpha/c)^\beta.$$

In the Tikhonov case, the bias decreases hyperbolically and then $M_\beta(\alpha) \leqslant \sup_{\lambda^2}\big[\frac{(\alpha/c)}{(\alpha/c)+\lambda^2}\big]^2\lambda^{2\beta}$. For $\beta < 2$, the supremum is reached for $\lambda^2 = (\beta\alpha/c)[2-\beta]^{-1}$ and thus

$$M_\beta(\alpha) \leqslant \lambda^{2\beta} \leqslant \big[\beta/(2-\beta)\big]^\beta(\alpha/c)^\beta.$$

As K is bounded, its largest eigenvalue is bounded. Therefore, for $\beta \geqslant 2$, we have

$$M_\beta(\alpha) \leqslant (\alpha/c)^2 \sup_j \lambda_j^{2(\beta-2)}. \qquad \square$$

PROPOSITION 3.12. *Let $K : \mathcal{H} \to \mathcal{E}$ be an injective compact operator. Let us assume that the solution φ of $K\varphi = r$ lies in the β-regularity space Φ_β of operator K, for some positive β. Then, if φ_α is defined by a regularization scheme geometrically unbiased at order β, we have*

$$\|\varphi_\alpha - \varphi\|^2 = O\big(\alpha^\beta\big).$$

Therefore, the smoother the function φ of interest ($\varphi \in \Phi_\beta$ for larger β) is, the faster the rate of convergence to zero of the regularization bias will be. However, a degree of smoothness larger than or equal to 2 (corresponding to the case $\varphi \in \mathcal{R}[(K^*K)]$) may be useless in the Tikhonov case. Indeed, for Tikhonov, we have $\|\varphi_\alpha - \varphi\|^2 = O(\alpha^{\min(\beta,2)})$. This is basically the price to pay for a regularization procedure, which is simple to implement and rather intuitive (see Section 3.4 below) but introduces a regularization bias which never vanishes completely.

Both the operator interpretation and the practical implementation of smooth regularization schemes (Tikhonov and Landweber–Fridman) are discussed below.

3.4. *Operator interpretation and implementation of regularization schemes*

In contrast to spectral cut-off, the advantage of Tikhonov and Landweber–Fridman regularization schemes is that they can be interpreted in terms of operators. Their algebraic expressions only depend on the global value of (K^*K) and (K^*r), and not of the singular value decomposition. An attractive feature is that it implies that they can be implemented from the computation of sample counterparts $(\hat{K}_n\hat{K}_n^*)$ and $(\hat{K}_n^*\hat{r}_n)$ without resorting to an estimation of eigenvalues and eigenfunctions.

The Tikhonov regularization is based on

$$(\alpha_n I + K^*K)\varphi_{\alpha_n} = K^*r \quad\Leftrightarrow\quad \varphi_{\alpha_n} = \sum_{j=1}^{\infty}\frac{\lambda_j}{\lambda_j^2 + \alpha_n}\langle r, \psi_j\rangle\phi_j$$

for a penalization term α_n and $\lambda_j = \sqrt{\lambda_j^2}$, while, for notational simplicity, the scaling factor c has been chosen equal to 1.

The interpretation of α_n as a penalization term comes from the fact that φ_α can be seen as the solution of

$$\varphi_\alpha = \arg\min_{\varphi} \|K\varphi - r\|^2 + \alpha\|\varphi\|^2 = \arg\min_{\varphi} \langle\varphi, K^*K\varphi + \alpha\varphi - 2K^*r\rangle + \|r\|^2.$$

To see this, just compute the Frechet derivative of the above expression and note that it is zero only for $K^*K\varphi + \alpha\varphi = K^*r$.

This interpretation of Tikhonov regularization in terms of penalization may suggest looking for quasi-solutions [see Kress (1999, Section 16-3)], that is solutions of the minimization of $\|K\varphi - r\|$ subject to the constraint that the norm is bounded by $\|\varphi\| \leqslant \rho$ for given ρ. For the purpose of econometric estimation, the quasi-solution may actually be the genuine solution if the specification of the structural econometric model entails that the function of interest φ lies in some compact set [Newey and Powell (2003)].

If one wants to solve directly the first-order conditions of the above minimization, it is worth mentioning that the inversion of the operator $(\alpha I + K^*K)$ is not directly well suited for iterative approaches since, typically for small α, the series expansion of $[I + (1/\alpha)K^*K]^{-1}$ does not converge. However, a convenient choice of the estimators $\hat{K}_n$ and $\hat{K}_n^*$ may allow us to replace the inversion of infinite dimensional operators by the inversion of finite dimensional matrices.

More precisely, when $\hat{K}_n$ and $\hat{K}_n^*$ can be written as in (2.21) and (2.22), one can directly write the finite sample problem as

$$(\alpha_n I + \hat{K}_n^*\hat{K}_n)\varphi = \hat{K}_n^* r \quad \Leftrightarrow \quad \alpha_n\varphi + \sum_{l,l'=1}^{L_n} a_{l'}(\varphi) b_l(\varepsilon_{l'})\eta_l = \sum_{l=1}^{L_n} b_l(r)\eta_l. \tag{3.16}$$

(1) First we compute $a_l(\varphi)$:
Apply a_j to (3.16):

$$\alpha_n a_j(\varphi) + \sum_{l,l'=1}^{L_n} a_{l'}(\varphi) b_l(\varepsilon_{l'}) a_j(\eta_l) = \sum_{l=1}^{L_n} b_l(r) a_j(\eta_l). \tag{3.17}$$

Equation (3.17) can be rewritten as

$$(\alpha_n I + A)\underline{a} = \underline{b}$$

where $\underline{a} = [\, a_1(\varphi) \quad a_2(\varphi) \quad \cdots \quad a_{L_n}(\varphi)\,]'$, A is the $L_n \times L_n$ matrix with principal element

$$A_{j,l'} = \sum_{l=1}^{L_n} b_l(\varepsilon_{l'}) a_j(\eta_l)$$

and

$$\underline{b} = \begin{bmatrix} \sum_l b_l(r)a_1(\eta_l) \\ \vdots \\ \sum_l b_l(r)a_{L_n}(\eta_l) \end{bmatrix}.$$

(2) From (3.16), an estimator of φ is given by

$$\hat{\varphi}_n = \frac{1}{\alpha_n}\left[\sum_{l=1}^{L_n} b_l(r)\eta_l - \sum_{l,l'=1}^{L_n} a_{l'}(\varphi)b_l(\varepsilon_{l'})\eta_l \right].$$

Landweber–Fridman regularization

The great advantage of this regularization scheme is not only that it can be written directly in terms of quantities (K^*K) and (K^*r), but also the resulting operator problem can be solved by a simple iterative procedure, with a finite number of steps. To get this, one has to first choose a sequence of regularization parameters, α_n, such that $(1/\alpha_n)$ is an integer and second the scaling factor c so that $0 < c < 1/\|K\|^2$. This latter condition may be problematic to implement since the norm of the operator K may be unknown. The refinements of an asymptotic theory, that enables us to accommodate a first step estimation of $\|K\|$ before the selection of an appropriate c, is beyond the scope of this chapter. Note however, that in several cases of interest, $\|K\|$ is known a priori even though the operator K itself is unknown. For example, if K is the conditional expectation operator, $\|K\| = 1$.

The advantage of the condition $c < 1/\|K\|^2$ is to guarantee a unique expression for the bias function $b(\alpha, \lambda^2) = (1 - c\lambda^2)^{1/\alpha}$ since all eigenvalues satisfy $\lambda^2 \leqslant 1/c$. Thus, when $(1/\alpha)$ is an integer:

$$\varphi_\alpha = \sum_{j=1}^{\infty} \frac{1}{\lambda_j} q(\alpha, \lambda_j^2)\langle r, \psi_j\rangle\phi_j$$

with

$$q(\alpha, \lambda_j^2) = 1 - (1 - c\lambda_j^2)^{1/\alpha} = c\lambda_j^2 \sum_{l=0}^{1/\alpha - 1} (1 - c\lambda_j^2)^l.$$

Thus,

$$\begin{aligned}\varphi_\alpha &= c \sum_{l=0}^{1/\alpha-1} \sum_{j=1}^{\infty} \lambda_j (1 - c\lambda_j^2)^l \langle r, \psi_j\rangle\phi_j \\ &= c \sum_{l=0}^{1/\alpha-1} \sum_{j=1}^{\infty} \lambda_j^2 (1 - c\lambda_j^2)^l \langle \varphi, \phi_j\rangle\phi_j \\ &= c \sum_{l=0}^{1/\alpha-1} (I - cK^*K)^l K^*K\varphi.\end{aligned}$$

Therefore, the estimation procedure will only resort to estimators of K^*K and of K^*r, without need for either the singular value decomposition or any inversion of operators. For a given c and regularization parameter α_n, the estimator of φ is

$$\hat{\varphi}_n = c \sum_{l=0}^{1/\alpha_n - 1} (I - c\hat{K}_n^* \hat{K}_n)^l \hat{K}_n^* \hat{r}_n.$$

$\hat{\varphi}_n$ can be computed recursively by

$$\hat{\varphi}_{l,n} = (I - c\hat{K}_n^* \hat{K}_n)\hat{\varphi}_{l-1,n} + c\hat{K}_n^* \hat{r}_n, \quad l = 1, 2, \ldots, 1/\alpha_n - 1,$$

starting with $\hat{\varphi}_{0,n} = c\hat{K}_n^* \hat{r}_n$. This scheme is known as the Landweber–Fridman iteration [see Kress (1999, p. 287)].

3.5. Estimation bias

Regularization schemes have precisely been introduced because the right hand side r of the inverse problem $K\varphi = r$ is generally unknown and replaced by an estimator. Let us denote by $\hat{r}_n$ an estimator computed from an observed sample of size n. As announced in the Introduction, a number of relevant inverse problems in econometrics are even more complicated since the operator K itself is unknown. Actually, in order to apply a regularization scheme, we may not need only an estimator of K but also of its adjoint K^* and of its singular system $\{\lambda_j, \phi_j, \psi_j\colon j = 1, 2, \ldots\}$. In this subsection, we consider such estimators $\hat{K}_n$, $\hat{K}_n^*$, and $\{\hat{\lambda}_j, \hat{\phi}_j, \hat{\psi}_j\colon j = 1, \ldots, L_n\}$ as given. We also maintain the identification assumption, so that the equation $K\varphi = r$ defines without ambiguity a true unknown value φ_0.

If $\varphi_\alpha = A_\alpha K^* r$ is the chosen regularized solution, the proposed estimator $\hat{\varphi}_n$ of φ_0 is defined by

$$\hat{\varphi}_n = \hat{A}_{\alpha_n} \hat{K}_n^* \hat{r}_n. \tag{3.18}$$

Note that the definition of this estimator involves two decisions. First, we need to select a sequence (α_n) of regularization parameters so that $\lim_{n\to\infty} \alpha_n = 0$ (possibly in a stochastic sense in the case of a data-driven regularization) in order to get a consistent estimator of φ_0. Second, for a given α_n, we estimate the second-order regularization scheme $A_{\alpha_n} K^*$ by $\hat{A}_{\alpha_n} \hat{K}_n^*$. Generally speaking, $\hat{A}_{\alpha_n}$ is defined from (3.9) where the singular values are replaced by their estimators and the inner products $\langle \varphi, \phi_j \rangle$ are replaced by their empirical counterparts (see Section 2.5.3). Yet, we have seen above that in some cases, the estimation of the regularized solution does not involve the estimators $\hat{\lambda}_j$ but only the estimators $\hat{K}_n$ and $\hat{K}_n^*$.

In any case, the resulting estimator bias $\hat{\varphi}_n - \varphi_0$ has two components:

$$\hat{\varphi}_n - \varphi_0 = \hat{\varphi}_n - \varphi_{\alpha_n} + \varphi_{\alpha_n} - \varphi_0. \tag{3.19}$$

While the second component $\varphi_{\alpha_n} - \varphi_0$ defines the regularization bias characterized in Section 3.3, the first component $\hat{\varphi}_n - \varphi_{\alpha_n}$ is the bias corresponding to the estimation of the regularized solution of φ_{α_n}. The goal of this subsection is to point out a set of statistical assumptions about the estimators $\hat{K}_n$, $\hat{K}_n^*$, and $\hat{r}_n$ that gives an (asymptotic) upper bound to the specific estimation bias magnitude, $\|\hat{\varphi}_n - \varphi_{\alpha_n}\|$ when the regularization bias $\|\varphi_{\alpha_n} - \varphi_0\|$ is controlled.

DEFINITION 3.13 *(Smooth regularization)*. A regularization scheme is said to be smooth when

$$\left\|(\hat{A}_{\alpha_n}\hat{K}_n^*\hat{K}_n - A_{\alpha_n}K^*K)\varphi_0\right\| \leqslant d(\alpha_n)\|\hat{K}_n^*\hat{K}_n - K^*K\|\|\varphi_{\alpha_n} - \varphi_0\|(1+\varepsilon_n) \tag{3.20}$$

with $\varepsilon_n = O(\|\hat{K}_n^*\hat{K}_n - K^*K\|)$.

PROPOSITION 3.14 *(Estimation bias). If $\varphi_\alpha = A_\alpha K^* r$ is the regularized solution conformable to Definition* 3.9 *and $\hat{\varphi}_n = \hat{A}_{\alpha_n}\hat{K}_n^*\hat{r}_n$, then*

$$\|\hat{\varphi}_n - \varphi_{\alpha_n}\| \leqslant d(\alpha_n)\|\hat{K}_n^*\hat{r}_n - \hat{K}_n^*\hat{K}_n\varphi_0\| + \left\|(\hat{A}_{\alpha_n}\hat{K}_n^*\hat{K}_n - A_{\alpha_n}K^*K)\varphi_0\right\|. \tag{3.21}$$

In addition, both the Tikhonov and Landweber–Fridman regularization schemes are smooth. In the Tikhonov case, $\varepsilon_n = 0$ identically.

PROOF.

$$\begin{aligned}\hat{\varphi}_n - \varphi_{\alpha_n} &= \hat{A}_{\alpha_n}\hat{K}_n^*\hat{r}_n - A_{\alpha_n}K^*r \\ &= \hat{A}_{\alpha_n}\hat{K}_n^*(\hat{r}_n - \hat{K}_n\varphi_0) + \hat{A}_{\alpha_n}\hat{K}_n^*\hat{K}_n\varphi_0 - A_{\alpha_n}K^*K\varphi_0.\end{aligned} \tag{3.22}$$

Thus,

$$\|\hat{\varphi}_n - \varphi_{\alpha_n}\| \leqslant d(\alpha_n)\|\hat{K}_n^*\hat{r}_n - \hat{K}_n^*\hat{K}_n\varphi_0\| + \|\hat{A}_{\alpha_n}\hat{K}_n^*\hat{K}_n\varphi_0 - A_{\alpha_n}K^*K\varphi_0\|.$$

(1) *Case of Tikhonov regularization*:

$$\hat{A}_{\alpha_n}\hat{K}_n^*\hat{K}_n\varphi_0 - A_{\alpha_n}K^*K\varphi_0 = \hat{A}_{\alpha_n}(\hat{K}_n^*\hat{K}_n - K^*K)\varphi_0 + (\hat{A}_{\alpha_n} - A_{\alpha_n})K^*K\varphi_0. \tag{3.23}$$

Since in this case,

$$A_\alpha = (\alpha I + K^*K)^{-1},$$

the identity

$$B^{-1} - C^{-1} = B^{-1}(C - B)C^{-1}$$

gives

$$\hat{A}_{\alpha_n} - A_{\alpha_n} = \hat{A}_{\alpha_n}(K^*K - \hat{K}_n^*\hat{K}_n)A_{\alpha_n}$$

and thus,

$$\begin{aligned}(\hat{A}_{\alpha_n} - A_{\alpha_n})K^*K\varphi_0 &= \hat{A}_{\alpha_n}(K^*K - \hat{K}_n^*K_n)A_{\alpha_n}K^*K\varphi_0 \\ &= \hat{A}_{\alpha_n}(K^*K - \hat{K}_n^*\hat{K}_n)\varphi_{\alpha_n}.\end{aligned} \tag{3.24}$$

Equations (3.23) and (3.24) together give

$$\hat{A}_{\alpha_n}\hat{K}_n^*\hat{K}_n\varphi_0 - A_{\alpha_n}K^*K\varphi_0 = \hat{A}_{\alpha_n}(\hat{K}_n^*\hat{K}_n - K^*K)(\varphi_0 - \varphi_{\alpha_n}),$$

which shows that Tikhonov regularization is smooth with $\varepsilon_n = 0$.

(2) *Case of Landweber–Fridman regularization*:
In this case,

$$\varphi_\alpha = \sum_{j=1}^{\infty}\left[1 - \left(1 - c\lambda_j^2\right)^{1/\alpha}\right]\langle\varphi_0, \phi_j\rangle\phi_j = \left[I - (I - cK^*K)^{1/\alpha}\right]\varphi_0.$$

Thus,

$$\begin{aligned}
&\hat{A}_{\alpha_n}\hat{K}_n^*\hat{K}_n\varphi_0 - A_{\alpha_n}K^*K\varphi_0\\
&\quad = \left[(I - cK^*K)^{1/\alpha_n} - (I - c\hat{K}_n^*\hat{K}_n)^{1/\alpha_n}\right]\varphi_0\\
&\qquad + \left[I - (I - c\hat{K}_n^*\hat{K}_n)^{1/\alpha_n}(I - cK^*K)^{-1/\alpha_n}\right](I - cK^*K)^{1/\alpha_n}\varphi_0\\
&\qquad + \left[I - (I - c\hat{K}_n^*\hat{K}_n)^{1/\alpha_n}(I - cK^*K)^{-1/\alpha_n}\right](\varphi_0 - \varphi_{\alpha_n}).
\end{aligned}$$

Then, a Taylor expansion gives:

$$\left\|I - (I - c\hat{K}_n^*\hat{K}_n)^{1/\alpha_n}(I - cK^*K)^{-1/\alpha_n}\right\| = \left\|\frac{c}{\alpha_n}(\hat{K}_n^*\hat{K}_n - K^*K)\right\|(1 + \varepsilon_n)$$

with $\varepsilon_n = O(\|\hat{K}_n^*\hat{K}_n - K^*K\|)$.

The result follows with $d(\alpha) = c/\alpha$. □

Note that we are not able to establish (3.20) for the spectral cut-off regularization. In that case, the threshold introduces a lack of smoothness, which precludes a similar Taylor expansion based argument as above.

The result of Proposition 3.14 jointly with (3.19) shows that two ingredients matter in controlling the estimation bias $\|\hat{\varphi}_n - \varphi_0\|$. First, the choice of a sequence of regularization parameters, α_n, will govern the speed of convergence to zero of the regularization bias $\|\varphi_{\alpha_n} - \varphi_0\|$ (for φ_0 in a given Φ_β) and the speed of convergence to infinity of $d(\alpha_n)$. Second, nonparametric estimation of K and r will determine the rates of convergence of $\|\hat{K}_n^*\hat{r}_n - \hat{K}_n^*\hat{K}_n\varphi_0\|$ and $\|\hat{K}_n^*\hat{K}_n - K^*K\|$.

4. Asymptotic properties of solutions of integral equations of the first kind

4.1. Consistency

Let φ_0 be the solution of $K\varphi = r$. By abuse of notation, we denote $X_n = O(c_n)$ for positive sequences $\{X_n\}$ and $\{c_n\}$, if the sequence X_n/c_n is upper bounded.

We maintain the following assumptions:

A1. $\hat{K}_n, \hat{r}_n$ are consistent estimators of K and r.
A2. $\|\hat{K}_n^* \hat{K}_n - K^* K\| = O\left(\frac{1}{a_n}\right)$.
A3. $\|\hat{K}_n^* \hat{r}_n - \hat{K}_n^* \hat{K}_n \varphi_0\| = O\left(\frac{1}{b_n}\right)$.

As before $\varphi_\alpha = A_\alpha K^* r$ is the regularized solution where A_α is a second-order regularization scheme and $\hat{\varphi}_n = \hat{A}_{\alpha_n} \hat{K}_n^* \hat{r}_n$. Proposition 4.1 below follows directly from Definition 3.13 and Proposition 3.14 (with the associated normalization rule $\alpha d(\alpha) = O(1)$):

PROPOSITION 4.1. *When applying a smooth regularization scheme, we get*:

$$\|\hat{\varphi}_n - \varphi_0\| = O\left(\frac{1}{\alpha_n b_n} + \left(\frac{1}{\alpha_n a_n} + 1\right)\|\varphi_{\alpha_n} - \varphi_0\|\right).$$

Discussion on the rate of convergence

The general idea is that the fastest possible rate of convergence in probability of $\|\hat{\varphi}_n - \varphi_0\|$ to zero should be the rate of convergence of the regularization bias $\|\varphi_{\alpha_n} - \varphi_0\|$. Proposition 4.1 shows that these two rates of convergence will precisely coincide when the rate of convergence to zero of the regularization parameter, α_n, is chosen sufficiently slow with respect to both the rate of convergence a_n of the sequence of approximations of the true operator, and the rate of convergence b_n of the estimator of the right-hand side of the operator equation. This is actually a common strategy when both the operator and the right-hand side of the inverse problem have to be estimated [see e.g. Vapnik (1998, corollary, p. 299)].

To get this, it is first obvious that $\alpha_n b_n$ must go to infinity at least as fast as $\|\varphi_{\alpha_n} - \varphi_0\|^{-1}$. For $\varphi_0 \in \Phi_\beta$, $\beta > 0$, and a geometrically unbiased regularization scheme, this means that:

$$\alpha_n^2 b_n^2 \geqslant \alpha_n^{-\beta}$$

that is $\alpha_n \geqslant b_n^{-\frac{2}{\beta+2}}$. To get the fastest possible rate of convergence under this constraint, we will choose:

$$\alpha_n = b_n^{-\frac{2}{\beta+2}}.$$

Then, the rate of convergence of $\|\hat{\varphi}_n - \varphi_0\|$ and $\|\varphi_{\alpha_n} - \varphi_0\|$ will coincide if and only if $a_n b_n^{-\frac{2}{\beta+2}}$ is bounded away from zero. Thus, we have proved:

PROPOSITION 4.2. *Consider a smooth regularization scheme, which is geometrically unbiased of order $\beta > 0$ with estimators of K and r conformable to Assumptions* A1, A2, A3, *and $a_n b_n^{-\frac{2}{\beta+2}}$ bounded away from zero. For $\varphi_0 \in \Phi_\beta$, the optimal choice of the* *regularization parameter is* $\alpha_n = b_n^{-\frac{2}{\beta+2}}$, *and then*

$$\|\hat{\varphi}_n - \varphi_0\| = O\big(b_n^{-\frac{\beta}{\beta+2}}\big).$$

For Tikhonov regularization, when $\varphi_0 \in \Phi_\beta$, $\beta > 0$, *provided* $a_n b_n^{-\min(\frac{2}{\beta+2},\frac{1}{2})}$ *is bounded away from zero and* $\alpha_n = b_n^{-\min(\frac{2}{\beta+2},\frac{1}{2})}$, *we have*

$$\|\hat{\varphi}_n - \varphi_0\| = O\big(b_n^{-\min(\frac{\beta}{\beta+2},\frac{1}{2})}\big).$$

Note that the only condition about the estimator of the operator K^*K is that its rate of convergence, a_n, is sufficiently fast to be greater than $b_n^{\frac{2}{\beta+2}}$. Under this condition, the rate of convergence of $\hat{\varphi}_n$ does not depend upon the accuracy of the estimator of K^*K. Of course, the more regular the unknown function φ_0 is, the larger β is and the easier it will be to meet the required condition. Generally speaking, the condition will involve the relative bandwidth sizes in the nonparametric estimation of K^*K and K^*r. Note that if, as it is generally the case for a convenient bandwidth choice (see e.g. Section 5.4), b_n is the parametric rate ($b_n = \sqrt{n}$), a_n must be at least $n^{1/(\beta+2)}$. For β not too small, this condition will be fulfilled by optimal nonparametric rates. For instance, the optimal unidimensional nonparametric rate, $n^{2/5}$, will work as soon as $\beta \geqslant 1/2$.

The larger β is, the faster the rate of convergence of $\hat{\varphi}_n$ is. In the case where φ_0 is a finite linear combination of $\{\phi_j\}$ (case where β is infinite), and $b_n = \sqrt{n}$, an estimator based on a geometrically unbiased regularization scheme (such as Landweber–Fridman) achieves the parametric rate of convergence. We are not able to obtain such a fast rate for Tikhonov, therefore it seems that if the function φ_0 is suspected to be very regular, Landweber–Fridman is preferable to Tikhonov. However, it should be noted that the rates of convergence in Proposition 4.2 are upperbounds and could possibly be improved upon.

4.2. *Asymptotic normality*

Asymptotic normality of

$$\begin{aligned}\hat{\varphi}_n - \varphi_0 &= \hat{\varphi}_n - \varphi_{\alpha_n} + \varphi_{\alpha_n} - \varphi_0 \\ &= \hat{A}_{\alpha_n}\hat{K}_n^*\hat{r}_n - A_{\alpha_n}K^*K\varphi_0 + \varphi_{\alpha_n} - \varphi_0\end{aligned}$$

can be deduced from a functional central limit theorem applied to $\hat{K}_n^*\hat{r}_n - \hat{K}_n^*\hat{K}_n\varphi_0$. Therefore, we must reinforce Assumption A3 by assuming a weak convergence in $\mathcal{H}$:

Assumption WC

$$b_n(\hat{K}_n^*\hat{r}_n - \hat{K}_n^*\hat{K}_n\varphi_0) \quad \Rightarrow \quad \mathcal{N}(0, \Sigma) \quad \text{in } \mathcal{H}.$$

According to (3.22), (3.23), and (3.24), we have in the case of Tikhonov regularization:

$$b_n(\hat{\varphi}_n - \varphi_0) = b_n \hat{A}_{\alpha_n}[\hat{K}_n^* \hat{r}_n - \hat{K}_n^* \hat{K}_n \varphi_0] \tag{4.1}$$

$$+ b_n \hat{A}_{\alpha_n}[\hat{K}_n^* \hat{K}_n - K^* K](\varphi_0 - \varphi_{\alpha_n}) \tag{4.2}$$

while an additional term corresponding to ε_n in (3.20) should be added for general regularization schemes. The term (4.1) can be rewritten as

$$\hat{A}_{\alpha_n}\xi + \hat{A}_{\alpha_n}(\xi_n - \xi)$$

where ξ denotes the random variable $\mathcal{N}(0, \Sigma)$ in $\mathcal{H}$ and

$$\xi_n = b_n(\hat{K}_n^* r_n - \hat{K}_n^* \hat{K}_n \varphi_0).$$

By definition

$$\frac{\langle \hat{A}_{\alpha_n}\xi, g\rangle}{\|\Sigma^{1/2}\hat{A}_{\alpha_n} g\|} \xrightarrow{d} \mathcal{N}(0, 1)$$

for all $g \in \mathcal{H}$. Then, we may hope to obtain a standardized normal asymptotic probability distribution for

$$\frac{\langle b_n(\hat{\varphi}_n - \varphi_0), g\rangle}{\|\Sigma^{1/2}\hat{A}_{\alpha_n} g\|}$$

for vectors g conformable to the following assumption:

Assumption G

$$\frac{\|\hat{A}_{\alpha_n} g\|}{\|\Sigma^{1/2}\hat{A}_{\alpha_n} g\|} = O(1).$$

Indeed, we have in this case:

$$\frac{|\langle \hat{A}_{\alpha_n}(\xi_n - \xi), g\rangle|}{\|\Sigma^{1/2}\hat{A}_{\alpha_n} g\|} \leqslant \frac{\|\xi_n - \xi\| \|\hat{A}_{\alpha_n} g\|}{\|\Sigma^{1/2}\hat{A}_{\alpha_n} g\|},$$

which converges to zero in probability because $\|\xi_n - \xi\| \xrightarrow{P} 0$ by WC. We are then able to show:

PROPOSITION 4.3. *Consider a Tikhonov regularization. Suppose Assumptions* A1, A2, A3, *and WC hold and* $\varphi_0 \in \Phi_\beta$, $\beta > 0$, *with* $b_n \alpha_n^{\min(\beta/2, 1)} \underset{n\to\infty}{\longrightarrow} 0$, *we have for any* g *conformable to* G:

$$\frac{\langle b_n(\hat{\varphi}_n - \varphi_0), g\rangle}{\|\Sigma^{1/2}\hat{A}_{\alpha_n} g\|} \xrightarrow{d} \mathcal{N}(0, 1).$$

PROOF. From (4.1) and (4.2), we have:

$$\begin{aligned}\langle b_n(\hat{\varphi}_n - \varphi_{\alpha_n}), g\rangle &= \langle \hat{A}_{\alpha_n}\xi, g\rangle + \langle \hat{A}_{\alpha_n}(\xi_n - \xi), g\rangle \\ &\quad + \langle b_n \hat{A}_{\alpha_n}[\hat{K}_n^*\hat{K}_n - K^*K](\varphi_0 - \varphi_{\alpha_n}), g\rangle \end{aligned} \tag{4.3}$$

in the case of Tikhonov regularization. We already took care of the terms in ξ and ξ_n, it remains to deal with the bias term corresponding to (4.3):

$$\begin{aligned}&\frac{b_n\langle \hat{A}_{\alpha_n}(\hat{K}_n^*\hat{K}_n - K^*K)(\varphi_0 - \varphi_{\alpha_n}), g\rangle}{\|\Sigma^{1/2}\hat{A}_{\alpha_n}g\|} \\ &\quad\leqslant \frac{b_n\langle (\hat{K}_n^*\hat{K}_n - K^*K)(\varphi_0 - \varphi_{\alpha_n}), \hat{A}_{\alpha_n}g\rangle}{\|\Sigma^{1/2}\hat{A}_{\alpha_n}g\|} \\ &\quad\leqslant b_n\|\hat{K}_n^*\hat{K}_n - K^*K\|\|\varphi_0 - \varphi_{\alpha_n}\|\frac{\|\hat{A}_{\alpha_n}g\|}{\|\Sigma^{1/2}\hat{A}_{\alpha_n}g\|} \\ &\quad= O\left(\frac{b_n\alpha_n^{\min(\beta/2,1)}}{a_n}\right).\end{aligned}$$

□

Discussion of Proposition 4.3

(i) It is worth noticing that Proposition 4.3 does not in general deliver a weak convergence result for $b_n(\hat{\varphi}_n - \varphi_0)$ because it does not hold for all $g \in \mathcal{H}$. However, the condition G is not so restrictive. It just amounts to assuming that the multiplication by $\Sigma^{1/2}$ does not modify the rate of convergence of $\hat{A}_{\alpha_n}g$.

(ii) We remark that for $g = K^*Kh$, $\hat{A}_{\alpha_n}g$ and $\Sigma^{1/2}\hat{A}_{\alpha_n}g$ converge respectively to h and $\Sigma^{1/2}h$. Moreover, if $g \neq 0$, $\Sigma^{1/2}h = \Sigma^{1/2}(K^*K)^{-1}g \neq 0$. Therefore, in this case, not only the condition G is fulfilled but the asymptotic normality holds also with rate of convergence b_n, that is typically root n. This result is conformable to the theory of asymptotic efficiency of inverse estimators as recently developed by Van Rooij, Ruymgaart and Van Zwet (2000). They show that there is a dense linear submanifold of functionals for which the estimators are asymptotically normal at the root n rate with optimal variance (in the sense of minimum variance in the class of the moment estimators). We do get optimal variance in Proposition 4.3 since in this case (using heuristic notations as if we were in finite dimension) the asymptotic variance is

$$\lim_{n\to\infty} g'A_{\alpha_n}\Sigma A_{\alpha_n}g = g'(K^*K)^{-1}\Sigma(K^*K)^{-1}g.$$

Moreover, we get this result in particular for any nonzero g in $\mathcal{R}(K^*K)$ while we know that $\mathcal{R}(K^*)$ is dense in $\mathcal{H}$ (identification condition). Generally speaking, Van Rooij, Ruymgaart and Van Zwet (2000) stress that the inner products do not converge weakly for every vector g in $\mathcal{H}$ at the same rate, if they converge at all.

(iii) The condition $b_n\alpha_n^{\min(\beta/2,1)} \to 0$ imposes a convergence to zero of the regularization coefficient α_n faster than the rate $\alpha_n = b_n^{-\min(\frac{2}{\beta+2},\frac{1}{2})}$ required for the consistency. This stronger condition is needed to show that the regularization bias multiplied by b_n converges to zero. A fortiori, the estimation bias term vanishes asymptotically.

The results of Proposition 4.3 are established under strong assumptions: convergence in $\mathcal{H}$ and restriction on g. An alternative method consists in establishing the normality of $\hat{\varphi}_n$ by the Liapunov condition [Davidson (1994)], see the example on deconvolution in Section 5 below.

5. Applications

A well-known example is that of the kernel estimator of the density. Indeed, the estimation of the p.d.f. f of a random variable X can be seen as solving an integral equation of the first kind

$$Kf(x) = \int_{-\infty}^{+\infty} I(u \leqslant x) f(u)\,\mathrm{d}u = F(x) \tag{5.1}$$

where F is the cdf of X. Applying the Tikhonov regularization to (5.1), one obtains a kernel estimator of f. This example is detailed in Härdle and Linton (1994) and in Vapnik (1998, pp. 308–311) and will not be discussed further.

This section reviews the standard examples of the ridge regression and factor models and less standard examples such as the regression with an infinite number of regressors, the deconvolution, and the instrumental variable estimation.

5.1. Ridge regression

The Tikhonov regularization discussed in Section 3 can be seen as an extension of the well-known ridge regression. The ridge regression was introduced by Hoerl and Kennard (1970). It was initially motivated by the fact that in the presence of near multicollinearity of the regressors, the least-squares estimator may vary dramatically as the result of a small perturbation in the data. The ridge estimator is more stable and may have a lower risk than the conventional least-squares estimator. For a review of this method, see Judge et al. (1980) and for a discussion in the context of inverse problems, see Ruymgaart (2001).

Consider the linear model (the notation of this paragraph is specific and corresponds to general notations of linear models):

$$y = X\theta + \varepsilon \tag{5.2}$$

where y and ε are $n \times 1$-random vectors, X is a $n \times q$ matrix of regressors of full rank, and θ is an unknown $q \times 1$-vector of parameters. The number of explanatory variables, q, is assumed to be constant and $q < n$. Assume that X is exogenous and all the expectations are taken conditionally on X. The classical least-squares estimator of θ is

$$\hat{\theta} = (X'X)^{-1}X'y.$$

There exists an orthogonal transformation such that $X'X/n = P'DP$ with

$$D = \begin{pmatrix} \mu_1 & & 0 \\ & \ddots & \\ 0 & & \mu_q \end{pmatrix},$$

$\mu_j > 0$, and $P'P = I_q$. Using the mean square error as measure of the risk, we obtain

$$\begin{aligned} E\|\hat{\theta} - \theta\|^2 &= E\big\|(X'X)^{-1}X'(X\theta + \varepsilon) - \theta\big\|^2 \\ &= E\big\|(X'X)^{-1}X'\varepsilon\big\|^2 \\ &= E\big(\varepsilon'X(X'X)^{-2}X'\varepsilon\big) \\ &= \sigma^2 \operatorname{trace}\big(X(X'X)^{-2}X'\big) \\ &= \frac{\sigma^2}{n}\operatorname{trace}\left(\left(\frac{X'X}{n}\right)^{-1}\right) \\ &= \frac{\sigma^2}{n}\operatorname{trace}\big(P'D^{-1}P\big) \\ &= \frac{\sigma^2}{n}\sum_{j=1}^{q}\frac{1}{\mu_j}. \end{aligned}$$

If some of the columns of X are closely collinear, the eigenvalues may be very small and the risk very large. Moreover, when the number of regressors is infinite, the risk is no longer bounded.

A solution is to use the ridge regression estimator:

$$\hat{\theta}_a = \arg\min_{\theta} \|y - X\theta\|^2 + a\|\theta\|^2 \quad \Rightarrow \quad \hat{\theta}_a = (aI + X'X)^{-1}X'y$$

for $a > 0$. We prefer to introduce $\alpha = a/n$ and define

$$\hat{\theta}_\alpha = \left(\alpha I + \frac{X'X}{n}\right)^{-1}\frac{X'y}{n}. \tag{5.3}$$

This way, the positive constant α corresponds to the regularization parameter introduced in earlier sections.

The estimator $\hat{\theta}_\alpha$ is no longer unbiased. Indeed we have

$$\theta_\alpha = E(\hat{\theta}_\alpha) = \left(\alpha I + \frac{X'X}{n}\right)^{-1}\frac{X'X}{n}\theta.$$

Using the fact that $A^{-1} - B^{-1} = A^{-1}[B - A]B^{-1}$, the bias can be rewritten as

$$\theta_\alpha - \theta = \left(\alpha I + \frac{X'X}{n}\right)^{-1}\frac{X'X}{n}\theta - \left(\frac{X'X}{n}\right)^{-1}\frac{X'X}{n}\theta = -\alpha\left(\alpha I + \frac{X'X}{n}\right)^{-1}\theta.$$

The risk becomes

$$
\begin{aligned}
E\|\hat{\theta}_\alpha - \theta\|^2 &= E\|\hat{\theta}_\alpha - \theta_\alpha\|^2 + \|\theta_\alpha - \theta\|^2 \\
&= E\left\|\left(\alpha I + \frac{X'X}{n}\right)^{-1} \frac{X'\varepsilon}{n}\right\|^2 + \alpha^2 \left\|\left(\alpha I + \frac{X'X}{n}\right)^{-1} \theta\right\|^2 \\
&= E\left(\frac{\varepsilon' X}{n}\left(\alpha I + \frac{X'X}{n}\right)^{-2} \frac{X'\varepsilon}{n}\right) + \alpha^2 \left\|\left(\alpha I + \frac{X'X}{n}\right)^{-1} \theta\right\|^2 \\
&= \frac{\sigma^2}{n} \operatorname{trace}\left(\left(\alpha I + \frac{X'X}{n}\right)^{-2} \frac{X'X}{n}\right) + \alpha^2 \left\|\left(\alpha I + \frac{X'X}{n}\right)^{-1} \theta\right\|^2 \\
&= \frac{\sigma^2}{n} \sum_{j=1}^{q} \frac{\mu_j}{(\alpha + \mu_j)^2} + \alpha^2 \sum_{j=1}^{q} \frac{((P\theta)_j)^2}{(\alpha + \mu_j)^2}.
\end{aligned}
$$

There is the usual trade-off between the variance (decreasing in α) and the bias (increasing in α). For each θ and σ^2, there is a value of α for which the risk of $\hat{\theta}_\alpha$ is smaller than that of $\hat{\theta}$. As q is finite, we have $E\|\hat{\theta}_\alpha - \theta_\alpha\|^2 \sim 1/n$ and $\|\theta_\alpha - \theta\|^2 \sim \alpha^2$. Hence, the MSE is minimized for $\alpha_n \sim 1/\sqrt{n}$. Let us compare this rate with that necessary to the asymptotic normality of $\hat{\theta}_\alpha$. We have

$$
\hat{\theta}_\alpha - \theta = -\alpha\left(\alpha I + \frac{X'X}{n}\right)^{-1} \theta + \left(\alpha I + \frac{X'X}{n}\right)^{-1} \frac{X'\varepsilon}{n}.
$$

Therefore, if X and ε satisfy standard assumptions of stationarity and mixing, $\hat{\theta}_\alpha$ is consistent as soon as α_n goes to zero and $\sqrt{n}(\hat{\theta}_\alpha - \theta)$ is asymptotically centered normal provided $\alpha_n = o(1/\sqrt{n})$, which is a faster rate than that obtained in the minimization of the MSE. Data-dependent methods for selecting the value of α are discussed in Judge et al. (1980).

Note that the ridge estimator (5.3) is the regularized inverse of the equation

$$
y = X\theta, \tag{5.4}
$$

where obviously θ is overidentified as there are n equations for q unknowns. Let $\mathcal{H}$ be $\mathbb{R}^q$ endowed with the euclidean norm and $\mathcal{E}$ be $\mathbb{R}^n$ endowed with the norm, $\|v\|^2 = v'v/n$. Define $K : \mathcal{H} \to \mathcal{E}$ such that $Ku = Xu$ for any $u \in \mathbb{R}^q$. Solving $\langle Ku, v\rangle = \langle u, K^*v\rangle$, we find the adjoint of K, $K^* : \mathcal{E} \to \mathcal{H}$ where $K^*v = X'v/n$ for any $v \in \mathbb{R}^n$. The Tikhonov regularized solution of (5.4) is given by

$$
\hat{\theta}_\alpha = (\alpha I + K^*K)^{-1} K^* y,
$$

which corresponds to (5.3). It is also interesting to look at the spectral cut-off regularization. Let $\{P_1, P_2, \ldots, P_q\}$ be the orthonormal eigenvectors of the $q \times q$ matrix $K^*K = X'X/n$ and $\{Q_1, Q_2, \ldots, Q_n\}$ be the orthonormal eigenvectors of the $n \times n$ matrix $KK^* = XX'/n$. Let $\lambda_j = \sqrt{\mu_j}$. Then the spectral cut-off regularized estimator is

$$\hat{\theta}_\alpha = \sum_{\lambda_j \geqslant \alpha} \frac{1}{\lambda_j} \langle y, Q_j \rangle P_j = \sum_{\lambda_j \geqslant \alpha} \frac{1}{\lambda_j} \frac{y' Q_j}{n} P_j.$$

A variation on the spectral cut-off consists in keeping the l largest eigenvalues to obtain

$$\hat{\theta}_l = \sum_{j=1}^{l} \frac{1}{\lambda_j} \frac{y' Q_j}{n} P_j.$$

We will refer to this method as truncation. A forecast of y is given by

$$\hat{y} = K \hat{\theta}_l = \sum_{j=1}^{l} \frac{y' Q_j}{n} Q_j. \tag{5.5}$$

Equation (5.5) is particularly interesting for its connection with forecasting using factors described in the next subsection.

5.2. Principal components and factor models

Let X_{it} be the observed data for the ith cross-section unit at time t, with $i = 1, 2, \ldots, q$ and $t = 1, 2, \ldots, T$. Consider the following dynamic factor model

$$X_{it} = \delta_i' F_t + e_{it} \tag{5.6}$$

where F_t is an $l \times 1$ vector of unobserved common factors and δ_i is the vector of factor loadings associated with F_t. The factor model is used in finance, where X_{it} represents the return of asset i at time t, see Ross (1976). Here we focus on the application of (5.6) to forecasting a single time series using a large number of predictors as in Stock and Watson (1998, 2002), Forni and Reichlin (1998), and Forni et al. (2000). Stock and Watson (1998, 2002) consider the forecasting equation

$$y_{t+1} = \beta' F_t + \epsilon_{t+1}$$

where y_t is either the inflation or the industrial production and X_{it} in (5.6) comprises 224 macroeconomic time-series. If the number of factors l is known, then $\Delta = (\delta_1, \delta_2, \ldots, \delta_q)$ and $F = (F_1, F_2, \ldots, F_T)'$ can be estimated from

$$\min_{\Delta, F} \frac{1}{qT} \sum_{i=1}^{q} \sum_{t=1}^{T} (X_{it} - \delta_i' F_t)^2 \tag{5.7}$$

under the restriction $F'F/T = I$. The F solution of (5.7) are the eigenvectors of XX'/T associated with the l largest eigenvalues. Hence $F = [Q_1 | \cdots | Q_l]$ where Q_j is jth eigenvector of XX'/T. Using the compact notation $y = (y_2, \ldots, y_{T+1})'$, a forecast of y is given by

$$\hat{y} = F\hat{\beta} = F(F'F)^{-1}F'y = F\frac{F'y}{T} = \sum_{j=1}^{l} \frac{Q'_j y}{T} Q_j.$$

We recognize (5.5). It means that forecasting using a factor model (5.6) is equivalent to forecasting Y from (5.4) using a regularized solution based on the truncation. The only difference is that in the factor literature, it is assumed that there exists a fixed number of common factors, whereas in the truncation approach (5.5), the number of factors grows with the sample size. This last assumption may seem more natural when the number of explanatory variables, q, goes to infinity.

An important issue in factor analysis is the estimation of the number of factors. Stock and Watson (1998) propose to minimize the MSE of the forecast. Bai and Ng (2002) propose various BIC and AIC criterions that enable us to consistently estimate the number of factors, even when T and q go to infinity.

5.3. Regression with many regressors

Consider the following model where the explained variable is a scalar Y while the explanatory variable Z is a square integrable random function w.r. to some known measure Π (possibly with finite or discrete support)

$$Y = \int Z(\tau)\varphi(\tau)\Pi(\mathrm{d}\tau) + U. \tag{5.8}$$

Moreover Z is uncorrelated with U and may include lags of Y and $E(U) = 0$. The aim is to estimate φ from observations $(y_i, z_i(\cdot))_{i=1,\dots,n}$. When Π has a continuous support, this model is known in statistics as the functional linear model. However, when Π has a discrete support, it corresponds to a regression with an infinity or a large number of regressors. For a broad review, see Ramsay and Silverman (1997). Various estimation methods of the function φ are discussed in recent papers including Van Rooij, Ruymgaart and Van Zwet (2000), Cardot, Ferraty and Sarda (2003), and Hall and Horowitz (2007).

First approach: Ridge regression

Equation (5.8) can be rewritten as

$$\begin{pmatrix} y_1 \\ \vdots \\ y_n \end{pmatrix} = \begin{pmatrix} \int z_1(\tau)\varphi(\tau)\Pi(\mathrm{d}\tau) \\ \vdots \\ \int z_n(\tau)\varphi(\tau)\Pi(\mathrm{d}\tau) \end{pmatrix} + \begin{pmatrix} u_1 \\ \vdots \\ u_n \end{pmatrix}$$

or equivalently

$$y = K\varphi + u$$

where the operator K is defined in the following manner:

$$K : L^2(\Pi) \to \mathbb{R}^n,$$
$$K\varphi = \begin{pmatrix} \int z_1(\tau)\varphi(\tau)\Pi(\mathrm{d}\tau) \\ \vdots \\ \int z_n(\tau)\varphi(\tau)\Pi(\mathrm{d}\tau) \end{pmatrix}.$$

As is usual in the regression, the error term u is omitted and we solve

$$K\varphi = y$$

using a regularized inverse

$$\varphi^\alpha = (\alpha I + K^*K)^{-1}K^*y. \tag{5.9}$$

As an exercise, we compute K^* and K^*K. To compute K^*, we solve

$$\langle K\varphi, \psi\rangle = \langle \varphi, K^*\psi\rangle$$

for ψ in $\mathbb{R}^n$ and we obtain

$$(K^*y)(\tau) = \frac{1}{n}\sum_{i=1}^n y_i z_i(\tau),$$
$$K^*K\varphi(\tau) = \int \frac{1}{n}\sum_{i=1}^n z_i(\tau)z_i(s)\varphi(s)\Pi(\mathrm{d}s).$$

The properties of the estimator (5.9) are further discussed in Van Rooij, Ruymgaart and Van Zwet (2000) and Hall and Horowitz (2007). Hall and Horowitz show that this estimator is more robust than the spectral cut-off estimator when the eigenvalues are close to each other.

Second approach: Moment conditions

As U and $Z(\cdot)$ are uncorrelated, we obtain the moment conditions:

$$E\big[YZ(\tau) - \langle Z, \varphi\rangle Z(\tau)\big] = 0 \iff$$
$$\int E\big[Z(\tau)Z(s)\big]\varphi(s)\Pi(\mathrm{d}s) = E\big[YZ(\tau)\big] \iff$$
$$T\varphi = r. \tag{5.10}$$

The operator T can be estimated by $\hat{T}_n$, the integral operator with kernel $\frac{1}{n}\sum_{i=1}^n z_i(\tau) \times z_i(s)$ and r can be estimated by $\hat{r}_n(\tau) = \frac{1}{n}\sum_{i=1}^n y_i z_i(\tau)$. Hence (5.10) becomes

$$\hat{T}_n\varphi = \hat{r}_n, \tag{5.11}$$

which is equal to

$$K^*K\varphi = K^*y.$$

If one preconditions (5.11) by applying the operator $\hat{T}_n^*$, one gets the regularized solution

$$\hat{\varphi}_n = (\alpha I + \hat{T}_n^* \hat{T}_n)^{-1} \hat{T}_n^* \hat{r}_n \tag{5.12}$$

which differs from the solution (5.9). When α goes to zero at an appropriate rate of convergence (different in both cases), the solutions of (5.9) and (5.12) will be asymptotically equivalent. Actually, the preconditioning by an operator in the Tikhonov regularization has the purpose of constructing an operator which is positive self-adjoint. Because $\hat{T}_n = K^* K$ is already positive self-adjoint, there is no reason to precondition here. Sometimes preconditioning more than necessary is aimed at facilitating the calculations [see Ruymgaart (2001)].

Using the results of Section 4, we can establish the asymptotic normality of $\hat{\varphi}_n$ defined in (5.12).

Assuming that

A1. u_i has mean zero and variance σ^2 and is uncorrelated with $z_i(\tau)$ for all τ.
A2. $u_i z_i(\cdot)$ is an i.i.d. process of $L^2(\Pi)$.
A3. $E\|u_i z_i(\cdot)\|^2 < \infty$
we have

(i) $\|\hat{T}_n^2 - T^2\| = O(\frac{1}{\sqrt{n}})$,
(ii) $\sqrt{n}(\hat{T}_n \hat{r}_n - \hat{T}_n^2 \varphi_0) \Rightarrow \mathcal{N}(0, \Sigma)$ in $L^2(\Pi)$.

(i) is straightforward. (ii) follows from

$$\hat{r}_n - \hat{T}_n \varphi_0 = \frac{1}{n}\sum_{i=1}^n y_i z_i(\tau) - \int \frac{1}{n}\sum_{i=1}^n z_i(\tau) z_i(s) \varphi_0(s) \Pi(\mathrm{d}s) = \frac{1}{n}\sum_{i=1}^n u_i z_i(\tau).$$

Here, $a_n = \sqrt{n}$ and $b_n = \sqrt{n}$. Under Assumptions A1 to A3, we have

$$\frac{1}{\sqrt{n}}\sum_{i=1}^n u_i z_i(\tau) \quad \Rightarrow \quad \mathcal{N}\big(0, \sigma^2 T\big)$$

in $L^2(\Pi)$ by Theorem 2.46. Hence

$$\sqrt{n}\big(\hat{T}_n \hat{r}_n - \hat{T}_n^2 \varphi_0\big) \quad \Rightarrow \quad \mathcal{N}\big(0, \sigma^2 T^3\big).$$

Let us rewrite Condition G introduced in Section 4.2 in terms of the eigenvalues λ_j and eigenfunctions ϕ_j of T

$$\frac{\|(T^2 + \alpha_n I)^{-1} g\|^2}{\|T^{3/2}(T^2 + \alpha_n I)^{-1} g\|^2} = O(1) \quad \Leftrightarrow \quad \frac{\sum_{j=1}^\infty \frac{\langle g, \phi_j \rangle^2}{(\lambda_j^2 + \alpha)^2}}{\sum_{j=1}^\infty \frac{\lambda_j^3 \langle g, \phi_j \rangle^2}{(\lambda_j^2 + \alpha)^2}} = O(1).$$

Obviously Condition G will not be satisfied for all g in $L^2(\Pi)$.

By Proposition 4.3, assuming that $\varphi_0 \in \Phi_\beta$, $0 < \beta < 2$ and $\sqrt{n}\alpha_n^{\beta/2} \to 0$, we have for g conformable with Condition G,

$$\frac{\langle \sqrt{n}(\hat{\varphi}_n - \varphi_0), g\rangle}{\|T^{3/2}(T^2 + \alpha_n I)^{-1} g\|} \xrightarrow{d} \mathcal{N}(0, 1).$$

The asymptotic variance is given by

$$\|T^{-1/2} g\|^2 = \sum_{j=1}^{\infty} \frac{\langle g, \phi_j\rangle^2}{\lambda_j}.$$

Whenever it is finite, that is whenever $g \in \mathcal{R}(T^{-1/2})$, $\langle(\hat{\varphi}_n - \varphi_0), g\rangle$ converges at the parametric rate.

A related but different model from (5.8) is the Hilbertian autoregressive model:

$$X_t = \rho(X_{t-1}) + \varepsilon_t \tag{5.13}$$

where X_t and ε_t are random elements in a Hilbert space and ρ is a compact linear operator. The difference between (5.13) and (5.8) is that in (5.8), Y is a random variable and not an element of a Hilbert space. Bosq (2000) proposes an estimator of ρ and studies its properties. An example of application of (5.13) is given in Kargin and Onatski (2004).

Kargin and Onatski (2004) are interested in the best prediction of the interest rate curve. They model the forward interest rate $X_t(\tau)$ at maturity τ by (5.13) where ρ is a Hilbert–Schmidt integral operator:

$$(\rho f)(\tau) = \int_0^\infty \rho(\tau, s) f(s)\,\mathrm{d}s. \tag{5.14}$$

The operator ρ is identified from the covariance and cross-covariance of the process X_t. Let Γ_{11} be the covariance operator of random curve X_t and Γ_{12} the cross-covariance operator of X_t and X_{t+1}. For convenience, the kernels of Γ_{11} and Γ_{12} are denoted using the same notation. Equations (5.13) and (5.14) yield

$$\begin{aligned}\Gamma_{12}(\tau_1, \tau_2) &= E\big[X_{t+1}(\tau_1)X_t(\tau_2)\big] \\ &= E\left[\int \rho(\tau_1, s)X_t(s)X_t(\tau_2)\,\mathrm{d}s\right] \\ &= \int \rho(\tau_1, s)\Gamma_{11}(s, \tau_2)\,\mathrm{d}s.\end{aligned}$$

Hence,

$$\Gamma_{12} = \rho\Gamma_{11}.$$

Solving this equation requires a regularization because Γ_{11} is compact. Interestingly, Kargin and Onatski (2004) show that the best prediction of the interest rate curve in finite sample is not necessarily provided by the eigenfunctions of Γ_{11} associated with the largest eigenvalues. It means that the spectral cut-off does not provide satisfactory predictions in small samples. They propose a better predictor of the interest rate curve based on predictive factors.

5.4. Deconvolution

Assume we observe i.i.d. realizations $y_1, \ldots, y_n$ of a random variable Y with unknown p.d.f. h, where Y satisfies

$$Y = X + Z$$

where X and Z are independent random variables with p.d.f. φ and g, respectively. The aim is to estimate φ assuming g is known. This problem consists in solving in φ the equation:

$$h(y) = \int g(y-x)\varphi(x)\,\mathrm{d}x. \tag{5.15}$$

Equation (5.15) is an integral equation of the first kind where the operator K defined by $(K\varphi)(y) = \int g(y-x)\varphi(x)\,\mathrm{d}x$ has a known kernel and need not be estimated. Recall that the compactness property depends on the space of reference. If we define as space of reference, L^2 with respect to Lebesgue measure, then K is not a compact operator and hence has a continuous spectrum. However, for a suitable choice of the reference spaces, K becomes compact. The most common approach to solving (5.15) is to use a deconvolution kernel estimator, this method was pioneered by Carroll and Hall (1988) and Stefanski and Carroll (1990). It is essentially equivalent to inverting Equation (5.15) by means of the continuous spectrum of K, see Carroll, Van Rooij and Ruymgaart (1991) and Section 5.4.2 below. In a related paper, Van Rooij and Ruymgaart (1991) propose a regularized inverse to a convolution problem of the type (5.15) where g has the circle for support. They invert the operator K using its continuous spectrum.

5.4.1. A new estimator based on Tikhonov regularization

The approach of Carrasco and Florens (2002) consists in defining two spaces of reference, $L^2_{\pi_X}(\mathbb{R})$ and $L^2_{\pi_Y}(\mathbb{R})$ as

$$L^2_{\pi_X}(\mathbb{R}) = \left\{\phi(x) \text{ such that } \int \phi(x)^2 \pi_X(x)\,\mathrm{d}x < \infty\right\},$$

$$L^2_{\pi_Y}(\mathbb{R}) = \left\{\psi(y) \text{ such that } \int \psi(y)^2 \pi_Y(y)\,\mathrm{d}y < \infty\right\},$$

where π_X and π_Y are arbitrary functions so that K is a Hilbert–Schmidt operator from $L^2_{\pi_X}(\mathbb{R})$ to $L^2_{\pi_Y}(\mathbb{R})$, that is the following condition is satisfied:

$$\iint \left(\frac{\pi_Y(y) g(y-x)}{\pi_Y(y)\pi_X(x)}\right)^2 \pi_Y(y)\pi_X(x)\,\mathrm{d}x\,\mathrm{d}y < \infty.$$

As a result K has a discrete spectrum for these spaces of reference. Let $\{\lambda_j, \phi_j, \psi_j\}$ denote its singular value decomposition. Equation (5.15) can be approximated by a well-posed problem using Tikhonov regularization

$$(\alpha_n I + K^* K)\varphi_{\alpha_n} = K^* h.$$

Hence we have

$$\begin{aligned}
\varphi_{\alpha_n}(x) &= \sum_{j=1}^{\infty} \frac{1}{\alpha_n + \lambda_j^2} \langle K^* h, \phi_j \rangle \phi_j(x) \\
&= \sum_{j=1}^{\infty} \frac{1}{\alpha_n + \lambda_j^2} \langle h, K\phi_j \rangle \phi_j(x) \\
&= \sum_{j=1}^{\infty} \frac{\lambda_j}{\alpha_n + \lambda_j^2} \langle h, \psi_j \rangle \phi_j(x) \\
&= \sum_{j=1}^{\infty} \frac{\lambda_j}{\alpha_n + \lambda_j^2} E\big[\psi_j(Y_i)\pi_Y(Y_i)\big]\phi_j(x).
\end{aligned}$$

The estimator of φ is obtained by replacing the expectation by a sample mean:

$$\hat{\varphi}_n = \frac{1}{n} \sum_{i=1}^{n} \sum_{j=1}^{\infty} \frac{\lambda_j}{\alpha_n + \lambda_j^2} \psi_j(y_i)\pi_Y(y_i)\phi_j(x).$$

Note that we avoided estimating h by a kernel estimator. In some cases, ψ_j and ϕ_j are known. For instance, if $Z \sim \mathcal{N}(0, \sigma^2)$, $\pi_Y(y) = \phi(y/\tau)$ and $\pi_X(x) = \phi(x/\sqrt{\tau^2 + \sigma^2})$ then ψ_j and ϕ_j are Hermite polynomials associated with $\lambda_j = \rho^j$. When ψ_j and ϕ_j are unknown, they can be estimated via simulations. Since one can do as many simulations as one wishes, the error due to the estimation of ψ_j and ϕ_j can be considered negligible.

Using the results of Section 3, one can establish the rate of convergence of $\|\hat{\varphi}_n - \varphi_0\|$. Assume that $\varphi_0 \in \Phi_\beta$, $0 < \beta < 2$, that is

$$\sum_{j=1}^{\infty} \frac{\langle \varphi, \phi_j \rangle^2}{\lambda_j^{2\beta}} < \infty.$$

We have $\|\varphi_{\alpha_n} - \varphi_0\| = O(\alpha_n^{\beta/2})$ and $\|\hat{\varphi}_n - \varphi_{\alpha_n}\| = O(1/(\alpha_n\sqrt{n}))$ as here $b_n = \sqrt{n}$. For an optimal choice of $\alpha_n = Cn^{-1/(\beta+2)}$, $\|\hat{\varphi}_n - \varphi_0\|^2$ is $O(n^{-\beta/(\beta+2)})$. The mean integrated square error (MISE) defined as $E\|\hat{\varphi}_n - \varphi_0\|^2$ has the same rate of convergence. Fan (1993) provides the optimal rate of convergence for a minimax criterion on a Lipschitz class of functions. The optimal rate of the MISE when the error term is normally distributed is only $(\ln n)^{-2}$ if φ is twice differentiable. On the contrary, here we get an arithmetic rate of convergence. The condition $\varphi_0 \in \Phi_\beta$ has the effect of reducing the class of admissible functions and hence improves the rate of convergence. Which type of restriction does $\varphi_0 \in \Phi_\beta$ impose? In Carrasco and Florens (2002), it is shown that $\varphi_0 \in \Phi_1$ is satisfied if

$$\int \left| \frac{\phi_{\varphi_0}(t)}{\phi_g(t)} \right| \mathrm{d}t < \infty \tag{5.16}$$

where ϕ_{φ_0} and ϕ_g denote the characteristic functions of φ_0 and g, respectively. This condition can be interpreted as the noise is "smaller" than the signal. Consider for example the case where φ_0 and g are normal. Condition (5.16) is equivalent to the fact that the variance of g is smaller than that of φ_0. Note that the condition $\varphi_0 \in \Phi_1$ relates φ_0 and g while one usually imposes restrictions on φ_0 independently of those on g.

5.4.2. *Comparison with the deconvolution kernel estimator*

Let $L^2(\mathbb{R})$ be the space of square-integrable functions with respect to Lebesgue measure on $\mathbb{R}$. Let F denote the Fourier transform operator from $L^2(\mathbb{R})$ into $L^2(\mathbb{R})$ defined by

$$(Fq)(s) = \frac{1}{\sqrt{2\pi}} \int e^{isx} q(x)\,\mathrm{d}x.$$

F satisfies that $F^* = F^{-1}$. We see that

$$F(g * f) = \phi_g F f$$

so that K admits the following spectral decomposition [see Carroll, van Rooij and Ruymgaart (1991, Theorem 3.1)]:

$$K = F^{-1} M_{\phi_g} F$$

where M_ρ is the multiplication operator $M_\rho \varphi = \rho\varphi$.

$$K^* K = F^{-1} M_{|\phi_g|^2} F.$$

We want to solve in f the equation:

$$K^* K f = K^* h.$$

Let us denote

$$q(x) = (K^* h)(x) = \int g(y - x) h(y)\,\mathrm{d}y.$$

Then,

$$\hat{q}(x) = \frac{1}{n} \sum_{i=1}^{n} g(y_i - x)$$

is a $\sqrt{n}$-consistent estimator of q.

Using the spectral cut-off regularized inverse of $K^* K$, we get

$$\hat{f} = F^{-1} M_{\frac{I\{|\phi_g| > \alpha\}}{|\phi_g|^2}} F \hat{q}.$$

Using the change of variables $u = y_i - x$, we have

$$(F\hat{q})(t) = \frac{1}{n}\sum_{i=1}^{n}\int e^{itx} g(y_i - x)\,\mathrm{d}x$$
$$= \frac{1}{n}\sum_{i=1}^{n}\int e^{it(y_i-u)} g(u)\,\mathrm{d}u$$
$$= \frac{1}{n}\sum_{i=1}^{n}\overline{\phi_g(t)}e^{ity_i}.$$
$$\hat{f}(x) = \frac{1}{2\pi}\int e^{-itx} I\{|\phi_g(t)| > \alpha\}\frac{1}{|\phi_g(t)|^2}(F\hat{q})(t)\,\mathrm{d}t$$
$$= \frac{1}{2\pi}\frac{1}{n}\sum_{i=1}^{n}\int e^{-it(y_i-x)} I\{|\phi_g(t)| > \alpha\}\frac{1}{\phi_g(t)}\,\mathrm{d}t.$$

Assuming that $\phi_g > 0$ and strictly decreasing as $|t|$ goes to infinity, we have $I\{|\phi_g(t)| > \alpha\} = I\{-A \leqslant t \leqslant A\}$ for some $A > 0$ so that

$$\hat{f}(x) = \frac{1}{2\pi}\frac{1}{n}\sum_{i=1}^{n}\int_{-A}^{A}\frac{e^{-it(y_i-x)}}{\phi_g(t)}\,\mathrm{d}t.$$

Now compare this expression with the kernel estimator [see e.g. Stefanski and Carroll (1990)]. For a smoothing parameter c and a kernel ω, the kernel estimator is given by

$$\hat{f}_k(x) = \frac{1}{nc}\sum_{i=1}^{n}\frac{1}{2\pi}\int\frac{\phi_\omega(u)}{\phi_g(u/c)}e^{iu(y_i-x)/c}\,\mathrm{d}u. \tag{5.17}$$

Hence $\hat{f}$ coincides with the kernel estimator when $\phi_\omega(u) = I_{[-1,1]}(u)$. This is the sinc kernel corresponding to $\omega(x) = \operatorname{sin}c(x) = \sin(x)/x$. This suggests that the kernel estimator is obtained by inverting an operator that has a continuous spectrum. Because this spectrum is given by the characteristic function of g, the speed of convergence of the estimator depends on the behavior of ϕ_g in the tails. For a formal exposition, see Carroll, van Rooij and Ruymgaart (1991, Example 3.1). They assume in particular that the function to estimate is p differentiable and they obtain a rate of convergence (as a function of p) that is of the same order as the rate of the kernel estimator.

By using the Tikhonov regularization instead of the spectral cut-off, we obtain

$$\hat{f}(y) = \frac{1}{n}\sum_{i=1}^{n}\int\frac{\overline{\phi_g(t)}}{|\phi_g(t)|^2 + \alpha}e^{-itx_i}e^{ity}\,\mathrm{d}t.$$

We apply a change of variable $u = -t$,

$$\hat{f}(y) = \frac{1}{n}\sum_{i=1}^{n}\frac{1}{2\pi}\int\frac{\phi_g(u)}{|\phi_g(u)|^2 + \alpha}e^{iu(x_i-y)}\,\mathrm{d}u. \tag{5.18}$$

The formulas (5.18) and (5.17) differ only by the way the smoothing is applied. Interestingly, (5.18) can be computed even when the characteristic function of Z vanishes but $\hat{f}$ is no longer consistent.

5.5. Instrumental variables

This example is mainly based on Darolles, Florens and Renault (2002).

An economic relationship between a response variable Y and a vector Z of explanatory variables is often represented by an equation:

$$Y = \varphi(Z) + U, \tag{5.19}$$

where the function $\varphi(\cdot)$ defines the parameter of interest while U is an error term. The relationship (5.19) does not characterize the function φ if the residual term is not constrained. This difficulty is solved if it is assumed that $E[U \mid Z] = 0$, or if equivalently $\varphi(Z) = E[Y \mid Z]$. However in numerous structural econometric models, the conditional expectation function is not the parameter of interest. The structural parameter is a relation between Y and Z where some of the Z components are endogenous. This is the case in various situations: simultaneous equations, error-in-variables models, and treatment models with endogenous selection, etc.

The first issue is to add assumptions to Equation (5.19) in order to characterize φ. Two general strategies exist in the literature, at least for linear models. The first one consists in introducing some hypotheses on the joint distribution of U and Z (for example on the variance matrix). The second one consists in increasing the vector of observables from (Y, Z) to (Y, Z, W), where W is a vector of instrumental variables. The first approach was essentially followed in the error-in-variables models and some similarities exist with the instrumental variables model [see e.g. Malinvaud (1970, Chapter 9), Florens, Mouchart and Richard (1974) or Florens, Mouchart and Richard (1987) for the linear case]. Instrumental variable analysis as a solution to an endogeneity problem was proposed by Reiersol (1941, 1945), and extended by Theil (1953), Basmann (1957), and Sargan (1958).

However, even in the instrumental variables framework, the definition of the functional parameter of interest remains ambiguous in the general nonlinear case. Three possible definitions of φ have been proposed [see Florens et al. (2003) for a general comparison between these three concepts and their extensions to more general treatment models].

(i) The first one replaces $E[U \mid Z] = 0$ by $E[U \mid W] = 0$, or equivalently it defines φ as the solution of

$$E\big[Y - \varphi(Z) \mid W\big] = 0. \tag{5.20}$$

This definition was the foundation of the analysis of simultaneity in linear models or parametric nonlinear models [see Amemiya (1974)], but its extension to the nonparametric case raises new difficulties. The focus of this subsection is to show how to address this issue in the framework of ill-posed inverse problems. A first attempt was undertaken by Newey and Powell (2003), who prove consistency of a series estimator of φ in Equation (5.20). Florens (2003) and Blundell and Powell (2003) consider various nonparametric methods for estimating a nonlinear regression with endogenous regressors. Darolles, Florens and Renault (2002) prove both the consistency and the asymptotic distribution of a kernel estimator of φ. Hall and Horowitz (2005) give the optimal rate of convergence of the kernel estimator under conditions which differ from those of Darolles, Florens and Renault (2002). Finally, Blundell, Chen and Kristensen (2003) propose a sieves estimator of the Engel curve.

(ii) A second approach called *control function approach* was systematized by Newey, Powell and Vella (1999). This technique was previously developed in specific models (e.g. Mills ratio correction in some selection models for example). The starting point is to compute $E[Y \mid Z, W]$ which satisfies:

$$E[Y \mid Z, W] = \varphi(Z) + h(Z, W), \tag{5.21}$$

where $h(Z, W) = E[U \mid Z, W]$. Equation (5.21) does not characterize φ. However we can assume that there exists a function V (the *control function*) of (Z, W) (typically $Z - E[Z \mid W]$), which captures all the endogeneity of Z in the sense that $E[U \mid W, Z] = E[U \mid W, V] = E[U \mid V] = \tilde{h}(V)$. This implies that (5.21) may be rewritten as

$$E[Y \mid Z, W] = \varphi(Z) + \tilde{h}(V), \tag{5.22}$$

and under some conditions, φ may be identified from (5.22) up to an additive constant term. This model is an additive model where the V are not observed but are estimated.

(iii) A third definition follows from the literature on treatment models [see e.g. Imbens and Angrist (1994), Heckman et al. (1998) and Heckman and Vytlacil (2000)]. We extremely simplify this analysis by considering Z and W as scalars. A *local instrument* is defined by $\frac{\partial E[Y \mid W]}{\partial W} / \frac{\partial E[Z \mid W]}{\partial W}$, and the function of interest φ is assumed to be characterized by the relation:

$$\frac{\frac{\partial E[Y \mid W]}{\partial W}}{\frac{\partial E[Z \mid W]}{\partial W}} = E\left[\frac{\partial \varphi}{\partial Z} \,\Big|\, W\right]. \tag{5.23}$$

Let us summarize the arguments which justify Equation (5.23).

Equation (5.19) is extended to a nonseparable model

$$Y = \varphi(Z) + Z\varepsilon + U \tag{5.24}$$

where ε and U are two random errors.

First, we assume that

$$E(U \mid W) = E(\varepsilon \mid W) = 0.$$

This assumption extends the instrumental variable assumption but is not sufficient to identify the parameter of interest φ. From (5.24) we get:

$$E(Y \mid W = w) = \int \big[\varphi(z) + zr(z, w)\big] f_Z(z \mid w)\,\mathrm{d}z$$

where $f_Z(\cdot \mid \cdot)$ denotes the conditional density of Z given W and $r(z, w) = E(\varepsilon \mid Z = z, W = w)$. Then, we have

$$\begin{aligned}\frac{\partial}{\partial w} E(Y \mid W = w) = &\int \varphi(z) \frac{\partial}{\partial w} f_Z(z \mid w)\,\mathrm{d}z \\ &+ \int z \frac{\partial}{\partial w} r(z, w) f_Z(z \mid w)\,\mathrm{d}z \\ &+ \int zr(z, w) \frac{\partial}{\partial w} f_Z(z \mid w)\,\mathrm{d}z,\end{aligned}$$

assuming that the order of integration and derivative may commute (in particular the boundary of the distribution of Z given $W = w$ does not depend on w).

Second, we introduce the assumption that $V = Z - E(Z \mid W)$ is independent of W. In terms of density, this assumption implies that $f_Z(z \mid w) = \tilde{f}(z - m(w))$ where $m(w) = E(Z \mid W = w)$ and $\tilde{f}$ is the density of v. Then:

$$\begin{aligned}\frac{\partial}{\partial w} E(Y \mid W = w) = &-\frac{\partial m(w)}{\partial w} \int \varphi(z) \frac{\partial}{\partial z} f_Z(z \mid w)\,\mathrm{d}z \\ &+ \int z \frac{\partial}{\partial w} r(z, w) f_Z(z \mid w)\,\mathrm{d}z \\ &- \frac{\partial m(w)}{\partial w} \int zr(z, w) \frac{\partial}{\partial z} f_Z(z \mid w)\,\mathrm{d}z.\end{aligned}$$

An integration by parts of the first and the third integrals gives

$$\begin{aligned}\frac{\partial}{\partial w} E(Y \mid W = w) = &\frac{\partial m(w)}{\partial w} \int \frac{\partial}{\partial z} \varphi(z) f_Z(z \mid w)\,\mathrm{d}z \\ &+ \int z\left(\frac{\partial r}{\partial w} + \frac{\partial m}{\partial w}\frac{\partial r}{\partial z}\right) f_Z(z \mid w)\,\mathrm{d}z \\ &+ \frac{\partial m(w)}{\partial w} \int r(z, w) f_Z(z \mid w)\,\mathrm{d}z.\end{aligned}$$

The last integral is zero under $E(\varepsilon \mid w) = 0$. Finally, we need to assume that the second integral is zero. This is true in particular if there exists $\tilde{r}$ such that $r(z, w) = \tilde{r}(z - m(w))$.

Hence, Equation (5.23) is verified.

These three concepts are identical in the linear normal case but differ in general. We concentrate our presentation in this chapter on the pure instrumental variable cases defined by Equation (5.20).

For a general approach of Equation (5.20) in terms of inverse problems, we introduce the following notation:

$$K : L^2_F(Z) \to L^2_F(W), \quad \varphi \to K\varphi = E\big[\varphi(Z) \mid W\big],$$
$$K^* : L^2_F(W) \to L^2_F(Z), \quad \psi \to K^*\psi = E\big[\psi(W) \mid Z\big].$$

All these spaces are defined relatively to the true (unknown) DGP (see Example 2.3 in Section 2). The two linear operators K and K^* satisfy:

$$\begin{aligned}\big\langle \varphi(Z), \psi(W)\big\rangle = E\big[\varphi(Z)\psi(W)\big] &= \big\langle K\varphi(W), \psi(W)\big\rangle_{L^2_F(W)} \\ &= \big\langle \varphi(Z), K^*\psi(Z)\big\rangle_{L^2_F(Z)}.\end{aligned}$$

Therefore, K^* is the adjoint operator of K, and reciprocally. Using these notations, the unknown instrumental regression φ corresponds to any solution of the functional equation:

$$A(\varphi, F) = K\varphi - r = 0, \tag{5.25}$$

where $r(W) = E[Y \mid W]$.

In order to illustrate this construction and the central role played by the adjoint operator K^*, we first consider the example where Z is discrete, namely Z is binary. This model is considered by Das (2005) and Florens and Malavolti (2002). In that case, a function $\varphi(Z)$ is characterized by two numbers $\varphi(0)$ and $\varphi(1)$ and L^2_Z is isomorphic to $\mathbb{R}^2$. Equation (5.20) becomes

$$\varphi(0)\operatorname{Prob}(Z = 0 \mid W = w) + \varphi(1)\operatorname{Prob}(Z = 1 \mid W = w) = E(Y \mid W = w).$$

The instruments W need to take at least two values in order to identify $\varphi(0)$ and $\varphi(1)$ from this equation. In general, φ is overidentified and overidentification is solved by replacing (5.25) by

$$K^*K\varphi = K^*r$$

or, in the binary case, by

$$\begin{aligned}&\varphi(0)E\big(\operatorname{Prob}(Z = 0 \mid W) \mid Z\big) + \varphi(1)E\big(\operatorname{Prob}(Z = 1 \mid W) \mid Z\big) \\ &\quad = E\big(E(Y \mid W) \mid Z\big).\end{aligned}$$

In the latter case, we obtain two equations which in general have a unique solution.

This model can be extended by considering $Z = (Z_1, Z_2)$ where Z_1 is discrete ($Z_1 \in \{0, 1\}$) and Z_2 is exogenous (i.e. $W = (W_1, Z_2)$). In this extended binary model, φ is characterized by two functions $\varphi(0, z_2)$ and $\varphi(1, z_2)$, the solutions of

$$\begin{aligned}&\varphi(0, z_2)E\big(\operatorname{Prob}(Z_1 = 0 \mid W) \mid Z_1 = z_1,\ Z_2 = z_2\big) \\ &\qquad + \varphi(1, z_2)E\big(\operatorname{Prob}(Z_1 = 1 \mid W) \mid Z_1 = z_1,\ Z_2 = z_2\big) \\ &\quad = E\big(E(Y \mid W) \mid Z_1 = z_1,\ Z_2 = z_2\big), \quad \text{for } z_1 = 0, 1.\end{aligned}$$

The properties of the estimator based on the previous equation are considered in Florens and Malavolti (2002). In this case, no regularization is needed because K^*K has a continuous inverse (since the dimension is finite in the pure binary case and K^*K is not compact in the extended binary model).

We can also illustrate our approach in the case when the Hilbert spaces are not necessarily L^2 spaces. Consider the following semiparametric case. The function φ is constrained to be an element of

$$\mathcal{X} = \left\{ \varphi \text{ such that } \varphi = \sum_{l=1}^{L} \beta_l \varepsilon_l \right\}$$

where $(\varepsilon_l)_{l=1,\dots,L}$ is a vector of fixed functions in $L_F^2(Z)$. Then $\mathcal{X}$ is a finite dimensional Hilbert space. However, we keep the space $\mathcal{E}$ equal to $L_F^2(W)$. The model is then partially parametric but the relation between Z and W is treated nonparametrically. In this case, it can easily be shown that K^* transforms any function ψ of $L_F^2(W)$ into a function of $\mathcal{X}$, which is its best approximation in the L^2 sense (see Example 2.4 in Section 2). Indeed:

If $\psi \in L_F^2(W)$, $\forall j \in \{1, \dots, L\}$

$$E(\varepsilon_j \psi) = \langle K\varepsilon_j, \psi \rangle = \langle \varepsilon_j, K^*\psi \rangle.$$

Moreover, $K^*\psi \in \mathcal{X} \implies K^*\psi = \sum_{l=1}^{L} \alpha_l \varepsilon_l$, therefore

$$\left\langle \varepsilon_j, \sum_{l=1}^{L} \alpha_l \varepsilon_l \right\rangle = E(\psi \varepsilon_j) \quad \Leftrightarrow \quad \sum_{l=1}^{L} \alpha_l E(\varepsilon_j \varepsilon_l) = E(\psi \varepsilon_j).$$

The function φ defined as the solution of $K\varphi = r$ is in general overidentified but the equation $K^*K\varphi = K^*r$ always has a unique solution. The finite dimension of $\mathcal{X}$ implies that $(K^*K)^{-1}$ is a finite dimensional linear operator and is then continuous. No regularization is required.

Now we introduce an assumption which is only a regularity condition when Z and W have no element in common. However, this assumption cannot be satisfied if there are some common elements between Z and W. Extensions to this latter case are discussed in Darolles, Florens and Renault (2002), see also Example 2.5 in Section 2.

ASSUMPTION A.1. The joint probability distribution of (Z, W) is dominated by the product of its marginal probability distributions, and its Radon Nikodym density is square integrable w.r.t. the product of margins.

Assumption A.1 ensures that K and K^* are Hilbert–Schmidt operators, and is a sufficient condition for the compactness of K, K^*, KK^* and K^*K [see Lancaster (1968), Darolles, Florens and Renault (2002) and Theorem 2.34].

Under Assumption A.1, the instrumental regression φ is identifiable if and only if 0 is not an eigenvalue of K^*K. Then, for the sake of expositional simplicity, we focus on the i.i.d. context:

ASSUMPTION A.2. The data (y_i, z_i, w_i), $i = 1, \ldots, n$, are i.i.d. samples of (Y, Z, W).

We estimate the joint distribution F of (Y, Z, W) using a kernel smoothing of the empirical distribution. In the applications, the bandwidths differ, but they all have the same speed represented by the notation c_n.

For economic applications, one may be interested either by the unknown function $\varphi(Z)$ itself, or only by its moments, including covariances with some known functions. These moments may for instance be useful for testing economic statements about scale economies, elasticities of substitutions, and so on.

For such tests, one will only need the empirical counterparts of these moments and their asymptotic probability distribution. An important advantage of the instrumental variable approach is that it permits us to estimate the covariance between $\varphi(Z)$ and $g(Z)$ for a large class of functions. Actually, the identification assumption amounts to ensure that the range $\mathcal{R}(K^*)$ is dense in $L^2_F(Z)$ and for any g in this range:

$$\exists \psi \in L^2_F(W), \quad g(Z) = E\big[\psi(W) \mid Z\big],$$

and then $\mathrm{Cov}[\varphi(Z), g(Z)] = \mathrm{Cov}[\varphi(Z), E[\psi(W) \mid Z]] = \mathrm{Cov}[\varphi(Z), \psi(W)] = \mathrm{Cov}[E[\varphi(Z) \mid W], \psi(W)] = \mathrm{Cov}[Y, \psi(W)]$, can be estimated with standard parametric techniques. For instance, if $E[g(Z)] = 0$, the empirical counterpart of $\mathrm{Cov}[Y, \psi(W)]$, i.e.:

$$\frac{1}{n}\sum_{i=1}^{n} Y_i \psi(W_i),$$

is a root-n consistent estimator of $\mathrm{Cov}[\varphi(Z), g(Z)]$, and

$$\sqrt{n}\left[\frac{1}{n}\sum_{i=1}^{n} Y_i \psi(W_i) - \mathrm{Cov}\big[\varphi(Z), g(Z)\big]\right] \xrightarrow{d} \mathcal{N}\big(0, \mathrm{Var}\big[Y\psi(W)\big]\big),$$

where $\mathrm{Var}[Y\psi(W)]$ will also be estimated by its sample counterpart. However, in practice, this analysis has very limited interest because even if g is given, ψ is not known and must be estimated by solving the integral equation $g(Z) = E[\psi(W) \mid Z]$, where the conditional distribution of W given Z is also estimated.

Therefore, the real problem of interest is to estimate $\mathrm{Cov}[\varphi(Z), g(Z)]$, or $\langle \varphi, g \rangle$ by replacing φ by an estimator. This estimator will be constructed by solving a regularized version of the empirical counterpart of (5.25) where K and r are replaced by their estimators. In the case of kernel smoothing, the necessity of regularization appears obviously. Using the notation of Section 2.5, the equation

$$\hat{K}_n \varphi = \hat{r}_n$$

becomes

$$\frac{\sum_{i=1}^{n} \varphi(z_i)\omega\big(\frac{w-w_i}{c_n}\big)}{\sum_{i=1}^{n} \omega\big(\frac{w-w_i}{c_n}\big)} = \frac{\sum_{i=1}^{n} y_i \omega\big(\frac{w-w_i}{c_n}\big)}{\sum_{i=1}^{n} \omega\big(\frac{w-w_i}{c_n}\big)}.$$

The function φ cannot be obtained from this equation except for the values $\varphi(z_i)$ equal to y_i. This solution does not constitute a consistent estimate. The regularized Tikhonov solution is the solution of

$$\alpha_n\varphi(z) + \frac{\sum_{j=1}^n \omega\left(\frac{z-z_j}{c_n}\right)\frac{\sum_{i=1}^n \varphi(z_i)\omega(\frac{w_j-w_i}{c_n})}{\sum_{i=1}^n \omega(\frac{w_j-w_i}{c_n})}}{\sum_{j=1}^n \omega\left(\frac{z-z_j}{c_n}\right)} = \frac{\sum_{j=1}^n \omega\left(\frac{z-z_j}{c_n}\right)\frac{\sum_{i=1}^n y_i\omega(\frac{w_j-w_i}{c_n})}{\sum_{i=1}^n \omega(\frac{w_j-w_i}{c_n})}}{\sum_{j=1}^n \omega\left(\frac{z-z_j}{c_n}\right)}.$$

This functional equation may be solved in two steps. First, the z variable is fixed to the values z_i and the system becomes an $n \times n$ linear system, which can be solved in order to obtain the $\varphi(z_i)$. Second, the previous expression gives a value of $\varphi(z)$ for any value of z.

If n is very large, this inversion method may be difficult to apply and may be replaced by a Landweber–Fridman regularization (see Section 3). A first expression of $\varphi(z)$ may be for instance the estimated conditional expectation $E(E(Y \mid W) \mid Z)$ and this estimator will be modified a finite number of times by the formula

$$\hat{\varphi}_{l,n} = (I - c\hat{K}_n^*\hat{K}_n)\hat{\varphi}_{l-1,n} + c\hat{K}_n^*\hat{r}_n.$$

To simplify our analysis, we impose a relatively strong assumption:

ASSUMPTION A.3. The error term is homoskedastic, that is

$$\operatorname{Var}(U \mid W) = \sigma^2.$$

In order to check the asymptotic properties of the estimator of φ, it is necessary to study the properties of the estimators of K and of r. Under regularity conditions such as the compactness of the joint distribution support and the smoothness of the density [see Darolles, Florens and Renault (2002)], the estimation by boundary kernels gives the following results:

(i) $\|\hat{K}_n^*\hat{K}_n - K^*K\|^2 = O(\frac{1}{n(c_n)^p} + (c_n)^{2\rho})$ where ρ is the order of the kernel and p the dimension of Z.
(ii) $\|\hat{K}_n^*\hat{r}_n - \hat{K}_n^*\hat{K}_n\varphi\|^2 = O(\frac{1}{n} + (c_n)^{2\rho})$.
(iii) A suitable choice of c_n implies

$$\sqrt{n}(\hat{K}_n^*\hat{r}_n - \hat{K}_n^*\hat{K}_n\varphi) \quad \Longrightarrow \quad N\big(0, \sigma^2 K^*K\big).$$

This convergence is a weak convergence in $L_F^2(Z)$ (see Section 2.4).

Using results developed in Section 4 and in Darolles, Florens and Renault (2002) it can be deduced that:

(a) If $\alpha_n \to 0$, $\frac{c_n^{2\rho}}{\alpha_n^2} \to 0$, $\frac{1}{\alpha_n^2 n c_n^p} = O(1)$, the regularized estimator $\hat{\varphi}_n$ converges in probability to φ in L^2 norm.

(b) If $\varphi \in \Phi_\beta$ $(0 < \beta \leqslant 2)$, the optimal choices of α_n and c_n are:

$$\alpha_n = k_1 n^{-\frac{1}{2\beta}}, \qquad c_n = k_2 n^{-\frac{1}{2\rho}}$$

and, if ρ is chosen such that $\frac{p}{2\rho} \leqslant \frac{\beta}{2+\beta}$, we obtain the following bound for the rate of convergence:

$$\|\hat{\varphi}_n - \varphi\| = O\big(n^{-\frac{\beta}{2+\beta}}\big).$$

(c) Let us assume that the penalization term, α, is kept constant. In that case, the linear operators $(\alpha I + K_n^* K_n)^{-1}$ and $(\alpha I + K^* K)^{-1}$ are bounded, and using a functional version of the Slutsky theorem [see Chen and White (1992), and Section 2.4], one can immediately establish that

$$\sqrt{n}\big(\hat{\varphi}_n - \varphi - b_n^\alpha\big) \quad \Longrightarrow \quad \mathcal{N}(0, \Omega), \tag{5.26}$$

where

$$b_n^\alpha = \alpha\big[(\alpha I + \hat{K}_n^* \hat{K}_n)^{-1} - (\alpha I + K^* K)^{-1}\big]\varphi,$$

and

$$\Omega = \sigma^2(\alpha I + K^* K)^{-1} K^* K (\alpha I + K^* K)^{-1}.$$

Some comments may illustrate this first result:

(i) The convergence obtained in (5.26) is still a functional distributional convergence in the Hilbert space $L_F^2(Z)$, which in particular implies the convergence of inner product $\sqrt{n}\langle\hat{\varphi}_n - \varphi - b_n^\alpha, g\rangle$ to the univariate normal distribution $\mathcal{N}(0, \langle g, \Omega g\rangle)$.

(ii) The convergence of $\hat{\varphi}_n$ involves two bias terms. The first bias is $\varphi_\alpha - \varphi$. This term is due to the regularization and does not decrease if α is constant. The second one, $\hat{\varphi}_n - \varphi_\alpha$ follows from the estimation error of K. This bias decreases to zero when n increases, but at a lower rate than $\sqrt{n}$.

(iii) The asymptotic variance in (5.26) can be seen as the generalization of the two stage least-squares asymptotic variance. An intuitive (but not correct) interpretation of this result could be the following. If α is small, the asymptotic variance is approximately $\sigma^2(K^* K)^{-1}$, which is the functional extension of $\sigma^2(E(ZW')E(WW')^{-1}E(WZ'))^{-1}$.

(d) Let us now consider the case where $\alpha \to 0$. For any $\delta \in \Phi_\beta(\beta \geqslant 1)$, if α_n is optimal $(= k_1 n^{-\frac{1}{2\beta}})$ and if $c_n = k_2 n^{-(\frac{1}{2\rho}+\varepsilon)}$ $(\varepsilon > 0)$, we have

$$\sqrt{\nu_n(\delta)}\langle\hat{\varphi}_n - \varphi, \delta\rangle - B_n \quad \Longrightarrow \quad N\big(0, \sigma^2\big),$$

where the speed of convergence is equal to

$$\nu_n(\delta) = \frac{n}{\|K(\alpha_n I + K^* K)^{-1}\delta\|^2} \geqslant O\big(n^{\frac{2\beta}{2+\beta}}\big),$$

and the bias B_n is equal to $\sqrt{\nu_n(\delta)}\langle\varphi_\alpha - \varphi, \delta\rangle$, which in general does not vanish. If $\delta = 1$ for example, this bias is $O(n\alpha_n^2)$ and diverges.
The notion of Φ_β permits us to rigorously define the concept of weak or strong instruments. Indeed, if λ_j are not zero for any j, the function φ is identified by Equation (5.25) and $\hat{\varphi}_n$ is a consistent estimator. A bound for the speed of convergence of $\hat{\varphi}_n$ is provided under the restriction that φ belongs to a space Φ_β with $\beta > 0$. The condition $\varphi \in \Phi_\beta$ means that the rate of decline of the Fourier coefficients of φ in the basis of ϕ_j is faster than the rate of decline of the λ_j^β (which measures the dependence). In order to have asymptotic normality we need to assume that $\beta \geqslant 1$. In that case, if $\varphi \in \Phi_\beta$, we have asymptotic normality of inner products $\langle\hat{\varphi}_n - \varphi, \delta\rangle$ in the vector space Φ_β. Then, it is natural to say that W is a strong instrument for φ if φ is an element of a Φ_β with $\beta \geqslant 1$. This may have two equivalent interpretations. Given Z and W, the set of instrumental regressions for which W is a strong instrument is Φ_1 or given Z and φ, any set of instruments is strong if φ is an element of the set Φ_1 defined using these instruments.

We may complete this short presentation with two final remarks. First, the optimal choice of c_n and α_n implies that the speed of convergence and the asymptotic distribution are not affected by the fact that K is not known and is estimated. The accuracy of the estimation is governed by the estimation of the right-hand side term K^*r. Secondly, the usual "curse of dimensionality" of nonparametric estimation appears in a complex way. The dimension of Z appears in many places but the dimension of W is less explicit. The value and the rate of decline of the λ_j depend on the dimension of W: Given Z, the reduction of the number of instruments implies a faster rate of decay of λ_j to zero and a slower rate of convergence of the estimator.

6. Reproducing kernel and GMM in Hilbert spaces

6.1. *Reproducing kernel*

Models based on reproducing kernels are the foundation for penalized likelihood estimation and splines [see e.g. Berlinet and Thomas-Agnan (2004)]. However, it has been little used in econometrics so far. The theory of reproducing kernels becomes very useful when the econometrician has an infinite number of moment conditions and wants to exploit all of them in an efficient way. For illustration, let $\theta \in \mathbb{R}$ be the parameter of interest and consider an $L \times 1$-vector h that gives L moment conditions satisfying $E^{\theta_0}(h(\theta)) = 0 \Leftrightarrow \theta = \theta_0$. Let $h_n(\theta)$ be the sample estimate of $E^{\theta_0}(h(\theta))$. The (optimal) generalized method of moments (GMM) estimator of θ is the minimizer of $h_n(\theta)'\Sigma^{-1}h_n(\theta)$ where Σ is the covariance matrix of h. $h_n(\theta)'\Sigma^{-1}h_n(\theta)$ can be rewritten as $\|\Sigma^{-1/2}h_n(\theta)\|^2$ and coincides with the norm of $h_n(\theta)$ in a particular space called the reproducing kernel Hilbert space (RKHS). When h is finite dimensional, the computation of the GMM objective function does not raise any particular difficulty, however when h is infinite dimensional (for instance is a function) then the theory of RKHS becomes very handy. A second motivation for the introduction of the RKHS of a self-adjoint operator K is the following. Let T be such that $K = TT^*$. Then the RKHS of K corresponds to the 1-regularity space of T (denoted Φ_1 in Section 3.1).

6.1.1. *Definitions and basic properties of RKHS*

This section presents the theory of reproducing kernels, as described in Aronszajn (1950) and Parzen (1959, 1970). Let $L^2_{\mathbb{C}}(\pi) = \{\varphi : I \subset \mathbb{R}^L \to \mathbb{C}\colon \int_I |\varphi(s)|^2 \pi(s)\,\mathrm{d}s < \infty\}$ where π is a p.d.f. (π may have a discrete or continuous support) and denote $\|\cdot\|$ and $\langle , \rangle$ the norm and inner product on $L^2_{\mathbb{C}}(\pi)$.

DEFINITION 6.1. A space $\mathcal{H}(K)$ of complex-valued functions defined on a set $I \subset \mathbb{R}^L$ is said to be a reproducing kernel Hilbert space $\mathcal{H}(K)$ associated with the integral operator $K : L^2_{\mathbb{C}}(\pi) \to L^2_{\mathbb{C}}(\pi)$ with kernel $k(t,s)$ if the three following conditions hold:

(i) it is a Hilbert space (with inner product denoted $\langle , \rangle_K$),
(ii) for every $s \in I$, $k(t,s)$ as a function of t belongs to $\mathcal{H}(K)$,
(iii) (reproducing property) for every $s \in I$ and $\varphi \in \mathcal{H}(K)$, $\varphi(s) = \langle \varphi(.), k(\cdot, s)\rangle_K$.

The kernel k is then called the reproducing kernel.

The following properties are listed in Aronszajn (1950) and Berlinet and Thomas-Agnan (2004):

(1) If the RK k exists, it is unique.
(2) A Hilbert space $\mathcal{H}$ of functions defined on $I \subset \mathbb{R}^L$ is a RKHS if and only if all functionals $\varphi \to \varphi(s)$ for all $\varphi \in \mathcal{H}$, $s \in I$, are bounded.
(3) K is a self-adjoint positive operator on $L^2_{\mathbb{C}}(\pi)$.
(4) To a self-adjoint positive operator K on I, there corresponds a unique RKHS $\mathcal{H}(K)$ of complex-valued functions.
(5) Every sequence of functions $\{\varphi_n\}$ which converges weakly to φ in $\mathcal{H}(K)$ (that is $\langle \varphi_n, g\rangle_K \to \langle \varphi, g\rangle_K$ for all $g \in \mathcal{H}(K)$) converges also pointwise, that is $\lim \varphi_n(s) = \varphi(s)$.

Note that (2) is a consequence of Riesz Theorem 2.18. There exists a representor k such that for all $\varphi \in \mathcal{H}$

$$\varphi(t) = \langle \varphi, k_t\rangle_K.$$

Let $k_t = k(t, \cdot)$ so that $\langle k_t, k_s\rangle_K = k(t,s)$. (5) follows from the reproducing property. Indeed, $\langle \varphi_n(t) - \varphi(t), k(t,s)\rangle_K = \varphi_n(s) - \varphi(s)$.

EXAMPLE (*Finite dimensional case*). Let $I = \{1, 2, \dots, L\}$, let Σ be a positive definite $L \times L$ matrix with principal element $\sigma_{t,s}$. Σ defines an inner product on $\mathbb{R}^L$: $\langle \varphi, \psi\rangle_\Sigma = \varphi' \Sigma^{-1} \psi$. Let $(\sigma_1, \dots, \sigma_L)$ be the columns of Σ. For any vector $\varphi = (\varphi(1), \dots, \varphi(L))'$, then we have the reproducing property

$$\langle \varphi, \sigma_t \rangle_\Sigma = \varphi(t), \quad \tau = 1, \dots, L,$$

because $\varphi \Sigma^{-1} \Sigma = \varphi$. Now we diagonalize Σ, $\Sigma = PDP'$ where P is the $L \times L$ matrix with (t, j) element $\phi_j(t)$ (ϕ_j are the orthonormal eigenvectors of Σ) and D is the diagonal matrix with diagonal element λ_j (the eigenvalues of Σ). The (t, s)th element of Σ can be rewritten as

$$\sigma(t, s) = \sum_{j=1}^{L} \lambda_j \phi_j(t) \phi_j(s).$$

We have

$$\langle \varphi, \psi \rangle_\Sigma = \varphi' \Sigma^{-1} \psi = \sum_{j=1}^{L} \frac{1}{\lambda_j} \langle \varphi, \phi_j \rangle \langle \psi, \phi_j \rangle \tag{6.1}$$

where $\langle , \rangle$ is the euclidean inner product.

From this small example, we see that the norm in a RKHS can be characterized by the spectral decomposition of an operator. Expression (6.1) also holds for infinite dimensional operators. Let $K : L^2(\pi) \to L^2(\pi)$ be a positive self-adjoint compact operator with spectrum $\{\phi_j, \lambda_j \colon j = 1, 2, \dots\}$. Assume that $\mathcal{N}(K) = 0$. It turns out that $\mathcal{H}(K)$ coincides with the 1/2-regularization space of the operator K:

$$\mathcal{H}(K) = \left\{ \varphi\colon \varphi \in L^2(\pi) \text{ and } \sum_{j=1}^{\infty} \frac{|\langle \varphi, \phi_j \rangle|^2}{\lambda_j} < \infty \right\} = \Phi_{1/2}(K).$$

We can check that

(i) $\mathcal{H}(K)$ is a Hilbert space with inner product

$$\langle \varphi, \psi \rangle_K = \sum_{j=1}^{\infty} \frac{\langle \varphi, \phi_j \rangle \overline{\langle \psi, \phi_j \rangle}}{\lambda_j}$$

and norm

$$\|\varphi\|_K^2 = \sum_{j=1}^{\infty} \frac{|\langle \varphi, \phi_j \rangle|^2}{\lambda_j}.$$

(ii) $k(\cdot, t)$ belongs to $\mathcal{H}(K)$.

(iii) $\langle \varphi, k(\cdot, t) \rangle_K = \varphi(t)$.

PROOF. (ii) follows from Mercer's formula (Theorem 2.42(iii)) that is $k(t, s) = \sum_{j=1}^{\infty} \lambda_j \phi_j(t) \overline{\phi_j(s)}$. Hence $\|k(\cdot, t)\|_K^2 = \sum_{j=1}^{\infty} |\langle \phi_j, k(\cdot, t) \rangle|^2 / \lambda_j = \sum_{j=1}^{\infty} |\lambda_j \phi_j(t)|^2 /$

$\lambda_j = \sum_{j=1}^{\infty} \lambda_j \phi_j(t)\overline{\phi_j(t)} = k(t,t) < \infty$. For (iii), we use again Mercer's formula. $\langle \varphi(\cdot), k(\cdot,t)\rangle_K = \sum_{j=1}^{\infty} \langle \phi_j, k(\cdot,t)\rangle \langle \varphi, \phi_j\rangle/\lambda_j = \sum_{j=1}^{\infty} \langle \varphi, \phi_j\rangle K\phi_j(t)/\lambda_j = \sum_{j=1}^{\infty} \langle \varphi, \phi_j\rangle \phi_j(t) = \varphi(t)$. □

There is a link between calculating a norm in a RKHS and solving an integral equation $K\varphi = \psi$. We follow Nashed and Wahba (1974) to enlighten this link. We have

$$K\varphi = \sum_{j=1}^{\infty} \lambda_j \langle \varphi, \phi_j\rangle \phi_j.$$

Define $K^{1/2}$ as the square root of K:

$$K^{1/2}\varphi = \sum_{j=1}^{\infty} \sqrt{\lambda_j} \langle \varphi, \phi_j\rangle \phi_j.$$

Note that $\mathcal{N}(K) = \mathcal{N}(K^{1/2})$, $\mathcal{H}(K) = K^{1/2}(L^2_{\mathbb{C}}(\pi))$. Define $K^{-1/2} = (K^{1/2})^{\dagger}$ where $(\,)^{\dagger}$ is the Moore–Penrose generalized inverse introduced in Section 3.1:

$$K^{\dagger}\psi = \sum_{j=1}^{\infty} \frac{1}{\lambda_j} \langle \psi, \phi_j\rangle \phi_j.$$

Similarly, the generalized inverse of $K^{1/2}$ takes the form:

$$K^{-1/2}\psi = \sum_{j=1}^{\infty} \frac{1}{\sqrt{\lambda_j}} \langle \psi, \phi_j\rangle \phi_j.$$

From Nashed and Wahba (1974), we have the relations

$$\begin{aligned} &\|\varphi\|_K^2 = \inf\{\|p\|^2\colon\ p \in L^2_{\mathbb{C}}(\pi) \text{ and } \varphi = K^{1/2}p\},\\ &\langle \varphi, \psi\rangle_K = \langle K^{-1/2}\varphi, K^{-1/2}\psi\rangle, \quad \text{for all } \varphi, \psi \in \mathcal{H}(K). \end{aligned} \tag{6.2}$$

The following result follows from Proposition 3.6.

PROPOSITION 6.2. *Let $\mathcal{E}$ be a Hilbert space and $T : \mathcal{E} \to L^2_{\mathbb{C}}(\pi)$ be an operator such that $K = TT^*$ then*

$$\mathcal{H}(K) = \mathcal{R}(K^{1/2}) = \mathcal{R}(T^*) = \Phi_1(T).$$

Note that $T^* : L^2_{\mathbb{C}}(\pi) \to \mathcal{E}$ and $K^{1/2} : L^2_{\mathbb{C}}(\pi) \to L^2_{\mathbb{C}}(\pi)$ are not equal because they take their values in different spaces.

6.1.2. RKHS for covariance operators of stochastic processes

In the previous section, we have seen how to characterize $\mathcal{H}(K)$ using the spectral decomposition of K. When K is known to be the covariance kernel of a stochastic process, then $\mathcal{H}(K)$ admits a simple representation. The main results of this section come from Parzen (1959). Consider a random element (r.e.) $\{h(t),\ t \in I \subset \mathbb{R}^p\}$ defined on a probability space $(\Omega, \mathcal{F}, P)$ and observed for all values of t. Assume $h(t)$ has mean zero and $E(|h(t)|^2) = \int_\Omega |h(t)|^2 \,\mathrm{d}P < \infty$ for every $t \in I$. Let $L_2(\Omega, \mathcal{F}, P)$ be the set of all r.v. U such that $E|U|^2 = \int_\Omega |U|^2 \,\mathrm{d}P < \infty$. Define the inner product $\langle U, V\rangle_{L_2(\Omega,\mathcal{F},P)}$ between any two r.v. U and V of $L_2(\Omega, \mathcal{F}, P)$ by $\langle U, V\rangle_{L_2(\Omega,\mathcal{F},P)} = E(U\overline{V}) = \int_\Omega U\overline{V}\,\mathrm{d}P$. Let $L_2(h(t),\ t \in I)$ be the Hilbert space spanned by the r.e. $\{h(t),\ t \in I\}$. Define K the covariance operator with kernel $k(t,s) = E(h(t)\overline{h(s)})$. The following theorem implies that any symmetric nonnegative kernel can be written as a covariance kernel of a particular process.

THEOREM 6.3. *K is a covariance operator of a r.e. if and only if K is a positive self-adjoint operator.*

The following theorem can be found in Parzen (1959) for real-valued functions and in Saitoh (1997) for complex-valued functions. It provides powerful tools to compute the norm in a RKHS.

THEOREM 6.4. *Let $\{h(t),\ t \in I\}$ be a r.e. with mean zero and covariance kernel k. Then*

(i) *$L_2(h(t),\ t \in I)$ is isometrically isomorphic or congruent to the RKHS $\mathcal{H}(K)$. Denote $J : \mathcal{H}(K) \to L_2(h(t),\ t \in I)$ as this congruence.*
(ii) *For every function φ in $\mathcal{H}(K)$, $J(\varphi)$ satisfies*

$$\big\langle J(\varphi), h(t)\big\rangle_{L_2(\Omega,\mathcal{F},P)} = E\big(J(\varphi)\overline{h(t)}\big) = \big\langle \varphi, k(\cdot,t)\big\rangle_K = \varphi(t), \quad \text{for all } t \in I, \tag{6.3}$$

where $J(\varphi)$ is unique in $L_2(h(t),\ t \in I)$ and has mean zero and variance such that

$$\|\varphi\|_K^2 = \big\|J(\varphi)\big\|^2_{L_2(\Omega,\mathcal{F},P)} = E\big(\big|J(\varphi)\big|^2\big).$$

Note that, by (6.3), the congruence is such that $J(k(\cdot,t)) = h(t)$. The r.v. $U \in L_2(h(t),\ t \in I)$ corresponding to $\varphi \in \mathcal{H}(K)$ is denoted below as $\langle \varphi, h\rangle_K$ (or $J(\varphi)$). As $L_2(h(t),\ t \in I)$ and $\mathcal{H}(K)$ are isometric, we have by Definition 2.19

$$\operatorname{cov}\big[\langle \varphi, h\rangle_K, \langle \psi, h\rangle_K\big] = E\big[J(\varphi)\overline{J(\psi)}\big] = \langle \varphi, \psi\rangle_K$$

for every $\varphi, \psi \in \mathcal{H}(K)$. Note that $\langle \varphi, h\rangle_K$ is not correct notation because $h = \sum_j \langle h, \phi_j\rangle \phi_j$ a.s. does not belong to $\mathcal{H}(K)$. If it were the case, we should have

$\sum_j \langle h, \phi_j \rangle^2/\lambda_j < \infty$ a.s. Unfortunately $\langle h, \phi_j \rangle$ are independent with mean 0 and variance $\langle K\phi_j, \phi_j \rangle = \lambda_j$. Hence, $E[\sum_j \langle h, \phi_j \rangle^2/\lambda_j] = \infty$ and by Kolmogorov's theorem $\sum_j \langle h, \phi_j \rangle^2/\lambda_j = \infty$ with nonzero probability. It should be stressed that the r.v. $J(\varphi)$ itself is well defined and that only the notation $\langle \varphi, h \rangle_K$ is not adequate; as Kailath (1971) explains, it should be regarded as a mnemonic for finding $J(\varphi)$ in a closed form. The rest of this section is devoted to the calculation of $\|\varphi\|_K$. Note that the result (6.3) is valid when t is multidimensional, $t \in \mathbb{R}^L$. In the next section, $h(t)$ will be a moment function indexed by an arbitrary index parameter t.

Assume that the kernel k on $I \times I$ can be represented as

$$k(s,t) = \int h(s,x)\overline{h(t,x)}P(\mathrm{d}x) \tag{6.4}$$

where P is a probability measure and $\{h(s,\cdot),\ s \in I\}$ is a family of functions on $L_2(\Omega, \mathcal{F}, P)$. By Theorem 6.4, $\mathcal{H}(K)$ consists of functions φ on I of the form

$$\varphi(t) = \int \psi(x)\overline{h(t,x)}P(\mathrm{d}x) \tag{6.5}$$

for some unique ψ in $L_2(h(t,\cdot),\ t \in I)$, the subspace of $L_2(\Omega, \mathcal{F}, P)$ spanned by $\{h(t,\cdot),\ t \in I\}$. The RKHS norm of φ is given by

$$\|\varphi\|_K^2 = \|\psi\|^2_{L_2(\Omega,\mathcal{F},P)}.$$

When calculating $\|\varphi\|_K^2$ in practice, one looks for the solutions of (6.5). If there are several solutions, it is not always obvious to see which one is spanned by $\{h(t,\cdot),$ $t \in I\}$. In this case, the right solution is the solution with minimal norm [Parzen (1970)]:

$$\|\varphi\|_K^2 = \min_{\substack{\psi \text{ s.t.} \\ \varphi = \langle \psi, h \rangle_{L_2}}} \|\psi\|^2_{L_2(\Omega,\mathcal{F},P)}.$$

Theorem 6.4 can be reinterpreted in terms of range. Let T and T^* be

$$T : L^2(\pi) \to L_2\big(h(t,\cdot),\ t \in I\big),$$
$$\varphi \to T\varphi(x) = \int \varphi(t)h(t,x)\pi(t)\,\mathrm{d}t$$

and

$$T^* : L_2\big(h(t,\cdot),\ t \in I\big) \to L^2(\pi),$$
$$\psi \to T^*\psi(s) = \int \psi(x)\overline{h(s,x)}P(\mathrm{d}x).$$

To check that T^* is indeed the adjoint of T, it suffices to check $\langle T\varphi, \psi \rangle_{L_2(\Omega,\mathcal{F},P)} = \langle \varphi, T^*\psi \rangle_{L^2(\pi)}$ for $\varphi \in L^2(\pi)$ and $\psi(x) = h(t,x)$ as $h(t,\cdot)$ spans $L_2(h(t,\cdot),\ t \in I)$. Using the fact that $K = T^*T$ and Proposition 6.2, we have $\mathcal{H}(K) = \mathcal{R}(T^*)$, which gives Equation (6.5).

EXAMPLE. The Wiener process on $[0, 1]$ has covariance $k(t, s) = t \wedge s$. k can be rewritten as

$$k(t,s) = \int_0^1 (t-x)_+^0 (s-x)_+^0 \, dx$$

with

$$(s-x)_+^0 = \begin{cases} 1 & \text{if } x < s, \\ 0 & \text{if } x \geqslant s. \end{cases}$$

It follows that $\mathcal{H}(K)$ consists of functions φ of the form:

$$\varphi(t) = \int_0^1 \psi(x)(t-x)_+^0 \, dx = \int_0^t \psi(x) \, dx, \quad 0 \leqslant t \leqslant 1$$
$$\Rightarrow \quad \psi(t) = \varphi'(t).$$

Hence, we have

$$\|\varphi\|_K^2 = \int_0^1 |\psi(x)|^2 \, dx = \int_0^1 |\varphi'(x)|^2 \, dx.$$

EXAMPLE. Let k be defined as in (6.4) with $h(t, x) = e^{itx}$. Assume P admits a p.d.f. $f_{\theta_0}(x)$, which is positive everywhere. Equation (6.5) is equivalent to

$$\varphi(t) = \int \psi(x) e^{-itx} P(dx) = \int \psi(x) e^{-itx} f_{\theta_0}(x) \, dx.$$

By the Fourier inversion formula, we have

$$\psi(x) = \frac{1}{2\pi} \frac{1}{f_{\theta_0}(x)} \int e^{itx} \varphi(t) \, dt,$$
$$\|\varphi\|_K^2 = \frac{1}{4\pi} \int \left| \int e^{itx} \varphi(t) \, dt \right|^2 \frac{1}{f_{\theta_0}(x)} \, dx.$$

6.2. *GMM in Hilbert spaces*

First introduced by Hansen (1982), the generalized method of moments (GMM) became the cornerstone of modern structural econometrics. In Hansen (1982), the number of moment conditions is supposed to be finite. The method proposed in this section permits dealing with moment functions that take their values in finite or infinite dimensional Hilbert spaces. It was initially proposed by Carrasco and Florens (2000) and further developed in Carrasco and Florens (2001) and Carrasco et al. (2007).

6.2.1. Definition and examples

Let $\{x_i: i = 1, 2, \ldots, n\}$ be an i.i.d. sample of a random vector $X \in \mathbb{R}^p$. The case where X is a time-series will be discussed later. The distribution of X is indexed by a parameter $\theta \in \Theta \subset \mathbb{R}^d$. Denote E^θ as the expectation with respect to this distribution. The unknown parameter θ is identified from the function $h(X; \theta)$ (called moment function) defined on $\mathbb{R}^p \times \Theta$, so that the following is true.

Identification assumption

$$E^{\theta_0}\big(h(X;\theta)\big) = 0 \quad \Leftrightarrow \quad \theta = \theta_0. \tag{6.6}$$

It is assumed that $h(X; \theta)$ takes its values in a Hilbert space $\mathcal{H}$ with inner product $\langle\cdot,\cdot\rangle$ and norm $\|\cdot\|$. When $f = (f_1, \ldots, f_L)$ and $g = (g_1, \ldots, g_L)$ are vectors of functions of $\mathcal{H}$, we use the convention that $\langle f, g'\rangle$ denotes the $L \times L$ matrix with (l, m) element $\langle f_l, g_m\rangle$. Let $B_n : \mathcal{H} \to \mathcal{H}$ be a sequence of random bounded linear operators and

$$\hat{h}_n(\theta) = \frac{1}{n}\sum_{i=1}^{n} h(x_i; \theta).$$

We define the GMM estimator associated with B_n as

$$\hat{\theta}_n(B_n) = \arg\min_{\theta\in\Theta}\big\| B_n\hat{h}_n(\theta)\big\|. \tag{6.7}$$

Such an estimator will in general be suboptimal; we will discuss the optimal choice of B_n later. Below, we give four examples that can be handled by the method discussed in this section. They illustrate the versatility of the method as it can deal with a finite number of moments (Example 1), a continuum (Examples 2 and 3) and a countably infinite sequence (Example 4).

EXAMPLE 1 *(Traditional GMM).* Let $h(x; \theta)$ be a vector of $\mathbb{R}^L$, B_n be a $L \times L$ matrix and $\|\cdot\|$ denote the Euclidean norm. The objective function to minimize is

$$\big\| B_n\hat{h}_n(\theta)\big\|^2 = \hat{h}_n(\theta)' B_n' B_n \hat{h}_n(\theta)$$

and corresponds to the usual GMM quadratic form $\hat{h}_n(\theta)' W_n \hat{h}_n(\theta)$ with weighting matrix $W_n = B_n' B_n$.

EXAMPLE 2 *(Continuous time process).* Suppose we observe independent replications of a continuous time process

$$X^i(t) = G(\theta, t) + u^i(t), \quad 0 \leqslant t \leqslant T,\ i = 1, 2, \ldots, n, \tag{6.8}$$

where G is a known function and $u^i = \{u^i(t): 0 \leqslant t \leqslant T\}$ is a zero mean Gaussian process with continuous covariance function $k(t, s) = E[u^i(t)u^i(s)]$, $t, s \in [0, T]$.

Denote $X^i = \{X^i(t)\colon 0 \leqslant t \leqslant T\}$, $G(\theta) = \{G(\theta, t)\colon 0 \leqslant t \leqslant T\}$, and $\mathcal{H} = L^2([0, T])$. The unknown parameter θ is identified from the moment of the function

$$h\big(X^i; \theta\big) = X^i - G(\theta).$$

Assume $h(X^i; \theta) \in L^2([0, T])$ with probability one. Candidates for B_n are arbitrary bounded operators on $L^2([0, T])$ including the identity. For $B_n f = f$, we have

$$\big\| B_n \hat{h}_n(\theta) \big\|^2 = \int_0^T \hat{h}_n(\theta)^2 \, \mathrm{d}t.$$

The estimation of model (6.8) is discussed in Kutoyants (1984).

EXAMPLE 3 *(Characteristic function).* Denote $\psi_\theta(t) = E^\theta[e^{it'X}]$ the characteristic function of X. Inference can be based on

$$h(t, X; \theta) = e^{it'X} - \psi_\theta(t), \quad t \in \mathbb{R}^L.$$

Note that contrary to the former examples, $h(t, X; \theta)$ is complex valued and $|h(t, X; \theta)| \leqslant |e^{it'X}| + |\psi_\theta(t)| \leqslant 2$. Let Π be a probability measure on $\mathbb{R}^L$ and $\mathcal{H} = L^2_{\mathbb{C}}(\mathbb{R}^L, \Pi)$. As $h(\cdot, X; \theta)$ is bounded, it belongs to $L^2_{\mathbb{C}}(\mathbb{R}^L, \Pi)$ for any Π. Feuerverger and McDunnough (1981) and more recently Singleton (2001) show that an efficient estimator of θ is obtained from $h(\cdot, X; \theta)$ by solving an empirical counterpart of $\int Eh(t, X; \theta)\omega(t)\, \mathrm{d}t = 0$ for an adequate weighting function ω, which turns out to be a function of the p.d.f. of X. This efficient estimator is not implementable as the p.d.f. of X is unknown. They suggest estimating θ by GMM using moments obtained from a discrete grid $t = t_1, t_2, \ldots, t_M$. An alternative strategy put forward in this section is to use the full continuum of moment conditions by considering the moment function h as an element of $\mathcal{H} = L^2_{\mathbb{C}}(\mathbb{R}^L, \Pi)$.

EXAMPLE 4 *(Conditional moment restrictions).* Let $X = (Y, Z)$. For a known function $\rho \in \mathbb{R}$, we have the conditional moment restrictions

$$E^{\theta_0}\big[\rho(Y, Z, \theta) \mid Z\big] = 0.$$

Hence for any function $g(Z)$, we can construct unconditional moment restrictions

$$E^{\theta_0}\big[\rho(Y, Z, \theta) g(Z)\big] = 0.$$

Assume Z has bounded support. Chamberlain (1987) shows that the semiparametric efficiency bound can be approached by a GMM estimator based on a sequence of moment conditions using as instruments the power function of Z: $1, Z, Z^2, \ldots, Z^L$ for a large L. Let π be the Poisson probability measure $\pi(l) = e^{-1}/l!$ and $\mathcal{H} = L^2(\mathbb{N}, \pi) = \{f : \mathbb{N} \to \mathbb{R}\colon \sum_{l=1}^{\infty} g(l)\pi(l) < \infty\}$. Let

$$h(l, X; \theta) = \rho(Y, Z, \theta) Z^l, \quad l = 1, 2, \ldots.$$

If $h(l, X; \theta)$ is bounded with probability one, then $h(\cdot, X; \theta) \in L^2(\mathbb{N}, \pi)$ with probability one. Instead of using an increasing sequence of moments as suggested by Chamberlain, it is possible to handle $h(\cdot, X; \theta)$ as a function. The efficiency of the GMM estimator based on the countably infinite number of moments $\{h(l, X; \theta): l \in \mathbb{N}\}$ will be discussed later.

6.2.2. Asymptotic properties of GMM

Let $\mathcal{H} = L^2_{\mathbb{C}}(I, \Pi) = \{f : I \to \mathbb{C}: \int_I |f(t)|^2 \Pi(\mathrm{d}t) < \infty\}$ where I is a subset of $\mathbb{R}^L$ for some $L \geqslant 1$ and Π is a (possibly discrete) probability measure. This choice of $\mathcal{H}$ is consistent with Examples 1–4. Under some weak assumptions, $\sqrt{n}\hat{h}_n(\theta_0)$ converges to a Gaussian process $\mathcal{N}(0, K)$ in $\mathcal{H}$ where K denotes the covariance operator of $h(X; \theta_0)$. K is defined by

$$
\begin{aligned}
&K : \mathcal{H} \to \mathcal{H}, \\
&\quad f \to Kf(s) = \langle f, k(\cdot, t)\rangle = \int_I k(t, s) f(s) \Pi(\mathrm{d}s)
\end{aligned}
$$

where the kernel k of K satisfies $k(t, s) = E^{\theta_0}[h(t, X; \theta_0)\overline{h(s, X; \theta_0)}]$ and $k(t, s) = \overline{k(s, t)}$. Assume moreover that K is a Hilbert–Schmidt operator and hence admits a discrete spectrum. Suppose that B_n converges to a bounded linear operator B defined on $\mathcal{H}$ and that θ_0 is the unique minimizer of $\|BE^{\theta_0}h(X; \theta)\|$. Then $\hat{\theta}_n(B_n)$ is consistent and asymptotically normal. The following result is proved in Carrasco and Florens (2000).

PROPOSITION 6.5. *Under Assumptions* 1 *to* 11 *of* Carrasco and Florens (2000), $\hat{\theta}_n(B_n)$ *is consistent and*

$$
\sqrt{n}\big(\hat{\theta}_n(B_n) - \theta_0\big) \xrightarrow{L} \mathcal{N}(0, V)
$$

with

$$
\begin{aligned}
V = {} & \big\langle BE^{\theta_0}(\nabla_\theta h), BE^{\theta_0}(\nabla_\theta h)'\big\rangle^{-1} \\
& \times \big\langle BE^{\theta_0}(\nabla_\theta h), (BKB^*)BE^{\theta_0}(\nabla_\theta h)'\big\rangle \\
& \times \big\langle BE^{\theta_0}(\nabla_\theta h), BE^{\theta_0}(\nabla_\theta h)'\big\rangle^{-1}
\end{aligned}
$$

where B^* is the adjoint of B.

6.2.3. Optimal choice of the weighting operator

Carrasco and Florens (2000) show that the asymptotic variance V given in Proposition 6.5 is minimal for $B = K^{-1/2}$. In that case, the asymptotic variance becomes $\langle K^{-1/2}E^{\theta_0}(\nabla_\theta h), K^{-1/2}E^{\theta_0}(\nabla_\theta h)\rangle^{-1}$.

EXAMPLE 1 *(Continued).* K is the $L \times L$-covariance matrix of $h(X;\theta)$. Let K_n be the matrix $\frac{1}{n}\sum_{i=1}^{n} h(x_i;\hat{\theta}^1)h(x_i;\hat{\theta}^1)'$ where $\hat{\theta}^1$ is a consistent first step estimator of θ. K_n is a consistent estimator of K. Then the objective function becomes

$$\langle K_n^{-1/2}\hat{h}_n(\theta), K_n^{-1/2}\hat{h}_n(\theta)\rangle = \hat{h}_n(\theta)' K_n^{-1}\hat{h}_n(\theta)$$

which delivers the optimal GMM estimator.

When $\mathcal{H}$ is infinite dimensional, we have seen in Section 3.1 that the inverse of K, K^{-1}, is not bounded. Similarly $K^{-1/2} = (K^{1/2})^{-1}$ is not bounded on $\mathcal{H}$ and its domain has been shown in Section 6.1.1 to be the subset of $\mathcal{H}$ which coincides with the RKHS associated with K and denoted $\mathcal{H}(K)$.

To estimate the covariance operator K, we need a first step estimator $\hat{\theta}^1$ that is $\sqrt{n}$-consistent. It may be obtained by letting B_n equal the identity in (6.7) or by using a finite number of moments. Let K_n be the operator with kernel

$$k_n(t,s) = \frac{1}{n}\sum_{i=1}^{n} h(t,x_i;\hat{\theta}^1)\overline{h(s,x_i;\hat{\theta}^1)}.$$

Then K_n is a consistent estimator of K and $\|K_n - K\| = O(1/\sqrt{n})$. As $K^{-1}f$ is not continuous in f, we estimate K^{-1} by the Tykhonov regularized inverse of K_n:

$$(K_n^{\alpha_n})^{-1} = (\alpha_n I + K_n^2)^{-1} K_n$$

for some penalization term $\alpha_n \geqslant 0$. If $\alpha_n > 0$, $(K_n^{\alpha_n})^{-1} f$ is continuous in f but is a biased estimator of $K^{-1}f$. There is a trade-off between the stability of the solution and its bias. Hence, we will let α_n decrease to zero at an appropriate rate. We define $(K_n^{\alpha_n})^{-1/2} = ((K_n^{\alpha_n})^{-1})^{1/2}$.

The optimal GMM estimator is given by

$$\hat{\theta}_n = \arg\min_{\theta\in\Theta} \| (K_n^{\alpha_n})^{-1/2}\hat{h}_n(\theta)\|.$$

Interestingly, the optimal GMM estimator minimizes the norm of $\hat{h}_n(\theta)$ in the RKHS associated with $K_n^{\alpha_n}$. Under certain regularity conditions, we have

$$\| (K_n^{\alpha_n})^{-1/2}\hat{h}_n(\theta)\| \xrightarrow{P} \| E^{\theta_0}(h(\theta))\|_K.$$

A condition for applying this method is that $E^{\theta_0}(h(\theta)) \in \mathcal{H}(K)$. This condition can be verified using results from Section 6.1.

PROPOSITION 6.6. *Under the regularity conditions of Carrasco and Florens (2000, Theorem 8), $\hat{\theta}_n$ is consistent and*

$$\sqrt{n}(\hat{\theta}_n - \theta_0) \xrightarrow{L} \mathcal{N}\left(0, \langle E^{\theta_0}(\nabla_\theta h(\theta_0)), E^{\theta_0}(\nabla_\theta h(\theta_0))'\rangle_K^{-1}\right)$$

as n and $n\alpha_n^3 \to \infty$ and $\alpha_n \to 0$.

The stronger condition $n\alpha_n^3 \to \infty$ of Carrasco and Florens (2000) has been relaxed into $n\alpha_n^2 \to \infty$ in Carrasco et al. (2007). Proposition 6.6 does not indicate how to select α_n in practice. A data-driven method is desirable. Carrasco and Florens (2001) propose to select the α_n that minimizes the mean square error (MSE) of the GMM estimator $\hat{\theta}_n$. As $\hat{\theta}_n$ is consistent for any value of α_n, it is necessary to compute the higher order expansion of the MSE, which is particularly tedious. Instead of relying on an analytic expression, it may be easier to compute the MSE via bootstrap or simulations.

6.2.4. Implementation of GMM

There are two equivalent ways to compute the objective function

$$\left\| \left(K_n^{\alpha_n}\right)^{-1/2} \hat{h}_n(\theta) \right\|^2, \tag{6.9}$$

(1) using the spectral decomposition of K_n, or
(2) using a simplified formula that involves only vectors and matrices.

The first method, discussed in Carrasco and Florens (2000), requires calculating the eigenvalues and eigenfunctions of K_n using the method described in Section 2.5.3. Let $\hat{\phi}_j$ denote the orthonormalized eigenfunctions of K_n and $\hat{\lambda}_j$ the corresponding eigenvalues. The objective function in Equation (6.9) becomes

$$\sum_{j=1}^{n} \frac{\hat{\lambda}_j}{\hat{\lambda}_j^2 + \alpha_n} \left| \langle \hat{h}_n(\theta), \hat{\phi}_j \rangle \right|^2. \tag{6.10}$$

The expression (6.10) suggests a nice interpretation of the GMM estimator. Indeed, note that $\langle \sqrt{n}\hat{h}_n(\theta_0), \phi_j \rangle$, $j = 1, 2, \ldots$, are asymptotically normal with mean 0 and variance λ_j and are independent across j. Therefore (6.10) is the regularized version of the objective function of the optimal GMM estimator based on the n moment conditions $E[\langle h(\theta), \phi_j \rangle] = 0$, $j = 1, 2, \ldots, n$.

The second method is more attractive by its simplicity. Carrasco et al. (2007) show that (6.9) can be rewritten as

$$\overline{\underline{v}(\theta)}' \left[\alpha_n I_n + C^2\right]^{-1} \underline{v}(\theta)$$

where C is a $n \times n$-matrix with (i, j) element c_{ij}, I_n is the $n \times n$ identity matrix and $\underline{v}(\theta) = (v_1(\theta), \ldots, v_n(\theta))'$ with

$$v_i(\theta) = \int \overline{h(t, x_i; \hat{\theta}^1)}' \hat{h}_n(t; \theta) \Pi(\mathrm{d}t),$$

$$c_{ij} = \frac{1}{n} \int \overline{h(t, x_i; \hat{\theta}^1)}' h(t, x_j; \hat{\theta}^1) \Pi(\mathrm{d}t).$$

Note that the dimension of C is the same whether $h \in \mathbb{R}$ or $h \in \mathbb{R}^L$.

6.2.5. Asymptotic efficiency of GMM

Assume that the p.d.f. of X, f_θ, is differentiable with respect to θ. Let $L^2(h)$ be the closure of the subspace of $L^2(\Omega, \mathcal{F}, P)$ spanned by $\{h(t, X_i; \theta_0): t \in I\}$.

PROPOSITION 6.7. *Under standard regularity conditions, the GMM estimator based on $\{h(t, x_i; \theta): t \in I\}$ is asymptotically as efficient as the MLE if and only if*

$$\nabla_\theta \ln f_\theta(x_i; \theta_0) \in L^2(h).$$

This result is proved in Carrasco and Florens (2004) in a more general setting where X_i is Markov of order L. A similar efficiency result can be found in Hansen (1985), Tauchen (1997) and Gallant and Long (1997).

EXAMPLE 2 *(Continued)*. Let K be the covariance operator of $\{u(t)\}$ and $\mathcal{H}(K)$ the RKHS associated with K. Kutoyants (1984) shows that if $G(\theta) \in \mathcal{H}(K)$, the likelihood ratio of the measure induced by $X(t)$ with respect to the measure induced by $u(t)$ equals

$$LR(\theta) = \prod_{i=1}^{n} \exp\left\{\langle G(\theta), x^i\rangle_K - \frac{1}{2}\|G(\theta)\|_K^2\right\}$$

where $\langle G, X\rangle_K$ has been defined in Section 6.1.2 and denotes the element of $L^2(X(t): 0 \leqslant t \leqslant T)$ under the mapping J^{-1} of the function $G(\theta)$ (J is defined in Theorem 6.4). The score function with respect to θ is

$$\nabla_\theta \ln\bigl(LR(\theta)\bigr) = \left\langle \nabla_\theta G(\theta), \frac{1}{n}\sum_{i=1}^{n}\bigl(x^i - G(\theta)\bigr)\right\rangle_K.$$

For $\theta = \theta_0$ and a single observation, the score is equal to

$$\langle \nabla_\theta G(\theta_0), u\rangle_K,$$

which is an element of $L^2(u(t): 0 \leqslant t \leqslant T) = L^2(h(X(t); \theta_0): 0 \leqslant t \leqslant T)$. Hence, by Proposition 6.7, the GMM estimator based on $h(X; \theta_0)$ is asymptotically efficient. This efficiency result is corroborated by the following. The GMM objective function is

$$\|h(x; \theta)\|_K^2 = \left\langle \frac{1}{n}\sum_{i=1}^{n}\bigl(x^i - G(\theta)\bigr), \frac{1}{n}\sum_{i=1}^{n}\bigl(x^i - G(\theta)\bigr)\right\rangle_K.$$

The first-order derivative equals to

$$\nabla_\theta \|h(x; \theta)\|_K^2 = 2\left\langle \nabla_\theta G(\theta), \frac{1}{n}\sum_{i=1}^{n}\bigl(x^i - G(\theta)\bigr)\right\rangle_K = 2\nabla_\theta \ln\bigl(LR(\theta)\bigr).$$

Therefore, the GMM estimator coincides with the MLE in this particular case as they are solutions of the same equation.

EXAMPLE 3 *(Continued)*. Under minor conditions on the distribution of X_i, the closure of the linear span of $\{h(t, X_i; \theta_0)\colon t \in \mathbb{R}^L\}$ contains all functions of $L^2(X) = \{g\colon E^{\theta_0}[g(X)^2] < \infty\}$ and hence the score $\nabla_\theta \ln f_\theta(X_i; \theta_0)$ itself. Therefore the GMM estimator is efficient. Another way to prove efficiency is to explicitly calculate the asymptotic covariance of $\hat{\theta}_n$. To simplify, assume that θ is scalar. By Theorem 6.4, we have

$$\left\| E^{\theta_0}\left(\nabla_\theta h(\theta_0)\right)\right\|_K^2 = \left\| \overline{E^{\theta_0}\left(\nabla_\theta h(\theta_0)\right)}\right\|_K^2 = E|U|^2$$

where U satisfies

$$E^{\theta_0}\left[U\overline{h(t;\theta_0)}\right] = \overline{E^{\theta_0}\left(\nabla_\theta h(t;\theta_0)\right)} \quad \text{for all } t \in \mathbb{R}^L$$

which is equivalent to

$$E^{\theta_0}\left[\overline{U(X)}\left(e^{it'X} - \psi_{\theta_0}(t)\right)\right] = -\nabla_\theta \psi_{\theta_0}(t) \quad \text{for all } t \in \mathbb{R}^L. \tag{6.11}$$

As U has mean zero, $\overline{U}$ has also mean zero and we can replace (6.11) by

$$\begin{aligned} & E^{\theta_0}\left[\overline{U(X)}e^{it'X}\right] = -\nabla_\theta \psi_{\theta_0}(t) \quad \text{for all } t \in \mathbb{R}^L \\ \Leftrightarrow \quad & \int \overline{U(x)} e^{it'x} f_{\theta_0}(x)\,\mathrm{d}x = -\nabla_\theta \psi_{\theta_0}(t) \quad \text{for all } t \in \mathbb{R}^L \\ \Leftrightarrow \quad & \overline{U(x)} f_{\theta_0}(x) = -\frac{1}{2\pi}\int e^{-it'x} \nabla_\theta \psi_{\theta_0}(t)\,\mathrm{d}t. \end{aligned} \tag{6.12}$$

The last equivalence follows from the Fourier inversion formula. Assuming that we can exchange the integration and derivation in the right-hand side of (6.12), we obtain

$$\overline{U(x)} f_{\theta_0}(x) = -\nabla_\theta f_{\theta_0}(x) \quad \Leftrightarrow \quad U(x) = -\nabla_\theta \ln f_{\theta_0}(x).$$

Hence $E^{\theta_0}|U|^2 = E^{\theta_0}[(\nabla_\theta \ln f_{\theta_0}(X))^2]$. The asymptotic variance of $\hat{\theta}_n$ coincides with the Cramer–Rao efficiency bound even if, contrary to Example 3, $\hat{\theta}_n$ differs from the MLE.

EXAMPLE 4 *(Continued)*. As in the previous example, we intend to calculate the asymptotic covariance of $\hat{\theta}_n$ using Theorem 6.4. We need to find U, the p-vector of r.v. such that

$$\begin{aligned} & E^{\theta_0}\left[U\rho(Y, Z; \theta_0)Z^l\right] = E^{\theta_0}\left[\nabla_\theta \rho(Y, Z; \theta_0)Z^l\right] \quad \text{for all } l \in \mathbb{N}, \\ \Leftrightarrow \quad & E^{\theta_0}\left[E^{\theta_0}\left[U\rho(Y, Z; \theta_0) \mid Z\right]Z^l\right] \\ & = E^{\theta_0}\left[E^{\theta_0}\left[\nabla_\theta \rho(Y, Z; \theta_0) \mid Z\right]Z^l\right] \quad \text{for all } l \in \mathbb{N}. \end{aligned} \tag{6.13}$$

Equation (6.13) is equivalent to

$$E^{\theta_0}\left[U\rho(Y, Z; \theta_0) \mid Z\right] = E^{\theta_0}\left[\nabla_\theta \rho(Y, Z; \theta_0) \mid Z\right] \tag{6.14}$$

by the completeness of polynomials under some mild conditions on the distribution of Z. A solution is

$$U_0 = E^{\theta_0}\big[\nabla_\theta \rho(Y, Z; \theta_0) \mid Z\big] E^{\theta_0}\big[\rho(Y, Z; \theta_0)^2 \mid Z\big]^{-1} \rho(Y, Z; \theta_0).$$

We have to check that this solution has minimal norm among all the solutions. Consider an arbitrary solution $U = U_0 + U_1$. U is a solution of (6.14) implies

$$E^{\theta_0}\big[U_1 \rho(Y, Z; \theta_0) \mid Z\big] = 0.$$

Hence $E^{\theta_0}(UU') = E^{\theta_0}(U_0U_0') + E^{\theta_0}(U_1U_1')$ and is minimal for $U_1 = 0$. Then

$$\begin{aligned}\big\| E^{\theta_0}\big(\nabla_\theta h(\theta_0)\big)\big\|_K^2 &= E^{\theta_0}(U_0U_0') \\ &= E^{\theta_0}\big\{E^{\theta_0}\big[\nabla_\theta \rho(Y, Z; \theta_0) \mid Z\big] E^{\theta_0}\big[\rho(Y, Z; \theta_0)^2 \mid Z\big]^{-1} \\ &\quad \times E^{\theta_0}\big[\nabla_\theta \rho(Y, Z; \theta_0) \mid Z\big]'\big\}.\end{aligned}$$

Its inverse coincides with the semi-parametric efficiency bound derived by Chamberlain (1987).

Note that in Examples 2 and 3, the GMM estimator reaches the Cramer–Rao bound asymptotically, while in Example 4 it reaches the semi-parametric efficiency bound.

6.2.6. *Testing overidentifying restrictions*

Hansen (1982) proposes a test of specification, which basically tests whether the overidentifying restrictions are close to zero. Carrasco and Florens (2000) propose the analogue to Hansen's J test in the case where there is a continuum of moment conditions. Let

$$\hat{p}_n = \sum_{j=1}^{n} \frac{\hat{\lambda}_j^2}{\hat{\lambda}_j^2 + \alpha_n}, \qquad \hat{q}_n = 2\sum_{j=1}^{n} \frac{\hat{\lambda}_j^4}{(\hat{\lambda}_j^2 + \alpha_n)^2}$$

where $\hat{\lambda}_j$ are the eigenvalues of K_n as described earlier.

PROPOSITION 6.8. *Under the assumptions of Theorem* 10 *of Carrasco and Florens (2000), we have*

$$\tau_n = \frac{\|(K_n^{\alpha_n})^{-1/2}\hat{h}_n(\hat{\theta}_n)\|^2 - \hat{p}_n}{\hat{q}_n} \xrightarrow{d} \mathcal{N}(0, 1)$$

as α_n goes to zero and $n\alpha_n^3$ goes to infinity.

This test can also be used for testing underidentification. Let $\theta_0 \in \mathbb{R}$ be such that $E[h(X, \theta_0)] = 0$. Arellano, Hansen and Sentana (2005) show that the parameter, θ_0, is locally unidentified if $E[h(X, \theta)] = 0$ for all $\theta \in \mathbb{R}$. It results in a continuum of moment conditions indexed by θ. Arellano, Hansen and Sentana (2005) apply τ_n to test for the null of underidentification.

6.2.7. Extension to time series

So far, the data was assumed to be i.i.d. Now we relax this assumption. Let $\{x_1, \ldots, x_T\}$ be the observations of a time series $\{X_t\}$ that satisfies some mixing conditions. Inference will be based on moment functions $\{h(\tau, X_t; \theta_0)\}$ indexed by a real, possibly multidimensional index τ. $\{h(\tau, X_t; \theta_0)\}$ are in general autocorrelated, except in some special cases, an example of which will be discussed below.

EXAMPLE 5 *(Conditional characteristic function).* Let Y_t be a (scalar) Markov process and assume that the conditional characteristic function (CF) of Y_{t+1} given Y_t, $\psi_\theta(\tau \mid Y_t) \equiv E^\theta[\exp(i\tau Y_{t+1}) \mid Y_t]$, is known. The following conditional moment condition holds:

$$E^\theta\left[e^{i\tau Y_{t+1}} - \psi_\theta(\tau \mid Y_t) \mid Y_t\right] = 0.$$

Denote $X_t = (Y_t, Y_{t+1})'$. Let $g(Y_t)$ be an instrument so that

$$h(\tau, X_t; \theta) = \left(e^{i\tau Y_{t+1}} - \psi_\theta(\tau \mid Y_t)\right)g(Y_t)$$

satisfies the identification condition (6.6). $\{h(\tau, X_t; \theta)\}$ is a martingale difference sequence and is therefore uncorrelated. The use of the conditional CF is very popular in finance. Assume that $\{Y_t,\ t = 1, 2, \ldots, T\}$ is a discretely sampled diffusion process, then Y_t is Markov. While the conditional likelihood of Y_{t+1} given Y_t does not have a closed form expression, the conditional CF of affine diffusions is known. Hence GMM can replace MLE to estimate these models where MLE is difficult to implement. For an adequate choice of the instrument $g(Y_t)$, the GMM estimator is asymptotically as efficient as the MLE. The conditional CF has been recently applied to the estimation of diffusions by Singleton (2001), Chacko and Viceira (2003), and Carrasco et al. (2007). The first two papers use GMM based on a finite grid of values for τ, whereas the last paper advocates using the full continuum of moments which permits us to achieve efficiency asymptotically.

EXAMPLE 6 *(Joint characteristic function).* Assume Y_t is not Markov. In that case, the conditional CF is usually unknown. On the other hand, the joint characteristic function may be calculated explicitly [for instance when Y_t is an ARMA process with stable error, see Knight and Yu (2002); or Y_t is the growth rate of a stochastic volatility model, see Jiang and Knight (2002)] or may be estimated via simulations [this technique is developed in Carrasco et al. (2007)]. Denote $\psi_\theta(\tau) \equiv E^\theta[\exp(\tau_1 Y_t + \tau_2 Y_{t+1} + \cdots + \tau_{L+1} Y_{t+L})]$ with $\tau = (\tau_1, \ldots, \tau_L)'$, the joint CF of $X_t \equiv (Y_t, Y_{t+1}, \ldots, Y_{t+L})'$ for some integer $L \geqslant 1$. Assume that L is large enough for

$$h(\tau, X_t; \theta) = e^{i\tau' X_t} - \psi_\theta(\tau)$$

to identify the parameter θ. Here $\{h(\tau, X_t; \theta)\}$ are autocorrelated. Knight and Yu (2002) estimate various models by minimizing the following norm of $h(\tau, X_t; \theta)$:

$$\int \left(\frac{1}{T} \sum_{t=1}^{T} e^{i\tau' x_t} - \psi_\theta(\tau) \right)^2 e^{-\tau'\tau} \, \mathrm{d}\tau.$$

This is equivalent to minimizing $\| B \frac{1}{T} \sum_{t=1}^{T} h(\tau, X_t; \theta) \|^2$ with $B = e^{-\tau'\tau/2}$. This choice of B is suboptimal but has the advantage of being easy to implement. The optimal weighting operator is, as before, the square root of the inverse of the covariance operator. Its estimation will be discussed shortly.

Under some mixing conditions on $\{h(\tau, X_t; \theta_0)\}$, the process $\hat{h}_T(\theta_0) = \frac{1}{T} \sum_{t=1}^{T} h(\tau, X_t; \theta_0)$ follows a functional CLT (see Section 2.4.2):

$$\sqrt{T} \hat{h}_T(\theta_0) \xrightarrow{L} \mathcal{N}(0, K)$$

where the covariance operator K is an integral operator with kernel

$$k(\tau_1, \tau_2) = \sum_{j=-\infty}^{+\infty} E^{\theta_0} \left[h(\tau_1, X_t; \theta_0) \overline{h(\tau_2, X_{t-j}; \theta_0)} \right].$$

The kernel k can be estimated using a kernel-based estimator as those described in Andrews (1991) and references therein. Let $\omega : \mathbb{R} \to [-1, 1]$ be a kernel satisfying the conditions stated by Andrews. Let q be the largest value in $[0, +\infty)$ for which

$$\omega_q = \lim_{u \to \infty} \frac{1 - \omega(u)}{|u|^q}$$

is finite. In the sequel, we will say that ω is a q-kernel. Typically, $q = 1$ for the Bartlett kernel and $q = 2$ for Parzen, Tuckey-Hanning and quadratic spectral kernels. We define

$$\hat{k}_T(\tau_1, \tau_2) = \frac{T}{T - d} \sum_{j=-T+1}^{T-1} \omega\left(\frac{j}{S_T} \right) \hat{\Gamma}_T(j) \tag{6.15}$$

with

$$\hat{\Gamma}_T(j) = \begin{cases} \frac{1}{T} \sum_{t=j+1}^{T} h(\tau_1, X_t; \hat{\theta}_T^1) \overline{h(\tau_2, X_{t-j}; \hat{\theta}_T^1)}, & j \geqslant 0, \\ \frac{1}{T} \sum_{t=-j+1}^{T} h(\tau_1, X_{t+j}; \hat{\theta}_T^1) \overline{h(\tau_2, X_t; \hat{\theta}_T^1)}, & j < 0, \end{cases} \tag{6.16}$$

where S_T is some bandwidth that diverges with T and $\hat{\theta}_T^1$ is a $T^{1/2}$-consistent estimator of θ. Let K_T be the integral estimator with kernel $\hat{k}_T$. Under some conditions on ω and $\{h(\tau, X_t; \theta_0)\}$, and assuming $S_T^{2q+1}/T \to \gamma \in (0, +\infty)$, Carrasco et al. (2007) establish the rate of convergence of K_T to K:

$$\|K_T - K\| = O_p\left(T^{-q/(2q+1)}\right).$$

The inverse of K is estimated using the regularized inverse of K_T, $(K_T^{\alpha_T})^{-1} = (K_T^2 + \alpha_T I)^{-1} K_T$ for a penalization term $\alpha_T \geqslant 0$. As before, the optimal GMM estimator is given by

$$\hat{\theta}_T = \arg\min_{\theta \in \Theta} \left\| \left(K_T^{\alpha_T}\right)^{-1/2} \hat{h}_T(\theta) \right\|.$$

Carrasco et al. (2007) show the following result.

PROPOSITION 6.9. *Assume that ω is a q-kernel and that $S_T^{2q+1}/T \to \gamma \in (0, +\infty)$. We have*

$$\sqrt{T}(\hat{\theta}_T - \theta_0) \xrightarrow{L} \mathcal{N}\left(0, \left(\langle E^{\theta_0}(\nabla_\theta h), E^{\theta_0}(\nabla_\theta h)' \rangle_K\right)^{-1}\right) \tag{6.17}$$

as T and $T^{q/(2q+1)}\alpha_T$ go to infinity and α_T goes to zero.

Note that the implementation of this method requires two smoothing parameters α_T and S_T. No cross-validation method for selecting these two parameters simultaneously has been derived yet. If $\{h_t\}$ is uncorrelated, then K can be estimated using the sample average and the resulting estimator satisfies $\|K_T - K\| = O_p(T^{-1/2})$. When $\{h_t\}$ are correlated, the convergence rate of K_T is slower and accordingly the rate of convergence of α_T to zero is slower.

7. Estimating solutions of integral equations of the second kind

7.1. Introduction

The objective of this section is to study the properties of the solution of an integral equation of the second kind (also called Fredholm equation of the second type) defined by

$$(I - K)\varphi = r \tag{7.1}$$

where φ is an element of a Hilbert space $\mathcal{H}$, K is a compact operator from $\mathcal{H}$ to $\mathcal{H}$ and r is an element of $\mathcal{H}$. As in the previous sections, K and r are known functions of a data generating process characterized by its c.d.f. F, and the functional parameter of interest is the function φ.

In most cases, $\mathcal{H}$ is a functional space and K is an integral operator defined by its kernel k. Equation (7.1) becomes:

$$\varphi(t) - \int k(t, s)\varphi(s)\Pi(\mathrm{d}s) = r(t). \tag{7.2}$$

The estimated operators are often degenerate, see Section 2.5.1 and in that case, Equation (7.2) simplifies into:

$$\varphi(t) - \sum_{\ell=1}^{L} a_\ell(\varphi)\varepsilon_\ell(t) = r(t) \tag{7.3}$$

where the $a_\ell(\varphi)$ are linear forms on $\mathcal{H}$ and ε_ℓ belongs to $\mathcal{H}$ for any ℓ.

The essential difference between equations of the first kind and of the second kind is the compactness of the operator. In (7.1), K is compact but $I - K$ is not compact. Moreover, if $I - K$ is one-to-one, its inverse is bounded. In that case, the inverse problem is well-posed. Even if $I - K$ is not one-to-one, the ill-posedness of Equation (7.1) is less severe than in the first kind case because the solutions are stable in r.

In most cases, K is a self-adjoint operator (and hence $I - K$ is also self-adjoint) but we will not restrict our presentation to this case. On the other hand, Equation (7.1) can be extended by considering an equation $(S - K)\varphi = r$ where K is a compact operator from $\mathcal{H}$ to $\mathcal{E}$ (instead of $\mathcal{H}$ to $\mathcal{H}$) and S is a one-to-one bounded operator from $\mathcal{H}$ to $\mathcal{E}$ with a bounded inverse. Indeed, $(S - K)\varphi = r \Leftrightarrow (I - S^{-1}K)\varphi = S^{-1}r$ where $S^{-1}K : \mathcal{H} \to \mathcal{H}$ is compact. So that we are back to Equation (7.1), see Corollary 3.6 of Kress (1999).

This section is organized in the following way. The next subsection recalls the main mathematical properties of the equations of the second kind. The two following subsections present the statistical properties of the solution in the cases of well-posed and ill-posed problems, and the last subsection applies these results to the two examples given in Section 1.

The implementation of the estimation procedure is not discussed here because it is similar to the implementation of the estimation of a regularized equation of the first kind (see Section 3). Actually, regularizations transform first kind equations into second kind equations and the numerical methods are then formally equivalent, even though the statistical properties are fundamentally different.

7.2. *Riesz theory and Fredholm alternative*

We first briefly recall the main results about equations of the second kind as they were developed at the beginning of the 20th century by Fredholm and Riesz. The statements are given without proofs [see e.g. Kress (1999, Chapters 3 and 4)].

Let K be a compact operator from $\mathcal{H}$ to $\mathcal{H}$ and I be the identity on $\mathcal{H}$ (which is compact only if $\mathcal{H}$ is finite dimensional). Then, the operator $I - K$ has a finite dimensional null space and its range is closed. Moreover, $I - K$ is injective if and only if it is surjective. In that case $I - K$ is invertible and its inverse $(I - K)^{-1}$ is a bounded operator.

An element of the null space of $I - K$ verifies $K\varphi = \varphi$, and if $\varphi \neq 0$, it is an eigenfunction of K associated with the eigenvalue equal to 1. Equivalently, the inverse problem (7.1) is well-posed if and only if 1 is not an eigenvalue of K. The Fredholm alternative follows from the previous results.

THEOREM 7.1 *(Fredholm alternative). Let us consider the two equations of the second kind*:

$$(I - K)\varphi = r \tag{7.4}$$

and

$$(I - K^*)\psi = s \tag{7.5}$$

where K^* *is the adjoint of* K. *Then*:

(i) *Either the two homogeneous equations* $(I - K)\varphi = 0$ *and* $(I - K^*)\psi = 0$ *only have the trivial solutions* $\varphi = 0$ *and* $\psi = 0$. *In that case,* (7.4) *and* (7.5) *have a unique solution for any* r *and* s *in* $\mathcal{H}$

(ii) *or the two homogeneous equations* $(I - K)\varphi = 0$ *and* $(I - K^*)\psi = 0$ *have the same finite number* m *of linearly independent solutions* φ_j *and* ψ_j $(j = 1, \ldots, m)$ *respectively, and the solutions of* (7.4) *and* (7.5) *exist if and only if* $\langle \psi_j, r\rangle = 0$ *and* $\langle \varphi_j, s\rangle = 0$ *for any* $j = 1, \ldots, m$.

(ii) means that the null spaces of $I - K$ and $I - K^*$ are finite dimensional and have the same dimensions. Moreover, the ranges of $I - K$ and $I - K^*$ satisfy

$$\mathcal{R}(I - K) = \mathcal{N}(I - K^*)^{\perp}, \qquad \mathcal{R}(I - K^*) = \mathcal{N}(I - K)^{\perp}.$$

7.3. Well-posed equations of the second kind

In this subsection, we assume that $I - K$ is injective. In this case, the problem is well-posed and the asymptotic properties of the solution are easily deduced from the properties of the estimation of the operator K and the right-hand side r.

The starting point of this analysis is the relation:

$$\begin{aligned}
\hat{\varphi}_n - \varphi_0 &= (I - \hat{K}_n)^{-1}\hat{r}_n - (I - K)^{-1}r \\
&= (I - \hat{K}_n)^{-1}(\hat{r}_n - r) + \big[(I - \hat{K}_n)^{-1} - (I - K)^{-1}\big]r \\
&= (I - \hat{K}_n)^{-1}\big[\hat{r}_n - r + (\hat{K}_n - K)(I - K)^{-1}r\big] \\
&= (I - \hat{K}_n)^{-1}\big[\hat{r}_n - r + (\hat{K}_n - K)\varphi_0\big]
\end{aligned} \tag{7.6}$$

where the third equality follows from $A^{-1} - B^{-1} = A^{-1}(B - A)B^{-1}$.

THEOREM 7.2. *If*

(i) $\|\hat{K}_n - K\| = o(1)$.

(ii) $\|(\hat{r}_n + \hat{K}_n\varphi_0) - (r + K\varphi_0)\| = O(\frac{1}{a_n})$.

Then $\|\hat{\varphi}_n - \varphi_0\| = O(\frac{1}{a_n})$.

PROOF. As $I - K$ is invertible and admits a continuous inverse, (i) implies that $\|(I - \hat{K}_n)^{-1}\|$ converges to $\|(I - K)^{-1}\|$ and the result follows from (7.6). □

In some cases $\|r - \hat{r}_n\| = O(\frac{1}{b_n})$ and $\|\hat{K}_n - K\| = O(\frac{1}{d_n})$. Then $\frac{1}{a_n} = \frac{1}{b_n} + \frac{1}{d_n}$. In some particular examples, as will be illustrated in the last subsection, the asymptotic behavior of $\hat{r}_n - \hat{K}_n\varphi_0$ is directly considered.

Asymptotic normality can be obtained from different sets of assumptions. The following theorems illustrate two kinds of asymptotic normality.

THEOREM 7.3. *If*

(i) $\|\hat{K}_n - K\| = o(1)$.
(ii) $a_n((\hat{r}_n + \hat{K}_n\varphi_0) - (r + K\varphi_0)) \Longrightarrow \mathcal{N}(0, \Sigma)$ *(weak convergence in* $\mathcal{H}$*).*

Then

$$a_n(\hat{\varphi}_n - \varphi_0) \Longrightarrow \mathcal{N}\big(0, (I-K)^{-1}\Sigma(I-K^*)^{-1}\big).$$

PROOF. The proof follows immediately from (7.6) and Theorem 2.47. □

THEOREM 7.4. *We consider the case where* $\mathcal{H} = L^2(\mathbb{R}^p, \pi)$. *If*

(i) $\|\hat{K}_n - K\| = o(1)$.
(ii) $\exists a_n$ *s.t.* $a_n[(\hat{r}_n + \hat{K}_n\varphi_0) - (r + K\varphi_0)](x) \xrightarrow{d} \mathcal{N}(0, \sigma^2(x)), \quad \forall x \in \mathbb{R}^p$.
(iii) $\exists b_n$ *s.t.* $\frac{a_n}{b_n} = o(1)$ *and*

$$b_n\hat{K}_n\big[(\hat{r}_n + \hat{K}_n\varphi_0) - (r + K\varphi_0)\big] \Longrightarrow \mathcal{N}(0, \Omega)$$

(weak convergence in $\mathcal{H}$*).*

Then

$$a_n(\hat{\varphi}_n - \varphi_0)(x) \xrightarrow{d} \mathcal{N}\big(0, \sigma^2(x)\big), \quad \forall x.$$

PROOF. Using

$$(I-K)^{-1} = I + (I-K)^{-1}K,$$

we deduce from (7.6) that

$$\begin{aligned} a_n(\hat{\varphi}_n - \varphi_0)(x) &= a_n\big\{(I-\hat{K}_n)^{-1}[\hat{r}_n + \hat{K}_n\varphi_0 - r - K\varphi_0]\big\}(x) \\ &= a_n(\hat{r}_n + \hat{K}_n\varphi_0 - r - K\varphi_0)(x) \\ &\quad + \frac{a_n}{b_n}\big\{b_n(I-\hat{K}_n)^{-1}\hat{K}_n(\hat{r}_n + \hat{K}_n\varphi_0 - r - K\varphi_0)\big\}(x). \end{aligned} \tag{7.7}$$

The last term in brackets converges (weakly in L^2) to a $\mathcal{N}(0, (I-K)^{-1}\Omega(I-K)^{-1})$ and the value of this function at any point x also converges to a normal distribution (weak convergence implies finite dimensional convergence). Then the last term in brackets is bounded and the result is verified. □

Note that condition (iii) is satisfied as soon as premultiplying by $\hat{K}_n$ increases the rate of convergence of $\hat{r}_n + \hat{K}_n\varphi_0$. This is true in particular if $\hat{K}_n$ is an integral operator.

We illustrate these results by the following three examples. The first example is an illustrative example, while the other two are motivated by relevant econometric issues.

EXAMPLE. Consider $L^2(\mathbb{R}, \Pi)$ and $(Y, Z(\cdot))$ is a random element of $\mathbb{R} \times L^2(\mathbb{R}, \Pi)$. We study the integral equation of the second kind defined by

$$\varphi(x) + \int E^F\big(Z(x)Z(y)\big)\varphi(y)\Pi(\mathrm{d}y) = E^F\big(YZ(x)\big) \tag{7.8}$$

denoted by $\varphi + V\varphi = r$. Here $K = -V$. As the covariance operator, V is a positive operator, K is a negative operator and therefore 1 cannot be an eigenvalue of K. Consequently, Equation (7.8) defines a well-posed inverse problem.

We assume that an i.i.d. sample of (Y, Z) is available and the estimated Equation (7.8) defines the estimator of the parameter of interest as the solution of an integral equation having the following form:

$$\varphi(x) + \frac{1}{n}\sum_{i=1}^{n} z_i(x) \int z_i(y)\varphi(y)\Pi(\mathrm{d}y) = \frac{1}{n}\sum_{i=1}^{n} y_i z_i(x). \tag{7.9}$$

Under some standard regularity conditions, one can check that $\|\hat{V}_n - V\| = O(\frac{1}{\sqrt{n}})$ and that

$$\begin{aligned}
&\sqrt{n}\frac{1}{n}\sum_i \left\{ z_i(\cdot)\left[y_i - \int z_i(y)\varphi(y)\Pi(\mathrm{d}y)\right] - E^F\big(YZ(\cdot)\big) \right. \\
&\qquad \left. + \int E^F\big(Z(\cdot)Z(y)\big)\varphi(y)\Pi(\mathrm{d}y)\right\} \\
&\quad \Rightarrow \quad \mathcal{N}(0, \Sigma) \quad \text{in } L^2(\mathbb{R}, \Pi).
\end{aligned}$$

Then, from Theorem 7.3,

$$\sqrt{n}(\hat{\varphi}_n - \varphi_0) \quad \Rightarrow \quad \mathcal{N}\big(0, (I + V)^{-1}\Sigma(I + V)^{-1}\big).$$

EXAMPLE *(Rational expectations asset pricing models)*. Following Lucas (1978), rational expectations models characterize the pricing functional as a function φ of the Markov state solution of an integral equation:

$$\varphi(x) - \int a(x, y)\varphi(y)f(y \mid x)\,\mathrm{d}y = \int a(x, y)b(y)f(y \mid x)\,\mathrm{d}y. \tag{7.10}$$

While f is the transition density of the Markov state, the function a denotes the marginal rate of substitution and b the dividend function. For the sake of expositional simplicity, we assume here that the functions a and b are both known while f is estimated nonparametrically by a kernel method. Note that if the marginal rate of substitution a involves some unknown preference parameters (subjective discount factor, risk aversion parameter), they will be estimated, for instance by GMM, with a parametric $\sqrt{n}$ rate of convergence. Therefore, the nonparametric inference about φ (deduced from the solution of (7.10) using a kernel estimation of f) is not contaminated by this parametric estimation; all the statistical asymptotic theory can be derived as if the preference parameters were known.

As far as kernel density estimation is concerned, it is well known that under mild conditions [see e.g. Bosq (1998)] it is possible to get the same convergence rates and the same asymptotic distribution with stationary strongly mixing stochastic processes as in the i.i.d. case.

Let us then consider an n-dimensional stationary stochastic process X_t and $\mathcal{H}$ the space of square integrable functions of one realization of this process. In this example, $\mathcal{H}$ is defined with respect to the true distribution. The operator K is defined by

$$K\varphi(x) = E^F\big(a(X_{t-1}, X_t)\varphi(X_t) \mid X_{t-1} = x\big)$$

and

$$r(x) = E^F\big(a(X_{t-1}, X_t)b(X_t) \mid X_{t-1} = x\big).$$

We will assume that K is compact through possibly a Hilbert–Schmidt condition (see Assumption A.1 of Section 5.5 for such a condition). A common assumption in rational expectation models is that K is a contraction mapping, due to discounting. Then, 1 is not an eigenvalue of K and (7.10) is a well-posed Fredholm integral equation.

Under these hypotheses, both numerical and statistical issues associated with the solution of (7.10) are well documented. See Rust, Traub and Wozniakowski (2002) and references therein for numerical issues. The statistical consistency of the estimator $\hat{\varphi}_n$ obtained from the kernel estimator $\hat{K}_n$ is deduced from Theorem 7.2 above. Assumption (i) is satisfied because $\hat{K}_n - K$ has the same behavior as the conditional expectation operator and

$$\begin{aligned}\hat{r}_n + \hat{K}_n\varphi_0 - r - K\varphi_0 = {} & E^{F_n}\big(a(X_{t-1}, X_t)\big(b(X_t) + \varphi_0(X_t)\big) \mid X_{t-1}\big)\\ & - E^F\big(a(X_{t-1}, X_t)\big(b(X_t) + \varphi_0(X_t)\big) \mid X_{t-1}\big)\end{aligned}$$

converges at the speed $\frac{1}{a_n} = \big(\frac{1}{nc_n^m} + c_n^4\big)^{1/2}$ if c_n is the bandwidth of the (second-order) kernel estimator and m is the dimension of X.

The weak convergence follows from Theorem 7.4. Assumption (ii) of Theorem 7.4 is the usual result on the normality of kernel estimation of conditional expectation. As K is an integral operator, the transformation by $\hat{K}_n$ increases the speed of convergence, which implies (iii) of Theorem 7.4.

EXAMPLE *(Partially nonparametric forecasting model).* This example is drawn from Linton and Mammen (2005). Nonparametric prediction of a stationary ergodic scalar random process X_t is often performed by looking for a predictor $m(X_{t-1}, \ldots, X_{t-d})$ able to minimize the mean square error of prediction:

$$E\big[\big(X_t - m(X_{t-1}, \ldots, X_{t-d})\big)^2\big].$$

In other words, if m can be any squared integrable function, the optimal predictor is the conditional expectation

$$m(X_{t-1}, \ldots, X_{t-d}) = E[X_t \mid X_{t-1}, \ldots, X_{t-d}]$$

and can be estimated by kernel smoothing or any other nonparametric way of estimating a regression function. The problems with this kind of approach are twofold. First, it is often necessary to include many lagged variables and the resulting nonparametric estimation surface suffers from the well-known "curse of dimensionality". Second, it is hard to describe and interpret the estimated regression surface when the dimension is more than two.

A solution to deal with these problems is to think about a kind of nonparametric generalization of ARMA processes. For this purpose, let us consider semiparametric predictors of the following form:

$$E[X_t \mid I_{t-1}] = m_\varphi(\theta, I_{t-1}) = \sum_{j=1}^{\infty} a_j(\theta)\varphi(X_{t-j}) \tag{7.11}$$

where θ is an unknown finite dimensional vector of parameters, $a_j(\cdot)$, $j \geqslant 1$ are known scalar functions, and $\varphi(\cdot)$ is the unknown functional parameter of interest. The notation

$$E[X_t \mid I_{t-1}] = m_\varphi(\theta, I_{t-1})$$

stresses the fact that the predictor depends on the true unknown value of the parameters θ and φ, as well as on the information I_{t-1} available at time $(t-1)$. This information is actually the σ-field generated by X_{t-j}, $j \geqslant 1$. A typical example is

$$a_j(\theta) = \theta^{j-1} \quad \text{for } j \geqslant 1 \text{ with } 0 < \theta < 1. \tag{7.12}$$

Then the predictor defined in (7.11) is actually characterized by

$$m_\varphi(\theta, I_{t-1}) = \theta m_\varphi(\theta, I_{t-2}) + \varphi(X_{t-1}). \tag{7.13}$$

In the context of volatility modeling, X_t would denote a squared asset return over period $[t-1, t]$ and $m_\varphi(\theta, I_{t-1})$ the so-called squared volatility of this return as expected at the beginning of the period. Engle and Ng (1993) have studied such a partially nonparametric (PNP for short) model of volatility and called the function φ the "news impact function". They proposed an estimation strategy based on piecewise linear splines. Note that the PNP model includes several popular parametric volatility models as special cases. For instance, the GARCH (1, 1) model of Bollerslev (1986) corresponds to $\varphi(x) = w + \alpha x$ while the Engle (1990) asymmetric model is obtained for $\varphi(x) = w + \alpha(x+\delta)^2$. More examples can be found in Linton and Mammen (2005).

The nonparametric identification and estimation of the news impact function can be derived for a given value of θ. After that, a profile criterion can be calculated to estimate θ. In any case, since θ will be estimated with a parametric rate of convergence, the asymptotic distribution theory of a nonparametric estimator of φ is the same as if θ were known. For the sake of notational simplicity, the dependence on unknown finite dimensional parameters θ is no longer made explicit.

At least in the particular case (7.12)–(7.13), φ is easily characterized as the solution of a linear integral equation of the first kind

$$E[X_t - \theta X_{t-1} \mid I_{t-2}] = E\big[\varphi(X_{t-1}) \mid I_{t-2}\big].$$

Except for its dynamic features, this problem is completely similar to the nonparametric instrumental regression example described in Section 5.5. However, as already mentioned, problems of the second kind are often preferable since they may be well-posed. As shown by Linton and Mammen (2005) in the particular case of a PNP volatility model, it is actually possible to identify and consistently estimate the function φ_0 defined as

$$\varphi_0 = \arg\min_{\varphi} E\left[\left(X_t - \sum_{j=1}^{\infty} a_j \varphi(X_{t-j})\right)^2\right] \tag{7.14}$$

from a well-posed linear inverse problem of the second kind. When φ is an element of the Hilbert space $L^2_F(X)$, its true unknown value is characterized by the first-order conditions obtained by differentiating in the direction of any vector h

$$E\left[\left(X_t - \sum_{j=1}^{\infty} a_j \varphi(X_{t-j})\right)\left(\sum_{l=1}^{\infty} a_l h(X_{t-l})\right)\right] = 0.$$

In other words, for any h in $L^2_F(X)$

$$\sum_{j=1}^{\infty} a_j E^X\big[E[X_t \mid X_{t-j} = x]h(x)\big] - \sum_{j=1}^{\infty} a_j^2 E^X\big[\varphi(x)h(x)\big]$$
$$- \sum_{j=1}^{\infty} \sum_{\substack{l=1 \\ l\neq j}}^{\infty} a_j a_l E^X\big[E[\varphi(X_{t-l}) \mid X_{t-j} = x]h(x)\big] = 0 \tag{7.15}$$

where E^X denotes the expectation with respect to the stationary distribution of X_t. As the equality in (7.15) holds true for all h, it is true in particular for a complete sequence of functions of $L^2_F(X)$. It follows that

$$\sum_{j=1}^{\infty} a_j E[X_t \mid X_{t-j} = x] - \left(\sum_{l=1}^{\infty} a_l^2\right)\varphi(x)$$
$$- \sum_{j=1}^{\infty} \sum_{l\neq j}^{\infty} a_j a_l E\big[\varphi(X_{t-l}) \mid X_{t-j} = x\big] = 0$$

P^X – almost surely on the values of x. Let us denote

$$r_j(X_t) = E[X_{t+j} \mid X_t] \quad \text{and} \quad H_k(\varphi)(X_t) = E\big[\varphi(X_{t+k}) \mid X_t\big].$$

Then, we have proved that the unknown function φ of interest must be the solution of the linear inverse problem of the second kind

$$A(\varphi, F) = (I - K)\varphi - r = 0 \tag{7.16}$$

where

$$r = \left(\sum_{j=1}^{\infty} a_j^2\right)^{-1} \sum_{j=1}^{\infty} a_j r_j,$$

$$K = -\left(\sum_{j=1}^{\infty} a_j^2\right)^{-1} \sum_{j=1}^{\infty} \sum_{l \neq j} a_j a_l H_{j-l},$$

and, with a slight change of notation, F now characterizes the probability distribution of the stationary process (X_t).

To study the inverse problem (7.16), it is first worth noticing that K is a self-adjoint integral operator. Indeed,

$$K = \left(\sum_{j=1}^{\infty} a_j^2\right)^{-1} \sum_{k=\pm 1}^{+\infty} H_k \left(\sum_{l=\max[1,1-k]}^{+\infty} a_l a_{l+k} \right)$$

and it follows from Section 2.2 that the conditional expectation operator H_k is such that

$$H_k^* = H_{-k}$$

and thus $K = K^*$, since

$$\sum_{l=\max[1,1-k]}^{+\infty} a_l a_{l+k} = \sum_{l=\max[1,1+k]}^{+\infty} a_l a_{l-k}.$$

As noticed by Linton and Mammen (2005), this property greatly simplifies the practical implementation of the solution of the sample counterpart of Equation (7.16). Even more importantly, the inverse problem (7.16) will be well-posed as soon as one maintains the following identification assumption about the news impact function φ.

ASSUMPTION A. There exists no θ and $\varphi \in L_F^2(X)$ with $\varphi \neq 0$ such that $\sum_{j=1}^{\infty} a_j(\theta)\varphi(X_{t-j}) = 0$ almost surely.

To see this, observe that Assumption A means that for any nonzero function φ

$$0 < E\left[\sum_{j=1}^{\infty} a_j \varphi(X_{t-j})\right]^2,$$

that is

$$0 < \sum_{j=1}^{\infty} a_j^2 \langle \varphi, \varphi \rangle + \sum_{j=1}^{\infty} \sum_{\substack{l=1 \\ l \neq j}}^{\infty} a_l a_j \langle \varphi, H_{j-l}\varphi \rangle.$$

Therefore

$$0 < \langle \varphi, \varphi \rangle - \langle \varphi, K\varphi \rangle \tag{7.17}$$

for nonzero φ. In other words, there is no nonzero φ such that

$$K\varphi = \varphi$$

and hence the operator $(I - K)$ is one-to-one. Moreover, (7.17) implies that $(I - K)$ has eigenvalues bounded from below by a positive number. Therefore, if K depends continuously on the unknown finite dimensional vector of parameters θ and if θ evolves in some compact set, the norm of $(I - K)^{-1}$ will be bounded from above uniformly in θ.

It is also worth noticing that the operator K is Hilbert–Schmidt and a fortiori compact under reasonable assumptions. As already mentioned in Section 2.2, the Hilbert–Schmidt property for the conditional expectation operators H_k is tantamount to the integrability condition

$$\iint \left[\frac{f_{X_t, X_{t-k}}(x, y)}{f_{X_t(x)} f_{X_t}(y)} \right]^2 f_{X_t}(x) f_{X_t}(y) \, \mathrm{d}x \, \mathrm{d}y < \infty.$$

It amounts to saying that there is not too much dependence between X_t and X_{t-k}. This should be tightly related to the ergodicity or mixing assumptions about the stationary process X_t. Then, if all the conditional expectation operators H_k, $k \geqslant 1$ are Hilbert–Schmidt, the operator K will also be Hilbert–Schmidt insofar as

$$\sum_{j=1}^{\infty} \sum_{l \neq j} a_j^2 a_l^2 < +\infty.$$

Up to a straightforward generalization to stationary mixing processes of results only stated in the i.i.d. case, the general asymptotic theory of Theorems 7.3 and 7.4 can then be easily applied to nonparametric estimators of the news impact function φ based on the Fredholm equation of the second kind (7.15). An explicit formula for the asymptotic variance of $\hat{\varphi}_n$ as well as a practical solution by implementation of matricial equations similar to those of Section 3.4 (without need of a regularization) is provided by Linton and Mammen (2005) in the particular case of volatility modeling.

However, an important difference with the i.i.d. case (see for instance Assumption A.3 in Section 5.5 about instrumental variables) is that the conditional homoskedasticity assumption cannot be maintained about the conditional probability distribution of X_t given its own past. This should be particularly detrimental in the case of volatility modeling, since when X_t denotes a squared return, it will in general be even more conditionally heteroskedastic than returns themselves. Such severe conditional heteroskedasticity will likely imply a poor finite sample performance, and a large asymptotic variance of the estimator $\hat{\varphi}_n$ defined from the inverse problem (7.15), that is from the least-squares problem (7.14). Indeed, $\hat{\varphi}_n$ is a kind of OLS estimator in infinite dimension. In order to better take into account conditional heteroskedasticity of X_t in the context of volatility modeling, Linton and Mammen (2005) propose to replace the least squares problem (7.14) by a quasi-likelihood kind of approach where the criterion to optimize is defined from the density function of a normal conditional probability distribution of returns, with variance $m_\varphi(\theta, I_{t-1})$. Then the difficulty is that the associated first-order conditions now characterize the news impact function φ as solution of a nonlinear inverse problem. Linton and Mammen (2005) suggest working with a version of this problem which is locally linearized around the previously described least-squares estimator $\hat{\varphi}_n$ (and associated consistent estimator of θ).

7.4. Ill-posed equations of the second kind

7.4.1. Estimation

The objective of this section is to study equations $(I-K)\varphi = r$ where 1 is an eigenvalue of K, i.e. where $I - K$ is not injective (or one-to-one). For simplicity, we restrict our analysis to the case where the order of multiplicity of the eigenvalue 1 is one and the operator K is self-adjoint. This implies that the dimension of the null spaces of $I - K$ is one and using the results of Section 7.2, the space $\mathcal{H}$ may be decomposed into

$$\mathcal{H} = \mathcal{N}(I - K) \oplus \mathcal{R}(I - K)$$

i.e. $\mathcal{H}$ is the direct sum between the null space and the range of $I - K$, both closed. We denote by $P_{\mathcal{N}} r$ the projection of r on $\mathcal{N}(I - K)$ and by $P_{\mathcal{R}} r$ the projection of r on the range $\mathcal{R}(I - K)$.

Using (ii) of Theorem 7.1, a solution of $(I - K)\varphi = r$ exists in the noninjective case only if r is orthogonal to $\mathcal{N}(I - K)$ or equivalently, if r belongs to $\mathcal{R}(I - K)$. In other words, a solution exists if and only if $r = P_{\mathcal{R}} r$. However in this case, the solution is not unique and there exists a one-dimensional linear manifold of solutions. Obviously, if φ is a solution, φ plus any element of $\mathcal{N}(I - K)$ is also a solution. This nonuniqueness problem will be solved by a normalization rule which selects a unique element in the set of solutions. The normalization we adopt is

$$\langle \varphi, \phi_1 \rangle = 0 \tag{7.18}$$

where ϕ_1 is the eigenfunction of K corresponding to the eigenvalue equal to 1.

In most statistical applications of equations of the second kind, the random element r corresponding to the true data generating process is assumed to be in the range of $I-K$, where K is also associated with the true DGP. However, this property is no longer true if F is estimated and we need to extend the resolution of $(I - K)\varphi = r$ to cases where $I - K$ is not injective and r is not in the range of this operator. This extension must be done in such a way that the continuity properties of inversion are preserved.

For this purpose we consider the following generalized inverse of $(I - K)$. As K is a compact operator, it has a discrete spectrum $\lambda_1 = 1, \lambda_2, \ldots,$ where only 0 may be an accumulation point (in particular 1 cannot be an accumulation point). The associated orthonormal eigenfunctions are $\phi_1, \phi_2, \ldots$. Then we define:

$$Lu = \sum_{j=2}^{\infty} \frac{1}{1-\lambda_j} \langle u, \phi_j \rangle \phi_j, \quad u \in \mathcal{H}. \tag{7.19}$$

Note that $L = (I - K)^{\dagger}$ is the Moore–Penrose generalized inverse of $I - K$, introduced in Proposition 3.3. Moreover, L is continuous and therefore bounded because 1 is an isolated eigenvalue. This operator computes the unique solution of $(I - K)\varphi = P_{\mathcal{R}} r$ satisfying the normalization rule (7.18). It can be easily verified that L satisfies:

$$\begin{aligned} &LP_{\mathcal{R}} = L = P_{\mathcal{R}} L, \\ &L(I - K) = (I - K)L = P_{\mathcal{R}}. \end{aligned} \tag{7.20}$$

We now consider estimation. For an observed sample, we obtain an estimator F_n of F (that may be built from a kernel estimator of the density) and then estimators $\hat{r}_n$ and $\hat{K}_n$ of r and K, respectively. Let $\hat{\phi}_1, \hat{\phi}_2, \ldots$, denote the eigenfunctions of $\hat{K}_n$ associated with $\hat{\lambda}_1, \hat{\lambda}_2, \ldots$. We restrict our attention to the cases where 1 is also an eigenvalue of multiplicity one of $\hat{K}_n$ (i.e. $\hat{\lambda}_1 = 1$). However, $\hat{\phi}_1$ may be different from ϕ_1.

We have to make a distinction between two cases. First, assume that the Hilbert space $\mathcal{H}$ of reference is known and in particular the inner product is given (for example $\mathcal{H} = L^2(\mathbb{R}^p, \Pi)$ with Π given). The normalization rule imposed on $\hat{\varphi}_n$ is

$$\langle \hat{\varphi}_n, \hat{\phi}_1 \rangle = 0$$

and $\hat{L}_n$ is the generalized inverse of $I - \hat{K}_n$ in $\mathcal{H}$ (which depends on the Hilbert space structure) where

$$\hat{L}_n u = \sum_{j=2}^{\infty} \frac{1}{1-\hat{\lambda}_j} \langle u, \hat{\phi}_j \rangle \hat{\phi}_j, \quad u \in \mathcal{H}.$$

Formula (7.20) applies immediately for F_n.

However, if the Hilbert space $\mathcal{H}$ depends on F (e.g. $\mathcal{H} = L^2(\mathbb{R}^p, F)$), we need to assume that $L^2(\mathbb{R}, F_n) \subset L^2(\mathbb{R}^p, F)$. The orthogonality condition which defines the normalization rule (7.18) is related to $L^2(\mathbb{R}^p, F)$, but the estimator $\hat{\varphi}_n$ of φ will be normalized by

$$\langle \hat{\varphi}_n, \hat{\phi}_1 \rangle_n = 0$$

where $\langle , \rangle_n$ denotes the inner product relative to F_n. This orthogonality is different from an orthogonality relative to $\langle , \rangle$. In the same way $\hat{L}_n$ is now defined as the generalized inverse of $I - \hat{K}_n$ with respect to the estimated Hilbert structure, i.e.

$$\hat{L}_n u = \sum_{j=2}^{\infty} \frac{1}{1-\hat{\lambda}_j} \langle u, \hat{\phi}_j \rangle_n \hat{\phi}_j$$

and $\hat{L}_n$ is not the generalized inverse of $I - \hat{K}_n$ in the original space $\mathcal{H}$. The advantages of this definition are that $\hat{L}_n$ may be effectively computed and satisfies the formula (7.20) where F_n replaces F. In the sequel $P_{\mathcal{R}_n}$ denotes the projection operator on $\mathcal{R}_n = \mathcal{R}(I - \hat{K}_n)$ for the inner product $\langle \cdot,\cdot \rangle_n$.

To establish consistency, we will use the following equality:

$$\hat{L}_n - L = \hat{L}_n(\hat{K}_n - K)L + \hat{L}_n(P_{\mathcal{R}_n} - P_{\mathcal{R}}) + (P_{\mathcal{R}_n} - P_{\mathcal{R}})L. \tag{7.21}$$

It follows from (7.20) and $\hat{L}_n - L = \hat{L}_n P_{\mathcal{R}_n} - P_{\mathcal{R}} L = \hat{L}_n(P_{\mathcal{R}_n} - P_{\mathcal{R}}) + (P_{\mathcal{R}_n} - P_{\mathcal{R}})L - P_{\mathcal{R}_n} L + \hat{L}_n P_{\mathcal{R}}$ and $\hat{L}_n(\hat{K}_n - K)L = \hat{L}_n(\hat{K}_n - I)L + \hat{L}_n(I - K)L = -P_{\mathcal{R}_n} L + \hat{L}_n P_{\mathcal{R}}$.

The convergence property is given by the following theorem.

THEOREM 7.5. *Let us define* $\varphi_0 = Lr$ *and* $\hat{\varphi}_n = \hat{L}_n \hat{r}_n$. *If*

(i) $\|\hat{K}_n - K\| = o(1)$.
(ii) $\|P_{\mathcal{R}_n} - P_{\mathcal{R}}\| = O(\frac{1}{b_n})$.
(iii) $\|(\hat{r}_n + \hat{K}_n\varphi_0) - (r + K\varphi_0)\| = O(\frac{1}{a_n})$.

Then

$$\|\hat{\varphi}_n - \varphi_0\| = O\left(\frac{1}{a_n} + \frac{1}{b_n}\right).$$

PROOF. The proof is based on:

$$\begin{aligned}\hat{\varphi}_n - \varphi_0 &= \hat{L}_n \hat{r}_n - Lr \\ &= \hat{L}_n(\hat{r}_n - r) + (\hat{L}_n - L)r \\ &= \hat{L}_n(\hat{r}_n - r) + \hat{L}_n(\hat{K}_n - K)\varphi_0 \\ &\quad + \hat{L}_n(P_{\mathcal{R}_n} - P_{\mathcal{R}})r + (P_{\mathcal{R}_n} - P_{\mathcal{R}})\varphi_0\end{aligned} \tag{7.22}$$

deduced from (7.21). Then

$$\begin{aligned}\|\hat{\varphi}_n - \varphi_0\| &\leqslant \|\hat{L}_n\| \big\|(\hat{r}_n + \hat{K}_n\varphi_0) - (r + K\varphi_0)\big\| \\ &\quad + \big(\|\hat{L}_n\|\|r\| + \|\varphi_0\|\big)\|P_{\mathcal{R}_n} - P_{\mathcal{R}}\|.\end{aligned} \tag{7.23}$$

Under (i) and (ii), $\|\hat{L}_n - L\| = o(1)$ from (7.21). This implies $\|\hat{L}_n\| \to \|L\|$ and the result follows. □

If $\frac{a_n}{b_n} = O(1)$, the actual speed of convergence is bounded by $\frac{1}{a_n}$. This will be the case in the two examples of Section 7.4.2 where $\frac{a_n}{b_n} \to 0$.

We consider asymptotic normality in this case. By (7.20), we have $\hat{L}_n = P_{\mathcal{R}_n} + \hat{L}_n\hat{K}_n$, hence:

$$\hat{\varphi}_n - \varphi_0 = P_{\mathcal{R}_n}\big[(\hat{r}_n + \hat{K}_n\varphi_0) - (r + K\varphi_0)\big] \tag{7.24}$$

$$+ \hat{L}_n \hat{K}_n \big[(\hat{r}_n + \hat{K}_n \varphi_0) - (r + K\varphi_0) \big] \tag{7.25}$$

$$+ \hat{L}_n (P_{\mathcal{R}_n} - P_{\mathcal{R}}) r + (P_{\mathcal{R}_n} - P_{\mathcal{R}}) \varphi_0. \tag{7.26}$$

Let us assume that there exists a sequence a_n such that (i) and (ii) below are satisfied

(i) $a_n P_{\mathcal{R}_n} [(\hat{r}_n + \hat{K}_n \varphi_0) - (r + K\varphi_0)](x)$ has an asymptotic normal distribution,
(ii) $a_n [\hat{L}_n \hat{K}_n (\hat{r}_n + \hat{K}_n \varphi_0 - r - K\varphi_0)](x) \to 0$, $a_n [\hat{L}_n (P_{\mathcal{R}_n} - P_{\mathcal{R}}) r](x) \to 0$,

and $a_n [(P_{\mathcal{R}_n} - P_{\mathcal{R}}) \varphi_0](x) \to 0$ in probability.

Then the asymptotic normality of $a_n(\hat{\varphi}_n - \varphi_0)$ is driven by the behavior of (7.24). This situation occurs in the nonparametric estimation, as illustrated in the next section.

7.4.2. Two examples: backfitting estimation in additive and measurement error models

Backfitting estimation in additive models Using the notation of Section 1.3.5, an additive model is defined by

$$(Y, Z, W) \in \mathbb{R} \times \mathbb{R}^p \times \mathbb{R}^q, \qquad Y = \varphi(Z) + \psi(W) + U,$$
$$E(U \mid Z, W) = 0. \tag{7.27}$$

It follows from (1.23) that the function φ_0 is solution of the equation

$$\varphi - E\big[E(\varphi(Z) \mid W) \mid Z\big] = E(Y \mid Z) - E\big[E(Y \mid W) \mid Z\big]$$

and ψ is the solution of an equation of the same nature obtained by a permutation of W and Z. The backfitting algorithm of Breiman and Friedman (1985), and Hastie and Tibshirani (1990) is widely used to estimate φ and ψ in Equation (7.27). Mammen, Linton and Nielsen (1999) derive the asymptotic distribution of the backfitting procedure. Alternatively, Newey (1994), Tjøstheim and Auestad (1994), and Linton and Nielsen (1995) propose to estimate φ (respectively ψ) by integrating an estimator of $E[Y \mid Z = z, W = w]$ with respect to w (respectively z).

We focus our presentation on the estimation of φ. It appears as the result of a linear equation of the second kind. More precisely, we have in that case:

- $\mathcal{H}$ is the space of the square integrable functions of Z with respect to the true data generating process. This definition simplifies our presentation but an extension to different spaces is possible.
- The unknown function φ is an element of $\mathcal{H}$. Actually, asymptotic considerations will restrict the class of functions φ by smoothness restrictions.
- The operator K is defined by $K\varphi = E[E(\varphi(Z) \mid W) \mid Z]$. This operator is self adjoint and we assume its compactness. This compactness may be obtained through the Hilbert–Schmidt Assumption A.1 of Section 5.5.
- The function r is equal to $E(Y \mid Z) - E[E(Y \mid W) \mid Z]$.

The operator $I - K$ is not one-to-one because the constant functions belong to the null space of this operator. Indeed, the additive model (7.27) does not identify φ and ψ. We introduce the following assumption [see Florens, Mouchart and Rolin (1990)], which warrants that φ and ψ are exactly identified up to an additive constant, or equivalently that the null space of $I - K$ only contains the constants (meaning 1 is an eigenvalue of K of order 1).

Identification assumption Z and W are measurably separated w.r.t. the distribution F, i.e. a function of Z almost surely equal to a function of W is almost surely constant.

This assumption implies that if $\varphi_1, \varphi_2, \psi_1, \psi_2$ are such that $E(Y \mid Z, W) = \varphi_1(Z) + \psi_1(W) = \varphi_2(Z) + \psi_2(W)$ then $\varphi_1(Z) - \varphi_2(Z) = \psi_2(W) - \psi_1(W)$ which implies that $\varphi_1 - \varphi_2$ and $\psi_2 - \psi_1$ are a.s. constant. In terms of the null set of $I - K$, we have

$$\begin{aligned} &K\varphi = \varphi \\ &\quad \Longleftrightarrow \quad E\big[E\big(\varphi(Z) \mid W\big) \mid Z\big] = \varphi(Z) \\ &\quad \Longrightarrow \quad E\big[\big(E\big[\varphi(Z) \mid W\big]\big)^2\big] = E\big[\varphi(Z)E\big(\varphi(Z) \mid W\big)\big] = E\big(\varphi^2(Z)\big). \end{aligned}$$

But, by Pythagore theorem

$$\begin{aligned} &\varphi(Z) = E\big(\varphi(Z) \mid W\big) + \upsilon, \\ &E\big(\varphi^2(Z)\big) = E\big(\big(E\big(\varphi(Z) \mid W\big)\big)^2\big) + E\upsilon^2. \end{aligned}$$

Then:

$$\begin{aligned} &K\varphi = \varphi \quad \Longrightarrow \quad \upsilon = 0, \\ &\quad \Leftrightarrow \quad \varphi(Z) = E\big[\varphi(Z) \mid W\big]. \end{aligned}$$

Then, if φ is an element of the null set of $I - K$, φ is almost surely equal to a function of W and is therefore constant.

The eigenvalues of K are real, positive and smaller than 1 except for the first one, that is $1 = \lambda_1 > \lambda_2 > \lambda_3 > \cdots$.[1] The eigenfunctions are such that $\phi_1 = 1$ and the condition $\langle \varphi, \phi_1 \rangle = 0$ means that φ has an expectation equal to zero. The range of $I - K$ is the set of functions with mean equal to 0 and the projection of u, $P_{\mathcal{R}}u$, equals $u - E(u)$.

It should be noticed that under the hypotheses of the additive model, r has zero mean and is then an element of $\mathcal{R}(I - K)$. Then, a unique (up to the normalization condition) solution of the structural equation $(I - K)\varphi = r$ exists.

The estimation may be done by kernel smoothing. The joint density is estimated[2] by

$$\hat{f}_n(y, z, w) = \frac{1}{nc_n^{1+p+q}} \sum_{i=1}^{n} \omega\left(\frac{y - y_i}{c_n}\right) \omega\left(\frac{z - z_i}{c_n}\right) \omega\left(\frac{w - w_i}{c_n}\right) \tag{7.28}$$

[1] Actually $K = T^*T$ where $T\varphi = E(\varphi \mid W)$ and $T^*\psi = E(\psi \mid Z)$ when ψ is a function of W. The eigenvalues of K correspond to the squared singular values of T and T^*.

[2] By abuse of notations, we denote the kernels associated with y, z, w by the same notation ω although they have different dimensions. Similarly, we denote all the bandwidths by c_n although they are equivalent up to a multiplicative constant.

and F_n is the c.d.f. associated with f_n. The estimated $\hat{K}_n$ operator satisfies

$$(\hat{K}_n\varphi)(z) = \int \varphi(u)\hat{a}_n(u, z)\,\mathrm{d}u \tag{7.29}$$

where

$$\hat{a}_n(u, z) = \int \frac{\hat{f}_n(\cdot, u, w)\hat{f}_n(\cdot, z, w)}{\hat{f}_n(\cdot,\cdot, w)\hat{f}_n(\cdot, z, \cdot)}\,\mathrm{d}w.$$

The operator $\hat{K}_n$ must be an operator from $\mathcal{H}$ to $\mathcal{H}$ (it is by construction an operator from $L^2_Z(F_n)$ into $L^2_Z(F_n)$). Therefore, $\frac{\omega(\frac{z-z_\ell}{c_n})}{\sum_\ell \omega(\frac{z-z_\ell}{c_n})}$ must be square integrable w.r.t. F.

The estimation of r by $\hat{r}_n$ verifies

$$\hat{r}_n(z) = \frac{1}{\sum_{\ell=1}^n \omega\left(\frac{z-z_\ell}{c_n}\right)} \sum_{\ell=1}^n \left(y_\ell - \sum_{i=1}^n y_i\omega_{\ell i}\right)\omega\left(\frac{z-z_\ell}{c_n}\right)$$

where $\omega_{\ell i} = \frac{\omega(\frac{w_\ell - w_i}{c_n})}{\sum_{j=1}^n \omega(\frac{w_\ell - w_j}{c_n})}$.

The operator $\hat{K}_n$ also has 1 as the greatest eigenvalue corresponding to an eigenfunction equal to 1. Since F_n is a mixture of probabilities for which Z and W are independent, the measurable separability between Z and W is fulfilled. Then, the null set of $I - \hat{K}_n$ reduces a.s. (w.r.t. F_n) to constant functions. The generalized inverse of an operator depends on the inner product of the Hilbert space because it is defined as the function φ of minimal norm which minimizes the norm of $\hat{K}_n\varphi - \hat{r}_n$. The generalized inverse in the space $L^2_Z(F)$ cannot be used for the estimation because it depends on the actual unknown F. Then we construct $\hat{L}_n$ as the generalized inverse in $L^2_Z(F_n)$ of $I - \hat{K}_n$. The practical computation of $\hat{L}_n$ can be done by computing the n eigenvalues $\hat{\lambda}_1 = 1, \ldots, \hat{\lambda}_n$ and the n eigenfunctions $\hat{\phi}_1 = 1, \hat{\phi}_2, \ldots, \hat{\phi}_n$ of $\hat{K}_n$. Then

$$\hat{L}_n u = \sum_{j=2}^n \frac{1}{1-\hat{\lambda}_j}\left\{\int u(z)\hat{\phi}_j(z)\hat{f}_n(z)\,\mathrm{d}z\right\}\hat{\phi}_j.$$

It can be easily checked that property (7.20) is verified where $P_{\mathcal{R}_n}$ is the projection (w.r.t. F_n) on the orthogonal of the constant function. This operator subtracts from any function its empirical mean, which is computed through the smoothed density:

$$P_{\mathcal{R}_n} u = u - \frac{1}{nc_n^p}\sum_i \int u(z)\omega\left(\frac{z-z_i}{c_n}\right)\mathrm{d}z.$$

The right-hand side of the equation $(I - \hat{K}_n)\varphi = \hat{r}_n$ has a mean equal to 0 (w.r.t. F_n). Hence, this equation has a unique solution $\hat{\varphi}_n = \hat{L}_n\varphi_0$ which satisfies the normalization condition $\frac{1}{nc_n^p}\sum_i \int \hat{\varphi}_n(z)\omega\left(\frac{z-z_i}{c_n}\right)\mathrm{d}z = 0$.

The general results of Section 7.4 apply. First, we check that the conditions (i) to (iii) of Theorem 7.5 are fulfilled.

(i) Under very general assumptions, $\|\hat{K}_n - K\| \to 0$ in probability.

(ii) We have to check the properties of $P_{\mathcal{R}_n} - P_{\mathcal{R}}$

$$(P_{\mathcal{R}_n} - P_{\mathcal{R}})\varphi = \frac{1}{nc_n^p}\sum_i \int \varphi(z)\omega\left(\frac{z-z_i}{c_n}\right)\mathrm{d}z - \int \varphi(z)f(z)\,\mathrm{d}z.$$

The asymptotic behavior of the positive random variable, $\|(P_{\mathcal{R}_n} - P_{\mathcal{R}})\varphi\|^2 = |\frac{1}{nc_n^p}\sum_{i=1}^n \int \varphi(z)\omega(\frac{z-z_i}{c_n})\,\mathrm{d}z - E(\varphi)|^2$, is the same as the asymptotic behavior of its expectation:

$$E\left(\frac{1}{nc_n^p}\sum_{i=1}^n \int \varphi(z)\omega\left(\frac{z-z_i}{c_n}\right)\mathrm{d}z - E(\varphi)\right)^2.$$

Standard computation on this expression shows that this mean square error is $O(\frac{1}{n} + c_n^{2\min(d,d')})\|\varphi\|^2$, where d is the smoothness degree of φ and d' the order of the kernel.

(iii) The last term we have to consider is actually not computable but its asymptotic behavior is easily characterized. We simplify the notation by denoting $E^{F_n}(\cdot \mid \cdot)$ the estimation of a conditional expectation. The term we have to consider is

$$\begin{aligned}
&(\hat{r}_n + \hat{K}_n\varphi_0) - (r + K\varphi_0)\\
&\quad= E^{F_n}(Y \mid Z) - E^{F_n}\big(E^{F_n}(Y \mid W) \mid Z\big) + E^{F_n}\big(E^{F_n}\big(\varphi_0(Z) \mid W\big) \mid Z\big)\\
&\qquad - E^F(Y \mid Z) + E^F\big(E^F(Y \mid W) \mid Z\big) - E^F\big(E^F\big(\varphi_0(Z) \mid W\big) \mid Z\big)\\
&\quad= E^{F_n}\big(Y - E^F(Y \mid W) + E^F\big(\varphi_0(Z) \mid W\big) \mid Z\big)\\
&\qquad - E^F\big(Y - E^F(Y \mid W) + E^F\big(\varphi_0(Z) \mid W\big) \mid Z\big) - R
\end{aligned}$$

where $R = E^F\{E^{F_n}(Y - \varphi_0(Z) \mid W) - E^F(Y - \varphi_0(Z) \mid W)\}$. Moreover, from (7.27):

$$E^F(Y \mid W) = E^F\big(\varphi_0(Z) \mid W\big) + \psi_0(W).$$

Then

$$\begin{aligned}
(\hat{r}_n + \hat{K}_n\varphi_0) - (r + K\varphi_0) &= E^{F_n}\big(Y - \psi_0(W) \mid Z\big)\\
&\quad - E^F\big(Y - \psi_0(W) \mid Z\big) - R.
\end{aligned}$$

The term R converges to zero at a faster rate than the first part of the r.h.s. of this equation and can be neglected. We have seen in the other parts of this chapter that

$$\big\|E^{F_n}\big(Y - \psi_0(W) \mid Z\big) - E^F\big(Y - \psi_0(W) \mid Z\big)\big\|^2 = O\left(\frac{1}{nc_n^p} + c_n^{2\rho}\right)$$

where ρ depends on the regularity assumptions. Therefore, condition (iii) of Theorem 7.5 is fulfilled.

From Theorem 7.5 and $nc_n^{p+2\min(d,d')} \to 0$, it follows that $\|\hat{\varphi}_n - \varphi_0\| \to 0$ in probability and that $\|\hat{\varphi}_n - \varphi_0\| = O\big(\frac{1}{\sqrt{nc_n^p}} + c_n^\rho\big)$.

The pointwise asymptotic normality of $\sqrt{nc_n^p}(\hat{\varphi}_n(z) - \varphi_0(z))$ can now be established. We apply the formulas (7.24) to (7.26) and Theorem 7.4.

(1) First, consider (7.26). Under a suitable condition on c_n (typically $nc_n^{p+2\min(d,d')} \to 0$), we have:

$$\sqrt{nc_n^p}\big\{\hat{L}_n(P_{\mathcal{R}_n} - P_{\mathcal{R}})r + (P_{\mathcal{R}_n} - P_{\mathcal{R}})\varphi_0\big\} \to 0$$

in probability.

(2) Second, consider (7.25). Using the same argument as in Theorem 7.4, a suitable choice of c_n implies that

$$\sqrt{nc_n^p}\,\hat{L}_n\hat{K}_n\big[(\hat{r}_n + \hat{K}_n\varphi_0) - (r + K\varphi_0)\big] \to 0. \tag{7.30}$$

Actually, while $E^{F_n}(Y - \psi_0(W) \mid Z) - E^F(Y - \psi_0(W) \mid Z)$ only converges pointwise at a nonparametric speed, the transformation by the operator $\hat{K}_n$ converts this convergence into a functional convergence at a parametric speed. Then

$$\sqrt{nc_n^p}\,\big\|\hat{K}_n\big[E^{F_n}(Y - \psi_0(W) \mid Z) - E^F(Y - \psi_0(W) \mid Z)\big]\big\| \to 0.$$

Moreover, $\hat{L}_n$ converges in norm to L, which is a bounded operator. Hence, the result of (7.30) follows.

(3) The term (7.24) remains. The convergence of $\sqrt{nc_n^p}(\hat{\varphi}_n(z) - \varphi_0(z))$ is then identical to the convergence of

$$\begin{aligned}
&\sqrt{nc_n^p}\,P_{\mathcal{R}_n}\big[E^{F_n}(Y - \psi_0(W) \mid Z = z) - E^F(Y - \psi_0(W) \mid Z = z)\big]\\
&\quad = \sqrt{nc_n^p}\bigg[E^{F_n}(Y - \psi_0(W) \mid Z = z) - E^F(Y - \psi_0(W) \mid Z = z)\\
&\qquad - \frac{1}{n}\sum_i (y_i - \psi_0(w_i))\\
&\qquad - \frac{1}{nc_n^p}\sum_i \int\!\!\int (y - \psi_0(w)) f(y, w \mid Z = z)\omega\Big(\frac{z - z_i}{c_n}\Big)\,dz\,dw\bigg].
\end{aligned}$$

It can easily be checked that the difference between the two sample means converge to zero at a higher speed than $\sqrt{nc_n^p}$ and these two last terms can be neglected. Then using standard results on nonparametric estimation, we obtain:

$$\sqrt{nc_n^p}\,(\hat{\varphi}_n(z) - \varphi_0(z)) \xrightarrow{d} \mathcal{N}\bigg(0, \operatorname{Var}(Y - \psi_0(W) \mid Z = z)\frac{\int \omega(u)^2\,du}{f_Z(z)}\bigg)$$

where the 0 mean of the asymptotic distribution is obtained thanks to a suitable choice of the bandwidth, which needs to converge to 0 faster than the optimal speed.

Note that the estimator of φ has the same properties as the oracle estimator based on the knowledge of ψ. This attractive feature was proved by Mammen, Linton and Nielsen (1999) using different tools.

Estimation of the bias function in a measurement error equation We have introduced in Section 1.3.6, the measurement error model:

$$\begin{cases} Y_1 = \eta + \varphi(Z_1) + U_1, & Y_1, Y_2 \in \mathbb{R}, \\ Y_2 = \eta + \varphi(Z_2) + U_2, & Z_1, Z_2 \in \mathbb{R}^p, \end{cases}$$

where η, U_i are random unknown elements and Y_1 and Y_2 are two measurements of η contaminated by a bias term depending on observable elements Z_1 and Z_2. The unobservable component η is eliminated by differentiation to obtain:

$$Y = \varphi(Z_2) - \varphi(Z_1) + U \tag{7.31}$$

where $Y = Y_2 - Y_1$ and $E(Y \mid Z_1, Z_2) = \varphi(Z_2) - \varphi(Z_1)$. We assume that i.i.d. observations of (Y, Z_1, Z_2) are available. Moreover, the order of measurements is arbitrary or equivalently (Y_1, Y_2, Z_1, Z_2) is distributed identically to (Y_2, Y_1, Z_2, Z_1). This exchangeability property implies that (Y, Z_1, Z_2) and $(-Y, Z_2, Z_1)$ have the same distribution. In particular, Z_1 and Z_2 are identically distributed.

- The reference space $\mathcal{H}$ is the space of random variables defined on $\mathbb{R}^p$ that are square integrable with respect to the true marginal distribution of Z_1 (or Z_2). We are in a case where the Hilbert space structure depends on the unknown distribution.
- The function φ is an element of $\mathcal{H}$ but this set has to be reduced by a smoothness condition in order to obtain the asymptotic properties of the estimation procedure.
- The operator K is the conditional expectation operator

$$(K\varphi)(z) = E^F\big(\varphi(Z_2) \mid Z_1 = z\big) = E^F\big(\varphi(Z_1) \mid Z_2 = z\big)$$

from $\mathcal{H}$ to $\mathcal{H}$. The two conditional expectations are equal because (Z_1, Z_2) and (Z_2, Z_1) are identically distributed (by the exchangeability property). The operator K is self-adjoint and is assumed to be compact. This property may be deduced as in previous cases from a Hilbert–Schmidt argument.

Equation (7.31) introduces an overidentification property because it constrains the conditional expectation of Y given Z_1 and Z_2. In order to define φ for any F (and in particular for the estimated one), the parameter φ is now defined as the solution of the minimization problem:

$$\varphi = \arg\min_{\varphi} E\big(Y - \varphi(Z_2) + \varphi(Z_1)\big)^2$$

or, equivalently as the solution of the first-order conditions:

$$E^F\left[\varphi(Z_2) \mid Z_1 = z\right] - \varphi(z) = E(Y \mid Z_1 = z)$$

because (Y, Z_1, Z_2) and $(-Y, Z_2, Z_1)$ are identically distributed.

The integral equation which defines the function of interest, φ, may be denoted by

$$(I - K)\varphi = r$$

where $r = E(Y \mid Z_2 = z) = -E(Y \mid Z_1 = z)$. As in the additive model, this inverse problem is ill-posed because $I - K$ is not one-to-one. Indeed, 1 is the greatest eigenvalue of K and the eigenfunctions associated with 1 are the constant functions. We need an extra assumption to warrant that the order of multiplicity is one, or in more statistical terms, that φ is identified up to a constant. This property is obtained if Z_1 and Z_2 are measurably separated, i.e. if the functions of Z_1 almost surely equal to some functions of Z_2, are almost surely constant.

Then, the normalization rule is

$$\langle \varphi, \phi_1 \rangle = 0$$

where ϕ_1 is constant. This normalization is equivalent to

$$E^F(\varphi) = 0.$$

If F is estimated using a standard kernel procedure, the estimated F_n does not in general, satisfy the exchangeability assumption ((Y, Z_1, Z_2) and $(-Y, Z_2, Z_1)$ are identically distributed). A simple way to incorporate this constraint is to estimate F using a sample of size $2n$ by adding to the original sample $(y_i, z_{1i}, z_{2i})_{i=1,\dots,n}$ a new sample $(-y_i, z_{2i}, z_{1i})_{i=1,\dots,n}$. For simplicity, we do not follow this method here and consider an estimation of F, which does not verify the exchangeability. In that case, $\hat{r}_n$ is not in general an element of $\mathcal{R}(I - \hat{K}_n)$, and the estimator $\hat{\varphi}_n$ is defined as the unique solution of

$$(I - \hat{K}_n)\varphi = P_{\mathcal{R}_n}\hat{r}_n,$$

which satisfies the normalization rule

$$E^{F_n}(\varphi) = 0.$$

Equivalently, we have seen that the functional equation $(I - \hat{K}_n)\varphi = \hat{r}_n$ reduces to a n dimensional linear system, which is solved by a generalized inversion. The asymptotic properties of this procedure follow immediately from the theorems of Section 7.4 and are obtained identically to the case of additive models.

References

Ai, C., Chen, X. (2003). "Efficient estimation of models with conditional moment restrictions containing unknown functions". Econometrica 71, 1795–1843.

Aït-Sahalia, Y., Hansen, L.P., Scheinkman, J.A. (2005). "Operator methods for continuous-time Markov processes". In: Hansen, L.P., Aït-Sahalia, Y. (Eds.), Handbook of Financial Econometrics. North-Holland. In press.

Amemiya, T. (1974). "The nonlinear two-stage least-squares estimators". Journal of Econometrics 2, 105–110.

Andrews, D. (1991). "Heteroskedasticity and autocorrelation consistent covariance matrix estimation". Econometrica 59 (3), 817–858.

Arellano, M., Hansen, L., Sentana, E. (2005). "Underidentification?". Mimeo. CEMFI.

Aronszajn, N. (1950). "Theory of reproducing kernels". Transactions of the American Mathematical Society 68 (3), 337–404.

Bai, J., Ng, S. (2002). "Determining the number of factors in approximate factor models". Econometrica 70, 191–221.

Basmann, R.L. (1957). "A generalized classical method of linear estimation of coefficients in a structural equations". Econometrica 25, 77–83.

Berlinet, A., Thomas-Agnan, C. (2004). Reproducing Kernel Hilbert Spaces in Probability and Statistics. Kluwer Academic Publishers, Boston.

Blundell, R., Chen, X., Kristensen, D. (2003). "Semi-nonparametric IV estimation of shape-invariant Engel curves". Cemmap working paper CWP 15/03, University College London.

Blundell, R., Powell, J. (2003). "Endogeneity in nonparametric and semiparametric regression models". In: Dewatripont, M., Hansen, L.P., Turnovsky, S.J. (Eds.), Advances in Economics and Econometrics, vol. 2. Cambridge University Press, Cambridge, pp. 312–357.

Bollerslev, T. (1986). "Generalized autoregressive conditional heteroskedasticity". Journal of Econometrics 31, 307–327.

Bosq, D. (1998). Nonparametric Statistics for Stochastic Processes. Estimation and Prediction. Lecture Notes in Statistics, vol. 110. Springer-Verlag, New York.

Bosq, D. (2000). Linear Processes in Function Spaces. Theory and Applications. Lecture Notes in Statistics, vol. 149. Springer-Verlag, New York.

Breiman, L., Friedman, J.H. (1985). "Estimating optimal transformations for multiple regression and correlation". Journal of American Statistical Association 80, 580–619.

Cardot, H., Ferraty, F., Sarda, P. (2003). "Splin estimators for the functional linear model". Statistica Sinica 13, 571–591.

Carrasco, M., Florens, J.-P. (2000). "Generalization of GMM to a continuum of moment conditions". Econometric Theory 16, 797–834.

Carrasco, M., Florens, J.-P. (2001). "Efficient GMM estimation using the empirical characteristic function". Mimeo. Université de Montréal.

Carrasco, M., Florens, J.-P. (2002). "Spectral method for deconvolving a density". Mimeo. Université de Montréal.

Carrasco, M., Florens, J.-P. (2004). "On the asymptotic efficiency of GMM". Mimeo. Université de Montréal.

Carrasco, M., Chernov, M., Florens, J.-P., Ghysels, E. (2007). "Efficient estimation of general dynamic models with a continuum of moment conditions". Journal of Econometrics 140, 529–573.

Carroll, R., Hall, P. (1988). "Optimal rates of convergence for deconvolving a density". Journal of American Statistical Association 83 (404), 1184–1186.

Carroll, R., Van Rooij, A., Ruymgaart, F. (1991). "Theoretical aspects of ill-posed problems in statistics". Acta Applicandae Mathematicae 24, 113–140.

Chacko, G., Viceira, L. (2003). "Spectral GMM estimation of continuous-time processes". Journal of Econometrics 116, 259–292.

Chamberlain, G. (1987). "Asymptotic efficiency in estimation with conditional moment restrictions". Journal of Econometrics 34, 305–334.

Chen, X., Hansen, L.P., Scheinkman, J. (1998). "Shape-preserving estimation of diffusions". Mimeo. University of Chicago.

Chen, X., White, H. (1992). "Central limit and functional central limit theorems for Hilbert space-valued dependent processes". Working paper. University of San Diego.

Chen, X., White, H. (1996). "Law of large numbers for Hilbert space-valued mixingales with applications". Econometric Theory 12, 284–304.

Chen, X., White, H. (1998). "Central limit and functional central limit theorems for Hilbert space-valued dependent processes". Econometric Theory 14, 260–284.

Darolles, S., Florens, J.-P., Gouriéroux, C. (2004). "Kernel based nonlinear canonical analysis and time reversibility". Journal of Econometrics 119, 323–353.

Darolles, S., Florens, J.-P., Renault, E. (1998). "Nonlinear principal components and inference on a conditional expectation operator with applications to Markov processes". Presented in Paris–Berlin conference 1998, Garchy, France.

Darolles, S., Florens, J.-P., Renault, E. (2002). "Nonparametric instrumental regression". Working paper 05-2002, CRDE.

Das, M. (2005). "Instrumental variables estimators of nonparametric models with discrete endogenous regressors". Journal of Econometrics 124, 335–361.

Dautray, R., Lions, J.-L. (1988). Analyse mathématique et calcul numérique pour les sciences et les techniques. Spectre des opérateurs, vol. 5. Masson, Paris.

Davidson, J. (1994). Stochastic Limit Theory. Oxford University Press, Oxford.

Debnath, L., Mikusinski, P. (1999). Introduction to Hilbert Spaces with Applications. Academic Press, San Diego.

Dunford, N., Schwartz, J. (1988). Linear Operators, Part II: Spectral Theory. Wiley, New York.

Engel, H.W., Hanke, M., Neubauer, A. (1996). Regularization of Inverse Problems. Kluwer Academic Publishers.

Engle, R.F. (1990). Discussion: Stock market volatility and the crash of '87. Review of Financial Studies 3, 103–106.

Engle, R.F., Ng, V.K. (1993). "Measuring and testing the impact of news on volatility". The Journal of Finance XLVIII, 1749–1778.

Engle, R.F., Hendry, D.F., Richard, J.F. (1983). "Exogeneity". Econometrica 51 (2), 277–304.

Fan, J. (1993). "Adaptively local one-dimensional subproblems with application to a deconvolution problem". Annals of Statistics 21, 600–610.

Feuerverger, A., McDunnough, P. (1981). "On the efficiency of empirical characteristic function procedures". Journal of the Royal Statistical Society, Series B 43, 20–27.

Florens, J.-P. (2003). "Inverse problems in structural econometrics: The example of instrumental variables". In: Dewatripont, M., Hansen, L.P., Turnovsky, S.J. (Eds.), Advances in Economics and Econometrics, vol. 2. Cambridge University Press, Cambridge, pp. 284–311.

Florens, J.-P. (2005). "Engogeneity in nonseparable models. Application to treatment models where the outcomes are durations". Mimeo. University of Toulouse.

Florens J.-P., Malavolti (2002). "Instrumental regression with discrete variables". Mimeo. University of Toulouse, presented at ESEM 2002, Venice.

Florens, J.-P., Mouchart, M. (1985). "Conditioning in dynamic models". Journal of Time Series Analysis 53 (1), 15–35.

Florens, J.-P., Mouchart, M., Richard, J.F. (1974). "Bayesian inference in error-in-variables models". Journal of Multivariate Analysis 4, 419–432.

Florens, J.-P., Mouchart, M., Richard, J.F. (1987). "Dynamic error-in-variables models and limited information analysis". Annales d'Economie et Statistiques 6/7, 289–310.

Florens, J.-P., Mouchart, M., Rolin, J.-M. (1990). Elements of Bayesian Statistics. Dekker, New York.

Florens, J.-P., Protopopescu, C., Richard, J.F. (1997). "Identification and estimation of a class of game theoretic models". GREMAQ, University of Toulouse.

Florens, J.-P., Heckman, J., Meghir, C., Vytlacil, E. (2003). "Instrumental variables, local instrumental variables and control functions". IDEI working paper No. 249, University of Toulouse.

Forni, M., Reichlin, L. (1998). "Let's get real: A factor analytical approach to disaggregated business cycle dynamics". Review of Economic Studies 65, 453–473.

Forni, M., Hallin, M., Lippi, M., Reichlin, L. (2000). "The generalized dynamic factor model: Identification and estimation". Review of Economic and Statistics 82 (4), 540–552.

Gallant, A.R., Long, J.R. (1997). "Estimating stochastic differential equations efficiently by minimum chi-squared". Biometrika 84, 125–141.

Gaspar, P., Florens, J.-P. (1998). "Estimation of the sea state bias in radar altimeter measurements of sea level: Results from a nonparametric method". Journal of Geophysical Research 103 (15), 803–814.

Guerre, E., Perrigne, I., Vuong, Q. (2000). "Optimal nonparametric estimation of first-price auctions". Econometrica 68 (3), 525–574.

Groetsch, C. (1993). Inverse Problems in Mathematical Sciences. Vieweg Mathematics for Scientists and Engineers, Wiesbaden.

Hall, P., Horowitz, J. (2005). "Nonparametric methods for inference in the presence of instrumental variables". Annals of Statistics 33 (6), 2904–2929.

Hall, P., Horowitz, J. (2007). "Methodology and convergence rates for functional linear regression". The Annals of Statistics 35, 70–91.

Hansen, L.P. (1982). "Large sample properties of generalized method of moments estimators". Econometrica 50, 1029–1054.

Hansen, L.P. (1985). "A method for calculating bounds on the asymptotic covariance matrices of generalized method of moments estimators". Journal of Econometrics 30, 203–238.

Härdle, W., Linton, O. (1994). "Applied nonparametric methods". In: Engle, R.F., McFadden, D.L. (Eds.), Handbook of Econometrics, vol. IV. North-Holland, Amsterdam, pp. 2295–2339.

Hastie, T.J., Tibshirani, R.J. (1990). Generalized Additive Models. Chapman and Hall, London.

Hausman, J. (1981). "Exact consumer's surplus and deadweight loss". American Economic Review 71, 662–676.

Hausman, J. (1985). "The econometrics of nonlinear budget sets". Econometrica 53, 1255–1282.

Hausman, J., Newey, W.K. (1995). "Nonparametric estimation of exact consumers surplus and deadweight loss". Econometrica 63, 1445–1476.

Heckman, J., Vytlacil, E. (2000). "Local instrumental variables". In: Hsiao, C., Morimune, K., Powells, J. (Eds.), Nonlinear Statistical Modeling: Proceedings of the Thirteenth International Symposium in Economic Theory and Econometrics: Essays in Honor of Takeshi Amemiya. Cambridge University Press, Cambridge, pp. 1–46.

Heckman, J., Ichimura, H., Smith, J., Todd, P. (1998). "Characterizing selection bias using experimental data". Econometrica 66, 1017–1098.

Hoerl, A.E., Kennard, R.W. (1970). "Ridge regression: Biased estimation of nonorthogonal problems". Technometrics 12, 55–67.

Horowitz, J. (1999). "Semiparametric estimation of a proportional hazard model with unobserved heterogeneity". Econometrica 67, 1001–1028.

Imbens, G., Angrist, J. (1994). "Identification and estimation of local average treatment effects". Econometrica 62, 467–476.

Jiang, G., Knight, J. (2002). "Estimation of continuous time processes via the empirical characteristic function". Journal of Business & Economic Statistics 20, 198–212.

Judge, G., Griffiths, W., Hill, R.C., Lutkepohl, H., Lee, T.-C. (1980). The Theory and Practice of Econometrics. John Wiley and Sons, New York.

Kailath, T. (1971). "RKHS approach to detection and estimation problems – Part I". IEEE Transactions on Information Theory IT-17, 530–549.

Kargin, V., Onatski, A. (2004). "Dynamics of interest rate curve by functional auto-regression". Mimeo. Columbia University, presented at the CIRANO and CIREQ Conference on Operator Methods (Montreal, November 2004).

Knight, J.L., Yu, J. (2002). "Empirical characteristic function in time series estimation". Econometric Theory 18, 691–721.

Kress, R. (1999). Linear Integral Equations. Springer, New York.

Kutoyants, Yu. (1984). Parameter Estimation for Stochastic Processes. Heldermann Verlag, Berlin.

Lancaster, H. (1968). "The structure of bivariate distributions". Annals of Mathematical Statistics 29, 719–736.

Linton, O., Mammen, E. (2005). "Estimating semiparametric ARCH(∞) models by kernel smoothing methods". Econometrica 73, 771–836.

Linton, O., Nielsen, J.P. (1995). "A kernel method of estimating structured nonparametric regression based on marginal integration". Biometrika 82, 93–100.

Loubes, J.M., Vanhems, A. (2001). "Differential equation and endogeneity". Discussion paper, GREMAQ, University of Toulouse, presented at ESEM 2002, Venice.

Loubes, J.M., Vanhems, A. (2003). "Saturation spaces for regularization methods in inverse problems". Discussion paper, GREMAQ, University of Toulouse, presented at ESEM 2003, Stockholm.

Lucas, R. (1978). "Asset prices in an exchange economy". Econometrica 46, 1429–1446.

Malinvaud, E. (1970). Methodes statistiques de l'econométrie. Dunod, Paris.

Mammen, E., Linton, O., Nielsen, J. (1999). "The existence and asymptotic properties of a backfitting projection algorithm under weak conditions". Annals of Statistics 27, 1443–1490.

Nashed, N.Z., Wahba, G. (1974). "Generalized inverses in reproducing kernel spaces: An approach to regularization of linear operator equations". SIAM Journal of Mathematical Analysis 5, 974–987.

Natterer (1984). "Error bounds for Tikhonov regularization in Hilbert scales". Applicable Analysis 18, 29–37.

Newey, W. (1994). "Kernel estimation of partial means". Econometric Theory 10, 233–253.

Newey, W., Powell, J. (2003). "Instrumental variables for nonparametric models". Econometrica 71, 1565–1578.

Newey, W., Powell, J., Vella, F. (1999). "Nonparametric estimation of triangular simultaneous equations models". Econometrica 67, 565–604.

Owen, A. (2001). Empirical Likelihood. Monographs on Statistics and Applied Probability, vol. 92. Chapman and Hall, London.

Pagan, A., Ullah, A. (1999). Nonparametric Econometrics. Cambridge University Press, Cambridge.

Parzen, E. (1959). "Statistical inference on time series by Hilbert space methods, I". Technical report No. 23, Applied Mathematics and Statistics Laboratory, Stanford. Reprinted in (1967), Time Series Analysis Papers, Holden-Day, San Francisco.

Parzen, E. (1970). "Statistical inference on time series by RKHS methods". In: Pyke, R. (Ed.), Proc. 12th Biennal Canadian Mathematical Seminar. American Mathematical Society, Providence, pp. 1–37.

Politis, D., Romano, J. (1994). "Limit theorems for weakly dependent Hilbert space valued random variables with application to the stationary bootstrap". Statistica Sinica 4, 451–476.

Polyanin, A., Manzhirov, A. (1998). Handbook of Integral Equations. CRC Press, Boca Raton, FL.

Ramsay, J.O., Silverman, B.W. (1997). Functional Data Analysis. Springer, New York.

Reiersol, O. (1941). "Confluence analysis of lag moments and other methods of confluence analysis". Econometrica 9, 1–24.

Reiersol, O. (1945). "Confluence analysis by means of instrumental sets of variables". Arkiv for Mathematik, Astronomie och Fysik 32A, 1–119.

Ross, S. (1976). "The arbitrage theory of capital asset pricing". Journal of Finance 13, 341–360.

Rust, J., Traub, J.F., Wozniakowski, H. (2002). "Is there a curse of dimensionality for contraction fixed points in the worst case?". Econometrica 70, 285–330.

Ruymgaart, F. (2001). "A short introduction to inverse statistical inference". Lecture given at the conference "L'Odyssée de la Statistique", Institut Henri Poincaré, Paris.

Saitoh, S. (1997). Integral Transforms, Reproducing Kernels and Their Applications. Longman, Harlow.

Sargan, J.D. (1958). "The estimation of economic relationship using instrumental variables". Econometrica 26, 393–415.

Schaumburg, E. (2004). "Estimation of Markov processes of Levy type generators". Mimeo. Kellogg School of Management.

Singleton, K. (2001). "Estimation of affine pricing models using the empirical characteristic function". Journal of Econometrics 102, 111–141.

Stefanski, L., Carroll, R. (1990). "Deconvoluting kernel density estimators". Statistics 2, 169–184.

Stock, J., Watson, M. (1998). "Diffusion indexes". NBER working paper 6702.

Stock, J., Watson, M. (2002). "Macroeconomic forecasting using diffusion indexes". Journal of Business and Economic Statistics 20, 147–162.

Tauchen, G. (1997). "New minimum chi-square methods in empirical finance". In: Kreps, D., Wallis, K. (Eds.), Advances in Econometrics. In: Seventh World Congress. Cambridge University Press, Cambridge, pp. 279–317.

Tautenhahn, U. (1996). "Error estimates for regularization methods in Hilbert scales". SIAM Journal of Numerical Analysis 33, 2120–2130.

Theil, H. (1953). "Repeated least-squares applied to complete equations system". Mimeo. Central Planning Bureau, The Hague.

Tjøstheim, D., Auestad, B. (1994). "Nonparametric identification of nonlinear time series projections". Journal of American Statistical Association 89, 1398–1409.

van der Vaart, A., Wellner, J. (1996). Weak Convergence and Empirical Processes. Springer-Verlag, New York.

Vanhems, A. (2006). "Nonparametric study of solutions of differential equations". Econometric Theory 22, 127–157.

Van Rooij, A., Ruymgaart, F. (1991). "Regularized deconvolution on the circle and the sphere". In: Roussas, G. (Ed.), Nonparametric Functional Estimation and Related Topics. Kluwer Academic Publishers, Amsterdam, pp. 679–690.

Van Rooij, A., Ruymgaart, F. (1999). "On inverse estimation". In: Ghosh, S. (Ed.), Asymptotics, Nonparametrics, and Time Series. Dekker, New York, pp. 579–613.

Van Rooij, A., Ruymgaart, F., Van Zwet, W. (2000). "Asymptotic efficiency of inverse estimators". Theory of Probability and Its Applications 44 (4), 722–738.

Vapnik, A.C.M. (1998). "Statistical Learning Theory". Wiley, New York.

Wahba, G. (1973). "Convergence rates of certain approximate solutions to Fredholm integral equations of the first kind". Journal of Approximation Theory 7, 167–185.

AUTHOR INDEX OF VOLUMES 6A AND 6B

n indicates citation in a footnote.

SUBJECT INDEX OF VOLUMES 6A AND 6B

C

E